ENCYCLOPEDIA OF
ARCHITECTURE
DESIGN, ENGINEERING & CONSTRUCTION

JOSEPH A. WILKES, FAIA
Editor-in-Chief

ROBERT T. PACKARD, AIA
Associate Editor

VOLUME 4
Pope, John Russell
to
Systems Integration

A WILEY-INTERSCIENCE PUBLICATION
JOHN WILEY & SONS
New York • Chichester • Brisbane • Toronto • Singapore

For her help in so many ways,
this encyclopedia is dedicated to
my wife Margaret.

Library of Congress Cataloging in Publication Data:

Encyclopedia of architecture.

"A Wiley-Interscience publication."
Includes bibliographies.
Contents: v. 4. Pope, John Russell to Systems Integration
1. Architecture—Dictionaries.   I. Wilkes, Joseph A.
II. Packard, Robert T.

NA31.E59   1988   720'.3   87-25222
ISBN 0—471–63245-7 (v. 4)
ISBN 0–471–63351–8 (set)

Printed in the United States of America

10 9 8 7 6 5 4 3 2 1

ENCYCLOPEDIA OF
ARCHITECTURE
DESIGN, ENGINEERING & CONSTRUCTION

EDITORIAL BOARD

EDITORIAL STAFF

Editor-in-chief: Joseph A. Wilkes, FAIA
Associate Editor: Robert T. Packard, AIA
Managing Editor: Stephen A. Kliment, FAIA
Editorial Supervisor: Samuel Christian

Production Manager: Jenet McIver
Production Supervisor: Jean Spranger
Production Assistant: Yvette Ho Sang
Designer: Jean Morley

CONTRIBUTORS

Sherry B. Ahrentzen, *University of Wisconsin, Milwaukee, Wisc.,* Single-Parent Housing

Russell E. Allen, *Cherry Hill, N.J.,* Power Generation, Fossil Fuels

William Allen, *Bickerdike Allen Partners, London, UK,* Profession in Contemporary Society

Joseph S. A. Amstock, *Bostik Construction Products, Huntingdon Valley, Penn.,* Sealants

Daniel Ancona, *Annadale, Virginia,* Power Generation, Wind, Ocean

Ronald D. Anzalone, *Advisory Council on Historic Preservation, Washington, D.C.,* Preservation, Historic

Christopher Arnold, *Building Systems Dev. Co., San Mateo, Calif.,* Seismic design

Henry Arnold, *Arnold Associates, Princeton, N.J.,* Shrubs and Trees

Peter Batchelor, *North Carolina State University, Raleigh, N.C.,* Regional Urban Design Assistance Teams (R/UDATs)

William B. Bechhoefer, *Bethesda, Md.,* Synagogues

Steven Bedford, *Middlebury, Conn.,* Pope, John Russell; Spence, Sir Basil; Stone, Edward Durrell

Steven L. Biegel, *Lawrence & Lawrence Architects, Warrenton, Va.,* Roofing Materials

Gregory J. Bocchi, *Powder Coating Institute, Alexandria, Va.,* Powder Coatings

Joseph V. Bower, *McGraw-Hill Information Systems Company, New York, N.Y.,* Sweet's Catalog Files

Kurt Brandle, *University of Michigan, Ann Arbor, Mich.,* Systems Integration

Susan Braybrooke, *London, UK,* Signing-Environmental Graphics

Janet Mackey Brown, *HOK Architects, St. Louis, Mo.,* Programming, Architectural

William Brubaker, *Perkins & Will Partnership, Chicago, Ill.,* Secondary Schools

Edward K. Budnick, *Hughes Associates, Inc., Wheaton, Md.,* Sprinklers and Other Fire Control Methods

Robert Burnham, *Kansas State University, Manhattan, Kans.,* Public Service Architecture

Donald G. Carter, *CT-PLUS Inc., Kensington, Md.,* Preventive Maintenance

Rico Cedro, *Brookline, Mass.,* Roche Dinkaloo

Clarence L. Chafee, *NCARB, Washington, D.C.,* Registration Examination Process, Architects

Joseph M. Chapman, *Joseph M. Chapman, Inc., Wilton, Conn.,* Security Systems

Jeffrey Christian, *Oak Ridge National Laboratory, Oak Ridge, Tenn.,* Radon Mitigation in Construction

Meredith Clausen, *University of Washington, Seattle, Wash.,* Shopping Centers

Kenneth Cooper, *Pool Pak, York, Penn.,* Refrigeration

Stanley W. Crawley, *University of Utah, Salt Lake City, Utah,* Steel in Construction

Manuel Cuadra, *Technische Hochschule, Darmstadt, FRG,* Scharoun, Hans

Robert Dillon, *Silver Spring, Md.,* Steel in Construction

P. J. DiNinno, *Hughes Associates, Wheaton, Md.,* Sprinklers and Other Fire Control Methods

Karen Dominguez, *Penn State University, State College, Penn.,* Sert, Jose Luis

Benjamin P. Elliott, *Rockville, Md.,* Religious Architecture

J. Jacek Figwar, *Jacek Figwar Associates, Inc., Concord, Mass.,* Sound Reinforcement Systems

Norman C. Fletcher, *The Architects Collaborative, Cambridge, Mass.,* Role of the Architect

Diane Yvonne Ghirado, *University of Southern California, Santa Monica, Calif.,* Rossi, Aldo

Harcharan S. Gill, *Trow Dames & Moore, Brampton, Ontario, Canada,* Soils Engineering

Gary Gordon, *Gary Gordon Architectural Lighting, New York, N.Y.,* Specialty Lighting

Shana Greenblatt, *Moshe Safdie Architect, Somerville, Mass.,* Safdie, Moshe

J. Russell Groves, Jr., *Johnson Romanowitz Architects & Planners, Lexington, Ky.,* Reasonable Care, Standards of

David Guise, *New York, N.Y.,* Salvadori, Mario, Structural Steel; Suspension Cable Structure

John Harkness, *The Architects Collaborative, Cambridge, Mass.,* Swimming Pools

Gregory Harrison, *Gaithersburg, Md.,* Stairs and Ramps, Safety Design Aspects

Kingston Heath, *University of North Carolina at Charlotte, Charlotte, N.C.,* Richardson, Henry Hobson

Mark A. Hewitt, *Columbia University, New York, N.Y.,* Soane, John

Gregory K. Hunt, *Alexandria, Va.,* Rogers, Richard; Schindler, R. M.

Richard Hyde, *National University of Singapore, Singapore,* Public Service Architecture

Gregory A. Johnson, *York International, Inc., Charlotte, N.C.,* Refrigeration

Earle W. Kennett, *Gaithersburg, Md.,* Research, Architectural

Douglas Kingsbury, *Kingsbury & Associates, Kansas City, Mo.,* Sports Stadia

Udo Kulterman, *Washington University, St. Louis, Mo.,* Southeast Asian Architecture

Ronald J. Labinski, *HOK Architects, Kansas City, Mo.,* Sports Stadia

Donald Levy, *The American Institute of Architects, Washington, D.C.,* Professional Development

Mark Loeffler, *Gary Gordon Architectural Lighting, New York, N.Y.,* Specialty Lighting

Dianne M. Ludman, *The Stubbins Associates, Cambridge, Mass.,* Stubbins, Hugh

Clark Lundell, *Auburn University, Auburn, Alabama,* Raymond, Antonin; Sasaki, Hideo

Robert McKowan, *Armstrong World Industries, Lancaster, Pa.,* Resilient Flooring

Angela Mace, *Royal Institute of British Architects, London, UK,* Royal Institute of British Architects

Thomas Mellins, *Robert A. M. Stern Architects, New York, N.Y.,* Stern, Robert A. M.

William C. Miller, *Kansas State University, Manhattan, Kans.,* Saarinen, Eliel

John E. Mocks, *Dept of Energy, Washington, D.C.,* Power Generation, Geothermal

Robert T. Packard, *Reston, Va.,* Root, John Wellborn; Sant'Elia, Antonio, Shepley, Bulfinch, Richardson and Abbott; Stirling, James

Peter C. Papademetriou, *Rice University, Houston, Texas,* Saarinen, Eero

Michael O. Pearce, *Nickel Development Industry, Toronto, Ontario, Canada,* Stainless Steels

Richard Penner, *Cornell University, Ithaca, New York,* Restaurants

Roscoe R. Reeves, Jr., *American Institute of Architects, Washington, D.C.,* Specifications

Elliot Paul Rothman, *Rothman & Rothman, Boston, Mass.,* Renderings, Architectural

John Sailer, *Stone World, Oradell, N.J.,* Stone, Natural Building

J. L. Schiffery, *Hughes Associates, Inc., Wheaton, Md.,* Sprinklers and Other Fire Control Methods

Norbert Schoenauer, *McGill University, Montreal, Quebec, Canada,* Residential Buildings

Joyce Pomeroy Schwartz, *Consultant, New York, N.Y.,* Public Art

Thomas L. Schumacher, *Washington, D.C.,* Scarpa, Carlo

Ronald Toms, *Department of Energy, Washington, D.C.,* Power Generation, Geothermal

Virginia Tortona, *Bechtel Power Corp., Gaithersburg, Md.,* Power Generation, Nuclear

Robert C. Twombly, *West Nyack, N.Y.,* Sullivan, Louis

Susan Ubbelohde, *Minneapolis, Minn.,* Solar Energy Efficient Design

Barbara L. Wadkins, *New School of Architecture, Chula Vista, Calif.,* Soleri, Paolo

Ralph Warburton, *Coral Gables, Fla.,* Review Boards; Single-Family Residences; Skidmore, Owings, & Merrill

Michael Wein, *Bellmore, N.Y.,* Stormwater Systems

Barbara Williams, *Kenney/Williams/Williams Inc., Maple Glen, Penn.,* Stucco, Synthetic

Mark Williams, *Kenney/Williams/Williams Inc., Maple Glen, Penn.,* Stucco, Synthetic

Forrest Wilson, *College Park, Md.,* Space Frames

Stephen J. Zipp, *Washington, D.C.,* Remodeling, Residential

Robert Zwirn, *Miami University, Oxford, Ohio,* Rudolph, Paul M.

CONTENTS

CONVERSION FACTORS, ABBREVIATIONS, AND UNIT SYMBOLS

Selected SI Units (Adopted 1960)

Quantity	Unit	Symbol	Acceptable equivalent
BASE UNITS			
length	meter†	m	
mass‡	kilogram	kg	
time	second	s	
electric current	ampere	A	
thermodynamic temperature§	kelvin	K	
DERIVED UNITS AND OTHER ACCEPTABLE UNITS			
* absorbed dose	gray	Gy	J/kg
acceleration	meter per second squared	m/s^2	
* activity (of ionizing radiation source)	becquerel	Bq	1/s
area	square kilometer	km^2	
	square hectometer	hm^2	ha (hectare)
	square meter	m^2	
density, mass density	kilogram per cubic meter	kg/m^3	g/L; mg/cm^3
* electric potential, potential difference, electromotive force	volt	V	W/A
* electric resistance	ohm	Ω	V/A
* energy, work, quantity of heat	megajoule	MJ	
	kilojoule	kJ	
	joule	J	N·m
	electron volt^x	eV^x	
	kilowatt hour^x	$kW·h^x$	
* force	kilonewton	kN	
	newton	N	$kg·m/s^2$
* frequency	megahertz	MHz	
	hertz	Hz	1/s
heat capacity, entropy	joule per kelvin	J/K	
heat capacity (specific), specific entropy	joule per kilogram kelvin	J/(kg·K)	
heat transfer coefficient	watt per square meter kelvin	W/(m²·K)	
linear density	kilogram per meter	kg/m	
magnetic field strength	ampere per meter	A/m	
moment of force, torque	newton meter	N·m	
momentum	kilogram meter per second	kg·m/s	
* power, heat flow rate, radiant flux	kilowatt	kW	
	watt	W	J/s
power density, heat flux density, irradiance	watt per square meter	W/m^2	
* pressure, stress	megapascal	MPa	
	kilopascal	kPa	
	pascal	Pa	
sound level	decibel	dB	
specific energy	joule per kilogram	J/kg	
specific volume	cubic meter per kilogram	m^3/kg	

Quantity	Unit	Symbol	Acceptable equivalent
surface tension	newton per meter	N/m	
thermal conductivity	watt per meter kelvin	W/(m·K)	
velocity	meter per second	m/s	
	kilometer per hour	km/h	
viscosity, dynamic	pascal second	Pa·s	
	millipascal second	mPa·s	
volume	cubic meter	m³	
	cubic decimeter	dm³	L (liter)
	cubic centimeter	cm³	mL

* The asterisk denotes those units having special names and symbols.
† The spellings "metre" and "litre" are preferred by ASTM; however "er-" is used in the Encyclopedia.
‡ "Weight" is the commonly used term for "mass."
§ Wide use is made of "Celsius temperature" (t) defined by

$$t = T - T_0$$

where t is the thermodynamic temperature, expressed in kelvins, and $T_0 = 273.15$ by definition. A temperature interval may be expressed in degrees Celsius as well as in kelvins.
ˣ This non-SI unit is recognized by the CIPM as having to be retained because of practical importance or use in specialized fields.

In addition, there are 16 prefixes used to indicate order of magnitude, as follows:

Multiplication factor	Prefix	Symbol
10^{18}	exa	E
10^{15}	peta	P
10^{12}	tera	T
10^{9}	giga	G
10^{6}	mega	M
10^{3}	kilo	k
10^{2}	hecto	h[a]
10	deka	da[a]
10^{-1}	deci	d[a]
10^{-2}	centi	c[a]
10^{-3}	milli	m
10^{-6}	micro	μ
10^{-9}	nano	n
10^{-12}	pico	p
10^{-15}	femto	f
10^{-18}	atto	a

[a] Although hecto, deka, deci, and centi are SI prefixes, their use should be avoided except for SI unit-multiples for area and volume and nontechnical use of centimeter, as for body and clothing measurement.

Conversion Factors to SI Units

To convert from	To	Multiply by
acre	square meter (m²)	4.047×10^3
angstrom	meter (m)	1.0×10^{-10}†
atmosphere	pascal (Pa)	1.013×10^5
bar	pascal (Pa)	1.0×10^5†
barn	square meter (m²)	1.0×10^{-28}†
barrel (42 U.S. liquid gallons)	cubic meter (m³)	0.1590
Btu (thermochemical)	joule (J)	1.054×10^3
bushel	cubic meter (m³)	3.524×10^{-2}
calorie (thermochemical)	joule (J)	4.184†
centipoise	pascal second (Pa·s)	1.0×10^{-3}†
cfm (cubic foot per minute)	cubic meter per second (m³/s)	4.72×10^{-4}
cubic inch	cubic meter (m³)	1.639×10^{-5}
cubic foot	cubic meter (m³)	2.832×10^{-2}
cubic yard	cubic meter (m³)	0.7646

To convert from	To	Multiply by
dram (apothecaries')	kilogram (kg)	3.888×10^{-3}
dram (avoirdupois)	kilogram (kg)	1.772×10^{-3}
dram (U.S. fluid)	cubic meter (m³)	3.697×10^{-6}
dyne	newton (N)	$1.0 \times 10^{-5\dagger}$
dyne/cm	newton per meter (N/m)	$1.0 \times 10^{-3\dagger}$
fluid ounce (U.S.)	cubic meter (m³)	2.957×10^{-5}
foot	meter (m)	$0.3048^{\dagger}$
gallon (U.S. dry)	cubic meter (m³)	4.405×10^{-3}
gallon (U.S. liquid)	cubic meter (m³)	3.785×10^{-3}
gallon per minute (gpm)	cubic meter per second (m³/s)	6.308×10^{-5}
	cubic meter per hour (m³/h)	0.2271
grain	kilogram (kg)	6.480×10^{-5}
horsepower (550 ft·lbf/s)	watt (W)	7.457×10^{2}
inch	meter (m)	$2.54 \times 10^{-2\dagger}$
inch of mercury (32°F)	pascal (Pa)	3.386×10^{3}
inch of water (39.2°F)	pascal (Pa)	2.491×10^{2}
kilogram-force	newton (N)	9.807
kilowatt hour	megajoule (MJ)	$3.6^{\dagger}$
liter (for fluids only)	cubic meter (m³)	$1.0 \times 10^{-3\dagger}$
micron	meter (m)	$1.0 \times 10^{-6\dagger}$
mil	meter (m)	$2.54 \times 10^{-5\dagger}$
mile (statute)	meter (m)	1.609×10^{3}
mile per hour	meter per second (m/s)	0.4470
millimeter of mercury (0°C)	pascal (Pa)	$1.333 \times 10^{2\dagger}$
ounce (avoirdupois)	kilogram (kg)	2.835×10^{-2}
ounce (troy)	kilogram (kg)	3.110×10^{-2}
ounce (U.S. fluid)	cubic meter (m³)	2.957×10^{-5}
ounce-force	newton (N)	0.2780
peck (U.S.)	cubic meter (m³)	8.810×10^{-3}
pennyweight	kilogram (kg)	1.555×10^{-3}
pint (U.S. dry)	cubic meter (m³)	5.506×10^{4}
pint (U.S. liquid)	cubic meter (m³)	4.732×10^{-4}
poise (absolute viscosity)	pascal second (Pa·s)	$0.10^{\dagger}$
pound (avoirdupois)	kilogram (kg)	0.4536
pound (troy)	kilogram (kg)	0.3732
pound-force	newton (N)	4.448
pound-force per square inch (psi)	pascal (Pa)	6.895×10^{3}
quart (U.S. dry)	cubic meter (m³)	1.101×10^{-3}
quart (U.S. liquid)	cubic meter (m³)	9.464×10^{-4}
quintal	kilogram (kg)	$1.0 \times 10^{2\dagger}$
rad	gray (Gy)	$1.0 \times 10^{-2\dagger}$
square inch	square meter (m²)	6.452×10^{-4}
square foot	square meter (m²)	9.290×10^{-2}
square mile	square meter (m²)	2.590×10^{6}
square yard	square meter (m²)	0.8361
ton (long, 2240 pounds)	kilogram (kg)	1.016×10^{3}
ton (metric)	kilogram (kg)	$1.0 \times 10^{3\dagger}$
ton (short, 2000 pounds)	kilogram (kg)	9.072×10^{2}
torr	pascal (Pa)	1.333×10^{2}
yard	meter (m)	$0.9144^{\dagger}$

† Exact.

Acronyms and Abbreviations

AA	Archigram Architects	AASHTO	American Association of State Highway and Transportation Officials
AAA	American Arbitration Association		
AACA	Architects Accreditation Council of Australia	AAT	Art and Architecture Thesaurus
AAL	Association of Architectural Librarians	ABA	Architectural Barriers Act
AAMA	American Architectural Manufacturers Association	ABC	Alternate birthing center; Associate Builders and Contractors
AASHO	American Association of State Highway Officials	ABNT	Associacao Brasileira de Normas Tecnicas

ABPMA	Acoustical and Board Products Manufacturers Association	APA	American Planning Association; American Plywood Association
ABS	Acrylonitrile–butadiene–styrene	APR	Air purifying respirators; Architectural program report
AC	Alternating current		
ACA	American Correction Association; Ammoniacal copper arsenate	APS	Arrival point of sight
ACEC	American Consulting Engineers Council	ARCC	Architectural Research Centers Consortium
ACI	American Concrete Institute	ARCUK	Architects Registration Council of the United Kingdom
ACS	Acrylonitrile–chlorinated polyethylene–styrene	ARE	Architect Registration Examination
ACSA	Association of Collegiate Schools of Architecture	ARI	Air-Conditioning and Refrigeration Institute
ADC	Air Diffusion Council	ARLIS/N	Art Libraries Society of North America
ADL	Activities of daily living	ARMA	Asphalt Roofing Manufacturers Association
ADPI	Air Distribution Performance Index	ARP	Air raid precaution
ADR	Alternative dispute resolution	ASA	Acoustical Society of America; American Subcontractors Association
AEC	Atomic Energy Commission		
AEG	Allgemeine Elektricitats-Geselschaft		
AEIC	Association of Edison Illuminating Companies	ASCE	American Society of Civil Engineers
		ASET	Available safe egress time
AEPIC	Architecture and Engineering Performance Information Center	ASHRAE	American Society of Heating, Refrigerating, and Air Conditioning Engineers
AFD	Air filtration devices		
AFL/CIO	American Federation of Labor and Congress of Industrial Organizations	ASHVE	American Society of Heating and Ventilating Engineers
		ASID	American Society of Interior Designers
AFNOR	Association Francaise de Normalisation	ASLA	American Society of Landscape Architects
AFUE	Annual fuel utilization efficiency		
AGA	American Gas Association	ASM	American Society for Metals
AGC	Associated General Contractors of America	ASME	American Society of Mechanical Engineers
AGIC	Architectural Group for Industry and Commerce	ASTM	American Society for Testing and Materials
AGTS	Automated guideway transit systems	ATA	Air Transportation Association of America
AHA	American Hardboard Association		
AHAM	Association of Home Appliance Manufacturers	AtBat	l'Atelier des Batisseurs
		ATBCB	Architectural and Transportation Barriers Compliance Board
AHU	Air handler unit		
AI	Articulation Index; Artificial Intelligence	ATC	Air Transport Command
		ATM	Automatic teller machine
AIA	American Institute of Architects	ATMA	American Textile Machinery Association
AIA/F	American Institute of Architects Foundation	A/V	Audio/video
AIAS	American Institute of Architecture Students	AWG	American wire gauge
		AWI	Architectural Woodwork Institute
AIA/SC	American Institute of Architects Service Corporation	AWPA	American Wood Preservers Association
AICP	American Institute of Certified Planners	AWPB	American Wood Preservers Bureau
AID	Agency for International Development	AWT	Advanced wastewater treatment
AIKD	American Institute of Kitchen Dealers	BBC	British Broadcasting Company
AIREA	American Institute of Real Estate Appraisers	BBN	Bolt Beranek and Newman
		BBP	Butylbenzyl phthalate
AISC	American Institute of Steel Construction	BCMC	Board for the Coordination of the Model Codes
AISI	American Iron and Steel Institute	BDA	Bund Deutscher Architekten
AITC	American Institute of Timber Construction	BEEP	Black Executive Exchange Program
		BEL	Bauentwerfslehre
ALS	American Lumber Standards	BEPS	Building Energy Performance Standard
AMA	Acoustical Materials Association		
AMCA	Air Moving and Conditioning Association	BFE	Base flood elevation
		BFSM	Building Fire Simulation Model
ANSI	American National Standards Institute	BH	Boxed heart
		BIA	Brick Institute of America

BJS	Bureau of Justice Statistics
BOCA	Building Officials and Code Administrators International
BOD	Biological oxygen demand
BOMA	Building Owners and Managers Association International
BOSTI	Buffalo Organization for Social and Technological Innovation
BPST	British portable skid tester
BRA	Boston Redevelopment Authority
BRAB	Building Research Advisory Board
BRB	Building Research Board
BRI	Building related illness
BS	Building standards
BSR	Board of Standards Review
BSSC	Building Seismic Safety Council
Btu	British thermal unit
BUR	Built-up roofing
BV	Bolt value
CA	Cellulose acetate
CAA	Clean Air Act
CABO	Council of American Building Officials
CACE	Council of Architectural Component Executives
CAD	Computer-aided Design
CADD	Computer-aided Design and Drafting
CAGI	Compressed Air and Gas Institute
CAJ	Committee on Architecture for Justice
CARF	Committee on Accreditation of Rehabilitation Facilities
CB	Cellulose butyrate
CBD	Central business district
CBR	California bearing ratio
CCA	Chromated copper arsenate
CCC	Civilian Conservation Corps
CCR	Ceiling cavity ratio
CCTV	Closed-circuit television
cd	candela
CDA	Copper Development Association
CDC	Community design center
CEC	Canadian Electrical Code; Consulting Engineers Council
cfm	cubic feet per minute
CFR	Airport Crash, Fire and Rescue Service; Code of Federal Regulations
CIAM	Les Congres Internationaux d'Architecture Moderne
CIB	International Council for Building Research, Studies, and Documentation
CIMA	Construction Industry Manufacturers Association
CKD	Certified kitchen designer
CLARB	National Council of Landscape Architectural Registration Boards
CLEP	College-level Examination Program
CLTD	Cooling load temperature difference
CM	Construction management; Construction manager
CMAA	Construction Management Association of America
CMU	Concrete masonry unit(s)
CN	Cellulose nitrate
COD	Chemical oxygen demand
COF	Coefficient of friction
CON	Certificate of need
CP	Cellulose propionate
CPD	Continuing professional development
CPE	Chlorinated polyethylene
CPM	Critical path method
cps	cycles per second
CPSC	Consumer Product Safety Commission
CPU	Central processing unit; Computer processing unit
CPVC	Chlorinated poly(vinyl chloride); Critical pigment volume concentration
CR	Cavity ratio; Condensation resistance
CRI	Color Rendering Index
CRREL	Cold Regions Research and Engineering Laboratory
CRS	Caudill Rowlett Scott
CRSI	Concrete Reinforcing Steel Institute
CRSS	Caudill Rowlett Scott Sirrine
CRT	Cathode ray tube; Computer relay terminal
CSI	Construction Specifications Institute
CSPE	Chlorosulfonated polyethylene
CSRF	Construction Science Research Foundation
CU	Coefficient of utilization
CUA	The Catholic University of America
CVS	Certified value specialist
DAL	Federation of Danish Architects
dB	decibel
DC	Direct current
DEW	Distant Early Warning
DHHS	Department of Health and Human Services
DOD	Department of Defense
DOE	Department of Energy
DOL	Department of Labor
DOP	Dioctyl phthalate
DOT	Department of Transportation
DP	Data processing; Degree of polymerization
DPIC	Design Professionals Insurance Company
DPLG	Diplome par le gouvernement
DPU	Data processing unit
DWV	Drain–waste–vent
DX	Direct-expansion
EDRA	Environmental Design Research Association
EENT	Eye, ear, nose, and throat
EER	Energy efficiency ratio
EERI	Earthquake Engineering Research Institute
EESA	Education Evaluation Services for Architects
EIP	Ethylene interpolymers
EJCDC	Engineers Joint Contract Documents Committee
ELR	Equivalent length of run
EMT	Electrical metallic tubing
ENT	Ear, nose, and throat
EP	Epoxies
EPA	Environmental Protection Agency

EPCOT	Experimental Prototype Community of Tomorrow
EPDM	Ethylene propylene diene monomer
EPI	Emulsion polymer/isocyanate
EPS	Expandable polystyrene
ERM	Escape and rescue model
ESD	Electrostatic discharge
ESI	Equivalent sphere illumination
ESP	Education Services for the Professions
ET	Evapotranspiration
ETP	Electrolytic tough pitch
ETS	Environmental tobacco smoke
E&B	*Environment and Behavior* (journal)
f	Fiber(s)
FAA	Federal Aviation Administration
FAIA	Fellow of the American Institute of Architects
FAR	Floor area ratio
FBI	Federal Bureau of Investigation
FBO	Foreign Building Operations
fc	footcandle(s)
FCARM	Federation of Colleges of Architects of the Mexican Republic
FCR	Floor cavity ratio
FEMA	Federal Emergency Management Agency
FG	Flat grain
FHA	Federal Housing Administration
FHWA	Federal Highway Administration
FIDCR	Federal Interagency Day Care Requirements
FIDIC	Federation Internationale des Ingenieurs-conseils (Federation of Consulting Engineers)
FIDS	Flight Information Display Systems
FIRM	Flood insurance rate map
FM	Fineness modulus
FmHA	Farmers Home Administration
FMRL	Factory Mutual Research Laboratories
FOHC	Free-of-heart center
fpm	feet per minute
fps	feet per second
FR	Flame retardant
FRP	Fiber glass-reinforced plastic
FRT	Fire retardant treated
FS	Factor of safety
FSES	Fire Safety Evaluation System
ft	foot (feet)
FU	Fixture units
GA	Gypsum Association
GAO	General Accounting Office
GATT	General Agreement on Tariffs and Trade
GDP	Gross domestic product
GFCI	Ground fault circuit interrupter
Glulam	Glued laminated wood
GMAW	Gas metal arc welding
GMP	Guaranteed maximum price
gpm	gallons per minute
GRP	Glass reinforced plastic
GSA	General Services Administration

GSIS	Government Service Insurance System
GTAW	Gas tungsten arc welding
h	hour(s)
HABS	Historic American Buildings Survey
HDO	High density overlay
HDPE	High density polyethylene
HEGIS	Higher Education General Information Survey
HEPA	High-efficiency particulate absolute
HGSD	Harvard Graduate School of Design
HHS	Department of Health & Human Services
HID	High-intensity discharge
HOK	Hellmuth Obata and Kassabaum
HPL	High-pressure laminate
HPS	High-pressure sodium
HUD	Department of Housing & Urban Development
HVAC	Heating, ventilating, and air conditioning
Hz	Hertz
I	Candlepower
IACC	International Association of Conference Centers
IALD	International Association of Lighting Designers
IAPS	International Association for the Study of People and their Physical Surroundings
IATA	International Air Transport Association
IBD	Institute of Business Designers
ICAO	International Civil Aviation Organization
ICBO	International Conference of Building Officials
ICEA	Insulated Cable Engineers Association
ICOR	Interprofessional Council on Registration
IDP	Intern–Architect Development Program
IDSA	Industrial Designers Society of America
IEC	International Electrotechnical Commission
IEEE	Institute of Electrical and Electronics Engineers
IES	Illuminating Engineering Society of North America
IF	Industrialization Forum
IG	International Group
IIC	Impact insulation class
IIT	Illinois Institute of Technology
ILS	Instrument landing system
in.	inch(es)
INCRA	International Copper Research Association
IP	Image processing
ir	infrared
IRA	Initial rate of water absorption
ISO	International Organization for Standardization

IUA	Institute Universitario di Architettura; International Union of Architects
JAE	*Journal of Architectural Education*
JAPR	*Journal of Architectural and Planning Research*
JCAH	Joint Commission on Accreditation of Hospitals
JEP	*Journal of Environmental Psychology*
JIS	Japanese industry standards
JIT	Just in time
JSAH	*Journal of the Society of Architectural Historians*
KCPI	Knife cuts per inch
KD	Kiln-dried
kg	kilogram
kip	1000 pounds
km	kilometer
kPa	kilopascal
ksi	kips per square inch
kW	kilowatt(s)
L	liter
lb	pound
LCC	London County Council
LDPE	Low density polyethylene
LDR	Luminaire dirt replacement; Labor/delivery/recovery
LDRP	Labor/delivery/recovery/postpartum
LFT	Laminated floor tile
LLDPE	Linear low density polyethylene
LLF	Light loss factor
LOF	Large ordering framework
LPS	Low-pressure sodium
LRI	Lighting Research Institute
LSC	Life Safety Code
m	meter
MAAT	Mean average air temperature
MAI	Member of the Appraisers Institute
MARTA	Metropolitan Atlanta Rapid Transit Authority
MBMA	Metal Building Manufacturers Association
MC	Moisture content
MDF	Medium density fiberboard
MDI	Methylene diisocyanate
MDO	Medium density overlay
MDP	Main distribution panelboard
MDPE	Medium density polyethylene
MERA	Man and Environment Research Association
MG	Motor generator
MGRAD	Minimum Guidelines and Requirements for Accessible Design
MH	Metal halide
MIA	Marble Institute of America
min	minute(s)
MIT	Massachusetts Institute of Technology
MLS	Master of Library Science
mm	millimeter
MOE	Modulus of elasticity
MOR	Modulus of rupture
MPa	Megapascal
MPS	Minimum property standards

mpy	mils per year
msec	millisecond(s)
MSHA	Mine Safety and Health Administration
MSR	Machine stress-rated
MV	Mercury vapor
μm	micrometer
NAAB	National Architectural Accrediting Board
NACA	National Advisory Council on Aging
NAEC	National Association of Elevator Contractors
NAHB	National Association of Home Builders of the United States
NAPF	National Association of Plastic Fabricators
NASA	National Aeronautics and Space Administration
NASFCA	National Automatic Sprinkler and Fire Control Association
NAVFAC	Naval Facilities Engineering Command
NBC	National Building Code
NBCC	National Building Code of Canada
NBFU	National Board of Fire Underwriters
NBM	National Bureau of Standards and Technology
NBS	National Bureau of Standards
NC	Network communications; Noise criteria
NCA	National Constructors Association
NCAR	National Council of Architectural Registration
NCARB	National Council of Architectural Registration Boards
NCEE	National Council of Engineering Examiners
NCIDQ	National Council of Interior Design Qualification
NCMA	National Concrete Masonry Association
NCS	Natural color system
NCSBCS	National Conference of States on Building Codes and Standards
NDS	National design specifications
NEA	National Endowment for the Arts
NEC	National Electrical Code
NECA	National Electrical Contractors Association
NEH	National Endowment for the Humanities
NEISS	National Electronic Injury Surveillance System
NEMA	National Electrical Manufacturers Association
NFIP	National Flood Insurance Program
NFPA	National Fire Protection Association; National Forest Products Association
NGR	National grading rule
NIBS	National Institute of Building Sciences
NIC	Noise insulation class
NIOSH	National Institute for Occupational Safety and Health

NKCA	National Kitchen Cabinet Association		psf	pounds per square foot
nm	nanometers		PSFS	Philadelphia Savings Fund Society
NMS	Nonmetallic sheathed		psi	pounds per square inch
NMTB	National Machine Tool Builders Association		PTFE	Polytetrafluoroethylene
			PTO	Power take-off
NPS	National Park Service		PTV	Passenger transfer vehicle
NR	Noise reduction		PUD	Planned unit development
NRC	Noise reduction coefficient		PVA	Paralyzed Veterans of America; Poly(vinyl acrylic)
NRCA	National Roofing Contractors Association		PVAC	Polyvinyl acetate
NSF	National Science Foundation; National Sanitation Foundation		PVAL	Polyvinyl alcohol
			PVB	Polyvinyl butyral
NSPE	National Society of Professional Engineers		PVC	Poly(vinyl chloride); Pigment volume concentration
NSSEA	National School Supply and Equipment Association		PVDC	Polyvinylidene chloride
			PVDF	Polyvinylidene fluoride
			PVF	Polyvinyl fluoride; Polyvinyl formal
oc	on center		PW	Present worth
OEM	Original equipment manufacturer		PWA	Present worth of annuity
OPLR	Office for Professional Liability Research		PWF	Permanent wood foundation
ORBIT-2	Organizations, Buildings and Information Technology (study)		RAIC	Royal Architectural Institute of Canada
OSA	Olefin–styrene–acrylonitrile		RBM	Reinforced brick masonry
OSB	Oriented strand board		RCR	Room cavity ratio
OSHA	Occupational Safety and Health Administration		REA	Rural Electrification Administration
			REI	Relative exposure index
			REIT	Real estate investment trust
PA	Polyamide		RF	Resorcinol–formaldehyde
P/A	Progressive Architecture (journal)		RFC	Reconstruction Finance Corporation
PACO	Probing Alternate Career Opportunities		RFP	Request for proposal
			rh	Relative humidity
PADC	Pennsylvania Avenue Development Corporation		RIBA	Royal Institute of British Architects
			RIM	Reaction injection molding
PAPER	People and the Physical Environment Research		RL, R/L	Random length
			ROI	Return on investment
PAT	Proficiency analytical testing		rpm	revolutions per minute
PB	Polybutylene		R/UDAT	Regional/Urban Design Assistance Team(s)
PBS	Public Building Service			
PBT	Polybutylene terephthalate			
PC	Personal computer; Polycarbonate; Polymer concrete		SAC	Sound absorption coefficient
			SAE	Society of Automotive Engineers, Inc.
PCA	Portland Cement Association		SAN	Styrene–acrylonitrile
PCB	Pentachlorobiphenyl		SAR	Stichting Architekten Research
PCC	Polymer cement concrete		SAVE	Society of American Value Engineers
PCD	Planned community development		SBCC	Standard Building Construction Code
PCEH	President's Committee for the Employment of Handicapped		SBCCI	Southern Building Code Congress International, Inc.
PCI	Prestressed Concrete Institute			
PE	Polyethylene		SBR	Styrene butadiene rubber
PEPP	Professional Engineers in Private Practice		SBS	Sick building syndrome
			SCFF	Silicone-coated fiber glass fabrics
PERT	Program evaluation and review technique		SCS	Soil Conservation Service
			SCSD	School Construction System Development
PET	Polyethylene terephthalate			
PIB	Polyisobutylene		SE	Service entrance
PIC	Polymer-impregnated concrete		sec	second(s)
PMMA	Polymethyl methacrylate		SERI	Solar Energy Research Institute
PMR	Protected membrane roof		SG	Slash grain
PMS	Pavement management system		SHHA	Self-help Housing Agency
POE	Post-occupancy evaluation		SIC	Standard Industrial Classification
PP	Period payment; Polypropylene		SIR	Society of Industrial Realtors
ppm	parts per million		SJI	Steel Joist Institute
PRF	Phenol–resorcinol–formaldehyde		SLA	Special Libraries Association
PS	Polystyrene		SMACNA	Sheet Metal and Air Conditioning Contractors National Association
PSAE	Production Systems for Architects and Engineers		SMH	Super metal halide

SMPS	Society for Marketing Professional Services		UFI	Urea–formaldehyde foam insulation
SMU	Southern Methodist University		UHMWPE	Ultra-high molecular weight polyethylene
SOCOTEC	Societe de Controle Technique		UIA	Union Internationale des Architects
SOM	Skidmore Owings and Merrill		UIDC	Urban Investment Development Company
SPD	Supply, processing, and distribution			
SPI	Society of the Plastics Industry		UL	Underwriters Laboratories
SPP	Speech privacy potential		ULI	Urban Land Institute
SPRI	Single Ply Roofing Institute		UNESCO	United Nations Educational, Scientific, and Cultural Organization
SSPB	South Side Planning Board (Chicago)			
ST	Structural tubing			
STC	Sound transmission class		UNS	Unified numbering systems
STD	Standard		UPS	Uninterruptible power supply
STL	Sound transmission loss		USCOLD	United States Committee on Large Dams
TAC	The Architects Collaborative		USDA	United States Department of Agriculture
TAS	Technical Assistance Series			
TCFF	Teflon-coated fiber glass fabrics		USIA	United States Information Agency
TDD	Telecommunication devices for deaf persons		USPS	United States Postal Service
			uv	ultraviolet
TDI	Toluene diisocyanate			
TEM	Transmission electron microscopy			
TH	Technische Hochschule		VA	Veterans Administration
THB	Technische Hochschule Braunschweig		VAT	Vinyl asbestos tile
TIMA	Thermal Insulation Manufacturers Association		VCP	Visual Comfort Probability Factor
			VCT	Vinyl composition tile
TL	Transmission loss		VDT	Video display terminal
T-PV	Temperature–pressure relief valve		VG	Vertical grain
TV	Television		VISTA	Volunteers in Service to America
TVA	Tennessee Valley Authority		VLH	Very low heat
TWA	Time-weighted average		VMA	Voids in the mineral aggregate
T & G	Tongue and groove		VOC	Volatile organic compound
T & P	Temperature and pressure		VU	Value unit(s)
UBC	Uniform Building Code		WAA	War Assets Administration; Western Association of Architects
UCC	Uniform Commercial Code			
UCI	Uniform Construction Index		WHO	World Health Organization
UDDC	Urban Design and Development Corporation		WMMA	Woodworking Machinery Manufacturers Association
UF	Urea–formaldehyde		WP	Word processing; Word processor
UFAS	Uniform Federal Accessibility Standards		WPA	Work Progress Administration; Work Projects Administration

POPE, JOHN RUSSELL

John Russell Pope's (1874–1937) architectural career typifies the practice of a successful academic classicist in the first half of this century. Contemporary critics even referred to Pope as the heir to the reputation and abilities of Charles McKim. Despite such an accolade, Pope's career has not received modern scrutiny, and his contribution to the development of U.S. architecture and city planning is only now becoming recognized.

Born in an age of nascent academic classicism, Pope received the perfect training to pursue a successful career in the practice of architecture during the period before World War II. After three years at the City College of New York, Pope entered the Department of Architecture in the School of Mines at Columbia University, New York. Under the tutelage of William Robert Ware, the founder of U.S. architectural education, Pope was instilled with principles that affirmed the inherent importance of historical precedent and encouraged strict adherence to the classical principles of design.

From the time of his graduation from Columbia in 1894, Pope began to establish himself as an important figure in the U.S. architectural world. In 1895, he was the simultaneous winner of the McKim fellowship and the first fellowship to the American School of Architecture in Rome (later the American Academy in Rome). After 18 months in Rome, he entered the Ecole des Beaux Arts. In completing his exposure to the principles and paradigms of a classical academic education, he was extremely successful. Pope returned to New York in 1900, and after three years in the firm of Bruce Price, began his own practice, as well as directing the Atelier McKim at Columbia's School of Architecture.

Pope then began a 34-year career of providing expression to the grandiloquent aspirations of private and public patrons. His designs for domestic architecture established him as a leader in the development of a highly refined and restrained classicism that came to distinguish U.S. architecture from that of its European contemporaries. Further, Pope was, in his work, able to penetrate beyond mere copyist approaches to any of various styles to absorb its underlying principles and then produce works that were perfect restatements of it. This ability instilled in his designs a credibility and solidity that was lacking in the work of his professional cohorts.

His residential work began with decidedly beaux-arts essays, including the Stowe (Roslyn, New York, ca 1903) and the Jacobs house (Newport, Rhode Island, 1905). The relative restraint of the houses' decoration was described by a critic as "[s]mart and gay; but also careful sober pieces of architectural design" (1). Pope's residential designs then embarked on two divergent courses. The first was a rather short-lived move to exuberant early northern Renaissance modes, in keeping with the then-popular styles and is best characterized by commissions such as that for the W. K. Vanderbilt gatehouse (Roslyn, 1905), the Stuart Duncan residence (Newport, 1911), and the country residence of Mrs. W. K. Vanderbilt, Jr. (Long Island, New York, ca 1913). This romantic vision of the appropriateness of such antique forms carried into some of Pope's work in the deep South, such as the Branch house (Richmond, Virginia, 1917), and on his own house in Newport (1928–1930). This aspect of Pope's work continued to surface occasionally and was expressed in a variety of modes. It can best be seen in Tenacre, the home of Joseph Knapp (Southampton, New York, 1920).

The second course, one for which Pope received greater critical approbation, was a restrained, severe approach to several architectural modes, varying from a vaguely Tuscan style through sternly Georgian and Adamesque forms. His avoidance of excess ornament and the severity of his adaptation of any stylistic mode created a casual dignity that especially appealed to clients who preferred to limit ostentatious expressions of wealth. The best-known residences include those for S. R. Hitt (Washington, D.C., 1908), Guy Fairfax Cary (Jericho, New York, 1915), and Marshall Field (Lloyds' Neck, New York, 1925).

Simultaneously with his success in the provision of refined domestic environments that appealed to those with a certain refined cosmopolitan taste, Pope was producing major public monuments. Starting with Freedman's Hospital (Washington, 1903–1908) and the Lincoln Birthplace Memorial (Hodgenville, Kentucky, 1908), Pope began to establish a reputation that later led *The New York Times* to remark that he was a leading "disciple of the neoclassical belief in both the rightness and practicability of perpetuating in America the ideals of an ancient world" (2). Following his success in Kentucky and Washington, Pope produced the powerfully severe Temple of the Scottish Rite (Washington, 1910) and then almost won the competition for the Lincoln Memorial (1911) in Washington with an extremely forceful composition, losing by only one vote to Henry Bacon. Pope continued to produce these images of looming force for such grand public buildings and memorials as the Theodore Roosevelt memorials in New York and Washington (1925), Plattsburgh City Hall (1917), The Daughters of the American Revolution Memorial Constitutional Hall (1925), the Richmond Terminal (1919), and the American Battle Monument at Monfaucon, France (1932).

Today, when one looks out from the upper floor of the Hirschorn Gallery on the south side of the Mall in Washington, one immediately realizes Pope's effect on one of the United States' most important public spaces. He was responsible for the removal of the trees and the design of the National Gallery of Art (1937), the National Archives (1929–1933), the American Pharmaceutical Association (1929), the Jefferson Memorial (1935–1937), and he served as a design critic for the Board of Architectural Consultants' work on the Federal Triangle (1929–1933). As a member of the Commission of Fine Arts (1917–1922), he passed judgment on several projects around the Mall. His planning skills also lay behind the campus plans for several major academic institutions, including Yale University (1917–1919) and Dartmouth College (1924).

Pope's success with his repertory of severe forms was the reason he was chosen by Lord Duveen to be the architect of large portions of the British Museum and the Tate Gallery in London (1929–1932). His subsequent commissions for the Frick Collection conversion (1932), the Baltimore Museum (1929), Metropolitan Museum additions (1930), The Cloisters (1930), the Art Institute of Chicago (1934), and finally, the National Gallery of Art in Washington established Pope as an important figure in the development of the art museum in the first half of the twentieth century.

In essence, Pope's career must be seen as the paradigm for the academically trained architect. Pope must be congratulated with "a sincere and reasoned enthusiasm [for] the fine consistency of purpose that animated him throughout his career" (2), that is, his firm adherence to a belief in the existence of an assemblage of ideal forms that were developed in the distant past and which continued to maintain validity as forms expressive of the spirit of the age.

This tenacious adherence produced "temples that sit serene in the moil and toil of modern commerce [and] belong to a specific period in our development as a nation: help express and interpret . . . the era through which we have just lived and in which we still strive to come to grips with our national soul" (2).

BIBLIOGRAPHY

1. H. Croly, "A New Use of Old Forms," *Architectural Record,* 273 (Apr. 1905).
2. Editorial, *New York Times* **IV,** 2 (Aug. 29, 1937).

Steven Bedford
Middlebury, Connecticut

PORTMAN, JOHN C.

John Calvin Portman, Jr. has gained an international reputation for his creative use of shared space and for his commitment to revitalizing the central business districts of major U.S. cities.

Born to John Calvin and Edna Rochester Portman on December 4, 1924 in Walhalla, South Carolina, he soon returned with his family to Atlanta, Georgia, where he was raised and educated.

Influenced by his mother's appreciation of art, he decided as a teenager to be an architect. At 15, rather than follow the typical college preparatory courses, he requested a transfer from O'Keefe High School to Atlanta's Tech High School to take architecture courses. Upon his graduation, he enlisted in the Navy and attended the U.S. Naval Academy. At the end of World War II in 1945, he transferred to the Georgia Institute of Technology, Atlanta, where he earned a Bachelor of Science degree in architecture in 1950.

As a student, he was strongly influenced by Frank Lloyd Wright, who was then a Visiting Lecturer at Georgia Tech. Portman adopted Wright's view that architecture is a comprehensive discipline that should give shape to all aspects of life. Wright awakened Portman to the writings of Emerson, whose self-reliant optimism is reflected in Portman's statements and actions, as is Wright's belief that the mission of architecture is to make a better world.

During that period, Portman worked part-time for New York architects Ketchum, Gina & Sharp, who were associated in Atlanta with H. M. Healy, architects. They were leading designers of department stores and shops, utilizing psychology in a very practical way, and making Portman mindful of how people react to their environment.

Upon graduation in 1950, he completed a three-year apprenticeship with Stevens and Wilkinson. At that point, he started his own firm with only one associate, John R. Street, Jr., now FAIA. In 1956, the firm merged with that of H. Griffith Edwards, a former professor of Portman's at Georgia Tech and an expert in construction specifications. The firm was Edwards and Portman until Edwards's retirement in 1968, after which it became John Portman & Associates.

In the early 1960s, two factors influenced Portman's career: his trip to Brasília and his combining the roles of architect and developer. In 1960, he was invited to attend the dedication of the new capital city of Brazil. Portman was eager to see the fully planned contemporary city, yet left sorely disappointed by its austerity and insensitivity to people. A strong statement of his design philosophy was articulated after that trip.

Successful architecture must be responsive to people and so recognize that people are all creatures of nature, drawn innately toward water, trees, and flowers. Portman also reflected on the architectural progression that had taken man from an agrarian society to an industrial one and had since progressed into an atomic age. The subject of the explosion of space and how to control it became extremely important in his work.

At the same time that Portman was clearly defining his design philosophy, he also took innovative business measures. He began to combine the roles of architect and developer. Eager to implement both design and business concepts, he built the Atlanta Merchandise Mart in 1961. The mart was the first building in Peachtree Center and became the key factor in the Atlanta Market Center complex, a separate Portman business enterprise, and an important factor in the architectural development of Portman's first mixed-use complex.

With the success of the Atlanta Merchandise Mart, followed by the construction of an adjacent office tower, Portman saw the need for a major downtown hotel. The construction of the Hyatt Regency Atlanta in 1967 revolutionized contemporary hotel design. Portman created a people-oriented place with great magnetic appeal. He "exploded" the interior of the 800-room hotel with a 22-story skylit atrium. He took the elevators out of their shafts and designed glass cabs that move like kinetic sculpture. The revolving rooftop restaurant was placed in a blue dome to give Atlanta's skyline a signature. The initial skepticism of hotel operators over the design concept was quickly outweighed by its huge financial success. Additions of 200 and 350 rooms were made to the hotel in 1972 and 1982, respectively.

While Portman was designing and developing Peachtree Center, he began work on two other large downtown complexes: Embarcadero Center in San Francisco, California, and Renaissance Center in Detroit, Michigan. They show the evolution toward integration of separate buildings into a single interdependent grouping or coordinate unit.

Portman's design for Embarcadero Center consists of a multilevel circulation spine connecting four office buildings, retail space, and a hotel with an enormous atrium, which plays an anchor role, analogous to that of a department store in a shopping center. The site was treated as a single entity, using broad pedestrian bridges to unify the retail space and decrease the vehicular congestion. Construction was phased over a 13-year period, from 1968 to 1981. The success of Embarcadero Center has had catalytic effect on the commercial development of that entire region of the city. In 1984, the Urban Land Institute recognized Embarcadero Center as the recipient of the prestigious Award of Excellence for Large Scale Mixed-Use Development.

Portman continued to design privately and developed an expansion to the project by adding a second hotel and a fifth office tower and by incorporating the refurbished Federal Reserve Building into the complex.

The Renaissance Center also had its beginnings in the early 1970s, when a consortium of 51 investors led by Henry Ford II asked Portman to design a complex that would rejuvenate the heart of Detroit. Portman created a 32-acre master plan that included office, retail, residential, and recreational components. The glimmering five-tower skyline signature included the 73-story Westin Detroit Plaza Hotel encircled by four 39-story office towers on a podium base of retail and parking space. The first phase opened in 1976. Two additional 22-story office towers were added in 1982, but the full master plan was not implemented.

In addition to large mixed-use complexes, Portman has designed individual buildings, which have also served as the impetus for urban redevelopment. Of note are the Westin Bonaventure Hotel in Los Angeles, a 1500-room convention hotel, and the New York Marriott Marquis, an 1877-room convention hotel in the heart of Times Square.

Portman's architectural career has been closely interfaced with his other business activities. As Chairman and Chief Executive Officer of ten firms within The Portman Companies, he has been able to expand his architectural concepts as well as direct their development and management.

In the 1980s, the companies placed a focused emphasis on East Asia and opened offices in Hong Kong, Singapore, and Shanghai, People's Republic of China. In addition to hotel and condominium projects, Portman designed and developed Marina Square (1987), a 4 million-ft² hotel/retail complex in Singapore, and Shanghai Centre (1989), a 2 million-ft² hotel, residential, office, exhibition, and recreational complex in Shanghai.

In the mid-1980s, Portman focused on his first major suburban project by beginning the design and development of Portman Barry Investments' first mixed-use complex, Northpark Town Center north of Atlanta.

In 1984, after years of designing hotels, Portman established the Portman Hotel Company to manage a select number of high-quality service-oriented properties. Its first hotel, The Portman-San Francisco, a Peninsula Hotel Group affiliate, opened in September 1987. The hotel company will also manage the hotels in Shanghai Centre and Northpark Town Center. Large or small, Portman's projects are focused on making a significant contribution to the communities they serve.

Portman is married to Joan (Jan) Newton, and they have six children: Michael, Jack, Jae, Jeff, Jana, and Jarel.

Portman serves as the Honorary Danish Consul. He has been the recipient of numerous awards and honors, including the AIA Medal for innovations in hotel design and the Silver Medal Award for innovative design from the Georgia Association of the AIA.

In 1976, Portman coauthored *The Architect as Developer* with Jonathan Barnett.

THE PORTMAN COMPANIES

The Portman family of companies began with John Portman's desire to create environments with a purpose—functional environments designed to lift the human spirit and satisfy human needs.

The Portman organization has grown from a two-man architectural firm in 1953 to a group of ten companies with over 1200 employees.

Working in response to client needs, the companies provide services tailored to varied situations. From architecture, engineering, and development to management and finance, many combinations of real estate-based services are available.

These companies combine a thorough knowledge of the marketplace with a commitment to quality service. Meeting the demands of the complex and competitive world of real estate, The Portman Companies stands as a leader in the industry.

THE PORTMAN COMPANIES
Atlanta, Georgia

POSTTENSIONED CONCRETE. See CONCRETE—POSTTENSIONING.

POWDER COATINGS

Powder coating is the fastest growing segment of the finishing industry today. Its share of the U.S. industrial coatings market is projected to more than double by 1995, with annual growth rates of 12–15% over the next 5 years. Currently, there are more than 2000 commercial powder-coating finishing lines in the United States, representing applications ranging from aluminum extrusions and cladding to metal furniture, appliances, automobile component parts and hundreds of other types of products. Between 3 and 5 million pounds of powder were used in 1987 by the U.S. architectural coating market, accounting for roughly 7% of the total powder-coating market.

A powder coating is a fine powder that fuses into a continuous film under heat. The dry powder is pneumatically fed from a supply reservoir to a spray gun, where a low amperage, high voltage charge is imparted to the powder particles. The powder is then sprayed onto the part to be finished (Fig. 1). The parts to be coated are electrically grounded so that the charged particles projected at them are firmly attracted to the part's surfaces and held there until melted and fused into a smooth coating in the baking ovens.

The coating process can be done manually or it can be a highly sophisticated automatic operation where computer programmed robots perform the spraying in booths up to 100 ft long. The wide variety of equipment available makes powder coating feasible for the small end-use manufacturer, as well as for the very large user who may require an extensive finishing operation for multiple products.

Recent improvements in application equipment and materials have enabled powder to produce smooth, durable finishes in thicknesses of 1–1.5 mils for building panels and aluminum extrusions. Powder coatings exhibit performance characteristics such as hardness, durability, and corrosion, chemical, and abrasion resistance that make them one of the most durable finishing options available.

Powder's durability and range of colors are helping it to gain popularity as a finishing technology for building components. In Europe, powder-coated architectural components dominate the market, but in the United States powder coating is still in its infancy in the architectural market. Although powder is already used on aluminum extrusions for a wide variety of high-performance applications, including window and door frames, interior partitions, ceiling panels, and shelving and ornamental facades and railings, more extensive use of the technology in building materials has been limited. One notable exception is a 27-story midrise office building in Oakland, Calif. Completed in 1985, the building contains a wide range of powder-coated components, including curtain walls, aluminum extrusions, door and window frames, and ceiling panels. Other buildings that extensively incorporate powder coatings include the Regents Two Building in La Jolla, California, which features powder-coated building panels, and the Embassy Suites Hotel in Birmingham, Alabama, featuring powder-coated railings (Figs. 2 and 3).

Powder coating's inroads into the U.S. architectural market have been fueled by increasingly stringent Environmental Protection Agency (EPA) regulations and escalating energy costs, which have prompted manufacturers to switch to more cost-effective compliance coatings such as powder.

Figure 1. Thermosetting powder coatings are typically applied using either automatic or manual electrostatic guns. Courtesy of the Powder Coating Institute.

ADVANTAGES

Manufacturers using today's powder coatings have realized a host of benefits. These are classified into what the Powder Coating Institute (PCI) terms, "The Four E's": excellence of finish, ecology, energy, and economy (1).

Excellence of Finish

Powder produces a uniform, durable finish with a deep color tone in just one coat and without the use of a primer. In addition to corrosion, chemical, and abrasion resistance, powder coatings resist handling abuse and adhere well to metal. Because powder is sprayed on in solid form and then melted, there are no drips and sags to cause rejects.

Ecology

Powder coating frees finishers from the environmental problems inherent in most liquid finishing systems. Powder contains no solvents, and thereby emits negligible if any, polluting volatile organic compounds into the atmosphere. Because oversprayed powder can be retrieved and recycled, hardly any solid waste is generated, eliminating the need to haul hazardous waste to burial sites.

Energy

Because venting of fumes from wet spray-paint solvent systems is not necessary, the need for air make-up—and

Figure 2. Regents Two Building, La Jolla, California. Courtesy of International Paint Company.

Figure 3. Embassy Suites Hotel, Birmingham, Alabama. Courtesy of International Paint Company.

the high costs for heating the air in colder climates—is greatly reduced, resulting in considerable energy savings.

Economy

The environmental advantages alone represent a significant economic advantage of powder, but many other on-line operating advantages combine with the environmental benefits to make powder even more cost-effective. Unused powder may be separated from the air stream by various vacuum and filtering methods and returned to a feed hopper for reuse, enabling efficiency-use rates to approach almost 100%. Labor costs run about 30% lower than with alternative solvent-based systems because the automated systems require less manpower. In addition, line speed can be increased because no drying or flash-off time is required; because there is no sludge or paint residue, clean-up costs are also significantly lower.

COMPARATIVE ECONOMICS

A model study of compliance technologies produced by the Powder Coating Institute for *Products Finishing* magazine illustrates powder's on-line operating advantages and favorable bottom-line economics. Using third quarter 1986 cost figures and economic data, PCI illustrated that the capital costs of powder were slightly higher than that of water-borne or high-solids systems (Table 1), yet the bottom-line operating costs proved to be less than the operating costs for conventional solvent, water-borne, and high-solids systems (Table 2) (2).

Table 1. Capital Costs

Type of Coating	Equipment	Installed Cost, $
Conventional solvent	2 Waterwash booths 1 Dry-filter booth 4 Automatic guns 2 Manual guns 2 Reciprocators Paint heating equipment Solvent recovery or burn-off equipment	150,000
Water-borne	2 Waterwash booths 1 Dry-filter booth 4 Automatic electrostatic guns 2 Manual electrostatic guns 2 Reciprocators Safety interlocks and stand-offs	110,000
High-solids	2 Waterwash booths 1 Dry-filter booth 4 Automatic electrostatic guns 2 Manual electrostatic guns Paint heating equipment	110,000
Powder	2 Powder spray booths 4 Automatic electrostatic guns 1 Manual electrostatic gun 2 Reciprocators or gun movers 2 Powder recovery systems with automatic recycle	120,000

PCI's study represented a standardized approach toward developing tangible costs on installing and operating VOC (volatile organic compounds) compliance lines. Operators of powder-coating lines continue to report a number of additional cost savings that are intangible and difficult to measure, such as minimum operator training and supervision for a powder line and employee preference in working with dry powder over other technologies.

TYPES OF POWDER COATINGS

Powder coatings fall into two broad categories: thermoplastic and thermosetting. Thermoplastic powders melt and flow under heat but do not change their chemical composition. Thermosetting coatings, on the other hand, change their chemical composition when heated.

Thermoplastic coatings are composed of high molecular weight resins that are difficult to grind to the small particles necessary for decorative applications and are predominantly used in functional applications where a thicker film is needed.

The majority of powder coatings used today are thermosetting powders based on epoxy, polyester, and acrylic resin systems. When heated in the presence of a curing agent, these low molecular weight resins fuse to a continuous film and then react chemically to form a smooth, uniform finish.

Thermosetting resins of different types are available to achieve the desired physical and decorative properties. Current resin technology provides coatings with abrasion resistance, scuff resistance, impact resistance, heat resistance, and outdoor weatherability. Thermosetting powder coatings are available in a variety of decorative finishes, including textured, low gloss, high gloss, wrinkle, smooth, clear, pigmented, and metallic.

Epoxy Resin Coatings

Epoxy powders are used for both functional and decorative coatings. The major functional applications are electrical-insulation coatings, pipe coatings, and coatings for the reinforcing steel bars used to support concrete bridges and decks. These functional coatings make the most of epoxy's outstanding insulative and corrosion-resistant properties.

Decorative epoxy coatings offer highly attractive coatings while still retaining the inherent toughness, corrosion resistance, flexibility, and adhesion characteristic of the epoxy family. Recent advances allow epoxy powder coatings to be cured at temperatures as low as 250°F for 20–50 min or for a very short time at higher temperatures. Epoxies are not recommended for use when the part is exposed to direct sunlight because of their tendency to chalk and discolor when exposed to ultraviolet radiation.

Polyester–Epoxy Hybrids

Hybrids offer better resistance to overbake yellowing and slightly better uv resistance than do standard epoxies.

Table 2. Total Annual Operating Costs Compared

Item	Conventional Solvent	Water-borne	High-solids	Powder
Material	$418,800	$427,200	$292,800	$327,600
Labor and clean-up	$141,900	$141,900	$141,900	$ 82,900
Maintenance	$ 24,000	$ 24,000	$ 24,000	$ 16,000
Energy	$ 30,500	$ 32,514	$ 28,300	$ 16,400
Sludge disposal	$ 48,758	$ 40,750	$ 31,500	$ 700
Amortization (10-yr straight line)	$ 15,000	$ 11,000	$ 11,000	$ 12,000
Total annual cost	$678,958	$677,364	$529,500	$455,600
Applied cost, ($/ft²)	0.0566	0.0564	0.0441	0.0380

They are softer than epoxies but maintain the good mechanical strength and corrosion resistance that is characteristic of epoxies. Hybrids have excellent transfer efficiency and penetrate well into the corners and recesses of a part that is difficult to coat.

Polyesters

There are two types of thermosetting polyester resins. The first is cured with a urethane cross-linker and produces smooth coatings in thicknesses ranging from 1 to 1.5 mils that demonstrate good adhesion, flexibility and corrosion and weathering resistance, making them excellent candidates for outdoor applications.

The second type of polyester is cured with TGIC (triglycidyl isocyanurate). It has been particularly popular in European exterior applications. Coatings formulated using polyester TGIC resins offer excellent outdoor durability and mechanical properties at high film thicknesses, good corrosion protection, good edge coverage, low temperature cure, and very good transfer efficiency performance.

Acrylic-Urethane Resins

Coatings formulated with acrylic resin cross-linked with isocyanates have excellent color, gloss, hardness, and outdoor exposure and chemical resistance. They are characterized by excellent thin-film appearance while maintaining good film flexibility. They do display less flexibility than polyesters, but in most cases will pass impacts that would deform the metal and ruin a fabricated piece.

Table 3 provides a general breakdown of the thermosetting coatings available on the market and their features (3). A powder-coating supplier should be consulted for specific information relevant to particular applications.

ARCHITECTURAL COATING SPECIFICATIONS

The Architectural Aluminum Manufacturers Association (AAMA) sets recommended standards for coatings used in residential and commercial building applications; AAMA 603 specifications apply to residential markets; AAMA 605 specifications provide guidelines for commercial markets.

Powder coatings can meet the AAMA 603 specifications and most of the AAMA 605 specifications except tests for 5-yr Florida exposure. Current testing indicates that acrylic and polyester systems will last at least 12–24 months in Florida while retaining acceptable gloss and color (4).

According to David E. Miles of The Glidden Company, "current powder technology can produce coatings with Florida durability of one to two years. . . . The European market, which is mainly high gloss colors and in the north latitudes, has powders that still look excellent after ten years in the field. The U.S. market, which has many locations which receive extreme sun, is more demanding. . . . The future calls for improved gloss reduction techniques and five years Florida durability." (4)

DEVELOPMENTS AND TRENDS IN POWDER-COATING MATERIALS

When powder coating was first used in the 1950s in North America, the technology was limited in terms of colors, thicknesses, exterior durability, and product applications. Today, manufacturers have developed solutions to earlier problems, and research continues at an impressive rate to refine and improve current technology.

Experimentation with resin systems have resulted in a number of specific advances including the following:

- *Thin layer powder coatings.* Thin-layer powder coatings based on epoxy–polyester hybrids provide applications in the range of 1–1.2 mils for colors with good hiding power. These thin coatings are suitable only for indoor applications.
- *Low temperature powder coatings.* Powder coatings with very high reactivity have been developed to cure at temperatures as low as 250°. Such low-curing powders makes it possible to run higher line speeds, thereby increasing production capacity. More systems are now relying on powders formulated to bake at low temperatures without sacrificing exterior durability.
- *Texture powder coatings.* Powder coatings have been developed in a variety of textures, from a fine texture

Table 3. Thermosetting Powder Coatings

Typical Properties	Epoxy	Polyester A[a]	Polyester B[a]	Epoxy/Polyester Hybrid	Acrylic
Application thickness	1–10 mils[b]	1–3.5 mils	1–10 mils	1–10 mils	1–3.5 mils
Bake cycle (metal temperature)	450°F, 3 min[c]	430°F, 7 min	430°F, 7 min	450°F, 3 min	400°F, 10 min
	250°F, 25 min	360°F, 16 min	350°F, 16 min	325°F, 25 min	350°F, 25 min
Outdoor weatherability	Poor	Good	Very good	Poor	Good
Pencil hardness	HB-5H	HB-2H	HB-2H	HB-2H	2H-5H
Impact resistance (in./lb)	60–160	60–160	60–160	60–160	20–120
Adhesion (without primer)	Excellent	Excellent	Excellent	Excellent	Excellent
Chemical resistance	Excellent	Excellent	Excellent	Excellent	Excellent
Solvent resistance	Excellent	Good	Good	Good	Good

[a]A—urethane cured. B—glycidyl (TGIC) cured.
[b]Thickness of up to 150 mils can be applied via multiple coats in fluidized bed.
[c]Time and temperature can be reduced via lower curing mechanisms yielding the same general properties.

with low gloss and high abrasion and scratch resistance to a rough texture useful for hiding the unevenness of substrates.

- *Low gloss powder coatings.* Today's technology makes it possible to reduce gloss values without diminishing the flexibility, mechanical properties, or appearance of powder coatings. Currently, it is possible to get gloss values down to 3% in pure epoxies. The lowest gloss in weather-resistant polyester systems is about 20%.

- *Metallic powder coatings.* A special process is now available in which metallic flakes are blended into the powder coating and sprayed onto a part. Many of these metallic systems are suitable for outdoor applications; but for superior exterior durability, a clear top coat is often applied over the metallic base. Lately, efforts are concentrated on developing perfect matches for standard anodizing colors to meet the needs of the aluminum extrusion market.

Powder manufacturers are continuing to work toward perfecting resin and curing-agent designs. Particular emphasis is being placed on developing exterior durable powders that meet 5-yr Florida exposure test requirements.

To date, a field application system has not been developed to apply thermosetting powder coatings at a site. However, a field application system for functional thermoplastic application has been recently put on the market and is undergoing tests.

TRENDS AND DEVELOPMENTS IN POWDER-COATING-APPLICATION EQUIPMENT

Improvements in powder-coating material have been accompanied by major advances in applications and recovery-equipment technology. Most anticipated changes will reduce the cost of powder-coating systems and make powder-coating spray and reclaim booths more compact. New booth designs now in use enable aluminum extrusions to be hung vertically for higher productivity and more efficient coating of extrusions up to 30 ft long (5).

Another major focus of equipment manufacturers has been increasing quick color-change capabilities. Because powder coating allows very favorable material use through the recovery of oversprayed material, it has been necessary to clean the booth and spray apparatus when changing colors. Previously, this color-change process could take as long as an hour, but recent breakthroughs in equipment design have greatly reduced color-change times.

Research and development efforts have also been focused on improving the transfer efficiency of electrostatic powder systems. New gun designs and improvements in charging methods have already increased the overall efficiency of powder systems. It is possible that new developments in application equipment will eventually eliminate the need for powder reclaim/recycling systems.

With the impetus provided by improved formulations and application characteristics, increasingly stringent EPA regulations that favor pollution-free powder coatings, and recognition that powder provides an outstanding combination of protective and decorative properties, powder is emerging as a significant finishing technology. Industry experts are optimistic that powder coating will become the finishing technology of choice within the metal building industry in the near future.

BIBLIOGRAPHY

1. Powder Coating Institute, *Powder Coatings,* Washington, D.C., 1984, reprinted 1987.
2. G. Bocchi, *Products Finishing,* 66 (April 6, 1987).
3. R. Farrell, *Products Finishing Directory 1988,* p. 41.
4. D. Miles, "High Performance Exterior Durable Powder Coatings," *Finishing '87 Conference Papers,* Society of Manufacturing Engineers Dearborn, Mich p. FC87-624-6.
5. D. Tyler, *Innovations in Powder Coating Booth Design for Architectural Aluminum Extrusions,* paper delivered at Aluminum Finishing '87, Ft. Mitchell, Ky. 1986.

General References

E. Miller, ed., *User's Guide to Powder Coatings, 2nd ed.,* Society of Manufacturing Engineers, Dearborn, Mich. 1987. One of the most comprehensive and easily understandable general references available.

Powder Coating Institute, *Technical Briefs,* Powder Coating Institute, Alexandria, Va., 1987. Concise briefs drafted by PCI's technical committee on topics including powder-coating materials, terms, and definitions and health and safety.

E. Bodnar, *Development of Polyester Powder Coating Systems for Outdoor Architectural Applications in Europe: A 15-Year Overview,* paper presented at the Fourth International Aluminum Extrusion Technology Seminar, Chicago, Ill, April, 1988. Good overview of European use of powder coatings in architectural market.

See also ALUMINUM; CORROSION; PAINTS AND COATINGS

GREGORY J. BOCCHI
Powder Coating Institute
Alexandria, Virginia

POWER GENERATION, FOSSIL FUELS

In the United States, the principal source of electric power is fossil-fired steam electric or thermal power stations. In these stations, the chemical release of heat is used to produce steam in a large steam generator. The steam is then used to drive a turbine–generator unit that produces the electricity. The chemical release of heat is achieved by the controlled burning of fossil fuels, such as coal, oil, or natural gas. Other heat sources have been used in the past, such as wood, and new sources are being considered for the future, such as trash and coal–water mixtures.

Fossil-fired thermal power stations have effectively provided the majority of electricity generation in the United States for many decades. In recent years, however, environmental concerns have been raised about their emissions of carbon dioxide (greenhouse effect), sulfur dioxide and oxides of nitrogen (acid rain effect), particulates, and other emissions produced by the combusted fuels. These concerns have led to significant changes and evolution in the configuration, design, performance, and cost of fossil power plants.

The type of fuel burned in a fossil-fired steam electric power plant has a significant impact on the plant design and on its construction and operating costs. Although coal is the cheapest fuel, its use requires major design features to handle the fuel and its wastes (scrubber sludge and ash) and to control the emission of pollutants. Natural gas, on the other hand, requires the simplest fuel-handling design features and burns cleanly, but is the most expensive fuel and requires the most sophisticated combustion control features.

Coal-fired Power Plant

Coal burning requires an extensive combustion control system, bulk materials-handling system, particulate removal system, flue-gas desulfurization system, and waste disposal system. The combustion control system, in addition to controlling the flow of fuel and air into the steam generator and the ignition of the fuel–air mixture, also controls the oxides of nitrogen by minimizing the excess air required for complete combustion. The materials-handling system provides high capacity coal receiving, storage, reclaiming, preparation (for firing), feeding, and consumption measuring facilities. The particulate removal system provides the facility to remove the required quantity of particulates and fines from the steam generator flue-gas stream. The flue-gas desulfurization system (scrubber) is a complex chemical process facility that removes the required quantity of sulfur from the flue-gas stream. The waste disposal system receives the collected particulates and scrubber residue, combines the ash and scrubber sludge, and processes the resulting mixture for off-site disposal in an approved disposal site. An additional burden is placed on the plant waste-water processing system in a coal-fired power plant because of the presence of the stored coal. This system's hold-up and processing capacity must be capable of handling the collected acidic rainwater runoff from the coal storage pile.

Generally, the above mentioned facilities increase the required power-plant land area by 2–3 times. These facilities also increase the electrical demand on the plant auxiliary power system, reducing the net plant output by several percent. The plant exhaust stack, which may have a total height of several hundred meters or more, may also be affected to the extent that an internal corrosive-resistant liner is required.

Oil-fired Power Plant

Fuel-oil burning requires a bulk materials-handling system that is less extensive than that for coal burning, and it may also require a particulate removal system. The materials-handling system provides relatively simple fuel-oil receiving, storage, feeding, and consumption measuring facilities. The particulate removal system, when required, collects the required quantity of particles from the flue-gas stream. These facilities generally increase the required land area for the power plant by ca 25–50% and have a power demand that decreases the plant net output by a fraction of a percent.

Gas-fired Power Plants

Natural-gas burning requires only a gas pipeline connection and a pressure reducing, regulating, and metering station. These facilities require no significant amount of additional land nor electric power. Consequently, the construction and operating (not including the cost of fuel) costs and the net plant output are not significantly affected by the fuel facilities in a natural-gas-fired power plant. Because of the potential hazards associated with using natural gas as a fuel, however, necessary safety features tend to make the boiler and combustion control system more complex than for either the coal or oil-fired units.

FOSSIL POWER PLANT DESIGN

Although the following discussion focuses on coal-fired power plants, it is also applicable to oil- and natural-gas-fired power plants except for the fuel-related differences discussed above.

Basic Power Plant

There are two major categories of fossil power plants in use today; those that operate at subcritical steam pressures and temperatures and those that operate at supercritical pressures and temperatures. Typical steam generator pressures and temperatures at rated load are

	Pressure, psig	Temperature, °F
Subcritical units	2400	1000
Supercritical units	3500–4000	1000–1100

Supercritical units generally have higher plant efficiencies than subcritical units but require the use of more expensive materials and larger wall sections on pressure-retaining parts to withstand the stresses imposed by the higher pressure/temperature regimes. In either type of unit, water is pumped through vertical tubes in the walls of the steam generator (water walls) where the heat of combustion of the fuel is transferred to the water primarily by radiation. The water is evaporated along the tubes and collected at the top of the steam generator. The saturated steam is then passed through additional tube bundles in the hot gas stream where it is superheated by radiation and/or convection. The superheated steam is then conveyed to the turbine–generator unit where it expands through the high pressure turbine yielding energy to provide the torque required to drive the electric generator. The steam is returned from the high pressure turbine to the steam generator for reheating in the reheater tube section and then expands through the intermediate and low pressure turbines, providing additional torque to drive the generator. Low pressure, low temperature steam exits from the low pressure turbines to the main condenser where it is condensed to water. The condensers are cooled by water in the condenser tubes, which is pumped from and is returned to a heat sink (a cooling tower, cooling pond, or river). The condensate is then pumped through feed-water heaters where it is gradually reheated and deaerated to the level required for injection into the steam generator water-wall tubes. The feed-water is heated by steam extracted at appropriate pressures and temperatures from various points on the main turbine.

Regulations

In the United States, the design of fossil power plants is based on rules, regulations, and requirements promulgated by the Environmental Protection Agency (EPA), the U.S. Corps of Engineers, various agencies of the states in which the power plants are located, mandatory codes, and national standards.

The most significant regulatory control is exercised by the EPA under the Environmental Policy Act of 1969. These regulations govern the discharge of pollutants from any point source into the air or water. Levels of pollutants are required to be controlled by the plant design and monitored for compliance during operation. A federal and/or state environmental impact statement must be developed by the EPA and/or state for each facility based on reports prepared by the facility owner. Other major regulatory programs affecting fossil power-plant design and construction include

- Prevention of Significant Deterioration (PSD) and New Source Performance Standards (NSPS) regulating air-quality impacts.
- State 401 Certification (water intake and discharge) and Corps of Engineers 404 permit (dredge-and-fill operation in navigable waterway) for impact to water and navigation.
- National (or State) Pollution Discharge Elimination System (NPDES/SPDES) permit for discharging liquid effluent into surface waters.

In 1979, the New Source Performance Standards, promulgated by EPA, introduced the concept of "Best Available Control Technology" (BACT). This set of regulations required that power-plant and other facility emissions must be controlled by the BACT that was commercially available at the initiation of plant design. A monetary level is set in dollars per ton of removed pollutant that establishes whether a BACT is cost effective and, therefore, mandatory to apply. The EPA has the option of adjusting this dollar value upward or downward, depending on a case-by-case evaluation of the existing pollution level, the potential for the facility to pollute, and the site conditions that might exacerbate the level of pollution.

In the plant design, various industry standards are applied to establish a basis for quality, maintainability, and operability or to meet personnel and property safety concerns. Such standards include those promulgated by the American Society of Mechanical Engineers (ASME), the American Society for Testing Materials (ASTM), the Institute of Electrical and Electronics Engineers (IEEE), and the National Fire Protection Association (NFPA). The ASME Boiler and Pressure Vessel Code and the NFPA National Electrical Code are examples of industry standards invoked as mandatory for safety considerations by local political jurisdictions.

Site Selection

The selection of a site for a power plant is a screening process that takes into consideration a variety of economic and technical concerns. The general geographic location is determined by transmission network (load-flow and system stability) considerations and the availability and cost of land. Specific considerations include suitability of soil conditions, site meteorology, availability of water, transportation and transmission line access, potential for support of construction by local political and social infrastructure, local tax rates, regional availability of construction craft skills, and regional labor relations and contracts. A variety of potential sites may be considered and evaluated over a 6- to 12-month period before a prime and alternative site are selected.

In many states, a site certification process is required, which adds another dimension to the site selection process. The site certification review may need to satisfy any or all of the following:

- Compatibility with the state's master plan for the development of energy resources.
- A demonstration that the power plant will be needed.
- A study showing that the selected power-plant site is preferable to other sites considered.
- Field monitoring and sampling data characterizing the environmental conditions at the site.

Fossil Power Plant Complex of Structures

A typical fossil power plant will include the following major structures and facilities:

- Steam generator building.
- Turbine, feed-water heater, and control building.
- Flue-gas desulfurization facilities (coal-fired).
- Fuel-handling and storage facilities (coal- or oil-fired).
- Stack structure.
- Circulating water pump house.
- Cooling towers and/or intake structure.
- Electrical switch-gear facilities (included in other buildings as required).
- Water treatment building.
- Waste-water treatment facility.

In support of these structures and facilities, additional facilities are provided in the above or in separate buildings for the following activities:

- Administration and operation (offices).
- Plant security (guard station).
- Warehousing (materials/equipment handling and storage).
- Maintenance (shops).
- Laboratories (water treatment, process sampling, etc).
- Personnel service (locker rooms, lunchrooms, showers).
- Effluent discharge monitoring.
- Meteorologic monitoring.

Design Bases

The various buildings that make up the fossil power plant complex are not all designed to the same criteria. The development of the configuration and the selection of the materials of construction for each building are based on the economical and safe operation of the plant and various combinations of the following criteria:

- Emission limitation requirements.
- Environmental protection (sun, rain, snow, heat, wind, dust).
- Flood protection or mitigation requirements.
- Fire protection.
- Noise abatement.
- Accessibility.

FACILITIES DESCRIPTION

Fossil power plant buildings are generally fully enclosed; however, in some mild climate regions of the United States, steam generators and turbine–generator decks are not enclosed. Superstructures typically have braced steel frames, insulated or uninsulated metal siding with an integral liner, and concrete channel plank roofs with elastomeric coatings. In some cases, roof decks may be cast-in-place concrete with waterproofing treatment or standing-seam metal type. Substructures may be reinforced concrete slabs or reinforced concrete spread footings. Grating floors supported on steel framing are used where possible to allow maximum air circulation. Office, locker room, and lunchroom areas generally have acoustical tile suspended ceilings. Buildings are ventilated by powered roof ventilators, supply/exhaust fan systems, or wall fans with or without filters as required. In coal and lime (scrubber sorbent) handling areas, electrical equipment rooms are kept at positive internal pressure to exclude coal or lime dust. Heating is often provided by steam unit heaters or steam coils in supply-air fan ducts. Supplemental heating is provided by electric baseboard, wall, and unit heaters. Air-conditioning, where required for personnel comfort or to meet material storage or equipment operating requirements, is provided by chilled water coils in supply-air fan ducts. Each building and the yard area is provided with drainage systems to provide controlled runoff of rainwater and collection of dirty, oily, or contaminated water for treatment before discharge from the site.

Yardwork

Figure 1 provides an overall plot plan of a typical 500-megawatt-electric (MWe) coal-fired power plant. Yard facilities include a coal storage area, fuel-oil storage tank (for the auxiliary/start-up boiler), condensate storage tanks, waste-water holding basins, sewage treatment facilities, plant switchyard, main transformer area, access roadways, rail sidings, outdoor lighting, plant fencing, and site access control.

Steam-Generator Building

The steam-generator building is the largest building on a fossil plant site and may reach heights on large units of 300–350 ft. This building is shown on the plot plan in Figure 1 and also in an enlarged cross section in Figure 2. In the design shown, the steam-generator building consists of the boiler house, auxiliary boiler room, air-compressor room, emergency diesel-generator room, and forced-draft fan room.

In a coal-fired power plant, the boiler house also contains the head end of the reclaim coal conveyors, day storage silos, coal feed and metering equipment, and the coal pulverizers. For oil-fired units, fuel oil pump and heater sets are contained in the boiler house. Coal-handling areas and storage silos are separately ventilated and provided with dust-suppression systems.

The auxiliary boiler room houses the auxiliary boiler and its accessory equipment. The auxiliary boiler provides steam to the auxiliary steam system during start-up and at other times when turbine extraction steam is not available. The auxiliary steam system distributes extraction or auxiliary boiler steam for building heating, miscellaneous heating, freeze protection, start-up services, and other needs for low pressure steam.

The air-compressor room houses the station air compressors, receivers, air driers and accessories, and the boiler roof fire water booster pumps In the case of coal-fired and oil-fired power plants, it may also house soot-blower air compressors (where steam soot-blowers are not used).

The emergency diesel-generator room houses the plant emergency power diesel-generator units and accessories. The forced-draft fan room houses the forced-draft (secondary air) fans, primary air fans for coal-fired units, inlet air silencers, combustion air preheating steam coils, and accessories. The room serves as an air plenum for the fans located therein.

Some major boiler equipment is located in the yard area just outside the steam-generator building. These include the primary air heaters for a coal-fired plant and secondary air heaters, the electrostatic precipitators for coal or oil-fired plants, the induced draft fans, the flue-gas desulfurization system booster fans, and the interconnecting ductwork.

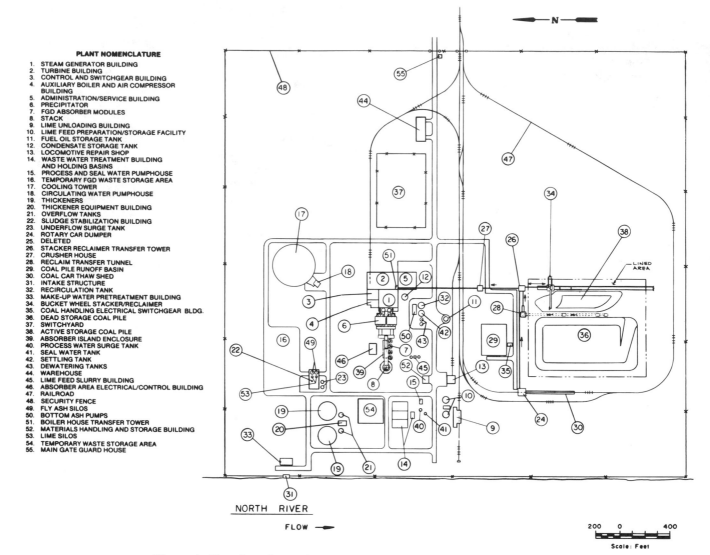

PLANT NOMENCLATURE

1. STEAM GENERATOR BUILDING
2. TURBINE BUILDING
3. CONTROL AND SWITCHGEAR BUILDING
4. AUXILIARY BOILER AND AIR COMPRESSOR
   BUILDING
5. ADMINISTRATION/SERVICE BUILDING
6. PRECIPITATOR
7. FGD ABSORBER MODULES
8. STACK
9. LIME UNLOADING BUILDING
10. LIME FEED PREPARATION/STORAGE FACILITY
11. FUEL OIL STORAGE TANK
12. CONDENSATE STORAGE TANK
13. LOCOMOTIVE REPAIR SHOP
14. WASTE WATER TREATMENT BUILDING
    AND HOLDING BASINS
15. PROCESS AND SEAL WATER PUMPHOUSE
16. TEMPORARY FGD WASTE STORAGE AREA
17. COOLING TOWER
18. CIRCULATING WATER PUMPHOUSE
19. THICKENERS
20. THICKENER EQUIPMENT BUILDING
21. OVERFLOW TANKS
22. SLUDGE STABILIZATION BUILDING
23. UNDERFLOW SURGE TANK
24. ROTARY CAR DUMPER
25. DELETED
26. STACKER RECLAIMER TRANSFER TOWER
27. CRUSHER HOUSE
28. RECLAIM TRANSFER TUNNEL
29. COAL PILE RUNOFF BASIN
30. COAL CAR THAW SHED
31. INTAKE STRUCTURE
32. RECIRCULATION TANK
33. MAKE-UP WATER PRETREATMENT BUILDING
34. BUCKET WHEEL STACKER/RECLAIMER
35. COAL HANDLING ELECTRICAL SWITCHGEAR BLDG.
36. DEAD STORAGE COAL PILE
37. SWITCHYARD
38. ACTIVE STORAGE COAL PILE
39. ABSORBER ISLAND ENCLOSURE
40. PROCESS WATER SURGE TANK
41. SEAL WATER TANK
42. SETTLING TANK
43. DEWATERING TANKS
44. WAREHOUSE
45. LIME FEED SLURRY BUILDING
46. ABSORBER AREA ELECTRICAL/CONTROL BUILDING
47. RAILROAD
48. SECURITY FENCE
49. FLY ASH SILOS
50. BOTTOM ASH PUMPS
51. BOILER HOUSE TRANSFER TOWER
52. MATERIALS HANDLING AND STORAGE BUILDING
53. LIME SILOS
54. TEMPORARY WASTE STORAGE AREA
55. MAIN GATE GUARD HOUSE

NORTH RIVER

FLOW →

200   0   400

Scale: Feet

Figure 1. Plot plan of typical 500-MWe high sulfur coal-fired power plant (1).

Turbine, Feed-Water, Heater, and Control Building

The turbine–generator hall and feed-water heater bay are located next to the boiler house. The building houses the turbine–generator unit, its condensers and associated equipment, feed-water and deaerating heaters, boiler feed-water pumps, condensate pumps, condensate polishing and demineralizing equipment, turbine electrohydraulic control and lubrication-oil equipment, and other auxiliary equipment. The turbine hall is served by a large bridge crane and a railroad receiving bay. The turbine, heater, and control building shown in Figures 1 and 2 has a volume of nearly 4 million ft³.

The turbine–generator unit pedestal is a generally massive reinforced concrete structure supported on a thick reinforced concrete slab (high-tuned pedestal) and is completely isolated from the remainder of the building for vibration control. The main condenser is supported by that part of the foundation that is below the low-pressure turbines. The high-tuned pedestal, in addition to supporting the turbine–generator unit and condenser, is designed with a natural frequency above the machine operating speed and to resist overturning moments created by elec-

trical faults. Low-tuned pedestals, which have a natural frequency below the machine operating speed, are not in general use in the United States.

The control and switch-gear building is located next to the turbine hall and adjacent to the steam-generator building. This building houses the main control room, instrumentation and control (I&C) cabinet room, computer room, cable-spreading room (below the main control and I&C cabinet rooms), shift offices, auxiliary power system main switch-gear area, and station battery rooms. The control-room equipment provides the human–machine interface between the station operators and the power plant systems and equipment. This interface provides control access and data displays for monitoring and protecting the plant, personnel, and equipment and for operating the various parts of the power plant for greatest efficiency and highest availability.

Flue-Gas Desulfurization Facilities

The flue-gas desulfurization (FGD) facilities are auxiliary to the boiler plant in a coal-fired power plant. (The FGD system discussed is a wet-lime type, which is currently the

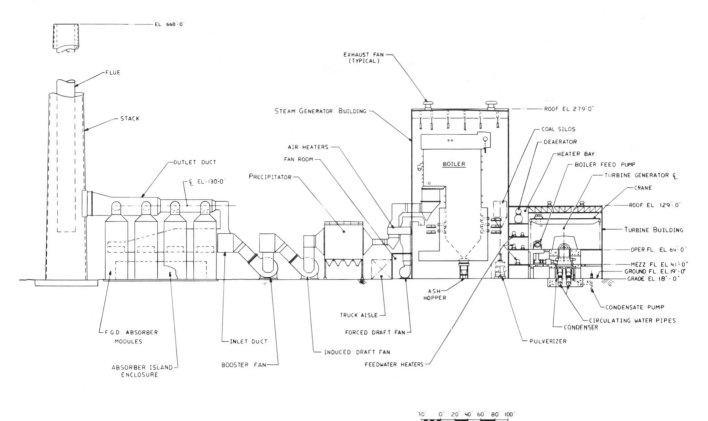

Figure 2. Cross section of typical 500-MWe high sulfur coal fired power plant (1).

most prevalent type in use; however, as technical problems are resolved, lower cost wet limestone scrubbers will increase in use.) They consist of the following buildings and structures:

- Lime unloading building.
- Lime feed-preparation and storage facilities.
- Lime preparation electrical and control building.
- Lime feed slurry building.
- Absorber island enclosure.
- Absorber island electrical and control building.
- Thickener equipment building.
- Sludge stabilization building and stack-out area.
- Process and seal water pump house.

The flue-gas desulfurization system is designed to remove sulfur dioxide (SO_2) from the flue-gas stream and produce a comixed fly ash/FGD waste product suitable for landfill disposal. The wet-lime process consists of a lime receiving and storage facility, a lime slurry preparation system, an SO_2 absorber system, a waste slurry thickening system, a waste stabilization system, and a water-distribution system. The wet-lime slurry is brought into intimate contact with the SO_2 in the flue gas in the absorber modules where 90% of the sulfur is absorbed and removed with the waste slurry. Some units have recently come on-line with removal efficiencies that are in the range of 95%.

Fuel-handling and Storage Facilities

The coal-handling and storage system is also auxiliary to the boiler plant and is composed of three parts: unloading, storage and stacking/reclaiming, and feed to the boiler. The system facilities consist of the following buildings and structures:

- Coal car thaw shed.
- Rotary car dumper and tunnel.
- Stacker/reclaimer transfer tower.
- Traveling stacker/reclaimer.
- Coal storage pile, liner and dikes, and water runoff holding basin.
- Dead storage reclaim hoppers and tunnels.
- Coal-crusher house.
- Boiler house transfer tower.
- Coal silos and feed equipment.
- Coal pulverizers (roller mills).
- Coal-handling/storage facility interconnecting conveyor galleries, support trusses, and bents.

The unloading facilities for the 500-MWe power plant are sized to unload a 100-car-unit train of 100-ton-capacity coal hoppers in an 8-h shift. The cars are thawed, if necessary, dumped one at a time without uncoupling (one end of each car is furnished with a rotating coupling), and the coal is conveyed to the stacker/reclaimer transfer tower. From that point it is conveyed to either the coal storage pile via the stacker/reclaimer or to the boiler house coal silos via the crusher house and boiler house transfer tower. The storage facilities are sized to store a 60-day supply of uncrushed coal. The coal pile is shaped, compacted, trimmed, and repiled as required by a 100-ton bulldozer and several smaller front-end loaders. The bulldozer and front-end loaders also assist in reclaiming operations. The traveling stacker/reclaimer feeds the storage pile with a boom conveyor fed from the reversible stacker/reclaimer conveyor. It also reclaims from the pile with a bucket wheel that feeds the stacker/reclaimer conveyor operating in the reverse direction.

Coal feed to the boiler is from storage via the stacker/reclaimer or from the car dumper. The coal passes through the crushers in the crusher house where it is reduced in size before being conveyed to the 8-h coal silos. Coal is fed from the silos by vibrating feeders and belt coal scales to the pulverizers in accordance with demand instructions from the combustion control system.

The fine-pulverized coal is blown from the pulverizers by heated air from the primary air fans through coal pipes to the coal burners. The burners are arranged in several rows on the front and rear of the boiler, with the burners in each row fed from a single pulverizer. The burner assemblies also contain igniters and fuel-oil guns for burner start-up and firing stabilization at low loads.

Other Major Buildings

The circulating water pump house is a reinforced concrete structure connected to the reinforced concrete cooling tower basin with a reinforced concrete flume. The structure provides separate bays for each of the vertical circulating water pumps and for the vertical service water pumps. A masonry equipment room is provided adjacent to the pump house that houses the circulating water chlorination system and required local instrument racks and electrical power-distribution equipment.

The cooling tower is generally a reinforced concrete structure and may be of either the natural or mechanical draft type. The natural draft type is hyperbolic in cross section, using natural circulation of air and a film-type fill to expose maximum surface of the hot water to the air. Air circulation in the mechanical draft type of tower is forced by the operation of large fans. Natural-draft towers are very large structures (the tower in Fig. 1 is 420-ft high and has a basin diameter of 350 ft) and are more expensive than mechanical draft towers. Mechanical draft towers reduce plant output, however, because of the power required to drive the fans.

The make-up water intake structure is located on a river or other body of water. Where a river is used as the source of circulating water, the circulating water pump house and make-up water intake structures would be combined and the cooling tower would be eliminated. The make-up water intake structure is of reinforced concrete construction and provides separate bays for the make-up water pumps and the plant fire pumps. Each bay is provided with a traveling screen and a trash rack to protect the vertical pump intakes from debris.

The make-up water pretreatment building is located near the intake structure. This building houses the strainers, clarifiers, chemical feed equipment, sludge dewatering equipment, circulating water system sulfuric acid feed equipment, and other components required for a complete water pretreatment system.

The waste-water treatment facility consists of three collection basins, a clarifier and various pumps, tanks, chemical feeds, mixers, pressure filters, and sludge dewatering devices. The treatment system treats normal operating wastes from the plant, rainfall runoff from contaminated areas, metal-cleaning wastes, and emergency FGD system blow down so that they will be suitable for discharge or re-use.

Support Buildings

The administration and service building houses the machine shop, equipment rooms, service shops, storage areas, locker and change rooms, showers, toilet rooms, lunchroom, laboratories, general offices, security offices, and conference rooms. The building also houses an on-site emergency vehicle.

The materials-handling and service building houses service shops, offices, storage areas, lunchroom, toilet rooms, and shower rooms. The building serves as a combined warehouse and heavy equipment repair and maintenance facility.

The vehicle repair shop and garage facility houses a repair area and garage facility for the on-site diesel-operated heavy equipment and service vehicles. A pit is provided for serving under the coal-pile bulldozer.

CONSTRUCTION CONSIDERATIONS

A median construction schedule for a 500-MWe coal-fired power plant is about 4 yr, based on a single 8-h daily work shift and a 40-h week. The associated average labor force is about 1000 with a peak force of about 1750. The construction phase of a coal-fired power plant is more predictable than the preconstruction (site certification and regulatory interface) activities because of decades of construction experience. Factors such as climate, geology, and fuel type, however, can affect the time required for construction.

The critical path for a coal-fired power plant runs through site selection and regulatory review up to the start of construction. Then it shifts to site preparation, boiler-house foundations and erection of the boiler, and preoperational testing. Construction of the other buildings and systems may be accomplished within the timing of the critical path. Circumstances can sometimes arise that cause the noncritical activities to become critical and extend the overall duration. These circumstances include late delivery of major equipment as a result of unavailability of raw materials, over-extended fabrication facilities, expiration of shop labor contracts, wildcat strikes, or failure of equipment under shop or acceptance tests.

BIBLIOGRAPHY

1. *Energy Economic Data Base (EEDB) Program, EEDB Program Technical Reference Book, Phase IX Update (1987),* United Engineers & Constructors Inc., Philadelphia, Pa., UE&C/ORNL-870615, *Martin Marietta Subcontract No. 30X-86004V,* June 1987.

General References

Ref. 1 is a good general reference.

Steam, It's Generation and Use, The Babcock and Wilcox Company, New York, latest edition.

A Reference Book on Fuel Burning and Steam Generation, Combustion Engineering, Inc., New York, latest edition.

Energy Technology Handbook, McGraw-Hill Inc., New York, latest edition.

Marks Standard Handbook for Mechanical Engineers, McGraw-Hill Inc., New York, latest edition.

Standard Handbook for Electrical Engineers, McGraw-Hill Inc., New York, latest edition.

See also POWER GENERATION–GEOTHERMAL, NUCLEAR, WIND, TIDAL

RUSSELL E. ALLEN
Cherry Hill, New Jersey

POWER GENERATION, GEOTHERMAL

Geothermal energy, the heat of the earth, originates in the earth's molten or near-molten interior and from the decay of radioactive materials in the earth's crust. Although geothermal energy can be found everywhere, because of its diffuse nature it can be extracted economically only where it is concentrated anomalously near the surface. Such concentrations are often manifested as hot springs, geysers, fumaroles, and volcanoes.

Geothermal fluids have been used since antiquity for bathing, heating, cooking, recreational, medicinal, and religious purposes. In the late 1800s, geothermal heat was first used in industry to evaporate water from geothermal brines at Larderello, Italy, facilitating the recovery of boron compounds. Electricity was produced for the first time from geothermal resources at Larderello in 1904 when a three-quarter horsepower generator was operated on dry steam from a geothermal reservoir. In 1913, a 250-kW plant was placed in commercial operation there. By 1940, the electrical-generating capacity at Larderello had increased to 130 MW; by 1985, it was more than 440 MW (the kilowatt (kW) and megawatt (MW) numbers given are the nameplate capacities of the generators installed, representing the maximum capacity of the plant; typical operating conditions may be somewhat lower). The first commercial geothermal electrical plant (12 MW) in the United States was installed in 1960 at The Geysers, located 120 km north of San Francisco, California (1,2). By 1985, The Geysers field had grown to approximately 1800 MW and was the largest geothermal power plant complex in the world.

The installed capacity of geothermal power plants throughout the world is shown in Table 1, taken from Ref. 3. The capacity increased from 1759 MW in 1979 to 4764 MW in June 1985, an annual growth rate of more than 17% (3). Most of this growth has occurred in the United States, the Philippines, Mexico, Italy, Japan, and New Zealand. Significant growth has also taken place in El Salvador, Kenya, Iceland, Nicaragua, and Indonesia.

TYPES OF GEOTHERMAL RESOURCES

Geothermal resources can be conveniently categorized into four principal types, according to physical characteristics and technological readiness for commercial exploitation. These are hydrothermal (water or steam), geopressured (water pressurized by overlying sedimentary rock), hot dry rock (with no fluid present), and magma (molten rock).

The geothermal resource base in the United States is extensive. The United States Geological Survey (USGS) provides two types of resource estimates: (1) the accessible resource base, which includes all geothermal resources shallow enough to be reached by production drilling in the foreseeable future, regardless of near-term economic viability; and (2) the resource, which includes only those geothermal resources that can be extracted from the accessible resource base at a production cost competitive with other forms of energy at a foreseeable time and under reasonable assumptions of continuing technological improvement. The best estimates of U.S. geothermal resources are shown in Table 2 (4,5). For comparison, the total consumption of energy in the United States in 1984 was approximately 75×10^{18} J, or 75 quads (a quad being 10^{15} Btu).

HYDROTHERMAL CONVECTION SYSTEMS

Hydrothermal resources, the geothermal resource base currently being exploited commercially, can be subcategorized as either liquid dominated (hot water) or vapor dominated (dry steam), according to the principal state of the fluid trapped in fractured or porous rock (6). Existing wells to recover hydrothermal resources are typically drilled to depths of 500–5000 m. The temperatures of the most useful resources generally range from 150 to 350°C. Commercially useful hydrothermal resources are scattered throughout the world. They are often found along the boundaries of tectonic plates, a notable example of which is the Circum-Pacific Belt (the so-called Ring of Fire). Other large hydrothermal areas are found around the Mediterranean Sea, in the Rift Valley of East Africa, and along the Mid-Atlantic Ridge, where it breaches the ocean surface, as in Iceland. In the United States, the highest-quality hydrothermal resources are located in the states of California, Hawaii, Oregon, Washington, Utah, and Nevada, where relatively young volcanoes or a thinning of the earth's crust are associated with the occurrence of high-temperature resources.

Table 1. Status and Projected Development of Worldwide Geothermal Power

Country	Megawatts			Megawatts to be Installed Each Year							Unspecified
	1985	1986	1987	1988	1989	1990	1991	1992	1993	1994	
United States	2022.11	137.62	115.0	241.4							815.0
Philippines	894.0			55.0	92.5						1155.0
Mexico	645.0	50.0	50.0	55.0	55.0	110.0	55.0	220.0	50.0		
Italy	519.2										380.0
Japan	215.1										108.0
New Zealand	167.2			116.2							
El Salvador	95.0										85.0
Kenya	45.0							60.0			
Iceland	39.0										
Nicaragua	35.0	35.0									
Indonesia	32.25		55.0	55.0	110.0	110.0	110.0	110.0	195.0	110.0	110.0
Turkey	20.6										
China	14.321										0.55
USSR	11.0					80.0					150.0
France (Guadeloupe)	4.2										
Portugal (Azores)	3.0										
Greece (Milos)	2.0										
Costa Rica	0				50.0						
Guatemala	0										15.0
Chile	0										15.0
Saint Lucia	0										30.0
India	0										1.0
Romania	0										1.0
Australia	0										0.5
Totals, each year		222.62	220.0	522.6	257.5	350.0	165.0	390.0	245.0	110.0	2866.9
Cumulative total	4763.981	4986.6	5206.6	5729.2	5986.7	6336.7	6501.7	6891.7	7136.7	7246.7	10113.6

Geopressured Geothermal Resources

Geopressured resources are geothermal brines containing dissolved methane (natural gas), generally at saturation concentrations of 20–60 SCF/barrel of fluid (equivalent to 20,000–60,000 Btu or 20–60 million J/barrel), depending on the temperature, pressure, and salinity of the fluid. These resources are characterized by anomalously high pressures, often twice that of normal hydrostatic pressure at an equivalent depth. Such resources, found extensively both onshore and offshore on the Texas and Louisiana Gulf Coasts, are quite large, typically located at depths of 3000–5000 m, with temperatures reaching 120–150°C.

Table 2. Estimated U.S. Geothermal Resources[a]

Type	Accessible Resource Base, 10^{18} J	Resource, 10^{18} J
Hydrothermal (T ≥ 90°C)	9,600	2,400
Geopressured		
Thermal energy	107,000	270–2,800[b]
Methane energy	63,000[c]	158–1,640[c]
Total	*170,000*	*428–4,440[b]*
Hot dry rock	450,000	Uncertain
Magma	500,000	Uncertain

[a] Ref. 5.
[b] Estimated range of resource values represents two different energy recovery plans used in USGS calculations.
[c] Assuming that the geothermal brine is fully saturated with methane, as found in practice.

Combined recovery techniques were being investigated in 1986 to obtain chemical energy (methane), hydraulic energy (from the abnormally high pressures), and thermal energy (hot brine) and to determine the economic feasibility of exploiting these resources (7).

Hot Dry Rock Resources

Hot dry rock resources consist of pockets of high-temperature, essentially nonporous, and impermeable rocks often associated with buried magma chambers. (A magma chamber consists of a large body of molten rock that has intruded upward from the liquid mantle below the earth's crust through a large crack in the crust or at the junction of two continental plates, often melting the neighboring rock to form a molten mass of dimensions of 1 km or more.) They can also occur associated with large radiogenic heat sources (uranium or thorium) buried at shallow depths or in areas where the earth's crust is thin over a wide area, giving high regional heat flow. The temperatures in these rock formations typically increase with depth and proximity to the heat source. The USGS estimates the resource base to be as much as 450,000 quads (Table 2). To extract usable energy, two wells must be drilled, the rock between them fractured, and a heat transfer fluid circulated between the wells through the induced fissure system to bring heat to the surface, where it can be used to generate electricity or for direct heat applications. Such systems are currently in the prototype stage.

Magma Resources

Magma resources consist of thermal energy contained in molten or near-molten rock at temperatures up to 1100°C. Such resources are found only in areas of recent volcanism; in the United States, such sites lie primarily in the western states, Hawaii, and Alaska. To extract energy from the liquid or partially solidified magma, wells must be drilled to considerable depths (and with great difficulty) into the magma chamber and a heat-transfer fluid cycled to extract heat and bring it to power-generating facilities located on the surface.

DESIGN OF GEOTHERMAL POWER PLANTS

Geothermal power plant design in the United States is changing as different resource types are exploited and as economic conditions change. The design of the power plant and other surface equipment varies with the heat cycle employed, which depends on the makeup of the geothermal fluid and on its physical and chemical state.

Design of Dry Steam Plants

Most of the operating plants at The Geysers dry steam field are similar in design. Figure 1 shows a simplified schematic. For a 55-MW plant, 10–20 production wells are drilled about 1000 m apart. These are equipped with valve assemblies providing a bypass to venting stacks that are lined with rock wool or rocks to act as mufflers and coupled directly into gathering pipelines. The gathering lines deliver steam at pressures of 1.2–1.5 MPa (12–15 atm) into cyclone separators for the removal of entrained particles and droplets. The separators are located near a central powerhouse that is the principal architectural element of the plant.

Most geothermal powerhouses are similar to the 50–250-MW powerhouses of small fossil fuel power plants using steam turbines. One or more large turbogenerators are mounted on a pedestal or pilings to provide space below for large condensation tanks. A full floor is provided at a level about 1 m below the horizontal axis of the turbogenerator; this floor is typically 8–10 m above ground. The generating room, a high bay of 8–10 m with a travel-ing gantry for installation and maintenance, is usually flanked by offices, a control room, and a fitting shop. The Northern California Power Administration (NCPA) plant at The Geysers has even provided a quiet room, soundproofed to allow off-duty relaxation for the staff.

The lower floor contains the condenser, steam ejectors to remove noncondensable gases, ancillary equipment including pumps and fluid monitoring equipment, and a fitting and repair shop. Condensed steam is used to replace water evaporated in the cooling tower, and the surplus is pumped through a delivery line to an injection well in a suitable part of the field. Injection can help maintain reservoir pressure, replace some lost fluid, and dispose of toxic wastes such as boron and arsenic. Cooling water passed through the condenser is pumped to a nearby cooling tower. Geothermal steam plants generally employ wet cooling towers, similar to those used in conventional fossil fuel steam plants, of the evaporative induced-draft type. A conventional substation or switchyard is provided close to the powerhouse to link the power output into the appropriate power transmission line system. Operational access to valves and monitoring equipment is provided throughout the lower level of the powerhouse. Access for routine cleaning of scale from the inside of valves, piping, the condenser, and other equipment and for both regular and emergency maintenance and replacement functions forms part of the design. Safety of all pressure vessels and pipework is ensured by applying additional corrosion allowances to the boiler code and providing inspection ports for monitoring the progress of corrosion at critical points.

Noise from the steam ejectors and bypass vents (used during plant outage) is minimized by mufflers. Contamination of surface aquifers is prevented by injecting waste fluids into deep aquifers in carefully cased and cemented injection wells. Geothermal operations can affect the surface of the land over some well fields by causing gradual subsidence, especially in sedimentary basins. Careful selection and control of injection of the condensate can mitigate this process, but some subsidence may be unavoidable. Buildings are usually rafted on large pads, and utility services are designed to accommodate the subsidence conditions anticipated at each site. Landscaping is necessary to enhance the appearance of the power plant and to recover from surface disturbance caused by drilling operations at the wellheads.

Gaseous emanations require control through chemical treatment to remove significant quantities of hydrogen sulfide and traces of boron, arsenic, and methane. Most of the plants at The Geysers use the Stretford process, in which the exhaust gases are scrubbed with a vanadium sulfate solution, forming insoluble vanadium sulfide that can be processed to regenerate the sulfate and provide solid elemental sulfur, which is trucked away to a waste site. The Stretford process is usually housed in a small free-standing building that contains the scrubbers, chemical processors, and storage for other chemicals. Alternative approaches include upstream scrubbing and even a condensing and reboiling system to clean the gaseous effluent.

In appearance, geothermal installations can be pleasing and no more intrusive than similar-sized oil- or gas-

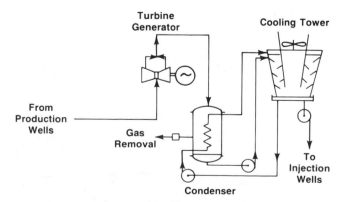

Figure 1. Dry steam schematic.

Figure 2. Geysers geothermal units 1 and 2 (11 and 13 MW) showing an early power house, separating tank, and cooling towers. Courtesy of Pacific Gas and Electric.

fired steam plants (Fig. 2). A particular feature of geothermal plants is the piping, which comes from each wellhead to the central powerhouse and has a series of expansion bends shaped as shown in Figure 3. These expansion bends are generally laid horizontally, but must be placed vertically over roadways. Geothermal engineers in Mexico have studied the cost of burying geothermal gathering lines, with appropriate insulation and corrosion protection. They have determined that it would be slightly more expensive, but desirable, to protect the environment and for aesthetics. To assist in noise abatement and to improve appearance in elevation, acoustic barriers can be provided in the form of walls or hedges. Acre-sized holding ponds for containment of the waste fluids from the scrubbers are sometimes placed for their ornamental value, reflecting the landscape to advantage. Solid waste or sludge re-

moved from the holding pond must be trucked from a dock or truck bay, usually sited at the small building provided to house pumps and filtering equipment.

The design of geothermal power plants is dictated not only by the type of geothermal resource, but by economics. Early plants were not designed for high efficiency because utilities purchased geothermal fluid from a supplier at a price based either on the price of electricity generated or on the amount of energy extracted from the fluid and could thus generate power from only the most economical fraction of the fluid's available energy. Recently, the trend has been toward plant builders owning the resource, making it important to design for higher efficiencies to conserve the resource. This trend is strongly encouraged by state public utility commissions. High efficiency has been achieved by the Sacramento Municipal Utility District Geothermal (SMUDGEO) in its plant (Fig. 4) by several techniques. Backpressure is reduced by following two stages of steam ejectors by a set of vacuum pumps. High velocities limit the blade length in large turbines so, instead of using a single turbine consisting of a double-ended turbine spool with central high-pressure entry and dual exhausts, SMUDGEO improves efficiency by using two such units to provide 72 MW of gross power, each unit having oversized turbines with a 63-cm blade length to maximize power extraction.

Design of Flash-steam Plants

The only dry steam field in the United States that can be exploited commercially is at The Geysers in California. Yellowstone Park in Wyoming is the only other steam field known to exist in the United States. It is treasured for its beauty as a national park; commercial development is prohibited there.

However, there are many liquid-dominated geothermal fields in the western United States that produce hot water at temperatures above 170°C and pressures above 10 atm, making them economically attractive for flash-steam plants. These plants typically have cyclone separators, or "flash tanks," in which the liquid (or two-phase fluid) flowing from the wellhead is subjected to a pressure drop, releasing saturated steam and noncondensable gases that

Figure 3. Geysers geothermal unit 18 (114 MW) showing a modern cooling tower, powerhouse, and gathering line with expansion bend. Courtesy of PG&E.

Figure 4. SMUDGEO Plant No. 1 (72 MW) showing powerhouse, cooling tower, and small exhaust scrubbing tower. Courtesy of Sacramento Municipal Utility District.

pass to power plants similar to those at The Geysers (Fig. 5).

Geothermal fluids from reservoirs with temperatures above 200°C contain large quantities of dissolved minerals. These minerals are most commonly silica (SiO_2) and calcium carbonate ($CaCO_3$), with smaller quantities of halite salts and traces of heavy metals, at concentrations of up to 35% by weight. The minerals can cause serious corrosion, scaling, and plugging of well casings, surface valves, piping, flash tanks, and turbines. They can also cause scaling and plugging of injection lines, the injection well, and nearby permeable rock into which the injected fluid must flow. Flash plants built to utilize such hot geothermal brines require chemical treatment facilities which make them resemble chemical plants (Fig. 6). The currently favored process is to precipitate much of the dissolved material, following a first-stage flash, in a reac-

tor vessel in which sludge from the waste extraction process is introduced. The brine with its suspended particles is transferred to a settling tank or clarifier. The wet sludge then passes to filter presses and, after dewatering, is trucked to a waste storage site. The brine often contains enough available energy for the process to be followed by a second flash stage, using flash tanks of a size similar to that for the first stage, but at lower pressure and smaller flow. The lower-pressure steam, often at pressures only slightly above 1 MPa (1 atm), is ducted to a low-pressure turbine or admitted to the low-pressure stages of a two-stage turbine. The quantity of fluid remaining after flashing is still over 70% of the initial flow, and reinjection underground is an important requirement. In order to recharge the reservoir, the design and placement of the necessary injection wells are more critical than for dry steam plants. Because of the large amount of solid waste or sludge, a large dock is required for articulated tankers to be filled many times a day, and a heavy traffic road with a turning circle is provided. The powerhouse and cooling tower are similar to those at dry steam plants.

U.S. design practice for flash plants has followed closely the earlier practices in Mexico and New Zealand, but with more concern for environmental protection. New Zealand uses river water for cooling at Wairakei, returning the warmed water to the river; Mexico discharges its spent brine into an open lagoon at Cerro Prieto. The use of wellhead generators or small "icebreaker" plants of 5–10 MW (to begin development of a well field and thus obtain both early revenues and early data on the nature of the reservoir) is growing and providing an incentive to develop new power conversion concepts. The energy lost in a flash tank when the high-pressure brine is injected into a cyclone separator can largely be recovered through a ro-

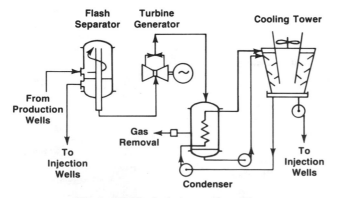

Figure 5. Flashed-steam schematic.

Figure 6. Salton Sea Geothermal Plant (10 MW) showing reactor/clarifying tanks to remove minerals from the geothermal fluid. Courtesy of UNOCAL.

tary separator driven as a water turbine. This provides additional shaft power for recovering pumping pressure, reinjection, or both, in an amount equivalent to about 15% additional energy recovery. The rotary separator turbine seems likely to be most practical in sizes of up to 10 MW and is likely to be used in modules of 5–10 MW for larger-scale power production. For small installations, the use of units that can be factory built and packaged in a shipping container tend to be optimum economically.

The developers of large well fields are finding economies in slant-drilling production and injection wells from one or more central islands. This avoids the time and cost necessary to dismantle and reerect the drill rig, move ancillary equipment to each new well site, construct new mud ponds, and restore each drilling site. Directional drilling equipment is becoming more readily available, and the U.S. Department of Energy is working with industry in the development of advanced geothermal drilling systems to reduce the cost of slant drilling.

Design of Binary Plants

When the temperature of the geothermal fluids is below about 170°C, the most efficient and economical plant is one employing a secondary working fluid in a binary cycle, as shown in Figure 7. Temperatures as low as 100°C and as high as 200°C are suited to binary operation, depending on the availability of cooling water, range of ambient temperatures, and depth of wells. The choice of working fluid depends on operating temperatures and ranges from mixtures of organic fluids (isohexane, isopentane, isobutane, and propane) to refrigerants (Freons and ammonia). The United States has the only commercial-sized geothermal binary plant built to date, the 45-MW plant at Heber, California, shown in Figures 8 and 9. It is more complex than a 49-MW flash plant built nearby on the same reservoir, but has higher efficiency. The cost of

plant construction was shared between the U.S. Department of Energy and a consortium of utilities to demonstrate its practicability and to obtain design and operating parameters. In order to maximize heat transfer, the geothermal fluid at 175°C is pumped from the wells by deep-set pumps and maintained at pressure so that it remains liquid as it passes through heat exchangers. The brine is injected into the reservoir without ever boiling or releasing its noncondensable gases. The absence of flash tanks, reactor clarifiers, steam ejectors, and effluent scrubbers, all of which would be required for a flash-steam plant, is readily apparent in Figure 10. Instead, there are additional pipes, tanks, pumps, and control systems. The heat exchangers and condenser are composed of modules small enough to be built off-site. The brine flows through the tubes of shell-and-tube heat exchangers, vaporizing the hydrocarbon, which passes to a turbine that is far smaller than a steam turbine of equivalent power. Leaving the

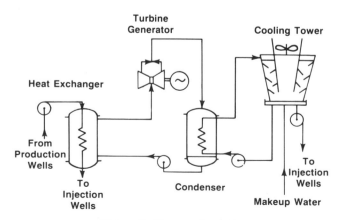

Figure 7. Binary schematic.

Figure 8. Heber binary plant (45 MW) showing heat exchangers, working fluid tank, powerhouse and cooling tower. Courtesy of San Diego Gas and Electric.

Figure 9. Heber binary plant showing working fluid tank. Courtesy of San Diego Gas and Electric.

turbine, the hydrocarbon is cooled in a water-cooled condenser and passed to the storage tank. The heated water from the condenser is pumped to a conventional cooling tower. In contrast to the steam and flash-steam plants, the binary plant must be supplied with makeup water to replace all the water evaporated in the cooling tower.

In spite of its greater complexity, the binary concept may be preferred over flash-steam, even for higher-temperature resources, because of its higher efficiency and environmental acceptability. One drawback is the requirement for cooling water since geothermal resources are most frequently found in arid areas. The 45-MW bi-

Figure 10. Heber binary plant aerial view. Courtesy of San Diego Gas and Electric.

nary plant at Heber is likely to be copied extensively, and the U.S. Department of Energy is funding research on many elements of a second-generation binary plant that can provide electricity much more economically in the next decade. Beyond the case of flash-steam plants, there is an advantage at some sites in using binary wellhead generators of 2–5 MW, or modules of up to 10 MW. For binary plants, the geothermal brine must be pumped to prevent flashing. Present technology uses shaft-driven downhole pumps, which are unsatisfactory in deep or slant-drilled wells. Pumps using submersible hydraulic or electric motors will soon become available with the needed capability. Meanwhile, several designs for small portable, or at least transportable, binary power plants are being installed in new well fields where growth to larger capacity may eventually be warranted.

The use of modules for the heat exchangers, condensers, and heat rejection units may grow even with that of central power stations. Because there is no other market at present for large turbines designed for operation with organic fluids, a single custom-built turbine can be expected to be more expensive than several batch-built smaller units. Whether to provide a single large generator or a modular one depends on the need for flexibility in power supply and growth. A central power station containing many modular binary plants will tend to have a low profile and be dominated by a central cooling tower. If newly designed fabric-covered, hyperbolic-shaped air-cooling towers can be built at low enough cost, they will become the most prominent architectural feature of most future geothermal power plants.

Geothermal development of hydrothermal resources has matured in the past decade from a fledgling technology to a well-established one supporting a growing industry. The architecture of the power plants is still evolving, following the trends described above, and the next decade can expect to see the designs refined and eventually stabilized. Geothermal energy will supply a significant portion of the nation's power by the next century, especially in the western United States.

BIBLIOGRAPHY

1. P. D. Blair, T. A. V. Cassel, and R. H. Edelstein, *Geothermal Energy: Investment Decisions & Commercial Development,* John Wiley & Sons, Inc., New York, 1982.

2. C. F. Budd, *Journal of Petroleum Technology,* 189 (Feb. 1984).

3. R. DiPippo in *Proceedings of 1985 EPRI/IIE Geothermal Conference and Workshop,* The Electric Power Research Institute, Palo Alto, Calif., June 1985.

4. L. J. P. Muffler, ed., *Assessment of Geothermal Resources of the United States—1978,* USGS Circular 790, United States Geological Survey, Reston, Va., 1979.

5. L. J. P. Muffler in L. Rybach and L. J. P. Muffler, eds., *Geothermal Systems: Principles and Case Histories,* John Wiley & Sons, Inc., New York, 1981.

6. S. L. Milora and J. W. Tester, *Geothermal Energy as a Source of Electric Power,* MIT Press, Cambridge, Mass., 1976.

7. E. Hughes in M. H. Dorfman and R. A. Morton, eds., *Geopressured—Geothermal Energy,* Pergamon Press, New York, 1985.

General References

J. Kestin, R. DiPippo, H. E. Khalifa, and D. J. Ryley, eds., *Sourcebook on the Production of Electricity from Geothermal Energy,* DOE/RA/4051-1, U.S. Government Printing Office, Washington, D.C., 1980.

H. C. H. Armstead, *Geothermal Energy,* 2nd ed., E.&F.N. Spon., New York, 1983.

E. W. Butler and J. B. Pick, *Geothermal Energy Development,* Plenum Press, New York, 1982.

JOHN E. MOCK
RONALD S. H. TOMS
Department of Energy
Washington, D.C.

POWER GENERATION, NUCLEAR

One of the most important technological advancements from the discovery of nuclear fission is the development of nuclear reactors. There are various uses for nuclear reactors such as biological research, materials testing, teaching aids, and electrical energy production. It is the electrical energy production (power plants) that has had the most impact on the economy and industrial development in the twentieth century.

A nuclear power plant is similar to a conventional thermal power plant. Each type uses steam to drive a turbine generator that produces electricity. In conventional thermal power plants, fossil fuel such as coal, oil, or natural gas is burned and the resulting heat is used to generate steam. In a nuclear power plant, no burning or combustion takes place. Nuclear fission is used instead to generate heat. This heat is sometimes indirectly transferred to the water, producing steam.

Although acid rain, as a long-term effect of coal-fired power plants, is a major concern in fossil plants, radiation contamination and the generation of radioactive materials are the major concerns in nuclear power plants. Herein lies the basic objective for all of the various criteria developed under which a nuclear power plant is designed and constructed. The safety implications of nuclear power plants does not depend on restraining the force of atomic energy but on containing the radioactivity it generates.

There are various types of nuclear power plant in use throughout the world. They include the boiling water reactor (BWR), pressurized water reactor (PWR), light water cooled graphite moderated reactor (LGR), gas cooled reactor (GCR), liquid metals fast breeder reactor (LMFBR), and variations thereof. The most widely used types are the PWR and BWR. Except for two prototype plants, the United States has mostly PWRs and BWRs. In the USSR, a majority are LGR, but the more recent ones are PWRs; this is also true in France, one of the major users of nuclear power plants today.

Generally, all nuclear power reactors operate similarly, ie, water is heated to produce steam, which turns the generator, thereby producing electricity. Differences between the various types of power reactor are distinguished by the following:

- Net consumption of nuclear fuel.
- Type of moderator.
- Type of containment (of reactor).

Net Consumption of Nuclear Fuel. There are reactors that have a high net consumption of nuclear fuel. PWRs and BWRs use up a high amount of nuclear fuel to produce electricity. On the other hand, there are reactors that have negative net fuel consumption. Typical of these are the "breeder" reactors. Breeder reactors produce new fissionable material that can be processed for use as its fuel. They produce more fuel than they use, thereby resulting in a negative net fuel consumption.

Type of Moderators. "Moderators" are materials that slow down neutrons quickly as well as absorb neutrons. In nuclear fission, the ability to slow down neutrons or absorb neutrons is necessary to maintain control of the chain reaction, necessary to control the heat produced. Materials containing a concentration of hydrogen are generally effective moderators. Materials used include ordinary water, heavy water (term used for water that contains a significantly higher proportion of heavy hydrogen atoms than ordinary hydrogen atoms), graphite, and certain organic compounds. In the United States, a majority of the commercial power plants use ordinary water, either as PWR or BWR; this is true in most plants around the world. France, second to the United States in nuclear power plant utilization, uses mostly ordinary water as the moderator in its PWRs while the USSR, which started with mostly graphite moderators, has in the last 10 years used ordinary water by building mostly PWRs. (Three Mile Island, TMI-2, in Pennsylvania, which suffered one of the major accidents known in U.S. commercial nuclear power reactor history, has an ordinary water moderator whereas the reactor suffering the worst worldwide accident so far, at Chernobyl in the USSR, has a graphite moderated reactor.)

Types of Containment. Prevention of the uncontrolled release of radioactivity is the major concern that has to be met in nuclear power reactor design. To determine whether releases are prevented, a designer needs to postulate credible accidents that could result in the escape of radioactivity to the atmosphere and surrounding areas and assess whether the barriers provided to prevent the release of radioactivity perform their function. These barriers include the fuel itself, the fuel cladding, the reactor vessel and associated piping and the reactor building (containment).

The critical barrier to the release of radioactivity from a nuclear power plant is the containment building. A containment structure must meet certain functional and service requirements, depending on the environmental conditions and the type of nuclear steam supply system (NSSS) (ie, the type of reactor) used. The structure must withstand the effects of such natural phenomena as earthquakes, tornadoes, hurricanes, and floods without loss of

capability to perform its safety functions and may also be required to withstand aircraft and missile impact generated by such postulated events and explosions near the site.

A description of the various types of PWR and BWR containments used in the U.S. is provided below.

PWR. Two types of PWR containment are in use:

- Large dry. This type of containment can be constructed as a domed cylinder or a sphere with a flat foundation. The walls are typically constructed using either postensioned prestressed concrete or reinforced concrete and are kept leaktight by a ¼–½ in. thick carbon steel plate (Fig. 1), or, free standing 1.5 in. thick steel plate surrounded by reinforced concrete shield wall (Fig. 2).
- Ice condenser (Fig. 3). This type of containment is constructed similar to the large dry containment. The ice condenser design is smaller than the large dry containment due to the use of ice to condense the steam generated following an accident.

BWR. BWRs use a pressure-suppression type containment. That is, the steam generated following an accident is forced through a pool of water to condense it. There are currently three variations in containment designs in the U.S. incorporating the pressure-suppression concept, which are described below.

- Mark I (Fig. 4a). This containment type is constructed in the configuration of an inverted lightbulb-shaped steel (drywell) connected to a torus-shaped steel vessel (suppression chamber). A reinforced concrete structure around the drywell provides shielding from radioactivity.
- Mark II (Fig. 4b). This containment type is constructed as a truncated cone (drywell) over a cylindrical suppression chamber. These two sections provide shielding from radioactivity and is comprised of a structurally integrated reinforced concrete pressure vessel and lined with welded steel plate.
- Mark III (Fig. 5). This containment type is constructed as cylindrical reinforced concrete containment. The suppression pool connects the two structures. The drywell provides the primary shielding from radioactivity.

Thus, the volume and construction of the reactor containment structure differs on the basis of potential radioactive vapor containment.

NUCLEAR POWER PLANT DESIGN

Basic Power Plant

Because most of the reactors in use (especially in the United States) are PWR and BWR, the typical plant described here is a PWR. The major difference between the PWR and BWR is the method of processing the water to produce the heat that creates the steam. In the BWR, as

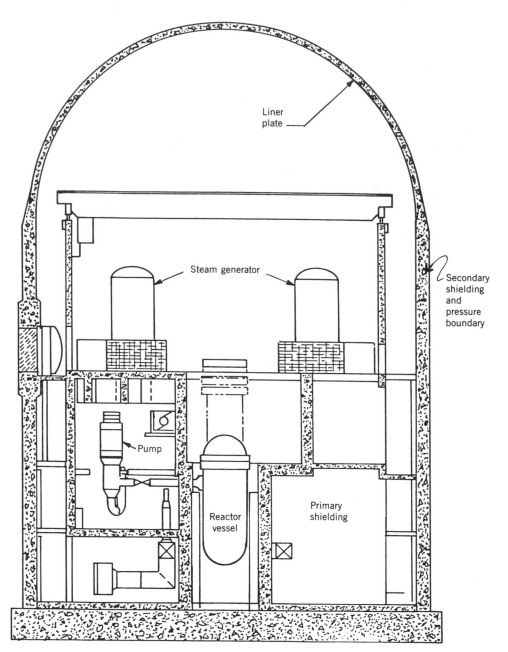

Figure 1. Typical dry containment.

the term suggests, the water is boiled inside the reactor. In this process, water passes through the reactor and is heated as it passes between the elements of nuclear fuel. The water in the reactor is kept at a very high pressure. The pressure raises the boiling point of the reactor water so that when steam is produced, its temperature and pressure are great enough for efficient use in the turbine. On the other hand, in the PWR, the water passing through the reactor does not boil. Rather, pressure in the reactor and the piping loop connected to it is much higher (more than twice) than that of a BWR. This very high pressure permits the water to be heated to a very high temperature without boiling. The heated water then goes through a steam generator that makes the steam that drives the turbine.

The major difference, then, between the PWR and BWR is the nuclear steam supply system (NSSS), which can easily be physically identified by the presence of a steam generator between the reactor process and the turbine process in PWRs. This, in addition to the method of vapor containment, establishes the major difference in the building volumes, safety implications, and criteria to be met in designing the various structures that make up a nuclear power plant complex. (Where a major difference in design clearly requires identification, this article will also identify the BWR requirement; otherwise, the typical plant described here is based on a PWR.)

Regulations

Nuclear power plant design, construction, and operation in the United States are under the surveillance and regu-

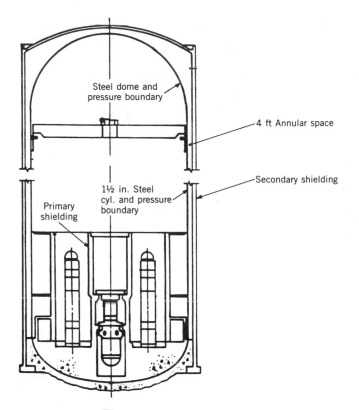

Figure 2. Dual containment.

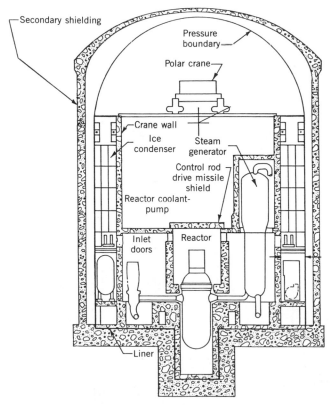

Figure 3. Cross-section of ice condenser containment.

latory control of the NRC. In 1954, the Atomic Energy Act was passed, establishing the government role in civilian nuclear power plants and creating the Atomic Energy Commission (AEC). The Energy Reorganization Act of 1974 established the NRC and abolished the AEC act of 1954, transferring all licensing and other related regulatory functions for civilian nuclear power plants to the NRC. The basic regulations promulgated by the NRC governing the design, construction, and operation of a nuclear power plant are contained in the Code of Federal Regulations, Title 10 (10 CFR), most specifically 10 CFR 50. The regulations contained in the 10 CFR are complemented by various guidelines and publications issued by the NRC from time to time, such as *Regulatory Guides* and *IE Bulletins*. In addition, various studies and component designs are sponsored by the NRC, which are utilized to support or be applied as a basis for the design, construction, and operation of the plant. There are, of course, various state and local codes and requirements that refer to standard building design and construction that are applicable and implemented, although should conflict arise with NRC regulations, the NRC regulations govern. Various industry standards are also applied to establish a basis of quality and acceptability. Such industry standards include those promulgated by the American Society of Mechanical Engineering (ASME), the American Society for Testing and Materials (ASTM), the National Fire Protection Association (NFPA), and others.

Except for nuclear liability, for which a special pool insurance among utilities with nuclear plants is provided, a nuclear power plant is also subject to the same requirements for insurability for personnel and property damage as any conventional power plant. As in conventional plants, life safety, maintenance, operational procedures and administration, health and safety in the workplace, and plant life are criteria used in the design and construction of a nuclear power plant.

Site Selection

Site selection for a nuclear power plant takes on a more critical importance than siting of a conventional power plant due to the safety parameters imposed. As in conventional power plants, operational requirements require its accessibility for both the workers and the equipment, especially heavy equipment. This means the availability of railroad spurs or water transportation near or adjacent to the site. Similarly, a large area is required to be available for all of the various support facilities, not to mention the facility itself.

Safety requirements imposed on nuclear power plants demand the need to locate the plant in remote, very low density areas due to the potential, no matter how low, of a radiation leakage from the plant. Distance provides dilution of airborne radiation. The utilization of the adjacent land is of equal importance due to the airborne leakage potential. The 10 CFR 100 also identifies the need to establish an exclusion area whereby necessary boundaries for the control of the area during an accident is defined. Another major consideration in nuclear power plant siting is the need for a substantial amount of water to cool and

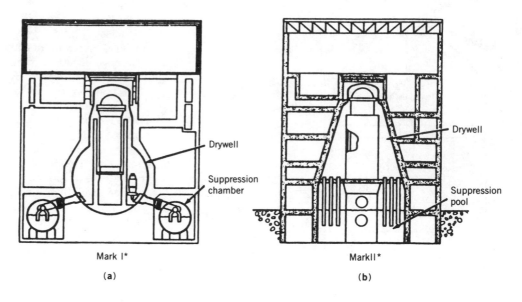

Figure 4. BWR containments.

(a)   (b)

control the fission in the reactor during operations and accident. An acceptable site, therefore, requires that it be close to a large body of water, remotely located in very low density (population) areas, yet accessible by water or land transportation.

Other critical siting criteria are the geological and seismic data on the proposed site. Considering the immensity of a nuclear power plant, the criticality of the nuclear reactor, and the precision involved in the instruments, it is of major importance to have a solid foundation, espe-

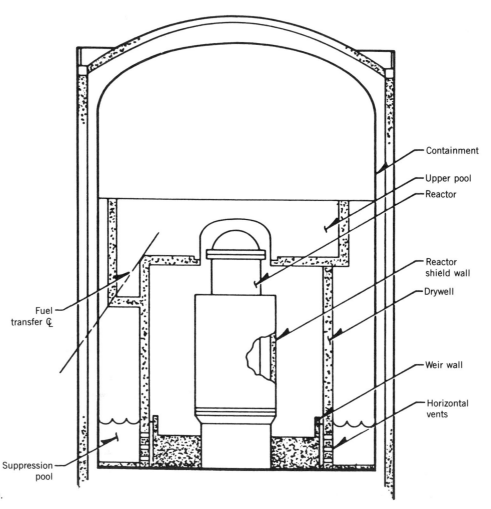

Figure 5. Reactor Building (Mark III).

cially at the location of the structure containing the reactor.

The proximity of an earthquake fault to the site is a major consideration, although design provisions could resolve any impact such faults may have on the plant. Economic considerations dictate that siting away from such locations is the more feasible and practical solution.

Nuclear power plants, especially those built in the United States, impose a tremendous load on the supporting soil foundation, especially the containment building that houses the reactor. This building alone, with its approximately 16-ft-thick concrete foundation and the containment shell of 2- to 4-ft-thick concrete wall and 8-in.-thick steel shell (not to mention the reactor itself), is a massive load to support. For this reason, the preferred site should have a rock-soil foundation, free of silty, clayey, sandy, or similar type soil.

Yet another important factor for a nuclear power plant site is flooding, whether due to normal site conditions or accidents caused by nature or by human error. The plant should be established above the maximum flood plain to protect from such incidents as failure of nearby dams, maximum precipitation, surges, tsunamis, etc. Protective barriers such as dikes installed around the plant or raising the plant level are two of the methods utilized where flooding is a site potential.

Nuclear Power Plant Complex of Structures

A typical nuclear power plant complex consists of the following structures collectively known as the power block.

- Reactor building.
- Auxiliary building.
- Control building.
- Radwaste building.
- Fuel handling building.
- Emergency diesel generator building.
- Switch gear facility.
- Turbine building.
- Intake structure.
- Water treatment building.

In support of the power block, facilities are required for the following activities.

- Administration and operation (office buildings).
- Plant security (guard stations).
- Warehousing (warehouse).
- Maintenance (shops).
- Laboratories (water treatment, process sampling, etc).
- Health physics operations.
- Personnel change facilities.
- Emergency operations facilities (EOF).
- Training and simulation facilities.

Depending on the site and on the designed process, other structures that may be required include:

- Cooling tower (in lieu of a cooling pond).
- Fire house.
- Low radwaste facility.

The function of the various buildings and the variation in the criteria under which the buildings are designed dictate the mass, configuration, and treatment of the building. The overriding parameter is the safe operation of the reactor.

Design Bases

The various buildings that make up the nuclear power plant complex are not all designed to the same criteria. The buildings are each designed to various combinations of the following functional criteria:

- Radiation shielding protection–containment.
- Seismic requirement.
- Tornado requirement.
- Flooding requirement.
- Pressure differential.
- Fire protection.
- Security requirement.
- Environmental protection, including sun, rain, snow, hail, wind, and dust.
- Noise abatement.
- Accessibility.

FACILITIES DESCRIPTION

Reactor Building

As noted earlier, the reactor building is the most critical structure in the entire nuclear power plant complex. The structure houses the nuclear reactor, the nuclear steam supply system, various process and operational support equipment, systems, and facilities. The containment structure is typically a round structure with a domed superstructure. The building is generally 130–140 ft in diameter and ranges in height from approximately 120–240 ft from the operating platform level. The operating platform level is that level where the reactor cover is located. Below the operating platform level is another 60–100 ft to the lowest foundation floor level, the level immediately above the foundation. Where vapor containment is used, the superstructure generally consists of a 2- to 4-ft-thick concrete shell located outside an 8-in.-thick steel shell liner. Where containment uses the dry well–wet well concept, the superstructure consists of the 8-in.-thick steel liner. A thinner concrete shell or a heavy-duty preformed metal enclosure may be used as the exterior envelope. Due to the need for the dry well–wet well for this configuration, a deeper volume for the basement levels of the structure is required.

Except for an equipment hatch and a personnel access hatch or door, there are no other openings through the reactor building wall and roof. Any penetration openings provided for equipment, such as cables, ducts, piping, etc, are sealed so that air leakage through these walls is virtually nil. The equipment hatch is a massive door opening that is used for equipment access during construction or maintenance. The nuclear reactor is shut down or not operating when this hatch is in use. This hatch is designed to function similarly to the wall shield during an accident. The hatch is provided with a seal to maintain the environment in the reactor building and to protect from any leakage. The door or hatch is provided with a density equivalent to the wall and is provided with a double seal at the perimeter of the hatch. The personnel access door is usually a set of tandem doors of normal size in heavy steel construction. The doors are configured so that both cannot be opened at the same time. As with the equipment hatch, the doors are constructed to a density equivalent to the shield wall. Double seals are also provided for each door leaf.

Inside the reactor building can be found not only the various equipment for the steam process, but also various equipment and facilities necessary for operational and maintenance activities. High above the nuclear reactor and located at the foot of the dome of the building is a polar crane. This crane is used mostly for lifting extremely sizable and heavy equipment such as the reactor head or cap, or the steam generator during construction and repairs. An elevator and stairs are provided for vertical communication and access. In addition, various platforms and ladders or stairs are located throughout the structure for access between equipment and short levels.

A negative pressure is maintained inside the reactor building to keep any radiation from leaking out of the building. Generally, the temperature inside the reactor building is approximately 120°F. Access to this structure is extremely limited. Workers are required to don protective clothing when entering the building. Besides the turbine building, the reactor building is one of the biggest and most massive structures in the power block complex. Exterior treatment of the structure is fairly limited due to its mass and its construction. Where metal enclosure is used, variation in colors, articulation, and profiles allow the designer some building treatment design flexibility. However, where a concrete shield wall is used, such flexibility is not available because the concrete is usually unpainted and articulation on the wall surface is limited to what economy and the construction technique will allow. The roof is generally provided with traditional roof covering that will require minimum maintenance. Roof drains are not allowed to penetrate the roof slab or reduce the thickness of the concrete shield requirement. A ladder with cage enclosure, as required by OSHA, is usually provided at the exterior of the structure to provide access to the roof.

Painting inside the reactor building takes on a variety of requirements that are not known to any other painting application. For this reason, a special coatings system with strict quality control is required. Interior finishes in the reactor building are limited to functional requirements that include potential decontamination of surfaces and the wearability and maintenance of surfaces such as floors. Painting inside the reactor building is required for the corrosion protection of steel structures and equipment

and to seal the porous surfaces of any concrete surface to allow for decontamination of the surfaces if necessary. Due to the environmental conditions inside the reactor building, corrosion protection of all steel structures is of paramount importance. In addition to the protective characteristics required of the coating system and its decontaminability, coating inside the reactor building is required to adhere to the subsurface during an accident where the temperature and pressure inside the structure could rise. The paint or coating cannot impact the operation of the various types of equipment inside the structure during such events. Coating systems used inside the reactor building are tested to provide assurance that the coating does not sufficiently delaminate during an accident to impact the sump or operations of sensitive instruments.

The reactor building is required to withstand the maximum seismic event that may occur at the given site. In addition, the reactor building envelope is required to resist penetration of various items transported by a tornado such as a pipe at high velocity or a small car at lower velocity. Combustible materials located inside the reactor building are held to a minimum to reduce the potential of a fire inside. All other materials used are required to pass a noncombustibility test.

Auxiliary Building

The auxiliary building is so called due to the various systems and equipment auxiliary to and in support of the nuclear reactor system located in the building. Various functions and support are housed within this structure, and the equipment and systems located here provide the interface between those functions required in the operation of the nuclear reactor. Included are mechanical and electrical systems and equipment associated with the steam supply to the turbine, the resulting radioactive waste being transported to the radwaste building, the emergency cooling system, and other process systems associated with the steam generation, the by-product of nuclear power generation and safety systems. In general, these systems and equipment are made up of various size tanks, motors, pumps, switch gears, batteries, instruments, etc. They also include hundreds of miles of cables, conduits, cable trays, and various size diameter pipes. The auxiliary building basically serves as the transition point for the mechanical and electrical systems from the nuclear reactor system to the operational, protective, and power-generation systems.

Nuclear power plant design is extremely conservative. This approach is evident in the size and configuration of the auxiliary building. The systems and equipment, under the defense in depth design approach, require system–equipment redundancy. This approach provides a higher level of confidence of system–equipment availability to shut down the reactor in case of accidents, equipment failure, or human error. This approach, however, not only complicates design but also increases the volume of the auxiliary building, which houses the primary and the redundant system. Due to the criticality of most of the system–equipment housed in the auxiliary building, the structure is designed to resist seismic loading, flooding, tornadoes, and generally the environmental, operational, and plant life degradation normal to the structure. In addition, a majority of the area within the auxiliary building is designed to contain radiation leakage. Although some equipment located in the auxiliary building need not be so protected, economy, design practicality, construction, operation constraint, and their potential impact on critical systems and equipment dictate their inclusion within such critically designed structures or boundaries.

Fuel Building

This structure is for temporary storage of used fuel awaiting transfer to permanent storage either within the plant compound or at a government-designated storage area. Because the used fuel, once removed from the reactor, requires immediate storage to protect against radiation contamination of the environmental and personnel, the fuel building generally has a direct fuel transfer provision from the reactor building; therefore, the location of this building should be as close as possible to the reactor building. A direct access to the exterior for vehicular transport of the fuel to permanent site storage is required for this building.

Control Building

The control building houses the main controlling instruments of the power plant. Within this structure is the heart–brain of the power plant. Generally, there is an area set aside within this structure, called the control room, that contains instrument panels and control boards. The panels and boards contain various indicators of the conditions or status of the systems, instruments, and equipment in the plant. This area is occupied 24 hours a day so that equipment, instrumentation, and personnel and administrative facilities are all located here. Personnel support facilities within this area include:

- Supervisor's office.
- Conference room.
- Chart room.
- Sanitary and janitorial facilities.
- Kitchen.

In addition, some plants provide a lounge or rest room for the operators to use whenever they must stay continuously in the control room such as during an accident or emergency. Within the control building, other facilities for support are provided.

The control room is maintained under a positive pressure to ensure habitability during a plant accident or chlorine release within the vicinity. In addition, due to the importance and criticality of the equipment within the control room, it is designed to resist earthquake, tornado, and all other environmental factors that could potentially damage the instruments.

Both for security reasons and for operational availability, the control building–control room is void of openings except doors for access and louvers as required by the HVAC. Even so, such openings are held to a minimum

number and size and are designed to incorporate the necessary security protection and meet the criteria to which the rest of the building area is subject to.

In the power plant complex, the support facilities and the control building–control room are the only areas provided with interior finishes for human occupancy and comfort. The use of decorative wall finishes, acoustical ceilings, carpeting, and the like provide comfort and psychological well-being to occupants of the room who are normally confined within the area during their working hours.

The exterior architectural treatment of this building is very limited. This building, being required to resist various impact loads such as tornado and flooding, generally has exterior walls of concrete 18–24 in. thick. In addition, its function necessitates its adjacency to the turbine building and the auxiliary building, thereby reducing the number of exterior walls available.

Radwaste Building

As a distinct building not found in conventional power plants, the radwaste building's function is to process both liquid and solid plant wastes contaminated with radiation. Waste processed in this building includes the plant process wastes such as liquids; it also includes wastes resulting from plant operations such as contaminated building, maintenance, or operational materials. Control of radioactivity and contamination is of paramount importance in this building resulting in the minimum use of penetrations.

Other Major Buildings

The other major buildings comprising the power block such as the turbine building, diesel generator building, and intake structure, are generally noteworthy more for their immense size than for any special functional design requirements. Their operational functions are exactly the same as those for a conventional power plant. In their immensity, the structural design, the ventilation system, and the general circulation requirement become compounded in terms of economy and conformity to average norms of buildings of similar types.

In a nuclear power plant, the diesel generator building and the intake structure take on a more critical role in that they are vital systems that may be required during shut-down operations of the plant to contain potential radiation hazard. As such, these structures are similarly designed as the auxiliary and containment buildings to resist loads such as tornado missile, seismic impact, etc. However, these buildings do not house equipment or processes that could potentially cause spread of radiation contamination.

The turbine building houses the turbine generator and the condenser. This massive structure does not require the protective function of the auxiliary or containment buildings except for environmental and safety protection. In some areas of the country, the turbine generator is left exposed to the elements for economic reasons. There is more flexibility in the architectural treatment of the turbine building than any other building in the power block.

Due to its mass, exterior treatment to visually reduce the overpowering size of the building is usually provided. In addition, the general materials used for the turbine building exterior are not limited to concrete as in the nuclear-related power block structures, thereby allowing material and design flexibility for the turbine building exterior walls. Where potential radiation contamination is present in the turbine building (such as in the BWR turbine building) such flexibility may be limited to materials that can easily be decontaminated and provide shielding characteristics. Still, the potential for architectural wall treatment is ever present.

Support Buildings

All other support buildings such as the administration buildings, training center, warehouse, shops, etc are all designed based on the governing codes of the locality and specific requirements of the owner and utility. Certain support structures, however, take on a more important role and complexity in nuclear power plant support than in conventional power plant operations. These structures include:

- Health physics and personnel change facilities.
- Warehouse and shops.
- Emergency response facilities.
- Plant security facilities.

Health Physics and Personnel Change Facilities. The health physics function is to control and monitor the spread of potential radiation contamination. A key operating and support facility for this purpose is the radiation access control area (RACA). This area is set aside for personnel who need to access areas that have potential for contamination such as those in the auxiliary building, containment, radwaste, and fuel buildings. Facilities are provided for personnel to change, dress, use sanitary facilities, and don protective clothing before entering the radiation-controlled areas. The RACA is also used for monitoring all access and egress of the controlled areas, which includes monitoring dosage received and supervisory decontamination. Preentry facilities normally provided include:

- Lockers.
- Toilets.
- Showers.
- Dressing area.
- Protective clothing storage.
- Administrative facilities.

Preegress facilities provided include:

- Disrobing areas.
- Decontamination shower.
- Monitoring equipment.
- Contaminated clothing holding area.
- Dirty (noncontaminated) clothing holding area.

Some plants may include laundry facilities, tailoring, health physics instrument issue, respirator repair facilities, and the like.

The HVAC and drainage of the preentry areas are completely separated from those in the preegress area for control of spread of potential contamination. This facility is best located as close to the auxiliary, containment, radwaste, and fuel buildings as possible. In some plants the RACA is an area set aside in one of those buildings. In addition, some plants provides a central RACA plus satellite RACAs for efficiency and special requirement.

Warehouse and Shops. Although the general functions of the warehouse and shops of a nuclear plant are the same as those for a conventional plant, the warehouse and shops for a nuclear power plant include operating requirements that render their design a little more complex. Warehouses for nuclear power plants require the storage of equipment, spare parts, and material so that immediate replacement and repair of equipment critical to safety can be performed. In addition, certain storage requirements to maintain spare parts, material, and equipment free from deterioration and damage for immediate use are required. Furthermore, it is important to maintain proper environmental control for some equipment and spare parts in the warehouse. Due to the need for immediate replacement for some spare parts and equipment, an inventory larger than a conventional power plant warehouse is maintained.

The shops for nuclear plants function similarly to conventional plants, including normal facilities for receiving, shipping, craneways, laydown, and tool storage. In addition, facilities for receiving, handling, and decontaminating equipment and pipes for shop repairs are provided. This entails control of potential radioactive airborne or waste contamination. For better control, some plants provide separate shops—one for repair of contaminated equipment and tools, another for normal (clean) plant repair needs. There is a need to locate the shop, or the part of the shop, that will provide the service for contaminated equipment or tools as close to the source building, ie, auxiliary building, as possible, to reduce the potential for spread of contamination and for handling efficiency.

Emergency Response Facilities. The Emergency Response Facilities (ERF) include the control room, on site Technical Support Center (TSC), onsite Operational Support Center (OSC) and near site Emergency Operations Facility (EOF). These are groups of habitable facilities required to be occupied or be available in case of an accident in the plant to assist in the operation and monitoring of the plant. Specific requirements as to their location and the relationship to the plant, their main functions, their design requirements, and their interface with plant operation are contained in an NRC document (NUREG 0696). The various facilities that make up the ERF are controlled areas for use of designated plant and NRC personnel. The TSC, however, generally house designated areas accessible to the public such as news briefing rooms, and display and exhibit areas.

Plant Security Facilities. Plant security in a nuclear power plant involves not only property protection and general health and safety provision but also provides protection capabilities from radiological sabotage. Due to the safety implication to the general public of a radiological occurrence in the plant, the security of vital or safeguard systems and equipment is of paramount importance in the design. Specific requirements in the Code of Federal Regulations are promulgated along with NRC regulatory guides with respect to the mission of the security provisions in a plant.

The physical security provided is mainly influenced by the site and plant design, the extent of utilization of guards, and the administrative procedures accompanying such a program. Specifics of security requirements are basically contained in 10 CFR 73, and are based on a defense in depth approach. Various portals, openings, and barriers are protected on a level relative to the importance of the equipment to the safe shutdown of the plant. In addition, a personnel screening facility is provided to screen and monitor access of all workers within the protected area of the plant. Documentation is an important activity of the security program and as such, facilities and systems provided are interfaced with such capabilities. The number of personnel who need access to the plant makes the security provisions more complex. Security provisions in a nuclear power plant respond to the requirement of detection, annunciation, deterrent or physical barrier, surveillance, and apprehension.

The guardhouse, or personnel-processing facility, located at the edge of the protected area of the plant is one of the major facilities provided for security. Its main function is to process personnel who require access into protected areas and structures of the plant. This facility design should consider the very high traffic and abuse the facility receives. There is flexibility in the design and architectural treatment of this structure. However, it is necessary that the peripheral area surrounding the structure should have a clear field of view for maximum efficiency of the security activities.

CONSTRUCTION MATERIALS

Nuclear power plants are generally constructed of concrete and steel. The various criteria that the structures have to conform to basically demand the use of these two building materials. Seismic loads, flooding, tornado resistance, pressure differential, maintenance, and permanence are some of the critical criteria that materials for use in the construction of nuclear power plants are required to withstand, whether alone or in combination. In addition, in certain buildings, such as the containment, auxiliary, fuel, and radwaste buildings, the need for the materials to withstand decontamination is paramount. Furthermore, materials in some areas are required to serve as barriers to radiation penetration or to be resistant to radiation to prevent early deterioration or degradation.

Various finish materials are utilized in power plant design and construction. The paramount criteria, however, in finish material selection are utilitarian or functional. The amount of architectural materials in a power plant varies extremely resulting in some difficulty or great expense in its procurement. It is normal to need 250–300 doors and frames for a one-unit power plant. At the same time, the amount of carpet that will be utilized within the whole power block is generally between 100–160 yd^2 with strict characteristics of fire resistance, static resistance, and maintenance. Given the general locations of nuclear power plants, the number of plants built, and material properties required, procurement of such material becomes very uneconomical and impractical. Such considerations limit the selection of materials for finishing and construction of nuclear power plants.

CIRCULATION

One of the most complex design problems in nuclear power plants is plant access: circulation and egress. Several plant functions contribute to such problems including:

- Very large areas or rooms.
- Containment of very large equipment or a number of pieces of equipment within the area or room.
- Very low ratio of personnel relative to floor area.
- Accessibility of areas to personnel.
- Containment function of barriers.
- Noise level in plants.
- Maze of equipment, cables, and pipings interlacing from one area to another.

In addition, conflicting functions of circulation are served by almost every portal within the buildings:

- For life safety purpose, should allow immediate exit from area or room.
- For radiological sabotage protection (security), should limit access to area or room.
- For radiological contamination safeguard, should limit access to certain areas.
- For operations and maintenance, should be accessible to workers and operators.

Additional functions that may complicate portal design include:

- Fire barrier requirement: containment (close portal).
- Radiation barrier requirement: containment (close portal).
- Equipment design performance: release of pressure (open portal).
- Environmental protection requirement: interior positive or negative pressure depending on the area.

To these ends, portals in a nuclear power plant are subject to extreme abuse, rendering a very high maintenance consideration.

CONSTRUCTION CONSIDERATIONS

The average nuclear power plant construction schedule is eight years from site preparation to commercial operation. Unlike a conventional power plant, the building of a nuclear power plant is not only impacted by the material and labor conditions, it is also impacted by the social and political climate relative to nuclear plants. The social and political attitudes of the locality, the state, or even the nation could indefinitely delay, or make costly delays to, the building of the plant. In addition, the constant changes in regulations brought about by the radiological safety considerations historically delays the completion of the plant.

Procurement for a nuclear power plant takes a long lead time, not only due to the complex equipment involved, but also due to the safety implications of the equipment's failure to operate or function. To provide safeguards, extensive testing and documentation is imposed on the majority of equipment and material used in the construction of a nuclear power plant.

Based on this, fast-track construction is the normal method utilized. Furthermore, the use of modular, or pre-engineered, systems is highly encouraged. Two-shift labor, or in some cases three-shift labor, is utilized and major subcontracts are let out. All of this results in a very complex construction schedule a need for a large project site, an extensive and well-coordinated project team, and a systematic network of labor and material suppliers.

Construction mobilization is as complex as the construction itself. At construction peak, an average of 3000 workers are at the site. Site mobilization includes providing structures and facilities that are semipermanent, including administrative and sanitary facilities, parking, access control, warehousing, shops, equipment and material laydown area, and site access.

In most instances, construction structures and facilities are utilized as permanent plant-support structures after construction is completed. Design and construction of these facilities are treated to be consistent with the permanent structures of the power plant.

BIBLIOGRAPHY

General References

"Nuclear Terms, A Brief Glossary," *Understanding the Atom Series,* U.S. Atomic Energy Commission, Division of Technical Information, Washington, D.C.

"Controlled Nuclear Fusion," *Understanding the Atom Series,* U.S. Atomic Energy Commission, Division of Technical Information, Washington, D.C.

"Atomic Power Safety," *Understanding the Atom Series,* U.S. Atomic Energy Commission, Division of Technical Information, Washington, D.C.

"Atomic Fuel," *Understanding the Atom Series,* U.S. Atomic Energy Commission, Division of Technical Information, Washington, D.C.

"Atomic Energy in Use," *Understanding the Atom Series,* U.S. Atomic Energy Commission, Division of Technical Information, Washington, D.C.

"Nuclear Reactors," *Understanding the Atom Series,* U.S. Atomic Energy Commission, Division of Technical Information, Washington, D.C.

"Nuclear Power Plants," *Understanding the Atom Series,* U.S. Atomic Energy Commission, Division of Technical Information, Washington, D.C.

VIRGINIA B. TORTONA
Bechtel Power Corporation
Gaithersburg, Maryland

POWER GENERATION, WIND, OCEAN

As solar energy is absorbed by the atmosphere, land, and sea, large predictable flow patterns are produced in the form of winds and sea waves and currents. Wind is created primarily by the uneven heating of the earth by the sun. Gravity interactions between the earth, moon, and sun provide additional flow in the oceans in the form of tides. Man has been using these kinetic energy sources for transportation and to perform mechanical tasks for more than 4000 years.

RESOURCE

The gross amount of kinetic energy in the earth's atmosphere is estimated to be 2.6×10^{21} kWh/yr. By capturing only the wind below the altitude of 300 m over the land masses in the United States, the entire electrical demand in the United States could be met. Such an ideal extraction of energy, of course, is not possible. However, there are many areas with annual average wind speeds of 6–10 m/s, which are considered to be excellent wind resources for generating electric power. Current wind energy turbines are approaching cost competitiveness with conventional energy sources for areas with these wind speeds.

The energy-producing potential of wind is defined in seven wind-power classes (Fig. 1) measured at standard reference heights of 10 and 50 m above the ground. At most sites, wind velocity increases with height in the earth's boundary layer. This is due to the frictional effect of wind blowing over the earth's surface. The wind velocity at the height of a wind turbine rotor hub, H, may be estimated by the following formula:

$$V_{\text{at hub height}} = V_{\text{ref}} \left(\frac{H}{H_r}\right)^N$$

where the reference velocity V_{ref} and height H_r, are normally measured 10 m above the ground. The wind shear exponent, N, varies considerably depending on the surface roughness and the site climatological conditions. Typically, an exponent of $N = 1/7$ is assumed over relatively flat and neutrally stable atmospheric conditions and increases with increasing suface roughness to $1/4$ for wooded areas and to $1/2$ or larger in very rough terrain.

Ocean energy resources are equally vast. On an average day, approximately 60 million km² of tropical seas

Classes of wind power density at 10 m and 50 m(a).

Wind Power Class	10 m (33 ft)		50 m (164 ft)	
	Wind Power Density (W/m²)	Speed(b) m/s (mph)	Wind Power Density (W/m²)	Speed(b) m/s (mph)
1	0	0	0	0
2	100	4.4 (9.8)	200	5.6 (12.5)
3	150	5.1 (11.5)	300	6.4 (14.3)
4	200	5.6 (12.5)	400	7.0 (15.7)
5	250	6.0 (13.4)	500	7.5 (16.8)
6	300	6.4 (14.3)	600	8.0 (17.9)
7	400	7.0 (15.7)	800	8.8 (19.7)
	1000	9.4 (21.1)	2000	11.9 (26.6)

(a) Vertical extrapolation of wind speed based on the 1/7 power law.

(b) Mean wind speed is based on Rayleigh speed distribution of equivalent mean wind power density. Wind speed is for standard sea-level conditions. To maintain the same power density, speed increases 3%/1000 m (5%/5000 ft) of elevation.

Figure 1. Wind power density classes.

absorb an amount of solar energy equivalent to the heat content of about 250 billion barrels of oil. This energy is stored in warm surface water, which could potentially be used to drive heat engines utilizing the temperature differential between the warm surface water and the cooler deep ocean water. Tidal energy and wave energy are other sources of ocean power. These resources are useful at sites with particular shore and terrain configurations. There has been some consideration given to harnessing the energy from ocean currents, such as the Gulf Stream. This is now considered to be impractical due to hardware design, anchoring problems, and the difficulties of transporting the power to shore.

Overall cost effectiveness of wind and ocean energy systems is improving. Projections show these systems can be economically competitive with conventional power sources depending on the availability of the renewable energy resource and on the cost of competing energy sources, especially oil and natural gas. Today, modern wind turbines, installed in clusters called wind power plants, are able to produce energy in the $0.08–0.15/kWh range at windy sites. This is approaching cost competitiveness for limited utility markets, but further improvements in the technology are expected to increase turbine energy capture and reliability and extend structural life. This should improve overall economics by a factor of two or more, opening large markets for power grid-connected and stand-alone applications around the world. Ocean thermal energy systems are still in the early stages of research and development, but projections show that they can eventually be built for $3200/kW, which will make them cost competitive for some tropical island applications. Tidal systems are useful today where shore configurations produce exceptionally high tides.

WIND ENERGY SYSTEMS

Historical Evolution

Clear evidence shows that as early as 13 B.C., wind power was used for transportation when Phoenician ships using

square-rig sails were prevalent in the Mediterranean. Sailing vessels dominated maritime transportation until the invention of the steam engine in the mid-nineteenth century. Following that period, fossil fuels became the dominant source of power for vessels, essentially eliminating the use of wind power for transportation. During the late nineteenth and early twentieth centuries, similar decline occurred in the use of wind power as a nontransportation energy source as shown in Figure 2. The advent of the Rural Electric Administration (REA) in the United States during the 1930s almost eliminated the use of wind power until its reemergence following the oil embargoes of

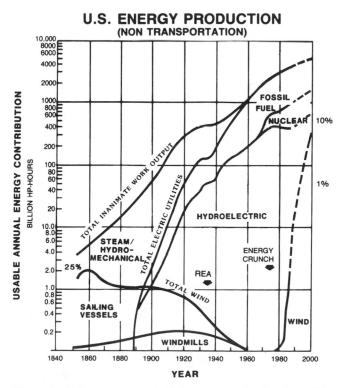

Figure 2. U.S. non-transportation energy production from 1840 to 2000.

the 1970s. In general, use of wind power is related to availability and cost of conventional sources of energy, principally fossil fuels.

The invention of the windmill is attributed to Heron of Alexandria almost 2000 years ago. These early machines, used for various mechanical tasks including grain grinding, were drag-type devices. They relied on the moving flow of air impinging on blades that rotated about an axis in order to produce usable torque. Many years later, sail-type devices were used to improve the efficiency of wind turbines by applying what is known today as aerodynamic lift principles. These concepts later led to the adaptation of the airfoil-shaped sail to marine applications.

Many variations of the windmill design occurred as the concept was applied in different parts of the world. The early Dutch windmills, used for grain grinding and water pumping, were typically very large in order to produce the required horsepower. Blades for these machines were developed with furling sails or wooden slats that could be used to change the amount of energy captured from the wind by controlling the amount of airfoil surface area. In many early machines, the entire windmill was rotated to allow the rotor to be pointed into the wind. In later designs and some early Mediterranean designs, only the top of the turbine building, which continued the main axis for the rotor, was rotated. With the introduction of electric-generating wind turbines, control systems had to be designed to limit the power levels achieved at very high wind speeds. This was accomplished by allowing either the turbine blades to feather out of the wind under the control of a mechanical actuator or by using a tail structure in order to turn the entire turbine partially out of the wind.

The number of blades on a wind turbine has also undergone evolution. Early grain-grinding and water-pumping applications used four or more blades in order to achieve the torque required to overcome high bearing frictions and pumping loads. For high speed electric power applications, wind turbines have evolved with three or fewer blades. Three blades have the distinct advantage of producing lower gyroscopic loads while one- or two-bladed machines have cost benefits and still achieve nearly the same energy extraction as the three-bladed machines. An experimental two-bladed, high speed, 100-kW turbine is shown in Figure 3. Today, many wind turbines are mounted on top of very tall, slender towers in order to take advantage of the higher wind velocities occuring above the boundary layer, while other machines use larger rotors in order to sweep a larger area of the wind stream in order to capture more energy.

The first use of wind energy for electric-power applications occurred in the United States in 1888, when electrical engineer Charles F. Brush, in Cleveland, Ohio, built a large wind turbine generator with a 56-ft-dia rotor that turned a 12-kW dc generator. Power was stored in lead acid batteries. Small wind generators became common on U.S. farms during the early twentieth century. Denmark, with good wind resources, used wind-generating turbines extensively, with electric output from thousands of machines totaling between 150 and 200 MW during the 1920s. Use of wind energy was nearly replaced by cheap

Figure 3. Experimental Department of Energy 100 kW experimental two-blade turbine located at the National Aeronautics and Space Administration (NASA) Plumbrook Station in Ohio.

fossil energy available during the early part of the twentieth century. Many of the water-pumping farm windmills were replaced by electric or diesel engine-driven pumps. The Rural Electrification Administration in the United States brought inexpensive electric power to many of the farms throughout the country. In most parts of the industrialized world, fossil-fueled, electric-generating stations replaced the wind turbine.

During World War II, the demand for electric energy and fossil fuels caused a reexamination of wind power. During the 1940s, in the United States, one pioneering wind energy project involved the construction of a 1.25-MW, 175-ft-dia wind turbine on Grandpa's Knob, Vt. This machine was operated until about 1945 when it suffered damage due to structural problems in one of its blades. Following the war, cheap fossil energy once again essentially eliminated the use of wind power around the world. During the 1970s, however, due to oil embargoes, the use of wind and other renewable energy sources was revived. Extensive research and development programs on wind, solar, and ocean energy were initiated in the United

States, and in many other countries around the world. The rapid development of dramatically improved wind turbines followed. Machines of various sizes were built and installed in many parts of the world, with the majority of these turbines being installed in the United States. The combination of financial incentives through tax credits, heavy dependence on expensive fossil fuels, and good wind resources combined to make the state of California the focus of this development effort. By the end of 1987, more than 16,000 wind turbines with a total capacity of nearly 1500 MW, were installed in California. During 1987 alone, these machines produced 1.8 billion kWh, the equivalent of burning 3 million barrels of oil. One example of a California wind farm is shown in Figure 4.

Modern Wind Turbines

Wind systems operate by extracting energy from a moving stream of air. Theoretically, the energy available from the wind is

$$\text{Kinetic energy} = \tfrac{1}{2}\,\rho\,A V^3$$

where ρ is the density of the air, A is the swept area of the turbine rotor, and V is the velocity of the wind. Well-designed and optimized turbines are capable of extracting 25–45% of the energy in the wind. Coefficients of performance, which reflect the efficiency of energy extraction from the wind over a variety of wind speeds, are shown in Figure 5 for the various types of machine. Because the energy in the wind is a cubic function of the wind speed, proper siting of wind turbines is extremely important. Doubling the wind speed increases the energy produced by a factor of eight.

Modern wind energy conversion systems are designed with two basic configurations: horizontal or vertical axis. The distinction between these two types relates to the position of the rotational axis of the machine. The horizontal axis machine, shown in Figure 6, consists of a large propeller with one or more blades mounted on top of a tower, providing sufficient clearance for the rotor above the ground. On the top of the tower is mounted a nacelle, which houses the support structure for the rotor, the gearbox to increase rotor speed to a level appropriate for con-

Figure 4. Wind power plant in Altamont Pass near San Francisco, Calif.

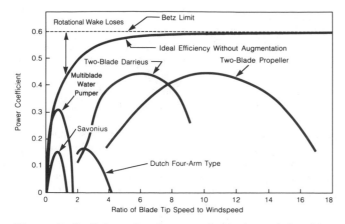

Figure 5. Coefficient of performance for various wind turbine types.

nection to a generator, and the generator itself. Horizontal axis wind turbines come in two varieties. Downwind machines, with the rotor blades turning downwind of the tower, have the advantage of being able to track the wind automatically by allowing the nacelle to rotate or yaw, thereby exposing the maximum rotor area to the wind. Upwind machines require either a tail to keep the rotor positioned upwind of the tower, or some other servocontrolled yaw drive system.

Vertical axis wind turbines, shown in Figure 7, have a

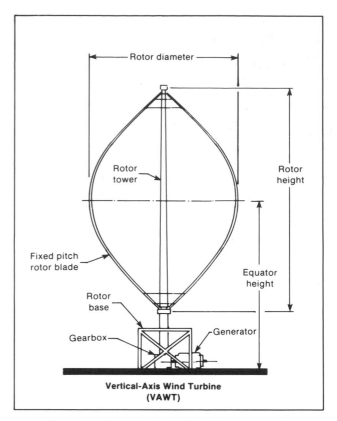

Figure 7. Vertical axis wind turbine components.

number of advantages. Because the power of the wind turbine is produced by the airfoil-shaped blades rotating around the vertical center axis, the wind turbine is insensitive to wind direction changes. Consequently, no yaw control system is required. In addition, much of the wind turbine machinery, gearbox, generator, or other drive system, is located on the ground, making servicing and maintenance simpler than on a horizontal axis machine.

Other types of wind turbines that have been investigated are shown in Figure 8. Shrouded turbines such as the diffuser-augmented wind turbine rely on a shroud structure to produce augmented flow through the wind turbine, allowing the size of the wind turbine to be reduced compared to a free-stream turbine of much larger diameter. This type of machine trades rotating structure for static structure; however, wind directionality requires that the shroud structure be repositioned to maintain a heading into the wind. This is a significant disadvantage in this type of machine. A derivative of the diffuser-augmented wind turbine is the tip-vane turbine, where small tip vanes are mounted on the end of the rotor blades, thereby producing augmentation. This kind of turbine has been investigated theoretically, but practical models have not proved to be economically competitive.

Another concept involves utilizing heat engines that produce wind inside a tall tower to be harvested by a small wind turbine. There are two basic concepts. One involving capturing solar energy in a greenhouse-type building, thus producing hot air that rises up a chimney. Wind energy is extracted by a small turbine in the base of the

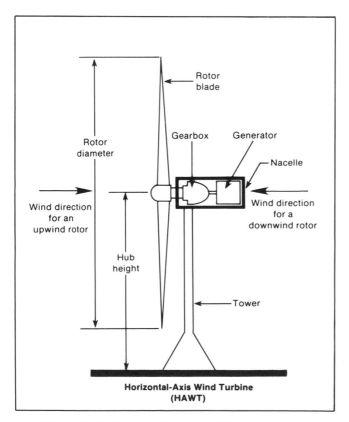

Figure 6. Horizontal axis wind turbine components.

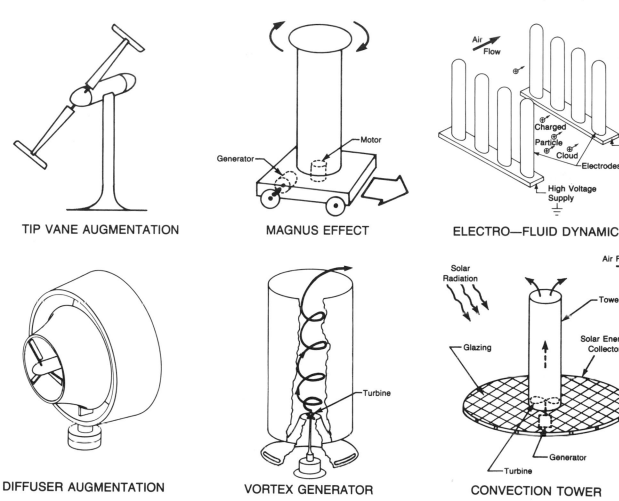

Figure 8. Taxonomy of innovative wind energy conversion systems.

tower. A related system takes air into the top of the chimney and chills it with the injection of water, which cools the air through the latent heat of vaporization, producing a downward flow in the column. These have been investigated theoretically, and practical experiments indicate that they are not expected to be competitive with other wind energy devices. Again, this type of device has not proven to be cost effective because of the large amount of structure involved in building the turbine and the tower.

One other tower device, sometimes called the vortex generator tower, uses slotted or airfoil-shaped entry ducts to route wind into a central tower producing a vortex flow in the center of the tower. This flow, with the resulting reduced pressure in the vortex, is used to produce flow through a small wind turbine mounted in the bottom of the tower.

Another type of wind machine is the electrofluid dynamic type, where charged particles are injected into the wind stream and transported by the wind from a cathode to an anode fence, thus producing an electrical potential. This kind of device has been investigated theoretically and has not yet proven to be economically competitive with other devices. Another tower concept is the Magnus effect rotor consisting of a rotating cylinder driven by a motor that, when operated in a wind stream, produces lift much like an airfoil. An example of this application is the Cousteau Society vessel *Alcyone*, which uses a Magnus effect rotor to power an oceangoing catamaran sailboat.

Wind energy is also being reexamined for applications in the marine transportation business. A number of countries have developed large merchant vessels from 300 to 45,000 tons, which have wind power augmentation systems in a variety of rig configurations. Most common are conventional lateen sails or large airfoil-shaped rigid sails mounted on one or more masts. Usually these are computer-controlled devices that are used to supplement conventional power plants when suitable wind is available. The cost effectiveness of this type of system is directly related to the competing cost of fuel for the ships.

OCEAN ENERGY SYSTEMS

Ocean energy systems have been used throughout history, principally by harnessing the tides to produce mechanical motion. Today, a variety of ocean energy resources have been recognized including tides, waves, currents, and thermal and salinity gradients. Ocean thermal and salinity energy conversion systems have the advantage of providing a virtually unlimited base-load power source that can operate continuously day and night throughout the year much as large coal or nuclear power plants do.

Ocean Thermal Energy Conversion Systems (OTEC)

OTEC systems operate on a heat engine principle using the temperature gradient of up to 20°C existing between warm surface water and colder water found at a depths of approximately 1000 m. This energy resource is particularly attractive for tropical islands with steep volcanic slopes, because they have both warm and cold water available near shore.

Ocean thermal energy systems operate on two basic cycles (Fig. 9). In the closed-cycle system, warm surface water is used to evaporate a working fluid such as Freon or ammonia, which then passes through a turbine driving a conventional generator. The working fluid then moves

through a condenser, which is cooled by seawater at 4–6°C brought up from the ocean depths. A pump then pressurizes the condensate and feeds it back into the evaporator, completing the cycle.

In open-cycle OTEC systems, the warm seawater itself serves as the working fluid. Warm surface water is pumped into a vacuum chamber evaporator to produce low pressure steam, which then passes through a multistage turbine that drives a generator to produce electricity. The steam is condensed using cold seawater pumped from the ocean depths. The open-cycle condensate, which is demineralized fresh water, can be used for drinking water. In both the closed-and open-cycles, cooling water from the condenser, which is nutrient-rich, sterile, deep-sea water, can also be used for mariculture and other applications. The triple products of electric power, fresh water, and nutrient-rich, deep-sea water make the open-cycle OTEC system particularly attractive.

The primary technical challenges in developing OTEC systems are in the need for extremely efficient and massive heat exchangers (evaporators and condensers), and the need for pumping large amounts of water from ex-

CLOSED CYCLE

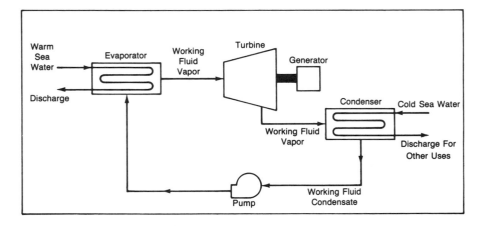

OPEN CYCLE

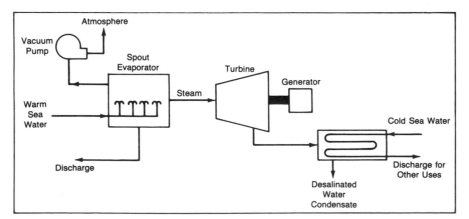

Figure 9. Ocean thermal energy conversion system cycles.

treme ocean depths, with pipes 2 km long and 1 m or larger in diameter. The turbines for open-cycle systems provide another technical challenge in that they must accommodate steam at extremely low pressures and correspondingly high volumetric flow rates.

In 1926, George Claude of France built an operating open-cycle OTEC plant off the coast of Cuba. Tremendous difficulties were encountered in the placement of the 2-km-long cold-water pipe. The plant was unable to produce net power because the cooling water temperature was about 10°C higher than expected. In August 1979, a demonstration closed-cycle OTEC plant called MINI OTEC operated for a short period of time off the coast of Hawaii, producing 50 kWe gross. The Japanese operated a 100-kWe-gross closed-cycle OTEC plant on the island of Nauru in 1981. Operation ceased when the cold-water pipe was damaged by a typhoon. Today, research is continuing with emphasis on the open-cycle concept, because this has the added benefit of producing desalinated water.

Salinity Systems

Power can be produced from two reservoirs of water having different salinity concentrations (such as the ocean and a river) through the use of pressure-retarded osmosis to develop a hydraulic pressure in the more concentrated solution. This pressurized solution can then be discharged through a hydraulic turbine, thus generating electricity. Ocean areas that experience low mixing and have little current, such as the Red and Dead seas, are potential sites for this approach.

Tidal Energy Systems

Tidal power systems were first recorded in the fourteenth century. Today, on the Rance River in France, a 240-MW tidal project produces 540 GWh of electricity annually. Other smaller tidal power systems are also operating in Norway, China, Canada, the UK, the USSR, and the United States. Tidal systems typically involve damming up a bay where there are naturally high tide conditions. The systems can be designed to operate while the tide is rising or dropping, or both. Parts of the world with unique, exceptionally high tides such as the Bay of Fundy in Canada make particularly attractive sites for tidal power systems.

Wave Energy Systems

Wave energy has been investigated in many countries, notably Japan, Norway, the UK, Canada, the USSR, and the United States. Wave energy extraction devices typically fall into three major categories: surface followers, pressure-activated systems, and focusing systems. Surface followers utilize two or more hinged sections that move relative to each other when subjected to wave motion. This relative motion can be harnessed mechanically to produce power. For presure-activated systems, wave power is used to compress air that in turn drives an air turbine. Pressure-activated pneumatic wave energy converters have been tested on a 500-ton Japanese research platform called the *Kaimei* in the Sea of Japan, under sponsorship of the International Energy Agency. Focusing systems use natural geographic features to concentrate the wave energy. One project, called the Tapered Channel Wave Focusing Experiment, is installed and currently under testing in Bergen, Norway. The primary disadvantage of wave energy systems is that in many parts of the world waves are not consistent energy sources. Furthermore, it is difficult to design a wave energy device that can survive the extreme conditions encountered during storms.

Today and in the future, ocean and wind systems can produce significant quantities of energy. U.S. Department of Energy studies project that early in the next century, these systems can be expected to produce more electric power from the wind and ocean than from all of the hydroelectric dams operating today.

BIBLIOGRAPHY

General References

Historical Statistics of the United States, Colonial Times to 1970, Part 2, Bicentennial Edition, U.S. Dept. of Commerce.

J. Reynolds, *Windmills and Watermills*, Praeger Publishers, 1970.

V. Torrey, *Wind-Catchers: American Windmills of Yesterday and Tomorrow*, The Stephen Greene Press, 1976.

G. W. Koeppl, *Putnam's Power from the Wind*, rev. ed., Van Nostrand Reinhold Co., Inc., New York, 1982.

P. M. Moretti and L. V. Divone, "Modern Windmills," *Scientific American* **254**(6), 110–116 (June 1986).

D. F. Ancona and J. B. Cadogan, "Wind Turbines at Work," *Institute of Electrical and Electronic Engineers, Spectrum* **19**(8), 46–51 (Aug. 1982).

Anderson and Romola, *The Sailing Ship: 6,000 Years of History*, rev. ed., Norton, 1963.

G. Claude, "Power from the Tropical Seas," *American Society of Mechanical Engineers, Mechanical Engineering* **52**(12), 1039–1044 (Dec. 1930).

R. Cohen, "Energy from the Ocean," *Philosophical Transactions of the Royal Society of London Series A* **307**(1499), 405–437 (Oct. 1982).

T. R. Penny and D. Bharathan, "Power from the Sea," *Scientific American* **256**(1), 86–92 (Jan. 1987).

See also Power Generation—Fossil Fuels; Power Generation—Geothermal—Power Generation—Nuclear

Daniel Ancona
U.S. Department of Energy
Washington, D.C.

PRECAST ARCHITECTURAL CONCRETE

Architectural precast concrete is a unique building product that offers many aesthetic and technical advantages for the project designer and owner. These include diversity in design expression, minimal maintenance, excellent durability, outstanding fire resistance, and superior quality control through factory production. Architectural precast concrete may be cast into structural elements, bearing-wall panels, or non-load-bearing cladding that is applied to a structural frame. Structural or architectural elements precast off site, in a controlled factory environment, offer some advantages over field-cast concrete. Precast plant production techniques are typically more efficient. Enclosed plant conditions afford greater quality assurance and better control of dimensional tolerances. Inclement weather has little impact on production, and on-site construction time should be reduced to field erection, cleaning, and minor patching.

Architectural precast concrete products consist of materials with unique properties having specific characteristics. As with most building materials, an understanding of material properties is essential to maximize the best qualities and minimize the weakest aspects.

MATERIALS

It is important to understand basic material properties and fabrication techniques that influence product performance and appearance. The concrete for architectural precast is composed of portland cement, aggregates (coarse and fine), water, and possibly certain admixtures. These materials will be examined individually.

Portland Cement

Portland cement is one of the principal materials required to produce architectural precast concrete. It is the binder that combines with fine aggregate and fills the spaces between pieces of large aggregate, bonding the large aggregate together. Cement is the primary material component affecting the color of smooth surface-as-cast finish architectural precast concrete. Therefore, consideration must be given to the color of portland cement specified.

The raw materials in cement are stone and sand, which are kiln fired and then ground into a powder. Because these materials may contain calcium, iron, magnesium, silica, and other elements (which vary by locale), the natural materials will influence the final color of the cement. Specifically, the content of iron and manganese oxides greatly affects cement color. Gray portland cement contains a high quantity of these elements, whereas white portland cement contains less iron and manganese oxide and is more consistent in color. If the designer requires reasonably uniform color, the specifications should require that all cement be obtained from a single manufacturer and produced from one source of raw materials during a specific time period. If the designer mandates absolutely uniform results, only white portland cement should be specified.

Aggregates

Aggregates are typically divided into two categories: coarse and fine. Sand, granite, quartz, limestone, and marble are materials commonly used as aggregates and found in architectural precast concrete.

While considering the factors that influence the selection of a particular aggregate, it is also necessary to determine the degree of exposure desired for a particular finish

and texture. If the coarse aggregate will be lightly exposed, the appearance of the concrete will be influenced by the remaining sand and cement, which is adjacent and bonded to the coarse aggregate. A medium exposure of coarse aggregate will have more influence on the final appearance. A heavy exposure of coarse aggregate will dominate the completed appearance of the finished panel. Exposing coarse aggregate produces one of the most readily achievable, reasonable, and consistent architectural precast concrete finishes. Considering the range of aggregates that are typically available (ie, granite, quartz, limestone, marble, plus other aggregates specific to a region), exposing coarse aggregate in architectural precast concrete offers many different visual solutions, finishes, and textures.

Coarse Aggregate. Coarse aggregate accounts for the greatest material bulk within architectural precast concrete. This type of aggregate typically exceeds the combined weight of portland cement and fine aggregate in the mix design. If the intended architectural precast concrete finish removes the portland cement paste and fine aggregates, the coarse aggregate will be the predominant material affecting color and texture. Coarse aggregate is available in a wide range of shapes, sizes, colors, hardness, and costs. Careful consideration must be given to all factors before making a final selection. If the coarse aggregate will be the primary factor influencing color and texture, it should be obtained from a single source for the entire project. It is a recommended practice that the project specifications include the purchasing and stockpiling of coarse aggregate to assure consistent results. Consideration must be given to the durability of particular aggregates in certain climatic conditions. The Mohs' scale identifies relative values of hardness for minerals. Talc is rated 1 (softest), and diamond is rated 10 (hardest). Typical architectural precast concrete aggregates are rated between 3 and 7 on this scale. In addition to aggregate hardness, the resistance of aggregate to multiple freeze–thaw cycles should be considered. This material property is directly related to absorption and retention of water.

Fine Aggregate. Fine aggregate, or sand, is the second most prevalent material in a typical architectural precast concrete mix. Fine aggregate will greatly influence the color and appearance of finishes where the portland cement has been removed but the large aggregate has not yet been exposed. Fine aggregate mixes with portland cement, thereby producing a paste that coats and bonds the large aggregate together. Fine aggregates are found in a natural state (sand with rounded edges) or may be manufactured (sand with angular edges). Fine aggregate is generally ¼–⅓ of the volume of total aggregate in the concrete, depending on whether it is natural or manufactured. Because of the rounded shape of natural sand, it is less likely to compact than is angular manufactured sand. Variations in color for both types of sand may occur because of inconsistencies at the source. The quantity, color, and type of sand will greatly affect the final appearance of lightly sandblasted (mechanically treated), light retarded (chemically treated), or acid etched (chemically treated) architectural precast concrete. Project designers should consider these influences and specify accordingly.

Water

Water must be added to the dry materials to produce a workable mix. For architectural precast concrete, the slump should be approximately 2 in. Because water will affect concrete slump, color, and texture, the quantity and quality of water must be controlled. Impurities and minerals in the water may affect the final appearance of the product. Therefore, all mix water should be potable and from a single source.

Admixtures

Admixtures are additives that, when combined with the previously listed raw materials, improve some aspect of the concrete. Such admixtures include superplasticizers (increase fluidity of concrete without adding additional water, resulting in stronger or more workable concrete), air entrainers (increase durability during freeze–thaw cycles), pigments (for achieving certain colors, which are not producible with natural materials), and retarders/accelerators (used to reduce or increase the working time and condition of concrete).

MIX DESIGN

The proportions of the previously mentioned materials will compose the mix design. Samples of four different mix designs for exposed aggregate concrete follow:

MIX 1

Cement, type I, gray (7½–8 bags)	705–752 lb
Masonry sand, minus No. 8 screen	925 lb
Crushed granite ½–¾ in.	2080 lb
Water	280 lb
Water–cement ratio	0.44
Sand, percent of total aggregate by volume	29
AEA as required to obtain approximately 6% air content	
Slump, approximately	2.0 in.

This particular mix design is appropriate for exposed granite aggregate, with most of the coarse aggregate of a single size. The surface of this mix could be exposed by chemical retarder, sandblasting, or acid washing.

MIX 2

Cement, type I, white (7½–8 bags)	750–752 lb
Sand (white silica), minus No. 16 screen	1070 lb
Crushed limestone, ⅜–¾ in.	1840 lb
Water	280 lb
Water–cement ratio	0.44
Sand, percent of total aggregate by volume	0.37
AEA	6%
Slump	2.0 in.

This particular mix design is used to achieve a white concrete surface with a light-to-medium surface texture. The

surface of this mix could be exposed by either a chemical retarder or sandblasting.

MIX 3

Cement, type 1, grey (7½–8 bags)	705–752 lb
White masonry sand, minus No. 8 screen	900 lb
Gravel, ⅜–¾ in.	2060 lb
Water	270 lb
Sand, percent of total aggregate by volume	30
AEA	6%
Pigment	9.26 lb
Slump	2.0 in.

This particular mix is suitable for all exposed textures. The mix uses grey cement with a small quantity of pigment to help reduce color differential throughout the matrix.

MIX 4

Cement, type 1, white (7½–8 bags)	705–752 lb
Masonry sand, minus No. 16 screen	1400 lb
Gravel ⅜–¾ in.	940 lb
Gravel ¼–⅜ in.	470 lb
Water	290 lb
Water–cement ratio	0.43
Sand, percent of total aggregate by volume	0.51
AEA	6%
Pigment	32 lb
Slump	2.0 in.

This particular mix design includes a considerable amount of pigment, white cement, and a high sand content. It would be used for smooth surface-as-cast finish or for a very light texture panel.

PRODUCTION CONSIDERATIONS

In addition to the material and mix consideration, certain production aspects must be included in the project design and planning phase.

Repetition of Panel Elements

For precast concrete components to be cost effective, repetition of elements is mandatory. Whether casting structural or architectural units, the most suitable designs will use the same form work (molds) for the maximum number of pieces. Variations in panel sizes and configurations may be accomplished with sufficient planning during the design phase. Ideal designs will incorporate block outs for specialty pieces within the typical panel form work. Although every project will have atypical conditions (which are unavoidable), the most successful and cost-effective projects will maximize the repetition of elements. This goal does not suggest that architectural precast concrete should be mundane or boring in the quest for simplicity and repetition. Many design variations may be developed by incorporating the basic architectural panel types (spandrel panels, floor-to-floor panels with or without openings, and column covers) on the same structure.

These panel types may also be varied with different architectural finishes and textures.

Size of Panel Elements

Because architectural precast concrete elements are factory produced, consideration must be given to the size and weight of each precast element. Hauling, handling, and erection of architectural precast concrete will greatly influence the unit cost. It is advisable to design the largest practical size, as hauling, handling, and erection costs are about the same for large and small pieces. It is important for the project design team to understand applicable trucking regulations for a particular region because factory-made elements are typically transported by truck to the site. Typically, panels should be less than 35 ft long, 12 ft high, and 10 tons in weight. Panel weight may be estimated based on the rough value of 155 lb/ft^3 (based on standard weight concrete), general reinforcing, and inserts and hardware.

Connections

Architectural precast concrete cladding panels are attached with special connections to the structure of the building. These connections must transmit live loads (wind, seismic forces) and dead load (weight of precast panels) back to the building's structure. One common approach for the connections is to attach the panel firmly to the structure at midspan and provide bearing points at panel ends. The bearing points are designed and constructed to permit expansion and contraction. Tie-back restraints are provided at upper panel points. Once in place, connections are either bolted (with provision for lateral movement) or welded. This scheme for connection places most of the concrete panel in compression, as the panel weight is supported near the bottom. With the panel midpoint fixed and the end point sliding, panel movement (due to thermal expansion and contraction) is reduced to one half of the panel length. Panel connections must also accommodate the necessary tolerances to erect a plumb exterior wall on structural columns that may be out of plumb but within the structural industry standards for erection.

Typical Panel Configuration

Architectural precast concrete cladding is typically classified as spandrel, floor to floor panels with or without openings, and column covers.

Spandrel panels span horizontally from column to column and vertically from window head to the window-sill above. Spandrel panels are commonly used in buildings that have a horizontal character, such as small and large office buildings and parking decks. If a window system is part of the design, erection of spandrel panels requires close attention to tolerances, because the window system must fit between upper and lower precast spandrel panels.

Floor-to-floor panels span horizontally from column to column and vertically from floor line to floor line. These precast panels may include windows, whose openings are

formed with block outs within the precast mold. Limitations for this system include a minimum dimension of 18 in. between panel edge and opening or 18 in. between adjacent panel openings.

Mold

Typically, panels are cast face down in an envelope mold. This mold is contained on the face and four sides. The back of the mold may be open or enclosed with special block outs to achieve a specific configuration on the back side of the panel. Because the architectural precast panel must be removed from the envelope mold, the sides of this mold must include a bevel or draft (minimum 1:12) to allow removing the panel from the mold. With certain panel configurations and openings, the mold draft may have to be increased, to facilitate panel removal. In special instances, the mold may be designed and constructed to come apart, using special hardware. This break-apart feature aids the removal of special-shaped panels or those panels that must be constructed. Molds are frequently constructed of plywood with an applied fiber glass resin finish. If considerable production is anticipated, steel molds may be used. These molds are more expensive, but have a significantly longer service life.

Other materials such as concrete, fiber glass forms, and urethanes have also been successfully used for architectural precast concrete molds. Whichever material is selected, the important issue is that the quality of the mold design and construction will directly influence the appearance of the final product.

FINISHES

Special finishes for concrete and adaptations to architectural precast concrete may be traced back to Roman times. Volcanic ash (pozzolana containing silica and alumina) was mixed with lime and water to create concrete. Shortly thereafter, mass concrete was combined with stone or brick to create rubble-and-concrete-filled walls. In some applications, mosaic tiles were placed in the concrete to camouflage and improve the appearance of raw concrete.

After the Roman period, composite concrete-wall technology can be traced into the Christian era typically as stone rubble and concrete construction. Thereafter, few advances were made until the late 1700s when portland cement was first commercially produced, thereby providing a greater consistency in materials.

By the late 1800s, Europeans found that concrete reinforced with steel mesh or bars would overcome the deficiencies of mass concrete in tension and shear. Although the steel added new structural properties to concrete, care in the placement of such reinforcing became a critical issue, because corrosion of the steel could cause concrete to spall. Attention to adequate concrete cover over the steel reinforcing in architectural precast concrete is still very important to prevent staining and spalling of the concrete surface.

Many variations occurred in the casting of mass concrete in the early to mid-1900s, demonstrating the potential of reinforced concrete for bridge construction and building enclosure and structure. In addition to the ongoing structural reinforcement, various types of finishes were explored to enhance the appearance of raw concrete. By the mid-1900s, precasting concrete into structural elements and cladding panels off-site was an approach that offered many technical and aesthetic advantages. Specifically, if the construction could be standardized components, considerable time and cost could be saved with repetitive elements.

It is evident from this brief historical overview that concrete is a very versatile material. With architectural precast concrete it is possible to achieve a large variety of colors, textures, and finishes by manipulating the key materials, molds or formwork, and casting techniques. The most typical architectural precast concrete finishes are outlined individually, with information that was provided by the Architectural Precast Association.

Smooth Surface, As Cast

Definition. Concrete is poured against hard, smooth form work to achieve a smooth "as-cast" finish on the precast unit (Figs. 1 and 2).

Reasons for Use. An as-cast finish shows the natural beauty of concrete without trying to emulate any other building product. A very clean definition of profile can be achieved with this surface. If the surface is to be painted,

this finish will provide an excellent surface, while keeping costs to a minimum.

Strengths. Cost is reduced by eliminating additional finishing steps after removal from the form. Sharp lines at intersecting planes can be achieved with this finish. The smoothness of this surface will self-clean more readily than an etched surface.

Weaknesses. The resulting surface of concrete will mirror the surface of the form it is cast against, showing even minor imperfections of the form. Because color is totally controlled by the cement, variations between pieces and within pieces will be more pronounced. The surface is difficult to repair. Air voids show more generally on this surface. Surface crazing (fine spider lines) may develop on the surface. Shadowing (stone or wire reinforcing showing through the surface) can occur with this finish.

Expectations. Color variations can be expected with this finish, but the variation can be minimized with careful selection of mix ingredients, combined with close control of the water to cement ratio and mixing time. All vertical casts will have small voids created by entrapped air or small water pockets. These voids can be minimized with proper mix design and casting procedures. White cement will achieve a greater uniformity of color than gray

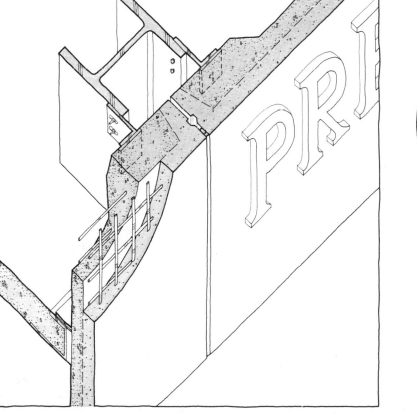
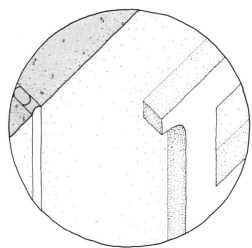

Figure 1. Smooth surface, as cast finish.

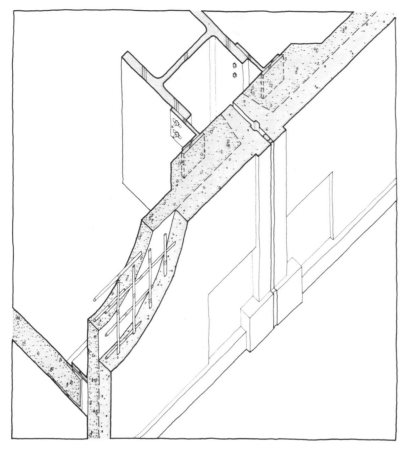
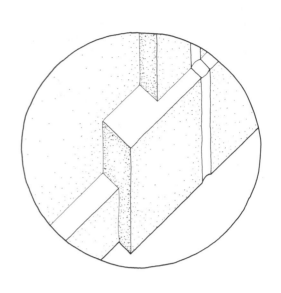

Figure 2. Smooth surface, as cast finish with reveals and surface articulations.

cement. Allowable color variation in gray cement is enough to cause noticeable color differences in precast panels.

To complete a project successfully with this finish requires considerable involvement before beginning actual production. Field trips to existing projects would demonstrate accepted finish expectations. Mock-ups should be made representing all configurations involved in the project. Mock-ups should be as cast for approval by the design team for acceptance of color variation, quantity of voids, and overall appearance of architectural design.

Smooth Surface, Light Sandblast

Definition. The smooth surface, light sandblast finish is achieved by casting concrete against a smooth, hard surface. After removal from the form, the product is given a light sandblasting. This light sandblasting will remove the laitence (cement skin) from the surface. The resultant finish is a smooth, sand-textured surface (Fig. 3).

Reasons for Use. Smooth cast, lightly sandblasted precast will give an appearance very close to natural stone. Because the surface is relatively smooth, it will tend to self-clean more readily than a deeply etched surface. Clean definition of a profile may be achieved with this surface.

Strengths. This is a common finish well within the capacity of all precast producers. Light sandblasting is a good method to remove the appearance of the poured concrete look. Crazing is minimized by removing the cement skin at the surface of the concrete. Color variation is reduced by removing the cement surfaces, allowing the sand to control the color to a greater degree.

Weaknesses. Smooth surfaces show imperfections more readily than do deeply etched surfaces. Damage to smooth, flat surfaces is more difficult to repair. Minor imperfections of the cast or form work show more quickly on this surface than on deeper etched surfaces. Variations in color show more quickly on smooth surfaces. Air voids, especially in the vertical portion of any cast, show more on smooth, flat surfaces.

Expectations. Any returns (turning vertically from a horizontal position while being cast) will have air holes. They would probably not be in excess of ¼-in. diameter and could be grouted if they are objectionable. White cement will achieve a greater uniformity of color than gray cement. Allowable color differences in gray cement are enough to cause noticeable color differences in precast panels. Sand is a very important ingredient in coloring light sandblasted finishes, as it is the predominant visual element on the finished surface.

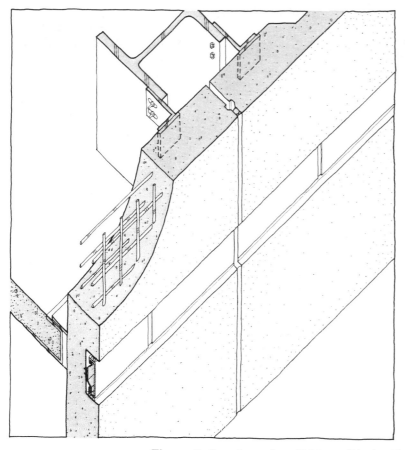
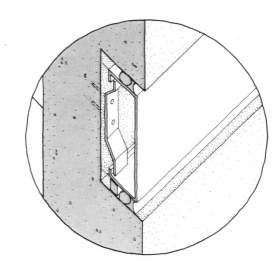

Figure 3. Smooth surface, light sandblast with metal band accent strip.

This finish can be used to achieve a natural-stone type finish. It will provide excellent detail; however, it is subject to some variation in color.

Smooth Surface, Acid Etch

Definition. This finish is achieved by casting concrete against a smooth, hard surface. After removal from the form, the piece is allowed to set to a uniform hardness. The product is then washed with an acid solution and scrubbed to remove the cement skin. The result is a smooth sand-textured surface.

Reason for Use. Acid etching produces a surface closely resembling natural stones such as limestone, brownstone, and sandstone. The preweathered surface will remain consistent for a very long time. Detail is not damaged with acid etching. Sand exposed retains more sparkle with acid etching than with sandblasting.

Strengths. Finer sand texture may be achieved with acid etching than with sandblasting. Brighter, deeper colors are achieved with acid etching. Retention of detail is best achieved with acid etching. Acid etching minimizes surface crazing by removing the cement skin on the precast.

Weaknesses. Acid etching should not be used on large panels. The method of applying and removing acid over a big area is difficult to achieve with great consistency. This surface is not as easy to patch as deeper etches; however, minor air voids are fairly easy to grout and refinish. Imperfections in the form show more readily than on deeper etches. Return, or vertical, casts will have air voids (probably ¼ in and under). If these are objectionable, they can be grouted and rewashed.

Expectations. As stated above, surfaces cast vertically will have minor air voids. These can be grouted and rewashed if they are objectionable. The color and nature of sand used is very important with acid-etched pieces. Acid etching is an important ingredient in controlling the appearance and color of the precast unit.

This finish is used to achieve a bright, sparkling natural-stone look. It is used successfully on smaller trim work such as sills, lintels, belt course, and similar decorative elements. It is not recommended for large panel work.

Exposed Aggregate, Sandblasted

Definition The exposed aggregate, sandblasted finish is achieved by casting concrete against a smooth, hard surface. After removal from the form, the finished surface is sandblasted to remove the matrix and expose, as well as etch, the coarse aggregate. The depth of the blast is determined by the desired texture and the target color, as influenced by the color of the matrix and the coarse aggregate. Three different types of exposures are possible. On light exposed surfaces, the skin of cement and sand is removed just sufficiently to expose the surface of the coarse aggregate. On medium exposed surfaces, further removal of cement and sand exposes approximately the same area of both coarse aggregate and matrix. On deep exposed surfaces, cement and fine aggregate are removed to a depth where the coarse aggregate becomes the dominant surface feature (Fig. 4).

Reasons for Use. A sandblasted finish can be used to achieve textured surfaces in which the coarse aggregate is exposed as well as etched by the blasting.

Strengths. Varying aggregate size and color with matrix color and sandblast texture provides flexibility for the final finish. Textured surfaces tend to distribute water runoff more evenly, thus reducing streaking from normal weathering patterns. Textured surfaces tend to forgive minor surface imperfections when observed at normal viewing distances. Damage is more easily repaired than on smooth finishes. The surface of the coarse aggregate is etched at the same time that it is being exposed by the blasting operation.

Weaknesses. Sandblasting hardened concrete is time-consuming and expensive. The deeper the blasting, the higher the cost. Damage to sandblasted surfaces, although easier to repair than on smooth surfaces, is more difficult to repair than chemically retarded surfaces. Air voids and uniformity of the aggregate density are difficult to control on vertical and sloped returns. Soft aggregates tend to erode at the same rate as the matrix and sometimes cannot be used. The exposure is influenced by the size of the sandblast sand and the skill of the sandblasting technician. Operating techniques must remain the same throughout the project to ensure uniformity.

Expectations. Good color uniformity can be achieved if care is taken in selection of the raw materials that contribute to the color of the product. Contrasting matrix and coarse aggregate colors should be avoided if uniformity of color is desired. The color of the finish will progressively change as the depth of the blast changes. The color will initially reflect the color of the matrix. As the coarse aggregate is exposed, the color will be influenced by the color of the coarse aggregate.

This finish is widely used for light and medium exposure. Labor expense usually prohibits its use for deep etches.

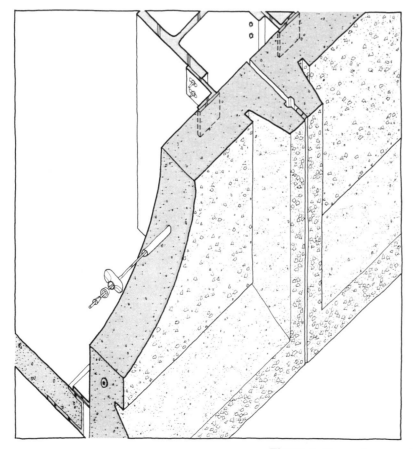
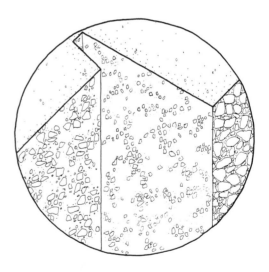

Figure 4. Exposed aggregate.

Exposed Aggregate, Chemically Retarded and Sandblasted

Definitions. The exposed aggregate, chemically retarded and sandblasted finish is achieved by casting against a form surface that has been painted with a retarder that slows the set of the concrete at its surface. After the panel is removed from the form, the retarder surface is removed by use of sandblasting. The result is a panel with coarse aggregate exposed to the degree called for by design.

Reasons for Use. Exposed aggregate finishes are achieved easily. Sandblasting allows for the correction of any variations in exposure, so this method will achieve a more uniform surface.

Strengths. Uniform exposure of stone aggregate is possible with minimum effort. Minor form imperfections do not impair the final surface. This method can achieve a very uniform surface.

Weaknesses. Any portion of the panel poured in a vertical position will not show the same concentration or positioning of aggregate as the flat surface. (This problem might be corrected by sequential casting, which allows all surfaces to be cast flat.)

Expectations. Color consistency is dependent on the consistency of the aggregate used. Consistency of surface can be controlled reasonably well. Sandblasting will dull the finish and color of the aggregate to a degree, depending on the hardness of the aggregate. If a strong, durable aggregate is used, this surface would not change over the years.

This finish should be used where the beauty of the aggregate or a textured surface is to be featured. The end result is a matte finish, as opposed to a brighter finish achieved with water blasting.

Exposed Aggregate, Chemically Retarded and Water-blasted

Definition. The exposed aggregate, chemically retarded and water-blasted finish is achieved by the application of a chemical retarder to the surface of the form. The retarder prevents the matrix from hardening at the surface of the panel to a specific depth (controlled by the strength of the retarder). After curing (normally overnight), the unhardened layer of matrix at the surface of the panel is removed by high pressure water blasting, thus exposing the aggregate.

Reason for Use. The natural beauty of the stone aggregate is displayed in its natural colors and finish without damage. This is an economical finish to achieve.

Strengths. The aggregate is not damaged or changed in this cleaning method. Minor imperfections in the form do not affect the final product. The finish is relatively easy to patch and tends to distribute water runoff more evenly, thus reducing the streaking that appears on smooth surfaces.

Weaknesses. The end result of chemical retardation removed by water blasting is controlled by the retarder; therefore, any variations in exposure are not as correctable as in sandblasting. Vertical, radius, or complicated surfaces are difficult because the retarder is subject to movement during casting on these surfaces and variation in etch can result.

Expectations. This finish will display the aggregate in its natural beauty. Control of mix, slump, retarder, and time of exposure is essential because there is very little correction allowed with the water-blasting method. Some variation will occur. Therefore, this should be minimized by having as little contrast between matrix and aggregate as possible.

If the bright, natural colors of the aggregate are the prime concern, water blasting is the best way to achieve this result.

Form Liners

Definition. This finish is achieved by the use of plaster, patterned rubber, grained wood, rope, or any other material as a liner in the casting mold to impart a particular finish to the face of the panel (Fig. 5).

Reasons for Use. Unlimited effects can be achieved by use of liners. This method can be combined with sandblasting and other techniques to achieve even greater variety of finishes.

Strengths. This method is extremely versatile.

Weaknesses. Commercially available liners are of fixed sizes. Joints from piece to piece are difficult to hide. The surface of the panel is usually difficult to repair. One-piece liners of plaster or rubber are expensive to produce.

Expectation. Because the detail of this finish is limited only by the imagination of the design team, it is hard to generalize on expectations. It is particularly important to develop samples, to be sure the end result is achieved in a satisfactory manner.

Use of liners opens an unlimited number of options on finish. However, use of this type finish requires close coordination between the design team and a precaster to be sure the end result is achievable.

Tooled Surfaces

Definition. Tooled surfaces are achieved by casting concrete against smooth or specially textured or patterned formwork and, after removal from the form, treating the hardened surface mechanically to create the desired effect. Fractured fin and bushhammered are two types of finish that employ tooling (Fig. 6).

Reasons for Use. This method is used solely to achieve a very special effect.

Strengths. Consistency (or lack of consistency if that is what is desired) is controlled by the artisan who finishes

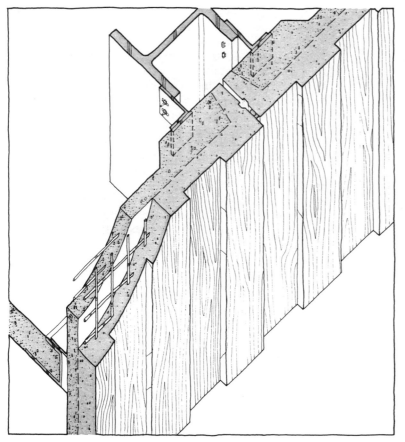
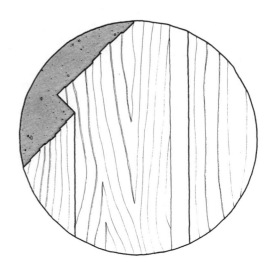

Figure 5. Form liners, finish with wood texture.

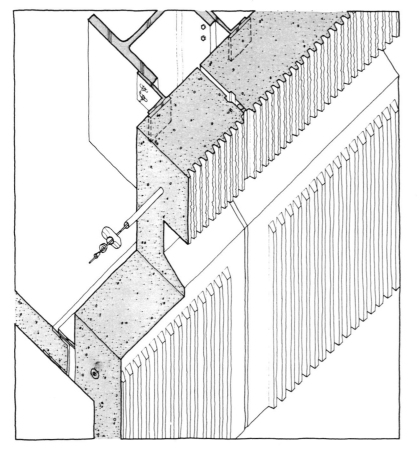
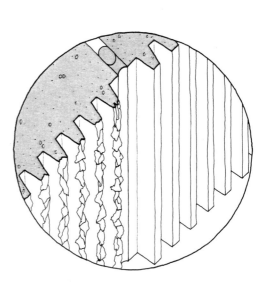

Figure 6. Tooled surface, fractured rib finish.

the panel. It is the effective way to achieve "broken stone" finishes that are sometimes required or desirable.

Weaknesses. This finish is probably the most expensive of the precast finishes. Variations due to more than one artisan working on the panel would be possible with this finish.

Expectations. This method allows the use of very different surfaces, such as split rib and broken stone. These surfaces closely resemble hand-tooled natural-stone faces.

Tooled surfaces allow many variations of precast panels. However, it is an expensive surface and it is very dependent on the caliber of the artisans. The result from tooled finishes is much more individual in nature than many other more standard finishes.

Veneers—Natural Stone

Definition. Natural-stone finishes are achieved by placing natural stone (limestone, granite, marble) pieces into a form and casting concrete behind it to achieve a large precast panel having a natural-stone face. The purpose is to create a natural-stone face on the building, while incorporating the efficiency of precast concrete (Fig. 7).

Reasons for Use. Veneers provide a natural-stone face while using the efficient methods of precasting panels. Stone-faced precast panels are far superior to individually set stones in achieving a watertight surface. Time and money are saved because the panels can be produced while the structure is being erected.

Strengths. Cast veneers provide safe, strong application of the natural stone to the face of the building. Panels can be prepared before completion of the structure of the building. Damage to the stone is minimized because the handling is all done on the ground.

Weaknesses. Some complicated, involved shapes do not lend themselves to casting into precast panels. Natural stone may have considerable variation in color, which must be evaluated before casting.

Expectations. Natural stone on precast will look exactly like field-set or frame-set stone.

Natural stone set on precast is an excellent option for achieving a natural-stone building with greater efficiency and far superior end result (safety, water tightness, etc). Almost without exception, time and money will be saved with this method over field-applied stone veneer.

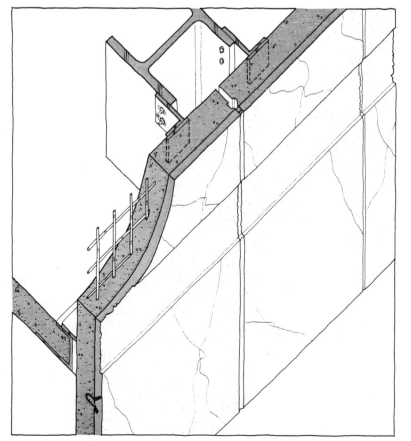

Figure 7. Veneer, natural stone finish.

Veneers—Brick or Ceramic Tile

Definition. This is a precast panel that has been specially cast so that brick can be set on the panel after its removal from the form (Fig. 8). Alternatively, thin brick or tile can also be set into a form and the concrete is cast behind it (Fig. 9). In this case, the comments on natural stone panels would apply more closely.

Reasons for Use. This method achieves a brick- or tile-veneered building with the efficiency of precast concrete. It is more economical to lay brick or tile on the ground as opposed to working from a staging. Panels can be prepared while the structure is being erected.

Strengths. This is an economical way to achieve an essentially brick or tile building. Precasting provides a better watertight skin than a conventionally set brick building.

Weaknesses. Extreme care must be taken to assure proper coursing when panels are installed on the building. Variations in brick or tile color may occur. All brick- or tile-facing materials must be blended when set in the molds to achieve uniform and consistent results. Extreme care must be taken in the placement of reinforcing bars to avoid having them directly behind the veneers.

Expectations. This method permits the combination of brick or tile veneer with precast trim. This approach is equal or superior to a conventionally set brick- or tile-veneer construction.

Brick or tile set into precast will achieve equal or superior workmanship and economy over conventionally set veneers. The end result will be a more watertight building. Preparation of the panel while the structure is being erected will save time and money.

COST INDEX

Considering the multiplicity of materials and casting techniques that are available to the project design team, the question of relative cost to achieve various finishes must be considered. The following cost information is very general. The charts are intended to provide relative costs of different materials and textures. The ratios shown are multiples of a theoretical plain-panel price. This plain panel is a flat 6-in.-thick precast concrete panel without any surface texture, made with gray cement and local aggregates. In 1988, this plain panel would cost approximately \$10/ft² delivered to the project site. This price may vary, depending on local labor rates.

Selection of other materials would multiply the applicable plain-panel price for an area by the following factors:

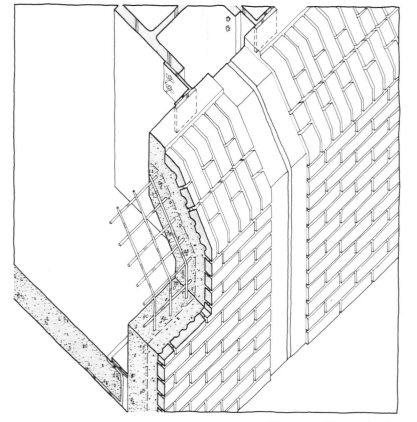
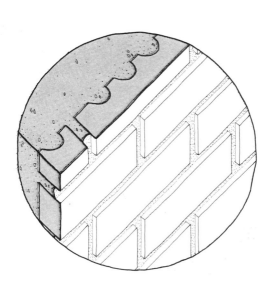

Figure 8. Veneer, brick finish.

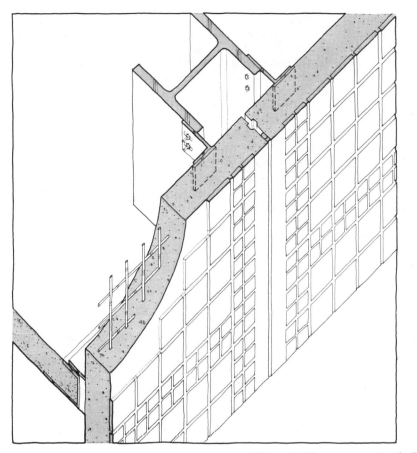
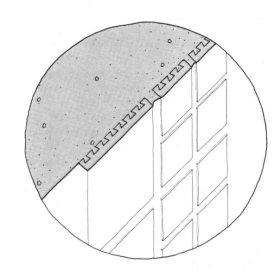

Figure 9. Veneer, ceramic tile finish.

White cement	1.07
Silica sand	1.06
Marble, coarse aggregate	1.15
Granite, coarse aggregate	1.20
Pigments	1.07

Selection of more elaborate textures would multiply the applicable plain-panel price for a specific locale by the following factors:

Form liners	1.06
Chemical retarder	1.06
Light sandblast	1.07
Acid etching	1.08
Heavy sandblast	1.15
Bushhammer, light	1.15
Hammered ribs with sandblast	1.17
Bushhammer, heavy	1.20
Smooth white	1.22
Tile/brick facing	1.24
Sand casting	1.27
Honing/polishing	1.55
Stone (veneer) facing	1.80

These factors are given to provide the project design team with a general overview of precast costs and how they are affected by materials and textures. The actual costs will vary somewhat with location. Plant labor, wastage factors, and plant material-handling charges are included in the cost estimates.

SAMPLE PANELS

Sample panels are a very important device to help achieve a satisfactory architectural precast project. The process should begin with the production of small pieces (3–5 units approximately 12–24 in. square) that show the general character and appearance of the desired architectural precast concrete finish. These pieces cannot represent an exact or final finish, as pouring concrete in such a limited size will not be equivalent to an entire full-scale panel. These units are frequently developed as part of the pre-bid process and will show the general finish and range of colors and textures.

Once general approval has been granted for the small pieces, two options exist. If necessary, intermediate-size pieces may be cast (3–5 units, approximately 48–60 in. square) to provide additional information regarding color range, distribution, texture, finishes, and so on. However, if all parties were comfortable with the small samples, the project team may proceed with casting the first full-size mock-up sample panel. The objective of this particular sample is to demonstrate all conditions that may be encountered in the project (recesses, reveals, outside/inside corners, multiple finishes/textures/veneers, etc). This particular sample may not be fully representative of the exact finishes that can be reasonably achieved during mass production.

To provide a sample panel standard for the entire production, it is recommended that 3–5 full-size panels be fabricated (once the previous mock-up has been approved). These full-size panels should be representative of the actual production run in every aspect, including maximum range of color; maximum number of acceptable imperfections, such as air-void holes; and maximum deviation in dimension and tolerances. These panels should be kept in a safe place in the precast plant, in order to evaluate the daily production. These sample panels may be incorporated in the building facade, assuming they are still in acceptable condition. All samples should be viewed in the sun and shade, with dry and wet surface finishes. In addition to these procedures, at the beginning of the project, the project team should visit other architectural precast concrete projects with similar finishes. These field trips help all parties to understand and observe the variations that may occur and help to define the overall appearance criteria that will be acceptable to the project team. Completing the sample panel process is extremely important and helps to develop communications among all parties.

CONCLUSION

Architectural precast concrete offers abundant technical and aesthetic opportunities, including a diverse range of finishes that are readily achievable. With an informed understanding of material advantages and limitations, the project team may achieve architectural precast concrete finishes that are aesthetically satisfying, economically produced, and durable over time.

MARK WILLIAMS
Kenney/Williams/Williams,
Building Diagnostics
Maple Glen, Pennsylvania

PRESERVATION, HISTORIC

Historic preservation in the United States and elsewhere in the world has come to mean a series of subtle and complicated design decisions, compromises, and protective mechanisms for old buildings, cultural landscapes, and entire urban and rural environments. Various public and private attitudes, legal and financial mechanisms, and planning processes undergird historic preservation as it has come to evolve in the late 1980s.

With the evolution of historic preservation, a number of terms have come into general use that are often ill-defined or unclear in context; therefore, a few working definitions are in order. Historic preservation is taken to mean the process of identifying, evaluating, treating, managing, and protecting historic sites, buildings, structures, districts, and objects. Rehabilitation means the remodeling or refurbishing of a building or structure to extend its useful life; adaptive use (or adaptive reuse) simply refers to accomplishing this modification with the intent of using the rehabilitated structure for new functions. Restoration in a preservation sense goes beyond rehabilitation by returning a building or structure to a close approximation of its original or historic condition, and conservation is the technical process of keeping old buildings, artwork, and their component parts from deteriorating to the point at which they lose their historic integrity and economic and social value. Thus, overall, the practice of "historic preservation" is simply one aspect of the modern design and urban-planning process concerned with protecting the richness and variety of the old and combining it with the new in ways that promote dynamic architectural environments and liveable communities.

FOUNDATIONS OF HISTORIC PRESERVATION

In 1926, John D. Rockefeller unveiled plans for the preservation and restoration of Colonial Williamsburg, Virginia. This event was followed shortly thereafter, in 1931, by the passage of the first local preservation ordinance for the Old and Historic District of Charleston, South Carolina; the second ordinance was passed for the Vieux Carre (French Quarter) of New Orleans in 1937, soon after Congress passed legislation to preserve and record many historic sites of national importance under the Historic Sites Act of 1935. The following 30 years saw little change in attitudes or moves toward widespread preservation efforts in the United States. To the contrary, the post-World War II years became a time of "urban renewal" as American communities sought to remove and remake decaying central business districts and inner-city neighborhoods, even while Europe and Asia were rebuilding war-damaged historic urban cores.

Partially in response to these developments, the acceleration of historic preservation interests and activities throughout the public and private sectors in the 40 years since World War II has made it increasingly incumbent on the architectural community and other participants in the design and construction fields to consider historic values in their work. Major public and private initiatives in the last two decades have helped bring this about; both economic changes and changes in attitudes in the design and development communities have also contributed. At the same time, the numerous and varied activist environmental and social movements of the 1960s and 1970s have given rise to an increasingly aware and community-conscious citizenry.

The early history of preservation, dating back at least to Roman times with their appreciation and borrowing from earlier civilizations, is well-recorded, and it is not the intention of this article to recite that history. Recent and excellent summaries include the works of Charles B. Hosmer (1) and James Marston Fitch (2) as well as several edited compilations (3–7).

It may be instructive, however, particularly in light of recent controversies over religious institutions' rights to develop their historic property (such as St. Bartholomew's Church in midtown Manhattan, New York City), to recall what may be the earliest recorded example of active historic preservation involving public controversy and differing government jurisdictions. In 1523, a local cathedral chapter in Spain wished to construct a new cathedral choir in an old church, formerly a mosque, over local city council opposition. As summarized by Ortiz (8), it did not seem right to the church officials that Christian worship should take place so far from the center of the old building, so they decided that a true cathedral should be built in the center of the old structure. Therefore, it was necessary to demolish a great number of arches. The work began that year; the local city government was so opposed to the demolition work necessary that it passed an ordinance to the effect that any worker taking part in this demolition would be sentenced to death. The ordinance included the following explanation: "This is because that which is being destroyed is of a quality which will not be possible to repeat in beauty or in the perfection in which it has been constructed (9)." Spanish ruler and Holy Roman Emperor Charles V granted permission for the work over the local government's objections; it was only later, on viewing the construction within the red and white striped forest of columns that had been the ninth and tenth century congregational area of the Great Mosque of Cordoba, Spain, that the Emperor declared that "if he had known what he had been dealing with, he would never have given permission for the work, as what they had constructed could be found in many places and [what] they destroyed could not be found anywhere else" (10).

In retrospect, from situations like the sixteenth-century battle over the fate of the Great Mosque of Cordoba, it is immediately apparent that such continuing conflicts involve a clash of different value systems and opposing views of the world. Architectural critic Ada Louise Huxtable has noted what she believes to be a fundamental different in perception between those regarding architecture principally as an investment and those concerned with "image, quality, and civic pride" (11). It is because of such differing perceptions and conflicting values that a system of checks and balances, imperfect as it may be in dealing with the diversity of economic, health and safety, and esthetic issues, has come about today to deal with the various problems surrounding historic preservation activities.

Some might assert that historic preservation in one form or another has always been in the forefront of architecture, as no design, or construction or engineering, for that matter, takes place in a vacuum. Each of the disciplines involving the built environment obviously draws on a considerable body of past work, past technology, and other historic, design, environmental, and technological contexts. At the same time, most design professionals, their clients, and those who review or regulate their work would probably agree that the process of sensitive and creative juxtaposition of the old and new is not an easy one and certainly that it is easier to judge through hindsight than foresight.

THE BASIS FOR MODERN HISTORIC PRESERVATION

Originally, most efforts at historic preservation were attempts to maintain and preserve the monuments and architectural landmarks associated with important people and historical events. George Washington's home at Mount Vernon, the earliest and best known example of a private preservation effort in the United States (1856), was saved because of its association with the life of an American founding father. Most elements of the National Park Service system that were established principally for their built environment were named by Congress because of their associative value of this kind and their connection to (and illustration of) major themes in American history.

In addition to the importance of associative values, many architectural historians have argued the value and importance of understanding the past in order to advance present and future design. In exploring historical examples of good architecture and the reason for particular forms during particular time periods, one is drawn to historical antecedents " that illustrate the relations between problems and solutions, and thus furnish an empirical basis for further work" (12). This is certainly one of the most compelling reasons for the architectural and design professions of why historic preservation is important. The aim is to preserve the best of the past in order to learn from it, as well as to appreciate its esthetic qualities. The establishment of the Historic American Buildings Survey (HABS) in 1935, and the succeeding Historic American Engineering Record, and their collections of measured drawings and other materials in the Library of Congress, were explicit attempts to record construction works threatened by neglect or destruction through demolition.

Newer buildings, too, may become worthy of preservation as outstanding examples of the best of architectural design, construction craftmanship, and ornamentation. Works such as the Solomon R. Guggenheim Museum, designed by Frank Lloyd Wright, or the Washington Dulles Airport terminal building, designed by Eero Saarinen, are recent examples of such works recognized as "historic" despite their recent construction.

The environmental value of old buildings is epitomized in such commercial urban redevelopment projects as Quincy Market, Boston, and South Street Seaport, New York; in the less commercial attempts to preserve a residential ambience in Savannah, Georgia or Charleston, South Carolina; and in the purposeful encouragement of sympathetic new construction and rehabilitation around Pioneer Square, Seattle, Larimer Square, Denver, and The Strand of Galveston, Texas (Fig. 1). Such examples, and numerous others across the United States in both large cities and in smaller communities, underscore the idea that keeping old buildings around because of the mi-

Figure 1. A 19th century historic residential area in Galveston, Texas continues to convey a strong sense of place and time. Photograph by: Marcia Axtmann Smith, Advisory Council on Historic Preservation, Washington, D.C.

lieu or environment they provide, because of the "sense of place" they convey, whether urban or rural, is also a worthy goal. Certain districts in places such as New Orleans, Louisiana, evoke a sense of time and place as a special kind of built environment that exists in the present, but relates to the past and echoes elements of it.

World Heritage Conventions and Charters

Several international organizations have been established over the years to deal with historic preservation issues. The United Nations Educational, Scientific, and Cultural Organization (UNESCO), established under UN charter in 1948 and headquartered in Paris, has a number of missions relevant to international preservation. It has promoted and had member states ratify several conventions related to international preservation interests; it has made recommendations for the use of member states in basic preservation policies, methods, and techniques; and it has helped to fund rescue and other special programs. The well-known attempts to save Nubian temples and other architectural and archaeological treasures from inundation by the Aswan High Dam on the Nile in 1960 was such a worldwide effort led by UNESCO.

The International Centre for the Study of the Preservation and Restoration of Cultural Property (ICCROM), also known as the Rome Center, was established and organized in 1958 under UNESCO auspices as a research center, training outlet, and clearinghouse for information on restoration and conservation. The Rome Center has 61 participating member nations, including the United States. U.S. membership is coordinated by the Advisory Council on Historic Preservation, working through a technical committee that makes recommendations on ICCROM activities.

In addition to training, principal ICCROM activities include special emergency and other missions by invita-

tion of host countries. Deterioration of the west front of the U.S. Capitol was one such problem for which ICCROM specialists were called in to make recommendations before its restoration. A principal training program includes instruction in techniques of architectural conservation.

ICOMOS, the International Council on Monuments and Sites, was founded in 1964 as an international, nongovernmental organization concerned with the conservation, protection, rehabilitation, and enhancement of monuments, groups of buildings, and sites. ICOMOS oversees international exchange programs and training in various historic preservation-related fields and in the development of recommendations on preservation issues of international concern.

Through UNESCO, nations have in recent years agreed on a number of general principles concerning historic preservation in the international community. The *World Heritage Convention for the Protection of the World Cultural and Natural Heritage* (1972), the UNESCO *Recommendation Concerning the Safeguarding and Contemporary Role of Historic Areas* (1976), and the UNESCO *Recommendation Concerning the Safeguarding of the Beauty and Character of Landscapes and Sites* (1962) embody the most important of these principles, along with the *International Charter for the Conservation and Restoration of Monuments and Sites* (1964), the so-called *Venice Charter*.

Generally, the UNESCO convention and recommendations and the Venice Charter recognize the importance of the historic built environment as part of the common heritage of all nations and underscore international agreements and national policies on the value of historic buildings and areas as part of the common cultural environment. The Venice Charter, developed at an international conference of architects and technicians of historic monuments, approved a "statement of principles guiding the preservation and restoration of ancient buildings" (13) (Table 1). The 1972 UNESCO Convention "set up a permanent legal, administrative, and financial framework for an international system that encourages and supports

Table 1. Principles Guiding the Preservation and Restoration of Ancient Buildings (Venice Charter)[a]

Art. 1. The concept of an historic monument embraces not only the single architectural work but also the urban or rural setting in which is found the evidence of a particular civilisation, a significant development or an historic event. This applies not only to great works of art but also to more modest works of the past which have acquired cultural significance with the passing of time.

Art. 2. The conservation and restoration of monuments must have recourse to all the sciences and techniques which can contribute to the study and safeguarding of the architectural heritage.

Art. 3. The intention in conserving and restoring monuments is to safeguard them no less as works of art than as historical evidence.

Art. 4. It is essential to the conservation of monuments that they be maintained on a permanent basis.

Art. 5. The conservation of monuments is always facilitated

Table 1. (*Continued*)

by making use of them for some socially useful purpose. Such use is therefore desirable but it must not change the lay-out or decoration of the building. It is within these limits only that modifications demanded by a change of function should be envisaged and may be permitted.

Art. 6. The conservation of a monument implies preserving a setting which is not out of scale. Wherever the traditional setting exits, it must be kept. No new construction, demolition, or modification which would alter the relations of mass and colour must be allowed.

Art. 7. A monument is inseparable from the history to which it bears witness and from the setting in which it occurs. The moving of all or part of a monument cannot be allowed except where the safeguarding of that monument demands it or where it is justified by national or international interests of paramount importance.

Art. 8. Items of sculpture, painting or decoration which form an integral part of a monument may only be removed from it if this is the sole means of ensuring their preservation.

Art. 9. The process of restoration is a highly specialized operation. Its aim is to preserve and reveal the aesthetic and historic value of the monument and is based on respect for original materials and authentic documents. It must stop at the point where conjecture begins, and in this case moreover any extra work which is indispensable must be distinct from the architectural composition and must bear a contemporary stamp. The restoration in any case must be preceded and followed by an archaeological and historical study of the monument.

Art. 10. Where traditional techniques prove inadequate, the consolidation of a monument can be achieved by the use of any modern technique for conservation and construction, the efficacy of which has been shown by scientific data and proved by experience.

Art. 11. The valid contributions of all periods to the building of a monument must be respected, since unity of style is not the aim of restoration. When a building includes the superimposed work of different periods, the revealing of the underlying state can only be justified in exceptional circumstances and when what is removed is of little interest and the material which is brought to light is of great historical, archaeological or aesthetic value, and its state of preservation good enough to justify the action. Evaluation of the importance of the elements involved and the decision as to what may be destroyed cannot rest solely on the individual in charge of the work.

Art. 12. Replacements of missing parts must integrate harmoniously with the whole, but at the same time must be distinguishable from the original so that restoration does not falsify the artistic or historic evidence.

Art. 13. Additions cannot be allowed except in so far as they do not detract from the interesting parts of the building, its traditional setting, the balance of its composition and its relation with its surroundings.

[a]Ref. 14.

the preservation of humanity's heritage, both natural and cultural. The chief components of the system are the World Heritage Committee, the World Heritage List, the List of World Heritage in Danger, and the World Heritage Fund" (14). Under contract with UNESCO, ICOMOS had a major role in the preparation of the 1972 Convention and has continued to play a part in coordinating nominations and listing of World Heritage sites as well as assisting in funding appeals for threatened or deteriorated sites.

Policies and Trends in Europe

Sometimes older than those in the United States, and occasionally borrowing from American experiences, individual national programs to identify and protect historic monuments or national landmarks exist and flourish in many nations. Consistent with the international policies and programs mentioned above, often these comprise some variation on the basic programs of national inventory of historic sites, registration, or "scheduling," to use the term in vogue in the United Kingdom, of significant monuments or areas and some form of national government oversight on planning coupled with restrictions on demolition or new construction affecting protected areas. Programs vary considerably from country to country, but the United Kingdom provides one example somewhat different from that of the United States. More specifically, in England (related but slightly different arrangements exist in Scotland, Wales, and Northern Ireland) the basic national legislation is contained in the Historic Buildings and Ancient Monuments Act of 1953; the Town and Country Planning Act of 1972, as amended; the Ancient Monuments and Archaeological Areas Act of 1979 (which superseded or amended portions of a number of ancient monuments and town and country planning statutes dating back to 1882); the Local Government Planning and Land Act of 1980; and the National Heritage Act of 1983 (15).

The monuments acts provide for scheduling of historic properties with resultant protections according to the properties' importance and a requirement that any activities that may affect scheduled monuments must have the appropriately conditioned written consent of the national government (the Secretary of State for the Environment). Compensation is payable by the government for certain circumstances where consent is denied or where the conditions would involve considerable private financial expenditures. The planning acts provide for appropriate preservation and development planning within both urban and rural historic areas in the country and local government participation in historic building repairs and similar conservation efforts.

The National Heritage Act of 1983 took that legislation a step further and established the Historic Buildings and Monuments Commission, otherwise known as English Heritage, as an independent, nongovernmental body to perform many of the functions previously pursued by the Department of the Environment. This includes the administration of the most important historic buildings and monuments in the country, along with provision of planning and restoration grants for local preservation activities and town planning in collaboration with local governments under the Town and Country Planning Act and its amendments. These activities are coupled with an ambitious program of public education and on-site interpretation for visitors, as well the provision of advice to the Cabinet Minister on applications for scheduled monument consent (see above). Stonehenge, Hadrian's Wall, Dover Castle, and Bury St. Edmunds Abbey are four examples of historic properties under English Heritage care (16).

As noted in a report prepared by the U.S. Advisory Council on Historic Preservation in 1975 at Congressional request, " . . . this successful governmental system for protection of Britain's cultural heritage is supplemented in the private sector by the very strong network of local amenity societies and pressure groups, the growth of which has increased greatly in recent years with the development of public interest in the conservation and protection of the heritage. Many of these societies work closely with local authorities to preserve the character of town and countryside" (17). Thus, public preservation in the United Kingdom rested, and continues to rely, on a strong foundation of private efforts.

National Policies and Trends in the United States

The involvement of private interest groups and organizations with public preservation efforts in the United States has a tradition and history not unlike that of the United Kingdom. Indeed, although the principal basis for national-level programs and policy began by focusing on federal lands and interests, the earliest preservation efforts to save places such as Mount Vernon, Independence Hall, and battlefields of the Revolutionary and Civil War originated with private initiatives.

Beginning in 1906 with the Antiquities Act and continuing into the post-World War I years with the Historic Sites Act of 1935, the federal government outlined the national interest in protecting antiquities on federal lands and established a systematic program through the National Park Service of the Department of the Interior to identify and designate nationally significant buildings, sites, and districts as National Historic Landmarks on both public *and* private lands. The Historic Sites Act, although providing work to numerous architects, historians, engineers, and draftsmen through the establishment of the Historic American Buildings Survey, carried no particular protections for designated National Historic Landmarks save their automatic inclusion in a list to be considered for National Park Service acquisition and administration. In other words, such properties became eligible to be added to the National Park system through legislation.

It was not until after World War II, with the establishment of the private National Trust for Historic Preservation under the National Trust Act of 1949 and the passage of the Surplus Property Act in the same year, that the national government considered supporting both private and federal efforts to protect historic properties and, in the case of the surplus property act, to restrict disposition and use of historic properties owned by the federal government that were declared surplus by giving the National Park Service and state and local government agencies opportunities to accept the properties for historic monument purposes.

Beginning in the 1960s and continuing to the present, the federal government took an increasingly active role in protecting historic properties and regulating the effects of development on them at all levels of significance. Until the late 1970s, most of the legislation applied only to federally owned properties or federally supported activities on properties in either public or private ownership. These included the Reservoir Salvage Act of 1960, which provided for salvage of sites of historic, archaeological, or scientific interest being destroyed by water projects; Section 4(f) of the Department of Transportation Act of 1966, which restricted planning of highway projects affecting historic properties unless there was no feasible and prudent alternative and the planning included all possible planning to minimize harm; the National Environmental Policy Act of 1969, which included consideration of effects of federal actions on historic properties among its overall environmental planning, review, and public disclosure requirements; and, most significantly, the National Historic Preservation Act of 1966 (Fig. 2).

The National Historic Preservation Act was and remains the most comprehensive piece of national historic preservation legislation and the foundation for much of the federal government's involvement in preservation activities at the federal, state, and even local level. Amended a number of times through 1980, it includes a number of key provisions. It established a National Register of Historic Places in the Department of the Interior to expand the original National Historic Landmarks list and to recognize historic districts, sites, buildings, structures, and objects at all levels of significance—national, state, and local. It authorized a Historic Preservation Fund administered by the Interior Department with a program of matching grants-in-aid to states, the National Trust for Historic Preservation, and local governments (through pass-through grants from the states), and it created the position of State Historic Preservation Officer to serve as the state-level preservation representative appointed by the governor of each state. Finally, it established a federal Advisory Council on Historic Preservation to advise the President and Congress on matters related to historic preservation and to administer a program of reviewing

Figure 2. The historic district of Crested Butte, Colorado, center of a popular and profitable skiing and recreation area, was threatened by nearby mineral development until the Federal government placed restrictions on the mining activities. Photograph by Walter Smalling, Jr., Heritage Conservation and Recreation Service (now NPS), Washington, D.C.

and consulting on federal, federally assisted, and federally licensed projects and other activities that could affect properties included or eligible for the National Register. Amendments to the law in 1980 provided for certification of local governments to carry out preservation administration and other activities and clarified federal agency responsibilities for historic preservation in their programs and, more specifically, on federal lands.

In 1974, the Housing and Community Development Act set up a program of community development block grants and other programs, including funds to local governments for rehabilitation of historic buildings as part of these community development activities. Finally, 1976 produced two important pieces of legislation more directly affecting the private sector. These were the Public Buildings Cooperative Use Act, which provided for federal government and private partnerships in the redevelopment and use of public buildings (the Old Post Office and Pavilion in Washington, D.C., is an example, as is Union Station in St. Louis, Missouri); and the Tax Reform Act of 1976, which provided for tax credits for rehabilitation work on income-producing properties certified by the National Park Service as meeting Interior Department standards (that legislation was amended and amplified by the Economic Recovery Tax Act of 1981, or ERTA, and subsequent tax system amendments, including the Tax Reform Act of 1986).

The policy direction embodied in this legislative summary is underscored in the language of Title I of the National Historic Preservation Act of 1966 (16 U.S.C. 470f) (18):

> . . . the historical and cultural foundations of the Nation should be preserved as a living part of our community life and development in order to give a sense of orientation to the American people; [and] the preservation of this irreplaceable heritage is in the public interest so that its vital legacy of cultural, educational, aesthetic, inspirational, economic, and energy benefits will be maintained and enriched for future generations of Americans . . . .

Federal policy was therefore established to:

> . . . use measures, including financial and technical assistance, to foster conditions under which our modern society and our prehistoric and historic resources can exist in productive harmony and fulfill the social, economic, and other requirements of present and future generations; [and] encourage the public and private preservation and utilization of all useable elements of the Nation's historic built environment . . . .

Over the past two decades, the rise of environmental awareness in the United States and the desire to preserve as much as possible of an irreplaceable past-built environment from irreversible decisions and commitments of resources has given rise to a series of federal, state, and local safeguards. Many of the laws, in essence, have established a planning and decision process that is designed to ensure that historic preservation and other environmental concerns are properly addressed and considered in new development projects. Most often, laws at the national or state levels provide not for absolute "preservation," as in the case of United Kingdom "scheduling" of nationally important monuments outside of government ownership, or even of restrictions on private development activities, but rather that a negotiated balance is struck between pro-development values and propreservation values when government assistance of some type for the development is involved. Sometimes these two sets of values are not in conflict, but often they are. In many instances, it has been left to local governments to create local ordinances restricting development in historic areas of their cities, towns, or counties (to the extent they are authorized to do so by state law) and to establish historic district commissions, design review boards, or some similar entity to review new construction and rehabilitation proposals and decide whether they are appropriate within the context of the historic areas given local restrictions.

HISTORIC PRESERVATION IN THE UNITED STATES TODAY

As one can surmise from the above summary, historic preservation activities in the United States today are therefore arranged in a complex federal/state/local/private partnership with a variety of incentives, controls, and other mechanisms at all levels. Although it is impossible to cover all these areas in detail, a thumbnail sketch of principal federal, state, local, and private involvement in historic preservation activities is briefly outlined below, followed by a discussion of how the process of historic preservation works in the three most important and far-reaching areas.

Federal Interests

At the federal government level, the two principal government bodies involved in historic preservation are the National Park Service of the U.S. Department of the Interior, and the Advisory Council on Historic Preservation. Important historic properties considered of national significance are often established by act of Congress as units within the National Park system; other nationally significant properties are designated National Historic Landmarks by the Secretary of the Interior and have some slight additional protection from federally assisted activities (but not from private actions). Both these groups of properties, as well as buildings and sites of state and local significance, are nominated to the National Register of Historic Places maintained by the National Park Service through the State Historic Preservation Officers or federal land-holding agencies. It is these properties, as well as those determined eligible for the National Register, that receive some measure of protection through review by the Advisory Council on Historic Preservation under Section 106 of the National Historic Preservation Act (known as Section 106 review) and that are also eligible for tax credits and other assistance.

At a broad-brush level, both the federal authorities and most state and local jurisdictions involved in overseeing construction through design review or similar mechanisms use the basic standards promulgated nationally by the Secretary of the Interior. There are two principal sets of standards; survey, evaluation, documentation, and consultant qualifications for many projects involving historic preservation are covered by the *Secretary of the Interior's Standards and Guidelines for Archeology and Historic Preservation* (19). Rehabilitation and new construction is covered by the *Secretary of the Interior's Standards for Rehabilitation and Guidelines for Rehabilitating Historic Buildings* (20). The latter were originally developed in 1979 (revised in 1983) to respond to the needs of tax-certification review and grants-in-aid under the Historic Preservation Fund.

State Interests

States are involved as partners in the various federal programs mentioned above; State Historic Preservation Officers (appointed by governors) and their staffs conduct historic survey activities, administer planning grants and other forms of local assistance, consider nominations to the National Register, assist in tax-certification review, and participate in review of federal and federally assisted projects by the Advisory Council. In addition, most states have their own historic preservation laws, often including State Historic Registers and other programs.

In Massachusetts, for example, the Massachusetts Historical Commission was established as an agency under its Secretary of State to set statewide preservation priorities, develop regional planning studies for areas particularly prone to development (eg, Greater Boston, Cape Cod), oversee and assist local historical commissions and local historic district commissions, designate properties to the State Register of Historic Places, administer grants and receive preservation donations and easements, and help protect state-owned or administered historic properties and properties that would receive state assistance. The Commission also participates in the federal programs of tax certification and Section 106 review.

Local Interests

At the local level, many communities have local zoning controls, historic preservation ordinances, or historic district commissions that oversee construction and other development activities in locally recognized historic districts. Where formally recommended by the state and certified by the federal government through the National Park Service to meet the criteria for certified local governments, such jurisdictions are eligible for pass-through grants and other assistance from the Historic Preservation Fund under the provisions of the 1980 amendments to the National Historic Preservation Act.

Currently, there are about 450 certified local governments and many more uncertified localities with some form of design review or other historic-area restrictions throughout the United States. Metro-Dade County, Florida, for example, which includes Miami and Miami Beach, has an ordinance that created a Historic Preservation Board under the auspices of the Department of Community and Economic Development. Local ordinances apply in some cities within the metro area; both these jurisdictions and those without local ordinances cooperate with the county board. The board and a small staff designate locally important historic properties, administer a loan program, provide information on tax and zoning incen-

tives and restrictions, and issue certificates of appropriateness for "substantial alterations" of the exterior appearance of designated buildings (21).

Privately Supported Preservation Efforts

Finally, private support for historic preservation has come through a series of nationwide programs operating through local sponsors, such as the National Trust for Historic Preservation's National Main Street Program and Endangered Properties Revolving Fund Program, as well as business investment in preservation efforts (Figure 3). The private business investment in historic preservation through both corporate philanthropy and the Tax Act for certified rehabilitation has been significant in recent years, although changes to the tax code in 1986 that reduced the percentage of rehabilitation costs eligible for tax credits substantially decreased much of this activity. Within the architectural profession, the American Institute of Architect's Committee on Historic Resources has been active since 1890, monitoring and encouraging historic preservation developments.

The National Trust's popular Main Street Program is one example of private support for historic preservation. Member organizations at the local level, supported by seed money from various federal and state programs, the Trust, and technical assistance through a Trust-developed network of state agencies, organizations, and community sponsors, undertake downtown economic revitalization demonstration projects and related activities in an effort to save and restore historic downtown areas. Originally launched in 1977 as a demonstration program in three towns, within 3 years the program was operating in more than 60 towns in Colorado, Georgia, Massachusetts, North Carolina, Pennsylvania, and Texas (22). Eventually, towns throughout the United States were participating; through the National Main Street Center the program remains an important one today for many smaller communities.

THE PROCESS OF HISTORIC PRESERVATION

Besides undertaking renovation or preservation work directly, most architects and design professionals come into contact with historic preservation needs and requirements in one of three ways: (1) as part of a tax-act project involving rehabilitation of a certified historic structure requiring certification for tax credits for a client; (2) as part of a federally supported or assisted project affecting a property listed in or eligible for listing in the National Register of Historic Places; or (3) as part of a project involving work in a local historic district that requires a certificate of appropriateness or permit from a local preservation or landmark commission. Each of these areas will be discussed in turn.

How Tax-Act Certification Works: Local, State, and Federal Cooperation Through Project Development

Federal historic preservation tax incentives are available for any qualified project that the Secretary of the Interior

Figure 3. A combination of Federal, State, local, and private preservation initiatives and assistance have contributed to revitalization of historic downtown commercial districts such as this one in Nashville, Tennessee. Photograph by Jack E. Boucher, Historic American Buildings Survey, NPS, Washington, D.C.

designates as a certified rehabilitation of a certified historic structure (23). These incentives were established and modified by the Tax Reform Act of 1976, the Revenue Act of 1978, the Tax Treatment Extension Act of 1980, the Economic Recovery Tax Act of 1981, as amended, and the Tax Reform act of 1986. The Tax Treatment Extension Act of 1980 also established permanent provisions affecting income and estate tax deductions for charitable contributions of partial interests in a historic property designated a certified historic structure. As of 1988, up to a 20% ITC (investment tax credit, reduced from a previous 25% in 1986) was available to developers for certified rehabilitation.

A "certified historic structure" is any structure, subject to depreciation (defined by the Internal Revenue Code) that is either listed individually in the National Register of Historic Places or located in a registered historic district and certified by the Secretary of the Interior as contributing to the importance of the district.

A "registered historic district" is any district listed in the National Register or any district designated under a state or local statute that has been certified by the Secretary of the Interior substantially to meet preservation purposes and that generally meets the requirements for listing in the National Register.

A "certified rehabilitation" is any rehabilitation of a certified historic structure that the Secretary has certified to the Secretary of the Treasury as being consistent with the historic character of the structure and, where applicable, with the district in which the building is located.

The tax code limits tax incentives for rehabilitation to depreciable structures ("buildings used in a trade or business or held for the production of income"), such as commercial or rental residential properties. Only charitable contributions of buildings are exempt from the "depreciable" restriction.

To qualify for the tax incentives, property owners must complete the appropriate part or parts of a Historic Preservation Certification Application. In participating states, completed applications are sent first to the State Historic Preservation Officer, who forwards applications to the National Park Service regional office (generally with a recommendation). In nonparticipating states, applications are sent to the appropriate NPS regional office. Applications may be sent at any time during the year. They consist of two parts, which may be sent separately or together (if sent separately, Part I must precede Part II).

Part I, Evaluation of Significance, is used to determine whether the property meets or does not meet the criteria for inclusion in the National Register or contributes to a listed historic district. Documentation in Part I applications must be sufficient to (1) make a judgment about how the building relates to the district as a whole and (2) determine what particular features of the building comprise its historic character. Part II, Description of Rehabilitation Work, is used to judge whether the project can be certified as "being consistent with the historic character of the structure and, where applicable, the district in which the structure is located." The criteria used to review Part II applications are the Secretary of the Interior's *Standards for Rehabilitation*.

The ten standards (Table 2) are broadly worded to guide the rehabilitation of all historic structures, such as industrial complexes, warehouses, schools, commercial structures, and residences. The underlying concern expressed in the standards, which are not dissimilar to the international principles contained in the Venice Charter (see Table 1), is the preservation of significant historic

Table 2. The Secretary of the Interior's Standards for Rehabilitation[a]

1. Every reasonable effort shall be made to provide a compatible use for a property which requires minimal alteration of the building, structure, or site and its environment, or to use a property for its originally intended purpose.

2. The distinguishing original qualities or character of a building, structure, or site and its environment shall not be destroyed. The removal or alteration of any historic material or distinctive architectural features should be avoided when possible.

3. All buildings, structures, and sites shall be recognized as products of their own time. Alterations that have no historical basis and which seek to create an earlier appearance shall be discouraged.

4. Changes which may have taken place in the course of time are evidence of the history and development of a building, structure, or site and its environment. These changes may have acquired significance in their own right, and this significance shall be recognized and respected.

5. Distinctive stylistic features or examples of skilled craftsmanship which characterize a building, structure, or site shall be treated with sensitivity.

6. Deteriorated architectural features shall be repaired rather than replaced, wherever possible. In the event replacement is necessary, the new material should match the material being replaced in composition, design, color, texture, and other visual qualities. Repair or replacement of missing architectural features should be based on accurate duplications of features, substantiated by historic, physical, or pictorial evidence rather than on conjectural designs or the availability of different architectural elements from other buildings or structures.

7. The surface cleaning of structures shall be undertaken with the gentlest means possible. Sandblasting and other cleaning methods that will damage the historic building materials shall not be undertaken.

8. Every reasonable effort shall be made to protect and preserve archeological resources affected by, or adjacent to, any project.

9. Contemporary design for alterations and additions to existing properties shall not be discouraged when such alterations and additions do not destroy significant historical, architectural or cultural material, and such design is compatible with the size, scale, color, material, and character of the property, neighborhood or environment.

10. Wherever possible, new additions or alterations to structures shall be done in such a manner that if such additions or alterations were to be removed in the future, the essential form and integrity of the structure would be unimpaired.

[a] Ref. 20.

materials and features of a building in the process of rehabilitation. The standards apply with equal force to both interior and exterior work. The NPS reviews the entire rehabilitation project (including any new construction on the site) rather than just a single segment of work. Certification is based on whether the overall project meets the standards.

For example, Macon, Georgia, has had a number of tax-act projects that have proceeded hand-in-hand with local

government and private preservation activities. A two-story commercial building at 609 Cherry Street, built in 1860, was purchased in 1981 for an architectural firm's office space. Project cost was $205,852; with rehabilitation expenditures equaling $150,000, the three partners were able to take a combined investment tax credit of $37,500 (25% at the time), or $12,500 each (24).

As a result of the Tax Reform Act of 1986, the reduction of the investment tax credit from 25 to 20% appears to have had considerable impact on rehabilitation investment. However, the magnitude of this impact is not fully known at this time, nor is it clear whether the tax change alone has had more to do with the slowing of rehabilitation investment than other aspects of the building economy. Figures available in 1987 do show a considerable drop from 1985 to 1986 in both numbers of projects and investment dollars (25).

How the Federal/State Oversight System Works: Planning Processes and Standards Involving Identification, Evaluation, and Protection

As defined by the expansion of the National Register of Historic Places following the passage of the National Historic Preservation Act in 1966, properties were deemed significant in relation to the following criteria (26) (Fig. 4):

The quality of significance in American history, architecture, archeology, and culture is present in districts, sites, buildings, structures, and objects of National, State, and local importance that possess integrity of location, design, setting, materials, workmanship, feeling, and association, and
a. That are associated with events that have made a significant contribution to the broad patterns of our history; or
b. That are associated with the lives of persons significant in our past; or
c. That embody the distinctive characteristics of a type, period, or method of construction, or that represent the work of a

Figure 4. The Mark Twain house in Hartford, Connecticut, designed by architects Edward T. Potter and Alfred H. Thorp in 1874, is a National Historic Landmark because of its association with the noted American author. Photograph by Robert Fulton, III, Historic American Buildings Survey, NPS, Washington, D.C.

master, or that possess high artistic values, or that represent a significant and distinguishable entity whose components may lack individual distinction; or

d. That have yielded, or may be likely to yield, information important in prehistory or history.

Section 106 of the National Historic Preservation Act (27) provides that

The head of any Federal agency having direct or indirect jurisdiction over a proposed Federal or federally assisted undertaking in any State and the head of any Federal department or independent agency having authority to license any undertaking shall, prior to the approval of the expenditure of any Federal funds on the undertaking or prior to the issuance of any license, as the case may be, take into account the effect of the undertaking on any district, site, building, structure, or object that is included in or eligible for inclusion in the National Register. The head of any such Federal agency shall afford the Advisory Council on Historic Preservation established under Title II of this Act a reasonable opportunity to comment with regard to such undertaking.

Under the 1986 regulations of the Advisory Council on Historic Preservation (Title 36 Code of Federal Regulations Part 800), the law is implemented in the following manner. First, the agency determines whether there are any historic properties in the area subject to effect by the undertaking. This usually involves consultation with the State Historic Preservation Officer (SHPO) and other interested parties and often requires field study and background research. Properties thought to be historic are evaluated by the agency in consultation with the SHPO. If questions exist about significance, the Department of the Interior is consulted.

Second, if properties already listed in the Register or eligible for it are identified, the agency applies criteria of effect and adverse effect as set forth in the regulations. Effects occur when the undertaking may alter characteristics of the property that may qualify it for inclusion in the National Register. For the purpose of determining effect, alterations to features of the property's location, setting, or use may be relevant, depending on the property's significant characteristics, and are considered accordingly. Adverse effects occur when the effect on a historic property may diminish the integrity of the property's location, design, setting, materials, workmanship, feeling, or association (see National Register criteria above). Such effects include, but are not limited to, (1) physical destruction, damage, or alteration of all or part of a property; (2) isolation of the property or alteration of the property's setting where that character contributes to the property's qualification for the National Register; (3) introduction of visual, audible, or atmospheric elements that are out of character with the property or alter its setting; (4) neglect of a property resulting in its deterioration or destruction; and (5) transfer, lease, or sale of the property (28).

If no effect will occur, the agency files documentation and the undertaking proceeds; if an effect will occur but it will not be adverse, a finding to this effect is made and sent to the Council for concurrence. If an adverse effect will occur, or if the Council objects to the no adverse effect determination, then the agency and SHPO, and sometimes the Council and other interested parties, consult to explore alternatives that would avoid or mitigate the adverse effect. If they agree, then a memorandum of agreement is executed stipulating the actions that will be taken and the undertaking proceeds. If no agreement is possible, a final Council comment is rendered, after which the agency makes the final decision about whether and how to proceed, taking the comment into account in making its decisions.

An example will help illustrate how the process works. In 1979, the city of Charleston, South Carolina, applied for funding from the U.S. Department of Housing and Urban Development's Urban Development Action Grant fund. In partnership with a private developer, a hotel, conference center, commercial retail space, and parking garage were proposed on the northern edge of Charleston's National Historic Landmark Old and Historic District. At the time of the original proposal, preservation groups condemned the mass and scale of the project as totally out of character with the historic area and likely to adversely change traffic circulation and other development-associated patterns within and around the historic area. Under the terms of the Urban Development Action Grant program (probably being phased out in 1989), the city assumed the role of federal agency for the purpose of meeting various environmental and other requirements, including Section 106 compliance. After a lengthy period of consultation, as well as lively input from hundreds of concerned citizens and all local preservation organizations, an agreement was concluded that provided for a somewhat scaled-down project and retention and rehabilitation of the existing surrounding buildings as part of the development. The hotel itself was reduced from 12 to 8 stories. Although critics differ about the success of the resulting design (29), the complex is now the heart of an economically successful redevelopment that includes the Charleston Omni Hotel and Charleston Center (a retail/office complex) and has helped provide a catalyst for individual rehabilitation projects and the overall revitalization of the adjoining King Street commercial corridor.

The Charleston case is instructive with regard to public participation in the historic preservation process. Citizen inquiry and the local public hearings mandated by the federal assistance requirements for the project brought local concerns to the attention of state and federal officials. Through petitions, letter-writing campaigns, and the threat of litigation on the adequacy of environmental studies, local preservation organizations and members of the general public put considerable pressure on the developers and the city to modify the project. When the project went to the Advisory Council for review, a special public information meeting was held to air views specifically related to historic preservation issues. The eventual compromise agreement, although unsatisfactory to those who were attempting to block the project entirely, reflected many of the public's views, particularly those expressed by members of the principal local historic preservation organization.

How a Local System Works: Comprehensive Plans, Historic District Ordinances, and Review Boards

Critics of design review boards or historic district commissions have sometimes suggested that resulting design and urban planning schemes look like they were arrived at by committee. Sometimes, this is almost literally true, owing to the nature of the review process. However, regardless of one's opinion of historic district commissions, historic area ordinances, and associating zoning requirements, it is clear that these local activities play perhaps the largest role in determining the relative success or failure of historic preservation within the local context (Figures 5 and 6).

Local ordinances and procedures vary widely, but they have some basic features in common. Based on creation of a historic review board of some sort, either integrated with or somewhat apart from the local government structure, construction and rehabilitation activities within locally designated historic districts are regulated. Most often, boards perform a function within the process of obtaining a local building permit or zoning variance by having the power to issue or deny certificates of appropriateness for the work. Depending on the state enabling legislation and specific local ordinances, restrictions may make distinctions between major and minor projects; minor work may only be reviewed by the local historic district commission staff, whereas major work would require a public hearing before the commission itself. An example of the system that includes both small towns and larger cities is that established for communities in Arkansas.

Under that state's Historic District Act, local historic district ordinances may be enacted. The purpose of this act is to promote "the preservation and protection of buildings, sites, places, and districts of historic interest . . . through the development of appropriate settings for such buildings, places, and districts." Thus, "No buildings or structures including stone walls, fences, light fixtures, steps and paving or other appurtenant fixtures shall be erected, altered, restored, moved or demolished within a historic district until after an application for a certificate of appropriateness as to exterior architectural features has been submitted to and approved by the Historic District Commission" (30).

In the city of Helena, Arkansas (population ca 10,000), the commission can thus regulate the exterior and grounds of any property within the boundaries of its local historic district. Exterior features are defined as "the architectural style, general design and general arrangement of the exterior of a structure, including the kind and texture of the building material and the type and style of all windows, doors, light fixtures, signs and other appurtenant fixtures. The style, material, size and location of outdoor advertising signs and bill posters within a historic district shall also be under the control of the Commission" (31). Table 3 outlines the basic procedure; commission procedures provide for some form of appeals process depending on the commission's action in a given case.

Usually, the local commission either relies on the *Secretary of the Interior's Standards* as its guidelines in making decisions about applications for certificates of appropriateness or develops its own guidelines. Some form of design criteria are essential to a legally enforceable ordinance, and they are best adapted to local situations, history, resources, and economics. In the state of California,

Table 3. Generalized Historic District Commission Review Process of Rehabilitation/Renovation Project

1. Decision by property owner to undertake rehabilitation of historic structure or contributing building within historic district.
2. Owner/architect meets with commission staff to discuss design guidelines and submission requirements.
3. Owner/architect finalizes rehabilitation plans with reference to guidelines and assembles materials necessary for submission of an application for a certificate of appropriateness.
4. Submission of application to commission staff.
5. Owner/architect, commission staff, and interested public make presentation before commission in public hearing.
6. Commission decision to grant or deny certificate.
7. Appeal of denial to city or other local authority.

Figure 5. Rehabilitation and adaptive use of architect Daniel H. Burnham's Union Station in Washington, D.C. (1903–1908) was undertaken as a joint Federal-private redevelopment to revive the original transportation facility by linking it to an upscale retail-entertainment complex. Exterior view of the project, completed in 1988 with architects Harry Weese & Associates and Benjamin Thompson & Associates (retail space). The project received funding support through Congress, and the work was reviewed by several local and Federal preservation agencies. Photograph by Marcia Axtmann Smith, Advisory Council on Historic Preservation, Washington, D.C.

Figure 6. Interior view of Union Station, Washington, D.C. Photograph by Marcia Axtmann Smith, Advisory Council on Historic Preservation, Washington, D.C.

more than 80 communities have adopted historic preservation ordinances of some type; these range from the special historic treasures ordinance protecting Greene and Greene houses in Pasadena, to design and demolition review of one-story brick structures in Colusa's Chinatown (32).

FORM, SUBSTANCE, ECONOMICS

Development Goals vs Preservation Goals

Preservation interests have collided in the past with development pursuits. The extreme tendency of some preservation groups to want to save everything because it is old is in direct contrast to the urban renewal philosophy of the 1950s and 1960s, continuing in some quarters to the present day, that everything old should be torn down. Coupled with such extremes of perception and philosophy, there have arisen many misunderstandings of the purposes of both new design and construction and preservation; such misunderstandings have produced facadism. They have also led to the sometimes regrettable creation of a false sense of the past that accompanies certain theme amusement park-type developments, with such new commercial developments as shopping centers and restaurants constructed in styles mimicking historic features in inappropriate ways and settings.

Conflicting Preservation Strategies: Incorporation vs Set-Aside

What are some of the reasons for the conflicts? As can be seen from the previous discussion, most efforts at preservation are aimed at one of two principal approaches. The first is the process of setting aside or "mothballing," in effect turning a building into a museum. Some notable examples in the United States of National Park system units created to preserve properties of architectural or engineering interest in this manner include the cliff dwellings in Mesa Verde National Park, Colorado; Sitka

National Historical Park, Alaska (19th-century Russian structures); San Juan National Historic Site, Puerto Rico (Spanish colonial fortress and urban plan), and Independence National Historical Park in Philadelphia, Pennsylvania (18th-century public buildings). Such places are clearly set aside as museums or collections of artifacts to appreciate and enjoy as specific preserved vestiges of the past. Until the last 20 years, this is the sort of historic preservation that most people understood the term to mean.

In direct conflict with this approach is the attempt to preserve properties through a strategy of incorporation (Fig. 7). Here the purpose is to incorporate historic buildings, planning principles, and design qualities more directly into everyday life. Adaptive use is relevant to this approach, but it is only one aspect of it. The process of incorporation requires many decisions and compromises in how old should relate to new: what are appropriate approaches to contextual design and infill construction; what changes in function are appropriate in adaptively using buildings and with what, if any, limits on the new uses; how and where is replication of missing historic features appropriate; how are building codes adhered to and how do they apply to historic structures being retrofitted; and, overall, what is the cost-effectiveness of the proposal in terms of short-term and long-term costs and returns?

Subjectivity of Design Review

Incorporation as a preservation approach, and the often conflicting goals of preservation desires and development

Figure 7. Results of the design process involving the juxtaposition of old and new, as here in the historic district of Old Town Alexandria, Virginia, involve compromises based on a complex mix of historic preservation concerns, community sentiment, city planning requirements, and development needs. Photograph by Jack E. Boucher, Historic American Buildings Survey, NPS, Washington, D.C.

needs, has combined with the growth of local and other governmental regulation of activities affecting historic properties to raise the further question of design review and its effect on the integrity and creativity of the architectural design process. Most recently, this debate has been aired over the proposed addition to Frank Lloyd Wright's Guggenheim Museum, where local preservation groups and the New York City Landmarks Preservation Commission have objected to the proposal on the basis of its compromise of Wright's design. Guggenheim project architect Charles Gwathmey has argued (33) that

> to a large degree, modern architects are being punished for sins of earlier decades. . . . I think there is an awareness among all good architects that history is critical, that the lessons of history are clear and that an understanding and interpretation of historical or existing elements in a city's infrastructure need to be primary considerations in new design. Interpretation of history is very different from imitation. Design review tends to applaud imitation and be very suspect of interpretation.

At the present juncture, the controversy over the Guggenheim addition remains unresolved, but questions raised during the design review process may force all sides to take a closer look at the operation and decisions of design review boards.

What is Worthy of Preservation?

Finally, debate continues on the twin questions of "what is truly historic" and "what is worthy of preservation?" John Morris Dixon (34), in an editorial in *Progressive Architecture*, has noted that "as architects' perceptions of landmarks change, we must realize that other groups recognize whole different sets of landmarks. [Ten] years ago some of us may have recognized the charms of Miami Beach's stucco Deco or Vancouver's sheet metal industrial sheds, but the public in general would not have supported government action to protect them; nor have they been attracted to places then perceived as inferior and expendable." This debate is not likely to be resolved; with the passage of time, attitudes change and perceptions of what qualifies as historic change with them. The generally applicable 50-yr cutoff for properties eligible for inclusion in the National Register of Historic Places expands with each passing year. In the meantime, communities searching for ways to revitalize their central business historic districts, or to ward off suburban and exurban development into rural areas, are pragmatically reexamining their own notions of what is historic in the context of protective laws or available economic incentives.

SUMMARY

Historic preservation, both on the international scene and, more specifically, within the United States in 1988, has become a part of everyday life. Nearly 450 local governments, each with a historic district commission or design review board, have been officially recognized and certified by the U.S. Department of the Interior. Fifty-seven state, district, commonwealth, and territorial jurisdic-

tions have historic preservation officers receiving some $25 million in federal assistance, and the National Trust for Historic Preservation receives close to an additional $5 million in federal assistance for its programs. Close to 50,000 properties have been entered in the National Register of Historic Places, many of these properties historic districts in local communities containing hundreds of individual buildings and sites. As of 1983, when a report was prepared for the Advisory Council on Historic Preservation, an estimated 3500–4000 rehabilitation projects were being received annually by the National Park Service for Tax Act certification, representing between $1.5 and $1.8 billion in investment.

As summarized by the annual report of the Advisory Council on Historic Preservation (35) on the 20th anniversary of the 1966 passage of the National Historic Preservation Act in 1986,

> . . .The late 1960s and 1970s saw struggles within the national program to establish the need for professional standards and oversight. The 1980s has seen this battle effectively won—though there is still room for debate about what professional standards should entail—and a shift back toward nonprofessional participation and leadership, particularly at the local level, and toward cooperation between professionals and nonprofessionals to advance the interests of preservation. . . .

Many community leaders have slowly recognized the need to address community problems in a broader and more integrated way. The Mayor of Charleston, South Carolina, noting his city's experience with historic preservation, has commented that "too often, preservation has been used to mask a fear of any change. A positive approach employs the preservation ethic as a tool to deal with a city's economic, housing, employment, and esthetic problems. This approach requires that the city be considered as a whole and saved and restored as a whole" (36).

This is not an easy task.

BIBLIOGRAPHY

1. C. B. Hosmer, Jr., *Presence of the Past,* The Putnam Publishing Group Inc., New York, 1965; *Preservation Comes of Age,* University Press of Virginia for the Preservation Press, Charlottesville, Va., 1981.
2. J. M. Fitch, *Historic Preservation,* McGraw-Hill Inc., New York, 1982.
3. J. Fawcett, ed., *The Future of the Past,* Whitney, New York, 1976.
4. N. Williams, E. H. Kellogg, and F. B. Gilbert, eds., *Readings in Historic Preservation,* Center for Urban Policy Research, Piscataway, N.J., 1983.
5. R. V. Keune, ed., *The Historic Preservation Yearbook,* Adler & Adler, Washington, D.C., 1985.
6. P. Thurber, ed., *Controversies in Historic Preservation,* National Trust for Historic Preservation, Washington, D.C., 1985.
7. J. C. Massey, *Readings in Historic Preservation,* National Preservation Institute, National Building Museum, Washington, D.C., 1986; an annotated bibliography.
8. J. Ortiz, *The Mosque-Cathedral of Cordoba,* Editions Luker, Saragosa, Spain, 1975.

9. *Ibid.,* p. 85.

10. *Ibid.,* p. 86.

11. A. L. Huxtable, *Kicked A Building Lately?,* Quadrangle/The New York Times Co., New York, 1976.

12. C. Norberg-Schultz, *Intentions in Architecture,* MIT Press, Cambridge, Mass., 1965, p. 23.

13. Ref. 5, pp. 33–53, especially pp. 40–41.

14. Ref. 5, p. 34.

15. Historic Buildings and Monuments Commission for England, *Report and Accounts, English Heritage, 1983–1985,* London, 1985.

16. Ref. 15, pp. 45–47.

17. Advisory Council on Historic Preservation, *The National Historic Preservation Program Today,* U.S. Government Printing Office, Washington, D.C., 1976.

18. Advisory Council on Historic Preservation, *National Historic Preservation Act of 1966, as Amended,* Washington, D.C., 1981.

19. U.S. Department of the Interior, National Park Service, *Secretary of the Interior's Standards and Guidelines for Archeology and Historic Preservation,* Federal Register, Vol. 48, pp. 44716–42, Sept. 29, 1983.

20. U.S. Department of the Interior, National Park Service, *The Secretary of the Interior's Standards for Rehabilitation and Guidelines for Rehabilitating Historic Buildings,* Washington, D.C., 1979, 1983.

21. Metropolitan Dade County, *Designating Historic Properties,* Miami, Fla., n.d.

22. Ref. 5, pp. 513–516.

23. U.S. Department of the Interior, National Park Service, *Historic Preservation Certification Application,* U.S. Government Printing Office, Washington, D.C., 1984.

24. Center for Business and Economic Studies, *Economic Benefits from the Rehabilitation of Certified Historic Buildings in Georgia,* Historic Preservation Section, Georgia Department of Natural Resources, Atlanta, Ga., June 1987, pp. 1–34.

25. M. Opsata, "How Pros Play the Rehab Game," *Historic Preservation* **39**(3), 38 (1987).

26. U.S. Department of the Interior, National Park Service, *National Register of Historic Places,* 36 CFR Part 60.

27. Ref. 18, Section 106.

28. Advisory Council on Historic Preservation, *Protection of Historic Properties,* 36 CFR Part 800.

29. J. M. Fitch, "Viewpoints: Design Review," *Preservation Forum,* 1(1) 5–7 (Fall 1987).

30. Arkansas Historic Preservation Program and City of Helena, *A Procedural Handbook for Local Historic District Commissions,* Little Rock, 1986.

31. Ref. 29, pp. 7–9.

32. California Office of Historic Preservation (Les-Thomas Assocs.), *Historic Preservation in California: A Handbook for Local Communities,* California Department of Parks and Recreation, Office of Historic Preservation, Sacramento, Calif., December 1986.

33. C. Gwathmey, In Ref. 29 pp. 2–4.

34. J. M. Dixon, "One Person's Landmark. . . ," *Progressive Architecture,* p. 7 (November 1982).

35. Advisory Council on Historic Preservation, *Twenty Years of the National Historic Preservation Act,* Washington, D.C., 1986.

36. J. Riley in N. Canty, "Happy Preservation Week," *AIA Journal,* p. 35 (May 1980).

General References

Preservation Bibliographies

Ref. 7 is a good source.

Advisory Council on Historic Preservation, *Where to Look: A Guide to Preservation Information,* Washington, D.C., 1982.

Preservation Assistance Division, Technical Preservation Services, *Publication Catalog,* Washington, D.C., 1987.

Books

C. Americus, ed., *Building Rehabilitation Research and Technology for the 1980's,* National Conference of States on Building Codes and Standards, Kendall/Hunt Pub. Co., Dubuque, Iowa, 1980.

D. Maddex, ed., *All About Old Buildings: The Whole Preservation Catalog,* National Trust for Historic Preservation, The Preservation Press, Washington, D.C., 1985.

National Trust for Historic Preservation, *Old and New Architecture: Design Relationship,* The Preservation Press, Washington, D.C., 1980.

Technical Preservation Services, National Park Service, U.S. Department of the Interior, *Respectful Rehabilitation,* The Preservation Press, Washington, D.C., 1982.

E. K. Thompson, ed., *Recycling Buildings,* Architectural Record, McGraw-Hill Inc., New York, 1977.

S. Timmons, ed., *Preservation and Conservation: Principles and Practices,* The Preservation Press, Washington, D.C., 1976.

Urban Land Institute, *Adaptive Use,* Urban Land Institute, Washington, D.C., 1978.

Periodicals

Selected articles in the following periodicals.

AIA Journal

Association for Preservation Technology Bulletin

Architectural Record (especially June 1986, October 1983, October 1986, November 1987)

Architecture (especially November of each year)

Historic Preservation

Landscape Architecture (especially January 1981, July, August 1987, September, October 1987)

Museum News (especially September 1980)

Preservation Forum

Preservation News

Progressive Architecture (especially November of each year)

Urban Land

Selected Government Publications of Particular Interest

Advisory Council on Historic Preservation, *Annual Reports* series and *Special Task Force Reports* on Urban Revitalization, Neighborhood Conservation, Energy Conservation, and other topics.

Anderson Notter Finegold, Inc., *Miami Beach Art Deco District: Preservation and Development Plan,* Metro-Dade County Office of Community and Economic Development, and Miami Beach Economic Development Department, Miami, Fla., January 1981.

J. O. Curtis, *Moving Historic Buildings,* Technical Preservation Services, National Park Service, Washington, D.C., 1979.

A. Derry, and colleagues, *Guidelines for Local Surveys: A Basis for Preservation Planning,* National Register Bulletin 24, National Park Service, Washington, D.C., 1977, 1985.

Preservation Assistance Division, National Park Service, *Interpreting the Secretary of the Interior's Standards for Rehabilitation,* Washington, D.C., 1982.

Preservation Assistance Division, National Park Service, *Preservation Briefs* series, *Preservation Case Studies* series, *Preservation Tech Notes* series, and *Technical Reports* series, Washington, D.C.

National Organizations (U.S.)

American Association for State and Local History, 172 Second Ave., North, Suite 102, Nashville, TN 37201.

American Association of Museums, 1225 "I" St., N.W., Suite 200, Washington, DC 20005.

American Institute of Architects, Committee on Historic Resources, 1735 New York Ave., N.W., Washington, DC 20006.

American Society of Landscape Architects, 4401 Connecticut Ave., N.W., Fifth Floor, Washington, DC 20008.

National Alliance of Preservation Commissions, Hall of the States, Suite 332, 444 North Capitol St., N.W., Washington, DC 20005.

National Conference of State Historic Preservation Officers, Hall of the States, Suite 332, 444 North Capitol St., N.W., Washington, DC 20005.

National Trust for Historic Preservation, 1785 Massachusetts Ave., N.W., Washington, DC 20036.

Preservation Action, 1350 Connecticut Ave., N.W., Suite 401, Washington, DC 20036.

Society for Industrial Archaeology, Room 5020, National Museum of American History, Smithsonian Institution, Washington, DC 20560.

Society of Architectural Historians, 1700 Walnut St., Room 716, Philadelphia, PA 19103.

Government Agencies (U.S.)

Advisory Council on Historic Preservation, Old Post Office Building, 1100 Pennsylvania Ave., N.W., Suite 809, Washington, DC 20004.

National Park Service, Department of the Interior, 1100 L St., N.W., P.O. Box 37127, Washington, DC 20013-7127 (includes Historic American Buildings Survey/Historic American Engineering Record; National Historic Landmarks Survey, History Division; National Register of Historic Places, Interagency Resources Division; Historic Preservation Tax Incentives and Technical Preservation Services, Preservation Assistance Division).

National Park Service Regional Offices (Tax Certification, Historic American Buildings Survey/Historic American Engineering Record, and Other Assistance).

National Park Service, Mid-Atlantic Region, 600 Arch Street, Rm. 9414, Philadelphia, PA 19106 (Connecticut, Delaware, District of Columbia, Indiana, Maine, Maryland, Massachusetts, Michigan, New Hampshire, New Jersey, New York, Ohio, Pennsylvania, Rhode Island, Vermont, Virginia, West Virginia).

National Park Service, Southeast Region, 75 Spring St., S.W., Atlanta, GA 30303 (Alabama, Arkansas, Florida, Georgia, Kentucky, Louisiana, Mississippi, North Carolina, Puerto Rico, South Carolina, Tennessee, Virgin Islands).

National Park Service, Rocky Mountain Region, 655 Parfet St., P.O. Box 25287, Denver, CO 80225 (Colorado, Illinois, Iowa, Kansas, Minnesota, Missouri, Montana, Nebraska, New Mexico, North Dakota, Oklahoma, South Dakota, Texas, Utah, Wisconsin, Wyoming).

National Park Service, Western Region, 450 Golden Gate Ave., P.O. Box 36063, San Francisco, CA 94102 (Arizona, California, Hawaii, Idaho, Nevada, Oregon, Washington).

National Park Service, Alaska Region, 2525 Gambell Street, Anchorage, AK 99503 (Alaska).

Selected Government Regulations (U.S., by subject)

(CFR citation = Title number, Code of Federal Regulations, Part number)

General Procedures for Protection (federal or federally assisted projects): 36 CFR Part 800

National Register of Historic Places: 36 CFR Parts 60, 63

National Historic Landmarks: 36 CFR Part 65

Standards for Preservation Projects: 36 CFR Part 68

State and Local Government Programs: 36 CFR Part 61

Tax Certification for Rehabilitation: 36 CFR Part 67

State Historic Preservation Officers (U.S.)

In the United States, 50 states and 9 additional jurisdictions that are part of the United States, its territories, possessions, and associated governments maintain Historic Preservation Officers appointed by the governor or chief administrative officer under Section 101 of the National Historic Preservation Act (16 USC 470a). These offices have architects and/or other design professionals and historic preservation experts on their staffs, and, outside of local government or professional consultants, should be the first point of contact for those seeking further information or technical advice on historic preservation issues. The address of each of these officers is provided below.

Alabama: SHPO, Executive Director, Alabama Historical Commission, 725 Monroe Street, Montgomery, AL 36130.

Alaska: SHPO, Division of Parks, Office of History and Archeology, P.O. Box 107001, Anchorage, AK 99510-7001.

American Samoa: HPO, Director, Department of Parks and Recreation, Government of American Samoa, Pago Pago, American Samoa 96799.

Arizona: SHPO, Arizona State Parks, 800 West Washington, Suite 415, Phoenix, AZ 85007.

Arkansas: SHPO, Arkansas Historic Preservation Program, The Heritage Center, Suite 200, 225 East Markham Street, Little Rock, AR 72201.

California: SHPO, Office of Historic Preservation, Department of Parks and Recreation, P.O. Box 942896, Sacramento, CA 94296-0001.

Colorado: SHPO, President, Colorado Historical Society, 1300 Broadway, Denver, CO 80203.

Connecticut: SHPO, Director, Connecticut Historical Commission, 59 South Prospect Street, Hartford, CT 06106.

Delaware: SHPO, Director, Division of Historical and Cultural Affairs, Hall of Records, P. O. 1401, Dover, DE 19901.

District of Columbia: SHPO, City Administrator, 1350 Pennsylvania Ave., N.W., District Building, Washington, DC 20004.

Florida: SHPO, Director, Division of Historical Resources, Department of State, R.A. Gray Building, 500 S. Bronough St., Tallahassee, FL 32399-0250.

Georgia: SHPO, Commissioner, Department of Natural Resources, Floyd Tower East, Suite 1252, 205 Butler Street, S.E., Atlanta, GA 30334.

Guam: HPO, Director, Department of Parks and Recreation, Government of Guam, 490 Naval Hospital Road, Agana Heights, Guam 96910.

Hawaii: SHPO, Chairperson, Department of Land and Natural Resources, P.O. Box 621, Honolulu, HI 96809.

Idaho: SHPO, State Historian, Idaho Historical Society, 610 North Julia Davis Drive, Boise, ID 83702.

Illinois: SHPO, Director, Illinois Historic Preservation Agency, Old State Capitol Building, Springfield, IL 62701.

Indiana: SHPO, Director, Department of Natural Resources, 608 State Office Building, Indianapolis, IN 46204.

Iowa: SHPO, Administrator, State Historical Society of Iowa, Capitol Complex, East Sixth and Locust Streets, Des Moines, IA 50319.

Kansas: SHPO, Executive Director, Kansas State Historical Society, 120 West Tenth, Topeka, KS 66612.

Kentucky: SHPO, Director, Kentucky Heritage Council, 12th Floor, Capitol Plaza Tower, Frankfort, KY 40601.

Louisiana: SHPO, Assistant Secretary, Office of Cultural Development, Division of Culture, Recreation and Tourism, P.O. Box 44247, Baton Rouge, LA 70804.

Maine: SHPO, Director, Maine Historic Preservation Commission, 55 Capitol Street, Station 65, Augusta, ME 04333.

Marshall Islands, Republic of: HPO, Alele Museum, P.O. Box 629, Majuro, Republic of the Marshall Islands 96960.

Maryland: SHPO, Executive Director, Historical and Cultural Programs, Department of Housing and Community Development, 45 Calvert St., Annapolis, MD 21401.

Massachusetts: SHPO, Executive Director, Massachusetts Historical Commission, 80 Boylston Street, Suite 310, Boston, MA 02116.

Michigan: SHPO, Director, Bureau of History, Department of State, 208 North Capitol, Lansing, MI 48918.

Micronesia, Federated States of: FSM HPO, Office of Administrative Services, Division of Archives and Historic Preservation, FSM National Government, Kolonia, Pohnpei 96941 (Note: the individual states have HPOs and programs as well, under a compact of free association with the United States).

Minnesota: SHPO, Director, Minnesota Historical Society, 690 Cedar Street, St. Paul, MN 55101.

Mississippi: SHPO, Director, Mississippi Department of Archives and History, P.O. Box 571, Jackson, MS 39205.

Missouri: SHPO, Director, Missouri Department of Natural Resources, 1915 Southridge Drive, P.O. Box 176, Jefferson City, MO 65102.

Montana: SHPO, Program Manager, State Historic Preservation Office, Montana Historical Society, 225 North Roberts, Helena, MT 59620-9990.

Nebraska: SHPO, Director, Nebraska State Historical Society, P.O. Box 82554, Lincoln, NE 68501.

Nevada: SHPO, Director, Department of Conservation and Natural Resources, Nye Building, Room 213, 201 South Fall St., Carson City, NV 89710.

New Hampshire: SHPO, Director, Division of Historical Resources and State Historic Preservation Office, Walker Building, State Office Park South, 15 South Fruit St., P.O. Box 2043, Concord, NH 03301.

New Jersey: SHPO, Commissioner, Department of Environmental Protection, CN 402, 401 East State St., Trenton, NJ 08625.

New Mexico: SHPO, Historic Preservation Division, Office of Cultural Affairs, Villa Rivera, Room 101, 228 E. Palace Ave., Santa Fe, NM 87503.

New York: SHPO, Commissioner, Parks, Recreation and Historic Preservation, Agency Building #1, Empire State Plaza, Albany, NY 12238.

North Carolina: SHPO, Director, Division of Archives and History, Department of Cultural Resources, 109 East Jones St., Raleigh, NC 27611.

North Dakota: SHPO, State Historical Society of North Dakota, Heritage Center, Bismarck, ND 58505.

Northern Mariana Islands, Commonwealth of the: HPO, Department of Community and Cultural Affairs, Commonwealth of the Northern Mariana Islands, Saipan, Mariana Islands 96950.

Ohio: SHPO, Ohio Historical Society, Historic Preservation Division, 1985 Velma Ave., Columbus, OH 43211.

Oklahoma: SHPO, Director, Oklahoma Historical Society, Wiley Post Historical Building, 2100 N. Lincoln, Oklahoma City, OK 73105.

Oregon: SHPO, Administrator, State Parks and Recreation, 525 Trade St., S.E., Salem, OR 97310.

Palau, Republic of: HPO, Director, Bureau of Community Services, Ministry of Social Services, P.O. Box 100, Koror, Republic of Palau 96940.

Pennsylvania: SHPO, Executive Director, Pennsylvania Historical and Museum Commission, P.O. Box 1026, Harrisburg, PA 17108.

Puerto Rico, Commonwealth of: HPO, Office of Historic Preservation, Box 82, La Fortaleza, San Juan, PR 00918.

Rhode Island: SHPO, Rhode Island Historic Preservation Commission, Old State House, 150 Benefit St., Providence, RI 02903.

South Carolina: Director, Department of Archives and History, P.O. Box 11669, Columbia, SC 29211.

South Dakota: SHPO, Office of History, South Dakota Historical Society, 900 Governors Drive, Pierre, SD 57501.

Tennessee: SHPO, Commissioner, Department of Conservation, 701 Broadway, Nashville, TN 37219-5237.

Texas: SHPO, Executive Director, Texas Historical Commission, P.O. Box 12276, Capitol Station, Austin, TX 78711.

Utah: SHPO, Director, Utah State Historical Society, 300 Rio Grande, Salt Lake City, UT 84101.

Vermont: SHPO, Director, Vermont Division of Historic Preservation, Pavilion Building, Montpelier, VT 05602.

Virgin Islands, Territory of: HPO, Director, Virgin Island Planning Office, Division of Archeology and Historic Preservation, 129-133 Chinnery Building, Sub Base, St. Thomas, USVI 00801.

Virginia: SHPO, Executive Director, Division of Historic Landmarks, 221 Governor St., Richmond, VA 23219.

Washington: SHPO, Director, Office of Archeology and Historic Preservation, 111 West 21st Ave., KL-11, Olympia, WA 98504.

West Virginia: SHPO, Commissioner, Department of Culture and History, Capitol Complex, Charleston, WV 25305.

Wisconsin: SHPO, Director, Historic Preservation Division, State Historical Society of Wisconsin, 816 State Street, Madison, WI 53706.

Wyoming: SHPO, Director, Department of Archives, Museums and History, Barrett Building, 2301 Central Ave., Cheyenne, WY 82002.

Certified Local Governments (U.S.)

There are, at present, approximately 450 local governments in the United States that have been certified by the National Park Service in the Department of the Interior. A current list of CLGs can be obtained from any of the regional offices or central offices of the National Park Service or from the National Alliance of Preservation Commissions (see above under National Organizations and Government Agencies).

International Agencies, Organizations, and Programs

Even a list of the principal government agencies in countries outside the United States would be too lengthy to include here; in addition, there are a great number of international and private organizations and special-interest groups dealing with some aspects of historic preservation. For further information on specific national programs or standards, or more detailed information on international activities, consult the following organizations. In the United States, additional bodies maintaining ties with other national programs, and sources of information on them include the National Trust for Historic Preservation (private) and the Advisory Council on Historic Preservation (federal government) (see above).

International Council on Monuments and Sites (U.S.), 1600 H Street, N.W., Washington, DC 20006.

Association for Preservation Technology, P.O. Box 2487, Station D, Ottawa, Ontario K1P 5W6 Canada.

International Centre for the Study of the Preservation and the Restoration of Cultural Property, Ospizio di San Michele, Via di San Michele 13, 00153 Rome, Italy.

Division of Cultural Heritage, UNESCO, Place de Fontenoy, 75700 Paris, France.

See also ADAPTIVE USE; FACADISM AND FACADE PRESERVATION; RESTORATION, HISTORIC

RONALD D. ANZALONE
Advisory Council On Historic
Preservation
Washington, D.C.

PRESERVATIVES.   See WOOD TREATMENT.

PRESTRESSED CONCRETE.   See CONCRETE— PRESTRESSED.

PREVENTIVE MAINTENANCE

The dual meaning of the word facility lends credence to its use in the expression that planned maintenance or preventive maintenance means "a facility for maintenance." As schools are said to be designed with a climate for learning, so too should multifamily, office, commercial, and industrial buildings have, by design, a facility for maintenance.

Preventive maintenance programs should not be thought of as spontaneous natural events that will occur in the passage of time to meet the needs of the systems in place. Preventive maintenance programs begin with the acceptance of a need and the development of a considered, planned program for addressing the individual and different needs of each specific unit or system in a project. Systems that receive little or no maintenance, or indifferent maintenance, fail more swiftly than systems that are well maintained. Most frequently, when a system fails, it is operating at its most stressful period. To lose any system at the time it is most needed certainly is a calamity.

The function of preventive maintenance is to extend the useful life of equipment and to minimize the breakdowns of systems from failures of maintenance. Good maintenance can take an expected boiler life of, say, 23 years for a cast-iron boiler, and extend it by another 50%, or almost 12 years of additional normal life. Poor maintenance, on the other hand, can subtract that same 12 years, so that the boiler might have 11 years of anticipated life.

Preventive maintenance activities can be separated into three groups: maintenance of the exterior of a structure, of the structure itself, and of the systems that function within the structure. Each of these three can be further separated into passive systems and active systems. Active systems are those that are movable, or consumers of energy. On the exterior of a structure, the sidewalks are considered passive, whereas the sprinkler system or exterior lighting devices are active. Dealing with the structure itself, the facade is generally passive, but the windows are active if they may be opened. Glazing is sometimes accompanied by active elements such as solar shading, screens, operable louvers, and the like. Within the structure are more systems that could be termed active. In fact, the passive interior system is more difficult to consider. Such systems could be carpeting, floor treatment, wall coverings, or ceiling tiles. These interact with the active elements of the interior systems that consume energy, move, create movement, make light, remove wastes, or serve for communication, and in so doing add dirt and wear to the passive elements.

A considered review of the facilities that require preventive maintenance or that will be enhanced by such a process should be undertaken to establish priorities. Priorities are not necessarily reflected in the frequency of attention, but they are important to recognize as minimum positions or minimum activity that must be done. Systems that are active rather than passive are generally given higher priority. The reasons for promoting any activity to the top of the priority list could involve security or comfort, life safety, the functioning of equipment, or the irreversible nature of a failure. Cost is not factored in the above; however, all parties should recognize that an underlying motive for preventive maintenance is the upholding of value in established systems.

CONSIDERATIONS

Preventive maintenance programs consider the personnel involved in any given plan, from housekeeping to maintenance, ranging from trainees and assistants, to operating engineers in various classifications, to contract employees and contract firms who perform specific functions, to consultants brought in for direction or redirection, and to the administration, which actively reviews the participation of all parties in the basic plan. It is the oversight and the demand for responsiveness by administration that sets the tone for preventive maintenance. Accountability and reportability are primary influences in establishing and holding appropriate work schedules and attention. The actual performance of maintenance tasks may range from observation around the site to manual inspection and adjustment without tools, to adjustments that require tools, to replacement of materials, and finally, to utilization of contractors with expertise and more sophisticated tools and equipment.

Regular training programs and demonstrations are an effective means of providing the training and education that foster a sense of professionalism in the staff. Manufacturers with products to sell are a frequent source of expertise in this area. One management firm brings a number of manufacturers and service agencies together each year. Its employees are required to spend the entire day participating in this valuable educational experience, hearing and seeing the suppliers and becoming exposed to state-of-the-art ideas.

Requirements

A good preventive maintenance program must include flexibility and accountability. Accountability is discussed first. All planned maintenance is presented in the belief that the individuals performing the maintenance have clear instruction, a known work site, an unconfused workplace, and nonhostile observers. In reality, these are infrequently experienced. Breakdowns demand time readjustment by the maintenance staff and attention to the panic of the moment. The maintenance program, which is frequently disrupted, is forgotten. If small, work tickets given out to the individuals are easily misplaced in any part of the chain of review and are inefficient in the long run.

Preventive maintenance instructions (work tickets) should be provided on full sheets of paper 8 ½ × 11 in., to be followed and countersigned for each activity, dated, kept clean and readable, and returned to the person in charge for the permanent files. Such instructions should be highly specific and list only the activities required at the time. The instructions should identify the equipment receiving the activity, its location, its description, and a short detail covering the work required. They must also have space for notes to be added by the worker, who can then report on actions worth reporting. The completed work ticket returned to the files is the administrator's guarantee of accountability, as well as a written history of work performed on any particular element of the system. It is an invaluable reference.

The second requirement of a good preventive maintenance program, flexibility, has an impact on a number of items dealing with timing, that is to say, the amount of time required for the activity, the date of the activity, and the flexibility to adjust the timing to suit available personnel, the scope of the work, its location, and crisis activity. Flexibility also allows the adaptation of preventive maintenance to the specific needs of a single project.

To meet the needs of the interrupted maintenance schedule, the planned maintenance program should offer a repeatable set of orders and an adjustable set of activities. A project with 75 large air-handling units does not maintain all of these in the same week. Having many fans demands that the activity of preventive maintenance be spread out. Fan coil units located around the periphery of the building can often be addressed floor by floor. It is unnecessary to identify each particular fan coil unit individually since frequently there are hundreds in place in large office buildings or apartment projects. Grouping like pieces of equipment into classes and concerted maintenance operations reduce the expense and increase the effectiveness of the work since the team charged with the effort gains greater facility as the work progresses.

Timing is important to the program. A boiler to be torn down and fully examined must be out of duty during inspection. Multiple boiler installations offer a better opportunity for maintenance in the summer, and this is the time when a complete overhaul should be scheduled. Should the boilers be used in the summer, multiple boilers allow the cooling down of one while the load is maintained by another. It may also be prudent to manage the load to facilitate good maintenance.

A good time to negotiate contracts with boiler maintenance personnel is immediately following the winter season, when memories of the year's events are most fresh. The firm providing the contract service should be called in, and the past year's performance reviewed in sufficient detail to encourage improvement in the following year. The amount of money charged can then be discussed, and a new contract negotiated with the successful previous firm. Should company policy or past practices require it, other bidders may be solicited to provide proposals for a clearly described scope of work. Tight specifications and a known series of activities are basic prerequisites for invitations for proposals.

Although spring is a good time to review a boiler contract, contracts for the maintenance and overhaul of centrifugal chillers are usually better negotiated in the fall, after the equipment has been shut down. This is also an appropriate time to establish contracts for the next season because it allows the greatest amount of time for planned performance by all parties. Consultants are frequently brought in at this stage to assist the administration in developing specifications for preventive maintenance contracts; however, not all professionals actively solicit this type of work. A list of those consultants that should be invited to respond can be developed through inquiries in any given city.

Estimates of the time required to lubricate a motor are adequate if the maintenance personnel are within sight of the motor and begin the work and return to their desks shortly thereafter. In a high-rise building in New York City or in a secure facility, perhaps as much as a half-hour may be required to make the round trip from the maintenance office to the motor that requires lubrication. Available personnel also have an impact on the specific needs of a program. A small hospital in Indiana may have two or three people on the maintenance staff and ask that each be a jack of all trades. A metropolitan hospital in Philadelphia might demand a large, regimented, and highly trained staff for the multiples of sophisticated equipment that would be found in such a facility.

Although flat roof maintenance can be performed in January in Florida, that same inspection should be scheduled for the summer in Minnesota. Fan inspections and maintenance procedures on roofs should be acceptable in July in moderate climates, but that same work should never be scheduled in, say, Oklahoma in July since the temperatures that develop on such equipment in the summer there do not encourage such activity.

IMPLEMENTATION

Implementation of a preventive maintenance program should take place after deliberations by a team consisting of property operations personnel, property management, a consulting engineer, and an architectural or structural expert. The team in turn utilizes the experiences and suggestions of professionals in the fields of elevators, boilers, cooling towers, water chillers, mechanical equipment, roofs, controls, garages, swimming pools, cleaning, and so forth. Bringing together all of these talents into a planned program ensures improved maintenance.

The cost of preventive maintenance ranges according to the intent of the plans this team develops. To set a budget for this type of work, one may estimate 5% of the present value of the building for preventive maintenance activity. Perhaps 1.5% of the value of the building may be estimated for simpler structures or systems. Just as the building value changes from year to year, the values of the systems escalate in response to general financial patterns. Replacement equipment, although purchased 20 years earlier, carries the price tag of today's economy rather than yesterday's. It is for this reason that tying the maintenance costs to a percentage of the ongoing building valuation makes sense. Life-cycle costing procedures address this through "present value" types of analyses, with a similar effect.

The professional in charge of distributing the funds for preventive maintenance activity should review the types of contracts to be done by consulting experts vs the types of activities in-house personnel should be directed to perform. The same budget can include updating of testing and maintenance equipment to augment the staff. Training and reeducation budgets should be factored in since personnel in this work often leave for other buildings.

Funding of continued annual activity should be a matter of high priority since the return on the investment can be enormous. Occupants rarely leave any structure because of their dissatisfaction with the color of the walls or the choice of fenestration. What causes dissatisfaction in a tenant is lighting that is ineffective, poorly spaced, or usually out; power that is insufficient, wrongly located, or unstable; air conditioning that is not cold enough or too humid, or is too cold or dry; a heating system that is too cyclical, too noisy, or too drafty; or elevators that are never on time, that are never fast enough, or whose doors are always malfunctioning. These and other factors are the expressed reasons for tenant dissatisfaction, which occurs every year in a crescendo of valid complaints. If a building does not turn to preventive maintenance to control these situations and provide a reasonably consistent level of satisfaction among the tenants, then the building will lose more than simply the equipment. It will also lose its financial reason for being.

RECORD KEEPING

In our discussion of accountability, record keeping was mentioned only briefly, although designated an invaluable reference. Record keeping by means of log sheets or data entry into a computer program serving as a database of activity should be a constant and consistent activity for proper management. The act of recording a reading (or function) or a verification of operability is important enough to require that an alert individual be physically present, be active, and make a written confirmation of the facts involved. Exception reporting falls within this activity, where readings or operations that fail to repeat earlier history or fall within identified limits, or failures to operate when commanded, all are entered into the book as exceptions and brought to the attention of the chain of command. Consistent record keeping provides the history that highlights an exception to routine operation. It pinpoints problems before they become failures. It also red-flags equipment or systems reaching their expected life so that replacement can become a budget consideration before failure requires emergency spending.

Entries into logs should be made carefully by a trained person. However, unless reviewed by a professional, such log sheets become a chore of less and less importance over the passage of time. The individual making the written record should understand that this is an important element. Accountability for the activities of the operating and maintenance personnel can be implemented through the sign-off procedure described earlier. Duplicate records should be kept in separate locations to guard against a total loss of information.

MONITORING

The cost of hiring a professional to perform the review may be paid back-monitoring through his efficiency in the preventive maintenance program and the project on an annual or spot basis. A survey noting deficiencies and comparing existing conditions with the plan for preventive maintenance can locate and enumerate areas of concern, where the program has not been followed or where a gap in the elements covered by the program exists. Such a professional review would employ various highly sensitive instruments to measure, for instance, heat flux, surface temperatures, sound, air flow, air pressure, boiler efficiency, lighting intensity, current flow, and voltage. One property management firm in the Washington, D.C., area retains a consulting engineer to visit its properties on a monthly basis to monitor the preventive maintenance programs in place on each project, to troubleshoot problems, and to advise on ways to improve the systems for energy conservation and cost-effectiveness.

An example of the kind of problem a professional might detect through preventive monitoring is roof leaks, which are frequently a matter of emergency attention rather than planned attention. An infrared thermometer or heat flux meter can scan the complete roof area in as little as half an hour. These devices function on the basis of temperature difference and are most accurate when employed during the winter. When temperature differences of greater than 10°F exist and snow cover does not confuse the issue, a scanning of the entire roof will quickly identify anomalies. A water leak into the roof insulation will show up as an area of increased heat-transfer rate. Such a problem can often be detected prior to the ceiling damage that is sure to follow. The wet spot on the roof may be the low point in the construction. This may be caused by a leak at another location.

The combustion efficiency of boilers can be monitored on a schedule or on a constant basis, with short payback periods. A boiler purchased with an 80% efficiency claimed and deliverable may be shown to operate on an annual basis at even less than 50% efficiency if effective maintenance procedures have not been followed. It is generally accepted that stressful operation, such as with the maintenance of supply water temperature near the limit of a boiler's rating, extreme and rapid fluctuations of the load impressed on a boiler, high quantities of makeup water, or faulty or no chemical treatment of the boiler water, can vary the life expectancy of the boiler by up to 50%. However, maintenance activity can change the life expectancy in that same range of plus or minus 50%. A boiler that has some of the negative characteristics mentioned above and might already have lost some percentage of its life expectancy, can have it further reduced when subjected to no maintenance. In cast-iron boilers, failure to blow down the boiler or the use of heavy oils while failing to maintain a clean condition within the flue passageways can result in serious damage to equipment.

In simple economics, a boiler may go from 23 to 14 years in life expectancy, a 40% reduction, through stressful operation and little or no maintenance. Replacement costs of the boiler should be estimated as approximately three times the raw cost of the boiler and fittings required. Maintenance costs for those reduced nine years, if based on 5% per year, would have cost 45% of the boiler cost. These simple facts illustrate a condition in which preventive maintenance is one-sixth as costly as replacement. Maintenance costs are known from several sources to be 1–5% of the equipment value.

COMPUTERIZED MAINTENANCE PROGRAMS

A computerized program providing instruction for preventive maintenance work is today's answer to the need for repeatability, considered actions, definitive lists of equipment, issuance of work orders, suggested times required, and correlation of dollars to work. Through a database management system, the returned work orders can contribute an understanding of failure patterns and maintenance patterns for future activity. Furthermore, computers are able to exhibit a perfect memory when frequent interruptions for emergency breakdowns occur. The standard situation in any operating engineer's office is one of daily crises, which, without the perfect memory, could break the orderly chain of maintenance procedures that are essential for the life of the equipment or systems.

Desktop computers are useful for the record keeping and work order issuance required in a full program. Most programs find the computer in the hands of the administration, which assists the operating personnel by doing the computer inputs. If the maintenance staff is large enough that the boiler room has its own administration,

obviously that can be the preferred location for a computer operating in the preventive maintenance mode.

Some computer programs allow adjustment and oversight of equipment with alarm reporting of exceptions to the norm. Many companies prefer to keep those controls separate from the preventive maintenance program since, although operations and maintenance are often considered as one, the two activities are not always compatible. A strange eye cast on equipment sees differently than the routine operator in judging the fitness of the equipment for the duty intended. The operator usually tries to make the installed equipment operate properly. The preventive maintenance individual frequently questions the application of that installed equipment to the need. With the cooperation but divergent views of these two, the maintenance of equipment is improved.

COMPUTERIZED PREVENTIVE MAINTENANCE

From experience with hundreds of buildings in the Washington, D.C., metropolitan area and around the nation (PM Analyst is in its fifth generation), CT Plus has developed a list of activities that can be rescheduled as required for a balanced effort in any project. This flexibility is necessary since no standard program can possibly predetermine the timing of work efforts, the types of equipment and their quantities, weather considerations, distances to travel, and the labor available. These factors force on any program elements that must be specific to the building itself. Extremely large projects should use a program that can issue weekly instructions for preventive maintenance. More modest buildings, such as a 100,000-ft^2 office building, can enjoy monthly instruction.

Example

The work sheets at the end of the article are for a particular building in the metropolitan Washington, D.C., area and serve to illustrate some of the principles stated above in practice. It should be understood that no two buildings are exactly alike, and this schedule may be completely unsatisfactory for some buildings. The challenge is to define the work tasks that are appropriate to a project's systems. To do this, it is necessary to contact the manufacturers of a project's equipment for advice and to review that advice with operating personnel and management to make certain that the final schedule is based on reality (see Work Sheets).

This operating system for preventive maintenance is presented to provide a model for activity. Any program employed should print the name of the property on every sheet so that order requests for similar buildings do not become confused and the work is performed on the correct building. Furthermore, a good preventive maintenance computer program should print two copies of any work order issued, an essential for success. One copy is for the operating engineer, and one copy goes to the property manager for oversight purposes. A side benefit of the requirement is in the educational opportunity it offers to the property manager. Most property managers have not been trained in the work that an operating engineer performs and typically have no idea at all of what the operating engineer is or should be doing. The second copy provides the property manager with a detailed knowledge of the operating engineer's work and the ability to evaluate that person's performance. The operating engineer can enjoy understanding, support, and even assistance from the front office. The work order, once completed, signed, and dated for each activity, should be filed and kept as a permanent hard-copy record apart from any data entry into the system that may result from the activity.

Initiating the Program

The basic program is typically applied by shifting applicable items from a master list in the program to the building's specific user list. Generic terms, such as "boiler, steam, year-round," are entered twice if a boiler room has a pair of boilers of that category. By entering them as "Boiler No. 1" and "Boiler No. 2" (common designations), the computer will, in the future, bring those boilers in for activity using the new names. It is essential to use those names with which the operating engineers are familiar in assigning work tasks. The boiler might be known as the "new boiler," "old boiler," "Boiler A," "Boiler B," "north boiler," "south boiler," and so forth. Large facilities with multiple equipment rooms find it useful to group the user lists by address. The operator should be able to input project-specific items not included in the more general master list (see Work Sheets 3, 4).

Entering the Equipment Data

Space should be provided to identify the age of the equipment in question and its condition, for instance, "1981 replaced." Such information is valuable in record keeping because of the tax laws regarding depreciation, because of the planning that may go into eventual replacement, and for insurance records that are brought up almost annually. The model number and serial number of the item are desirable, and space should be provided on a form for those types of identification. A boiler might be entered as a Scotch marine boiler, 200-hp, low-pressure steam, gas- and oil-fired, with firing rates included.

Assembling the Tasks

Master programs, in the case of a boiler, suggest retubing at, perhaps, five-year intervals. The operator should enter the last year in which the boiler was retubed so that the user can determine, year after year, the upcoming work that may be required. The operator may make that determination or request some outside advice to find out when the retubing would be most appropriate. The timings for the maintenance tasks should be adjustable by the user, although the program may contain general suggestions for each item. A good preventive maintenance computer program requires the kind of flexibility that allows an operating engineer to reschedule work activity rather than be impacted in any one time period with more work than can be handled. It should be understood that standard span-of-work times suggested in a program are based on the personnel in proximity to the equipment being

serviced. High-rise buildings in a metropolitan area require the use of an elevator for some tasks, passkeys, security doors, and the transport of tools to aid in the work. A bearing located in the vicinity of the operating engineer's desk may be lubricated in a matter of 5 min, whereas a bearing in a remote location may require 45 min to lubricate.

Boilers tend to be high-priority items in any maintenance program, for compelling reasons. Boilers are frequently worked on in alternate months so that constant operability of the system is achieved. No less important are the burners that function with a boiler. These tend to be separated as discrete items for maintenance purposes. Just as a chain is no stronger than its weakest link, one must also consider such things as condensate pumps, steam traps, automatic control valves, strainers, blow off valves, relief valves, makeup water connections, steam heat exchangers or coils, steam grid humidifiers, piping systems, insulation, and so forth. The list is seemingly endless, yet to provide heat from the boiler to the building, all such components have to be in working condition. A fan system connected to ductwork is likewise subject to the vagaries of fan belts, motors, dampers, inlet vanes, controls, supply outlets, exhaust returns, time clocks, etc. In air handling, just as with forced water or steam, the "goes-into's" must equal the "goes-out-to's." The return systems must never be overlooked since dysfunctions in returns are reflected in the supply system as well.

The computer program should allow the operator to print a summary of the user list of maintenance items, tasks, and schedules in a choice of formats: one form for a simple equipment inventory, useful in many ways to property management and operating personnel as in Work Sheet 5. Use a longer form for a detailed writeup of the projects maintenance schedule. On this printout, adjustments to schedules, noted and routed for approvals (Work Sheets 6, 7).

Work Orders

Work orders must be printed on full-size sheets of paper, specify the maintenance item and location, and include any elaborating comments the operator feels are appropriate. The specific maintenance tasks for a month are then identified. Again, a long and a short form are desirable, although experience recommends using the long form to refamiliarize the operating engineer with the particular item to be serviced. Once the activity is completed, the work order is signed, dated, and returned for the permanent record (Work Sheets 1–4).

Summary

Computerized preventive maintenance programs help the administration to collect and organize building maintenance information, keep a current equipment inventory, identify key periodic facility maintenance tasks, set task schedules, and issue work orders on a regular basis. They further provide an invaluable reference tool in analyzing maintenance history on a project or equipment-specific basis, assist in budget planning, and are a cost-effective means of following and maintaining a planned preventive maintenance schedule.

WORK SHEETS

The illustrations that follow have been taken from a preventive maintenance program copyrighted by CT Plus, a Washington, D.C., firm, with their permission. A standard work sheet measures 8½″ × 11″.

Work Sheet 1

PM ANALYST MONTHLY PREVENTIVE MAINTENANCE TASK SHEETS
November 1988

****

BUILDING MANAGEMENT INFORMATION

****

PROPERTY NAME: ABC INC.
STREET: 100 MAIN STREET
CITY/STATE: NEW YORK, N.Y.
OWNER: CT PLUS
MANAGEMENT FIRM: CEI

PROPERTY MANAGER: JOHN SMITH   Tel: 123-456-7890
BUILDING MANAGER: BETSY ADAMS   Tel: 234-567-8901
BUILDING ENGINEER: TOM BROWN   Tel: 345-678-9012
CONSTRUCTION DATE: 1970   RENOVATION/CONVERSION DATE: N.A.

COMMENTS:
HOSPITAL WITH 250 BEDS PLUS 300 BED EXTENDED CARE SECTION;
ONE CENTRAL SYSTEM LOCATED IN REMOTE BUILDING WITH TUNNEL.

****

ABC INC.
100 MAIN STREET
November 1988

                                              DATE   INITIALS

Work Sheet 2

Item: SERVICE CONTRACTS   Location:
Comments:
SCHEDULE A CONFERENCE TO REVIEW LAST YEAR'S PERFORMANCE AND NEGOTIATE
A NEW CONTRACT, OR SOLICIT PROPOSALS FROM OTHER SUPPLIERS.

ELEVATORS (MFR. MULTIYEAR CONTRACT ENDING 1989)   _____   _____
COMMENT:_____

EMPLOYEE REVIEW   _____   _____
COMMENT:_____

AIR QUALITY SAMPLING FOR RADON AND CONTAMINANTS   _____   _____
COMMENT:_____

GARAGE DOOR AND THREE GATES   _____   _____
COMMENT:_____

****

Work Sheet 2 (*Continued*)

Item: BOILER NO. 1   Location: BLR. RM.
Comments:
GAS- AND OIL-FIRED LOW-PRESSURE STEAM BOILER, SCOTCH MARINE TYPE,
PIPED AS SECONDARY CIRCUIT OFF THE PRIMARY MAIN.

PERFORM EFFICIENCY TEST; TUNE AS NEEDED   _____   _____
COMMENT:_____
_____

BLOW DOWN BOILER   _____   _____
COMMENT:_____
_____

TEST RELIEF VALVE   _____   _____
COMMENT:_____
_____

TAKE WATER SAMPLE FOR CHEMICAL ANALYSIS   _____   _____
COMMENT:_____
_____

READ AND RECORD STACK TEMPERATURES   _____   _____
COMMENT:_____
_____

****
Item: BURNER NO. 1   Location: BLR. RM.
Comments:
#2 FUEL OIL AT 100 GPH, LOW-PRESSURE NATURAL GAS AT 12-MMBTUH INPUT.

OBSERVE FLAME SHAPE ON HIGH AND LOW   _____   _____
COMMENT:_____
_____

****

Work Sheet 3

PM ANALYST MONTHLY PREVENTIVE MAINTENANCE TASK SHEETS
November 1988

****
BUILDING MANAGEMENT INFORMATION
****

          PROPERTY NAME: ABC INC.
          STREET: 100 MAIN STREET
          CITY/STATE: NEW YORK, N.Y.
          OWNER: CT PLUS
          MANAGEMENT FIRM: CEI

    PROPERTY MANAGER: JOHN SMITH   Tel: 123-456-7890
    BUILDING MANAGER: BETSY ADAMS   Tel: 234-567-8901
    BUILDING ENGINEER: TOM BROWN   Tel: 345-678-9012
    CONSTRUCTION DATE: 1970   RENOVATION/CONVERSION DATE: N.A.

       COMMENTS:
              HOSPITAL WITH 250 BEDS PLUS 300 BED EXTENDED CARE SECTION;
              ONE CENTRAL SYSTEM LOCATED IN REMOTE BUILDING WITH TUNNEL.
****

Work Sheet 4

Property Name: ABC INC. _____   November 1988
Maintenance Item: SERVICE CONTRACTS   Status: ANNUAL
Specific Identity: Location:
Manufacturer: Model #:
Comments:
SCHEDULE A CONFERENCE TO REVIEW LAST YEAR'S PERFORMANCE AND NEGOTIATE
A NEW CONTRACT, OR SOLICIT PROPOSALS FROM OTHER SUPPLIERS.

MAINTENANCE TASKS THIS MONTH	DATE	INITIALS
ELEVATORS (MFR. MULTIYEAR CONTRACT ENDING 1989)	_____	_____
EMPLOYEE REVIEW	_____	_____
AIR QUALITY SAMPLING FOR RADON AND CONTAMINANTS	_____	_____
GARAGE DOOR AND THREE GATES	_____	_____

****

Property Name: ABC INC. _____   November 1988
Maintenance Item: BOILER, STEAM, YEAR-ROUND USE   1980 Status: REPLACED
Specific Identity: BOILER NO. 1   Location: BLR. RM.
Manufacturer: CLEAVER BROOKS   Model #: CL350-W
Comments:
GAS- AND OIL-FIRED LOW-PRESSURE STEAM BOILER, SCOTCH MARINE TYPE,
PIPED AS SECONDARY CIRCUIT OFF THE PRIMARY MAIN.

MAINTENANCE TASKS THIS MONTH	DATE	INITIALS
PERFORM EFFICIENCY TEST; TUNE AS NEEDED	_____	_____
BLOW DOWN BOILER	_____	_____
TEST RELIEF VALVE	_____	_____
TAKE WATER SAMPLE FOR CHEMICAL ANALYSIS	_____	_____
READ AND RECORD STACK TEMPERATURES	_____	_____

****

Property Name: ABC INC. _____   November 1988
Maintenance Item: BURNER, DUAL FUEL   1980 Status: REPLACED
Specific Identity: BURNER NO. 1   Location: BLR. RM.
Manufacturer: PEABODY GORDON PIATT   Model #: GO-22222
Comments:
#2 FUEL OIL AT 100 GPH, LOW-PRESSURE NATURAL GAS AT 12-MMBTUH INPUT.

MAINTENANCE TASKS THIS MONTH	DATE	INITIALS
OBSERVE FLAME SHAPE ON HIGH AND LOW	_____	_____

****

Work Sheet 5

Item: SERVICE CONTRACTS   Year: Status: ANNUAL
Name: Location:
Manufacturer: Model #:
Comment:
SCHEDULE A CONFERENCE TO REVIEW LAST YEAR'S PERFORMANCE AND NEGOTIATE
A NEW CONTRACT, OR SOLICIT PROPOSALS FROM OTHER SUPPLIERS.

****

Item: BOILERS, STEAM, YEAR-ROUND USE   Year: 1980   Status: REPLACED
Name: BOILER NO. 1   Location: BLR. RM.
Manufacturer: CLEAVER BROOKS   Model #: CL350-W
Comment:
GAS- AND OIL-FIRED LOW-PRESSURE STEAM BOILER, SCOTCH MARINE TYPE,
PIPED AS SECONDARY CIRCUIT OFF THE PRIMARY MAIN.

****

Work Sheet 5 (*Continued*)

Item: BURNER, DUAL FUEL   Year: 1980   Status: REPLACED
Name: BURNER NO. 1   Location: BLR. RM.
Manufacturer: PEABODY GORDON PIATT   Model #: GO-22222
Comment:
#2 FUEL OIL AT 100 GPH, LOW-PRESSURE NATURAL GAS AT 12 MMBTUH INPUT.

****

Item: CENTRIFUGAL CHILLERS   Year: 1970   Status: NEW
Name: CHILLER A   Location: BLR. RM.
Manufacturer: TRANE   Model #: CTV-4F
Comment:
TWO-PASS EVAPORATOR AND CONDENSER WITH MARINE WATER BOXES ON 460-V
SYSTEM WITH PART-WINDING STARTER, IN PARALLEL WITH CHILLER B.

****

Item: COOLING TOWER   Year: 1970   Status: NEW
Name: Location: BLR. RM. ROOF
Manufacturer: MARLEY   Model #: AQUA-400
Comment:
DOUBLE-FLOW AQUATOWER WITH GEAR DRIVE AND WOOD FILL, LADDERS AND
COVERS OVER PANS.

****

Item: LIFE SAFETY SYSTEM   Year: 1979   Status: NEW
Name: Location: OFF LOBBY
Manufacturer: ELLENCO   Model #:
Comment:
SYSTEM CONFORMS TO 1978 LIFE SAFETY CODE, HAS EXTERIOR DOOR FOR THE
FIREMEN FROM THIRD DISTRICT. TEL. 911.

****

Work Sheet 6

****
                          BUILDING MANAGEMENT INFORMATION
****

PROPERTY NAME: ABC INC.
STREET: 100 MAIN STREET
CITY/STATE: NEW YORK, N.Y.
OWNER: CT PLUS
MANAGEMENT FIRM: CEI

PROPERTY MANAGER: JOHN SMITH   Tel: 123-456-7890
BUILDING MANAGER: BETSY ADAMS   Tel: 234-567-8901
BUILDING ENGINEER: TOM BROWN   Tel: 345-678-9012
CONSTRUCTION DATE: 1970   RENOVATION/CONVERSION DATE: N.A.

COMMENTS:
          HOSPITAL WITH 250 BEDS PLUS 300 BED EXTENDED CARE SECTION;
          ONE CENTRAL SYSTEM LOCATED IN REMOTE BUILDING WITH TUNNEL.
****

Work Sheet 7

Item: SERVICE CONTRACTS	Year:	Status: ANNUAL
Name:		Location:
Manufacturer:		Model #:

Comment:
SCHEDULE A CONFERENCE TO REVIEW LAST YEAR'S PERFORMANCE AND NEGOTIATE A NEW CONTRACT, OR SOLICIT PROPOSALS FROM OTHER SUPPLIERS.

```
MAINTENANCE TASKS                                    SCHEDULE:   J F M A M J J A S O N D
CHILLER (DEF CO. 1988 = $21,500, 1987 = $16,800)                 . . . . . . . . . X . .
BOILERS (GHI CO. 1988 = $12,200, 1987 = $12,100)                 . . . . . X . . . . . .
WATER TREATMENT (JKL CO. 1988 = $8000, 1987 = $6850)             . . . . . . . . . X . .
ELEVATORS (MFR. MULTIYEAR CONTRACT ENDING 1989)                  . . . . . . . . . . X .
THERAPY POOL AND EQUIPMENT                                       . . . . . X . . . . . .
MASTER TV SYSTEM AND RENTAL SETS (HOURLY)                        . X . . . . . . . . . .
TRASH DISPOSAL (BY CITY)                                         . . . . . . . . . . . .
GROUNDS MAINTENANCE (BY STAFF)                                   . . . . . . . . . . . .
GUARD SERVICE (MNO CO. $11.87/H/MAN PLUS 18%)                    . . . . . . . X . . . .
EMPLOYEE REVIEW                                                  . . . . . . . . . . . X
AIR QUALITY SAMPLING FOR RADON AND CONTAMINANTS                  X X X X X X X X X X X X
LAUNDRY EQUIPMENT (BY STAFF)                                     . . . . . . . . . . . .
EVERY FIVE YEARS, TESTING AND BALANCE OF HVAC, 1991 NEXT         . . . . . X . . . . . .
ROOF WARRANTY REINSPECTION                                       . . . . . . . . . . . X
GARAGE DOOR AND THREE GATES                                      . . . . . . . . . . X .
```

****

Item: BOILER, STEAM, YEAR-ROUND USE	Year: 1980	Status: REPLACED
Name: BOILER NO. 1		Location: BLR. RM.
Manufacturer: CLEAVER BROOKS		Model #: CL350-W

Comment:
GAS- AND OIL-FIRED LOW-PRESSURE STEAM BOILER, SCOTCH MARINE TYPE, PIPED AS SECONDARY CIRCUIT OFF THE PRIMARY MAIN.

```
MAINTENANCE TASKS                                    SCHEDULE:   J F M A M J J A S O N D
PERFORMANCE EFFICIENCY TEST; TUNE AS NEEDED                      . . . . . . . . . . X .
CLEAN FIRE SIDE                                                  . . . X . . . . . . . .
BLOW DOWN BOILER                                                 X X X . X X X X X X X X
TEST RELIEF VALVE                                                X X X X X X X X X X X X
TAKE WATER SAMPLE FOR CHEMICAL ANALYSIS                          X X X X X X X X X X X X
TEST SAFETY CONTROLS                                             . X . X . X . X . X . X
CALIBRATE PRESSURE GAUGES AND THERMOMETERS                       . . . X . . . . . . . .
INSPECT COMBUSTION CHAMBER AND FLUES                             . . . X . . . . X . . .
DRAIN AND FLUSH, REFILL, RETREAT WATER                           . . . X . . . . . . . .
CONFIRM ALL SERVICE VALVES                                       . . . X . . . . . . . .
CONFIRM FILL VALVE FUNCTIONS                                     . . . X . . . . . . . .
**EVERY FIVE YEARS BOIL WATERSIDE**DUE IN 1990                   . . . X . . . . . . . .
**EVERY 15 YEARS INSPECT FOR RETUBING**DUE IN 1995              . . . X . . . . . . . .
READ AND RECORD STACK TEMPERATURES                               X X X X X X X X X X X X
                                                                 . . . . . . . . . . . .
```

****

BIBLIOGRAPHY

General References

"Equipment Life and Maintenance Survey," *ASHRAE Journal* (1978).

PM Analyst, software program by CT Plus, Inc., Kensington, Md.

DONALD G. CARTER
CT Plus, Inc.
Kensington, Maryland

PRISONS. See JUSTICE BUILDINGS—LAW ENFORCEMENT, COURTS, AND CORRECTIONS.

PROFESSIONAL DEVELOPMENT

The practice of architecture has long been recognized as a curious amalgam of art and science, sociology and commerce, creation and craft. Although the laws of physics determine with precision the skeletons that support the buildings that cultures create, there are no formulas that define the shapes the buildings take. Rather, within the limits imposed by gravity and materials, the shapes of structures and the philosophies that bring them into being are never fixed, but continually reflect like a moving river those for whom the buildings are constructed.

The creation of an architect, similarly is not a fixed process, for there are no instances of identical skills, vision, talent, resources, energy, or opportunity. Each architect, like the culture that produces him or her, is a product of a dynamic combination, shifting, growing, changing, adapting, and reacting to forces from within and without, simultaneously immersed in the private creation of a public product. Because of this dynamic synergism that underlies the process of architecture, indeed is the process of architecture, it is impossible to identify the moment when an individual may truthfully be called an architect, in spite of laws that tie that moment to a licensing examination. Because of the organic manner of the process, it is also impossible to determine when the education of an architect is complete, if it can ever be considered complete. An architect's education can be considered concluded only when the individual sees no more buildings, discovers no new combinations of shape and texture, defines no new purpose or process, or encounters no new materials or techniques. The education of an architect is never complete; it is by definition a continuous evolution.

It is the purpose of this article to examine the nature of this evolution, known popularly as continuing professional education (CPE) and within the industry as professional development.

HISTORICAL CONTEXT

Like most of today's professions and trades, architecture traces its origins to the craft guilds of the thirteenth century. During that period, expertise within a craft area was divided into three levels: apprentice, journeyman, and master. An architect was essentially a master builder, a tradesperson well practiced in the construction of buildings, usually for private patrons or the local or regional government or church. In the earliest stages, there was little, if any, formalized education; young boys were taken into apprenticeship by masters, who agreed to provide instruction in return for the boys' labor. This on-the-job-training would eventually lead to the journeyman level, when general competence was recognized by the master and the young man was accepted by other journeymen as a peer. The processes by which a journeyman was elevated to the master level varied among guilds, but was generally achieved through the completion of a masterwork and subsequent recognition by other masters of the individual's accomplishment and talent. There was no set duration for either the apprentice or journeyman level; one simply kept at it until hard work and learning were recognized by those in a position to assess competence.

The practice of architecture as a discipline grew out of increasingly complex construction forms, increasingly refined materials and technologies, and an expanded level of construction activity. Master builders, called on to produce more and more sophisticated structures, necessarily devoted increasing amounts of time and energy to determining what the journeymen and apprentices would build, defining the general plan, selecting materials and the methods by which they would be combined, and engaging the client in discussions to decide what could be built, what would be built, and in what manner. The study of geometry, drawing, static mechanics, and the compo-

nents of contemporary architectural practice all found their origins centuries earlier at the hands and in the hearts and minds of the master builders.

The earliest organized program for training apprentices in architecture appears to have been developed in Prague by Peter Parler in 1353. As court architect to Emperor Charles IV, Parler sought to provide more structure to apprentice training in order to improve the quality and increase the number of buildings being undertaken for the throne.

During the late sixteenth century and accelerating through the seventeenth, more formalized approaches to design education began to play an increasingly important role in architecture. The Academy of Design was formed in 1562 in Florence, and in 1593 the Academy of St. Luke's offered drawing, perspective, and architecture (1).

Architecture, traditionally the craft-based province of the master builder, began to assume a more scholarly mien. Many professions gathered credibility in the eighteenth century, and the industrial revolution marked a dramatic shift. Cyril O. Houle recognized the shift in his *Continuing Learning in the Professions,* observing that "[b]oth theoretical and practical knowledge began to be built into complex systems. Simple skills taught by apprenticeship grew more refined; engineering, architecture, pharmacy, and nursing emerged as clear-cut separate occupations" (2). Increasingly complex structures, a more urban development pattern, and improvements in building technologies and tools contributed to the transformation of the master builder into a designer–manager–aesthete.

In 1671, the Royal Academy of Architecture, the first institution dedicated to the study of architecture and the education of the practitioner, was founded in Paris. The two-year program, headed by Jacques-François Blondel, consisted of both classes and studio work under the faculty. The program included semiweekly classes in arithmetic, geometry, perspective, stereotomy, mechanics, architectural theory, gnomics, hydraulics, military architecture, and fortifications. The academic curriculum was viewed as a supplement to studio preparation, not as a substitute; faculty selected the students from their own apprentices and continued their education in their studios. The advent of the comprehensive class schedule was seen as a time saver for the faculty. Architecture had by then developed a codifiable body of knowledge, and the essential precepts, known to active practitioners, could most efficiently be transferred to students in larger groups, freeing the practitioner–faculty member to devote greater time to higher-level work and teaching. The reliance on the studio as the principal focus for the higher preparation of architects-to-be was a recognition that architecture could not be taught effectively as a dispassionate academic discipline. Although requiring a solid foundation in physics, mechanics, mathematics, and history, the real education of a practitioner lay in the integration and application of those studies in a creative, artful whole.

The early eighteenth-century UK saw a shift from the apprentice system to an approach that reinforced the studio as the principal focus of instruction in architecture. Architects provided instruction in return for fees (as opposed to service), and tutors began to offer completely independent classes in architecture and drawing. Elsewhere in Europe, all-inclusive programs began to produce students who met with success; Blondel founded a two-year, 8-h/day program of classes, and specialized schools of engineering began to appear in both France and Germany. Although the advantages of the collegiate setting were real, the education of the practitioner never concluded with schooling. Graduates still undertook work in the field under seasoned professionals before taking on works of their own. The movement up the ladder of success was, as it is today, an evolutionary, ongoing process dependent on skill, talent, hard work, and good fortune. In Prussia, practical experience was a prerequisite for advanced study and was gained through employment with the Department of Public Works, the first formalization of schooling and practice/office experience as a cooperative, interrelated, and interdependent effort (3).

The continued recognition of the essential interdependence of formal schooling and practical experience today underscores the acceptance that preparation for the practice of architecture is necessarily more than a static, academic process. Following graduation from an accredited professional degree program, an aspiring architect typically must spend three years in an active field and gain office experience under a licensed practitioner before being allowed to sit for the registration examination (licensure regulations vary somewhat from state to state, but usually require an internship). It is during this period that the apprentice architect develops skills in the practice of the profession. The American Institute of Architects (AIA) has recognized the importance of this period by establishing, in collaboration with the National Council of Architectural Registration Boards (NCARB), the Intern Development Program (IDP). The IDP provides a voluntary structure for the internship period.

Advances in materials and technologies, shifting social and cultural patterns, and mounting environmental pressures dictate that the competent professional grow professionally throughout his or her career, not only through schooling and internship.

The AIA, in its "Study of Education for Environmental Design," concluded that (4)

> . . . the knowledge explosion demands that the individual who wants to learn how to make a contribution to society through environmental design subject himself to a two-way stretch. He must stretch his mind in breadth to learn how his design decisions interact with the design decisions of others and also how they interact with the structure of men's lives in the nonphysical realm. At the same time, he must stretch in depth to keep up with an ever-increasing body of research that can help him to make the most effective decisions about any single detail of the physical environment . . .

LICENSURE

Although the licensure of architects, initiated in the United States in 1897, establishes minimum standards for independent practice, increases in state legislation concerned with ensuring the continued competence of professionals suggest that continued professional growth requires continuing professional education. The mechanism employed to ensure competence usually takes either of two principal forms: mandatory continuing educational activities or reexamination. Analysis of the regulations in place suggests that when state licensing boards are given the responsibility for the task, a reexamination mechanism is put in place, and when professional societies are charged with the responsibility, continuing education is instituted. In a few instances, membership requirements for professional associations have been altered to include continuing education, and when membership in those societies is a de facto practice requirement, continuing education also becomes a requirement.

MANDATORY CONTINUING EDUCATION

In an ongoing study of mandatory continuing education in the United States, a survey of the legislation at the state level and across 16 licensed professions suggests that mandatory continuing education for licensure maintenance is increasing. In the study, the 16 professions and 51 licensing jurisdictions (50 states and the District of Columbia) form a matrix of 816 potential mandatory continuing education situations ($16 \times 51 = 816$). In 1980, there were 278 (34.04%) instances where continuing education was required; by 1984, that figure had increased to 322 (39.46%), and by 1988 it had grown to 386 (47.3%). The number of jurisdictions with enabling legislation in place increased from 21 to 31 (by 47.62%) by 1984 and had receded to 26 by 1986 as legislation became active. Virtually every state requires continuing education for at least three of the occupations studied. However, of the 16 professional areas studied, architecture, engineering, and physical therapy have the fewest requirements for continuing education for the retention of licensure (1 and 8 requirements in place, respectively). Certified public accountants, optometrists, and nursing home administrators are the most heavily regulated, with 48, 48, and 45 requirements, respectively; the remaining 10 occupational groups have from 16 to 39 requirements each (5). In 1977, Iowa passed omnibus legislation that required all 23 of its licensed professions to undertake continuing education, consequently becoming the only state to have such a requirement for architects. Of the 6 states with enabling legislation in place for continuing architectural education, the responsibility has been remanded to the licensing boards.

RELICENSURE

The relicensure issue is an ongoing topic of discussion in itself; although there is increasing pressure from legislators and the public to mandate continuing professional education or reexamination to maintain licensure, the professional societies themselves are the driving forces behind mandatory continuing professional education (6). Although there is no conclusive evidence that either compulsory continuing education or periodic reexamination assures competence in a practice, the professional societies in general have embraced CPE (6). It has been written that (7)

> There is considerable support among practicing professionals for mandatory continuing education in spite of increasing recognition of its limitations. Whether this represents an acceptance of professional responsibility for continual learning or the inevitability of changes in the relicensure process, after years of debate, professionals appear to be accepting such mandates more readily.

The National University Continuing Education Association (NUCEA), in a paper published in 1984, reinforced this conclusion by stating that ". . . few providers [of CPE] can demonstrate that specific educational programs affect practitioner performance or enhance competency . . ." (8). Additionally, the NUCEA observed that (9)

> The relationship between mandatory continuing education and professional practice is not fully understood. Therefore, emphasis should be placed on individual professional responsibility for maintaining their ability to work competently throughout their career rather than on mandated continuing professional education.

AIA POLICY ON CPE

The AIA has long asserted that (10)

> . . . the ultimate responsibility for professional development lies with the individual architect. Professional development occurs properly in both formal continuing education and less formal learning experiences, including everyday professional practice. The AIA advocates the professional development of its members and is committed to provide resources and services in its support.

In light of its assertion that the responsibility for continuing professional education rests with the individual, and recognizing that mandating continuing education can neither assure competence nor guarantee improved client service, the AIA has long lobbied against mandatory CPE requirements. The policy also takes a broad interpretation of continued professional development, consistent with those of other professional societies, concluding that continued professional growth occurs not only through educational programs, but as a result of a wide range of activities, such as reading, interaction with peers, membership in professional associations, conducting and reporting research, involvement with local agencies and related professional groups, teaching, preparing and submitting works for juried competitions, and conducting the ongoing business of active professional practice.

The final report of the AIA's Professional Development Evaluation Task Force cited seven elements of an ideal professional development program (11):

1. It should be based on a tradition of professional development, the collecting, improving, and sharing of professional information among colleagues, a tradition that must be fostered in the schools of architecture and continue throughout the architect's professional life.
2. It should be responsive to membership needs, from internship throughout career development.
3. It should be responsive to the public's expectation of professional accountability.
4. It should respect the requirements of regional and component (state and local AIA organization) interests and capabilities.
5. It should maintain currency with the rapidly changing circumstances that influence architecture.
6. It should accumulate and provide rapid access to a body of knowledge related to architecture and the practice of architecture.
7. It should be accepted by the membership as being indispensable.

In creating its Professional Development Committee, the AIA confirmed the organization's role in providing educational resources for the practitioner. The Committee was "committed to nurture and encourage a lifelong learning attitude for the architect . . . [and to] implement professional development programs which reflect society's changing needs and new technologies" (12).

In developing the plan, the Committee identified the possible phases of an architect's career (13):

Prearchitecture Student. This typically refers to a student in grades 1–12. It also includes junior and community college students planning a career in architecture, but not yet registered in a professional degree program.

Architecture Student. This is a student in an accredited professional architecture program.

Architecture Graduate. This is a graduate of an accredited professional program.

Intern Architect. An intern architect is a graduate of an accredited professional degree program working toward licensure under the guidance of a licensed architect; an alternative path to licensure has been maintained for those without an accredited degree. The joint AIA–NCARB IDP provides a voluntary structure for the internship period.

Nonproprietary Architect. This is a licensed architect not in a position of ownership or responsible management of a firm.

Career Practitioner. This is a licensed architect working in a practitioner capacity; it includes nonproprietary and proprietary architects.

Architect in Nonpractice Role. This is a licensed architect working in a role outside traditional practice; examples include architects in government, academic, regulatory, or research roles.

Architect in Career Transition. This is a practitioner considering or making a substantial alteration in a typical career path, for example leaving active practice to accept a teaching position or to seek elective public office.

Senior Architect. This is a practitioner nearing the conclusion of an active professional career, preparing for retirement and/or involved less with daily practice and concerned with ownership–management transition.

Retired Architect. This is a practitioner who has concluded his or her active career.

The Committee affirmed that each role constituted a legitimate target audience for CPE programs and developed a comprehensive plan to assess current offerings for each phase and recommend programs where opportunities exist. The "several audiences" conclusion of the committee is supported by the NUCEA in its general principles (14):

> The educational demands of the professional who is a seasoned veteran differ markedly from the midcareer professional's needs. These in turn are sharply different from the requirements of professionals holding their first jobs. Similarly, the mix of new information, experiential knowledge, and wisdom will be quite different at each of these career stages.

Research undertaken in support of the Continuing Professional Education Development Project resulted in profession-wide consensus that practitioners are interested in continuing education and will become involved in programs independently of external mandates (15). In developing its program, the study undertook the creation of a useful assessment tool for the guidance of education providers. Traditional providers' assessment methods involved little more than "asking them what they want" and were at the same time criticized for not providing "programs that are directly related to practice" (16). In order to address this apparent inconsistency, a correlative approach was developed that included a traditional needs assessment tool and an innovative Practice Audit Model, a series of simulated practice exercises and case studies, which were completed by representatives of the professional areas under study. The results are of substantial importance to program providers and professional associations. The study reported that (17)

> Several outcomes of the audit sessions are particularly noteworthy. They demonstrated, for example, that practicing professionals do have performance deficiencies in the basic skills they perform on a daily basis, and that these deficiencies can be addressed by continuing education programs. In addition, the audit data strongly suggest that the learning needs identified through a performance assessment are substantially different from perceived learning needs of professionals. Finally, participants in the audit sessions seemed to view them as a learning experience providing them with insights into their practice deficiencies.

This conclusion is supported in part by an independent research survey conducted for the AIA by the MGI Management Institute as part of its ongoing professional development program (18).

The Pennsylvania State University (Penn State) study isolated four areas of practice that would be the pilot assessment areas: cost estimation, programming, construction administration, and project scheduling. In the AIA–

MGI survey, only one topic, cost estimation, appears in the top 15 topics (from a field of 74), although it appears twice. Most other topics fell into the business development-oriented category. The study team chose to focus on the cost estimation and project scheduling areas because these topics were rated as high self-perceived needs on the correlation instrument, and a successful education program was developed in 1984.

THE ROLE OF THE ACADEMIC COMMUNITY

The interest of the academic community in providing comprehensive continuing professional education programs to the practicing community is just beginning to gain substantial focus. The work accomplished by the Penn State project initiated a structured collaboration between the academic and practitioner communities that has not, on a broad scale, been fully exploited by either group. The successful results of the collaborative effort should result in increased ventures in this critical area. Research accomplished by the AIA's Division of Professional Development in 1985 suggests that although there is only modest involvement of schools of architecture in providing meaningful and comprehensive programs for the practitioner, an overwhelming majority of schools responding indicated that they intend to expand offerings in the future (19) (Table 1). This was reinforced by the NUCEA when it concluded that (20)

> Collaboration between continuing education departments, professional schools, and professional associations in the design and provision of continuing professional education is highly desirable . . . The role of the academic faculty in the provision of continuing professional education requires university recognition, definition, and clarification.

The need for this collaboration is underscored by the "1986 Planning Report" of the AIA, which placed substantial importance on both architectural education and professional development (CPE), with approaches targeted at strengthening the linkages between the AIA, the schools of architecture, the national and local AIA organizations, and practitioners (21).

Architecture is only one of a number of professions coming to grips with the issue of compulsory CPE. As has been outlined earlier, all major professional and licensed occupations operate under mandatory regulations in at least 1 (and as many as 46) licensing jurisdictions, with enabling legislation in place to extend that base. The broader issue of continued professional competence in an increasingly complex and competitive practice environment is leading many professions to reassess the nature of their practices. The American Medical Association (AMA), for example, is engaged in a broad-ranging self-analysis in order to define the role of the physician and the manner in which services are provided. There is a shift from traditional, entrepreneurial medical practice toward group practice; the business environment in which the services are provided is forcing changes in the way those services are brought to the public. The impact of malpractice insurance rate increases is forcing many sole practi-

Table 1. Summary of Responses to AIA Survey on Continuing Architectural Education[a,b]

Does your institution currently provide continuing education programs for licensed architects?

Yes	No	Number of Responses
27	33	60
45.0%	55.0%	96.77%

Types of Programs Offered	Typical Fees by Event	Number of Programs/Yr	Average Number of Participants/Program
Evening programs, single events			
	Free	3	15
	75	2	95
	Free to AIA	2	60
	200	4	20
	Free	10	100
	Free	18	250
	Free	6	10
	Free	4	150
	5–10	4–5	5–10
	Free	6	10–20
	25	4	20
		10	125
	30–50	Varies	15–25
	25	1	30
	75	3–5	35
	Free	15	30
	Free	6–9	8–10
Evening programs, serial schedule			
	300	1	10
	200	60	1500
	Free	10–15	5–10
	125	4–6	15–25
	150	2	20
Weekend programs, single events			
	75	3–5	60
	270	10	10
	500	1	10
	20–150	2–5	20–70
	100	4	40
Weekend programs, serial schedule			
	200	4	60
	85	1–2	30
Full-day programs, single events			
	100–200	2–5	15–30
	120	1	75
	100–200	2–3	20
	150	2	180
	50–85	10–12	25–50
	20–150	2–5	20–70
	Free	1–2	Varies
	20	7	25 (State subsidy)
	195	3	20–30
	300	2–3	20
	150	2–4	75
Full-day programs, serial schedule			
	50–100	1–3	10–30
	295	3	50
Special sessions (summer design symposia, charettes, conferences on specific topics, etc)			
	100	1	50
	150	1–2	20
	100	1–2	40
	1200	2	15
	85	3	30
	150	1	150
	Free	2	20
	200	1	10
	500	30	700
	700	1	40
	50	1	40

Table 1. (Continued)

	150–300	1–2	50–100
	100–400	1–2	20
	100	1	40
	Varies	1	20–25
Video cassette-based programs			
		1	30
Audio cassette-based programs			
Correspondence courses			
External/off-campus programs			
	Free	2	40
	75–95	3–4	25–50
	0–50	1	50
	125	1	30
Teleconferences			
	35	1	150
	30	1	30
	125	1	600
Other			
Four 1–2 h/wk with professional schools	50	1	6–10
Audio-cassette correspondence courses	200	1	30
Architecture workshops for high school students	25	10	10
Exam preparation workshops	50	1	50
Mock exams	50	2	50
State contract seminars	25–35	4–5	25–40
Outside contracts/big cities	75–85	25	25 (1985–1986 only)
3–5-day summer CADD courses	300	6	6
Extension	500/		
	Semester	3–4	20

Into which content categories are the bulk of your continuing education programs placed?

Design	Technical	Business/Office Practices	Number of Responses
13	20	9	31
42.94%	61.52%	29.03%	50%

Personal Skills-Based	Professional Skills-Based	Number of Responses
2	12	15
13.33%	80%	24.19%

Likely future trend for your institution?

More Programs	Fewer Programs	About the Same	No Programs	Number of Responses
25	1	20	11	57
43.86%	1.75%	35.09%	19.03%	91.94%

Do you anticipate mandatory continuing education in your state?

Yes	No	Already in Place	Number of Responses
7	42	1	50
14%	84%	2%	80.65%

Does your institution have teleconferencing capabilities?

Yes	No	Number of Responses
26	26	52
50%	50%	83.87%

Have you ever developed/implemented programs with state/local AIA organizations?

Frequently	Occasionally	Seldom	Never	Number of Responses
5	27	16	7	55
9.09%	49.09%	29.09%	12.73%	88.71%

[a] Preliminary summary of professional development programs from Ref. 19.
[b] The institutions surveyed were 105 architecture schools in the United States and Canada that are member institutions in the Association of Collegiate Schools of Architecture. Responding were 62 (59.05%) institutions, representing 55 schools in the United States and 7 in Canada.

tioners to abandon their practices, a trend which crosses professional boundaries.

At a meeting held at AIA headquarters in late 1985, the directors of the continuing education departments of the AIA, AMA, the American Bar Association (ABA), and the American Institute of Certified Public Accountants (AICPA) discussed current programming and projected trends. The organizations represent well-established professions with solid professional associations long in place, yet the nature of their responses to the issues and the environments in which they are operating are substantially dissimilar. The AIA represents approximately 45,000 members, and the ABA has a membership of about 625,000 members. Forty-three states require continuing education for accountants, whereas only one state has such a requirement for architects. The AIA has an extensive member review and approval mechanism that approves individual programs for continuing education unit (CEU) credit, the AMA approves providers but not individual programs, and the ABA has no centralized approval system whatever (CEU approval is the responsibility of the state bar associations). However, all four associations recognize an increase in the movement toward mandatory continuing education, in spite of the absence of conclusive evidence that it assures competence or improves an individual's ability to practice. All organizations also noted an increased interest in continuing education from their members. The kinds and speed of changes in the professional practice environments have forced corollary changes in the manner in which continuing education is provided; all four associations are involved in assessing or are using advanced delivery technologies, such as teleconferences, audio and videotape, computer databases, etc, in the provision of CPE. All four association educators reported pressure to have their programs be self-sustaining financially, and all four expressed difficulty in doing so in light of nonrevenue-producing service responsibilities attached to each department (22). The financial issue has been addressed by the Penn State Continuing Professional Education Project as well, which has asserted that monetary pressures can have a negative impact on the quality of the CPE brought to the practitioners. In an effort to maintain an acceptable bottom line, providers are forced to minimize investments in their products or to drive up tuition and fees. This can result in either lower-quality educational experiences or programs beyond the financial reach of those they target (23).

CONTINUING PROFESSIONAL EDUCATION IN CONTEXT

Any meaningful discussion of continuing architectural education must necessarily be placed within the context of both the nature of professionalism and the current practices and trends in CPE as a discipline in its own right. Both are undergoing important evolutionary changes, which have an impact on continuing architectural education and consequently on those actively practicing in a changing professional environment.

Although virtually every profession has long recognized the need for its practitioners to keep abreast of new developments in its field, the processes by which that continued development is directed have only recently taken on enough of a shape that they can be viewed as an educational discipline with an increasingly important theoretical and practical structure. It is difficult to identify the origin of CPE—both the horse and the cart lead and follow, depending on the vantage point of the observer. Has increased involvement in CPE created the discipline, or has the evolving discipline led to increased activity? In large part, the question is moot; there are at least 15 million workers identified as professionals, with some estimates closer to 20 million (24), and it is clear that continuing education for professionals is here to stay. It is more useful, especially for the purposes of this article, to examine the context in which continuing professional education is placed and to review and project the resulting impact on the architectural profession.

The rapidly increasing activity in continuing education (estimates by the U.S. Office of Personnel Management suggest that $80 million was spent in 1979 on training programs (25)) has grown faster than its skeleton, for although adult education has a discernible body of knowledge, continuing education for the professions lacks a corollary scholasticism (26). As Milton Stern observed, "[e]ducationally, continuing professional education is an infant . . . this multibillion dollar activity has no educational precedent and is a field emerging and still to be defined" (27). Lack of scholarly structure notwithstanding, the pressures to develop and deploy CPE activities come from a variety of sources. In addition to the long-accepted individual professional responsibility to keep up with advances in professional practice, today's professional also faces pressures from other directions, such as increasingly sophisticated clients, government regulators, professional competitors, emerging specialists, aggressive courts, and changing practice environments and technologies. CPE is one of several responses to the issue of maintenance of professional competence; other approaches include the periodic reexamination of professionals, peer reviews and assessments, performance evaluations, and specialty certifications.

In large part, certain vocations have derived their status as professions by virtue of their being licensed by a regulatory body, generally to ensure the maintenance of the public health, safety, and welfare. Although commonly accepted by contemporary society, the licensure of professionals has emerged only within the last 100 years. The medical community, long recognized as an ancient and scholarly profession, found itself embroiled in a passionate discussion in 1910, when it was trying to decide if a physician needed to be a high school graduate in order to be licensed (28). That was a comparatively short time ago, and the changes in the medical profession, the knowledge and technology explosion, and the practice environment have taken the discussion far beyond that seemingly absurd discussion. Certifications are now required of some occupations that did not exist ten years ago, such as nuclear medicine, biomedical engineering, and international satellite communications law. These new occupations cross professional boundaries and have specialties so narrow that they nearly defy organized attempts for regulation, much less for effective CPE. Efforts expended in continuing education, recertification procedures, and membership in specialized societies all have as their goals the assurance that practitioners will deliver competent service to the clients they serve. Developing that assurance is certainly and obviously a worthwhile endeavor; arriving at a conclusive mechanism is not so easily accomplished.

Discussions of this sort must necessarily distinguish between education and training. Education, generally, is understood to mean the broader development of the critical mind—exposure to the great thinkers, an appreciation of history, a grasp of the unifying principles that comprise intellectual development. Training, in contrast, focuses more on the acquisition of specific skills and knowledge that enable someone to perform certain tasks or render a service in a particular manner. Education can be said to strive toward an intrinsic goal, learning for the sake of knowing; training is said to be instrumental, possessing "utility of content, skills, and principles applied to practical ends" (29). As such, CPE is more strongly grounded in the training arena and is intended to equip the practitioner with the tools necessary to render competent service. Although it does not ignore broader educational goals, CPE is actually more accurately termed continuing professional training. However, inasmuch as the milieu in which today's professionals practice demands more than mere technical proficiency of its professionals, the term education will be generalized to include both intrinsic and instrumental meanings.

THE GOALS OF CPE

The increased activity in CPE has been noted elsewhere in this article; notice has also been made of the field of CPE as an emerging profession apart from the vocations it serves. It is interesting to note that although there has been tremendous growth in continuing education in general and CPE in particular, there has not been a corollary refinement of the expressed goals of CPE; there are numerous viewpoints, differing aspirations, conflicting regulations, disparate providers, variations in methodologies, and a wide and expanding set of boundaries. As Stern observed, in 1983, it is a "disorderly market" where "everyone has gotten on the bandwagon, but not everyone is playing the same tune" (30).

What then is the goal of CPE? Who does it serve? What purpose is intended? What are its limitations and liabilities, its problems, and its prospects? By what measure is it evaluated?

Houle, in his seminal work, *Continuing Learning in the Professions*, listed 14 characteristics of educational programs that can be said to comprise goals (31):

1. To clarify the functions that define the profession.
2. To master theoretical knowledge.
3. To develop the capacity to solve problems.
4. To use practical knowledge to solve problems.
5. To provide self-enhancement of the participant.

6. To provide formal training.
7. To lead to some type of certification or credential.
8. To reinforce the creation of a (professional occupational) subculture.
9. To reinforce the assertion of legal rights in a vocational arena.
10. To obtain public acceptance or affirmation.
11. To evolve and reinforce standards of ethical practice.
12. To provide a mechanism to implement sanctions or penalties, including revocation of the right to practice, against practitioners not meeting standards of acceptable or ethical practice.
13. To establish, enhance, or differentiate relationships or roles within occupational areas.
14. To establish relationships between practitioners and the users of the professional service.

Houle further lists 11 stimuli that encourage individual involvement in CPE activities (32):

1. A search for information concerning a specific problem.
2. As a response to a felt crisis of self-identification and/or stress.
3. As part of the informal collective life of the professional.
4. To provide or enhance social status.
5. As a vehicle of professional collegiality.
6. To secure expert consultation.
7. To seek or provide role models.
8. As an element of an institutional climate.
9. To seek consensus or derive a decision.
10. To avoid exclusion from practice.
11. To ameliorate the distance from contemporary practice that increasing age implies.

In 1982, five principal aims of adult education were identified (33):

1. Cultivation of intellect.
2. Facilitation of individual self-fulfillment.
3. Promotion of personal and societal improvement.
4. Catalyzing social transformation.
5. Advancement of organizational effectiveness.

Apps's "Typology of Continuing Education Learning Models" identifies three basic goals: acquiring content, solving problems, and attaining self-actualization (34).

There is obviously, a wide range of goals that can be ascribed to CPE, and involvement can be motivated from within the individual as well as from without. Most professions have long recognized the individual practitioner's responsibility to remain abreast of current developments in practice, and most responsible professionals have made noble efforts to do so. Most continuing education activities have traditionally been offered on a voluntary basis, and it is only comparatively recently that additional goals have been articulated and have been increasingly mandated for the professions, to ensure the delivery of competent service and to protect the public health, safety, and welfare. Stern, in *Power and Conflict in Continuing Professional Education* asserts that competence is the whole point of CPE, for it is the delivery of competent service that is the driver (35).

REGULATION OF PROFESSIONAL COMPETENCE AND SERVICE

Traditionally, the regulation of the professions by licensing boards operating in the public interest has, in whole or in part, been delegated to the professions. Who else but the professionals themselves could possibly understand the intricacies of professional practice and determine appropriate requirements and standards? Although this delegation has generally resulted in reasonably effective mechanisms to qualify licensees for practice, the approach is not without its critics. It has been wryly observed that (36),

> The hoary story of the fox guarding the henhouse surely illustrates the conflict of interest inherent in asking professionals to regulate themselves for the purpose of protecting the public. It is in the fox's interest to be selective and to guard the henhouse against other predators. Like the hens, the public appears to be ignorant and vulnerable, not able to protect itself or to distinguish its fair weather friends from its genuine allies. Given a choice between self-regulation by the professionals (that is, the foxes) and no regulation, Western societies have usually chosen self-regulation.

However, the increased sophistication of consumers in the last 20 years has placed mounting pressure on regulatory agencies (generally composed of practitioners) to assure the delivery of competent service by the professionals regulated. Increased participation in regulatory boards by nonprofessionals and a shift to statewide, centralized licensing and regulatory agencies have somewhat reduced the power of profession-dominated regulation (37). State regulation by initial licensing examinations attests only an individual's ability to pass the examination, and is at best only a minimal index of the individual's ability to enter professional practice. Only recently has what has amounted to licensure for life come into question.

Houle discusses three broad areas of criticism of the professions by the public (38):

1. "[T]he alleged failure of the professions to develop comprehensive service systems to care for all of the people who need help, particularly the poor and the socially least franchised."

2. The assertion by the public that the professionals tend to place their own interests before those relating to the public's welfare; included in the specific charges are "conspiring to inhibit or prevent competition; protecting erring colleagues; charging excessive fees; and trying to have all the economic advantages of trade unionism while retaining professional status."

3. A general feeling that the professions are incompetent, inattentive, dogmatic, lacking in feeling, or malevolent; specific charges include "conservatism; faddism; coldness and impersonality; recommendation of unneeded procedures; experimentation at the expense of the public or the persons who should be served; adherence to unnecessary and time-wasting rigidities of procedure; mindless and continued enforcement of regulations that are intended to work in one way but actually work in another: ignorance of new ideas and practices; and failure to develop adequate systems of monitoring quality."

Without the implementation of ongoing recertification of professionals, the public is forced to accept the licensure for life of the professions. As a control, the typical examinations that qualify an applicant for professional licensure serve only as a check on entry into the professional ranks. Critics argue that this entry hurdle in fact protects the interests of the profession's practitioners by limiting access to the practice arena; if the number of practitioners were to increase, the critics argue, competition would also increase, prices would fall, and income would fall (39). The licensing laws are largely written by practitioners in concert with legislators, who are forced to rely on the guidance of the professional associations for the development of the regulations. Additionally, "[t]here is little evidence that licensing contributes positively to fulfilling such functions as effective monitoring of continued competence, discipline of errant practitioners, facilitation of the distribution of licensed professionals to needy areas and populations, or utilization of individuals from related fields or paraprofessionals where such persons are as or more competent and less costly than professionals . . . no relationship, positive or negative, has been demonstrated between licensing and quality" (40).

Faced with increasing public pressure, the professions have opted for the institution of mandatory CPE, especially when contrasted to reexamination or peer evaluation. Here again, the majority of the mandatory regulations, authored in many cases by members of the professions, have established substantial latitude in what is acceptable as continuing education; in addition to traditional formal coursework, credit is allowed for attending professional meetings (conventions, etc), conducting and reporting research, producing articles for publication, making presentations and giving lectures, self-study, and being engaged in active professional practice. Hours of involvement range from a minimum of 4 per year to a maximum of 50. Matters get confusing when reciprocal licensing is sought by a practitioner holding licenses in states with dissimilar requirements (41). Most state boards are not equipped to administer more complex forms of recertification or reexamination; if controls tighter than the perfunctory administrative processes typical of most recertification procedures are sought, most boards will select the continuing education avenue; although still substantial, the effort (and expense) necessary to record participation in CPE is far less than that of periodically writing examinations and retesting hundreds or thousands of professionals (41).

Three patterns of CPE participation have emerged and seem to occur sequentially:

1. Voluntary participation (the preferred and predominant mode for most professions).
2. Conditional participation, as a requirement for membership in a professional association (but not for practice), special certifications, or credentials.
3. Mandatory participation, which is clearly increasing and is seen as the emerging pattern.

Most professionals support the notion of CPE, and although more support voluntary programs than mandatory approaches, they generally accede that the practitioners, and consequently clients and society, benefit from the involvement. In certain occupations, the majority opinion has shifted to support mandatory CPE. The central paradox of this evolution of opinion lies in the fact that there are no empirical data that suggest that participation in continuing education programs assures competence; indeed, there is precious little research that demonstrates any impact on practice whatsoever.

PROGRAM DESIGN, IMPLEMENTATION, AND EVALUATION

The development and deployment of CPE programs and products mirrors the diversity of users, professions, and the goals they serve. As has been noted earlier, without a widely accepted organized body of knowledge concerned with CPE (as contrasted with adult education or vocational training), there is little cohesion drawing together the providers, programs, and users in a systematized manner; the professional is, in large part, left alone to select from an extremely broad array the programs that will answer some felt deficiency or provide additional professional skills.

Three essential differences between the general adult population and the professional population have been outlined (42):

1. *Differences in the Basic Characteristics of the Populations Served.* Professionals tend to be more homogeneous (at least within the context of their professions) than the general population, have a higher educational level, and have a different occupational status.
2. *Nature of Participation.* Professionals are generally more limited in the arrays of choices available to them than the general population, and mandated continuing education (where in place) further limits the selection to approved or qualified offerings.
3. *The Beneficiaries.* In adult continuing education, the participant is the direct beneficiary of the program; in CPE, the real beneficiary is not the professional, but rather the client, society, or the profession.

The Participation Reasons Scale (PRS), developed by The Office of the Study of Continuing Professional Education, University of Illinois, Urbana-Champaign, explores the reasons practitioners elect involvement in CPE. The 30-element instrument (19- and 35- element surveys were tested; the 30-element survey is the most recent and is held to be the most useful) asks participants to respond to statements concerned with participation in CPE by ranking each element on a 7-point Likert scale, from "not important" to "very important." The most frequently studied profession is medicine; the findings, however, are at least indicative of the opinions of licensed professionals, although differences were noted within subgroups of some professions as well as between professions. In sum, (1) professional improvement and development is only one of many reasons for participation; (2) professionals differ in the importance they ascribe to these reasons, both across and within professional groups; (3) longitudinal analysis suggests that professional perceptions shift or evolve with respect to educational expectations; and (4) educational expectations vary with characteristics specific to individual professions (43).

The development of effective CPE programs and products is necessarily by an amalgam of a variety of approaches. The responses must match the needs, and the needs have been shown to be many and diverse. In addition to the many differing needs of the population served, more basic philosophical issues must be discussed and identified as the foundation for programming. It has been suggested that there are basically two camps in the philosophical arena: those that assert that continuing education works for the ultimate benefit of society by improving the quality of service delivered to the client and (conversely) those that assert that CPE reinforces and perpetuates the stratified, educationally based caste system, which is ultimately harmful to society (44). Programs that benefit the individual participant alone are at one end of a continuum, and programs serving society are at the other. Bisecting that continuum is another that defines the concept of professionalism, which ranges from the traditional (exclusive body of knowledge, legal autonomy of action, distinctive occupational culture, and recognition by society and law that the occupation is a profession, with a norm of authority over clients that the public feels is its duty to obey) to the revisionist (in which it is the perception fostered by the practitioners that convinces the public, law, etc, that it is different from other occupations, and which ultimately concludes that "[a] profession is not, then, an occupation but a means of controlling an occupation" (45)). The intersection of these two continua forms a biaxial matrix, resulting in four distinct viewpoints concerning the relationship of the providers of the programs to the professions served. Briefly, the four viewpoints are summarized in the following manner (45):

1. *Individual, Traditional.* This viewpoint is focused on providing programs to the individual that will enhance his/her service skills.
2. *Social Structural, Traditional.* CPE programs (providers) are full partners in the process by which competent service is rendered to society by the pro-

fessionals served; educators, therefore, serve the profession but are not subservient to it.

3. *Individual, Revisionist*. This viewpoint seeks to demystify the professionals' services and encourages the client to accept greater responsibility and to work together with the professional for an improved society.

4. *Social Structural, Revisionist*. Like viewpoint 3, this view places increased responsibility on the client to redress the "balance of power" between client and professional and additionally asserts that it is the profession's responsibility (not the practitioner's) to work toward the benefit of society.

An additional view is that CPE programs are grouped into two basic camps: those that relate to licensure (and relicensure) and those that do not (46). It was also suggested that, although mandatory CPE is an important driver of continuing professional education, those programs and participation therein that do not have a direct impact on licensure are more significant, for they reflect a growing awareness and acceptance of the lifelong learning responsibility of the practitioner (46).

In addition to addressing the philosophical issues, the provider of CPE must also consider the practical elements present in any educational effort. Identifying goals, developing materials, assessing learning levels, focusing on audiences, determining learning outcomes, training faculty, executing promotion and marketing plans, keeping a watchful eye on the budget, and evaluating not only the program or product but the result of the undertaking are all integrated parts of the educational whole. Without appropriate attention to the myriad details, the project is subject to failure.

It is not the purpose of this article to explore in detail complex learning theory or to provide critical analyses of existing program efforts. However, it is appropriate to examine briefly a model by Houle and to compare it with a model developed by the AIA, both of which describe general operating frameworks. By combining one with the other, it is possible to develop a model that usefully describes educational efforts at the professional level.

In his landmark book, Houle outlines three modes of learning: inquiry, instruction, and performance. The inquiry mode is "the process of creating some new synthesis, idea, technique, policy, or strategy of action." This mode can be either structured or informal and includes activities such as discussion or encounter groups, roundtables, seminars, informal presentations, focus groups, and similar activities. Although precise learning outcomes are difficult to predict, issues will be presented, opinions heard, concepts discussed, and (possibly) consensus developed. This is a discovery mode and is an essential element of learning.

Houle's second mode is that of instruction, "the process of disseminating established skills, knowledge, or sensitiveness." This mode is the mainstay of most educational endeavors. The teacher (whether person, book, machine, panel of experts, etc) is presumed to possess the knowledge, skill, or sensitivity sought; learning outcomes/goals are known in advance, and learner success is measured

against those outcomes/goals. The educational effort proceeds along a path known to the instructor, although it may be modified en route.

The third mode Houle articulates is that of performance, "the process of internalizing an idea or using a practice habitually, so that it becomes a fundamental part of the way in which a learner thinks about and undertakes his or her work" (47). In the performance mode, the learner typically performs under the supervision of an authority (be it employer, teacher, licensing board, or peer group) and comes to exhibit the behavior not as an isolated response to a particular situation, but rather as an integrated response that has become part of the learner's response pattern. In the architectural profession, the clearest example is that of student charrettes, where the student is expected to react to the problem statement as an architect could be expected to react; the student leaves behind his or her "studentness" and (it is hoped) exhibits "architectness."

In 1985, the AIA, through an education policy task force, articulated three levels of learning that parallel (but do not exactly replicate) Houle's model. The AIA's model included awareness, information, and education. The awareness mode creates the realization that an issue, policy, skill, development, etc, exists, and the learner is expected to describe, recall, or define the item with a reasonable specificity. In this mode, a complete understanding of the subtleties or of all the component parts is unnecessary; it is only necessary to know that the issue, etc, exists.

The second level suggested by the AIA task force is that of information, the ability to cite statistics, identify elements, suggest resources, or in some other manner describe and relate pertinent data. Included in this level are knowledge of sources of information, the identities of component elements, and the manner in which the components relate.

The third level identified by the AIA is that of education, the traditional model in which the learner is changed through a structured sequence of exercises. The learner becomes able to recognize the problem, identify the resources necessary to evolve a solution, and demonstrate an adequate level of ability to use the information to develop an appropriate solution.

Although both models succeed in discussing in the broadest sense the levels of most learning situations, by combining both models a more comprehensive approach is developed. The AIA model outlines the first and primary element, awareness; without an awareness of the problem, further educational efforts will fail for lack of foundation. Houle's model provides the second level, inquiry, ie, seeking context, identifying scope, and exploring avenues. The third level, instruction and education, is discussed in both models; conceptually, the two elements, respectively, represent the micro- and macroelements of the process. Instruction is the vehicle by which education is accomplished. Houle's third level, performance, is the test of the effectiveness of the undertaking. If learning has occurred and the student is changed, performance will reflect the learning or change. The AIA's second level, information, is a critical element of all four levels: information flows through each level and provides fuel for the success of the undertaking.

EVALUATION OF CPE PROGRAMS

There is no question that continuing education for professionals is now firmly planted in professional practice; indeed, it is now required for many of the licensed professions. The larger issue then becomes one of evaluating participation. What is the impact of the program, product, or service? Who has benefited and how? What has been changed? Is the practitioner better able to serve clients and society?

Houle outlines four bases for evaluation (48):

1. *Extent of Participation.* A simple record of activities undertaken by the practitioner; generally ineffective as an evaluative tool because mere participation does not ensure educational benefit.

2. *Extent of Learner Satisfaction.* Not particularly effective in determining actual change; satisfaction actually evaluates the program, not the extent of educational change.

3. *Accomplishment of a Learning Plan.* A demonstration that the participant has successfully completed a series of educational modules that have, collectively, been recognized as effective educational "steps" toward the stated goal and that imply that the successful completion of the series constitutes adequate preparation for the task.

4. *Measurement of Performance.* A competence-based goal in which a specific learning situation seeks to alter behavior; more important than the completion of the educational program is the degree of integration the participant achieves with respect to the program's content.

In addition to evaluations of learning resulting from involvement in individual programs, there are other factors that must be part of the evaluation equation. Included in these considerations are the relationship of the specific program to the broader educational view; the cost- and time-effectiveness; the use of individual and organizational resources; and the generalized impact on the professional's ability to render competent service. A critical element often overlooked by evaluators is the use to which the evaluations will be put: How risky are the decisions in which the evaluation findings are to be used, and how much is already known (49)?

Evaluations can examine program elements (participants, instructors, materials, topics, and context) as well as planning elements (goals, plan, implementation, and outcome) (50). Determining standards of an achievable best practice can be an additional form of evaluation where the participant's performance is based on a normative "best" scale.

An evolving and increasingly important form of evaluation is individual self-assessment. In light of the general consensus that places the responsibility for continued competence on the individual, the ability of the individual to assess learning needs effectively becomes critical. Many needs assessment tools are little more than menu approaches, where the individual selects appealing programs for reasons that may or may not be valid. The research undertaken by Penn State (cited earlier) suggests that practitioners know what they want, but not necessarily what they need. The importance and utility of self-assessment tools are therefore apparent.

THE PROVIDERS

The substantial increase in CPE programs for an increasing range of professions (and vocations seeking professional status) has brought with it a corollary increase in the number and kinds of providers of educational programs. The field of CPE, as a profession in its own right, has grown to embrace a varied and aggressive body of providers; with the continuing expansion of existing and emerging professions, it is logical to assume that the concomitant growth in the number of providers will also continue.

Possibly the most obvious of the providers of CPE are the colleges and universities, which have traditionally provided the professional preparatory education. Possessing the libraries, faculties, facilities, and administrative mechanisms to provide logistical support, their suitability to the task is apparent. Yet it has been argued that universities, by their very nature, are not particularly well suited to the task and have not been particularly successful in providing CPE to the practicing community (51). The university setting is not at all similar to the practice setting; rather, the two are seemingly at opposite ends of a spectrum. The university education takes the broad view, seeks to develop the critical faculties, and fosters learned inquiry. The rigors of daily professional practice, however, demand practical, immediate solutions to problems faced on the firing line of professional commerce. Although there is a desire on the part of many universities to generate much-needed revenues by expanding the utilization of their resources, the nature of the institutions serves to proscribe their success in the expanding CPE market.

Additionally, as many professions continue to evolve increasingly narrow specialties, university programs will be forced to provide increasingly narrow professional education for their principal audiences, undergraduate and professional degree candidates, which will further separate the university from the practitioner community. To further complicate matters, the university community is under economic, political, and academic pressures of its own, which detracts from a concerted effort to provide appropriate CPE. Centralized continuing education departments vie with professional schools for the same markets; university administrations are increasingly dependent on external means of support for programs, seeking funding directly from business, government, and associations, and are forging ties that force the faculties into reactive positions. Universities typically do not have the flexibility to react to rapid changes in the practice environment and have a tendency to relate to only the immediate vicinity, thereby limiting their markets to local practitioners. This is not to say, however, that effective CPE programs have not been developed at the university level; cooperative programs and collaborative efforts have been successful in some cases. But informed opinion suggests that neither the universities nor the professional schools are to be the principal providers of CPE.

The professional associations have played, and will continue to play, a leading role in the CPE arena. As organizations ostensibly existing for the benefit of their members, professional societies have derived much of their status by providing programs that respond to the pressing needs of the professions they represent. However, association-sponsored education departments are subject to the pressures of dues-based, volunteer-led organizations; shifts in focus and direction brought on by changes in leadership and political climates often force premature alterations in educational efforts. Subject to broad and frequently contradictory expectations, the "educational committee or division has responsibility for only a few specific activities, often characterized in terms of methods or processes, such as short courses, telelectures, or programs carried out by the mass media. The resulting divided authority often leads to ambiguity and imprecision" (52). Pressure to generate revenues force education departments to develop and deploy the programs that have the greatest, broadest market appeal, detracting from their ability to serve the more complex and specialized needs of small segments of the populations they represent.

The fact that the membership of the American Society for Training and Development has grown at a relatively constant 15% per year is testimony to the interest of employers in furthering the education and training of employees (53). The employer is substantially interested in providing CPE when it will serve the best interests of the organization; industry is less interested in the intellectual growth of staff and more interested in developing solutions to problems faced daily in commerce. Less inclined to turn to the colleges and universities for education and training assistance, employers are more likely to develop in-house training departments or to turn to consultants to develop programs that exactly match their needs. Employers are more interested in practical results than they are in the educational trappings (diplomas, credentials, certificates, CEUs, etc), which have been the mainstay of traditional educational institutions and which are frequently sought by licensing boards and other regulatory bodies.

Because a building is essentially an amalgam of parts, the manufacturers of building products have historically made a substantial effort to provide the practitioner with information about their products. Although initially suspect because of their interest in having the architect pick their product over a competitor's, manufacturers have frequently provided an important part of the continuing education of practitioners, especially when generically discussing specific applications of types of products. Because the product manufacturers are frequently the leading edge of innovation, they fill an important role in keeping the practitioner up to date; the learning levels of awareness and information mentioned earlier are areas in which the manufacturers are important players. This is especially true in the case of isolated practitioners who do not have other forms of education immediately and conveniently available. Efforts by groups like the Construction Product Manufacturers Council to provide information to the profession have brought a measure of uniformity and objectivity to manufacturer-supported education, but in large part this group of providers is diverse and without significant cohesion. With effective organization and the support of professional organizations, however, product manufacturers could assume a critical role in CPE. Manufacturers of office products, computer systems, drafting and technical equipment, etc, are also potentially important providers of education and training in office practices and related areas. However, as with construction product manufacturers, issues of vested interests and a lack of coordinated approaches have restricted their effectiveness.

Like product manufacturers, publishers have an interest in having practitioners select their products over their competitors'. But, unlike manufacturers, the publishing industry has a reputation for a more scholastic and impartial viewpoint and is therefore free of many of the "vested interest" allegations. Publishers are particularly well suited to provide information in specialized areas. They know who the experts are and have access to the specialized lists that narrow-cast marketing requires. Publishers have a tendency to have a limited view of education products (printed works) and will therefore probably not be an important innovator or provider of CPE to large portions of the professional population.

Perhaps the fastest-growing and potentially most responsive group of providers is the independent, the education company that assesses needs and develops and delivers programs targeted at specific groups of practitioners. They range from sole proprietor consultants to large multidisciplinary organizations. These for-profit firms have tremendous advantages over the groups cited above: they have more flexibility than the universities, lack the political and financial constraints of the associations, are free of the "vested interest" issues of the product and supplies manufacturers, and are more innovative in delivery mechanisms than the publishers. They are quick to sense shifts in practitioner needs and can devote start-up capital to the rapid development of programs that respond to the immediate needs of the professionals they serve. Programs developed by the independents are generally targeted to specific markets and are frequently developed in collaboration with professional associations to penetrate those populations, returning (in many cases) important revenues to the cosponsoring organization. The independents can devote time and dollars to develop needs assessment tools that increase the likelihood of success in a competitive marketplace and aggressively pursue those avenues that will provide profits.

The independent provider can also play an important role in bringing narrowly focused education and training to firms and organizations, custom tailoring the programs to the specific needs of the group. Few, if any, of the organizations mentioned earlier can provide this kind of assistance.

There are a variety of providers in addition to those discussed above, such as consulting and accounting firms; laboratories and research organizations; local, state, and national agencies; industrial and academic consortia; and professional associations acting collaboratively. Each of these providers has strengths and weaknesses. They provide (and presumably will continue to provide) a wide variety of programs and educational materials to the professions. These organizations, like the others, will continue to fill roles as they are identified and will have both successes and less successful conclusions.

The issues facing all providers of CPE are related to the issue of professionalism: To what degree are these providers self-regulating? From whom do they receive their credentials? By what mechanisms and under whose authority are the programs deployed? Who is responsible for the maintenance of records, and to what ends will those records be put? Who is responsible for the establishment of standards, and how will those standards be maintained? What sanctions will be imposed in cases of less than adequate performance? Should the development and deployment of those programs be funded by the individual practitioner, the employer, the professional society, or the licensing body? How will the effectiveness of the programs be measured? What mechanisms will be used to settle disputes?

There does not seem to be, at present, uniformity among the professions in their responses to these questions. In large part, the issues have been resolved on a case-by-case basis as the need arose, and the resolutions have been subjected to various interpretations over time, depending on current trends. Responses are frequently developed with *sub rosa* agendas.

When all the players in this rapidly evolving arena are viewed side by side, the associations and the independent providers will, in all likelihood, emerge as the principal providers of CPE (54). The associations are generally seen as representing informed opinion concerning standards of professional conduct and responsibility for the maintenance of the public welfare and safety. The independent providers are able to respond most effectively when the needs are clear and sufficient interest is articulated.

SUMMARY AND CONCLUSIONS

In the final analysis, architecture is a craft-based profession, possessing the elements that entitle its practitioners to adopt professional status in contemporary society. These elements include the provision of essentially intellectual services with substantial individual responsibility and a definable body of knowledge that is put toward practical ends. Further, the profession is governed by state regulatory agencies and is empowered by virtue of licenses granted by those agencies to practitioners to assume certain responsibilities for the maintenance of public safety and welfare.

Architecture is one of the ancient arts, having found its earliest expression when humans adopted life in social tribes and began to fashion even the most rudimentary dwellings. Formally, the profession is known to have had its roots in the craft guilds of the Middle Ages. Young men were apprenticed to experienced craft masters, exchanging labor for instruction and progressing to the journeyman level only at the discretion of the master tradesperson. There were no classes, no preset curricula, and no examinations; transition from the first level to the next was a function of performance evaluated by the master of the guild.

The first formal program for the instruction of apprentices was developed by Peter Parler, court architect to Emperor Charles IV in 1352. Through the sixteenth and into the seventeenth centuries, more formalized approaches were instituted, generally to free master builders from the nettlesome task of teaching the most basic theory and application to apprentices. In 1671, the Royal Academy of Architecture in Paris instituted a two-year comprehensive preparatory program that offered arithmetic, geometry, perspective, stereotomy, mechanics, architectural theory, gnomics, hydraulics, military architecture, and fortifications. This first formalized architecture curriculum was intended to supplement studio preparation, not replace it, and it was in the studio, under the watchful eye of the master, that the application of the classroom material took shape; the apprentice-to-journeyman-to-master approach was still the accepted path to practice. Without studio instruction and practical experience under the tutelage of the master, the academic exercises would have been useless.

The interdependence of academic and studio preparation has continued through the years and is today an essential element of preparation for professional practice.

Entrance into the profession of architecture is marked by the passage of the architectural licensing examination and typically follows five or six years of academic preparation and a three-year internship under a licensed architect, who must vouch for the applicant's general preparedness. With the exception of the state of Iowa, no licensing jurisdiction requires any subsequent demonstration of a practitioner's continued competence. Iowa's relicensure regulations require only attendance at approved CPE programs, which have not been shown to assure competence or fitness for practice.

Regardless of motivation, architects have traditionally been substantially involved in continuing education activities, whether formal or informal, and this continued involvement suggests that most practitioners recognize the dynamic nature of the profession. Changing materials, technologies, and modes of practice by themselves virtually require that architects continue their education; architects realize that to remain the same is to be left behind. "It is clear that the nature of the enterprise will change and the existence of the profession of architecture should not be thought to depend upon its identification with a particular form of business enterprise which is solely architectural" (55).

The AIA has long asserted that each practitioner has a responsibility to stay up to date and that it is this individual responsibility, and not mandatory education or reexamination regulations, that keeps the professional informed of changes in the occupation and the context in which the profession is practiced. Even though the license grants the right of practice, architects accept that the passage of the examination is not the end point of their education, but merely an index by which the attainment of essential individual skills and the acceptance of individual responsibilities are measured. It is the ongoing maturation of each practitioner, throughout all phases of his or her career, that complements academic preparation and supervised internship and, in total, leads to the artful expression of the practitioner's vision. Although participation in CPE programs does not guarantee competence, the absence of continuing individual professional growth virtually rules it out.

Developments in all professions, including architecture, suggest that some sort of demonstration of continued competence, whether by participation in continuing education programs or passing a relicensure examination, will be increasingly demanded by licensing agencies acting on behalf of the public. Additionally, the increases in complexity of certain professions, including architecture, have given rise to emerging professional specializations within traditional occupational boundaries. The combination of these two elements implies changes in the conduct of professional services and the methods by which competence is assessed and assured.

BIBLIOGRAPHY

1. T. C. Bannister, ed., *The Architect at Mid Century: Evolution and Achievement,* Reinhold Publishing Corp., New York, 1954, p. 83.
2. C. Houle, *Continuing Learning in the Professions,* Jossey-Bass Publishers, San Francisco, Calif., 1980, p. 21.
3. Ref. 1, p. 85.
4. *The Princeton Report,* American Institute of Architects, Washington, D.C., p. 2.
5. L. E. Phillips, *Status of Mandatory Continuing Education for Selected Professions,* University of Georgia, Athens, Ga., 1986.
6. L. E. Phillips, "Trends in State Relicensure," in M. R. Stern, ed., *Power and Conflict in Continuing Professional Education,* Wadsworth Publishers, Belmont, Calif., 1983, p. 203.
7. *Ibid.,* p. 213.
8. *The Role of Colleges and Universities in Continuing Professional Education,* National University of Continuing Education Association, Washington, D.C., 1984, p. 5.
9. *Ibid.,* p. 6.
10. *Comprehensive Education Policy,* American Institute of Architects, Washington, D.C., 1983, p. 18.
11. *Final Report,* Professional Development Evaluation Task Force, American Institute of Architects, Washington D.C., 1981, p. 5.
12. *Five Year Plan,* Professional Development Committee, American Institute of Architects, Washington, D.C., 1983, p. 1.
13. *Ibid.,* p. 2.
14. Ref. 8, p. 4.
15. *Annual Narrative Report for the Period July 1, 1984–June 30, 1985,* Center for the Study of Higher Education, Office of Planning Studies, Pennsylvania State University, University Park, Pa., 1985, p. 1.
16. *Ibid.,* p. 3.
17. *Ibid.,* p. 4.
18. *Final Report on the Survey of AIA Member Interests in Professional Development Opportunities,* American Institute of Architects, Washington, D.C., and the MGI Management Institute, Harrison, N.Y., 1984, p. 3.
19. *Initial Data Survey—College and University Continuing Education,* Division of Professional Development, American Institute of Architects, Washington, D.C., 1986, p. 3.
20. Ref. 8, p. 8.
21. *1986 Planning Report,* American Institute of Architects, Washington, D.C., 1986, pp. 55, 59.
22. Discussion, American Institute of Architects Headquarters, Washington, D.C., Dec. 1985, with directors of continuing professional education of ABA, AIA, AICPA, and AMA.
23. Ref. 15, p. 24.
24. M. R. Stern, ed., *Power and Conflict in Continuing Professional Education,* Wadsworth Publishers, Belmont, Calif., 1983, p. 5.
25. Arnstein in Ref. 24, p. 227.
26. C. L. Scanlan in R. M. Cervero and C. L. Scanlan, *Problems and Prospects in Continuing Professional Education,* Jossey-Bass, Inc., San Francisco, Calif., 1985, p. 7.
27. Ref. 24, p. 9.
28. C. O. Houle in Ref. 24, p. 263.
29. Ref. 26, p. 10.
30. H. Kempfer, cited by C. L. Scanlan in Ref. 26, p. 5.
31. Ref. 2, p. 35.
32. Ref. 2, p. 106.
33. Darkenwald and Merriam, cited by C. L. Scanlan in Ref. 26, p. 7.
34. J. W. Apps, *Toward a Working Philosophy of Adult Education,* Syracuse University Publications in Continuing Education, No. 36, Syracuse, N.Y. 1973.
35. Ref. 24, p. 8.
36. S. J. Gross in Ref. 24, p. 172.
37. Ref. 6, p. 202.
38. Ref. 2, p. 271.
39. S. J. Gross in Ref. 24, p. 175.
40. S. J. Gross in Ref. 24, p. 176.
41. Ref. 6, p. 207.
42. A. D. Grotelueschen in Ref. 26, p. 34.
43. A. D. Grotelueschen in Ref. 26, p. 37.
44. R. M. Cervero in Ref. 26, p. 22.
45. T. J. Johnson, cited by Cervero in Ref. 26, p. 26.
46. R. W. Kenny in Ref. 26, p. 48.
47. Ref. 2, p. 31.
48. Ref. 2, p. 238.
49. A. B. Knox in Ref. 26, p. 64.
50. A. D. Grotelueschen, cited by A. E. Knox, Ref. 26, p. 64.
51. L. Berlin in Ref. 24, p. 119.
52. L. Berlin in Ref. 24, p. 173.
53. H. R. Shelton and R. L. Craig in Ref. 24, p. 161.
54. A. Suleiman in Ref. 24, p. 141.

55. M. G. McCue and W. R. Ewald, Jr., *Creating the Human Environment,* University of Illinois Press, Urbana, Ill., 1970, p. 309.

General References

References 1, 2, 4, 5, 8, 10–12, 15, 18, 19, 21, 26, and 55 are good general references.

Architecture Education, Careers, and Opportunities, Association of Collegiate Schools of Architecture, Washington, D.C., 1985.

See also ASSOCIATION OF COLLEGIATE SCHOOLS OF ARCHITECTURE (ACSA); EDUCATION, ARCHITECTURAL

DONALD R. LEVY
The American Institute of
Architects
Washington, D.C.

PROFESSION IN CONTEMPORARY SOCIETY

THE PROFESSIONAL CONCEPT

The term "profession" has a generalized definition as given by dictionaries, but a specific meaning depends on the nature of the activity concerned. In its earliest form it was simply a descriptive term for people "professing" religious faith (1). Gradually, however, the term was adopted by other groups laying claim to widening areas of advanced learning, and as the application of learning to practical affairs developed, proficiency and skill became ingredients of the concept. This, in turn, was followed by the idea of monetary rewards and eventually by ethical considerations, contractual arrangements, and in the present century, liability for the competence and care exercised by professional people in their work.

Few professions incorporate all ingredients, and the individual importance of those ingredients within the different bodies varies greatly. How greatly becomes apparent by the range of activities now claiming to be professional, among which are such fields as teaching, art, writing, hairdressing, sport, and even burglary and that which is said to be the oldest in the world. There is no simple definition of professionalism that can encompass such a disparate array of human endeavors. The question to be examined here is what it means today for those who design buildings.

THE EARLY STAGES

The earliest of mankind's specialties recognizable today as forms of professional activity are those that serve four fundamental needs: a priesthood to minister to the soul, medicine men to minister to the body, lawgivers to see fair play in society, and people to contrive shelter and symbolic enclosures. To some extent the priesthood initially provided all such skills, but by at least 5000–6000 years ago their separate identities had begun to become evident in some civilizations. In architecture, Imhotep, the architect–engineer for the first of the true pyramids, the Stepped Pyramid at Saquara (2778 B.C.) and for much else in that astonishing development, is the most familiar of the early practitioners of building design in the western world.

Greece, Rome, Judaism, and the Islamic world between them later provided about 1000 years of distinctively professional people of several kinds, architect–engineers, medical practitioners, writers, philosophers, scientists, and lawgivers. But this greatly creative millenium in turn fell away to a prolonged period of generally lower levels of civilized activity (although the "Dark Ages" is no longer an appropriate descriptive for a time of which so much is now known and that created so much beauty), until the beginnings of the present society took shape, 11 or 12 centuries ago.

Western Europe was the nursery of contemporary society and the leading "profession" there at that time was the priesthood of Christianity, the senior members of which formed part of the political establishment and had power and influence sometimes nearly equal to that of kings. The leading figures were relatively well educated, although within the constraints of a system of patronage for selected young individuals that clustered them in "courts" around great personalities in ecclesiastical establishments. There they acquired their value system, administrative skills, and personal recognition for advancement.

They also learned to call on art and architecture to buttress their political needs of personal status, power, and authority by castles, palaces, cathedrals, churches, monastic establishments, fine furnishings, and personal adornments—the Church and royal authority made visible as the chief instruments of government. The monasteries were the principal centers of learning to support this mechanism, and they provided elementary social services as well as nourishing the early strivings of two other specialized areas of learning, medicine and law. The trinity of divinity, medicine, and law were the first to be described as "learned" professions.

Architecture was different. It was a practical activity, creating durable and capital assets; using contracts; controlling expenditures; and employing assistants, skills, and labor, often "unionized" in guilds. The terms architect and engineer were both in use but were not always differentiated. When large programs of construction were put in hand, the overall control was sometimes exercised by persons known as Clerks of the Works—a term still in use, particularly in the UK, although now usually applied to architects' representatives on site for day-to-day inspection rather than as the executive controllers of projects.

Architects continued to develop, mainly as lay practitioners, throughout the Middle Ages. Harvey (2) identifies by name more than 150 "architects and artists," a few in the thirteenth century, but mostly in the fourteenth, fifteenth, and early sixteenth centuries carrying on business chiefly in London, York, and Bristol in a manner recognizably similar in its essentials to that in use today. Occasionally an evolutionary thrust forward was given to the process, notably perhaps by John of Gaunt, the vigorously creative second son of Edward III who, in the late years of the fourteenth century, had under his patronage the great architect Henry Yevele and the poet Geoffrey Chaucer, both leading spirits in his drive to develop "Englishness" as a distinctive national attribute in place of the hitherto fashionable "Frenchness" of higher society. Significantly, perhaps, Harvey's list shows as many as 90 architects practicing in the century following Yevele's death in 1400, developing and refining that very British form of Gothic, the perpendicular style.

THE BEGINNINGS OF THE MODERN WORLD

The identification of professions as a distinct estate of society must gradually have been coming into focus as the early sounds of liberal debate began to be audible during the 1400s and into the 1500s. Colleges and universities had come into existence under royal or religious patronage and were spreading secular as well as religious learning, aided greatly by the development of printing. In Great Britain, a decisive step toward the identification of modern professionalism was taken when Henry VIII (d. 1547) granted a charter to the Royal College of Physicians in 1518 (3). Meanwhile, civil architecture was working its way down the social scale.

Henry's reign marked significantly the transition of the medieval world to the modern, the shift that in oversimplified terms is sometimes described as the movement from faith to reason, taking visible form as the end of the long classical-to-Gothic evolution and the beginning of the Renaissance. King's College Chapel in Cambridge, the last major building of the gothic era in the Western world, was given its great Renaissance organ screen by Henry VIII, and it carried his and Anne Boleyn's initials. In a sense, therefore, this building marks the fulcrum of architectural history, the end of one long, continuous evolution over several millenia, and the beginning of developments still unfolding today.

Henry VIII may have had foresight for which he is given little credit, because he took great care to ensure that his daughter Elizabeth received a liberal education of exceptional quality. She had five tutors from Cambridge University led by Sir Robert Ascham, and under Elizabeth's inspiration and tolerant rule (1558–1603) the modern world blossomed. Shakespeare, Marlowe, Bacon, Raleigh, Drake, and Harvey (the discoverer of the circulation of blood) are representative names from this half-century of heroic intellectual and physical innovation, and half a century onward from them the idea of the Royal Society of London, the first of the great English-speaking scientific institutions, emerged in the aftermath of the British Civil War. It was formally founded by Charles II; significantly for architecture, Christopher Wren was one of its initial members.

The creative momentum was high and sustained in science and philosophy and within another half-century had taken root strongly in the New World as well, marked *inter alia* by the founding of colleges that subsequently have become great universities. After another half-century, technology in Europe and the New World began to consolidate the practical uses of science by the development of the manufacturing industry, with iron casting providing the cutting edge.

Professionalism was also spreading and developing, and at intervals throughout the eighteenth century, people with similar "professional" interests were meeting in clubs or societies to discuss common concerns. Architecture clubs came on the scene from 1791 onward.

THE NINETEENTH AND EARLY TWENTIETH CENTURIES

Up to this time, the growth of the concept of professionalism had taken place among practitioners themselves, seeking to formulate some sort of special identification for the role that they recognized for themselves in society. The number of practitioners was growing as wealth and education was spreading and the market for their services increased and became predominantly secular. But they were also beginning to experience criticism of deficient or fraudulent service from a society newly capable of expressing discontent and with a rising set of values by which to judge it. This external pressure was forcing recognition of the necessity for practitioners to identify and cultivate more explicitly the quality of the special service that they purported to offer. Sir John Soane, the architect of the Bank of England, identified the role of the architect in the early years of the nineteenth century (4).

> That he was "to make designs and estimates, direct works, measure and value the parts" and act as intermediary agent between the client "whose honour and interest he is to study" and the "mechanics," i.e. those doing the construction, "whose rights he is to defend."

Soane was a rigorously "professional" man and he was giving identity to certain "natural" and specifically noncommercial characteristics of professionalism as he already saw them and as they can be seen today—that it should be a solid assurance to the public of competence, honesty, and independent integrity among those calling themselves professional, founded on a specialized education, a sense of responsibility, and what is now called, in legal language, the duty of care.

In response to the new mood, the Law Society in Britain, after nearly a century in an earlier form, was reformed in 1825 and received a royal charter in 1845. "Civil" engineers in Britain first got together in 1818 and were chartered in 1828, while the architects graduated from club to institute in 1834 and received their first royal charter in 1837. Interestingly enough, apothecaries initiated reforms among medical people and sponsored a bill in Parliament in 1815 to get them implemented. Moves generally similar to these took place in the United States; the American Society of Civil Engineers was formed in 1852 and the American Institute of Architects in 1857, the latter after a club existence as in the UK. It was a natural extension of the early nineteenth century spread of education, wealth, industry, and organization.

The later years of the century saw consolidation of the idea of professionalism and the proliferation of other aspirants to professional status handling new bodies of knowledge and accepting by inference society's right to know that they were doing it responsibly. Several new branches of engineering formalized themselves in this way—mechanical, electrical, mining, sanitary, and heating and ventilating along with naval architecture, consulting chemists, surveyors, actuaries, and accountants. Early in the twentieth century, automobile and aeronautical engineers joined the list, and more recently the lighting and acoustic communities and electronic engineers coalesced in this way. No doubt the spread will continue as science extends the knowledge base and new or greater degrees of specialism become desirable. Like-minded people instinctively group together to advance their subject and mutual interests.

Occasionally the direction of development was arrested and changed, and the reasons for it give further information about the "natural" meanings of professionalism. Chemical science had its origins among alchemists and later developed among chemical philosophers. Chemistry's industrial importance became evident early in the nineteenth century and created a need for industrial chemists and later for public safety inspection. A professional outlook was needed. A scientific society had been formed in 1841 but proved insufficiently professional, prompting, in 1879, the then Board of Trade in the UK (the counterpart of the modern American Department of Commerce or the contemporary British Department of Trade and Industry) to promote the formation of a professional institute. By this case, a distinction between two kinds of scientist was made, some concerning themselves with knowledge and its acquisition by research, and the "professionals" concerned with the application of knowledge and its use for practical purposes; government recognition of the distinctive function and value system of professionalism and the necessity to nurture it can also be seen in this example.

In what ways does the distinction between the scientists matter? Why should one scientist be a professional in this sense and another not, though both have the same education? The question goes to the heart of what professionalism has come to mean, at least in subject areas requiring learning, and it can be put briefly. A person who in public holds himself or herself out to be professional in this sense is claiming to be competent in the practical application of a specific body of knowledge, to offer for reward in the open market to put such competence at the disposal of others, and to be accountable for the discharge of the duties he or she thereby contracts to undertake. With respect to the uses of a science, it is a very different kind of activity from that of the academic or even the industrial research laboratory, calling for a different set of values, different ways of thinking, and above all, a background of practical experience in the use of the knowledge and the recognition of accountability when offering a public service.

Then what distinguishes this from other kinds of professionalism, such as sport or, say, entertainment? The example of the chemists showed the use of a specialized body of learning; what the definition implied, therefore, is that it describes a specifically "learned" profession. However, this is not one of the historic trilogy of divinity,

medicine, and law, and it is therefore in question whether this group now has any exclusive right to such a description: in logic the answer in the modern world must be no. Medicine, law, architecture, engineering, and other activities requiring a lengthy higher education, with a period of supervised experience in practice preceding a qualifying examination and typically taking altogether some seven years, reflect the fact that modern science has created a hugely increased knowledge base, and that the custody and development of certain parts of it to meet the practical needs of society has been placed in the hands of organized bodies of qualified practitioners, and that individually and collectively they have had to accept accountability for the way they discharge the related duties. They might properly be thought of now as the learned and accountable professions.

ACCOUNTABILITY

Accountability requires some further explanation. In particular, to whom is it due, how is it exercised and who decides if the duties have been discharged? For individuals in the accountable professions answers have been given sharply in recent years in litigation about alleged negligence of various kinds, and for professional institutes it has long been reflected in the acceptance of the need for ethical codes and the necessity to police their memberships to ensure conformity to defined standards of performance and behavior, the prime purpose of which is to protect the public interest.

Individual professionals receive the sharpest reminders of accountability in the form of the necessity for indemnity insurance. Before long it may well become a prerequisite for practice in order to give the public further protection.

For professional institutions, accountability includes responsibility for the supervision of education to ensure its quality and for the proper custody and cultivation of the professional subject areas, which includes the attention that must be given to the advancement of the knowledge base by research and the collation of experience. By custom, the advancement of the subject areas has usually taken the form of papers read to the institutions and published in their journals, confirming their claim to be learned societies, but today this is increasingly found to be inadequate to keep up a professional learning rate commensurate with the growth of the knowledge base. Therefore, a systematic approach to midcareer learning is developing, commonly known as Continuing Professional Development (CPD). Its importance is increasing and is already attracting forms of credits by which to mark the maintenance of competence. Probably it will also support the cultivation of greater specialization within individual professions.

Government interest in these matters has grown as society's dependence on learned professional expertise has developed. Henry VIII's charter for the medicals was apparently the earliest example, but he did not function in a democracy; in modern times chartering has become not merely a recognition by society of a body operating in a satisfactory way to provide it with a specialized service, but also an instrument for governmental leverage by which to instigate reforms when they seem to become necessary and are not initiated internally.

The most formal recognition now of the right to practice as a professional occurs when a registration body or a licensing authority is set up by government as part of the machinery of authorization. It may be operated directly by the government, as is done in some European countries, or the power may be delegated to a registration or licensing body that has a membership reflecting the public as well as the professional interest. Either way it can apply a sanction for impropriety by withdrawing a practitioner's license or right to practice or to use the title of the profession concerned. In the UK, this is exercised by the Architect's Registration Council. This council has policing powers, control over admission to the Register, and supervisory duties concerning education. It publishes an ethical code and was set up by two Acts of Parliament in the 1930s. In the United States, the states themselves have licensing powers, exercised through registration boards, and there is a National Council of Architectural Registration Boards to provide certain central facilities. The National Council and the UK's Registration Council have reciprocal arrangements to facilitate practice in each other's country of properly qualified individuals.

THE INFLUENCE OF THE COURTS

One source of pressure for continuing professional education has begun to come from courts in their evaluations of shortcomings of professional people with respect to what they should reasonably have known at any given time in relation to the service they purport to provide. For example, in the event of a litigious claim for redress when a building has a technical fault, the courts will ask whether the knowledge necessary to avoid it was available at the time (the state-of-the-art argument) and if so, whether it was in language appropriate for professional use and had been published in a manner and place customary for professional communication. If these conditions were met and yet an architect or one of his consultants had not known of it, he or she may be held responsible, for the courts currently and logically take it to be a professional duty to keep up with the growth of knowledge relevant to the proper discharge of the duty of care.

In ways such as this the courts of the modern world act to protect the public interest against shortcomings in individual professional services but, as remarked above, when an entire profession, as embodied in its chartered formation, becomes open to general criticism for inadequate standards of performance, society may use its collective powers through government to effect large scale reform. The action taken by the government in the UK about the chemists was only the initial example. Today it would usually be done by what is known in the UK as a Royal Commission, a body appointed under the authority of Parliament specifically for one inquiry and report and having extensive powers to call for evidence. Other countries use equivalent mechanisms for reform. The truism is that the more dependent society becomes on the service provided by a profession, the more entitled it becomes to ensure that the service is of acceptable quality.

RECENT CRITICISM

The justice and logic of this is clear enough, but in recent years the learned and accountable professions in the English-speaking world have come under attack from governments holding two beliefs that appear to be essentially political in character and less evidently justifiable. They do not directly criticize the quality of service provided, but base their criticism on an assumption that professions create closed communities in order to protect a privileged and noncompetitive way of life that, by their criteria, must militate against efficient service to the community and should therefore be corrected. The proper correction is assumed to be by exposure to market forces.

At an early stage in the development of this viewpoint in the 1960s, one specific criticism was that these closed communities were kept as such by having control, wrongly, of their own education and admission systems and in particular by restricting entry through the requirement to qualify by examination. To practitioners within these communities the idea that membership creates a privileged and protected way of life is unimaginably different from reality, not least with respect to the education and admission systems. These originated as a response to the early nineteenth-century demands from the public for reliability in professional services and for trustworthy ethics; self-evidently the only way of ensuring this was by a qualifying examination and acceptance of an agreed upon ethical code. The development of education has been an accepted concern by all learned professions since that time, moving gradually from its earliest form, pupilage, in which practical experience with an established practitioner was predominant, to full-time schooling for several years accompanied by a period of supervised practical experience before becoming entitled to take the qualifying examination. It is therefore somewhat ironic to find that the actions taken by professions to develop and discharge these duties responsibly have themselves been attacked 150 years later for allegedly creating antisocial exclusivity. The criticisms are misplaced and their evident illogicality has perhaps undermined them, for they seem now to have fallen into what Churchill once aptly termed desuetude.

Governments have persisted, however, in their pressures on professions to expose themselves to commercial market forces, most specifically by removing restrictions on fee competition and advertising. The interest of governments springs perhaps as much from their immediate concern that they should not be thought lacking in zeal for control of the public purse when they commission design work, as from ideological belief that competition is fundamentally good for society and should therefore pervade all sectors of it.

Soane identified the necessity for the profession to be noncommercial, and what history may judge to be peculiar about this contemporary development is that no evidence apparently existed and none seems to have been sought to establish whether or in what forms competition might already exist among professionals, or what levels of efficiency might already be prevalent, or whether commercial competition in these matters would be beneficial or harmful to professional services.

In fact, competition is and always has been endemic among professionals such as architects and engineers where those who want their services can pick and choose to whom they will go; their initial choice has commonly depended on either an established professional track record or on recommendations from third parties who have had favorable experience in working with them, or on the principle of "like choosing like," or a shared interest of some kind, or quickness of service or known expertise in the type of project that it is intended to develop, or because the practitioner is local in an area where few of his or her kind are in practice, or, in architecture, by winning a design competition. In real life, a competitive price for professional service seems seldom to have been sought except by clients who do not care about its quality or cannot discriminate, or who are under some public requirement to get the best price they can for a service and who may give no thought to the risk of lower quality or of losing accountability.

It should seemingly be evident, therefore, that in principle the arguments are sound for encouraging the traditional basis of competition by competence. It encourages the discriminating selection of professional advisers by their evident quality of service and capacity to carry the relevant responsibility where competition by fee cutting tends to lead away from this, tempting professionals to cut corners, take risks, and minimize service, and thereby reducing their regard for responsibility. The argument has often been advanced in contemporary litigation that pressure on fee rates undermines the ability to discharge properly the duty of care, although the courts usually take the hard view that this was paramount and not to be debased by consideration of profit. It is undoubtedly correct but can force hard decisions on practitioners, and not to any apparent social good.

It is difficult, therefore, to understand why this readily foreseeable pattern of undesirable consequences was not persuasive in counteracting the pressure for open-ended fee competition, but fortunately the intelligence of clients is doing this to a useful and apparently reasonable extent, for there is a widening appreciation among them now of the ways in which competently imaginative design can increase the value of a constructed asset, and clients' briefing of their chosen architects has become better informed and more explicit, so that overall there is greater recognition of the work input needed for good professional service and for the reliable discharge of the responsibility carried by a design team. These are creating a beneficial climate for the negotiation of fair rates of reward and this is particularly relevant where architects of exceptional ability find their services sought even at exceptional fees.

Is the enforced removal of professional constraints on advertising likely to have adverse consequences? Originally the restriction was laid down in codes of professional ethics to serve two purposes, the encouragement of clients to choose on quality of service rather than in response to marketing skills, and to protect smaller practices from being undesirably overshadowed by those that are large and powerful. Professional institutes have generally preferred to maximize the total market for their memberships' services by appropriate publicity, rather than to permit individual advertising, and much success has attended such endeavors.

There is little evidence in the late 1980s to show that practices are in fact doing much advertising of their individual services; many find it distasteful and persist in the belief that it is not professional and that it brings no significant practical benefits. Good clients know the difference between a commercial attitude and that of a professional, and want the latter from their chosen practitioner. But the relaxation of the restraint is evidently being used considerably by architects as a freedom to approach existing or potential clients on a personal basis with information about the services a practice can provide, and especially when they have ideas for new projects. Usually, however, such an approach is preceded by a request to be allowed to make it, another reflection of instinctive professionalism, and both sides seem to be finding it an acceptable and useful freedom. Where the projects are speculative, architects are now sometimes taking a share in the equity to benefit directly from their own ideas, or are even moving into development themselves. When present trends become history this may prove to have been the biggest influence in these times for change in the traditional values of professionalism, but it needs watching to see that its advantages are not accompanied by undesirable side effects, which clearly is a possibility. If it proves to be so, it will doubtless be corrected in the course of time because, of all sectors of society, professions exercise the highest standards of public responsibility.

WIDENING ACTIVITIES OF ARCHITECTS

This does not complete the catalog of changes taking place today in architecture. Among the skills that an architect's education develops are systems thinking (all buildings are compatible assemblies of subsystems of one kind or another) and the handling of complex three-dimensional design. Such skills have wider potential use than just for buildings and, as a result, architects are seeking, finding, and being invited into extended markets for their services. These skills are capable of strengthened development in schools of architecture when these new horizons are scanned thoughtfully by educators and no doubt the movement will continue. Some boundaries between architecture and other related professions will soften, although the courts can be expected to exercise a watchful influence on clarity of accountability.

As part of this extension of activity, a tendency has been developing to form multiprofessional practices or groups of practices of differing kinds of work together for particular types of project or service, eg, leisure facilities or interior design. Some large-building contractors develop in-house architectural facilities to provide comprehensive design-and-build services; they serve useful but limited purposes. In all such developments, the boundaries of accountability have to be kept clear. That is the present and necessary emphasis.

Yet another facet of this widening outlook is the development of technical specialties within the profession. Acoustics consultancy by architects now has a history of nearly 75 years. Within the past 25 years, energy conservation, lighting, fire prevention, construction technology, and project management have come into the architectural fold as well. Because these all have a bearing on design, specification, and the quality and value of the buildings built, it is proving valuable to have these specialized consultancy capabilities within the profession as well as being independently available. This implies a need for specific developments in education, now overdue.

KNOWLEDGE COMMUNICATION

Technologies have their origins in the world of scientific research and development and it is self-evident today that all learned and accountable professions, being the instruments by which specialized knowledge is given application in the public domain, face similar problems of ensuring the operation of effective transfer mechanisms from laboratory to practitioner. The difficulties are familiar but are not proving easy to surmount. Traditionally and naturally, research is organized in single disciplines, but real-life technical problems are never solvable within one discipline. The solutions call on many sources of knowledge in constantly changing mixes, so that effective application becomes a matter of providing the mental reservoirs of practitioners with information from many sources, processed so that it is relevant to professional use and can, therefore, more readily be called into action as the problem-solving mechanisms go to work in designers' minds.

Science-based industry has a problem similar in principle; in using knowledge to develop new or improved products or to get rid of shortcomings that are discovered in existing products, the concept of the research and development team has been cultivated successfully. What one might call bridgehead scientists of various relevant disciplines are put together to address real-world problems, keeping their lines of communication open to their scientific peers so that they can both receive and send messages while having team goals of usage on which to focus joint creative endeavor. The professions use the products of this technique but have not yet brought into clear focus their own problems of communication with the scientific world. As a result, they have not yet developed processing mechanisms of equivalent effectiveness. This appears to be an area needing vigorous attention in order to maintain proper standards of service.

Among the building professions, the problems are admittedly severe because the knowledge base of design and construction technology that is deemed "reasonable" in law for professionals to possess, which has always had a wide spectrum, has been growing, through research, at a rate that could not have been imagined as little as 50 or 60 years ago and that has proved to be much greater than they or the construction industry, with its large learning

inertia, could match. Communication and technology transfer between the producers of the new knowledge and its users has not been good. The producers have not adequately processed their material for use, packaged it well for transfer, or tested the success of transfer endeavors, while schools have been slow to take up their own responsibilities as recipient users and midcareer education is not yet out of its experimental stage.

The problem is perhaps currently to be seen in its most acute form in the UK. It began with the initiation of comprehensive building research in 1919 and was followed less than 20 years later by the concept of a performance-based regulatory system to allow easier introduction of research-based innovation than was possible under the constraints of the traditional prescriptive form of control. The new form of regulation was implemented in stages after 1945, and the innovation that was encouraged by postwar reconstruction needs has led, in turn, to numerous and often unforeseeable defects from the late 1960s onward. This, in turn, has prompted the initiation of litigation on a substantial scale. Clients, naturally, are often the plaintiffs and the defendants are the professionals, the contractors, and sometimes the product manufacturers. The same pattern is to be found in other countries but seemingly not yet on the same scale as in the UK.

As noted earlier, there is an important proportion of this litigation in which key questions concern the state of the art at the time when the decision making was done, which later proved to be faulty. Did the necessary knowledge exist at the relevant time, and if so, had it been processed to the point of readiness for use, and had it been communicated effectively? The test of proper processing would be that it was couched in language appropriate to the type and quality of education that practitioners had been given and, as noted above, whether publication had taken place in the manner and places customary for professional reading.

These are reasonable criteria and they apply to all learned and accountable professions and their supporting service industries, but they carry a considerable burden of implication. First, these criteria identify the fact that in this age of science there is a continuous production of new knowledge. Second, there is a duty on the part of its producers to see that this new knowledge is properly processed for use and that it is transmitted effectively. Third, those who must make decisions for which they are accountable must be willing to read, listen, and discuss.

Underlying these implications, however, serious as they are, lies a still more fundamental issue, because the knowledge base of the design professions, the construction industry, and the product makers has now been enlarged so greatly that it is far beyond the scope that any single individual can encompass, unlike the position of 50 or 75 years ago, and this widened knowledge base exposes the problem of who along the line in the production of a building should reasonably be responsible for knowing what. How is this body of information now to be divided up?

The problem has scarcely been recognized yet, let alone solved, but some glimpses of the future appear first in the changing nature of design teams for advanced projects and second in the clearer migration of responsibilities to subcontractors. The design teams for such projects now comprise a much greater array of specialist advisers than formerly, with more sharply defined responsibilities, while subcontractors, by their nature specialists, have now to be expected not merely to provide a skill but to be the most knowledgeable people in the project about their specialty, and therefore the most accountable for it. Design teams, implicitly recognizing this, are sometimes proceeding by writing performance specifications for the parts of construction projects that can be treated as subsystems and inviting subcontractors to provide competitive specifications to meet them, underwritten by guarantees. In such situations, the subcontractor must obviously be knowledgeable in ways not formerly needed when he had only to offer a skill and meet someone else's specification. The writing of these performance specifications is itself a challenging technology and will enlarge the present responsibility of professional specification writers. These are logical directions of development, and a natural counterpart of a regulatory system, which itself reflects the new problems presented by the developing knowledge base by being couched as performance requirements.

There is one final aspect of this important area of change to be noted. Performance requirements of a technical nature cannot only be specified with increasing precision now, but the technology of testing proposals in advance and of evaluating the results *in situ* is developing in parallel. Even some matters that do not lend themselves to exact prediction and measurement can be predicted reasonably accurately by skilled judgment and the desired performance can be similarly well evaluated.

An example in this slightly gray area is to be found in acoustics. No auditorium today need be an acoustic failure, but failures still occur as judged by, say, musical opinion or the views of critics or by public consensus, and the financial loss due to the shortcomings may be real and substantial. No litigation on such an acoustic misfortune appears to have been initiated thus far, but in some cases it has come close. Success in auditorium acoustics is essentially a matter of architectural design, and if litigation does begin, the vital questions will probably therefore relate to the quality of the interaction between the architect and the acoustic consultant and the extent to which the design embodied the consultant's advice.

Acoustics is not alone as an example. Safety in respect of human life in fires and often the survival of buildings depends on good judgment in design, although again the area is gray due to gaps in the system of information that has emerged thus far from laboratories (5). Conservation for museums and art galleries is in this category too, and there are others. Such subject areas are approaching or have reached the point where the knowledge necessary to avoid loss of some kind is sufficiently developed and available for professional shortcomings to be the subject of legitimate complaint.

One of the contemporary reactions to the pitfalls of modern and innovative construction is an attempt to turn back the pages of history and revert to what are imagined to be safe traditions. Safety is unlikely to be found now in this direction because the technical world of building has changed too fundamentally and pervasively. Regulatory requirements are different and so are the knowledge requirements, the materials, and their interactions. Even in the conservation of buildings a specialized technology has had to be developed in order to work reliably; research laboratories have been organized specifically for this purpose.

The fact is that in every direction thrusts of research and development occur in contemporary culture and attempt to create change toward greater economy and more precise predictability; as predictability has seemed to become more accurate, factors of safety have been eroded and replaced by dependence on this greater knowledge and precision. It is a condition in which casualties are unavoidable for, with all its advances, the knowledge base grows unevenly and its imbalances at any given time can create risks of misfortunes, which in buildings are usually slow to reveal themselves for correction. The fact that it takes three to five years to create a building is one cause of inertia. Statistically, risks are therefore much higher than they were and are to some degree inescapable; the modern world responds by the development of insurance techniques. These form an area of difficulty for professional people, but while professions must obviously make every reasonable effort to surmount technology-induced problems, it would seem reasonable that insurance protection against loss should not be borne entirely by them. Client insurance of new buildings for some reasonable period has become a logical necessity, and professions need to address this problem urgently at an institutional level.

COMPUTERS

Computer-aided design and drafting is now commonplace in large and medium-sized practices and it is working its way further down the scale rapidly. Software, which carries architecturally valuable information for computer-aided design and for other purposes in architectural practice, is at this date only moderately developed, but is gradually being extended. A cause for concern is that its development is not being guided or promoted by the profession; it is just happening by thrusts here and there from interested organizations of various kinds. The potentially very valuable form known as expert systems is still in its infancy for architecture, although relatively well advanced in the medical world and in some aspects of engineering. Expert systems appear at present to be the most powerful and direct aid for informing design. Their knowledge-bearing capacity is very high, and they teach as the user uses them.

However, relatively little computer technology has any bearing on professionalism as such, with one exception, the area of accountability. Software by its nature carries a great deal of information that is not apparent to the user and what he or she cannot know is whether it is correct and comprehensive, contains errors, or is only partial and therefore out of balance. The question that arises is whether the practitioner, who uses faulty software and creates a defective design as a result, is then liable for the defect or the software producer or marketer is at fault.

In some leading engineering circles, faced with technically challenging problems where an error could lead to an environmental disaster, the opinion seems to be that liability lies with the user and not with the organization producing the software, unfair as this may seem to be, and it appears rather naturally to be putting a brake on movement. The matter has not had a ruling in court up to now. Apparently there are not as yet any independent bodies recognized for certification in this area, but something of the sort is badly needed. It is another of the problems created for designers by the world of the laboratory, which the learned and accountable professions have yet to confront effectively.

CONCLUSION

Professionalism has been a distinctive factor in social evolution and its essentials have survived all of society's vicissitudes of development. This argues forcibly that its fundamentals are logically sound and that society needs them and their value system. The descriptive term professional has been adopted by or applied to people in an increasing variety of activities when one or other parts of the concept of professionalism have been borrowed for some identifying purpose, and attention has been drawn to the fact that the traditional trilogy of learned professions—divinity, medicine, and law—has now widened to embrace not only the building professions but a large number of other fields that require an advanced education and a period of controlled practical experience before candidates can become recognized as being competent for practice.

These learned professions have now themselves become divisible into two kinds, those that do not offer any sort of public service for reward and those that do, such as medicine, the design of buildings, or accountancy, in other words, where other peoples' health, welfare, or money will be placed in their hands. Professions practicing such activities by their nature take on responsibilities for which they can be held to account in law, and for this reason, it seems best now to regard them specifically as the learned and accountable professions.

Professionals are custodians and users of particular bodies of knowledge. Consequently, they have the counterpart duty to care for its cultivation and to use it properly and with integrity. For their use of it, individual practitioners claim a fair reward, neither so low that it undermines their duty of care nor so high as to be a possibly corrupting influence. Integrity is at the heart of it all, for trust is the basis of professional relationships.

It is matters such as these that cause accountable professional people to eschew the value system of commerce and the marketplace. Each is right in principle for its purpose but they are not interchangeable. If market competition has seemed necessary to some critics as a spur to efficiency, it must answer to the claim that accountability is more effective to that end and serves clients' interests better.

In order to protect the public against bad service, professionals of a kind must gather or be brought together to form collective organizations that have the responsibility for ensuring the existence of a satisfactory, up-to-date education system, supervising the acquisition by entrants of initial experience, and examining candidates for entry. Such a body also has the inherent duty of developing the knowledge base, which is the intellectual capital on which its members draw for the service they offer to the public, because professionals must continuously learn collectively from other members' experience and from research. When such bodies are seen to be performing these duties properly they may be given recognition by the state in a form such as a charter, but by such an instrument they, in turn, become accountable to society for the general competence and responsible behavior of their members. It is society's way of protecting itself against bad service.

As for architecture specifically, it has changed in one major respect in the modern world; it has almost entirely given up the concept of patronage of a kind that formerly implied a market mainly of perceptive and perhaps ambitious individual patrons who would select the services of a small number of designers to provide great "set pieces" of architecture. Instead, the idea has developed of architecture as a professional service to society, with the profession becoming the normal agency for procuring the structures that comprise the built environment and give it its social investment value. This, in turn, has moved the profession as a whole into a position of very great financial responsibility, providing and certifying in some countries a larger sector of fixed capital formation than does any other single profession or industry.

This applies particularly to the English-speaking world where architects have the duty of final certification of the satisfactory completion of contracts. Other arrangements prevail elsewhere but cannot be explored here. In any case, they do not alter the central idea of accountable professionalism, that it provides expert application of specialized knowledge to practical purposes, and from this flows the duty of care, the requirement for reasonable proficiency, and the need for integrity, all of which must be exposed to the critical gaze of society, exercised in respect of individuals by the courts and of a profession as a whole by governments.

For any such learned profession today the most difficult problems are presented by the pervasive influence of science. This mainly functions in a fragmentary manner by research, creating states of knowledge that at any moment are out of balance, thrusting strongly in different directions as time passes. The professional has always to seek a balance in his or her use of knowledge, attempting constantly to correct the imbalancing thrusts of science by judgment based on experience and informed observation.

For architects, then, the challenges are particularly testing because the products of their imagination determine the quality of the built environment and its social and monetary investment value. These are the criteria by which history will judge professionals' performances both as individuals and as associations.

BIBLIOGRAPHY

1. *Shorter Oxford English Dictionary,* Clarendon Press, Oxford, 1973, Vol. II, p. 1680.

2. J. Harvey, *The Perpendicular Style,* Batsford, London, 1978, pp. 301–304.

3. A. M. Carr-Saunders and P. A. Wilson, *The Professions,* Oxford University Press, 1933, p. 68.

4. T. Bolton, *Life and Work a Century Ago; An Outline of the Career of Sir John Soane,* Soane Museum Publications, London, 1923, No. 11, p. 5.

5. W. A. Allen, "Fire and the Architect: The Communication Problem," *The George Nice Memorial Lecture,* Building Research Establishment, Garston, Watford, UK, 1988.

General References

Ref. 3 is a good general reference.

A. Saint, *The Image of the Architect,* Yale University Press, New Haven, 1983. Includes a large body of bibliographical references.

A. Saint, *Towards a Social Architecture,* Yale University Press, New Haven, 1987. Story of the postwar school development in the UK.

P. du Prey, *John Soane: The Making of an Architect,* University of Chicago Press, Chicago, 1982.

W. A. Allen, "The Profession in Contemporary Society," *Royal Institute of British Architects Journal* **67**(7) 251–264 (May 1960).

W. A. Allen, "A Sense of Direction," *Journal of the New Zealand Institute of Architecture,* **32**(5) 163–168 (June 1965).

B. Kaye, *The Development of the Architectural Profession in Britain,* George Allen & Unwin, London, 1960.

M. S. Briggs, *The Architect in History,* Clarendon Press, Oxford, UK, 1927.

Handbook of Professional Practice, American Institute of Architects, Washington, D.C., 1987.

Handbook of Architectural Practice and Management, 4th ed., RIBA Publications Ltd., London, 1980.

See also AMERICAN INSTITUTE OF ARCHITECTS (AIA); EDUCATION, ARCHITECTURAL; NATIONAL COUNCIL OF ARCHITECTURAL REGISTRATION BOARDS (NCARB); PROFESSIONAL DEVELOPMENT; ROLE OF THE ARCHITECT; ROYAL INSTITUTE OF BRITISH ARCHITECTS (RIBA).

WILLIAM ALLEN, CBE, RIBA,
HON. FAIA
Bickerdike Allen Partners
London, UK

PROGRAMMING, ARCHITECTURAL

Programming is that part of the design process where the quantitative and qualitative requirements of a design project are defined and documented. When done well, it can improve the efficiency of the design process, strengthen the architect–client relationship, and promote buildings that better facilitate the goals and objectives of their users and owners.

Architects have long seen themselves as problem solvers and referred to their designs as solutions. William Pena, an architectural programming pioneer, defined programming as problem seeking, the part of the process where the problem that the designer is to solve is identified (1). A well-organized problem definition, based on systematically collected information, lets designers respond more effectively, efficiently, and creatively to the client's requirements and constraints (2).

Traditionally, programming has focused on the space program, listing the items to be included in a specific design project, with an estimate of how much area should be provided for each component. A traditional program might also include information about how the components need to relate to each other spatially; information about people and materials flow; identification of special conditions, such as exceptional parking demands, unusual floor loads, special plumbing or electrical requirements, or special fittings for a workstation. These traditional programs are usually developed in preparation for a specific design or construction project. Figure 1 illustrates a sample traditional program.

A site analysis (3,4) and a project budget and schedule (1) are necessary additions to this spatial and functional program in the predesign package. Traditionally, this predesign package has been called "The Architectural Program," a complete document handed off to the designer before design work begins. This document is intended to contain all of the information the designer needs to design the building.

As client organizations become more dynamic and as buildings and the organizations who use them become more complicated, however, the need increases for functional and spatial information management to continue throughout the project and into the operation and management of the building and its occupants. The program then is more than a problem definition at one point in time: it is a dynamic information system with more and more information layered on as a project develops and progressively more detailed decisions are made. Changes in the client's organization and requirements that occur during the project are also documented, and appropriate responses are made in frequently adjusted new problem statements and criteria. The architectural program then becomes a living, changing information resource to both the designer and the client.

These information management capabilities can also be developed into the ability to offer nontraditional services that are often natural and welcome adjuncts to a traditional practice. These services might expand the depth and richness of the problem definition for a particular forthcoming project or might be outside of the usual program–design–build cycle. For example, the programmer might consult with a client concerning the relative advantages of leasing rather than owning buildings, the establishment of an appropriate facility image for a network of facilities, the development of an appropriate facility management data base, or an evaluation of the appropriateness of an existing facility.

In any case, the programming process includes system-

CAFETERIA PROGRAM

Mission
- To serve lunches to employees and seminar participants in the north part of the campus. May also be used for occasional evening social functions.

Image
- Equal but different than the existing cafeteria
- Lively, fun, energizing
- Intimate
- Appealing to scientists

Criteria
- Quiet
- Bulletin boards
- Dance floor
- Orient dining area to allow for expansion at a later date
- Cafeteria area can be separated into seminar seating on an as-needed basis (e.g., movable plants, portable screens, or by planning concept)
- Speaker support (Screen, A/V hook-ups, light control, acoustical control, electrical outlets)
- Furniture: easily movable, stowable, tables for 4-6, chalk board, tables that can be pulled together

Planning Assumptions
- Total capacity - 450 persons
- Outdoor dining, seating 20-30, in addition to 450 (not included in the space program)
- Cashiers similar to existing cafeteria
- Staff of approximately 35
- Cafeteria seating for 400, restaurant seating for 50
- Full menu
- Self-busing
- All private dining is in existing cafeteria
- Sundry store will carry 'daily use' products only - no perfume

Issues
- Restaurant service
- Private dining

(a)

SPACE PROGRAM

	AREA (SF)
Dining	
● Cafeteria dining (seating for 400 people at 15 SF each)	6,000
-furniture storage	700
● Restaurant(seating for 50 at 18 SF each)	900
-waitress station	50
● Servery	2,300
-dish return	108
KITCHEN	
● Main kitchen	1,750
● Dish wash	550
● Restaurant kitchen	875
● Freezer storage	425
● Dry storage	600
● Coffee service set-up	150
● Extra dish storage	275
● Office area	
-Manager	100
-Bookkeeper (2 at 64 SF each)	128
-Secretary	64
Files (2 5-drawer lateral files at 13 SF each)	26
Bookcase	13
● Rest rooms/lockers	500
● Time clock/receiving area	150
● Sundry shop	225
-storage	75
SUB-TOTAL	16,014
Circulation (15% of Sub-total)	2,402
TOTAL Useable Square Feet	**18,416**

(b)

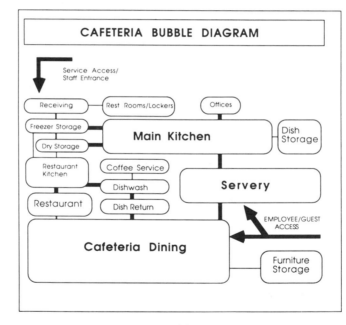

(c)

Figure 1. A traditional program might include: (**a**) notes on the mission, image, criteria, assumption, and issues; (**b**) a space list with the area required by each; (**c**) An adjacency or bubble diagram.

atically collecting information, organizing and storing the data for easy access and manipulation, analyzing the information's relevance to the facility problem, and communicating the information to the client for decisions and often to other members of the design team.

The involvement of the client and the future building users is extremely beneficial to the programming process. They know their own purposes, goals, biases, operations, culture, resources, and constraints better than the designer. Their involvement in the programming process increases the chance of identifying the real issues and therefore increases the chance of ultimately producing a building that is right for them. Client and user involve-

ment minimizes the real possibility of producing an otherwise ipmressive solution that solves the wrong problem.

Clients who manage an organization are particularly enthusiastic about participating in the programming process if they recognize that the physical environment can contribute to making their organization work better. An organizational development specialist has stated that "influencing behavior is almost all of what management is about, and buildings influence behavior"(5).

Another benefit of a well-documented programming effort is that it gives the client (as well as the design team) a rational basis on which to evaluate a proposed design. Clearly established criteria become the standard with which a proposed solution is compared, and it is deemed a good solution to the extent that it meets the programmatic criteria.

Emphasizing the programming phase offers benefits to architects and other design professionals as well. The design process is more efficient since the number of versions that must be designed to get client approval is minimized by avoiding a trial-and-error approach as much as possible. It is also typically easier to get clients to approve designs when they are involved in the programming process. First, they understand the logic of how and why the design is the way it is, and second, they are more likely to support something they have helped create.

Programs are often developed by the same person who will design the building. This approach minimizes communication difficulties and is ideal for relatively simple problems, especially if the designer is as skilled in and enthusiastic about problem defining as problem solving. As problems become larger and more complex, projects are rarely handled by a single individual. In this case, programming specialists who are trained in applied research methods can add quality and sophistication to the design team while freeing designers to do what they do best— design.

Some programming specialists are experts in one type of building where the operations are sufficiently complex and specialized to require an expert with experience in that particular building type (eg, a hospital, prison, library, etc).

For those responsible for developing the program, it is important to do everything possible to maximize the potential for creative problem solving. The first impediment to creative problem solving is the natural inclination of both client and designer to assume solutions prematurely without identifying the problem and evaluation criteria. A client may, for example, want a building like one that its competitor has built, or an architect may be intrigued by an unusual building form. These kinds of presumptions are likely to preclude the possibility of finding a design more fitting to the particular circumstances.

Creative problem solving is also hampered by assuming that clients know what kind of building would best serve their purposes. Most clients are not trained in facilities planning. If they are forced to define their facility needs, they naturally rely on their own frame of reference, which is usually their existing facility, which may be inadequate, or some other organization's facility which may not be relevant. This approach is likely to result in a status quo solution, if not an inappropriate one.

What clients do know better than anyone else are their own operations. Creative problem solving is promoted by asking the client and future users about themselves, what they and their organization are trying to achieve, what tasks need to be performed, how those tasks are performed now and the problems with those operations and how they envision their organization in the future. It can then be determined what environmental qualities would best support the individuals and/or organization that they hope to become.

Converting behavioral goals into environmental support requirements is no easy chore. Fortunately, program-

mers can draw on a large and growing body of environment–behavior research that can inform this difficult task (6–10). Unfortunately, architects have not always taken advantage of this research resource. It has been noted that "although competent research on environment and behavior has appeared in journal and book form, many architects designing buildings for organized activity have not been led to employ this growing body of knowledge"(5).

The remainder of this article focuses on programming applications, including discussions of client types, processes, methods, products, and applications.

CLIENT TYPES

Clients vary significantly in their experience with building projects and in their ability and willingness to become involved in the programming process. The programming products that are developed as well as the procedures for developing them should vary as well.

The key to designing an appropriate program is to ask what information the designer needs to design an environment that will best serve the client's interest, and then what information the client needs in order to make decisions that are as thoughtful as possible. It is the programmer's responsibility to design a process that gets the right information to the right person at the right time.

Some clients, such as developers, are in the business of building buildings. Typically, they do not use the buildings themselves, so their interest is to have facilities designed that will sell well to their clients and to build them at a cost that will make them profitable. In this case, the programmer's role may be to conduct market studies of the supply and demand for such facilities in a particular area or perhaps to interpret the results of this kind of study supplied by the client. The client may be well informed, and here the programmer's primary responsibility may be to document the requirements and their cost implications.

At the other end of the spectrum is the client who wants a new home for an organization and has had little, if any, experience with acquiring a major facility or having one designed and built. The programmer should not expect this client to know all of the facility requirements. In this case, one of the programmer's roles is to facilitate the process, making the client feel as comfortable and secure as possible. This can be accomplished by letting the client know what decisions need to be made, when each needs to be made, what the repercussions of each decision are, and in some cases, how similar organizations have handled this decision.

With the inexperienced client, it is particularly important to help the client think about and articulate the purpose of the project. What are the organization's mission, values, and culture, and how can a new facility help it realize its goals? Without this contemplative phase, it is likely that good opportunities to provide facilities that actually promote organizational goal achievement will be lost.

Client involvement varies from project to project.

Ideally, the people who will use the facility have an opportunity to influence the problem definition by sharing their hopes, problems, goals, tasks, and attitudes. Fortunately, many clients encourage broad participation; however, some clients feel that their employees should tend to their own duties and that the design consultants, who have been hired for their expertise, should not have to ask many questions. In this case, the programmer should explain that the designer needs to understand the particular client's operations, goals, etc., in order to design an optimal environment for the organization. If the client still wants to limit user involvement, the programmer should meticulously document every planning assumption and explicitly point out the implications of that assumption. If those assumptions prove to be correct, then there is no problem. If they are wrong, the client may catch the mistake early. For example,

> *Assumption.* All mail will come to one central mail area in the main building, where it will be sorted by department and delivered.
>
> *Advantage.* One mail room needs less space than many, special equipment does not need to be duplicated, and one staff is responsible for all mail.
>
> *Disadvantages.* Mail delivery may be slow, and the opportunity to have the post office presort it may be lost.

Some clients may be willing to participate fully, but may not be able to provide the needed information. In some cases, plans to add a new function that will require a new facility may precede adding the staff who would represent that interest. For example, a corporate client might consider adding day care to a new headquarters project. Clearly, the facility decision is secondary to the many other decisions that need to be made, such as the kind of day care, the number of children, the operating policies, etc. The architectural programmer cannot be expected to clarify all of the issues, but providing a model program for a typical day-care facility, with clearly documented planning assumptions, can be a useful planning tool for the client. The architectural programmer may also be asked to work with a nonarchitectural consultant who is a specialist in a particular field such as physical fitness or training.

The differences in clients, from building experts to building novices and from very participative to minimally participative, are only some of the variables to which the architectural programmer needs to respond. Virtually every programming assignment must be accomplished within the context of time constraints, fee constraints, zoning and code constraints, limited information, etc. No single programming process works best for all clients and all situations. The process must be tailored to the needs of each project.

THE PROCESS

Traditionally, programming has been considered a predesign service, with the completed program developed, documented, and delivered in its entirety to the designer or client before the start of design. It is becoming more common, however, to view programming as an integral component of the design process with continual iterations between programming and designing.

Producing a program before design begins has a few advantages. First, it ensures that the problem definition phase will get complete attention before solutions are sought. This discourages the real possibility of either the designer or the client becoming committed to a design thrust before the problem is defined and criteria are established. Second, a predesign program can be a useful planning tool for a client who may want to consider various facility options based on a preliminary program, such as whether to lease space or to build a new building. Third, some agree that there are valuable checks and balances in a decentralized approach, where one party is wholly responsible for the program and another is wholly responsible for the design.

A more nonlinear, integrated approach, where the programmer stays one step ahead of the designer and continues as a member of the team throughout the design process, has many advantages. An integrated approach allows for more feedback, and therefore more responsiveness, throughout the project's development. The program is not frozen in time, so that as information and design opportunities become apparent as the project develops, the program can grow, becoming richer and more detailed. Also, the programming specialists can make an ongoing contribution to the design effort in their role as program advocates.

A more pragmatic advantage of an integrated approach is that the program does not have to be completed before design work can begin. When time is a constraint, as is often the case, it can be helpful to fast track the programming and design process. (It should never, however, be used as an excuse to shortchange the programming effort.)

U.S. manufacturers have borrowed from the Japanese the concept of "just-in-time" (JIT) delivery of parts to the manufacturing floor. The point of JIT is to avoid the wasted space and capital of having huge stocks of components warehoused on the assembly floor before they are needed. The components are delivered just in time to be added to the assemblage. Similarly, a designer does not need every bit of information in order to begin to design a project. It is not important, for example, to know whether the cafeteria will provide table service when making the decision to have three buildings or four. Nor is it important to know which laboratories have hoods that need venting when deciding how the laboratory staff parking should relate to the laboratories. What is critical is that the programming process be designed so that needed information is identified and that a detailed schedule be developed so the information is available just in time to keep the design process progressing smoothly. This information layering gives the client time to make decisions without deluging the designer with unneeded data.

The programming process, then, can occur entirely before design begins, or it can be integrated with the design work. In either case, the programmer's primary functions are to collect data, analyze them, and pass the results on to the designer. The next section emphasizes the importance of research methods to the programming process.

PROGRAMMING METHODS

Good programming methods are systematic, orderly, and methodical. They avoid the temptation to collect information randomly and haphazardly until something inspires a design idea and/or to include in the analysis only information that supports preconceived design directions or personal biases.

A broad range of methods is available to help the programmer accomplish the tasks of collecting, analyzing, and communicating information. It is important that the programmer know at least enough about available methods to be able to evaluate their usefulness to a particular problem. Numerous methods, referred to collectively as the programmer's "kit of parts," are reviewed in ref. 11. Each method can be a useful tool in certain situations. The well-armed programmer develops a kit of parts based on personal knowledge and experience with a broad variety of tools. In virtually every programming effort, common data collection methods are used either exclusively or in conjunction with more sophisticated and specific tools. It is particularly important to become skilled in these techniques.

The easiest way to get information is to gather existing data—information developed for some other purpose. For example, a corporation's materials-handling staff may track the schedule of truck deliveries in order to justify its staffing level. These data may be used incidentally to determine the number of docks needed. Alternatively, the reprographics staff may track photocopy facilities' use per department in order to calculate chargebacks. This information could help the interior designer locate copiers in a new office environment. Found information is particularly valuable for broad-brush planning when information that is quick and inexpensive to gather can be used for preliminary planning purposes in the short run and then verified and refined before final commitments are made.

The ability to uncover an organization's information resources is valuable. The creative programmer considers it a challenge to determine who has useful data.

Published materials are another readily available information resource. These might include articles about the client's organization or its people, articles about the industry or the region, and articles or books on the building or population type. This information is also quick and easy to obtain and can provide useful background at the beginning of the programming effort.

In virtually all cases, additional information is needed. Typically, this is acquired through a combination of observations, interviews, questionnaires, and group work sessions.

Generally, a broad range of information is required to complete a program. It can range from the organization's vision of the future to mundane administrative issues, such as where office supply stock is stored. The programmer should identify the information needed and the best source for that information, as well as choosing an appropriate data-gathering method. For example, hospital administrators are responsible for guiding a health-care organization into the future, so they are the best source of input on the kinds of changes likely to need accommodation in 5 or 10 years. On the other hand, to ask chiefs of staff where laundry is collected for pick-up would waste their valuable time, and they would be poor and unreliable sources for such information.

As a practical matter, the programmer should seek information at the lowest level at which the information is reliable. Since executives' time is generally the most limited, the programmer should ask for their input only on the topics, values, and forecasts that they alone can address as leaders and strategists. Lower-level employees typically are under less time pressure, and they often know more about day-to-day operations. Their input should be used as much as possible.

Data Collection Methods

The programmer can learn much about an organization and its culture simply by looking at the existing facility and personally experiencing the ambience, activity level, attitudes of the users, etc. Tours should be carefully planned to include all relevant areas or at least a good cross section. They should not be random and haphazard. Particular attention should be paid to "traces," evidence that users have modified their space to correct problems. A photographic record of the tour can serve as a reminder to the programmer. Photographs can also be used to explain and document observations to both the client and the designer.

Questionnaires. Questionnaires are useful if many people need to provide information and if the information is primarily of a factual nature, as opposed to highly subjective and philosophical. Care should be taken in the design of the questionnaire.

- The questionnaire should be as simple and user-friendly as possible. Filling out a questionnaire is not a popular task. It helps if it is attractively packaged, asks for only the information that is required, and clearly and simply explains what is expected of the respondent.

- The questions should be as unbiased as possible. The way a question is asked clearly has an impact on the answer. For example, the questions "Do you need your own copier?" and "Could you share a copier?" are both likely to be answered "yes." In the first case, respondents may fear that no copier will be provided if the answer is "no," whereas the second question makes it clear they would have access to a copier, which would simply be shared. The programmer should make every effort to write questions that do not predispose the respondent to make certain replies.

- If the respondent misinterprets what is being asked, then the response is not meaningful. The best way to prevent this kind of misunderstanding is to pretest the questionnaire on some uninvolved parties, asking them if the questions are clear and what they think is being asked of them.

- More objective answers result if behavior is questioned rather than directly asking what spaces are required. For example, asking how many meetings a department has and how many people attend those meetings produces fairly objective answers. The programmer can easily determine how large to make the group's conference room from this information. It is much more subjective to ask the respondent how big a conference room is needed. Asking directly for space requirements tends to promote empire building and presumes that the client understands space usage well enough to make that determination.

In many cases, the head of every department or unit is asked to complete a questionnaire for the group, but in some cases, a sample of respondents are questioned, and their responses are generalized, inferring that they fairly represent a larger group (7). In general, the more random the sampling techniques, the better, with each individual having the same chance of selection as every other individual.

It may be necessary to use a stratified sampling technique, where the members of each class are identified and a random sample is generated from within the class. This technique is appropriate if the proportions of the population in the various categories are not equal. For example, few of the residents in a low-cost housing project may be middle aged, so a large random sample would be needed to get a representative from this category. In this case, random samples of young residents, of middle-aged residents, and of elderly residents might be generated.

The constraints of real-world projects often make research rigor difficult to achieve. It is important to keep in mind that the more rigorous the research design, the more reliable the results, but this must be balanced by realizing too that standards that are too high can immobilize an effort.

Interviews. The most common form of data collection is the interview. Interviews may be loosely structured meetings where casual, free-flowing conversation can be useful for developing personal bonds between interviewer and interviewee and can bring out issues, biases, and preconceptions. Usually, however, the interview schedule or agenda should be planned with the same care and attention used in developing a questionnaire. In either case, it is the interviewer's responsibility to use the time well. The goal of the interview should be absolutely clear to the interviewer and usually should be articulated to the interviewee as well.

Interview questions can be either open- or closed-ended. With open-ended questions, the interviewee is allowed a broad latitude in answering. These are particularly appropriate when the topics are subjective and philosophical and/or where the goal is to learn more about the interviewee's style, values, interests, etc. Closed questions ask for specific answers to direct questions. These are appropriate when the goal is to get more factual information and/or when time is limited.

One distinct advantage of interviews over question-naires is that misunderstandings and miscommunications can be clarified immediately. To this end, the interviewer should feel free to ask for clarification and, when in doubt, restate impressions and understandings for verification.

Another advantage of interviews is that the interviewee can be told how the information will be used. Interviewees often speak more candidly if they know whether they will be quoted and who will have access to the information. The presence of another in-house person can also influence an interviewee's willingness to speak openly with the programmer. For example, a manager may not be ready to share certain plans for the organization with subordinates, and yet those plans may have a dramatic impact on future programmatic requirements.

Interviews should always be documented in a format that is appropriate for the problem. This might include meeting notes, diagrams, and data sheets. The documentation should be as complete and self-explanatory as possible. When time allows, the interviewee should be given the opportunity to review and correct products before they are distributed, and before design commitments are made in response to the information.

Work Session Methods. Group programming sessions are appropriate when planning programmatic issues are not clear-cut and/or when many people will be affected by the results. For example, a cross section of employees might be brought together to talk about their collective values and preferences for a newly planned fitness center, or a group of manufacturing engineers might come together to discuss how their divisions might share resources if their functions were brought together in the same factory. Focus groups and work sessions are particularly effective in generating a broad range of new ideas, as well as when broad participation is particularly valued in the client organization. Reference 12 is a good source on group session methods.

Data Analysis

The next step in the process is to analyze the data that have been collected. The actual process varies significantly from one project to another, but generally the objectives are to cull out the information that has facility implications from that which does not, to put as much creative thought into exploiting the available data as would be put into the design process, and to present the results in as simple and straightforward a manner as possible.

For the most part, descriptive statistics, such as ranges, averages, medians, and frequencies, are sufficient to describe the data. Some examples are "Departments have from 1 to 12 computer terminals," "The average number of visitors per day is 36," "The median filing requirement for directors is 76 in.," and "Walk-in refrigerator units are required in 8 of the test kitchens."

Content analysis can be used effectively to produce a composite of all facts or opinions generated by a number of people in response to a particular question, especially if a structured interview schedule is used.

Executive summaries are especially important. They enable the client and designer to see quickly the bottom line without reading all of the detailed backup information from which it was produced.

Explicit lists of the implications of the findings, the issues that have been raised, and the assumptions and alternative directions, with their advantages and disadvantages, are products of analyses that clearly inform both the client and the designer.

Results can be presented in tabular, verbal, and/or graphic form. The representation should be as clear, simple, and self-explanatory as possible. Never in the practice of architecture is Mies van der Rohe's motto "less is more" better advice than it is to the programmer preparing the products of the data analysis phase. It is often tempting to include everything that is known and to show every relationship and complication. Succumbing to this temptation invariably results in documents that few people are willing to even try to comprehend.

Typically, the data contain inconsistencies. This should be viewed as a natural part of a complex problem. For example, top management's vision of the future may be vastly different from the existing organization. When forecasting staffing levels, managers are predicting what will be in a future of which only they are aware. When line managers forecast staffing levels, they have their own concept of what the future will bring. Their staffing plans may quite naturally differ substantially from those of their superiors. Neither body of information should be ignored. The various predictions should be presented to the decision makers along with the facility opportunities and risks that might be the result of using alternative planning assumptions.

The Role of the Computer

The most important products the programmer produces are creative conclusions based on systematically gathered data that have been meticulously organized and accurately manipulated. The computer cannot be relied on to yield a creative interpretation of data, but it is an invaluable tool in providing the accurate, credible, quantitative information that is a necessary part of each programming effort.

A good computerized database permits easy access to data in various configurations, as well as easy and accurate updating. Global changes can be made that can show the implications of certain policy decisions. For example, if office standards are adjusted to fit a 4-ft building module rather than a 5-ft module, this has an impact on the total space requirements. These two scenarios can be tested simply and accurately if the data are accessible to a good, flexible database management system, whereas the process is laborious and error prone if done manually.

Normative Databases

A normative database, information about how others have solved similar problems, is another useful tool. Relying too heavily on the status quo can hamper creative, fresh thinking, but knowing the range and distribution of solutions that occur in other situations is useful background. For example, knowing that 100 insurance companies have office areas of 146–238 sq ft per person would help an

other insurance company evaluate the appropriateness of its programmatic numbers.

PROGRAMMING PRODUCTS

Space Program

The basic product of programming is a space program that lists the components that are to be included, along with the area allocated to each. The space allocations are then summed to indicate the total space required. To the list of each workstation, support space, or piece of equipment, circulation space is added for movement between areas. The sum of the areas required plus the circulation space equals what the Building Owners and Managers Association (BOMA) (13) calls usable square feet (USF). In order to provide a certain amount of usable square feet (or meters), a building must be built that is larger still, to allow space for stairways, large circulation spaces such as elevator lobbies, janitors' closets, mechanical shafts, and often toilets. A "gross-up factor," a percentage of the usable square feet added to the base requirement, is typically used to estimate the total space or gross square feet (meters) that must be built to meet the program requirements. For example, if an additional 33% of the usable square feet needs to be added, then the gross square feet (GSF) needed can be estimated by multiplying 1.33 times the usable square feet (eg, USF × 1.33 = GSF or [USF × 33%] + USF = GSF).

Another term that is used to define space, especially in buildings other than office buildings, is "net assignable area" (1). This is similar to usable square feet and includes all spaces that are required by the user, but does not include the circulation areas, mechanical shafts, general toilets, etc.

Adjacency Information

The designer also needs to know how the components of the program need to relate to each other spatially. This information can be stored in an interaction matrix such as the one shown in Figure 2. A bubble diagram such as the

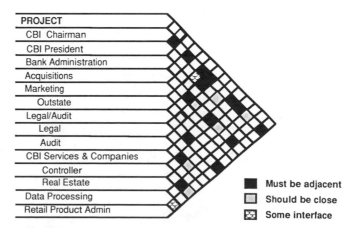

Figure 2. An interaction matrix stores the adjacency requirements of various groups or spaces. The shading in the square where two groups intersect indicates the strength of their relationship.

one in Figure 3 can be used to show the relationship of organizational units, or the relationship of spaces can be illustrated as in Figure 4. Reference 14 is a good source on methods of communicating adjacency requirements.

Image Program

It is often important to develop a facility image program along with the space and relational program. A facility image program might consist of a statement of the organization's mission; a list of the organization's goals and objectives; a list of the organization's strengths and weaknesses, as perceived by those within the organization; the organization's existing image, as perceived by various constituencies in and out of the organization; an explicit review of the constituencies that might be targeted by an image program; and finally, a list of image criteria.

Blocking and Stacking Diagrams

The programming effort may go so far as to produce stacking diagrams that show how the units of an organization should occupy a building or buildings by floor and blocking diagrams that show how floor space is to be allocated. These planning concepts are based on the area requirements of each group and their adjacency requirements.

Architectural requirements, such as utility service, floor loading, and bay size, are often considerations as well. The section diagrams in Figure 5 illustrate stacking plans, and the plan views in Figure 6 illustrate blocking plans.

Inventory

A programming study may include quantitative inventories of facility resources range from buildings in various locations to particular secretarial chairs. These inventories can be simple and straightforward or extremely complex and data-intensive, depending on the problem.

Evaluation Criteria

Explicitly articulated evaluation criteria are important program products. They can range from design specifications (eg, classrooms must be at least 25 ft (10 m) wide) to more subjective criteria such as that the facility should not make any user feel like a second-class citizen.

APPLICATIONS

The process, methods, and products mentioned above can be part of many kinds of programming efforts. This section briefly describes some types of programming projects.

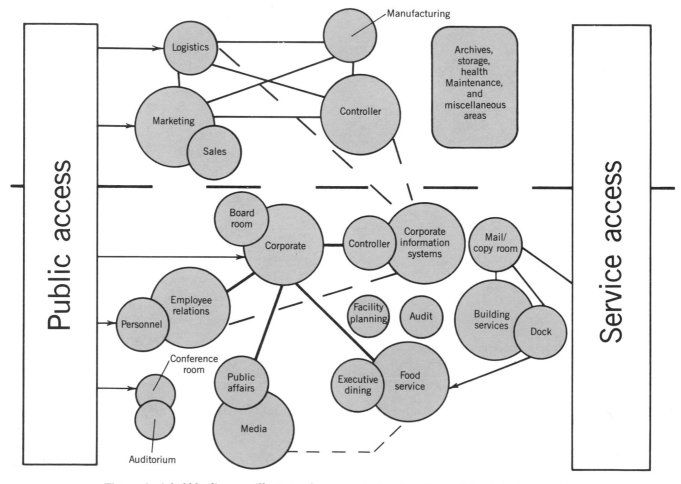

Figure 3. A bubble diagram illustrates how organizational units need to relate to each other spatially.

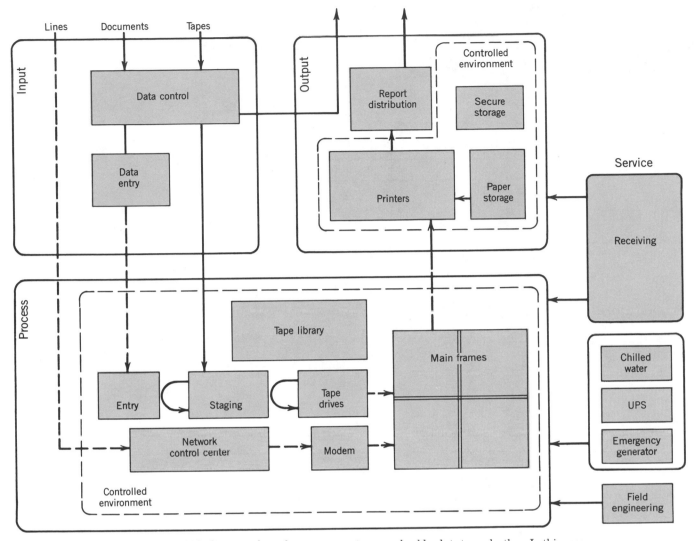

Figure 4. A bubble diagram shows how component spaces should relate to each other. In this case, the diagram shows the relationships in a data center.

Strategic Programming

As organizations make their plans for the future, they might well consider how to position themselves to manage what are often their largest single capital assets—their facilities. Strategic facility programming involves working with clients to evaluate various facility strategies for accommodating possible future scenarios. The goal is to ensure that appropriate facilities will be available where and when the organization needs them and at an acceptable cost.

Financial Analysis

Cost is almost always a factor in any facility decision, and clients often need assistance in analyzing the short- and long-term cost implications of alternative facility proposals. They may also need help analyzing the economic interactions of various factors over time. For example, purchasing an inexpensive site may save money in the short run, but the undesirability of the location may have

a negative impact on the building's appreciation in the long run. A good introduction to financial analysis can be found in Ref. 15.

Master Plan Programming

The development of a master plan program is an integral part of managing a large facility. It includes an occupancy and facility plant over time and is an important partner to a physical master plan that shows how and where a site will be developed. A master plan program may include plans for occupying a facility in various stages as an organization grows and changes. It typically uses gross cut information. For example, a master plan statement might be as follows. "70,000 GSF of laboratory space will be required by 1995. Building A will be used exclusively for laboratories by then, and a 20,000-GSF addition will have been added along with an additional parking structure." A master plan program may pertain to a single building or to multiple buildings. In most cases, more detailed pro-

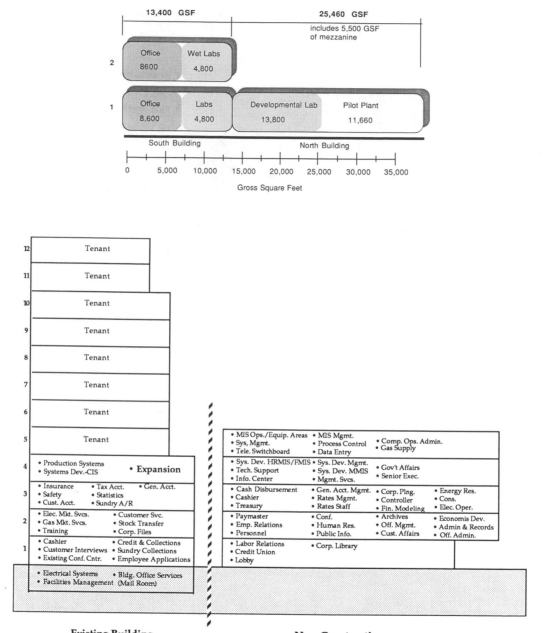

Figure 5. Stacking diagrams show how groups or functions will occupy a building or buildings.

gram information needs to be layered on before the plan can be implemented.

Base Building Programming

Before a building is designed, the designer needs to know what size it should be, what the major component parts will be and how they should be organized, how many parking spaces are required, what kinds of materials handling and servicing the building users require, the owner's attitudes about first cost versus operating costs, the desired image, the users' maintenance attitudes and resources,

the local codes that constrain the design, etc. A good base building programming effort supplies this information to the designer in a clearly understandable, timely fashion.

Detailed Programming

The data needed to plan and design an interior space are somewhat similar to the elements mentioned above, but are in much greater detail and on a much smaller scale. Here, each workstation (or nurses or waiter station or laboratory bench) must be enumerated, and its design criteria and adjacency requirements described.

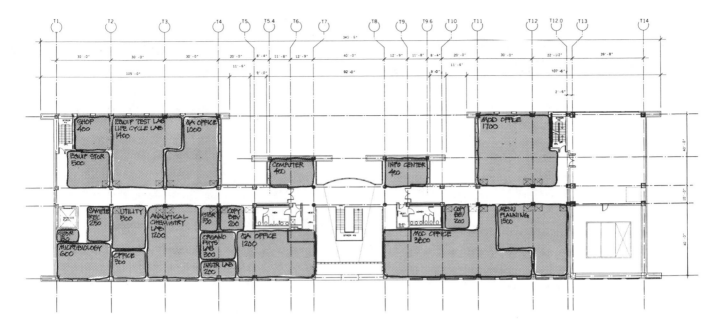

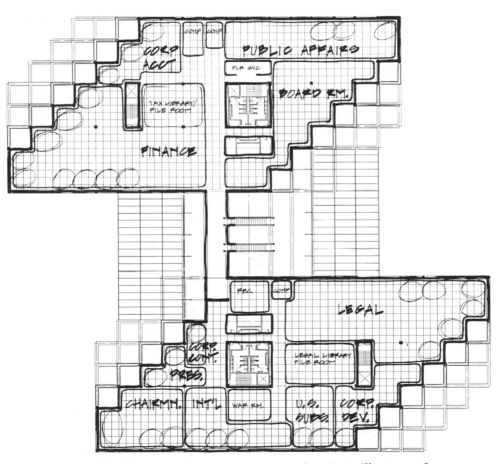

Figure 6. Blocking diagrams show how groups or functions will occupy a floor.

Workstation Studies

At a still smaller and more personal level is the study of the programmatic requirements of individuals' workstations. The issues here include privacy, flexibility, standardization, storage, work surface, lighting, guest accommodation, and personalization. A program could be developed and a workstation custom-designed for a specific individual, but more often a group of individuals is studied to develop workplace standards. Workplace studies are becoming more prevalent as evidence mounts that workplace design affects workers' productivity, and as automation, reorganization, and other changes make managing the workplace more complex and expensive (10).

Post-occupancy Evaluation and Building Audits

The evaluation criteria produced as a part of the programming process are an ideal tool in evaluating an existing facility since they articulate what the facility should be. An existing facility is good to the extent that is meets those criteria and bad to the extent that it does not meet those criteria. Reference 16 is a good introduction to the topic.

Facilities Management

An expanded, nontraditional definition of programming makes programming services integrally related to facilities management. Much of facilities managers' efforts are the continual and ongoing definition of facilities' requirements and the testing of those requirements against existing facilities. All of the processes, methods, and products described above can be used to proactively manage facilities, as well as to design them.

CONCLUSION

Architectural programming is the part of the design process where the problem that the design effort is to solve is identified. A wide range of applications outside of the program–design–build cycle use basically the same methods and can expand the services traditionally offered by an architectural firm. Active participation of the user and rigorous data collection and analysis contribute to providing environments that better meet the users' and client's goals and requirements.

BIBLIOGRAPHY

1. W. Pena and J. Focke, *Problem Seeking: New Directions in Architectural Programming* 3rd ed., American Institute of Architects Press, Washington, D.C., 1987.
2. M. Palmer, *The Architect's Guide to Facility Programming,* McGraw-Hill Inc., New York, 1981.
3. E. T. White, *Site Analysis: Diagramming Information for Architectural Design,* Architectural Media, Tuscon, Ariz., 1983.
4. F. Zimmerman and co-workers, *Site Analysis,* American Institute of Architects, Washington, D.C., 1987.
5. J. A. Seiler, "Architecture at Work," *Harvard Business Review,* **62**(5), (Sept.–Oct. 1984).
6. R. Sommers, *Personal Space: The Behavioral Basis of Design,* Prentice-Hall, Inc., Englewood Cliffs, N.J., 1969.
7. E. T. Hall, *The Hidden Dimension,* Doubleday & Co., Garden City, N.Y., 1966.
8. C. Alexander, *Notes on the Synthesis of Form,* Harvard University Press, Cambridge, Mass., 1971.
9. F. I. Steele, *Physical Settings and Organization Behavior,* Addison-Wesley Publishing Co., Inc., Reading, Mass., 1973.
10. M. Brill and co-workers, *Using Office Design to Increase Productivity,* Workplace Design and Productivity, Inc., Buffalo, N.Y., 1985.
11. H. Sanoff, *Methods of Architectural Programming,* Dowden, Hutchinson & Ross, Inc., Stroudsburg, Pa., 1977.
12. S. A. Olssen, ed., *Group Planning and Problem Solving Methods in Engineering Management,* John Wiley & Sons, Inc., New York, 1982.
13. "Standard Methods for Measuring Floor Area in Office Buildings," Building Owners and Managers Association International, Washington, D.C., 1981.
14. C. Jones, *Design Methods: Seeds of Human Futures,* Wiley Interscience, London, 1970.
15. *Life Cycle Cost Analysis: A Guide for Architects,* The American Institute of Architects, Washington, D.C., 1977.
16. C. Zimring and J. Reizensteins, "A Primer on Post-occupancy Evaluation," *AIA Journal* **70** (13), 52 (Nov. 1981).

General References

W. G. Cochran, *Sampling Techniques,* John Wiley & Sons, Inc., New York, 1953.

L. Kish, *Survey Sampling,* John Wiley & Sons, Inc., New York, 1965.

See also CONSTRUCTION FUNDING; LIFE CYCLE COSTING; OFFICE BUILDINGS

JANET MACKEY BROWN, PhD
Hellmuth, Obata &
Kassabaum, Inc.
St. Louis, Missouri

PROJECT MANAGEMENT, MANUAL DELIVERY.   See CONTRACT ADMINISTRATION; INSPECTION, OBSERVATION AND SUPERVISION.

PROMOTION OF ARCHITECTURAL SERVICES.   See COMMUNICATIONS IN ARCHITECTURE.

PUBLIC ART

Public art is created to communicate with a large audience. Works in public places are scrutinized by those educated and uneducated in the arts. A criterion for its publicness is its appropriate siting in an architectural or landscape environment.

Although sculpture is the most frequent form of public art; terra–cotta and stone reliefs, frescoes, murals, as well as architectural ornament have equally rich histories. Sculpture and painting are an enduring universal lan-

Figure 1. Tivoli, Italy. Photograph by Joyce P. Schwartz.

guage that draws its vocabulary from the forms of nature and, more recently, technology. Hills, valleys, plants, air, and water have been used by artists as inspirations to create personal statements as well as expressions of a particular culture.

Art in public places, a more accurate phrase than public art, has existed in different forms from antiquity to the present day according to the needs of the culture producing it. The pyramids in Egypt and Mexico, and decorated Carolingian and Gothic cathedrals, attest to the leading role public art played in the lives of people in highly religious societies.

Gardens containing art and amenities used as public and private places of pleasure may have originated with the sacred grove consecrated to a spirit or divinity, with trees, rocks, and water surrounding a shrine or an altar in a temple, grotto, or cave. The temple of the Sibyl near Tivoli built in the first century B.C. perched on a cliff over the falls of the Arno River was frequently imitated in European gardens (1). (Fig. 1)

In Roman times the god Priapus was responsible for overseeing gardens, and a statue of him would be placed to frighten elves, birds, or mischievous youths. Plautus wrote of gardens watched over by Venus. Sculptures of the god Terminus marked boundaries of states and rural properties. Pliny described the carefully arranged arbor, colonnade, or walkway that offered a sheltered sunny promenade in winter, the refreshment of shade in the heat of summer, and all the while a variety of views as one moved along the walk. Such an idea goes back to the *peripaton*, the walk or promenade of the Greek garden. As garden

ornaments, to line a walkway, or to close a vista, garden sculptures have survived into modern times (1).

In classical Greece, religious and political masterpieces of art and architecture were produced at public expense for the edification and pleasure of the public. Both the wealthy and the indigent had access to visual and performance art. The theater was free; any Athenian could walk through the agora and view the sculpture of Greek heroes and look up to gaze at the glories of the Parthenon (Fig. 2). The best art was public. The populace of different Greek city-states regularly commissioned artists to create works to adorn their cities. Pericles, in a formal oration after the Peloponnesian Wars, declared that beautiful Athens should be a model for other city-states. American democracy may now be looking at Greece for a model of egalitarian access to culture.

The Renaissance introduced the concept of secular public art, usually intended to glorify the wealth of a patron or the status of a city. Donatello's equestrian sculpture the *Gattamelata* was commissioned by the Paduan commune to honor their most famous war hero.

Historically, the church, royalty, government, and private wealthy families commissioned the many examples of art in public places in Europe, Asia, and America. The still existing and much visited grand public gardens of Europe and Asia were more often than not created for the privileged.

Figure 2. Parthenon, Greece.

Figure 3. Bernini Fountain, Versailles, France.

Coleridge's *Kubla Khan* offers Marco Polo's view of the Mongol ruler's Kuhilai, a huge palace of marble and ornamental stones. In a poem by the poet Chong' Jian, a garden is described as having a square pavillion, a summer lodge, a flowering arch, and a round belvedere. "A straw-thatched cot . . . a temple nestling beneath a hill . . . a dry stone wall . . . a straight gallery . . . a crooked cane (1)."

The ideal of the formal French garden as designed by Le Notre—the Tuileries, Versailles, and Vaux-le-Vicomte—are now grand public places. They are distinguished by terraced parterres designed as part of a unified general plan related to the house or building. Beyond are walks and fences, with walks almost always terminated by a fountain or statue on a pedestal. Aviaries, waterworks, and ornamental statues are placed in balanced, symmetrical patterns.

Versailles was conceived as a great water garden. Italy's greatest sculptor, Bernini, created its greatest fountains (Fig. 3). The public display of water may be seen today only on specific days.

The Italian Renaissance gardens, still existing, are now among the most visited grand public gardens. The Villa d'Este at Tivoli is the most exuberant and complete water garden in the world (Fig. 4). It includes an extravagant multiplicity of jets, sprays, and streams of an incredible one hundred fountains to tranquil fish ponds to the fecund statue of a many-breasted Diana with streams of water gushing from each nipple.

In nineteenth-century America, the grand sculpture gardens were mostly private and were not distinguished for art. It was the town center of colonial times that became the setting for commemorative statues, obelisks, and stelae emblazoned with names of war heroes. Gazebos functioned as bandstands. In this century, World War I cannons were often used as "sculptures" decorating the lawns of town centers.

The idea of monument in late nineteenth-century and early twentieth-century America has evolved. The man-on-a-horse or the figure on a pedestal still administers to the designation of a public place as commemorative. These traditional monuments begin to look vigorous and

energetic once again in the 1980s (Fig. 5). The pluralistic concepts of war memorials for Vietnam, Korea, and the Holocaust have revived interest in classical commemoratives.

In America, Vaux and Olmsted's parks around the country functioned as bits of country in the city and as a repository of neoclassical sculpture, fountains, and formal

Figure 4. Villa d'Este, Rome, Italy.

Figure 5. Saint Gaudens, "General Sherman Led By Justice." Base: McKim, Mead & White. Photograph by Joyce P. Schwartz.

public spaces. In addition to allees of trees and sculpture on pedestals, there are natural lakes, cottages, rustic loggia, seating, and bridges. Central Park's great centerpiece is Bethesda Fountain, a grand public living room (Fig. 6).

PUBLIC ART IN THE TWENTIETH CENTURY

Public art of the 1980s grew out of innovative advances in sculpture by the cubists and constructivists and the environmental site-specific sculpture earlier in the twentieth century. With the decorative arts movements, Weiner Werkstätte (begun in 1903), de Stijl (1917–1931), Bauhaus (1919–1933), arts and crafts, in the first half of the twentieth century, came an interest in making functional art and the impulse to integrate art and architecture. Many artists in the 1970s and 1980s worked on site-specific projects by investigating not only physical location, but also sociohistoric context. Contemporary artists integrate their art into the surrounding social fabric by expanding their knowledge of anthropology, history, philosophy, and the sciences as content for their art.

In America there was a radical change in the appearance of public art from that of academic nineteenth-century monuments. Galleries and museums held performances and showed photographs of work no longer in existence. Art and technology were celebrated as public events. In 1960, the Swiss artist Jean Tinguely built an elaborate machine that self-destructed in the open garden behind the Museum of Modern Art in New York. Ironically, Tinguely's works are now a permanent part of the Museum sculpture collection.

CONTEMPORARY SOURCES OF ART IN PUBLIC SPACES

Conceptual art, environmental art, earthworks, and reclamation monuments brought art out of the cloistered museum and gallery orbit into public spaces—from vast rural American landscapes to urban streets. Parks, plazas, waterfronts, airports, train stations, hospitals, hotels, schools, courthouses, playgrounds, shopping malls, street corners, and parking lots became suitable sites for museum-quality artworks.

American artists perceived the monumental American natural landscape as primary inspiration for their art concepts. The most important spokesperson for the art of reclamation and earthworks was Robert Smithson. Smithson's appreciation of natural wonders and awareness of the dangers of potential devastation by industry as well as thoughtless misuse of American resources allied artists and scientists in a common cause. Smithson's *Spiral Jetty* in Utah's Great Salt Lake (now under water) became symbolic of this aesthetic environmental consciousness. Smithson articulated a vision of the American landscape and established environmental awareness as purpose of contemporary art in public places.

Smithson's monumental earthworks and those of his artistic and social circle—Nancy Holt, Michael Heizer, Charles Ross, Robert Morris, Sol LeWitt, and Richard Serra—anticipated the functional and accessible public

Figure 6. Bethesda Fountain, Central Park, New York. Photograph by Joyce P. Schwartz.

art of the 1980s. These artworks, in addition to their conceptual basis also required knowledge and understanding of the disciplines of engineering, construction, architecture, and landscape design.

Whereas in the 1960s and early 1970s artists sought out rural landscape sites to make art, in the 1980s artists began to work primarily in an urban context.

AN AMERICAN PUBLIC ART EVOLVES

Since the nineteenth century, America and Europe have developed more democratic sponsorship and funding of public art. In America, steps were initiated by the government and institutional groups with the Works Project Administration (WPA). Where in the past public art was conceived for higher purposes of commemoration of events or people, art in America generally was viewed with puritanical suspicion. The successive waves of immigrants from abroad assimilated this point of view. It was not until Franklin Delano Roosevelt established the WPA in 1935 as an emergency support program for artists that a large body of public art emerged. John F. Kennedy in 1961 was an advocate of the arts, and Lyndon Johnson established the National Endowment for the Arts in 1965. The Nixon administration embraced and supported the new cultural policy. Thus White House support has proved the guarantee of an arts program.

GOVERNMENT PUBLIC ART PROGRAMS

In 1966, René d'Harnoncourt, curator of the Museum of Modern Art, proposed that the National Endowment for the Arts (NEA) give an award of excellence that would take the form of a major public art commission. This idea eventually evolved into the works of art in public places program.

Henry Geldzahler, the first director of the visual arts program of the NEA, visited Grand Rapids, Michigan, and suggested that an application be made to the NEA to erect a major sculpture on a downtown renewal plaza. A $45,000 matching grant was approved, and a panel composed of local representatives and national experts in art and architecture met at Grand Rapids, viewed the site, and selected Alexander Calder to execute the sculpture (2). *The Grand Vitesse* was dedicated in June 1968 and became the logo of the city, "a coat of arms," appearing on the official city letterhead, on street signs, and on city sanitation trucks. President Ford is widely quoted as having said "I didn't know what a 'Calder' was." But that "Calder" in the center of a city in an urban redevelopment area helped to regenerate a city. For Grand Rapids the Calder plays a traditional role as a civic monument (2).

The Calder is a model of successful assimilation of a work of advanced art by a community that prepared itself to receive it. It fulfilled the necessities of various groups. The art community was delighted with the choice. Cultural leaders applauded its symbolism for all the arts. The downtown renewal was on its way, and the city continued to select major visual artists for public sites (2).

Six years later, Robert Morris's first earthwork in the United States reclaimed an area in Grand Rapids that became a park—a most exceptional gesture toward advanced public art made by a community (2) (Figure 7).

The development of quality in the public arts that takes cognizance of the most innovative contemporary artists is always a difficult issue. One is reminded 20 years after these early great works were installed that the issue of quality has more to do with establishing high standards by art professionals who involve the community on an active level than a patronizing attitude toward community involvement.

The arts endowment program giving matching grants of up to $45,000 to hundreds of communities placing public works of art was perhaps the single most significant factor in the recent emergence of art in public places. A professional artist-selection process was originally of primary importance to this program and established ground rules for percent-for-art programs yet to come. Richard Koshalek (Director of the Museum of Contemporary Art in Los Angeles) and Brian O'Doherty (NEA Director of Film and Video), who were early directors of the Visual Art programs, and the late Nancy Hanks (second chairman of the Arts Endowment, 1969–1977) set goals for the art in public places program that have been maintained. There is today in Washington, D.C., a national organization of civic visual arts agencies that meets regularly and disseminates information to artists, the public, and public arts agencies.

The Arts Endowment public art commitment has an effective design arts advocacy program combining architecture, urban design, and the visual arts. Symposia, books, and articles proliferate, offering information and guidance. In addition, public art consultancy is a recognized profession.

The 1960s ushered in an era of renewed interest in public art. At the request of President Kennedy a report was issued, *Guiding Principles for Federal Architecture,* charging: "Where appropriate, fine arts should be incorporated in the designs of new Federal buildings with the emphasis on the work by living American artists" (3). In 1963, the administrator of the General Services Adminis-

Figure 7. Robert Morris, "Grand Rapids Project," asphalt, Grand Rapids, Mich., 1974. Courtesy of Castelli/Sonnabend Galleries, New York.

tration (GSA) responded with a direct policy order establishing an allowance for fine arts of 0.5% of the estimated cost of construction of each new federal building. The order also initiated a new program, art-in-architecture, created to carry out the policy and to develop the procedures for its implementation. Its momentum was halted in 1966, when a sudden rise in construction costs caused a shift in national spending priorities. In 1972, Congress gave new emphasis to the art-in-architecture program (3).

The program expanded the original approach to include the active participation of the NEA and the project architect in the selection process. The architect is encouraged to submit an art-in-architecture proposal as part of his or her overall design concept. This proposal must include a description of the location and nature of the artwork(s) to be commissioned. Shortly after the award of the construction contract, GSA requests NEA to appoint a panel of qualified art professionals to meet with the project architect for the purpose of nominating three to five artists for each proposed artwork (3).

At least one of the panelists is to be from the area of the project. Then the panel, including the architect, meets at the project site with representatives of GSA and NEA to analyze sites for art and to review visual materials of

Figure 8. Louise Nevelson, "Bicentennial Dawn," white painted wood, 15 × 30 × 90 ft, James A. Byrne Federal Courthouse, Philadelphia, Pa., 1976. GSA Commission. Courtesy of The Pace Gallery, New York and Chase Manhattan Bank, New York. Photograph by Tom Crane.

artists whose work would be appropriate for the proposed commission. The artist is then selected by the administrator of GSA, after which GSA and the artists negotiate a fixed-price contract for the design, fabrication, and installation of the artwork. The artist's concept is reviewed and approved by GSA's art-in-architecture design review panel. An architect, Donald W. Thalacker, was put in charge of the renewed program. Under his energetic leadership from 1972 to 1988 more than 300 projects were completed; thus the program has been an active catalyst for public art. This GSA program gave many artists their first opportunity to create a permanent work of public art, including many nationally known artists, such as Louise Nevelson (Fig. 8), Tony Smith, Isamu Noguchi, Jack Beal, and also regional artists of established reputation. The GSA program became the role model for an enlightened process that demanded responsibility on the part of artists yet nurtured their personal vision for creative freedom.

PERCENT-FOR-ART LEGISLATION

The Arts Endowment established professional standards for all arts groups, not only for all their funded projects, but also those of the GSA and other federal agencies. Public art is not new in this country, but a widespread commitment for art in local and government buildings has come with the proliferation of percent-for-art legislation in hundreds of cities, counties, and states. Europe has concurrently seen the growth of percent-for-art programs, although 2%, which is customary there, provides them with a more generous art budget. Early advocates of percent-for-art wanted to create better architecture. But the fullest meaning encompasses both architecture and the art that surrounds and enhances the architecture. Percent-for-art allocates money from already appropriated public construction budgets. It circumvents the need to seek money from already small civic budgets, and it safeguards the money set aside for art, which often decreases as construction costs run over budget.

Advocates believe percent-for-art legislation has created real improvement in the design quality of public buildings and is a powerful force in support of a nation's artists and craftspeople. This increased government involvement recognizes that art and cultural development are vital to the economic and social well-being of cities and towns. Percent-for-art programs are an approach integrating the artistic and utilitarian into one humane and responsive form of public architecture.

Percent-for-art laws vary at state, county, and city levels but share some common vital components. Categories of public construction either above or below grade can be included. In Seattle "'Construction project' means any capital project paid for wholly or in part by The City of Seattle to construct or remodel any building, structure, park, utility, street, sidewalk, or parking facility, or any portion thereof, within the limits of the city of Seattle." This creates a larger overall art budget that has given the city more art and greater commitment to art. The law is administered by existing public agencies: The Public Works Department, Buildings Department, and Cultural

Figure 9. Giuseppe Penone, "A Forked Branch and Three Landscapes," bronze, plants, water, clay pots, Sheraton Society Hill Hotel, Philadelphia, Pa., 1986. Rouse and Associates and the Redevelopment Authority of the City of Philadelphia. Courtesy of the Marian Goodman Gallery, New York.

Department. Procedures are developed to select the art and artists (4).

The State of Washington requires that its State Art Commission approve the selection of the various agencies, each of which has its own art acquisition resources. To ensure the highest quality and most appropriate art, the composition and size of selection panels is determined by law (4).

Baltimore has a civic Design Commission that is comprised of a representative of the Baltimore Museum of Art, an architect, a recognized artist or teacher of art located in Maryland, and a citizen who is actively interested in civic improvement (4).

Colorado's percent program is based on variables such as feasibility, budget allocation, complexity of the project,

and location and function of the facility. Methods of selection can include one or a combination of the following: direct purchase, direct commission, limited competition, and open competition (4).

National standards for the percent-for-art legislation in America were established in 1959 by the first percent-for-arts program, established in Philadelphia. This unusual mandate states that 1% of all building construction costs on land assembled and conveyed by the Redevelopment Authority of the City of Philadelphia must be budgeted for the acquisition of original works of art created specifically for public spaces within the development.

Philadelphia achieved one of the most successful early urban redevelopment programs under the guidance of city planner Edmund N. Bacon, executive director of the City Planning Commission. Philadelphia has one of the largest quality public art collections in the country, including sculpture by three generations of Calders. Although local and regional artists have benefited from this program, the Authority seeks artists internationally. More than 300 works have been installed in such diverse developments as high-rise commercial and residential towers, housing for low-to-moderate income families, and in housing for the elderly. Industrial plants, universities, hotels (Fig. 9), hospitals, libraries, and schools have also benefited. Paralleling this program is that of the City of Philadelphia that requires inclusion of 1% for fine arts in all new public construction and one of the oldest private programs supporting art in public places, the Fairmount Park Association (Fig. 10).

Percent-for-art programs such as the one in Philadelphia mandate that the developer, architect, and artist work together from the inception of each construction project, selecting a public art consultant or panel of art professionals to guide the process. The site for art, the artists selected, and their proposal must be approved by the Fine Arts Committee of the Redevelopment Authority, which

Figure 10. Jody Pinto, "Fingerspan," Corten steel, 9 ft × 4 ft 10 in. × 59 in. Fairmount Park, Philadelphia, Pa., 1987. Courtesy of the Hal Bromm Gallery, New York, the Marian Locks Gallery, Philadelphia, Pa. and the Fairmount Park Art Association. Photograph by Wayne Cozzolino.

includes at least one contemporary art professional, architect, landscape architect, artist, and several lay-citizens with an interest in the arts. What is unique is the active role of the developer in the process.

The city of Baltimore was the second to legislate percent-for-art in support of these programs. William Donald Schaefer, then Mayor of Baltimore said: "The question of financing art in new construction is not a matter of can we afford the experience of art in our new buildings, but rather, can we afford not to finance art . . . Art gives meaning to life, and art must be seen to have meaning (5)."

Percent-for-art legislation usually happens after years of hard work by a few dedicated, persevering citizens. Doris Freedman, founder of the Public Art Fund, was New York City's advocate for a percent-for-art law. In 1982 the law passed. Projects completed and in progress in New York City mirror places for art in many cities: zoos and aquariums, transportation facilities, public schools, libraries, government office buildings, parks, firehouses, sanitation garages, and revitalized waterfronts. For example, for a recreational pier at 107th Street, Manhattan artist Andrea Blum and architects Cavaglieri & Sultan worked as a team to renovate the historic pier.

Other communities and states having active, well-conceived percent-for-art programs include Metro-Dade County (Florida), Alaska, Connecticut, San Francisco, Minneapolis, Hawaii, Seattle, Wilmington (Delaware), New Jersey, Massachusetts, Cambridge (Massachusetts), Phoenix, Albuquerque, Pittsburgh, Santa Monica (California), Chicago, New York, and Los Angeles. Today it is a rare community that does not have some form of sponsorship for art in public places. Often it is a specific government agency that conceives of a public art program.

PLACES FOR ART IN TRANSPORTATION FACILITIES

Transportation facilities are a major venue for introducing public art in cities. Commitment to art in transportation facilities received encouragement from the Department of Transportation (DOT). In 1981 it instituted a design-for-transportation national awards program to honor both design and design management by giving recognition to outstanding design and art in transportation that improves the quality of the nation's environment.

The DOT instituted a combined city/DOT program that gave impetus to projects in airports and rail facilities. Joan Mondale, the wife of then Vice-president Walter Mondale, took a leadership position in the selection of major artworks for Atlanta's International Hartsdale Airport.

In 1978 the Cambridge (Massachusetts) Arts Council and the Back Bay Transportation Authority with funding from the U.S. Department of Transportation became partners in a public arts program "Arts-on-the-line" that selected 20 artists for four new stations. The art was conceived as environmental and intimate. Four criteria were established: artistic excellence, appropriateness to the site, durability of design and materials, and minimum maintenance. Aesthetic decisions were made by art professionals, with artists involved at early design stages with architects.

In Pittsburgh, the Allegheny Transit Authority received additional monies from corporations having buildings near a particular station. The Heinz foundation helped fund a 203-ft. Sol LeWitt wall relief at the Wood Street station. The site for art was selected by the Pittsburgh Art Commission with the help of the architects for the station, Parsons-Brinckerhoff Quaide & Douglas. The surface material for the wall was left unspecified, intentionally awaiting the artist's choice. LeWitt selected white marble to contrast with black slate geometric reliefs. LeWitt's understanding of scale and proportion and the dramatic black and white make this successful aesthetically and environmentally (Fig. 11).

For more than 15 years the New York/New Jersey Port Authority has had an art program that incorporates all forms and media in airports, bus terminals, and their office buildings. People line up behind George Segal's waiting line of people at the bus terminal in New York (Fig. 12).

Kinetic, reflective light installations have proven popular in transportation systems across the country.

Major art programs are calculated to encourage more pleasurable public use of rail systems. Detroit, Buffalo, San Francisco, Miami-Dade County, Baltimore, New York City, and Los Angeles have modern art programs integrating art and architecture.

Figure 11. Sol Lewitt, "Thirteen Geometric Figures," slate on marble, 203 × 9 ft, Wood Street Station, Pittsburgh, Pa., 1984. Courtesy of the Pittsburgh Art Commission. Photograph by Clyde Hare.

Figure 12. George Segal, "Next Departure," bronze, metal, plastic, wood, paper and vinyl. 84 × 72 × 96 in., New York/New Jersey Port Authority Bus Terminal, New York City, 1979. Courtesy of the Sidney Janis Gallery. Photograph by Allan Finkelman.

Figure 13. Joyce Kozloff, Wilmington Delaware Train Station, glazed ceramic tiles, 30 × 20 × 15 ft, 1984. Courtesy of the Barbara Gladstone Gallery, New York. Photograph by Eugene Mopsik.

The Northeast Corridor Transit System (Washington-to-Boston) is one of the most ambitious, involving artist-and-architect collaborations. Skidmore Owings & Merrill and artist Joyce Kozloff participated in a restoration of architect Frank Furness's Wilmington Station. Kozloff researched the lost imagery of Furness's great ornamented buildings that had been destroyed; she created hand-painted tiles covering the interior entrance walls thus keeping forever these designs in an appropriate place (Fig. 13).

Artist Robert Irwin has articulated a philosophy of public art themes, purpose, and management that has been influential and effective. For Miami's International Airport, Irwin master planned an innovative visual arts program involving many artists. He established criteria for the projects' management as well as concepts for unusual art sites.

Although advances have been made, none of the American transportation projects approaches the scope of the art in several European train systems, including exceptional programs in Brussels, Amsterdam, and Stockholm. For the Stockholm subway the two architects who headed

the design division believed that "only art could transform the underground station (6)." Architects Michael Granit and Per Reimers contrasted walls of concrete with smooth steel and terrazzo floors. Entire spaces were created by blasting rock; walls, floors, and ceilings are given over to the artists. The resulting works of art gave each station its identity and helped passengers find their way in it (6).

Construction of the Brussels metro system began in 1965. Under Herman Leibears, the seven-member artistic commission worked to humanize the underground life of the Brussels commuters by setting aside 2–3% of the construction budget to pay for art. Artists, generally Belgians—Paul Del Vaux, Michel Folon, Pol Bury, Pierre Aleschinsky—were allowed as much freedom as possible. Limitations came in the form of size or shape of wall or space to be decorated. Sometimes, limitations became inspiration. The metro station Horta, completed in 1988, named for Victor Horta the Belgian Art Nouveau architect, was planned around a staircase saved from Le Maison du Peuple designed by Horta before the turn of the century.

Automobile freeways, highways, and roads, long considered destructive to the visual environment, are being scrutinized as overdue for aesthetic embellishment. An enlightened program in France has corporations contributing 2%-for-art on their particular stretch of road for beautification.

In America, in 1976 the Nebraska State Arts Council formulated a percent-for-art competition, inviting artists to create work for truck stops on the long, flat stretches of I-80. In 1988, artists and design professionals were asked to collaborate in a competition seeking art for Houston highways. Also in 1988, Phoenix developed a public art program master plan for the city's infrastructure, notably encouraging opportunities for art with special attention to vantage points from which art may be viewed (ie, airplanes, automobiles, freeway overpasses), and by pedestrians.

THE INDIVIDUAL AS ART PATRON

The wealthy patron of the arts is a continuing phenomenon. Private art collectors are innovative and adventurous, free of restraints imposed by corporate or government bureaucracies. In Mountainville, New York, Storm King Art Center was originally a private estate. It was purchased in 1960 by businessman Ralph Ogden to create an open-air sculpture garden. He was inspired by photographs of Henry Moore sculptures on a rural sheep farm in Glen Kiln, Scotland. Ogden was an admirer of David Smith, one of America's seminal modern sculptors. Ogden visited Bolton Landing, New York, where Smith had created large welded-steel sculpture, installing them in the natural landscape surrounding his studio. His work was intended as corollary to nature and to architecture. In 1967, Ogden acquired 13 of Smith's sculptures and sited them at Storm King on the terraces and lawns near and inside the manor house (7).

Before site-specific was an art word, Ogden commissioned artists to create sculpture at Storm King that related specifically to a landscape site of the artist's own choosing. The sculptor David von Schlegell, using modern materials and technology, created five environmental sculptures that took landscaping and topography as their inspiration. Storm King continues to commission major contemporary sculptors.

Art collector Lewis Manilow, an advocate of art-for-architecture in Chicago, established The Nathan Manilow Sculpture Park at Governors State University in Chicago. This collection on the cutting edge includes works by Bruce Nauman, Martin Puryear, Jene Highstein, Mary Miss, and Mark di Suvero (Fig. 14). Manilow is one of several major collectors who advised Chicago about buying art for public spaces. Major works by Calder, Picasso, Miró, Nevelson, Dubuffet, and Chagall continue the tradition of public art-for-architecture in Chicago from Louis Sullivan's ornamental buildings to Claes Oldenburg's *Bat Column*. The commissioned art identifies the city of Chicago, with, for example, Picasso's controversial Corten

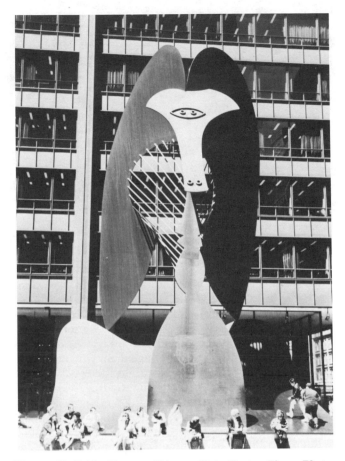

Figure 15. Pablo Picasso, Chicago Civic Center Plaza. Photograph by Jeffrey Wilkes.

steel sculpture, which is instantly recognized as being in Chicago (Fig. 15).

Villa Celle, near the Tuscan town of Pistoia, a great European contemporary sculpture garden, was founded by art patron Giuliano Gori. An Italian industrialist, he sought to provide an organic place for avant-garde art. Beginning in 1982, under the direction of curator Amnon Barzel, leading international artists were invited to create outdoor projects challenged by the topography, vegetation, historical remnants, and cultural contexts of Villa Celle (Figs. 16–18).

Figure 14. Mark Di Suvero, "For Lady Day," 54 × 50 × 35 ft Nathan Manilow Sculpture Park, Governor's State University Foundation, University Park, Ill., 1968–1969. Courtesy of Governor's State University and the Oil and Steel Gallery, New York.

Figure 16. Magdalena Abakanowicz, "Catharsis," 33 bronze figures, Villa Celle, Frattoria d'Pistoia, Italy, 1985. Courtesy of Giuliano Gori, and Marlborough Gallery, New York.

Figure 17. Robert Morris, "Labyrinth," green/white marble, Villa Celle, Italy, Frattoria d'Pistoia, Italy, 1981–1983. Courtesy of Giuliano Gori.

Works in the open air are situated, each of them, in a space within the large space of the park. Although a "civilized nature" as planned and planted over the last two centuries, the park is thus transformed by nature and works by artists Richard Serra, Dani Karavan, Alice Aycock, Dennis Oppenheim, Magdalena Abakanowicz, Ulrich Ruckreim, Robert Morris, Anne and Patrick Poirier, Max Newhaus, Alan Sonfist, George Trakas, and Mauro Staccioli. The artists brought their own personal vocabularies to the place, adapting and modifying in keeping with *genus loci*.

Begun in 1969, the Hakone Open-Air Museum in Japan is a complete inventory of twentieth-century modern international sculpture. Under the patronage of the Fuji-Sankei group, it includes artists from Rodin to Jean Tinguely. It is dedicated to contemporary sculptors and environmental art in arcadia and is a bridge between East and West.

The Stuart Collection of sculpture, on a 1200-acre campus at the University of California, San Diego in La Jolla,

Figure 18. Alice Aycock, "The Nets of Solomon," Villa Celle, Frattoria d'Pistoia, Italy, 1983. Courtesy of Giuliano Gori. Photograph by Alice Aycock.

Figure 19. Richard Fleischner, La Jolla Project, limestone, Stuart Collection, University of California, San Diego, at La Jolla, 1984. Courtesy of the University of California, San Diego.

is being created through an imaginative and perhaps unprecedented collaboration between James Stuart DeSilva, art patron and businessman, and the University. Its stated purpose is to enrich the cultural, intellectual, and scholarly life of the campus while it provides a range of opportunities for artists pursuing new approaches to public art. Works are commissioned that specifically address a site, a context, or a functional need. The campus contains natural chaparral-filled canyons, eucalyptus groves, urban plazas, and green lawns. An advisory committee of art professionals of international standing selects the artists. The first work commissioned was *A Sun God* by Niki de St. Phalle. It has become a mascot for the student body. Other provocative art works are by Robert Irwin, Bruce Nauman, Ian Finley Hamilton, Richard Fleischner, Jackie Ferrara, and art using sound, light, and video by Terry Allen, Bruce Nauman, and Nam June Paik (Fig. 19).

The university as a place for experiment with temporary projects has therefore become a repository of innovative permanent art in the campus environment. MIT has long had a commitment to major contemporary sculpture, believing that engineering-science students would not necessarily expose themselves to art and the humanities, therefore the university would bring it to them. Through

Figure 20. Tony Smith, MIT Sculpture Collection, Corten steel, Massachusetts Institute of Technology, Cambridge, Mass. Courtesy of the Paula Cooper Gallery, New York and the Tony Smith Estate. Photograph by Joyce P. Schwartz.

Figure 21. Vito Aconci, "Face of the Earth," astroturf, 28 × 20 × 12 ft. Courtesy of the Rhona Hoffman Gallery, Chicago.

Gyorgy Kepes, Director of the Department of Visual Studies, and its sculpture collection MIT has done just that (Fig. 20).

C. W. Post College in Long Island funded the cost of an environmental work by Vito Acconci exhibited at the Museum of Modern Art in New York in May 1988 and thus was able to install the eccentric participatory artwork permanently on campus (Fig. 21).

CORPORATIONS AND DEVELOPERS AS ART PATRONS

Corporations and developers are considered modern Medicis. One of the greatest art and architecture projects conceived by a corporate developer is Rockefeller Center in New York. In 1931, although the Rockefeller building design was well-advanced, the architect Wallace Harrison suggested to John D. Rockefeller that someone be employed to advise on the decoration of the building. They did not seek simple embellishment of the architecture, but the development of a theme that would unify the art and decoration and allow it to communicate an uplifting message. A philosopher, Huntly Burr Alexander, developed the theme and advised the artists on subject matter, decorative motifs, colors, and symbols (8).

Those influencing the art and decoration of the building were champions of corporate good taste and competent mediocrity in art. The exception was young Nelson Rockefeller, who originated the proposal to invite artists of international standing. Although Picasso and Matisse declined his invitation, other great artists accepted the challenge. Among them were José Luis Sert, Paul Manship, Gaston Lachaise, Giacomo Manzu, William Zorach, Yasao Kuniyashi, Stuart Davis, Lee Lawrie, and a 32-year-old Isamu Noguchi, who won a competition to create a realistic relief in stainless steel for the Associated Press building. Today Rockefeller Center's ornamentation, sculptures, murals, mosaics, friezes, and landscaping program add up to an exciting art-informed urban experience. The promenade is in the European tradition of an art-filled urban landscape.

Rockefeller Center inspires corporations today to be progressive in their art selection. The Equitable Life As-

surance Society chose to make a similar commitment to the visual arts in their building in New York's Times Square area on a suggestion of architect Edward Larrabee Barnes. Benjamin D. Holloway, Chairman of Equitable's real-estate group and one of the art project's founders, gave reasons for a corporate involvement to a *New York Times* art critic: "This is investment real estate. We are doing these things because we think it will attract and hold tenants, and they will pay us the rents that we are looking for (9)." Holloway has said that the arts and good restaurants will get them Park Avenue prices on Seventh Avenue. The arts complex includes a midtown branch of the Whitney Museum, which guided the art selection of many commissioned artworks.

Scott Burton, an articulate public artist known for his sculptural furnishings, was given major spaces and autonomy to create for the lobby a huge semicircular green marble sculptural seating, including plants, paving and lighting. In addition, he designed two eccentric street-side plazas of chairs, tables, and planters. Roy Lichtenstein painted a billboard-sized mural in the lobby overlooking Broadway, while Sol LeWitt and Barry Flanagan executed murals and sculptures, respectively, for the arcade. A vibrant mural by the Italian artist Sandro Chia celebrating the medieval Sienese horserace, the Palio, surrounds the lobby of a restaurant whose name and decor are inspired by the art and the event.

The New York branch of The First Bank of Chicago in the same complex followed Equitable's lead. To enhance their image, their entrance lobby in the building is transformed by artist Agnes Denes's pink rosa etched glass ceiling (Figs. 22–24).

Banks have always been among the most dedicated corporate collectors of museum-quality art. Chase Manhattan Bank, one of the first to do so, entered the world of art collecting more than 25 years ago. In 1972, Chase, under the guidance of architect Gordon Bunshaft of Skidmore, Owings & Merrill commissioned French artist Jean Dubuffet to enliven and humanize their new huge plaza in

Figure 22. Scott Burton, Urban Plaza North and South, 80 × 80 × 15 ft. Equitable Center, New York. Courtesy of the Max Protech Gallery, New York and the Equitable Life Assurance Society of the U.S. Photograph by Joyce P. Schwartz.

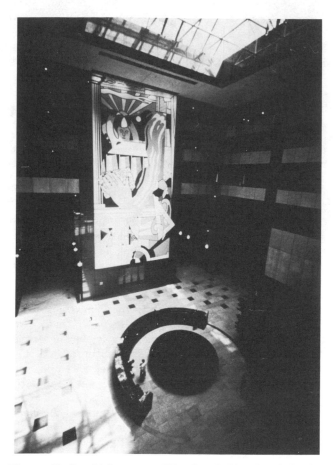

Figure 23. Roy Lichtenstein, "Mural with Blue Brush Stroke" Equitable Center, New York. Courtesy of the Leo Castelli Gallery, New York. Photograph by Scott Burton. Courtesy of the Equitable Life Assurance Society of the U.S.

lower Manhattan. The artist's *Group of Four Trees*, created to bring nature to a cold international-style building, identifies Chase Manhattan Bank and is a popular contemporary public work (Fig. 25).

NCNB Corporation, a regional bank with headquarters in Charlotte, North Carolina, has made their major commitment to art and architecture of quality symbolic of their "caring for their employees and the surrounding community (10)." For their Florida headquarters in Tampa, NCNB commissioned large-scale, site-oriented sculptures by major contemporary artists Manuel Neri and George Sugarman (Figs. 26, 27). Chairman of the Board Hugh McColl gave guidance to an art committee of bank officials, developers (Faison Associates), and architects (Odell Associates) who recommended that the bank use a professional public art consultant to coordinate the selection process and commit sufficient funds for major works.

Many banks and corporations have art collections to enhance their employees' surroundings. Commissioned or sited art in major public spaces, particularly on exterior plazas or landscaped areas, gives corporations a highly visible civic identity, not unlike that of their building, which affects the public environment.

General Mills Corporation in Minneapolis, in recognition of its parklike office environment of 85 acres, embarked on an outdoor sculpture project. By 1982 the program was redefined to use sculptures, plantings, and landforms to soften and shield various unattractive aspects of the site—parking lots, ramps, loading docks, and service areas—as well as to direct those entering and leaving. Landscape architect William A. Rutherford created a landscape sculpture plan. Richard Fleischner, Scott Burton, Jonathan Borofsky, Richard Serra, Jackie Ferrara, and Jene Highstein are among the artists commissioned (Fig. 28).

In rural areas a sculpture collection can become a community resource. For example, the excellent PepsiCo sculpture garden in Purchase, New York, is on art tours for art, charitable, and civic organizations (Fig. 29).

Prudential Corporation has one of the more venturesome public art commission programs for each of its new buildings around the country. They commission museum-credible emerging artists to create ornament and sculpture that is integral to architecture. Floors, walls, ceilings, entranceways, and dining rooms are places for art effectively executed under the direction of an in-house art professional staff closely cooperating with the architects and interior designers for each building (Figs. 30, 31).

Figure 24. Agnes Denes, "Hypersphere—The Earth in the Sphere of the Universe," 24 × 24 × 43 ft, 144 panels of carved, frosted pink rosa glass in two layers, 1300-ft² bronze mirrors, Equitable Center, New York, 1987. Photograph by Peter Mauss/ESTO.

Figure 25. Jean Dubuffet, "Group of Four Trees," 42 ft, Chase Manhattan Plaza, New York, 1972. Courtesy of The Pace Gallery, New York and Chase Manhattan Bank, New York.

Figure 26. Manuel Neri, "Espanola," marble, 12 × 3 ft, NCNB National Bank Headquarters, Tampa, Fl., 1988. Commissioned by NCNB. Photograph by Joyce P. Schwartz.

PUBLIC ART AND THE MUSEUM AS PATRON

Although the phrase "public art" implies continuous accessibility, the popularity and significance of public art installations has necessitated the creation of public art environments in museums. This is especially ironic as many of the public artists of the 1960s and 1970s created public art specifically so it could not be collected and housed in museums. Robert Smithson censured museums as collections of useless void and anachronisms (11). Yet soon museum sculpture gardens and even outdoor museums began to proliferate. Storm King Art Center in New York, The Louisiana Museum in Denmark, the Kröller-Muller in the Netherlands, Millesgarten in Sweden, the Vigeland Sculpture Park in Norway, the Billy Rose Sculpture Garden in Israel, and the Hakone Open-Air Museum in Japan are just a few institutions designed to house public art in its natural environment rather than in the "void" of Smithson's description. Museums and universities in 1988 routinely collect large-scale art and commission artists to create specific works for their new or renovated buildings and gardens. Museums therefore have set high standards for public art that influence the government and corporations when they become purchasers of public art.

Museums have also assumed the role of warehouses for former public works of art. Some architectural sculpture and ornament that might have been destroyed in the process of urban development have been rescued by museums and given permanent homes in their collections. The Chicago Stock Exchange Buildings, designed in 1893 by the firm of Adler & Sullivan was, until its demolition in 1972, a major contribution to the Chicago school of architecture. Having failed to designate the building as an architec-

Figure 27. George Sugarman, "Untitled," NCNB National Bank Headquarters, Tampa, Fl., 1988. Commissioned by NCNB. Photograph by Jim Chandler.

Figure 30. Ned Smyth, "A Part of the Whole," marble and terrazzo columns, glass and gold leaf, Prudential Insurance Company California, 1982. Courtesy of Ned Smyth.

Figure 28. Jonathan Borofsky, General Mills Corporation, Minneapolis, Minn., 1988. Courtesy of the Paula Cooper Gallery, New York. (*General Mills Collection*)

tural landmark, the city of Chicago offered The Art Institute of Chicago its choice of artifacts from the building. In 1976 The Art Institute began reconstructing Adler & Sullivan's Trading Room within the new east wing of the museum; in 1977 the Trading Room was reopened to the public.

Museums have also provided havens for public works of art that have proven too controversial for a public audience. Frederick William MacMonnies gave a gift of the first cast of his *Bacchante with an Infant Faun* to the architect Charles F. McKim, who placed it in the courtyard of the new public library McKim and associates had designed for Copley Square in Boston. The trustees saw the sculpture as an image of "wanton nudity and drunkenness" and demanded its removal. McKim withdrew the sculpture and offered it to the Metropolitan Museum of Art in New York, which accepted it and promised never to remove MacMonnies's *Bacchante* from public view. Simi-

larly, several museums offered a permanent site for Richard Serra's *Tilted Arc* if it were removed from its original site in New York City's Federal Plaza. Later the museums rescinded their offer, respecting Serra's opinion that his work would be incomplete if not located in its original site.

City agencies are also working collaboratively with museums to create public sculpture gardens. The Minneapolis Sculpture Garden was the result of efforts made by the Walker Art Center, the Minneapolis Park and Recreation Board, and the Minnesota Landscape Arboretum at the University of Minnesota. As the landowners, the Park and Recreation Board maintain the sculpture garden while the Walker Art Center organizes all the curatorial and educational activities. The Minneapolis Sculpture Garden is one example where a museum has augmented its collection by incorporating public art works.

The garden's focal point is the fountain sculpture *Spoonbridge and Cherry* by Claes Oldenburg and Coosje van Bruggen. The huge aluminum spoon holds a red cherry with a black stem arching from the shore to an island in a free-form pond. The architect Frank Gehry's

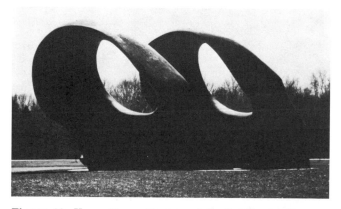

Figure 29. Henry Moore. Photograph by the Pepsico Corporation, Purchase, New York.

Figure 31. Robert Stackhouse, "Prudential Installation," wood boat and etched shadow, 55 × 15 ft. Prudential Insurance Company, New Jersey. Courtesy of Robert Stackhouse.

Figure 32. Siah Armajani, Irene Hixon Whitney Bridge, Walker Art Center, 1988. Courtesy of the Walker Art Center. Photo by Glenn Halvorson.

22-ft. glass fish rises from a pool of white water lilies. Siah Armajani designed a footbridge to link the garden to Young Park and downtown Minneapolis (Fig. 32). Martin Friedman, the Director of the Walker Art Center, said the garden and its sculptures are meant to attract art lovers and people who do not normally visit museums.

The Prato Museum for Contemporary Art, near Florence, Italy, which opened its doors in 1988, is yet another example of a museum expanding its collection to include public art. Sculptures by the artists Anne and Patrick Poirier, Mauro Staccioli, and Enzo Cucci define the perimeters of the museum's property. Not only do these sculptures act as signposts announcing the presence of the museum, but, because they are visible from two major highways, the works of art attract visitors to the museum and enhance the civic landscape.

PUBLIC ART AS PUBLIC PROCESS

Although many projects today are funded by percent-for-art legislation, others are funded by developers or corporations to cite a building's uniqueness and high quality and enhance the surrounding community and the working space of employees. Ideally, the budget is a percentage of the entire construction budget, planned for early in the project's conception. Spending 0.5–2% is customary and realistic. The actual amount can be calculated based on the square-foot rental or sales costs of the building. High rents in an upscale building mandate a higher percentage of the funds be spent on art. No matter how a project is funded, planning a budget is a responsibility shared by all participants. The artist requires sufficient money to create and construct a work of appropriate, durable, and maintainable materials on a scale relevant to the architectural site. Treating the artist as a working professional gives art dignity and value that is reflected ultimately in public acceptance and appreciation of art. The budget is apportioned to cover artist's fees, materials, fabrication, administrative costs, legal fees, travel, engineering, site preparation, installation, shipping, and insurance. The client's payments in progress are protected by product insurance because artists require substantial start-up funds.

Contracts between the artist and client are best written in clear language and signed before any work begins. Contracts state responsibilities of all parties and anticipate problems with sensitive mechanisms for solving them. In disagreements, contractual arbitration is the method of choice. Copyright and reproduction rights customarily stay with the artist, with use of the image for public relations a client right. Maintenance instructions must be given by the artist. Responsibility for restoration or repairs is the client's, who is required to seek the advice of the artist, thus ensuring the integrity of the art, the artist's reputation, and the value of the artwork.

Contrary to popular myth, artists are disciplined workers who are focused on their art. They will keep realistic budgets and time schedules. As professionals, they learn about the technical aspects and material requirements of the work and site. Unique about artists who work in a public context is their conviction that people can be educated by the artwork. Robert Irwin, one of the major public artists working today says "my highest ambition . . . is, to make you see a little bit more tomorrow than you saw today" (12).

Defining clearly the requirements and roles of participants as part of the commission process is the way for all to understand and appreciate each other's role. In many cities, contemporary-art curators at museums are asked to advise or act as panelists on public art committees, thus directly influencing the quality of art selected. The client as an individual supporter of a project seeks to place art in a public area for reasons of civic philanthropy and as a statement of one's own importance. The government has a dual role as a supporter of artists and of the arts constituency and has responsibility for community enhancement. The developer and corporation that place the art in a publicly visible and accessible place support art with enlightened self-interest. A beautiful and exciting artwork can attract affluent tenants, encourage employee creativity and productivity, and demonstrate corporate interest in the community and the environment.

THE COMMISSION PROCESS AFFECTS THE QUALITY OF ART

Successful public art projects do not happen by chance. They are planned, and the procedures followed affect the quality of the art commissioned. Of equal importance are the artist selection process and management of the project as it is implemented and installed. Public art is public event, and the public is served when it is considered and communicated with during the entire process from inception to dedication (13).

The commission process engages all the players—the artist, the architect, the client, and the community. Inherent in it are all the frustrations, achievements, and satisfactions one can imagine would happen before contemporary art of museum quality is brought into the daily lives of the general public.

Selection of the artist is the most important decision in the commission process. The quality of the art, its creative integrity, and its appropriateness to the architecture, spatial environment, and function are essential. Accessibility for the user community is an additional critical factor for public success.

The experience gained by the Arts Endowment and GSA with selecting artists through panels has proved invaluable to the commissioning agencies; civic and corporate. They recommend that each panel include art professionals with curatorial knowledge of contemporary regional, national, and international artists. Architects and landscape architects can bring knowledge of appropriate scale, siting, and materials to the panel's evaluation of artists. Analyzing sites for public art is best accomplished as a collaborative function, including the art and architect professionals and the public—the ultimate user or viewer.

Artist selection evolves through a series of educational presentations of many kinds of art projects, historical and contemporary. The actual selection may be based directly on past work of artists or a competition. Limited competitions ask a selected number of qualified artists. Open competitions advertise publicly and, for government groups, are politically viewed as more democratic.

As with architectural competitions, art competitions for public art can inspire adventurous and unusually imaginative entries. More often, it has been documented, the mediocre, familiar entry can become the winning choice. Competitions, if well-conceived, have value as community events that draw positive attention to public art. They are administratively expensive and can deplete funds better spent for artwork.

Competitions offer inexperienced younger artists great challenge and visibility. However, mature, highly qualified artists often refuse to compete. For them, competitions are expensive and time-consuming. Thus projects based on competitions may lose the participation of more qualified artists.

Crucial to a successful project is its management. Public art consultants or coordinators have the pivotal role of guiding the process from selection of artists to installation. They try to synthesize all the participants needs. They help to identify the human factors, establish and maintain a positive climate, and expedite contract negotiations, fabrication, site planning and preparation, shipping, insurance, and installation, acting as liaison between everyone from lawyers to artists, to clients to engineers and fabricators. The consultant, in the interests of the project, communicates with appropriate government agencies or construction company subcontractors.

The coordinator can be an independent public art consultant or a staff person in the government or corporation. The coordinator has the role of helping the client and/or community to realize that the creation of an artwork from maquette to installation at the site entails awareness of the fabrication process, as well as a leap of faith in the artist's evolution of the final work.

The commission process anticipates problems inherent in the uniqueness of the art commission and recognizes appropriate solutions. Appreciated artists and satisfied clients more often make public art of lasting value. Creative tension is not always a negative. Michelangelo and Pope Julius were known to argue continuously, perhaps energizing creativity. They both sought excellence.

Artists, traditionally solo workers, find it stimulating to work in the public context and in collaboration with other art professionals. It can propel their work in significant new and fresh directions and media. Artists, furthermore, are challenged by the social, political, and psychological aspects of the public art process that enhances the content and fecundity of their art.

CHRISTO'S PROJECTS DEFINE THE ART OF THE COMMISSION PROCESS

Christo, the artist who surrounded eleven islands, ran 24.5 miles of fence over hills and valleys, and will place in 1991 thousands of umbrellas simultaneously in Japan and the Western United States, took over 10 years to gain permission to wrap the historic Pont Neuf bridge in Paris in 1985. As with all of Christo's monumental environmental projects, it was commissioned by the artist and was a premiere cultural event for Parisiens and art people who flew in from all over the world.

Wrapping the bridge involved thousands of fabric weavers, laborers, environmentalists, and engineers. It spawned museum exhibitions and television coverage worldwide. The Pont Neuf is now unwrapped, but postcards of the event sell along with those of the Eiffel Tower and Notre Dame (Fig. 33).

Christo's art is all about the politics of public art commissions. The public or private process he undertakes with patience and meticulous planning involves lawyers,

Figure 33. Christo, "Pont Neuf Wrapped," Paris, France, 1975–1985. Copyright Christo 1985. Photograph by Wolfgang Volz.

environmentalists, government agencies, officials, and citizens as participants and viewers. The art event is managed and orchestrated by Jeanne-Claude, his wife. The project is funded solely by the artist through the sale of his drawings of the projects. Christo never takes funds from any other sources. The art of Christo is a model of public art as public process and mirrors the psychological, sociological, and political aspects of every public art commission as well as being feats of engineering and aesthetics that articulate the landscape or urban environment.

ARTISTS AND ARCHITECTS—CHALLENGES IN COLLABORATION

Collaboration between artists and architects is a significant issue in public art. Of note is the important role architects have and continue to play in the selection and installation of public art. Among the best projects are those that have been conceived by artists and architects during the early design stages, resulting in successfully integrated artworks. Because of the enormous undertaking, expense, and public nature of such projects, they depend on the goodwill and cooperation between artists, architects, engineers, city officials, and business and community members. Such collaborations foster provocative ways of spatial perception and imaginative solutions to urban dilemmas.

Historically, architects selected the sites, the media of the artwork, and an artist whose work conformed to the limitations of the site. Robert Smithson was one of the first modern public artists to collaborate with architects as part of a conceptual design team. In 1966, Smithson was paid a stipend by architects Tibbets-Abbott, McCarthy to help them develop a master plan for the Dallas/Ft. Worth airport as a place for the exhibition of artwork. Although much of what was planned for that facility never happened, 20 years later transportation facilities are pursuing similar collaborative planning.

Art that is created collaboratively establishes a new goal for the art of our time. The goal is not to display works merely because they are decorative adjuncts in an urban environment, regardless of their merit, but rather to create situations that represent qualitative involvement in the use of space at the public's disposal: "In other words . . . urgently find new approaches and perspectives in order to redefine the artists' contribution to the utilization of public space" (13). Jean-Christophe Ammann, the critic, lists the few projects that in his view meet these criteria for art in public spaces (14): works by Robert Morris, Siah Armajani, Maria Nordman, and Jean Tinguely. It is these and other publicly-oriented artists, working as creative equals in an atmosphere of mutual respect with other professionals of similar standards, such as architects or urban designers, who establish the new criteria.

One of the earliest collaborations was David von Schlegell's monumental sitework done in 1972 with Henry Cobb of I. M. Pei & Partners for Harbor Towers Apartments on Boston's waterfront. "The buildings came first and I adapted to what was given," said von Schlegell, "but Cobb involved himself in my choices, and I responded to

his thoughts. He rejected my first proposal. It was a mistake and I will always be grateful for his insight" (15) (Fig. 34).

Procedures that inhibit excellence and deactivate creative energy can discourage the best artists and architects from the idea of conceptual collaboration. In addition, there are forces weighing heavily against artists who move into areas traditionally reserved for architects and landscape architects. Several years ago, at a joint conference of the Skowhegan Art School and the AIA Design Committee, artist Richard Serra established the tone of the meeting by stating flatly, "the architect is the enemy" (15). He was referring, no doubt, to his confrontation with architect Robert Venturi over their conflicting proposals for the Pennsylvania Avenue Redevelopment in Washington, D.C. Venturi pushed his own design, two pylons, as an urban design solution; Serra proposed a sculptural one. In 1988, another solution was found for the Pennsylvania Avenue site. Artist Vito Acconci and architect Stephen Holl are conceptually collaborating on a functional and environmental artwork. According to Acconci (15):

Collaboration, while bringing roles together, is forced to separate roles and define them, in order to prevent slippage from one to the other (since, if the roles are the same to begin with, you couldn't tell one from the other, there'd be no one left to collaborate). Collaboration is a conservative impulse, it retains definition, preserves the traditions of a particular discipline. Collaboration is analytic and not mystical (by definition it keeps to two, it never comes down to one).

The architect defends to the death the notion of "space" (and, hence, the notions of expansiveness, expansion, abstraction); the sculptor defends to the death the notion of "statue," (and, hence, the notions of condensation, home, figuration).

Plan, the bird's-eye view (represented by architecture) collides with monument, the close-up (represented by sculpture). "Beings" (sculpture) come into collision with "being there" (architecture). (Of course, all the while, the roles of artist and architect might be shared by one and the same person; and, of course, all the while each participant might be despising his/her own discipline and dreaming of the other.)

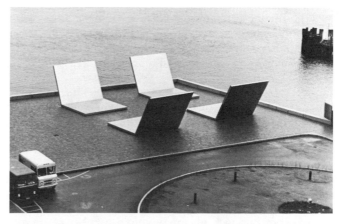

Figure 34. David Von Schlegell, "Harbor Towers," stainless steel, 60 × 60 × 16 ft, 1973. Commissioned by the Boston Redevelopment Authority. Architect: I. M. Pei. Courtesy of David Von Schlegell.

Originality as individual characteristics is also de-emphasized. The differing beliefs of many artists and architects are also problematic. For the Jerome Weisner Center at MIT, I. M. Pei and partners collaborated with three artists: Kenneth Noland, Scott Burton, and Richard Fleischner. It was said about the project that the artists tended to engage the space directly, whereas the architects conceived and refined their designs and plans (16). Architects are accustomed to creating over a long period of time, accommodating the stops and starts inherent in the building process. Artists usually cannot, or will not, work for years on a single concept. The artist Jackie Ferrara speaks for many artists when she says "As soon as I visit a site I cannot help but begin to think about solutions (15)." Unlike architects, Ferrara finds it difficult to postpone action or plan to work intensively to create within a limited, designated time period.

How can architects assist artists in fully expressing their ideal works of art? Lee Harris Pomeroy, architect for the landmark Fulton Street subway station in Manhattan, recognized early on that an environmental artist could bring a fresh and unencumbered viewpoint to the design of the station without compromising the integrity of the historic tile motifs depicting Fulton's steamboat. "Where the architect stresses social and technical issues, artists can supply the intuitive substance that comes from their more abstract thinking," said Pomeroy (15). Having been included in the beginning of the design process, the artist Nancy Holt was able to develop an integrated "light" system that was a functioning artwork for the ceiling of the subway corridor (Fig. 35). Although not a conceptual collaboration, this project allowed the artist and architect to inform each other's creative viewpoint. Pomeroy was also able to intervene for the artist with the subway authorities, explaining technically how the eccentricities of the artwork were possible.

Holt, who has completed many public art projects, defines three different modes of collaboration. In the first, two equal professionals conceptually collaborate to create a unique work that is greater than each could have done separately. The second is a correlative relationship, in which the artist and architect inform each other's work and each brings his or her own special training, ability, and intelligence to the project. The third mode is cooperative collaboration, a working team including construction people, fabricators, architects, landscape architects, engineers, community workers and representatives of civic institutions (15).

Holt's *Dark Star Park* in Rosslyn, Virginia, is a primary example of this form of collaboration—one that Holt considers particularly productive and satisfying. Mark Wilkenson, Gunite specialist of Paddock Pools who helped fabricate the sculptural spheres for the park, said, "When Nancy walked through the door, the fun started" (17). Nancy's workmen/collaborators felt that she added another dimension to their lives.

The NOAA (National Oceanic and Atmospheric Administration) project, also involving a number of artists, was successful both visually and functionally. It strayed, however, from the original intentions of being a collaboration. Instead, there is a synthesis of landscape amenities

Figure 35. Nancy Holt, "Astral Grating," lights and grating. Fulton Street Station, MTA New York, 1987. Architect: Lee Harris Pomeroy. Courtesy of Nancy Holt.

and individual site-specific works, including seating, waterfront landings, sound sculpture, a viewing place, and a pedestrian bridge. Each of the five artists (Scott Burton, Siah Armajani, Doug Hollis, Martin Puryear, and George Trakas) staked out their own territory after a few meetings. The harmony of the waterfront environment may be a result of the sensitivity of the selection committee and its knowledge about these artists' work and the procedures that involved the community as advisers to the artists from the beginning (Fig. 36, 37). Therefore artists can act as design catalysts for architectural planning groups by challenging current thinking about art in the environment: the workspace, civic space, or play space.

LANDSCAPE ARCHITECTS AS COLLABORATORS

Ideal collaborators for artists are landscape architects, who are accustomed to being supporters and embellishers of larger design ideas. For example, the Dutch developers Savage/Fogarty Companies decided to incorporate art into the design of a waterfront plaza for the Transpotomac Canal Center, a four-building office and retail complex in Alexandria, Virginia, after the design was completed. After consulting with a committee composed of Washington-based museum curators and Donald Thalacker, Director

Figure 36. Doug Hollis, "A Sound Garden" (detail), National Oceanographic and Atmospheric Agency (NOAA) Seattle, Wash., 1983. Courtesy of Doug Hollis.

of the GSA Fine Arts Program, the developers selected French artists Anne and Patrick Poirier, whose mythologically inspired marble and bronze sculptures they thought ideally suited to the classical style of the Washington, D.C. area.

"The Poiriers didn't simply put sculptures in the landscape," asserts M. Paul Friedberg, the landscape architect who collaborated with them from the beginning. "In fact, it was the re-formation of the landscape, a complete narrative of birth and regeneration experienced through waterways, pools, and cascading falls" (18).

Figure 37. George Trakas, "Berth Haven," (detail) National Oceanographic and Atmospheric Agency (NOAA), Seattle, Wash., 1981–1983. Courtesy of George Trakas. Photograph by Colleen Chartier, *Art on File*.

Figure 38. Anne and Patrick Poirier with M. Paul Friedberg, "Promenade Classique," marble, bronze, water, Transpotomac Canal Center, Alexandria, Va., 1986. Courtesy of the Savage Fogarty Companies.

Comprising a sequence of sculptural elements, fountains, brick-paved paths, cascading stairwells, and enveloping trees, the Poiriers' waterfront plaza is the centerpiece of Transpotomac Canal Center. The work offers the pedestrian an invitation to stroll down to the waters of the Potomac (19).

The artists took full and fitting advantage of the chance to relate the Virginia shoreline to the not-so-distant artifacts of the capital city. Consequently, the park now moves to the river in axial gesture reminiscent of L'Enfant's plan of Washington. From a birch-tree island in the center of the building complex, the eye is led on a straight line toward the tip of the obelisk at riverside. And where the eye leads in this case, feet will certainly follow, for the sequence of spaces is at once enticing and clear. A reflecting pool framed by paved walkways and double rows of cherry trees progresses to an overlook where the view is further framed by two large slabs of marble silhouetted against the sky. Two sweeping stairwells lead down to a grotto pool from which a semicircle of amphitheater seats/steps leads to the 30-ft. high marble obelisk (19) (Figs. 38 and 39).

Figure 39. Anne and Patrick Poirier with M. Paul Friedberg, "Promenade Classique," marble, bronze, water, Transpotomac Canal Center, Alexandria, Va., 1986. Courtesy of the Savage Fogarty Companies. Photograph by Joyce P. Schwartz.

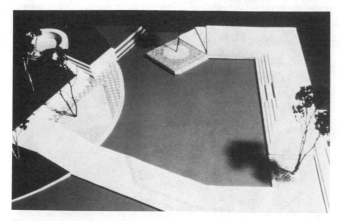

Figure 40. Jackie Ferrara with M. Paul Friedberg, "Belvedere" (model). Courtesy of J. Ferrara.

M. Paul Friedberg, has designed several projects with artist Jackie Ferrara (Fig. 40). He also worked in unison with Scott Burton, Siah Armajani, and architect Cesar Pelli in New York City's Battery Park City: a public/private mixed-use development where intent is to provide residents, office workers, tourists, and visitors the pleasures of a variety of public areas and major amenities as a coordinated sense of unified yet distinct spaces.

At Battery Park City, artist Mary Miss collaborated with Susan Child, landscape architect, and Stanton Eckstut, architect, to design a 3-acre site at South Cove that invites the public to walk on the waterfront. A sculptural *Widow's Walk* in the configuration of the *Statue of Liberty's* crown is the best vantage point to see that Lady and New York harbor (Fig. 41).

THE ROLE OF ART IN URBAN PLANNING

Percent-for-art legislation affects the economies of cities. David Rockefeller, President of Chase Manhattan Bank, said: "Diminished cultural activity can bring economic chaos to a city, affecting not only business specifically dependent on tourism such as hotels, restaurants and stores, but all commercial enterprises (5)." In further support of percent-for-art legislation as a way of improving the economy of cities, Robert Montgomery and Patricia C. Jones, President and Vice-president of the Alliance for the Arts said (20): "The arts generate six billion dollars a year for New York City . . . It is not a frill. The arts attract more than 13 million tourists to the city . . . they are one of the main reasons that corporations and their highly skilled, tax-paying employees move to and remain in the area."

Combined public and private funding is becoming a major spur for the acquisition of public art. Art and cultural development are centerpieces of urban renewal and development of the multiuse community. A system of joint policy-making that includes the artist as a peer with architects, city planners, landscapists, and developers is becoming a reality as requests for urban-planning proposals include artists and public art consultants as team members.

That artists predicted their ability and willingness to participate in public art was summarized by Carl Andre at the time of The Jewish Museum's exhibition "Primary Structures" in 1966. Andre defined sculpture's past, present, and future: sculpture as form, referring to traditional studio object sculpture prior to minimalism; sculpture as structure, alluding to the work of the day included in the exhibition; and, finally, sculpture as place, defining his own sculptural concerns at the time and accurately forecasting the direction to be pursued by sculptors over the next two decades. The progression from form, to structure, to place conveys an increasing engagement of space that parallels twentieth-century sculpture's development from the discrete object removed from its pedestal, to the minimal structure that shares or crowds the space, to environmental or site sculpture that is integrated with the space and transforms it in a way that creates a new place for the viewer (21).

(a)   (b)

Figure 41. Mary Miss, The South Cove, Battery Park City, New York, 1988. **(a)** Aerial view; **(b)** ground view. Architect: Stanton Eckstut. Landscape Architect: Susan Child. Courtesy of Mary Miss.

PUBLIC ART AND THE REVITALIZATION OF URBAN LIFE

The development of percent-for-art legislation closely followed the evolution of contemporary urban renewal in the 1980s; the revitalization of main streets lost in the suburbanization of America during the 1950s, and renewed townscapes viewed as stages for art, architecture, and landscape. The town square, with its bandstand and war memorial, is redesigned as a communal center. There is a return to main street, away from the decentralized, homogeneous suburban malls that had become America's town centers.

The urban planner Kevin Lynch has perhaps influenced the direction of urban design more than anyone else in America. He understands that "city-making is a fine art . . . the city is an intended landscape . . . Paris, Rome are cities that are deliberate acts of city design . . . (26)." He describes the artist as someone who creates an object or event to convey meanings or feelings to a critical audience. He speaks of "city design as concerned with continuous change, a plurality of clients, conflict and participation . . . leaving room for the creative act and the aesthetic response. It should be possible to create new forms and styles and to convey meanings and feelings worthy of critical judgement. . . . Programs and criteria are effective ways of improving the quality of everyday life even if their composition is a rational exercise rather than a creative act. Creative artists work within them, and are supported by them. I am convinced of their importance, and city planning is at least beginning to move in this direction" (22).

Lynch describes a rationale for urban design that must include the visual artist. He identifies the special thinking of artists as necessary in creating great cities. Great cities link citizen and place, enhance the significance of everyday life, and reinforce the identity of the group and self: "I am the citizen of no mean city" (22). Ordinary citizens participate in making special city images: "Images that arise from changes in perception as well as physical changes. Newspaper critiques, town trails, new view points or entrances, painters' or designers' visions, or the enthusiasms of renovators, all remold a city's image" (22). Gyorgy Kepes, Director of Visual Studies at MIT has said (23):

> Art is both a way to relate to life and a way to improve it. It is best experienced not only in the historical categories of a museum, but in the actual situations in which people live. *Our lives should become more artful.* Everyone should become involved not only in the possession or experience of art works but also in the process of creating art. The way to learn about making (or undertaking) art is through contact with artists and art processes. The goal is the development of individual creativity. When art is examined for its own sake outside the competitive institutional context, collaboration between artists offers reward possibilities.

PUBLICLY ACCESSIBLE ART IN URBAN PLACES: LIGHT, WATER, SOUND

Categories of artwork that are accessible to the public and particularly relevant to the experience of public urban spaces are artworks involving water, sound, and light. Gyorgy Kepes says that sensory quality is a legitimate and necessary concern of city planning. Criteria for the immediate, sensuous, psychological effects of the environment should certainly be added to all those other effects that are considered when setting city policy. Area programs should deal with shape, sound, smell, climate, color, texture, symbols, space, and sequence, as well as with use, access, bulk, and the like. Fountains and sound and light art take on contemporary meaning when thought of in terms of urban and civic problems such as pollution, visual blight, and sensory deprivation. Public monuments directed toward the future not the past see water-purification and waste disposal as functions of art, fountains, and earthworks (23): "The urban world is a fabric of acoustical experience with contrasts, complementary harmonies and thresholds of entrances at both the loudest and quietest of the acoustical spectrum." Artists such as Max Neuhaus, Doug Hollis, and Liz Phillips create visual sound works for inner cities, parks, transportation facilities, universities, and other sites.

Great fountains and intimate waterworks are found throughout Europe. In the 1920s the enlightened businessman J. Nicholas visited Spain and came home to Kansas City, Missouri, to build County Club Plaza, America's first shopping mall. He copied decorative Moorish tiles and installed multiple fountains, making his city second only to Rome in the number of its fountains. Great contemporary fountains include the active water-spouting machines of Jean Tinguely who with Niki de St. Phalle, the *Stravinsky Fountain* at Centre Georges Pompidou in Paris (Fig. 42). Cesar Pelli commissioned Tinguely to create a fountain for a mall in Columbus, Indiana; it is Tinguely's only public work in America.

Light artists such as Chryssa identified city lights as subjects for neon art. Stephen Antonakos, a minimalists sculptor, has created monumental neon works in cities around the world for airports, train stations, theaters, office buildings, and schools (Fig. 43). Charles Ross transforms public places with multiprism light sculptures. In Dallas, Wynn-Jackson Corporation commissioned Ross to

Figure 42. Jean Tinguely and Niki de St. Phalle, "Fontaine Stravinsky," Centre Pompidou, Paris, France. Courtesy of Jean Tingueley. Photograph by David T. Schwartz.

Figure 43. Stephen Antonakos, "Neon for Charles Street Station," Baltimore MTA, Baltimore, Md., 1979–1983. Courtesy of Stephen Antonakos.

build a 36-prism sculpture at the Plaza of the Americas, a retail–hotel–office complex. The ever-changing color spectrum unifies and activates the total environment (Fig. 44).

CONTROVERSY IN PUBLIC ART

A statue of Captain Alfred Dreyfus, the nineteenth-century victim of French anti-Semitism, was completed in

Figure 44. Charles Ross, "Lines of Light/Rays of Color," 36 plexiglass prisms, Plaza of the Americas, Dallas, Texas, 1985. Courtesy of Charles Ross. Photograph by Elizabeth Ginsberg.

Paris in 1985. It was stored by the mayor of Paris, Jacques Chirac for two years while Jack Lang, the French Minister of Culture (1981–1986) who commissioned the work and others by Anne and Patrick Poirier, Gerard Garouste, and Pol Bury was out of office. When the Socialists returned, the statue by Tim, a French political cartoonist, was immediately installed by the returning Lang in the Tuileries' City Gardens. "I wanted to repair an injustice. The right of an artist is to be seen by the people, and Tim was refused this right," said Lang (16).

Lang's office overlooks the architectural spaces of the colonnaded Palais Royale, where he had commissioned Daniel Buren's contemporary sculpture of varied sized, boldly-striped columns that inflamed many. Visitors to Palais Royale see an environment that invites people to sit, skate, walk, and cycle around and note similarities and differences between modern art and historic architecture (Fig. 45).

One of France's most controversial works is I. M. Pei's glass pyramid, "a structure that has been denounced by many critics as destroying the beauty of the Louvre." This is a controversy, however, that despite his mood of conciliation, Mr. Lang welcomed. "I think that when people see the pyramid they will say: 'It is only this? It is not bigger?' And perhaps they will protest because it is not sufficiently high. And in ten years they will organize a committee to ask the Minister of Culture to protect this pyramid as a historical monument." (16) That this glass pyramid closely resembles a well-known sculpture concept by contemporary artist Agnes Denes adds an additional controversy over both the aesthetic idea and their source.

Politics as a cause of public art controversy in France has a long history. Clemenceau, when Prime Minister of France, asked Claude Monet to create a series of paintings to be installed in the Hôtel de Ville, a government building, Monet proceeded, only to find when Clemenceau was in the project was on again. When Clemenceau was out, the project was off. For world art lovers the timing was bad. Clemenceau died before the paintings could be installed permanently.

Rodin, the master of modernist sculpture, had his share of public art controversy. His *Balzac* was much maligned in all its versions, robed and unrobed. Fifty-one years passed between the completion of the model and the unveiling of the bronze *Balzac*. It was installed at the corner of Boulevards Montparnasse and Raspail in Paris on July 2, 1939—18 years after Rodin died. While the controversy was still raging, Rodin told his friends (25): "I no longer fight for my sculpture. It has been able to defend itself for a long time . . . if truth is imperishable, I predict that my statue will make its own way . . . This work that men ridicule . . . is the result of my whole life."

The Calais Municipal Art Committee was offended by the attitude struck by the six figures in Rodin's *Burgers of Calais*. The committee wanted Rodin to vary the sizes of the figures, and to stick more closely to accurate historical depictions of the figures (25). Of art historical significance is that Rodin took this monument off the pedestal. He wanted the six burgers at the ground or human level (Fig. 46). The project was put off until 1893. It was installed in Calais in 1895.

Figure 45. Daniel Buren, "Palais Royale," Paris, France. Courtesy of the John Weber Gallery. Photograph by Joyce P. Schwartz.

Bronze versions of *Burgers of Calais* now exist in public and private collections throughout the world: Brussels, Copenhagen, Paris, London, Basel, Tokyo, Los Angeles, Philadelphia, and Washington, D.C.

THE TILTED ARC CONTROVERSY

Richard Serra's monumental sculpture *Tilted Arc* may become the landmark case regarding contemporary public art controversy (Fig. 47). It is sited on the plaza of the Jacob Javits Federal Building in New York City, a not very distinguished public space.

Morris Ordover, a Social Security Administrator at the public hearings seeking removal of the sculpture may have had Rodin's sculptures in mind. He testified "art is liked or disliked according to individual taste. . . . yet no one can dispute that our museums are filled with art that has survived public opinion" (26).

Figure 46. Auguste Rodin, "Burghers of Calais." Courtesy of Rosenthal Art Slides.

Figure 47. Richard Serra, "Tilted Arc," steel, Foley Square, New York. Photograph by Richard Serra.

Commissioned by the federal government under procedures established by the art-in-architecture program of the General Services Administration, *Tilted Arc* became an embarrassment to the government when the employees of the Javits office building decided they did not want that enormous wall of steel cutting across their plaza. Complaints ranged from its being an eyesore, an attraction for vagrants, and that it prevented public use of the plaza. A petition with 1300 signatures of federal employees requested removal of the sculpture (26).

The New York Regional Head of GSA, William Diamond, an avowed critic of Serra's work, convened a hearing that lasted 3 days, March 6–8, 1985, in Manhattan. A five-member panel selected by Diamond, who acted as chairman, heard the testimony of 181 people, 118 spoke in favor of retaining the sculpture at the site; 63 urged removal. The final decision shocked the art world but not the public: the panel recommended four-to-one that the sculpture be relocated. In the aftermath of the hearings, issues of history, ideology, public policy and the legal and moral rights of artist intersect and diverge in confusion and disagreeable debate in which underlying issues are never made explicit. The tribulation of *Tilted Arc* brings into focus the attitudes and institutions that have emerged in the past 25 years to serve a national audience for the arts.

It was officially recommended that *Tilted Arc* be relocated. The then GSA Commissioner, Dwight Ink, asked the National Endowment for the Arts to establish a committee to review proposed new sites.

Serra's attorney, Gustave Harrow, filed a 30 million dollar lawsuit against the GSA. The resolution of Serra's case was still unclear in late 1988. Serra's lawsuit has been rejected. Regarding relocation, self-respecting museums or universities with the space for a monumental work will not take it without Serra's approval. And he was not inclined to give it.

Is the artist right to insist on retention, if the immediate public is offended? Conversely, should public art be subjected to pressures of public opinion when relocation threatens freedom of art? Will the opposition disappear with the passage of time as with Rodin? Other cases are coming up before the courts. A park official plowed under an environmental sculpture by Alan Sonfist in St. Louis. In the state of Washington, murals in the legislature chambers by Michael Spofford were covered with draperies by lawmakers. Alden Mason's murals were removed because they did not match the color scheme. In 1987, in a court case, Judge Terence Carroll rendered in favor of the artist saying that site-specific art is owned by the public independent of the artist and has a right to be displayed aesthetically (27): "In our society which values free expression, art has a right to exist." Public art is on trial. The issues remain to be resolved.

THE VIETNAM MEMORIAL

The controversy over the Vietnam Veterans Memorial in Washington, D.C., is still crucial and unresolved. The work was installed in 1982 after an open, nationwide com-

Figure 48. Maya Lin, Vietnam Veterans Memorial, Washington, D.C. Photograph by Joyce P. Schwartz.

petition for which there were 2573 entries. A professional committee selected and commissioned the first-prize winner, Maya Lin, a 21-year-old Chinese-American woman studying architecture at Yale University. Its minimalist form, "entering the earth rather than skyward," resembled a Richard Serra work (Fig. 48). Serra was, in fact, one of Lin's teachers (28).

This memorial is public art in the truest sense. It is on shared public ground and implies a consensus of values about patriotism and honor among and toward those who served in combat. Its designated site, by congressional legislation, is on the mall in West Potomac Park, 600 ft from the Lincoln Memorial. The work of grand materials, integral and harmonious with the site, "frees visitors from the site and sound of traffic" (28).

Lin's design has been praised by the art community and many veterans and their families who visit seeking out names written chronologically, referring to date of death, rather than alphabetically.

Some veterans envisioned a more heroic work, and a group lobbied for a figurative work of three soldiers by sculptor Frederick Hart, the third-prize winner. It was finally installed, in view of but away from the black granite wall (Fig. 49).

What is disturbing to some is that the Veteran's Committee was willing to sacrifice the integrity of its visual statement, to satisfy a small, vocal constituency. In 1988, lobbying for a female nurse's statue was begun. At no time has the artist been consulted about any additions or changes.

There is a boundary between rejecting work outright, which was not done here, or altering it to a degree affecting its original concept. However, the power of Maya Lin's memorial seems to be such that it withstands these intrusions.

One of the most important components of the moral right concept is the integrity of the art. "Distortion or misrepresentation of the work," according to John Henry Merryman (29), "affects the artist's artistic identity, personality and honor and thus imparts a legally protected personality interest." California and New York have a

Figure 49. Frederic Hart, Vietnam Veterans Memorial, bronze, Washington, D.C. Photograph by Joyce P. Schwartz.

form of moral right laws. Other states are considering it. In Europe such laws are more common.

Attorney Barbara Hoffman, who headed a subcommittee on public art law for the Association of the Bar of the City of New York, says (26) "You have the government owning works of art, so the question is: what limitations are imposed . . . when that property is art? Are there limitations that arise from artists' rights? . . . Community concerns? We are talking about private property concepts as they relate to government ownership of art that has to include public intent as well as artists."

Furthermore, controversy sparks great awareness on the part of the many commissioning parties. Pressures are exerted on artists to give away these rights if the client, public or corporate, is concerned about their property rights.

Lawyers reviewing a contract between artist Vito Acconci and Coca-Cola, U.S.A. Atlanta, cited the Serra controversy when they refused to agree to the site-specific sculpture's right to permanence if the chairman of the board wanted it removed for any reason. The artist's model had been completed and approved. Anxious to realize this work, Acconci reluctantly agreed to sign away his "moral right." The only condition he insisted on, and it was agreed to, was his having the opportunity to address Coca-Cola employees about the work before it was removed. Fortunately, the sculpture was positively received. Because it was designed around existing architectural columns in the space, removal would have totally destroyed the work. The corporation believed that although it was conceptually a "public" work, it was in the interior of one of their buildings, therefore not truly "public" (Fig. 50).

THE FUTURE OF PUBLIC ART

Art of our time has been characterized as pluralistic (having many images). Public art is no less so. Where functional urban art has prevailed in the 1980s, artists are again making objects that can become monumental.

As American artists seek to inspire, they once again make monuments that, compete with the land, which is monumental; the deserts, national parks, prairies, and mountains. Earthworks may be the significant contribution, but the remaking of cities moves artists to create the civic monument again. The artist Marisol has considered creating a contemporary man (or woman) seated on a horse.

The Basque sculptor Chillida built a sculptural plaza for a Spanish town square to display his own sculptures as well as create spaces for pedestrian activity (Fig. 51).

The young artists of the 1980s reflect a contemporary dependence on a media-oriented society where they get

Figure 50. Vito Acconci, "Garden of Columns," 13 painted fiber glass columns, goldfish, water, plants, lights, Coca Cola USA Town Square, Atlanta, Ga., 1986. Courtesy of the Barbara Gladstone Gallery.

Figure 51. Chillida, "Plaza de los Fuevos," Vitoria Basque Country, Spain, 1973–1980. Courtesy of the José Tasende Gallery, La Jolla, Calif.

information from moving signs of light and billboards, as well as television. For artist Jenny Holzer, her private art is public art. At the Las Vegas airport she recreated ticker-tape signage (Fig. 52). Les Levine and Keith Haring put art in subways and buses that appears to be no different from advertising. Nam June Paik's video installations mimic involvement with quickly moving images as content. His works appear in airports and hotels, a reminder of Marshall McLuhan's "the medium is the message."

Public art is for everyone. It is not elitist. It is environmental, architectural, functional, monumental, commemorative, and communicative, when it is made by artists of unique personal vision and content who prefer to work in a public context. They are artists who understand scale, proportion, and durability of materials.

Public art can have lasting value to society. Controversy slows its progress, but when the art meets quality as a criterion, it merely draws attention to it and educates. Benign, insignificant art rarely becomes controversial. "Just as mediocre, crude architectural structures have a pernicious importance in our environment (for they shape the world around us), works of art in public spaces that are second-rate imitations add to a dismal landscape (31)."

Figure 52. Jenny Holzer, "Selections from *Truisms*" 1986 at Baggage carousel, McCarran International Airport, Las Vegas, Nevada. Courtesy of the Barbara Gladstone Gallery, New York.

BIBLIOGRAPHY

1. C. Thacker, *The History of Gardens,* University of California Press, Berkeley, 1979.
2. B. O'Doherty, "Public Art in The Government: A Progress Report," *Art in America* (May 1974).
3. Art-in-Architecture Program, General Services Administration, Washington, D.C., 1978.
4. From testimony in favor of percent-for-art legislation, New York City, 1982.
5. D. Green, *Percent for Art New Legislation Can Integrate Art and Architecture,* Western States Arts Foundation, Denver, 1976.
6. L. Lerup, "Below Surface," *Places* 1 (3) (Spring 1984).
7. J. C. Brown, H. P. Stom, D. Collens, *Sculpture at Storm King,* Cross River Press, Ltd., New York, 1980.
8. A. Balfour, *Rockfeller Center Architecture as Theater,* McGraw-Hill Inc., New York, 1978.
9. *The New York Times.*
10. S. Craig, "The Artist's Signature," *Piedmont Airline Magazine,* 30 (Oct. 1987).
11. N. Holt, ed., *The Writings of Robert Smithson,* New York University Press, New York, 1979.
12. M. Esterow, "How Public Art Becomes a Political Hot Potato," *Art News* (January 1986).
13. J. P. Schwartz, "Practice: Make that Percent for Art Pay Off," *Architectural Record* (May 1988).
14. J. C. Amman, "Art in Public Places," *Parkett* 2 (July 1984).
15. J. P. Schwartz, ed., *Artists and Architects, Challenges in Collaboration,* Cleveland Center for Contemporary Art, Cleveland, Ohio, 1985.
16. M.I.T. Committee for the Visual Arts, *Artists and Architects Collaborate: Designing the Weisner Building,* M.I.T. Press.
17. "Rossylyn's New Parks," *Washington Post* (Sept. 17, 1983).
18. G. Sargeant, "Promenade Classique," *Sculpture International Magazine* (Jan./Feb 1987).
19. B. Forgey, "The Winning Waterfront," *Washington Post* (October 18, 1986).
20. "Art Complex Planned in New Tower," *The New York Times* (May 14, 1985).
21. D. Bourdon, *The. . . .Art of Carl Andre,* La Jolla Museum of Art, La Jolla, Calif., October 1986.
22. K. Lynch, "The Immature Arts of Urban Design," *Places,* 1 (3) (Spring 1984).
23. G. Kepes, "Art and the Ecological Consciousness," *Arts of the Environment,* George Braziller, New York, 1970.
24. "Jack Lang, Creatively Engage, Plots France's Cultural Future, *The New York Times* (July 26, 1988).
25. J. F. Chabrun, *Auguste Rodin,* Viking Press, New York, 1967, pp. 107, 115.
26. S. Jordan, L. Parr, R. Porter, G. Storey, eds., "The Tilted Arc on Trial," in *Public Art/Public Controversy,* ACA Books, New York, 1987.
27. *Ibid.,* p. 184.
28. J. Pachner, Treatise on the Vietnam Memorial, 1982, "Whose Memorial is It Anyway?" (Unpublished document, 1982).
29. J. H. Merryman and A. Elson, "Law, Ethics, and the Visual Arts," in *Public Art and Public Controversy,* ACA Books, New York, 1987.
30. P. Goldberger, *The New York Times* (November 24, 1985), Section 2, p. 35.

General References

J. Beardsley, *Earthworks and Beyond: Contemporary Art in the Landscape.* Abbeville Press, New York, 1984.

P. Conway and R. Jensen, *Ornamentalism.* Clarkson N. Potter, New York, 1982.

J. L. Cruikshank and P. Korza, *Going Public: A Field Guide to Developments in Art in Public Places,* Arts Extension Service, Amherst, Mass., 1988.

A. O. Dean, "Art in Environment," *AIA Journal* (October 1973).

P. Fuller, ed., *Five Architects at NOAA: A Casebook on Art in Public Places,* Comet Press, Seattle, 1985.

A. L. Harney, ed., *Art In Public Places, A Survey of Community Sponsored Projects Supported by the National Endowment for the Arts,* Partners for Liveable Places, Washington, D.C., 1981.

S. P. Harris, *Insights/On Sites, Perspectives on Art in Public Places.* Partners for Liveable Places, Washington, D.C., 1984.

R. Irwin, *Being and Circumstance: Notes Toward a Conditional Art,* The Lapis Press, Larkspur Landing, Calif., 1985.

J. Kardon, ed., "Urban Encounters" in *Art and Architecture,* Institute of Contemporary Art, University of Pennsylvania, 1980.

L. Lippard, *Overlay,* Pantheon Books, New York, 1983.

M. Lipske, *Places as Art,* Publishing Center for Cultural Resources, New York, 1985.

M. A. Robinette, *Outdoor Sculpture: Object and Environment,* Whitney Library of Design, New York, 1976.

J. P. Schwartz, *Art in the Environment,* Boca Raton Museum of Art, Boca Raton, Fla., 1986.

Stroll, The Magazine of Outdoor Art and Culture, New York,

D. W. Thalacker, *The Place of Art in the World of Architecture,* Chelsea House Publishers, New York, 1980.

J. Wines, *De-Architecture,* Rizzoli International Publications, Inc., New York, 1987.

S. Yard, ed., *Sitings,* La Jolla Museum of Contemporary Art, La Jolla, Calif., 1986.

New York City Department of Cultural Affairs, *Projects and Proposals* (Percent for Art).

See also ORNAMENT IN ARCHITECTURE

JOYCE POMEROY SCHWARTZ*
Public Art Consultant
New York, New York
* with research and clerical
  assistance from Jordana
  Pomeroy, Brece Honeycott,
  Cynthia Abramson

PUBLIC SERVICE ARCHITECTURE

The notion of public service architecture is at first difficult to grasp. It conjures images of prestigious public buildings and schemes developed by organizations such as cities and states throughout the world. These projects are often monumental in nature, representing the power and authority of these community organizations. Yet the images characterize a public architecture that is distinct from public service architecture. If this idea is accepted, then public service architecture should perhaps be examined more in terms of the process of design as opposed to the product. Public service architecture is therefore the architecture that results from the services provided by the architect for the community. Indeed, this definition causes some problems since most of the architect's activities are of this nature, and public service architecture is therefore rather broad and ill–defined. In order to define it further, it is necessary to examine it in the context of the architect's relationship with the client, the contractor, and the various public agencies that regulate the building process. In fact, the way in which the architect operates in this context defines the type of public service provided.

In the traditional relationship among these various groups, the architect acts as a mediator between client and builder. Simply, the architect represents the client's interests in the design of a building and in negotiations with the various public agencies, such as those for planning and building control. Clearly, this role is an important public service, is widely recognized, and is one for which the architect receives remuneration. It could be argued, and rightly so, that this is the main form of public service that the architect provides.

There are, in addition, many services to the community that the architect provides for which little or no remuneration is received.

Architects work as advisors or counselors for various agencies and professional bodies for the advancement and regulation of architecture. In the United States, these include agencies such as architectural registration boards, local state review boards, accreditation boards for schools of architecture, expert witnesses in litigation and arbitration activities, as well as regional and urban design assistance teams. In the United Kingdom, they include organizations such as the Royal Institute of British Architects (RIBA) and the Architects Registration Council. This type of work involves a more formal relationship between architect and agency. In addition, the architect often works in a more informal, ad hoc way, giving advice to the public. This may be through educational establishments such as universities or schools, regarding a variety of topics. In schools, architects are often called upon to give career advice or become involved in projects dealing with the built environment. In universities, particularly in schools of architecture, career advice is often required, but in addition, assistance with design projects is often undertaken. This type of work, whether informal or formal, requires close ties with the community. From the architect's standpoint, it gives a better understanding of the needs of the public, but also gives the layperson a better understanding of architecture. This is in addition to the benefits to the environment from the counseling work.

Thus, public service architecture can be examined in terms of two main dimensions: the degree of commercial orientation or the degree of voluntary orientation taken by the work. Furthermore, there is a range of separate aspects exclusive of these activities that have to do with the advancement and regulation of the profession vis-à-vis the architect's work in the various professional organizations and in education.

There is a range of aspects that have a more social

orientation, social in a political and philanthropic context of providing services to a section of the community that does not normally utilize professional architectural services. In the United States, this is represented by various community design centers and community aid organizations. In the UK, it is represented by various community architecture groups and practices. These groups operate on a voluntary basis or are subsidized by governmental agencies.

To summarize, there are three main thrusts to public service architecture in a broad sense:

1. The traditional work of an architect in commercial practice for the community.
2. The voluntary work in which the architect can be involved in the advancement and regulation of the profession for the community.
3. The voluntary and commercial work of the architect in a more social context, providing services to sections of the community that do not normally utilize the services, which is commonly called community design or community architecture.

It is this final thrust of public service architecture that is of the most interest for a number of reasons.

First, the former aspects of the traditional work of the architect and regulation of the profession are well documented and critically analyzed in many well-known texts.

Second, from the architect's standpoint, the motivations for this type of work require more of an altruistic nature than a commercial concern. This reflects the need for concern for sections of the community that are disadvantaged or displaced. In this respect, the appropriate ideological beliefs as well as skills and knowledge are a prerequisite for work in this area.

Third, the methods and processes of design in the area of community design represent new paradigms in design thinking. The traditional theories of design and methods may not be appropriate in this situation.

Fourth, the organizations that have developed provide new ways of providing a community architecture service.

Fifth, the product of community architecture is developing its own aesthetic or style of architecture. It often has a particular regional quality or a quality specific to the location. Thus, it reflects a contrast to the universal nature of the international style.

The focus of this article is an examination of the nature of the social orientation of public service architecture. Also, in particular, on its form and historical development; the motivation, ideology, skills, and knowledge required of an architect to work in this area; the methods and processes used; new ways of solving problems in the environment; and finally, the new aesthetic conditions that have developed. The article explores practices in both the United States and the UK.

COMMUNITY DESIGN

Community design has been given many names: advocacy planning, social architecture, social design, architecture for the people (1), and community architecture (2). As will be seen further, it differs from traditional commercial practice in its aims and methods.

These aims are perhaps best encapsulated in sections of a speech given by the Prince of Wales. The Prince has become an advocate of community architecture in the UK and has made many critical comments on modern architecture (3):

> We all recognise the contribution of professional expertise to society but there has been a real danger of professional arrogance developing (and not just in architecture) the "we know best" approach. This must be fought at every turn because it makes people dependent rather than independent and can lead directly to the nightmare of the "well intentioned" concrete jungle, with all its human frustrations and dangers.
>
> Talking to the residents of community architecture schemes on my visits during the past year I have heard again and again that their community architects have helped find a way out by enabling them to create the kind of surroundings they are proud to live in and wish to care for. (If only it had been tried 30 years ago, there might have been fewer concrete carbuncles.)

Community architecture is proving to be a practical alternative to traditional practice, although some would not agree. Protagonists argue that it is similar to traditional practice. Architects always consult their clients in a way similar to that of community architects, to shift all the decision making regarding the building to the client abdicates professional responsibilities (4).

These are some of the issues facing community architecture in the UK; a similar situation exists in the United States. Community architecture is now approximately 30 years old and is being seen as a serious development to fill the vacuum left by the modern movement (5). Furthermore, to reveal the background to these issues, it is interesting to trace the development of the approach.

HISTORICAL DEVELOPMENT

Community architecture seems to have started earlier in the United States than in the UK. Both movements started primarily in the decaying areas of many large cities as a means of improving the derelict areas accommodating the urban poor. In the United States during the 1960s, it grew specifically out of the realization that much of the philanthropic legislation under the Kennedy and Johnson administrations was unsatisfactory in combating the problems of the U.S. urban poor. Many of the urban renewal strategies of this era had negative effects on communities. Professionals working in these areas started to combine into groups to present the case for these communities and redress some of the negative aspects of these strategies. These professional groups were nonprofit and called community design centers (CDCs).

One of the first recorded CDCs was in New York in 1963. The Architects Renewal Committee in Harlem (ARCH) was set up to fight a proposed freeway in upper Manhattan. These early types of CDCs were made up of young professionals, all-volunteer staffs who took to the streets with residents to protest projects proposed by government without consulting the residents.

The period from 1968 to 1972 saw a further increase in the number of these centers, resulting from public dissatisfaction with the Vietnamese war and other social issues. Various multidisciplinary teams were set up in the CDC, comprising architects, urban planners, and sociologists.

By 1983, there were 60 CDCs opening around the United States. Their role had changed from the initial activist role of many of the early centers. Many diverse modes of operation were found. Some centers emphasized commercial and economic renewal. Others specialized in housing rehabilitation in large urban areas where economic decline and depopulation due to migration to the sunbelt had caused a growing stock of dilapidated and vacant buildings. Centers were set up in rural areas where similar economic and social problems had occurred.

With the advent of the Reagan era, much of the funding of such organizations as the Community Development Block Grant program of the U.S. Department of Housing and Urban Development and the federal CETA and Action programs has been cut back (5). The effects of this are unclear, but it is inevitable that the growth of these organizations will be limited unless funds from alternative sources can be found.

In the UK, many inner city areas in the 1960s suffered problems similar to those found in the United States. These were exacerbated by many areas still suffering from war damage to the building stock.

The community architecture movement developed from three main factors:

1. The increased social concern felt by architects for the views of users.
2. Changes in legislation that led to the emergence of user client groups.
3. Support for the movement from royal patronage and other sources, such as the RIBA.

The first of these factors came about as an extension of the Welfare State System in the United Kingdom; the benevolent society became incorporated in the architects' belief systems. The architect became the benevolent architect with a social conscience. A change of view took place. In large government bodies, a distinction is now made between the client and user, and it is recognized that often each has views and objectives regarding the built environment that are different and possibly contradictory. In public housing, this is very apparent: the user is a tenant, and the client a housing department. It is often found that the architect is responding to the requirements of the housing department and not the tenants. In this way, debate occurs as to who is the real client, the people using the building or those responsible for the construction and maintenance (6). The latter view became more prevalent in many areas of the UK during the 1970s, with the aim of synthesizing the needs of both client and user through a process of dialogue.

This concern for the opinions of the user had a profound effect on urban development in the period after 1960 in the UK. It was one of the main factors contributing to changes in legislation for tackling the problems of urban decay and social deprivation in many inner city areas in the United Kingdom. In the period up to the 1960s, the general planning policy was to demolish the areas of the inner cities that were the worst affected and then to rebuild them. Often, this was particularly unpopular with the residents of these areas, as it broke up existing communities. There was resistance to slum clearance, even though the living conditions were poor. People preferred to retain the social structure of the community.

After this period, the policy changed to one of urban renewal. This involved the renovation of areas with a view to retaining the social structure of the area. Many areas had been built in the Victorian era, and although the basic building fabrics were sound, the buildings lacked basic amenities such as adequate toilets, kitchens, and bathrooms. Also, many areas suffered planning "blight." This was a situation where many owners thought their properties would be compulsorily purchased for redevelopment and so did not carry out proper maintenance on their properties. Generally, a lack of confidence developed in the area, this resulted in businesses moving away. These are just some of the problems that still face architects and planners working on urban renewal in inner city areas in the UK.

The implementation of this urban renewal policy came from the 1969 and 1974 Housing Acts, which enabled local authorities to divide inner city areas into zones for rehabilitation. These are called Comprehensive Development Areas (CDAs), Housing Treatment Areas (HTAs), Housing Action Areas (HAAs), and General Improvement Areas (GIAs) depending on the type of rehabilitation provided. For example, HAAs provide basic amenities to houses in the area and can be upgraded to GIAs.

In 1975, 30–40 HAAs had been developed, and for the next 10 years this number grew (2). In addition, architectural practices of the public sector department within local government agencies and housing associations developed their own forms of community architecture. By 1985, it was estimated that 500–1000 architects in the UK were working on community architecture-type work (7).

A significant boost to the movement was given by the patronage of the Prince of Wales, who hails this type of architectural approach as an important new direction for architects in solving urban problems. Furthermore, to advance the cause of community architecture, the RIBA Community Enterprise Scheme has been developed. It is aimed, through an award scheme, at "encouraging community involvement in the process of commissioning and managing buildings of all types, particularly in the regeneration of towns and cities." The award is for the "most imaginative, need fulfilling community projects" (8).

This type of work, to provide imaginative and viable community projects, requires particular skills and training for architects. The work of the community architect is a specialized activity; some of this training comes from work in practice, and some through the formal education process. Some schools of architecture now have programs that involve community architectural issues.

COMMUNITY ARCHITECT'S SKILLS

The way in which community architects practice is different from traditional practice in many respects, although there are similarities. Many of the laypeople involved in community projects have no experience in working with an architect, are unsure of their role, and are unsure of the appropriate questions to ask or how to explain their ideas.

Many of the views of the communities are identified through resident group meetings; in this situation, laypeople have difficulty understanding the issues and articulating their views.

As a consequence, architects working in this area require particular skills. These can be formulated into five main areas. A community architect needs to (9)

1. Ask the right question and be able to orchestrate the discussion on any issues raised.
2. Be a good listener and observer sensitive to people's views.
3. Have an understanding of the future implications of people's decisions and advise accordingly.
4. Be a good translator of people's needs into buildable architectural solutions.
5. Have a sense of appropriate design through evolution of the building through discussion.

These kinds of skills should be linked to an interest in people and in helping to solve problems in the environment. Clearly, the level of architectural need is often fairly basic to the architect, but to the resident these architectural needs and the means of satisfying them appear to be major difficulties. The sense of achievement in working in these areas comes in part from solving the architectural problems, but there is also a great sense of achievement and satisfaction from helping residents solve these problems. To a large extent, this sense of achievement comes from the resolution of the management problem rather than the architectural problem. In this respect, there should be a keen interest in the management aspects of architectural design and in the design process involved. It is the effectiveness of these procedures that leads the architect to a successful solution to the problems encountered in this kind of work.

THE DESIGN PROCESS IN COMMUNITY ARCHITECTURE

One of the key words in the design process of a community architect is "participation." This process starts with the client and/or user participating with the architect and client in solving an environmental problem. It could be argued that traditional design does this already, in that the architect solicits information from the client about the building before the design commences and during the design process. In small projects where the client and user are the same person or group, this is clearly the case, but with large government or locally organized projects where

the client and user are different, the situation is more complicated.

Furthermore, the nature of participation is perhaps appreciated by examining it in relation to the nature of the environmental problems that are to be solved. Participation grew out of the way reconstruction of large urban areas was taking place in the 1960s. For example, the method used for the development of the Inner Belt Highway in Boston, Massachusetts, or the Yenerka Buena project in San Francisco, California, and others was a more centralized organizational process and endangered local communities affected by the proposals. This process is called the top-down approach to the design of urban projects because of the primary concern for the goals and objects of the central agency rather than the communities affected (Table 1). As a counterforce to this, community groups developed effective methods of organization to promote their own views. This has become known as a bottom-up approach, in which the citizens' goals and objectives for the area represent the starting point in the design process.

This approach clearly represents a shift in the decision-making process away from centralized agencies to a sharing between centralized agencies and community groups. This move represents a change from a *representative* democratic process, where architects work primarily with elected representatives of the citizens, to a participatory democratic process. The representative democratic process is seen as more hierarchical, where the citizens' representatives often decide policy independently. In contrast to this, participatory democracy is more interactive: all parties are involved in the decision-making process as far as possible (10).

This approach of using participation with the community has been seen to have a number of benefits for solving inner city problems.

First, through participating in decision making with citizens, planners and architects become better informed. Also, the process is reciprocated with citizens. They begin

Table 1. Comparison in Process of Design

Community Design (as practiced by community designers)	Traditional Design (as practiced by larger architecture and planning firms)
Small scale	Large scale
Local	National/international
Appropriate technology	High technology
Human oriented	Corporate or institutionally oriented
Client redefined to include users	Single-client oriented
Process and action oriented	Building and project oriented
Concerned with meaning and context	Concerned with style and ornament
Low cost	High cost
Bottom-up design approach	Top-down design approach
Inclusive	Exclusive
Democratic	Authoritarian

to appreciate some of the problems architects and planners have in tackling the problem of urban decay.

Second, the dialogue process is normally resolved in a solution to which both parties subscribe. This process legitimizes and endorses the design solution, avoiding the acrimonious criticism often found when centralized planning decisions are made.

Third, the processes of participation and organization often awaken further interest by the local residents, create greater links between all parties, and most of all, engender greater confidence in an area again. Many of these urban areas have been blighted for many years, and the generation of community action signals that an area will be improved rather than demolished. This indication of confidence in an area is very important.

Unfortunately, the participatory approach has met with some problems of which the architect should be aware when working in this manner. The system of residence participation is often troubled by an overly bureaucratic administration. The procedures for participation can be uniform throughout the city, yet there is a wide range of different groups and situations that require a unique approach rather than a standard procedure. Also, the different parties involved in the participation process often polarize and work against each other. Debate is a necessary part of this participation process, and often, strong views are held by those concerned, but in some cases the participation system is open to political manipulation. This is often counterproductive and leads to difficulty in achieving a consensus for action in an area (11).

This process of participation should vary with the type of project. Also, the organizational approach taken by the architect, citizens group, and central agency should reflect the type of user group and project.

COMMUNITY ARCHITECTURE ORGANIZATIONS

In the area of community architecture, a range of organizational structures has been devised to carry out this work. This is particularly apparent when a comparison is made between practices in the UK and the United States. This difference appears to result from the way these organizations have developed, the type of work carried out or services provided, and the financial structure.

In the United States, the main type of organization for carrying out community architecture work is the CDC. These organizations started as centers for advocacy planning in the early 1960s, as has been described earlier. Today, these centers have expanded and diversified their spheres of operation to include a wide range of professional activities, such as feasibility studies for urban development, rehabilitation, commercial development, small town redevelopment, historic preservation, landscaping, and appropriate energy projects. Many of these centers are attached to architectural education establishments through an affiliation system. This enables the centers to draw on volunteer students, who are assigned to them. The students receive course credits and gain valuable on-site professional experience. In these cases, the center operates with a full-time director and some qualified architects and planners, who form a core staff, in addition to the volunteer help of the student assignees. In this way, the center can operate on a nonprofit basis.

The financial support comes from federal grants and contracts, private foundations, banks, and local and state government sources.

The Pratt Institute Center for Community and Environmental Development in New York is a good illustration of a CDC. As one of the oldest CDCs, it takes students from the local schools of architecture and planning. It has three main areas of work. Mainly, it provides architectural and planning assistance to nearly 80 organizations in areas such as housing rehabilitation, neighborhood surveying, reuse of community facilities, and economic development. The Center also provides close coordination between these groups. It also acts as a watchdog, monitoring and evaluating city, state, and national urban programs and providing a strong lobbying force for local resident views.

It should be recognized that not all CDCs are urban based. The Cornell Regional Community Design Assistance Program serves the villages and small cities of upstate New York. The center is affiliated with the Cornell College of Architecture, Art and Planning. A three-tiered approach operates in the areas of historic preservation, downtown revitalization, and design education in public schools (12).

In the UK, the organization of community projects is also varied. Some originated as project groups affiliated with schools of architecture (13), but these projects often remained academic. Plans and proposals were developed with residence groups and then left to be implemented by local councils.

Other, more active community architecture groups set up either as in-house architectural departments for local councils or as community design practices. The former groups often set up area offices in improvement areas. Multidisciplinary teams composed of architects, planners, environmental health officers, engineers, and quantity surveyors work in these areas with local residence groups. These teams discuss plans for upgrading the area with the residents and, when agreed on, the proposals are put before a public meeting of the area residents for ratification. Once agreement is reached, the proposals are placed before the local council for approval.

The environmental improvement included in this type of work is wide ranging. It covers aspects like the relocation of industries incompatible with the residential function of the area, road improvements and closures to provide quiet cul-de-sacs, housing modernization, and development of social amenities such as community centers and play areas.

Fees for this work come from central government and local councils and through the grants system for house improvement under the relevant housing acts.

This kind of work is also carried out by the community architect, who often sets up local offices in these areas of development. A recent practitioner in the field made the following suggestion (14):

What makes the community architect different from the traditional architect is that he is available, he's there seven days a week, 24 hours a day to feel the vibration and pulse of the community . . .

This is the kind of missionary zeal with which many community architects see their work. Private firms of architects are normally small practices that work with residence groups in conjunction with local councils or housing associations. Housing associations are nonprofit organizations in the UK. The associations purchase and renovate properties and rent them to tenants, particularly those in need.

In recent years, more innovative ways in which architects work in this area have been established. Architects have become more entrepreneurial in attempting to solve community problems. Rod Hackney, often recognized as the pioneer of community architecture in the UK, has developed several initiatives in this area.

First, in Burnley, Lancashire, the District Council commissioned Hackney's firm to provide a development strategy for a decaying cotton weaving area. The strategy formulated departed from the normal practice of simply drawing plans for the area. It first involved discussion with the owners, tenants, amenity societies, potential investors, developers, and employers. Second, using a building company, Hackney purchased a derelict property in the area for proposed conversion to a mixed-use development including the architect's site office. Finally, feasibility studies for development of the area were prepared and then placed before the District Council (15).

In other schemes, architects work with the community in self-build schemes. Self-builders range from those who renovate a flat to those who build a new home on a prelaid slab. Illustrative of this is a scheme developed with the Stirling District Council and made financially viable with the support of various building societies, who are prepared to grant mortgages on the self-build properties. Self-builders can choose to do the whole house or selected parts. Even unemployed people are able to participate in the scheme. In this situation, calculations have shown that a maximum of 28% of the overall building cost can be saved (15).

The process of self-building requires further explanation. This type of construction is becoming a more popular form of community architecture. This has occurred through basic changes in the social structure, such as increased leisure time, which has spawned crude forms of self-help such as do-it-yourself (DIY) building, where the layperson carries out minor home building or repair projects. Some innovative architects have seen the potential for this and developed a more extensive form of self-building for housing. In this type of work, future owners come together in a cooperative group to purchase a site and build their homes. This is a form of the maximum approach to self-help housing. Essentially, the owners rely on "sweat equity" from their own labor to reduce the cost of their housing (16).

The architect in this situation has to be concerned about a number of factors. First, the building system should be technically as simple as possible, as this reduces the training and site supervision required. Also, the types of components used are important. Early schemes used timber frame construction with off-the-shelf pieces to ease utilization. Illustrative of this is the use of standard timber lengths and sections to minimize the need for cutting. In addition, these types of self-build houses are designed with a number of options regarding room layout, so that occupants can select an arrangement to suit their needs (17).

In recent years, self-building has become more complex. Some schemes offer solar heating. This provides a low-cost house, and also lower operating costs. In this type of project, as with any self-build operation, the training of the group is critical to the success of the operation. The architect in this situation should make sure the self-builder is aware of the logic of the construction, the geometric and dimensional criteria for site layout, planning, and structure. Also, methods of work should consider psychological factors as well as technical aspects of the project. For example, it is necessary to consider the morale of the builders. Building systems that show quick results are favored. In this respect, timber frame construction is appropriate since the structure can be built quickly (18).

Finally, although the group approach to self-building is a common form of organization, some developments have favored an individual self-builder approach. In this case, the architect may act more entrepreneurially, providing a housing development with a range of options (19).

Clearly, these forms of self-building require a different approach to public service architecture. Yet the philosophy remains the same: to serve the interests of the community in a professional manner whether by providing design services or just by providing the technical and organizational skills of the architect.

COMMUNITY DESIGN AESTHETICS

At present, community design is changing not only the process of design, but also the product. The style of community architecture is now perhaps just a vision. Some glimpses of the type of architecture that can come from this process are possible, but a unique style of community architecture has yet to crystalize fully.

There are some emerging characteristics. The products of community design are often personalized structures produced and appreciated by the residents. These types of structures are visually "rough and ready" in nature and may contrast greatly with the simple clean aesthetic of modern buildings (11). Some projects use second-hand materials and temporary buildings. These are reworked for a new use in the community. Illustrative of this is a recent community workshop at Wester Hailes in the UK. There, the community architect worked in a modern estate that lacked community facilities. There were no redundant buildings to utilize. The new community building was formed from a plentiful supply of "prefabs" (temporary relocatable buildings) (20).

Although the aesthetics of some community architecture can be regarded as ad hoc, many well-recognized ar-

Figure 1. Exterior view of the Byker "wall" by Ralph Erskine. A symbol of identity for community architecture.

chitects can be labeled community architects through their use of participatory methods and also because of their distinctive styles of building. Ralph Erskine, Walter Segal, and Christopher Alexander are useful examples. Some of the distinctive characteristics of form that might represent a style of community architecture can be analyzed in the work of one of these architects, Erskine. His housing project at Byker, Newcastle-upon-Tyne, UK, is a notable example (21) (Figs. 1 and 2).

The project is a "new build" housing development on a south-facing hill. The design uses a mixture of high-rise and low-rise development. The high-rise development forms a wall between a proposed motor way and the low-rise development. The wall, conceived as a noise barrier, in fact gave great identity to the development and a sense of place to the residents (22).

Materials such as brick patterning, timber balustrades, as well as asbestos and colorful metal sheeting are blended together to reduce the scale of the development. The image is a combination of modern and vernacular expressions, which perhaps reflects most appropriately the style for community architecture.

Finally, community architecture may in the future present a more pervasive style, a form of regionalism that reflects local taste. It may also represent a style for the future that has as its objective not making new architecture, but making a new form of architecture that uses the new to unify the existing architecture to provide a coherent community environment (23).

ROLE OF PUBLIC SERVICE ARCHITECTURE

Public service architecture, in its broad sense, encompasses many areas, such as the commercial practice of architecture, the volunteer work of regulating the profession, as well as commercial and volunteer work in the community. The last is an emerging area of architecture that seeks to provide professional services to sections of the community that would not normally utilize them. This role is particularly significant in that it attempts to bring architects and architecture closer to society, in the sense that the design process encompasses the users' views in

Figure 2. Interior view of the Byker "wall" showing contrasting use of materials.

situations where they are not normally directly represented, eg, in urban planning or rehabilitation of decaying areas. Also, it seeks to retain the social structure of communities rather than destroying it and refurbishes the existing fabric rather than demolishing and rebuilding. This type of architecture is one that often requires much voluntary activity, and many organizations in these areas are not profit making. It requires of the architect an altruistic view of the world of design and an honest concern for human needs, particularly for those sections of the population that are disadvantaged or displaced. The role of the architect in this area therefore is distinctly different from that of the traditional practicing architect with a commercial orientation.

The achievements of this type of architecture have been in the areas of providing alternative methods of design to solve the problems of urban decay in many cities, particularly in the UK and the United States. It provides an excellent way for students, through community projects related to educational institutions, to learn about community needs and to gain practical experience. It is starting to produce new organizations, new processes of design, and new styles of architecture that relate more specifically to the needs of the common person.

BIBLIOGRAPHY

1. M. Francis, "Community Design," *Journal of Architectural Education,* **37**(1), 14–19 (1983).
2. R. Hackney, "Architect Aspects: 3 Organising," *Royal Institute of Britsh Architects' Journal* **83**(7), 283, 284, (1976).
3. C. Knevitt, "Architectural Consultants: The People," *The Times* (Sept. 17, 1985).
4. P. Buchanan, "With Due Respect: Regionalism," *Architectural Review* **173**(1035), 15 (May 15, 1983).
5. P. M. Sacher, "Still Planning with the Poor Community Design Centres Keep Up the Good Work," *Architectural Record,* (171), 26 (Jan. 1983).
6. T. Wolley, "Community Architecture," *Open House International* **10**(1), 22, 23 (1985).
7. C. Knevitt, "A Prince Among Architects," *Art and Design* **1**(3), 20 (1985).
8. Ref. 3, p. i.
9. Ref. 1, pp. 14, 15.
10. H. G. Rikhof, "Self-help Housing and Citizen Participation," *Open House International* **8**(3), 39 (1983).
11. *Ibid.,* pp. 37, 38.
12. Ref. 5, pp. 127–129.
13. C. Abel, "Camber Redevelopment Project (Portsmouth)," *Building Design* (87), 24–27 (1978).
14. N. Wates, "The Hackney Phenomenon," *Architects' Journal* **181**(8), 48 (Feb. 20, 1985).
15. N. Wates, "Architect as Entrepreneur," *Architects' Journal,* **181**(8), 51–53 (Feb. 20, 1985).
16. Ref. 10, pp. 41, 42.
17. C. Ellis, "Self Build: Lewisham by Walter Segal," *Architects' Journal,* **179**(4), 36–39 (Jan. 25, 1984).
18. D. Raven, "Green Energy," *RIBA Journal,* 25–27 (1985).
19. Ref. 15, p 61.
20. T. Wolley, "The Prefab. Pioneers," *Architects' Journal* **176**(42), 54, 58 (Oct. 20, 1982).
21. Ref. 1, p. 19.
22. C. Jenks, *Language of Post Modern Architecture,* 85 (1977).
23. E. Galea, "First 10 Finalists," *A Style for the Year* 2000' 15 (1985) Rizolli Publications, New York.

General References

R. Hester, Jr., "Process Can Be Style: Participation and Conservation in Landscape Architecture," *Landscape Architecture,* **2**(3) 49–55 (May 1983).

M. R. Behesht and D. J. M. Dinjens, "Review of the Design Participation Conference 1985," *Open House International* **10**(1), 3, 4 (1985).

N. Wates and C. Knevitt, "Community Architecture: How People are Creating Their Own Environment," *Penguin* (1987).

See also CAREERS IN ARCHITECTURE; HOUSING-SELF HELP; REGIONAL/URBAN DESIGN ASSISTANCE; REVIEW BOARDS—ARCHITECTURAL; USER PARTICIPATION

RICHARD HYDE
National University of
    Singapore
Singapore

PUBLIC TRANSPORTATION.   See BUS MAINTENANCE FACILITIES; TRANSIT SYSTEMS.

PUD (PLANNED URBAN DEVELOPMENT).   See CLUSTER DEVELOPMENT.

PVC.   See PLASTICS.

Q-R

QUALITY CONTROL. See Diagnostics, Building; Value Engineering.

QUANTITY SURVEYING. See Supplement.

QUARRY TILE. See Ceramic Tile.

RADON MITIGATION IN CONSTRUCTION

Radon is rapidly diluted in the outdoor air, but indoors radon can accumulate to significant concentrations. With an atomic weight of 222, it is a naturally occurring decay product of radium-226, which is in turn a decay product of uranium-238. Both uranium-238 and radium-226 are present in most soils and rocks in widely varied concentrations. As radon forms from the decay of radium-226, it can leave the soil or rock and enter the surrounding air or water. Radon is a colorless, odorless, tasteless, inert, radioactive gas. It can travel through the soil and into a building through very small cracks, joints, and other openings in the foundation floor and wall.

The predominant source of indoor radon in most single-family housing in the United States is the soil adjacent to the house substructure (1). Building materials and well water are sometimes contributors to radon levels in indoor air, but generally to a lesser extent than the soil. It is widely believed that for every 10,000 pCi of radon in a liter of water, the indoor concentration will be raised 1 pCi of radon per liter of air (2). The incremental radon due to most building materials is believed to be less than 1 pCi/L. A picocurie of radon per liter of air represents a level at which 2.2 alpha particles are ejected per minute. Radon concentrations are also expressed in becquerel per cubic meter (Bq/m^3). Thirty-seven Bq/m^3 is equivalent to 1 pCi/L.

Radon in the home may be the single largest source of lung cancer among nonsmokers. With people quitting smoking, eating better, exercising more, and in general trying to live safer, healthier lives, they do not want radon killing them, especially because it is no fault of their own lifestyle choice. In 1984, the discovery of residences with indoor levels of radon far in excess of those equivalent to federal limits for occupational exposures to short-lived progeny of radon raised public interest in how to fix existing homes with elevated radon levels and how to build new homes that are radon resistant.

HEALTH EFFECTS OF RADON EXPOSURE

Radon decays with a half-life of 3.82 days into a series of solid, short-lived radioisotopes collectively referred to as radon daughters or progeny. Two of these daughters, polonium-218 and polonium-214, emit alpha particles. The al-pha particles are ejected at high speed (with high energy levels). When these alpha particles (helium atoms stripped of their two electrons) are emitted in the lung, their energy is deposited in the cells lining the airways. This interaction causes cell damage. The alpha particles lose energy as they pass through material. They gradually slow down (lose energy) and acquire two electrons, becoming atoms of helium gas in thermal equilibrium with the surrounding material. The resulting biological changes in the cells that slowed down these alpha particles can ultimately lead to lung cancer.

The National Academy of Sciences has recently issued a detailed review of human health effects called "Biological Effects of Ionizing Radiation IV" (3). The consequences of lung cancer are severe—death occurs in more than 9 cases in 10 within five years after the cancer is detected (4). The length of life lost by those who actually die of lung cancer is typically about 15 years.

Among all sources of naturally occurring radiation that deliver significant doses to the tissues or cells of the respiratory tract, inhaled radon progeny are dominant. A current issue in the scientific community is not whether radon progeny cause lung cancer in humans, but how strong a carcinogen it is for the general population, who vary in some respects from miners (3). Numerous studies of underground miners exposed to radon daughters in the air of mines have shown an increased risk of lung cancer in comparison with nonexposed populations. Laboratory animals exposed to radon daughters also develop lung cancer. Predicted levels of exposure, are frequently converted to levels of associated risk. Predicting health risks always has some degree of uncertainty. However, because the data on radon exposure risk are based on human studies and in some cases at exposure levels comparable to those in domestic environments, the accuracy and reliability of the risk estimates are better for radon than for many chemical carcinogens.

Some of the major uncertainties involve the extrapolation of radon progeny impacts from mines to domestic environments and the interaction between smoking and exposure to radon progeny. The risk associated with radon daughter exposure has not typically taken age into account either. Dosimetric models for radon daughters, however, project greater risks associated with exposure during childhood (5). Analysis of the epidemiological studies suggests that the incidence of fatal lung cancers in underground miners increases according to cumulative exposure to radon progeny; however, at lower concentrations is mostly due to the synergistic effect of cigarette smoking and radon exposure. The increased risk of lung cancer due to elevated radon exposure is about 10 times greater in smokers than in nonsmokers.

A male nonsmoker exposed to only average outdoor radon progeny levels has an 11 in 1000 chance of lung cancer; a female nonsmoker has a 6 in 1000 chance. The increased lifetime risk of a male nonsmoker getting lung cancer living in a house an average of 12 hours per day, with an average radon level of 4 pCi/L is 5 in 1000 (female nonsmoker 3 in 1000) compared to the increased risk of a male smoker, 50 in 1000 (female smoker 25 in 1000) (3). These same data suggest that a male who smokes but is not exposed to elevated radon progeny has an increased risk of 123 in 1000 chance of lung cancer mortality (female smoker, 58 in 1000).

RADON MEASUREMENT LEVEL GUIDELINES

In August 1986, the U.S. Environmental Protection Agency announced that radon gas is a significant health threat (6). In September 1988, the Public Health Service announced in a national health advisory that "radon-induced lung cancer is one of today's most serious public health issues" (7). As a national policy, the public has been urged to consider 4 pCi/L as an "action level" for both new and existing buildings. The ASHRAE Standard 62–1981R, "Ventilation for Acceptable Indoor Air Quality," has also adopted 4 pCi/L as a guideline (8).

The working level (WL) is defined as the amount of radon daughters in 1 L of air that results in the ultimate release of 1.3×10^5 MeV of potential alpha energy. One working level in a domestic environment is approximately the amount of alpha energy emitted by the radon daughters in 50% equilibrium with 200 pCi/L of radon. Radon exposure is defined as the product of concentration and time. The unit of exposure to radon progeny commonly used by health physicists is the working-level-month (WLM). Because radiation exposure concerns in the past have been occupation related and because the average number of hours on the job in a month is around 173, the block of time in a WLM is defined as 173 h. In addition, to make a conversion from measured radon concentration levels in a mine to the home requires a home occupancy rate. Assuming an occupancy of 50% and an average radon concentration of 4 pCi/L in a house, the WLM/yr exposure is equal to 0.5 WLM/yr. An occupancy rate of 75% and an average radon concentration of 4 pCi/L, would result in an exposure of 0.75 WLM/yr.

Radon can be found in any building, but most of the high exposures levels have been found in single-family detached houses. Residential buildings typically have a larger percentage of total surface area in contact with the earth and tend to be occupied for a larger percentage of the day than most commercial buildings.

WHY RADON ACCUMULATES IN HOUSES

The rate of radon movement into a house depends on the source strength in the soil, permeability of the soil (grain size distribution and percent of moisture), surface area in contact with the ground, air exchange rate in the house, tightness of the foundation, ambient conditions (wind, rain, and temperature), and the presence of a driving force caused when the pressure inside a home is lower than the pressure outside or in the surrounding soil. A lower pressure inside a home may result from the following:

1. Heated air rising, which causes a stack effect.
2. Wind blowing on the exterior envelope of the build-

ing that results in high pressure relative to indoor pressure on one side and low pressure on the other surfaces.

3. A vacuum effect can be induced by operation of fireplaces and furnaces vented to the outside, but without an outdoor air intake, as well as clothes dryer and exhaust fans in bathrooms, kitchens, or attics. In homes, where a partial vacuum exists, outdoor air and soil gas are driven into the home. Surveys of houses show that radon concentrations have little correlation with energy efficiency or ventilation rates within the range found in current housing construction (9).

4. Leaky supply heating and air-conditioning ducts located in the attic. Significant depressurization can occur when supply ducts are located outside the conditioned space.

GENERAL CONSTRUCTION GUIDELINES

Based on what is known about radon entry into homes, the following construction principles should be applied to the design of mitigation systems: (1) minimize foundation pathways for soil gas to enter; and (2) strive to achieve as small a negative pressure differential between indoors and outdoors as possible. Eliminating radon entry pathways and pressure differentials is seldom if ever fully achieved in typical construction. Missing even minor cracks in the foundation sealing process compromises the entire radon reduction effort. Furthermore, houses experience minor movement throughout the year. Unless the sealant adheres perfectly to the floors and walls, is able to flex with the seasons, and even has the attribute of being self-healing, new cracks will appear.

SITE EVALUATION

It is usually less expensive to provide the basic radon control measures than to make the soil tests to determine if they are necessary, particularly because many of the basic control measures are desirable for moisture and energy control. If the planned source of water to the site is a local or on-site well, it should be determined whether excessive levels of radon have been detected in other wells within the same geologic area. (Levels of 40,000 pCi/L of water could produce indoor radon concentrations of about 4 pCi/L.) State health services, departments of natural resources, and environmental protection offices may be able to assist in providing this information. If excessive radon levels are confirmed, a granular-activated carbon filtration system might be considered. However, carbon filters may become difficult to discard on saturation because of their own radiation level. Aeration and long-term (greater than half-life) storage may also be considered.

NEW CONSTRUCTION MITIGATION TECHNIQUES

Construction techniques for minimizing radon entry fall under three basic approaches: radon barrier, air management, and subslab depressurization. Radon barrier techniques are the first level of defense and generally can also help minimize potential moisture problems. Many of the radon barrier techniques are common building practices in many areas and are less costly if accomplished during construction. Air management techniques can alleviate other indoor air quality problems besides radon. The sub-slab depressurization is done exclusively to intercept soil gas. However, soil gas may have other potentially harmful compounds such as termiticides and other lawn chemicals.

THE RADON BARRIER

The same construction techniques that keep radon out usually benefit moisture and humidity control (10). Air contained in the soil is almost always at 100% relative humidity; therefore, if a barrier is built that reduces the infiltration of soil gas, indoor humidity levels can be lowered as well. Barrier techniques minimize cracks, joints, and other openings through the foundation to the soil. Waterproofing membranes on the exterior wall surface and under the floor are excellent barriers that, if performing properly, cover cracks and joints. The following barrier design approaches are for the most part taken from the EPA "Radon Reduction in New Construction: An Interim Guide" (11) and the "Building Foundation Design Handbook" (10). Buildings built with careful application of the barrier techniques listed below will be less likely to accumulate radon and have ground source moisture problems.

Slab

The resistance of radon and soil moisture infiltration through both slabs-on-grade and slabs-below-grade can be increased by the following measures and as shown in Figure 1.

1. Use solid pipes for floor discharge drains to daylight or valved traps designed for radon control that discharge to subsurface drains.

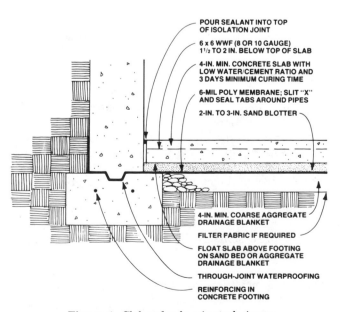

Figure 1. Slab radon barrier techniques.

2. Where client, site, and climatic conditions permit, design monolithic slab-on-grade foundations to eliminate the perimeter joint between the slab and foundation wall. If properly insulated below grade level, shallow monolithic foundations can be poured even in cold climates.

3. Lay a 6-mil (minimum) polyethylene film layer on top of the gravel drainage blanket. This film serves as both a radon and moisture retarder. Slit an "x" in the polyethylene membrane to receive penetrations. Turn up the tabs and tape them. Care should be taken to avoid unintentionally puncturing the barrier. Consider using washed and sized river bed gravel if possible. The round river bed gravel allows for freer movement of the soil gas as well as offering no sharp edges to penetrate the polyethylene. The edges of the membrane should be lapped at least 12 in. Avoid or carefully seal all necessary grade stake punctures of the vapor barrier. Wooden grade stakes that are subject to decay should be removed from the slab or driven at least 1 in. below the surface so a clean, formed opening with a minimum depth of 1 in. is created. Once the concrete has cured, the gap should be filled to a minimum depth of 1 in. with a polyurethane sealant. The polyethylene should extend over the top of the footing, be sealed to the foundation wall, or extend to the bottom edge of a monolithic slab-grade beam or patio. It is recommended that patios, carports, and garages be included in barrier installations due to the frequency with which they become homeowner-enclosed living space. A 2-in.-thick sand blotter on top of the polyethylene improves concrete curing and reduces cracking. Special care must be exercised not to puncture or tear the vapor barrier when placing the sand. The sand should be dampened, but not saturated, before the concrete is poured. Using concrete with a low water to cement ratio may make the sand layer less important. However, the sand will offer some protection from puncture of the polyethylene during the concrete pouring operation.

4. Provide an isolation joint between the wall and slab floor where vertical movement is expected. The joint may be sealed as shown in Figure 2. Be sure to clean and dry surfaces for proper bonding of the sealant. After the slab has cured for several days, pour polyurethane or similar caulk into the ½-in. channel. Polyurethane caulks adhere well to masonry and are long lived. They do not stick to polyethylene.

5. Avoid edge channels that allow water to drain from the floor and wall to beneath the slab by providing adequate subslab and footing drainage.

6. Minimize shrinkage cracking by keeping the water content of the concrete as low as possible. If necessary, use plasticizers to increase workability, not water.

7. Reinforce the slab to reduce shrinkage cracking with wire mesh or fiber. Consider control joints or additional reinforcing near the inside corner of L-

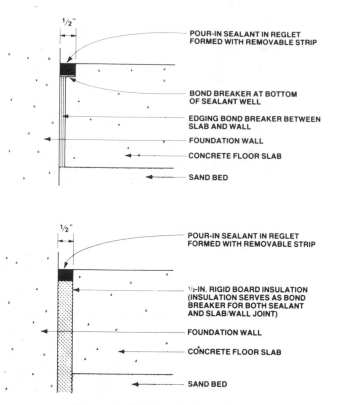

Figure 2. Wall/floor isolation joint.

shaped slabs. Two pieces of #4 reinforcing bar, 3 ft long and 12 in. on center across areas where additional stress is anticipated, should reduce cracking.

8. Control joints should be finished with a ½-in. depression and this recess fully filled with polyurethane or similar caulk.

9. Minimize the number of pours to reduce the number of cold joints. Begin curing the concrete immediately after the pour, according to recommendations of the American Concrete Institute (12,13). At least three days are required at 70°F, longer at lower temperatures. Use an impervious cover sheet or wetted burlap.

10. Form a gap of at least ½-in. width around all plumbing and utility lead-ins through the slab to a depth of at least ½ in. Fill with polyurethane or similar caulking.

11. Cover sump pits with a sealed lid and vent to the outdoors. Use submersible pumps to minimize pump corrosion.

12. Install well-sealing valved traps at all floor drains.

13. Condensate drains should connect to air outside the perimeter of the building envelope. Condensate drains that connect to dry wells or other soil may become direct conduits for soil gas and can be a major entry point for radon.

14. Concrete cracks greater than 1/16 in. that occur within 28 days of pouring the concrete slabs should be sealed by widening to form a minimum gap of approximately ¼ × ¼ in., and cleaning and filling it with polyurethane sealant.

Basement and Crawl Space Walls

The following measures are derived largely from Ref. 8 and are shown in Figure 3.

1. Reinforce walls and footings to minimize shrinkage cracking and cracking due to uneven settlement.

2. Seal the top of hollow masonry walls with a solid block, bond beam, or cap block.

3. Parge the exterior face of concrete masonry walls in contact with the soil. Drainage boards could be applied to permit an airway for soil gas to reach the surface outside the wall rather than being drawn through the wall. These products could serve to aid moisture control and reduce heat loss.

4. Install a continuous waterproofing membrane on the exterior of the basement wall or unvented crawl space wall.

5. Paint the interior face of the foundation wall with an epoxy or other high quality water-resistant paint. Its effectiveness depends on the wall material and the extent and quality of the exterior moisture proofing. Wait 30 days after wall construction to permit drying of the concrete. In retrofit applications, painting the inside surface of porous concrete block walls has been found to be largely unsuccessful in reducing soil gas entry (2).

6. Seal around plumbing and other utility and service lead-ins through the wall with polyurethane or similar caulking.

7. Install airtight seals on doors and other openings between basements and adjoining crawl spaces.

8. Seal around ducts, plumbing, and other service connections between basements and crawl spaces.

9. Concrete cracks greater than 1/16 in. should be sealed by widening to a minimum gap of approximately ¼ × ¼ in., and cleaning and filling with polyurethane sealant or equivalent.

Crawl Space

1. Place a 6-mil polyethylene vapor barrier over all exposed soil floor areas. Overlap edges 12 in. and seal. Seal edges to the foundation wall. Figure 1 shows the details of one method for installing a continuous barrier at the time of construction. It is difficult to adhere tightly to interior surfaces.

2. Ventilate crawl spaces in high radon risk areas. Unless some other provisions are provided to mitigate radon infiltration if needed, such as a reliable radon barrier at the earth contact surfaces, provide pressurization of the crawl space or subcrawl space depressurization. Consider designing the crawl space with the same moisture and radon barrier techniques described above for basements. This includes pouring a concrete slab over a gravel pad for the floor.

3. Construct floors above unconditioned spaces with an air infiltration barrier. Tongue-and-groove plywood floor decking should be applied with butt joints con-

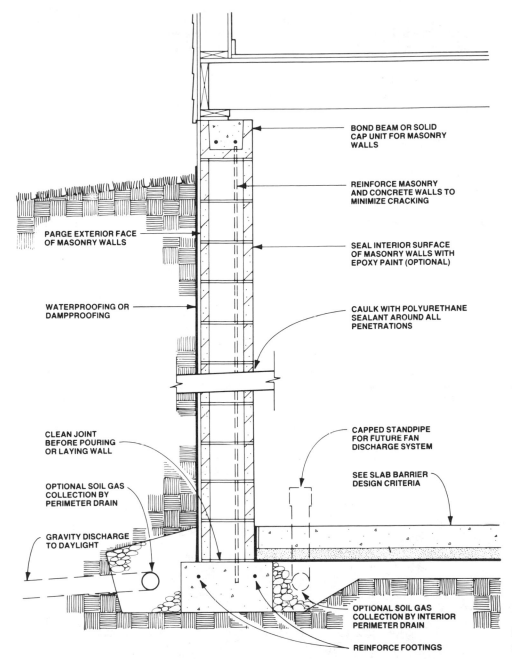

BOND BEAM OR SOLID
CAP UNIT FOR MASONRY
WALLS

REINFORCE MASONRY
AND CONCRETE WALLS TO
MINIMIZE CRACKING

SEAL INTERIOR SURFACE
OF MASONRY WALLS WITH
EPOXY PAINT (OPTIONAL)

PARGE EXTERIOR FACE
OF MASONRY WALLS

WATERPROOFING OR
DAMPPROOFING

CAULK WITH POLYURETHANE
SEALANT AROUND ALL
PENETRATIONS

CLEAN JOINT
BEFORE POURING
OR LAYING WALL

CAPPED STANDPIPE
FOR FUTURE FAN
DISCHARGE SYSTEM

SEE SLAB BARRIER
DESIGN CRITERIA

OPTIONAL SOIL GAS
COLLECTION BY
PERIMETER DRAIN

GRAVITY DISCHARGE
TO DAYLIGHT

OPTIONAL SOIL GAS
COLLECTION BY INTERIOR
PERIMETER DRAIN

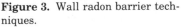

REINFORCE FOOTINGS

Figure 3. Wall radon barrier techniques.

tinuously glued to floor joists with a waterproof construction adhesive. All penetrations through the subfloor should be sealed. Large openings such as at bathtub drains should be enclosed with sheet metal or other rigid material and sealants.

MANAGEMENT OF INDOOR AIR

Air management techniques may be used first to minimize the suction applied to the surrounding soil gas by the building and second to dilute indoor radon concentrations by ventilating with outdoor air. Dilution of indoor radon is generally energy intensive, even with heat recovery, and not particularly effective, especially at higher radon concentrations.

In order to control the pressure differential between indoors and outdoors, it is desirable to make the entire building envelope airtight and control the amount of incoming fresh air, exhausted inside air, and supply air for combustion devices. The principles applied to minimize indoor–outdoor pressure differences are essentially the same as those recommended for moisture vapor control and energy-efficient design.

1. Reduce air infiltration from the unconditioned spaces (crawl spaces, attics, and unconditioned basements) into the occupied space by sealing openings and cracks around flues, vent stacks, attic hatchways, plumbing, wiring, and duct penetrations.

2. To reduce the stack effect of a house, reduce air exfiltration routes. Consider locating the attic access outside conditioned space, and avoid recessed ceiling lights.

3. Seal all openings in top and bottom plates of frame construction, including interior partitions.

4. Provide separate outdoor air intakes for combustion equipment.

5. Install air infiltration barriers in all above-grade exterior walls.

6. Adjust ventilation systems to help neutralize imbalances between indoor and outdoor air pressures. Keeping a house under continuous slight positive pressure is a difficult technique to accomplish. At this time, whole house, basement, or crawl space pressurization is not a recommended solution to radon control, unless these spaces have been built extremely airtight.

7. Avoid pressurizing basement space or crawl spaces with moist warm indoor air that could condense on cool below-grade surfaces, causing wood decay, masonry spalling, and propagation of mold and mildew.

8. Modest elevated radon levels can be controlled by increasing the whole house ventilation, but avoid exhaust fan depressurization. Figure 4 shows the effect of ventilation under balanced indoor and outdoor pressures on indoor radon concentrations (14). Dilution can cause significant energy cost penalties, because the added ventilation air must be conditioned most of the year in many climates.

9. Return air ducts should not be located in a crawl space or beneath a slab. Placing the HVAC ducting inside the conditioned space will have energy savings benefits as well.

10. Supply ducts should not be located below concrete slabs-on-grade or slabs-below-grade.

11. Seal all supply ductwork located in crawl spaces.

12. Balance the HVAC ducts. System imbalance can lead to pressurization in some zones and depressurization in others.

INTERCEPTION OF SOIL GAS

Up to this point all of the suggested radon minimizing techniques contribute to other desirable features such as energy efficiency, moisture control and improved general indoor air quality. Subslab depressurization has repeatedly proven to be an effective technique for reducing radon concentrations to acceptable levels, even in homes with extremely high concentrations (2). This technique results in lowering the pressure outside the foundation, causing the soil gas to be routed into a collection system, thus avoiding the inside spaces by being discharged to the outdoors. This system can be installed in two phases. The first phase is the collection system located on the soil side of the foundation, which should be done during construction. The collection system can be installed at little or no additional cost in new construction. The second phase is the discharge system, which can be installed later if necessary at the homeowner's expense.

A foundation with good subsurface drainage already

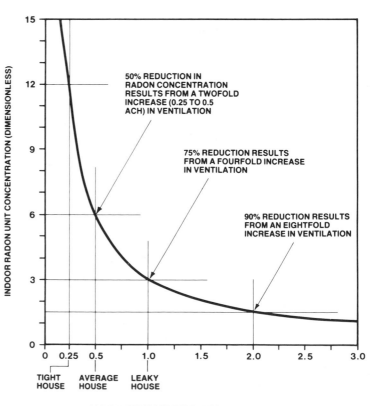

Figure 4. Effect of ventilation on indoor radon concentrations.

has a collection system. The underslab gravel drainage blanket can be used to collect soil gas. It should be at least 4 in. thick and of clean aggregate of no less than ½-in. dia. If groundwater is likely to rise above the slab level, a suitable filter fabric should be installed to prevent the gravel from clogging with soil fines. Crossover pipes through the footing or a gravel bed extending beyond the foundation wall will help ensure good air communication between the foundation perimeter soil and the underside of the slab. The gravel should be covered with a polyethylene radon-and-moisture barrier, which in turn should be covered with a 2-in. sand bed.

A continuous loop of perforated 4-in.-diameter drainpipe can be installed around the perimeter on the inside, outside, or both sides of the footing. It can be vented to a closed sump or left with good air communication with the gravel bed under the slab. A sump system with an exterior footing drain is shown in Figure 5. If a sump is not in-

stalled prior to pouring the slab, consider inserting one or more short (12-in.) lengths of 4-in. minimum diameter PVC pipe vertically into the subslab aggregate and cap the top end. Standpipes can also be installed horizontally through below-grade walls to the area beneath an adjoining slab. A single standpipe is adequate to sufficiently mitigate the radon infiltration for typical house basement-size floors with a clean, course gravel layer. After construction, if necessary, these standpipes can be uncapped and connected to the discharge system. Additional standpipes can be installed by drilling 4-in. holes through the finished slab. The standpipes should be positioned for easy connection to discharge vents run to the roof through plumbing chases, interior walls, or closets.

The subslab depressurization system requires the floor slab to be nearly airtight so that collection efforts are not short-circuited by drawing excessive room air down through the slab and into the system. Cracks, slab pene-

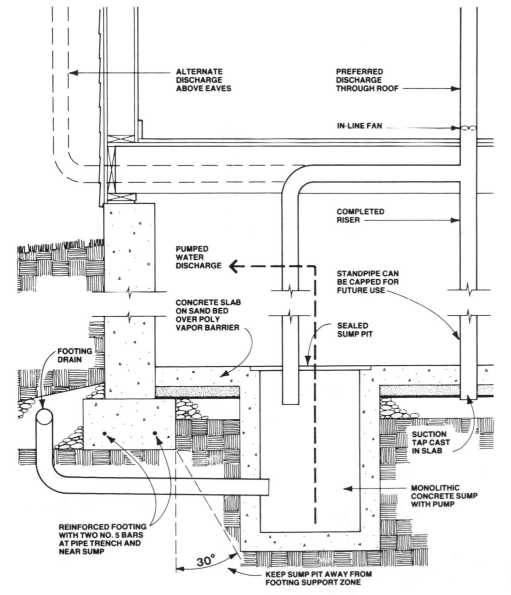

Figure 5. Soil gas collection and interior discharge techniques.

trations, and control joints must be sealed. Another potential short circuit can occur if the subdrainage system has a gravity discharge to an underground outfall. This discharge line may need to be provided with a water trap. Another consideration is to use this line for the discharge system as shown in Figure 6. However, the need for keeping water in the trap and the unlikelihood of regular inspection is a major disadvantage of combining the radon interception system with a gravity water-drainage system. The subsurface drainage discharge line, if not run into a sump, should be constructed with a solid glued drainpipe that goes to daylight openings.

Passive discharge systems have not been effective in achieving acceptable radon reductions on a year-round basis. Performance is improved to some degree by using a 6-in. diameter vent routed straight from the floor through

the roof, with minimum bends (11). The stack should be insulated where it passes through an uninsulated attic space.

To consistently achieve radon levels below 4 pCi/L in all seasons, active discharge systems are needed. Active systems use quiet, in-line duct fans to draw gas from the soil. The fan should be located in an accessible section of the stack so that any leaks from the positive pressure side of the fan are not in the living space. Ideally, the stack should be routed up through the building and should extend 2–4 ft above the roof. It can also be carried out through the band joist and up along the wall, to a point at or above the eave line.

A fan capable of maintaining 0.2 in. of water suction under installation conditions is adequate for serving both perimeter and subslab collection systems for most houses

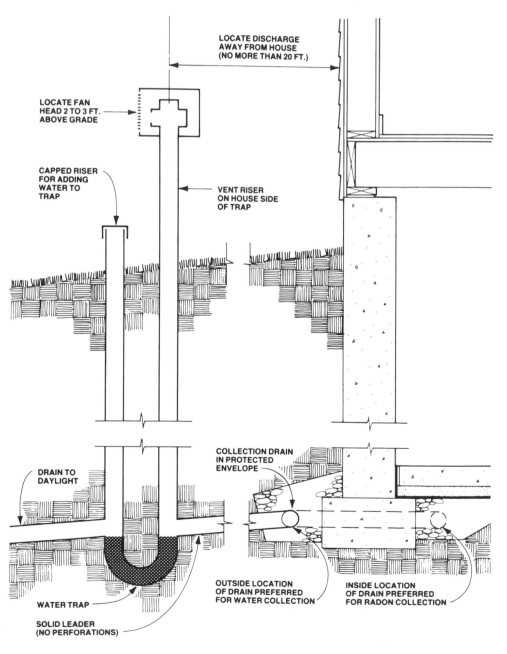

Figure 6. Soil gas collection and exterior discharge techniques.

(8). This is often achieved with a 0.03-hp (25W), 160-cfm centrifugal fan (maximum capacity) capable of drawing up to 1 in. of water before stalling. Under field conditions of 0.2 in. of water, such a fan operates at about 80 cfm.

It is possible to test the suction of the subslab system by drilling a small (¼-in.) hole in an area of the slab remote from the collector pipe or suction point and measuring the suction through the hole. A suction of 5 Pa is considered satisfactory. The hole must be sealed after the test.

Subslab depressurization does raise some long-term concerns that at this time are not fully understood. In some areas, this system could dry out the soil and raise the permeability such that, if the fan should be turned off, the radon flow into the building could be even higher than before the system was activated. In warmer climates, where the slab is below the soil temperature, this system could cause excessive moisture to condense on the underside of the slab and cause problems. If the radon barrier techniques are not fully utilized along with the subslab depressurization, considerable indoor air could be discharged, resulting in a large energy penalty. System durability is of concern, particularly with respect to motor-driven components. This system is also susceptible to owner interference.

CONCLUSION

At this time, the best strategy for building radon-resistant homes seems to be to build a tight foundation and make sure a radon collection system and provisions for a discharge system are integral parts of the foundation. This has the appeal of an insurance policy at very low cost. If on completion radon levels are higher than desired, a discharge system can be completed at a reasonable cost. With some uncertainty about what is an acceptable radon concentration level for domestic environments, it would be prudent to build foundations with some means for active removal of radon in case this becomes necessary or desirable.

Radon must be taken seriously, and potential mitigation design considerations must be worked into the foundation design of almost all new housing in the future. At this time, radon mitigation could be perceived for new construction as having engineering solutions that work, such as subslab depressurization. If the foundation is constructed with adequate subdrainage and reasonable waterproofing techniques, the added cost of radon resistant features should be minimal. Foundation systems should reflect integration of structural integrity, moisture control, radon mitigation, and energy efficiency.

BIBLIOGRAPHY

1. R. G. Sextro, B. A. Moed, W. W. Nazaroff, K. L. Revzan, and A. V. Nero "Investigations of Soil as a Source of Indoor Radon," in *ACS Symposium Series No. 331, Radon and Its Decay Products Occurrence, Properties, and Health Effects,* 191st Meeting of the American Chemical Society, 1987, pp. 10–29.
2. C. S. Dudney, L. M. Hubbard, T. G. Matthews, R. H. Scolow, A. R. Hawthorne, K. J. Gadsby, D. T. Harrje, D. L. Bohac, D.
L. Wilson "Investigation of Radon Entry and Effectiveness of Mitigation Measures in Seven Houses in New Jersey," ORNL–6487, draft, Sept. 1988.
3. "Health Risks of Radon and Other Internally Deposited Alpha-Emitters," *BEIR, Committee on the Biological Effects of Ionizing Radiations Board on Radiation Effects Research Commission on Life Sciences,* National Research Council, National Academy Press, Washington, D.C. 1988, p. 56.
4. *Statistical Abstracts of the United States,* U.S. Bureau of the Census, 107th ed., U.S. Government Printing Office, Washington, D.C., 1987.
5. *Evaluation of Occupational and Environmental Exposures to Radon and Radon Daughters in the United States,* NCRP Report 78, National Council on Radiation Protection and Measurements, Washington, D.C., 1984.
6. U.S. EPA, "A Citizen's Guide to Radon, What It Is and What to Do About It," OPA–86–004, Office of Air and Radiation, Aug. 1986.
7. EPA press conference at EPA held by Lee Thomas, Administrator, U.S. EPA and Vernon Hough, Assistant Secretary General, U.S. Public Health Service, Sept. 1988.
8. ASHRAE Standard 62–1981R, "Ventilation for Acceptable Indoor Air Quality," American Society of Heating, Refrigerating, and Air-Conditioning Engineers, Inc., draft, Atlanta, Ga., 1987.
9. A. V. Nero, "The Indoor Radon Story," *Technology Review* **89**(1), 28–31, 36–40 (Jan. 1986).
10. K. Labs, J. Carmody, R. Sterling, L. Shen, Y. J. Huong, and D. Parker, "Building Foundation Design Handbook,"ORNL/Sub/86–72143/1, Oak Ridge National Laboratory, Oak Ridge, Tenn., May 1988.
11. "Radon Reduction in New Construction: An Interim Guide," OPA–87–009, United States Environmental Protection Agency, Offices of Air and Radiation and Research and Development, Washington, D.C., 1987.
12. *Guide to Concrete Floor and Slab Construction,* 302.1R–80, American Concrete Institute (ACI), Detroit, Mich., 1980.
13. *Construction of Slabs on Grade,* SCM4–83, American Concrete Institute (ACI), Detroit, Mich., 1983.
14. "Radon Reduction Techniques for Detached Houses: Technical Guidance," EPA/625/5–86/019, Environmental Protection Agency, Washington, D.C., 1986.

JEFFREY CHRISTIAN
Oak Ridge National Laboratory
Oak Ridge, Tennessee

RAPID RAIL TRANSIT SYSTEMS.   See TRANSIT SYSTEMS.

RAYMOND, ANTONIN

Antonin Raymond (1888–1976) was a Czech born, American architect who introduced the modern architecture of the first half of the twentieth century to Japan. He was one of the first Western architects to see an inherent sympathy between traditional Japanese aesthetics and the new modernism of the Western world. His collaboration with Japanese architects united the two cultures and created the rich and fertile soil from which contemporary Japanese architecture has grown. He is considered to be the father of modern architecture in Japan by both Japanese and American architects.

Raymond wanted to see architectural values return to the fundamental principles of good design. He believed that good architecture could be appreciated through the elimination of the unnecessary, that the best design is arrived at through the simplest, most direct, and economical solution. He developed what might be called a functionalist style.

Raymond's new functionalism combined elements of traditional Japanese minimalism and the tenets of the international style. He believed that the modern floor plan should be freed from the imposition of structure, materials should be natural and expressive, interior and exterior spatial relationships should be clearly established, and that architectural form of lasting value comes only from new developments in technology and changes in the structure of a society. The direct application of stylistic developments leads to false values and a misinterpretation of modernism.

Antonin Raymond was born Antonin Rajman on May 10, 1888, in Kladno, Bohemia (present-day Czechoslovakia). He came from a Bohemian peasant family. His original name was Rajman. He studied at the Czechoslovakian Higher Technical Institute in Prague from 1906 to 1910, during which time the work of Otto Wagner and the Viennese Secession movement was very influential. Raymond came to America in 1910 and worked for Cass Gilbert in New York. While in Gilbert's office he became involved with the construction supervision of the Woolworth Building.

On December 15, 1914, Antonin Raymond married Noemi Pernessin. It was about this time that Raymond's studies took him to Italy. He returned to the United States and became a naturalized citizen in 1916, at which time he met Frank Lloyd Wright and joined his group of disciples in Wisconsin. Raymond remained with Wright for only one year before returning to New York to open his own office. His professional practice struggled for two years, when in 1919 Frank Lloyd Wright offered Raymond the opportunity to accompany him to Japan to help in the construction and site supervision of Wright's Imperial Hotel in Tokyo. Wright returned to the United States leaving Raymond in charge of the incompleted hotel.

After the completion of the hotel, Raymond remained in Tokyo where he was ultimately to accomplish most of his professional work. In these difficult first years of practice he struggled to develop his own design philosophy. Raymond's approach to architecture was essentially functional, European, and urban, and was influenced greatly by the new international style of the Bauhaus and the traditional minimalism of the Japanese.

One of Raymond's first projects in Japan was the Women's Christian College designed in 1921. The building complex, made up of dormitories, a gymnasium, teachers' residences and dining facilities, clearly shows the influence of Wright and of the French architect August Perret.

The Kanto earthquake of 1923 did substantial damage to the buildings of Tokyo, but helped support Raymond's

position of recognition in his association with one of the few buildings that remained undamaged, the Imperial Hotel.

Shortly after the earthquake Raymond completed his own residence in Tokyo. His innovative design utilized exposed reinforced concrete, a free plan, proper orientation, generous natural lighting and aeration, rubber flooring, and roof gardens. The house was clearly done in the international style with its flat roofs, bold planes, and metal window frames, while also demonstrating the Japanese influence in its simplicity of surface treatment, oriental gardens, and horizontal emphasis of the window mullions. The interior furnishings were also designed by Raymond in conjunction with his wife, Noemi. These features included light fixtures, rugs, and tubular steel furniture, all in the aesthetic of the Bauhaus.

In 1926, Raymond's firm designed the office building for the Rising Sun Petroleum Company in Yokohama. The structure combines the use of steel and reinforced concrete in an innovative effort to create an antiseismic form of construction. The building also accommodates the then new technology of air conditioning. The exterior fenestration is designed with the first and third floor windows recessed from the building facade, while the second floor windows project out from it. The projected windows visually appear as traditional Japanese wall screens. The building is viewed by contemporary architectural critics as having set the foundation for Japanese modernism and the Japanese New Wave architecture of the late 1970s.

A number of service-station prototypes were developed by Raymond for the Sun Petroleum Company. In these designs he again incorporated the antiseismic technology he had developed in their large office building. These prototypes, built in the early 1930s, have a strong visual affinity to the work accomplished 50 years later by the American post-modernist architects.

In 1928, Raymond became involved with the design for St. Luke's International Hospital Center. The center had received significant damage during the 1923 earthquake and major reconstruction and renovation was needed. Raymond applied the technology of steel-reinforced concrete construction pioneered by August Perret. His design was a serious attempt at a modern (the first in Asia), rational hospital. He replaced pretension and sentimentality with common sense and efficiency. Sadly, after its construction the building was modified and decorated by other architects.

Raymond introduced the European aesthetics of the Bauhaus to a generation of Japanese architects who worked for him during this time. The two most notable are Kunio Maekawa and Junzo Yoshimura, both of whom were to have a great impact on the evolution of Japanese modern architecture. Maekawa had worked for Le Corbusier in Paris (1928–1930) before returning to Japan and working in Raymond's office.

In 1937, Raymond left Japan to work on a dormitory complex in French India. One of the main considerations in the design was the need for the building to moderate, without mechanical means, the extremely hot, damp climate of Ponicherry, India. This building complex remains one of Raymond's purist works. The plan is strikingly simple. The buildings are made up of a series of single rooms facing a southern galley. The two long elevations of the multi-story buildings are equipped with operable louvers to accommodate light, shade, and ventilation. There is no glazing. The structure of the building is exposed reinforced concrete.

Because of the deteriorating political relations between the United States and Japan, Raymond returned to the United States where he entered into a partnership with L. L. Rado in New York City. Raymond maintained this partnership from 1939 until his death. During World War II the firm worked on a number of projects for the U.S. Army both in the United States and overseas.

In 1947, Raymond returned to Japan to rebuild his home and practice. In 1949, he completed the Reader's Digest Building in Tokyo. This award-winning building is considered a landmark postwar building by many Japanese architects. It established the aesthetic of the international style in the mind of the postwar Japanese construction industry.

The Gunma Music Center is a demonstration of Raymond's ability to manipulate his chosen medium of reinforced concrete. Built in 1962, the folded plate construction served both the aesthetic and acoustic levels of design that he was attempting to achieve and also the structural requirements for an open span interior space. The building is expressive in its efficient application of the structural system.

Raymond authored a number of publications during his long career and published his autobiography in 1973. After the war, he maintained a home and office in both New York and Tokyo.

Raymond had a confident and vigorous personality and held strong opinions concerning the shortcomings of others. He had a profound influence on the development of modern architecture in Japan. In many ways his architecture served as a bridge between the Eastern and Western cultures. Certainly he had an important impact on the architecture of Japan, but at the same time he provided the opportunity for the inherent aesthetics of the Japanese culture to be recognized by the West.

BIBLIOGRAPHY

General References

Antonin Raymond, His Work in Japan 1920–35, *Architectural Record,* (1936).

Antonin Raymond, Architectural Details, *Architectural Forum,* (1938).

CLARK LUNDELL
Auburn University
Auburn, Alabama

REASONABLE CARE, STANDARD OF

The legal standard of reasonable care, which is also called the community standard, has received increased emphasis in recent years as the yardstick against which the actions and decisions of design professionals are measured. Claims and litigation involving design professionals frequently examine the standard of reasonable care as part of the claims resolution process. The standard of reasonable care is based on a process in which a community of professionals gives its opinions as to whether a specific action of a fellow or allied professional was reasonable. A judge, jury, or arbitration panel may make the final decision. In large part, the decision results from testimony based on specific circumstances and actions that were or would have been reasonable under those circumstances.

The actions of those in virtually all the professions can be evaluated by the community standard. In this sense, an examination of a generic community standard transcends that of any particular profession. However, the attempt here is to answer certain basic questions about the importance of the community standard to the design professions and how it can be applied in daily practice. A knowledge of the community standard can help practitioners to understand better the risks of practice and apportion them as necessary. The result can be a proactive practice that anticipates, manages, and controls risks and produces more effective professional services.

The community standard refers to actions that are reasonable under a given set of circumstances. The reasonableness of those actions is determined by the testimony of other professionals, legal writings, and case law, in the context of the time, place, and location out of which a claim has arisen. In recent years, many legal commentators have sought, through reviews of case law and scholarly writings, to provide better insight into the community standard. It could be presumed that the goal of these efforts is to answer the question, "Might I be successfully sued for a given act or under certain circumstances?"

This question goes to the heart of possible litigation that may result from certain actions or inactions by design professionals. Some commentators contend that the most that can be said about the process are merely generalizations about phenomena that unfortunately never quite operate according to the laws of reason. To a degree, this is true. However, these generalizations can be of value if used in context.

The community standard has been and will continue to be a statement of policy. It can be helpful to practitioners in providing probable answers to questions about potential claims and liability. It has as its essence the professional judgment of peers and colleagues and the decisions of judges and lay juries. The community standard rests on an examination of an always unique set of facts and circumstances at a given point in time, with the change of one small condition or fact having the potential to bring about different outcomes from otherwise similar situations.

Throughout case law and the literature pertaining to the community standard, the term judgment is common. As such, application of the community standard inevitably includes elements of subjectivity. As the body of case law has expanded, it has become apparent that attempts to quantify, make objective, and attach specific performance criteria to the community standard frequently collide with subjective judgment. Application of the community standard brings into being a hypothetical practitioner whose professional behavior, although not perfect, is always reasonable and prudent and never negligent. Unfortunately, the actions of real practitioners may be less than reasonable and prudent. Claims and litigation are often the result. It may then be through application of the community standard that the claim is resolved.

What guidance can then be given to design professionals who at times may face uncertainty on the matter of the community standard? In addition, what can be the response to the public, which seeks to know in advance what is to be expected from architects, engineers, and others who are providing services to which the community standard applies? In advance of formally utilizing a claims resolution process such as litigation or arbitration, the community standard can provide only speculative answers. The answers may have a high probability of being proven accurate by the claims resolution process. However, definitive answers can result only from the claims resolution process running its course.

An erroneous dimension on a plan prepared by a design professional may or may not be within the community standard, depending on an almost infinite set of circumstances. The same holds true for a statement in the specifications that is at variance with the drawings. Production of a faulty wiring diagram by an electrical engineer or miscalculation of the amount of structural steel shown in concrete reinforcing is another example.

Decisions made by design professionals and placed in the contract documents, as well as decisions made in the field during construction, are all subject to the community standard. The amount of successful construction attests the fact that the majority of decisions made by design professionals are within the community standard.

The community standard can be described graphically as a region of behavior, the center of which is the ideal or perfection. As one moves from the center in any direction, one approaches the boundary between the community standard and the realm of liability. The precise location of the disputed act is based on the specific set of circumstances. Prudence and reasonable behavior exist within the boundary, but crossing it means liability. Negligent acts can exist on either side of the boundary. Negligent acts can occur from which no liability results. Under these conditions, the negligent act may yet remain within the community standard. However, when a negligent act results in damages, the result is likely to be liability.

Practitioners want to be assured that their actions conform to the community standard. Receiving that assurance is perhaps best achieved through a process of informed and enlightened self-evaluation that can be applied both consciously and subconsciously. Through its application, design professionals can seek to affirm their actions with the following declarations: "What I am about to do is the right thing. I know it to be best for the circumstances. I can explain my reasoning to others. The decision is defensible in litigation if necessary. If there is an element of risk in making the decision, it is one with which I can genuinely say I am comfortable and the outcome of which will be favorable. I have apportioned the risk properly and have not unnecessarily taken (or been unreasonably forced to take) too much risk on myself."

These statements can seldom be made with formality. The process is nonetheless a part of the exercise of judgment normally associated with the design professions. It is one reason that the majority of construction projects are completed without claims. As stated earlier, assurance that all decisions will prove to be within the region of the community standard cannot be given in advance any more than an architect or engineer can know the exact construction cost for a given project prior to the taking of bids. However, as design professionals know, it is possible to come close.

Dwelling for a moment on this example, as the difference between the design professional's cost estimate and the actual construction cost increases, so does the figurative distance from the center of the region of the community standard (perfection) to the graphic location of the estimate until the boundary surrounding and defining the standard of care is crossed, with the possible result being a claim and liability. A reasonable and acceptable explanation for the disparity between the design professional's estimate and the actual construction cost may be possible. However, locating the estimate in relation to the region of the community standard and determining its proximity to perfection or liability requires an application of the community standard.

Where then are the interests of the public to be placed, and how is the matter of public expectations to be addressed? Through the application of the community standard, virtually any set of circumstances can be analyzed using the testimony of professionals and authoritative witnesses, one goal of which is to reveal a condition as it should have been, rather than as it turned out to be. The extent of deviation from the community standard, if a deviation is found, can then be evaluated. A deviation from the community standard implies liability, the extent of which may be affected by the amount of resulting loss or damages.

The community standard is established by opinions and judgments brought to bear on a given set of circumstances that occurred at a given point in time. Establishing the reasonableness of actions within that set of circumstances may require an analysis of both technical and aesthetic matters and a wide range of issues in between. Certainly, opinions may vary on the use of one technical method or means over another. For this reason, attempts to establish precise performance requirements in professions that involve technical judgments often encounter difficulty, although achieving consensus on a technical matter, or at least a preferred or standard technique, is common. Generally, however, the greater the subjectivity associated with a decision by a design professional, the wider the potential range of views that are likely to result in an attempt to establish a community standard. It is possible that no community standard may be found. The outcome may instead be a collection of opinions based on preferences and little else.

Written contract obligations are intended to leave no doubt about the rights and obligations of the contracting parties. The AIA contract documents follow that principle.

However, at the heart of the standard AIA contract documents is the recognition that design professionals are not expected to be perfect in the discharge of their professional duties. As a result (implied by the documents), any evaluation of services rendered should be based on the community standard, rather than rigid criteria that are not project specific and carry implications of strict liability.

There may be events adverse to the owner for which no one is at fault. For example, an owner may retain an architect for the design of a residence. The architect's efforts in developing and translating the owner's requirements into a solution satisfactory to the owner may fail. The owner may simply not accept the architect's solution. Is this a case of violating the community standard? Arguably, the outcome represents a loss to the owner. Should the owner pay for services rendered? Should the architect be allowed to continue to seek a solution acceptable to the owner? Under these circumstances and without knowing more, it could be said that no one has acted in bad faith and no mistake has been made by either the architect or the owner. Can it be said that the standard of care mandated the production of an acceptable solution by the architect? The probable answer is no, unless the concept of design as a personal and subjective process is to be discarded.

Is it possible to say there are acts that, without exception, will always be within the practice standard? The answer is, arguably, no. For every attempt to place even the most simple, straightforward, and commonplace professional act within or outside the region of the community standard, there will be an exception. An infinity of countervailing possibilities can affect any situation, a condition that the volume of construction case law overwhelmingly attests.

Even under these ambiguous circumstances, it is possible to locate the boundary of the community standard with reasonable certainty. To say that the boundary is totally nebulous and defies description is inaccurate. Likewise, it is incorrect to say that the boundary can be described with precision and that previous decisions will automatically lead to the same answer for the next similar question. The boundary of the community standard is not rigid. It changes with the evolution of public policy found in legislation, regulations, and case law.

One result of this condition is that efforts to legislate or mandate conclusions that are characterized chiefly by the exercise of professional judgment will often be reconsidered and revised. What is legally determined to be reasonable and prudent behavior today may not be tomorrow.

Building codes are an example. Design professionals know that building codes convey, with as much precision as is possible through use of the written word, the requirements necessary for safety and comfort in buildings, and yet there is still the question of how those codes are applied. Initially and ultimately, the application is one of human judgment, often with a recognizable bias on the part of the design professional, the enforcement official, or both. All involved with the application of building codes seek predictability and consistency. At the same time, no building code ever written can be applied without the intervention of a person who brings to the process a unique collection of training, education, experience, and persuasion.

Once again, despite every effort to maintain objectivity, human judgment is the final determinant. Thus, applying the community standard brings the outcome of specific issues into focus, but the big picture is forever in the process of coming into focus. The public should be able to consult architects, engineers, physicians, attorneys, accountants, and all others who occupy positions of special trust with reasonable reliance. The public is entitled to expect and demand that those providing the services enumerated should be able to do the job. However, perfection is not yet, and is not likely to be, the rule in providing professional design services. Therefore, a lack of perfection cannot always be equated with liability.

Not every attorney wins every lawsuit. Not every patient fully recovers after having received the best medical treatment. Not every mechanical and plumbing system functions without flaw, nor are all architectural services performed with the total absence of errors or omissions. As history has shown, most of the time the process produces the desired result. The participants do the job that was intended, and the imperfections in the process are far overshadowed by the actions and decisions that fall within the community standard.

Attempts to develop strict and objective performance criteria for the services of design professionals always require the exercise of judgment. For design professionals, apportioning risks with an understanding of the community standard, along with candid discussions between design professionals and their owner/clients concerning the nature of the services to be provided, including appropriate supporting contract language, can do much to reduce claims and litigation at a later date. Understanding the community standard can add to the overall success in the design and construction of the built environment.

BIBLIOGRAPHY

General References

Architects and Engineers Legal Newsletter and Guidelines for Improving Practice, Architects and Engineers Professional Liability Division, Victor O. Schinnerer & Co., Inc., Washington, D.C., 1972.

J. Acret, *Architects and Engineers: Their Legal Responsibilities,* McGraw-Hill Inc., New York, 1978.

J. Acret, *Architects and Engineers,* Shephards/McGraw-Hill, Colorado Springs, Colo., 1984.

A. Dib and J. K. Grant, eds., *Legal Handbook for Architects, Engineers and Contractors,* Clark Boardman Co., New York, 1985.

M. S. Simon, *Construction Contracts and Claims,* McGraw-Hill Inc., New York, 1985.

J. Sweet, *Legal Aspects of Architecture and Engineering,* 3rd ed., West Publishing Co., St. Paul, Minn., 1985.

"AIA Plans 'Standard of Care' Document to Assist Architects," *American Institute of Architects Newsletter* **37**(10), 1 (Nov. 1986).

"Toward a Standard of Care," *American Institute of Architects Newsletter,* Special Issue 7 (Dec. 1986).

J. R. Franklin, "An Architect Looks at the Standard of Care," American Institute of Architects, Washington, D.C., 1988.

A/E Legal Newsletter, Office for Professional Liability Research, Victor O. Schinnerer & Co., Inc., Washington, D.C., periodically updated.

Guidelines for Improving Practice: Architects and Engineers Professional Liability, Office for Professional Liability Research, Victor O. Schinnerer & Co., Inc., Washington, D.C., supplemented regularly.

The Schinnerer A/EGIS, Victor O. Schinnerer & Co., Inc., Washington, D.C., quarterly report.

The following periodicals are good general references:

Architecture Magazine

Architectural Record Magazine

Architectural Technology

See also Arbitration In Construction; Construction Law; Contract Administration; Liability Insurance; Mediation In Architectural And Construction Disputes

J. Russell Groves, Jr., AIA
Johnson Romanowitz
Architects & Planners
Lexington, Kentucky

RECREATIONAL FACILITIES.   See Supplement.

REFRACTORIES

Refractory means stubborn; unresponsive; difficult to fuse, corrode, or draw out (fiberize); capable of withstanding high temperature. Synonyms include intractable and obstinate. "Refractories virtually laugh at fire," according to the Dictionary of Ceramic Science and Engineering (1).

Refractories include a wide variety of nonmetallic materials that can be creatively formulated and processed into shapes and forms as required to meet specific construction industry requirements. The four main requirements refractories must meet are: (1) the ability to retain their physical shape and chemical identification when subjected to high temperatures; (2) the possession of suitable physical and chemical characteristics to withstand abrasion from hot gases, flames, and mechanical abuse; (3) the ability to resist sudden changes in temperature; and (4) the ability to withstand chemical corrosion.

Until recently, the most common use of refractories as building materials was in the form of firebrick in industrial furnaces and residential fireplaces; as a fire-resistive medium around structural steel; and as a thermal- and chemical-resistant additive to mortars, concrete, and cement panels.

Many materials have been used to protect structural steel from fire damage. Concrete was used for years. Sprayed mineral fiber and gypsum board were developed as inexpensive lightweight protections. Calcium silicate panels also have served well for this purpose. Other products used for steel protection include cementitious insulating castables, mineral wool blankets, and intumescent coatings. (These coatings remain specialty products used where saving space is of paramount importance.)

Refractory materials are better known in industrial and aerospace settings than in construction. Gradually, specialized uses have been found in construction for these fire-resistors.

Fire protection refers to methods of (1) retarding the spread of fire; (2) lengthening the time a structural item can withstand high temperatures; or (3) reducing the flammability of materials.

Refractories are valuable in construction because they are truly incombustible, that is, when subjected to extremely high temperatures or direct flame, they do not burn or contribute to the combustion's environment. They are also completely resistant to thermal shock and are used in severe applications such as furnace doors or stairwell fire doors.

Calcium silicate boards and refractory fiber blankets are being used to protect cable trays for limited periods of time. Such protection of critical electrical wiring extends circuit continuity, which in the past could fail before significant damage occurred. Similar refractories are being specified as fire barriers preventing flame spread between floors. Flexible refractories are packed into void spaces around cables or pipes penetrating ceilings and floors.

Construction conditions demand that in addition to fire resistance, all types of refractories meet other considerations including the ability to withstand various loads and pressures, weight of the material used, thickness control, and ease of maintenance or replacement.

HISTORY OF DEVELOPMENT IN THE UNITED STATES

The earliest type of refractory used in the United States was mica schist, or siliceous rock, as furnace stone in early iron furnaces and forges.

The first successful furnace was built in 1645 at Saugus, Mass.; the next year another was operating at Braintree (2).

Fireclay brick, manufactured from native clays, made an appearance in the 1790s in New Jersey and Massachusetts. Probably the first silica bricks made in the United States were manufactured by J. P. Alexander of Akron, Ohio around 1866. These were produced primarily for the steel industry.

Bauxite was first discovered in the United States near Rome, Georgia during 1888 and led to the first production of high-alumina refractories.

In 1942, a pure silica fiber was created and was used widely as jet engine insulation during World War II and thereafter. Refinements of this high-purity silica fiber have been used for jet engines and early space vehicles and was chosen for the tiles which formed the first reusable thermal-protection system on the NASA space shuttles. These fibers, however, were far too expensive to be used as construction materials.

Mineral or rock wool, was developed as a low-cost, insulating and fireproofing material and has been widely used in construction. These fibers are melted and fiberized from blast furnace slag or native rock generally having calcium–aluminum–silicate chemistry.

Many developments have occurred rapidly since the mid-1960s that have solved problems related to energy efficiency and the demands of the aerospace industry. This research and development has led to the creation of refractories that withstand direct contact with flame and sustained exposure to temperatures in excess of 1649°C (3000°F) while maintaining their physical and chemical properties.

The success of researchers' abilities to combine these materials to yield ever-increasing fire resistant properties, and the demands for better fire protection in public buildings, has led to the use of better refractories as building materials at all levels of construction from residential to industrial.

USES IN CONSTRUCTION AND AVAILABLE FORMS

Wherever high temperatures from 1600–3000°F are encountered in the construction industry, some form of refractory envelope or platform is required to contain and control the heat and its effects.

Refractories for use in the construction industry can be organized into three basic categories (3):

1. Clay brick: fireclay brick; insulating firebrick.
2. Bulk fibers: calcium silicate and mineral wool boards and blankets; refractory fiber felts and blankets.
3. Concrete and mortars: panels; mixture additives; artificial stone and joint compounds.

The following summary describes the components and current uses of refractories in construction.

Clay Brick

A. Fireclay Brick, also known as fired-clay brick, is for use in temperatures up to 3300°F. It has high strength and medium thermal conductivity and is relatively inexpensive on first installation.

Uses in Construction. Building and facing brick, arches, furnace linings, piers, firestops, solar heat storage.

Components. Low-purity quartzite, dolomite, olivine, graphite, zircon sand, fireclay, bonding clays.

Available Forms. All international brick equivalents.

B. Insulating firebrick is available to 3300°F and generally weighs less than fireclay brick. The product has much better insulating qualities because it is two to four times more resistant to heat transmission, but it is not as strong as fireclay.

Uses in Construction. Industrial furnace linings, prefabricated fireplaces, piers, firestops, solar heat storage.

Components. High-purity kaolin, diatomite clays.

Available Forms. Brick equivalents, blocks, wedges, slabs. All can be machined to various shapes.

Bulk Fibers

A. Calcium silicate and mineral wools are used at the lower fringe of refractory-temperature ranges often because of their combination of qualities. Calcium silicate usually offers structural-strength and high thermal-insulating values and is not affected by humidity. Mineral wools generally combine the properties of light weight, heat resistance, low conductivity, and high sound absorption.

B. Refractory fibers are available up to 3000°F with three major advantages: excellent insulating values, ease of application, and low heat storage.

Uses in Construction. Emergency repairs to brick, joint fireproofing, cavity fills, wrappings, lightweight firestops, door linings, trough linings, replacement for asbestos, shields against molten metal spills, protection of cable trays.

Components. Purified minerals such as titania, zirconia, silica, alumina, and chromium oxide.

Available Forms. Felts, papers, blankets, boards, bulk, textiles, vacuum-formed shapes.

Concretes and Mortars

Uses in Construction. Special facings, firestops, joints, coatings, panel or poured-in-place roof decks.

Components. Various combinations of the above components, calcium aluminade cements.

Available Forms. Concrete panels, artificial stone, mortar additives.

PHYSICAL AND CHEMICAL PROPERTIES

The most important properties of a refractory are its high-temperature stability, hot strength, resistance to chemical corrosion, and resistance to spalling.

High-temperature stability is a measure of the volume change (or the linear change) of a material that has been heated at specific temperatures for known lengths of time. Most refractories have no true melting point; the change from solid to liquid takes place over a range of temperatures.

Hot strength is determined by measuring the modulus of rupture at elevated temperatures and is sometimes known as the transverse breaking strength. The tests may be carried out at room temperature or at various elevated temperatures.

Refractories are chemically classified according to their impurity content, particularly reactive impurities such as iron oxide in clays; alumina and alkalies in silica refractories; and silica or boron in basic refractories (4).

Refractory fibers are desirable in situations requiring resistance to chemical corrosion. A general indication of resistance to chemical corrosion is demonstrated in Table 1. The test results show the percentage of weight loss of four refractory fibers after immersion in various acidic and one basic solution for four hours.

Spalling means to break or crack in service to such an extent that pieces separate or fall away, exposing new surfaces of the refractory. Spalling may be thermal, mechanical, or structural. It is caused by nonuniform temperature distributions within the material sufficient to set up stresses between areas not expanding or contracting at the same rate. Mechanical spalling is caused by stresses resulting from impact or pressure. Structural spalling is

Table 1. Percentage of Weight Loss after Four Hours at 90°C in Solution[a]

Acid	Concentration	A	B	C	D
H_2SO_4	1.0 N	5.0	2.9	0.8	0.4
H_2SO_4	0.02 N	1.5	0.7	0.4	0.7
HCl	1.0 N	5.7	2.0	0.5	0.4
HCl	0.02 N	1.5	0.7	0.5	0.6
H_3PO_4	1.0 N[a]	6.6	1.0	0.3	0.1
H_3PO_4	0.02 N	0.1	0.4	0.3	0.4
HNO_3	0.02 N	1.66	0.8	0.5	0.2
HF	0.02 N	6.0	5.7	0.4	1.7

[a] Weight loss values in this acidic condition may have been reduced because of the formation of salts on the fiber surface. A represents bulk refractory fiber; B, C, and D represent various zirconia-stabilized refractory fibers.

caused by chemical changes, usually in brick, that alter physical properties. Weathering of brick is an example of structural spalling caused by reaction of brick and airborne chemicals.

Another characteristic of refractories frequently stated is density, expressed as the weight of material required to fill 1 ft³. This measurement is necessary to determine the amount of material needed for a particular installation. It is also useful in determining the total load that a refractory will place on the supporting structure.

In certain service conditions, a minimum transmission of heat to the outside is desired. Therefore a refractory with a low thermal conductivity factor must be selected for those conditions. Other applications require a refractory with a high conductivity value.

The coefficient of thermal conductivity is usually expressed in the English system of units by k indicating the number of BTUs per hour that will pass through a 1-ft² area, 1-in. thick, when there is a 1°F temperature difference between the two surfaces of the material. (SI conversion: amount of heat in watts per hour through a 1-m² area, 1-cm thick, with 1°C temperature difference.)

$$k = q \times l/A(t_2 - t_1)$$

where q = BTU per hour (or W),

l = thickness in inches (or cm),

A = area in square feet (or m²),

t_2 = temperature of hotter surface, °F (or °C),

t_1 = temperature of cooler surface, °F (or °C).

The coefficient of thermal conductivity varies with the temperature, and usually increases with increasing temperatures. Thermal conductivity normally is reported at various mean temperatures, which are simply the average temperatures between the hot and cold faces (5).

Thermal conductivity in refractory fibers is affected by the bulk density of the material, the fiber diameter, the amount of unfiberized material (shot), and the mean temperature of application (Fig. 1). With such a wide range of shot contents and fiber diameters, the thermal conductivity of equivalent bulk-density blankets or felts made from different fiber can differ significantly (Fig. 1).

Table 2 compares the generalized properties of the major refractory categories. Because of the large number of products in each category, and because each manufacturer

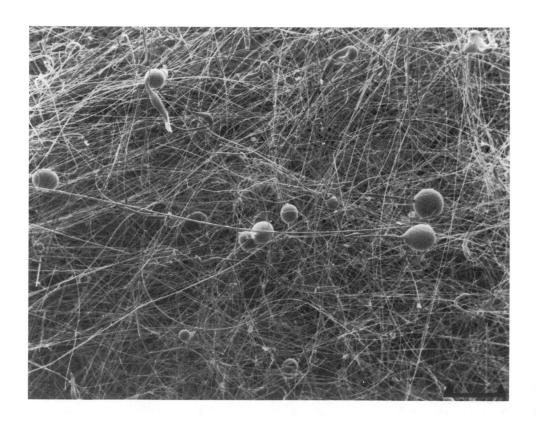

Figure 1. Refractory fibers.

Table 2. Generalized Properties of Major Refractories

Property	Silicate Block	Insulating Firebrick	Mineral Wool Board	Refractory Fiber Blanket
Weight	Low	Med	Very Low	Very Low
Temperature limit °F	2000	3200	1500	2600
Temperature limit °C	109	176	82	143
Heat storage	High	Med	High	High
Thermal conductivity	Low	Low	Very Low	Very Low
Thermal shock resistance	Low	Med	Low	High
Compressive strength	Low	Med	Low	Low
Flexibility	Med	Low	High	High
Resistance to abrasion	Med	Med	Low	Low
Chemical resistance	Low	Med	Low	Med
Acoustical effect	Med	Med	Med	High

uses different formulations, specific values or ranges are impossible to list. Specific values are available from any manufacturer.

DESIGN AND SELECTION STRATEGY

Rather than concentrating on refractory material properties, the design engineer should consider refractories as a strategy for slowing the transfer of heat. This point of view will guide the engineer through problems of material incompatibility, space limitations, and so on. The strategy begins with keeping in mind the three modes through which heat is transferred: radiation, conduction, and convection. The design strategy is to minimize radiation transfer, minimize convective transfer, and introduce a minimum of solid conduction media.

The compromise required for a given set of conditions is further affected by the need to solve problems related to temperature limitations, thermal-shock resistance, coefficient of expansion, strength, hardness, compressibility, specific heat, erosion resistance, chemical resistance, environmental resistance, space limitations, and installed cost.

The study of a refractory system should involve three specific areas, whether a system is being designed or a specific material is being evaluated: (1) the refractory system must resist the attack of the heat that is expected; (2) the refractory structure must be mechanically sound; and (3) the system must resist the attack of whatever chemicals, solids, or gases may be present.

In an effort to strike the best bargain among desired qualities of mechanical strength, chemical compatibility, weight, compactness, and so forth, with the least heat conductivity at the best possible cost, insulation manufacturers engineer their insulations toward particular applications. Extensive details are available from individual manufacturers for each of their products.

METHODS OF MANUFACTURE

Essentially, refractories can be used in bulk or preformed shapes. The range of sizes and shapes is almost infinite and therefore standardization throughout the industry is not always possible.

Most manufacturers of major refractory products stock high-request sizes and have facilities to produce special shapes to individual specifications. The larger manufacturers are also constantly researching special blends of clay and fiber materials to respond to special situations.

Clay Brick

The production of brick generally involves five stages: mining, mixing, molding, drying, and firing. Raw materials are mixed to meet requirements such as moldability and bonding. The blend can be pressed, fired, or chemically bonded into some final form.

The purpose of firing is to produce a ceramic bond. The degree of firing enhances the bond, which improves the refractoriness of the final brick. Special chemical bonds eliminate the need for firing and may improve the refractory quality of the brick. This process is more expensive but can yield superior properties, such as resistance to spalling.

Raw clays are mixed and crushed to size and, generally, calcined fireclay (grog) is added to reduce shrinkage during burning. Intricate shapes are hand-molded. Standard shapes are usually machine-molded by the power-press process.

The bricks are fired in kilns, following various air-drying processes, at temperatures ranging from 1148–1621°C (2100–3000°F).

Bulk Fibers

Most refractory ceramic fibers produced today are manufactured by two melt-fiberization techniques.

In the steam-blowing process the desired materials are melted in an electric furnace and the glassy melt is released as a stream, or streams, through a hole in the bottom of the furnace. The falling stream is blasted by compressed air or steam and literally blown into fine fibers. These fibers are then processed into various forms for distribution (Fig. 1).

In the spinning process, the molten material is dropped on the periphery of a rotating disk and is spun off this surface into fibers by centrifugal action. Mineral wool is made in a similar spinning process, yielding a less refractory (lower temperature) glass than ceramic fibers.

HEALTH AND SAFETY ASPECTS

Clay brick, mortars, and concrete refractories do not pose any known health problems at the application and use levels. However, dust generated by cutting these materials contains respirable silica, and consequently proper precautions must be taken to avoid inhalation (6–9).

Bulk fiber refractories are not currently regulated in the occupational environment by any federal or state health agency except as a nuisance dust. There are no known published reports in the medical literature dealing with the health experience of workers who come in contact with refractory ceramic fibers. Conflicting information has been developed as part of two animal inhalation studies, raising the question as to whether high-dose exposure in animals may cause lung disease, including cancer. Several studies have been designed and funded by the Thermal Insulation Manufacturers Association (TIMA). Until more is known concerning the possible health effects of bulk fibers, it is advisable to follow certain common-sense work practices designed to minimize exposure.

As are many other vitreous fibers, refractory fibers are irritants to the skin, nose, and throat. This irritation can be minimized by taking the precautions of wearing long-sleeved shirts, loose-fitting clothing, gloves and eye protection; using a respirator; washing exposed areas with soap and warm water; and washing work clothes separately from other clothing.

Alumina–silica refractory ceramic fiber that has been in service at elevated temperatures (greater than 871°C (1600°F)) may undergo partial conversion to cristobalite, a form of crystalline silica known to cause the respiratory disease silicosis. This may present a health hazard to unprotected workers tearing out after-service refractory ceramic fibers.

STANDARD TESTS AND CODES

Refractory materials are compared by the use of standard tests. Some data is supplied by the manufacturer, but because of differences in testing procedures the data cannot be compared quantitatively.

The American Society for Testing and Materials (ASTM) has standard testing methods that allow data comparison. ASTM frequently publishes new standards that may assist refractory manufacturers in standardiz-

ing testing and that may be used as a guide to the selection of the required product.

More sophisticated building specifications, the increasing popularity of coatings, and the relative lack of standards in the area led ASTM to form the Committee E-6 on Performance of Building Constructions in 1966. The committee began writing standards for fire-resistive materials and has completed details for seven testing methods in the area of fire resistance. The first two methods are for both field and laboratory applications; the rest are for laboratory use only.

E605, Tests for Thickness and Density of Sprayed Fire-Resistive Material Applied to Structural Members.

E736, Test for Cohesion/Adhesion of Sprayed Fire-Resistive Materials Applied to Structural Members.

E759, Test for Effect of Deflection on Sprayed Fire-Resistive Materials Applied to Structural Members.

E760, Test for Effect of Impact on Bonding of Sprayed Fire-Resistive Material Applied to Structural Members.

E761, Test for Compressive Strength of Sprayed Fire-Resistive Material Applied on Structural Members.

E859, Test for Air Erosion of Sprayed Fire-Resistive Materials Applied to Structural Members.

E119, Test for Fire Resistance.

Special tests measuring the thermal conductivity of refractories include ASTM C201, ASTM C177, ASTM C518, and ASTM C892-78, which is a general specification for ceramic fiber blankets.

In addition to material controls, codes and regulations also use the design features of a building as intervention strategies in an attempt to prevent ignition and to control the growth and spread of fire in such a way as to provide maximum time for occupants to reach an exit or a safe refuge.

Virtually all modern buildings in the United States are required to be compartmentalized, that is, divided into zones by fire resistive partitions designed to stop the passage of fire and smoke.

BIBLIOGRAPHY

1. L. S. O'Bannon, *Dictionary of Ceramic Science and Engineering,* Plenum Press, New York, 1984.

2. F. H. Norton, *Refractories,* 2nd, 4th eds., McGraw-Hill, Inc., New York, London, 1942, 1968.

3. J. E. Neal and R. S. Clarke, "Saving Heat Energy in Refractory-Lined Equipment," *Chemical Engineering* **88**(9), 56 (May 4, 1981).

4. W. C. Miiller [sic], *Kirk–Othmer: Encyclopedia of Chemical Technology,* Vol. 20, 3rd ed., John Wiley & Sons, Inc., New York, 1982, p. 65.

5. A. P. Mills et al., *Materials of Construction, their Manufacture of Properties,* 6th ed., John Wiley & Sons, Inc., New York, 1955, Chap. 20.

6. J. M. G. Davis, *Proceedings of the World Health Organization Conference on the "Biological Effects of Man-Made Mineral Fibers,"* Copenhagen, 1982.

7. *The Occupational Safety and Health Administration (OSHA)*, U.S. Department of Labor, 29 CFR 1910.1000, Table Z-3, Mineral Dusts (Cristobalite).

8. P. E. Enterline and G. M. Marsh, International Agency for Research on Cancer (World Health Organization), Scientific Publication No. 30, *Mortality of workers in the man-made mineral fibre industry,* 1980, pp. 965–72.

9. Manville Corporation, Bulletin HSE-66, 5-85, *Health and Safety Aspects of Refractory Ceramic Fibers,* Denver, 1985.

General References

C. Hornbostel, *Construction Materials; Types, Uses and Applications,* John Wiley & Sons, Inc., New York, 1978.

Shoub, National Bureau of Standards, *"Early History of Fire Endurance Testing in the United States,"* ASTM STP No. 301, 1961.

Underwriters Laboratories Inc., *Fire Protection Equipment Directory,* 333 Pfingsten Rd., Northbrook, Ill.

M. R. Harrison and C. M. Pelanne, "Cost-effective Thermal Insulation," *Chemical Engineering* **84**(27), 62 (Dec. 19, 1977).

See also Fire Control Systems; Fireproofing; Life Safety

Manville
Denver, Colorado

REFRIGERATION

Refrigeration is the use of mechanical or heat-activated machinery for freezing or cooling purposes. The production of extremely low temperatures (less than $-150°C$) is referred to as cryogenics (1). The use of refrigeration equipment to provide human comfort is known as air conditioning. This article emphasizes applications of refrigeration for food storage which would normally be found in buildings designed by architects—although refrigeration, used in its broadest sense, covers such diverse uses as food processing and storage, biomedical applications, refrigerated display cases and ice manufacture. For a more complete coverage of the field, refer to the general references.

Refrigerated storage units are used in food-service facilities such as institutional and commercial kitchens in hospitals and restaurants. Refrigerated display cases, which hold foods such as dairy products, desserts, and frozen foods at the proper temperature, are used in many restaurants, supermarkets and cafeterias. Common household-type refrigerator-freezers may be used for temporary storage of medicine in patient areas at large hospitals. Table 1 provides a glossary of the common types of refrigeration equipment with a brief definition of each.

Thermodynamic principles govern all refrigeration processes. For a review of the basic laws of thermodynamics and the nature of the reverse Carnot cycle, ie, the refrigeration cycle, refer to the general references. Refrigeration is accomplished in this cycle by using a fluid usually called the refrigerant, that evaporates and condenses at suitable pressures. The vapor cycle is illustrated by a pressure–enthalpy diagram in Figure 1.

The compressor raises the pressure of the refrigerant vapor so that its saturation temperature is slightly above the temperature of an available cooling medium (such as air or water). This difference in temperature allows heat to transfer from the vapor to the cooling medium so that the vapor can condense. The liquid's pressure is then lowered so that its saturation temperature is slightly below the temperature of the product to be cooled. This difference in temperature allows heat to transfer from the space or product to the refrigerant, causing the refrigerant to

Table 1. Commercial Refrigeration Equipment Types

Type	Comment
Walk-in cooler	Generally used for long-term storage of bulk quantities or short-term storage of individual servings on carts. Mostly constructed on site to meet varying requirements.
Chilling	Processing hot, precooked foods through the 55 to 7°C danger zone. Convertible to 3°C conventional storage.
Thawing or tempering	Thaw frozen foods quickly and evenly with air at 7°C.
Mechanical air blast freezing	Uses −40 to −29°C high velocity air to freeze quickly.
Dual temperature	Separate refrigeration and freezer compartments for limited spaces.
Self-contained	Generally located close to the point of use for short term storage.
Upright	Temporary storage of limited quantities in preparation and storage areas.
Reach-in	Shelf or pan slide storage for storage and preparation areas.
Roll-in	Mobile carts for easy storage of large quantities.
Undercounter	Under preparation, assembly, and serving areas.
Griddle stand	Short order items under cooking equipment.
Display/merchandising case	Temporary storage for prepared foods such as salads or desserts.
Mobile	Self-contained on wheels for transport and distribution.
Doors	
Full length	Large access area.
Half length	To reduce cold air spillage due to frequent access.
Pass through	Access from either side of cabinet.
Extra wide	Double-width carts for increased tray-holding capacity.
Strip curtain	Hanging plastic strips in the doorway to provide ready access but keep most of the cold air inside the cooler.
Sliding	Use where space for a conventional swinging door is a problem.

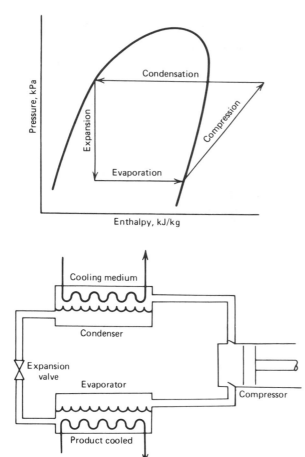

Figure 1. Basic vapor compression cycle (1)

evaporate. The vapor formed must be removed by the compressor at a sufficient rate to maintain the low pressure in the evaporator and keep the cycle operating.

All mechanical cooling results in the simultaneous rejection, somewhere else, of a greater amount of heat that is transferred out of the system by the condenser section. For refrigeration equipment contained entirely within a building, this heat rejection must be accounted for when designing the ventilating and air conditioning system. This heat can often be put to good use if provision is made to recover it from the condenser. A good example of this is the use of waste heat from supermarket refrigeration equipment to help heat the store in cold weather.

Refrigeration may also be produced using thermal energy from absorption systems. Large, water-cooled absorption systems are generally not used for refrigeration applications because of the difficulty of producing temperatures below freezing. A second type—the continuous, air-cooled absorption-refrigeration apparatus utilizing ammonia, water, and hydrogen as its working mediums—can produce lower temperatures. Refrigerant is boiled off in the generator with a gas flame or electric heater and rises to the condenser where it is liquefied as indicated in Figure 2. Liquid refrigerant flows from the condenser to the evaporator by gravity where the liquid refrigerant flows in the presence of the inert gas (hydrogen). Absorp-

tion of heat through the evaporator walls causes the refrigerant to evaporate and mix with the hydrogen. In the absorber, the weak solution becomes heated due to absorption of refrigerant vapor from the gas mixture formed in the evaporator. This heat must be removed through the absorber. The rich solution leaving the absorber flows back to the generator where the cycle starts over. This type of absorption system was originally used in household refrigerators. Today it is used primarily in refrigerators for recreational vehicles, and there is only one U.S. manufacturer of this type of refrigerator.

SYSTEM COMPONENTS

Cooler Storage Area

Refrigeration equipment uses electrical energy to produce a cooling effect. To minimize the cost of operation, the cold-storage area must be sized properly. A storage area that is too large wastes energy, whereas one that is too small or is improperly loaded with products will prevent air from circulating properly throughout the product zone and hinder the maintenance of proper temperatures inside the storage space. For energy conservation, all refrigerated spaces should have the best insulation possible. Generally, the lower the storage temperature, the better the insulation should be. Wall, floor, and ceiling insulation used for walk-in coolers are typically 10 cm (4 in.) thick, foamed-in-place urethane panels. In addition to being insulated, the walls must be constructed with a vapor barrier to prevent moisture from penetrating the insulation and reducing its effectiveness. For foamed-in-place panels the outer skin of the insulation normally serves as the vapor barrier. One should design a refrigerated storage space to have the smallest access door that is practical for the operation to reduce the amount of heat entering the system when the door is open. Proper door seals are another area of importance for energy conservation.

The cooler section of all refrigeration systems needs to be cleaned periodically to comply with sanitation regulations. The construction of the storage unit should lend itself to ease of cleaning through the use of well-rounded corners and no exposed fasteners or screwheads. Sanitation codes prohibit the use of floor drains inside a walk-in unit used for food storage; the drain should be properly located in the floor just outside the cooler. The construction materials should be able to withstand moisture and the chemicals used for cleaning. Type 302 stainless steel, at least 18 gauge, is an excellent material for large kitchen equipment. It is, however, also the most expensive. Aluminum may be used for the finish walls in larger-size coolers. High impact plastic is used for small reach-in refrigerators.

Larger walk-in and roll-in rack refrigeration systems should be constructed with the top of the insulated cooler floor flush against the outside floor, allowing racks and carts to be moved in and out without tipping over. This requires a recess of about 13 mm (5 in.) to allow for the cooler floor insulation and a level bed of sand. A built-in floor ramp can be used if a recessed floor cannot be provided. Door openings should be wide enough so that the

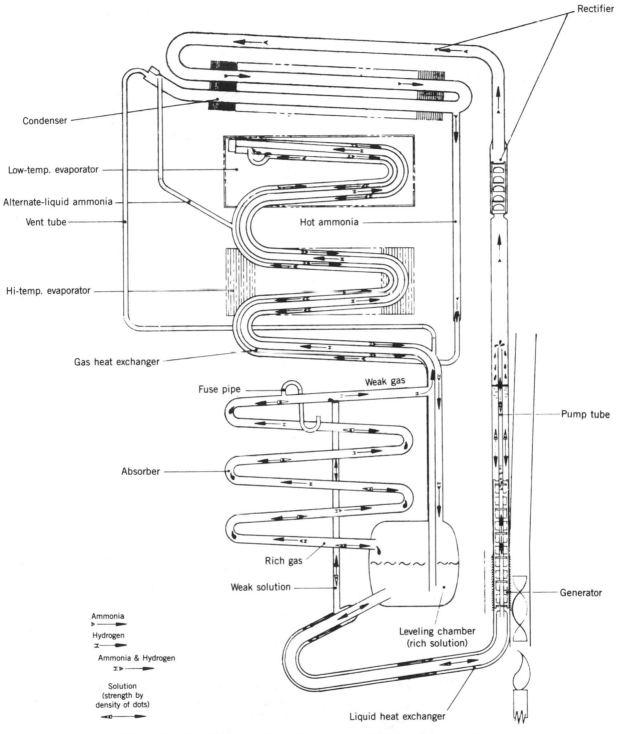

Figure 2. Air cooled absorption cycle. Courtesy of Preway Industries, Inc.

racks and carrying carts can enter without excessive maneuvering. These systems may be of modular construction to allow for future expansion if room is left during the facility design.

There are many specialized refrigeration units to cover nearly any application. Table 1 lists some of the more common types, and Figure 3 shows an example of a walk-in cooler. Manufacturers' literature will describe them in more detail. A partial list of manufacturers includes:

Alco/The Delfield Co.

Bally Case and Cooler, Inc.

Hobart Corp.

Hussman Refrigeration

Figure 3. Walk-in cooler. Courtesy of Bally Engineered Structures, Inc.

Kelvinator Commercial Products, Inc.

Leer Mfg. Co., Inc.

Penn Case and Cooler, Inc.

Traulsen

Tyler Refrigeration Div., Clark Equipment Co.

Compressor and Condensing Unit

A refrigerant compressor is used to raise the pressure and temperature of the refrigerant vapor returning from the evaporator. The condenser consists of one or more finned coils in which the high temperature refrigerant is condensed, and the heat is rejected outside the storage area by a fan blowing air across the coils. These components are generally located close to each other in what is known as an air-cooled condensing unit as shown in Figure 4.

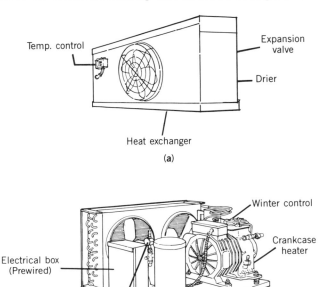

Figure 4. Typical refrigeration system components. **(a)** Evaporator assembly; **(b)** Condensing unit assembly. Courtesy of Bally Engineered Structures, Inc.

In a self-contained system, the condensing unit is an integral part of the refrigerated storage cabinet. This is desirable for upright refrigeration systems because it makes the unit easy to relocate; it does, however, require proper ventilation for the heat to be rejected by the condenser. Manufacturers' literature gives the minimum clearances required around the unit.

With walk-in coolers and freezers, the condensing unit usually is located outside (eg, on the roof or in a separate condenser equipment room) to save space, to reduce the noise level inside the building and to keep the heat being rejected from adding to the cooling load. Alternatively, the condensing unit may be attached to the wall or located directly on top of the ceiling of the cooler. These types of systems must be designed by a qualified refrigeration consultant and installed by a competent refrigeration mechanic. They are not easy to relocate once installed. When designing a remote condensing unit, consideration must be given to locating the refrigerated cabinet and condensing unit for efficient installation and shortest distance between the two units for the necessary piping and wiring.

Evaporator Coil and Fan

An evaporator coil-and-fan assembly, shown in Figure 4, is located within the storage area. Typically it is hung from the ceiling with sufficient clearance for air circulation through the assembly. The evaporator is connected to the condensing unit by refrigerant piping. In the evaporator coil, the refrigerant changes from a liquid to a vapor and removes heat from the air passing through the coil. A fan moves the air from the storage area through the evaporator coil, where it is cooled and circulated back to the cold-storage area to remove the heat transferred into the cooler. The temperature of the air leaving the coil will be between -25 and $-20°C$ for a freezer and between -2 and $2°C$ for a cooler. The manufacturer of the walk-in unit will generally supply or recommend an appropriate evaporator coil-and-fan assembly for the storage unit. The evaporator coil-and-fan are integral parts of a self contained system.

In addition to maintaining the proper temperature in the storage unit (-23 to $-18°C$ for a freezer and 2 to 5°C for a cooler), the evaporator will also remove moisture from the air. This moisture will come from the items stored in the cooler and from air entering the cooler when the door is opened. The water (either liquid or frozen) that collects on the outside of the evaporator tubes is known as condensate and must be removed. The manufacturer will provide a means for defrosting the coil, if needed, and collecting the condensate as well as a means of draining it from the refrigerated space. Self-contained units may have a tray underneath the unit to hold the water and evaporate it.

Refrigerants

Refrigeration equipment for cold-storage applications is usually of the closed cycle type and uses any one of a number of common refrigerants. All refrigerants have a common numbering system described by ASHRAE Standard 34–78 that uniquely specifies the chemical compound without the use of cumbersome chemical names (2). In refrigeration systems normally used in a building, refrigerants R22 and R502 are common, however, R12 is sometimes used. Very large refrigeration systems may use ammonia as the refrigerant; however, these systems are always constructed for a specific purpose and are usually in a building by themselves. These refrigerants are not interchangeable. Because they have boiling points ranging from −30 to −45°C, they are pressurized at normal temperatures and require special cylinders for containment. Each refrigeration-system manufacturer designs his system using the best refrigerant for the temperature to be maintained. For example, R12, R22, or R502 may be used when the storage temperature is near −20°C, but R502 is recommended at lower temperatures. All systems in buildings use common refrigerants that are available to the dealer who services the equipment. Since most systems in buildings only use between 1 kg and 50 kg of refrigerant, extra refrigerant normally is not stored on site but is supplied by the servicing dealer. All of the common refrigerants in use, except for ammonia, fall into the American National Standards Institute (ANSI) Group 1 class which means that they are nontoxic and nonflammable (3). Special precautions are necessary when installing and maintaining a refrigeration system using ammonia as the refrigerant.

CAPACITY REQUIREMENTS

The most important decision in the design of a refrigerated food-storage system is the selection of the layout and capacity of the storage unit. Many different sizes and layouts are available for storing different types of fresh foods, packaged foods and liquids. The architect/consultant must find out the size, shape, weight and amount of the material to be stored before selecting a suitable refrigeration system. The volume needed to store foods properly depends entirely on the types of foods to be served as well as the size of the operation. When allocating storage space for refrigeration systems used in food service, consider the following (4):

- Type of menu
- Frequency of delivery
- Purchasing policy
- Style of service
- Clientele
- Size of operation or seating capacity
- Way foods are purchased (fresh vs frozen)
- Storage-container sizes
- Quality storage life of the various food products

When foods are purchased in bulk, such as meat by the side, the storage requirements increase owing to the unusable portions of the bulk-purchased items and the need to provide additional storage for the trimmed parts. Table 2 summarizes the approximate percentage of total cold-storage needs for various types of foods. Many of these foods require isolation from one another, so the storage cannot

Table 2. Food Storage Space Requirements

Food	Total Storage Need, %
Meat and poultry	35 to 40
Dairy	20 to 25
Fruit and vegetable	20 to 25
Fish	10 to 15
Bakery, salad, dessert, ingredients	up to 10
Deep freezer storage	up to 40

be all in one cabinet. A food-service design consultant is best equipped to determine the sizes and types of cold-storage required for each application and should be engaged to help design all but the simplest installations.

Sizing Walk-in Coolers and Freezers

Walk-in coolers and freezers are typically constructed with prefabricated panels to provide the required storage capacity. They are usually made in three standard heights: 2.28 m, 2.59 m, and 3.2 m (7 ft 6 in., 8 ft 6 in. and 10 ft 6 in.) with various standard lengths and widths, in 29.2 mm increments (11.5 in.) for modularity. The American Gas Association recommends that the storage capacity be based on the number of meals served between food deliveries (4). Meats range from 0.0003 to 0.0009 m³ (0.01 to 0.03 ft³) per meal, whereas dairy products range from 0.0002 to 0.0004 m³ and vegetables and fruits from 0.0006 to 0.0012 m³ per meal. Generally, the lower ranges are for schools, middle ranges for hospitals, and the high ranges for "fine dining" restaurants. Once the total food-storage volume has been determined, this figure should be multiplied by approximately 2.5 to determine the actual size of the refrigerated area owing to unusable storage space between shelves and in aisles.

Sizing Upright Coolers

Upright refrigeration cabinets are made in many styles and configurations to serve specific needs. The space is used efficiently provided that a proper assessment of need has been made. To estimate the storage need, allow from 0.03 to 0.045 m³ (1 to 1.5 ft³) of storage space per person per 3 meals daily plus allow 0.03 m³ of storage space per 14 to 16 kg of food to be stored (4).

EQUIPMENT SELECTION

The refrigeration equipment required for a walk-in cooler or freezer will generally be selected by the manufacturer of the unit based on the room characteristics provided in the plans generated by the food-service consultant or facility designer.

Walk-in Coolers and Freezers

Most manufacturers provide forms to help in the selection of the proper equipment. The following information is generally required to select a walk-in cooler or freezer designed to store perishable foodstuffs:

Design Data
Dry-bulb temperatures in the area surrounding the cooler.
Room-temperature conditions required for the cooler.
Size of the storage area (length × width × height).
Number of doors and average time open (min/h).
Insulation type and thickness.

Electrical Service
Power characteristics.
Service availability (amperes available)

Information on Product to be Stored
Container type and material.
Package size and weight of product.
Entering temperature of product.
Final temperature of product.
Retention time of the product.

Storage Technique
Number and size of shelving.
Size of aisle.

Condensing Unit
Location relative to the cooler.
Ambient air temperature at the condensing unit.

Upright Coolers

Upright coolers and refrigerators are generally available for specific applications. Sizes range up to approximately 2 m³ (83 ft³). These units are normally self-contained and the floor space and ceiling height requirements vary considerably from one type to another. Consult manufacturers literature for actual sizes and clearances required.

INSTALLATION REQUIREMENTS

Once the type of refrigeration system needed has been determined using a design consultant or the procedures suggested above, potential suppliers of the equipment should be contacted to determine the exact installation needs for their equipment. When designing a new facility that uses refrigeration or remodeling an older facility, the following checklist will help to estimate the new installation needs:

1. *Floor Load Capability.* The floor should be vibration free and able to support the cabinet weight plus the maximum product load. Walk-in coolers usually require special floor preparation such as insulation or floor warming using thermostatic heat tape in conduit below the floor to prevent damage due to the temperature differences.
2. *Clearance.* Make the space for the cooler about 10 cm (4 in.) larger than the nominal cooler dimensions to allow for irregularities in construction.
3. *Ventilation.* Check proximity to heat or smoke generating equipment such as ovens and fryers. Leave proper space around equipment as specified by the manufacturer to ensure adequate ventilation for air-cooled condensers.

4. *Humidity.* Locating refrigeration equipment in hot, humid areas will degrade the system performance.
5. *Electrical.* Be sure that proper voltage and sufficient electrical service (wire size and ampere rating) is installed. If the electrical service is too small, the system life will be degraded because of hard starting and overheating of the refrigeration compressor owing to excessive voltage drop.
6. *Maintenance Access.* Be sure that there is adequate access for refrigeration system repair. Locate large processing equipment such as blast freezers and walk-in coolers where service and maintenance can be performed easily. This may mean that they should be located near an outside wall that has an access door.
7. *Access.* Be sure that there is adequate space around the refrigeration unit so that traffic patterns are not impeded. Consider the maneuverability of the storage and transport carts as well as the proposed traffic flow.
8. *Drainage.* Consider the need for condensate drainage as well as floor drains for use in sanitation cleaning. Many upright and self-contained systems provide for evaporation of condensate but may still need a trapped floor drain for efficient cleanup of the cooler. Sanitation codes prohibit drains inside the food-storage area.
9. *Door and Sill Warming.* Walk-in freezers require heating of the door-jamb and window-sill area to prevent frost formation. The heating element is usually thermostatic heat tape behind the door jamb, in the door and around the window sills. The manufacturer normally provides this heating element as part of the freezer.
10. *Interior Lighting.* Determine the proper placement of lighting within the cooler or freezer. Generally, incandescent lighting is provided with a wall switch located at eye level just inside the access door.
11. *Defrost.* After installation the defrost times should be adjusted so that defrosting occurs when there is little activity in the cooler. Defrost times can be set using the provided time clock. Typical times are after the day shift and in the middle of the night.

BIBLIOGRAPHY

1. *ASHRAE Handbook,* American Society of Heating, Refrigerating, and Air Conditioning Engineers, Inc., Publication Dept. Atlanta, Ga., 1982, Chapt. 49.
2. *ASHRAE Std. 34-78, Number Designations of Refrigerants,* ASHRAE, Inc., Publications Dept., Atlanta, Ga., 1978.
3. *ASHRAE/ANSI Standard 15-1978, Safety Code for Mechanical Refrigeration* ASHRAE, Inc., Publications Dept., Atlanta, Ga., 1978.
4. S. J. Levy, *Food Service Refrigeration,* CBI Publishing Co., Boston, Ma, 1980.

General References

K. W. Cooper and K. E. Hickman, "Refrigeration," in M. Grayson, ed., *Kirk-Othmer Encyclopedia of Chemical Technology,* 3rd ed., Vol. 20, Wiley-Interscience, New York, 1982, pp. 78–107.

F. C. McQuiston and J. D. Parker, *Heating, Ventilating and Air Conditioning, Analysis and Design,* John Wiley & Sons, Inc., New York, 1977.

ASHRAE Handbooks, American Society of Heating, Refrigerating and Ventilating Engineers, Inc., Publications Department, Atlanta, Ga. 4 volumes: Fundamentals, Equipment, Systems, Applications, one volume revised each year.

See also MECHANICAL SYSTEMS; RESTAURANT AND SERVICE KITCHENS

KENNETH W. COOPER
Pool Pak, Inc.
York, Pennsylvania

GREGORY A. JOHNSON
York International, Inc.
Charlotte, North Carolina

REGIONAL AND URBAN DESIGN ASSISTANCE TEAMS (R/UDATS)

In 1967, James Bell, President of the Rapid City, South Dakota, Chamber of Commerce, was in Washington, D.C., for a meeting of the U.S. Chamber of Commerce. He stopped at the headquarters of the American Institute of Architects (AIA) to visit with Andy Euston, then Director of Urban Programs. Bell, a practicing engineer, had a keen interest in what makes cities work and a deep dedication to his home town.

After he articulated a few of Rapid City's problems and some intense talk, the architects present from the Urban Design and Planning Committee offered to gather a small group of experienced professionals to go to Rapid City as volunteers and confer with local government officials and citizens on site, if Rapid City would put together enough funds to pay their expenses.

Soon after Bell's visit to Washington, a formal request for an assistance team came to the AIA from the Rapid City Chamber of Commerce. The Urban Planning and Design Committee met, and a visit was committed.

Four team members, two architects and two planners, were selected, and a packet of maps, aerial photographs, statistics, and other background information about Rapid City was sent to each.

The team met with the Mayor and Council, local architects, the media, and key citizens. It tried to keep its meetings informal and to hear all sides of the various issues that were raised, reviewing the data for Rapid City in the light of what it heard. At the end of the visit, the team made a verbal presentation of its findings. A week or so later, it mailed to Rapid City a brief written report and recommendations.

The results, over time, were powerful. A planning commission was established, with one of the local architects as a member. The city hired a full-time planner and engaged a consultant to help. Citizens and officials became aware of the issues and learned to debate them jointly as part of the planning process. Everyone involved, including the visiting team, came to see in a few short, busy days that the community, with stimulus and help from the outside, had resources that it could learn to harness in the public interest. Businesspeople, citizens, and government joined forces for the first time. The value of the process was clear, and it was decided to offer the idea to other communities, thus, the R/UDAT was born.

DEFINITION

R/UDAT is the acronym for Regional and Urban Design Assistance Team. This title was derived from those of two AIA national committees: the Regional Planning Committee and the Urban Planning and Design Committee, which shared responsibility for the program when it was first started.

THE FIRST R/UDAT IN ITS NATIONAL CONTEXT

Rapid City's R/UDAT occurred over 20 years ago. That was a period of great urban renewal activity. Suburbs were expanding. New urban growth was at the edges of cities large and small, spreading out into the open countryside. Everyone who could afford it in the 1950s and 1960s moved outward, particularly young, college-educated families. Cars and gas were cheap. Highways and interchanges were under construction. New strip shopping centers, the forerunners of today's enclosed malls, were steadily draining the strength of traditional downtowns. Offices and light industry had begun moving to suburban industrial parks.

The architectural language of the new suburban schools, offices, and industries, sited on wide lawns with neat parking areas landscaped with trees, was of a bright technological future; it was spacious, open, and optimistic. Those who were left behind in the older neighborhoods were most often the people who could not afford to move: the old, the minorities, the unskilled, and the poor. The usual cure for the problem areas of the inner city was to declare them blighted and to demolish them, leaving churches without congregations and cities with declining tax bases to maintain their streets, parks, hospitals, libraries, utilities, and services.

Today's attitudes make it difficult to believe how many politicians and department heads at the national level were then declaring that the old and traditional city was dead and that new decentralized urban forms would replace it. Metropolitan growth was seen as radial extensions along highways like the spokes of a wheel. Forecasts of urban growth showed these lineal extensions of metropolises becoming linked to form urban corridors. Two well-known studies in the 1960s showed city corridors linking Boston, Providence, New York, Philadelphia, Baltimore, and Washington in a northeast coastal system and Chicago, Detroit, Toledo, Cleveland, Erie, and Buffalo in a Great Lakes system. The traditional centers of cities were perceived as "islands of excellence," commuter cores of high-density office towers reached by limited-access high-speed highways and rapid transit lines. Along the radials were suburban nodes—decentralized office and industrial parks and shopping centers. Under urban renewal, the older residential areas of the center city would be cleared and would become building sites for the expansion of high-density cores or park land.

REDISCOVERY OF THE CITY

Many historic inner-city areas were declared blighted and demolished. Because it is now known that they could have been rehabilitated, the loss is recognized. Enough of the older neighborhoods remain to be able to work with the urban inheritance, socially as well as physically, and to graft new urban futures onto the old historic stems. A great interest in the redevelopment of the inner city has come about.

Art museums, universities, and historic buildings are being rediscovered. The energy crisis of the 1970s brought the realization of the need for alternative energy sources. Costs of family travel to work, shop, school, and leisure have soared, particularly for people who live in the suburbs and commute to the city. Housing shortages have led to a rediscovery of older city neighborhoods and to satisfactory remodeling and gentrification.

Developers and local governments are realizing that rebuilding old neighborhoods offers economic advantages over building suburbs because roads, sewers, utilities, shops, schools, and all other amenities already exist. People in ever-increasing numbers are interested in the roots, or ethnic origins of cities. However, intense urban problems still remain unsolved. Cities still house the poor and the segregated. In a world of rapid technological change in industry, the problems of unemployed men and women who lack the technical skills for the new employment markets are intense and real.

THE BIRTH OF A NEW CONSCIOUSNESS

The Rapid City R/UDAT occurred at a moment of historical importance for cities. The civil rights movement was gathering momentum. Martin Luther King, Jr. was assassinated in 1968, and burnings, lootings, and riots broke out in the black ghettos of several cities, including Detroit, Chicago, Pittsburgh, and Washington, D.C. Perhaps the racial riots in Washington, the nation's capital, were the biggest surprise.

Urban design was little known in the United States. The words were not a phrase in the vocabulary as they are today. If anyone thought about urban design at all, it was taken to mean the formal beaux-arts design of civic spaces. Certainly, it was not geared to grapple with the social, economic, and political forces that underlay the urban problems that erupted in U.S. cities in the 1960s.

In contrast with later R/UDATS, which became much more sophisticated as a result of dealing directly with these difficult issues in more complex cities, the Rapid City R/UDAT was simple and, in light of current events,

patently lacking in consequence. As it turned out, Rapid City taught a revealing and basic lesson.

A NEW KIND OF URBAN DESIGN TAKES SHAPE

Architects, by training, measure success in physical terms. Design to the architectural world means the design of physical environments and buildings.

It is not surprising, therefore, that virtually every urban renewal clearance in the 1950s and 1960s was accompanied by official plans and models showing new buildings, boulevards, parks, and schools. The graphics were beautiful and idealistic. New buildings stood out like sharp cubes in the sun, surrounded by trees and grass. Cars were parked neatly in lots, and street intersections were free of congestion. Usually, the graphics were drawn by architects and planners who worked in offices that were remote from the sites they drew. Sometimes these offices were in distant cities. It is understandable that the architects' designs for these urban renewal areas in the hearts of cities resembled suburbs. After all, the suburbs were the older inner city's competition, and they were successful.

DESIGN WITHOUT PEOPLE

Seldom were the citizens who lived in inner-city communities asked by the official designers what their perceptions and goals were. The thought that the inhabitants might have different values and priorities from those of the planners and architects, and the government agencies that hired them, did not occur to anyone. It seemed ludicrous that the citizens might want to retain the character and density of an inherited city that had so clearly become obsolete and failed. The plans were objectively thought out in terms of public budgets, health standards, zoning regulations, demographic projections, new employment, and tax benefits. Fortunately, the plans were seldom built; the few that were tended to be cold and impersonal.

DESIGN WITH PEOPLE

It turned out that the most significant achievement of the Rapid City R/UDAT was not physical at all. It lay in a different kind of design: the design of public policy, arrived at through a process of democratic exchange.

Five months after the one at Rapid City, there was a second R/UDAT in Frankfort, Kentucky, in November 1967. There were two more in 1968, three in 1969, and three more in 1970. In all of these early R/UDATs, many of the same characteristics recurred. When a team came to town, communication channels opened.

Businesspeople, government employees, and neighborhood people, came to the same open meetings to talk about their aspirations and the obstacles that stood in the way of achieving their goals. Problems were debated from every angle. There was no concealing any of the issues that were important to the citizens.

Some meetings started as confrontations. But most of

the time, people could see that confrontation was really a measure of passion. People released their frustrations by shouting at one another and making accusations. Meetings tended to become discussions, and the discussions began to reveal a wealth of information in the form of local input and perceptions. The team would learn about the issues and about the history of local places and buildings in an entirely new way, not from books or reports, but firsthand, from people's voices, in open and free public exchange.

Far more importantly, the people themselves learned from one another about the issues in this new way and saw within each issue, each perception, each piece of information and insight a gist of political signficance, a detailed piece in the jigsaw puzzle of policy and consensus. Agency representatives were asked to provide detailed explanations of how a property came to be zoned a certain way, how an intersection would operate when rebuilt, or how state and federal funding for a particular project would be regulated, and through their explanations, citizens began to understand government better. Documents of many different kinds, some of which might not have been made public, or been of particular interest if they had, gained meanings that were not perceived before.

IMPACT ON DESIGN

As the members of the professional teams began intensive discussions about what they had heard and learned, interrelationships among issues became apparent. Recommendations in one area became linked with those in another. Networks of recommendations would be set up, anchored solidly in local contexts. When the citizens who had participated perceived in the team's recommendations a true responsiveness to their concerns and inputs, local pride and commitment began to surface.

The focus of the architects and planners on these early assistance teams was not primarily on design, at least not in the old sense, but on making recommendations that would affect policy. When they drew their recommendations, they found that they were drawing in ways that differed from those of urban renewal planners and the majority of professional architects. Instead of inserting hard new buildings into old streets or replacing entire city blocks, they found themselves treating urban communities like pieces of old and treasured quilts, picking up threads of meaning and value, patching, and stitching. They tried to find the implicit, the particularity of inherited structure, texture, and scale. They introduced new buildings sensitively into old contexts and elicited new vocabulary from a sense of local place and heritage.

As they drew, the architects explored the meanings of their drawings with the other professionals on these early R/UDATs, the economists, engineers, sociologists, and historians. A sense began to emerge that drawings could become vehicles by which the whole team could work together to explore alternatives and define recommendations, and in this way, economic and social policies became as much part of the content of drawings as the physical concern for local fit.

So much has changed in the past 20 years in the way architecture is taught and practiced that much of this can be taken for granted now. But in the 1960s and early 1970s, it was not. Architects and other professionals 20 years ago did not think that anything was to be gained from listening to ordinary citizens. R/UDAT has been an important influence in bringing about this change.

R/UDAT: HOW IT WORKS

Growth of an Idea

From the primitive beginning in Rapid City nearly 20 years ago, R/UDAT has grown. In the 100 or more communities that have now had R/UDATs, millions of dollars worth of professional services have been volunteered, and more than one-tenth of the nation's urban population has in one way or another been affected by R/UDATs. The program itself has profited with each succeeding experience. Logistics have been refined to enable teams to have more creative time. With experience, capacities for sensitive response to delicate local issues have developed.

Today's R/UDAT

Although the processes vary as much as the communities, certain elements have become fairly constant. R/UDATs are always invited. A R/UDAT is never forced on any community. A team of about eight people comes to a town. They are drawn from all over the country. They are from different disciplines, but all are leaders in their fields. They have been carefully selected for their capacity to deal with the specific problems at hand and their ability to work effectively in an interdisciplinary setting. They have been briefed with materials that spell out the key local issues and provide essential technical information. They volunteer their time. Only their expenses are reimbursed, and to ensure their objectivity, they may not accept commissions for work that results from study recommendations. They are joined by at least an equal number of students from nearby schools of architecture, urban design, and planning.

THE TEAM IN ACTION

Arriving from all over the nation, a group of persons prepares for a R/UDAT project. Their mission is to give design and planning assistance to a community. They receive a package of material in advance of the visit in order to familiarize themselves with the characteristics of the community and the problems they are likely to encounter.

Their professional backgrounds are diverse, yet they all have one thing in common: a strong commitment to improving the quality of life in cities. The R/UDAT visit that brings them together will result in proposals that reflect the diversity of value systems on the team.

One of the team members is designated as a leader. This person is carefully chosen to manage the R/UDAT event so that it is productive and meaningful to the participants. The team leader must represent the findings of the team to the community and must be able to organize the effort internally. Such a person requires enormous amounts of energy, patience, and good humor. Not surprisingly, a few natural leaders have emerged in the R/UDAT process, and their skills are called upon with great frequency.

Over the course of several months, perhaps even as much as a year or more, a task force prepares for the event. Reconnaissance visits are made to the community for the purpose of meeting local officials and assessing the nature of the issues to be addressed. Local committees and contacts are established, and a list of key actors (businessmen, politicians, professionals, and community leaders) is prepared. The local chapter of the AIA is involved in planning for the visit, and where possible, schools of architecture and city planning are invited to send faculty and students to assist in R/UDAT sessions. Much time and energy is spent on preparing for a visit because it is essential to secure the active support and participation of the community and because the team can spend its time more effectively responding to the local problems if sufficient background information is available. The existence, for example, of a properly scaled set of reproducible base maps has a dramatic impact on the output of a team and the specificity of the product.

At some point late in the preparatory phase, a team is identified by both the R/UDAT task force and the team leader. The unique strengths of a pool of several hundred volunteers are known, and individuals are selected on the basis of their ability to contribute to specific planning and design issues. Also important is the ability of the team member to contribute to the success of the visit, a factor that places cooperation on an equal footing with individual creativity and skill. Out of the process of selection is forged a team whose separate strengths are brought to focus on a common problem.

The R/UDAT is a unique assembly of talented people. It meets for four or five days at one location in the United States. Some team members may know each other or may have heard of each other through professional practice, but for most, it is the first time they have assembled as a group. The convergence of these skilled professionals at a particular location and time in history is an event never to be repeated. It is bound to influence some aspect of community development, and yet its principal actors are only required to make a short-term commitment.

GENERAL STRUCTURE AND PROBLEM-SOLVING PROCESS

R/UDAT workshops tend to follow a fairly well-defined format. The first day is usually given over to meeting representative community groups and becoming familiar with the physical environment. On the second day, public hearings and reviews of available and recently gathered data tend to sharpen the team's perception of the main issues. By the midpoint of this day, preliminary problem statements and programs are defined, and by the end of the day, a strategy for approaching the problem is established. The third day is essentially an in-house problem-solving work session. Finally, during the evening of the

third day, or on the following day, recommendations are given to the community during a public presentation.

The problem-solving methodology of a R/UDAT workshop is based on team discussion of concepts, followed by a work in joint or individual groups assigned to specific segments of the program. The assignment process tends to be a voluntary act on the part of a team member with expertise and interest in a specific aspect of the program. After about two to four hours, the team is called together again, and a new round of presentations is started. This recycling of concepts brings about a steady inflow of new ideas and a modification of previous ones, as well as a large amount of drawing and writing. The team often works around the clock to put the final documents and public presentation together.

A TYPICAL R/UDAT SCHEDULE

The following itinerary reveals a general pattern of activities common to all R/UDAT sessions. On the first morning, a bus loaded with officials, team members, and students makes a tour of the region, followed by a drive through the town itself. This serves to introduce the team to the regional problems and to reveal the nature of the urban and rural landscapes. The afternoon is a mixture of meetings with town officials, walking tours, and photographic surveys of the environment. An evening presentation by the secretary of the department overseeing natural and economic resources gives the team an overview of the state's role in land development.

During the morning of the second day, special interest groups present a picture of housing, employment, and social conditions to the team. Public officials are requested to stay away from this meeting so that discussion can be relatively uninhibited.

The second and third days of the workshop produce a large variety of planning and design concepts. Drawing boards and work surfaces are set up. By the end of the third evening, the team produces the main portion of the report and accompanying design concepts. The production of a slide show for presentation to the public on the fourth evening and the printing of copies of the report are the only tasks left for the final day.

GENERATION AND COMMUNICATION OF IDEAS

Although the organizational structure of a R/UDAT visit follows a predictable course, the origins and flow of ideas are highly variable phenomena. Team members bring to each R/UDAT visit personalized approaches to issues of urban design, which tend to act as filters for sifting through and discarding or incorporating information. There are, in addition, some recurring themes, not necessarily conscious ones, which have a tendency to predispose conceptual ideas to an array of acceptable alternatives. Finally, the technique of communicating the ideas acts to shape the nature of the ideas. All of these factors depend on the composition and skills of the team, the imaginableness of the issue to be studied, and the manner in which information about the study problem is obtained. Since no two situations are alike, the conceptualization of ideas does not unfold in a steady, step-by-step fashion. Consequently, a R/UDAT visit is a highly creative affair, proceeding as much by inspiration as by conscious management.

Ordinarily, an overview or official presentation is given to team members before they have any contact with the actual site. Many civic groups assume a positive attitude about the community in an attempt to maintain a progressive spirit. Most teams are careful to question speakers at this stage and to examine disparities between documented material and official views of the community. It is a period in the process in which intuition comes into play; clues are sought that throw light on conflicts between civic agencies or on evasive behavior over specific planning and design issues. During informal conversations and social events, team members receive a more personal set of perceptions of local problems, thus modifying the official view. Ultimately, individual and collective opinions are held concerning planning issues, and these may be widely divergent from the official view.

A tour of the site provides additional information of a contextual nature, supplementing diagrams and maps provided by civic and local officials. Depending on the size of the problem area, a means of transportation that affords a comprehensive view of the community is provided. In the case of a suburbanizing region, or a large city, it is not uncommon to utilize airplanes and helicopters.

The two methods of gathering site information, vehicular and pedestrian, serve two distinct purposes. The former affords a broad view and enables team members to comprehend the complete urban fabric without being distracted by details. The latter permits involvement with the textures and details of the urban landscape, such as buildings, trees, signs, street furniture, etc. Architects are trained to work from a total concept down to details, and the R/UDAT process follows traditional problem-solving methods fairly closely when it comes to dealing with cities. One scale of analysis clearly imparts a sense of structure to the proceedings, whereas the other provides the content.

At this stage of the R/UDAT visit, verbal and statistical descriptions of the problem become infused with graphic and photographic imagery. Subsequent meetings with special interest groups, interested citizens, and individuals create an understanding of the priority of issues, which is the final step before the generation of new ideas. It is usually at this point that conceptual solutions begin to emerge from the team.

Many of the popular conceptual solutions of the R/UDAT process owe their form and structure to recurring themes in the literature of urban design. Linear organizing concepts, such as malls, boardwalks, riverfront greenways, arcades, and so on, apparently strike the imagination of designers with greater intensity than other formal ordering systems. For example, in a city possessing an undifferentiated grid, the tendency is to favor those solutions that emphasize linear segments over those that treat the grid as an entire structural system. A similar tendency to favor concentrated cores can be found in the conceptual diagrams of a R/UDAT team. The sheer

physical dominance of a downtown area overrides the importance of suburban cores, even if economic evidence demonstrates that the downtown plays a subordinate role. It could be argued that a professional bias operates in favor of the downtown, but it is also possible that it is easier to conceptualize and to reproduce in graphic terms such a tightly knit accretion of built space.

Linear form connotes growth, expansion, and adaptability. It suggests linkage and continuity, characteristics deemed desirable in contemporary cities. The core implies density and multiple uses, which in turn suggest high levels of human interaction. In their simplest form, lines and cores can be organized into graphic constructs of just about any conceivable type of urban structural system. Therefore, a city with a strong central core and one or more linear organizing systems possesses a higher level of imaginableness than either a suburban region or a typical small town with a dispersed population.

Aerial drawings, plans and perspective, are printed most often in the official reports to communicate ideas to the public. Aerial relief plans, also known as shadow plans, allow the designer to give a sense of mass, and therefore density, to large sections of a city with comparatively few lines. These types of drawings also permit the forms of buildings to be outlined, even if the plan arrangements are unknown. In addition, landscape details can be executed as masses of foliage or planes of uniform texture. Aerial perspectives are extremely useful for describing the physiography of regions or large cities and for visualizing the sculptural qualities of downtown cores and other urban concentrations. Both types of aerial drawings are used to describe complex urban environments in broad, structural terms so that the whole city is perceivable, or so that some large part of a city can be comprehended.

R/UDAT team members distill the unique visual attributes of cities into a language of design through rapid sketching techniques. These sketches take the form of either ground-level views, usually made during the traditional tour of the site, or conceptual diagrams. Executed with a drawing pen in five minutes or less, ground-level drawings reduce vistas, buildings, or building details down to their essential formal characteristics with only a minimum amount of detail. Conceptual diagrams are usually an abstraction, in plan form, of some aspect of the city that will later become a structuring device for recommendations. For example, the leftover spaces in a city block might be organized into a pedestrian-oriented park system through a diagrammatic interpretation of built and open space. Similarly, the ragged edge of an urban grid system as it makes contact with a meandering river might become a visual pattern for riverfront housing. The reductionist element of these drawings feeds the creative component of the R/UDAT process and simultaneously allows communication of imaginable ideas among team members.

Finally, some mention of the process diagram should be made. It is a complex flow diagram in which a series of actions is mapped out. Utilized most often in conjunction with implementation strategies, the process diagram is the urban designer's equivalent of written instructions. Process diagrams can be found in many R/UDAT reports, leading a community through various stages of a comprehensive plan or outlining a plan to rebuild a downtown area.

As stated previously, the generation and communication of ideas are subject to highly variable factors: the composition of the team and the skills its brings to bear upon the problem, the nature and imaginableness of the problem itself, and the manner in which information is obtained. The following section examines these issues in greater detail.

CRITICAL DIMENSIONS OF THE CREATIVE PROCESS

Nothing is more important to the success of a R/UDAT mission than the composition of the team. Apart from social compatibility and mutual respect, team members must possess the ability to grasp the essence of a problem, often on the basis of fragmented and incomplete information, and to understand differences in point of view between themselves and their colleagues. This latter quality requires breadth of knowledge in many fields, and the composition of the team typically reflects the complexity of the problems studied, including building design, landscape design, transportation planning, urban land economics, project financing and development, urban administration, land-use control systems, urban sociology, and other disciplines. Whatever their backgrounds may be, all team members have a special interest in urban issues, and their training probably includes experience in the resolution of problems by drawing on knowledge from this diverse array of disciplines. The architect as urban designer has, for example, most likely received some sort of formal training at the introductory level in all of these disciplines, and it is equally likely that information originating in these disciplines is brought to bear on the architect's problem-solving activities in professional practice.

Understanding all of the fields of study involved in the R/UDAT problem to be investigated, and possessing depth and creative skills in at least one such field, is the prerequisite for membership on the team. This precludes a narrow specialist from being a team member because it is unlikely that such a person could respond to the intuitive processes at work in the concentrated, charette type atmosphere of a R/UDAT mission. A R/UDAT team therefore tends to be a group of creative generalists, with each member having a rather special skill to contribute to the problem-solving process.

Over the years, a pool of talent has been organized by the AIA's R/UDAT Administration. In its published material, the AIA has identified 572 team members from 23 professions during the first 19 years of operation of the R/UDAT program.

In addition, 65 schools of architecture have provided 360 students as resource personnel for 89 R/UDAT projects. Teams are assembled on the basis of exposure to and performance in previous projects, contact with colleagues within the AIA and its Urban Design and Planning Committee, professional practice, and recommendations.

Each new R/UDAT mission has a documented inheritance of urban design projects whose collective effect is to raise the effort and output successively. In this regard, a steady improvement in the quality of R/UDAT projects as judged by the reports has been observed over time, based on both quality of graphic and written material and depth of investigation.

All of the attributes of a successful team member apply to its leader, the chairperson. This person must be resourceful and compassionate in managing people, especially under the stressful conditions of a high-pressure R/UDAT mission, and sympathetic to the needs of the community. Although the chairperson is just as capable of formulating creative solutions to problems as any team member, it is necessary to play this down in order to maximize the contributions of others. Consequently, the chairperson encourages, supports, sympathizes, and even exhorts, but rarely becomes involved in committing conceptual statements to paper.

Another critical dimension of the problem-solving process is the imaginableness of the problem under investigation. Just as the words "linear" and "core" are able to evoke images of form, the words and phrases "downtown," "historic preservation," and "waterfront" have the power to evoke the physical environments of cities. The associative aspects of words can shape attitudes, both positive and negative, among urban designers and consequently predispose team members to the acceptance or rejection of a concept.

The phrases "commercial strip" and "suburban development" have never enjoyed a favorable position in the literature on urban design, and these serious urban development problems are rarely utilized as thematic material for a R/UDAT mission. It is not so much a matter of rejection of fact as of imagery. Both of these phrases generate images of confused or unrelated forms, or perhaps a lack of visible structure, a characteristic that makes the urban designer uneasy. Those words and phrases that indicate a highly structured content or suggest a concentration of buildings, such as "riverfront development" or "downtown," give the designer an immediate mental construct on which to build a formal design statement. Although it is difficult to prove, it seems that the imagery of a problem can provide intuitive access to a means for resolution and that this accessibility is somehow shaped by professional attitudes toward key words and phrases.

The manner in which information is obtained by team members is also important in the creative process. The team is usually provided with a package of information prior to a site visit. Contextual information, which is important to the comprehensive design and planning processes of the R/UDAT methodology, cannot easily be provided through words and drawings. Consequently, a great deal of useful information is obtained through actual inspection of the site. During this time period, team members may make sketches, take photographs, or simply commit to memory a set of visual impressions.

Physical contact with the site enables team members to develop design criteria for future proposals. It is during this period that value judgments concerning the appropriateness of form, detail, texture, color, density, and other environmental variables are made. Naturally, each team member makes the assessment independently, and an open discussion or presentation is needed to discover those ideas that reinforce each other or those that are in conflict. This occurs in the R/UDAT meeting place or workplace. The team pins up sketches, looks at slides, makes comments about maps, and generally exposes its collective intelligence to general scrutiny. A half dozen or more environmentally perceptive people are able to amass a great deal of useful information through such an informal data-gathering process. More importantly, open discussion serves as a kind of filter in which idiosyncracy is separated from constituent knowledge.

Organizing and assessing information in this fashion is characteristic of the R/UDAT problem-solving process. It is probably the most effective way to interpret the issues of complex environments in a short period. Patterns of recognition and the recurrence of physical attributes take precedence over the abstract identity of numbers. Visual information can be translated into action without the necessity for rigorous analytic tools.

THE R/UDAT's IMPACT ON URBAN DESIGN

The impact of the R/UDAT program on the nation's cities is unequaled by any other urban design activity over the past decade. No consultant organization has worked so closely with so many communities, and no government agency has dealt with such a rich variety of issues. The breadth, quantity, and quality of experienced talent in the R/UDAT process exists in no institution or consultant organization.

The R/UDAT can therefore be considered an encapsulation of urban design. All of the fundamental elements of the discipline exist in the R/UDAT. The extent and activity of this program have not only taught lessons for the improvement of the program, but have also exposed the bare bones of urban design. Almost every planning and architectural office in the nation that practices urban design, whether in the public or the private domain, has been directly affected by the R/UDAT.

THE R/UDAT's THREE INGREDIENTS

It is possible to conclude from the R/UDAT experience that the three ingredients for successful urban design are as follows:

1. The Process. First, the process by which the effort takes place is as important as its product. Making urban democracy work is a critical demonstration in the R/UDAT program, as it engenders a sense that ordinary people can and do affect urban change. The urban design process must openly involve all elements in the community, from the decision-making structure to the neighborhood organization, and from the first perceptions of goals and objectives through the development of implementation strategies. To be successful, urban design must be sensitive to the people in the community and its physical fabric, as well as to the culture and history of the place, its political framework, and the events that produced the existing climate. The process must contain feedback techniques so that decisions reached in one stage can be evaluated and adjusted against criteria established earlier.

2. Interdisciplinary Teams. The second requirement for successful urban design is that the work be performed by an interdisciplinary group so that not only all of the issues, but also all of the angles on those issues can be explored at a professional level. Today's issues in urban design are far too complex to be understood and addressed by any single profession. Although a sociologist and an economist may understand each other's products, neither has the skill to perform the other's work. The sensitive meshing of the interdisciplinary team is vital to ensure not only the quality of its work, but also its credibility in the community. The dialogues among professionals with different backgrounds and areas of expertise can grow tougher, more sophisticated, and more meaningful as recommendations are challenged and hashed out within the team. Healthy urban design recommendations and stronger projects for each particular context spring from such a dialogue.

3. Citizen Participation. The key ingredient of urban design is citizen participation. The citizen's movement is no longer the scattered local voices it was only a few decades ago. Neighborhood organizations have new strength and are being heard in city halls across the nation.

BIBLIOGRAPHY

General References

S. Arnstein, "A Ladder of Citizen Participation," *Journal of the American Institute of Planners* **35**, 216–224 (1969).

P. Batchelor and D. Lewis, *Urban Design in Action*, The Student Publication of the School of Design, North Carolina State University, Raleigh, North Carolina, 1985.

R. L. Cole, *Citizen Participation and the Urban Policy Process*, Lexington Books, Lexington, Mass., 1974.

P. Davidoff, "Advocacy and Pluralism in Planning," *Journal of the American Institute of Planners* **31**, 331–337 (1965).

M. Fagence, *Citizen Participation in Planning*, Pergamon Press, Oxford, UK, 1977.

L. Halprin and J. Burns, *Taking Part: A Working Approach to Collective Creativity*, the MIT Press, Cambridge, Mass., 1974.

J. G. Hurwitz, "Particapatory Planning in an Urban Neighborhood, Soulard, St. Louis Missouri: A Case Study," *DMG Journal 9* **4**, 348–357 (1975).

S. Williams, "City Participation in City and Regional Planning: An Effective Methodology," *Town Planning Review* **47.4,** 349 (1976).

PETER BATCHELOR, AIA/AICP
North Carolina State
   University
Raleigh, North Carolina

DAVID LEWIS, FAIA
UDA Associates
Pittsburgh, Pennsylvania

REGISTRATION EXAMINATION PROCESS—ARCHITECTS

One of the most difficult tasks associated with regulation and licensure of any profession is determining whether applicants are sufficiently knowledgeable to practice the profession without endangering the health, safety, or welfare of the public. To accomplish this often highly subjective task, the state regulatory agencies or boards charged with licensure have usually sought to quantify "minimum competency" and to establish objective standards that applicants must meet prior to licensure. Without such standards, it would be difficult, if not impossible, to evaluate individuals fairly and without bias.

In architecture, as in most professions, the boards have established minimum standards in areas of education and training, or internship. In order to ensure that individuals have acquired the required knowledge through education and internship, the boards have also required a demonstration of portions of that knowledge through some form of examination.

This article explores the development of registration examinations in architecture and attempts to identify the objectives, the development process, and the strengths and the weaknesses of the examinations of the past and of the present. It also explores the possibilities for examinations of the future.

THE EVOLUTION OF THE REGISTRATION EXAMINATION

To understand the evolution of the architectural registration examination, it is necessary to first understand that, due to the political environment in which registration takes place, differences in requirements from state to state and changes in requirements over time are both inherent parts of the process. Of particular importance are the facts that each state is totally autonomous in the registration of its professionals and that there is no federal government registration authority. States register architects on the basis of statutes adopted by their legislatures. Most of these statutes are fairly general in terms of requirements and call for the establishment of a regulatory board to develop and enforce specific rules and regulations for registration. These boards are of varying size and composition but most often consist of experienced architects. Members of related professions, such as engineers and public members, are also now commonly found on architectural registration boards. Board members are appointed by the governor or the legislature of the state for specific terms and tend to change as the governors or legislatures change. As the board members change, attitudes and interpretations of requirements may also change.

Prior to the adoption of registration laws, individuals were free to call themselves architects and to practice the profession whether or not they had any experience or ability in the field. An article in *The Journal of the American Institute of Architects* (*AIA Journal*) in 1917 summed up the need for registration as follows (1):

> The truth is that an architect, in order to do the work which belongs to his name, should have special ability and special

training backed up by a broad general education; and the further sad fact is that, up to the present, anyone in New York State could assume the title of architect without let or hindrance, even if he were lacking in any one or all three of these qualifications—general education, special ability, and special training. Anyone with a flattered knowledge of drawing but without taste; anyone with a T-square and a triangle, a little knowledge of carpenter work and none of the vital elements of construction; anyone shrewd enough to hire a draughtsman but not to know a Corinthian capital from a Gothic vault—any of these may (and all of them do) go to the public which builds usually only once and under false pretenses claim a commission to design a building. The client, imbued with thrift, knows that he has secured his building for one percent instead of five or ten. He may never have the taste to realize that he has committed a crime against his neighbors, but when he completes his building is only confirmed in his belief that six percent architects are robbers.

> The function of the registration law, so far as the public is concerned, is to say, "If you want an architect, the man who may use that title is sure to know something about his business."

A fundamental aspect of registration noted by the author, D. Everett Waid, is that the work of an architect affects not only the specific client, but also the general public. Registration laws reflect this attitude and charge registration boards with the responsibility of protecting the public health, safety, and welfare by permitting only those individuals who possess the necessary knowledge, skills, and abilities to use the title "architect" and to practice architecture.

The registration board's primary responsibility was the evaluation of applicants for architectural registration. As stated in an article in the October 15, 1913 issue of *The American Architect* concerning the newly adopted New York State registration law (2),

> The primary purpose of the bill is the protection of the public against the unscrupulous and incompetent practitioner of architecture. To this end it provides for the appointment of a board of examiners who shall determine the qualifications of each applicant to practice.

The concept that a board of examiners would determine who should and should not be registered was consistent with the U.S. system of justice in that applicants for registration would be evaluated by a jury of their peers. Applicants presented documentation of their background and submitted samples of their work for the review of the jury. The examiners could also conduct oral examinations to further determine an applicant's knowledge.

The early examiners, however, soon discovered that they were faced with the problems of evaluating the abilities of applicants with widely divergent educational and training backgrounds. Although most of the registration laws required some amount of technical education and professional experience as prerequisites to registration, standards applied by the examiners varied widely through the use of numerous exemptions. Exemptions were made based on the reputation of an applicant's school or employer or even on the region of the state in which the applicant proposed to practice architecture.

By 1917, the registration process in Illinois, which had

enacted the first registration law in 1897, had already undergone a major revision. The lack of consistent standards and the vulnerability of the previous system to political and personal bias were major factors contributing to this change. An article in the May 1917 issue of the *AIA Journal* reported (3) that

> This reform is the result of many years of dissatisfaction with the work of the old board of examiners—though not always expressed with due respect for justice—which never was free from political appointees in its membership, and which for some years past has lacked the respect and support of the best element in the architectural profession.

It was obvious that more formalized standards and examinations were necessary to ensure a fair and consistent evaluation process. Several boards developed two basic types of examination called Junior and Senior examinations. The Junior Examination was a written examination on the technical subjects thought necessary to practice architecture. It was an essay and graphic type exam that often included provisions to conceal the identity of the applicant until after the grade had been given and was usually required for candidates who had not previously practiced architecture as a principal. The Senior Examination was intended for architects who had practiced architecture as a principal for at least ten years. This examination, like the previous examination, consisted of an oral exam as well as a review of an architect's background and work samples.

Boards were also faced with the fact that while architectural registration was regulated by independent states, architectural practices were often far ranging, crossing into several states. Architects with such interstate practices sought to obtain registration by reciprocity based on their initial license and without additional examination. Although most boards generally agreed that an architect completely examined and of good standing in one state should not be required to be reexamined in other states, the boards realized that requirements and examinations varied greatly from state to state and that the registration standards of other states were not always equal to their own.

To address this problem, representatives from nineteen registration boards met in November 1920 to discuss the problems of reciprocal registration. The boards decided to create a permanent forum for continuing the discussion of reciprocity. Titled the National Council of Architectural Registration Boards (NCARB), the purpose of the new organization was the enactment of uniform architectural laws, equality of standard examinations of applicants for state registration or licensure, and the establishment and maintenance of reciprocal registration between states having registration laws.

One of the first actions of the new organization was the creation of a committee to create a standard NCAR Examination that could act as the common denominator for all examinations and afford a standard medium of exchange between states. This committee recommended that standardized Junior Examination and Senior Examination formats be followed. The Senior Examination was a standardized oral exam requiring the applicant to present

evidence of ten years of "honorable and discreet practice." The recommended syllabus for the Junior Examination was a written examination of 29 hours given over a four-day period consisting of the following parts.

Day One
    Architectural Composition—4 h
    History of Architecture—4 h
Day Two
    Design Problem—9 h
Day Three
    Practice and Supervision—4 h
Day Four
    Reinforced Concrete Design, Structural Steel Design, and Details of Fire Proof Construction—4 h
    Graphic Statics and Truss Design—4 h

Although this syllabus was recommended to all states as the basis for their own Junior Examinations, NCARB also wrote an NCAR Examination. This exam was an optional Junior Examination that had to be taken in addition to the examination of the applicant's state. Applicants who passed the NCAR Examination, however, were assured that the exam satisfied the requirements of every state and was in excess of the requirements of many states. Applicants, therefore, could be reasonably assured of reciprocal registration on the basis of that examination.

Although there was some success in having states adopt the form of the NCAR Examination, there was little success in having applicants take two examinations in order to assure reciprocity. Furthermore, even between states using the NCARB syllabus, there continued to be significant differences in the difficulty of examinations and the grading procedures of the various states' examinations. As stated by a delegate to the 1928 annual meeting of NCARB (4),

> Some states have an examination that would be a discredit to a high school student if he could not pass it. Other states consider their examinations very carefully. When young men are examined on questions which are not qualifying, and, because of such, are denied admission to other states they cannot understand it.

Debate also continued over the type and extent of examination required of an applicant with a college degree in architecture. In many states, college graduates were exempt from the examination requirements and were registered on completion of the required internship period. Individuals registered by these exemptions were not eligible for reciprocal registration until they had acquired the ten years of experience necessary to complete the Senior Examination or until they completed the Junior Examination in another state. Other states felt that a college graduate should only be examined in professional practice areas and should be exempt from examination in the academic and technical areas that were taught in college. These differences continued to restrict reciprocity between states.

The status of examinations continued along these same lines for several years with each state continuing to write and grade its own examinations and with NCARB continuing to encourage states to use the NCARB Examination syllabus. By 1954, most state boards were developing their examinations based on the NCARB syllabus, which at that time had been revised to contain the following sections.

A. Education and experience—board review of background.
B. Personal audience—board interview of applicant to determine eligibility for examination.
C. History and theory of architecture—3-h written examination.
D. Site planning—5-h written and graphic examination.
E. Architectural design—12-h graphic examination.
F. Building construction—3-h written examination.
G. Structural design—5-h written examination.
H. Professional administration—3-h written examination.
I. Building equipment—5-h written examination.

Although this format was widely used, the level of examination difficulty and the grading standards applied varied widely. The examinations were often not accepted from state to state reciprocally. The NCARB member boards decided that the only way to ensure acceptability of examinations was for all states to utilize the same examinations. In 1962, NCARB committees again began writing sections of the examination. Unlike the NCAR Examination of the 1920s, however, this examination was not required in addition to the state registration exam but was used by the states in lieu of their own examination sections.

NCARB was writing examinations for all sections of the exam syllabus by 1966 and the entire examination, called the 7-Part Examination, was adopted for use in all states by 1968. This exam was based on the 1954 Junior Examination syllabus but differed from previous examinations in that, with the exception of the graphic sections, NCARB also graded the examinations for the state boards. The availability of a national examination, uniformly graded across the country was a major advancement in easing reciprocity between states. The 7-Part Examination was the registration examination in all states from 1968 to 1973. During this time refinements continued to be made in the writing and grading process of the exam to improve exam validity and reliability.

The United States underwent a number of social and political changes in the 1960s. Of particular importance to architecture was the public's heightened awareness of the environment and a growing demand for improvements in the quality of the built environment. Architectural schools, architectural practice, and the registration examination were all affected by these changes. As a result, a new examination format was implemented in 1973. Like the 7-Part Examination, it was a national examination written by NCARB; however it was substantially different from that exam in both concept and format. This new examination was divided into two distinct sections, the Equivalency Examination and the Professional Examination. As the name implies, the Equivalency Examination

was intended for those candidates who had not graduated from an accredited school of architecture and was designed to test them in technical areas they would have otherwise learned in school. It consisted of the following parts.

Architectural theory—2 h.
Construction theory and practice—8 h.
Architectural design and site planning—10 h, graphic exam.

Once an applicant passed the Equivalency Examination, he or she was permitted to sit for the Professional Examination. Based on the assumption that an applicant acquired knowledge in the technical areas of architecture while completing an accredited architectural degree program or demonstrated this technical knowledge through passage of the Equivalency Examination, the Professional Examination did not concentrate on these aspects of architecture, but rather focused on the ability of the candidate to demonstrate the knowledge and professional judgment necessary to practice architecture. Specifically, candidates were expected to demonstrate the ability to

1. Make strategic decisions relative to a major environmental issue or project.
2. Synthesize basic general knowledge.
3. Exercise environmental value judgment.
4. Show understanding of responsibility to the public, to the client, and to the profession.

The philosophy of the new examination was expressed by NCARB's then president-elect E. G. Hamilton, FAIA, in a 1971 *AIA Journal* article (5).

> NCARB holds that the protection of the public's health, safety and general welfare means providing no less than a satisfactory environment, that such an environment means not only one which is clean and safe, but also one which is functional and beautiful. Judging from the profession's favorable response to the Model Exam, most architects today clearly subscribe to an enlarged concept which asks of the profession that it accept leadership accountability for the quality of the manmade environment. This consensus signifies a revolutionary change in the profession's attitude toward itself. Never before has any recognized profession in our society ventured from the well-marked path of demonstrable objectivity to assume stewardship responsibilities for the psychological and aesthetic qualities of the man-made environment. In declaring itself concerned with the "functional and the beautiful" in a proprietary sense, NCARB has introduced a new and higher standard of sensitivity as a condition of admission to the practice of architecture.

The Professional Examination consisted of four 4-h sections given over a two-day period. The sections were as follows:

I. Environmental analysis.
II. Architectural programming.
III. Design and technology.
IV. Construction.

In an effort to reduce the human decision-making process in the grading of the examination, the entire exam was multiple choice and graded by machine.

Although the Professional Examination was installed as the registration examination in all states by 1975, there was disagreement among some state boards over whether or not college graduates should be examined in the technical subject areas. Four states continued to require the graphic design test in addition to the Professional Examination for all applicants and 14 states continued to require the entire Equivalency Examination in addition to the Professional Examination for all candidates. These divergent views meant that the examination requirements were still not uniform in all states and that candidates registered in one state could be required to sit for additional examinations if they desired registration in those states with different standards.

The Equivalency and Professional examinations went through a series of refinements and adjustments over the following few years, and in 1977, the Equivalency Examination was renamed the "Qualifying Test." Subject material was rearranged into the following parts:

A. Architectural history—2 h.
B. Structural technology—3 h.
C. Materials and methods of construction—2 h.
D. Environmental control systems—2 h.
E. Principles of site planning and architectural design—2 h.
F. Design/site planning—10 h.

All sections were multiple-choice examinations except for section F, which was a graphic examination. In 1978, section E was discontinued and section F became an 11-h examination.

The number of boards that believed that a graphic design test should be a part of the examination requirements for all applicants continued to grow, and in 1978, every state added the design test as a requirement for all applicants. In 1979, section F of the Qualifying Test was renamed section A of the Professional Examination. The now 12-h design test differed from the previous design exams, however, in that the examinations from all state boards but one were graded under the direction of NCARB at regional grading sessions. For the first time, all graphic examinations were graded under the same criteria by jurors who did not know the identity of the applicant or the applicant's state of origin. Factors such as personal bias and differences in the application of the grading criteria from state to state were thus eliminated from the grading process.

Also in 1979, NCARB undertook a project to analyze and define the knowledge, skills, abilities, and functions necessary for minimum competence for the practice of architecture in the United States and to evaluate the effectiveness of the current examinations in testing for the knowledge, skills, abilities, and functions necessary. NCARB first sought to list the services that architects were called on to render through a major study, not only of 12,000 architects from across the country, but also of frequent users of architectural services from both the private and public sectors. From this list of 164 services, 128 "knowledges" and 14 skills were identified. These were further refined to determine those that were necessary to protect the public health, safety, and welfare. The Qualifying Test and Professional Examination were then evaluated to determine the extent to which the resulting 29 "knowledges" and 4 skills were being tested. The study concluded that, although the then-current examinations were reasonably related to the practice of architecture, improvements could be made. As a result, a new examination format was adopted based on the following knowledge and skills.

1. Skills
   a. Conceptual, creative
   b. Management, coordination
   c. Analytical, perceptual
   d. Communication
2. Knowledge
   a. Social, cultural
      (1) Humanities
      (2) History and theory of architecture
   b. Natural and physical forces
      (3) Natural forces
      (4) Environmental theory
      (5) Acoustics
      (6) Moisture and thermal forces
      (7) Soil protection and treatment
      (8) Topographical factors
   c. Design Process
      (9) Aesthetics
      (10) Proximity relationships
      (11) Spatial relations
      (12) Circulation
      (13) Site planning
      (14) Landscape design
      (15) Interiors
      (16) Documentation methods
   d. Building systems, methods and materials
      (17) Energy utilization and conservation
      (18) Structural systems
      (19) Security systems
      (20) Fire protection systems
      (21) Plumbing systems
      (22) Environmental control systems
      (23) Electrical systems and illumination
      (24) Utility and civil systems
      (25) Construction materials and assemblies
      (26) Construction industry operations
   e. Legal constraints
      (27) Laws and regulations
      (28) Contract law
   f. Management
      (29) Business principles

The new examination, titled the Architect Registration Examination (ARE), was a nine-division examination based on an exam specification developed from the following group of previously identified knowledge and skills.

a. Predesign—Division A
   (1) Design objectives

    (2)   Space requirements
    (3)   Space relationships
    (4)   Flexibility, expansibility
    (5)   Site requirements
b.   Site Design—Division B
    (1)   Land utilization
    (2)   Structures placement
    (3)   Form relationships
    (4)   Movement, circulation, parking
    (5)   Utility systems
    (6)   Surface, subsurface conditions
    (7)   Ecological requirements, climate
    (8)   Deeds, zoning, construction
    (9)   Topography, relations to surroundings
    (10)   Architectural management and coordination
    (11)   Cost
c.   Building Design—Division C
    (1)   Building sections, elevations, plans
    (2)   Selections, layout of building systems
    (3)   Structural considerations
    (4)   Mechanical considerations
    (5)   Electrical considerations
    (6)   Civil considerations
    (7)   Interior considerations
    (8)   Documentation (design)
d.   Building Systems—Divisions D, E, F, G, H
    (1)   Structural, general, Division D
    (2)   Structural, lateral forces, Division E
    (3)   Structural, long span, Division F
    (4)   Mechanical, electrical, plumbing, Division G
    (5)   Miscellaneous systems, life safety, Division G
    (6)   Materials and methods, Division H
e.   Construction Documents and Services—Division I
    (1)   Architectural drawings
    (2)   Structural drawings
    (3)   Interior drawings
    (4)   Specifications
    (5)   Cost estimates
    (6)   Bidding documents
    (7)   Organization, handling bids
    (8)   Bids evaluation
    (9)   Coordination, management
    (10)   Construction administration, office
    (11)   Construction administration, field
    (12)   Field tests
    (13)   Quotation requests, change orders
    (14)   Construction cost accounting
    (15)   Project close-out

The ARE was administered for the first time in 1983 and until 1987 was the only registration examination given in all states and five jurisdictions in the United States. All jurisdictions required candidates to pass the complete examination and each board participated in the regional grading process. The goal of a nationally accepted registration examination to serve as the basis for reciprocity, which had been established in the first meeting of the state registration boards of 1920, had for the first time been completely realized.

However, this significant achievement was short lived. In June 1987, the state of California began administering its own examination, requiring architects seeking reciprocity in California to complete their state examination in addition to the national exam. California will return to the national exam in 1990.

THE PURPOSE OF THE ARE

Although every individual in the United States has the right to apply for registration as an architect, such registration is a privilege reserved for those who meet certain qualifications. To ensure that individuals who receive registration as architects are qualified to provide architectural services, states adopt standards including proper and appropriate education, appropriate and adequate training, and passing a related and appropriate examination.

The Architect Registration Examination is intended to screen out those individuals whose education and training have not adequately prepared them for registration. The exam tests for the adequacy of knowledge, skill, and ability necessary to provide the services required in the design and construction of the built environment. Although the examination does test for factual knowledge, it is primarily concerned with testing the ability of candidates to assess a situation and, using their understanding of the factual and conceptual processes involved, determine a correct response or action. In attempting to test for such professional judgment, the examination concentrates on practice-related situations and problems.

When registration is granted by a governmental authority, it is that jurisdiction's method of announcing to the public that the holder thereof has been found to be reasonably competent in the expertise for which the registration was issued. The ARE, or any examination, cannot be so exhaustive that it alone can determine the eligibility of an individual to practice architecture. However, when taken in conjunction with the other registration requirements of education and experience, it provides a jurisdiction with a fair degree of certainty that the individual is sufficiently competent to enter the practice of the profession.

SCOPE OF THE ARE

The ARE has been developed with specific concern for its fidelity to the practice of architecture. Its content relates as closely as practicable to the actual practice of architecture. To meet this objective of testing for the knowledge, skills, and abilities required in the practice of architecture as an integrated whole, the examination is arranged into nine distinct divisions that relate directly to the various phases of the practice of architecture. The examination is administered once a year over a four-day period. The divisions of the ARE, their subject matter and duration as described in the 1988 NCARB Circular of Information No. 2 are as follows (6).

Division A: Predesign

This division requires responses to questions presented mostly in the multiple-choice format. Tasks in Predesign require the candidate to apply factual practical knowledge, understanding, and experience to the subjects of design objectives, space requirements, space relationships, adjacencies, flexibility and expansibility, and site considerations, and to apply the theories and principles from architectural history relating to the usual services provided by architects in the Predesign phase of project development. Functional, physical and technical, economic, legal, and perceptual issues form the content areas of questioning in this division.

Division B: Site Design

This division will combine written and graphic problems, using multiple-choice and written simulation questions, as well as problems that require the candidate to produce vignette (small, limited) graphic answers. The graphic portion will be graded holistically. Division B is primarily oriented to conceptual-creative skills, with which the candidate demonstrates a knowledge of and ability to handle land utilization; structures placement; form relationships; movement, circulation, and parking; utility systems; surface and subsurface conditions; ecological considerations; deeds, zoning, and construction; topography and relations to surroundings; architectural management and coordination; and costs.

Division C: Building Design

This division concentrates on conceptual-creative and communications skills. Candidates are expected to resolve the issues of function, physical and technical, economic, legal, and perceptual aspects in developing a satisfactory solution to a building design problem. Candidates are also expected to be able to graphically communicate building sections, elevations, and plans; and selection and layout of building systems including structural considerations, mechanical considerations, electrical considerations, civil considerations, and interior considerations (Fig. 1).

Division D/F: Structural Technology—General and Long Span

The problems and questions in this division are mostly presented in the form of multiple choice; however, written identification type questions will also be used. Like divisions E, F, G, and H, this division is organized around tasks demanding a considerable store of factual knowledge combined with analytical ability. Some conceptual and creative skill is also applicable. The candidate will be asked questions in the areas of analysis and selection of appropriate structural systems and components, complex structural systems, structural connections, loading, code requirements, costs, structural construction methods, materials and safety, the impact of structure on the design of buildings, and the historical aspects of architecture as related to structural theory and design (Table 1).

Division E: Structural Technology—Lateral Forces

Division E uses multiple-choice questions to examine the candidate's ability to identify and calculate lateral loads as well as to apply factual knowledge about designing systems to accommodate lateral loads, materials, methods, finances and costs; and laws and regulations. Conceptual-creative aspects are also tested, as

Table 1. Typical Questions from Division D—General Structures of the Current ARE

Division D/F—Structural Technology—General and Long Span

1. The numerical value in pounds per square inch for the stress allowed in structural timber is LEAST for
    (A) compression parallel to the grain.
    (B) compression perpendicular to the grain.
    (C) extreme fiber stress in bending.
    (D) horizontal shear.
2. What is the nature of the inertial forces in a building that result from an earthquake?
    (A) They remain constant throughout the duration of the earthquake.
    (B) They are always horizontal in direction.
    (C) They become greater at longer periods of vibration.
    (D) They vary according to the weight and period of the building.
3. On a small flat-roofed, one-story building, the pressure produced by wind forces on the roof is
    (A) neutral.
    (B) inward.
    (C) outward.
    (D) torsional.
4. Factors that can contribute to the vulnerability of long-span structures to collapse include which of the following?
    I. Relatively few major structural elements.
    II. Different safety factor values for different structural materials.
    III. Failure of a joint tending to spread to other joints.
    (A) I only
    (B) I and III only
    (C) II and III only
    (D) I, II, and III
5. Which of the systems listed below would minimize both site construction time and costs?
    (A) Lift-slab construction with steel columns.
    (B) Cast-in-place concrete prestressed folded plate system.
    (C) Open-web steel joists with metal decking.
    (D) Long-span, post-tensioned concrete waffle system.

these relate to the impact of lateral forces on architectural design.

Division G: Mechanical, Plumbing, and Electrical Systems

This division will use predominantly multiple-choice questions. Questions will be presented to ascertain the candidate's abilities as related to the functional, physical and technical, economic, legal, and perceptual aspects of environmental controls and life safety in the design and construction of buildings. This examination will incorporate such subjects as natural forces, moisture and thermal forces, energy use and conservation, environmental controls, acoustics, fire-prevention systems, electrical systems, illumination, security systems, sound control, environmental theory, building enclosure systems and their relation to mechanical systems, use of tables and charts relating to environmental systems, costs, life safety systems and mechanical and electrical facilities for handicapped persons, humanities, aesthetics, and the history and theory of architecture as related to the design of mechanical, plumbing, electrical, and life safety systems for buildings.

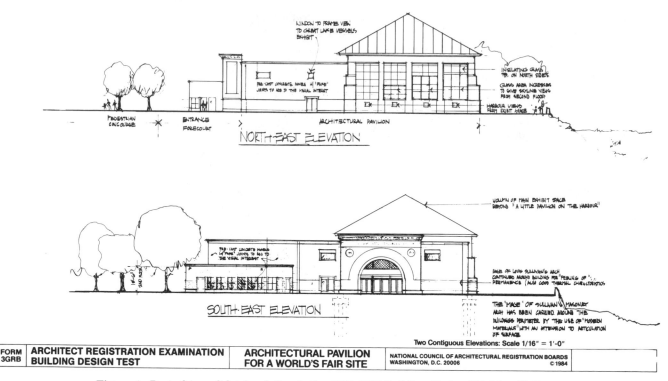

| FORM 3GRB | ARCHITECT REGISTRATION EXAMINATION BUILDING DESIGN TEST | ARCHITECTURAL PAVILION FOR A WORLD'S FAIR SITE | NATIONAL COUNCIL OF ARCHITECTURAL REGISTRATION BOARDS WASHINGTON, D.C. 20006   ©1984 | |

Figure 1. Part of a candidate's solution to the 1985 ARE Building Design (Division C) Test.

Division H: Materials and Methods

Division H uses a combination of multiple-choice, written simulation, and written identification forms of questioning. Factual knowledge and understanding, the application of knowledge and conceptual/creative abilities are tested as they relate to the functional, physical and technical, economic, legal, and perceptual content areas of this test subject. Test questions will emphasize such subjects as environmental theory, energy use and conservation, construction materials and assemblies, construction industry operations, natural forces, soil properties and treatment, topographic factors, moisture and thermal forces, structural systems, history and theory of architectural materials and methods, costs, business operations, building and life safety codes, handicapped provisions, humanities, aesthetics, utility and civil systems, and laws and regulations.

Division I: Construction Documents and Services

The orientation of this division is heavily toward the ability of the candidate to apply his or her factual knowledge. Composed of multiple-choice and written simulation questions, this division tests a candidate's ability to work from and with architectural drawings; structural drawings, mechanical, electrical, and plumbing drawings; interior drawings; specifications; cost estimates; bidding documents; the organization and handling of bids; the evaluation of bids; coordination and management; project administration in the office and in the field; field tests; quotation requests and change orders; construction cost accounting; and project close-out.

PREPARATION OF THE ARE

The ARE is very much a product of the joint effort of all of the registration boards in the United States. These boards acting together provide the direction for the ARE at the annual meeting of NCARB where they formulate and vote on policy decisions. Committees comprised of members from these registration boards are formed to work on the details of actually drafting, reviewing, and refining the questions for each year's examination. The process involves the efforts of over 50 committee members over a nine-month period. Although a testing consultant is used to advise the committee members as to appropriate test development and scoring procedures, the committee members are the only individuals who actually write examination questions. To say that NCARB prepares the ARE is to say that the examination is the result of the endeavors of the registration boards of the United States acting together.

EXAMINATION ADMINISTRATION

Although all boards work together through NCARB to write each examination and to establish standard examination administration policies, each board is responsible for the actual administration of the examination in its state. Each board establishes its own application procedures, standards for admission to the examination, and fee structure. The state boards also arrange for the locations in which the examination will be administered and the proctors for the exam. The duration of each examination and the materials that may be used

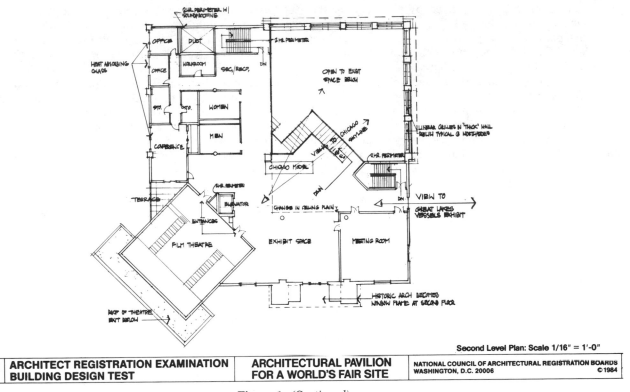

Second Level Plan: Scale 1/16" = 1'-0"

| FORM 3GRB | ARCHITECT REGISTRATION EXAMINATION BUILDING DESIGN TEST | ARCHITECTURAL PAVILION FOR A WORLD'S FAIR SITE | NATIONAL COUNCIL OF ARCHITECTURAL REGISTRATION BOARDS WASHINGTON, D.C. 20006 ©1984 |

Figure 1. *(Continued)*

during the examination, however, are established by NCARB.

GRADING THE ARE

Examinations from all jurisdictions administering the ARE are scored by NCARB and their testing consultants using the same scoring criteria. Regardless of the state in which an individual takes an examination, it will always be scored in exactly the same way. In all cases, the identity and all other personal information concerning the candidate are concealed during the scoring process.

In divisions A, D/F, E, G, H, and I of the ARE, candidates record all of their answers on machine-scorable answer sheets. Answers for the first part of division B are also recorded on machine-scorable answer sheets. The second part of division B and all of division C required candidates to present graphic solutions that are graded by registered architects at grading sessions conducted by NCARB in accordance with established NCARB grading criteria.

CONVERTED SCORES

The scores reported to candidates for all divisions of the ARE, with the exception of division C, are "converted scores." The minimum converted score required to pass any division of the ARE is 75. Converted scores are determined in the following manner: answer sheets are scanned by computers that record and tally the number of correct responses for each answer sheet, and the number

of correct responses is converted to a scale of 1 to 99 with a predetermined minimum number of correct answers set as the passing point of 75 on the scale. Setting the minimum number of correct answers required to pass an examination, like setting any standard, involves a certain amount of professional evaluation and judgment. This judgment is carefully exercised by the examination writers and experts in the various subject areas of the ARE prior to the administration of the examination. The passing points are the same for each board administering the ARE and are not affected by the number of people who pass or fail divisions of the examination.

GRADING THE GRAPHIC EXAMINATIONS

At the NCARB grading sessions, during which the graphic portions of divisions B and C are graded, registered architects from each jurisdiction are trained by NCARB in the application of the examination grading criteria and the "holistic grading process." The grading criteria are established by the examination committees who prepare the examinations and describe for the graders the various aspects of the examination that they are to evaluate. The holistic grading process requires the grader to examine each of these aspects and to ultimately determine whether or not the candidate has successfully demonstrated minimum competency in the subject area.

The holistic grading method also involves the independent grading of each solution by two or three graders. No grader knows the candidate's name, the name of the state in which the examination was taken or the grade assigned to a solution by previous graders. Borderline cases are resolved by a fourth grading given by a member of the Master Jurors' Committee.

It is not possible to write two different examinations and have them be of exactly the same difficulty. In order to be certain that the applicants for registration this year must pass an examination of the same level of difficulty as the candidates did last year, statistical methods of measuring the difficulty of each year's examination are used. The required number of correct responses needed to pass each examination is adjusted as necessary by the relative difficulty of the examination. This means that, contrary to some beliefs, the registration examination does not become harder or easier to pass from year to year. It also means that state boards cannot control the number of individuals who pass the examination from year to year.

EXAMINATION FEEDBACK

Feedback from the registration boards to the candidates taking the ARE consists primarily of the candidates' converted scores. These scores are an indication to candidates of their overall performance on each division of the examination in relation to the established minimum level represented by the passing score of 75. For the graphic portions of the examination, candidates also receive reports identifying the general areas of the grading criteria in which their solution was found to be weak.

Candidates for architectural registration who are unsuccessful in passing the examinations are often of the belief that the registration boards should provide them with feedback as to the specific subject matter in which they performed poorly. Such candidates are accustomed to an examination system in which examination feedback is an important part of the educational process. However, the registration examination is not intended as an educational experience, but rather as a tool used by the registration boards to determine the extent to which an individual's education and experience has prepared him or her for architectural practice. The primary responsibility of the registration boards is the protection of the public from incompetent practitioners. Architectural schools and internship are responsible for the education of examinees.

Furthermore, the examination is not designed or intended to be used as a diagnostic examination in identifying areas of weakness in a candidate. Examinations may be written to either determine an applicant's ability or to determine an applicant's areas of weakness. No examination can do both and do them well. The registration examination, therefore, is written specifically with the intent of separating as accurately as possible those individuals who have acquired sufficient knowledge from those who have not. The responsibility rests with the candidates to examine their own backgrounds and experiences and determine the areas in which they have not yet acquired sufficient knowledge or ability.

PREPARING FOR THE ARE

The process of preparing for the registration examination is, in fact, the same as preparing for the practice of archi-

tecture. It begins with architectural education and continues throughout internship. An individual who has not had sufficient education and training will not be able to pass the registration examination regardless of the extent of pre-examination preparation. Therefore, the first step every individual should take in preparing for the ARE is to conduct a thorough, accurate self-evaluation of his or her education and internship. Individuals must honestly evaluate whether or not they have a complete and well-rounded background and whether they have learned and experienced the significant theoretical and practical aspects of architectural practice. For instance, an individual whose only experience has been with a single building type or construction material will not be qualified to assume the role of an architect ready to undertake a variety of diversified projects on a day-to-day basis. The registration examination tests for the general practice of architecture, not for practice specialties. An individual with limited experience should seriously consider obtaining other types of architectural experience prior to attempting the registration examination. Likewise, individuals who do not have a complete educational background in architecture may wish to take additional coursework prior to sitting for the ARE.

The type of preparation necessary to practice architecture is not learned in a weekend seminar or even in a few months of concentrated study, but rather over all of the years that an individual contributes to the study and practice of architecture. Contrary to the claims of many who seek to profit from examination preparation books or seminars, there are no secret clues or rules of thumb that will help a candidate pass the examination if he or she has not already acquired the necessary skills and abilities. An accurate self-evaluation will identify those areas in which an individual has had the least recent exposure. Individuals who have not been recently exposed to a particular area of architecture may wish to take a refresher course and concentrate their studying in that area. Applicants who have had sufficient education and experience and have brushed up on those subject areas in which they have not been recently involved should have little difficulty in passing the examination.

It is also of great importance for individuals to familiarize themselves with the ways in which the examination will be conducted and the ways in which the exam questions will be asked. Any examination is an attempt to elicit a desired response from a candidate using a controlled stimulus. Examinations, therefore, are not natural environments in which discussion can take place to determine the meaning of a question. Examination writers must be extremely accurate in the wording and presentation of each examination question in order to be certain that examinees clearly understand the information presented. For this reason, examination questions often may not be worded in everyday terms commonly used in an examinee's office. Because the examination is administered over the entire country, many regional terms or practices will not be used if they are not commonly understood across the country. Candidates should expect that exam questions may be worded in a manner that may be unnatural to them but they should not try to infer meaning from a question due to such wording. The obvious meaning is the intended meaning.

Examinees should carefully review all pre-examination information made available to them so they may become completely familiar with the examination wording and administration procedures. They will find that an understanding of what to expect will help them avoid some of the anxiety that is a natural part of the examination process. The goal of both NCARB and the state boards is to determine an examinee's ability, not to confuse examinees or make it difficult for them to perform to the best of their ability.

THE EXAMINATION OF THE FUTURE

As has been the case in the past, registration examinations of the future will continue to change as the practice of architecture and the political environment in which registration takes place continue to change. The registration examinations will undoubtedly also be affected by the use of new technology including computers, laser disks, and video disks in the examination administration process. The use of computers in the administration of future tests is virtually assured. The areas of greatest promise offered by the incorporation of this new technology into test administration are as follows.

The ability to make examinations more closely simulate actual practice in order to be able to measure complex skills such as professional judgment.

The ability to distinguish between those applicants who have acquired the necessary knowledge and skill from those who have not more accurately and in less time.

The ability to offer the examinations at any time and to provide candidates with their scores instantly.

The ability of a computer-administered examination to adjust its questioning to concentrate on those areas where the candidate does not clearly fall into either the acceptable or the unacceptable range.

In 1988, a pilot computerized exam was offered, C/ARE and is scheduled to used nationally by 1992.

The very first registration examinations were based on the logical belief that individuals should be examined for their overall ability to practice the profession without endangering the health, safety, and welfare of the public. Present registration examinations are restricted by their formats to the evaluation of an individual's abilities in a number of very specific areas. They are based on the assumption that this series of "still photographs" represents a fairly accurate picture of the ability of an individual as a functioning whole. Examiners have often wished that they could actually observe individuals in the performance of day-to-day architectural work and thus be able to determine their eligibility to practice architecture. In many ways, the registration examinations of the future may be able to use computer technology to simulate that same kind of complete view of each candidate.

BIBLIOGRAPHY

1. D. E. Waid, "A Review of the Operation of the Registration Law in the State of New York," *The AIA Journal* **5**, 159–160 (Apr. 1917).
2. "State Registration Laws, Need for Uniform Legislation," *The American Architect* **104**, 151–152 (Oct. 15, 1913).
3. D. E. Waid, "Idaho's New Registration Law and the Proposed Law of Pennsylvania," *The AIA Journal*, 239 (May 1917).
4. National Council of Architectural Registration Boards, *1928 NCARB Annual Meeting Minutes*, **3**, Book C, 9 (May 15, 1928).
5. E. G. Hamilton, "The New Exam," *AIA Journal*, 41–43 (Oct. 1971).
6. National Council of Architectural Registration Boards, *NCARB Circular of Information No. 2* (Jan. 1988).

General References

National Council of Architectural Registration Boards, *1920 NCARB Annual Meeting Minutes*, St. Louis, Mo., 1920, 1 p. 428.

Architectural Registration Handbook, National Council of Architectural Registration Boards, Washington, D.C., 1973.

"The Qualification of Architects," *The American Architect and Building News* **2**, 215–216 (July 7, 1877).

W. Wagner, "Progress Report on NCARB's Astonishing Effort to Improve the National Exam," *Architectural Record*, 13 (Jan. 1982).

See also EDUCATION, ARCHITECTURAL; INTERN PROGRAMS; NATIONAL COUNCIL OF ARCHITECTURAL REGISTRATION BOARDS (NCARB); PROFESSIONAL DEVELOPMENT; PROFESSION IN CONTEMPORARY SOCIETY

CLARENCE L. CHAFFEE
National Council of
Architectural Registration
Boards
Washington, D.C.

REGISTRATION OF PROFESSIONALS IN CONSTRUCTION.   See SUPPLEMENT.

REGULATIONS.   See SUPPLEMENT.

REINFORCED CONCRETE.   See ENTRIES UNDER CONCRETE.

REINFORCED MASONRY.   See BRICK MASONRY; CONCRETE MASONRY.

RELIGIOUS ARCHITECTURE

Religious architecture is a phrase commonly used to describe buildings used as places of worship, such as temples, shrines, synagogues, churches, and cathedrals. To be exact, the phrase suggests that the building is religious. The term religious (an adjective) means adherence to religion or a religion. The definition of architecture (a noun) is the science, the art, or profession of designing and constructing buildings. It may, therefore, be assumed that buildings constructed to shelter those who gather together for worship may be labeled religious buildings. Professor Joseph Sittler once said, "It is no more logical to call a church building religious architecture because it encloses religious people than to call a monk's trousers religious pants." The fact that a church or synagogue might use a house, school, or theater in which to worship does not immediately transform any of those places into what might be termed religious architecture. However, the term is widely used and understood, is useful, and does define structures built specifically for worship.

Man's recognition of a God or gods seems to be universal; the places at which worshipers assemble have almost always been set apart from other structures. Hindu temples were designed to enshrine the images of gods or saints, their architecture was entirely different from Hindu homes, and they were always located in dominating situations, as were Greek and Roman temples, which are superb examples of excellence in design and construction for their era.

Cathedrals, temples, shrines, and churches may seem to be religious because of a certain indefinable quality that sets them apart from other structures. An example is Stonehenge located on Salisbury Plain in Wiltshire, UK. It has been defined as sacred circles of massive monoliths supporting horizontal slabs. Some have speculated that this and other such structures of the period (c. 2000 B.C.) were temples of the Druids. Another example, the pyramids in Egypt (before 3700 B.C.), may be classified as having a religious quality. In fact, the vast majority of prehistoric and historic structures standing today were in some way related to religion by practice or man's belief in God or gods.

From the time man first discovered fire, and perhaps earlier, he felt the need to recognize the existence of a God or gods. Rituals of some sort became an outward expression of his belief. Families and others gathered to practice these rituals using both movement and utterances. Stones were arranged as a focal point and tree trunks may have been placed around the area's perimeter to set apart the place. A sacrifice of some type was or became a part of the ritual to appease the gods. The concept of sacrifice still prevails in many religions and the sacrifice is very often the focus of the ritual. That the act of worship was of singular importance in the history of mankind is evident by the special attention and prominence given places of worship.

Historically, regardless of his particular religious belief, mankind has set places of worship apart from places of shelter, has designed them with great care, and has used those materials and technologies that have resulted in a lasting physical and artistic quality. The importance of places of worship in the community of man is also apparent in the early Spanish and English colonies in the United States. It was often the case that the first reasonably permanent structures built in the Colonies were churches, usually situated in a prominent or central location within the community.

Historically, religious buildings have been planned to accommodate the form of worship, whether it be private or corporate. With the development of man's skill, the structures became more elaborate, reflecting the finest and most advanced skills in both creative concept and execution. The same is true for art; the history and the development of all art forms at their finest level seem to have been dominated or influenced by belief in God or gods. Thus, for centuries, buildings identified with religion have been a most dominant influence on all of architecture and building technology.

BIBLIOGRAPHY

General References

Religious Buildings for Today, F. W. Dodge Corp., New York, 1957.

American Institute of Architects, Committee of Religious Architecture, *Guide to Successful Planning of Religious Buildings,* Washington, D.C., 1966.

T. D. Atkinson, *A Key to English Architecture,* M. S. Mill Co., Inc., New York, 1936.

D. J. Bruggink and C. H. Droppers, *Christ and Architecture,* William B. Eerdman's Publishing Co., Grand Rapids, Mich., 1965.

T. F. Bumpus, *Cathedrals and Churches of Rome and Southern Italy,* E. P. Dutton & Company, New York (n.d.).

A. Christ-Janer and M. M. Foley, *Modern Church Architecture,* Dodge Book Dept., McGraw-Hill, Inc., New York, 1962.

Constitution on the Sacred Liturgy, (Sacrosanctum Concilium), Guild Press, New York, 1966.

C. J. Cormick, *Adventures in Light and Color,* Random House, New York, 1937.

B. Fletcher, *A History of Architecture,* Charles Scribner's Sons, New York.

P. Hammond, *Liturgy and Architecture,* Columbia University Press, New York, 1961.

B. H. Hayes, *Tradition Becomes Innovation,* The Pilgrim Press, New York, 1983.

C. E. Hiller, *Caves to Cathedrals,* Little, Brown, and Company, Boston, 1974.

M. Lavanoux, "Religious Architecture," *J. American Institute of Architects,* 1953.

M. Halverson, "Religious Architecture," *J. American Institute of Architects,* 1953.

H. M. Prince, "Religious Architecture," *J. American Institute of Architects,* 1953.

S. Kostof, *A History of Architecture: Settings and Rituals,* Oxford University Press, New York, Oxford, 1985.

E. C. Lynn, *Tired Dragons,* Beacon Press, Boston, 1972.

M. E. Schoen, *The American Synagogue, a Progress Report,* Union of American Hebrew Congregations, New York, 1958.

E. H. Short, *A History of Religious Architecture,* Norton, New York, 1951.

E. A. Sovik, *Architecture for Worship,* Augsburg Publishing House, Minneapolis, Minn., 1973.

P. Thiry and H. L. Kamphoefner, *Churches and Temples,* Reinhold Publications Corp., New York, 1954.

Union of American Hebrew Congregations, *Contemporary Synagogue Designs,* New York, 1957.

R. B. Wischnitzer, *The Architecture of the European Synagogue*, Jewish Publication Society of American, Philadelphia, 1964.

Faith & Form, Journal of the Interfaith Forum on Religion, Art and Architect, Washington, D.C., (in publication since 1967).

Stained Glass, Journal, Stained Glass Association of America, St. Louis, Mo., (published quarterly).

BENJAMIN P. ELLIOTT, FAIA
Rockville, Maryland

See also CATHEDRALS AND ABBEYS; CHURCH ARCHITECTURE; MOSQUES; ORIENTAL ARCHITECTURE; SYNAGOGUES

RESIDENTIAL REMODELING

A home remodeling project can vary from the remodeling of interior spaces such as baths and kitchens or entries and closets, which are usually termed alterations, to the design of an addition to the house with one or more stories of new construction. Homeowners who have decided that they would benefit from a change in their living space with either a rearrangement for more convenience or an enlargement for more room, have two options with which to proceed. They can deal directly with a contractor who can provide design services and construction if the scope of the project is limited so that professional drawings will not be required for a building permit, or they can engage an architect to provide comprehensive design services.

WORKING DIRECTLY WITH A CONTRACTOR

Some contractors sell design-and-build services and have designers on their staffs, who may or may not be trained architects, who can provide design services and construction drawings. Many contractors are architects by training who prefer to work in the field. Kitchen-cabinet suppliers are usually well equipped to supply the design services and drawings required for a kitchen renovation and to provide construction services to make the necessary alterations. The homeowner who has a strong design sense, knows what he or she needs and where it is needed, and has some graphic ability may be able to communicate his or her ideas directly to the contractor without difficulty, and the result will be a successful project. This procedure will certainly work best when a contractor is known to the homeowner or is selected without bidding competition. For any project in which the scope of the work or the budget dictates that professional drawings are necessary for a permit or for the purposes of selecting a contractor through the bidding process, the homeowner should secure the names of one or more architects who can provide the necessary design services. The owner may get the name of an architect from friends who have completed similar projects, from a realtor if they are buying the house, or perhaps from a local contractor. In addition, most local chapters of the American Institute of Architects will provide a list of names from the chapter membership of architects who do home-remodeling design work.

WORKING WITH AN ARCHITECT

The owner and an architect schedule an initial interview at the site at a mutually convenient time. This would ideally be a time when all family members who will use the addition can be present so that the prospective architect will get an idea of the number, ages, sexes, etc of the family members for whom he or she will be designing. During this interview the architect will want to learn why the owners want to remodel or add to their home, to learn something of the living habits of the potential clients, how they use the existing spaces, and what they hope to gain from the alterations or addition contemplated. The architect should understand these requirements in addition to hearing the owner's specific ideas such as "we need a new bedroom for Junior over the garage."

During the initial interview, the architect will make a tour of the existing house to develop an idea of the type of project that might best meet the owner's program goals. This is not an opportune time for "off-the-cuff" design solutions for a project of any size. Homeowners frequently ask for some indication of design direction at this early stage, but the architect should resist the temptation to design on the spot, beyond the most elementary discussion of possibilities. It is important from the outset for prospective clients to be aware that they will be asked to pay for design work as the job progresses.

During the initial meeting the owner's proposed budget should be discussed. The homeowner who has not previously undertaken a remodeling project will more than likely have little idea of project costs. It will be the architect's responsibility to suggest a budget range. This can best be done, after thorough consideration, in the follow-up proposal letter rather than at the interview. For a very small project, however, an experienced architect can use judgment about this.

During the initial meeting the architect should take the opportunity to survey the house generally to become familiar with the condition of the structure, problems of settlement, and age and wear of the mechanical systems. In addition, the architect should anticipate potential zoning problems either through observation of the placement of the house on the property or through the owner's disclosure of covenants or set-back restrictions that are not immediately apparent.

If an addition or remodeling project involves baths or the kitchen, the preliminary survey will indicate what work will be required on the existing plumbing system. As an example of mechanical conditions that will affect design thinking, galvanized steel water-supply piping may have severely restricted water pressure on the upper floors of a house from the buildup of corrosion in the pipes. Also, an older hot-water heating system may be much more likely to accommodate a new addition than a forced hot-air system of the same age, which may need to be replaced. Frequently, houses older than 30 years will have an inadequate electrical service that will need to be increased during the construction project to supply sufficient power for new lights and appliances. Structural bearing walls can be removed without great expense, and a built-up wood or steel beam can be installed to open up small areas into larger ones.

The Proposal for Services

At the conclusion of the initial interview, the architect will usually indicate that he or she will send the owner a proposal for architectural services either in the form of an AIA contract document or, for a small project, in the form of a simple letter. The AIA documents, called *Standard Form of Agreement Between Owner and Architect,* cover the responsibilities of both parties to the agreement and are published in a variety of forms to cover all types of construction projects, from those of limited scope to large projects requiring the full range of architectural and engineering services. For most home remodeling projects, the *Abbreviated Form of Agreement* will be adequate.

If the proposal and agreement are in the form of a letter, the letter will outline the program that was discussed and note the budget figure. If no budget figure has been discussed, or if the owner is unsure of what budget figure to use, the proposal letter will establish an estimated range of costs that may be required to complete the construction work, as stated above. The proposal letter will then outline the fees to be charged for comprehensive architectural services and describe the services to be offered. The fees can vary from a fixed percentage of the project construction cost to an hourly fee for services, billed monthly. This latter method of determining fees, usually given an upset limit or percentage, provides the owner with a tracking method for the fees when billed on an hourly basis. Additionally, the architect might indicate the number of hours he or she estimates will be required to reach one or more of the design service goals such as preliminary or schematic design, design development, and completion of contract documents.

After receiving the proposal and having had an opportunity to review it and to have raised any questions with the architect, the owner will have an opportunity to make additions or deletions to the program based on projected cost or reconsidered requirements and to consider the proposed fee structure. If the client is not already familiar with the architect's work, he or she may at this time be given a list of completed projects to see. It is more than likely that the owner may be considering two or more architect's proposals and will make a decision based on a review of the proposal, reaction to the design work or completed projects the owner has seen, as well as reaction to the architect and how well the owner feels he or she and the architect will be able to work together. Often, too, the client makes a selection based solely on the fee proposed.

Preliminary Work at the Site

After notification to proceed, the architect will arrange a time to measure the existing structure. This should be done even if the owner has the original drawings for the house. Having the original drawings available will save considerable time, but checks will need to be made to determine if the existing structure was built in general conformance with the drawings and that changes made during construction were noted on the drawings. If no drawings of the house exist, the house will be measured. This need not be time consuming. After the architect has gained experience in this task, he/she will be able to measure and record the existing structure in a minimum

of time. At the time the agreement for architect's services is signed, the architect should request that the owner supply a plat survey of the property if one is available or, if not, arrange with a surveyor to have one made. A plat is a survey drawing of the size and dimensions of a property showing the house and other accessory structures located on the site.

Preliminary Work at the Office

When the measuring of the house has been completed, the architect will check the house for compliance with the zoning restrictions of the locality. At the initial interview the architect will have noted the building's placement on the property and advised the owner of any apparent zoning-restriction conflicts such as side-yard or rear-yard encroachments that would clearly limit the proposed project. The owner should make the architect aware of any known zoning problems such as covenants. Final zoning checks will be made with the local jurisdictions when the measured drawings are complete; any conflicts that will require approval or variance action must be brought to the owner's attention and discussed.

The feasibility of obtaining a variance will depend on the local jurisdiction. The variance process is easy in some localities and difficult in others. The architect's previous experience may be a helpful guide in determining whether or not to pursue a variance. In many instances a variance, which is usually time consuming and expensive to obtain, may be indicated only if there is no other way to achieve the program goals.

Snapshot photos of the house should be taken for the file when the house is measured. These are helpful later in recalling existing conditions and details while design work is progressing at the office. Once the existing conditions have been thoroughly recorded and zoning, structural, and mechanical restraints have been determined, the architect can begin the design work.

Schematic Design Work

Using as-built drawings of the structure that have been produced from the measurements, the architect will prepare schematic designs that coalesce the owner's program, the structure, and his or her own design ideas. Unlike for the new house or new building project in which the client and the architect together work out program requirements and design ideas, in the home remodeling or addition project, working within the constraints of an existing house imposes another demand on the design process in that aesthetic and structural design consideration must be given to the peculiar characteristics of the existing structure. These characteristics or constraints often control the design to a large extent. Some architects and their clients may want to add on to a structure with a "statement"—an addition that explores new design thinking and does not attempt to match the existing structure, whereas others may prefer to design in a contextual manner, adding onto the structure with an addition that appears to have always been a part of the house.

At the first design conference, the architect may present the owner with more than one design solution. These may be schemes of equal merit, or perhaps there will be one best scheme with some alternatives. It is helpful for the owner to see in this way the thinking that went into the work and that a number of approaches to a solution were considered. The advantages and disadvantages of these schematic designs are discussed, and one scheme will be selected with modifications as appropriate.

Design Development

Following the selection of the general design direction for the project, the architect will proceed with the design development phase of the work. During this phase, the selected design-scheme plan is refined according to the owner's requirements or reactions and the design schemes are developed in three dimensions. Elevations of an addition will be drawn; concept perspective sketches of interiors and exterior views will be made as appropriate. A study model of the project might be made at this time either for the architect's own use in clarification of design thinking or for presentation of the design to the owner.

The refined design ideas will be presented to the client at the second design conference, and the design concepts developed will be discussed. This meeting is also a good opportunity to discuss the construction materials to be used. The choice of exterior materials may be decided by the materials used on the existing house or they may be limited by the construction budget. Interior finishes are generally less inhibited by the existing finish materials and may offer a vehicle for a change in design tone from the original house. The greatest variety will probably be found in flooring materials, which can range from low-cost vinyl-asphalt tile to higher priced wood, ceramic tile, or natural stone flooring.

Following the second design meeting the architect will have an opportunity to develop details of the design scheme and the owner will make further choices among the alternatives presented, perhaps in one or more subsequent conferences. During the design development phase of the work, the architect will consult with a structural engineer if the project is of a size and complexity to require an engineer's expertise or if there are existing structural or settlement problems. An experienced architect will have sufficient knowledge to enable him or her to design the new structural system of the typical small-home remodeling project. A mechanical contractor's services are useful in the design of a heating and cooling system for the new addition or newly remodeled space or for modifications to the existing system to accommodate the new addition. A good mechanical contractor can help to design the system and will present a proposal to the owner that will contain a description of the new work and a price for installing the system. For a complex or large job, a mechanical engineer's design services may be required.

Preparation of Construction Documents

When the owner has made the requisite choices and the design of the alterations or addition is set, work on the construction documents can begin. Construction documents include drawings, sufficient to describe the project in plan, elevation, section, and detail, and schedules or lists in tabular form describing kind, size, etc of various materials and components such as windows and doors. In addition to the drawings, the construction documents will include specifications for the quality of workmanship and materials, often in the form of construction notes on the drawings, or, for a larger project, in the form of a separate document. The contract for construction, usually an AIA document, in which the agreement between owner and contractor is set out, also forms a part of the construction documents. A standard proposal form used by many home-improvement contractors may serve as a contract form for a small construction project.

FINDING THE CONTRACTOR

When the construction drawings and specifications are complete and have been reviewed by the owner to ensure that they encompass his or her program goals, the project will be sent for bid by two or more general contractors or will be sent to one contractor for price negotiation.

In the latter case, the contractor will usually be someone known to the owner through previous work and in whom the owner has confidence. Regardless of the method of securing a construction price, the architect will help in advising the client, will be required to meet the potential contractors on the site and will need to answer questions as to the intent of various details during the bidding process.

In many instances the homeowner can act as the general contractor, arranging for the carpentry work as well as the work of the various subcontractors such as the electrician and the plumber. The advantage provided by the general contractor is in organization and a timely job schedule, weighed against the money saved, often as much as 15% of the construction cost, when the homeowner acts as the general contractor. Experienced general contractors have a number of subcontractors with whom they usually work and on whom they can usually depend to be prompt. A homeowner may find that the subcontractors are not as responsive as they might be for a well-known contractor. On the small job where the subcontractor may only make a single visit to complete the work, delays will not be a problem.

When contractor's bid prices are received, the architect will help the owner review the bids and qualifications and decide on the contractor to perform the work. This may not ultimately be the lowest bidder for any number of reasons. Usually, however, the lowest bidder will be awarded the work.

CONSTRUCTION OF THE PROJECT

The owner and the contractor will sign an agreement. Either the contractor's proposal form or an AIA document as outlined above can be used, and the construction work itself can begin. As the construction work progresses, the architect will make periodic visits to the job site to inspect the work to ensure that the intent of the construction documents is being carried out. The architect is not a construction supervisor and will not be at the job every day. The architect is responsible for certifying to the owner that the materials and labor being billed by the contractor have in fact been provided and installed. From time to time the architect will be called on to negotiate differences between the contractor and the owner and to design changes in the work requested by the owner or required by job conditions.

The owner has a responsibility to make observations of the job as the work progresses and to call to the attention of the architect and the contractor any questions he or she may have about the work. The owner is responsible for maintaining a floater insurance policy that should be written to cover all work and materials the owner has paid for. Also, a part of the owner's responsibility is notifying the architect of any changes in the work that have been negotiated directly with the contractor.

The contractor is responsible for the general progress of the job, for maintaining the schedule set out in the contract, for keeping an adequate work force on the job, for directing the work of the subcontractors, for keeping the job site clean and secure, and for on-the-job safety. The contractor is responsible for delivery of a completed job of the quality and quantity described and specified in the documents. At the completion of the job, the contractor is required to provide operating instructions and warranties for all equipment installed and to provide the owner with the standard 1-yr trade warranty on the whole project.

Toward the end of the project, the architect, owner, and contractor will meet at the substantially complete job to make a final punch-list inspection for items of work to be finished and to agree on a time for final payment. The substantially complete job is one where some work may need to be completed, such as touch-up painting or installing pieces of trim, but where the owner nevertheless has beneficial occupation.

With the completion of the final punch list by the contractor, the final bills will be submitted for payment to the owner by the contractor and by the architect. Following successful completion of the home remodeling construction project, the architect may continue to provide services to the owner in the form of interior design or landscape design consultation and the owner may be asked on occasion to allow the architect to show the completed project to prospective clients.

STEPHEN J. ZIPP, AIA
Washington, D.C.

REMUNERATION

Appropriate professional remuneration is important in allowing architects and other design professionals to meet their goals. It assures the type and level of service needed to fulfill clients' expectations.

How much clients should expect to pay an architect relates to the types and levels of professional services provided. The more service needed and the more complex or experimental the project, the more should be budgeted for architectural services. Of the methods of compensation available, the following are the most common:

1. A stipulated sum per unit, based on what is to be built (eg, the number of square feet, apartments, rooms).

2. A percentage of the construction cost.

3. A stipulated sum based on the architect's compensation proposal.

4. Hourly rates.

5. Combinations of the above.

When a project is characterized by repetitive units (beds, rooms, apartments), it sometimes makes sense to use these units as a basis for compensation, for example, when the probable number of units (or, alternatively, the highest and lowest probable numbers) is known.

Percentage of construction cost has been a simple and popular method of compensation. However, it requires a rigorous determination of what "construction cost" includes and does not include. The result may be too high or too low given the complexity of the project and the professional services needed to accomplish it. Finally, this method may penalize the architect for investing extra effort to reduce construction cost on behalf of the owner.

What is included in the stipulated-sum method is a matter of negotiation with the architect, but generally it includes the architect's direct personnel expenses (salary and fringe benefits), other direct expenses chargeable to the project (such as consultant services), indirect expense or overhead (costs of doing business not directly chargeable to specific projects), and profit.

It sometimes makes sense to consider hourly billing methods. Again, this is a matter of negotiation, but it may be used when there are many unknowns. Indeed, many projects begin this way, continuing until the scope of services is determined and it is possible to establish a stipulated sum. Some also use this approach for construction contract administration and special services, such as energy and economic analyses.

Other costs to the client are reimbursable expenses. These are out-of-pocket expenses incurred by the architect on behalf of the project. They usually cannot be predicted at the outset. They include long-distance travel and communications, reproduction of contract documents, and authorized overtime premiums. Detailed in the agreement between the owner and architect, they are usually outside the stipulated sum or hourly billing rate and are as a rule billed as they occur.

Once the method and amount of compensation have been established, the architect provides a proposed schedule of payments. Such a schedule helps the client plan cash requirements for the project.

The owner can expect to pay other expenses. The owner–architect agreement outlines a number of owner responsibilities, some of which will require financial outlay. These include site surveys and legal descriptions; soils-engineering services (eg, test borings or pits); required technical tests during construction (eg, concrete strength tests); an on-site project representative, and the necessary legal, auditing, and insurance counseling services needed to fulfill the owner's responsibilities.

If owner and architect cannot agree on compensation, they are advised to keep talking, so that each understands the other's basis for negotiation. Often, differences result from incomplete or inaccurate understandings of project scope or services. Perhaps some services can be performed by the architect on an hourly basis, or by the owner. On occasion, coordination of owner forces, special consultants, or other individuals mandated by the owner add to the architect's costs. When even after this there is no agreement on compensation level, both the owner and the architect have no choice but to discontinue negotiation.

BIBLIOGRAPHY

General References

S. A. Kliment, *Compensation Guidelines for Architectural/Engineering Services,* The American Institute of Architects, Washington, D.C., 1978.

P. Piven, *Compensation Management: A Guide for Small Firms,* The American Institute of Architects, Washington, D.C., 1982.

The American Institute of
Architects
Washington, D.C.

RENDERINGS, ARCHITECTURAL

DEFINITION

Architectural rendering is a form of visual communication in which the architect or artist represents an architectural building design for acceptance by the owner. Although delineation is generally associated with line drawings and rendering, with the application of tones, in this discussion delineation is used to describe both.

Delineation is representational and purports to accurately identify what the architectural building or monument will look like when it is completed (Fig. 1). The architectural rendering is also a work of art. It is undertaken by the delineator as an artistic expression, the pragmatic objectives notwithstanding. The art of the delineator is considered to be an independent artistic act. When used by the architect to produce "atmospheric visions of a building" as he or she sees it, the mood created by the renderings provides an image that drives its creator through the design process. Of his renderings for the Provincetown Playhouse and Eugene O'Neill Archival Center, Provincetown, Massachusetts, Turner Brooks writes (1):

> The drawings make a project palpable and real in a way that line drawings and even models cannot. They are atmospheric visions of a building as I see it—here the image of a ship steaming through the night, lights reflecting off water, mist and steam. There is much more to designing than this, but it is image more than anything else that takes possession of me and drives me through the design process.

Architectural rendering may be represented in a variety of graphic media, including pen and ink, pencil, direct color application, and computer-aided design delineation. The representation may be in black and white or in color.

Black and white representations are normal for newspaper reporting; color representations are often desirable for communications to owners and their representatives in order to simulate reality.

Architectural delineation has been used through the centuries to communicate design intent, and a variety of delineators utilizing a wide range of media have succeeded in doing so. A brief review of the history of architectural delineation illustrates the progression and the range. The history of drawing as seen through the eyes and hand of the architectural delineator is a history of technique through history, of the evolution of perspective, and the aspirations of the society for its built environment.

HISTORICAL REVIEW OF ARCHITECTURAL DELINEATION

Architectural delineation exists where the art of building exists. The history described in this discussion is the history of delineation in Western culture.

This discussion will not address the diverse non-Western cultures and societies in which masters of architectural delineation produced building delineation of quality equal to that in the Western societies to be cited. For example, a detail from *Shokunin-zukushi-zu* by Kano Yoshinobu (1552–1641), a drawing of carpenters constructing a traditional Japanese house shows them working with an orthographic drawing of a Japanese house poised in the middle of the construction work. In this case, the architectural delineation was actually used to explain how similar buildings should be designed and constructed (2).

In *Masterpieces of Architectural Drawing* (3), Helen Powell and David Leatherbarrow have classified periods of drawings, beginning with Medieval drawing, in which the delineation occurred before construction. In the Middle Ages, drawings, for the most part, represented "as built" details and elevations.

The Italian Renaissance and Perspective Theory

Perspective theory was developed in the Italian Renaissance, largely through the seminal work of Filippo Brunelleschi (1377–1446), who initiated practical experiments and identified one-point perspective; Leon Battista Alberti (1404–1472), who relied on three-dimensional models rather than drawings; and Leonardo Da Vinci (1452–1519), who introduced the bird's-eye view. Donato Bramante (1444–1514) recognized the artistic intent of architectural delineation and introduced sketches as a means of further working out solutions. Raphael (1483–1520), who succeeded Bramante as the architect responsible for constructing St. Peter's, Rome, used separate ground plans, elevations, and sections, which were then drawn in multiple perspectives to provide a greater sense of the interior spaces (3).

Sixteenth-Century Publications

In the sixteenth century a series of publications that formalized classical delineation had wide influence. They include:

Figure 1. Rendering of the appearance of the West elevation of the Washington Cathedral, Washington, D.C., when completed in the year 2000. Renderer: Paul Stevenson Oles. Media: Black prismacolor on strathmore board. Architect: D. C. Frohman. Courtesy of Paul Stevenson Oles.

1. Sebastian Serlio, *L'Architettura (1537–1551),* providing a comparative analysis of the architectural orders showing plates from Bramante and Peruzzi. Sections are combined with interiors drawn in perspective.
2. Giacomo Barozzi da Vignola, *Regole delle Cinque Ordini* (1562), copper-engraved plates showing a simplified method for drawing the orders.
3. Andrea Palladio, *Quatro Libri dell'Architettura* (1570), woodcuts showing plans, elevations, and sections, but not perspectives. The plates were re-engraved on copper in eighteenth-century editions. Palladio's buildings and drawings influenced Thomas Jefferson and American architecture.
4. Jacque Androuet Du Cerceau, *Les Plus Excellents Bastiments de France (1576, 1579),* showing bird's eye topographical perspectives and precise building detail on copper engravings.
5. Jacques Perret, *Des Fortifications et Artifices Architecture et Perspective* (1601), whose "cut-away and oblique projections of Mannerist designs . . . prefigures the axonometric view, which is the modern draughtsman's system of detachment" (4).

The Italian Baroque

Italian baroque architects developed the techniques of perspective by using additional vanishing points, multiple objects, corner views, and contrasts of light and shade as the battle raged between the "painters" who emphasized perceived relationships and the "architects" who developed perspectives on the basis of exact measurements. Gianlorenzo Bernini's (1598–1680) and Francesco Borromini's (1599–1667) superb draftsmanship permitted them to develop the concepts they ultimately built in Rome.

Carlo Fontana (1634–1714) further developed techniques used in Bernini's workshop (5). His drawings, now in the Royal Library at Windsor, show an increasing isolation of the drawing on the page. Geometrical guidelines are laid out in black chalk. Brown ink is then applied to show the outlines of the buildings, with grey wash used for shading. A greater range of colour was used than previously, but conventionally rather than representationally, with existing fabric shown in yellow or brown, proposed building in grey, water in blue and brickwork in elevation or plan in red.

At the end of the seventeenth century architectural delineation began to be formalized on the basis of regularized requirements, including competition requirements.

French Drawing: Topography and Decoration

The French tradition of architectural topographical draftsmanship focused on perspectives of great houses. The horizon line was moved up to produce bird's eye perspectives. This was also symbolic of an age of great scale, which emphasized formal views and vistas.

Architectural Drawing in England

Inigo Jones (1573–1652) created perspective drawings for his stage design, but his architectural drawings relied more on the nonperspective drawings of Palladio and others. "He learnt the discipline of orthogonal drawing in plan, section and elevation, all of which he executed with a fine pen delicate washes or with a lively pen, sepia ink, and cross-hatched shadows" (6). Jones and his successors, including Sir Christopher Wren (1632–1723), tended to emphasize models and simple orthogonal drawings.

Rococo and Palladian Drawing

Cartouche sketches, which emphasized scroll-like ornamentation, detail, and light and shadow, characterized the Rococo period. In England, the Palladian influence, with its emphasis on simple shapes and forms, dominated, as in the work of William Kent (1685–1748) (7):

To show the effect of decoration in a room, Kent used the technique of a plan, with elevations projected outwards in four directions, like a cut-out model. As architects began to be more concerned with the internal arrangements of houses, and the desire to control the details of panelling, chimneypieces and other important constituents of rooms, this technique was increasingly adopted.

Kent's proposals for chambers of the House of Commons exemplify this approach.

The Revival of Antiquity

Giovanni Battista Piranesi (1720–1778) created imaginative reconstructions of classical Rome through romantic drawings, which showed how architectural delineation can create moods and stimulate attitudes about buildings. Massive scale, light, shade, and shadow were all used to produce the desired emotion. Piranesi's work influenced the twentieth-century renderers M. Murray Leibowitz and Hugh Ferriss, whose original visions of the contemporary skyscraper were based on romantic optimism about the new building form. Piranesi collections are in the Sir John Soane museum in London and at Columbia University in New York.

Charles de Wailly

In his design for La Comedie Francaise (1776), in collaboration with Marie-Joseph Peyre (1730–1785), Charles de Wailly drew the building section and perspective from the courtyard outside into the grand galleries and the theatre itself (8). By identifying the pedestrian flow through the building, Wailly was one of the first delineators to address the dynamic experience desired while walking through architectural space. His successors in the twentieth century use movie techniques and sequential-flow perspectives generated by computer-aided design.

Space and Simple Geometric Forms

Romantic designers in the early eighteenth century, who sought to identify architecture with primitivism, simple periods, and simple forms also were concerned with color, light, and environmental ambience. The aquatint technique was developed and reinforced this attitude. Aquatint is "a process by which spaces rather than lines are etched with acid, producing tones that give the effect of a wash drawing or watercolor"(9).

Architectural delineation found its ultimate poetic expression license in the visionary drawings of Etienne-Louis Boullee (1728–1799), who emphasized basic geometric forms—the sphere, cube, cylinder, cone, and pyramid.

Joseph Michael Gandy (1771–1843), Sir John Soane's (1753–1837) draftsman, was an outstanding exponent of the effects of light on geometric (largely Romanesque) forms. His ingenious renderings created a world of design that was purely the renderer's art. An example is his synthesis of Soane's work, *A Composition of Various Designs Executed by Sir John Soane.*

Neo-Classical Germany and the Outline Style

Bare-bones delineation was introduced by Karl Friedrich Schinkel (1781–1841), who developed an outline technique in which shadow is minimized and light is bright and constant. In his drawing of the Altes Museum, Berlin (10), Schinkel also illustrates people moving through the space. The outline style has been adopted by many twentieth-century renderers.

The Ecole des Beaux Arts

The Ecole des Beaux Arts, founded in 1818, formed the basis for European and American architectural education until the beginning of World War II. Walter Gropius revolutionized architectural education in Germany in the 1920s and 1930s and at Harvard in the 1940s and 1950s, and Frank Lloyd Wright's Taliesin schools represented breaks from architectural dependence on the beaux-arts system, in which drawings (11) were produced as artistic objects on their own right, . . . acknowledged conventional means of representation: plans, sections and elevations, not perspectives . . . . they are nearly always Neo-Classical in style, and reflect a consistent doctrine of axial planning, and a particular attention to the artistic quality of the plan as a piece of graphic design.

The beaux-arts approach was also concerned with the experience of the sequence of spaces in a building (the *marche*). This has proved to be a recurring theme in the efforts of delineators to represent the emotional impact of buildings under design. In 1971, Paul Stevenson Oles sought to accomplish this in his drawings of the East Wing of the National Gallery in Washington (Fig. 2).

Works by M. Murray Leibowitz are particularly exemplary of student beaux-arts work in late 1920s, bearing all of the traditional aspects of the beaux-arts competitions, as in his rendering of a planetarium and observatory on the Hudson River Palisades (Fig. 3).

Richard Morris Hunt (1827–1895) remains one of the preeminent renderer architects of American architecture. His pencil and watercolor renderings epitomize the nineteenth century as well as the beaux-arts classicism. Among his renderings, the elevation of the Administration Building of the World's Columbian Exposition in Chicago provides a significant example of pencil and watercolor overlay.

Late Nineteenth-century Drawing

Henry Hobson Richardson (1838–1886) developed miniature rough studies, sketch renderings, which he communicated to his staff, including Standford White (1853–1906), who formed McKim, Mead and White. Louis Sullivan (1856–1924) developed a soft-pencil technique for designing his ornamentation.

Nineteenth-century Reproduction Techniques

The nineteenth century saw the proliferation of new construction drawing techniques, including working drawings, and new reproduction techniques, such as blueprinting. Lithography was introduced, and chromolithography was used to produce color prints.

"In lithography, a greasy image on smooth limestone is moistened and inked, the image repelling water and accepting ink; the stone accepting water and repelling ink. Chromolithography (was) a slow and painstaking process for producing coloured prints, in which flat colours were printed with tonal effects achieved by stippling or by zigzag lines; by local shading, colour, and tone; and by use of transparent and graduated tints" (12).

The development of photolithography and photography permitted direct reproduction of pen and ink images.

Fin de Siecle: Drawing in Europe

In the early twentieth century, a style of delineation developed ". . . with a sparse outline and flat washes of color which suited . . . a graphic style of architecture" (13). Innovators and followers included Rennie Mackintosh, M. H. Ballie Scott (1865–1945), Otto Wagner (1841–1918), Josef Maria Olbrich (1867–1908), and Josef Hoffman (1870–1956). Tony Garnier's (1869–1948) drawings for Une Ville Industriele are memorable for their three-point perspective and linear simplicity.

Frank Lloyd Wright

Few practicing architects have exploited the emotional impact of architectural delineation through the means of evocative drawings as well as has Frank Lloyd Wright (1869–1959). Wright used delicate color, often colored

Figure 2. Rendering of the East Wing, National Gallery of Art, Washington, D.C. Renderer: Paul Stevenson Oles. Media: Black prismacolor on strathmore board. Architect: I. M. Pei. Courtesy of Paul Stevenson Oles.

Figure 3. Rendering of Planetarium and Observatory located on the Palisades, Hudson River, New York. Renderer: M. Murray Leibowitz. Media: Washes using hand ground ink finished with charcoal and lithograph pencils and erasers. Architect: M. Murray Leibowitz. Courtesy of M. Murray Leibowitz.

pencil, with pencil line to enhance the ephemeral quality of his buildings while at the same time emphasizing their linear qualities, unique forms, and delicate use of materials.

Wright's classicism begins with the plan, sharply pochéd, and evolves into the three-dimensional spatial interpretation, usually in perspective. The "Design for House and Temple, Unity Church, Oak Park, Illinois" illustrates the strength of his plan and the linear clarity of his delineation (14).

The drawing of the stable for the Winslow house further identifies the strong correlation between plan and perspective formulation that identifies proportion, materials, and architectonic intent (15).

The Renderers

In the twentieth century a tendency toward specialization led architects to engage professional renderers, many of whom were also architects, to communicate their proposals. Some of the renderers used the dazzle technique, which "relied on the effect of strong light created by wavy lines (15)."

Practitioners of the dazzle technique in pencil included Martin Rico and Henry P. Kirby (1853–1915) in the United States and C. E. Mellows (1864–1915) and his pupil Robert Atkinson (1883–1952) in England. Practitioners of the dazzle technique in watercolor included William Walcot (1874–1943) in England and Henry van Buren

Magonigle (1867–1935) in the United States, who rendered "large areas of cool colours, often with deep blue skies" (16).

M. Murray Leibowitz of Boston bridged the classical standards and developed a handsome pencil and charcoal overlay technique as evidenced in his rendering of a skyscraper, now part of the collection of the Boston Museum of Fine Arts (Fig. 4). Leibowitz combined the emotional impact of delineation with accurate representation.

The renderings of Hugh Ferriss of New York in the 1930s communicated innovations in architecture—in particular in the skyscraper—and social ideas associated with building. His visions of the skyscraper in charcoal and pencil are unforgettable leaps of imagination and optimism, despite his written concerns that the proliferation of skyscrapers could eliminate light in the cities.

The Modern Movement and Expressionism

Powell and Leatherbarrow (17) contrast the concept diagrams produced by the architect LeCorbusier (1887–1965) with his technical construction drawings, calling them, respectively, the "poetic" and "technical aspects of design." It is this same tension that has existed in the history of architectural delineation—the need to describe the proposed subject accurately and the need to idealize it, even if artistic license is required.

The sketches of Erich Mendelsohn (1887—1953) evoke

Figure 4. Rendering of Skyscraper. Renderer: M. Murray Leibowitz. Media: Washes using hand ground ink finished with charcoal and lithograph pencils and erasers. Architect: Mr. Murray Leibowitz. Courtesy of Museum of Fine Arts, Boston, gift of M. Murray Leibowitz.

clear concepts. Each transmits a direct and dramatic message of the proposed building.

The de Stijl movement of Holland emphasized the axonometric and the graphic nature of design. Theo van Doesburg and Cornelis van Eesteren's 1923 plan for an artist's house separates the elements in an axonometric drawing in order both to communicate its intent and to identify the nature of the construction elements (18).

Louis Kahn's sketches communicate conceptual and technical intent in a freehand form. His use of charcoal on yellow tracing paper is both tentative and forceful in perspective and massing. The sketches for the Salk Institute for Biological Studies (1962) convey the strength of informal delineation just as do Paranesi's drawings (9).

Twentieth-century Drawing

Paul Stevenson Oles is the most imaginative, disciplined delineator-renderer of the 1960s to 1980s. His wax-base

(Prismacolor) overlay techniques and architectural perceptions are used not only to render the final conception but also to assist the architect in the developmental studies of the spaces through which people move. The team of I. M. Pei and Oles synthesized two great contemporary talents in the development of the East Wing of the National Gallery in Washington, D.C. and in the Dallas Symphony Hall (Fig. 5). In these renderings Oles follows in the tradition of Charles De Wailly.

In the latter part of the twentieth century Parisian architect Georges Maurios' residential developments are clearly articulated in competitions that he has won (Fig. 6).

The postmodern movement, spearheaded by Robert Venturi and Denise Scott-Brown (late 1960–1980s), has brought with it a new painterly quality to orthographic drawings. By contrast, in his drawings Richard Meier expresses the aspirations of Walter Gropius's Bauhaus.

The opportunities for computer-aided design are not yet fulfilled, as the architectural profession and its renderers proceed to invent, explore, and develop more sophisticated programs and create new reproduction techniques. Yet the purpose of architectural delineation, in its highest form, has not merely been to communicate the dimensional accuracy of a building, but also to present a building as a reflection of society's progress.

CONSTRUCTING DRAWINGS FOR ARCHITECTURAL DELINEATION

Architectural delineations depict buildings or monuments from many points of view. They include direct orthogonal representation and isometric and perspective representations. See Ref. 20 for a complete treatment of this topic.

The direct orthogonal drawing depicts the elevation or elevations of a building as though one were viewing each part of the building from exactly the same viewing position and viewing angle instead of standing at one point and seeing the building diminish in perspective. The horizontal and vertical dimensions remain true to the exact scaled dimensions of the building.

The isometric drawing is a method by which the horizontal and vertical planes remain true to the exact scaled dimensions of the building as in an orthogonal drawing, but the building is drawn at a 30° angle to the ground plane. Axonometrics are a form of isometric drawing in which only the angle between the front plane and the side planes is distorted for the drawing.

Perspective drawings depict a building from the viewpoint of one position. From a single position, the viewer can encompass a building or monument within the direct cone of vision. The cone of vision is usually 45° off the centerline of the eyes. A cone of vision of 45° represents normal vision. Thirty degrees is like a telephoto lens. A cone of vision of 60° would tend to distort the external edges of a building. It is a like a wide-angle lens. The dimensions of the building diminish and vanish with the perspective as it is drawn.

The elements that are required to construct the base for an architectural delineation are

Figure 5. Rendering of Dallas Symphony Hall, Dallas, Texas. Renderer: Paul Stevenson Oles. Media: Black prismacolor on strathmore board with dry mounted vellum. Architect: I. M. Pei. Courtesy of Paul Stevenson Oles.

1. The ground plane, which is the ground level.
2. Location of the eye, the horizon line. Normally, the eye level is 5 ft from ground level. Eye level is usually called the horizon line.
3. Location of the station point, which is the place where a person stands in relation to the building.
4. Location of the picture plane, which is the vertical plane located anywhere in front or behind the object. The picture plane may be located between the viewer and the building or behind the building. If between the viewer and the building, the final drawing will be smaller than the building image; if behind the building, the building will be projected larger.

5. The vanishing points, which are the points in a perspective, located on the horizon line, toward which all lines diminish. In a one-point perspective, all lines diminish (vanish) to one point. In a two-point perspective, all lines in a building diminish to either a left point or a right point. In a three-point perspective, all lines vanish to a left point, a right point, and an overhead point.

Basic constructions assume 90° angles at corners. Parallel lines not perpendicular to station points also vanish to vanishing points. One-point or two-point perspectives are normal viewing perspectives. The three-point perspective is usually associated with aerial perspectives and tall buildings.

Figure 6. Rendering of urban center, Belfort, France. Renderer: Georges Maurios. Media: Line drawing in pencil. Architect: Georges Maurios. Courtesy of Georges Maurios.

6. The measuring point, which is the vanishing point of a series of parallel lines that cut off equal distances on another series of parallel lines and on the picture plane.

The method for constructing a two-point perspective is as follows:

1. The plan is drawn to scale.
2. The elevations are drawn to scale.
3. The viewer is located on the plan according to a preconceived image of what view of the building is desired.
4. The picture plane is located between the viewer and the building, which is the typical relationship.
5. Lines are drawn from the viewer (one point between the eyes) to every point on the plan. These lines will intersect the picture plane.
6. Directly below the plan the picture plane, the right and left vanishing points, and the location of the observer are located.
7. A line is projected vertically from the intersection of the picture plane on the plan to the vertical picture plane which is located below. The heights along the picture plan are measured and projected through to the vanishing points. This will provide accurate measurements for the perspective or for the isometric. It identifies the location of the major vertical elements of the building.
8. Projection of light, shade, and shadows is related to an assumed direction and altitude of the sun. One altitude of light chosen for use in casting shadows in orthographic projections is the diagonal of a cube or 35° 16′. The azimuth used was 240°. This fixed altitude and aximuth is used because of its ease for casting shadows in plans and elevations in the northern hemisphere. Shadows cast in the Southern hemisphere are cast from the north rather than from the south.
9. Steps 1–8 are hand methods that have been calculated into computer aided design programs.

MEDIA USED IN ARCHITECTURAL DELINEATION

Many media are used by architectural delineators. Each technique conveys different feelings of light, texture, and depth. They are used according to availability of materials, appropriateness for the depiction of the building type, ease of reproduction, and requirements of the owner. Original drawings may be reproduced by many techniques, including photo reproduction, half-tone prints, and letterpress reproduction. The focus of this discussion is the original drawing.

1. *Ceramic Mosaic and Stone.* Ancient delineators incorporated ceramic mosaics to depict their existing buildings such as the famed Jerusalem mosaic that depicted the original city plan. The Mayans carved their buildings into their stone edifices. The Governor's Palace at Ixmal, for example, shows the domestic houses of the citizens carved into the frieze.
2. *Ink.* Inks have been available for centuries. India ink was a favored medium of the beaux-arts period, during which the ink was hand ground and used for line drawings and washes.

• Ink line provides a clear, sharp image. Ink lines may be ruled or drawn at different thicknesses. Repetition of ink lines and overlaying of ink lines provides tones, density, and shading.
• Ink wash is created by applying and overlaying flat tones of ink as in watercolor, but smoothly and consistently.
• Ink line applied with watercolor provides a sharp background line with the benefits of the many colors available in watercolor pigments. Colored washes are used with black ink washes.

3. *Graphite.* Graphite is used alone or with other media, and is equally useful for sketching existing buildings and for architectural renderings. There is variety in the weights of graphite used. Graphite is readily available, requires no penetration for its use, can be easily erased, and has great flexibility.

• Linear representation in graphite is softer than pen and ink. Line weight can vary with pressure and create light and darks within the same line.
• Tones can be created by increasing the density of lines of the same weight or by drawing with the side of the graphite pencil, thus creating areas of tones. Graphite can be overlaid to create increasing depths as a result of greater density.
• A drawing can be delineated in graphite using watercolor washes with accents.

4. *Charcoal.* Charcoal is a soft organic material, usually dark gray or brown, used to create dark, highly contrasting images. Charcoal is applied in pencil or crayon form and can be rubbed, erased, and overlaid to create density. Hugh Ferriss, active in the 1920s to 1940s, was a master of the charcoal medium.
5. *Wax-Base Overlay (Prismacolor).* Wax-base overlay applied with Prismacolor or similar pencils can be built up in layers to provide depth, texture, and light. This technique was expertly pioneered and refined to a high art by Oles in the 1970s and 1980s.
6. *Tempera.* In painting, tempera is an opaque water-base paint, but when tempera is used for architectural delineation, pigments are mixed with sizing casein, or egg to create a dull finish. Tempera is applied with ruling pen, brush, or airbrush. It is a commercially popular medium, for it simulates color photographic quality.
7. *Applied color tones.* Applied color tones are trans-

parent colored films that can be applied directly to ink or graphite drawings. They provide a mechanical but consistent image.

8. *Felt pens.* Felt pens used in architectural delineation generally consist of oil-based inks impregnated in felt rolls or strips. They can be applied in broad lines that produce tones and are available in a variety of colors, grays, and blacks. Application is rapid and diagrammatic, but effective for large presentations.

9. *Computer-aided Drawing.* Computer-aided drawings provide the delineation technology for the computer age. Because computer-aided drawings provide a data base for calculating viewing angles of a building, part of a building, a group of buildings, a city block, or an entire city, the opportunity to select a favorable viewing angle is rapid, accurate, and effective. Perspectives, once created, can be rotated on the screen in order to select a single image or identify the many images for the final building. Images can be produced as a basis for an architectural delineator using the media discussed previously to complete the rendering; they can be an end in themselves either by printing an image directly in line, in tone, or in color, or by having the photographic image on the computer's screen reproduced and using that image.

Many current computer programs provide delineation bases. In the United States, the firm of Skidmore, Owings and Merrill has been an innovator in the use of computer-aided renderings for design.

M. Morse Payne of The Architects Collaborative, Inc. had developed earlier techniques for simulating a final building for IBM in the 1950s using motion pictures.

BIBLIOGRAPHY

1. G. Allen and R. Oliver, *Architectural Drawing: The Art and the Process,* Whitney Library of Design, Watson–Guptill Publications, New York, 1981, p. 166.
2. H. Engle, *The Japanese House: A Tradition for Contemporary Architecture,* Charles E. Tuttle Company, Rutland, Vt., 1964, plate 2, p. 177.
3. H. Powell and D. Leatherbarrow, *Masterpieces of Architectural Drawing,* Abbeville Press Publishers, New York, 1982.
4. Ref. 3, p. 23.
5. Ref. 3, p. 27.
6. Ref. 3, p. 30.
7. Ref. 3, p. 34.
8. Ref. 3, p. 109.
9. D. B. Guralnik, ed., *Webster's New World Dictionary of the American Language,* 2nd college ed., Simon & Schuster, New York, 1980, p. 69.
10. Ref. 3, p. 41.
11. Ref. 3, p. 42.
12. Ref. 3, p. 50–51.
13. Ref. 3, p. 55.
14. F. L. Wright, *Drawings and Plans of Frank Lloyd Wright:* *The Early Period (1893–1909),* Dover Publications, New York, 1983, plate LXIII9a.
15. *Ibid.,* plate III.
16. Ref. 3, p. 53.
17. Ref. 3, p. 58.
18. H. L. C. Jaffe, *De Stijl,* Harry N. Abrams, New York, p. 31.
19. R. S. Wurman and E. Feldman, *The Notebooks and Drawings of Louis I. Kahn,* MIT Press, Cambridge, Mass., 1973, drawing 59.
20. M. G. Mayo, *Working Manual: Shade and Shadow on Orthographic, Isometric and Perspective Projections,* Unpublished document, Carnegie Institute of Technology, Carnegie-Mellon University, Pittsburgh, Pa., 1953.

General References

F. Ching, *Architectural Graphics,* Van Nostrand Reinhold, New York, 1975.
A. L. Guptill, *Rendering in Pen and Ink,* Watson-Guptill Publications, New York, 1976.
E. F. Sekler and W. Curtis, *Le Corbusier at Work,* Harvard University Press, Cambridge, Mass., 1978.
S. R. Stein, *The Architecture of Richard Morris Hunt, the catalogue of the travelling exhibition,* The University of Chicago Press, Chicago, 1986.
S. Simmons III and M. S. A. Winer, *Drawing: The Creative Process,* Prentice–Hall, Englewood Cliffs, N.J., 1977.
Architecture in Perspective, American Society of Architectural Perspectivists, Boston, Mass., 1986.

ELLIOT PAUL ROTHMAN, AIA
Rothman Rothman Heineman
Architects Inc.
Boston, Massachusetts

RESEARCH, ARCHITECTURAL

This discussion of architectural research is meant to provide practicing professionals, academicians, and students in architecture and the related design fields with a survey of, and reference to, the rapidly emerging field of architectural research.

It will define architectural research and explain why it is important to the architectural profession, schools of architecture, and the building industry, as well as to the public. The brief history of architectural research in the United States will be discussed within the framework of The American Institute of Architects and the schools of architecture. The present nature and current methods of architectural research will be examined. A taxonomy of needed areas of research will be presented, as well as a listing of organizations involved in architectural research.

DEFINITION

Architectural research is systematic inquiry directed toward the creation and development of knowledge so that it can be used to understand or change in a positive manner the production of architecture. This inquiry may be in the form of knowledge development in order to solve a problem (applied research) or in the form of knowledge development for the sake of knowledge (basic research). Both types can be seen throughout the spectrum of architectural research, from energy research to historical research.

Frequently, the various methods of inquiry are described as two, often conflicting, ways at looking for knowledge. These have been described as the romantic and classic paths of seeking objective truth. The romantic view is based on knowledge through experience, intuition, and feeling. In contrast, the classic view is based on knowledge via reason and laws. This latter view is articulated as empirical or scientific inquiry, whereas the former is represented as creative and inspirational.

Unfortunately, the experiences accumulated through academic institutions and professional careers tend to place people in one camp or the other. Those who rely on romantic views for understanding tend to believe that inquiry through classic or scientific means is mechanical and constraining and does not account for many factors found in the real world. Those who rely on scientific inquiry often view romantic inquiry as irrational and without substance. In fact, both views are integral parts of systematic inquiry and knowledge building. Inquiry follows a path of hypothesizing or intuitive understanding, deduction or reasoning, experimentation, and inference or concluding. Beliefs or theories are tested, substantiated, and added to the body of knowledge. An accepted set of rules must govern the process; acceptability depends on a rigorous methodology of inquiry and the ability to validate the findings or conclusions. In other words, intuition and inspiration can generate the relationships that must then be tested objectively. The development of knowledge depends on both the romantic and classic views of seeking truth.

IMPORTANCE OF ARCHITECTURAL RESEARCH

The desire to understand is a fundamental attribute of humanity. Obviously the architectural profession desires to understand, to have knowledge. However, the process of gaining knowledge in the architectural profession through architectural research is more a question of the responsibility of various parties to create as well as to apply this knowledge.

There is a growing awareness among the building industry and the public that the built environment too often fails—in aesthetic, functional, social, and economic performance—and that the industry has not developed socially or technologically as well as other industries and components of society. In the past, the body of knowledge grew at a pace that could be internalized by solid vocational training and professional experience. The fundamentals covered in universities spanned most of the professional's life. However, the increasing pace of postindustrial technological change has exploded the knowledge base. Traditional forms of professional and institutional information and knowledge transfer can no longer cope with these rapid advancements. The world in which the architectural profession designs is simply too complex; this requires more and better knowledge more rapidly developed and transferred to the architectural profession.

This creation of knowledge must become an integral part of the architectural profession. Architects must be educated to become a profession of both knowledge creators and knowledge appliers. This is the model for most professions and universities. However, neither the building industry, the architectural profession, nor the schools of architecture are structured in a way that facilitates or promotes systematic inquiry for the purpose of building knowledge.

First, the building industry, unique among the nation's industries, is large, yet fragmented. The value of new construction put in place in 1986 is estimated to be over $243 billion not including value added. Total industry in the United States comprises 32% of the Gross Domestic Product (GDP), while over 19% of the industry sector is composed of the construction industry (and this does not include the large sector of product manufacturers who are considered part of the building industry). Thus, over 6% of the United States' total economy is based on the building industry. However, the building industry is composed of a large number of small, labor-intensive firms with local area markets. More than any other industry in the United States, it is modeled after the craft system, with each trade essentially self-employed. Because each event is unique, bringing a mix of participants together, the roles of participants are governed by years of tradition and practice. Thus, the industry is disaggregated into a large number of relatively small entities, which in turn act independently with little or no knowledge for industry-wide research or knowledge development. New research and technology is driven largely by the product development efforts of manufacturers and the development of building standards.

Architectural firms, like other industry participants, are numerous and small. While there are over 10,000 architectural firms in the United States, well over half employ less than 4 persons, and less than 100 firms have more than 100 employees. Thus only a few firms are large enough to achieve a critical mass of research-oriented personnel; most rely on consultants for specialized technical knowledge. Knowledge is therefore built within firms through a progression of architectural commissions and reliance on technical consultants. There is little systematic contribution to, or reliance on, a larger knowledge base.

Education and training in architecture in the United States is the function of approximately 100 accredited university schools of architecture. Architectural education focuses primarily on design and technology, with a strong emphasis on studio experience. That is, a major educational effort occurs in an integrative design studio, where students work with faculty on various architectural design problems on an individual or small group basis. The intellectual tradition or architectural education emphasizes precedent and adaptation rather than actual knowledge development. Only a handful of schools of architecture have moved away from this tradition of professional design education toward the more prevalent university mode of knowledge development.

In the United States, the building industry, the architectural profession, and the schools of architecture are all relatively weak contributors to new knowledge. However, over the last 20 years, a few of the schools and a small part of the architectural profession have begun accepting the responsibility, common to other professions, for research. In fact, a fundamental change is occurring in architectural practice and in professional architectural education: the inclusion of research as an integral part of architecture.

HISTORY OF ARCHITECTURAL RESEARCH IN THE UNITED STATES

The short history of architectural research can be documented by looking at the fluctuations of research programs within The American Institute of Architects, the professional society representing architects in the United States, and through the schools of architecture. In the late 1960s and early 1970s, a small architectural research program existed within the AIA. Its primary purpose was that of interaction with the various other institutions and organizations that developed knowledge and information that was usable by and transferable to the architectural profession. It also attempted to promote architectural research. However, the resources allocated to the program were meager, and during this period, architectural research was not seen as an integral part of the practice of architecture.

In 1974, the AIA formed the AIA Research Corporation, a separate nonprofit organization. This organization saw as its main purpose the promotion, development, and performance of architectural research. Later, in the early 1980s, the AIA Research Corporation was merged into the AIA Foundation; however, its purpose remained the same. Over these 12 years, this organization managed over $25 million of architectural research on a range of research issues including natural hazards, energy, health, fire, and occupant behavior. Over 1000 consulting professionals were used in these projects, which began building a group of architects within the profession interested in both performing and applying architectural research. The dissemination of this research came in the form of reports, conferences, educational seminars, and a magazine, *Research and Design*. One of its major efforts was the dissemination of much of its energy research through the development of the successful AIA Energy Professional Development Program.

In 1983, the AIA Foundation formed the Architectural Research Council composed of representatives from the AIA's design and practice committees. The purpose of this council was to ensure that the direction of research efforts were responsive to the needs of the architectural profession and to assist in disseminating the results through the committees. The Architectural Research Council developed an annual listing of needed research, which was published as the AIA's *Architectural Research Priorities*. In 1985, it conducted a major national conference attended

by over 500 professionals and covering over 120 architectural research papers. This conference, "Research and Design 85," was the first time in which a major effort brought together the existing communities of researchers, architectural practitioners, and professors of architecture under a distinct program of architectural research.

In 1985, the AIA transferred its architectural research program to the newly formed Council on Architectural Research, which was a joint program between the AIA and the Association of Collegiate Schools of Architecture (ACSA). This council is composed of members appointed by and representing both the AIA and the ACSA. Its primary purposes are similar to the earlier Architectural Research Council from which it was derived. Various research programs exist under its auspices. One in particular is the Health Facilities Research Program. This research program, which is supported by the AIA's Committee on Architecture for Health, solicits outside funding and directs architectural research projects aimed at the development of knowledge important in the design and operation of health-care facilities. Other programs concerned with natural hazards and energy exist within the council.

During this period, the schools of architecture were also experiencing similar changes regarding architectural research. In the early 1980s, the ACSA formed a committee on research that represented those faculty members involved and interested in architectural research. The ACSA conducted various institutes where current architectural research was presented to architectural faculty for inclusion in the educational system.

Parallel to this effort, the Architectural Research Centers Consortium (ARCC) was formed, representing the schools of architecture that had formed research units or centers within their schools. ARCC, which presently represents over 30 schools, brought together the research community in order to promote architectural research through an interaction between the various centers involved in research. They have held numerous workshops and developed a number of reports, primarily documenting architectural research and future needs and directions.

The late 1970s and 1980s saw a dramatic growth in research projects being performed in the schools of architecture. Surveys in 1981 by the ACSA and in 1984 by the AIA Architectural Research Council indicated several hundred research projects totaling between $10 and 15 million per year for each of the surveys.

Hundreds of architectural research projects performed by hundreds of researchers worth millions of dollars is now the norm. Although small in comparison to the other professions, it is nonetheless a beginning. It is hoped that the next 10 years will see it grow into a recognized and integral part of the profession of architecture.

THE NATURE OF ARCHITECTURAL RESEARCH

Architectural research freely borrows from a range of other fields. While this has paid off in the form of acquisition of considerable new knowledge, it has taken its toll on the efforts to integrate that knowledge into the practice and education of architecture. The introduction of methods from "foreign" fields has caused a degree of incompatibility between the research findings and their application in architecture. Of course there is value in importing research methods and results and then assimilating them into the field where they become a part of architecture. However, there is greater value in developing methods that are indigenous to the field of architecture.

The present nature of architectural research, including the methods employed in the research and the results derived from the research and applied to the profession, comes primarily from four areas: the humanities, the natural sciences, the social sciences, and the management sciences. The humanities are those fields that have primarily a cultural character and include mathematics, philosophy, history, and languages (or modern linguistics). The methods traditionally used by these fields have historically been integrated with architectural inquiry. History and philosophy have long been associated with the development of architectural knowledge and criticism. The logic of mathematics and use of scale has been associated with the building of a base of knowledge central to architecture. Mathematics has most recently begun to play an increasingly important role in the acquisition of new knowledge in the area of architectural computer applications including the development of expert systems. Also recently, modern linguistics has introduced new ways of representing architectural knowledge.

The natural sciences are those fields that deal with matter, energy, and their interrelations and transformations and include physics, chemistry, and biology. Particularly since the emergence of the engineering professions, the natural sciences have become strong allies in the development of architectural knowledge. The natural laws of physics (statics, dynamics, and thermodynamics) that dictate the behavior of the building physically have been applied directly into the profession within the structural, material, energy, and lighting aspects of building design. To a lesser degree, the development of knowledge of natural forms and growth has been transferred from the field of biology into architecture. The emerging interests in the physical health effects of buildings are intertwined with the field of chemistry.

The social sciences are those fields that deal with the institutions and functioning of human society and with the behavior of members of society; they include sociology, psychology, anthropology, political science, and economics. The recent fervor over environmental studies has resulted in the application of social science methods in the development of architectural knowledge. The use of behavioral science (psychology) to understand the effects of a building on its occupants and vice versa has become a major component of architectural research over the last 10 years. The effects of the urban environment on society through studies in sociology and anthropology have been studied for application in architecture and urban design. The systematic study of economics to understand the consequences of the application of new knowledge and technologies is playing a larger and larger role in architectural research.

The management sciences are those fairly new fields that deal with business and financial management. The areas of importance to the architectural profession that have emerged include decision theory, operations research, simulation techniques, cost–benefit analysis, critical path management, and dynamic programming. Knowledge in these fields has found its way and continues to find its way into architecture and offers assistance to the profession in terms of financial and management complexities.

All of these fields and disciplines have been instrumental in the formulation of architectural inquiry and the development of knowledge that is used daily in the practice of architecture and in the education of architects. With any transfer of information from separate disciplines to a new field there is a transformation that occurs with the integration of this knowledge. Within architectural research, this transformation has been the emergence of new methods of research and new ways to present the findings for more responsive application in the profession.

THE METHODS OF ARCHITECTURAL RESEARCH

Applied architectural research is undertaken to produce knowledge to promote informed action. This knowledge has clear uses within the programming, designing, building, operating, and evaluating processes. Architectural research not linked specifically to stages in that process runs the risk of being irrelevant in the eyes of the practitioner and educator.

The process of architectural research to fulfill this need usually consists of five distinct phases: measurement of performance, prediction of performance, generation of alternative solutions, selection of alternative solutions, and measurement of performance achieved. This process attempts to follow the path of scientific inquiry. The measurement of performance consists of either using the data to generate hypotheses or hypothesizing first and measuring the data to substantiate the hypothesis, the prediction of performance based on reasoning and deduction applied to the measured data, the generation of alternative solutions to provide the basis for an experiment or for comparisons of potential solutions to particular problems identified by the data, the final selection of alternative solutions that correspond to the findings and conclusions of the research, and the eventual evaluation and measurement of the performance attained by these solutions in order to sustain, modify, or refute the hypotheses.

Measurement of performance of buildings is the critical step in this process. As the ability to measure how buildings perform under varying conditions is improved, the ability to produce buildings that deliver more to society under most conditions is improved. However, one of the fundamental problems of architectural research is the absence of relevant, quantitative data and the relevant indicators to measure the data. Methodological problems are serious in every subject area of architectural research. The case study approach so well used in the educational process and in practice is only a prelude to more rigorous methods of inquiry. Advancement beyond the intuitive, descriptive case study to a more rigorous and quantitative recording of performance observations, allowing for the comparison between cases and controlled experimentation, is essential for the progress of this discipline.

AREAS OF ARCHITECTURAL RESEARCH

Various taxonomies of architectural research have been developed over the years. All of them have some validity based on the group developing the research needs or areas, whether practitioners, educators, researchers, client groups, or sponsors of research. They can be vastly different in detail but most approach the same general areas of architectural research. These needs are characterized by research into the process of design, conservation of resources, occupant behavior, human safety and health, building technology, and the process of construction occupancy. Of course, the research may be at the building scale or the urban scale, it may deal with one particular building type or buildings in general, it may focus on one particular user category or the general public, or it may concern itself with developing knowledge for application at any of the various stages of design, construction, and occupancy.

Architectural research on the process of design typically looks at the entire process of the delivery of design in order to understand the relationships so that better technologies and management techniques can be brought to bear on the design of the built environment. Architectural research on the conservation of resources attempts to understand the use of resources (energy, water, lighting, building materials) in the building in order to identify and develop more efficient ways to use these resources. Architectural research in occupant behavior explores the various factors that cause satisfaction and dissatisfaction and a range of behaviors in various occupancy groups (general, elderly, disabled, children, sick, incarcerated) in order to produce more pleasing and appropriate environments.

Architectural research for human safety and health investigates the various hazards to occupants in buildings (fire, earthquakes, winds, floods, indoor air quality, collapse) in order to produce safer environments. Architectural research into building technology examines the performance and use of various building technologies (systems, components, materials, equipment) in order to recommend or develop more appropriate technologies to fulfill design requirements. Architectural research into the construction–occupancy process looks into the various elements of construction and occupancy (construction methods, construction delivery processes, diagnostic and evaluative techniques) in order to ensure the efficient production of buildings and effective evaluation of problems after construction.

The development of any research agenda or taxonomy is fraught with difficulties. The real world will just not submit to the compulsive need to classify it. However, there is a real need to demonstrate the breadth of architectural research, the large number of severe problems that wait to be solved, and the large amounts of knowledge that wait to be found.

PROFESSIONAL ORGANIZATIONS INVOLVED IN ARCHITECTURAL RESEARCH

There are various organizations involved in architectural research. A few relate exclusively to architectural research, but for most architectural research it is only one (and many times a small) component of their overall program. The AIA/ACSA Council on Architectural Research directs all architectural research activities of the American Institute of Architects and the Association of Collegiate Schools of Architecture. Several programs are currently underway (primarily health facilities, earthquake, and energy research), and others are planned. The Council plans to hold an annual Research and Design Conference in order to promote the transfer of architectural research to the architectural profession and schools.

AIA/ACSA Council on Architectural Research and the Architectural Research Center Consortium (mentioned previously) are the only ones that presently exist that are involved exclusively in architectural research. However, a number of national organizations exist that in one form or another are involved in architectural research as part of their program. They include the following:

The American Consulting Engineers Council (ACEC) Research and Management Foundation is the research arm of ACEC, which is a membership association of engineering and architectural firms that undertakes projects that will benefit the engineering profession as a whole. The American Society of Civil Engineers (ASCE) is the professional society for civil engineers with some application to architecture.

The American Society of Heating, Refrigerating, and Air-conditioning Engineers (ASHRAE) is a membership organization composed of engineers and architects interested in energy design and mechanical engineering. Its research program seeks to advance the arts and sciences of heating, ventilation, refrigeration, air-conditioning, and the related human factors. Although focused primarily on engineering, it does involve architectural researchers and has some projects directly applicable to architecture.

The American Society of Plumbing Engineers (ASPE) Research Foundation coordinates and sponsors research in plumbing systems. The Architectural and Engineering Performance Information Center (AEPIC) is an organization supported by the American Society of Civil Engineers and the National Society of Professional Engineers through the University of Maryland, which collects and analyzes building performance data.

The Building Research Board (BRB) of the National Research Council was established by the National Academy of Sciences to further the development of knowledge and advise the federal government in areas of importance. The program has a heavy emphasis on architectural research integrated with other allied disciplines. The Building Seismic Safety Council (BSSC) is a national organization that fosters the improved seismic safety of the built environment. The program relates to and involves all professions involved in the earthquake safety of buildings, including the architectural profession.

The Environmental Design Research Association (EDRA) is a national membership association of researchers and practitioners including the disciplines of architecture, behavioral science, planning, interior design, and other allied fields. The organization seeks to promote the field of environmental design research and conducts annual conferences aimed at cross-fertilization and information transfer.

The Earthquake Engineering Research Institute (EERI) is a national membership association of structural engineers, geologists, architects, social scientists, and others involved in earthquake mitigation research. Although heavily engineering oriented, the organization does have an architectural research component.

The Intelligent Buildings Institute (IBI) is a nonprofit professional association that seeks to serve all sectors of the intelligent buildings community through market information, training, research, guidelines, and standards. The International Technology Council (ITC) of the Building Research Board of the National Academy of Sciences represents, encourages, facilitates, and develops United States participation in the technical activities of the International Council for Building Research, Studies, and Documentation (CIB). The ITC serves as the mechanism through which U.S. and international building communities exchange building and construction research findings.

The Lighting Research Institute (LRI) is a research organization supported by the Illuminating Engineering Society (IES), the International Association of Lighting Designers (IALD), and other groups to foster and promote lighting research. Architectural research is seen as an integral part of this program.

The National Association of Home Builders (NAHB) Research Foundation is the research arm of the NAHB and is interested in the introduction of significant new developments in residental building products and manufacturing practices. The National Fire Protection Association (NFPA) Research Foundation is the research arm of the NFPA, a membership organization made up of fire protection engineers, architects, client groups, and others. Architectural research is one component within their broader field of fire protection.

The National Institute of Building Sciences (NIBS) is a membership organization of disciplines in the building industry. They offer a forum for programs and projects of interest to the building industry. Architectural research plays an important role in their overall program.

The Urban Land Institute (ULI) is a membership association of developers, financiers, officials, and designers in the property development field. Their research program is primarily focused on research applicable to development; however, architectural research does play a role in the development of information.

Substantial support for the development of architec-

tural research has come from federal agencies, primarily in terms of research funding, but also in terms of cooperative efforts in structuring the field. Three federal agencies stand out that have probably done more to promote and foster architectural research through their funding strategies than any others.

The Department of Energy (DOE) has two programs that contain large components of architectural research applied to the energy problem. The conservation program supports research on the envelope, various building types, design and analysis tools, and systems. The solar program supports research on renewable technologies including active and passive energy systems. DOE has a number of laboratories each with separate research programs on specific areas of interest to architectural research including Lawrence Berkeley Laboratory, Pacific Northwest Laboratory, Oak Ridge National Laboratory, Solar Energy Research Institute, and Brookhaven National Laboratory.

The National Science Foundation (NSF) has two programs that have supported architectural research. The earthquake program has long been a supporter of architectural research, and the newer buildings program also has an architectural component.

The Department of Defense (DOD) has funded a multitude of architectural research areas including research in computer design, housing, health facilities, and energy. Each service (U.S. Army Corps of Engineers, Naval Facilities Engineering Command, and U.S. Air Force Logistics Command) has its own research program and laboratories.

Other federal agencies continue to sponsor architectural research. These agencies include the Agency for International Development (AID), which has funded international disaster mitigation and recovery projects in the architectural research field; the Environmental Protection Agency (EPA), which has funded a number of projects primarily focused on the effects of acid rain on buildings; the Federal Emergency Management Agency (FEMA), which has funded various national disaster mitigation projects in the architectural research field; the General Services Administration (GSA), which has funded a range of design research projects on a number of topics concerning office buildings; the Department of Health and Human Services (HHS), which has funded architectural research projects in health-care facilities and health-delivery systems; and the Department of Housing and Urban Development (HUD), which has a research program primarily dealing with housing research.

The National Bureau of Standards (NBS), now the National Institute of Standards and Technology (NIST), has funded a range of projects of interest to architectural research. These include fire, structural, energy, acoustics, lighting, and behavioral research.

The National Endowment for the Arts (NEA) has funded a number of architectural research projects on a varying range of subjects. The National Endowment for the Humanities (NEH) has funded architectural research primarily in architectural history, and the Veterans Administration (VA) has funded a number of research projects concerned with hospital design and construction.

ACADEMIC ORGANIZATIONS INVOLVED IN ARCHITECTURAL RESEARCH

The following universities have programs that perform architectural research usually affiliated with their architectural departments or colleges:

Carnegie-Mellon University
  Center for Building Diagnostics
University of California-Berkeley
  Center for Environmental Design Research
  Institute for Urban and Regional Planning
University of Colorado
Columbia University
  Center for Preservation Research
Georgia Institute of Technology
  Architectural Research Laboratory
  Center for Architectural Conservation
Harvard University
University of Illinois
Illinois Institute of Technology
University of Maryland
  Architecture and Engineering Performance Information Center
Massachusetts Institute of Technology
  Laboratory of Architecture and Planning
University of Michigan
  Architecture and Planning Research Laboratory
University of Minnesota
State University of New York
Ohio State University
University of Oregon
Princeton University
Rensselaer Polytechnic Institute
  Center for Architectural Research
University of Texas at Austin
  Center for the Study of American Architecture
Virginia Polytechnic Institute and State University
University of Washington
  Center for Planning and Design
University of Wisconsin
  Center for Architecture and Urban Planning Research

INTERNATIONAL ORGANIZATIONS INVOLVED IN ARCHITECTURAL RESEARCH

The following international organizations are concerned with areas involved in architectural research:

1. International Council for Building Research, Studies, and Documentation (CIB) located in the Netherlands is an international, nongovernment, nonprofit organization whose purpose is to encourage, facilitate, and develop international cooperation in building, housing and planning research, studies, and documentation, covering not only the technical but also the economic and social aspects of building and the related environment.

2. Council on Tall Buildings and Urban Habitat, an international activity sponsored by engineering, architectural, and planning professionals, was established to study and report on all aspects of the planning, design, construction, and operation of tall buildings.

3. International Energy Agency (EIA) is an autonomous agency, represented by a number of countries, that collects and analyzes energy data, reviews member countries' domestic energy policies and programs, makes energy forecasts, and undertakes and publishes special studies.

4. United Nations Centre for Human Settlements (UNCHS, Habitat) works in the field of human settlements in the areas of policies and strategies, planning, community services, land, low-cost housing and infrastructure, and human settlements institutions and management.

FOREIGN NATIONAL ORGANIZATIONS INVOLVED IN ARCHITECTURAL RESEARCH

The following foreign national organizations are recognized leaders in the fields of building and construction research:

1. Commonwealth Scientific and Industrial Research Organization's (CSIRO) Division of Building Research is a statutory agency of the government of Australia whose activities range from basic studies in building materials through such design disciplines as structural engineering, acoustics, and building services, to planning activities, operations research, and social and economic studies related to the built environment.

2. Centre Scientifique et Technique de la Construction (CSTC) (Belgian Building Research Center) is an industrial technical center, created to promote the technical progress of construction by all means including research, documentation, assistance, education, etc.

3. National Research Council of Canada's Division of Building Research is a government institution that provides a national research facility for the Canadian construction industry to perform basic studies, field or performance studies, and standards development.

4. Staten Byggeforskningsinstitut (SBI) (Danish Building Research Institute) is an independent public institute working for the Danish building sector and serving all parties from legislators to public users.

5. Valtion teknillinen tutkimuskeskus (VTT) (Finland Technical Research Center's Division for Building Technology and Community Development) is a governmental research and testing institute with the purpose of maintaining and rais-

ing the level of technology in Finland and of meeting the research and testing needs of the construction industry including the public and private sectors.

6. Centre Scientifique et Technique du Batiment (CSTB) (Scientific and Technical Building Center) is a public organization sponsored by the French government, which performs building research, technical, sociological, and economic projects for government and private organizations.

7. Informationszentrum RAUM und BAU (IRB) (Information Center for Regional Planning and Construction) is entrusted by the government of the FRG with the function of a central information agency in the fields of planning, housing, and engineering including the collection and dissemination of technical and scientific information.

8. Epitestudomanyi Intezet (ETI) (Hungarian Institute for Building Sciences) is the central research institute of the Hungarian building industry, which carries out research for the government, the building industry, and other branches of the national economy.

9. Instituto Centrale per l'Industrializzazione e la Tecnologia Edilizia (ICITE) (Italian Building Research Station) is an institute of the National Research Council of Italy whose aims are the standardization and qualitative control of building component requirements and performance.

10. Building Research Institute's (BRI) (Ministry of Construction is the building research organization of the government of Japan whose research results are used to give scientific and technical support for new policy, to ensure public welfare, and to contribute to the international research community.

11. Plancommissie Bouwresearch (TNO) (Planning Committee for Building Research of the Netherlands) coordinates the research activities of various divisions and institutes partly or entirely engaged in building and living research including not only buildings but also offshore construction, environmental aspects, working conditions, and economy.

12. Norges byggforskningsinstitutt (NBI) (Norwegian Building Research Institute) is a semigovernment organization that performs building research at the disposal of central and local authorities, the construction industry, and private individuals.

13. Staten institut for byggnadsforskning (SIB) (National Swedish Institute for Building Research) is a state-financed research organization that is used to analyze shortcomings and qualities within the building sector in order to promote improvements to buildings and living conditions and provide a factual basis for a debate on better ways to plan and build.

14. Building Research Establishment's (BRE) Building Research Station of the UK is a government research establishment that carries out research

and development in building and construction and allied fields primarily for the needs of the government.

CONCLUSION

Most fields of professional practice have evolved during the course of the twentieth century from total reliance on intuitive understanding, experience, and historical precedent to a significant emphasis on research and scholarship as a basis for practice. This progression can clearly be seen in the professions of law, medicine, and engineering. Such changes have had profound impacts on their training and practice.

This evolution seems to have progressed much more slowly in the field of architecture. The call for such an expanded and deepened knowledge base has received only limited support from most of the profession. But there are signs that a tradition of research within architecture is slowly beginning to evolve.

Architecture cannot be based entirely on intuition, experience, and precedent. It must also be based on knowledge carefully acquired through research. The belief is not that such knowledge can replace individual architectural creativity, but that it can inform and improve both the design process and the final architecture.

BIBLIOGRAPHY

General References

Research and Design: General Proceedings, The American Institute of Architects, Washington, D.C., 1985.

American Institute of Architects Research Council, *Architectural Research Priorities,* The American Institute of Architects, Washington, D.C., 1984.

G. T. Moore and J. A. Templer, eds., *Doctoral Education for Architectural Research,* Architectural Research Centers Consortium, Inc., Washington, D.C., 1984.

G. T. Moore, D. P. Tuttle, and S. C. Howell, *Environmental Design Research Directions: Process and Prospects,* Praeger, New York, 1984.

R. L. Schluntz, *Survey of Sponsored Architectural Research,* The Association of Collegiate Schools of Architecture, Washington, D. C., 1981.

J. C. Snyder, ed., *An Agenda for Architectural Research,* Architectural Research Centers Consortium, Inc., Washington, D.C., 1982.

J. C. Snyder, ed., *Architectural Research,* Van Nostrand Reinhold Co., Inc., New York, 1984.

See also American National Standards Institute (ANSI); Architecture and Engineering Performance Information Center (AEPIC); Behavior and Architecture; Computerization; Diagnostics, Building; National Bureau of Standards (NBS); Regional/Urban Design Assistance Teams (R/UDAT); Theory of Architecture; Value Engineering

Earle W. Kennett
Nanita/Kennett Associates
Gaithersburg, Maryland

RESIDENTIAL BUILDINGS

In most climates shelter is a basic requirement of human existence. As the need for food is primordial, however, the means by which food is procured usually determines the nature of human dwellings. Thus, dwellings reflect like mirrors the living conditions of their builders. Nomads, for example, need different types of dwellings from those of sedentary societies, and rural homes of folk societies naturally differ greatly from those of urban dwellers. Adding further variables such as climate, topography, and availability of building materials to these basic distinctions has resulted in a very rich spectrum of residential building types over the past millenia.

THE GENESIS OF HUMAN SHELTER

The true origins of residential buildings must be sought in the obscure early stages of human evolution. Nevertheless, it is possible to formulate a reasonable picture of the humble beginnings of domestic architecture by using archaeological findings of prehistoric cultures in combination with anthropological descriptions of isolated contemporary societies that until recently lived much as their ancestors did in the Stone Age.

Although it is tempting to assume that human shelters had but a single origin, a more realistic assumption is that they had various roots. Despite the popular acceptance that caves were the primordial dwellings of paleolithic people, this belief seems untenable because it implies that human evolution was at the outset restricted to those geographic areas where caves existed. This is not to deny the evidence found in many caves that they were used by prehistoric humans as domestic shelters, but it is likely that they were merely one alternative when available to the more prevalent beehive huts and windbreaks. The inherently permanent nature of caves ensured the survival of middens and paintings left behind by their early occupants, whereas the fragility of ephemeral dwellings for the most part precluded, over the span of several millenia, the survival of any traces of their occupancy. Hence, evidence favors the assumption that caves rather than other forms of shelter were mankind's original dwellings.

It is generally acknowledged that the most ancient economy of human subsistence was based on food gathering and primitive hunting, which implies a nomadic existence in other than paradiselike environments, because the inevitable exhaustion of food resources in almost any other environment enforced migration.

RURAL DWELLINGS

Shelters of Food Gatherers and Hunters

Food gatherers and lowly hunters inhabiting less than ideal regions must be constantly on the move in an endless pursuit of food. In the absence of caves, these nomads must build ephemeral shelters. The huts are small in size and constructed solely of materials collected in the vicinity of their temporary campsite. They are usually circular in shape with a beehive-type roof structure and are erected in a few hours. They provide only the most elementary form of interior climate control with an open fire outside the shelter giving the necessary comfort on cool nights.

The Bushmen of the Kalahari Desert and the pygmies of the Ituri Forest, both in Africa, as well as the Australian aborigines, still use dome-shaped beehive-type huts in their natural habitat. Judging by archaeological evidence, this dwelling type has been in use for more than a quarter of a million years. The U.S. anthropologist Carleton S. Coon asserts that this type of "domed hut is as specific to man, in a cultural sense, as the oriole's special kind of nest is instinctively specific to orioles" (1).

Because primitive nomads subsist on the game and plants that nature provides, they must follow a seasonal pattern of movement—within a given territory—related to the availability of food and water. As soon as their food resources within walking distance are exhausted, they abandon their hut and temporary campsite. The *skerm* (Fig. 1) or grass hut of the Bushmen may serve as a prototype of an ephemeral dwelling. After the women have collected some tree branches and a pile of grass, they erect these small shelters in 1 or 2 hours. Branches are driven upright into the ground in a circular pattern and then opposites are arched overhead and fastened to form a skeletal lattice structure that will support the grass covering. After thatching is completed, the shelter is then tied around once with a sinew string.

The huts of the pygmies and Australian aborigines are similar in form and construction to the Bushman skerm. Shelters used long ago by the American hunter-gatherers, such as the Karankawa and Ute of North America and the Pelche, Ona, and Yaguans of South America, were also similar to the skerms of the present-day African Bushmen.

Shelters of Skilled Hunters

More complex forms of shelters are the episodical dwellings of nomadic bands or tribes of skilled hunters and fishermen. Although these shelters are still erected within an hour or two, the period of their use extends to several weeks rather than mere days. Usually the plan of these dwellings is still circular, but the space enclosure may be either dome-shaped or conical. A further distinction of the episodical dwellings is their relative sizes, since both the surface area and the height of the interior are considerably greater than in the ephemeral shelter. The

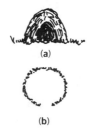

(a)

(b)

Figure 1. Bushmen skerm. **(a)** Elevation; **(b)** plan.

interior is divided into sleeping and cooking areas with a designated place for the hearth. A more sophisticated interior climate control as well as the reuse of some building materials that are transported to new campsites when the band moves are other characteristics.

The Inuit (Eskimo) igloo and the Plains Indians tepee are the most familiar forms of episodical dwellings. Others are the tepee-like tents of the Tungus who roam the eastern Siberian taiga, as well as the *kota* used by the Lapp reindeer herders of Northern Europe.

The Inuit igloo is perhaps the most fascinating dwelling, because it is built of snow, seemingly the most unlikely building material for protection against the cold Arctic weather. Working from the inside, the Inuit places one snow block tipped slightly inward next to another in upward spiraling rows until a dome structure with a key closing block results. With this method of construction, scaffolding is not required but, once the dome is finished, the porous snow blocks must be solidified. Blubber lamps are lit in the interior until the inside walls start to sweat and the blocks absorb this moisture. When the dome appears to have absorbed enough moisture, a door and a vent hole are cut so that cold air can rush into the structure, chill the surface, and freeze the water-permeated walls into a solid, monolithic structure.

Although snow has good insulating qualities, the interior climate of the igloo is further improved by lining the inside dome surface with caribou hides and seal skins. Similarly, skins also cover the raised sleeping platform, which is placed fronting the entrance; cooking shelves flank the entry.

The main dome of the igloo is frequently extended by additional vaulted structures, such as a tunnel passageway, or domed antechamber, and numerous storage vaults abutting the main dome and its antechambers. In summer, when the igloo begins to melt, it is abandoned and replaced by a seal-skin tent called a *tupiq*. In contrast to the igloo, the *tupiq* (Fig. 2) is a portable dwelling like the tepee that consists of a framework of poles covered with skins.

Tepees of the North American Plains Indians are equally ingenious episodical shelters. These skilled hunters, who followed the immense bison (buffalo) herds that roamed the plains, lived in portable dwellings consisting of a skeletal structure of poles with a tailored buf-

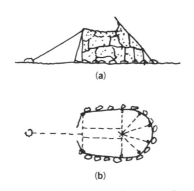

Figure 2. Inuit tupiq. **(a)** Elevation; **(b)** plan.

falo-hide cover. A tripod or tetrapod tied together at the top was first erected with up to 20 additional poles placed against it outlining a horseshoelike circular floor plan. The cover was then placed on this skeleton with a smoke hole at the top, the size of which could be controlled with the help of two "ears" or flaps, each attached to a separate free-standing pole. The fire was built near the center, below the smoke hole, and bedsteads were placed around the periphery of the tent, except at the doorway, which normally faced the rising sun. In winter the tepee cover was staked or weighted down with stones all around the bottom edge, and to prevent draft, an inner skin lining covered the ground and ran up the tepee's sides about 4–5 ft.

Tepees were pitched by women, usually within an hour's time, and dismanteled in less than that. Interestingly, the poles were then used to form travois to transport both personal belongings and the tent cover itself. Initially, Plains Indians used dogs to drag the travois; later, horses were used for this purpose.

The prehistoric dwellings of some Eurasian skilled hunters show many similarities with the *tupiq* and tepee. For example, the Mammoth Hunters of the Don River basin in Russia lived in tepeelike compound structures.

Portable Dwellings of Nomadic Pastoral Societies

Periodic dwellings of pastoral nomads represent the ultimate evolutionary stage of indigenous portable shelters. The primary characteristics that set these nomads apart from hunters and food gatherers are, first, their economic dependence on domesticated animals, and, second, the possession of some form of political tribal organization that controls their cyclical or seasonal migration pattern.

There are three inherent requirements that portable dwellings must possess. First, building materials must be lightweight so that they can be easily transported from one periodic settlement to another. Second, they must possess a low heat-storage capacity, ensuring quick heat response in winter and preventing heat build-up in summer. Finally, the structural system must be stable, and is ideally composed of a skeleton of compression members covered by a tensile membrane.

The Kirgizian yurt of Central Asia and the Bedouin black-tent are two illustrative prototypes of portable shelters. The former is a weatherproof dwelling that affords its occupants a remarkable degree of protection against the inclement weather of the Asian steppes. The latter, in contrast, is primarily a sun shade against intense solar radiation and a windscreen against sand storms.

The yurt (Fig. 3) has a circular plan and is a dome-shaped structure consisting of a skeleton and membrane cover, resulting in a minimum exposed surface with maximum stability. Its walls consist of willow latticework sections and a door frame lashed together that support curved roof poles radiating toward the center, with their top ends fitted into a wooden compression ring defining a smoke hole. A tension band tied around the top of the peripheral wall neutralizes the outward thrust of the roof poles. Over the entire framework of the yurt, layers of large pieces of heavy felt are fastened in accordance with

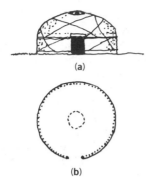

Figure 3. Kirgizian Yurt. (a) Elevation; (b) plan.

appropriate seasonal protection required. A felt curtain, often ornamented, is hung over the door.

Fire is made in the center of the yurt, and the smoke escapes through the central hole in the roof, which can be controlled from the inside by a movable felt cover. When open, the smoke hole also acts as a sundial, because sun-rays penetrating through it show the time of day. Storage boxes, carpets, and bedding are placed against the walls. The setting up and the dismantling of the yurt are always done by the women, which is also the case with the Bedouin black-tent.

Black-tents do not accentuate the boundaries between outdoors and indoors to the same degree as the yurts do, making it difficult sometimes to define where the true boundaries of the dwelling lie. Weather permitting, women in fact do many chores under the open sky.

Like its cover, the floor plan of the black-tent is rectangular. In pitching a tent, the first step entails the spreading of the cover on a cleared and level site, followed by pulling out and staking its ropes at an appropriate distance. Then, starting from one corner, poles are pushed up one by one until the tent roof is aloft. Next, the rear and side walls as well as the dividing curtain between the women's and the men's sections are pinned in place. This total operation may be completed within an hour.

The Bedouin black-tent is an efficient tensile structure with a flat roofline to minimize resistance to winds and sandstorms. Its poles are mere compression members supporting the weight of the roof cover; lateral wind forces are borne by the cover itself and its stays.

The women's side of the tent is the living and working area of the family, whereas the carpeted men's section is mainly used for receiving visitors. The contents of the tent are usually scanty, consisting mainly of bedding, cooking utensils, water skins, pack saddles, wheat bags, looms, and various weapons.

Periodic shelters like the yurt and black-tent were used in the distant past. The descriptions of the Scythians' tents by Herodotus and the biblical accounts of Abraham's tent suggest that the former resembled yurts and the latter, black-tents.

Communal Dwellings of Quasisedentary Societies

The discovery of the ability to domesticate plants initiated the neolithic revolution and a new economy of subsistence based on cultivation. By necessity, the most ancient cultivators augmented their food production with hunting and food collection, which often implied a semisedentary existence in contrast to a nomadic one, but gradually, with the improvement of agricultural technology, cultivators evolved into sedentary societies, first using semipermanent dwelling forms and later permanent ones.

"Slash-and-burn" or shifting cultivation represents one of the simplest, most ancient and least productive uses of cropland. Only a few implements such as the axe, the machete, and a digging-planting stick are employed. Because labor energy is provided solely by human effort, a large collective labor force is a necessity; it is also important to have access to a large amount of reserve land to allow for the customary fallows. Indigenous to tropical forest regions, this slash-and-burn technique of cultivation is called *milpa* in Latin America and *ladang* in Indonesia. In keeping with their collective economy, the dwellings of these rudimentary cultivators are large detached communal structures, of a circular, doughnut, oval, or rectangular plan. In South America, a communal dwelling is called either a *bohio* or *maloca*.

The indigenous dwelling of the Wai-Wai (Fig. 4) forest Indians of Guyana in South America may serve as an example of the communal habitation of shifting cultivators. The dwelling is a large circular hut with exterior walls built of vertical poles; the interior is divided into compartments by freestanding posts supporting a cone-shaped thatched roof. Each compartment accommodates one family, with the sleeping hammocks draped between

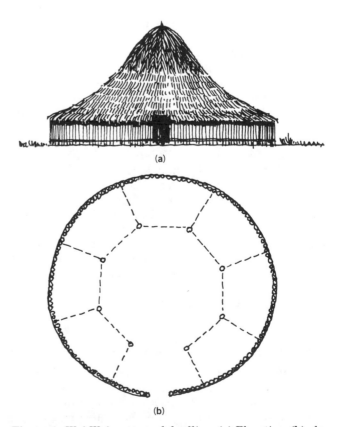

Figure 4. Wai-Wai communal dwelling. (a) Elevation; (b) plan.

the hut's posts; each family has its own hearth for cooking, with the smoke escaping through apertures in the thatched roof. Providing maximum shade and good ventilation, this building, with its low-heat capacity walls, responds well to the climatic realities of the tropical rain forest, which is the habitat of the Wai-Wai.

After a few years, when the soil of the forest clearing ceases to be productive, the Wai-Wai abandon their fields and their dwelling, and move to a new area to clear a new plot and build a new house, usually in a distant enough location to offer better hunting opportunities.

At the time of the discovery of America, several agrarian tribes of North American Indians, such as the Onandaga, Oneida, Seneca, Mohawk, and Iroquois, lived in communal long houses. These dwellings sometimes reached 125 ft in length and consisted of two facing rows of bays or compartments with sleeping platforms separated by a central corridor. Each compartment was occupied by one family and had a hearth in the corridor shared by the family opposite. It was not unusual for 20 families to live in one communal house. The building was constructed of a series of poles arched to form a barrel vaultlike skeleton supporting the bark roof shingles and the matting of the walls. These buildings were not substantial because their inhabitants frequently had to move to a new locality after a few years when tilling their fields without subsequent fertilization produced scanty crops.

Similar communal dwellings were also used by the coastal Indians of the Northwest inhabiting a temperate climate and an abundant maritime habitat where the sea and rivers teemed with fish; a rain forest supplied not only ample edible plants and fruits but also an inexhaustible supply of good building materials. This economy of plenty of the Haida, the Kwakiutl, and Salish, among others, depended primarily on fishing and food gathering. They lived in low pitched gable-ended rectangular long houses with a layout similar to that used by the agrarian Indians. Constructed of cedar planks and posts, the dwelling's interior was subdivided into a number of bays, each compartment having a low sleeping bench against the outside wall. Between facing bays ran a wide corridor down the length of the building. The smoke of the numerous hearths tended by each family escaped through the gaps between the roof planks when thrust aside by means of a pole. Most of these communal buildings had but a single entrance in the center of one of the gable ends.

Prehistoric communal dwellings used by primitive agrarian people existed also in northwestern Europe during the fifth millenium B.C., and were used by the Danubians who introduced a rudimentary agricultural technology to this region. Their dwellings were large rectangular multifamily structures built of timber and with a thatched roof.

Communal Dwellings of Sedentary Societies

A unique and very picturesque collective dwelling form is the pueblo of the American Pueblo Indian tribes of New Mexico and Arizona. These tribes cultivate staple crops on lands that are marginal because of limited rainfall and growing seasons curtailed by frost. They have a collective economy and live in multistoried buildings of many dwelling units arranged in tiers. These adobe buildings are usually three to five stories high and often enclose one or more plazas. Usually, each flat-roofed and terraced upper story on the plaza side is set back from the one beneath it, but they end in the rear in a multistoried perpendicular fortresslike wall.

The pueblo is composed of numerous rooms, sometimes hundreds, with each dwelling unit consisting of several rooms arranged two or three deep and connected to each other by small doors. A fireplace with a chimney is usually found in one corner of the main room and mealing bins with stone metates for grinding corn in another. The innermost rooms are usually used for storage. Peeled cedar beams span the rooms, with small poles placed transversely and close together supporting a layer of bark, brushwood, and grass, as well as a 3- to 4-in. coat of adobe. Being a precious building material, floor beams are never trimmed but are allowed to penetrate beyond the face of the exterior wall, thereby creating a visual feature characteristic of these dwellings.

Traditionally, the pueblo dwellings had no external doors; access to the peripheral rooms was gained through an opening in the roof through which ladders permitted passage. The wide roof terraces were used for sitting, sleeping, winnowing grain, drying crops, and as viewing platforms to observe dance performances and religious ceremonies held in the plaza below. The pueblo is an additive and cumulative building structure that periodically changes its mass and shape as the result of demolition of dilapidated sections followed by new construction in another part of the pueblo.

Seasonal Dwellings

Societies with an economy based on crop cultivation and animal husbandry often use two distinct type of seasonal dwellings, a substantial one for the sedentary period of their life and a temporary structure for the periods of migration. The *hogan* and the *ramada,* two distinct house types of the Navaho Indians, are good prototypical examples of seasonal dwellings. The traditional, and more substantial, dwelling is the hogan (Fig. 5), a low, one room,

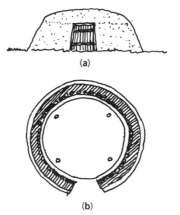

(a)

(b)

Figure 5. Navaho hogan. (a) Elevation; (b) plan.

mud-covered log hut built over a 2-ft deep, excavated pit. Each hogan is occupied by a single family; several hogans grouped together house a clan or extended family. Hogans usually have a circular plan with forked posts supporting a roof structure of beams and brushwood and side walls of inclined poles. The entire structure is covered with moist desert earth scraped up in baskets after a rain. Facing the east, a door opening just high enough for a man to crawl through gives access to the dwelling. The smoke from the central hearth escapes through a smoke hole above the door. Because the diurnal extremes of temperature are evened out by the lag in heat gain and heat loss of the thick layer of mud covering, the hogan is a comfortable indigenous dwelling.

The summer home of the Navaho is the *ramada,* essentially a roof shade structure with four or six upright posts supporting a flat roof of poles and brush. At times, a pole-and-brush wall is erected on the windward side to give greater comfort to its dwellers.

Hoganlike structures were widespread dwelling types used not only by other North American Indian tribes, but also in many other regions of the world. Near the village of Pan-p'o, in China, a hoganlike dwelling was found dating from about 4000 B.C. Similar dwellings were also used in Japan and Europe, as well as on the African continent.

Semipermanent Dwellings of Subsistence Agrarian Societies

Agrarian "folk" societies cultivate their land through regular planting of assorted seeds, tubers, or cuttings in fields that are prepared to yield staple crops. Unlike the rudimentary agrarians previously described, they no longer use digging sticks for cultivation but use hoes or even plows pulled by domesticated animals. However, they have not yet reached the advanced stage of agriculture in which more sophisticated plows and other technologies are used to go beyond a subsistence economy.

A wide range of physical environments, coupled with a greater variety of crops, organizations of manual labor, and cultural background bring about many types of settlement patterns and dwelling forms. The basic dwelling types of these societies are the cylindrical hut with a conical roof, the oval house, and the rectangular dwelling, the last-named usually with rounded corners, and a saddle-type roof. The walls of dwellings in arid tropical and subtropical regions are built of adobe, while in hot and humid climes, of vertical stalks with narrow gaps in between to ensure good cross ventilation; roofs of both types are invariably thatched. In its simplest form, the semipermanent dwelling has only one room, which the human occupants often share with small domesticated animals, but more frequently are compound or cluster dwellings consisting of several structures, each designated for certain functions; for example, some huts are built for sleeping, others for cooking, storage, or as pens or stables.

A typical semipermanent compound dwelling is the Mesakin Quisar cluster (Fig. 6) built by a Nuba people of the Sudan. It consists of five or six windowless adobe round huts, each with stone foundations and conical thatched roofs, enclosing a courtyard, the center of which is the family cooking area. Connecting walls between the

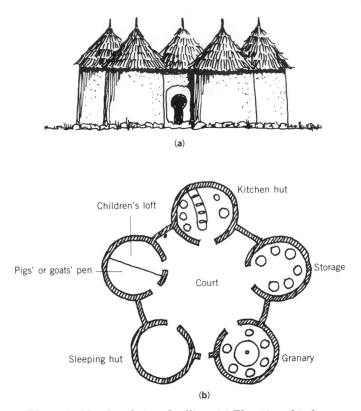

Figure 6. Masakin Quisar dwelling. **(a)** Elevation; **(b)** plan.

turretlike huts provide security and privacy to the occupants. The courtyard is often covered with a sun shade of loosely woven grass and boughs.

A keyhole-shaped entrance door in one of the connecting walls gives direct access to the courtyard of a five-hut cluster, whereas in a cluster dwelling of six huts, entry is gained through a large hut also used as a guest house. At the left side of the entrance is usually located the main sleeping hut; next to it is the animal pen with a loft at a higher level used as a sleeping platform for the young boys of the family; this is followed by a kitchen hut and two storage huts which complete the circle. Each hut is illuminated by daylight through its doorway, a small round or oval opening with high mud threshold. Wooden pegs are set into the smoothly plastered interior walls for hanging utensils such as calabashes used as containers. Particularly smooth and ornate are the hand-rubbed walls of the bathroom, which has a simple shower consisting of a calabash cradled on a pair of antelope horns mounted on the connecting wall between the kitchen hut and the pen.

The central space of this dwelling is the courtyard used for most social activities, as well as eating and cooking. Moreover, because every hut is entered from this space, the courtyard also functions as a hallway. This rural courtyard dwelling probably antedates in evolutionary terms the prototypical urban courtyard house so familiar from antiquity.

The Mesakin cluster dwelling is only one example of many similar rural courtyard houses found in the African continent. The indigenous dwellings of the Awuna people of Ghana, for example, have a similar arrangement of

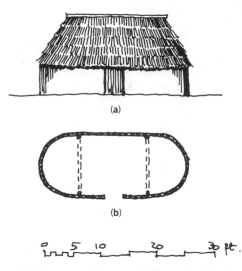

Figure 7. Mayan oval house. (a) Elevation; (b) plan.

huts surrounding a courtyard. Also similar, at least conceptually if not in detail, are the cluster dwellings of the Dogon people of Mali and the Gurunsi of the Upper-Volta region.

Another prototypical semipermanent dwelling is the Mayan oval house (Fig. 7) of the Yucatan peninsula in Mexico. This is usually a one-room house having corn stalks or wattle and adobe walls and a thatched roof. This windowless house is entered through a door placed in the center of one of its broad sides. The interior of the dwelling with its tamped dirt floor is scantily furnished with sleeping hammocks and small wooden benches for sitting. Cooking is done on a small stone hearth.

Circular semipermanent dwellings were common during the pre-Roman Iron Age in many parts of the British Isles. A circular dwelling from this period was excavated at Little Woodbury in Wiltshire, and other circular dwellings and farmhouses were found over wide areas of the northern and western Scottish highlands and islands. The latter are called wheelhouses and take their name from the radial, buttresslike piers inside the circular stone walls.

Permanent Dwellings of Advanced Agricultural Societies

Agricultural societies that permanently farm the land build permanent rural dwellings constructed from durable building materials such as wood or masonry. In contrast to previous prototypes, the effective use period of these buildings is that of a lifetime or, indeed, of several generations. The permanent character of the house is also reflected in better workmanship and detailing made possible through the specialization of labor in the wake of a surplus food economy. Interior climate control is no longer designed to the criterion of survival but to that of comfort—with doors, windows, floors, roofs, and chimneys all well built. Permanent dwellings are also generally more spacious and are predominantly multiroom structures.

Traditionally, permanent rural dwellings were built of local materials indigenous to a given region, resulting in

harmony with its surroundings. And, it becomes obvious that, with the number of variables, including building materials, climate, topography, crop cultivation, and cultural heritage, there is a multitude of permanent-dwelling prototypes ranging from cave dwellings to complex compound farmsteads.

Extensive villages of cave dwellings are found in the Matmata region of Tunisia, in Andalusia in Spain, in Cappadocia in Turkey, and the Honan district of China, to name just a few. The troglodyte caves of Matmata and Honan are very similar in concept and consist of a deep central crater scooped out of the ground and left open to the sky. A descending open trench, which turns into a tunnel near the bottom, gives access to this "court." Several subterranean rooms carved into the walls of the crater surround the court. These cave dwellings are far from primitive and are climatically well suited to their particular region because the thermal mass of their walls assures relative comfort in summer and winter alike.

Cave dwellings, however, are not common permanent dwellings; by far most agriculturalists live above ground in buildings of various sizes and forms. Two generic types of permanent homesteads can be distinguished, one composed of the house and auxiliary functions, such as stable, barn, and hayloft in one structure, and the other in various structures. In the case of the latter, the siting of buildings can be random, linear, L-shaped, U-shaped, or quadrangular, and the units may be detached or attached. Although the rectangular form predominates in permanent buildings, exceptions do exist. One exceptional indigenous permanent dwelling is the *trullo* used by the inhabitants of the central region in Apulia in southeastern Italy. This typical multiroom farmhouse has several rectangular rooms enclosed by thick stone walls with alcoves and niches; above each room the walls support a conical dome built with overlapping flat stones. Both the walls and the capstones of the trulli are whitewashed.

The largest room is the main living space; off of it open bedrooms and a kitchen, each with its own dome. The dome above the large open kitchen hearth ends in a chimney. During the long summer season the stone trulli are comfortably cool, but in winter they can be damp and cold.

Barns and stables have a similar form, so that larger farmsteads are built as continuous trulli clusters with domes numbering up to two dozen. Hay barns have a truncated roof cone with a hatch on top, capped with a large and flat removable stone; steps built into the sides of the cone allow the farmer access to the hatch to fill the barn. Large homesteads are usually linear clusters of trulli where each unit is attached to the next in an agglutinative way, resulting in a very picturesque building form.

A trulli-like form of permanent dwelling is also found in the western part of Syria. These buildings are often built of adobe bricks, with each room constituting a square base with rounded corners, and roofed by a conical vault.

By far the most frequent prototype of rural permanent dwellings is the rectangular structure. In China, the descendants of this very ancient agricultural society believe that the square or rectangular shape has a mythical dimension, and the design of their traditional rural dwellings reflects this adherence to rectangularity.

The basic composition of a Chinese farmhouse consists of a south-facing main building with two detached side wings enclosing a court that on the fourth side is defined by a masonry wall with a gate. The main building contains a central large room, the ancestral hall, flanked on both sides by one or two pairs of rooms, some of which are used as bedrooms. One side wing may be used as a kitchen and the other as a stable or storage room. With the growth of the family, the U-shaped basic unit is extended, first by a fourth building at the south side of the court followed by other side wings, and so on. With expansion, the functions of the first side wings change and become dwellings for the younger family members. The axially central ancestral hall, however, remains in perpetuity the most venerable place in the building complex.

The typical Japanese farmhouse also has a formal room with an alter for the family's ancestors, but otherwise the arrangement of their dwellings differs considerably from those of the Chinese. Essentially, the Japanese farmhouse has two parts, one with a ground-level earth floor used for house- and farm-related work and an elevated section with a wooden floor covered with tatami mats. Cooking is done in the ground-level section of the house; the upper level is used for receptions, dining, and sleeping. The elevated section of the house has typically four rooms, with one south-facing one called zashiki equipped with a tokonoma (alcove for the family alter).

A stove, called a kamado, is used in the ground-level section of the house for cooking, and, having no chimney, the smoke rises into the loft space, where it escapes through an opening.

The eastern European farmstead is usually built in a village settlement and consists often of an L-shaped building enclosing a farmyard. A Hungarian farmstead may serve as an illustrative example. The front room of this two-room house is used as a multifunctional family room and is followed sequentially by the kitchen, a storage room, and the stable; an arcaded gallery links the various spaces of this linear building to each other. The barn with its threshing floor and hayloft is at a right angle to the linear main building and defines the rear end of the yard. The street side of the property is fenced in. Access to the yard is through a large portal; a neighbor's building usually defines the fourth side of the farm yard. The typology of western European farmsteads is very rich, and many of these came to the North American continent with the colonists.

Naturally, the early settlers continued to build in the way they were accustomed to do in the old country. Hence, one can trace French, Dutch, German, Scandinavian, Spanish, and, above all, English influences in rural domestic architecture in North America.

Both the Cape Cod-styled farmhouse and the salt box (Fig. 8) type have their origins in Lowland England, especially in the Eastern Counties. Their main feature is a massive central chimney with several fireplaces at its base, as well as on the upper floor level in a two-story structure. The entrance to the house is central and leads to a vestibule flanked by two front rooms both with fire-

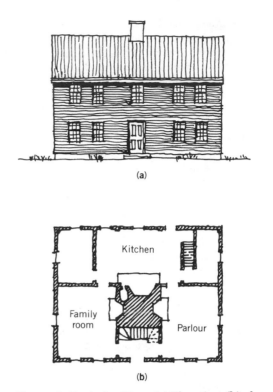

(a)

(b)

Figure 8. Typical saltbox. (a) Elevation; (b) plan.

places. One of these rooms was used as a parlor and the other as a family room. In a two-story building the vestibule also had a staircase that led to the upper-story bedrooms. The two-room deep building had a kitchen in the rear with its own fireplace built into the central chimney and additional stairs giving access not only to the upper floors but also to the cellar. A pantry and another smaller room flanked the central kitchen at the rear. Ancillary buildings were usually detached structures placed around a farmyard.

The early Cape Cod-style and saltbox houses were built of heavy post and beam frames filled in with wattle and daub, which proved to be inadequate in regions with a harsher climate than that of England. Invariably, these structures had to be covered with wooden clapboard for additional protection, which led to the abandonment of wattle and daub in newer building construction in favor of wood plank or brick infill.

A scattered arrangement of farm buildings proved to be inconvenient in the northern parts of New England where winters are severe. To facilitate communication between buildings during the cold winter, a linear form of farmstead was developed, with the main house being connected to all ancillary structures. This arrangement is known as big house, little house, back house, barn. The "big house" in this linear sequence was a Cape Cod or saltbox building type as described above, but it was connected to a "little house" with a large winter kitchen, a smaller summer kitchen, and a woodshed; the "little house," in turn, was attached to a "back house" containing a large workshop and a privy; the last building was a "barn" with a hayloft, threshing floor, and a stable. By using setbacks for the little house and back house, two yards were defined, namely the front yard next to the big house and the dooryard fronting on the other three buildings; a third yard, the barnyard, was at the rear of the barn.

During the seventeenth century, dwellings of notched logs were introduced to the United States by Swedish settlers in Delaware. German, Russian, and other settlers introduced their own forms of one or two room log cabins in the timber-rich frontier land.

With the settlement of the St. Lawrence River valley, early French Canadian settlers created a new building tradition reminiscent of the rural domestic architecture of their homeland but using local building materials. The first dwellings were constructed of wooden planks with a shingled high-pitched roof and gable verges. These low rectangular buildings were divided into two rooms of unequal size, with a large masonry chimney rising from the cross wall. Gradually, plank walls gave way to masonry walls, floor levels were raised above the snow level, gable verges were superseded by gables and, with the introduction of a second fireplace, chimneys were now placed at the gable ends. Finally, eaves were extended over a front porch, which became the Quebec veranda house with its typical bell-cast roof.

Sedentary agriculturists who permanently cleared the land for cultivation succeeded in surpassing the subsistence level of agricultural production, and thereby initiated a surplus agricultural economy enabling people to specialize in endeavors other than that of food production. Only at this stage of socioeconomic development were the basic prerequisites provided to foster urban development, and with it a new form of domestic architecture: urban housing.

URBAN DWELLINGS

Ancient Urban Dwellings

Four early cradles of civilization gave rise to urban development and with it the emergence of ancient urban dwelling forms. All four ancient civilizations evolved from agrarian societies settled in fertile alluvial river valleys that enabled their inhabitants to go beyond subsistence farming. Apart from providing continuous fertility to their valleys, these rivers also facilitated communication between the settlers and thereby exerted a unifying influence on the people living alongside them. The alluvial regions of these four civilizations were

1. The Tigris–Euphrates valleys in Mesopotamia.
2. The valley of the Indus River and its tributaries in India and Pakistan.
3. The valley of the Nile River in Egypt.
4. The networks of the Hwang Ho and Yangtze rivers in China.

In all four of these urban civilizations an inward-oriented urban house form evolved that featured attributes essential to their occupants at the dawn of urban settlements. First, the inward-oriented courtyard house provided pri-

vacy and security to its occupants. Second, it was an economical house form that required relatively little land. Third, being attached to other dwellings on three sides, the inward-oriented house had a minimal exposure to the elements and its protected courtyard afforded favorable microclimates through the use of water and planting. Fourth, the enclosed and protected courtyard, or courtgarden, of the ancient urban house had an affinity with humanity's image of paradise; its lateral dimensions were defined, but its third dimension, its height, was limitless.

Another common feature shared by all ancient urban dwellings was an offset main entrance, designed to provide privacy. Invariably, interior screen walls faced the entrance to block the view from the public street into the private house and its courtyard.

Ancient urban houses dating from about 2400 B.C., were excavated in the Sumerian city of Ur, in Mesotamia. Typically, these urban dwellings were two-story courtyard houses with a reception room, kitchen, and ancillary rooms at ground level and private family rooms and bedrooms on the upper level, all facing the courtyard. A staircase, usually near the entrance with a protective screen wall, led to the upper floor and to the roof. Occasionally, houses of well-to-do families had two courtyards (Fig. 9), and the rooms around one court were probably used for public functions, whereas those around the other court were the exclusive private domain of the family.

Urban dwellings of the ancient Indus Valley civilization dating from about 3000 B.C. were excavated in Mohenjo-Daro; they show a great similarity to the Mesopotamian dwellings just described. A large urban house located near the main thoroughfare of Mohenjo-Daro, but fronting on a narrow residential lane, was entered through a small front courtyard with a porter's lodge from which a short passage led to the large main courtyard. All rooms on the ground floor and upper level were grouped around this central open space. The ground level rooms included a guest suite off the entrance passage, a kitchen, bedrooms for servants, and a bathroom adjacent to a well chamber. The bathroom was accessible by a private staircase from the upper level, and a narrow aperture between the well chamber and the bathroom permitted small vessels to be passed between them. The private family quarters, both living rooms and bedrooms, were located on the upper story and were reached through the main staircase located on the north side of the courtyard.

Of course, most dwellings in Mohenjo-Daro were much smaller than this example, but the design principle of

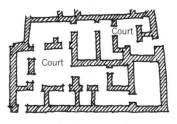

Plan
Ur: Ancient urban dwelling

Figure 9. Ancient urban dwelling plan in Ur.

grouping rooms around an open courtyard was shared by every urban house, although in smaller homes rooms occupied only two sides of the courtyard.

The ancient urban dwellings of Egypt were also predominantly courtyard houses. Dwellings excavated in Kahun, a town site built for people engaged in the construction of a pyramid around 2670 B.C., show the design of both small workmen's houses and palatial residences. The smallest houses had rooms on three sides of the courtyard with a staircase on the fourth side leading to the roof, which would have been used as additional living and sleeping space during the warm season. Larger workmen's houses had two courtyards and 11 rooms around the courts. The palatial residences of the western sector of Kahun had more than 20 rooms and a large north-facing reception room opening on a large courtyard. These large homes had a tripartite division, with a public reception area, a private family quarter, and a service section.

Urban dwellings of the ancient Chinese civilization were also courtyard houses, a tradition that has survived into the twentieth century in the so-called Beijing house.

The Greek Peristyle House

From about the fifth century B.C. onward, urban houses in Greek cities combined two earlier traditions of domestic architecture, the Greek indigenous hall-type house, the *megaron,* and the ancient oriental urban house (Fig. 10). The central space of this urban dwelling was an open courtyard, usually surrounded on several sides by colonnades, which in turn gave access to the adjacent rooms. The courtyard sides not defined by rooms were screened by a masonry wall, the *herkos,* which provided privacy. As in the ancient urban house, the open courtyard was an indispensible part of the home; apart from serving as a source of light and air for its surrounding rooms, the courtyard also served as an outdoor room in which the occupants of the house could carry out many household activities. The pillared portico usually faced south, which gave the advantage of providing shade in summer but allowing sun penetration in winter when the sun had a low altitude. Generally, the Greek urban house was a single-storied dwelling built of adobe, bricks, or stone, with floors of hardpacked earth, but mosaic was frequently used in representational rooms. Occasionally, larger homes had two stories, with a two-tier colonnade facing the courtyard.

The principal rooms were the family room, called the *oecus,* and the dining room, called the *andron.* Together with the bedrooms, kitchen, and bath, the oecus formed part of the private section of the home, the *gynaikonitis,* whereas the andron, the exclusive domain of men, the public section, the *andronitis.* The main entrance to the dwelling was usually through a door placed in a recess, called the *prothyron,* which gave shelter to anyone waiting to be admitted. On entering, one came to a short corridor or colonnade that led to the courtyard.

The Roman Domus and Insulae

There were two types of Roman urban dwellings, the *domus* (Fig. 11), a single-family house, and the *insula,* or tenement building. The former was predominant in provincial towns, whereas the latter was predominant in large cities, such as Rome.

Like the Greek urban dwelling, the prototypical Roman *domus* was a composite derived from the traditional Etruscan and classical Hellenistic house forms. Usually, the Etruscan *atrium* section constituted the public part of the dwelling, whereas the Greek peristyle section served as the family quarters. Thus, the typical urban house that emerged during the Late Roman period featured two courtyards, an atrium court in the front part of the dwelling and a peristyle court-garden in the rear. Larger dwellings had a third outdoor space, a secluded rear garden called the *hortulus.*

In keeping with the previously described ancient urban dwellings, the Roman domus had an unassuming street facade, as most rooms opened onto the courtyards or garden. In contrast to the exterior simplicity, however, the interior of the urban dwelling was often sumptuous.

The main entrance was set in a recess called the *vestibulium* and led to a small hallway or *fauces,* usually guarded by a porter, a slave. From the *fauces* one entered the atrium, which was flanked by a number of small rooms that served as bedrooms for guests (*hospitia*) or slaves (*ergastuae*). The principal room of this public section of the dwelling was the *tablinum,* or reception room. Next to the tablinum was frequently located a dining room, called a *triclinium,* with raised platforms on three

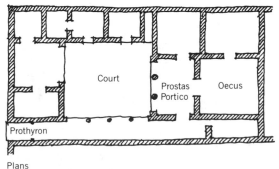

Plans
Priene: Greek house

Figure 10. Greek house plan in Priene.

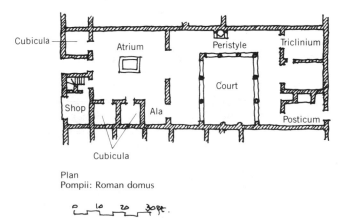

Plan
Pompii: Roman domus

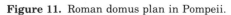

Figure 11. Roman domus plan in Pompeii.

sides to serve as couches. Finally, two alcoves called *alae* at the far corner of the atrium were used as waiting or conversation rooms. Of course, the central space of this room assembly was the atrium, with a catch basin or *impluvium* sunk in the pavement and lit from above through an aperture corresponding in size to that of the basin. The atrium was protected by a roof or *compluvium* supported on brackets projecting from the wall, and rainwater was shed into the basin, which was linked to a cistern below.

A narrow passageway next to the *tablinum* connected to formal part of the dwelling with the family quarters surrounding the peristyle garden. This courtyard also had a basin for rainwater, but here the inclined roofs were supported by a colonnade with red-dyed veils called *courtinae* hung between the columns in summertime to provide shade. In contrast to the hard-surfaced Greek courtyard, the Roman peristyle court was made into a garden with climbing vines, flower beds, and numerous potted plants. The principal rooms that surrounded the peristyle were the family reception room or *oecus*, the dining room or *triclinium*, bedrooms called *cubicula*, a bathroom or *balneum,* and the kitchen or *culina* with its ancillary storage rooms. A rear service entrance called a *posticum* often led to a secondary street.

Dwellings along main streets frequently had shops, bakeries, and other commercial spaces along the sidewalks incorporated in them, with small residential accommodation for the shopkeepers above them. The most common commercial space was the *taberna*, often a two-story barrel-vaulted space with a wooden mezzanine level above the shop serving as lodging for the shopkeeper's family.

Insulae probably evolved from the *tabernae,* or small shop-and-dwelling adjuncts, of the Roman dwellings described above. These multistory tenements were often built by entrepreneurs as rental accommodation not only for the lower-income groups, but also for those in the middle range. Their height varied, but six- and seven-storied insulae were not uncommon, with *tabernae* at grade level surmounted by several stories of flats, often arranged around an interior courtyard. At first, construction of these tenements was rather shabby, but later more solid materials, such as brick and concrete, were used as a measure to prevent their collapse or destruction by fire.

The *piano nobile* just above the *tabernae,* often with a balcony on the street side, was usually occupied by a more prosperous tenant. These decorative balconies were too narrow to be useful as outdoor extensions of the dwellings, but they provided some shade and protection from falling objects to shoppers using the sidewalk. The upper-level flats of the *insulae* were rented to lower-income tenants.

After the gradual decline and eventual collapse of the Roman Empire, the Oriental urban-dwelling tradition survived in the Near East and in North Africa, but in Western Europe it came to a sudden end. In Byzantium and the world of Islam sedentary urban life continued, but in the Occident it virtually came to a standstill during the Dark Ages, a period that was characterized by a maelstrom of migration and barbaric assaults. During these centuries of chaos, foundations were laid for a new urban house form, the Occidental urban house.

The Occidental Medieval Urban House

In an age marked by ongoing hostilities, defense was of primary concern, and this is clearly reflected in medieval domestic architecture. It is particularly evident in the castles or fortified habitations of feudal lords, as well as in the burghers' dwelling towers (Fig. 12) built in medieval cities.

The principal elements of the Early Middle Ages castle were the keep and the hall, surrounded by fortifications, with the former being spacious enough to accommodate the living quarters of the lord's family and his garrison. The massive keep, or donjon, was the last stronghold defended during a siege, but after the introduction of firearms during the Late Middle Ages this tower lost its effectiveness.

The dwelling towers were the urban counterparts of the keep. They served as fortified residences of well-to-do burghers. Because the medieval city, not unlike the castle, was usually surrounded by fortification walls reinforced by bastions and gatetowers, dwelling towers did not have to duplicate these installations. The main doorway to the towers was often one story above ground level; access to it was by a ladder that could be withdrawn when necessary to make entry nearly impossible. Dwelling towers usually had narrow loophole-like windows, a crenellated parapet, and sometimes even machicolation, the

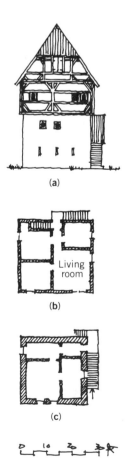

(a)

(b)

(c)

Figure 12. Medieval dwelling tower. (**a**) Elevation; (**b**) 2nd upper floor; (**c**) 1st upper floor.

last-named an overhanging structure with floor openings through which boiling water or missiles could be dropped on attackers, to enhance their defensiveness. In contrast to the Roman *domus*, this defensive medieval urban dwelling was an outward-oriented building, in many ways the complete opposite in terms of physical design, as it was multistoried, frequently detached, and had fenestration on all four exterior sides.

Of course, the majority of medieval urban dwellers could not afford the luxury of having individual fortress dwellings but had to rely on the collective defense provided by the city they lived in—gabled houses built on narrow street-front building lots within the city walls. This second medieval urban-dwelling prototype had its roots in indigenous rural dwellings and were often timber-framed small, detached buildings. Few of these wooden structures have survived.

Residences and workshops of medieval urban dwellers were complementary rather than incompatible elements, a concept that was similar to the notion that homestead and farmstead in rural societies were synonymous. In fact, many urban dwellers also had fields outside the city gates and practiced agriculture as a sideline to their main occupation, which meant that many urban dwellings had regular farmyards at the rear with at least a stable and haybarn above.

The relative width of a building's street frontage was a clear indication of the wealth of its owner, and in the case of half-timber construction, street frontage was expressed in terms of bays. A bay represented a module of vertical timber supports with the space between them occupied by windows, doors, or masonry infill panels. The gable-ended front symbolized the individuality and freedom of the medieval city dweller.

The hall-type medieval dwelling in the British Isles was the typical merchant's home. It usually occupied a narrow but deep building lot and was a multistoried structure with a hall sandwiched between the street-front shop and a chamber block in the rear. The hall, with a fireplace, was the principal room of the dwelling and was often a two- or three-story space open from the ground floor to the roof. A narrow passage led from the front door to the hall and to an upper-level gallery, reached through an open stair from the hall, and connected the jettied chambers above the shop to the chambers of the rear block. An undercroft or basement was usually used for commercial purposes.

Although overhanging upper stories gave some protection from the elements to shoppers below, a more efficient shelter was provided by the arcaded medieval houses that became prevalent in the late Middle Ages. Arcaded buildings were usually erected along main streets and town squares by wealthy merchants and had shops and workshops at ground level and dwelling accommodations above. Of masonry construction, the upper story walls were supported on heavy arched piers. Noted examples of arcaded homes can be found in Bern, Switzerland, in Monpazier, France, and in numerous Silesian and East European medieval towns.

The Rows, in Chester, England, is a unique example of arcaded buildings. These buildings have the singular

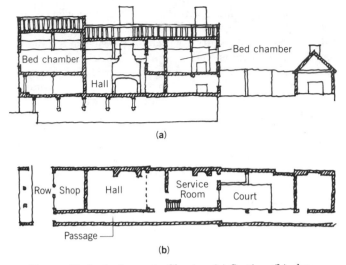

Figure 13. Leche house in Chester. (**a**) Section; (**b**) plan.

characteristic that sidewalks, shops, and dwellings are elevated one story above ground level and are perched on top of vaulted undercrofts also used for commercial purposes. The elevated public walkways on top of these undercroft substructures replace the sidewalk and continue along the entire stretch of the main street with intermittent public stairways giving access to it. Leche House (Fig. 13) on Watergate Street illustrates clearly the spatial arrangement of these hall-type urban dwellings.

Most medieval urban homes had interior courtyards, but the function of these outdoor spaces was different from that of an atrium or peristyle court. The medieval courts were basically service yards rather than court-gardens. They were used for the loading and unloading of goods in merchant houses or as outdoor workplaces for artisans and farmyards for cultivators. Thus, in the outward-oriented medieval home the courtyard ceased to be the focal point. No doubt, climatic considerations contributed to this departure from ancient traditions, at least in Northern Europe.

The Renaissance Town House

The close relationship between home and workplace in the medieval urban house was gradually abandoned during the Renaissance period. This separation first appeared in the homes of wealthier urban dwellers, but by the nineteenth century it had reached most city inhabitants. From this time onward, the dwelling was a place for entertaining, eating, sleeping, and child rearing, but not where one worked to support the family. And, because the dwelling was outward oriented, the quality of public open spaces adjacent to one's home became increasingly important.

At the beginning of the transition from the Medieval period to the Renaissance, some urban characteristics of the previous epoch were retained, such as, for example, arcaded street fronts, as can be seen in Paris in the Place des Voges and in London's Covent Garden. But these two examples also illustrate other characteristics that had no precedents: first, a uniform treatment of the facade, which simulated a palatial front while in reality covering an assembly of many diverse buildings, and, second, the creation of residential squares, which, in the case of the Place des Voges, was envisaged as a place for tournaments and jousting before it became a landscaped park.

The prototypical English town house of the Renaissance period was a three- or four-story dwelling with a three-bay front (Fig. 14). It was a refined building type, often built by developers who paid considerable attention to its aesthetic appearance and spatial organization. The entrance was a few steps above street level and was reached by a bridge spanning an area well that separated the lower floor of the house from the sidewalk. The ground floor had a vestibule and a parlor in the front section and a dining room in the rear. The parlor was used as a reception room for visitors other than relatives and close

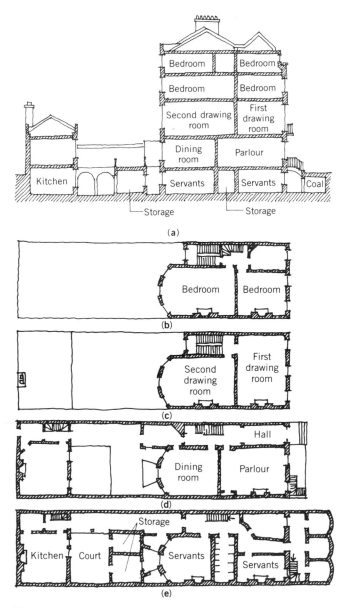

Figure 14. Typical town house in London. **(a)** Section; **(b)** 2nd upper floor; **(c)** 1st upper floor; **(d)** ground floor; **(e)** basement

friends. A central hall, often with a curved or spiral staircase, led to the other floors. The position of the dining room on the ground floor was determined by the fact that the kitchen occupied the basement and faced the rear service yard, which was frequently half a level or more below street level; the front part of the basement floor was in fact a cellar and contained most ancillary service rooms as well as the service door opening on the area well. A narrow service stair led from the area well to street level, and below the sidewalk were dug the coal and dust bins.

The second level of the town house, the *piano nobile*, contained two drawing rooms in addition to the stair hall. The first drawing room, occupying the entire front of the house, was used predominantly by men; the narrower second drawing room, facing the yard—and where smoking was not permitted—was reserved for women. On the third level above the drawing rooms were the family bedrooms, with the master bedroom at the front of the house. Finally, in the garret were the servants' bedrooms lit through dormer windows. To the rear of the property and served by a narrow lane or mews was the coach house with stables and related facilities, including the living quarters of the coachman.

Bedford Square in London is a good illustration of a residential square with its fenced-in landscaped park reserved for the exclusive use of the occupants of houses around the square who possessed a key to one of its small gates. The use of this park for outdoor recreational needs but in full view of the public is just the opposite of the Oriental court-garden tradition of ancient times.

Town-house living was initially exclusive to the aristocracy and to the wealthy bourgeoisie, but gradually this terraced house form was adopted by others as well. Houses on Munster Square, St. Pancras, London, were designed for artisans by the architect John Nash. These town houses were only two bays in width and three stories high, with smaller and less luxurious accommodations, but, apart from the elimination of the piano nobile drawing rooms and the servants' quarters in the garret, the basic design remained unchanged.

The town-house concept also found application in many European countries, but there the dwellings differed from their English counterparts in several respects. First, European town-house developments were not built on the same large scale as they were in London, resulting in less formality and lacking the uniformity of palatial facade treatment. Second, in the absence of landscaped residential squares, most town houses had small private gardens at the back of the property. Finally, area wells were seldom built because the kitchen was most frequently placed at ground level behind the dining room.

In North America, town-house living and residential squares became popular during the eighteenth and nineteenth centuries. In 1683, when Thomas Holme laid out the plan for Philadelphia, and in 1733, when James Oglethorpe and his colonists settled in Savannah, Georgia, the concept of residential squares was the basis for the plan of their new city. And, although the London town-house plan served as a model, U.S. builders introduced some changes, the most significant being that no cellar or basement accommodation was provided. The U.S.

town house was entered through a stoop, or flight of stairs leading to the front door nearly a full story above sidewalk level. Through a vestibule one entered a stair hall located, as was the front door, near one of the party walls. A parlor occupied the front section of the house. It was frequently linked through a central wide opening with sliding doors to a dining room in the rear. The parlor and the dining room had identical fireplaces along the party wall. By opening the sliding doors between them, the two rooms could be made into a single space. A butler's pantry equipped with a dumbwaiter and a service stair linked the dining room to the kitchen below. An intrinsic feature of the kitchen was an alcove flanked by masonry piers supporting the fireplace of the room above; a coal stove with an oven was fitted between the piers and vented into the chimney flue. Additional spaces at ground level were servants' parlor, storage rooms, and a service entrance located below the front stoop.

Above the parlor was the master bedroom, and over the dining room a smaller bedroom facing the rear yard, with a bathroom in the corner behind the staircase. The clothes closets between the two bedrooms acted as acoustic barriers. A similar floor plan was repeated on the top floor of the town house with the exception that a small bedroom replaced the bathroom.

The early New York town houses were typically 25 ft in width, but with the mounting pressure of increased land costs, it became common to build three town houses on two lots, resulting in a narrow front urban house 16 ft 8 in. in width (Fig. 15).

The town house with its outward orientation established a new urban house-form tradition in the Occident, but in the Near East, North Africa, India, China, and

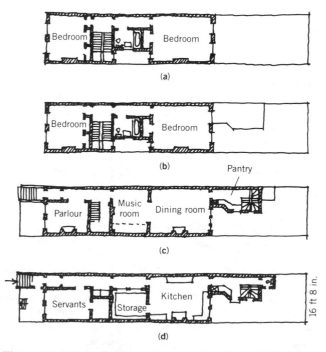

Figure 15. Narrow front town house in New York. (a) 2nd upper floor; (b) 1st upper floor; (c) ground floor; (d) basement

Japan the ancient inward-oriented urban dwelling traditions prevailed. In fact, the Spanish and Portuguese patio houses and their Latin American counterparts represented a continuation of the ancient urban house tradition and are to a large extent a legacy of the centuries-long domination of the Hispanic Peninsula by Islam during the medieval period.

The Islamic House

The medieval Islamic urban house had its roots in the ancient urban dwellings of Mesopotamia and Egypt and was, no doubt, influenced by the Greco-Roman urban dwelling. Being more recent, the Islamic house is, of course, more sophisticated than its precursors. Nevertheless, the basic design principles, such as the provision of maximum privacy, the division of the home into a public and private section, the humble appearance of the exterior of the home, and the central court-garden as the principal space of the dwelling remained unaltered.

The traditional Islamic house had a spatial organization that reflects a different perception of a home's function from that held in the West. The various spaces of an urban house were not designated as living room, dining room, or bedroom, but were viewed in the light of their optimum usefulness to their users in winter or summer, in the morning, at noon, in the evening, or at night. Accordingly, most principal spaces had multiple uses. Because food was served on large metal trays placed on a low stool, it was consumed by diners in any room that was comfortable. In summer time the cool roof terraces were used at night for sleeping; during the hot midday, a cool basement room offered the greatest comfort for a siesta.

The heart of the Islamic house was the open courtyard, the *hosh,* with its intrinsic attribute, the provision of favorable microclimatic conditions. Moreover, the walls of the square courtyard inherently offered exposure in four different directions, thereby enabling optimal orientation of various rooms of the house without limitation by external constraints. And, because most habitable rooms faced on it, this central and private courtyard invariably functioned as a patio or small garden, in great contrast to the service yard of the Occidental urban house.

Naturally, there are some regional variations in the spatial organization and building construction technology of the Islamic urban house, but two examples illustrate the indigenous characteristics that are rooted in climatic forces as well as in cultural heritage.

The first example is the prototypical Baghdad house (Fig. 16), which, although about six millenia removed in time, bears an uncanny similarity to the Sumerian urban house excavated in the ancient city of Ur. The entrance to the two-storied traditional Baghdad house was through a *mudshahs,* an angular entrance hall with a privacy wall facing the main door. Benches in alcoves were provided in this entryway for a doorman and for visitors waiting to be admitted into the house. Through the hall one entered the courtyard from which all other parts of the house were accessible.

The ground floor of the house served as the *diwanchane* or public section and the upper story as the *harem.* At

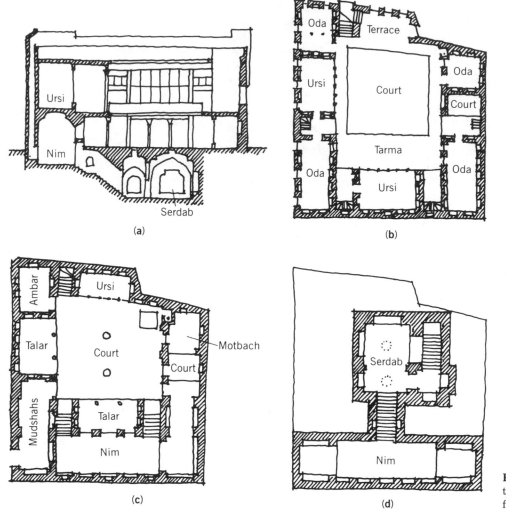

(a)

(b)

(c)

(d)

Figure 16. Baghdad house. (a) Section; (b) upper floor; (c) ground floor; (d) basement.

ground level, an open alcove called a *talar* served as a summer reception room, and a sliding window walled *ursi* fulfilled a similar function in winter. Both of these reception rooms were arranged to derive the optimum benefit from their orientation, namely the *talar* facing north or east, and the ursi facing south. A *motbach,* or kitchen, with its own light well, was in the northeast corner of the courtyard. Finally, at ground level were also the *ambar* or storage room, an *adebchane* or toilet, tucked in a corner, and several stairways to the harem upstairs, and others leading down to the basement rooms.

The typical Baghdad house also had a semibasement living room called the *nim* and a cellar room or *serdab,* both of which offered comfort when the midday temperature was extremely warm. Located below the courtyard, the subterranean *serdab* was a domed living space with several recesses; it was usually lit from above through skylights and had a fountain, a *faskije,* placed in a central octagonal basin.

The upper floor of the house had a gallery around the periphery of the courtyard, which gave access to both common and reception rooms of the harem. The most common room was the *oda,* frequently without windows and lit—like the Roman domus' *cubicula*—by a transom above the

door. The reception rooms of the harem were similar to the ground floor *ursi* but, if located on the street side, these upper-story rooms had additional openings in the form of trellised bay windows called *mushrabiyyahs,* which enabled the occupants of the harem to view street activities in privacy. Moreover, these mushrabiyyahs eliminated glare and provided a pleasant level of illumination to the interior.

Air circulation in the dwelling was enhanced by the use of wind traps or *badgirs* (*malqafs* in other parts of the Islamic world), placed above the roof parapet and linked to vertical air ducts equipped with water filled jars to humidify and cool the fresh-air intake. A disproportionately high ceiling in most rooms enhanced air circulation, and by sitting close to the floor level their occupants enjoyed the coolest indoor environment.

The second example is a Cairo house that also consists of two distinct parts, a *salamlik,* or public section of the house, and a *haremlik,* or private section of the house, each with its own street entrance in larger and wealthier homes.

The public section of the house was invariably located on the ground-floor level and consisted of a formal suite of reception spaces, called collectively a *mandara.* A multistory space, a *durqa,* occupied the center of the *mandara* and was flanked by reception alcoves called *liwanat,* each with symmetrical wall recesses or *sidillahs* in the traditional North African Islamic fashion. The *durqa* functioned as a hallway and most often had a marble mosaic floor with a sunken basin and fountain placed in its center. A narrow and bent passageway usually linked the *durqa* to both the courtyard and the kitchen. During receptions, servants were stationed in the *durqa.*

The principal living quarters of the family were on the upper level of the dwelling and were reached from the courtyard, or *hosh,* through adorned portals giving access to two main staircases. One staircase led to an open reception porch, the *maq'ad,* reminiscent of the talar of Baghdad, while the second set of stairs, restricted to private use, led to the *qa'a,* the secluded living quarters of the harem's occupants. In the style of the *mandara,* the *qa'a's* central space was also a *durqa* lit from above through a windowed wooden dome, and two *liwanat* faced each other across this central space. The window openings of the *qa'a* were invariably trellised bay windows whether they faced the street or the courtyard. As in the Baghdad dwelling, *mushrabiyyahs* enabled the occupants of the haremlik to observe public activities in the street and in the courtyard of the house without being seen.

Most ground-floor rooms surrounding the central courtyard were used as storage spaces. The kitchen, also at ground level, was ventilated through another small courtyard.

In general, the typical Islamic urban house has a simple and unpretentious street facade that reflects the social values of its inhabitants; public ostentation is shunned to the extent that even the building height is modest. Accordingly, the exterior walls of dwellings of well-to-do people are often subdued and even hidden behind secondary structures, whereas the interior facades facing the private courtyard are lavished with the most exquisite architectural details, invisible from the street. The desire to remain unostentatious is carried beyond the boundaries of the home into the urban residential environment and manifests itself in a random mix of both rich and poor homes in precinctual communities called *mahallahs.*

The Haveli of India

Urban houses, or *havelis,* in the Indian subcontinent also display a strong sense of anonymity and, like the Islamic house, they are built back-to-back and side-to-side in dense city blocks to protect as many outside surfaces as possible from direct sun radiation, leaving essentially only a small courtyard, the roof, and a narrow street facade exposed. True to the Oriental urban house form, the courtyard functions as the central core of the house, providing lighting, ventilation, and privacy to the dwelling's occupants. Because the courtyard is usually small and deep, the hot sun is prevented from penetrating into the rooms opening on it.

Most rooms and spaces of the *haveli* change their use seasonally and diurnally in accordance with specific needs and desired comforts. Thus, in the late summer morning, kitchen activities usually spill over into the courtyard,

and in winter they are often moved to the roof terrace. In contrast, roof terraces serve in summer for sleeping under the cool night sky, while in winter, interior spaces on the ground floor, or even in the basement, may serve as bedrooms.

The Rajasthani *havelis* of Jaisalmer are good examples of urban house forms in India. The typical Jaisalmer *haveli* is attached on both sides and at the back to its neighbors, leaving only a narrow facade with screened openings exposed to the street. The ground-floor entrance is raised a few feet above the street and is often flanked by platforms for viewing street activities, and within the doorway a privacy wall usually blocks a direct view of the interior. The entrance hall or *moda* is a spacious room serving primarily as a transitional area leading to the courtyard. The ground floor accommodates most activities and is designed as an open living area with a raised veranda opening on the courtyard. At the side of the veranda is the kitchen alcove and in the rear a storage room or bedroom. A staircase leads to the upper stories from the court.

The upper floor layout is similar to that of the ground floor with the exception that the front part of the house is occupied by a large living room with projecting screened oriels called *zarookhas* allowing women to view street life unobserved. These screened oriels are more efficient than windows because they afford side views down the length of the narrow street and, in addition, provide welcome shade over the street. The top floor of every house is a roof terrace surrounded by a parapet wall for privacy.

The homes along the streets of Jaisalmer vary considerably in size according to the wealth of their occupants, with the larger homes having several courtyards and many *zarookhas* on the street facade. Because most houses are built of local yellow sandstone and such prefabricated building elements as *zarookhas* and shade canopies called *chajjas,* which are acquired from stone carvers, the streetscape has a pleasing balance between similarity and diversity.

The Beijing House

The traditional Chinese urban house is also a courtyard house, but, in contrast to previous examples, it is most frequently a compound consisting of several single-story buildings. The court is the heart of this compound dwelling and its poetic name is *t'ien chin,* which, translated, is "the well of heaven"; this well provides the occupants of the house with sunlight, air, and rainwater. The organization of the Beijing urban house resembles the traditional Chinese family structure, which was an extended family, both patriarchal and patrilocal. Unmarried children and married sons with their families lived with their parents and occupied houses in the compound in a hierarchic order, with the innermost and most private section belonging to the head of the family.

The typical single-courtyard house was the *szu-ho-yuan* or "four-compound-yard," a walled enclosure consisting basically of four buildings around a rectangular court with a north-south axis. The south building, adjacent to the street and facing north, was the least important in the hierarchic arrangement and usually accommodated the servants' quarters and ancillary household functions. The two side buildings were occupied by the married sons of the family, with the oldest son and his family living in the east building. Finally, the main building at the rear of the property and facing south was inhabited by the head of the family and enjoyed the highest status in the hierarchic sequence.

The entrance to the compound was usually at the southeast corner of the property and led to a paved entrance hall that was slightly raised above street level. Facing the door was a "screen wall," or *ying-bi*, which inhabited a direct view from the street into the courtgarden. It was believed that a screen wall prevented the entry of evil spirits into the home, as they could only move along straight lines. Thus, evil spirits were stopped by the screen wall, just as peering eyes of envious neighbors were. The front door of the well-to-do was often painted red and studded with bolts in a decorative manner.

Each building was built on a slightly raised rammedearth platform. On this platform, timber columns of a post-and-beam structure were placed on carved stone bases or dome-shaped bronze disks to protect the wood columns from the dampness of the ground. The columns supported a lintel, which in turn supported a tiered-beam frame system to span the building. The panels between the columns were of masonry infill, and the roof was tiled, with the projecting eaves supported on intricate composite brackets called *tou-kung*. Broad steps led to the centrally located main door of each building of a dwelling compound. The windows and the transom light above the door were latticed. Portable charcoal braziers supplied the necessary heat for most rooms during the winter, but another method of heating was the *k'ang* or raised heated dais extending over part of the room, which served as a sitting area during the day and sleeping platform at night; the *k'ang* was usually heated from the outside of the house. The most venerated room of the traditional Beijing urban dwelling was the ancestors' hall with the family altar located in the central space of the south-facing main building.

Merchants' urban dwellings or shop houses naturally had a narrow street frontage and were built on deep lots similar to the medieval urban houses of Western Europe, but, in contrast to the service yard of the Occidental merchant's house, the Chinese shop-house usually had a court-garden as an outdoor extension of the dwelling.

The Kyoto Urban House

The traditional urban house of Kyoto was the *machiya*, used by merchants and artisans alike. Like the Chinese shop-house, these dwellings usually had a narrow street frontage and were built on a deep urban lot. The narrow front was not only derived from land use efficiency but also from a former taxation policy based on the extent of street frontage. These elongated dwellings acquired the popular name "eel nests."

The front room was the shop, or *mise*, where goods were displayed and sold. In linear sequence it was followed by the *nakanoma,* or middle room, with a staircase leading to

the upper floor, which had a similar layout to that of the ground floor. Next to the nakanoma was the back room, or *zashiki,* which was the formal reception room as well as the master's room. The spine of the *machiya* was a side corridor called *tooriniwa,* which ran from the street entrance hall to the backyard garden, a multipurpose space open to the rafters that, apart from acting as a passageway to most of the rooms, also accommodated kitchen facilities and a water well. The floor of the *tooriniwa* had a tamped earthen floor about 20 in. below the *tatami* covered floors of the various rooms accessible from it.

Being the most formal room, the *zashiki* contained the alter box of the family's ancestors as well as the symbolic alcove space called the *tokonoma,* the latter invariably adorned with beautifully arranged *objets d'art* or flowers. A wooden terrace or veranda acted as a transition space between the *zashiki* and the backyard garden called the *senzai.* The exterior panelled sliding wall of this formal room varied with the seasons. In winter a wooden lattice covered on one side with translucent white rice paper called a *shoji* was used, whereas in summer reed screens or bamboo blinds were used.

Most rooms were multipurpose spaces. Bedsteads were absent in the Japanese house; mats called futons that could be folded up and stored in closets were used. The toilet and bathroom were located in a rear narrow wing projecting into the backyard and were accessible both from the veranda and the spine corridor. It is interesting to note that well-to-do merchants also built a detached fireproof masonry storehouse called *dozoh* in the rear of the property as a precaution against fire in a vulnerable timber-built urban area.

Larger and more elaborate urban houses often had an interior courtyard called a *tsuboniwa* demarcating the boundary between the commercial front section of the house and the dwelling. Moreover, a detached *zashiki* may also have been built in the back garden, where the master of the house could hold the tea ceremony for his guests. The back garden is designed to be enjoyed from indoors when the *shoji* is opened to permit a garden view. Along the borders of the garden, fencing or hedge planting ensures complete privacy from the neighbors. The elements of the garden may include stepping stones, a water basin, and plants graduating in height as they approach the property line, but equally important vistas are the rooftops of the neighbors, the distant mountains, and, above all, the sky.

THE NINETEENTH CENTURY URBAN DWELLING

In the Occident, the nineteenth century witnessed a significant departure from the housing design traditions that were rooted in the Middle Ages and modified in the Renaissance period. These changes are mainly attributable to the social and economic developments that followed in the wake of unprecedented growth in industrialization and urbanization.

During the nineteenth century, urban housing—and living conditions generally—deteriorated, giving rise to the emergence of slums and related disease and crime areas in industrialized and overpopulated cities. In an attempt to improve these living conditions, new forms of housing were introduced, such as back-to-backs, lodging houses, tenements, and bylaw-houses in Great Britain, and dumbbell tenements in North America. All the above dwelling types were built as minimum standard-living accommodations for low-wage earners. More commodious detached villas in suburbs and apartment buildings, catering flats, and apartment hotels in cities were designed for middle- and upper-income groups.

From the middle of the nineteenth century onward, several social reformers called attention to the devastating impact of the Industrial Revolution on the city and on the housing conditions of its underprivileged inhabitants; they rallied to combat the seemingly inevitable deterioration of urban life, but no real improvement was to follow until the twentieth century.

Back-to-Backs, Lodging Houses, Tenements, and Bylaw-Housing

A building process developed in Great Britain for middle-class town-house developments in the seventeenth and eighteenth centuries, and based on speculation, became the vehicle for the construction of workers' housing in the nineteenth century. But there was a significant difference, namely the original high standard of construction was replaced by shoddy building practices resulting from the ever increasing demand for living accommodation by migrants settling in urban areas.

Exploitation of urban land led to the development of the back-to-back dwelling, a row-house development in which all dwelling units with the exception of the end units were attached on three sides to neighboring units, which made cross ventilation of most dwellings impossible. To maximize land-use efficiency, rows of back-to-backs were frequently built by "jerry-builders" at right angles to the street and were separated from each other by narrow and ill-ventilated alleys or, at best, narrow courts with communal privies at a ratio of about seven households to one earth closet.

The back-to-back dwelling consisted of a living room and a scullery at ground level and two small bedrooms on the upper level. The dwelling had but one entrance and windows were all on the entrance side. The absence of adequate open space combined with poor sanitary facilities made back-to-back housing developments the most unhealthy of urban living environments.

Housing for single men and women also became a serious urban problem during the nineteenth century, because hitherto single employees had been accommodated on the premises of their respective employers. However, with the emergence of large factories, industrialists no longer felt obliged to provide lodgings for their single workers as medieval artisans and merchants had done for their apprentices or servants. Under these circumstances, most single workers had to board with the families of other workers who were already living under very crowded conditions.

In response to these dire conditions, some charitable organizations built lodging houses for single people in large cities. The typical lodging house consisted of a large kitchen and washhouse in the cellar, a steward's flat and a large common room on the ground floor, with several dormitory floors above. A central core formed by a stair hall, with rudimentary sanitary facilities consisting of six washbasins and one toilet for 25 lodgers, linked the dormitories to each other. The dormitories were divided into a dozen or more cubicles of about 40 ft^2, but the thin dividing partitions did not extend to the ceiling, in order to make possible the sharing of the heat generated by a single fireplace in each dormitory.

During the middle of the nineteenth century, multistoried model tenements for workers' families were introduced by charitable organizations in the city of London. These buildings provided more reasonable accommodation for their tenants and consisted of a series of flats accessible from an open gallery in the rear.

Model tenements built by philanthropic organizations were supposed to establish housing standards for the working class, but these standards were rarely followed by the builders. Most tenements continued the practice of providing communal toilet facilities near the stair hall; dwelling units were designed as clusters of small rooms linked by a narrow corridor, enabling each room to be let singly or in a variety of combinations, which exacerbated the existing overcrowdedness and unsanitary conditions. Tenements for the working class were also built in several large European cities, including Berlin, where industrial development attracted a large labor force.

During the second half of the nineteenth century, local governments began to curtail the construction of sub-standard housing and adopted bylaws that ensured a minimum health standard in newly constructed housing. Builders complied with these minimum standards and developed two-story row houses with small backyards with privies and coal bins at the rear of the property. Although modeled on Georgian town houses, these miniscule bylaw-houses (Fig. 17) had little in common with their precursors and created a monotonous, uninspiring urban environment consisting of endless rows of houses with dreary facades lining the treeless streets, block after block.

Bylaw-houses had no entrance hall; the front door led directly into the living room or "parlor," which was lit by a single window facing the street. This parlor had to be crossed in order to reach the kitchen, where a narrow, winding staircase led to the upper floor. Behind the kitchen was the scullery with a sink, and through the scullery one entered the rear yard with the privy and the coal-storage shed.

The upper floor usually had a bedroom in the front and a smaller one in the rear. A marked improvement was the fact that all rooms had a fireplace. Moreover, bylaw-houses were well built, and many survive today in industrial towns in Britain.

Railroad Flats and Dumbbell Tenements

During the nineteenth century, New York City also experienced a deterioration in housing conditions precipitated by an unusually large demand for living accommodation that could not be met by traditional housing. First, large

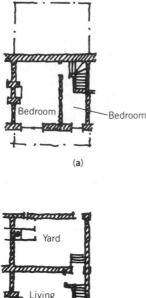

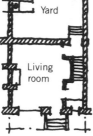

Figure 17. English bylaw house. **(a)** Upper floor; **(b)** ground floor.

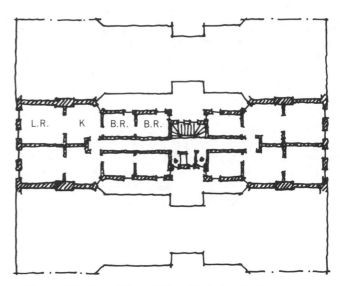

Figure 18. Typical floor of New York dumbbell tenements.

homes abandoned by well-to-do owners who had moved to the country were converted into tenant houses by partitioning the large rooms into several small rooms without regard to light and ventilation. Thus, several dwellings were created from a single home and, to further increase the rentability of the conversion, additional accommodation was built at the rear of the property. It was not uncommon for a town house originally built for a single household to become, with its infamous "rear house," a tenement for 10 families.

The conversion of old houses, however, could not satisfy the demand for dwellings. This led to the building of new multistory tenements on 25-ft-wide and 100-ft-deep city lots. These early tenements employed a central staircase and hall that gave access to four flats on each floor. Each apartment was three or even four rooms deep, with only the living room at front having direct access to daylight or fresh air. Not only dingy, these railroad flats were no less crowded than their predecessors.

In 1867, the Tenement-House Act by the New York Health Board prevented the further construction of unventilated railway flats and prescribed the use of air shafts for the ventilation of the innermost rooms. Generally, tenements were built five stories high above a basement; an apartment consisted typically of a front living room on the street or on the backyard side, followed by a kitchen and one or two bedrooms. Both the kitchen and the bedrooms were lit and ventilated from a narrow air shaft. The indentation of the air shaft at the center of the building block led to the dumbbell configuration and to the name dumbbell tenements (Fig. 18). Toilets were usu-

ally communal and were located either in the basement or along the stair hall; the latter solution included two toilets per four apartments. New York City dumbbell tenements were constructed extensively during the last two decades of the nineteenth century in clusters of four on a 100-ft-wide lot, but a new Tenement House Law passed in 1901 marked their demise.

The Villa in the Country

As urban life in overcrowded cities began to deteriorate during the nineteenth century, well-to-do families gradually abandoned their urban town houses and fled to the nearby countryside to live in villas (Fig. 19). In its standard form, the detached villa occupied a large plot of land and was set back from the roadway. The size of the plot now permitted the planning of the house so that the principal rooms, such as the parlor, dining room, and drawing rooms, could occupy the ground-floor level, and even the kitchen with its ancillary spaces could be accommodated at grade level, albeit often in a single-story wing that projected into the garden area. In its classic form, the villa emerged as a symmetrical two-story house with a central pillared porch and main entrance leading to a central stair hall flanked by a set of two formal rooms. The second floor had a similar layout to that of the ground floor and contained the family bedroom suites with bathrooms.

In England, by the middle of the nineteenth century the detached house was adopted by ever-larger groups of middle-income families as the preferred house form; this trend manifested itself in the emergence of suburbs, as well as in the pairing of villas as semi-detached dwellings to increase their affordability.

Similar developments also occurred on the North American continent, where available land for urban expansion was most abundant. Andrew Jackson Downing, a landscape architect from Newburgh, New York, became a celebrated protagonist of "tasteful cottages" with "smiling lawns." New York urban dwellers who were longing to leave the grime and crime ridden city for a healthier coun-

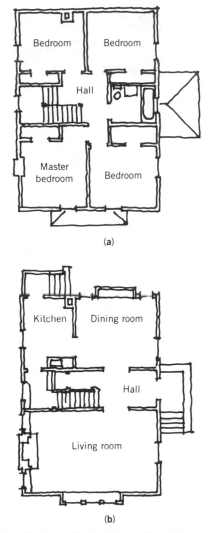

Figure 19. Typical villa. (a) Upper floor; (b) ground floor.

try environment were easily persuaded, and thereby launched a trend that eventually resulted in the proliferation of dormitory suburbs around large cities.

Apartment Dwellings

Although in Britain the middle-class ideal was the single-family dwelling, this was not the case in several European countries. The European bourgeois family was content to live in "flats" or apartments, but building regulations ensured in most cities a relatively high standard in multiple-housing construction. In Paris, for example, the maximum height of apartment buildings was limited during the nineteenth century to about 65 ft or 20 m, which resulted in buildings that rarely exceeded six stories in height. Along major city thoroughfares, apartment buildings often contained a few shops at sidewalk level, a practice of mixed land use inherited from the Middle Ages.

The size of the Parisian apartment building was relatively small in today's terms, but the dwellings themselves were quite large with a generous ceiling height. At ground-floor level was the elaborately adorned entrance lobby, supervised by the concierge. A grand stairway, well lit, gave access to the various upper levels. Typically, each upper-floor level had only two large apartment units, with all principal rooms facing the wide avenue or street.

The principal rooms were linked axially to each other in an *en suite* arrangement, but a hall running parallel with the main rooms enabled their independent use if so desired. Bedrooms often had a private dressing room or bathroom adjacent, and light shafts ensured ventilation and daylighting to toilets and other ancillary rooms. Smaller bedrooms, kitchens, and bathrooms faced the courtyard, and each apartment had access to a service stair that led to the attic floor where the servants' quarters were located.

The street elevations of apartment buildings in nineteenth-century Paris were often palatial in appearance, in marked contrast to the monotonous and dreary facades of tenements. Apartment buildings built for the middle-class in other large European cities were equally well designed and enjoyed a popularity similar to the Parisian ones. This approach to the design of apartment buildings was also adopted in North American cities, but here the single-family detached house enjoyed the greatest popularity.

The first apartment house in New York City was built in the mid-1850s and was followed by others, as exemplified by Richard Morris Hunt's Stuyvesant apartment house built in 1869. Although influenced by Parisian flats, these early apartment houses did not initially project the formality and grandeur of their French counterparts, but by the end of the century several luxury apartment houses were built in New York City. The forerunner of these was The Dakota, built in 1884 and emulating the château-esque style of medieval architecture. Like a true château, The Dakota was originally surrounded by copious parklike grounds, but most of the grounds, including the tennis courts, were later turned into building sites.

Usually, luxury apartment houses had few, but very large dwelling units on each floor, as exemplified by Alwyn Court, a French Renaissance luxury building at 180 West 58th Street. This building, like many others, was later modifed to contain more apartments per floor. Where there had previously been only two very large ones, each with a library, billiard room, music room, reception room, salon, and personal maids' rooms in addition to living room, dining room, bedrooms, or chambers complemented by dressing rooms, bathrooms, kitchens, and several servants' rooms, now there were six still generous apartments per floor.

A dwelling unit whose rooms were all on a single floor was very unlike the traditional house or villa in which there were invariably several stories. To simulate the house atmosphere, duplex apartments were developed in New York with living room, dining room, library, and kitchen on one floor and bedrooms and bathrooms on the floor above. As in the villa, the first floor level had a higher ceiling than the second one, and an internal, often monumental, stair connected the two.

To reduce the excessive height of kitchens and ancillary rooms, such as the butler's pantry, on the first floor, an economical solution was developed by grouping three floor levels with lower ceiling heights, containing kitchens, pantries, bedrooms, and bathrooms, behind two floor levels of 15-ft-high living and dining rooms, the former, of course, in the rear of the building, and the latter along the street front. Not only were duplex apartments more homelike, but they were also more attractive for artists' studio apartments. This artistic dimension eventually led to the fad of "studio-apartment" living by the middle-class, but, unlike artists, they understandably preferred south-facing studios.

Catering Flats and Apartment Hotels

During the second half of the nineteenth century a new residential building type emerged in London. Called catering flats, these luxurious apartment buildings were developed to fulfill the demands of a certain segment of society, namely well-to-do single or elderly people without children who sought the "homelike" quality of a dwelling with the household services offered in a hotel. The evolution of this building type was attributed to the increasing difficulty in obtaining good servants, but another reason was the demand for an agreeable form of dwelling for affluent people who were willing to pay for the conveniences they desired.

Catering flats consisted of a number of self-contained apartment suites of various sizes, usually with a pantry but without a kitchen and servants' rooms. Household services and meals in the common dining room were paid for at a fixed charge, whereas the use of all other common rooms such as the billiard room were included in the rent.

The central kitchen with its ancillary rooms was located either in the basement or in the garret of the apartment building. It was not compulsory for the tenants to consume their meals in the common dining room, as arrangements could be made to have meals served in a private dining room. Three noted examples of catering flats built around the turn of the century were Queen Anne's Mansions, Camden House Chambers, and Marlborough Chambers, the last considered at the time to have had some of the best and most expensive suites in London.

A similar evolution of a new residential building type occurred on the North American continent with the development of apartment hotels. Like their English counterparts, these buildings were also inhabited exclusively by the well-to-do.

As its name implies, an apartment hotel was a cross between a hotel and an apartment building. At ground-floor level, with the foyer, lounge, and dining room, the similarity with the hotel was greatest, although the common spaces in the apartment hotel were more informal and less stately but, on the upper-floor levels, the building more closely resembled an apartment building, because the dwelling suites of its permanent residents had to be much larger than rooms for transient guests.

The concept of collective habitation where resources were pooled in order to eliminate the numerous duplications of household work had many advocates during the nineteenth century. Social reformers, such as Fourier, Kropotkin, Wells, and others extolled the virtues of centralized kitchens not merely for the well-to-do, but for all segments of society. This movement led during the twentieth century to some experimentation with collective apartment-house living where centralized kitchens and housekeeping services were offered to middle- and lower-income groups mainly in Denmark, Sweden, Germany, and Russia. The first Kollektivhus was built in 1903 by Otto Fick in Copenhagen, a prototype that served as a model for the Swedish collective house Hemgaard in Stockholm, as well as the German Einküchenhaus in Berlin. The Russian experiments with collective habitation based on similar principles commenced in the late 1920s with Moses Ginzburg's Dom-Kommuna apartment building called Narkomfin in Moscow.

THE TWENTIETH-CENTURY SUBURBAN AND URBAN DWELLING

More significant for the evolution of contemporary housing were the urban reform movements of the turn of the century, of which Ebenezer Howard's Garden City concept must be singled out as the one with the most far-reaching consequences on twentieth-century housing. Because the Garden City movement advocated starting anew with building "new towns" in virgin green fields protected by "green belts," it was essentially a confirmation of a trend that had manifested itself decades before when well-to-do families abandoned the city and built their homes in the countryside. Moreover, the Garden City movement inadvertently avoided the problems of the nineteenth-century industrialized city with its deteriorating housing conditions, slums, pollution, and disease, and provided instead an escape from the harsh realities of city living for a large segment of citizens who otherwise, in their self-interest, would have had to improve the physical and social conditions of their cities. This task was left to housing reformers of the twentieth century, who stressed the importance of hygiene and wholesome dwellings for everyone.

The craving for open space and nature became an obsession for most late-nineteenth-century urban dwellers living in cities adversely affected by large-scale industrial development. A marriage of town and country became a logical objective to most housing reformers of this century, regardless of whether they advocated, on the one hand, low-density nucleated Garden Cities such as Howard's, the Linear Towns proposed by Don Arturo Soria y Mata, and Broadacre Cities by Frank Lloyd Wright, or, on the other hand, high-density Vertical Garden Cities, such as the Cité Jardin Vertical by Le Corbusier, their most famous protagonist.

These housing-reform movements brought about a significant departure from traditional housing design during the course of this century and, with the emphasis placed on open space and nature, the single-family detached house was universally perceived as the dream house of Occidental countries. Although at the beginning of the Garden City movement, both semi-detached and attached single-family dwellings were also built in order to meet the demands of the various income groups acquiring houses outside the city, the detached house represented the ideal.

The dream of the single-family house, whether in a Garden City or a mere suburb, proved to be very seductive, as it offered the tranquility of the country and the convenience of the city; above all else the detached house was perceived as the desirable dwelling for child-oriented family living. During the twentieth century, the suburban detached house indeed became affordable to an ever wider range of income groups, especially on the North American continent, with the result that the parent cities gradually lost a large segment of their population to their respective suburbs.

Along with the proliferation of single-family dwellings in the suburbs, multifamily residential buildings in cities also underwent radical changes during this century. To spread the higher costs of urban land, dwelling-unit densities were gradually increased in the city by building higher and higher buildings, which led to a polarization of the housing stock between two extremes, namely low-density single-family houses in the suburb on the one hand, and high-density multifamily housing in the city on the other. As could be expected, multifamily residential accommodations also presented extremes, with luxury apartment buildings for the upper-income group and public-housing tenements for underprivileged citizens representing opposite poles.

The Bungalow and the Suburban Home

An unprecedented single-story suburban detached house called the bungalow became popular during the twentieth century in North America. This prototype had its roots in the Orient and was derived from the indigenous Bengali hut called bangla (bangala). The bungalow was first adopted by European colonial officials in India as a dwelling admirably suited for the hot climate with its front and rear shaded verandas and high-ceilinged rooms lit and ventilated by clerestory windows. Later, retired British colonial officers adopted the bungalow, in a more modest version, in England, primarily as a second home for summer use only. Eventually, the convenience of the single-level bungalow was discovered to be more advantageous in a permanent dwelling than the two- or three-storied traditional villa, especially at a time when servants were increasingly unavailable to help with household chores. Thus, the bungalow was adopted as a new type of suburban home, and, after its introduction to North America it was embraced by a wide range of income groups. It was the most common suburban dwelling during the post-World War II period, and, with the inevitable picture window and garage door facing on a tree-lined avenue, it became the American dream house, at one extreme of the income groups a modest house, and at the other, a luxurious rambling estate.

The bungalow, like all other dwelling prototypes popular during this century, was subjected to the influences of a new architectural trend, the so-called modern movement of the early decades of this century, which later became known in the United States as the International style. Although each protagonist of the modern movement had an identifiable individual style, each also subscribed to some commonalities governing domestic architectural design. These commonly shared features were primarily hygiene, functionalism, informality, and a closer relationship between house and garden.

The first common emphasis was on hygiene, a natural reaction to the crowded, ill-ventilated, and dismal dwelling conditions so prevalent during the nineteenth century. Healthful living conditions implied ample living space, access to sunlight and fresh air, clean heating, and good sanitary services, with potable water supply to each dwelling and sanitary sewer disposal. In this century the privy was replaced with the water closet, and individual bathrooms became an accepted standard for each dwelling unit; similarly, hot-air or hot-water central heating systems replaced fireplaces as the main heat source for a dwelling just as the wood or coal-fired kitchen range gave way to gas and, later, electric stoves and cooking appliances.

The second common emphasis on functionalism was the result of new socioeconomic realities brought about by a generally servantless open society that insisted on home comfort. The functional house was designed not so much to impress occasional visitors, but to comfort with the least amount of effort. Le Corbusier's definition of the house as a "machine to live in," became a motto of many architects and resulted in new layouts of dwellings.

The design, size, and location of the kitchen in modern houses perhaps best illustrates the impact of functionalism on housing. No longer was the kitchen relegated to the basement or to an obscure corner of the house, as indeed it had been in the past, but instead was designed as a well-equipped sunny and efficient space adjacent to the dining area, or often even combined with it.

Similarly, greater attention was given to the design of bedrooms, with the provision of ample storage for clothing in built-in closets. Moreover, the layout of bedrooms and bathrooms was designed so that reasonable privacy could be enjoyed by each member of the family.

The third common emphasis in housing design was on informality, in great contrast to the formal Victorian dwellings of both middle- and upper-income groups. Thus, the en suite arrangement of the drawing and dining room, or that of the double parlor, was replaced by a less formal open plan, where the principal living spaces flowed into each other. This design trend was also largely attributable to the unavailability of servants and, hence, the redundancy of sculleries, butlers' pantries, and service corridors, all of which had a liberating influence on house design.

Finally, ornamentation in domestic architectural interiors was also shunned and replaced by pristine (and, by the way, easy to clean) architectural details; "ornament is crime," a slogan by Adolf Loos, and "less is more," a phrase attributed to Mies van der Rohe, best express the modern architects' attitude toward "superficial" ornamentation.

Finally, a new emphasis was placed on the complementary relationship between house and garden, which is partly attributable to Japanese influence and partly to the extensive use of glass in domestic architecture. Perhaps Frank Lloyd Wright was the most successful interpreter of this trend to bring nature into the house and the house to nature. As a proponent of "organic architecture" and "the natural house," it is not surprising that he, above everyone else, accomplished a pleasing balance between openness and closure, nature and house, in all of his celebrated domestic architecture (Fig. 20). In fact, Wright suggested that the integration of a house with its building site is achieved when "the garden be the building as much as the building will be the garden" (2).

A new focus on views and a greater awareness of the outdoor environment led to extensive use of terraces, patios, and gardens as outdoor extensions of the home; in addition, more consideration was given to landscape design. The suburban sprawl of the postwar period resulted

in ever increased distances between the city where one worked and the suburb where one lived.

To economize on land, in the late 1950s alternatives to the bungalow were introduced in many suburbs, such as the split-level house, followed more recently by a return to two traditional house forms, the two-story cottage and the town house. The town house concept received an additional boost during the energy crisis of the 1970s, because of its superior energy efficiency in comparison to all other single-family housing prototypes.

The Multistory Apartment Building and Tenement

Apartment houses continued to attract some urban dwellers who were not family-oriented and who preferred to live in the city for proximity to work and entertainment. As a result of the attempt to reduce the high cost of urban land per dwelling unit, coupled with greater demands for communal amenities, such as swimming pools and security installations, apartment houses evolved during this century into ever-larger building complexes. Greater sophistication in structural design and construction, new types of building materials, and mechanical improvements such as high-speed elevator services as well as the pressurization and air-conditioning of buildings, made it possible for the first time ever to exceed 100 stories in height not only for office towers but residential towers as well. As technologic achievements, true skyscrapers like Chicago's Hancock Tower are awe-inspiring, but hardly affordable for most tenants.

With higher buildings, upper-story apartments offered more dramatic views, and the ultimate in urban luxury living became the penthouse apartment, simulating a villa or bungalow on a roof. With heights in excess of 60 stories, outdoor terraces in penthouse apartments are no longer feasible because of unpleasant climatic conditions.

The physical layout of a typical apartment unit followed principles similar to those in suburban houses, an open plan with an L-shaped living room with the short leg of the L serving as a dining area, the latter in proximity to a well-equipped but tight galley-type kitchen. From the central entrance hall, access was gained to the living room section of the apartment and to a corridor leading to bedrooms and bathrooms. In one important respect, however, apartments differed from detached houses because, by confining most dwelling units to a single aspect, the double-loaded corridor access made cross ventilation impossible. However, in luxury apartments these shortcomings were offset by air conditioning.

High-rise apartment buildings proved to be both popular and prestigious living accommodations for the well-to-do, not only because of the extensive amenities such as swimming pools and saunas offered in luxury apartment buildings, but also because of the security provided. In essence, contemporary high-rise apartment towers fulfill a function similar to that which tower dwellings of patrician families provided during the Middle Ages; they ensure safety and prestige for their occupants. In fact, the two 60-story residential towers of Marina City in Chicago are veritable fortresses as is the case with most other prestigious high-rise buildings.

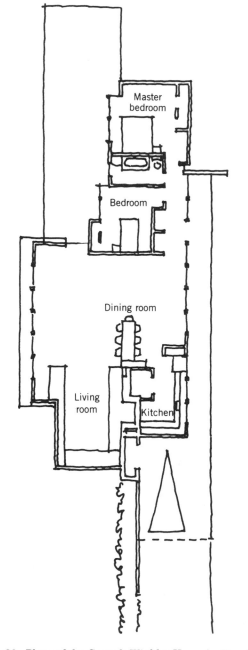

Figure 20. Plans of the Goetsch-Winkler House by Frank Lloyd Wright.

In the absence of proper security provisions and lack of collective amenities, high-rise dwellings built for the lower-income group proved to be disastrous. In extreme cases, such as the Pruitt-Igoe public-housing development built in 1955 by the city of St. Louis, all 17 blocks, containing a total of 2764 dwelling units, had to be demolished, despite the fact that large sunny open spaces separated the buildings of this development and that its density was quite moderate, at about 50 dwelling units per acre. This final remedy became necessary because of excessive vandalism, crime, and social problems in the development. Such drastic intervention was not unique to this continent, but was also necessary for some high-rise tenements in Great Britain.

CONCLUSION

During this century the choice of housing accommodation on the North American continent has become polarized, with low-density single-family suburban houses at one extreme and high-density multifamily apartment towers in both urban and suburban settings on the other. However, with the emergence of demographic and socioeconomic changes in today's society, coupled with a new awareness of the need for energy efficiency, new housing trends that are a departure from both extremes are emerging.

The energy crisis that began in the early 1970s stirred the consciousness of many architects to design energy-effective housing. The simplest approach was to increase the insulation of external walls and to use passive solar energy by means of an optimum orientation of the dwelling toward the sun. Another approach entailed the active collection of solar energy through solar panels and storing it in some form of thermal mass until required.

The need to increase the energy efficiency of single-family detached houses also led to the earth-shelter movement that promised warmth, quiet, and energy efficiency in subterranean dwellings. But underground homes have yet to gain popularity. Similarly, the ecological solutions of the counterculture, as exemplified by the dome shelters of Drop City, Colorado, proved to be too radical to be generally acceptable.

A more reasonable and successful alternative to suburban detached houses are attached cluster houses and town houses in suburban settings conceived as planned unit developments. Attached houses inherently require less energy for heating and cooling and, if ground-related with private outdoor extensions, they offer most of the advantages associated with the bungalow.

An alternative to high-rise living is represented by medium-rise housing, from six to eight stories high, with a high proportion of ground-related dwellings at the base and equally desirable penthouse units at roof level. Coupled with perimeter planning, medium-rise housing can provide similar densities to that of most high-rise developments, admittedly with higher ground coverage but with adequate outdoor spaces both private and public. Medium-rise housing inherently promotes greater opportunity for self-policing and is more affordable in terms of building construction.

Another emerging housing trend involves mixed land use, in which housing is built in combination with commercial and office buildings. It has become apparent that housing in urban areas enhances the attractiveness and vitality of the city, whereas its absence often diminishes these qualities. Perhaps during business hours, when office workers and shoppers crowd the streets, the additional activity generated by urban dwellers is less significant to street life, but after hours—when shops are closed and office buildings deserted—the 24-hour use of apartment buildings (and hotels) adds life to the city core, not to mention creating a sense of street safety. In fact, residential land use in a three-dimensional fashion with shops and restaurants at sidewalk level, office floors above, and apartments in the uppermost floors of a building results in greater abundance of sunshine, air, and view for the dwellings and at little distance from the crowded street, but proximity nevertheless to the urban and cultural facilities offered by the city. Moreover, mixed land use makes economic sense by more efficient use of infrastructure and municipal services. Finally, mixed land use reduces the tendency of over centralization of development and a more equitable distribution of development opportunities over a large area of the city.

During the twentieth century most "modern" architects avoided whimsy, color, and embellishment in housing because of their rational design approach with an emphasis on hygiene, functionalism, and informality. In opposition to the starkness of modern architecture, two new design trends have recently emerged that reemphasize the very qualities of architecture that were rejected by the early modernists. First, the "vernacular" movement advocates the rediscovery of time-proven building traditions as exemplified by *A Pattern Language,* by Christopher Alexander and co-workers (3), and, second, the postmodern movement, which propounds design tenets based on classical architecture. Not unlike the nineteenth century's battle of styles, the protagonists of these two movements reach back into history for inspiration to satisfy not only physical needs in housing design but also aesthetic aspirations.

BIBLIOGRAPHY

1. C. S. Coon, *The Hunting Peoples,* Little, Brown, Boston, 1971, pp. 28–29.
2. F. L. Wright, *The Natural House,* Mentor Book, New York, 1963, pp. 46–47.
3. C. Alexander and co-workers, *A Pattern Language: Towns—Buildings—Construction,* Oxford University Press, New York, 1977.

General References

M. W. Barley, *The House and Home,* Vista Books, London, 1963.
A. F. Bemis and J. Burchard, II, *The Evolving House,* Vol. 1, The Technology Press, Cambridge, Mass., 1933.
A. Boyd, *Chinese Architecture and Town Planning,* Tiranti, London, 1962.
S. Cantacuzino, *European Domestic Architecture,* Studio Vista/Dutton Pictureback, London, 1969.

S. Davis, *The Form of Housing,* Van Nostrand Reinhold, New York, 1977.

J. Ford, *Slums and Housing,* Harvard University Press, Cambridge, Mass., 1936.

D. P. Handlin, *The American Home: Architecture and Society, 1815–1915.* Little, Brown, Boston, 1979.

D. Hayden, *Redesigning the American Dream: The Future of Housing, Work, and Family Life,* W. W. Norton, New York, 1984.

T. C. Hubka, *Big House, Little House, Back House, Barn: the Connected Farm Buildings of New England,* University Press of New England, Hanover, N.H., 1984.

R. W. Kennedy, *The House and the Art of its Design,* Reinhold Publishing, New York, 1963.

A. G. McKay, *Houses, Villas and Palaces in the Roman World,* Thames and Hudson, London, 1977.

C. Moore, G. Allen, and D. Lyndon, *The Place of Houses,* Holt, Reinhart, & Winston, New York, 1974.

S. Paul, *Apartments: Their Design and Development,* Reinhold Publishing, New York, 1967.

S. Perks, *Residential Flats of All Classes including Artisan's Dwellings,* Batsford, London, 1905.

D. Procos, *Mixed Land Use: from Revival to Innovation,* Dowden, Hutchison & Ross, Stroudsbourg, Pa., 1976.

A. Rapoport, *House Form and Culture,* Prentice-Hall, Englewood Cliffs, N.J., 1969.

N. Schoenauer, *6000 Years of Housing:* Vol. 1 *The Pre-Urban House,* Vol. 2 *The Oriental Urban House,* and Vol. 3. *The Occidental Urban House,* Garland STPM Press, New York, 1981.

J. Summerson, *Georgian London,* Pleiades Books, London, 1945.

M. Wood, *The English Mediaeval House,* Phoenix Press, London, 1965.

See also ADOBE ARCHITECTURE; HIGH RISE APARTMENTS; HOTELS; INDUSTRIALIZED CONSTRUCTION; MULTI-FAMILY RESIDENCES; NOMADIC ARCHITECTURE; PLANNED COMMUNITIES; SINGLE FAMILY RESIDENCES; SINGLE PARENT HOUSING; TIME-ADAPTIVE HOUSING.

NORBERT SCHOENAUER
McGill University
Montreal, Quebec, Canada

RESILIENT FLOORING

Resilient flooring has been in use for more than a century. Its wear resistance, ease of maintenance, and attractive appearance make resilient flooring an ideal choice for office and institutional buildings, hospitals and other health care facilities, stores and shopping malls, schools, banks, and residential buildings.

Resilient flooring has undergone many changes since its beginning as a relatively simple floor covering. Today's resilient flooring is the result of extensive research, new raw materials, improved manufacturing techniques, and innovative design treatments. Its use is extensive. In 1985, resilient flooring accounted for 25–30% of the 450-million square yards of floor space in the commercial and institutional building markets alone.

Even though resilient floors have been around for more than 120 years, there is still some confusion about this classification of flooring. Resilient flooring describes a family of products that includes such materials as linoleum, asphalt tile, rubber sheet and tile, and vinyl tile and sheet products. The word resilient connotes the ability to recover from deformation, ie, recover from indentation that may be created by the heel of a shoe, a table leg, or a wheel. This separates the family from other products used for flooring such as carpeting, wood, ceramics, and stone.

HISTORY

The earliest "resilient" flooring product consisted of canvas or other fabric coated with oxidizing oils or oil paints (1,2). These were called floor cloths or oilcloths. In 1844 Elijah Gallaway developed a product called "Kamptulicon," which was a mixture of India rubber, sawdust, and cork. Its relatively high cost led to the development in 1860 of a product named "linoleum" by its inventor, Frederick Walton, which essentially launched the resilient-flooring industry. Linoleum in its earliest form consisted of layers of linseed oil compounded with cork dust, wood flour, whiting, and pigments applied to fabric and cured by air oxidation. Later refinements included the partial preoxidation of the drying oils, linseed and others, blended with gums and resins, to make a linoleum cement that was compounded with cork dust, wood flour, whiting, and pigments. This heavy stock could then be processed by calendering or molding to create heavy-gauge flooring with inlaid designs or solid colors.

Felt-Base Linoleum

A variation of linoleum, which had great success in the residential flooring market, was called felt-base linoleum. It consisted of a resin or asphalt saturated rag felt base with a pattern, usually applied by woodblock printing, of alkyd paints. This product was very popular in the 1940s and 1950s, filling the need for a low cost, decorative floor covering for almost any room in the house.

Asphalt Tile

Because linoleum was subject to degradation (hydrolysis) by alkaline moisture, it was suitable for use only on dry suspended subfloors. For on- or below-grade concrete subfloors, asphalt tile was used. This product was introduced in 1922 as a spinoff from attempts to create a synthetic roofing tile to simulate slate. By 1947 it was a major item in the floor-covering market. Asphalt tile, as the name implies, was originally based on an asphaltic binder filled with limestone, asbestos, and pigments. Later, other resinous materials, including coal-tar-derived coumarone indene resins, and petroleum-derived hydrocarbon resins, were used to produce lighter-colored tiles. Deficiencies in the intrinsic properties of asphalt tiles, such as color restrictions, and poor resistance to oils and greases, led to the development of vinyl asbestos tiles and ultimately the vinyl composition tile of today.

Modern Floor Coverings

Linoleum and asphalt tile are now considered virtually obsolete in the U.S. flooring market. The manufacture of linoleum in the United States was discontinued in 1974; however, it is still manufactured in Europe. Much of the imported linoleum is used not for flooring but for desk-top material. Asphalt tile is currently manufactured domestically by one producer.

The major forms of resilient flooring used today are based on either rubber or poly(vinyl chloride).

CLASSIFICATION OF RESILIENT FLOORING

The American Institute of Architects provides the following classifications of resilient flooring in the AIA "Masterspec" 09650, (1984):

Asphalt tile
Rubber tile
Rubber sheet flooring
Raised profile rubber tile
Vinyl tile
Vinyl composition tile
Vinyl sheet flooring
    Filled vinyl sheet with backing
    Filled vinyl sheet without backing
    Filled vinyl sheet with foam backing
    Unfilled vinyl sheet with foam interlayer and backing
    Unfilled vinyl sheet with vinyl backing
    Unfilled vinyl sheet with reinforced vinyl interlayer and backing
    Unfilled vinyl sheet flooring with reinforced vinyl backing
    Unfilled vinyl sheet flooring with reinforced vinyl interlayer and foam backing
    Raised profile vinyl sheet with backing
    Raised profile vinyl sheet without backing

As can be seen from this list, there is a wide variety of structures of sheet vinyl flooring. The more predominant types will be described later.

Vinyl Flooring

By far, the predominant form of resilient flooring used today is of the vinyl type, ie, having a binder system based on poly(vinyl chloride) commonly abbreviated as PVC.

This polymer by itself is a very hard, tough, virtually intractable, thermoplastic material that must be compounded with various additives to produce commercially useful products. It is one of the most adaptable polymeric materials and is used for applications as widely divergent as rigid pipe and almost jellylike fishing lures. Because of this adaptability, it is well suited to the manufacture of both flexible and semirigid flooring materials.

PVC's high molecular weight and chemical and physical nature allow it to accommodate relatively large amounts of inert filler. It can be plasticized effectively and permanently to create materials with a wide range of flexibilities.

PVC is inherently resistant to acids and alkali and many organic solvents, and it does not hydrolyze even when in continuous contact with moisture. It is attacked by some organic solvents, including ketones, low molecular weight esters, aromatic hydrocarbons, and chlorinated hydrocarbons.

Because of the chlorine content of PVC, it is also inherently fire resistant and as a plastic material is classed as self-extinguishing. Plasticized PVC is less fire resistant than rigid PVC, but it can be formulated to pass the flame-spread and smoke-generation requirements of most building codes for use as floor covering.

When properly compounded and processed, PVC is a clear, colorless material and can be pigmented to produce the full range of colors in transparent or opaque forms.

GENERAL COMPOUNDING INGREDIENTS USED IN VINYL FLOORING

PVC Resins. The vinyl resins used in flooring may be "homopolymers", ie, polymers containing only vinyl chloride units, or "copolymers" consisting of vinyl chloride and vinyl acetate units. The molecular weights of the resins range from 40,000 to 200,000. The higher molecular weight polymers have greater ultimate tensile strengths and abrasion resistance and are generally used in flooring wear layers, whereas the lower molecular weight polymers are most useful in producing foams for cushioned flooring. As a general rule, vinyl homopolymers are primarily used in sheet flooring and solid vinyl tiles; vinyl composition tiles usually contain copolymers of vinyl chloride and vinyl acetate.

Stabilizers. To protect the PVC from degradation during processing and during its use as flooring material, vinyl compounds must be stabilized against the effects of heat and ultraviolet (uv) light. The most common stabilizers used in flooring are soaps of barium, calcium, and zinc; organo-tin compounds; epoxidized soybean oils and tallate esters; and organic phosphites.

Plasticizers. Flooring compounds, even the relatively rigid vinyl composition tiles, contain plasticizers to provide flexibility and to facilitate processing. The most frequently used plasticizer is dioctyl phthalate (DOP). Others that may be found in flooring use include butylbenzyl phthalate (BBP), alkylaryl phosphates (used primarily as flame retardants), other phthalate esters of both aliphatic and aromatic alcohols, chlorinated hydrocarbons, and various other high boiling esters. The selection of the proper type and amount of plasticizer is critical in the formulation of flooring compounds because of the interaction of flexibility requirements, resistance to staining, reaction with maintenance finishes, and processing requirements.

Fillers and Pigments. In tile and sheet flooring (with the exception of the clear wear layer on some types of flooring) the stabilized and plasticized vinyl formulation is mixed with varying amounts of inorganic filler to provide mass and thickness at a reasonable cost. The most common filler found in flooring is limestone (calcium carbonate). Others that may be used include talcs, clays, and feldspars.

In addition to providing bulk at reasonable cost, inorganic fillers in flooring structures provide increased dimensional stability, resistance to cigarette burns, improved flame-spread ratings, and reduced smoke generation.

Pigments used in flooring provide both opacity and color to the finished product. The preferred white pigment is titanium dioxide. Colored pigments are preferably inorganic. However, certain colors are only available as lakes, such as the phthalocyanine blues and greens. They must be resistant to the effects of alkali and light fading.

Other Compounding Ingredients. To pass certain code requirements with regard to fire and smoke properties, various additives may be employed to reduce flame spread and smoke generation ratings. These compounds may include alumina trihydrate, antimony trioxide, phosphate or chlorinated hydrocarbon plasticizers, zinc oxide, and boron compounds. Cushioned flooring containing chemically expanded foam usually is compounded with azobisformamide blowing agents. Some compounds may also contain processing aids and lubricants.

TYPES OF FLOORING TILE PRODUCTS

Vinyl Composition Tile

The most widely used resilient flooring product today is vinyl composition tile (VCT), described by Federal Specification SS-T-312b, Composition I. It has superseded the asbestos-containing composition referred to as VAT.

Manufacture. A typical formulation for VCT is

Ingredient	Wt %
Vinyl resin (copolymer blend)	12.5
Processing aid (hydrocarbon resin)	2.5
Plasticizer (phthalate esters)	4.0
Stabilizer	1.0
Fillers/pigments	80.0

As can be seen from the above, vinyl composition tile is highly filled. The primary filler is limestone. Other proprietary fillers and reinforcements may also be used.

Manufacturers carefully guard their actual formulations, particularly with regard to fillers and stabilizers, because of their effect on performance properties.

The ingredients are mixed in a high power, high shear, heated mixer, such as a Banbury mill, to fuse them into a heavy doughlike mass. This mass is then banded on a two-roll mill. Accent colors of the same or similar composition may be added to the mill nip in the manufacture of grained or jaspéd tile.

The mix is then cut off the mill roll in the form of thick slabs that may be folded to create more uniform graining. These folded "blankets" are then passed through a sheeting calender to form a continuous web close to the final

gauge of the tile. The web is then passed through a second calender to reduce to the final gauge and provide a smooth face. For the production of tile having a surface pattern, usually for residential use, previously prepared accent chips are applied to the face of the tile between the first and second calender. Tile having an embossed surface texture will be embossed by passing between another pair of rolls with tooled embossing on the top roll.

After exiting the finishing calender or, if used, the embosser, a factory finish may be applied to the hot sheet to provide uniform gloss and prevent blocking in storage. The sheet is then cooled and die cut in a punch press to the finished size. The cut tiles are then inspected and packed. Rejected tile and frame scrap from the punching operation are recycled to the mix operation.

Characteristics. Vinyl composition tile is offered in several gauges and sizes, depending on intended end use. For residential applications, VCT is offered in "service" gauge, which is approximately 1/16-in. thick. These tiles are frequently embossed and may contain surface-applied patterns and grainings. A modern variation of residential tile is the use of rotogravure-printed overlays protected by a wear layer of clear vinyl.

For the commercial market, VCT is offered in 3/32- and 1/8-in. thicknesses, the latter being most frequently specified for heavy traffic. The standard size of VCT is 12 in. × 12 in., although other sizes may be available from various suppliers.

The performance requirements outlined in Federal Specification SS-T-312b include size, thickness, squareness, and dimensional stability tolerances. These factors are critically important in the finished appearance of the installed tile floor. Other characteristics contained in the specification are solvent resistance, indentation requirements, deflection, volatility, and impact resistance.

Two other important attributes of vinyl composition tile that should be considered are as follows:

1. *Consistency of shade and graining from tile to tile, and within each tile from face to back.* Tile used in high traffic areas will eventually wear, and if the graining is not consistent throughout the thickness of the tile, obvious traffic lanes may appear long before the tile is worn through (Fig. 1).
2. *Tightness of face and back.* All vinyl composition tile has some surface porosity. If it is excessive on the face, more sealer and/or polish will be required to prepare it for commercial traffic. If it is excessive on the back, the tile will be more subject to water absorption from concrete slabs on or below grade, resulting in a greater tendency to grow, curl, or peak at the joints after installation on damp subfloors.

Vinyl composition tile is a fairly rigid material, and at room temperature it will not bend acutely without breaking. However, if deflected very slowly, it will bend. This attribute is necessary to install the material successfully over normal subfloors that are not perfectly flat, allowing it to conform to subfloor irregularities. Because of this

Figure 1. End mill turn down to show through-grain tile.

feature, its resistance to indentation from static loads is not as great as that of other vinyl flooring.

Commercial installation of VCT is usually done with a full spread of cut-back asphalt adhesive that is applied with a finely notched trowel. After the solvent has evaporated, the tile is set into the adhesive. The open time of the adhesive can be designed to accommodate spreading on 1 day and installing the next for large installation areas.

Also available are solventless adhesives containing emulsified asphalt and resins for areas where solvent vapors are undesirable. Rubber latex adhesives also are used where black asphalt adhesives would be undesirable and for use over preexisting tile floors.

Uses. Vinyl composition tile is considered the standard or base grade commercial finish flooring. It has the lowest relative installed cost and has performed in these environments satisfactorily for many years. The major market today is the mercantile market. It is used almost exclusively for the general floor area of grocery stores, supermarkets, and department stores. It also is used extensively in schools, health care facilities, and, to a lesser extent, in offices, banks, and light industry.

Vinyl Tile

Vinyl tile is called variously "solid vinyl tile," "homogeneous vinyl tile," and even "pure vinyl tile." The primary difference between vinyl composition tile and vinyl tile is the binder level. The Federal Specification SS-T-312b, Type III, requires that the minimum binder level for a

vinyl tile shall be not less than 34%. The binder is defined as the vinyl resin(s), plasticizers, and stabilizers. There is no minimum binder level requirement for Type IV (Vinyl Composition Tile).

Manufacture. A typical formulation for a solid vinyl tile is as follows:

Ingredient	Wt %
Vinyl resin (homopolymer or low acetate copolymer)	25
Plasticizer (phthalate esters)	9–10
Stabilizer/processing aids	1–2
Filler and pigments	65

Many proprietary methods are used for the production of vinyl tiles, so it is not possible to provide a specific manufacturing process here. A very generalized process might consist of the following steps:

1. High intensity mixing of compounding ingredients.
2. Sheeting through a two-roll mill.
3. Combining sheets with accent colors to produce mottled or marbled designs, or combining sheets of different colors to produce appliqué tiles.
4. Pressing or molding in a continuous or intermittent press.
5. Oversize punching, back sanding, and applying factory finish.
6. Annealing.
7. Die cutting or block sanding to final size.

Characteristics. Vinyl tile is available in 9 in. × 9 in. and 12 in. × 12 in. sizes usually ⅛ in. thick. Among the different styles are through-grained marble or mottle designs, solid color pavers, and appliqué tile, which consists of a base color overlaid with a differently colored layer cut to resemble brick or pavers.

Vinyl tile is considerably more flexible than vinyl composition tile and has different specification requirements, as outlined in Federal Specification SS-T-312b, Type III, particularly with regard to recovery from indentation and flexibility. The size, squareness, thickness, and dimensional stability requirements are the same as for vinyl composition tile (Type IV). Because of its high binder level, it has significantly higher resistance to abrasive wear and is more resistant to impact damage. Conversely, its higher binder level makes it less resistant to damage from accidental cigarette burns.

Vinyl tiles are installed with a full spread of rubber or resin latex adhesive applied with a notched trowel and allowed sufficient open time to allow most of the water to evaporate. Some applications require the use of reactive epoxy adhesives.

Uses. The initial cost of vinyl tile is significantly higher than VCT, but because of its flexibility and high degree of abrasion resistance and resilience, this product is very suitable for areas subjected to high pedestrian and cart traffic. Many vinyl tiles are offered in imitative patterns of brick, slate, and ceramic pavers and are frequently used in mercantile settings to highlight special merchandising areas in the store.

Rubber Tile (and Sheet)

Rubber tile and sheet flooring was introduced in the 1920s and was widely used through the 1950s, particularly for applications unsuited to linoleum and asphalt tile. Its popularity declined through the 1960s and 1970s owing to the relative success of vinyl tiles and sheet flooring. Today it is enjoying a comeback in certain specific applications, primarily because of the popularity of the raised disk design.

Manufacture. Modern rubber tile and sheet is based primarily on styrene-butadiene rubber (SBR). Other rubbers that may be incorporated with the SBR include neoprene and nitrile rubbers. A typical rubber flooring formulation will contain the rubber or rubber blend, a high styrene resin as a hardener, hydrocarbon oil extender, inert fillers such as clays, talcs, and limestone, and vulcanizing agents such as sulfur and zinc oxide.

The ingredients are blended in a Banbury mixer followed by sheeting through a two-roll mill. The sheet from the mill is rolled into a "pig" with previously compounded accent colors for production of marbleized or grained flooring. The pig is fed to a four-roll calender in which the accent colors form the graining and a relatively smooth sheet approaching the final gauge of the product is achieved.

In the manufacture of tile and nonroll goods, this sheet is cut into slabs that are press-cured at elevated temperature for 10- to 12-min in multiple or stack presses. Sheet flooring is cured in a continuous press such as a Rotopress.

After cure, the material is allowed to age a day or two before cutting to the finished size. The tile may have embossed ribbing on the back to enhance adhesive grab, or may simply be sanded. The face of the goods may be smooth or have a molded embossing such as round disks, raised squares, or other configurations.

Characteristics. Rubber tile is a very durable flooring product, with excellent wear characteristics, resilience, quietness under foot, and the best resistance to cigarette burns of all the generally available resilient flooring products. It also has better resistance to polar organic solvents, such as acetone and other ketones, esters, and cyclic ethers. However, it has poorer resistance to aliphatic and aromatic hydrocarbons and vegetable oils than do vinyl products.

Rubber tile is more costly to install than vinyl flooring of similar physical appearance, is limited in design capabilities, and is difficult to produce in light, bright colors.

Uses. Smooth-surface rubber flooring is frequently specified in light industry and laboratories because of its unique solvent resistance. It is used in health care facilities and schools where its good wear resistance and resilience are required. The raised-disk rubber flooring has found widespread acceptance in areas where wet slip re-

sistance is required or where that particular decorative effect is desired.

Rubber flooring is used extensively for stair treads and risers and for landings in stairways. Stair-tread material is usually molded into shapes specifically for this application.

SHEET VINYL FLOORING

As shown in the classification system used by AIA Masterspec, there are many structural variations for sheet vinyl products. Only the major ones will be covered here. They will include the unfilled wear layer with foam interlayer and backing, commonly referred to as cushioned rotovinyl; filled vinyl wear layer with backing; and filled vinyl without backing. These are the major types of sheet flooring structures manufactured domestically.

Cushioned Rotovinyl

The structure of cushioned rotovinyl products usually consists of an organic or inorganic felt composition backing or an extensible vinyl backing, coated with a foam layer for cushioning and to facilitate pattern embossing, a rotogravure-printed pattern, and a transparent or translucent unfilled vinyl wear layer (Fig. 2).

Manufacture. The manufacture of these products employs a dispersion of very finely divided vinyl resin particles, pigments, stabilizers, and other additives in a liquid matrix of plasticizer(s) to form a material called a "plastisol." Plastisols are fluid at room temperature and can be coated onto a web by various standard coating methods. When heated to approximately 360–380°F, they fuse to form a tough plastic film.

The backing felt or carrier is coated with a foamable plastisol containing a blowing agent, usually an azobisformamide compound, which decomposes at elevated temperatures to create nitrogen and other gases. After coating, the foamable plastisol is gelled at a temperature below the decomposition temperature of the blowing agent to form a smooth, printable substrate.

The gelled foam coat is then printed by rotogravure process to create the decorative pattern. Some of the printing inks may contain agents that interfere with the expansion of the foam coat to create pattern embossing in the finished product (3).

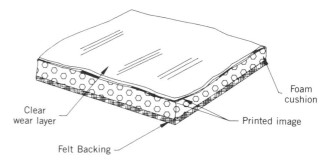

Figure 2. Typical cushion rotovinyl structure.

The printed sheet is then coated with a clear plastisol, and the entire structure is heated to a temperature adequate for complete fusion of the plastisols and expansion of the foam layer to produce the final product. Some manufacturers may use mechanical embossing techniques to create overall textures in this final step.

Characteristics. Cushion rotovinyls are usually produced in 12-ft widths, although 6-, 9-, and 15-ft widths may be available. The backings, foam layers, and wear layers are available in a variety of thicknesses, depending on the intended applications.

Federal Specification LF-001641 specifies that for commercial spaces, the minimum wear-layer thickness shall be not less than 0.020 in.; and for residential spaces, 0.010 in. Because they are decorated by rotogravure printing, virtually any color and design can be produced.

Cushioned rotovinyls are quite flexible and lightweight and can therefore be handled easily in wide widths and are relatively easy to cut and fit for installation. They are normally installed with full spread of a rubber latex base adhesive, although some varieties are designed to be loose laid (no adhesive) or adhered only around the perimeter, seams, and field cuts.

By virtue of the fact that the wear layer is unfilled vinyl, the abrasion resistance is excellent and even relatively thin wear layers have a reasonable wear life. The major weakness is that because the wear layer and printed image are supported only by foam, there is relatively less resistance to damage by cuts and punctures than for nonfoam-containing products, and greater susceptibility to damage by accidental cigarette burns.

Uses. Most cushion rotovinyl is used residentially and is today the most popular resilient flooring product in this market. The foam interlayer is fairly effective in reducing impact sound transmission from the floor to the space below. Combined with appropriate subfloor structures, it can be used to achieve certain impact isolation class requirements in multifamily housing units. Variations of this product contain a polyurethane coating to provide a "no wax" finish.

For commercial spaces, products having a wear-layer thickness of 0.020 in. or greater and that meet the requirements of FS LF-001641, Grade 1, may be used.

Filled Vinyl Sheet Flooring with Backing

Products in this category are described by Federal Specification LF-475a and comprise a felt composition backing with an inlaid vinyl wear layer of varying thickness dependent on intended end use. (Fig. 3)

Manufacture. The filled formulation would typically be similar to the formula given for vinyl tile. It is mixed and fused in a high intensity mixer such as a Banbury mill or a reciprocating screw extruder and milled and/or calendered into sheets of plain or jaspéd color that are then fractured or cut into various shapes and sizes, depending on the finished design. These "chips" are cast onto the

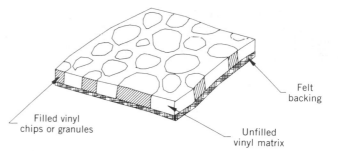

Figure 3. Typical structure of filled vinyl with backing sheet flooring.

backing carrier and fused with or without an unfilled vinyl matrix surround to create a random inlaid design, or they may be positioned by various methods to create specific patterns.

Characteristics. Products of this type are sturdy and durable. Their more massive wear layer supported directly by the felt backing provides increased resistance to damage by cuts and punctures over the cushioned rotogravure products. The abrasion resistance of the filled composition is not as great as the unfilled vinyls, and this is reflected in the wear-layer gauge requirements of the Federal Specifications for equivalent traffic classes.

Applications	LF-475a Filled Vinyl, Wear Layer	LF-001641 Unfilled Vinyl, Wear Layer
Commercial traffic	Grade A, 0.050 in.	Grade 1, 0.020 in.
Residential	Grade B, 0.030 in.	Grade 2, 0.014 in.
Residential	Grade C, 0.020 in.	Grade 3, 0.010 in.

These filled vinyl sheet floorings are available in 6-ft widths only and generally require more skill in fitting and installing. They are installed with a rubber latex adhesive in the field area with a two-part epoxy adhesive frequently used at the seam.

Uses. This type of sheet flooring, meeting the Grade A requirements, has found widespread use in health care facilities, and to a lesser extent in schools and institutions. The Grades B and C type are used in abusive residential applications such as dormitories and military housing.

Filled Vinyl Sheet without Backing

This category identifies products variously called "solid vinyl sheet flooring," "PVC sheet flooring," or "homogeneous vinyl." It has been popular in Europe for many years, particularly for commercial and institutional applications and is now increasingly popular in the United States. There is no Federal Specification to cover this type of product at the present time, but both LF-475a and SS-T-312b are used as reference standards for many of its performance characteristics.

Manufacture. Solid vinyl sheet flooring is normally manufactured by combination of calendering, consolidating, and/or laminating. The compounding ingredients are mixed and fused in a high intensity, high shear mixer, sheeted through a two-roll mill, and calendered with previously prepared accent colors to produce sheets with the desired graining. If these resulting sheets are not as thick as the required finished gauge, they may be laminated together in a continuous or intermittent pressing operation to obtain the desired thickness.

The formulation is similar to that used in solid vinyl tile; however, it is more highly plasticized to make it more flexible and the filler level may vary from 20 to 65% by weight of the composition.

Characteristics. These floors are available in rolls and, from some manufacturers, in sheets, usually 3-ft square or in tile sizes (12 in. × 12 in.). Roll widths vary from 4- to 6.5-ft wide. The most frequently specified thickness for commercial applications is 0.080 in. (2 mm) although 0.060 in. (1.5 mm) is also available from some manufacturers. Depending on the structure and process employed in manufacture, the pattern and graining is more or less consistent throughout the thickness of the product. Some laminated structures, while being of solid vinyl construction, may have the pattern only in the top layer.

Solid vinyl or PVC sheet flooring is the most durable sheet flooring available today. It is formulated with fairly high molecular weight homopolymer and contains relatively little inert filler that, combined with its thickness and through color construction, gives it excellent resistance to abrasion and other mechanical damage from punctures, cuts, and gouges. This composition also provides it with good chemical resistance.

Because it does not have a felt composition backing, it is also more resistant to indentations from heavy loads, both static and dynamic. However, this lack of a backing felt results in more critical subfloor requirements, particularly with regard to moisture and smoothness.

PVC sheet flooring has a unique seaming system that has been employed in Europe for many years. The flooring is adhered with a full spread of adhesive, usually a pressure-sensitive resin emulsion or in some cases an epoxy, and after laying, the seams are heat-welded together using a rod of plasticized vinyl. Recent developments have provided PVC sheet flooring that does not have to be heat-welded, resulting in almost invisible seams.

Uses. These products, because of the factors mentioned above, are used in commercial and institutional areas having rigorous performance requirements such as industrial, medical, and educational laboratories and clean rooms, veterinary clinics, outpatient health care clinics, and hospital procedure rooms including surgeries.

Specialty Flooring Products

In addition to these basic flooring products discussed above, there are a variety of specialty products for various applications. The more important ones are as follows:

Conductive Flooring: Used in areas where explosive or flammable vapors or dusts may exist, or where control of static electricity for sensitive electronic equipment is needed. These products obtain their conductivity by the use of conductive carbon black in the formulation, which somewhat limits the color and design capabilities. Conductive flooring is manufactured to meet the requirements of the National Fire Protection Association (NFPA) for explosive or flammable environments.

Slip-Retardant Flooring: Used in areas where slip-retardant properties above that of traditional flooring are required, such as ramps, wet areas, and vestibules. These usually have raised areas or deep embossing to help prevent hydroplaning when wet and/or mineral particles such as carborundum, quartz, or other mineral aggregates in the surface to provide increased friction with shoe soles.

FLOORING ACCESSORIES

In addition to the flooring material itself, accessories such as wall base and transition or reducer strips are included in the same specification division.

Wall base is used to provide a trim accent at the floor/wall juncture, filling the same role as baseboard and quarter round did in the past. Today, wall base is fabricated out of rubber or vinyl in a variety of contrasting and complementary colors for all types of flooring products and wall treatments.

Top-set wall base for use with resilient flooring is molded with an integral toe and finished top edge. It is available in standard lengths, usually 4 ft, or in rolls. The standard heights are 2-½ and 4 in. Some colors may also be available in 6-in. heights. Wall base for carpet applications generally does not have a toe and is referred to as "straight" base.

Transition strips are used to provide a transition between floor coverings of two different thicknesses, or to provide a small ramp from an existing floor level to the top surface of a flooring applied to that substrate. The latter is called a zero reducer. These strips are usually made of vinyl composition.

Feature strips are used to provide special design opportunities for custom-inset flooring effects. They are made of the same material and thickness as the flooring with which they are intended to be used, in solid contrasting or complementary colors.

GENERAL PERFORMANCE ATTRIBUTES OF RESILIENT FLOORING

Flooring products, in performing their function of providing a decorative, durable, easy to clean and maintain finish, are subjected to many actions and agents to which other interior finishes are not exposed. Therefore, they must be designed, formulated, and structured to withstand these forces and abuses acting on them and still retain their functional purpose and appearance for many years of service.

A resilient flooring must be resistant to the effects of abrasive and other forms of wear, cuts, punctures, and gouges from objects dropped or slid across the floor, indentations and fractures from the impact of stiletto heels and the pressures of rolling loads, degradation from the environment both above and below the floor covering, frequent scrubbing with strong detergent solutions, and stains from spills and tracked-in soil. All these factors must be considered in the application of a finish flooring.

Wear Resistance and Durability

Unfortunately, wear resistance is frequently considered synonymous with abrasion resistance, which it is not. Abrasion is only one factor of wear. Other factors not usually measured or reported include adhesive and corrosive wear and surface fatigue. However, abrasion resistance is an important consideration in selection of flooring materials, and it is relatively simple to measure; it is just not a good predictor of service life.

An investigation performed by the International Study Committee for Wear Tests of Flooring Materials (4) compared the wear resistance of a wide variety of flooring materials when installed in elevators, which are subject to concentrated shuffling, scuffing, and pivotal pedestrian traffic. The overall result of the study was a ranking of the different flooring products with regard to thickness loss. The bar graph shown in Figure 4, generated from data given in the report, illustrates the relative performance of the products tested.

The primary source of abrasion on flooring is the action of grit particles worked against the floor by shoe soles. The abrasion test that most resembles this action is the Taber Abraser with leather wheels and a carefully controlled feed of loose aluminum oxide grit particles that are continuously applied and removed during the test. Although there are a number of tests that are available for abrasion

testing for various materials, this is the only abrasion test specifically designated for resilient flooring products by the American Society for Testing and Materials and is described in ASTM Test Method F-510 (6,7).

In comparing resilient flooring variations within a given material group (ie, vinyl flooring), the most significant formulation variable affecting abrasion is the amount of limestone filler in the composition (8). For example, unfilled vinyl, such as the relatively thin wear layers applied to rotogravure flooring, has higher intrinsic abrasion resistance than does highly filled vinyl composition tile. This difference is, of course, compensated for by the relative thickness of the wear layers. The following wear layer thicknesses are about equivalent in potential abrasive wear resistance:

Unfilled vinyl clear coat	0.025 in. (0.63 mm)
Moderately filled vinyl (~60%)	0.050 in. (1.27 mm)
Highly filled vinyl (~80%)	0.125 in. (3.16 mm)

However, abrasion resistance is only one factor in the durability of flooring, and with well-maintained flooring in normal traffic situations it is a relatively insignificant factor. Flooring seldom fails from abrasive wear-through. Usually failure is due to other forms of traumatic damage. Although filler reduces the inherent abrasion resistance, it does provide thickness and mass to the flooring to provide durability against cuts, punctures, and gouges at a reasonable cost. Filler also provides increased dimensional stability and resistance to accidental burns from dropped cigarettes.

Resilience

The resilience of a flooring material is assessed by the amount of deformation created by a given load related to its ability to recover from that deformation. It is determined by an indentation test, in which a load is applied to the flooring material via a small diameter flat or hemispherical indenter for a specified length of time; the amount of penetration is then measured. The load is then removed, and the material is allowed to recover for another specified length of time after which the amount of residual indentation is measured.

Federal specifications for each type of flooring material have indentation requirements, and, with the exception of vinyl composition and asphalt tile, a residual indentation requirement.

Vinyl tile meeting the requirements of SS-T-312b, Type III must pass the most stringent residual indentation test; after being exposed to a load of more than 5000 pounds per square inch (psi) it has to recover to 92% of its original thickness in 1 hour.

Flooring products behave differently to different durations of loading. Short-term, or dynamic, loading is experienced by the flooring from foot fall, wheeled vehicles, and impacts, whereas long-term, or static, loading is the result of stationary or occasional furnishings.

Vinyl composition tile has excellent recovery from dynamic loads but a relatively low resistance to permanent

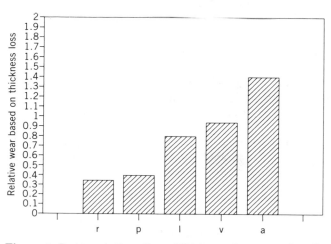

Figure 4. Representation of loss of thickness due to actual traffic wear (5). r = rubber tile; p = PVC sheet flooring; l = linoleum; v = vinyl composition tile; a = asphalt tile.

indentations from static loads, which is reflected in its usually reported recommended load limit of 50 psi. Conversely, some felt-backed sheet-flooring products having recommended static load limits of 100 psi, may have poorer recovery from heavy dynamic loads. Solid vinyl sheet and tile products generally have the best overall resilience, with excellent recovery properties from both dynamic and static loads.

Particularly severe dynamic loads can be applied to a floor from small diameter heels, common in ladies high- or stiletto-heeled shoes, and protruding nailheads and heel shanks in worn shoes. A $\frac{1}{4}$-in. diameter heel supporting a 125-lb woman can exert more than 2000 psi, and a $\frac{1}{8}$-in. nailhead exposed by a worn heel pad can exert more than 8000 psi. Wheeled vehicles with hard composition, small diameter wheels can also produce very high pressures at the line of contact of the wheel and the floor. These loadings and pressures should also be kept in mind for the selection of underlayments and floor fills, especially for commercial spaces.

The design of the flooring material employed will have an effect on the visual appearance of a floor subjected to heavy loads and indentations. A very smooth surface with little or no pattern, maintained at a high gloss level, will tend to show the inevitable dents and dings from traffic more than will a busy pattern, with a textured surface, maintained at a lower gloss level. The same holds true for hiding subfloor irregularities.

Flame and Smoke Properties

Flooring used in many commercial applications, particularly hospitals, nursing homes, and other areas where the mobility of the occupants may be limited, must meet the flammability and smoke-generation requirements of certain federal, state, and local building codes.

The most widely accepted test for flammability of flooring today is the Flooring Radiant Panel Test, ASTM E-648, which assesses the amount of radiant energy required to cause the flooring material to sustain combustion. It is generally recognized that traditional resilient flooring materials, regardless of the origin of the fire, do not significantly contribute to the fire until the space in which it is located is fully involved. The flooring radiant panel test then looks at the floor's behavior when located proximate to a room at flash-over to estimate its propensity to spread the fire to other areas.

Two categories of product performance are recognized by the National Fire Protection Association (NFPA):

Class I Critical radiant flux of 0.45 W/cm² or greater
Class II Critical radiant flux of 0.22 W/cm² or greater

In this test, higher numbers indicate more energy is required to sustain combustion.

Smoke generation is most frequently measured in the National Bureau of Standards (NBS) smoke chamber. A specific optical density of 450 or less is required by most codes in use today. This relates to the amount of vision that would be obscured for escape from the space.

Chemical and Stain Resistance

As discussed under the basic properties of PVC and rubber flooring, these materials have good resistance to a wide variety of chemical agents and stains. However, there are some specific agents that the specifier should be aware of in selecting resilient flooring.

It is almost axiomatic that a white flooring will, with use and age, drift toward yellow. This is due to the accumulative effects of tracked in coal-tar derivatives from paved parking areas, tannins from shoe leather, antioxidants from rubber heels and soles, minor degradation from light and heat, and gradual oxidation from the atmosphere. Because of this, most flooring manufacturers, much to the chagrin of some interior designers, soften the original white colorations to the yellow side.

Although most modern resilient floor coverings have good resistance to dilute acids and alkali, strong acids and alkali can react with the fillers and pigments used in the formulation to change the color and appearance of the flooring. Where spills of these powerful agents can normally be expected, such as in laboratories and areas where battery-operated equipment might be used, flooring specifically designated as acid resistant should be used.

In many areas of hospitals and other health care facilities, there are strongly colored reagents and dyes used that could be spilled on the floor. No known floor covering is resistant to discoloration by some of these agents. The best protection in these cases is to provide a good coating of strippable floor polish that can be periodically removed and reapplied.

INSTALLATION CONSIDERATIONS

The quality of the finished flooring installation is the sum of several factors, including the quality and workmanship of the products employed, the quality of the subfloor on which it is installed, and the craftsmanship of the installer. Since the individual flooring products have already been discussed, the latter two considerations are now addressed.

SUBFLOORS

For the purpose of these discussions, subfloors are defined as the structural floor and are usually classified by their relationship to the ground:

1. Suspended floors are defined as being separated from the ground by at least 18 in. of ventilated space.
2. On-grade floors are in contact with the ground at or above the surrounding grade level.
3. Below-grade floors are in contact with the ground below the surrounding grade level.

Suspended subfloors are normally constructed of wood, concrete, or, more rarely, steel, whereas on- or below-grade subfloors are nearly always concrete.

The general requirements for a substrate to receive a resilient flooring, indeed any permanent floor finish, are that it be clean, dry, smooth, structurally sound, and free from foreign materials such as paints, varnishes, oils, and waxes. The following discussion focuses on the various subfloors and substrates to receive resilient flooring.

Wood Subfloors

Wood construction subfloors are found in many single- and multiple-family dwellings and some commercial spaces. Resilient flooring can be successfully installed only on wood structures that meet the definition of suspended floors. It is not advisable to install resilient flooring on wood over unventilated space, or on sleeper construction on or below grade. The resilient flooring prevents these wood structures from "breathing," resulting in moisture saturation of the wood, flooring adhesive failure, and ultimately rotting of the wood structure.

An important point to remember is that wood is not dimensionally stable to changes in ambient humidity. In some areas of the country there are wide swings in seasonal humidity within habitable structures resulting in significant subfloor movement. Floor coverings should have some extensibility and compressibility to comply with this movement, and flooring panels and construction techniques should be chosen to provide the maximum dimensional stability achievable. The American Plywood Association (APA) provides specific recommendations regarding panel grades and their installation (9).

Additional underlayment panels, designated as such by the APA, are frequently recommended for use over wood subfloor structures to provide a smooth substrate for the installation of the flooring. These usually comprise plywood, wafer board, oriented strand board, or untempered hardboard. For use over plywood or other panels, or tongue-and-groove strip wood with less than a 3-in.-wide face, they should have a minimum thickness of ¼ in. For use over non-tongue-and-groove single-layer strip wood or strip-wood subfloors with wider than 3-in. face, ½ in. or heavier plywood is recommended.

In some multifamily residential buildings, wood subfloors are sometimes capped with lightweight concretes or gypsum-based cements to provide certain acoustic or fire-performance characteristics. For use as underlayment for resilient flooring, these materials should have a minimum density of 90 lb/ft³ and have compressive and cohesive integrity commensurate with the floor loadings and type of traffic expected.

Concrete Subfloors

Commercial and institutional spaces usually have concrete subfloors at all grade levels. When properly proportioned, mixed, placed, finished, cured, dried, and—for slabs in contact with the ground—protected from the ingress of groundwater, concrete is an excellent substrate for resilient flooring.

Concrete when poured contains the water needed for hydration of the cement and some extra water to provide fluidity required for the placement and finishing of the concrete. Before any finish flooring can be installed, the concrete must cure and dry sufficiently to allow adhesives to set. The suitability of the slab to receive flooring is established by tests recommended by the flooring manufacturers and may employ moisture meters, measurement of the rate at which moisture is emitted from the slab, or actual bond tests of the product to be installed (10).

The time needed to meet the suggested requirements will vary with the location of the slab, the ambient temperature and humidity, the type of aggregate used, method of cure, and the water : cement ratio used in the mix. A typical, standard density, 6-in. suspended concrete floor, exposed both sides, may take 60 days after placement to dry adequately. Concretes containing lightweight aggregates, cured with combination cure and seal compounds, or exposed on only one side, may require longer drying times.

Floor slabs in contact with the ground (5,11) and exposed to ground moisture may take very long times to dry because water that evaporates may be partially replaced by the influx of moisture from the ground. Improper placement and proportioning of the concrete, particularly the water-to-cement ratio, can result in slabs that will never be dry enough to receive floor finish (11) (Fig. 5).

Most flooring manufacturers will recommend that the slab in contact with the ground be protected from the ingress of moisture by the use of capillary breaks and moisture vapor barriers (Fig. 6).

The curing of concrete to be used in areas designed for the subsequent application of finish flooring should be accomplished by damp curing or protecting with waterproof papers or plastic films (5). Curing compounds, sealers, and hardeners are not generally recommended because of their tendency to interfere with adhesive bonds and, in some cases, they retard the drying process.

Subfloor Preparation

Substrates for resilient flooring should be smooth and flat, structurally sound, and free from foreign materials that may interfere with the adhesive bond or show through the

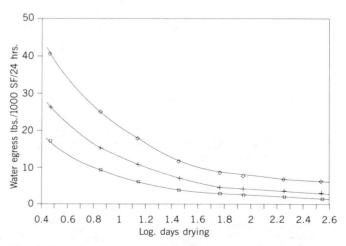

Figure 5. Drying rate of concretes in contact with ground water (11). □: water/cement = 0.4; +: water/cement = 0.5; ◇: water/cement = 0.6.

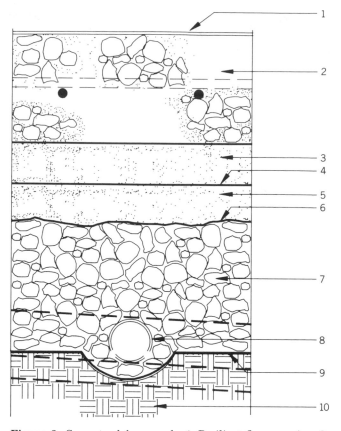

Figure 6. Concrete slab on grade. 1, Resilient floor covering. 2, Reinforced concrete slab. 3, 2 in. sand. 4, Vapor barrier. 5, 1 to 2 in. sand. 6, Geotextile filter. 7, 4 to 8 in. ¾–¼ in. Graded washed drain rock. 8, Perforated drain tile. 9, Geotextile filter. 10, Grade sloped to drain. Courtesy of Craig Henry, Architect.

installed floor. Careful subfloor preparation is an important step in the realization of a successful flooring installation. All protuberances should be ground down; minor depressions, construction joints, and crack relief cuts filled with patching compounds; and overall roughness or irregularity smoothed with mastic underlayment preferably of the latex/portland cement type. Any curing compounds, sealers, or other coatings and treatments not known to be compatible with the installation system should be removed.

SEAMS AND WALL/FLOOR JUNCTIONS

In addition to previous installation information given with the different types of flooring, more information on seaming and wall/floor junctions will be helpful.

Sheet Flooring Seaming Systems

A primary reason for using sheet flooring instead of the generally less expensive tile, aside from aesthetics, is the reduction or elimination of joints. Several different methods are used to produce tight seams that resist the natural tendency of vinyl flooring to shrink and the penetration of liquid spills and cleaning solutions.

Adhesive-Bonded Seams. Seams that are held together by the shear strength of the adhesive used for the installation or specifically for the seam are called bonded seams. Filled wear layer felt-backed products can produce a fairly high tensile force from even small strains induced by subfloor or product dimensional changes. Bonded seams for these products are accomplished with the use of epoxy adhesives applied at the seam area. The normally recommended field adhesive is usually adequate for bonding the seams of rotogravure flooring, but the top of the seam is normally sealed (see below). Some PVC sheet flooring products may be seamed by adhesive bonding when wet-lay, hard-setting adhesives are employed for the installation.

Solvent-Welded Seams. Flooring products with substantial unfilled vinyl wear layers are seamed by solvent welding adjacent wear layers together. These seam sealers contain an organic solvent that is capable of dissolving the vinyl and may also contain some dissolved PVC and plasticizer. The combination of the installation adhesive and seam sealer maintain the integrity of the seam and prevent water penetration.

Heat-Welded Seams. Many solid vinyl sheet-flooring products are installed with pressure-sensitive adhesives that have relatively low long-term shear strength. To assure the integrity of the seams, they are fused together with the help of a vinyl welding rod. After installation, the juncture between two adjacent sheets is routed with a special tool through about two-thirds to three-fourths of its thickness to provide a bed for the welding rod. Then, with the use of a special hot-air heating gun, the welding rod is fused into this routed seam and later skived off level with the flooring surface. These seams, while producing a functionally seamless installation, are quite visible (Fig. 7).

Treatment of Wall/Floor Junction

Most flooring installations are finished with a decorative and functional wall-base treatment. In earlier residential installations, the flooring was installed to the "baseboard" and the fitted edge of the flooring was covered with quarter-round molding. Today, most wall-base coverings are of resilient material, vinyl or rubber, supplied in a range of colors compatible with the installed floor. There are three basic techniques used today to finish the wall/floor junction: top-set wall base, border cove or butt-to-base, and integral or flash coving (Fig. 8).

Top-set base is employed in residential and commercial spaces where normal floor maintenance is used and flooring sanitation is not critically important. The border cove and integral cove are essentially equal in helping to maintain the cleanliness of the flooring perimeter, with the choice between them based primarily on aesthetics.

MAINTENANCE

Flooring maintenance is a significant economic factor in the life of a flooring product. The maintenance procedures,

Routed seam

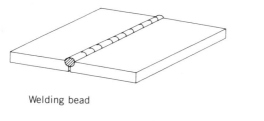

Welding bead

Finished seam

Figure 7. Hot weld procedure.

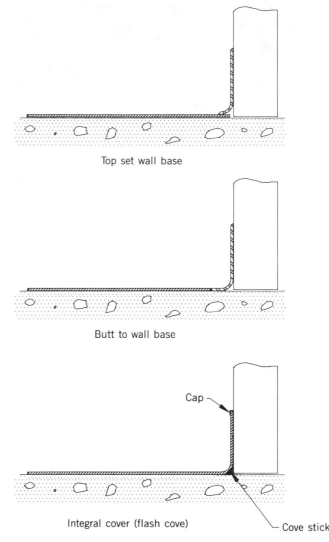

Top set wall base

Butt to wall base

Cap

Integral cover (flash cove)   Cove stick

Figure 8. Floor/wall treatment. **(a)** Top set wall base. **(b)** Butt–to–wall base. **(c)** Integral cove (flash cove).

chemicals, and equipment have changed radically over the past 10 years. For residential applications, many flooring products sold today have a "no-wax" feature. Some may have a factory-applied coating of urethane or urethane/acrylic polymers that have a very high resistance to gloss loss under normal use. Others may have a tough unfilled vinyl wear layer that, although not as resistant to deglossing as the urethane, can still function well without the use of applied waxes or polishes. After all, the major reason for applying wax or polish to a floor is to provide a uniform high gloss. Incidentally, this was not true of the older products of linoleum and asphalt tile, which actually required wax just to provide adequate service performance.

The polishes used on resilient floors also have changed. They are no longer "waxes"; they are sophisticated polymeric films that contain reversible ionic bonds and are referred to as metal cross-linked acrylic polishes. They are tough, detergent resistant, usually nonyellowing films that, when desired for refurbishing, are easily removable with alkaline detergents (stripping solutions).

Although some commercial flooring products have promoted "no-wax" features, it is generally more economically effective to use protective maintenance polishes for general commercial applications (12). The use of modern polishes protects the flooring from abrasive wear, embedment of soil particles, many stains, and the leaching effects of frequent washing, and provides a surface that is easy to maintain at a uniform high gloss.

Three basic maintenance systems are employed in commercial spaces: washing and recoating, spray buffing, and burnishing or dry buffing (13,14).

Washing and Recoating. Initial maintenance consists of building a foundation of polish consisting of sealer, if required, and several coats of polish. Routine maintenance includes sweeping or dust mopping and occasional damp moppings. Periodically the floor is scrubbed and recoated with polish when and where needed to replace worn polish and restore gloss. Stripping and rebuilding foundation are performed when polish buildup becomes excessive or when the surface becomes irreversibly soiled. This procedure is most effective in small or obstructed areas.

Spray Buffing. Initial and routine maintenance are essentially the same as above; however, periodically the floor will be "spray buffed," ie, buffed with a standard or high-speed floor machine while wet with a spray of diluted polish or special restorer, to return the surface to its original gloss. This reduces the frequency of recoating, thereby reducing the rate of polish buildup and subsequently the frequency of stripping. This latter procedure is the single most expensive maintenance operation.

Figure 9. A vinyl sheet floor developed especially for areas where slip resistance is important. The raised disks are embedded with thousands of mineral aggregate particles to aid slip resistance.

Burnishing or Dry Buffing. Again the initial and routine maintenance procedures are similar to the other techniques. However, the foundation consists of at least five coats of high solids polish designed specifically for high-speed maintenance. When it is desired to restore the gloss, the clean floor is burnished at 1500 to 2000 rpm. Restorer solutions or polish coatings applied to areas of heavy wear, unlike spray buffing, must dry before buffing. Dry buffing with ultra-high-speed machines consumes only about one third the time of spray buffing, and with a well-balanced and controlled maintenance system, stripping can be delayed for several years. High-speed burnishing is most cost-effective in large, unobstructed areas.

SUMMARY

Resilient flooring is a unique group of floors that are better suited for certain areas than any other material. In some areas they offer wear resistance and ease of maintenance that would be difficult to achieve with comparably priced materials. In other areas, their qualities, such as cleanliness and resistance to acids and stains, would be almost impossible to duplicate.

In addition to many functional attributes, resilient flooring also offers modern designs and colors that are compatible with almost any interior decorating scheme. They are designed not only for traditional areas but also specialized locations such as ramps requiring slip-retardant surfacing and laboratories and hospitals requiring stain and chemical resistance (Fig. 9). There is a resilient floor for almost any need.

BIBLIOGRAPHY

1. R. F. Lanzillotte, *Hard Surface Floor Covering*, State College of Washington Press, 1955.
2. B. Berkley, *Floors; Selection and Maintenance*, LTP Publishers, Chicago, 1968.
3. U.S. Pat. 3,293,094 and 3,293,108 (Dec. 1966), F. Nairn, and co-workers.
4. International Study Committee for Wear Testing of Flooring Materials, *Wear*, 4(4), 479–494 (1961).
5. American Concrete Institute, ACI 302 IR.80, 1980.
6. American Society for Testing and Materials, Test Method F-510, Philadelphia, Pa.
7. W. E. Irwin, Development of a Test Method to Measure Wear on Resilient Flooring, *Journal of Testing and Evaluation*, 1, 15–20 (1976).
8. A. W. McKee, Study of the Effects of Fillers in Compounding Plastics Flooring, *Society of Plastics Engineers Journal*, 2, 186–190 (Feb. 1962).
9. American Plywood Association, *Product Guide—Performance Rated Panels*, APA F 405F, Jan. 1986.
10. S. H. Kosmata, Floor Covering Materials and Moisture in Concrete, *Concrete Technology Today*, Portland Cement Association, Sept. 1985.
11. H. W. Brewer, *Moisture Migration—Concrete Slab on Ground Construction*, Portland Cement Association, Bul. D89, (May 1965).
12. Booz, Allen, and Hamilton, Inc., *Performance of No-Wax Flooring in the Institutional and Industrial Environment*, Chemical Specialties Manufacturers Association, 1979.
13. C. Zackrison and M. Gindling, The RPM Race—Is It for You?, *Sanitary Maintenance*, (May 1985) pp. 27–29.
14. R. R. Falconio and co-workers, *Resin Review* 35(3), 19–27 (1985); 36(1), 19–24 (1986).

See also WOOD STRUCTURAL PANEL COMPOSITES.

RICHARD MAZZUR
Armstrong World Industries
Lancaster, Pennsylvania

RESTAURANTS AND SERVICE KITCHENS.   See SUPPLEMENT.

RESTORATION, HISTORIC.   See SUPPLEMENT.

RETIREMENT HOUSING.   See HEALTH CARE FACILITIES.

RESTAURANTS

Restaurants, rooms or buildings in which food is served to the public, cover a broad spectrum, from the efficient quick service restaurant, to the flamboyant California coffee shop of the 1950s, to such sophisticated urban restaurants as New York's The Four Seasons. Throughout the world, distinctive restaurants help set or reflect the mood of the country, from European bistros and *trattoria,* to Middle Eastern *tavernas* and *iskembeci,* to Asian *sashimi* or *dim-sum* shops. Whatever the location or setting, each is tailored to meet the specific objectives of the operator and the expectations of the dining public. Each calls for consummate skill from the architect or designer not only to create an image, often a fantasy environment, but also to meet stringent requirements for operation.

Somewhat surprisingly, restaurants, unlike many other building types, are a relatively recent phenomenon, little more than 200 years old. Inns and taverns—Roman thermopoliums, church-run hospices, and British ale-houses—have existed for thousands of years as places for travelers to stop overnight and take refreshment. Yet no restaurants offering food without lodging or bars are recorded. For example, in colonial America inns were established along the post roads and in the larger towns to provide overnight accommodations, and taverns, offering drinks (occasionally food was given away with the purchase of liquor), were common; a 1656 Massachusetts law required that every town establish a tavern. But public restaurants, dining rooms unconnected to hotels or bars, were unknown. However, during the early eighteenth century most towns established an "ordinary," a tavern that offered at a set time a single meal at a fixed price. Eventually, in both Europe and the American colonies, restaurant operations developed to meet growing social needs.

Parisian A. Boulanger in 1765 established a "restorative," generally considered the first true restaurant, which immediately gained great popularity (Table 1). A sign in Latin over the door urged potential customers to "[c]ome to me all whose stomachs cry out in anguish and I shall restore you" (1). Following this modest beginning, the luxury Grande Taverne de Londres opened in 1782. The culinary movement had begun. Throughout Europe and eventually in the American colonies, restaurants were established, often by Huguenot chefs fleeing the French Revolution. Despite the increasing sophistication of both restaurateur and customer, however, any public meal, whether in a tavern, coffeehouse, or hotel dining room, for the most part was poorly prepared and hurriedly eaten amid strangers.

Among the earliest U.S. restaurants of the nineteenth century were the Union Oyster House (Boston, Mass., 1826), Delmonico's (New York, 1827), the Tremont House (Chicago, Ill., 1838), and Antoine's (New Orleans, La., 1840). However, only a small percentage of the population, the very wealthy, ever ate in these elegant and expensive restaurants; there were practically no restaurants other than bars or taverns available to the general public. Travelers dined in their hotels, families ate three meals at home, and workers usually returned home for lunch. Not until the Industrial Revolution, following the Civil War, did the burgeoning working and middle classes provide clientele for public restaurants. The earliest types of res-

Table 1. Restaurant Milestones

Before 1875

1634 Samuel Cole opened first tavern, or ordinary, in Boston, Mass.
1765 A. Boulanger established restorative in Paris.
1782 Grande Taverne de Londres offered luxury dining in Paris.
1827 Delmonicos opened wine and pastry shop in lower Manhattan, New York.
1865 Bookbinder's Restaurant, still family-operated at the same location, opened in Philadelphia, Pa.
1872 Lunch wagon first served factory workers in Providence, R.I.

1875–1900

1876 Fred Harvey opened first depot restaurant on Atchison, Topeka, and Santa Fe Railroad in Topeka, Kans.
1882 Luchow's opened in New York.
1898 Louis Sherry opened new restaurant on Fifth Avenue across the street from Delmonico's.
1898 Child's Cafeteria opened in New York.
1898 Horn & Hardart opened first Automat in Philadelphia.

1900–1925

1903 Hamburgers first served on bun at St. Louis World's Fair.
1919 Allen and White opened first A&W root beer stand; first franchised restaurant company.
1919 Conrad Hilton purchased Mobley Hotel in Cisco, Tex.; beginning of the modern hotel chain.
1919 Volstead Act established prohibition of liquor.
1921 Pig Stand restaurant opened on Dallas–Ft. Worth highway; first drive-in with curb service.
1921 White Castle hamburger chain founded in Wichita, Kan.
1925 Howard Johnson opened first restaurant in Wollaston, Mass.

1925–1950

1928 J. W. Marriott opened A&W stand in Washington, D.C.; converted it to Hot Shoppe in the winter.
1933 Prohibition repealed.
1939 McDonald brothers opened drive-in restaurant in San Bernardino, Calif.; converted in 1948 to self-service, limited-menu operation.
1949 John Lautner designed Googie's and Douglas Honnold designed Tiny Naylor's, among the first flamboyant California coffee shops.

1950–1975

1952 First Holiday Inn opened by Kemmons Wilson in Memphis, Tenn.
1954 J. McLamore and D. Edgerton franchise first Burger King.
1955 Ray Kroc opened his first McDonald's restaurant in Des Plaines, Ill.
1958 Thomas Wells designed Snack Shop in Honolulu, Hawaii predecessor of restaurants emphasizing natural materials.
1959 The Four Seasons restaurant opened in New York, designed by Philip Johnson with others.
1962 Chart House restaurants founded in Aspen, Col.
1968 McDonald's changed building prototype to more restrained brick and mansard style.
1969 Theme restaurant chain Victoria Station founded.
1971 Wendy's founded, incorporating drive-through window in all stores.
1973 Oil embargo: quick service restaurants expand in urban areas.

1975 to present

1976 Warren Platner designed Windows on the World in New York.
1987 Joe Baum reopened the Rainbow Room at Rockefeller Center, New York/Hugh Hardy, architect.

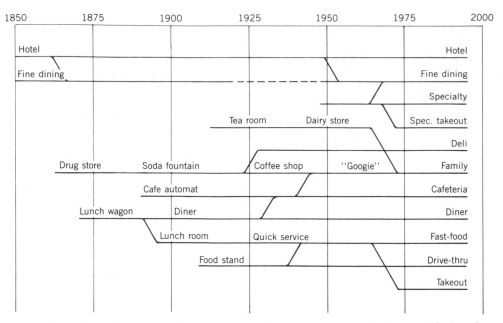

Figure 1. Restaurant evolution: diagram represents the evolutionary development during the late 19th and 20th centuries of restaurants.

taurants offering inexpensive meals were horse-drawn lunch wagons parked outside factories, soda fountains, and cafeterias. These food service innovations, which identified and met the specific needs of new markets, heralded the beginning of a period of constant innovation in the restaurant industry (Figure 1).

In the United States, restaurants have undergone explosive growth in this century, increasing from only a few thousand mostly independent operations in 1900 to almost 300,000 units in 1985. Restaurants today range from quick service to full service, takeout to luxurious dining rooms, theme menu and motif to classical cuisine and decor. Restaurants are classified by type of food service: quick service, cafeteria, family restaurant/coffee shop, specialty/theme restaurant, and fine dining restaurant. In some cases, these distinctions are blurred as new concepts develop that cross over conventional definitions. By all accounts, the restaurant industry is an immense business; for example, the National Restaurant Association estimates that 1985 sales in restaurants in the United States exceeded $110 billion and by 1990 will exceed $150 billion. Also, it has become an industry ruled by national and regional chains. More than 150 companies operate at least 200 individual restaurants (McDonald's alone has over 9500 outlets worldwide and revenues of nearly $13 billion), 1400 companies manage some type of quick service unit, and 350 run fine dining establishments (2).

EVOLUTION OF RESTAURANT TYPES

The scores of different types of restaurants around the world attest to the creativity of both the restaurant operator and the architect or designer. In addition, the elements that combine to give a restaurant its character and ambiance are so complex, and affect each other so differ-

ently, that innovations in concept and design continue to blossom. Although restaurant architecture and interior design is fundamental to establishing the concept, the restaurateur first must define a number of important factors, such as those included later in the restaurant concept checklist (Table 2). These variations in menu, price, service, etc, can help to define the different categories discussed below. Other types of restaurants, such as delicatessens, cafes, brasseries, and gourmet takeout operations, in fact, bridge the classifications provided here and offer unique characteristics of their own.

In addition to the independent or chain restaurants are such other types of food service operations as those for hotel dining; corporate and industrial feeding; museum, sports, and other recreational outlets; and colleges, hospitals, and other institutions. No matter what the setting, however, these exhibit many of the same characteristics as the individual restaurants; hotels, for example, usually include an informal restaurant (hoteliers disdain the term coffee shop), a speciality or theme restaurant, and in the larger cities, a fine dining outlet. Museums and corporate offices offer upscale cafeterias, and practically everywhere some variety of quick service eating is available.

Quick Service Restaurants

The quick service restaurant, familiar to diners in every corner of the world, is exemplified by its limited menu (often preprepared), low price, and self-service layout, generally represented by customers ordering at a counter and taking their meal to a seating area or outside. Today's quick service or fast-food outlets, which have evolved from food stands, lunchrooms, and drive-ins, are undergoing a revolution in menu and design. Competing with hamburger and chicken outlets are restaurants serving healthier or upscale foods in distinctive, creative settings.

Most quick service restaurants still have fairly small seating capacities, under 100 seats, although in the large chains the trend is toward larger in-store dining rooms, with room for more than 150. Architecturally, fast-food restaurants are generally in free-standing structures, surrounded by parking, and although once characterized by a bold, assertive design in the 1950s and 1960s, they now exhibit crisper lines and subdued colors and materials. The bright interiors, which typically include easily maintained materials and finishes, are not intended to make the customer so comfortable as to linger after a meal. Recently, quick service restaurants have been more commonly housed within shopping centers or tucked into city storefronts, forcing on the architect a more constrained facade design.

Quick service restaurants have developed from a variety of basic, highly space-efficient operations that were established in the late nineteenth century to meet the needs of U.S. factory workers. The first of these was the lunch wagon (1872), a horse-drawn cart barely large enough for the operator to prepare sandwiches and dispense them through a window; larger versions had room sufficient to accommodate four or six customers at a narrow counter inside the wagon. The assembly-line wagons were a forerunner of such prefabricated restaurants as White Castle (1928) and Krystal (1932). As the demand for meals increased, larger prefabricated restaurants resembling railroad dining cars were permanently located at busy sites. The additional room in these diners provided for a kitchen along one side, separated from the customers by a linear counter and an expanded menu, which allowed them to compete with luncheonettes and coffee shops.

Increasing demand during the period from 1880 to 1920 saw the growth of low-priced, large-volume lunchrooms in nearly every city. The usual procedure was for customers to walk to the rear, select their food, and carry a tray to a seat. The larger lunchrooms were designed with several parallel rows of small tables, sometimes supplemented with counter seating; smaller operations provided tablet-arm chairs or one-person booths to accommodate the demand yet maximize the turnover for single diners. Practically all lunchrooms were located on street level in urban areas; their only architectural feature was some minimal signage on the facade; their Spartan interiors had few amenities and easily maintainable finishes.

Restaurants began to take on a stronger identity when they were developed as free-standing operations. White Castle, which erected its first white enameled-block outlet in 1921, no more than 10 × 15 ft, was remarkable for gaining almost immediate public acceptance for a level of quality and consistency of product in a period when low-priced restaurant food was suspect. Clearly, the standardized building design, with gleaming white surfaces and a view of the kitchen, was an essential element of the chain's success (Figure 2).

After World War I, local residents established food stands along the highways, little more than sheds decorated with advertising, with windows through which simple sandwiches and drinks could be served. They were far from distinguished, either by architecture or food. A few of the owners, however, playfully constructed structures

Figure 2. White Castle (c. 1932). The chain moved from enameled-block buildings to prefabricated, demountable, metal-panel structures in the early 1930s, still exhibiting the crenellations and other castlelike details of the first stores. Courtesy of White Castle.

that advertised their offerings: buildings in the shape of ice cream cones, milk cans, coffee pots, fish, burgers, and the like. As highway traffic increased, larger roadside eateries opened. The Pig Stand, along the Dallas–Ft. Worth highway, was the first to offer curb service, in 1921. Others quickly copied the ideas; A&W root beer had tray girls serve customers from drive-ins shaped like root beer barrels. Drive-ins developed most quickly in California, a natural result of the automobile-oriented lifestyle and the mild climate. Eventually, the restaurants were designed in an octagonal or circular shape with sweeping roof overhangs to let cars pull up around them more easily and featured brightly lit signs, often on vertical pylons, and art deco or modern details.

In the 1940s and 1950s, the phenomenal increase in automobile ownership as well as suburban development fueled the expansion of more elaborate drive-ins in all parts of the country. In contrast, simpler restaurants, little more than refreshment stands, such as Dairy Queen, opened relatively plain one-story buildings. The McDonald brothers, operating a drive-in in San Bernardino, Calif., realized that many more customers could be served more quickly with takeout service; as a result, in 1948 they changed their concept; eliminated carhops; simplified the menu to hamburgers, drinks, and french fries; and renovated their building. Their model introduced the concept of the modern fast-food restaurant (3,4).

The McDonalds refined a system that provided quick service at low prices, created high profits, and satisfied customers. Their first franchise prototype building, in 1952, set a standard too. Richard McDonald himself designed the key elements: the sloping roof visually supported by illuminated yellow arches, the red and white tile cladding, and bands of neon lighting (Figure 3). In the late 1950s and in the following decade, dozens of fast-food

Figure 3. McDonald's (Downey, Calif., 1953). The original McDonald's prototype, designed by Stanley Meston, features stripes of red and white tiles, soaring yellow arches, upturned roof, and a curtain wall facade to attract the highway customer. Photograph by Alan Hess.

Figure 4. Jackets (New York City, 1985). The quick service, limited menu restaurant featuring stuffed potato skins shows the use of bold graphic and visual images—neon signage, "roughly torn potato skin" walls, and blue "sky" beyond the lighting grid—which create a lively dining environment. Courtesy of Arlen & Fox, Architects. Photograph by Jim D'Addio.

chains were established, many copying the operational concept and design elements of the McDonald's prototype. Most companies experimented primarily with the design of the roof line, including signs and features that would make it more visible and identifiable along the growing commercial strips. Carrols and Burger King built crisp angular wings; Kentucky Fried Chicken designed a tall red-and-white-striped pyramidal roof; Pizza Hut conceived a double-gambrel shape. In the mid-1960s, many of the original takeout restaurants added enclosed seating and, by the 1970s, drive-through service, although it had been a part of earlier Pig Stand restaurants and smaller West Coast chains of the 1950s.

The 1970s and 1980s have shown continued development and refinement of the chain quick service restaurant and innovation and architectural creativity in the newer quick service concepts. Partly in response to a growing concern about the visual environment, chain designers modified their prototype designs by simplifying the roof lines, incorporating such natural materials as brick and wood, choosing subtler earth-tone colors, reducing the impact of signage, and adding landscaping. For example, Burger King replaced its painted metal roof and walls with cedar shakes and brick and established extensive standards for plantings, paving materials, site lighting, and signage. As these restaurants moved into malls and downtown locations, their designs carefully echoed the surrounding environment. McDonald's architectural department has promulgated an extensive array of designs, including colonial designs in New England, art deco at Rockefeller Center, and glass pavilions in suburban shopping centers.

Independent quick service restaurants do not have the advantage of a chain identity and national advertising campaign. Instead, their design must establish an immediate impression of the menu and environment through the creative use of materials, lighting, color, and graphics. Usually, these restaurants also stand out because they focus on an inventive food concept that is reinforced in the interior design (Figure 4). At Quincy Market in Boston, scores of mostly independent quick service operations, each with its own creative identity, are housed in the central building of a primary shopping and tourist destination. With the increased cultural emphasis on snacking or "grazing," the consumption of smaller amounts of food throughout the day or evening rather than the three traditional meals, newer quick service concepts should continue to grow.

Cafeterias

Cafeterias offer several key departures from the usual quick service restaurant: a much more extensive menu, a style of self-service by which the customers pass down a long line selecting from displayed items, and generally a much larger seating capacity. Two key segments, the commercial cafeteria and the subsidized or institutional operation, have enjoyed quiet growth over the past several decades. Most successful commercial cafeterias today are one-story, free-standing buildings, often located in or near shopping centers or along commercial strips. In the 1980s, some cafeteria operators are expanding to other sites, often to locations that attract an older clientele. Others aim to grow by offering upscale food to young adults. Subsidized cafeterias occur not only in schools and similar institutions, but also in such upscale locations as museums, universities, and corporate offices, for which high-quality interior design and food presentation are essential.

Among the earliest cafeterias were those developed by the YWCA (Kansas City, Mo., 1891) and other philanthropic organizations late in the nineteenth century. Before the turn of the century, commercial restaurant entrepreneurs opened the Exchange Buffet near the New York Stock Exchange and the first Child's Cafeteria in New York (1895). At that time, there were few alternatives between lunch wagons or low-priced lunchrooms and elegant private or hotel restaurants. Partly because of their large menu and lack of effective competition, the innovative cafeteria operations immediately became successful and remained the primary type of restaurant well into the 1920s.

At the turn of the century, the Horn & Hardart Co. created a special type of cafeteria, the Automat, where customers placed coins into slots next to an item, opened the glass door, and carried the food to their seats, in a system not unlike that of modern vending machines. The Philadelphia Automat glittered with polished glass and tile, oak paneling, and brass hardware. Horn & Hardart expanded rapidly, primarily to New York, where they constructed a series of elegant, marble- or tile-floored, high-ceilinged halls to house their innovative food dispensing machinery. Architecturally, the Automats were the first restaurants to establish a large-scale treatment of the facade, the stone and plate glass elevations providing the customer with a grand view of the sparkling interior and the gleaming machinery. Other restaurant types began to recognize the merchandising value of both a higher-class exterior design and of visible and inviting sanitary interiors (5).

Cafeteria chains have continued to evolve, although with less publicity and fanfare than quick service and other types of restaurants. Early regional chains such as Bishop's Buffets and Morrison's, both still in existence, continually change their menus to attract large numbers of customers. (Other types of restaurants find it much more difficult to modify their menus quickly to respond to changing tastes in the industry.) For example, Morrison's has begun to emphasize takeout food in many of its locations. In the subsidized cafeterias of such operations as museums or corporate offices, the design of the servery and dining room are considered among the more important public areas. They provide one of the principal locations for informal interaction among employees. As a result, although some cafeterias are used for a variety of eating, meeting, and lounge purposes, designers often are called upon to provide a restaurantlike ambiance, with visually separate seating areas for privacy, greater attention to lighting and acoustics, and interior materials that convey an upscale image (6).

Coffee Shops and Family Restaurants

Family restaurants introduce a number of amenities not found in the first two restaurant types. The mid-priced family restaurant, in some classifications a coffee shop, offers a moderately large menu served at a counter and at booths or tables in a separate dining room. Its design introduces the clear separation between public and service areas, with the kitchens usually fully hidden from the public's view. This permits a much different ambiance in the dining room, which leads to a longer stay and more relaxed dining experience.

Among the first restaurant organizations in the United States was Harvey House, which operated restaurants and hotels at railroad depots throughout the Southwest, opening 45 restaurants between 1876 and the turn of the century. Many were simple outlets with nothing more than counter service, the predecessors of later low- and moderate-priced coffee shops; others offered full dining rooms with table service. The buildings were straightforward and functional; however, later projects, which usually included a depot hotel, were imaginative, elegant, and sophisticated, frequently based on Spanish or Indian themes and design motifs.

The key elements of the coffee shop developed in the later part of the nineteenth century as a response to a growing working population and expanding eastern and midwestern cities. The drug store/soda fountain, which initially served sweet beverages, became immensely popular after the invention of the ice cream soda. As more and more opened (reportedly, 75,000 were in operation soon after the turn of the century, with more than 3,500 in metropolitan Chicago), operators expanded their counter offerings, and they began to function as restaurants (7). These luncheonettes gained popularity in cities and small towns. Helped by Prohibition beginning in 1919, when full-service restaurants suffered a substantial loss in business, medium-priced restaurants, more often called coffee shops, flourished. Chock Full o' Nuts's graphic logo complemented the modern glass, stone, and metal facades, opening up the New York storefronts visually and encouraging customers to enter.

In the same period, the diners improved their quality and expanded their menus. To better compete, newer diners added architectural enhancements: stainless steel sides, plate glass windows, parapets to obscure a raised roof profile, and greatly expanded seating, particularly booths and tables to supplement the earlier counter.

In the 1920s, as the United States began to take to the roads, the need arose for family dining in more rural areas. In small communities, tearooms opened in a variety of rustic or quaint settings. At the same time, the modern chain restaurant was established when, in 1925, Howard Johnson took over the operation of a drug store/soda fountain outside Boston. Soon he added ice cream stands during the summer season and a full-service restaurant. In 1935, he franchised his first restaurant, according to his design and operating standards; within five years, he added more than 125, each displaying some combination of typical colonial New England features: small-paned windows, gabled roofs capped by cupolas, and dormers. Balustrades, shutters, and weathervanes added detail (Figure 5). Johnson recognized the need to make his restaurants stand out along the highways and sheathed the roofs with orange porcelain tiles, a trademark that continued even as the prototype restaurants were redesigned into modern Florida and California styles. The exterior had a stately presence. The restaurant interiors were de-

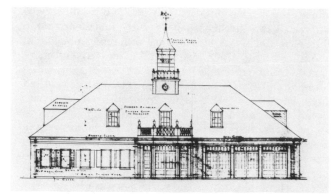

Figure 5. Howard Johnson's (1937). Design by Joseph G. Morgan incorporating the use of Georgian details, cupola, dormers, and a high level of ornamentation, makes a dignified and substantial looking restaurant. The second floor was generally used for offices or storage. Courtesy of Philip Langdon.

Figure 6. Norm's (Los Angeles, Calif., 1954). The California coffee shop features the usual over-scaled roof and signage to attract attention on the commercial strip and soaring windows to present views into the brightly lit interior. Armet and Davis Architects. Courtesy of Alan Hess.

signed flexibly enough to appeal to varying markets. One side featured counter seating for breakfast or light meals, which was used for ice cream in the afternoon; the dining room had a comfortable feel, with wood-beamed ceilings and paneling, not unlike the rural tearooms; often, a second room contained a bar or was used for banquets or overflow. In the postwar period, Howard Johnson's architects developed a series of designs more appropriate to the period and to expansion outside the Northeast: low-hipped roofs overhanging plate glass windows, materials other than clapboard, and stylized cupolas or spires. The interiors were also modernized: plastic laminate replaced the wood surfaces, and such accessories as clocks and lamps were updated (8,9).

A wholly different type of modernization took place in California in the 1940s and 1950s with an exuberant style featuring sharply angled roof shapes, bold signs thrusting skyward, and brightly colored and illuminated interiors seen through full-height plate glass windows (Figure 6). The jumble of shapes and materials, although derisively hailed at first, had significant assets: the soaring roof lines raised high the front facades, increasing natural light and views both in and out. The interiors were similarly dramatic, yet functional. With a variety of counter, booth, and table seating, often the layouts were organized to provide privacy or views to the street or of such inside activity as that of the grill area. Several architects gained national attention: John Lautner for Googie's and Armet and Davis for literally dozens of dramatic California coffee shops, including later prototype designs for Bob's Big Boy and Denny's (10,11).

The flamboyant California coffee shops were appropriate for some sites, but by the mid-1960s, communities began to resist the bright colors and strange conglomerations of shapes, in coffee shops as well as fast-food restaurants. Architect Tom Wells created several restaurants featuring natural materials and flowing, open spaces. Colwell and Ray developed a more residential prototype for Denny's, with a brick exterior, a low tiled gable roof, interior wood beams and paneling, a fireplace, and full carpeting for the dining room. For the next decade, family res-

taurants and coffee shop chains remodeled to bring earlier outlets into line with the current more reserved mood of the country.

Family restaurants continue to serve a large segment of the dining public. However, in the 1980s, most of the architectural innovation has been to other types of restaurants, primarily the specialty and theme restaurants, which by their nature are highly differentiated and focused on specific preferences in food, service, or ambiance.

Specialty and Theme Restaurants

Specialty restaurants include a wide range of different types of outlets, but are distinguished by a special menu, an unusual style of service, or a distinct theme, such as the railroad cars of the Victoria Station chain. For the most part, the restaurants offer a limited menu, moderate to high average check, liquor, and usually, full table service. Unlike other restaurant types, specialty and theme restaurants are open only during one or two meal periods daily.

Most early twentieth-century restaurants focused on efficiency and on adapting technology or building materials to the food service industry; few focused on any sort of special theme. However, in Boston, William Childs (the cafeteria innovator) created a series of novel restaurants, not unlike modern Disney creations, with dining rooms thematically decorated to give the appearance of a variety of European settings. Meanwhile, across the continent, in Los Angeles, Clifton Cafeterias were designed around such fantasy settings as a redwood forest and a Polynesian paradise (12).

There was little development of new theme or specialty restaurants for three decades, until the mid-1960s, when a number of new chains became popular. Some, such as steak houses (Steak & Ale) or seafood restaurants (Brighton Fish Pier), established limited menus; others emphasized nostalgic decor and artifacts (TGI Friday's and Houlihan's); a few were constructed in highly thematic settings (Victoria Station); whereas others featured innovative service or presentation (Benihana of Tokyo and Fuddruckers). Victoria Station, which grew in the 1970s to over 100 units, clustered 4 or 5 railroad cars around a waiting room/bar to create a variety of dining and drinking spaces, which seated over 200 and were connected to a kitchen built in a new structure (Figure 7). The theme was reinforced by a myriad of accessories from the British railways, such as authentic baggage carts, lamps, and signs; the refurbished boxcars were finished with wood paneling and timbered ceilings. A red London phone booth stood outside the entrance.

While restaurant design has often been criticized for its lack of architectural quality, some specialty restaurant companies have built their reputation at least in part on ambitious design standards. Chart House has constructed more than 50 units, most of them remarkably different in design, including renovated boathouses (Annapolis, Md. and San Diego, Calif.), a remodeled 200-year old New England Home (Simsbury, Conn.), an adapted coal bin (Newport, R.I.), and such sensuous new restaurants as the Kendrick Kellogg-designed restaurant with its sweeping wood roof in Rancho Mirage, Calif. (1980) (Figure 8). Chart House executives are convinced of the value of architectural quality in restaurants today: "If you compromise the design then you dilute the success factor" (13).

Figure 8. Chart House (Rancho Mirage, Calif., 1980). Organic design for Southern California specialty restaurant exemplifies use of natural materials and respect for the landscape; the building, fit into the hillside, and featuring massive cantilevered roofforms, brings exterior desert gardens and water features into the dining areas. Courtesy of Kendrick Bangs Kellogg.

Specialty restaurants can be of almost any type: the design theme might be nautical, recreate the mood of a racetrack or diner, or surround the customer with life-sized cartoon figures. The ethnic menu may suggest a highly thematic native decor, Mexican or Japanese for example, or an architectural approach using understated motifs or decorative patterns. Many restaurants include takeout food using displays of fresh vegetables, fruits, and baked goods or stacks of packaged gourmet delicacies or wine as the visual focus of the entry or dining room (Figure 9). These operations combine profitable and visually stimulating aspects of both food retailing and restaurants.

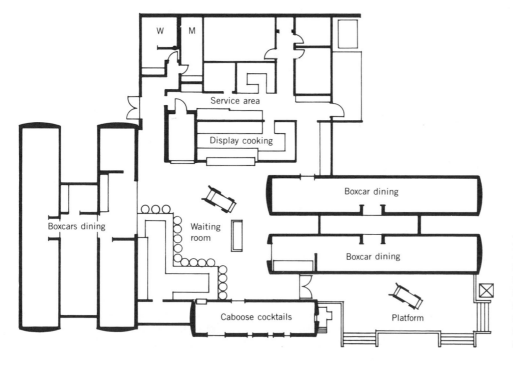

Figure 7. Victoria Station (1970). Plan of highly thematic dinnerhouse seating about 220 people composed of British railroad cars and numerous artifacts used both decoratively and functionally, for example, baggage carts are adapted as salad bars. Courtesy of Victoria Station.

Figure 9. DDL Foodshow (Beverly Hills, Calif., 1985). A combination of gourmet takeout and sit-down restaurant celebrates the colorful presentation of fresh food in a theatrical setting; more than 10,000 ft² and a two-story volume provide opportunities for drawing customers past the displays to the mezzanine restaurant at the rear. Courtesy of Adam D. Tihany International. Photograph by Toshi Yoshimi.

Fine Dining Restaurants

Fine dining restaurants are the most complex type in many ways, in part because they are practically always individually designed and operated; they do not benefit from the standardization of the chain restaurants. Fine dining represents an extensive menu and full service, sometimes including the tableside preparation of special items, and a relatively high check average. The size of the restaurant is perhaps the most variable characteristic: intimate restaurants may have fewer than 50 seats, whereas others, which also still offer superb food and service, may have several hundred seats and additional banquet rooms.

The best dining rooms were found originally in the elegant hotels of large cities. Eventually, restaurants opened nearby to compete. In New York, John and Peter Delmonico in 1827 opened a modest cafe in lower Manhattan, little more than a wine and pastry shop occupying a single room with half a dozen plain tables. The restaurant was an immediate success, and several generations of Delmonicos over nearly 100 years opened a succession of 11 different restaurants moving northward as the city grew. That their names soon became synonymous with fine dining reinforced Brillat-Savarin's earlier definition of a restaurateur (1825): "a person whose trade consists in offering to the public an ever-ready feast, the dishes of which are served in separate portions, at fixed prices, at the request of each consumer" (14). Generally, however, the middle half of the last century offered few dining alternatives to hotels, taverns, or the few elegant and expensive restaurants. Later in the century, though,

European immigrants established taverns in their neighborhoods. These occasionally evolved into drinking halls with free buffets, and soon ethnic restaurants such as Luchow's (1882) opened. Competition was intense. To compete with the grand hotels and Delmonico's, Louis Sherry established a world famous restaurant in a 12-story Stanford White building on Fifth Avenue.

The early twentieth century brought major changes to the fine dining restaurants. Chains of low- and medium-priced restaurants eroded the business, followed by World War I and, in 1919, the Volstead Act prohibiting the sale and service of alcoholic beverages, which caused nearly every elegant restaurant to close. During Prohibition, New Yorkers flocked to small, ethnic, family-owned restaurants with minimal amenities, better equipped to survive than the grander establishments uptown. The dining traditions established in those elegant restaurants for the rich were lost.

In the decades following World War II, restaurateurs reestablished in the larger cities elegant restaurants catering primarily to business people at lunch and society at dinner. Among the best-known restaurants in the world is The Four Seasons, designed by Philip Johnson for the first floor of the Seagram Building in New York (Figure 10). Opened in 1959, The Four Seasons, with more than 500 seats in 2 dining rooms, 3 banquet rooms, and a bar, combines impeccable food and service with an understated and elegant interior that is legendary. The main dining room features a central 20 × 20-ft pool of Italian marble and window coverings made of chains of alternating brass, copper, and aluminum, which shimmer and ripple from the air movement of the HVAC system. Artwork is prominent: an immense Picasso painting hangs in the gallery between the two dining rooms, and a Lippold sculpture of brass rods is suspended above the bar, effectively lowering the ceiling height. Every detail—the table settings and accessories, printed graphics, plantings, the chairs designed by Mies van der Rohe, Charles Eames, and Eero Saarinen—complements the architecture. The Four Seasons, as much as any other single restaurant, satisfies Frank Lloyd Wright's axiom for a successful restaurant: "to give the people something better and more beautiful than they have ever seen or had" (15).

A second large New York restaurant of first-class design is Windows on the World, designed by Warren Platner for the 107th floor of the World Trade Center in lower Manhattan (Figure 11). Platner arranged a marvelous variety of public spaces around the perimeter of the building: reception lounges, the City Lights Bar, the Cellar in the Sky (wine room), a restaurant seating 350, and 17 private dining rooms. Most of the dining and lounge spaces are tiered to provide views and added privacy to those tables away from the exterior windows. Among the most impressive spaces is the Gallery, an interior corridor leading to the dining rooms, which combines photographic images of international scenes with multiple reflections from glass and mirror surfaces to create the impression of a bridge.

More common are smaller destination restaurants, each designed with a carefully conceived mix of food, service, and ambiance. The design concept can be practically

Figure 10. The Four Seasons (New York City, 1959). The classic design of the main dining room by Philip Johnson and William Pahlmann, focused around a marble fountain anchored by four fig trees, endures unchanged after 30 years of continual refurbishment. Courtesy of The Four Seasons. Photograph by Louis Reens.

anything, given *haute cuisine* and attentive service. Although a number of these restaurants may be oriented towards a view, the great majority are introverted designs, emphasizing the interiors and a memorable restaurant experience. Many are trendy; those that are designed to last, however, attempt a more classic design (Figure 12).

RESTAURANT PLANNING

The critical elements of a restaurant, whatever the type, are food, service, and ambiance. The restaurant developer or operator generally approaches the new or renovation project from the operational viewpoint, considering how the market, competition, dining habits, and trends influence the range of choices among menu, type of service, price, and hours. The restaurant design, architectural and interior, follows the operational concept. Design professionals, on the other hand, may first approach the project as a design problem, allowing the operational concept to

follow the physical solution. Restaurant designers must understand the needs of and accept a close working relationship with the restaurateur, whose interests and efforts are entrepreneurial.

Developing the Restaurant Concept and Program

The restaurant industry has shown amazing vitality and creativity over the past decade, during which both chain and independent operators have developed a myriad of new concepts. Often, the developer may undertake substantial amounts of research, even test-marketing a prototype before introducing the product more widely. Developing a concept requires several steps and a combination of talents. The need for consultants abounds. In addition to the usual project team, including the owner or developer, architect, interior designer, and food service consultant, such specialties as lighting, graphics, menu concept development, and marketing may be added to help ensure success. The accompanying checklist briefly identifies the variety of organizational, operational, and design issues that the project team must confront (Table 2).

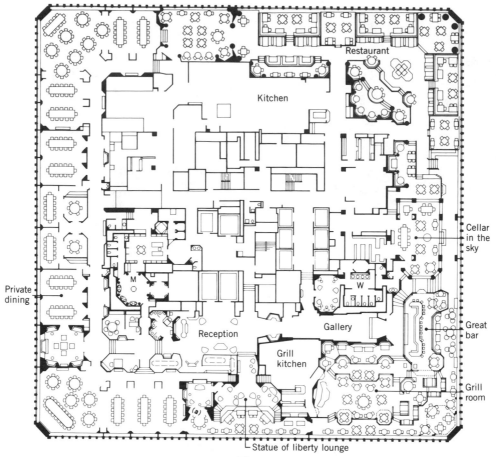

(a)

Figure 11. Windows on the World (New York City, 1976). (a) Plan: the rooftop complex combines a myriad of dining and drinking spaces around the perimeter of the World Trade Center; for example, the restaurant overlooks the length of Manhattan stretching to the north, the Grill and Statue of Liberty Lounge feature views of New York harbor. (b) The Great Bar: ceiling finishes and mirrored panels reflect the city lights below. Courtesy of Warren Platner Associates. Photograph by Alexandre Georges.

(b)

(a)

(c)

(b)

(d)

Figure 12. (a) Le Bernardin (New York City, 1986). Dining room within the Equitable Center seating 110 is luxuriously furnished with such residential touches as porcelain lamps, features a carefully detailed teak ceiling, and showcases the owners' art collection. Courtesy of The George Office. Photograph by Peter Paige. (b) The Remington (Houston, Texas, 1982). The luxury hotel incorporates brightly daylit public spaces whose architectural details and furnishings recall English garden rooms. Courtesy of Intradesign. Photograph by Jaime Ardiles-Arce. (c) Spring Green (Spring Green, Wisc., 1954): a late design of Frank Lloyd Wright (yet not completed until 1967). The restaurant combines the classic prairie materials, low gabled roof, and clerestory windows with soft-colored finishes and diffused lighting. Courtesy of Taliesin Associated Architects. Photograph by John Amarantides. (d) Prospect Centre (Princeton, N.J.). The understated dining room of the graduate and faculty center serves as background to the views of manicured gardens on the Princeton campus. Courtesy of Warren Platner Associates. Photograph by Ezra Stoller.

The programmatic requirements for restaurants vary according to the type of outlet. For some, the architecture, or at least the street facade, is crucial for establishing an image and attracting customers; for others, the principal requirement is efficient planning of the kitchen facilities to produce a large number of quick service meals throughout the day. The program is intimately tied to the business plan prepared by the owner or operator. This, of course, includes an analysis of the local market conditions and financial projections. But it also must focus in detail on the specifics of the proposed restaurant and the costs involved in development and operation. The development costs are based, in part, on the restaurant facilities that are required to meet the market's expectations (Table 3).

Table 2. Restaurant Concept Checklist

Organizational Concept
- ☐ Type of restaurant
- ☐ Chain or independent
- ☐ Name of outlet
- ☐ Location
- ☐ Market description
- ☐ Financial projections
- ☐ Capital requirements
- ☐ Staffing

Operational Concept
- ☐ Menu
- ☐ Capacity
- ☐ Operating hours
- ☐ Style of service
- ☐ Off-site dining (drive-through, takeout)
- ☐ Use of service staff
- ☐ Pricing philosophy
- ☐ Merchandising opportunities
- ☐ Entertainment
- ☐ Separate bar/lounge
- ☐ Cash settlement

Architectural Concept
- ☐ Building form
- ☐ Siting
- ☐ Image
- ☐ Materials
- ☐ Plan organization
- ☐ Entry
- ☐ Interior design

Dining Room Concept
- ☐ Entry sequence
- ☐ Food/wine display
- ☐ Self-service/buffet
- ☐ Decorative treatment
- ☐ Atmosphere
- ☐ Seating type and mix
- ☐ Lighting
- ☐ Level changes
- ☐ Tabletop design
- ☐ Uniforms

Table 3. Restaurant Functions

Public (front of the house)

Reception	Vestibule, foyer (waiting, display, takeout), support (toilets, coats, phones, vending), office
Dining room	Host, seating, merchandising elements (food display, exhibition cooking, self-service buffet) support (wait station, service bar, cashier)
Banquet rooms	Foyer, seating, banquet office
Bar/lounge	Bar, seating, stage, dance floor, support (bar storage, sound equipment)

Service (back of the house)

Kitchen	Servery, hot foods production, cold foods production, prepreparation, dishwashing, pot washing, bakery, storage (clean dishes, silver), drive-through station
Receiving	Receiving, refuse, storage (dry and refrigerated food, liquor, wine, paper goods)
Support	Mechanical rooms, employee areas (lockers, toilets, training room), utility room (cleaning supplies, furniture storage, etc)

After establishing the concept in general terms, based on the operational requirements of the owner or operator, the architect or designer must establish an appropriate relationship among the restaurant functions, depending on the type of operation. For example, the planning requirements for a quick service operation, with a relatively open kitchen and self-service by the customer, are quite different from those for a fine dining restaurant in which the kitchen is fully separated and the wait staff provides every need (Figure 13).

In addition, conceptual planning requires an estimate of the total amount of floor area required. The design team must establish the space program, remembering to allocate sufficient area to support functions, in both the front and back of the house. Table 4 provides space requirements, per seat, for three distinct levels of restaurant operation. Although these guidelines are representative of most restaurants of each type, developers need to use them with caution and adjust them to meet the specific requirements of a particular project. The table illustrates a number of rules of thumb that the restaurant operator and architect should recognize.

1. Dining room seating varies substantially from as little as 10 ft^2/seat in quick service operations to over 20 ft^2 for luxury dining with tableside service.
2. The ratio between the public and service areas is approximately 60:40 for a full-service restaurant; for takeout, quick service, and limited-menu table service restaurants, it can vary from 25:75 to 75:25, depending on the amount of kitchen storage and production space.
3. The public support functions require 10–15% of the area of the public spaces; the service support functions require about 25% of the kitchen and food storage area.

Designing the Restaurant Exterior

Restaurant images are established by a balance of the interior design and the exterior architecture, in addition to the food, service, and other operational elements. Certainly, in quick service outlets, and many other chain restaurants, the building shape, color, materials, and signage create a single image that may be duplicated hundreds of times and may be the most important marketing tool of the company. The design of the building's exterior has several goals: to communicate correctly the type of restaurant, to attract customers, to set a mood or theme, and to establish an identity. In the 1930s, for example, Howard Johnson founded the first large roadside family restaurant chain behind a facade of traditional architectural details, whereas Chock Full o' Nuts established a group of urban coffee shops featuring crisp, contemporary facades of polished stone, glass, and mirror. The former was intended to catch the eye of the motorist seeking a

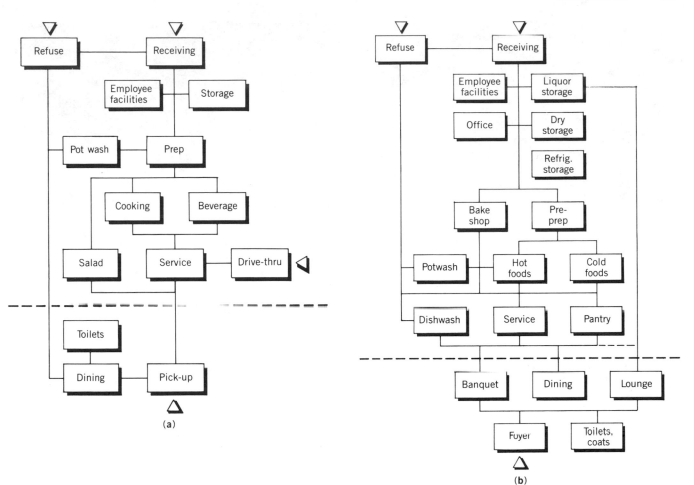

Figure 13. Schematic diagrams. (**a**) Quick service restaurant; (**b**) fine dining restaurant.

secure and safe restaurant, the latter the pedestrian who could view the spotless interiors through the visually open storefronts.

Restaurants in the 1980s include chain operations that have moved beyond the national prototype to offer a range of exterior designs that better fit particular regions or individual sites. McDonald's, for one, designed restaurants for a renovated colonial house (Freeport, Me.), the concourse at Rockefeller Center, and a floating barge

(Vancouver, B.C., Canada, Expo). These newer chain designs, although responsive to local demands or desires, tend to be highly restrained and feature familiar materials and motifs. Despite this, restaurants may offer the architect more latitude in design than practically any other building type. New operations, not affiliated with chains, must stand out among the competition, and architectural design offers unique opportunities. There is no single approach: some architects incorporate bold and

Table 4. Restaurant Space Requirements

	Quick Service, ft²/seat	Family/ Coffee Shop, ft²/seat	Fine Dining ft²/seat
Public (front of the house)			
Dining room	10–12	14–16	20–24
Bar		14–18	16–20
Banquet		10–14	12–20
Pickup	2–3	2–3	
Support	1	2	2–3
Service (back of the house)			
Kitchen	5–8	6–8	7–10
Receiving/storage	3–5	2–3	2–3
Support	2–3	2–3	3–4
Total	*22–30*	*24–32*	*35–40*

(a)   (b)

Figure 14. **(a)** Domino's Pizza (Jackson, Mich., 1988). A prototype for future freestanding stores which are intended to be recognized from a great distance, the building has a semicircular roof line with a wedge slightly removed. Courtesy of Gunnar Birkerts and Associates. Photograph by Randall Mascharka. **(b)** Fishdance (Kobe, Japan, 1987). A fantasy construction combining an industrial shed (dining room), a ziggurat-shaped, copper-clad structure representing a coiled snake (bar and lounge), and a sculptural wire-mesh fish provide a variety of interior dining environments. Courtesy of Frank O. Gehry and Associates.

bright forms, much like those of the original quick service outlets and California coffee shops, or postmodern or other fashionable but short-lived architectural details; others introduce a clever graphic or name trick (Franks for the Memory); many design unexpectedly high-quality materials, lighting effects, or furnishings to make the restaurant stand out (Figure 14).

In addition to the purely aesthetic decisions, the architect must deal with several practical problems in the building and site design. All restaurants require attention to the entrance facade, whether along a commercial strip, on an urban street, on a country road, or inside a shopping mall. In some cases, a single flat facade can define the type of operation. But free-standing restaurants require careful attention to all sides: motorists approach at highway speeds, pedestrians approach more slowly, and customers park beside the service entrance. Operators of most restaurants, except for the more expensive ones, insist that the elements of the interior design and operation be visible to potential customers outside.

Planning the Restaurant Interior

Once the overall operational and architectural concepts have been established, the design team focuses on two principal tasks: functional planning and interior design. The latter is the more visible, of course, yet the former often more fully influences, in a less conscious way, the guests' reactions to the restaurant (Figure 15). There are five critical issues in planning:

1. Organization of the entrance sequence.
2. Arrangement of the dining room(s) and lounge.
3. Layout of the tables.
4. Connection between the dining room and kitchen.
5. Design of the kitchen and back of the house.

Other issues, although potentially important, are certainly less critical to the operating and experiential success of a restaurant.

The entrance foyer or reception space offers the designer a number of opportunities for establishing the mood and ambiance of the restaurant, while at the same time solving a variety of functional requirements. The reception area may include or have adjacent to it such ancillary functions as a weather vestibule, toilets, coats, vending, phones, office, host/maitre d', cashier, food display, or takeout counter. Several of these are best grouped together, whereas others should be the visual focus or immediately identifiable. The restaurant customers arrive with certain expectations for the ambiance, service, and food, and the designer must try to anticipate these; the plan should lead the guests to the host, to the coat room and toilets, or to the bar or dining room.

The arrangement of the dining room(s) and lounge is a second planning consideration. Larger-capacity restaurants should be broken up into smaller intimate areas to enhance the dining experience and to provide greater privacy. This arrangement also offers the opportunity to use only certain rooms or areas, depending on the meal period or the demand for seating; separate rooms are often required for private functions. The dining rooms should be clustered closely around the kitchen to facilitate service and must have supplemental service areas within the public area. The cocktail lounge or bar might be somewhat more removed from the kitchen and relate more to the entrance.

The table arrangement is usually determined by the interior designer or the operator, but the architect should consider the implications of the design on the eventual layout. Certainly, the mix of tables for two ("deuces"), four, or six or more must be based on the anticipated business. In addition, the restaurateur wants every table to be desirable to potential customers. Some guests, depending on the type of operation, prefer tables by the windows or

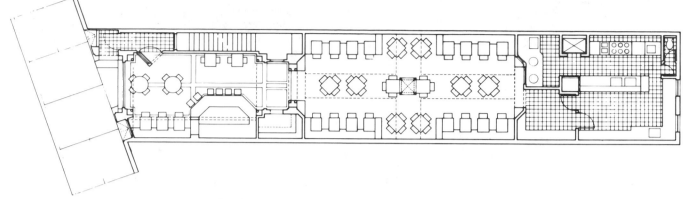

(a)

(b)

Figure 15. Indian Oven (New York City, 1985). **(a)** Plan: a series of architectural volumes, linked by gateways, organize a long, narrow space into separate bar and dining room. **(b)** Interior: the Indian motif is expressed by the procession of arches and the refined use of millwork trim. Courtesy of Peterson/Littenberg Architects. Photograph by Peter Margonelli.

next to a display, against the wall (privacy), away from the kitchen and aisles, near the entrance (to be seen), and so forth. The larger tables, for six or eight diners, may best be relegated to the less desirable locations in the dining room. Table 5 illustrates common table sizes and their space requirements for three levels of restaurants.

The architect should clearly define the relative separation of the public and service functions, especially the con-

nection between the dining room and the kitchen. Of course, in quick service, cafeteria, and coffee shop operations, the cooking or serving areas are purposely integrated into the dining room. But in other types of restaurants, the customer should perceive only the public areas. Service traffic should be contained in the back of the house; no direct sightlines into the kitchen should be permitted; and noise, light, and odors form the kitchen must be controlled.

Table 5. Restaurant Table Sizes

	Quick Service, in.		Coffee Shop, in.		Fine Dining, in.	
	Table	Space[a]	Table	Space[a]	Table	Space[a]
	24 × 24; 24 dia	60 × 24	30 × 24	72 × 24	34 × 30	84 × 30
	24 × 42	60 × 42	30 × 48	72 × 48	34 × 54	84 × 54
	30 × 30; 30 dia	60 × 60	36 × 36; 36 dia	72 × 72	40 × 40; 42 dia	78 × 78
	24 × 60	60 × 60	30 × 72	72 × 72	34 × 84	84 × 84
	30 × 60	60 × 90	36 × 60	78 × 102	40 × 72	90 × 120
	42 dia	72 × 72	48 dia	90 × 90	54 dia	102 × 102
	24 × 84	60 × 84	30 × 96	72 × 96	34 × 108	84 × 108
	30 × 72	60 × 102	36 × 84	78 × 126	40 × 96	90 × 144
			60 dia	102 × 102	66 dia	114 × 114

[a] Space is the area required for the table and chairs, excluding major aisles.

Usually, a food service consultant is retained to design the kitchen and storage areas. The kitchen planner attempts to meet several functional objectives to simplify the operation and to reduce eventual staffing needs. These planning goals include providing a straight-line flow of food from storage to the service area, eliminating cross traffic, minimizing the distance between the kitchen and dining room, and providing necessary service support in the public areas. The kitchen design also influences sanitation practices, employee safety and productivity, and energy use of several utilities. The capital costs of the kitchen exceed those of any other portion of the restaurant.

No single part of the restaurant design may be as important as proper lighting, which allows the customer to see the space, food, and dining companions. The lighting designer's task is to consider four important lighting needs:

1. Effect of light on the restaurant space, especially the walls, ceiling, and other surfaces.
2. Effect of light on the food presentation, including any food displays.
3. Effect of light on the diners, especially their appearance to their companions.
4. Functional requirements, including the ability to read the menu, move through the space, serve, and clean.

Of course, the type of restaurant greatly influences the type of lighting solution and, in fact, the relative importance of lighting as a design element. In quick service outlets, cafeterias, and coffee shops, where the interior design is generally less carefully conceived and where the budgets are lower, lighting is a less important design tool. For other restaurant types, where lighting is critical to the success of the concept, most restaurant lighting consultants consider the interplay of two equally important lighting approaches: the need for general overall illumination and the impact of special lighting effects. The basic lighting must be fairly even, whether at a high or low lumen level, in order to minimize high contrasts. One goal is to try to light the surfaces of the room, realizing that these create the mood and ambiance and that reflected light is probably sufficient for most specialty and fine dining requirements. The lighting must be highly adjustable, so that the mood can be changed from breakfast, when it should be brightest, to lunch, tea, cocktails, dinner, and after-dinner periods, the most intimate and dimly lit. If the dining room has large amounts of natural light, the overall lighting scheme must be designed to compensate for the resulting uncomfortably bright areas of the room, possibly by increasing the light level in the areas removed from the windows. For example, preset dimmer systems are available that automatically adjust the lighting levels based on the meal period, desired mood, or outdoor lighting conditions.

The restaurant is enhanced if the lighting design creates such special effects as patterns on the walls or ceiling and highlights on sculpture or other art, bars, pools or other focal points, food displays, or exhibition cooking areas. Such special lighting sources as wall sconces, chandeliers, table lamps, or candles may be appropriate to the type of restaurant and the overall lighting and design concept.

Many low- and medium-priced restaurants use overall fluorescent lighting; some newer operations have added high levels of incandescent lighting to attract attention to entrances, order or pickup areas, menu boards, or food displays. Often, an important goal is to highlight the interior so that as a merchandising tool it is brightly visible to those outside. In addition, as more attention is placed on the importance of the facade and the overall architectural treatment of restaurants, and as the public becomes more sophisticated, exterior illumination is increasingly used as a design element.

Future development and design innovation should continue in all categories of restaurants; each plays an important role in serving the members of the community. Imaginative architects and designers, creative operators, and enterprising developers and owners will continue to collaborate on original restaurant concepts. The increasingly sophisticated dining public seeks out the bold and innovative on the one hand and crisp, elegant, classic design on the other. Each can be as appropriate for the quick service outlet as it is for fine dining—it depends entirely on the skills of the architect and the clarity of the design and operational concept.

BIBLIOGRAPHY

1. A. Harael, "Food Service: How It All Began," *Nation's Restaurant News*, 72 (Sept. 15, 1975).

2. *Directory of Chain Restaurant Operators*, Business Guides, Inc., New York, 1987.

3. P. Langdon, *Orange Roofs, Golden Arches*, Alfred A. Knopf, New York, 1986, pp. 81–109.

4. C. Liebs, *Main Street to Miracle Mile, American Roadside Architecture*, New York Graphic Society, New York, 1985, pp. 212–216.

5. Ref. 3, pp. 13–24.

6. S. Colgan, *Restaurant Design, Ninety-five Spaces That Work*, Whitney Library of Design, New York, pp. 215–218.

7. Ref. 3, p. 9.

8. Ref. 3, pp. 46–55.

9. Ref. 4, pp. 199–204.

10. A. Hess, *Googie, Fifties Coffee Shop Architecture*, Chronicle Books, San Francisco, Calif., 1985, pp. 61–95.

11. Ref. 3, pp. 113–129.

12. Ref. 3, pp. 23–25.

13. "Chart House, A Corporate Overview," *Restaurant Design*, 36 (summer 1981).

14. J. Jacobs, *New York a la Carte*, McGraw-Hill Inc., New York, 1978, p. 2.

15. "Frank Lloyd Wright on Restaurant Architecture," *Food Service*, 17 (Nov. 1958).

Comprehensive and fully referenced histories of specific types of restaurants include Langdon (U.S. chain restaurants), Liebs (roadside restaurants), Gutman and Kaufman (diners), and Hess (California coffee shops). Recent restaurant surveys including color photographs and plans are books by Alejandro, Cohen and Emery, Colgan, frequent volumes published by Shotenkenchiku (Tokyo), and all issues of *Restaurant/Hotel Design International* magazine. Earlier surveys including many international restaurants are Aloi, Atkin and Adler, Dahinden and Kuhne, Fengler, and Schirmbeck. Somewhat more technical information and planning data are in Lawson (newly revised and expanded), Rutes and Penner, Wilkinson, and Baraban and Durocher.

General References

W. Atkin and J. Adler, *Interiors Book of Restaurants*, Whitney Library of Design, New York, 1960.

M. Fengler, *Restaurant Architecture and Design, An International Survey of Eating Places*, Universe Books, New York, 1971.

G. Aloi, *Restoranti*, Ulrico Hoepli Editore, Milan, Italy, 1972.

J. Dahinden and G. Kuhne, *New Restaurants, An International Survey*, Verlag Gerd Hatje, Stuttgart, FRG, 1973.

J. Wilkinson, ed., *The Anatomy of Foodservice Design 1*, Cahners Books, Boston, Mass., 1975. Includes chapters on coffee shops, fast service, and institutional food service.

J. Wilkinson, ed., *The Anatomy of Foodservice Design 2*, CBI Publishing Co., Boston, Mass., 1978. Includes chapters on cafeterias, specialty restaurants, and hotel food service.

R. Gutman and E. Kaufman, *American Diner*, Harper & Row, New York, 1979.

E. Schirmbeck, *Restaurants, Architecture and Ambience*, Architectural Book Publishing Co., New York, 1983.

E. Cohen and S. Emery, *Dining by Design*, Cahners Publishing Co., New York, 1984.

W. Rutes and R. Penner, *Hotel Planning and Design*, Whitney Library of Design, New York, 1985.

F. Lawson, *Restaurants, Clubs and Bars*, Van Nostrand Reinhold Co., New York, 1987.

R. Alejandro, *Restaurant Design*, PBC International, New York, 1987.

R. Baraban and J. Durocher, *Successful Restaurant Design*, Van Nostrand Reinhold, New York, 1989.

See also RESTAURANT AND SERVICE KITCHENS

RICHARD PENNER
Cornell University
Ithaca, New York

REVIEW BOARDS, ARCHITECTURAL

Writing in Daniel Burnham's legendary *Plan of Chicago* in 1909, (which clearly advocated the need for overriding some property ownership freedoms in the interest of a designed "city beautiful"), attorney Walter L. Fisher predicted: ". . . there is every reason to believe that any method of taking . . . land justified by the reasonable purpose of controlling the environs of a public place would withstand the scrutiny of the United States Supreme Court. . . ." (1).

This proved to be true, as 45 years later Justice William Douglas was to write in the majority opinion in the case of *Berman v. Parker:* "The concept of the public welfare is broad and inclusive. . . . The values it represents are spiritual as well as physical, esthetic as well as monetary. It is within the power of the legislature to determine that the community should be beautiful as well as healthy, spacious as well as clean, well balanced as well as carefully patrolled" (2).

Significant other developments were occurring during this time. The first comprehensive zoning ordinance was enacted in New York City in 1916, and the concept of zoning was declared constitutional by the Supreme Court in *Euclid v. Ambler Realty Company,* 1926. Private regulation of land in the form of restrictive convenants was also maturing, primarily in connection with residential developments and large retail projects.

Also, important performance-oriented criteria were beginning to emerge in new federal legislation relating to historic preservation, environmental quality, air pollution, water pollution, noise, etc. These were founded on the rediscovery of Renaissance principles of urban design, the increasing body of research in both the physical and social sciences, the invention of new means of measuring visual and other environmental phenomena, and improved microprocessor-based analytical equipment.

Although the greater use of objective criteria will

greatly assist the regulated achievement of design quality, it has been recognized by public and private entities alike that a design review board is usually necessary for sensitive and realistic application of this information for quality control in specific cases.

ROLE OF COMMUNITY ASSOCIATIONS: PRIVATE DESIGN REVIEW

Presently there are more than 125,000 private community associations in the United States, of which 95% have restrictive design covenants enforced by a design review process. Community acceptance of covenant-based design review appears to be most successful if the community affected contains no more than 5000 dwelling units. Problems occur if the covenants are too restrictive, unenforced, or if review decisions are inconsistent.

One of the largest community associations with covenants establishing a design review process is the new town of Reston, Virginia, with more than 15,000 residential units, where design review is a function of the Reston Association. Its design review board is composed of seven registered architects, most of whom are currently town residents, and two lay members, Reston residents not trained in the fields of architecture or land planning.

THE AIA STUDY: PUBLIC DESIGN REVIEW

In 1968, the AIA Committee on Design commissioned a survey of the policies and practices of 221 then-existing local government design review boards. One finding correlated with the legal background outlined above: most of the 101 responding design review boards has been in existence less that 10 years, and only one fourth had been operating for more than 20 years. The Committee also found that architects made up 97% of the representation on such boards, ". . . followed by landscape architects, 'property owners,' 'citizens,' artists-designers, and engineers, in that order" (3).

The study identified several challenges in implementing the review-board process. First was the problem of assuring procedural fairness in a system dependent on discretionary authority. Another was the issue of how much room to leave for freedom of project design expression. And there was the matter of assuring equal protection and precluding exclusionary practices.

URBAN DESIGN

A solution to these and other concerns will be found in the adoption of a community design at an influential scale; such a design may already be evident or prepared with relative ease in the case of historic districts or large new proposals. It can require both uniformity and, in other cases, variety—in manageable degrees. This professional urban design would be consistent with a larger scale city plan and, in turn, would take precedence over all the smaller scale project designs in the subject community. It

would take great care to avoid racial bias and to ensure that the needs of all envisioned economic groups could be accommodated.

Such a urban design would then be administered with a review board selected for its competence (education and experience) in performing at that scale with regard to the matters being regulated, with significant conflict of interest procedures in operation. Composition of the board can include "citizen" members, but state professional licensing statutes and legal case precedents suggest that a design review board quorum should contain at least a majority of qualified designers.

SCOPE OF REVIEW

Successful project plans in some well-regulated communities may pass through two or more review boards. For example, a house design in a subdivision might need to be reviewed by a private-sector developers' or a community association's review board to determine conformance with restrictive covenants that may more permanently control items not then regulated by the local government. These could include landscaping concerns, orientation of garage doors, and style. To avoid a conflict between review boards, most communities require that a design pass a developers' review board before it is accepted for review by the government review board and that the covenanted design standards have previously been approved by the community.

The best review board procedures require that all submitted work be prepared and sealed by a registered architect or other licensed design professional as appropriate, even if not so required by other state or local statutes or regulations, and additional designers may have advised on the quality of that aforementioned house through review board processes by the time it is erected.

Public review boards need not limit their review to private sector development or to elements placed by a traditional architect–builder process. Local government boards of design review regularly handle such issues as the development of land within the community owned or controlled by other governments and the design of such elements as traffic control equipment containments, power transformer screening, telephone booths, vending machines, automatic teller machines, signs, and lighting, all of which are visible to the public.

With the advance of technology and increasing leisure time, review boards are often called on to consider design approaches to manufactured housing; on-site parking of recreational vehicles such as motor homes and trailered boats; solar collectors; radio and satellite TV antennas; and building accessories such as awnings, window air conditioners, additional site lighting; and exterior shutters or blinds.

Some of these are especially serious matters for building and community appearance with respect to tall residential condominium structures, where individual-unit-owner proposals for modifications may occur after the original architect–builder group has completed its work.

At least one government permits no such additions without association and community review board approval of a prototype; it also requires re-approval if it is proposed to remove an architectural element or change the approved exterior colors of any development.

MAINTENANCE OF QUALITY

Maintenance of quality falls under the general category of regulating the quality of the building stock over time, which to date has been addressed by very few local governments. Dade County, Fla., the most advanced in this respect, requires most buildings above the scale of a single-family house to be reviewed at age 40 years (and every 10 years thereafter) to determine whether its certificate of occupancy should be withdrawn.

This recertification review, paid for by the owner and conducted by a private-sector design professional, does not yet extend directly to review board aesthetic matters, although it may portend another aspect of activity in the future so that the design quality of the community is fully protected over time.

BIBLIOGRAPHY

1. W. L. Fisher, "Legal Aspects of the Plan of Chicago," in D. H. Burnham and E. II. Bennett, *Plan of Chicago*, The Commercial Club, Chicago, 1909, pp. 127–156.
2. *Berman v. Parker,* 348 U.S. 26 (1954).
3. Committee on Design, *Design Review Boards: A Handbook for Communities,* The American Institute of Architects, Washington, D.C., 1974.

General References

Ashley/Myer/Smith, Signs/Lights/Boston Project, *City Signs and Lights,* The Boston Redevelopment Authority, Boston, Mass., 1971.

J. Barnett, in F. So and J. Getzels, eds., *The Practice of Local Government Planning,* 2nd ed., International City Management Association, Washington, D.C., 1988, pp. 187–191.

B. Bookin and L. Epstein, *Regulating Radio and TV Towers,* Planning Advisory Service Report Number 384, American Planning Association, Chicago, Ill., 1984.

A. Bowsher, *Design Review in Historic Districts,* The Preservation Press, National Trust for Historic Preservation, Washington, D.C., 1978.

M. Brodeur, "Preparing Urban Design Guidelines," *Florida Planning* 8(10) (June 1988), pp. 5–6.

C. Browne, *The Mechanics of Sign Control,* Planning Advisory Service Report Number 354, American Planning Association, Chicago, Ill., 1980.

C. J. Duerksen, *Aesthetics and Land Use Controls,* Planning Advisory Service Report Number 399, American Planning Association, Chicago, Ill. 1986.

W. R. Ewald, Jr. and D. R. Mandelker, *Street Graphics,* The American Society of Landscape Architects Foundation, Washington, D.C., 1971. Revised edition: D. R. Mandelker and W. R. Ewald, Jr. *Street Graphics and the Law,* Planners Press, American Planning Association, Chicago, Ill., 1988.

P. Glassford, *Appearance Codes for Small Communities,* Planning Advisory Service Report Number 379, American Planning Association, Chicago, Ill., 1983.

R. Hedman with A. Jaszewski, *Fundamentals of Urban Design,* Planners Press, American Planning Association, Chicago, Ill., 1984.

Junkyards, Geraniums and Jurisprudence: Aesthetics and the Law, American Bar Association, Chicago, Ill., 1967.

L. Kendig, *Performance Zoning,* American Planning Association, Chicago, Ill., 1980.

J. L. Nasar, "Viewpoint," *Planning* (May 1988), p. 46.

R. Roddewig, *Preparing a Historic Preservation Ordinance,* Planning Advisory Service Report Number 374, American Planning Association, Chicago, Ill., 1983.

W. Sanders, *The Cluster Subdivision: A Cost-Effective Approach,* Planning Advisory Service Report Number 356, American Planning Association, Chicago, Ill., 1980.

W. Sanders, *Regulating Manufactured Housing,* Planning Advisory Service Report Number 398, American Planning Association, Chicago, Ill., 1986.

W. Sanders and D. Mosena, *Changing Development Standards for Affordable Housing,* Planning Advisory Service Report Number 371, American Planning Association, Chicago, Ill., 1982.

H. Shirvani, *Urban Design Review,* Planners Press, American Planning Association, Chicago, Ill., 1981.

R. Tseng-yu Lai, *Law in Urban Design and Planning: The Invisible Web,* Van Nostrand Reinhold, New York, 1988.

C. Tunnard and B. Pushkarev, *Man-Made America: Chaos or Control?,* Yale University Press, New Haven, Conn., 1963, reprinted 1966; Harmony Books, New York, reprinted 1981.

Urban Renewal Administration, Housing and Home Finance Agency, *Design Review in Urban Renewal, Technical Guide 15,* U.S. Government Printing Office, Washington, D.C., 1965.

M. Vance, *Building Laws: A Bibliography,* Vance Bibliographies, Monticello, Ill., 1985.

M. Vance, *City Planning and Redevelopment Law: Monographs,* Vance Bibliographies, Monticello, Ill., 1985.

M. Vance, *Zoning and Zoning Law,* Vance Bibliographies, Monticello, Ill., 1985.

R. Warburton, *A Model Recertification of Buildings Process,* University of Miami, Coral Gables, Fla., 1982.

R. Warburton, "A Progressive Approach to Zoning and Building Codes," *Systems Building News* (July 1971), pp. 42–49.

R. Warburton, "Evaluation of Proposals for Operation Breakthrough," *Industrialization Forum* 1(4) (July 1970), pp. 9–17.

R. Warburton, "Recertification of Buildings—An Idea Whose Time Has Come," *Technology Talks Conference,* The American Institute of Architects, Washington, D.C., 1983.

R. Warburton, "Toward a Systematic Approach to Design Values," *High Speed Ground Transportation Journal* (January 1972); reprinted in The Open University, *Urban Development,* The Priory Press, St. Albans, UK, 1973.

See also FINE ARTS COMMISSION; URBAN DESIGN—ARCHITECTURE AT URBAN SCALE; URBAN DESIGN—CREATION OF LIVABLE CITIES

RALPH WARBURTON, FAIA,
F.ASCE, AICP
University of Miami
Coral Gables, Florida

RICHARDSON, HENRY HOBSON

Henry Hobson Richardson was born at the Priestly Plantation in Louisiana on September 29, 1838. During his brief but productive career of 21 years he had perfected building solutions and design formulas for a wide range of building types, many of which were new to his age: small-town and large-scale libraries, campus buildings, train stations, cathedrals, courthouses, city halls, state capitals, the commercial block, and the suburban home. As a gauge to the important role Richardson attained in his day, the *Amercian Architect and Building News* in 1885 polled its readers for, "the ten buildings which the subscriber believes to be the most successful examples of architectural design in the country." Of the top 10 choices, half were by Richardson. Trinity Church, Boston (1872–1877) was voted first (nominated by 84% of the voters). Also on the list were these works by Richardson: Albany City Hall, Albany, N.Y. (1880–82); Sever Hall, Harvard University (1880–1882); New York State Capital (1867–1898); Town Hall, North Easton, Mass. (1879–1881).

At the time of his death in April 1886 at the age of 47, Richardson was at the peak of his career, and the architecture that he had raised to a national style and that bore his name—Richardsonian Romanesque—could not be ignored by aspiring young architects who hoped to fall heir to his architectural dynasty. However, as evidenced by the assortment of buildings selected as Richardson's best, there was no consistent agreement as to what constituted the basis for his achievements even by his peers. Much, then, that would be mimicked in Richardson's work did not strike at the heart of his style.

Today, the term Richardsonian Romanesque is perhaps one of the most generalized stylistic categories in architecture; its vagueness allows one to apply the term to nearly any structure from the mid-1870s to the turn of the century that used rock-faced granite ashlar, one or more apparent arches, or a host of architectural features that one associates automatically with the master, namely, eyebrow windows, octagonal library rooms, short stubby columns, or the so-called "Loire dormers." Oddly, the term maintained as much latitude at the end of the nineteenth century as it does today, and an architect who mimicked all or any of these typologic elements could legitimize his end product by referring to it as Richardsonian. But these disparate parts in themselves do not begin to constitute the essence of Richardson's style; they are simply part of the design vocabulary that accompanies a more vital grammar. Instead, these design elements are synthesized into a powerful language that emerges from a very conscious and consistent design process that most Richardsonians failed to perceive.

Richardson's architecture, when analyzed according to the basic forms it assumed, presents a reliable key to the underlying creative formulas that would lend his total work the qualities of consistency, strength, clearness of conception, and repose (1). This article will provide a formalistic study of Richardson's architecture based on an examination of his preliminary sketches and completed work as abstract forms in an attempt to establish what patterns emerge in his work and to identify the essential qualities that make Richardson's reinterpretation of historic styles (such as the Romanesque) distinctive. Through such a study, it will be seen that Richardson's approach remains relatively static and (after Sever Hall, 1878) responds little to changes in material or civic or domestic programs, because what is given from the first sketch is a Richardsonian formula—a consistent aesthetic response applied to five architectural formats, within which all functions are sensitively arranged and clearly expressed. It is inappropriate, then, to make distinctions of substyles within Richardson's mature work (ie, the Queen Anne, the shingle style, or Romanesque) on the basis of the materials used or the typologic elements employed—they are simply Richardsonian.

Richardson developed many of his design principles and his design process while at the Ecole des Beaux Arts (from 1859 to 1865, but principally in 1861). He was the second American to study at the Ecole (preceded only by Richard Morris Hunt). There, a student was required (generally within a day's time) to establish a *parti* or schema that incorporated the required program and to present an *esquisse* (quick sketch). Both the *parti* and the *esquisse* would then be developed into scaled and tinted drawings and be presented to the *patron* of the *atelier* for criticism, the final presentation having not deviated at all from the primary elements of the original *esquisse*.

A perusal of Richardson's sketches reveals that he maintained his quick sketch technique throughout his career. W. A. Langdon, who had functioned as Richardson's local superintendent in Washington, recalls Richardson's design process in an essay of 1900 (2,3):

> Often done in bed, where the state of his health obliged him to spend much of his time . . . a plan two or three inches square embodied his idea. The ultimate result of his study was inked in over the mass of soft pencil marks with a quill pen, and sometimes principal dimensions were figured. That was usually the end of his work on paper.

It seems appropriate to examine these first impulse sketches in order to arrive at those qualities that best define the essence of Richardson's work, for these sketches provide the viewer with direct insight into the creative process and aid in establishing what elements Richardson felt most comfortable with and relied on constantly for massing and program solutions.

Through a study of the various schemes for buildings, which are recorded on the numerous sketches by Richardson (mainly in the possession of Harvard's Houghton Library), certain observations can be made. One notices, for example, the tendency to rely on imposing rooflines (which after 1875 are usually unbroken along the ridge) as an organizing element and as a means of achieving repose (Fig. 1). The roofline, by providing a strong visible statement, lends unity to the design as a whole as opposed to the nervous profiles of Queen Anne and Victorian Gothic forms; this is found to be true even in his Watts–Sherman house of 1874, where there is a piling up of rooflines. The front gable in this structure, nevertheless, rules supreme in the hierarchical arrangement of forms and establishes a focal point. By stretching the roof out-

Figure 1. Roof as a symbol and unifying element. Through the use of roof forms Richardson "domesticates" his monuments and "monumentalizes" his domestic scale structures. **(a)** Emmanuel Episcopal Church, Allegeny City., Penn., 1883–1886. **(b)** North Easton railroad station, North Easton, Mass., 1881. **(c)** J. J. Glessner House, Chicago, Ill., 1885–1887. **(d)** Watts Sherman House, Newport, R.I., 1874. **(e)** Sever Hall, Harvard, Cambridge, Mass., 1878–1880. **(f)** Chamber of Commerce, Cincinnati, Ohio, 1885. By A. Ioannou.

line nearly two stories down to the masonry construction of the first floor, it visually unites the home with the earth and reinforces the human scale of the structure. This "hovering" quality of the roof is especially apparent in Richardson's designs for the North Easton and Chestnut Hill railroad stations. In these examples, the roof fully embraces (and nearly smothers) the structure below as it overtly expresses its function to shield passengers and carriages from the elements.

The roof, then, lends monumentality as well as unity (compositional, spatial, and textural) by its forceful presence and at the same time becomes a symbol of home or shelter. This play of monumentality and domesticity can be merged (as in the Watts–Sherman house) or manipulated for its associative aspects to achieve the desired

results. Richardson effectively used roof forms as a symbol to temper or reinforce the impact he desired in a building. For example, he would use a very apparent hip roof to temper the impersonal quality of a tall and expansive civic building, such as the Cincinnati Chamber of Commerce (1886–1888), or to help stretch the horizontal lines of Harvard's Sever Hall while serving to relate it conceptually to colonial structures nearby. When unbroken rooflines were coupled with uniform surface treatment and tight wall surfaces, Richardson had achieved the basic ingredients of his mature style. Note the powerful image of the Glessner house. The long gable ridge line, parallel rows of rock-faced granite ashlar, and forceful expanse of uninterrupted wall (150 ft long) all serve to reinforce horizontality and continuity of planar surfaces while establishing a weighty and rooted presence. Yet, the house form, when viewed abstractly, takes on the appearance of a simply central-hall eighteenth-century Colonial domestic structure with an attached ell. This visual alignment with familiar Colonial house forms was an attempt to balance the assertive design gestures of the explosion of scale, rugged wall surface, and inordinate length that otherwise counter the associations of home. It was Richardson's ability to pull forms across the surface of the building and to use expressive building materials skillfully that transformed this simply domestic outline into a monumental structure. At the same time, Richardson's handling of uniform surface texture within a unified wall plane preserved visual unity despite the variety of features and demonstrates how Richardson had reconciled the use of singular picturesque elements of Queen Anne styling to be compatible with his design philosophy of a unified whole. The window and door openings in the Glessner house, for example, withdraw into the wall mass, allowing the wall to assert itself even further as a singular element. Individual elements (such as the Saracenic arch that leads to the service wing) maintain their own

life and personality, but not just as singular sensational elements that call out for attention (as in Queen Anne styling); instead, they become subordinate parts of a larger compositional scheme. Richardson, having relied heavily on Queen Anne design features and handling earlier in his career, resists (after 1878) sacrificing the whole to the power of its parts.

Richardson, then, through the manipulation of rooflines and materials, is able to lend his domestic structures monumentality and his monuments, domesticity. The use of the roofline as a domineering and symbolic element provides the viewer with the simplest (though perhaps the most forceful) organizing scheme (see Fig. 1). Close observation of Richardson's sketches also reveals that except for his earliest works, such as the Unity Church (Springfield, 1866–1869), and when it was necessary to compromise his design for economic reasons, as in the case of the Emmanuel Episcopal church (4), Richardson generally avoided placing entrances at the gable end of a building, preferring instead to place the entrance on axis with the long side of a building (Fig. 2). The gable entrance structures generally signal the still immature

Figure 2. Tower–gable–arch. *Church format.* **(a)** Unity Church, Springfield, Mass., 1866–1869. Entry on gable end, arched entry integrated with tower. **(b)** Grace Church, Medford, Mass., 1867–1869. Octagonal apse, tower separate from gabled porch and arch entrance. **(c)** Winn Memorial Library, Woburn, Mass., 1877–1878. Octagonal museum wing, tower and gable merged archway off to side. Latin cross design with entry through side porch. *Large scale library format.* **(d)** Billings Memorial Library, Burlington, 1883. Features now integrated in compressed form. Perfected format for large scale libraries. *Small town library format.* **(e)** Ames Memorial Library, North Easton, Mass., 1877–1879. Tower–gable–arch merge, L-shape plan. **(f)** Crane Memorial Library, Quincy, Mass., 1880. Perfected format for small town libraries. By A. Ioannou.

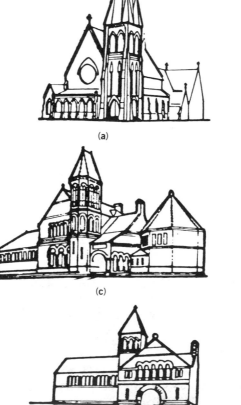
(a)

(b)

(c)

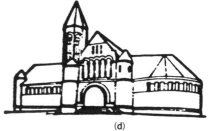
(d)

(e)

(f)

phase of his work when in 1865, having returned from his studies at the Ecole des Beaux Arts, the young architect was groping for architectural inspiration. Having had little practical experience designing churches while in Paris (5), Richardson relied on English precedents for parish churches built by architects such as Butterfield and Burgess whose works were constantly illustrated in English periodicals.

What quickly developed, however, from these early church formats, when combined with the rationalist training at the Ecole in cross-axial planning, was merely a reorientation of focus in the nave–transept–apse arrangement. The standard cruciform format was later merely shifted so that one enters through the "transept" and a long horizontal wall is allowed to assert itself. This orientation was actually prompted by the predilection of English Gothic churches to have the primary entrance through the side (north porch) rather than the front portals (as the French prefer). One notices in the massing for the Grace Church in Medford, Massachusetts, as early as 1867–1869 (see Fig. 2b) that Richardson is already well on his way to establishing the basis for his later library *parti*—employing the tower–gable–arch grouping (still separate elements in Grace Church) on axis with the long side of the building and using the apse area as a reading room Fig. 2c–f, especially the Winn and Billings libraries).

Once Richardson established this format (1877) of tower–gable–arch meeting the building at right angles (and placed visually off-balance to the long side of a structure), he was able to consistently tap these features for planning solutions in other building types as well by sliding features all along the long horizontal stretch of wall and adding on or dropping off others. The same features and formats are used over again along with the same approach to surface treatment by simply reshuffling the parts and materials and shifting the focus. The repetition of such schemes allowed Richardson to arrive at programmatic massing and siting solutions in a relatively short time. J. J. Glessner, for example, notes that after seeing the Prairie Avenue building site for his home only a few minutes, Richardson drew a sketch during dinner of the L-shaped plan (that would be tucked into the rectangular lot) with boxed-off spaces for interior volumes, and said, "If you won't ask me how I get into it, I will draw the plan for your house." "The first floor plans," Glessner notes were "almost exactly as it was finally decided on (6)." In essence, it was the Stoughton House and Converse Library schemes reversed and backed against a two-story blank wall of a proposed house to create an enclosed courtyard reminiscent of a palazzo *cortile*. Additionally, the Winn Public Library (March 1877) becomes the Billings Library of April 1883 by centering the portal in the gable and adding the end turret, which 4 months later would be grafted onto the Converse Library in Malden, Massachusetts (August 1883) (Fig. 3).

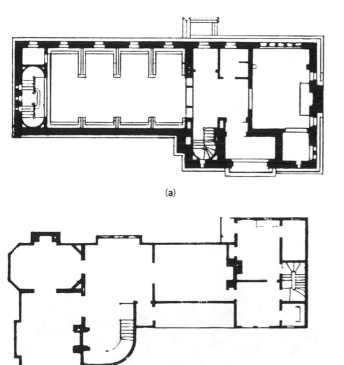

(a)

(b)

(c)

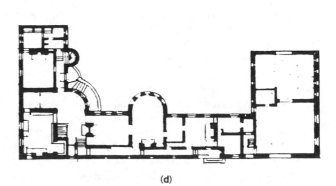

(d)

Figure 3. L-shape plan of residences and libraries. Compact to projecting entry of libraries. Frontal to inside court entry for residences. **(a)** Ames Memorial Library, North Easton, Mass., 1877–1879: compact frontal entry. **(b)** Converse Memorial Library, Malden, Mass., 1883–1885: projecting entry. **(c)** Stoughton House, Cambridge, Mass., 1882–1883: entrance at inside corner; tower projection completely merged with the general massing. **(d)** Glessner House, Chicago, Ill., 1885: entrance through enclosed court and frontal arch.

The Billings Memorial Library (1883–1887) in Burlington, Vermont, was specifically designed to mirror the Winn Library at the request of the president of the University of Vermont. Van Renssalaer argues that this gave Richardson the unique opportunity to improve his original inspired design. The Billings Library reflects an even closer affinity to the design elements of the Winn Library in earlier project sketches in which the tower is retained to the right of the gable instead of being shifted to the left of the gable and is loosely contained by two stubby turret forms. The oversized stair tower, the indefinite entry, and the picturesque grouping of features of the Winn Library are rethought and refined in the later library. In the Billings Library, the polygonal reading room (housing the Marsh Collection) is firmly integrated into the major fabric of the elevation. The ridge line, too, is allowed to continue in an unbroken line on the other side of the entrance grouping to connect with the apsidal form instead of allowing it to exist as an awkward appendage to the main structure as is the case in the Winn Library. In the Billings Library, compositional and spatial unity have been achieved through the adjustment of massing while establishing the dominance of the entrance feature. The perfected formula for a large-scale library in Richardson's oeuvre had now been achieved.

The Ames Library (1877–1879), on the other hand, represents a consolidation of the library format and a simplification of the plan over what was presented in the Winn Library 6 months earlier; it offers a more practical and economical scheme for small town libraries that required less book space, but still provided ample space for a reading room while eliminating the museum special collections addition (Fig. 2e). As opposed to the Winn format, the polygonal museum space was simply lopped-off. The entrance porch became less of a distinct and isolated element and was absorbed into the center of the tower-gable complex (as in the later Billings Library). The entrance grouping is allowed to assert itself more and is pushed forward. This is the same general arrangement as for the Crane Library (1880–1883); in both cases, the fireplaces that previously were placed in the central hall crossing (the far "transept" wall) of the Winn and Billings libraries are redirected to the short reading-room space to the right of the entrance; the reading-room fireplaces are now in direct line with the long alcove book collection area. This adjustment of format plan from continuous cross axis to that more resembling an "L" shape allowed Richardson to exaggerate in later schemes the subtle format gestures present in the Ames Library to those more in keeping with the picturesque open planning of Queen Anne house forms and indicates that even in his more elaborate structures he was often thinking in terms of domestic planning and features. In this regard, the homelike ambiance of the interior reading-room space of even the large-scale libraries (such as the Billings Memorial) harkens back to the gentleman's library tradition. Such private estate libraries of the Colonial era in the United States are visually referred to in the selected design features used by Richardson to bridge the new "public" library movement. This new building type (as part of the larger cultural revolution in America that produced public museums, opera

Figure 4. New England saltbox house, Little Compton, Mass. Photograph by Heath.

halls, parks, and public school buildings throughout the second half of the nineteenth century) was sponsored largely by Richardson's design solutions and programs for large and small town libraries (7).

Richardson (whose office after 1874 was located in Brookline, Mass.) provided a scale that was public, but at the same time mitigated the "public" aspects by inserting potent domestic references familiar to the New England consciousness. The massing profile of the Crane Memorial Library in Quincy, Massachusetts, for example, assumes the character of a New England saltbox house (Figs. 4 and 5). On the interior of the Billings Memorial Library one finds a seventeenth-century New England style hearth (complete with built-in settles, andirons, cooking cranes) and a personalized version of a Colonial-era grandfather clock nearby. All these features, although based on New England vernacular traditions, are elevated to the level of a conscious work of art—what might be appropriately termed high-style vernacular; the chimney lintel, for example, historically used for hanging cooking utensils now celebrated a stylized floral carving that anticipated Sul-

Figure 5. Saltbox profile of Richardson's Crane Memorial Library, Quincy, Mass. 1880. Perfected small town library scheme. Photograph by Heath.

Figure 6. Richardson's firehearth, Billings Memorial Library, Burlington, Vt., 1887. Photograph by Heath.

livan's Auditorium period (Figs. 6 and 7). Hence, the vernacular domestic medieval (not just the ecclesiastical medieval) often served Richardson as a starting point for progressive, high style design.

When Richardson was called on to design more monumental structures, such as large university buildings, civic and commercial structures, or cathedrals of the magnitude of Trinity Church, his elevations became more symmetrical (often relying on projecting end pavilions to contain the mass of the block and a central tower to mark monumental entry), and his planning became more formal. In the Harvard University structures of Sever Hall (1878) and Austin Hall Law School (1881), French classical planning of the type similar to the project for the Worcester General Hospital of the late 1860s was revived. As in the hospital plan, one enters on axis through a clearly marked entrance and is struck by the apparent flow of the cross-axial movement. In Sever Hall, circulation patterns are clearly evident on entering: One may pass directly through the structure and leave through an equally balanced facade in the rear, choose the vertical circulation up

a stairway opposite the entrance to the upper stories, or proceed laterally into the first-floor classroom area. In Austin Hall, a large lecture hall was needed; thus, in lieu of a stairwell space, the rear of the building is projected out in the manner of the Worcester General Hospital plan except that in the law school the space radiates inward to provide space for lecture-hall seating. As in Sever Hall, the cross axis again leads to classrooms and to upstairs stairwells.

A reading of the elevations of the two Harvard structures provides nearly all of the monumental design dictums of the Ecole: simplicity of form, majesty of scale, a central mass to express clarity of intention, and formal massing stressing good proportion. Again, one observes the general tendency to begin with a spreading horizontal form that is organically rooted to the ground line by a flaring base and is entered on axis (in this case, a purposefully centered axis) to stress formality. As is typical with Richardson's large-scale structures, an imposing hip roof is relied on to tame impersonal formality and to present a domestic association. The uninterrupted roofline, however, maintains the geometric qualities of the form as a whole (providing visual unity) and provides it with the monumentality it seeks by extending its lines. The organizing principles inherent in these two stylistically divergent buildings generally establish the massing patterns of other diverse buildings such as the Cincinnati Chamber of Commerce and the New York State Capital (Fig. 8); a

(a)

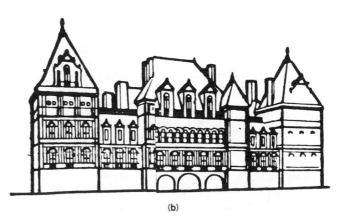

(b)

Figure 8. Projecting tower forms: to define the entrance, contain the building block and give formality and focus. Hip roof as organizing element and domestic symbol; **(a)** Sever Hall, Harvard, Cambridge, Mass., 1878–1880. **(b)** N. Y. State Capitol, Albany, 1875. By A. Ioannou.

Figure 7. New England seventeenth century firehearth. Photograph by Heath.

simple horizontal form is reinforced visually by a prominent hip roof and is consistently bounded by towers or projecting bays that serve to contain the block and give it formality, focus, and marked symmetry.

As a variation of Figure 8, structures seeking added monumentality were given centered groupings of a projecting pavilion, chateau roof, or tower bounded by two vertical forms (side towers or pavilions), and the entrance was given visual focus by being centered and accented by either one large arch or a grouping of three. Hence, while it is accurate to speak of the Worcester High School format (1869–1871) as using a palazzo organizing scheme for the elevation, augmented by Second Empire massing, and High Victorian Gothic coloration, what results is the adoption of a central tower form (now buttressed by side pavilions) for large municipal structures such as the Allegheny County Court House (1884–1888) (Fig. 9). Similarly, for planning schemes in larger structures, such as Trinity Church (1872) and Albany Cathedral (not built), Richardson condensed the *parti* and turned more-or-less to a contained, compact block surmounted by built-up pyramidal massing elements over a Greek cross plan. Because the Brattle Square Church, Boston (1866–1873) was originally conceived in a cruciform plan, O'Gorman believes that in plan and in styling (the first appearance of the Romanesque in Richardson's work) that Brattle Square anticipates Trinity. But, although the German Romanesque provided a turning point in Richardson's search for an appropriate architectural language, Trinity's powerful, simple massing led Richardson more clearly along the path of a personal style that would be independent of historical sources. Richardson's search for a new style was attained more through massing solutions and surface treatment that would provide simplicity of form and wholeness of conception than the prominence of any one style. Even though his formats and individual features might be derivative, Richardson was successful in fitting new and challenging building programs into massing schemes rich in historical associations compatible with it and making an architectural statement totally his own.

The basic qualities of mass, simplicity, proportion, and concentration were clearly seen by some of his contemporaries, and it was these same qualities that Richardson seemingly used with a vengeance in the Marshall Field Warehouse (begun 1885, Fig. 10), in Chicago, when he clarified his format for the "commercial box." The Marshall Field building represents a continual process of simplification of form and a paring away of excessive eccentric details present in earlier commercial formulas. The Cheney Building of 1875, for example, shunned the use of the mansard roof of the Union Express Company Building, Chicago (1872) but retained two slightly projecting pavilions. The basic cubic quality and visual alignment of windows under attenuated arches (which unite several stories and then divide at the top floors into two smaller arches) already signaled the refined format of the Marshall Field Warehouse. The single "tower" that asserts itself in the side elevation of the Cheney Building scheme disrupts the organization achieved in the cubic section and is a residue of the older formula of the Union Express Company.

Richardson's use of a hierarchic arrangement of arches

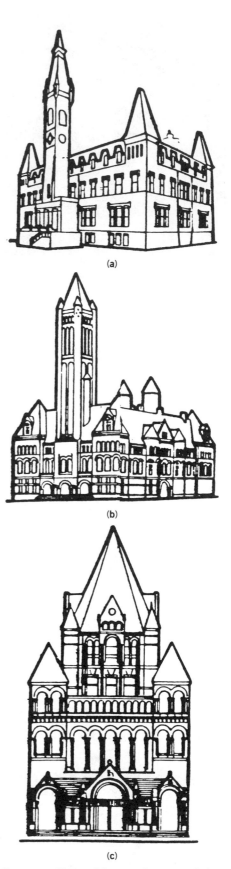

Figure 9. Corner pavilions with central tower; to define entrance and establish monumentality. Buttressing towers provide central focus for formality. (a) Worcester High School, Mass., 1869–1871: Allegeny County Courthouse, Pittsburgh, Penn., 1883–1886. (b) Trinity Church, Boston, Mass., 1872. By A. Ioannou.

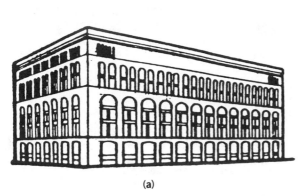

(a)

(b)

Figure 10. Commercial block, arranges the building on horizontal zones, uses rhythm of arches, uses rational and decorated schemes. **(a)** Marshall Field Warehouse, Chicago, Ill., 1885–1887. **(b)** Chamber of Commerce, Cincinnati, Ohio, 1885. By A. Ioannou.

for decorative effect and to unite the surface design as a whole relies basically on the Italian Renaissance palace tradition—a popular symbolic reference for the association of a commercial structure. Such Renaissance arch organization had been employed for commercial structures since the mid-nineteenth century and had been used with much success even more recently in the 1870s in large commercial buildings by George Post (whom, interestingly, Richardson had replaced in Charles Dexter Gambrill's office in 1867). The reliance on arcuated formulas to discipline the facade is used by Richardson almost exclusively for commercial structures; the interior courtyard of the Allegheny County Courthouse offers a rare exception. In applying this formula, Richardson is searching for decorative unity without detracting from the sobriety of the pure form of his structures. At its extreme, and the Field building qualifies, the commercial block was merely an austere (yet monumental) geometric envelope to shelter a diversity of functions. Both Post and Richardson successfully arrived at a desirable solution for the commercial block by the mid-1880s (Post's Produce Exchange Building, 1884, in New York and Richardson's Field Warehouse, 1885). These structures avoid the trappings of a "commercial palace" that were looked down on by some contemporary architectural critics, such as Montgomery Schuyler, and produced instead a severely simple form boldly expressive of its utilitarian purpose. Schuyler's comments on the Field Warehouse are especially revealing in light of the unique qualities he thought this work possessed (8):

> . . . a huge warehouse covering a whole square, and seven stories high. With such an opportunity, Mr. Richardson could be trusted implicitly at least to make the most of his dimensions and large as the building is in fact, it looks interminably big. Its bigness is made apparent by the simplicity of its treatment and the absence of any lateral division whatever. Simplicity indeed, could scarcely go further. . . . The great pile is one of the most interesting as it is one of the most individual examples of American commercial building. In it the vulgarity of the "commercial palace" is gratefully conspicuous by its

absence, and it is as monumental in its massiveness and durability as it is grimly utilitarian in expression.

It is in this observance of the properties of commercial architecture, and in this self-denying rejection of an ornateness improper to it, that the best of the commercial architecture of Chicago is a welcome surprise to the tourist from the East.

But what happened to this "simplicity of treatment" and this sense of pure form only 4 months later (August 1885) when Richardson designed the Cincinnati Chamber of Commerce Building? Was it a step backward in Richardson's supposed quest for a progressive architecture of his times—"an unfortunate abberation defying rational explanation" as some suggest? Or, is it essentially a dual view of the concept of "reality" that was present throughout Richardson's career, as Gowans suggests (9).

One definition of reality (that sponsors the creation of such elevations as the Field Building) holds that reality in architecture is "an expression of the intrinsic qualities of stone: its texture, its capacity to carry weight, the constructional techniques appropriate in such a medium;" the other definition of reality, as Gowans sees it, means "archaeological accuracy—the demonstration of how forms of a past style may be adapted to modern uses with minimum sacrifice of historical reference." This later definition gives birth to such structures, Gowans feels, as the Cincinnati Chamber of Commerce building. Gowans stated that, "essentially both buildings proceeded from the same impulse and premises." However, these two structures are not essentially different, except in intent. The Chamber of Commerce building is not an anomaly in Richardson's work that stands as a blaring impasse to his more progressive developments. It comes from the same conscious selection of forms and design formulas he had consistently drawn on throughout his career. In fact, one can view the Chamber of Commerce Building as the Marshall Field Warehouse "softened" by the associational (not necessarily "historical") qualities of the hip roof to meet the demands of his client (see Fig. 10a). Despite the fact that Richardson may borrow French Renaissance or Romanesque elements, or even Colonial features, this does not make him an historical or revivalist architect; this, essentially, is the shortcoming of such terms as Richardsonian Romanesque. He uses these elements in a fresh and original manner often purely for compositional or associational qualities, as in the brick "sidelights" or stretched dormers of Sever Hall. These elements become "found objects" (to use Marcel DuChamp's meaning of the phrase) and possess vitality and meaning that is "Richardsonian"—not historic. Therefore, the character of the Chamber of Commerce building does not reflect another view of "reality," as Gowans proposes, but a consciously conceived format that has been manipulated for a desired effect. What Richardson has done in the Cincinnati Chamber of Commerce is to merge the hip roof—the two buttressing towers vocabulary of the State Hospital, Buffalo with the Renaissance design formulas of his earlier commercial structures (see Fig. 9) to yield a formal yet "humanistic" structure. Or seen another way, the Chamber of Commerce Building stands as a bridge between the more "romantic" massing of the earlier Merchant's Union Express Office with its French roof and side pavilions and the later "rational" massing and design features of the Field building. Simply flatten the roof of the Chamber of Commerce Building and remove or recess the side towers, and the remaining elements speak with the same power and simplicity as does the Field building.

This dual sensitivity toward romantic and rational schemes runs throughout Richardson's career and accounts for the disparity of judgment among what contemporary critics saw as Richardson's "best" work—works that seemingly drew from inspiration far afield from one another. Richardson's broad-based popularity, then, likely stems from the dual nature of his designs. Coeval architects, who held widely divergent design biases, could each find something they could draw from in the rich and varied offerings within Richardson's oeuvre.

The difference in handling of these two structures results from a difference in intent. The Field Warehouse was designed as a utilitarian, investment structure with no pressure to present a corporate image and, therefore, could afford to be severely simple, whereas the problem presented by the Chamber of Commerce building, as Van Rensselaer states (10),

> had not the hampering monotony of a simple commercial building but it was quite as modern in its own way. American merchants, like their far-off predecessors in Belgium and Holland, want a great and dignified hall of assemblage; but with a keener eye to revenue, they demand that it shall be combined with an "office building"—that every possible foot of space shall be put to use in ways that are often quite at variance with the chief use of a building, and that as many such feet as possible shall be secured by vertical extension.

The form that the Chamber of Commerce takes, it appears, results from a desire to satisfy the demands for "dignity" (in its use of the hip roof and side turrets) and the desire for utility (in its compactness and expressed separation of parts).

As O'Gorman is quick to inform us, Richardson's quest for a personal style does not reflect a direct development.

Although there are consistencies in format applications and spatial arrangements, his path is less than direct in synthesizing the "derivative and often awkward eclecticism" of the late 1860s to the mid-1870s into the "profound and powerful" language of his maturity (11). The key to Richardson's eventual success, however, has less to do with coming to grips with any *one* style than with the final resolution of his design process and aesthetic philosophy with which he could address *all* of his styles. Richardson gained full command of his resources, as O'Gorman put it, in 1878. Oschner recounts (12):

> Richardson's professional maturity was marked by a series of projects beginning in 1878: Sever Hall, Cambridge; The John Bryant House, Cohasset; the Ames Monument, Wyoming; and the Crane Library, Quincy. In these projects Richardson began to simplify form and to eliminate archeological detail. He turned instead to basic shapes, continuous surfaces, and the innate qualities of his buildings.

In this manner, buildings from widely divergent stylistic roots became swatches from the same design fabric. Stoughton is the Glessner House rendered in granite instead of shingles; Ames Gate is Sever formed out of glacial boulders in lieu of brick. Sweeping surfaces allow for the synthesis of form and feature into a unified whole.

It was Richardson's unique ability to manipulate masses imaginatively into functionally distinct volumes, design within a fixed framework of several formats, and apply a consistent aesthetic philosophy to the surface treatment that defines the essence of his mature style. The end result is a highly powerful and original architectural statement free of historical precedent. After 1878, America had its first original style—Richardsonian. American architecture had come of age.

BIBLIOGRAPHY

1. M. G. van Rensselaer, *Henry Hobson Richardson and his Works*, Dover Publications, Inc., New York, 1888 and 1969, p. 126.
2. W. A. Langdon, "The Method of H. H. Richardson," *The Architect and Contract Reporter* LXIII, 156–158 (March 9, 1900).
3. J. F. O'Gorman ed., *H. H. Richardson and his Office, A Centennial of his Move to Boston*, Harvard College Press, Cambridge, Mass., 1974, p. 60.
4. *Ibid.*, p. 60.
5. H. H. Hitchcock, *The Architecture of H. H. Richardson and his Times*, Hamden, 1961.
6. J. J. Glessner, "Why we built this house and how we came to select this architect," (a four-page typescript, only two printed), reproduced in full in Ref. 5, pp. 328–330.
7. W. Jordy, *American Buildings and their Architecture: Progressive and Academic Ideals of the Turn of the Twentieth Century*, Vol. 3, Doubleday, New York, 1976, pp. 314–375. A good background on the development of library formats in the United States.
8. M. Schulyer in W. Jordy and R. Coe, eds., *American Architecture and Other Writings*, Atheneum, New York, 1964, pp. 97–99.

9. A. Gowans, "High Victorian Art as Personal Expression," in *Images in American Living*, Lippincott, Philadelphia, Pa, 1964, pp. 360–361.

10. Ref. 1, p. 98.

11. J. F. O'Gorman, *H. H. Richardson: Architectural Forms for an American Society*, The University of Chicago Press, Chicago, Ill., 1987, pp. 29, 42.

12. J. K. Oschsner, *H. H. Richardson, Complete Architectural Works*, M.I.T. Press, Cambridge, Mass., 1982, p. 3.

KINGSTON HEATH
University of North Carolina, Charlotte
Charlotte, North Carolina

RIVETING.   See STRUCTURAL STEEL.

ROADS, HIGHWAY.   See PAVING SYSTEMS, ASPHALT.

ROCHE DINKELOO

The firm Kevin Roche (1922–), John Dinkeloo (1918–1981) and Associates has produced some of contemporary America's most significant and influential civic and corporate architecture. Recognizing new social conditions within postindustrial society, the firm has designed buildings that focus on the changing role of public space and its relationship to the individual. Working primarily in the established centers of older American cities and their vast emerging regional fringes, the firm has contributed to the transformation and maturity of such basic twentieth-century building types as the corporate headquarters and the skyscraper. Informing this typological research is a continuing free manipulation of the legacy of modern architecture. Consistently choosing an outlook both pragmatic and visionary, the firm has shunned conventional solutions, pursuing instead technological and social innovation patiently within the context of present cultural conditions.

Kevin Roche (1922–) was born in Dublin, Ireland, where he received a Bachelor of Architecture from the National University of Ireland in 1945. After professional experience in Dublin with Michael Scott and in London with Maxwell Fry, he came to the United States in 1948, spending one semester in the Illinois Institute of Technology Master's program with Ludwig Mies van der Rohe. After a short time at the United Nations Planning Office, Roche in 1950 joined Eero Saarinen and Associates at Bloomfield Hills, Michigan. By 1954 he was Saarinen's principal design associate.

John Dinkeloo (1918–1981) received a degree in architectural engineering from the University of Michigan in 1942, subsequently becoming the chief of production at the Chicago office of Skidmore, Owings and Merrill. Also joining the Saarinen office in 1950, Dinkeloo became a partner in 1956. Like Roche, he began his Saarinen years working on the enormous General Motors Technical Cen-

ter in Warren, Michigan (1948–1956), one of the most important and technically advanced projects of the postwar years. With Saarinen's untimely death in 1961, as the office was moving to Hamden, Connecticut, Roche and Dinkeloo, along with senior partner and administrator Joseph Lacy, continued under Saarinen's name, finishing projects and securing new work, most notably the Oakland Museum (1961–1968) in Oakland, California. In 1966, with Saarinen's work complete, the office adopted the present name.

Once established, Roche Dinkeloo continued and expanded on the legacy of Saarinen, particularly in the area of large urban and suburban projects. Beginning with the Ford Foundation Headquarters (1963–1968) in New York City, the firm demonstrated its mastery of evolving modern building types. An L-shaped 12-story office building, enclosing an equally tall glass-roofed garden, the Ford Foundation Headquarters transformed the typical postwar office building lobby into a potent design element. Now it became capable of responding to new concerns for the public realm, which emerged from the destruction of public space during the urban renewal interventions of the 1950s and 1960s. Extending this exploration in the renovations and extensions of the Metropolitan Museum of Art (1967–1985) in New York City, Roche Dinkeloo created a network of large atrium gardens and courts that configure entire sections of a vast museum complex. In addition to solving the practical issues of orientation and relief in the gallery experience, these elements have emerged as significant and vibrant public spaces within the life of the city on par with Central Park and Manhattan's other outdoor rooms.

While the expansive glass spaces emblematic of Roche Dinkeloo's urban buildings have endeavored to invigorate the expression of community in older U.S. cities, their use in the firm's suburban buildings have created a vision of public life where none previously existed. The John Deere & Company West Office Building (1975–1979) in Moline, Illinois, an addition to an earlier Saarinen masterpiece, is typical of the suburban variation. A large winter garden, a full one quarter of the building footprint, establishes a central void, in what otherwise is a low-rise extension of the existing building. Containing a cafeteria, the garden represents the public life of the corporate workplace, while providing a link to the other parts of the Deere complex for which Roche Dinkeloo have added or proposed several other buildings. More than just an amenity, these spaces in principal designer Roche's hands have changed the form and perception of the corporate office building from a serial grouping of single office units into a hierarchical environment capable of supporting a full range of experiences from the solitary to the communal.

Concurrent with the transformation of the internal nature of the corporate office building, Roche Dinkeloo has significantly altered its external relationship to the suburban automobile landscape. A striking result of this investigation is the General Foods Corporation Headquarters (1977–1982) in Rye, New York. (Fig. 1.) Raised on a three-story podium of structured parking, its symmetrical composition culminates in a six-story rotondalike dining atrium. Clad in panels of white aluminum siding and re-

Figure 1. General Foods Corporation Headquarters (1977–1982), Rye, New York. Courtesy of Roche Dinkeloo.

flective glass, the building successfully dominates a large portion of the scattered Westchester County suburban countryside. Elevated to almost monumental status, General Foods Corporation offers a highly visible image to passing motorists and an island of stability to smaller developments surrounding it. No longer a skyscraper transposed to the country and lain on its side, the corporate headquarters through the work of Roche Dinkeloo has emerged as an important modern building type—the corporate villa.

The involvement of the firm with these suburban modifications has not deterred it from investigating the older, although still significant, urban skyscraper type. Perhaps most indicative of Roche Dinkeloo's skill at manipulating the high-rise office building is the United Nations Plaza (1969–1983) in New York City. Actually a complex of two 39-story hotel and office towers connected by a one-story base, these buildings deviate with spectacular results from the two zoning paradigms of New York skyscrapers. Neither a step-backed pyramid nor a sheer tower, they are gridded green reflective glass volumes that are tapered and chamfered to imply with subtle but effective means a base, middle, and top.

Although references to traditional architectural language have always been part of the firm's work, they have emerged with greater force in its most recent high-rise projects. Projecting an overt classical profile, the Morgan Bank Headquarters (1983) in New York City rises from a four-story arcaded base, terminating in a copper mansard roof supported by glass window bays configured like columns. Variations in other projects include the skyscraper as a column or spire. It is perhaps too early to judge whether these figurative investigations are a turn away from the use of modern elements and the minimalist references that have previously characterized the firm's high-rise work.

In general, Roche Dinkeloo's relationship to modern architecture and theory as established in the 1920s and 1930s is a curious one. Inheriting from Eero Saarinen a skepticism about the universal pronouncements of the CIAM urbanism and international style architecture, the work of the firm has at times demonstrated an almost Beaux-Arts sense of composition and proportion. Early projects such as the Richard C. Lee High School (1962–1967) in New Haven, Connecticut, and later work such as Bouygues Headquarters (1983) Paris, France, demonstrate a continuing use of axial procession, the origins of which can be traced to Roche's early academic training and his contact with the American work of Mies van der Rohe. Nevertheless, in the broad view, the buildings of Roche Dinkeloo share some key tenets of modernism. For example, through the efforts of John Dinkeloo, important building technology innovations have merged from the present firm and its predecessor. Most notable are the development of weathering steel and the perfection of the reflective glass curtain wall and its gasketing system. But such technical advances, like those involving building types described above, have primarily been responses to practical problems, infused with a modest vision of seeking a better solution. Although borrowing from a variety of modern vocabularies—Constructivism, Rationalism, and even Corbusian forms as at the Fine Arts Center (1968–1974), University of Massachusetts, Amherst—the firm is at odds with the various social and political programs these branches of modernism represent. Through this disengagement from theory as ideology, Roche Dinkeloo has continued, although with much more rigor, the wide-ranging even eclectic experiments of Saarinen.

Avoiding the narrow formal and theoretical strictures of the modernist agenda, Roche Dinkeloo has been free to accept present conditions with the proviso that they can be gradually modified within existing architectural, technical, and social conventions. The design of Union Carbide Corporation World Headquarters (1976–1982), Danbury, Connecticut, demonstrates this point of view. Beginning with extensive employee interviews, the architects produced a building that makes use of freeway-type access, decentralization of departments, and individual preferences for office styling. From these familiar elements and experiences an extraordinary work environment resulted. Perched at tree-line on *pilotis,* the four-story low-rise building makes a minimal impact on the countryside, wrapping in on itself to disguise a central 2850 car parking garage. Such pragmatism coupled with aspirations for an improved future is squarely in line with an American architectural tradition stretching from Thomas Jefferson's tinkerings at Monticello through the development of the skyscraper in Chicago to Albert Kahn's industrial sheds. Roche Dinkeloo's search, like theirs, is for evolutionary possibilities instead of the creation of revolutionary inevitabilities.

The working methods of Roche Dinkeloo are somewhat unique to U.S. architectural practice in that they allow the time necessary to explore innovative design strategies. Given the scale of the projects, it is a small office—usually about 60 architects—where design is pursued at a comfortable pace, each part from overall planning to interior materials and furnishings receiving Roche's attention. However, models and not drawings play the critical role in the design development process. Frequently built at large scale, with simulated materials, and later photographed under exacting conditions, the models are almost interchangeable with the finished buildings. Such observations have led to criticism that the work of Roche Dinkeloo lacks spontaneity and human scale. Although this is certainly characteristic of some early work such as the New Haven Veterans Memorial Coliseum (1965–1972), the technique of models and full-size mock-ups has produced such finely scaled work as the Central Park Zoo (1980–1988), in New York City.

For a firm that has produced significant work for more than 25 years, Roche Dinkeloo has only relatively recently attracted the focus of critical attention. Emerging from the bulk of current civic and corporate architecture, the work of Roche Dinkeloo has received international recognition for its excellence, integrity, and style. Among the numerous honors awarded to Kevin Roche, the Pritzker Architecture Prize in 1982 is foremost. Despite John Dinkeloo's death in 1981, the firm continues to prove that within the context of present social life, the automobile landscape and corporate capitalism can produce architecture worthy of society's most stringent expectations. In doing so, Roche Dinkeloo has neither discarded modernism and its forms nor engaged in a futile revision. By avoiding the entanglements of current debate—Roche neither writes nor teaches—the firm is able to maintain a clear outlook directed to the pursuit of architecture as a constructive and ennobling act.

BIBLIOGRAPHY

General References

J. W. Cook and H. Klotz, *Conversations with Architects,* Praeger, New York, 1973, pp. 52–89.

F. Dal Co, *Kevin Roche,* Rizzoli, New York, 1985.

P. Drew, *Third Generation: The Changing Meaning of Architecture,* Praeger, New York, 1972, pp. 160–171.

Y. Futagawa, *Kevin Roche, John Dinkeloo and Associates, Vol. One 1962–1975,* ADA, Tokyo, 1975.

P. Heyer, *Architects on Architecture: New Directions in America,* Walker, New York, 1966, pp. 355–361.

"In Memoriam: John Dinkeloo 1918–1981," *Skyline,* 10, (Oct. 1981).

"Kevin Roche and John Dinkeloo: 1964–1975," *Architectural Forum,* **140,** 16–85. (March 1974) Articles by Ludwig Glaeser, Paul Goldberger, Vincent Scully, and Suzanne Stephens.

K. Roche, "A Conversation," *Perspecta 19,* Perspecta and MIT Press, New Haven, 1982, pp. 164–171.

RICO CEDRO
Brookline, Massachusetts

ROEBLING, JOHN. See BRIDGES.

ROGERS, RICHARD G.

Born on July 23, 1933 in Florence, Richard George Rogers spent his early childhood as a member of an affluent upper middle class British family living in Italy. As the political climate under Fascism deteriorated, the Rogers family emigrated to England in 1938, where he spent the remainder of his youth. It was through frequent visits to the studio of his Italian cousin, Ernesto Rogers, that he eventually decided to become an architect. Ernesto was a highly influential architect, writer, and editor, and his fervent promotion of the modern movement in Italy provided an inspired foundation for his younger cousin's desire to enter the profession. On his advice, Rogers entered the Architectural Association (AA) in London to pursue his architectural studies, and it was there that he came under the influence of Peter Smithson, with whom he studied. Smithson was one of the founders of New Brutalism, an architectural movement promoting the design of buildings of uncompromising clarity and honesty in the presentation of structure, characteristics that Rogers himself would later strive to achieve in his own work.

After receiving his AA diploma in 1959, Rogers worked briefly with the Middlesex County Council's architects' department before beginning graduate studies in architecture at Yale University as a Fulbright scholar in 1961. At Yale, Rogers experienced the ideas and theories of a number of influential teachers, including historian Vincent Scully, who introduced him to the work of Frank Lloyd Wright; Serge Chermayeff, whose views on public and private space were to have lasting impact; and Craig Ellwood, who familiarized him with the experimental steel structures of postwar California. It was also at Yale that Rogers met fellow British student Norman Foster, with whom he worked on joint school design projects, and together they absorbed the work of the leading contemporary American architects, most importantly that of Louis Kahn. On completion of his studies, Rogers moved to San Francisco, where he worked in the office of Skidmore, Owings & Merrill.

Rogers returned to England in 1962 and in the following year established Team 4, an architectural office with the husband-and-wife teams of Richard and Su Rogers and Norman and Wendy Foster. Team 4 produced a number of inventive residential designs that displayed sensitive building-to-site relationships and uses of traditional building materials and construction techniques.

The Creek Vean House at Feock, Cornwall (1963) consisted of an enfilade of irregularly-shaped rooms arranged along a continuous skylit picture gallery. With its deft siting and planted roofs, the house merged gracefully with its cliff-side setting, and it was the first private residence to receive a 1969 RIBA (Royal Institute of British Architects) Award "for work of outstanding quality."

The Jaffe House in Radlett, Hertfordshire (1966) employed a system of parallel masonry walls in a spatial organization that offered ease of subdivision and extendibility, as well as potential application as a high-density housing system. Thus its design foreshadowed principles of flexibility and expansion that would be investigated in nearly all of Rogers's later work.

Team 4's most important achievement was the construction of the Reliance Controls Electronics Factory in Swindon, Wiltshire (1967), a one-story building that provided flexible industrial space within a clearly articulated building shell of exposed steel structure, external diagonal wind bracing, and profiled steel cladding. Responding to a restricted budget and limited construction time, Team 4 abandoned the constraints of traditional construction methods in favor of industrially produced, readily available building components that offered speed of erection, systematized assembly, and flexibility for future change. Inspired by the visual and constructional clarity of Alison and Peter Smithson's steel skeleton Hunstanton School in Norfolk (1949–1954) and by Ray and Charles Eames's own house in Pacific Palisades, Calif. (1949), with its *ad hoc* use of standard, economical, industrial building components, the design of Reliance Controls was based on a clear ideological and architectural rationale. Reliance Controls received the *Financial Times* Award for "the most outstanding work of industrial architecture" in 1967, and is a pivotal building in Rogers's career.

In 1967, the Team 4 office was dissolved, the Fosters separated to establish their own architectural practice, and the partnership of Richard and Su Rogers was formed. The Rogers office continued to investigate the use of structure as a fundamental discipline in a building's overall design, as a means of attaining flexibility of use, and as the generator of an architectural aesthetic that reflected its primary role. By the end of the 1960s, Rogers had formulated the basis of a design rationale that stressed "general-purpose rather than tailor-made building designs; maximum flexibility for future growth and change; speed of erection; minimum maintenance; use of the minimum number of prefabricated steel components; and the use of maximum spans with minimum internal structure to obstruct flexibility of partitioning" (1). Both the Spender House in Ulting, Essex (1968) and the Rogers House in Wimbleton, London (1969), designed for his parents, displayed the rigorous application of these precepts with their use of clear-span, welded portals of standard steel sections, factory-fabricated wall and roof panels, and

provision for expansion and internal change. Intended to be prototypes, these completed houses demonstrated a studied application of industrial building techniques and new materials to residential design, and they were both selected to represent contemporary British architecture at the Paris Biennale of 1969. Research into new building technologies and materials also led to designs for two prototypical "Zip-up" Houses (1968, 1971) which were based on a system of structural aluminum sandwich panels assembled to form continuous-surface wall and roof components joined with neoprene gaskets.

Rogers's interest in industrialized building techniques and lightweight components brought him in contact with Renzo Piano, whose architectural practice in Genoa had produced a series of innovative structures based on advanced building technologies, and in 1971 they formed the partnership of Piano + Rogers. With their winning entry in the international competition for the design of the Centre National d'Art et de Culture Georges Pompidou (Pompidou Center) in Paris that same year, both architects received worldwide notoriety and acclaim for what many consider one of the most notable achievements of contemporary architecture. Anxious to avoid producing a hermetic and static monument to "culture," the architects proposed a building that would be "both a flexible container and a dynamic communications machine" (2). Their design emphasized programmatic change, impermanence, and indeterminacy, and its fundamental concept echoed earlier projects by English architects Cedric Price (Fun Palace, London, 1967) and Peter Cook, founder of the Archigram group (Plug-in City, 1964–1966).

Pompidou Center, completed in 1977, accommodated its various museum, library, exhibition, and support facilities within superimposed, column-free loft spaces interconnected by a primary movement system of external, glazed, circulation galleries and multiple escalators (Fig. 1). Assembled from a kit of highly engineered industrial parts, it was an enormous, multifunctioning, flexibly serviced container that achieved its memorable aesthetic through the precise articulation of its interdependent structural, mechanical, enclosure, and movement systems. As an act of urban design, Pompidou Center today serves as a kinetic backdrop to its large public piazza and reciprocates with its site to produce a highly active urban place in the heart of Paris. Piano + Rogers also explored the design of flexible, highly serviced shells in industrial and commercial buildings that frequently incorporated wide-span, exposed steel structures with expandable envelopes of various modular panel systems (Factory for Universal Oil Products, Tadworth, Surrey, 1973; PA Technology Laboratory, Melbourn, Hertfordshire, 1975). In a proposal for Millbank Riverside Housing (1977), a luxury waterfront housing development projected for Pimlico, London, their design was based on the concept of the building as a large terraced pier with high-level river walks, and its lightweight, open structural framework was intended to allow flexibility and variety in the mix and placement of accommodations.

The partnership with Renzo Piano ended in 1977, and with the formation of the new firm of Richard Rogers and Partners, Rogers proceeded to expand the application of

Figure 1. Pompidou Center, Paris, France. Courtesy of Martin Charles and *The Architectural Review*.

the architectural precepts that had permeated his previous work. A number of designs for research and production facilities reflected a continued interest in adroitly engineered and fully expressed structural, service, and enclosure systems, and he carried the exploratory architectural vocabulary of the earlier Reliance Controls Factory to new levels of complexity and sophistication.

Beginning with a project for NAPP Laboratories in Cambridge (1979), he created a series of one- and two-story buildings with long-span, suspended steel roof systems hung from exterior structural masts. This design approach resulted in economies of enclosed volume, flexibility of mechanical servicing, ease of expansion, and aesthetic clarity, and it marked the emergence of a new type in Rogers's architectural repertoire. The Fleetguard Factory in Brittany, France (1981) used a square grid of tubular steel structural masts and suspension rods to form a bright red structural web beneath which sat a readily-expandable volume in silver-colored profiled steel cladding. In 1982 it received a Premier Award as "the most exceptional steel structure built in France in 1981–1982." In the design of a large low-cost shopping center in

Nantes, France (1987), Rogers employed the structural, economic, and functional advantages of a similar roof system, again reflecting his interest in developing general-purpose building designs. Both the Inmos Microprocessor Factory in Gwent, South Wales (1982) and the PA Technology Laboratories in Princeton, N.J. (1982) utilized standard, prefabricated steel components and suspended roof systems, but here the primary structural masts became an integral part of the central circulation and service spines along which both buildings were designed to expand. Systems of tension tie rods branched off from these spine towers to assist the long-span tubular steel roof trusses, providing uninterrupted, column-free floor space for maximum internal flexibility. As with Fleetguard, the use of color on these buildings artfully heightened the clear visual articulation of the component parts and reinforced their interdependent role in these carefully orchestrated, precisely-engineered assemblies.

Several large-scale urban design and planning projects in the 1980s have required Rogers to deal with the problems of urban intervention on a number of scales. His proposed designs for singular urban buildings have nearly always exhibited their vertical circulation and mechanical servicing functions in separate "servant" towers, resulting in highly expressive urban assemblages (National Gallery Extension, London, 1982; First United Methodist Church Office Building, Seattle, Wash., 1984). At the same time, his projected schemes for mixed-use developments have revealed the potential for large public, interior, glazed urban rooms that serve as enriching features of the contemporary city (Coin Street Development, London, 1979–1984); Pater noster Square Development, London, 1987). Proposals for a new pedestrian realm along the banks of the River Arno in Florence, Italy (1983–1984), a Master Plan for the Royal Docks in London (1986),

and urban design schemes for a mixed-use development on Brunswick Wharf, London (1986) are among the largest urban projects in the Rogers office during the 1980s.

The building that perhaps most comprehensively illustrates Rogers's current ideas on architecture and urbanism is the remarkable high-rise headquarters for Lloyd's of London, completed in 1986 on a site in London's central financial district. Organized as a series of superimposed, concentric, gallery spaces overlooking a spectacular central, glass-roofed atrium that rises to a height of 12 stories, Lloyd's of London is a *tour de force* of engineering precision and technological poetry (Fig. 2). By placing all

Figure 2. Lloyd's of London, London. UK. Courtesy of Richard Bryant.

elevators, stairs, lavatories, and mechanical equipment outside the building in six independent service towers, he achieved a rectangular envelope that allowed greater flexibility of interior planning and mechanical servicing.

As were the Japanese Metabolists of the 1960s, Rogers is very aware of the relative life cycles of various parts of contemporary buildings: "Whereas the frame of the building has a long life expectancy, the servant areas, filled with mechanical equipment, have a relatively short life . . ." (3). For Rogers, these freestanding service towers express the faster rate of change of these elements, and their juxtaposition with the permanent rectangle of the main building presents an expanded interpretation of Louis Kahn's seminal concept of "servant" and "served" spaces. As with all of his previous work, the legibility of each functioning part of the building is paramount: "Thus one may recognize in each part, its process of manufacture, erection, maintenance, and finally demolition: the how, why and what of the building" (4). Lloyd's of London displays its concrete frame, innovative glazing system, stainless steel cladding, and exposed mechanical services with elegant clarity and compositional brilliance. In its urban context, Lloyd's is a high-rise building that offers several scales of rich visual engagement from varying perspectives, and it is one of Rogers's most significant accomplishments.

Richard Rogers has created an architecture that celebrates process and technique through the discipline of engineering and the performance of technology, and he has continuously sought to amplify the credo of early modernism in a variety of building types, scales, and contexts. His many national and international accolades include the Gold Medal of the Royal Institute of British Architects of 1985, and numerous publications, exhibitions, and overseas commissions (France, the United States, Japan) have impressively disseminated his highly emblematic architecture. Rogers's architectural ideology is firmly rooted in the promise of technology and its application to contemporary life, and his practice will undoubtedly continue to develop an architecture that reflects this commitment as society moves toward the twenty-first century.

BIBLIOGRAPHY

1. B. Appleyard, *Richard Rogers—A Biography,* Faber & Faber Ltd., London, 1986, p. 139.
2. B. Cole, and R. Rogers, eds., *Richard Rogers + Architects,* Architectural Monographs, Academy Editions, London, 1985, p. 91.
3. T. Nakamura, ed., "Richard Rogers Partnership: Lloyd's of London," *Architecture and Urbanism,* No. 198, A+U Publishing Co., Ltd., Tokyo, March 1987, p. 41.
4. *Ibid,* p. 93.

General References

Refs. 1, 2, and 3 are good general references.

"'Centre Georges Pompidou,' Paris", *Global Architecture* 44: *Piano & Rogers,* A.D.A. Edita Tokyo Co., Ltd., Tokyo, 1977.

A. Morgan and C. Naylor, *Contemporary Architects,* 2nd ed., St. James Press, Chicago, London, 1982, pp. 755–756.

D. Sudjic, *Norman Foster, Richard Rogers, James Stirling: New Directions in British Architecture,* Thames and Hudson, Inc., New York, 1986.

GREGORY K. HUNT
Virginia Polytechnic Institute
and State University
Alexandria, Virginia

THE ROLE OF THE ARCHITECT

This article defines how the role of the architect has changed over time, from that of anonymous craftsman and mason, to acknowledged artist working for princes of state, to corporate professional managing large offices and producing huge sets of drawings, utilizing computers, and administering legal contracts. While the architect struggles for identity, the world and society around him are constantly developing and changing. Feudal states with their princes and barons have changed to nations with kings and queens and then to democracies. Mainly a cathedral builder in Gothic times, the architect now serves many different clients both public and private, designing structures from prototypical pizza parlors to giant buildings for the Federal Reserve system. The physical world has changed too. It has become more connected through sophisticated transportation and communications systems. Materials once obtainable in only one part of the world, such as teak from Indonesia or granite from India, have become accessible and eventually almost universally available. Steel from Belgium or Korea competes with that from the United States. Contractors from Korea compete with contractors from Sweden or Germany in the Middle East. All of this has an impact on design, tending to make buildings in one place look like buildings in any other place. Questions arise about style. How should design reflect the culture of the region? To what extent should the ethic of reflecting the vernacular of the region prevail? How at the same time should the architect express the standards of the high level of technology and engineering available almost universally in the late twentieth century?

THE ARCHITECT AS MASON

Tombs, Temples, and Palaces

Humanity's greatest monuments were built in the Nile Valley 4000–5000 years ago. The names of the architects or designers who conceived these immense structures are lost in the sands of time. Many of the monuments are attributed to pharaohs such as Snefru (Third Dynasty) and Ramses II (Nineteenth Dynasty). However, Imhotep, the architect for King Zoser, was revered in his own times and in later dynasties. In fact, he was deified in the Twenty-sixth Dynasty. His great monument was Zoser's Step Pyramid at Saqqara and its surrounding complex. Built over Zoser's mastaba; the pyramid was the first sizable stone structure ever erected. It went through five alterations, the first of which was the enlargement of the mastaba and the building of a pyramid with four steps. Later, one with six steps was built. The whole complex is enclosed by a wall 1790 ft long and 912 ft wide. There are many tomb passages under the pyramid, and within the enclosures are other subsidiary buildings. It was built of limestone quarried nearby, but the facing is of white Tura limestone from the other side of the Nile. The casing had to be fitted carefully and covered 70,000 m² of surface.

Building a pyramid was a great engineering challenge, and merely piling up large blocks of stone in horizontal layers was not the solution. Great lateral thrusts developed near the base, and these forces could push out and collapse the pyramid, as happened at the Pyramid at Meidum. To build these steep mountains of stone, it was necessary to use inwardly inclined buttress walls with downward-sloping stones of sufficient strength and number. The stability and permanence of Zoser's Pyramid prove Imhotep's genius (1).

It took thousands of laborers to build this and the other great pyramids, such as those at Giza. Mendelssohn, in his book *The Riddle of the Pyramids,* proposes an interesting theory as to why the pharaohs devoted so much human effort and resources to these monumental tombs. He says the urge to build monuments is an extrapolation of the child's fundamental desire to build castles out of sand. He quotes the ancient cry from the book of Genesis, "Let us build us a city and a tower whose top may reach into heaven; and let us make a name." Mendelssohn then goes on to say that these pyramids were really huge public works jobs organized by a king at a time when he was struggling to create a unified state. Thousands of people working together for a common goal lessened their differences and helped unify the nation, even though it was by building a largely useless object. The point of the effect, therefore, was not finishing the pyramid, but the process of building as a political strategy (2).

The earlier tomb structures of the Third Dynasty were largely walled structures with columns rarely freestanding. Centuries later, in the temple complexes of Ammon, Karnak, and Luxor at Thebes, great columned halls, called hypostyle halls, were developed. Perhaps Karnak is the greatest of these. It was built by many kings, starting in 1530 BC and ending in 323 BC. It is placed in an immense enclosure including many courts and temple structures. The great hypostyle hall built by Seti I and Ramses II is 338 × 170 ft internally. The roof is supported by enormous slabs of stone sitting on columns 11.75 in diameter with papyrus bell capitals. There are 134 columns in 16 rows. The three central aisles are wider and higher than the side aisles and permit clerestory light to filter in between the two heights. The clerestory is made of pierced slabs of limestone, and heralded a method of lighting that would be highly developed in the Gothic and early Christian styles.

Ramses II was an indefatigable builder, and many tombs and temples bear his name. The most impressive was the Great Temple at Abu Simbel (1301 BC), cut into the rock on a dramatic hillside, with a smaller temple to his queen Nefertari standing nearby. The imposing facade consists of four rock-cut seated colossal statues of Ramses 65 ft high. Behind the statues are various tomb chambers (3).

When Lake Nasser was built, an international effort to move the temple to higher ground was mounted to avoid the submerging of this great monument. This nearly impossible task was finally accomplished, and the rebuilt temple sits not far away, crowning an artificial hill. The technology and skill used in rebuilding it are almost as impressive as the creation of the original temple.

The history of tombs, temples, and palaces is really a history of materials and methods of building. For example, in the Assyrian culture, which flourished between 1859 and 539 BC in the northern reaches of the Tigris and Euphrates Rivers, the available material was mud bricks. Stone and timber were relatively unobtainable. Their architecture was a walled architecture set on large terraces and forming a series of large and small courtyards. The walls were very thick, 20 ft on the average in the Palace of Sargon at Khorsabad, and rooms were narrow, carrying brick barrel vaults. The chief temples had sacred "ziggurats," which were like artificial mountains rising in rectangular tiers up to seven levels. Burnt brick was used for special facings, and walls were plastered and painted with polychrome decorations in glazed brick. The Assyrians did use stone for wall reliefs and for huge winged bulls that guarded the entrances to their palaces. These winged bulls and reliefs, which tell the history of their conquests, lion hunts, and building, are among the most impressive early works of art in existence and are shown in a magnificent collection at the British Museum in London. The Assyrian civilization centered around the ancient cities of Nimrud, Nineveh, Ashur, and Khorsabad in northern Iraq.

The Persians had available to them cedar from Lebanon and teak from the Zagros Mountains. This made it possible for them to build columned halls like the "Hall of a Hundred Columns" at the Palace of Persepolis (518–460 BC). The roofs were framed in wood, the columns were slender and graceful, and the architecture looked much lighter than the heavy barrel-vaulted spaces of the Mesopotamian cultures. They also borrowed craftsmen from the Assyrians, Babylonians, Egyptians, and Ionians. This availability of craftsmen and materials led to a rich architecture.

Credit for building these big palace complexes, as in Mesopotamia, went to their great leaders. For example, the Palace of Persepolis, begun in 518 BC by Darius I, was largely built by Xerxes I from 486 to 485 BC and was finished by Artaxerxes in 460 BC. Who the real designers were is lost in history. Many great artists worked to create the glazed brick and stone sculptures that decorate the palace. The monumental stairs are lined with reliefs, and these reliefs picture processionals with nobles, courtiers, warriors, and tribute-bearers advancing in dignified fashion, all originally in brilliant colors.

The major buildings of Mesopotamia and Iran exemplify the two main building traditions of the Middle East as a whole: the clay brick architecture of the alluvial river plains of the fertile crescent and the addition of wood and increasing use of stone in the highland zone of Iran.

The character of Greek architecture from 650 to 630 BC,

like that in Mesopotamia, developed from the materials and techniques available. Largely a wood architecture to begin with, it was essentially columned and trabeated (beamed). The method of construction is immediately clear and uncomplicated by arches, vaults, or domes. Since triangulation was unknown, its gabled roofs were built of wood purlins and rafters propped up by vertical struts sitting on crossbeams.

These forms were translated into stone about 600 BC, and the translation was quite direct. Marble began to be used and finally became the material for whole temples in the fifth century BC. Sometimes, stone slabs spanning the roof over colonnades surrounding the temples were coffered to imitate timber detailing. The finest temples had beautiful sculpture, and the earlier stone sculptures were highly colored, but as marble began to be used, color was applied only to selected parts, keeping the qualities of the marble more natural.

Greek architecture, particularly of the Hellenic period in the fifth century BC, produced architectural forms and orders that strongly inspired the Romans, Renaissance Europe, and then, later into the nineteenth century, cultures all over the western world. The artistic qualities developed during that period were the source for much of the artistic and literary greatness that followed.

The Greeks developed the orders, the type forms of the simple Doric, the more slender Ionic, and the later Corinthian, which was used widely by the Romans as the standard for all classic architecture. The refinements they developed, such as entasis on columns, the curving of the stylobate upwards at the middle by a few inches to correct the optical illusion of sagging, the spacing of columns closer to the ends to strengthen the illusion of evenness, and many others, indicate subtleties in design rarely achieved again.

The peak of the Greek achievement was the Acropolis and the Parthenon. The Parthenon (447–432 BC), built under Pericles, was designed by Ictinus and Callicrates, with Phidias as the master sculptor. This building established for its architects their reputation as being among the finest ever. The 42-ft high gold and ivory statue of Athena Parthenos of Chryselephantine standing in the middle and the famous Elgin marbles of the Panathenic procession sculptured into the frieze and pediments established Phidias as a great sculptor. The Parthenon stands as the prototypical classical temple studied by all young architects as they aspire to perfection (3).

THE ARCHITECT AS SERVANT OF GOD

The Medieval Architect

The cathedrals of France, Germany, and the United Kingdom, perhaps the grandest spaces the world has ever known, were obviously designed by gifted architect-designer-engineers, but there is little agreement about who the actual individuals were. Perhaps this is due in part to the length of the construction process and possibly to the lack of printing to record accurately the history. There is much debate about the authors of these magnificent structures. The anonymity of the artists may be at-

tributable, on the one hand, to a fear of offending God by too great an individual artist on the side of the monks and, on the other, to the brotherhood of the guilds on the side of the masons. In any case, the soul of the individual architect was struggling to emerge, and in some rare shafts of light there is a glimpse of that individual.

For the young Goethe, traveling about Germany in 1772, the Strasbourg Cathedral was the most awesome thing he had ever seen. In a book he wrote called *Von deutscher Baukunst (On German Architecture)*, he praises the architect Master Erwin (Von Steinbach) as superhuman and as a genius. The debate about genius immediately began, with the eternal problem of the inspired artist vs the practical man who builds the cathedral. Actually, Erwin appeared after the nave was built in 1284 to build the rose window and redesign the west front to fit the nave. The tower and spire admired by Goethe were not designed by Erwin. It seems that the theory that the great Gothic architecture rose out of individual fiery instantaneous inspiration was a long way from the truth (4).

Andrew Saint in his book entitled the *Image of the Architect* calls attention to some of these myths about architects. Early nineteenth century authors like Cunningham, in *Lives of the Most Eminent British Painters, Sculptors and Architects*, have few doubts about the monks. He ascribes all sorts of buildings to William of Wykeham, Bishop of Winchester, buildings like Winchester Cathedral, Windsor Castle, and New College, Oxford. This was the ideal of the architect–priest who built or erected cathedrals. On the other hand, it appears that a nonpriest, William of Wynford, was the person who actually executed and supervised the work. Assigning professional responsibility for this or that design became an increasing problem for succeeding generations (4).

After the French Revolution, the churches and abbeys were returned to the State, and in France the state began to restore them. There was a strong Catholic sentiment that wanted the Gothic monuments to be returned to the Church, but famous secular architects like Viollet-le-Duc were against it. They developed all the arguments they could to show that the lay craftsmen had created the Gothic.

Other views appeared in the mid-nineteenth century in the UK in Ruskin's writing. His view was a reaction to the social ills of the time, which he said could be cured if only people could devote themselves to the holiness of the work ethic. He believed that proper work to build beautiful houses and churches was important to the social health of the nation. He went further to suggest, in the *Seven Lamps of Architecture*, that the greatness of the Gothic sprang ultimately from the spiritual contentment of its builders. His was a romanticized social and political ideal: he was trying to eliminate the difference between the thinking gentleman and the master architect. Each should have expert hands-on experience, whether a master-manufacturer in the mills or an architect in the mason's yard. Thus there would be an egalitarian peace between the two (5).

The records on masons go back to 1400, and there was a good deal of writing about the traveling bands of Freemasons who went from nation to nation selling their expertise on building churches. Interest in the freemasonry myth grew, and William Morris arrived on the scene in the 1880s to extol the lifestyle of the working craftsman of the medieval age as preferable to the burgeoning capitalism. He reinforced strongly Ruskin's view of the medieval architect and craftsman. He pictured a true and equal contribution of collaborative artists skilled in all their trades. The beauty of Gothic art was a product of their love of their work and a socialist ethic. The collaborative ideal is that "each man feels responsible for the whole," that "no part is unimportant," and that "men work not like ants or live machines, or slaves to a machine—but like men" (6).

Certainly, the Gothic was, for all kinds of craftsmen, one of the most hands-on building periods in history. First, the master builder was brought in and hired all the craftsmen, who formed their own workshops. The master builder had gained his experience working on other cathedrals and visiting and examining other sites. He brought in the quarriers who quarried the rough stone; the stone cutters, who cut the stone down into the proper sizes; the mortar makers; the master mason, who had many assistants; the blacksmith; the master carpenter, who made the scaffolding, centering, gabled roof structure, and machines for lifting; the master roofer; and, finally, the sculptor and stained glass artisans. The master builder probably presented the plans on two slabs of plaster, one to lay out the plans and vaulting and the other to describe in elevation the typical bay of the cathedral from the ground up to the roof showing the three levels of nave arcade, triforium, and clerestory.

Building a Gothic cathedral could take from 40 to 80 years, and in the process, the master builder could be succeeded by one or two other master builders. Also, several bishops could reign over the same project. Obviously, building such a structure meant the succeeding architect had to continue with the same overall plan and details. The architect had to suppress personal ego for expression and make it part of a contribution to community and to the glory of God (7).

The key development of the Gothic architects was the creation of *la voûte sur croisée d'ogives,* a vaulting framework of intersecting stone pointed arch ribs, which support thin stone filler panels. In the earlier Roman and Romanesque methods of vaulting, the vaulting compartments were square, and the vaulting heavy continuous stonework was more or less integral with the walls. With the development of the pointed ribs, differences in arch widths could be accommodated, and the ribs could still meet at the center at the same height. This allowed much greater freedom in planning with rectangular vault compartments. Also, with the stone ribs and lighter stone infill panels between ribs the vaults could be made much lighter. Abbé Suger is generally given credit for beginning the ogival system in the choir roof of the Benedictine Abbey on the outskirts of Paris (1144). Gravity loads were taken straight down the large piers, and the outward thrust of the arch voussoirs was collected at the meeting points of the ribs of adjoining compartments, carried to the ground by buttresses, and weighted by stone pinnacles. Since walls were now discontinuous in the form of large piers, the infill between the piers could be traceried stained glass windows, the most glorious being the windows of Chartres, and the most totally transparent and graceful example of stained glass being that in the Gloucester Cathedral in England.

Some of the famous maston—architects, such as those of the Reims Cathedral (1211–1290) in France, are known. The western facade of the Reims Cathedral (1255–1290) was done by Bernard de Soissons and is more ornate than that of Notre Dame in Paris. Amiens Cathedral (1220–1288) began with the nave designed by Robert de Luzarches and was completed in 1236. Next, the choir (1236–1270) was designed by Thomas and Regnault de Cormont, father and son. In the UK, the beginning of a separate development was started by William of Sens in the rebuilding of the choir of Canterbury Cathedral in 1174 (3).

THE ARCHITECT AS DESIGNER FOR RULING FAMILIES, POPES, AND KINGS

The Renaissance Architect

With the beginning of the Renaissance in the fifteenth century in Florence, there was no longer any doubt of the identity of the individual architect. The anonymity of the medieval architect was gone forever. Instead of the master mason, there was the architect as a master artist accomplished in the arts of sculpture and painting as well as architecture, like Michelangelo, Brunelleschi, and Bernini. It was commonplace for artists to be distinguished in several arts, and social prestige accompanied ability in the crafts and arts. Great artists achieved a higher social status than in previous periods.

The patrons of these artists were ruling families such as the Medicis and the Pittis. These families achieved great commercial success and were the heads of various city-states. The Medici family, founded in 1424 by Giovanni de Medici, was the first; Giovanni's son Cosimo founded many Florentine institutions and was the patron of Brunelleschi, Michelozzi, Donatello, Masaccio, and Lippi. Cosimo's grandson Lorenzo the Magnificent (1449–1492) devoted his life to the arts and brought Florence to its cultural zenith.

The rediscovery of classical literature created a wave of interest in old Roman architecture, but the new movement approached the "orders" with great freedom, using them decoratively rather than academically. In their palaces, the heavy, rusticated facades are without pilasters, leaving the expressions of colonnades for the courtyards or cortiles within. Columned arcades were a popular feature in streets as well as in courtyards, and the architectural character owes much to the contributions of sculptors and painters such as Luca della Robbia, Ghiberti, and Donatello. The freedom with which the architect approached designs and the turning away from the Gothic are almost reminiscent of the present struggle of the postmodernists to escape the straitjacket of the modernist approach.

Examples of palaces in the early Florentine period are the Riccardi, the Pitti, and the Strozzi. Typically, their facades were divided into three large stories, divided by horizontal stone courses, punctuated with arched windows, and topped by huge cornices.

The high Renaissance developed in Rome and borrowed much from the Florentine architects who went to work there. The grandest example there is the Cathedral of St. Peter (1506–1626). Pope Julius II had the idea to build a tomb house for himself that would express his personality as a great pontiff and statesman and would be the most magnificent monument of the Christian religion. Bramante won the initial competition, but was succeeded by Giuliano San Gallo, Fra Giocondo, Raphael, and others. Finally, Michelangelo, at the age of 72, produced a more dense composition using a Greek cross plan with four giant bays leading up to the cupola. He designed the dome, which was carried out after his death. In order to keep the giant dome from thrusting off its drum, a series of tension chains were wrapped within the circumference of the dome to keep the dome from spreading. This ingenious Renaissance structural solution was used in the Duomo in Florence by Brunelleschi and later by Christopher Wren in St. Paul's Cathedral in London.

As the Renaissance developed in France in the sixteenth century, it exhibited marked differences from the Italian. In France, there was more a grafting of classic details onto Gothic features, producing picturesque ensembles. In Italy, the major buildings were built in cities such as Florence, Rome, Venice, and Genoa for popes and nobles, whereas in France they were built in the countryside around Paris and the Loire for kings and courtiers. The Italian Renaissance was more horizontal and stately, whereas in France there was more a feeling of verticality.

Although at first Italian architects produced the Renaissance buildings in France, gradually the School of Fontainebleau took over in 1535. The French began to produce their own style, and the leaders were Jean Goujon (1505–1568), Pierre Lescot (1510–1578), Philibert de L'Orme (1512–1570), Jean Bullant (1520–1578), and Jacques du Cerceau the Elder (1520–1585).

In the later classical period (late sixteenth and early seventeenth centuries), many of the great palaces, such as those in the Loire valley, Blois for Louis XII and Francis I and Chenonceaux for Henry II, were built. The great palaces of the Louvre in Paris and Versailles just outside Paris are literally a history of the kings of France and such great French architects as Jacques Le Mercier, Lescot, Le Vau, J. A. Gabriel, Jules Mansart, and Charles Le Brun. The gardens of Versailles were by André Le Nôtre. They are grand in scope and among France's finest gifts to the culture of Europe (3).

THE ARCHITECT BECOMES PROFESSIONAL

The Eighteenth and Nineteenth Centuries

During the eighteenth century in the UK, architects came from two different classes. They were talented amateurs like Wren or Vanbrugh or they were building craftsmen, masons, or carpenters with a reputation for design, like Hawksmoor and Ware. The educated amateurs did a small portion of all work, concentrating on churches and public works or expensive houses for themselves or their friends. The craftsmen were the profession proper and did the bulk of the work. They also made a living by acting as surveyors, builders, house agents, materials suppliers, etc.

There was another type of architect that had a great impact in the gradual shaping of the profession. They were entrepreneur–architects like John Wood the Elder and John Wood the Younger in Bath, England, John Nash in London, and Charles Bulfinch in Boston, Massachusetts, who put their own money at risk in city building.

In the early eighteenth century, John Wood the Elder wanted to transform Bath into a second Rome, embracing the ideals of classical architecture following Andrea Palladio. After executing a number of private commissions, he became an entrepreneur. He would acquire a piece of land, and then invite builders to build houses and lodgings to suit individual clients behind a facade of his design. His first masterpiece was Queen Square in 1729, followed by Prior Park. He culminated his life's work with the famous Circus in 1754. Today, walking up through the city and into the Circus, one is surrounded by the artistic greatness of John Wood the Elder.

During the latter half of the eighteenth century, Bath experienced a building boom. John Wood the Younger took the opportunity to continue in his father's tradition in the expansion of Upper Bath and built the Royal Crescent between 1767 and 1774 (8).

In early eighteenth-century London, developer–architect John Nash stood in sharp contrast to an architect such as Sir John Soane, who personified the ideal of the individual architect that was eventually to survive as the primary image (Soane was to be the great "consolidator of British architectural professionalism"). Nash proved that the entrepreneur–architect, like John Portman today, can be a great force in the building of cities. At age 58, Nash changed from being a country house architect to being a city planner, builder, and promoter. He was appointed architect for the Office of Woods and Forests, and as such was asked to prepare plans for the crown lands of St. Mary-le-Bone connecting to Westminster. He threw himself into this with vigor and, having developed the government plan, proceeded to accomplish the Regent Street development, using his own money when other means failed. Just above Piccadilly, a section called the Great Quadrant needed to be developed as a unit, but other speculators were reluctant to put in the large sums necessary. Undaunted, Nash built this part with a large injection of his own funds (Fig. 1).

The idea of Regent Street was to create a series of normal building lots for separate financing. Since many of these sites were designed by Nash and others who were connected with and influenced by him, strong architectural coherence was achieved along the street. With remarkable vision and will, Nash created the whole connecting urban fabric from his Regents Park design, with Cumberland Terrace and other terraces around the park, through Regent Street to the Quadrant, to Waterloo Place, down to St. James Park (designed by him) and then along the Mall to Buckingham Palace (for which he made the original design) (9).

In a similar period in the United States, there was

Figure 1. The Great Quadrant, Regent Street by John Nash.

another remarkable speculator architect, Charles Bulfinch (1793–1844), who is generally recognized as Boston's first true architect.

Born on August 8, 1763, Bulfinch had observed the beginning of the Revolutionary War and remembered the Boston Tea Party and the encampment of UK troops on Boston Common.

Building in Boston was at a virtual standstill after the war, and Bulfinch took the opportunity, with an inheritance of 200 £ sterling, to go to Europe and travel for two years, visiting the great buildings and absorbing the culture of the UK, France, and Italy. He came home to Boston committed to specializing in architecture. His early designs met with universal approval, and soon commissions came to Bulfinch in increasing numbers. By 1787, Boston was beginning to be a thriving city, and Bulfinch had the opportunity to design many public buildings, churches, educational institutions, and homes for prosperous merchants. Later, he was even asked to be the architect for the Capitol in Washington, D.C.

He gave Boston much of its architectural significance through his sound judgment, discriminating taste, and wide variety of designs. Perhaps his greatest talent was his instinctive ability to select and adopt a style appropriate to each building. His genius was untutored. He relied on his own taste, a few books brought back from Europe, and memories of all the marvelous things he had seen.

As a planner and developer, Bulfinch helped transform the neglected acreage known as Copley's pasture on the southern slope of Beacon Hill into a district of quiet, tree-shaded streets lined with fine houses of generous proportions. He combined with a group of five men known as the Mount Vernon Proprietors to buy 18 acres of land from John Singleton Copley on what is known as Beacon Hill. He transformed the Beacon Hill area as well as streets around the Common.

Another of Bulfinch's developments was the Tontine Crescent on Franklin Place. The crescent shape was influenced by Wood and Nash. There were 16 connecting town-houses. This was a bold attempt to create a fashionable residential area using undeveloped marshland. The project failed, and Bulfinch's partners bowed out. He was unable to borrow the necessary funds and went bankrupt, but later on the project made money for others and was successful.

He also developed Colonnade Row on Tremont Street in 1810, a row of connecting mansions. Although successful and popular, it was torn down in 1855.

Among other things, Bulfinch was a tireless public servant, serving as Great Selectman in 1791–1795 and 1799–1817. He started Boston's police force and was the first Chief of Police. He established a municipal court, devised a plan for collecting taxes, and created Boston's first budget.

In the UK after such speculator builder–architects as Adam Brothers, Holland, and Nash, master builders (building companies) encompassing all trades took over the action from the architect–developer. Architects often made elevations for them for sales appeal, but large London companies like William Cubitt and Co. ran good architectural offices with able designers and, without any independent architect, even built houses for grand clients, like the Osborne House (1845–1850) for Victoria and Albert. This made the Victorian architect feel painfully redundant.

The ensuing struggle for registration silhouetted the positions of different sides of the profession. Opposing registration were two groups. The first was the older generation, the editors of *Architecture a Profession or an Art*, T. G. Jackson and Norman Shaw. As artist-architects, they opposed registration on the rather quixotic view that art and professionalism were incompatible. The second was the arts and crafts movement centered on Lethaby, which wanted to give substance to idealistic ideas about the sacredness of labor and to the nonstylistic ideas about architecture espoused by Ruskin and popularized by Morris.

By 1890, architects had become the dictators and the

craftsmen their servants. The autonomy of the latter dwindled, and they came more and more under the direction of the architect.

The older members of the Royal Institute of British Architects (RIBA), who were well established and had large practices, wanted registration under RIBA control, but were in no hurry. The younger group pushed for action and wanted to see its qualifications recognized. Finally, it forced RIBA to adopt registration as its official policy in 1890. Only a quarter of British architects were members of RIBA in 1911, but by the 1920s this had risen to half, and full registration was finally achieved in 1931 (10).

It is largely recognized that Ithiel Town and Alexander Jackson Davis, who started their office in 1829, were New York's first true architectural practice. After Town took the younger Davis in as partner, he went off to Europe to study the buildings of London, Paris, and Italy, hoping to gain advantage by learning about the fashions and building methods there. Touches of Nash's terraces and other European house planning began to appear in their work around Lafayette Square in New York City, builders requested more and more designs from them, and many students hurried to study under them. No doubt they even earned modest fees for their work. By 1844 when Town died, the profession was well established.

The following generation of New York architects was working to establish its professional integrity and status as artistic arbiters. One facet of this was the establishment of the science of ecclesiology. This placed on a high pedestal the serious designer of sacred buildings. Richard Upjohn, a Gothic revivalist, was a prominent ecclesiologist and designed the famous Trinity Church in New York City in 1839. He did much for the profession and crusaded against the inequities of architectural competitions and for the merits of a uniform fee schedule.

A solid citizen, conservative designer, and solid churchman, Upjohn rallied New York architects to form a professional body. On February 23, 1857, 13 architects, including Richard Morris Hunt and Upjohn's son, Richard M. Upjohn, met and formed the New York Society of Architects, soon to become the American Institute of Architects (AIA). Upjohn served as President for 18 years, and the Institute's first secretary was Hunt.

Ecclesiology as the mainstream ideal of architects grew weaker, and New York grew more secular and cosmopolitan. Ideally suited to lead the profession after these early beginnings was Hunt. He had the charisma and the right social and artistic pedigree for the challenge. He was also unique in that he was trained at the Ecole des Beaux Arts in Paris and was born rich.

Hunt's influence was enormous in the profession. He even set up an informal atelier following the beaux-arts method and he and his disciples set the direction of architectural thinking for the next 75 years. The beaux-arts ideal spread throughout the United States in the newly established schools led by Hunt's followers at the Massachusetts Institute of Technology (MIT) (1865) and Columbia University (1881) and then in many others, such as Yale University and the University of Illinois, up until the 1930s. These University beaux-arts architects, even while hard, pragmatic priorities were developing, were

openly on the artistic side of architecture at the expense of practicality. Hunt himself was well known for exceeding estimates, disregarding instructions, and neglecting supervision.

But Hunt was also a great enthusiast, educator, and strong professional voice. He led one of the early battles to get a decent fee for architects' work. He was commissioned by Eleazar Parmly, a real estate speculator, to design a studio and residence for Parmly's son-in-law T. P. Rossiter. Rossiter had met Hunt in Paris and discussed the house with him. Hunt's advice was to get an architect and pay him 5% of the cost of construction. Hunt was hired, and made some sketches that pleased Rossiter and Parmly, and then went on to complete working drawings and specifications. Parmly had another architect, Thomas Thomson, make a new set of drawings based on the Hunt design, but reducing the size and cost. Parmly paid Hunt only half his fee, saying that he had only used Hunt's general drawings, not his details or specifications.

The case went to the Superior Court in New York, and many important architects came to Hunt's defense, citing the fact that 5% of a building's cost had been the regular charge for at least 10–12 years. The judge drew attention to the fact that "Hunt did render most important and extensive services in and about the building. The enormous mass of plans spread before you shows you the great extent of the labor that the plaintiff performed. . . ." The jury rendered a verdict awarding Hunt the balance claimed, 2½% on $40,000 with four years' interest.

By the 1880s, the U.S. Renaissance was flowering, architectural offices were humming, the railroads had tied the country together, and there was building everywhere. While Hunt was providing his clients with Moorish rooms, Byzantine rooms, and Palm courts and grand staircases, H. H. Richardson was busy recreating the ponderous Romanesque architecture of Southern France for New England churches and libraries, such as Trinity Church in Boston. The battle of the styles was on. Great country homes, city houses, and public buildings were being built in the Renaissance style by McKim, Mead and White and the firm of Carrère and Hastings. The rich could order adaptations of Georgian, French Renaissance, or Colonial architecture, or they could order a Renaissance palace worthy of the Medicis, as the Henry Villards did at the corner of Madison Avenue and 50th Street in New York City.

The Columbian Exposition of 1893 was perhaps the apogee of the flowering of the beaux-arts in the United States. Plans by Frederick Law Olmsted and his assistant, Henry Codman brought order out of the wasteland along the lake shore of Chicago, Illinois. The architects John Wellborn Root and Daniel H. Burnham, the most famous professionals in Chicago, were given supervision over the plans, and they brought in famous architects from all over. The result was called "The White City." "It was an array of beaux-arts classicism as white and richly ornamented as a congregation of royal brides" (12).

The influence of the architects who catered to the upper class and their tastes in the East was now to give way to a new and vital thrust from the practical needs of the commercial world in Chicago. Fire, boom, and bust started a revolution in building in Chicago in the 1880s. Contractors knowledgeable about management, foundation conditions, and steel frames began to make the first skyscrapers possible. A new pragmatic profession was emerging. Administrative ability became more important in these more complex buildings, and the architect had to accept the conditions imposed on him by the speculators.

The two strong leaders of the profession, coming out of commercial practices, were Dankmar Adler, of Adler and Sullivan, and Burnham, of Burnham and Root. They and other Chicago architects were tired of the ineffectiveness of the AIA's Chicago chapter, and they organized a meeting of 150 practitioners in 1884 to form the Western Association of Architects (WAA). The WAA and its constituent associations wanted three things: effective rules on competitions, a share in government commissions, and architectural licensing. Adler and Burnham presented two reports on these subjects at the historic second convention of the WAA, held in St. Louis, Missouri in 1885. The Illinois State Licensing Law was passed in 1897, largely owing to Adler's lobbying efforts. It was the first one, and not until 1951 were all the states covered.

The WAA lost some of its radicalism, and finally both Adler and Burnham, seeing the profession from a more national perspective, advocated the absorption of the WAA into the national AIA. In 1899, as Burnham had suggested, the now more vigorous AIA transferred its headquarters from New York to Washington D.C., where it has been since then (13).

The fight between the artistic and the business sides of architecture still goes on, but the AIA generally contends the two are not mutually exclusive. In some of the biggest and most successful practices, the managerial and artistic sides have healthily coexisted.

THE ARCHITECT AS SERVANT OF SOCIETY

Once the architect was established as a real professional in the late nineteenth century, with percentage-type fees, commissions by contracts, production offices, and achieved status in society, there was bound to be a gradual diversification of what the ideal of the architect should be. Architecture had been gaining confidence in its newly recognized professionalism, and individual architects stood out: Richardson; Hunt; McKim, Mead and White; Louis Sullivan; and Burnham and Root. That recognition was bound to continue and grow until, late in the second half of the twentieth century, there is a plethora of superstars: Pei, Jahn, Graves, Venturi, Meier, and others. It was not until World War II, also, that another trend asserted itself, that is, the emergence of offices known by their acronyms, the most famous of which is probably SOM (Skidmore, Owings and Merrill), the initials standing for partners or principals in the firm. These are a different type of firm, sometimes with well-known designers, such as Gordon Bunshaft or Walter Netsch of SOM or Paul Kennon of CRS (Caudill Rowlett Scott), and they are made up in different ways. They are sometimes made up of a designing partner, with other partners doing managerial or marketing tasks, or they may be a combination of generalist architects, as is TAC (The Architects Collaborative). Other such firms are CUH2A, HOK, and H2L2.

In any case, such firms are often large and handle large projects. They are able to design for some of the complex needs of modern society, such as hospitals, large schools, and sometimes very large multiuse projects. Their emphasis is often on a broad practice and enhancement of the firm's name, with less emphasis on the glorified individual architect.

There is no guarantee that firms emphasizing anonymity will sacrifice the reputations of individuals in favor of a more unselfish approach to architecture and a service-to-society attitude. Some of the firms mentioned above have in fact devoted a large part of their practice to work for large corporate clients or big-moneyed institutions such as insurance companies, which most would not put in the first rank of social need. Nevertheless, the idea of an abstract idea for a name or the idea of anonymity itself leads to intimations of the potential of an ideal for the architect as a servant of society.

The emergence of the ideal that the architect should be in service to social need received great impetus in the social upheavals after World War I, dramatized first by the depression in socialist Germany, then by the Great Depression of 1929 in the United States. In Germany, pioneering housing projects such as the Siemensstadt project by Walter Gropius and the housing by Bruno Taut, Mart Stam, and Hannes Meyer were significant. The Siemensstadt project sought to ensure minimum standards of spacing between buildings to guarantee adequate space and sun at all times for all inhabitants. The orientation of the slab buildings on the east–west axis was also important to ensure sun for all dwellers in the housing. It was at this time that Gropius made one of the first attempts at prefabrication in the Toerten group, an essay on prefabrication using copper-covered panels. Prefabrication has been the dream of providing low-cost housing, scientifically designed, like a car, for many years. Essentially aimed at meeting the needs of the masses, it is a dream that still evades successful realization, although it is by no means dead.

Architects such as Meyer, Ernst May, and Stam interpreted social service and the means to accomplish it as a transition to the left, if not actually communist at least very sympathetic to it. Some of these Bauhaus architects actually went to the USSR after the Bauhaus to escape Fascism and to practice. As a footnote, in the late 1930s and early 1940s the Harvard School of Architecture published a magazine called *TASK*, which had its main emphasis on architecture for people and was considered quite left in its total approach. These were war days, when political position was much in architects' thoughts and fascism was an overwhelming enemy to be faced. Frank Lloyd Wright, a populist from the Midwest, took a political stance on the right with his acolytes as an American Firster, a rightist group emphasized isolationism just before World War II.

With the Great Depression of 1929 and the parallel disaster of the Dust Bowl a few years later, new social programs had to be created to save the nation. Franklin Roosevelt stepped into the breach and created such innovative alphabetic programs as the NRA, the WPA, and many others. Under the Works Progress Administration (WPA), with the thrust to create millions of new jobs, hundreds of new post offices and public buildings were created, with jobs for architects and artists. Artists such as Stuart Davis and Ben Shahn found the U. S. government a handsome patron. Projects like the seminal and now famous San Antonio riverwalk system were established during this period.

In an attempt to attack the gigantic problems of erosion from river valleys in Oklahoma and the south, a new agency was designed to develop the Tennessee River into an integrated system of dams for power and flood control, forest conservation to protect the hillsides, lakes to provide recreation, and new cities and industries. It was called the Tennessee Valley Authority (TVA). It created a whole new standard of unified river valley development, not to be equaled by other large regional river developments, even the immense Columbia River System (14).

The head architect for the TVA was Roland Wank, and under him, a high level of architectural design was achieved throughout the valley for many types of buildings. Young architects such as Abraham Geller produced imaginative designs for trailer-built temporary communities for the building of the dams.

On the west coast, the government created another public service agency called the Farm Security Administration. It was designed to provide economical housing for migratory workers in the southwest and in the Central Valley of California. Burton Cairns and Vernon DeMars headed the architectural office in San Francisco and created some pioneering housing designs for projects such as the adobe row houses at Chandler, Arizona, near Phoenix, and others in the Central Valley of California. They were economical, inventive, and imaginative. The site plans were beautifully designed, and it was here that the well-known landscape architect Garrett Eckbo did much of his early work (15).

Architecture that serves the people can be defined as architecture that needs to be built to meet an important social need, whether it yields a profit or not. It should be noted here that, depending on the party in power, Republican or Democratic, some government programs encourage private initiative for public-oriented projects for rental programs such as the infamous 608 rental apartments program and the more current program for old-age housing. Private developers in these programs are encouraged to participate with profit as the incentive.

In a symposium held in 1983 by the Carnegie-Mellon University Department of Architecture in Pittsburgh, Pennsylvania, some interesting insights on the servant role of the architect were presented. The meeting was called "The Role of the Architect in Society." Most or all of the participants agreed with the AIA, which stated in its bylaws of 1981 that "the purpose of the organization is to ensure the advancement of the living standards of people through their improved environment; and to make the profession of ever-increasing service to society." However, there was much analysis of how to improve that service.

As a basis for a critical look at how well the architect has served the public, work on housing and redevelop-ment was closely scrutinized. Housing projects, undertaken with idealistic fervor and imagination, have rarely met the social goals that were intended (16).

There were some fine public housing projects built in the 1930s, such as the Harlem River Houses in New York City. Two notably successful projects for a slightly higher income bracket were the low-rise Chatham Village Homes in Pittsburgh and Baldwin Hills Village in Los Angeles. These last two are still viable and pleasant environments. In Baldwin Hills Village, two-story units are arranged around open pedestrian spaces, and the individual units have their own walled patios. It is the handsome land-scaped open space that is the beauty of this project (17).

In general, however, housing projects were seen as failures. They had become alien and dangerous places. The social upheavals of the 1960s and the deterioration of social ethics in the underprivileged classes hastened the rapid deterioration of these environments. They were seen as environments in which crime could fester and drugs could prosper. High-rise solutions no longer seemed good for families. Corridors and hidden corners became threats to personal safety. In the book *Defensible Space*, a whole set of negative standards for planning was developed (18).

Projects such as the high-rise Pruitt-Igoe in St. Louis, a project that not long before had received a high architectural honor and was designed by the prestigious firm of Hellmuth, Yamasaki and Leinweber, was finally destroyed by dynamiting because the whole environment had become such a threat to life and safety. The condition of the Columbia Point Housing project in Boston poses a continual challenge to rescuing that highly threatened project. It was not long before postmodernist critic Charles Jencks, Peter Blake in his book *Form Follows Fiasco*, and Tom Wolfe in his book *From Bauhaus to Our House* pounced on the failure of Pruitt-Igoe. It was final proof that modern architecture had failed, they said, and that modern architecture's claim to be able to serve society was totally false. Urban renewal projects stimulated by and funded under the Federal Housing Administration and urban renewal programs bulldozed ahead through old neighborhoods, where many fragile human relationships were destroyed. It was unclear whether all of this urban renewal, meant so well, was really being done in the public interest. Jane Jacobs criticized the architects for destroying the U.S. city, and she had a tremendous impact on the awareness of the profession and also on the negative perception of urban renewal on the part of the public. The destruction of the historic West End in Boston by development and urban renewal was a black mark on the history of such renewal and heralded a gradual turning away from such solutions toward more sympathetic restoration and rehabilitation (19).

In 1978, Herbert Gans, a socialist, approached the question from a slightly different direction. He said that all professions that seek to do good do it in ways that follow their own definition of good, but always so as to create more "power, status, and income" for their members, leading to a "benevolent, professional imperialism." This somewhat cynical view pictures the architect as satisfying self-expression in aesthetic values and with a paternalistic view toward society in attempts to do good (20).

What went wrong with the architects' attempts to design successful environments for these social programs? Have the attitudes that have developed been wrongheaded or lacking seriously in some way? Some insight is gained by a review of the Carnegie-Mellon conference.

Two role models were suggested by James Ackerman in an article titled "Listening to Architects" (1969). They were the egoist and the pragmatist. The egoist places his or her own freedom high and equality low. The attitude is paternalistic, and according to this breakdown, such an architect responds only superficially to relevant value systems. The architect produces what he or she wants. The pragmatist places equality high and freedom low. Such an architect is entrepreneurial and gives clients exactly what they want, totally accepting the value system. Burgess, Littman, and Mayo, in a 1981 article called "Political Knowledge and the Architectural Studio" developed a third role, where freedom and equality (equality with the value systems of the client and user) were valued equally. This role was called that of facilitator. The facilitator, in contrast to the egoist or the pragmatist, gives them what he or she can (21).

Interesting here is that, although the architect has to be very responsive and this can help to create better architecture, it is clear that "good processes don't guarantee good buildings" as Stefani Ledewitz pointed out in the symposium. There is a need to be sensitive, but finally the architect has to turn these thorough and well-intentioned processes into better and inspiring environments. The pragmatic architect listens well to the clients, but being underprivileged does not mean that they can convey or articulate their needs, except in a primitive way, or what is really required for healthy living ambience. The pragmatic architect, in giving clients exactly what they want, may be giving them the minimum of what is possible. Ledewitz notes the difference between a skilled occupation which caters to a client who "determines what services and/or commodities he/she wants," and a professional, who takes some responsibility for what is good or bad for a client. Obviously, this latter role places on the architect greater accountability and greater risk in taking positions not always within the total consensus of the client. The architect who wants to work in the community design tradition should have greater sensitivity to user needs and a stronger theoretical foundation (22).

Out of the social upheavals of the late 1950s and 1960s, the civil rights movement produced chaos in major U.S. cities. As Ledewitz pointed out, the "urban poor became politically active and vocal," and the Johnson administration initiated the Community Action Program, which asked for the "maximum feasible participation of residents of the areas and members of the groups" in local programs.

Many architects responded in community design centers. Some centers were offshoots of universities, like the Pratt Institute community design center (serving poor sections of Brooklyn) and the Urban Field Service program under Chester Hartman at Harvard University, and others were groups such as the Architects Renewal Committee for Harlem (ARCH). These architects and planners gave free technical service, providing architectural, planning, and other services for an underprivileged community.

Architects gave their time as technical experts, as advocates, and sometimes as *facilitators* helping to manage a process where decent housing or recreational facilities could be achieved.

The Builders of New Towns

After World War II, in many countries of Europe, the rapid growth of population and the phenomenal rise in traffic caused by the increased use of the automobile created severe congestion on the highways and in the cities and growing sprawl in the countryside as people fled the cities to find space. Earlier, architects such as Eliel Saarinen in Finland and Le Corbusier in France had advocated new plans for cities, trying to give order to the circulation and green space between sectors. In 1943, Saarinen, in his book *The City*, advocated decentralization of cities. Le Corbusier, in *Ville Radieuse*, proposed a plan for Paris that had long rectangular buildings in a continuous zigzag over the landscape with a high density. The higher density relieved much of the land for open space, gardens, and recreation. He separated the car from the pedestrian with raised motorways, and people were free to circulate safely in any direction (23). Lewis Mumford criticized Le Corbusier's designs as being too dense, too monumental, and therefore inhuman, but the basic search for open space and the idea of freeing pedestrians from the increasing menace of the automobile became a basic theme through all new planning (24).

In the UK in the 1950s, a New Towns policy was initiated, and 20 or more New Towns were actually built. Most are very rational, humane, and pleasant environments, but in achieving their open space goals those towns became very spread out, lacking the focus and cohesiveness that a higher density might have given.

In order to correct this, a plan for a New Town called Hook was developed for 100,000 inhabitants in a valley. It featured a spine with multilevel separation of cars and people with housing for 100 persons per acre along the spine and was somewhat less dense (40 persons per acre) farther from the spine. Distances were short, and all community facilities were easily reached. The open space of the countryside was never far from the center (25).

Hook was never built, but a successor design, the New Town of Cumbernauld near Glasgow, was built and embodies many of these principles. The town and commercial center are a concentrated megastructure with many kinds of facilities, a retail mall, hotels, theaters, cafes, and town government and social services. Buses, cars, taxis, and service vehicles all circulate at a lower level, and pedestrian activities take place on several levels above the vehicles. This creates a radical, urbane quality for a town in the country. Other housing is dispersed around the center, with green open space intervening between neighborhoods. Housing is provided for several different lifestyles, from patio rowhouses to mid-rise towers.

Vallingby, near Stockholm, Sweden, is an example of a satellite town depending on its mother city for industry and workplaces. Road and rail connect it to Stockholm.

Although somewhat lower in density than Hook or Cumbernauld, it still provides rail connections beneath the center of the town. High towers surround the center, and many types of housing are provided in the various development sectors, with open space between.

In the United States, some attempts to solve the problem of urban congestion without producing more suburban sprawl were made by semipublic groups such as the Town of Benjamin (near Minneapolis, Minnesota). Funding for the infrastructure was to be provided by the federal government. Most of these attempts were unsuccessful, but two more privately financed and promoted projects, Columbia, Maryland, and Reston, Virginia, were successful. Columbia was developed by the Rouse group, a large shopping center developer. Reston, in the suburbs of Washington D.C., planned its town center at one end of a large lake. Housing is of various types, including apartment towers, and it is rather dense overall. Again, the planning is aimed at concentrating amenities and housing to produce a more urban quality and provide for convenient movement from one area to another. Conklin and Rossant were the architects for the central portion and master plan, and other architects designed the various sectors.

Under the leadership of Edward Logue, the Urban Development Corporation of New York State as part of its overall housing development program embarked on the creation of three new towns: Lysander, near Syracuse in upper New York, which was based on its location near industry (master plan by David Crane); Audubon Village a satellite town for the State University of New York at Buffalo (master plan by the office of Llewelyn-Davies); and Roosevelt Island, in the middle of the East River in New York City (original master plan by Philip Johnson).

Roosevelt Island is the most complete, the most dense, and perhaps the most interesting of these. Logue's mission was to create a high-density, completely integrated town with schools and all amenities, but with a human scale and generous open space. Roosevelt Island is reached at the south end by a cabled gondola car from Manhattan at about 60th Street, and cars cross a bridge at the north end and park in a huge garage there. Transportation in the town is by public minibus. The central spine street bends around in an interesting fashion, with high-rise apartments on each side. Shops and amenities line the street level. The apartment buildings cascade in terraces down on each side toward the East River. There is ample open space between blocks. The town is high in the middle and low at its edges. It is a lively, entertaining place to live in the middle of New York City.

Architecture for People

Housing for the Poor—Undeveloped Countries. With the continuing growth of industrialization, combined with high birth rates and a perception that the city can offer more than the abject poverty of the rural areas, a tidal wave of poor migrants has invaded the major cities of the developing world. Two to three hundred million people in the developing world have moved into cities as squatters and have found conditions better than the poverty and lack of natural resources in the rural areas. The developing nations had 16 cities of 1 million or more 25 years ago. Now there are 60 such cities. Squatter communities are growing at an annual rate of 6% or more, whereas the rest of the developing communities are increasing at 3%, just half of the squatter growth. These squatters make up from 25 to 50% of the population of cities such as Ankara, Turkey; Caracas, Venezuela; Jakarta, Indonesia; and Lima, Peru.

These bloated urban areas have become concentrations of unemployment, hunger, disease, crime, and pollution. The squatters live in dilapidated houses that are unsafe and where there are not adequate sewers or water supply. These people come to the cities often lacking skills to support themselves, and they have not for the most part found a satisfactory adjustment to urban life. Much of their work is part time, and they live by their own efforts. The challenge to the architect is to improve their conditions through housing and community life.

For governments to provide conventional housing for all of these people is far beyond the resources available, but the solution may be found in the squatters themselves. Although they create the problem, they may, through proper organization of self-help and community, point the way toward improved conditions. They may be poor, but they often are resourceful, have free time, and are willing to work. They also have another important attribute: they have a strong sense of community with strong ties to one another, sharing common goals and a willingness to sacrifice to achieve their ends.

Architects searching for a way to contribute to solving these problems realize that the usual approach to housing, worked out to the last detail and with conditions imposed by the heavy hand of the state or municipality, is not going to work in this context. The architect must think of means for community organization and development and develop principles of housing rather than create detailed, completed designs. The role of the architect in working toward a housing solution in developing countries is new in history. Helping squatters build their own houses and communities is a more subservient role and is the opposite of the grand architect role. There is some analogy to medieval history, when hundreds of craftsmen working anonymously on a cathedral were more important than the individual architect.

Although the World Bank and the U.S. Agency for International Development have made attempts to improve housing conditions throughout the world, there has been little opportunity for architects to participate as a group. With this in mind, the Habitat Conference—Exposition on Human Settlements held in Vancouver, B. C., Canada, in June 1976 inspired the staffs of the magazines *Architectural Record* and *L'Architecture d'Aujourd'hui* to contribute to the conference by forming the International Architectural Foundation, a nonprofit organization, which then sponsored the International Design Competition for the Urban Environment of Developing Countries Focused on Manila. More than 2500 architects from all over the world learned about the squatter problems of the Tondo area of Manila, the Philippines, and 500 completed the competition.

The Tondo area of Manila is a marshy area of Manila Bay, has a density of 460 people per acre, is the largest slum area of Manila, and as such, is prototypical of slums of many cities in the developing countries. The winner of the competition was Ian Athfield of New Zealand. A key element in Athfield's solution was the belief that squatters' problems would not be solved without providing new job opportunities. He proposed workplaces in the form of continuous linear buildings surrounding each *baranguay*, or neighborhood, for cottage and other light, nonpolluting industries. They have community gardens on top. These buildings also supply centers for energy conservation. The proposed housing ideas emphasize the vernacular roots and self-help. The jury thought his designs struck the right balance between traditional materials and innovative methods. Athfield's design has not been implemented, but it is hoped that the Philippine Government will demonstrate its sincerity and commitment by going forward (26).

Through this competition, architects had to think deeply about their own role. To provide what the community needed, they could not intervene in a total way and had to perceive themselves as helpers and facilitators rather than being in control of the whole design process.

One of the most noted architects to devote his life to providing adequate housing for the poor is Hassan Fathy, an Egyptian architect. He is a deep believer in the idea that the most practical solution for this housing is in using immediate and ready-at-hand materials like mud brick in the Middle East and wood in Southeast Asia. He believes that combining these materials with regional and local ways of capturing ventilation and shading the sun and then planning villages that reflect local planning traditions can yield the most satisfying social and aesthetic environments for these people.

Early in his career, Fathy began to believe that mud brick, the humblest of all materials, dug out of the earth and dried in the sun, was a key to his housing goals. Unfortunately, even though he designed a number of handsome mud brick residences in the 1930s, they were just as expensive as normal houses because of their expensive timber roofs. If he could use mud brick vaulting for the roof, he might have an answer. To this end, he did research in Egypt to see if they had any experience with brick vaulting. Contrary to the theory that the Romans had invented the first arch, Fathy found evidence at the granaries of the Ramasseum at Luxor, at Touna el Gebel, and at Aswan that vaulting and dome techniques were familiar to Egyptians as early as the Twelfth Dynasty.

The ancient technique for building mud brick vaults required no centering (formwork) and the vaults spanned 3 m. Essentially, the vaulting bricks were laid against each other to form a parabolic curve, not on a vertical plane with the walls, but on a slight diagonal so that one ring of brick was leaning against another, ending up on a vertical wall face.

Through the Egyptian Department of Antiquities, Fathy was asked to undertake the design of a whole village, the village of Gourna, opposite Luxor. This was a sensitive situation because the 7000 inhabitants of Gourna were essentially squatters, building on and around the ancient tombs of the Valley of the Kings and Queens. The Gournis had for 50 years been living on the past, robbing the rich graves of their ancestors and then being exploited by clever dealers in Cairo. A new 50-acre site was selected, not on the hills where there were still many undiscovered tombs, but on agricultural land a few miles away protected by dikes from flooding.

In his designs, Fathy emphasized the individuality of the houses, as opposed to mass-produced objects. He said that in mass production the individual puts less and less into the product. Machine-made products are impersonal, whereas the craftsperson brings irregularity, oddities, and differences into the result.

Fathy does not believe that mass-produced housing can house the peasant cheaply enough or humanely enough. He believes that it is more practical to involve the people in building their own houses.

In his houses for Gourna, Fathy incorporated many ingenious local traditions and persons. The keynote idea was the pigeon tower, which was originally the way the villagers kept pigeons. Fathy also used the *maziara*, the vaulted structure that shaded the place where the villagers got water, and the *malkaf*, or wind catch. This last device has a part of the room catch the wind high up and lets the hot air escape through the top. It is specially oriented to catch the breeze regardless of the grid alignment of the house. On top, a sloping metal tray is wetted by a tap and cools the air before it enters the room. The houses were designed to capitalize on their thick wall insulating values during the day, and the dwellers lived on the roof at night to avoid the buildup of heat in the lower level during the day. A light structure covers the roof, shading the bottom part during the day and providing mosquito protection during the night.

In the urban planning of the village, inspiration was taken from the idea of the sky as the home of God. For the desert dweller, the desert is a hostile, difficult environment. It is a cruel enemy. The sky is clear, promising coolness and water with its clouds. A house with a courtyard frames the sky and focuses on its beneficence. Such a house became a planning module. Fathy used these houses to create, at intervals in the plan, an outside public square, which the houses face and so partake in the life of the village. These squares form a social focus for the *badina*, the familial group with cafés, bakeries, and grocers' shops. It is the socioeconomic group of the community for celebrations and feasts (27).

Unfortunately, bureaucratic red tape and other problems prevented the completion of New Gourna, but it points to a way of dealing with the problems of housing for the poor.

Prefabrication

In the industrialized countries of the western world, a growing disparity between the need for housing and the capacity of the housing industry became evident. With the population growth after World War I and the later population explosion after World War II, a substantial proportion of the whole was ill housed. Prefabrication, or industrialized housing, was seen as a solution to the mass-housing problem. Quantity could be combined with quality. In contrast to the antiquated methods of building houses on the site, the whole process could be industrialized in controlled conditions in the shop, prefinished and completed with hardware and equipment. There was a good deal of romantic appeal to a rational mind in this prospect.

One of the early attempts to build cheap industrialized houses was the joint effort between the Hirsch Copper Works in Germany and Walter Gropius. Hirsch was an old, established manufacturer of copper products, including many building products, and came out with its own version of an industrialized house made of copper modular panels over wood frames, shown at the German Building Exhibition in May 1931. The space between the panels was filled with an insulated material consisting of a series of airtight cells, and care was taken to prevent a heat bridge between inner and outer surfaces. However, the architectural character was entirely conventional and in no way expressed its functional character. Gropius, although generally approving the technical quality of the panels and their weather resistance, had his own reservations about the architectural design.

Gropius prepared some material for the Bauwelt Catalogue on the Hirsch Houses, with technical details and publicity supplied by Hirsch. Soon after, Gropius prepared a paper with both technical and merchandising recommendations on the potential development of the houses. These recommendations became policy, and Gropius went to work for Hirsch in the development and refinement of the copper houses.

An intensive series of tests was conducted on the quality of the materials, acoustics, thermal characteristics, and fire safety of the houses. A constant dialogue between the factory and Gropius's designers was maintained. A sort of ideal interaction between architect and industry developed, as envisaged by the Deutsche Werkbund and the Bauhaus.

Gropius's three themes for the design emphasize the flexibility and dynamic qualities of the system. These themes are mobility, or the ease of transportation and adaptation to various locations and climes; adaptability, or the capacity to generate many house types and variations through the interplay of standardized components; and growth, or the expandability of the house. Designs were developed for several prototypes, from a minimum 36.9-m^2 house to one of 111.82-m^2.

Thirty houses were built by the end of 1931, and Gropius was part of the entire process. The culmination of the design effort was the erection of two developed houses for Hirsch at the Building for All exhibition in Berlin in May 1932. The houses were functionally and aesthetically in the best Bauhaus tradition and received the most acclaim. They had a flat roof, clearly expressed their modular character, and were elegantly detailed, inside and out.

In spite of this initial success, however, Gropius's dream of at last producing a salable prefabricated house was not to become reality. There had been many contacts for possible projects using these houses not only in Germany, but in Budapest and the USSR. But the Great Depression in the United States tended to undermine the

optimistic hopes for large projects, and the desperate growth of Hitler in Germany put an end to hopes for the copper house project, particularly since Hirsch was a well-known Jewish industrial leader. Hirsch was faced with many problems larger than the copper house project (28).

In February 1943, Gropius and Konrad Wachsmann, under the name of the General Panel Corporation, came out with a wood panel prefabricated house system and a model house (29). Wachsmann, like Gropius, had worked on prefabricated houses in Germany; however, he had worked with wood for the firm of Christoph and Unmack, the largest producers of wooden houses on the continent. Wood was plentiful in the United States and seemed a natural material to use. Not only was Wachsmann an expert in wood panel design, but he developed ingenious joints for the attachment of the panels. The connectors were a special metal clip with wooden wedges. Four, six, or eight were used per panel, and together with the nails used to secure the surfacing material to the wooden frames, these constituted much less metal than the maximum allowed by the government at that time. The only tool needed for the attachment of the panels was a hammer, and for disassembly a pair of pliers. No nails or screws were required, except for a limited amount of trim.

All panels were 40 in. wide and varied in length from 40 to 80 to 120 in. They were interchangeable as floor, wall, and ceiling panels. Also, door and window panels were typically 40 in. wide. They were covered with vertical siding, and all panels were flush at the joints with filler strip identical to the siding. There were no projections to interfere with shipping (30).

Thus Gropius's ideal of a standardized, modular product used to build houses with an infinite variety of plan variations was achieved. The system even had possibilities for different types of buildings far beyond the modest dwellings originally built to meet the requirements of the Federal Housing Administration.

After World War II, Consolidated Vultee Aircraft Corporation, seeking to take up the slack after the huge war production programs, and aiming at the mass market for a low-cost, small house, commissioned industrial designer Henry Dreyfuss and architect Edward L. Barnes to design a competitive, industrialized house.

In contrast to Gropius and Wachsmann's efforts, the house was designed to be site specific, in this case to southern California, and model specific; that is to say, the unit was the house itself. It was not panelized, like the General Panel design; rather it was a specific design for an 804-ft^2, two-bedroom, one-bath house aimed at a specific market.

A three-bedroom model was planned as well, and some variety could be achieved with different orientations of the house in the site plans and with the location of a patio wall designed as an integral part of the house (31). However, in spite of the excellence of the design, these houses never went into real production.

By 1969, the United States had, according to the U.S. Department of Housing and Urban Development (HUD), a shortage, and the need was for 26 million new or rehabilitated dwellings, or a 10-yr program for 2.6 million units/yr. There was a deficit between existing capabilities and need, which was sure to grow larger in the following decade. HUD sought to attack this problem by initiating an industrialized housing program called Breakthrough. It sought to answer the questions of outmoded laws and codes and to remedy the fragmentation of the market, which made impossible the large-scale procurement of materials and scheduling of labor forces. It was designed as a three-part program. First, private industry would compete for contracts to design industrialized housing systems. Then, significant numbers of units would be built to these designs and demonstrated on several prototype sites across the country. Finally, successful systems would go into volume production.

Twenty-two systems finalists were finally selected out of thousands of original competitors. They included designs that ranged from split-level to high-rise proposals. Materials specified included wood, concrete, metal, and plaster.

Eventually, 2000 units were built on 9 sites, but the program never graduated into large-scale production. Initiated by HUD Secretary George Romney, it was never carried through with the conviction and commitment of money necessary to acquire the sites and stimulate the building of large numbers of units.

The dream of industrialized housing to solve the need of the ill housed of the nation goes on today, however, and in the private sector several companies are producing whole trailer-built units that can be assembled like building bricks into houses. These companies are beginning to vary the box dimensions up to 12 ft wide and higher than the usual 8 ft, which may widen the appeal of such houses to a much bigger market.

The Conserver of Energy

The oil shortage of the late 1970s served to dramatize a trend that had escalated steadily since the early 1950s, particularly in the United States. A population increase of 45% and the resultant demands on energy through the growth of industry, transportation, and housing were producing disastrous consequences. The current way of building, the overdependence on the automobile, and the reliance of industries in the midwest on huge quantities of high-sulfur coal produced pollution problems of crisis proportions. Moreover, the high cost of nonrenewable fuels such as oil and coal resulted in great economic and political consequences. The oil crisis of the late 1970s only heightened the huge problem that existed and will continue to exist. As mechanical systems are developed to answer the increased standards formulated for comfort and new materials become acceptable, more energy will be used per square foot each year. Electrical energy usage in the 1980s is roughly six times that used in 1950, and 50% of it goes to keep buildings running, including lighting. "Our buidings alone consume about twice the electricity that was used 25 years ago for all purposes" (32).

The architect has been largely responsible for creating the problem. Commercial buildings and towers that face equally north, south, east, and west create large heat loads for cooling the buildings. These buildings are uncomfortable to live in. Although glass technology has struggled to keep pace with these problems, it does so at a large increase in the cost per square foot, and windows are designed with reflecting or tinted glass dark enough to make a clear, sunny day seem like twilight. Views have been sacrificed in favor of uniform curtains or louvers fully drawn. Moreover, the architect, more and more dependent on mechanical systems, has created deeper interior space, putting greater strain on the cooling systems. It has become impossible to open windows in an office even on a good spring day.

The large increase in energy consumption is closely tied to the creation of sprawling suburbs. These suburbs need extended lines of services to provide electricity, telephones, sewers, and water. The planning decisions of the architect, eager to build huge suburban malls have increased the scale of the problem.

However, the architect is in a prime position, by a fundamental and radical change in approach, to help moderate the continuing crisis. Intelligent decisions about orientation must be made, with particular attention to different elevations of buildings. Using strategies for saving the sun's heat or alternatively forms that shade and reject unwanted sun, using current strategies for insulating to a greater degree than ever before, using methods for storing energy in the form of chilled or heated water, and borrowing the earth's mass as a thermal heat sink and insulator, along with many other strategies, the architect can lead the way toward a rational use of resources and conservation of the environment.

Many of these strategies are not new. Over many centuries, societies have developed shelter methods in many diverse climates to save heat, to shade from the heat, and to use winds for cooling. Heavy masonry walls have been used to store heat and to cool in hot weather; in the Southwest, heavy walls of adobe brick are used to slow down the extreme changes between heat gain in the day and coolness in the evening. The Indian dwellings in Mesa Verde, Colorado, are sheltered with a huge rock overhang, which shades the dwellings in the summer, but permits the sun's penetration in the winter. The traditional Japanese house, with its large overhangs, sliding exterior panels, light *shoji* to filter the light, solid panels to protect against the weather, and *tatami* (straw mats) to cover and insulate the floor, is a very good example of design that responds to the environment.

More recently, in the 1930s, George Fred Keck in Chicago designed a series of solar houses. They are generally narrow, oriented east–west on their long axis, and designed to get the maximum sunlight and heat gain naturally, but protected from the south by a carefully designed overhang that is just deep enough to let the winter sun in and keep the summer sun out. This simple and basic principle has been exploited by many contemporary architects, and a whole technology of predicting sun angles for different seasons and latitudes has developed.

Architects in recent years have made significant advances in the development of energy-saving strategies. Active strategies include solar water collectors, which have been successful in many installations, although not always cost-effective. The simplest type is the so-called flat plate collector, which allows the sun through two layers of glass into a metal panel painted black. The heat is trapped between the second layer of glass and the metal panel and transmitted to pipes attached to the plate. Insulation is added to the back of the plate. Although some collectors have generated up to 350°F, 140°F is a more average temperature. The hot water generated can then be used for domestic hot water or residential heating. Some effective solar air heating designs have been developed, doing away with the maintenance problems of water piping. One residential scheme lets the sun in through a pitched glass roof facing the sun and pushes the heated air down into joist spaces of the first and second floor, using these spaces as duct systems. Then the residual warm air is stored in a rock storage area in the basement and re-used. Electric resistance heating in the joist duct spaces is used as a booster system.

Recently, there has been an accent on passive solar heating strategies. In residential work, a greenhouse design on the south side of a house, often in connection with the kitchen, can act as a collector and as a buffer between the cold outside and the living areas. Combined with a vertical space connecting the living with the bedroom areas and with wood stoves at the lower level, the heat generated can heat bedrooms and, through the chimney action, the whole house. In commercial and larger structures, there has been an increasing accent on the maximum use of natural light to minimize the energy used for lighting, which turns out to be the largest user of energy in most commercial buildings. In the 1950s and 1960s, in school and office design it became apparent that a reasonable lighting environment does not need 100 fc of light, as the Illuminating Engineering Society long recommended, but rather more between 50 and 75 fc. These standards, combined with extreme air change regulations in schools, were a tremendous energy drain. These realizations, combined with the redirecting of natural light into the interior of the work space by means of light shelves, slightly higher ceilings, and flat, reflecting ceilings, can produce designs that sharply cut electricity consumption for lighting.

Many other strategies have developed, such as the use of reclaimed heat from the plenum space surrounding the lights in an office building, the reclaiming of heat from the exhaust ducts of laboratory fume hoods, and the use of double walls surrounding a building to control the temperature fluctuations around the exterior skin as in the brilliant design for the Hooker Building in Niagara Falls, New York, by the Cannon Design Group. The *trombé* wall, which captures heat coming in through a window in a thick concrete or masonry wall; the storage of large quantities of cooled water in underground concrete tanks, the cooling being generated in off-peak hours by the electrical system; and sophisticated new heat-conserving strategies such as earth berm architecture or geothermal heat pump systems that use the earth as a heat sink, a constant source of heat that can be used for heating or cooling, all present options worth exploring.

Perhaps the most dramatic form-making idea that has resulted from attempts to conserve energy is the acceptance of the idea of atria, roofing over spaces between wings of buildings with a skylight to create a year-round protected environment. The idea is as old as civilization; it was used in the Roman house with its roofed-over central court or atrium, in the Glazed Courts of Covent Garden in London by Inigo Jones, and later in the glazed, barrel-vaulted Galleria in Milan, Italy, providing year-round shopping.

Initially conceived as protecting the pedestrian from the vicissitudes of the weather in hot areas such as Georgia or in cold countries such as Canada, the idea of atria has had larger dimensions. It has spread to temperate climates as well and has been used to create glamorous and lovely environments in buildings serving many functions, such as museums, office buildings, and apartment buildings. It has been particularly useful in hollowing out deep old warehouse-type buildings, letting light in and creating a new central focus for new uses.

The atrium was an idea whose time had come and was coincident with or even preceded the energy crisis. The creation of large interior atriumlike spaces brought a new visual and sensual dimension to many buildings. Such spaces could be wonderfully landscaped (albeit at the expense of heavy banks of artificial lighting focused on the plants at odd hours), and they could house dining, library, and many other human activities. Architect John Portman, creating first his dramatic spaces at the Hyatt Regency Hotel in Atlanta, Georgia, and then following with other great spaces at the Hyatt Regency in San Francisco, California, and the Renaissance Center in Detroit, Michigan, led the way in showing how exciting such spaces could be. But this was not architecture for the people—it was sheer visceral excitement, luxurious, sensual, and satisfying. As public relations, it was unbeatable. It had overtones of expressing the cultural soul of the people, but the value of atria in modifying and upgrading shelter and controlling the environment is addressed next.

There is one imaginative urban design idea that is indicated in Cesar Pelli's design for a Winter Garden in Niagara Falls. It is a totally glass-enclosed multiuse environment that can be plugged into on all sides by owners. Thus the Winter Garden has become a possible spark for downtown renewal. No doubt, these environments go beyond mere utility.

Atriums as energy-conserving shelter address two important energy thrusts. One is to maximize the use of natural light to save on electrical energy. Since the biggest single user of energy in modern workplaces is artificial lighting, this is an extremely important factor. The second is that atria are buffer zones between the actual workplaces and the extremes of the climate outside. The economy of buffer spaces is negated if the spaces themselves are fully air-conditioned. The logic of their economy is that they are "lightly constructed, and are colder in winter, hotter in summer than the fully comfort-conditioned spaces they protect." Such spaces basically create double, or triple-glazed insulated zones. The walls of the workplaces need not be as well insulated as if they were outside, and this is an economy (33).

The need for control of natural light coming into an atrium to prevent glare and the need to reject the heat from the southern side have produced ingenious shading devices, from motorized louvers on the outside, which are the most effective, to a plastic solar veil, which is a white

Figure 2. TVA Headquarters Office Building, Chattanooga, Tennessee, by The Architects Collaborative, Caudill, Rowlett, and Scott and Van der Ryn, Calthorpe, and Partners. Photograph by Steve Rosenthal.

translucent fabric that is pulled across the inner face of the glass when the automated system responding to light and sun tells it. To enhance the flow of natural light into the work spaces, systems of horizontal light shelves at the transom level can deflect the light from skylights deep onto the ceilings of the office space.

Examples of this are the TVA Complex (Fig. 2) in Chattanooga, Tennessee (designed by TAC, CRS, and Van der Ryn Calthorpe and Partners) and the Solar Energy Research Institute Headquarters in Golden, Colorado (by CRS and Dubin-Bloom Associates) (34).

THE ARCHITECT AS DESIGNER FOR THE NEW PRINCEDOM

Corporations and Financial Institutions

Some of the most beautiful architecture in the United States, and indeed the western world, has been produced for corporate clients such as IBM or AT&T and even for governmental financial giants such as the Federal Reserve System (35). Much of this corporate building has been in the suburbs of large metropolises, where these buildings can find space. Magnificent examples of modern architecture, they sit in spacious green landscapes within tailored gardens. The triple attractions of planning horizontally for flexibility, the comparatively economical

handling of parking and circulation, and the beauty of the natural landscape make an appeal that is hard to refuse.

The many examples of superb design are a result not only of the skill of architects confronted by wonderful natural environments, of which the United States has many, but also of the combination with, in many cases, knowing clients. Corporate clients such as AT&T, working with Eero Saarinen, Kevin Roche, and others, and IBM's Facilities Division helped sponsor good design, as did individuals such as Irwin Miller of Cummins Engine Co., Columbus, Indiana; William Hewitt of the Deere Co., Moline, Illinois; and Edward Logue of the New York State Urban Development Corporation. All of these people were somehow persuaded that excellence in design was important and used their power and influence to ensure it.

Starting with the Connecticut General complex in Bloomfield, Connecticut, near Hartford, by SOM, these examples raise site planning to a high level. The Bloomfield complex is a taut steel composition punctuated with courtyards and enclosed with cool green Solex glass. It provides a complete lifestyle with cafeterias, shops, and athletic facilities set in a sylvan landscape. Challenging but imaginative sites were chosen by the Deere Co. in Moline and the Weyerhaeuser Corp. outside of Seattle, Washington. They both span valleys with their buildings, with water as an integrated component (36).

Parking has been and is a primary motivator of site planning. Modern office complexes demand approximately 3–3.5 cars/1000 ft^2 of work space. Thus a complex of 1 million ft^2 must have 28.5 acres or more of parking space at 350 ft^2/car. This is a huge site planning and engineering problem. The problem has been handled beautifully at the Thomas J. Watson IBM Laboratories in Yorktown, New York, where Eero Saarinen designed a great arched building to house the laboratories and offices. It is a very large building and deep enough to house all functional spaces inside the curved glass envelope. Views are from the radial corridors rather than from the spaces themselves. This concept, with its buttoned-up interior environment and back-to-back laboratories with a 7-ft service corridor between, has turned out to be a popular laboratory planning concept. The parking has been organized on the uphill and outer side of the curving building, and views downhill into the natural landscape are beautiful. Judicious planting in the parking softens the paved areas.

The Johns-Manville project by TAC in the foothills of Denver, Colorado, places an 800-ft long gleaming aluminum curtain wall building against a magnificent mountain landscape. It concentrates its 750,000-ft^2 office spaces against the hills, leaving the great range of the Ken Caryl ranch in front of it looking toward Denver. The cars are placed in a bowl-shaped set of terraces on the side toward the hills and on the roof of the building. On approaching the building, the vast complex of parking associated with the building is imperceptible (37).

One project that deserves special mention was an outgrowth of the Yorktown IBM project. This is the Bell Laboratories Research Center at Holmdel, New Jersey. Designed by Eero Saarinen and following the same conceptual planning as in Yorktown, it is a heroic mirror glass box 800 ft long and five stores high. It houses some of the most advanced telecommunications research in the world. The whole complex is penetrated by a monumental five-story atrium running its entire length. Recently, Roche has added at least another third in length to this minimalist reflective box. The handling of the circulation of the road system, the parking, and the general site plan challenge the grandeur of Versailles. To come upon this mirror glass building in the midst of the verdant mid-New Jersey landscape is a cultural shock, but the building is classic in its serenity (38).

Increasing attention is being paid to the interior working environment of these buildings as computerized information systems begin to play a larger role in all office and research and development activity. Word processors, with their terminal readouts and printers, are becoming commonplace in the standard office environment. Computer capability through a multitude of software programs and minicomputer capability on a per-person basis and with random connections to a mainframe computer are becoming commonplace in research and development buildings. Power and cabling requirements have escalated astronomically. Whereas formerly a figure of 4–5 W/ft^2 would have been sufficient, in today's world electronic flexibility requires a minimum of 6.5 W/ft^2 and a capability of up to 12 W/ft^2. This power requirement fights the need to conserve energy and additionally creates greater cooling loads. Moreover, ceiling heights in office buildings are increasing from 12.5 ft floor to floor to 14 or 15 ft to provide for 18–24 in. raised floors for cabling.

The human result of this is the need to consider the working environment of a person sitting in front of a VDT for eight hours a day. Eye strain, back fatigue, and other ailments have been developing. Unions for workers are concerned by these problems. Designers, particularly industrial designers, are paying increasing attention to these questions. The design of the display, whether light letters against dark or dark letters against light, the tilt of the keyboard and the height, the adjustability of the seating, and the planning of the work surface all play a role. The number of hours of concentrated work are being surveyed to arrive at reasonable standards for work intervals with rest periods in between. All of this is part of the new world of ergonomics, the study of equipment design in order to reduce operator fatigue and discomfort. Designers such as Niels Diffrient are producing revolutionary chairs such as the Jefferson Chair, a totally flexible chair that is really a machine providing different positions for sitting and for working with computers (39).

Towers for the Merchant Princes

As the cost of real estate has escalated enormously in the inner city since the late nineteenth century, the architect has sought solutions in designing higher and higher buildings. William LeBaron Jenney, a Chicago engineer, designed the first skyscraper in 1885 and started a development that now envisages superskyscrapers up to 150–200 stories high. The first skyscraper was made possible through the design of a steel frame, the use of which makes feasible the soaring towers of today. A few years later, the electric elevator came in and heralded a new

era. The progression began, punctuated by buildings like the 60-story Woolworth Building (New York, 1913), the 77-story Chrysler Building (New York, 1929), and the 102-story Empire State Building (New York, 1931). Since that time, only small increases in height have been made, in the twin towers of the World Trade Center in New York and the 110-story Sears Tower in Chicago, the tallest building in the world. However, there have been dramatic advances in engineering in that period, such as the decrease in the pounds of steel per square foot. The Empire State Building required 42.2 lb steel/ft,^{2} whereas the John Hancock Tower in Chicago has only 29.7 lb/ft^2 (40).

High land values in dense metropolitan areas drive developers to stack as much as possible on a given piece of land, but there is additional human motivation to build high. Like the merchant princes who built the medieval masonry towers of San Gimmignano, modern merchant princes want to demonstrate their prestige and power. John Hancock competes with another insurance giant in Boston, Prudential. Citicorp in New York looks for an image with its slanted, pointed top. Donald Trump in New York, not content with the fame of his present Trump Tower, has announced plans to build a still higher superskyscraper. The urge to build higher and higher is like the desire to climb Mount Everest.

Most interesting is the architect's, and particularly the engineer's, ingenuity in overcoming the forces that high-rise buildings generate. Gravity loads have not been the driving force in design since both steel and concrete resist compressive loads very well. But wind loading, resulting in lateral thrust, is important since wind loads increase geometrically with height. The history of the skyscraper is a story of how these lateral loads have been overcome.

Since the stability of a tower depends on the ratio of the width of the base to the height of the tower, most high-rise buildings have heights that are no more than six to eight times the width of the base. This is called the aspect ratio, and much of the effort in superskyscraper design is devoted to building a tower stable and rigid enough to withstand the vibrations of high winds with an aspect ratio of 10. With a base of 400 ft, it would be theoretically possible to build up to 160–200 stories, but a 400-ft base is impractical to rent or to work in. The Sears Tower has an aspect ratio of 6.4.

A skyscraper subjected to the wind acts like a cantilevered beam anchored in the ground. The sides perpendicular to the wind are in compression and tension, and the two sides parallel to the wind are subjected to shear forces. The shear forces must be counteracted by internally strong solid walls or walls that are often X-braced around the elevator core or braced by poured reinforced concrete core walls. The vertical forces are then carried down by the more flexible exterior columns. This structural approach has reduced the weight of skyscrapers substantially.

Further advances have been made in buildings such as the John Hancock Tower in Chicago, where the outer walls have been designed to take the wind loads through a system of large diagonal wind braces. Although these diagonals cross many office windows per side per floor, the owner has capitalized on this in his public relations advertising and actually charges more for offices having a diagonal window brace. This structural concept has been developed further in the tubular concept, where the exterior takes the lateral loads by having closely spaced columns around the perimeter connected by broad spandrel beams. The whole building acts like a giant hollow tube. The most refined version of this is the World Trade Center. The exterior columns are only 3 ft apart and serve as the window mullions. Fazlur Khan, a Pakistani engineer with SOM in Chicago, in designing the 1454-ft high Sears Tower, employed nine modular tubes bundled together at the base in a 3×3 matrix. Each tube is $75'$ on a side with columns 15 ft apart. Various floor plans are created as the building sets back on the way up (41).

William LeMessurier of Cambridge, Massachusetts, has taken this concept further with a theoretical design called Erehwon Center. It has a base of 220 ft and an aspect ratio of 12, providing space practical to lease. He carries the vertical loads down in four giant reinforced concrete corner columns. The tower consists of a series of clusters of 18-story modules having diagonal external braces. Interior steel superdiagonals resist wind loads and conduct gravity loads to the four massive corner columns.

Building these huge monuments would not have been possible without equal advances in other technologies. Elevators have been developed as double deckers, serving odd and even floors simultaneously. Of course, the lobby must also have a two-level loading scheme. Another option is dividing the building into vertical zones. Express elevators, moving at 2000 ft/min, go to "sky lobbies" at intermediate stops and go by slower local elevators to individual floors.

In contrast to former high-rise buildings, where large central ventilation fan rooms blow air down shafts, very high buildings have separate fan rooms on each floor. Cooling plants at the top, middle, and bottom send chilled water to these fan rooms.

Finally, these buildings depend on advances in fire protection. Since in a very high building it is impossible to evacuate thousands of people down the stairs, the occupants are led to the next sealed off protected zone or refuge area until the fire is brought under control. More and more buildings are becoming fully sprinklered, and sophisticated smoke exhaust systems are switched on automatically under emergency power when a fire starts.

THE ARCHITECT AS EXPRESSIVE ARTIST

Nowhere is the difference between the architect and other professionals expressed so much as when the architect reinterprets cultures and traditions of other lands and gives them new life. Debussy, who never set foot in Spain, wrote a piano piece called "La Soirée dans Grenade" ("Evening in Granada"). "The power of evocation integrated in the few pages of the "Evening in Granada" borders on the miracle when one realizes that this music was composed by a foreigner. . . . There is not one bar of this music borrowed from Spanish folklore, and yet the entire composition, in its most minute details, admirably conveys Spain" (42).

An example from architecture is the Imperial Hotel by Frank Lloyd Wright (Tokyo, 1923). Using native Oya stone (lava) and Hokkaido oak for the interior finish, Wright produced a huge complex of buildings in which no single form is distinctly Japanese, but according to Louis Sullivan, is an "epic poem, addressed to the Japanese people, their inmost thought. It is characterized by the quality *Shibui*, a Japanese word, signifying the reward of earnest contemplation" (43).

Another example is the Barnsdall Residence ("Hollyhock House") in Hollywood, California, by Wright. Although Wright was probably never in Yucatan, this dramatic complex lives and breathes the Mayan spirit of Uxmal, Mexico, in its Governor's Palace and the Nunnery quadrangle, yet its forms are unique.

Le Corbusier in his Notre-Dame du Haut in Ronchamp, France, created an unforgettable experience by combining the image of a nun's hat with the great roof, and the forms of the exterior shell and the vertical light unmistakably recall the M'Zab area of North Africa in Ghardaia, Algeria. The building, with its mysterious enclosed space, conveys an atmosphere of Catholic devotion and deep religiosity (44).

The architect as philosopher–artist has through the years struggled to articulate beliefs in words as well as form. In many cases, as in Louis Kahn's, those articulations have changed and developed over the years. Wright came to realize that the essence of a building is not the walls, but the space within, only to find that Lao Tze developed that concept hundreds of years before. Starting with Sullivan, his *Liebemeister*, Wright, in the Sulgrave Lectures at RIBA in May 1939, developed at length the idea of integrity as a cornerstone of the architect's belief. "Let us express our time as it wants to be; the American architecture cannot copy from Europe. Even Britain with its Georgian is copying from Italy and France, and even though dead this is more legitimate than the American copies. Let America find its own 'organic' architecture, something that springs indigenously from the prairies and the true American experience" (45).

That dedication to integrity has carried through in the fabric of thought of most of the great modern leaders in architecture: Mies van der Rohe in his dramatization of the glories of structure, Le Corbusier in his radical approaches to the modern skyscraper and aggressive solutions to sun shading through his designs for *brise soleil*, Gropius in his naked expression of the curtain wall of glass in the Bauhaus, and, later on, Kahn in his search for expressing "what the building wants to be."

The realization of structure as a poetic element in architecture has reached great heights in such work as Mies van der Rohe's at the Illinois Institute of Technology in Chicago and the apartment houses at 860 Lake Shore Drive; Kenzo Tange's National Gymnasium for the 1964 Olympic Games and his St. Mary's Cathedral, thoroughly modern in concept, but somehow mysteriously recalling Japanese tradition; and Eero Saarinen's masterpiece of compression and tension, the Dulles Airport in Washington, D.C. (46).

An architect who has searched his soul as hard as anyone to find the truth about design is Kahn. From humble beginnings, he developed into a great philosopher, always struggling to articulate his thoughts. Students recognized the devotion of this man and worshipped at his feet. He sought without reliance on academic references to find his own way to the altar of truth in architecture. He sought first the poetic essence of form, of "what a building wants to be," a library, a laboratory, or a seat of government. He recognized order as a way of structure and systems to achieve that essence, and he recognized natural light as a supreme delineator of space. He continued to address the problem of light and shading throughout his career, evoking new ways of handling the problem in later years, as at the First Unitarian Church, Rochester, New York, and at the Kimbell Museum, Fort Worth, Texas (47).

He somehow managed to convey the feeling of great mass and the monumentality of the architecture of older traditions by using double wall spaces in the form of "servant spaces and served spaces." Recognizing that massive wall structures at column points of large spans are no longer needed, but that spaces to house mechanical ducts, pipes, and cables are, he developed column points that are essentially hollow square shells that give room for these servant facilities. He combined his original thinking with influences from Wright and other modern architects with the historic architecture of the world, such as that in India and Spain, more perhaps than most other giants of architecture (48).

In an attempt to extend further the expressiveness of later modern architecture and enlarge its vocabulary, two thrusts have appeared since about 1970. They are late modernism, a term coined by Charles Jencks, and postmodernism. The first is an extension of the extremes of modern architecture in form, materials, and detail, as witnessed by the evolution of the many sides of modern architecture developed in The Museum of Modern Art's show "Transformations" in the spring of 1979. Postmodern design founds its fragile framework on the theoretical demise of modern architecture. Modern architecture has failed sociologically, according to Jane Jacobs's 1961 book *The Death and Life of Great American Cities.* It has failed economically, as evidenced by the cost of such structures as the Boston City Hall. "What we need is the 'decorated shed,'" said Robert Venturi. And modern architecture has failed to meet the emotional needs of people. Postmodernists call for more decoration and more history since, after all, people are familiar with the monuments of the past (49).

Under the first group of modernists, in their reaching for greater expressiveness, some imaginative structures have been created, stretching technical capabilities to the limit. The Pompidou Centre in Paris (by Rogers and Piano), with its exposed structure and ducts and expressed exterior escalators, is one of the most exciting of these. Its neutral glass envelope houses a multitude of art, music, and research activities. It attracts many more people than even the Louvre. Strangely enough, as it sits enclosed in its twenty-first century skin in the midst of a great stone plaza and surrounded by traditional French townhouses, a new harmony has been created.

Norman Foster, a British architect, has been a leader in expressing technology and logic to its limits. His Sains-bury Center at the University of East Anglia (Norwich, UK, 1974–1978) houses visual arts in what looks like a giant airplane hangar. The aluminum grid panels are repeated endlessly on the roof and walls. The structure is the decoration. Foster carries exposed construction and detail even further in his Hong Kong superskyscraper. The latter takes the Pompidou aesthetic into a super-high-rise (50).

Another aspect of this movement exploits the technology of glass, which has advanced immeasurably. With the ability to make the color of vision glass and the spandrel glass between floors look the same, a monolithic surface divided only by a constant window module can be designed. The result is a continuous geometric surface defined only by shape. Such a building is the United Nations Plaza Hotel in New York City by Roche, where the chamfered slopes of the tower play against each other. The Dallas Hyatt Hotel by Welton Becket and the Renaissance Center in Detroit by Portman are similar examples of continuous surface geometries. In Detroit, instead of triangular forms, Portman used cylinders, and in Dallas, Becket used rectangular articulated boxes.

One of the big opening guns of the postmodernist movement, although he probably would not have called it postmodern, was Venturi's book *Complexity and Contradiction in Modern Architecture,* published in 1966 by The Museum of Modern Art. Venturi's references to traditional styles and inferences of a more subtle, undogmatic approach awakened a whole generation of younger architects to the possibilities of historicism (51).

As a result, postmodernism has had a great deal of appeal in the architectural press, and some of the leaders, such as Venturi and Graves, have achieved gurulike status. Even some of their drawings, shown in important New York galleries, earn large sums of money. Architecture, more than ever before, has become recognized as a valid museum subject.

There is no doubt that under the banner of contextualism many new forms and different ways of looking at architecture have been developed. This approach, freed from the dogmas of modern architecture, has some merit in its exploratory attitude. New forms, not necessarily tied to function, decorative two-dimensional layering, and different color approaches generate visual challenges. Charles Moore has done some interesting work in this school. His Piazza D'Italia in New Orleans, Louisiana, is a brilliant fountain framed with a series of arcades of different classic orders and paved with a mosaic map of Italy. At the University of Santa Cruz, Kresge College exploits his sense of whimsy in the composition of a Mediterranean hill town. For a college on the Pacific coast on a hilly site, with a white-painted collection of buildings wandering back and forth on the slope, this metaphor is quite appropriate.

Sometimes, these architects use open frameworks to create context and symbol. Venturi, in his Franklin Court in Philadelphia, Pennsylvania, a park scheme, uses a stainless steel frame to approximate Benjamin Franklin's old mansion. Franklin's memorabilia are housed there, and the surrounding buildings have been restored, altogether a knitting of the old and new.

Other architects, like Leon and Bob Krier, emphasize city building as a return to old values, as in the plan of Paris or Hadrian's Villa. This latter has become a reference point for many architects with its fascinating series of set buildings colliding in different grids. The Kriers seek a new emphasis on the spaces between, emphasizing the public forum and symbolic public buildings. Outside of Paris, in St. Quentin-en-Yvelines, Ricardo Bofill has designed a large housing development that could be a part of one of these classic cities. It is called Les Arcades du Lac. It is extremely formal and classical in plan, and although it is made of precast concrete, it does not reveal its technology and has all of the embellishments of classic orders.

It was natural in this search for contextualism that some of the old traditional vernacular forms would be copied and refashioned. Examples of this have been particularly successful in existing villages and towns. The Pershore Housing (UK, 1976–1977) by Darbourne and Dark fits particularly well with its pitched roofs and brick into its traditional village setting. The Zwolle Housing (the Netherlands, 1975–1977) by Aldo Van Eyck and Theo Bosch has continuous blocks of housing knitted into traditional urban patterns and articulated with lopped-off Dutch gables. The narrow Dutch facades fit in well with the old neighborhood. The Byker Housing Estate for 7000 people (Newcastle-upon-Tyne, UK, 1974) by Swedish architect Ralph Erskine combines brick, concrete, wood, metal, and bright color to break down the scale of this large development. Patterned brick, gables, decorative end walls, and an overall plan that is broken down into small neighborhoods combine to destroy the monotonous character common in most housing projects.

Architect Michael Graves has taken postmodernism to its most visible stage. His Public Service Building, which won a competition in Portland, Oregon, has stimulated national notoriety and debate. Graves, for his contextualism, uses distinctly classic formulas to produce an overpowering square bulk and almost Roman posture. The building has a dark, stepped, overscaled base like a Greek stylobate. The middle part of the building flares out into an outwardly stepped, crownlike form with a keystone that looks more Egyptian than Roman. The keystone sticking out resembles the headdress on an Egyptian pharaoh. The facade envelope is covered with three type forms: walls with punched holes, vertical striped windows, and typical curtain walls. Huge stucco swags decorate the two side elevations.

Grave's work is much more intimate in his San Juan Capistrano Library, which also won a competition. The character of the exterior combines the closed wall, covered in white stucco, with controlled smaller openings characteristic and expressive of the California mission style, of which San Juan Capistrano is one of the finest examples. The gables covered with tile and the skylight structures with their little tiled tops are consistent in furthering the expression. Inside, the tightly gridded spaces feel more like a Roman villa, with deep colors almost Pompeian in character. The highly organized composition, with a multitude of axes, is relieved by an arcaded central garden court.

There is no doubt that Graves, with his little towers, closely spaced column style, sense of color, and stylistic sense of freedom has influenced a whole generation of students and younger architects.

THE ARCHITECT IN THE TWENTY-FIRST CENTURY

What will the role of the architect be in the twenty-first century, as there are greater and greater concentrations in the cities, with 150-story superskyscrapers? Can the continued health of cities in the northwestern, north central, and northeastern United States be ensured as growth shifts to the south and southwest? As the demographic balance changes to a greater percentage of the elderly, can garden suburbs be provided for the aged that are still well integrated with society as a whole? Can the needed technology in health care and social services be supported as society with increased longevity demands more and more services? In spite of courageous attempts to improve public transportation, such as the BART system, the Washington, D.C. subway system, and the new Red Line in Cambridge, Massachusetts, the use of the automobile continues to grow. The motor car becomes more and more a part of society, and workplaces are being swallowed up by an asphalt sea. The saturation point is not far away. The present world of motor cars and highways makes Eero Saarinen's exhibit of the future for the General Motors Pavilion in the 1939 World's Fair in New York City pale by comparison with the reality of the present.

The architect, in the late twentieth century, has developed skills to handle these complex problems of the future, becoming an administrator and, in the change from a production to an information society, an information administrator. The architect has lost the hands-on skill of the craftsperson, but is skillful in delegating tasks to a multi-headed team to bring information from hundreds of components. The architect is as adept as an assembler of manufactured parts. The architect is aware of the manufacturers of curtain wall components, knows the different types of tinted or mirror glass available, knows where to get precast components, and knows how to order acres of dry wall gypsum board partitions (which takes no great brains). Hardware is delegated to a consultant, and the lighting, mechanical, and life safety systems are all delegated to the proper professionals. The architect's greatest talent is in getting all of these professionals together in one room to make sure all the parts fit together (which does take skill). The architect also grows as a manager of larger and larger offices capable of handling billion dollar jobs.

With this rather cynical picture of the developing architect as a professional getting further and further from design, or design humans can touch, another great component appears on the scene, namely, computer-aided design and drafting (CADD). CADD is a huge force for the future. Most firms have passed the stage where word processing, specifications writing, schedule charts, and cost control spreads are commonplace. Architects are now entering a stage where graphic design and production drawings by computer are routine. By the year 2000, the acceleration of use will pass from an evolutionary stage to a revolutionary stage. In graphic designs, the ability of the computer to provide design variables in interior layouts, to develop shadow patterns of urban complexes, and to draw three-dimensional massing studies on large complexes, which can be called up in seconds from matrix plans, is nothing but astounding. Young people, not university graduates, but computer draftspersons, are turning out production and contract drawings for major buildings. This may present a great threat to employment for architects in the years to come since a large proportion of the effort in an architect's office is devoted to working drawing production (52). If this portion of an architect's production can be done by younger, less educated professionals skilled in only this one aspect of architecture, the skilled working drawing architect, or the "old shiny pants draftsman" who has virtually disappeared anyway, will finally meet his demise. However, as Gropius used to say, "[t]he machine need not be an enemy of man; it's all in how you use the machines and to what ends." The CADD capability is almost unlimited, but it still needs human imagination to drive it.

As the twenty-first century approaches, it is important that the architect, who has become an administrator, delegator, and assembler of parts, recognize with trepidation the erosion of the profession's essential being, that of the designer.

The architect is the one professional component who can act the part of humanist with regard to density of site and scale for the pedestrian, who can envision great site compositions, who knows what ceiling, floor, and mechanical systems can yield real integrated quality, and who chooses the color of the mortar of the brick joints, the joints of the precast, the shape of the handrail, and the proportion of tread to riser. The architect who walks into the twenty-first century, or the twenty-second century for that matter, should give up these choices with great reluctance.

It is imperative that architecture retain its important heritage and ascendency with pride and conviction as the profession uniquely qualified to build the peaceful civilization of the future.

BIBLIOGRAPHY

1. M. Miller, *The Splendour That Was Egypt*, Praeger Publishers, Inc., New York, 1969.
2. K. Mendelssohn, *The Riddle of the Pyramids*, Thames and Hudson, London, England, 1975.
3. B. Fletcher, *A History of Architecture*, Charles Scribner's Sons, New York, 1975.
4. A. Saint, *The Image of the Architect*, Yale University Press, New Haven, Conn., 1983.
5. J. Ruskin, *The Stones of Venice*, John Wiley & Sons, Inc., New York, 1876.
6. W. Morris, *"The Gothic Revival II,"* E. D. Le Miro, ed., *Unpublished Lectures*, Detroit, Mich., 1969.
7. D. Macaulay, *Cathedral*, Houghton Mifflin Co., Boston, Mass., 1973.
8. *Golden Hart Guides, Bath*, Sidgewick and Jackson, London, 1983.
9. E. Bacon, *Design of Cities*, Viking Press, New York, 1967.
10. Ref. 4. chapt. III.
11. "The AIA's First Hundred Years," *Journal of the AIA* 4 (May 1957).
12. R. Lynes, *The Tastemakers*, Dover Publications, Inc., New York, 1980 p. 134.
13. Ref. 4. chapt. IV.
14. S. Chase, *Rich Land, Poor Land*, A. M. S. Press, New York, reproduction of 1936 edition.
15. A. Roth, *The New Architecture*, Dr. H. Girsberger, Zurich, Switzerland, 1940.
16. P. Burgess, ed., *The Role of the Architect in Society*. Department of Architecture, Carnegie-Mellon University, Pittsburgh, Pa., 1983.
17. D. Gebhard and R. Winter, *A Guide to Architecture in Los Angeles*, Peregrine Smith, Inc., 1977.
18. O. Newman, *Defensible Space*, Macmillan Publishing Co., Inc., New York, 1972.
19. J. Jacobs, *The Death and Life of Great American Cities*, Random House, New York, 1961.
20. Ref. 16, flyleaf.
21. Ref. 16, pp. 24, 25.
22. Ref. 16, pp. 57–59.
23. Le Corbusier and P. Jeanneret, *Oeuvre Complet 1910–38*, Dr. H. Girsberger, Zurich, Switzerland, 1939, 1941, 1943.
24. A. Blowers, C. Hammett, and P. Saare, eds., *The Future of Cities*, Hutchison Educational Ltd., London, England, 1974.
25. P. Spreiregen, *Urban Design*, McGraw-Hill Inc., New York, 1965.
26. M. Seelig, *The Architecture of Self Help Communities*, Architectural Record Books, 1978.
27. H. Fathy, *Architecture for the Poor*, University of Chicago Press, Chicago, Ill., 1973.
28. G. Herbert, "Graphics, Hirsch & the Saga of the Copper Houses," Israel Institute of Technology, 1980.
29. S. Giedion, *Walter Gropius, Work and Teamwork*, Reinhold Publishing Corp., New York, 1954.
30. "General Panel House," *New Pencil Points* 4 (1943).
31. H. Dreyfus and E. Barnes, "House in a Factory," *Arts and Architecture* 9 (1947).
32. R. Stein, *Architecture and Energy*, 1st ed., Anchor Press/Doubleday, Garden City, N.Y., 1977.
33. R. Saxon, *Atrium Buildings*, Van Nostrand Reinhold Co., Inc., New York, 1983.
34. "Chattanooga Office Complex," *AIA Journal* 9 (1979).
35. "IBM," *Building Design & Construction* 12 (1979).
36. "John Deere's Sticks of Steel," *Architectural Forum* 7 (1964).
37. "The Johns-Manville World Headquarters," *Architectural Record* 9 (1977).
38. "The Biggest Mirror Ever," *Architectural Forum* 4 (1967).
39. S. Hauserman, *Leading Edge* 1(5) (1984).
40. M. Salvadori, *Why Buildings Stand Up*, W. W. Norton & Co., New York, 1980.
41. "Superskyscrapers," *High Technology* 5(1) (Jan. 1985).
42. M. de Falla, *Claude Debussy. Piano Music*, vol. 1, Vox Records.
43. *The Work of Frank Lloyd Wright*, Wendingen ed., Bramhall House, New York, 1965.
44. M. Roche, *Le M'Zab*, B. Arthaud, France, 1973.
45. F. L. Wright, "The George Watson Lectures at the RIBA," Lund Humphries & Co., Ltd., London, 1939.

46. R. Boyd, *New Directions in Japanese Architecture,* George Braziller, New York, 1968.

47. V. Scully, Jr., *Louis I. Kahn,* George Braziller, New York, 1962.

48. A. Tyng, *Beginnings, Louis I. Kahn's Philosophy of Architecture,* John Wiley & Sons, Inc., New York, 1984.

49. C. Jencks, *The Language of Post Modern Architecture,* Rizzoli International Publications, Inc., New York, 1977.

50. C. Jencks, *Late Modern Architecture,* Rizzoli International Publications, Inc., New York, 1980.

51. R. Venturi, *Complexity and Contradiction in Architecture,* Museum of Modern Art and Graham Foundation, New York, 1966.

52. H. Mileaf, *Techpointers,* Construction Industry Group, McGraw-Hill Information Systems Co., New York

See also ADAPTIVE USE; AMERICAN INSTITUTE OF ARCHITECTS; ATRIUM BUILDINGS; BUILDING TEAM; CAREERS IN ARCHITECTURE; HOUSING IN DEVELOPING COUNTRIES; INDUSTRIALIZED CONSTRUCTION; PLANNED COMMUNITIES (NEW TOWNS); PROFESSION IN CONTEMPORARY SOCIETY; PUBLIC SERVICE ARCHITECTURE; REGIONAL/URBAN DESIGN ASSISTANCE TEAMS (R/UDAT); ROYAL INSTITUTE OF BRITISH ARCHITECTS; SOLAR DESIGN

NORMAN C. FLETCHER, FAIA
The Architects Collaborative
Cambridge, Massachusetts

ROOFING MATERIALS

Roofing is one of the most critical building components. It is also one of the least understood aspects of building science. Roofing failures are commonplace and become the subject of intense litigation. The roof assembly is a product of many trades and pinpointing responsibility for roof failure is difficult, if not impossible. The science of designing a roof system is complex, involving interactive components of the building envelope and wide-ranging weather conditions. For each specific project, the best roof design will result from a synthesis of many physical and environmental properties.

A roof is a system that must respond to many influences from both outside a building enclosure and inside. In addition, the roofing system must combine with other building envelope systems, such as walls, windows, structure, and interior finishes, to ensure the safety of building occupants and maintain some preestablished level of thermal and moisture integrity. The roof will probably have to satisfy requirements imposed by the local building code as well as an insurance company's estimation of longevity and wind and fire resistance. Designers should familiarize themselves with all local conditions including climate, materials, regulatory requirements, and capacities of runoff and storm sewer systems before undertaking a new roof design. As a critical element of any enclosure, a roof provides shelter and protection from environmental forces.

Unlike other building enclosure surfaces, the roof must perform many difficult functions such as shedding moisture, retaining established temperatures within the enclosure, supporting horizontal ceiling finishes below, and providing a surface for some mechanical and electrical equipment. Roofs are also subject to a much broader attack from natural forces than other building components. In some parts of the continental United States, roof surfaces experience annual temperature changes exceeding 200°F and daily changes exceeding 100°F. Rain, snow, sleet, and hail pound the roof surface while acid mists, other airborne pollutants, and animals assault the roof.

The roof of a building carries a huge economic burden, as a roof failure can often mean destruction of materials and furnishings beneath. Building owners should recognize the importance of a roofing system and understand that penny-wise and dollar-foolish decisions may lead to premature roofing failure. For slight additional cost during roof replacement or new roof design, building owners may extend the useful life of the roof and, for that matter, the entire enclosure. Costs of premature roofing failure can be staggering and the legal threat to building owners, architects, contractors, and manufacturers is potentially devastating. Without a doubt, roofing is one of the most litigious aspects of architectural and engineering practice.

Considerations for new or replacement roofing include a complex list of qualitative performance attributes. Although emphasis may vary depending on what type of roofing material is selected by the designer, the successful roof responds to minimum requirements for the following:

- Wind resistance (uplift).
- Fire resistance.
- Moisture control.
- Environmental agents (ultraviolet light, temperature swings, ozone, etc).
- Compatibility with adjacent materials.
- Movement and deflection.
- Loads (static and dynamic).
- Dimensional stability.
- Maintenance.

From a performance standpoint, the ultimate goal of the roof designer is to provide a means to protect a building's interior from the weather by creating a physical separation of the building's interior from the exterior. Given the practical difficulties of achieving a design that satisfactorily responds to all of the above characteristics, market opportunities exist for manufacturers of new products that attempt to combine several performance attributes. For example, several manufacturers of bituminous felts now sell modified bituminous membrane used in single and two-ply configurations and a few sell an ethylene proprylene diene monomer or terpolymer sheet as well.

A roof is a custom "product" constructed at the job site. Many different roof types may be used to accomplish the same general objective of preventing moisture from penetrating an enclosure. Roofing procedures vary considerably in different parts of the United States. Appropriate procedures depend on climatic conditions, the type of roof system selected, the materials that may be used in the system, and the availability of skilled labor. Built-up systems are predominantly selected and specified in larger commercial, industrial, and office building projects.

The complexity of a roof requires knowledge in many areas of physics, materials science, and climatology. However, the science of roofing is also dependent on tradespeople who consider their work an art. Therefore, roofing is both a science and an art and must be approached by a designer with both scientific precision and an understanding of building trades.

TYPES OF ROOFING

Built-up Roofing (BUR)

The traditional BUR system, like all low slope roofing systems, is custom built at the job site and composed of a structural deck, thermal insulation, and multilayered membrane. Most BUR systems also include flashings for waterproofing joints, penetrations, stops, walls, curbs, vents, and drains. All of these components work together as the system functions to keep moisture out and maintain a comfortable interior environment.

The National Roofing Contractors Association has indicated that BUR is now used in 46.4% of cases where flat roofing is required. Compared to other types of flat roofing (new and reroof), BUR is used more frequently than any other flat roofing systems. BUR has a long track record of trustworthy service. Contractors have been installing built-up systems since 1844. The Asphalt Roofing Manufacturer's Association (ARMA) estimates that the amount of BUR currently in use exceeds 50 billion ft².

Each component in a BUR system performs a specific function. The structural deck carries and transmits the membranes' weight, as well as dynamic forces, to the roof frame and the building's structural membranes. Thermal insulation reduces energy loss, increases interior comfort, and prevents condensation on interior surfaces. Insulation also resists horizontal shearing, which helps relieve stresses transferred to the membrane from movement in the structural deck. The membrane is the most critical element in the system as it protects not only the interior of the building but all roofing system components as well.

BUR membranes contain several alternating layers of bitumen and felt capped by a surfacing material. The asphalt or coal-tar-pitch is the membrane component that actually makes the system waterproof. It is also the adhesive that binds the system together.

There are four types of asphalt available, each with a different softening point. Refiners alter asphalt's properties such as the softening point to control the product's tendency to flow at normal outdoor temperatures. A low softening point asphalt, which flows more readily than a high softening point product, may last longer because in cold temperatures it is less brittle and in warm temperatures it will flow together to repair small surface cracks. Low softening point asphalt's tendency to flow, however, can allow felts to slip downslope on steeper roofs. To avoid membrane slippage and still obtain the longest roof life possible, the specifier will use the asphalt with the lowest softening point the roof slope will permit.

Besides reinforcing the roofing systems, felts do the following: (1) enable roofing contractors to apply several thin bitumen layers rather than one thick layer (several layers restrict bitumen flow, and make a more durable

membrane) and (2) protect the bitumen from water degradation.

Fiberglass felts represent the latest innovation in BUR technology and are the most widely used felts today. Although glass felts have supplanted organic felts (which are made of wood pulp) in the marketplace, organic felts are still available. Glass felts are known to have superior strength when compared to organic felts.

Mineral aggregate surfacing, usually gravel, slag, or crushed rock, protects the top bitumen layer from destructive ultraviolet (uv) radiation; provides fire resistance; and guards the bitumen from wind, rain, and foot traffic. In some parts of the country, mineral-surfaced cap sheets are often used in place of aggregate embedded in a bitumen "flood coat" (Fig. 1).

Application of BUR. Three things are essential for long roof life: good design, good materials, and good workmanship. Because the BUR membrane is essentially manufactured at the job site, good workmanship is especially important.

Despite new techniques such as use of mechanical equipment, tankers, pumping hot bitumen, etc, the methods used to construct a BUR have changed only moderately in over 140 years. They continue to be efficient and economical, in part because roofing material manufacturers have kept their product lines compatible with changing construction industry practices and technologies. When properly installed by a skilled roofing contractor, a BUR should provide many years of trouble-free service.

Proper BUR installation begins at the deck. BURs can be applied over a variety of roof deck types, including steel, wood, concrete, and gypsum. Steel decks are the most commonly specified for new flat roof construction. On new buildings with steel decks, the contractor will probably install two layers of insulation, mechanically fastening the first layer to the deck and adhering the second layer to the first with hot bitumen. Mechanically attaching the first layer of insulation firmly anchors the roofing system to the deck, preventing blowoffs. In fact, Factory

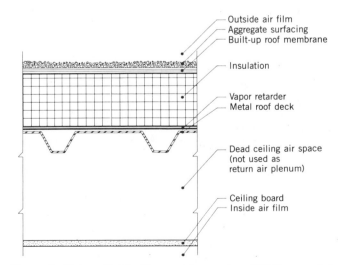

Figure 1. Hot-applied built-up roofing system (BUR) on metal deck.

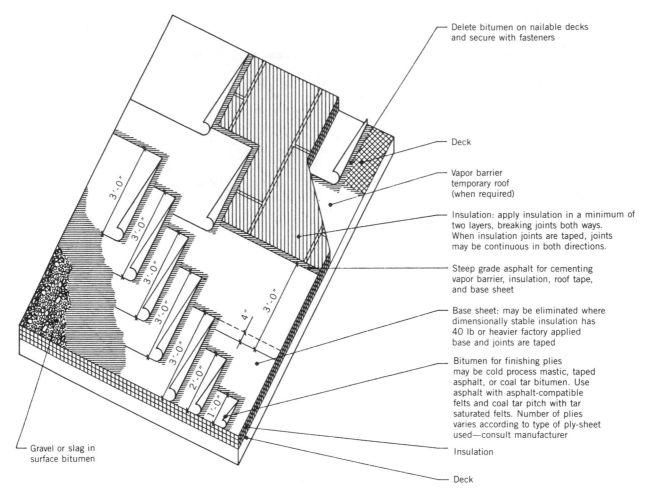

Delete bitumen on nailable decks
and secure with fasteners

Deck

Vapor barrier
temporary roof
(when required)

Insulation: apply insulation in a minimum of
two layers, breaking joints both ways.
When insulation joints are taped, joints
may be continuous in both directions.

Steep grade asphalt for cementing
vapor barrier, insulation, roof tape,
and base sheet

Base sheet: may be eliminated where
dimensionally stable insulation has
40 lb or heavier factory applied
base and joints are taped

Bitumen for finishing plies
may be cold process mastic, taped
asphalt, or coal tar bitumen. Use
asphalt with asphalt-compatible
felts and coal tar pitch with tar
saturated felts. Number of plies
varies according to type of ply-sheet
used—consult manufacturer

Insulation

Deck

Gravel or slag in
surface bitumen

Figure 2. Construction sequence for hot-applied built-up roofing system. Edges of felts should be turned up on all but not cemented to all vertical surfaces to a height of 6 in. and should overhang all roof edges a similar amount. Before application of the roofing, the 6 in. of felt must be returned over the insulation and mopped solidly.

Mutual, an organization that rates building materials for insurance purposes, requires that insulation over steel decks be installed this way.

Achieving the desired insulation thickness with two layers of insulation rather than one may also provide more effective thermal resistance. By offsetting the joints of the second layer from those of the first, heat loss through the insulation joints is minimized. When a building is to be reroofed with BUR, roofing contractors often apply the required insulation with hot bitumen rather than mechanically fastening the first layer as they do in new construction.

Once the insulation is in place, the roofing contractor can proceed to build the membrane. The first step is to heat the bitumen, which is relatively solid at normal outdoor temperatures. By carefully monitoring the bitumen's application temperature, the contractor can control the amount of bitumen laid down in each layer. Thin, continuous bitumen coatings, called moppings, between each layer of felt ensure proper adhesion. The bitumen may be mechanically applied or hand mopped onto the roof.

While the bitumen is still hot, a ply of felt is rolled into it either by hand or with a mechanical felt layer. BURs typically contain between three and five felt plies. Gener-

ally, three plies is considered a minimum for a BUR membrane. After rolling the felts into place, roofers broom in the felts to embed the material into the bitumen. Some applicators do not broom in fiberglass felts because the material is porous and usually bonds automatically to the bitumen.

Adding a fourth or fifth layer can increase the roof's useful life. Four or five plies provide a thicker, heavier, more waterproof system that is more resistant to cracking, splitting, and puncturing than a thinner membrane. It may be useful to note that accepted roofing practices vary from one section of the country to another. For example, a four-ply BUR in southern California can, and often does, differ from the one described above.

When surfacing with aggregate, roofers cover the top surface of the roof membrane with a flood coat of hot bitumen. This becomes the membrane's first line of moisture protection. The aggregate is embedded in the hot bitumen.

Along the Gulf Coast, proper application of the aggregate surfacing is particularly important. Roofs there are exposed to more intense sunlight during more of the year than in most other parts of the country and must be able to resist ultraviolet radiation to perform effectively. This precaution is important everywhere, however (Fig. 2).

Cold-applied Roofing

Historically, cold-applied roofing is assumed to be a patch, repair, or maintenance method where a temporary solution was gained by the use of cold-applied mastics or coatings. For many years, asphalt emulsions, asphalt and coal-tar cutbacks, and aluminum-fibered coatings were available. These materials were destined for use in repairing or helping to maintain both gravel- and smooth-surfaced roofing. Metal roof systems were also recoated with aluminum coatings once their primary weathering surface broke down.

By definition, cold-applied roofing is the use or application of a waterproofing material in liquid form at ambient temperature. Normally, the waterproofing material does not require heating in order to achieve performance. However, under certain conditions, the liquid may be mildly heated for application purposes only.

Cold-applied roofing systems may or may not incorporate reinforcing materials. If they do not use reinforcing materials, they are usually referred to as liquid membrane systems. All cold-applied systems are designed for use in new construction (depending on type of deck), maintenance activities, repair efforts, and recovering existing roof membranes. To a large part, the selection of a specific cold-applied material depends on the primary goal of reroofing, maintaining, or repairing; a secondary concern is the compatibility between the cold-applied materials and the existing roof system.

Resaturants and special surface coatings are also considered to be cold-applied roofing systems. These are put down as a primary liquid over a preexisting roof system that already contains some type of reinforcement in it.

If an existing gravel-surfaced BUR is to be recovered with a cold-applied system, a thorough inspection must be made of the roof. The existing BUR may be in a deteriorated state, but it must be repairable. All dirt, dust and loose gravel must be removed; otherwise, areas of poor bonding will occur. It is best to use an asphalt cutback if the existing roof is asphalt based. Tar cutbacks should be used on old coal-tar pitch roofs. Once the roof is clean and prepared, the cold-applied liquid is put down at the rate of 5–7 gal/ft² into which a layer of spun-laced polyester is then embedded. After the spun-laced polyester is embedded, the heavy second coating is used to complete the waterproofing membrane. A finish coating may then be applied; normally, it is best to wait for several days while the solvent or water evaporates from the system.

Cold-applied materials are widely used to make emergency repairs. They can help get a roof through bad weather. Long-term repairs can also be made with cold-applied materials. Additives can be used that help the material adhere to wet or damp roofs during low temperatures. There are many "cut-and-patch" materials available on the market. Many are fiber reinforced; plastic roof cement will become unworkable during cold weather.

Cold-applied roofing is yet another option available to specifiers of roof systems. While cold-applied systems are attractive in cost, they do require a cure time. Heavy rooftop traffic must be avoided during the initial cure.

The polyester reinforcements that have become available offer new dimensions to the cold-applied process and

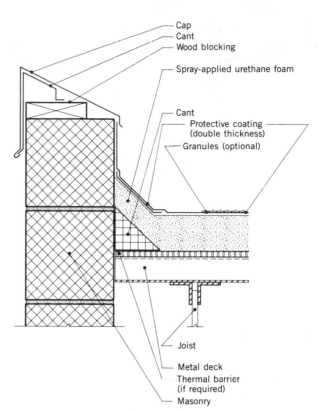

Figure 3. Cold-applied, polyester reinforced membrane applied over spray-applied polyurethane foam insulation.

offer the largest growth potential. Both new construction and reroofing efforts may utilize polyester along with a cold-applied material to provide a flexible membrane that has good strength and high elongation properties. (Fig. 3).

Metal Roofing

Standing-seam metal roof systems require unique details to maintain their high performance and to ensure an architecturally attractive appearance. Unlike other roofing systems, standing-seam metal roofs are designed to move in response to the forces induced by changing outdoor temperatures and the resultant thermal expansion and contraction of the roofing material itself.

Movement transverse to the metal panel corrugations is absorbed in the accordion-type action of the panel rib itself. In the longitudinal direction, the panel floats across the building roof structure. The panels are attached to the structure with clips, which allow this movement to occur. At the free-floating end most manufacturers provide specific components to take this movement with the use of flashings, flexible sealant membranes, or both.

Similar provision must be made for panel movement at the perimeter of the metal roof along the side of the panels. Usually this consists of a counterflashing lapped over a vertical extension of the roof panel. The roof panel and its extension are usually allowed to slide underneath the counterflashing. This required detail is necessarily vulnerable to weather penetration because no complete seal can be made in such a sliding connection.

The sliding action of the basic panel clip itself is the responsibility of the panel manufacturer. However, the architect–engineer has the task of evaluating alternative systems in order to have some assurance that the system used will, in fact, perform as desired. The most favorable location for the sliding to occur is as high up on the clip as possible, near to the point of contact with the seam, but other locations appear to work well with some systems.

A simple examination of sample roof panel assemblies will often reveal the adequacy of a design. An even better test is to evaluate random samples from a box of clips, because sales samples can sometimes be specially prepared to demonstrate sliding action that may not be representative.

There are other detail situations that may require design attention for specific projects. These include the following: roof curbs for mechanical equipment, penetrations for pipes, and various corner conditions where the sliding action must be maintained.

With most systems, the panel end at the gutter is fixed to the structure and the upper end is allowed to move for thermal expansion and contraction. The amount of movement expected is determined by the coefficient of expansion of the metal and the length of panel run. Many standard details for this condition allow up to 2 in. of panel movement. In southern regions of the United States, this is usually more than adequate and in northern regions it may be inadequate for a very long run of paneling. In such cases the roof is separated into two or more lengths of panel, and expansion flashings are provided at the top end of each panel run.

Individual panel lengths are usually limited to 40 ft for ease of shipment, and rigid splice connections are made between the ends of panels. It is important that this splice connection also be allowed to float freely over the structure. If this condition is made with fasteners penetrating into the building structurals, the roof movement requirement is destroyed (Fig. 4).

Some panel designs employ a support strap beneath the lapped panels to receive fasteners and a strap on top to press the two panels tightly together against a sealant. This joint is located away from a supporting structure to avoid any interference or connection with the structure (Fig. 5).

The flashing detail at the movement end of the panel may incorporate only an overlapping metal flashing, or in some instances a metal flashing and a flexible membrane seal. The flashing alone can allow melting snow or other moisture to enter the building by capillary action or wind pressure. Most manufacturers provide a predesigend detail and manufactured components for this important condition, along with explicit instructions for proper installation. However, some manufacturers leave this detail up to the roof designer. The designer, in these instances, must not only come up with a typical detail that works, but must also anticipate the transition of this detail at corners.

Side–edge details are extremely important. This is the condition where the side–edge of the roof panel must be free to slide behind a counterflashing. Usually the manufacturer provides a vertical flashing extension under the counterflashing. This extension of the basic panel should be as high as possible, as this provides the main assurance

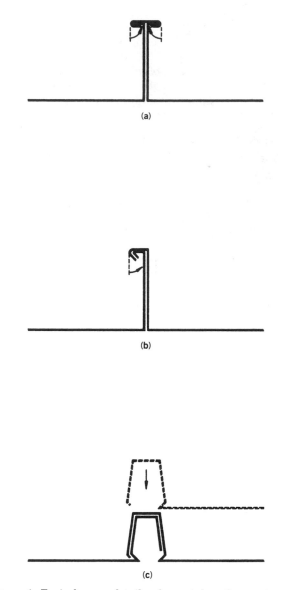

Figure 4. Typical seam details of a metal roofing system. (**a**) Upturned edge with seam cap; (**b**) upturned edge with interlocking seam; (**c**) snap-together battens.

against weather penetration (Fig. 6). Details of this condition must clearly indicate the sliding nature of the flashing. It is probably a good idea to add a note to the detail indicating that fasteners must not connect the counterflashing to the sliding flashing. Any gaps should be filled to combat air infiltration. In some instances, flexible membranes may be adequate for this side condition rather than using sliding metal flashings. However, the flexible membrane approach is limited to fairly small runs and depends on exceptional long-term performance of the membrane.

Roof curbs and pipe flashing require a designer's close attention. Large openings for mechanical equipment, or for ductwork for mechanical equipment, require roof curbs. When the weight on the curb is not excessive and when the connection from below to the curb has some capacity for movement, the roof curb may be allowed to float along with the roof.

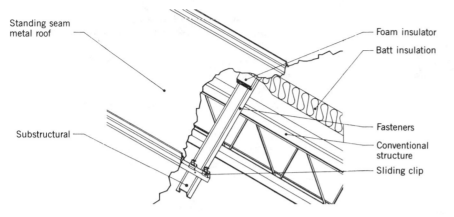

Figure 5. Construction detail for standing seam metal roofing system on light structural steel framing.

Curbs for large and heavy equipment may require a double curb: one curb is fixed to the building structure and the equipment, while the other curb is allowed to float with the roof. Flexible or overlapping flashings connect the two curbs. Large equipment is frequently mounted on pipe supports above the roof, and only the ductwork pene-

trates through curbs. Flexible pipe flashings are available for these pipe supports and for other pipe penetrations such as vent stacks.

Corner conditions are critical. Two-way movement must be accommodated at corners where the sliding side detail meets the panel end movement joint. This compound movement is handled for some systems with molded rubber parts. With some manufacturers this important requirement is ignored. Occasionally even the most sophisticated manufacturers will handle difficult corner requirements with evasive notations such as, "to be specified in field." Corners remain a potential problem area for various types of application, especially on complicated building shapes.

General approaches to problem corner conditions can be suggested by the building designer, but the installer or manufacturer is usually in a better position to anticipate and provide workable solutions. Their responsibility should be clearly stated in the drawings. Even basic details may be omitted on the architectural drawings if the roofing contractor accepts complete responsibility for proper design and installation. The shop drawings, however, should at least show the methods used for key conditions and be subject to the architects approval.

Batten Seam. The batten-seam roof is chosen when strong vertical lines are desired. Batten seams create a bold linear appearance that adds depth and beauty to any roofing installation. The batten-seam roof has as its characteristic feature evenly spaced battens running with the slope of the roof. These battens are usually about 2-in. square and are spaced about 20 in. apart.

Batten seam is not the least expensive type of metal roofing because it uses more material and requires more labor than standing seam. But batten has its own dignity, character, and beauty, and by its very construction, provides against expansion and contraction. On large steep roof areas, such as mansards and gables, and for public buildings, churches, or large residences, it gives dignity and character to the structure, lending itself easily to rich ornamentation (Fig. 7).

Color. Color, for some roofs, is a planned process of weathering and corrosion. As exposed aluminum, copper, and zinc react to chemicals in the atmosphere, each forms

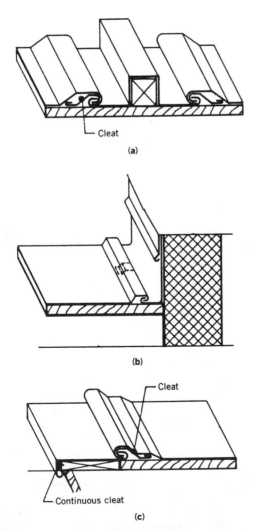

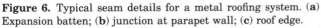

Figure 6. Typical seam details for a metal roofing system. (a) Expansion batten; (b) junction at parapet wall; (c) roof edge.

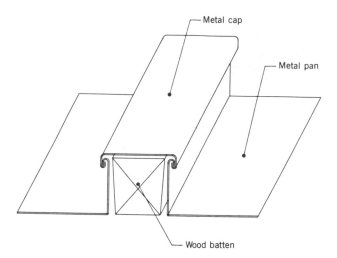

Figure 7. Batten-cap detail for a metal roofing system.

a thin film of oxides on its surface. The corrosion not only causes the roof to change color, but also helps to inhibit further corrosion as well. As the rich patina develops, the metal's protection against pitting and chemical consumption increases.

Copper, one of the most durable metals, goes through many stages of corrosion on its way to the mottled green of fully aged metal. Starting out salmon pink, copper moves through various shades of brown as first oxides and then sulfides form on its surface. The basic blue-green patina is actually copper sulfate and is the only copper film that is truly corrosion resistant.

Copper may take from 25 to 30 years to reach the final stages of weathering. This time frame depends on the amount of sulfur and moisture in the atmosphere where the roof is located. Copper may be chemically aged to take on the blue-green patina in a matter of weeks rather than years. Alternatively, the bright color of new copper may be preserved with special coatings.

Zinc and aluminum form oxides that inhibit further corrosion. In fact, the oxidation rate for aluminum is actually faster than that of iron. The oxide film that forms is so impervious, however, that further corrosion is quickly stopped. Aluminum changes little in color as it weathers. Zinc, on the other hand, ages to a uniform gray in about a year. Preweathered zinc alloy panels are also available.

Stainless steel, another metal that may be left exposed, protects itself slightly differently. While the chromium in the alloy forms a protective shield on the surface, the nickel the metal contains provides further rust protection. Because of this added defense, stainless steel changes little in appearance as it weathers.

Plain carbon steel, the most widely used roofing metal, must be coated with another material to withstand corrosion. Paint, other metals, and ceramic coatings are all used, and their choice, like the choice of metal itself, will determine the appearance and performance of the roof.

Installation. Installing a metal roof system can be a simple operation with preengineered materials. Manufacturers, working from building specifications, are able to preform panels and, in some cases, flashings and details as well. For the work crews, the job is simply putting the pieces together.

To help the crews form strong, watertight seams, electric seam formers have been developed. These small electric machines straddle the seam and crimp the edges together as they roll along the seam's length.

Contractors with sheet metal experience, on the other hand, may choose to form the entire system, including the panels and flashings, at the site. This allows the contractor to custom form the roof to the building. It also eliminates the problem of transporting long, preformed panels to the site.

The ease of preengineering and the quality of job-site custom fitting may be combined in a couple of ways. Some contractors may use their own crews to install preengineered panels, but leave the intricate flashing details to sheet metal mechanics. Manufacturers may also provide on-site engineering services. In this case, the manufacturer uses mobile equipment to form the metal components.

With the look of metal roofing becoming popular, more and more metal roof systems are being used on reroofing jobs as well as new construction. In many cases, the support system provides the necessary pitch to avoid standing water on the metal panels. With the advent of preengineered, easy-to-install metal roof systems, it is now possible for most contractors to enter the growing metal roofing market. Carefully scrutinizing the different manufacturers and systems will help find the one most suitable.

Single Plies

The use of single-ply roof membranes has grown considerably in the last decade. Current data available from the Single Ply Roofing Institute set the market share of "in-place" single-ply roofing at just under 30% of total roofing installations. Demand for reroofing, together with actions by code committees, standards groups, and manufacturers, will enhance the desirability of single plies on into the future.

The synthetic materials that are used today as single-ply roofing membranes have a long history of use in other types of product; for example, synthetic rubber sheeting has been used to make tarpaulins and tires, and vinyl products have been used for window framing and exterior siding. The specific formulations of these materials are determined by the way they will be used.

The roof membrane must be able to accommodate anticipated structural movement without splitting or cracking. Furthermore, it must retain these properties over a reasonable period of time. The material's properties must be consistent from batch to batch. Manufacturers adhere to strict quality control programs to ensure that minimum physical properties are achieved and maintained.

Single-plies, as they are commonly known, refer to all poly(vinyl chloride) (PVC), chlorinated polyethylene (CPE), or any other polymeric alloy or blend of thermoplastic polymers as plastic membranes. The unique feature of the plastomeric materials is the weldability of the material, either by solvent or heat welding.

The elastomeric or thermoset materials include ethylene propylene diene terpolymer, neoprene, and chlorosulfonated polyethylene (CSPE). These elastomers are normally referred to as synthetic rubber membranes. It is possible to have a cured or vulcanized sheet such as EPDM while most CSPE materials are referred to as uncured elastomers. They will cure or cross-link after a period of time with the application of heat promoting the cure. This is why a cured EPDM sheet can only be glued together with an adhesive while some CSPE membranes can be heat welded and then allowed to cure in place on the roof (Fig. 8).

Polyisobutylene (PIB) is also referred to as an uncured elastomer and utilizes a self-adhering butyl rubber lap. Modified bitumen membranes primarily use a plastic or elastomeric modifier (atactic polypropylene or styrene–butydiene–styrene) materials to blend with a select grade of asphalt. These sheets have polyester or glass reinforcement and may be plain, granule surfaced or metal foil surfaced.

According to the National Roofing Contractors Association, the roofing industry consumed somewhere between 650 and 750 million ft^2 of this material in 1984. This compares with 450 million ft^2 reportedly used in 1983. The majority of EPDM membranes were utilized in a ballasted or mechanically fastened roof system, and they were also used in fully adhered situations. This usage includes black and white EPDMs.

The plastomeric membranes were also in demand for ballasted, mechanically fastened, or fully adhered configurations. While there are no figures available at this time, it is anticipated that an increase in the use of white reinforced plastomeric-type membranes will be seen, especially for mechanically fastened use. Nonsupported or plain PVC membranes were also being specified but not to the extent of EPDM membranes, especially for ballasted roof systems.

Modified bitumen membranes are perhaps the largest growth area, along with EPDM. These materials are more correctly identified with built-up roof systems and, in many cases, have been installed as part of a BUR.

Building code authorities are typically concerned with the fire and wind performance of roof systems; usually roof systems must undergo a series of fire tests at Underwriters Laboratories (UL). Due to the large number of membrane manufacturers now actively marketing roof membranes, there is a backlog of fire-testing work at UL and elsewhere.

Depending on the generic materials and the system in which they are used, many single-ply membranes will easily pass the UL Class A fire test, in some cases up to slopes of 3 in. to the horizontal foot, unless otherwise indicated. Such materials as CPE, PIB, and CSPE pass the UL Class A fire test, while EPDMs and PVCs need a flame retardant (FR) additive to achieve a Class A rating. Modified bitumen systems sometimes have a more difficult time achieving the Class A rating due to the asphalt or modifiers used. As a result, intensive research is currently underway with the hope of achieving a Class A fire rating without the use of a coating or gravel covering. A Class B rating can be achieved in many instances with a coated emulsion. However, the service life of the coating is difficult to predict.

Perhaps the most important consideration in single ply is the effects of wind, especially with ballasted single-ply membranes. Manufacturers, contractors, and code officials are concerned with several items including wind scour; ballast size, gradation, and coverage; roof edge design; and design wind speeds.

In regard to wind scour, the National Roofing Contractors Association indicates that the following wind scour speeds should be considered:

Stone Diameter, in.	Scour Speed, mph
1/2	64
1	76
1 1/2	88

The wind scour speeds may cause individual ballast particles to move and become airborne. These data were derived from wind tunnel testing and limited full-scale tests. The full-scale experiments involved aircraft-type engines mounted on an elevated platform with a prototype roof deck assembly.

Two different independently conducted field studies have shown that wind scour is occurring on some of the ballasted roofs currently in place. The wind scour noted is, in many cases, insignificant and involves localized ballast movement in the extreme corners of the roof or along the perimeter. In many cases, the roof had experienced high wind forces (in excess of 40 mph) and minimal scouring at these locations. These studies as well as individual observations made by others during periods of high wind activity on ballasted roofs have shown that in some instances building height, edge detail, and internal pressure can contribute to a wind scour problem.

Of interest, is the current ballast size used on loose-laid roofs. One study reports that the average stone diameter is slightly in excess of 1 in. when considering the range of stone diameters received from specification calling for 1 3/4- to 1 1/2-in. stone.

ASTM Committee D-8 on Roofing, Waterproofing, and Bituminous Materials has approved material and application standards. The Rubber Manufacturers Association has completed a material standard for EPDM and neoprene via the American National Standards Institute

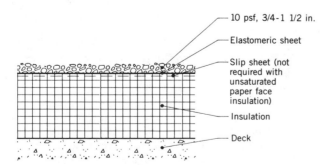

Figure 8. Single-ply elastomeric sheet applied over foam insulation.

10 psf, 3/4-1 1/2 in. — Elastomeric sheet — Slip sheet (not required with unsaturated paper face insulation) — Insulation — Deck

(ANSI) process. The ASTM and RMA standards are similar. The joint CIB–RILEM International Committee on Single Layer Roofing is also interested in both material and performance standards. The Single Ply Roofing Institute (SPRI) also continues to develop material and application guidelines for different generic systems.

Manufacturers continue to strive for improvement in the membrane material, application techniques, and component design. New seaming techniques have been introduced for EPDM roofs. Continuing development work on mechanically fastened single-ply roofing continues to grow. Insulation suppliers now recognize the special features of single ply. New facers along with fire-rated insulation materials will probably be introduced soon.

The four groups of single-ply products, defined by their chemical nature are as follows:

1. Vulcanized elastomers are also referred to as thermosets. Both terms relate to the chemical cross-linkage of the polymers, which occurs during the manufacturing process. Once the linkages have been formed, a process also termed curing there cannot be changed. A distinguishing characteristic of a vulcanized elastomer is that it can only be bonded to itself (for example, to seam overlapping sheets) by the use of an adhesive because, once cured, new molecular linkages cannot be formed.

2. Nonvulcanized elastomers, also referred to as uncured elastomers, are not physically cured during manufacture. However, they may cure or vulcanize naturally over some period of time, on exposure to the elements. Once they have cured, their behavior is similar to that of the vulcanized elastomers, and they have become thermosets.

3. Thermoplastic materials, distinguished from thermosets in that there is no cross-linking or vulcanization, can be welded together with heat or solvent and develop, in these welds, bond strengths that equal or surpass the strength of the base material.

4. Modified bitumen roofing membranes are composite sheets consisting of bitumen, polymer modifiers, and reinforcement. The term modified bitumen encompasses a broad range of materials, and each specific material differs from the others with respect to the modifiers and reinforcements used. They exhibit the thermoplastic behavior of being softened by heat, but are separated into their own generic category because of the significant differences in chemical makeup from the other thermoplastic materials.

Recognizing that no two products are identical even if they consist of the same predominant polymeric composition, the following descriptions provide some general information about each generic product type.

Vulcanized Elastomers. *EPDM.* EPDM is an elastomeric compound synthesized from ethylene, propylene, and a small amount of diene monomer. It is generally used for roofing as a vulcanized material, although it is also possible to formulate EPDM membranes that are non-

vulcanized. Used as a roofing material in the United States since the early 1960s, EPDM sheets range in thickness from 30 to 60 mil and are usually black in color. White colors are also available. EPDM membranes exhibit a high degree of ozone, ultraviolet, weathering, and abrasion resistance as well as good low temperature flexibility. EPDMs properties of resilience, tensile strength, elongation, and hardness are largely retained in aging tests at elevated temperatures. Resistance is excellent to acids, alkalies, and oxygenated solvents such as ketones, esters, and alcohols. On the other hand, exposure to aromatic, halogenated, and aliphatic solvents should be avoided to prevent swelling and distortion of the membrane.

Neoprene. Neoprene, or chloroprene rubber, is the first commercially available synthetic rubber product. Neoprene is formulated from polymers of chloroprene and may be used in a variety of elastomeric applications. Neoprenes may be calendered into sheets that vary in thickness from 30 to 120 mil and it is in this form that neoprene is used for roofing membranes. Chloroprene synthetic rubber sheets have been used as a single-ply roofing membrane since 1957. Sheets are available plain or with a reinforcing fabric. Neoprene roof membranes have excellent resistance to weather, heat, oils, solvents, and abrasion. The characteristics of neoprene adhesives allow fabrication of field splices that achieve high seam strength to provide a reliable continuous weatherproofing membrane. Some formulations are available that will receive a coating of liquid Hypalon synthetic rubber when a stable uniform color is desired for the roof membrane. These special nonstaining neoprene products require such a coating for weather protection.

Nonvulcanized Elastomers. *CSPE.* Chlorosulfonated polyethylene, a synthetic rubber, was introduced in 1951 under the trade name Hypalon, (Hypalon is a registered trademark of DuPont.) It is a self-curing nonvulcanized elastomer and is available as a liquid coating or in sheet form for single-ply membrane application. CSPE sheet roofing membranes have been in use since 1966. They may be reinforced with polyester scrim or laminated to felt backing materials and have a finished thickness of 30–60 mil. CSPE is a nonvulcanized product that exhibits thermoplastic qualities during processing and field installation. During roof exposure, curing or cross-linking occurs. CSPE exhibits strong resistance to weathering and a broad range of chemicals and pollutants, as well as being inherently ozone resistant. It may be produced in many colors and offers design versatility because of its adaptability to a variety of roof shapes and substrates.

CPE. Chlorinated polyethylene was first introduced to the single-ply membrane roofing market in 1964. CPE may be formulated for use as roofing membranes as both cured and uncured elastomers. They may be nonreinforced or reinforced with scrim and may range in thickness from 40 to 48 mil. They are inherently flexible and do not require the addition of plasticizers in their formulations. CPE exhibits strong resistance to oils and chemicals, excellent weatherability, and ozone resistance. CPE membranes are also resistant to bitumen and can therefore be installed directly over existing asphalt or coal-tar pitch roofs. Although usually produced in white or light gray for reflectivity and energy efficiency, CPE can also be pigmented to a variety of colors.

PIB. PIB (polyisobutylene) is an elastomeric compound, composed of isobutylene and other polymers, which was first used as a roofing membrane in Europe in the 1960s. It has been available in the United States in the form used today since the mid-1970s. The 60-mil PIB membrane is laminated to a 40-mil nonwoven synthetic fleece backing, with an unbacked prefabricated sealing edge for the side laps. PIB exhibits good resistance to weathering, ultraviolet light, and radiant heat. It is compatible with asphalt, but is not resistant to petroleum distillates, organic oil and fats, or substances containing tar.

NBP. NBP nitrile alloy membranes are compounded from butadiene–acrylonitrile copolymers with other proprietary ingredients. They are typically reinforced with polyester and range in thickness from 30 to 45 mil. First developed in the mid-1960s, nitrile alloys have been used in engineering applications in the aircraft, automotive, and geomembrane industries. Used extensively for weatherproofing and waterproofing applications since the mid-1960s, NBP-reinforced single-ply membranes exhibit excellent tear and puncture resistance, good weatherability, good flexibility at low temperatures, and low water vapor permeability. They are resistant to most chemicals but are sensitive to aromatic hydrocarbons.

Thermoplastics. *PVC.* PVC, or poly(vinyl chloride), polymers, originally produced in the FRG almost 30 years ago, are among the most versatile of thermoplastics for industrial and commercial application. They are produced by the polymerization of vinyl chloride monomer, a gaseous substance resulting from the reaction of ethylene with oxygen and hydrochloric acid. In its most basic form, the resin is a relatively hard material that requires the addition of other compounds, commonly plasticizers and stabilizers as well as certain other ingredients, to produce the desired physical properties for end use. PVC membranes may be produced by calendering, extruding, or spread coating, and they may be nonreinforced or reinforced with glass fibers or polyester fabric. They are usually 40–48 mil thick. PVC membranes are available that have provided up to 20 years of service life as exposed roofing. They are resistant to bacterial growth, industrial chemical atmospheres, root penetration, and extreme weather conditions. PVC membranes, properly formulated, have shown excellent fire resistance and seaming capabilities. PVC membranes are chemically incompatible with bituminous materials.

EIP. EIP are thermoplastic compounds consisting of ethylene interpolymers, stabilizers, pigments, antioxidants and modifying polymers. EIP membranes are generally reinforced with polyester fabric and are usually 32 mil thick. They possess good resistance to fire, chemicals, and oils and have high tear strength.

Modified Bitumens. Polymer-modified bituminous membranes were developed in Europe in the mid-1960s and have been in use in the United States since 1975. Both the bitumen and polymers used in these systems have been carefully selected and combined to result in an engineered coating that is coupled with various reinforcements to form a membrane specifically designed to meet the requirements for successful performance in a roofing system. The modifying compounds, such as styrene butadiene or atactic polypropylene, impart flexibility and elasticity, and improve cohesive strength, resistance to flow at high temperatures, and toughness. Reinforcing materials consist variously of plastic film, polyester mat, glass fibers, felt, or fabric; they may be embedded within or laminated to the surface of the modified bitumen membrane. The membrane may be surfaced with liquid coatings, metallic laminates, ceramic granules, or mineral aggregates to enhance ultraviolet and fire resistance. Modified bitumen membranes range in thickness from 40 to 160 mil.

Properties. Although it is difficult to directly correlate physical property data with actual performance or life expectancy, manufacturers typically utilize such data in their quality-control programs to ensure the suitability of the compound for its end use. The following is a list of 12 basic material properties that the Single Ply Roofing Institute's Technical Commitee has identified as being pertinent to all roofing membranes.

1. Thickness.
2. Tensile strength.
3. Ultimate elongation.
4. Modulus.
5. Tear resistance.
6. Water vapor transmission rate.
7. Water absorption.
8. Dimensional stability.
9. Factory seam strength.
10. Low temperature resistance.
11. Results after heat aging.
12. Results after accelerated weathering.

The relationship of thickness to actual performance is not entirely clear, and membranes are available in thicknesses ranging from 30 mil to as much as 160 mil. This rather significant variance may be accounted for by such factors as the polymer type and formulation, method of manufacture, physical construction of the finished sheet (eg, surfacing reinforcements, etc), as well as the intended method of application. The performance-related factors usually associated with membrane thickness are its resistance to mechanical damage, hail, traffic, and surface wear, although there are certainly other factors, such as compressibility of the substrate, that also contribute to all of these. In other words, the susceptibility of a membrane to damage does not in any way rely solely on the thickness of the material.

Tensile strength relates to the ability of a membrane to withstand stresses that might be imposed by such things as building movement, wind uplift, and thermal loading. The presence and type of reinforcing material may also affect tensile strength.

The elongation of a membrane may contribute to its ability to accommodate movement in the substrate or structure without rupturing. Elongation varies from product to product depending on chemical composition and sometimes on the presence of reinforcing materials. In some cases, a reinforcing material may break internally at a low strain level without affecting the integrity of the sheet, thereby allowing the membrane itself to stretch and achieve its elongation property. In other cases, the reinforcement has a high resistance to elongation and imparts this characteristic to the finished sheet, producing a membrane with a low elongation property. The selection is made by the manufacturer and is based largely on the manner in which the material will be installed.

Because polymeric materials do not exhibit traditional elastic behavior over their entire range of elongation, the modulus is not a constant; instead, it is reported as the tensile stress required to produce a prescribed elongation. When the modulus at 50% elongation is reported for a number of products, it allows for a comparison of their relative stiffness. This is expressed as pounds per square inch (psi) at a given percent elongation.

The presence of reinforcement affects the modulus of a material by significantly increasing its stiffness; it may also affect the elongation properties in the direction of the reinforcing medium. Like elongation, this property is an indicator of the suitability of the formulation for use as a roofing membrane, but is not a direct predictor of its performance once installed. However, modulus, in combination with other factors such as coefficient of thermal expansion and dimensional stability, may have an effect on the manner of attachment of the membrane at terminations.

Tear resistance indicates a membrane's ability to resist initiation and propagation of a tear. Recognizing that mechanical damage occasionally occurs that results in a tear or puncture, it is important that during installation, or membrane expansion and contraction due to structural or substrate movement or wind uplift pressures, the membrane be able to resist further tearing. Resistance to tear is also of importance in mechanically attached membrane systems in which the membrane is penetrated by fasteners and wherever penetration of the membrane occurs at terminations. Different test methods are used to test the tear resistance of reinforced and nonreinforced membranes.

The actual water vapor transmission rate of a specific membrane is important in the design of the total roofing assembly with regard to the vapor retarder. The membrane must be resistant to water absorption from continuous submersion in water due to ponding, whether because of poor drainage or snow and ice buildup. A significant loss or gain of weight during immersion would indicate that the membrane may not perform satisfactorily over a long period of time. This water absorption may affect dimensional stability and membrane thickness and may cause internal stress that could lead to cracking.

In most cases, standard test methods to evaluate material properties are available. When using physical property data to compare various single-ply roof membranes, consider the test methods used to determine those data. Different tests produce different results.

Fabric Roofing

Fabric roofing is used to cover large spaces and involves both structural considerations and moisture control. Architectural fabrics are relatively new and are just becoming recognized as permanent and legitimate building materials. Today, four major criteria have been established for fabric structures:

- *Solar optical properties, transmission and reflectance.* Light transmission equals cost savings associated with lower artificial light requirements and high reflectance of radiant heat equals lower air-conditioning costs.
- *Durability.* Major strength properties, tensile and tear strength, are affected little by outdoor exposure. During the first year or two, a modest decrease (20%) in properties usually takes place, but thereafter no significant change occurs.
- *Safety.* Fabric structures must meet fire code regulations.
- *Technology.* An established manufacturing technology is needed for coating glass cloth with Teflon, using reliable raw materials readily available worldwide. Teflon-coated fiberglass, silicon-coated fiber glass, and vinyl-coated polyester are the most popular coating fiber combinations in use today.

Two technological breakthroughs have made fabric roofs viable. First, computer analysis allows the mathematical modeling of complicated surfaces. Second, woven materials that are fairly inert and of high strength and durability enable architects and engineers to design efficient, durable fabric roofing systems.

Asphalt, Slate, Clay, Concrete Tile and Wood Shingles

Slate and tile products are generally used in steep roofing applications. Concrete tile is occasionally selected when the weight of the roof is particularly important as a design criterion.

Asphalt. The most frequently used shingle material on sloping roofs in the United States is asphaltic shingles. Formed in strips of asphalt-impregnated organic or fiber glass felts, they are surfaced with slate granules in a variety of colors: black, red, green, brown, and off-white. They can be applied to roof slopes as low as 2 in. in 12 in., but are used more commonly with slopes of 4 in. and above (Fig. 9).

Slate. Roofing slate is a dense, durable rock material that is practically nonabsorbent, having a porosity generally of 0.15–0.4%. The principal property of slate is its natural "cleavage," which permits it to be easily split in one direction. A second direction of fracture, usually occurring at right angles to the cleavage is called the "grain." Roofing slates are commonly split so that the length of the slate runs in the direction of the grain (Fig. 10). The surface texture of slate after it is split for commercial use depends on the characteristics of the rock from which it is quarried. Many slates split to a smooth,

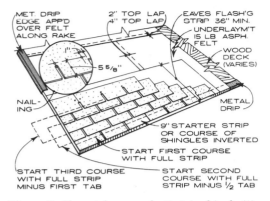

Figure 9. Three tab square butt strip shingle (1).

practically even, uniform surface while others split to a surface that is somewhat rough and uneven. As a result, a wide range of surface effects is available for the appearance of slate roofs.

Some slate contains narrow "ribbons" of rock that are different in chemical composition and color from the slate itself. If the chemical composition of these ribbons does not weaken the slate and if the color is not objectionable, ribbon slates are acceptable for use. Slate that has been trimmed so that the ribbons are eliminated is known as "clear slate." Slate that contains acceptable ribbons is sold as "ribbon stock."

The color of slate is determined by its chemical and mineralogical composition. Because these factors differ in various regions, it is possible to obtain roofing slates in a variety of colors and shades. To relieve the monotony of a flat uniform roof color, various shades of the same colored slate may be used to provide interesting color patterns when applied up and down the roof, across the roof, or interspersed throughout the roof. The diversity in shades of color makes slate a valuable material in the creation of an aesthetically appealing roof.

Exposure to weather causes all slate to change slightly in color. The degree of color change varies with different slates. Those slates that exhibit minimal color change are classified as permanent or unfading slates. Those slates that exhibit a more obvious color change are known as weathering slates. Weathering slates offer the designer

another variation in roof color. For the purpose of classifying the basic natural colors of roofing slate now available in large quantities for general use, the Division of Simplified Practice of the Department of Commerce recommends the following color nomenclature for slate materials.

Basic Slate Colors

Black	Gray	Purple	Green
Blue-black	Blue-gray	Mottled purple and green	Red

When selecting a slate color from a manufacturer, the color should be preceded by the word unfading or weathering to designate the color change that may be expected for a particular material.

Slate roofs may be classified into three general categories:

- Standard slate roofs.
- Textural slate roofs.
- Graduated slate roofs.

Standard slate roofs are those roofs composed of standard commercial slate (approximately 3/16 in. thick), having one uniform length and width and having square tails or butts laid to a line. Standard commercial slate may be used to form a variety of designs on the roof and are suitable for any building where a permanent roofing material is desired at a minimum cost. Standard slate roofs differ from other slate roofs only in the texture or appearance of the roof. If desired, the butts or corners of each slate may be trimmed to give a diamond, hexagonal or Gothic pattern for all or part of the roof. Variety in the pattern of standard slate roofs is sometimes attained by laying two or more sizes of standard commercial slate over the same area (Fig. 11).

Textural slate roofs are composed of textural slate, which is usually rougher in texture than standard slate.

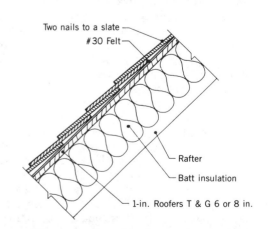

Figure 10. Slate shingle on pitched roof.

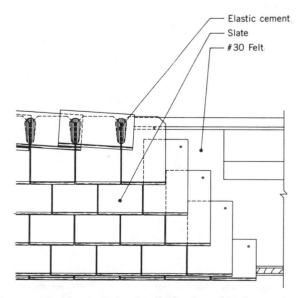

Figure 11. Ridge detail of a slate shingle.

Textural slates are produced with uneven butts and with variations in thickness and size. In general, the term textural slate is not applied to slate over ⅜ in. in thickness. Varying shades of textural slate are frequently used to enhance the color effect of the roof. In addition to the basic colors of textural slate, other colorings, such as bronze or orange, may also be obtained in limited quantities. Textural slate roofs are aesthetically pleasing due to the variations in texture and color attainable with textural slate.

Graduated slate roofs combine the artistic features of the textural slate roof with variations in thickness, size, and exposure. In graduated slate roofs, the thickest and longest slates are placed in the eaves. As the slate courses progress to the ridge, slates of gradually diminishing size and thickness are used, creating the graduated effect. Slates for roofs of this type can be obtained in any combination of thickness from ³⁄₁₆ to 1½ in. Heavier slates are available if desired.

Clay. Clay roofing tile is produced by baking plates of molded clay into tile. The density of the tile is determined by the length of time it is heated and by the heating temperature employed. Clay tile offers a wide range of design possibilities for residential roofs due to the large variety of tiles available for use (Fig. 12).

Clay tile may be classified into two categories:

1. *Roll Tile.*

- Pan shape (either curved or flat and available with or without interlocking features).
- Cover (or barrel) semicircular shape.
- Pan and cover shape.
- S shape.

2. *Flat Tile.*

- Flat shingle shape.
- Flat ribbed shape (with interlocking features).

To ensure proper fit and appearance of clay tile, each tile should be aligned so that horizontal joints are parallel to the eaves and vertical joints are at right angles. Care should be taken to remove all foreign material from the interlocking ribs and grooves of interlocking tiles to ensure uniform contact between the tiles. Tiles installed at hip and valley locations should be cut to match the angle of the hip or valley in a manner that will maintain the watertight integrity of the hip or valley.

In order to ensure a watertight roof, the following minimum slope requirements should be strictly applied.

Type of Tile	Roof Slope
One-piece barrel tile	4 in./ft
Two-piece barrel tile	4 in./ft
Flat shingle tile	5 in./ft
Interlocking flat ribbed tile	4 in./ft

Whenever clay tile is laid on a roof with a minimum slope of 4 in./ft or less, a double layer of felt set either in mastic or hot asphalt is recommended to ensure a watertight roof.

On wood plank or plywood roof decks, the sheathing should be tight and covered with a No. 30 or a No. 40 asphalt saturated or asbestos saturated felt. If the roof deck is made of concrete, a surface must be provided on which the tiles may be applied. To create this surface, 1 × 2 beveled wood nailing strips, running from the eaves to the ridge, should be embedded in the concrete, spaced according to the size of the tile to be installed. Felts should then be nailed to these nailing strips. Lengths of lath should be nailed directly above the nailing strips through the felt. Horizontal battens (stringers), spaced according to the type of tile to be used, should then be nailed across the lath. In this way a simulated wood surface is created to accommodate the application of tiles.

More tiles are broken in transit and on the ground than are broken on the roof. Therefore, great care must be taken in unloading tile at the job site. Tile should be unloaded as near as possible to the building and distributed to points where delivery to the roof will be convenient. To prevent tiles from becoming soiled, they should be piled not more than four rows high, on edge, and on strips of lumber. Nails, cement, and coloring material should remain covered until needed.

After about 75 or 100 tiles have been installed, a visual inspection of the tile application should be made from ground level and at a distance from the building to see that the tile course follows straight and true lines and that the colors of the tile blend well. This procedure should be repeated at regular intervals during tile installation to ensure an attractive and acceptable roof. The blending of the tile shades is particularly important to avoid streaks or "hot spots." Tiles that have been preblended at the factory can be obtained from some manufacturers. Blending may also be performed in the field.

During the application of flat tile, the spacing of the tiles may need to be adjusted to provide a uniform exposure beneath dormer windows. Although normal practice with flat tile is to drain water into a hanging gutter, a concealed gutter may be constructed by building a lead- or copper-lined box into the roof. When this is done, the bottom tiles (or "pans") of the first and second tile courses

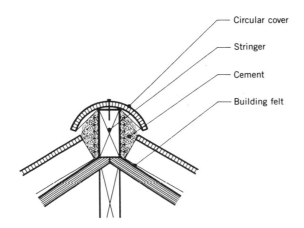

— Circular cover

— Stringer

— Cement

— Building felt

Figure 12. Ridge detail of a clay tile roofing system.

should be cut short or omitted to leave a gap through which water may drain from the roof. The application of roll tile involves similar details to those described above for flat tile.

Concrete Tile Shingle. Concrete roofing tile is composed of portland cement, sand, and water, mixed in varying proportions. These materials are mixed and extruded on individual molds under high pressure to form the tile product. The exposed surface of the tile is finished with a cementitious material colored with synthetic oxides. Tiles are placed in curing chambers under controlled humidity and temperature conditions to reach a required strength prior to shipment (Fig. 13). Consideration should be given to using concrete tile products that meet the moisture absorption requirements for a particular area. If concrete tiles absorb moisture, structural roof problems may result.

Concrete tile may be classified into two categories:

1. *Roll Tile.*

- Pan shape (either curved or flat and available with or without interlocking features).
- Cover (or barrel) semicircular shape.
- Pan and cover shape.
- S shape.

2. *Flat Tile.*

- Flat shingle shape.
- Flat ribbed shape (with interlocking features).

To ensure proper fit and appearance, each tile should be aligned so that horizontal joints are parallel to the eaves and vertical joints are at right angles. Care should be taken to remove all foreign material from the interlocking ribs and grooves of interlocking tiles to ensure uniform

contact between the tiles. Tiles installed at hip and valley locations should be cut to match the angle of the hip or valley in a manner that will maintain the watertight integrity of the hip or valley.

In order to ensure a watertight roof, the following minimum slope requirements should be strictly applied:

Type of Tile	Roof Slope
One-piece barrel tile	4 in./ft
Flat shingle tile	5 in./ft
Interlocking flat ribbed tile	4 in./ft

Whenever concrete tile is laid on a roof with a minimum slope of 4 in./ft or less, a double layer of felt set either in mastic or hot asphalt is recommended to ensure a watertight roof.

Modern concrete tiles are produced in a variety of colors, which may be attractively arranged on the roof. To guard against a spottily colored roof, tiles should be mixed in the correct color arrangement on the ground and sent up to the roof in bundles with strict instructions that application must follow the color order already arranged in each bundle of tiles. For instance, if the color scheme calls for 10% of one color, 30% of another color and 60% of a third color, the tile should be sent up to the roof in bundles of 10 tiles, with each bundle having 1 tile of the first color, 3 of the second color and 6 of the third color. In this way the tiles may be applied in the order in which they are bundled and no time will be wasted on the roof for color selection.

Wood Shingle Roofs. Wood shingles are produced almost entirely from cedar, because of its natural splitting characteristics, its natural resistance to rot and insect infestation, and its aesthetic characteristics. The shingle is manufactured in machine sawn, machine split, or hand split shakes in lengths from 18 to 24 in. It may be applied over No. 30 or No. 40 building felt, often with a plastic-

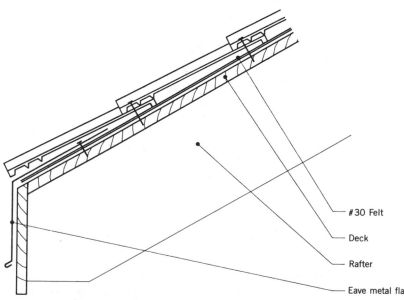

#30 Felt

Deck

Rafter

Eave metal flashing   **Figure 13.** Eave detail of concrete roofing tile.

coated steel foil layer, to a plywood or wood panel sheathing or to wood strips nailed to the rafters (Fig. 14).

Spray-applied Foams

There are a number of qualified system suppliers of spray-applied foams; however, no two systems are alike. A wide range of foam systems is available in variable densities, with different temperature limitations, combustibility characteristics, etc. The use of these systems in combination with each other or with conventional insulation products offers an unlimited range of economical installations.

It is necessary to understand that most published properties are run on laboratory-produced samples. The thickness of foam sprayed, number of passes, temperature of substrate, ambient temperatures, etc, have a pronounced effect on all properties.

Chemical resistance should be considered in the selection of the proper foam system. The degree of possible damage is determined by the amount of the chemical, its type, and duration of contact. In regard to fire safety, foam can be used safely.

When spray-applied urethane foam is applied externally, as an integral part of the roofing system, it must be given a protective covering due to the fact that the foam is subject to degradation from ultraviolet radiation. In some instances, conventional building materials may constitute a protective covering. However, typically the required protection is attained through application of an elastomeric liquid-applied coating system.

As in the case of foam systems suppliers, there are a number of protective coating suppliers. Protective coating performance is directly proportional to the applied film thickness. Minimal film thickness should be avoided as coating service life will be poor. Consider the following items in the proper selection of the coating material:

1. Environment in which it is to be used (abuse, hail, resistance, etc).
2. Life expectancy.
3. Ease of maintenance.
4. History of similar applications or laboratory data relating to the application in question.
5. Water vapor permeance.
6. Application conditions (temperature, etc).
7. Cost vs performance.
8. Tension and elongation strength.
9. Adhesive to the urethane foam.
10. Retention of physical properties on aging.
11. Ability to withstand normal, short-term ponding water.
12. Opacity to light.
13. Combustibility characteristics, individually and in combination with the selected foam systems.
14. Ability to withstand normal foot traffic.
15. Aesthetic qualities.
16. Warranty.
17. Compression strength.

On all coating applications, the foam should be dry, clean, and free of dust, dirt, or foam overspray before application. If the insulation has been left uncoated for more than three days, the surface should be brushed or air blown before applying the coating.

A minimum of 15 dry mils, or as recommended by the protective coating manufacturer, should be spray applied to cover the foam in a crisscross technique. The coating can be installed in one or more coats. However, if more than one coat is specified, contrasting colors should be used with the final coat being the finish color. It is also good practice to install additional mils around heavily worked areas, such as equipment, etc.

GLOSSARY

Aggregate. (*1*) Crushed stone, crushed slag, or water-worn gravel used for surfacing a built-up roof; (*2*) any granular mineral material.

Alligatoring. The cracking of the surfacing bitumen on a built-up roof, producing a pattern of cracks similar to an alligator's hide; the cracks may or may not extend through the surfacing bitumen.

Application Rate. The quantity (mass, volume, or thickness) of material applied per unit area.

Area Divider. A raised, double wood member attached to a properly flashed wood base plate that is anchored to the roof deck. It is used to relieve the stresses of thermal expansion and contraction in a roof system where no expansion joints have been provided.

Asbestos. A group of natural, fibrous, impure silicate materials.

Asphalt. A dark brown to black cementitious material in which the predominating constituents are bitumens, which occur in nature or are obtained in petroleum processing.

Asphalt, Air Blown. An asphalt produced by blowing air

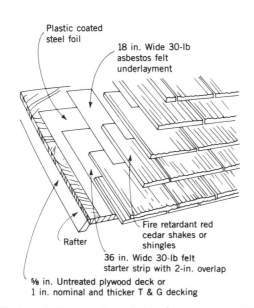

Figure 14. Fire-rated wood shingle construction (2).

Plastic coated steel foil

18 in. Wide 30-lb asbestos felt underlayment

Fire retardant red cedar shakes or shingles

Rafter

36 in. Wide 30-lb felt starter strip with 2-in. overlap

⅝ in. Untreated plywood deck or 1 in. nominal and thicker T & G decking through molten asphalt at an elevated temperature to raise its softening point and modify other properties.

Asphalt Felt. An asphalt-saturated felt or an asphalt-coated felt.

Asphalt Mastic. A mixture of asphaltic material and graded mineral aggregate that can be poured when heated but requires mechanical manipulation to apply when cool.

Asphalt, Steam Blown. An asphalt produced by blowing steam through molten asphalt to modify its properties, usually used for highway bitumen.

Backnailing. The practice of blind nailing (in addition to hot mopping) all the plies of a substrate to prevent slippage (See Blind Nailing).

Base Flashing. *See* Flashing.

Base Ply. The first ply of roofing material in a roof membrane assembly.

Base Sheet. A saturated or coated felt placed as the first ply in some multiply, built-up roof membranes.

Bitumen. The generic term for an amorphous, semisolid mixture of complex hydrocarbons derived from any organic source. Asphalt and coal tar are the two bitumens used in the roofing industry.

Bituminous. Containing or treated with bitumen. Examples: bituminous concrete, bituminous felts and fabrics, bituminous pavement.

Bituminous Emulsion. (1) A suspension of minute globules of bituminous material in water or in an aqueous solution; (2) A suspension of minute globules of water or an aqueous solution in a liquid bituminous material (invert emulsion).

Bituminous Grout. A mixture of bituminous material and fine sand that will flow into place without mechanical manipulation when heated.

Blind Nailing. The practice of nailing the back portion of a roofing ply.

Blister. A spongy raised portion of a roof membrane, ranging in area from 1 in. in diameter and of barely detectable height upward. Blisters result from the pressure buildup of gases entrapped in the membrane system. These gases most commonly are air and water vapor. Blisters usually involve delamination of the underlying membrane plies.

Bond. The adhesive and cohesive forces holding two roofing components in intimate contact.

Brooming. Embedding a ply of roofing material by using a broom to smooth out the ply and ensure contact with the adhesive under the ply.

Btu. British thermal unit—The heat energy required to raise the temperature of 1 lb of water 1°F.

Built-up Roof Membrane. A continuous, semiflexible roof membrane assembly, consisting of plies of saturated felts, coated felts, fabrics, or mats between which alternate layers of bitumen are applied, generally surfaced with mineral aggregate, bituminous materials, or a granule surfaced roofing sheet (Abbreviation: BUR).

Cant Strip. A beveled-shaped strip of wood or wood fiber that fits into the angle formed by the intersection of a horizontal surface and a vertical surface. The 45° slope of the exposed surface of the cant strip provides a gradual angular transition from the horizontal surface to the vertical surface.

Cap Flashing. *See* Flashing.

Capillarity. The action by which the surface of a liquid (where it is in contact with a solid) is elevated or depressed, depending on the relative attraction of the molecules of the liquid for each other and for those of the solid.

Cap Sheet. A granule-surfaced coated sheet used as the top ply of a built-up roof membrane or flashing.

Caulking. A composition of vehicle and pigment, used at ambient temperatures for filling joints, that remains plastic for an extended time after application.

Coal-tar Bitumen. A dark brown to black, semisolid hydrocarbon formed as a residue from the partial evaporation or distillation of coal tar. It is used as the waterproofing agent in dead-level or low slope built-up roofs. It differs from Coal-tar Pitch in having a lower front-end volatility. (For specification properties, see ASTM Standard D450, Type III.)

Coal-tar Felt. *See* Tarred Felt.

Coal-tar Pitch. A dark brown to black, semisolid hydrocarbon formed as a residue from the partial evaporation or distillation of coal tar. It is used as the waterproofing agent in dead-level or low slope built-up roofs. (For specification properties, see ASTM Standard D450, Types I and II.)

Coated Base Sheet (or Felt). A felt that has been impregnated and saturated with asphalt and then coated on both sides with harder, more viscous asphalt to increase its impermeability to moisture; a parting agent is incorporated to prevent the material from sticking in the roll.

Cold-process Roofing. A continuous, semiflexible roof membrane, consisting of plies of felts, mats, or fabrics that are laminated on a roof with alternate layers of cold-applied roof cement and surfaced with a cold-applied coating.

Condensation. The conversion of water vapor or other gas to liquid as the temperature drops or the atmospheric pressure rises (*See* Dew Point).

Coping. The covering piece placed on top of a wall that is exposed to the weather. It is usually sloped to shed water.

Counterflashing. Formed metal or elastomeric sheeting secured on or into a wall, curb, pipe, rooftop unit, or other surface to cover and protect the upper edge of a base flashing and its associated fasteners.

Course. (1)The term used for each application of material that forms the waterproofing system or the flashing; (2) One layer of a series of materials applied to a surface (ie, a five-course wall flashing is composed of three applications of mastic with one ply of felt sandwiched between each layer of mastic).

Coverage. The surface area (in square feet) to be continuously coated by a specific roofing material, with allowance made for a specific lap.

Crack. A separation or fracture occurring in a roof membrane or roof deck, generally caused by thermally induced stress or substrate movement.

Creep. The permanent deformation of a roofing material or roof system caused by the movement of the roof membrane that results from continuous thermal stress or loading.

Cricket. A superimposed construction placed in a roof area to assist drainage.

Cutback. Any bituminous roofing material that has been solvent thinned. Cutbacks are used in cold-process roofing adhesives, flashing cements, and roof coatings.

Cutoff. A material seal that is designed to prevent lateral water movement into the edge of a roof system where the membrane terminates at the end of a day's work or used to isolate sections of the roof system. Cutoffs are usually removed before the continuation of work.

Dampproofing. Treatment of a surface or structure to resist the passage of water in the absence of hydrostatic pressure.

Dead Level. The term used to describe an absolutely horizontal roof. Zero slope (See Slope).

Dead-level Asphalt. A roofing asphalt that has a softening point of 140°F (60°C) and that conforms to the requirements of ASTM Standard D312, Type I.

Dead Loads. Nonmoving rooftop loads, such as mechanical equipment, air-conditioning units, and the roof deck itself.

Deck. The structural surface to which the roofing or waterproofing system (including insulation) is applied.

Delamination. Separation of the plies in a roof membrane system or separation of laminated layers of insulation.

Dew Point. The temperature at which water vapor starts to condense in cooling air at the existing atmospheric pressure and vapor content.

Drain. A device that allows for the flow of water from a roof area.

Dropback. A reduction in the softening point of bitumen that occurs when bitumen is heated in the absence of air (See Softening Point Drift).

Edge Sheets. Felt strips that are cut to widths narrower than the standard width of the full felt roll. They are used to start the felt-shingling pattern at a roof edge.

Edge Stripping. Application of felt strips cut to narrower widths than the normal width of the full felt roll. They are used to cover joints.

Edge Venting. The practice of providing regularly spaced protected openings along a roof perimeter to relieve moisture vapor pressure.

Elastomer. A macromolecular material that returns rapidly to its approximate initial dimensions and shape after substantial deformation by a weak stress and the subsequent release of that stress.

Elastomeric. The term used to describe the elastic, rubberlike properties of a material.

Embedment. (1) The process of pressing a felt, aggregate, fabric, mat, or panel uniformly and completely into hot bitumen or adhesive; (2) the process of placing a material into another material so that it becomes an integral part of the whole material.

Emulsion. The intimate dispersion of an organic material and water achieved by using a chemical or clay emulsifying agent.

Envelope. A continuous felt fold formed by wrapping and securing a portion of a base felt back up and over the felt plies above it. Envelopes help prevent the seepage of bitumen.

Equilibrium Moisture Content. (1) The moisture content of a material stabilized at a given temperature and relative humidity, expressed as percent moisture by weight; (2) the typical moisture content of a material in any given geographical area.

Expansion Joint. A structural separation between two building elements designed to minimize the effect of the stresses and movements of a building's components and to prevent these stresses from splitting or ridging the roof membrane.

Exposure. (1) The transverse dimension of a roofing element not overlapped by an adjacent element in any roof system. The exposure of any ply in a membrane may be computed by dividing the felt width minus 2 in. by the number of shingled plies; thus, the exposure of a 36-in. wide felt in a shingled, four-ply membrane should be 8½ in.; (2) the time during which a portion of a roofing element is exposed to the weather.

Fabric. A woven cloth of organic or inorganic filaments, threads, or yarns.

Factory Mutual (FM). An organization that classifies roof assemblies for their fire characteristics and wind uplift resistance for insurance companies in the United States.

Factory Square. 108 ft² (10 m²) of roofing material.

Felt. A fabric manufactured from vegetable fibers (organic felts), asbestos fibers (asbestos felts), or glass fibers (glass fiber felts). The manufacturing process involves mechanically interlocking the fibers of the particular felt material in the presence of moisture and heat.

Felt Mill Ream. The mass in lb of 480 ft² of dry, unsaturated felt; also termed point weight.

Fine Mineral Surfacing. A water-insoluble, inorganic material, more than 50% of which passes through the No. 35 sieve, that may be used on the surface of roofing material.

Fishmouth. (1) A half-cylindrical or half-conical opening formed by an edge wrinkle; (2) in shingles, a half-conical opening formed at a cut edge.

Flashing. The system used to seal the edges of a membrane at walls, expansion joints, drains, gravel stops, and other areas where the membrane is interrupted or terminated. Base flashing covers the edges of the membrane. Cap flashing or counterflashing shields the upper edges of the base flashing.

Flashing Cement. A trowelable mixture of cutback bitumen and mineral stabilizers, including asbestos or other inorganic fibers.

Flat Asphalt. A roofing asphalt that has a softening point of approximately 170°F(77°C) and that conforms to the requirements of ASTM Standard D312, Type II.

Flood Coat. The top layer of bitumen into which the aggregate is embedded on an aggregate-surfaced built-up roof.

Fluid-applied Elastomer. An elastomeric material, which is fluid at ambient temperature, that dries or cures after application to form a continuous membrane.

Glass Fiber Felt. A felt sheet in which glass fibers are bonded into the felt sheet with resin. They are suitable for impregnation and coating. They are used in the manufacture and coating of bituminous waterproofing materials, roof membranes, and shingles.

Glass Fiber Mat. A thin mat composed of glass fibers with or without a binder.

Glaze Coat. (1) The top layer of asphalt in a smooth-surfaced built-up roof assembly; (2) a thin protective coating of bitumen applied to the lower plies or top ply of a built-up roof membrane when application of additional felts or the flood coat and aggregate surfacing are delayed.

Grain. The weight unit equal to 1/7000 lb; used in measuring atmospheric moisture content.

Gravel. Coarse, granular aggregate, containing pieces approximately 5/8–1/2 in. in size and suitable for use in aggregate surfacing on built-up roofs.

Gravel Stop. A flanged device, frequently metallic, designed to provide a continuous finished edge for roofing materials and to prevent loose aggregate from washing off of the roof.

Headlap. The minimum distance, measured at 90° to the eaves along the face of a shingle or felt, from the upper edge of the shingle or felt to the nearest exposed surface.

Holiday. An area where a liquid-applied material is missing.

"Hot Stuff" or "Hot". The roofer's term for hot bitumen.

Hygroscopic. The term used to describe a material that attracts, absorbs, and retains atmospheric moisture.

Incline. The slope of a roof expressed either in percent or in the number of vertical units of rise per horizontal unit of run.

Inorganic. Being or composed of matter other than hydrocarbons and their derivatives, or matter that is not of plant or animal origin.

Insulation. A material applied to reduce the flow of heat.

Knot. An imperfection or inhomogeneity in materials used in fabric construction, the presence of which causes surface irregularities.

Live Loads. Moving roof installation equipment, wind, snow, ice, or rain.

Manufacturer's Bond. A security company's guarantee that it will stand behind a manufacturer's liability to finance membrane repairs occasioned by ordinary wear within a period generally limited to 5, 10, 15, or 20 years.

Mastic. See Flashing Cement and Asphalt Mastic.

Membrane. A flexible or semiflexible roof covering or waterproofing layer, whose primary function is the exclusion of water.

Mesh. The square or circular opening of a sieve.

Metal Flashing. See Flashing; metal flashing is frequently used as through-wall flashing, cap flashing, counterflashing, or gravel stops.

Mineral Fiber Felt. A felt with mineral wool as its principal component.

Mineral Granules. Opaque, natural, or synthetically colored aggregate commonly used to surface cap sheets, granule-surfaced sheets, and roofing shingles.

Mineral Stabilizer. A fine, water-insoluble inorganic material, used in a mixture with solid or semisolid bituminous materials.

Mineral-surfaced Roofing. Built-up roofing materials whose top ply consists of a granule-surfaced sheet.

Mineral-surfaced Sheet. A felt that is coated on one or both sides with asphalt and surfaced with mineral granules.

Mole Run. A meandering ridge in a roof membrane not associated with insulation or deck joints.

Mop-and-flop. An application procedure in which roofing elements (insulation boards, felt plies, cap sheets, etc) are initially placed upside down adjacent to their ultimate locations, are coated with adhesive, and are then turned over and applied to the substrate.

Mopping. An application of hot bitumen applied to the substrate or to the felts of a built-up roof membrane with a mop or mechanical applicator. 1. *Solid Mopping.* A continuous mopping of a surface, leaving no unmopped areas. 2. *Spot Mopping.* A mopping pattern in which hot bitumen is applied in roughly circular areas, leaving a grid of unmopped, perpendicular bands on the roof. 3. *Sprinkle Mopping.* A random mopping pattern wherein heated bitumen beads are strewn onto the substrate with a brush or mop. 4. *Strip Mopping.* A mopping pattern in which hot bitumen is applied in parallel bands.

Nailing. (1) In the exposed nail method, nail heads are exposed to the weather; (2) in the concealed nail method, nail heads are concealed from the weather (See also Blind Nailing).

Neoprene. A synthetic rubber (polychloroprene) used in liquid-applied and sheet-applied elastomeric roof membranes or flashings.

Nineteen-inch Selvage. A prepared roofing sheet with a 17-in. granule-surfaced exposure and a nongranule-surfaced 19-in. selvage edge. This material is sometimes referred to as SIS or as Wide-selvage Asphalt Roll Roofing Material Surfaced with Mineral Granules.

Organic. Being or composed of hydrocarbons or their derivatives, or matter of plant or animal origin.

Perlite. An aggregate used in lightweight insulating concrete and in preformed perlitic insulation boards, formed by heating and expanding siliceous volcanic glass.

Perm. A unit of water vapor transmission defined as one grain of water vapor per square foot per hour per inch of mercury pressure difference (1 in. of mercury = 0.491 psi). The formula for perm is

$$P = \text{Grains of Water Vapor/ft}^2 \cdot \text{hour} \cdot \text{in. Mercury}$$

Permeance. An index of a material's resistance to water vapor transmission (See Perm).

Phased Application. The installation of a roof system or waterproofing system during two or more separate time intervals.

Picture Framing. A rectangular pattern of ridges in a roof membrane over insulation or deck joints.

Pitch Pocket. A flanged, open-bottomed, metal container placed around columns or other roof penetrations that is filled with hot bitumen or flashing cement to seal the joint. The use of pitch pockets is not recommended.

Plastic Cement. See Flashing Cement.

Ply. A layer of felt in a built-up roof membrane system. A four-ply membrane system has four plies of felt. The dimension of the exposed surface (the "exposure") of any ply may be computed by dividing the felt width (minus 2 in.) by the number of plies; thus, the exposed surface of a

36-in. wide felt in a four-ply membrane should be 8½ in. (*See* Exposure).

Point Weight. *See* Felt Mill Ream.

Pond. A roof surface that is incompletely drained.

Positive Drainage. The drainage condition in which consideration has been made for all loading deflections of the deck, and additional roof slope has been provided to ensure complete drainage of the roof area within 24 h of rainfall precipitation.

Primer. A thin, liquid bitumen aplied to a surface to improve the adhesion of subsequent applications of bitumen.

Rake. The sloped edge of a roof at the first or last rafter.

Reentrant Corner. An inside corner of a surface, producing stress concentrations in the roofing or waterproofing membrane.

Reglet. A groove in a wall or other surface adjoining a roof surface for use in the attachment of counterflashing.

Reinforced Membrane. A roofing or waterproofing membrane reinforced with felts, mats, fabrics, or chopped fibers.

Relative Humidity. The ratio of the weight of moisture in a given volume of air-vapor mixture to the saturated (maximum) weight of water vapor at the same temperature, expressed as a percentage. For example, if the weight of the moist air is 1 lb and if the air could hold 2 lb of water vapor at a given temperature, the relative humidity (rh) is 50%.

Reroofing. The practice of applying new roofing materials over existing roofing materials.

Ridging. An upward, "tenting" displacement of a roof membrane, frequently occurring over insulation joints, deck joints, and base sheet edges.

Roll Roofing. The term applied to smooth-surfaced or mineral-surfaced coated felts.

Roof Assembly. An assembly of interacting roof components (including the roof deck) designed to weatherproof and, usually, to insulate a building's top surface.

Roofer. The trade name for the worker who applies roofing materials.

Roof System. A system of interacting roof components (not including the roof deck) designed to weatherproof and, usually, to insulate a building's top surface.

Saturated Felt. A felt that has been partially saturated with low softening point bitumen.

Screen. An apparatus with apertures for separating sizes of material.

Seal. (*1*) A narrow closure strip made of bituminous materials; (*2*) to secure a roof from the entry of moisture.

Sealant. A mixture of polymers, fillers, and pigments used to fill and seal joints where moderate movement is expected; it cures to a resilient solid.

Selvage. An edge or edging that differs from the main part of (*1*) a fabric or (*2*) granule-surfaced roll roofing material.

Selvage Joint. A lapped joint designed for mineral-surfaced cap sheets. The mineral surfacing is omitted over a small portion of the longitudinal edge of the sheet below in order to obtain better adhesion of the lapped cap sheet surface with the bituminous adhesive.

Shark Fin. An upward-curled felt side lap or end lap.

Shingle. (*1*) A small unit of prepared roofing material designed to be installed with similar units in overlapping rows on inclines normally exceeding 25%; (*2*) to cover with shingles; (*3*) to apply any sheet material in overlapping rows like shingles.

Shingling. (*1*) The procedure of laying parallel felts so that one longitudinal edge of each felt overlaps and the other longitudinal edge underlaps an adjacent felt (*See* Ply). Usually, felts are shingled on a slope so that the water flows over rather than against each lap; (*2*) the application of shingles to a sloped roof.

Sieve. An apparatus with apertures for separating sizes of material.

Slag. A hard, air-cooled aggregate that is left as a residue from blast furnaces. It is used as a surfacing aggregate and should be surface dry and free of sand, clay, or other foreign substances at the time of application.

Slippage. The relative lateral movement of adjacent components of a built-up roof membrane. It occurs mainly in roof membranes on a slope, sometimes exposing the lower plies to the weather.

Slope. The tangent of the angle between the roof surface and the horizontal in in./ft. The Asphalt Roofing Manufacturers Association (ARMA) ranks slope as follows:

Level slope	up to ½ in./ft
Low slope	½ to 1½ in./ft
Steep slope	over 1½ in./ft

Smooth-surface Roof. A built-up roof membrane surfaced with a layer of hot-mopped asphalt, cold-applied asphalt–clay emulsion, cold-applied asphalt cutback, or sometimes with an unmopped inorganic felt.

Softening Point. The temperature at which bitumen becomes soft enough to flow. The softening point of asphalt is measured by the "ring-and-ball" test (ASTM Standard D2398). The softening point of coal-tar pitch is measured by the "cube-in-water" test (ASTM Standard D61).

Softening Point Drift. A change in the softening point of bitumen during storage or application (*See* Dropback).

Solid Mopping. *See* Mopping.

Special Steep Asphalt. A roofing asphalt that has a softening point of approximately 220°F (104°C) and that conforms to the requirements of ASTM Standard D312, Type IV.

Split. A separation in roofing material resulting from movement of the substrate (*See* Crack).

Split Sheet. *See* Nineteen-inch Selvage.

Spot Mopping. *See* Mopping.

Sprinkle Mopping. *See* Mopping.

Square. The term used to describe 100 ft² of roof area.

Stack Vent. A vertical outlet in a built-up roof system designed to relieve any pressure exerted by moisture vapor between the roof membrane and the vapor retarder or deck.

Steep Asphalt. A roofing asphalt that has a softening point of approximately 190°F (88°C) and that conforms to the requirements of ASTM Standard D312, Type III.

Strawberry. A small bubble or blister in the flood coating of a gravel-surfaced roof membrane.

Strip Mopping. See Mopping.

Stripping or Strip Flashing. (*1*) The technique of sealing a joint between metal and the built-up roof membrane with one or two plies of felt and hot-applied or cold-applied bitumen; (*2*) the technique of taping joints between insulation boards on deck panels.

Substrate. The surface on which the roofing or waterproofing membrane is applied (ie, the structural deck or insulation).

Superimposed Loads. Loads that are added to existing loads. For example, a large stack of insulation boards placed on top of a structural steel deck.

Tapered Edge Strip. A tapered insulation strip used to (*1*) elevate the roof at the perimeter and at curbs that extend through the roof; (*2*) provide a gradual transition from one layer of insulation to another.

Taping. See Stripping.

Tar. A brown or black bituminous material, liquid or semisolid in consistency, in which the predominating constituents are bitumens obtained as condensates in the processing of coal, petroleum, oil shale, wood, or other organic materials.

Tarred Felt. A felt that has been saturated with refined coal tar.

Test Cut. A sample of the roof membrane, usually 4 × 40 in. in size, that is cut from a roof membrane to determine the weight of the average interply bitumen poundages and diagnose the condition of the existing membrane (eg, to detect leaks or blisters). It is recommended that the test cut procedure not be used as a means of determining the quality of a roof system.

Thermal Conductance (C). A unit of heat flow that is used for specific thicknesses of material or for materials of combination construction, such as laminated insulation. The formula for thermal conductance is

$$C = \frac{k}{\text{thickness in inches}}$$

Thermal Conductivity (k). The heat energy that will be transmitted by conduction through 1 ft^2 of 1-in.-thick homogeneous material in 1 h when there is a difference of 1°F perpendicularly across the two surfaces of the material. The formula for thermal conductivity is

$$k = \text{Btu/ft}^2/\text{in.}/\text{h}/°\text{F}$$

Thermal Insulation. A material applied to reduce the flow of heat.

Thermal Resistance (R). An index of a material's resistance to heat flow; it is the reciprocal of thermal conductivity (*k*) or thermal conductance (*C*). The formula for thermal resistance is

$$R = \frac{1}{C} \text{ or } R = \frac{1}{k} \text{ or } R = \frac{\text{thickness in inches}}{k}$$

Thermal Shock. The stress-producing phenomenon resulting from sudden temperature changes in a roof membrane. (For example, when a rain shower follows brilliant sunshine.)

Through-wall Flashing. A water-resistant membrane or material assembly extending through a wall and its cavities, positioned to direct any water entering the top of the wall to the exterior.

Underwriters Laboratories (UL). An organization that classifies roof assemblies for their fire characteristics and wind uplift resistance for insurance companies in the United States.

Vapor Migration. The movement of water vapor from a region of high vapor pressure to a region of lower vapor pressure.

Vapor-pressure Gradient. A graph, analogous to a temperature gradient, indicating the changes in water vapor pressure at various cross-sectional planes through a roof or wall system.

Vapor Retarder. A material designed to restrict the passage of water vapor through a wall or roof. In the roofing industry, a vapor retarder should have a perm rating of 0.5 or less.

Vent. An opening designed to convey water vapor or other gas from inside a building or a building component to the atmosphere, thereby relieving vapor pressure.

Vermiculite. An aggregate used in lightweight insulating concrete, formed by the heating and consequent expansion of a micaceous mineral.

Water Cutoff. See Cutoffs.

Waterproofing. Treatment of a surface or structure to prevent the passage of water under hydrostatic pressure.

BIBLIOGRAPHY

1. J. R. Hoke, ed., *Ramsey/Sleeper Architectural Graphic Standards,* 8th ed., John Wiley & Sons, New York, 1988, p. 386.
2. *Ibid.,* p. 341.

General References

C. W. Griffin, *Manual of Built-up Roof Systems,* 2nd ed., McGraw-Hill Inc., New York, 1982.

M. C. Baker, *Roofs,* Multiscience Publications Ltd., Montreal, Quebec, 1980.

Publications are available from the following organizations:

Asphalt Roofing Manufacturing Association
Single Ply Roofing Institute
Roofing Industry Educational Institute
National Roofing Contractors Association

See also INSULATION, THERMAL; MEMBRANE STRUCTURES; METALLIC COATINGS; POWDER COATINGS

STEVEN L. BIEGEL, AIA
Lawrence & Lawrence,
Architects
Warrenton, Virginia

ROOT, JOHN WELLBORN

John Wellborn Root was born in 1850 in Lumpkin, Georgia. Later, his family moved to Atlanta. His future as an architect was a family goal. For his first 10 years, he was educated at home. To escape the draft during the Civil War, John left for study in Great Britain in 1864. At the end of the Civil War, the family moved to New York, and John was called home in 1866; he earned his degree in science and civil engineering from the University of the City of New York in 1869. After graduation, he was taken into the office of Renwick & Sands, without pay. After about a year, he moved to the office of J. B. Snook, with a small salary. He was Snook's superintendent of construction for the first Grand Central Station in New York (1869–1871). The glass and iron vault was similar to that of St. Pancras Station in London.

Root had met the architect Peter B. Wight in New York. After the great Chicago fire of 1872, Root went to Chicago to be foreman of a new architectural office including Wight, Asher Carter, and William H. Drake. The amount of rebuilding was immense. The young draftsman Daniel Burnham entered the firm that year and undertook promotion of his own clients. Burnham convinced John Root to join him as partner for design in a new firm in 1873. The financial panic of 1873 caused cancellation of most of their projects. What they considered their first project was a house for John B. Sherman in 1874. Throughout the 1870s, commissions were small and far between. Most commercial building in Chicago was based on East Coast prototypes. The first new work of importance came from the office of William Le Baron Jenney in the first Leiter Building of 1879–1880.

Between 1880 and Root's early death in 1891, the firm of Burnham and Root quickly rose to an important role in the development of the high-rise commercial building made possible by the development of the elevator. Their first commercial building, the Grannis block (demolished), was followed by a long series of works, among which the most interesting are the Rookery of 1885–1888 and the Monadnock building of 1889–1892, both commissioned by the investors Peter and Shepherd Brooks and Owen Aldis.

The architects had their offices on the eleventh floor of the Rookery, at the corner of LaSalle Street and Adams Street in Chicago. The interior light court and its oriel stair were above the glass-roofed two-story entrance court of the building. The exterior was masonry with large window openings. Framing was of wrought-iron beams supported on a single line of interior columns, about 20 ft on center. The wall of the interior court was separately framed, with terra-cotta and glazed brick finish. Later alterations to the interior of the building have obscured much of Root's design, which survives in such items as the stair with its decorative rails and perforated risers. Original photographs published in the magazines of the period provide an historic record of the building (1).

The Monadnock Building received more of Root's design attention than any other project. Under development for several years, the program for the building was revised continuously. Additional property was added, and, when it was decided to widen Dearborn Street, the site was re-duced in width from 100 ft to 66 ft. The height of the building was undecided, finally increasing from 12 stories to 16 stories.

The inspiration for the design was the "Egyptian Style," without applied ornament. Root constantly adjusted the design as the property changed. Molded brick was used to soften corners, and a curved wall was used to meet the base, echoed at the top of the building with a similar curved profile replacing the typical cornice details used on other buildings. The bay windows were adjusted to different widths to suit various elevations, and by use of softened corners appear to grow organically from the wall. The material was a dark brick, which changes appearance depending on lighting and time of day.

Root believed that the building design was suited to the marshy Chicago site. The difficulty of building on the lakefront property was resolved by shallow mat foundations. The building was framed in steel. His design inspiration was derived from plants native to such land, such as the Egyptian papyrus or Chicago's wild onion. Although the project was not particularly well reviewed in the press, the architectural critic Montgomery Schuyler was the first to recognize the success of Root's design (2), and the project was admired by Louis Sullivan and Frank Lloyd Wright.

Although named consulting architect to the World's Columbian Exhibition of 1892, on Chicago's lakefront, Root did not live to complete more than early designs with Frederick Law Olmsted, landscape architect for the fair. The work on the Exhibition continued under Burnham's direction, who continued practice for many years.

A great deal is known about Root's design ideas from a book written in 1896 by the poet Harriet Monroe, whose sister Dora Louise Monroe was John Wellborn Root's second wife, whom he had married in 1882. His first wife, Mary Louise Walker, had died 6 weeks after their marriage.

With the other firms of the Chicago School, Burnham and Root were among the first who investigated the design of the high-rise commercial building. Many of the buildings designed by the firm have been destroyed in the intervening years. Root's fame as a designer has been overshadowed by that of Louis Sullivan. Had Root lived longer, his design contributions would have been seen more clearly.

BIBLIOGRAPHY

1. D. Hoffman, *The Architecture of John Wellborn Root*, Johns Hopkins University Press, Baltimore, 1973, Figures 44–56.
2. M. Schuyler, "D. H. Burnham & Co.," *Architectural Record* **5**, 59 (Dec. 1895).

General Reference

H. Monroe, *John Wellborn Root*, Houghton Mifflin, Boston, 1896. Reprinted with an introduction by Reyner Banham, The Prairie School Press, Park Forest, Ill., 1966.

ROBERT T. PACKARD, AIA
Associate Editor

ROSSI, ALDO

Aldo Rossi (b. 1931), one of the most influential architects during the period 1972–1988, has accomplished the unusual feat of achieving international recognition in three distinct areas: theory, drawing, and architecture. After receiving his architecture degree at the Polytechnic University in Milan in 1959, Rossi served as a course assistant to prominent architects Ludovico Quaroni and Carlo Aymonino. He became a faculty member in the School of Architecture in Milan in 1965 and at the University in Venice in 1975. In addition to these regular appointments, his growing fame brought him positions as a professor in Zurich, Spain, and the United States.

Rossi's career as a theorist began to take shape during the years he worked with Ernesto Rogers on the leading Italian architecture magazine *Casabella-Continuità* (1955–1964). In 1966 he published the book *The Architecture of the City*, which subsequently was translated into several languages and enjoyed enormous international success. Spurning the then fashionable debates on style, Rossi instead criticized the lack of understanding of the city in current architectural practice. Rossi argued that a city must be studied and valued as something constructed over time; of particular interest are urban artifacts that withstand the passage of time. Despite the modern movement polemics against monuments, for example, Rossi held that the city remembers its past and uses that memory through monuments; that is, monuments give structure to the city.

This understanding of the city and its elements, its monuments, and its permanences, informed Rossi's own designs for public buildings. One of his earliest major public buildings was the addition to the existing cemetery of the city of Modena in northern Italy. Perceiving the cemetery as a repository of social meaning, Rossi conceived of it as a house for the dead, indeed, a city of the dead. The elemental architectonic forms, as in the elegant stereometric volumes of the ossuary with its chamfered windows, reflect his ongoing investigations into building typology, that which remains beyond the particular and the concrete.

The primary elements of architecture are repeated again and again in his work as he engages in a determined search for essential forms based on what he refers to as "repetition and fixation." He attempts to recover the "immovable elements of architecture," not as empty catalogs of forms but as a search for an ageless originality found in formal types. Understood in this fashion, architecture, Rossi claims, helps make sense of the lived reality of the world. It also provides the fixed scene of human events, which the architect historically has not been able to foresee. The most enduring architecture has been that which, in Rossi's words, "stopped short of the event." He gave these ideas built form in the school at Fagnano Olona, for example, where the grand stepped podium leads to the gymnasium and provides a place where class photographs can be taken, a school ritual in both Italy and the United States. Such rituals, says Rossi, give the "comfort of continuity, repetition, compelling us to an oblique forgetfulness"; the architecture should provide the backdrop against which they can be played out.

In the project for the Carlo Felice Theater in Genoa, Rossi's task was to replace the theater that was bombed in World War II. His project leaves the old facade intact but accommodates a full complex of new functions and spaces. The stereometric architectural forms convey an originality that at the same time transcends time and asserts a powerful presence in the urban fabric. Here and elsewhere Rossi avoids historical and technological detailing in favor of preserving the integrity of the volumes, which then convey the quality of structures that have stood since antiquity.

For Rossi, public buildings often become miniature versions of the city, particularly his schools and his Teatro del Mondo for the 1980 Venice Biennale. At Fagnano Olona, he organized a series of elements (rotunda, cubic block, conical smokestack) around a central court and approached along linear elements such as a street, a bridge, or a wall axially aligned with the central elements, a disposition that recalls Italian city planning. Such an organization also characterizes the school in Broni, where the library recalls historic models such as the anatomical thoaters of Padua and Bologna. In turn, these types informed his Teatro del Mondo floating in the canals of Venice; like the city, the theater is also a stage, and simply miniaturizes the activity and organization of the city. In the same way, Rossi denies that he creates the elements that regularly recur in his work; instead, he discovers them in the city, especially the cities in Italy that he knows and loves best; Milan, Mantua, and Venice.

Even before the success that he has enjoyed in the last decade with projects underway from Japan to Germany, Rossi achieved singular distinction for his drawings. Although one of his professors tried to discourage him from studying architecture on the grounds that he drew as if he were a rural builder, Rossi was not discouraged. Inspired by the urban landscapes of Italian painters Mario Sironi and Giorgio Morandi, Rossi produces haunting images in which his buildings and others in the city shrink, while everyday objects such as coffeepots and cigarette packs swell to fill the frame. The drawings conflate historical buildings, built and unbuilt projects by Rossi, mundane utensils, and shadowy figures occupying tiny cabins or yellow windows, and the same images, combined and reshuffled, reappear regularly, just as the cube and the cone reappear in his buildings.

The recurrence coffeepots in his increasingly well-known drawings eventually induced the Italian firm Alessi to commission him to design a line of coffeepots and even, eventually, a watch that recalls those of his childhood schoolrooms.

Although Rossi's first projects, for a housing complex on the outskirts of Milan (Gallaratese, 1969–1974), the San Cataldo cemetery in Modena (begun 1972), and Fagnano Olona School in Varese (1972–77), were contemporary with the publication of his most important theoretical works, only in the late 1970s and 1980s did his building work begin in earnest, and only in the last few years has his fame brought him a significant number of commissions in Italy.

Two civic center projects in Italy indicate the range of his responses to a similar program. In Perugia, a large civic center (1988), with town hall, theater, and housing

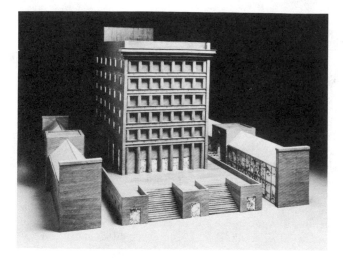

Figure 1. View of Fukuoka Hotel and restaurant project model. Courtesy of Ned Matura.

project, is elevated on a parking podium and mediates between the historic city and the postwar business center. The U-shaped Town Hall, with shops below and offices above, is bisected by a galleria raised high on slender piers. Adjoining the town hall but irregularly placed on the parking podium are the theater, with its freestanding conical entrance tower, and a long, slender housing block. The disposition suggests an accretion of disparate buildings over time rather than a complex planned for uniformity. Although here as elsewhere drawing on simple local types, Rossi also transforms them, as he does with the public arcade that slices through the town hall.

The town hall for the small village of Borgoricco demanded an altogether different response. Although he adopted the U-shaped plan again, Rossi opens it up here with a south-facing courtyard framed on one end by copper clad, barrel-vaulted roofs that cascade down over the meeting room and the archives. The simple elemental forms of the massive Perugia project give way here to a more complex massing and a greater play of materials. Each of the three principal views is articulated in markedly different ways, yet ordered and related by such elements as the narrow brick walls that rise through the full two stories.

Two other major recent private commercial projects in Italy are worth noting. For the GFT fashion group in Turin, Rossi designed an office building on an L-shaped site with an angled corner entrance of smooth brick. Rossi repeats a motif from Borgoricco when he anchors the entrance with giant double columns surmounted by a green steel I-beam lintel. By incorporating a smaller version of the double column I-beam lintel motif in the auditorium, Rossi emphasizes the parallel between public, urban scale and the theater as a smaller version of the city. Street elevations of the two lateral wings incorporate stone porticoes, a traditional urban element in the Piedmontese city, but he also modulates the surface by extending the stone revetment up to the first floor and framing the stone piers with green steel I-beams. A regional shopping center outside Parma rises up out of the flat plains with 50-ft-high brick towers that both carry the name of the center and provide a setting for billboards and advertising.

A hotel complex in Fukuoka, Japan (Fig. 1), an architecture school for the University of Miami, Florida (Fig.

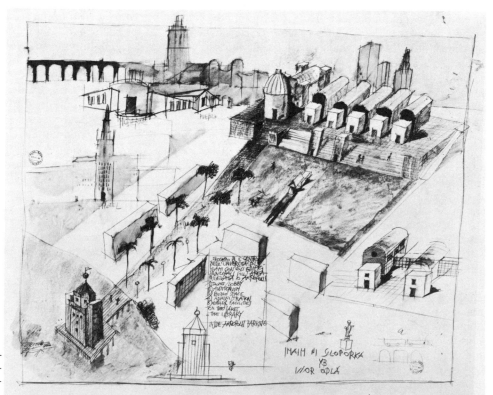

Figure 2. Aldo Rossi drawing of University of Miami, new school of architecture project. Courtesy of Ned Matura.

2), and a victory in a major competition for the Museum of Natural History in Berlin promise further opportunities to render the ideas Rossi explored in *Architecture of the City* in built form.

DIANE GHIRARDO, PhD
University of Southern
California
Los Angeles, California

ROYAL INSTITUTE OF BRITISH ARCHITECTS

The Royal Institute of British Architects (RIBA) is a professional institution with more than 27,000 corporate members and 1500 student members. It is a registered charity with a royal charter that defines its purposes as "for the general advancement of civil architecture and for promoting and facilitating the acquirement of the knowledge of the various arts and sciences connected therewith."

At the time of the Institute's foundation in London in 1834, the building industry was riddled with dishonest practices and incompetence and there was an urgent need to establish and maintain professional and ethical standards of practice among those who called themselves architects. The members of the new institute were elected by ballot into three classes, Fellows, Associates, and Honorary Members, and were governed by an elected council of Fellows, which was subject to the control of the General Meetings. Any Fellow or Associate could be expelled

> For having engaged since his election in the measurement, valuation or estimation of any works undertaken or proposed to be undertaken by any building artificer, except such as are proposed to be executed or have been executed under the member's own designs or directions; or for the receipt or acceptance of any pecuniary consideration or emolument from any builder or other tradesman whose works he may have been engaged to superintend; or for having any interest or participation in any trade, contract or materials supplied at any works; or for any conduct which, in the opinion of the Council, shall be derogatory to his professional character.

Lord de Grey, a member of the government and an influential Privy Councillor, was elected the first President. The institute took as its motto "*Usui civium decori urbium*," which was rendered in the royal charter granted by King William IV in 1837 as "to promote the domestic convenience of citizens and the public improvement and embellishment of towns and cities." Further royal favor was granted in 1847 when Queen Victoria announced that, under the guidance of the RIBA, she would award a Royal Gold Medal each year to "such distinguished architect or man of science of any country as may have designed or executed any building of high merit or produced a work tending to promote or facilitate the knowledge of architecture or the various branches of science connected therewith." This coveted award still continues today. The founding members of the Institute, one of the most active of whom was Thomas Leverton Donaldson, the first Hon-

orary Secretary, had four main objectives in mind: to improve the reputation and status of architects by promoting "uniformity and respectability of practice"; to become a learned society; to work for the cultivation and improvement of architecture; and to become a body representing the architectural profession in Britain.

One of the first problems to be addressed was the very unsatisfactory state of the system of architectural competitions. The Institute proceeded to publish a set of general regulations for the conduct of competitions, which led eventually to the development of the present RIBA regulatory system. A major advance was made in 1862 with the publication of the Institute's first recommended scale of charges for professional services, forerunner of the Architects Appointment, as the present conditions of engagement are called. This was followed in 1870 by the publication of recommended general headings to be used for clauses of contract, which eventually led to the Standard Form of Contract and the establishment of the present Joint Contracts Tribunal to administer it. From the 1880s onward, the Institute closely monitored the professional conduct of its members, and from 1923 it published in the annual *RIBA Kalendar* "Suggestions governing professional conduct and practice of architects," which developed into the present RIBA Code of Conduct. Important influence was exerted by the Institute on the development of the laws and bylaws concerning the regulation of building; it was appointed the statutory body for examining the competence of local authority building surveyors. Concern for the preservation and correct restoration of ancient and historic buildings was also shown by the Institute, which in 1865 published its first guide sheets for builders and others engaged in repairs and restoration of such buildings. It was perturbed, too, by the widespread demolition of historic buildings. It campaigned to save several of them and encouraged the collection of measured drawings and other architectural records.

From the early days, the objective of becoming a learned society was actively pursued. The members were constantly exhorted to donate books, pamphlets, manuscripts, prints, drawings, models, casts of classical details, and specimens of building materials to the Institute's library and museum. Their generosity laid the foundations of the magnificent collections held by the present British Architectural Library at the RIBA. It was also the custom from the beginning for learned papers on a great variety of aesthetic, archaeological, historical, scientific, and technical subjects related to architecture and construction to be read at the Institute's meetings and published in *RIBA Transactions*, which later amalgamated with *RIBA Proceedings* to become the *RIBA Journal*. From the 1870s onward, the Institute called general conferences of British architects every 2 or 3 years, when matters of interest to the profession as a whole were discussed. Since the 1920s, these conferences have been held annually.

Probably the most important achievement of the RIBA in the nineteenth century, however, was the development of a comprehensive system of architectural education. Previously, prospective architects usually obtained training, often very incomplete and unsatisfactory, as apprentices with practicing architects, supplemented if they were fortunate by a few lectures and evening classes. Dissatisfaction with the state of architectural education was the main cause of the formation in 1847 of the Architectural Association, which in 1855 petitioned the RIBA Council to introduce examinations certifying qualification to practice as an architect. In 1863, the RIBA introduced voluntary examinations, and from 1882 it began to develop a national system of obligatory progressive examinations (preliminary, intermediate, and final). Later developments included the establishment in 1904 of the Board of Architectural Education and the active fostering of architectural schools by a system of formal RIBA recognition.

This development of architectural education and examination went hand in hand with the controversial question of whether or not statutory registration of architects should be introduced in Britain and, if so, whether or not the RIBA should be the body that controlled such registration. This topic was hotly disputed for more than 50 years from the 1880s onward, and the controversy was one of the causes of the formation in 1884 of the breakaway Society of Architects. This society eventually amalgamated with the RIBA in 1925, and the matter was finally resolved by the passing of the registration acts in the 1930s and the establishment of the Architects Registration Council of the United Kingdom (ARCUK).

During the first half of the twentieth century the RIBA widened its horizons. In 1906 it played host to the Seventh International Congress of Architects, and from 1907 to 1939 the British Section of the Comité Permanent International des Architectes met at the RIBA, as did the British Section of the Franco-British Union of Architects from 1922 to 1939. During the 1930s and 1940s, the RIBA was active in aiding refugee architects fleeing from Nazi-occupied territories. In 1948 the Union Internationale des Architectes was formed and its UK Committee met under the auspices of the RIBA. By 1939 there also existed throughout the British dominions and colonies a large network of architectural societies and institutes in formal alliance with the RIBA. In 1959 the RIBA set up a committee to prepare for a conference of these overseas allied societies to discuss forming a new federation and to consider ways in which standards for qualification as an architect might be unified throughout the Commonwealth. The conference was held in 1963 and was followed by the formation of the Commonwealth Association of Architects and the establishment of a Commonwealth Board of Architectural Education to take over the RIBA's role as a regulatory body among Commonwealth schools of architecture.

In the decade before World War I the Institute began to play an important role in the development of town planning and public housing. The first of its many influential planning committees was appointed in 1907. Its chairman was Sir Aston Webb. Other figures who played an active part on this committee during the 1920s and 1930s were S. D. Adshead, Patrick Abercrombie, and Sir Raymond Unwin. A new field of interest was slum clearance and the provision of new housing developments. The first of many RIBA working groups on housing was appointed in 1917. The main concerns were national housing policies, campaigning for the increased employment of architects in the design of local authority housing, raising housing standards, and eliminating "jerry-building" and setting up, in conjunction with the Council for the Preservation of Rural England and the Institute of Building, a system of panels of architects and others to advise local planning authorities on the quality of planning applications. In a further effort to improve the standards of design and increase public interest in architecture, the Institute started in the 1920s its Bronze Medal Awards Scheme for new buildings of merit, which continued until 1965 when it was replaced by the present RIBA Architecture Awards.

In the period after World War II there was a great increase in the employment of architects by the public sector. By the early 1950s half the registered architects in the United Kingdom were in salaried employment, and there was some demand for the Institute to engage in collective bargaining on behalf of its members for improvements in their salaries and conditions of employment. Inhibited by its charter and bylaws from performing these functions in any formal way, the Institute encouraged the formation in 1959 of the Association of Official Architects as a focus for the consideration of matters affecting terms and conditions of service in the public sector.

A major task of the Institute after the war was to help architects keep abreast of the rapid rate of change in scientific and technical matters and managerial techniques. The need to promote architectural and building research and develop technical information services for architects had led during World War II to the establishment, in cooperation with the Building Research Station, of the Architectural Science Board. Following this, the Institute in the 1950s set up an Economics Research Department with a Statistics Section and, in the 1960s, a Professional Services Department that performed a wide range of technical and professional services, many of which in the 1970s became part of newly formed commercial companies of the RIBA.

In the 1960s the constitution of the RIBA was amended to create a new national, regional, and branch organization to replace what had essentially been a central metropolitan body in alliance with dozens of provincial architectural societies that had come to be financed largely from the national membership subscriptions. Regional constituencies for Council elections were established, and a three-tier structure adopted: nationally the Institute is governed by the RIBA Council, a third of whose members are elected nationally and two-thirds regionally; the 13 regions are governed by regional councils; and the 80 or so branches are governed by branch committees.

In 1969–1970 the RIBA set up three commercial companies to provide practices and members with services for which they could be expected to pay and which should not fall as a charge on general subscriptions. Profits were covenanted back from the companies to the RIBA, as a charity. RIBA Services Ltd provides technical and other services that include the publication of RIBA Product Data and the RIBA Product Selector, the RIBA Office Library Service, the Appointments Bureau, Standard Building Plaques, Product Literature Advisory Service, Computer

Services, and Mailing Activities. National Building Specification Ltd published the first edition of the National Building Specification in 1973 and now actively promotes its use in the form of a subscription service. RIBA Publications Ltd publishes the basic legal and professional documents used by architects as well as a range of textbooks and provides a personal and mail-order service through the RIBA Bookshop. A fourth company, RIBA Magazines Ltd, was formed in 1981 to take over the publication and develop the commercial potential of the *RIBA Journal,* now *The Architect,* and to undertake other publishing ventures in the architectural field.

In the late 1970s and first half of the 1980s several new initiatives have been taken by the Institute. It has set itself to influence the adverse way in which successive governments have handled demand on the building industry. Severe fluctuations in the workload of the industry have been extremely harmful to the cause of good architecture and have prompted the RIBA to set up and lead the Group of Eight, a pressure group composed of organizations in the construction industry, which has become the industry's principal channel of contact with the government on strategic matters. The Institute has also embarked on a program of continuing professional development to complement its involvement with undergraduate education and on a program to advance energy conservation in building, undertaken with the support of the fuel industry. Increased attention has been devoted to the problems of urban regeneration, particularly in the inner cities, and to encouraging the various forms of practice described by the term "community architecture," whereby users are involved in the design and management of the buildings and places they inhabit.

Under the chairmanship of the President, the Council manages the affairs of the Institute through standing committees whose work is coordinated by the Policy Committee comprising the President, the Institute's honorary officers, and the chairmen of the standing committees. The Secretary heads a staff of permanent officials who service the Institute's Council and committees and provide continuity and consistency in the implementation of Council policy. The Education and Professional Development Committee has the responsibility for the collective development of policy on such matters as course framework, postgraduate specialization, and career-long continuing education; for the inspection of architectural schools for the purposes of RIBA recognition; and for the conduct of the RIBA's own examinations. The Practice Committee is concerned with the broad issues of competence among architects in practice and with the conditions in which they work. Among other things, it monitors the operation of the conditions of engagement (Architects' Appointment) and the effects on architectural practice of technical change. It develops support services for practices and formulates Institute comment and influence on government legislation affecting architectural practice. The RIBA's Legal Adviser works closely with both the Education and Practice departments, advises the Disciplinary Committee, and acts as joint secretary to the Joint Contracts Tribunal. The Public Affairs Committee is concerned with stimulating public understanding and enjoyment of architecture and is responsible for the Clients' Advisory Service, the Architectural Awards Scheme, the monitoring and promotion of competitions, the sessional program of meetings at the RIBA, and the annual RIBA Conference. A considerable amount of public relations work is carried out by the regions and branches of the Institute through the regional offices, whose activities are supervised by the Membership Committee, of which the Regional Chairmen are members. The Membership Committee is also responsible for the Salaried Architects Group and the Women in Architecture Group. The Overseas Affairs Committee is responsible for the Institute's international relations, including liaison with the Commonwealth Association of Architects and the International Union of Architects. The issues associated with British membership of the European Economic Community are dealt with by a joint committee of ARCUK and the RIBA. In addition to the work of these committees, there are a number of activities that are directly responsible to the Institute's Policy Committee. These include the work of the Research, Energy and Statistics Office, which is responsible for the collection and analysis of statistics on workload and earnings and on the changing pattern of practice and which is concerned with relations with other organizations engaged in architectural research and the administration of the RIBA Research Awards Scheme. The Central Services Department is responsible for the general administration of the Institute and its premises and also reports directly to the Policy and Finance Committees.

The Institute's library, which started as a special collection for the exclusive use of its members, has developed into the British Architectural Library, probably the largest and finest architectural library in the world. It holds outstanding collections of printed works, manuscripts, and archives; architectural drawings; photographs; models; architectural drawing instruments; and medals. The Library, which is open to all, mounts regular exhibitions, publishes the *Architectural Periodicals Index,* and provides an information service by mail and telephone.

BIBLIOGRAPHY

General References

C. L. Eastlake, An Historical Sketch of the Institute, *RIBA Transactions,* 1st Ser., **26,** 258–272, (1875–1876).

J. A. Gotch, ed., *The Growth and Work of the Royal Institute of British Architects. A Centenary Guide,* RIBA, London, 1934.

"Inside the RIBA," *RIBA Journal* **76,** 409–451 (1969).

B. Kaye, *The Development of the Architectural Profession in Britain,* Allen & Unwin, London, 1960.

I. Macalister, The History and Work of the RIBA, *Architectural Association Journal* **50** 425–434 (May 1935).

A. Mace, *The Royal Institute of British Architects. A Guide to Its Archive and History,* Mansell Publishing Ltd, London and New York, 1986.

The Work of the RIBA, *RIBA Journal* **55** 483–489, 526–533 (1948).

See also the following regular publications of the RIBA: *The Architect, Directory of RIBA Members,* and *Guide to RIBA Practices.*

See also AMERICAN INSTITUTE OF ARCHITECTS

ANGELA MACE
Royal Institute of British
Architects

RUDOLPH, PAUL

Paul Rudolph was born in Elkton, Kentucky, in 1918. His father was a Methodist minister; the family moved from parish to parish throughout the Southeast. Although his father hoped his son would carry on the clerical tradition, Rudolph seems to have chosen his profession at an early age. In 1935 he entered the architecture program at the Alabama Polytechnic Institute (since 1960, Auburn University) in Auburn, Alabama. The oldest architectural program in the South, the A.P.I. program offered a traditional 5-year curriculum befitting a land grant college whose original mission was to offer agricultural and engineering training to the young men of Alabama. Over the years, Rudolph has had little to say about his undergraduate education. In the introduction to *The Architecture of Paul Rudolph* (1970), Sibyl Moholy-Nagy quotes Rudolph as saying that the faculty at A.P.I. "was best when they left you alone." The reaction was spawned, perhaps, by Rudolph's discovery, in his first job in an architect's office, that the 5 years at A.P.I. had given him little preparation to make buildings. Working drawings, site supervision, the nature of materials—seemed overwhelming. E. B. Jan Kueren, his first employer, reports that the 22-year-old Rudolph was devastated by this realization.

He did, in fact, find, in the Art Department, a mentor and champion in department head Frank Appelbee for whom he would later design a house. In addition to the Appelbee residence (1956), he also designed the Kappa Sigma fraternity house (1961) at Auburn. In 1972, he was welcomed back to his alma mater to receive an honorary degree.

After graduation from A.P.I. in 1940, Rudolph moved to Cambridge, Massachusetts, to begin work on a graduate degree at Harvard. This was interrupted by naval service during World War II, but he returned to Harvard in 1946 to finish his graduate work. This was the Harvard of Walter Gropius and other refugees from Germany's Bauhaus. Rudolph studied alongside many of the so-called "second-generation modernists" including Philip Johnson, Victor Lundy, Edward Larrabee Barnes, Ulrich Franzen, and John Johansen. Through these and others of his students, Gropius and the functionalist ideals of the Bauhaus would become the most important force in American architecture of the postwar period. The naval experience, where Rudolph was assigned to shipbuilding, and the Harvard years proved to be a combination that would serve Rudolph well. Perhaps his early work with the wartime bureaucracy gave him the ability and confidence to be one of the few "star" designers of his generation who could work with relative ease on government projects.

After receiving his master's from Harvard, Rudolph returned to the South where he worked with partner Ralph Twitchell in a Sarasota, Florida, practice from 1948 to 1952. During these years the firm had a significant number of residential commissions. Almost all of these early buildings were clearly products of Rudolph's Harvard training—unadorned, planar compositions devoid of ornamentation. A few also illustrated Rudolph's navy training and fascination with materials and technology. In the Healy guest house in Siesta Key (Sarasota), the structural tour-de-force of exposed columns, floor beams, and tension rods is enhanced by a composite roof of board, fiberglass, and plastic; materials that had been used by the navy in both producing and mothballing ships. This would be the beginning of Rudolph's career of combining the learned and experienced elements of his past.

On the one hand, he was fascinated by materials and technology. He recognized, perhaps earlier than many of his Harvard classmates, that the lessons of Gropius and Siegfried Giedion fell short of their professed goal of a "new architecture" born of technical advance. His native American interest in experiment, combined with his naval experiences probably served him better. Furthermore, as an American individualist he had a difficult time with the team approach and collaborative dicta being preached at Harvard. A brief fellowship in Europe, prior to his partnership with Twitchell, further convinced him that Gropius's notion of leaving urban design to the planners was wrong. Consciously and unconsciously, Paul Rudolph was already embarking on an architectural career in which Wrightian individualism would dominate his education in Bauhaus functionalism.

The 4 years with Twitchell in Sarasota were, by any criterion, a success. The work was plentiful, the commissions were well received critically, and, unlike many young practices, the firm made money. Yet, by 1952 the relationship between the two men came apart. As Rudolph later observed, "architects were never meant to design together . . . architecture is a personal effort, and the fewer people coming between you and your work, the better."

In 1954 Rudolph was awarded the distinction of Outstanding Young Architect at an international competition in Sâo Paulo, Brazil. Shortly thereafter, he received two commissions that would lead him to leave the South. His design for the U.S. Embassy in Amman, Jordan, was a problematic effort that seems awkward in its attempt to combine "early Assyrian architecture" with better understood elements of modernism. The design was never built. The Mary Cooper Jewett Arts Center at Wellesley College was; and it is a far clearer break from the International Style coming out of the Harvard/Gropius generation. The collegiate Gothic campus at Wellesley was a powerful force that Rudolph could not ignore. He attempts, in the Art Center, to bridge the gap between old and new was a notion certainly not a part of his Harvard training. The site, not far from Lake Waban, is developed as a quadrangle/camp ideal, whereas the buildings themselves combine a dominant red brick with a secondary overlay of metal grillwork to echo the material and scale of detail of its neogothic neighbors. The vast expanses of brick and the introduction of a somewhat brutalist entrance stair detract from Rudolph's intentions to create an environment that would be context sensitive.

At this point Rudolph was splitting his professional time between offices in New Haven and Sarasota, where he was busy designing Riverview High School. The Riverview commission led to the larger Sarasota High School project largely through the influence of Philip Hiss, a wealthy builder and chairman of the Sarasota School Board. Utilizing the planar concrete forms he had employed in the earlier house projects, Rudolph achieved a repetitive, but powerfully formal, building, which despite the waferlike slabs, has a good deal more solidarity than the slightly earlier tensile forms at Riverview.

In 1957 came an offer to Chair the School of Architecture at Yale University. With the offer, came the promise of total freedom in shaping the curriculum and the possibility of designing the new Art and Architecture Building. Although there is strong evidence that Rudolph pushed for the commissioning of Le Corbusier, the Art and Architecture project was, eventually, his along with the chairmanship.

The years at Yale (1957–1965) were among the most controversial and widely debated in the annals of architectural education. Prior to his time at Yale, Rudolph had been an active guest critic at a number of schools of architecture. These associations with the educational community appear to have been very successful. His strong showing on the lecture/critic circuit was, in part, responsible for his being chosen to head the program at Yale. Yet despite his previous educational forays, his strength as a designer, and his relative youth (he was not yet 40 when he went to New Haven), the 8 years at Yale were often trying and difficult. To be sure, Rudolph's time at Yale, particularly the last few years, were congruent to the period of sharp questioning and occasional upheaval that would become standard fare at many U.S. universities by the end of the 1960s. Not quite the enfant terrible, but certainly no diplomat, Rudolph exacerbated the mood of the time by the sweeping curriculum changes, the new building, and his own practice.

The so-called humanistic-scientific framework of the U.S. university has been called to task by Sibyl Moholy-Nagy in her writings on Rudolph. Paul Rudolph, she contends, tried to make Yale's school of architecture "an ideal office." This meant the coalescence of lecturers and critics from all over the country. Many of them, like Ulrich Franzen, had been Rudolph's classmates at Harvard. Rudolph's own dissatisfaction with the Gropius/Giedion line was apparent in his efforts to involve actively the students in urban concerns as the head of a consultant team, not simply a part of one.

Rudolph turned to talking about proportions, sequence, scale, and volume at a time when student interest was beginning to move toward sociopolitical arenas that Rudolph would dismiss as "peripheral matters." An architectural individualist, in an era when ego was under severe scrutiny, Rudolph found the going rough. The Yale years saw his own practice grow not only in its size, but in its

movement away from the structuralist and regionalist constraints. Ironically, as he broke from his teachers, finding their lessons too constricting and narrow, so his own students often broke with him, finding his example socially insensitive and politically incorrect.

Part of the problem was the Art and Architecture Building. Painstakingly planned, it, like other Rudolph efforts, came only after detailed site analysis. Six versions were designed and debated—from a boxlike series of concrete planes much reminiscent of the work in Sarasota, to the final project of massive, vertical, ribbed concrete solids tied together with smooth concrete beams and framing sheets of glass. What is most striking about this evolution is that the earlier composition relies so heavily on two-dimensional elements whereas the final version is a highly articulated composition of solids and voids with intricate volumetric relationships. Superficially, it most closely resembles the late work of Le Corbusier, but without Corbu's power and directness. The building, like much of Rudolph's work of the 1960s, has both a heroic and picturesque quality. No longer content with the structural dominance of the Sarasota and earliest Yale work (Greeley Memorial Lab and Temple Street parking garage), Rudolph embarked on a series of projects that are remarkable in their massiveness and volumetric complexity. Largely of exposed concrete, the buildings often combine a Wrightian adherence to pinwheel plan with a fascination for the light, shadow, and texture of the post-Ronchamp work of Corbusier.

At the Tuskegee Chapel, at Tuskegee Institute in Eastern Alabama, the combination works best. The singular function of the building and its largely symbolic role on the campus augur well for the kind of powerful, fortresslike statement Rudolph was noted for in the 1960s. Originally planned as a concrete building, the Chapel was ultimately rendered in brick, which gives it a warmth that the scale and intricacy of the plan would belie.

In other projects, notably the Boston Government Center and the Orange County Office and Courthouse in Goshen, New York, the complexities of plan and volume create many interior and exterior spaces of visual delight and even mystery. At the Christian Science Center at the University of Illinois Champaign-Urbana and the Endo Laboratories in Garden City, New York, the massing and volumetric intricacies—the Chinese puzzle qualities—are replaced with large, unbroken ribbed concrete walls and fortresslike projections. At Illinois, the vertical shafts, with their upper, narrow openings resemble Renaissance watchtowers and seem to be attenuated derivations of the cratelike Southern houses. At Endo Labs, the walls are punctuated by a series of turretlike projections creating a medieval castle quality.

Much more successful is the Creative Arts Center at Colgate University in Hamilton, New York. Here a far-more delicate series of vertical supports forms a powerful, but not overwhelming, rhythm between which Rudolph spans the many functions of the building. This less-contrived series of volumes would later influence some of the institutional work of I. M. Pei, in such projects as the arts building at Choate School and museums at Cornell and in Syracuse. All these buildings possess a power and delicacy that would mark the best work of the modern movement in the 1960s and 1970s.

Rudolph completed other projects in New Haven during his Yale years. Most notable are the married student housing (1960–1961)—brick boxes set in a tiered arrangement along a gentle slope—and Crawford Manor (1962–1966) a high-rise housing project for the elderly made of a series of precast, ribbed concrete units of rather unusual configuration. Like others of Rudolph's high rise projects [Tracey Towers of Bronx, New York (project 1967)] Crawford Manor has been sharply criticized for its relentless massiveness and banal repetition of indelicate projections.

In 1967, Rudolph, still fascinated by the technically advanced and seduced by the idea of a plug-in city, created a design for a graphic arts center on the waterfront in Manhattan. Here a series of prefabricated units would form a megastructure stretching both vertically and horizontally to form a marina in the Hudson River. The drawings, like all of Rudolph's graphic production are extremely seductive, but this notion of an assembly-line production method combined with a formal architectonic construct was never built.

Rudolph did get to try this idea at the Oriental Gardens Housing near the Merritt Parkway in West Rock, Connecticut. The 148-unit project was a mere speck of the graphic arts design, but it did afford Rudolph the opportunity to put into action a prefabricated housing scheme. The wooden-clad units were manufactured in Baltimore and shipped to Bridgeport harbor as part of the Operation Breakthrough project of the early 1970s. Sponsored and approved through the Department of Housing and Urban Development, the project, which leaks badly and has poor "defensible space" according to HUD, is slated to be demolished. Ironically, Oriental Gardens, a government-sponsored project, would have been politically correct in the eyes of Yale's architecture students of the 1960s in contrast to many of the more well-to-do clients/users for whom Rudolph has worked.

Over the last two decades, Rudolph has worked as a late-modernist, shunning the historicism of many of his contemporaries and former students whom he referred to, in a 1985 interview with *Architectural Record,* as the "paint-modernists." Although the hyperproductive years of the 1960s and early 1970s seem to be over, Rudolph continues to execute large projects in a practice that is now worldwide, with projects in Singapore, Indonesia, and Texas. Although he has continued to work with concrete, his more recent works have included glass curtain wall, high-rise projects.

Eschewing the cladding of buildings in stone, Rudolph contends, "I still think buildings should . . . show how they are constructed and what they are made of." In that regard, Rudolph has remained true to his earliest beliefs, and continues to be an architect whose best work is a product of his modernist schooling and practical bent.

BIBLIOGRAPHY

General References

From Object to Space: An Interview with Paul Rudolph, *Architectural Record,* (June 1985).

S. Moholy-Nagy, *The Architecture of Paul Rudolph,* Praeger Publishers, New York, 1970.

R. Spade, *Paul Rudolph,* Simon & Schuster, New York, 1971.

ROBERT ZWIRN
Miami University
Oxford, Ohio

RUGS AND CARPETS.   See SUPPLEMENT.

S

SAARINEN, EERO

Eero Saarinen (1910–1961) shared both the same birthday and career with his father, Finnish architect Eliel Saarinen. This coincidence of birth foreshadowed a complex relationship as well as the artistic and professional distinction of a son seeking identity independent from the distinguished recognition of his father during a period characterized by radical ideological and aesthetic change. Saarinen's career in architecture spanned the Depression through the Kennedy years, a period during which the philosophy of modernism entered the American professional mainstream. Saarinen sought an appropriate design process that was derived from the perceived new programs of a new society and whose artistic variety came to embody the "search for form" in the 1950s. His coming of age as a recognized leader in design was in part symbolic of changes in U.S. architectural practice as well. It was through the realization of unity in diversity that his mature work brought Saarinen into his own right: from the minimalist perfection of the General Motors Technical Center to the sculptural baroque forms of the Trans World Airlines Flight Center at Idlewild (now Kennedy) Airport, to the innovative architectural technology of the John Deere and Company Administrative Center (Fig. 1) and the Bell Telephone Laboratories Development Center, the conceptual and programmatic innovations of the Washington Dulles International Airport (Fig. 2), and the abstract monumental symbolism of the Jefferson National Expansion Memorial in St. Louis (Fig. 3). Eliel Saarinen's practice in the United States must acknowledge the strong influence of his son's design interests after 1935; their partnership was a reality until the elder's death in 1950. This makes Eero Saarinen's autonomous career of slightly more than a decade all the more remarkable when measured against the influence he exerted on the U.S. architectural scene during the 1950s and subsequently by virtue of his completed works.

Eero was the second child of Eliel Saarinen and the sculptor Loja (Louise) Gesellius, born in Kirkkonummi (Kyrkslätt), Finland, on August 20, 1910; his sister Pipsan (Eva-Lisa) had been born in 1905.

Eliel Saarinen achieved international notice by winning second prize in the competition for the Chicago *Tribune* Tower in 1922. On the strength of the *Tribune* publicity, and because of a severe economic depression in Finland, Eliel Saarinen came to the United States, where he undertook a milestone study of the Chicago Lakefront and was eventually joined by his family. They settled briefly in Evanston, Illinois. By 1924, the elder Saarinen had been invited to teach architecture at the University of Michigan, and the family moved to Ann Arbor, returning to Finland in summers on a regular basis until World War II. Among his students were J. Robert F. Swanson, who became his son-in-law, and Henry S. Booth, son of George Gough Booth, publisher of the Detroit *News*. In a project initiated by the Detroit chapter of the American Institute of Architects, Saarinen proposed an extensive civic center for the city. Booth was impressed by the elder Saarinen, and retained him to undertake designs for a group of educational institutions at Cranbrook, his estate in Bloomfield Hills near Detroit. By late 1925, the Saarinens relocated after Booth established a $12 million foundation to implement the Cranbrook concept; Eero entered Baldwin High School in nearby Birmingham, from which he graduated in February 1929.

In many ways, Cranbrook was an Americanized version of "Hviatträsk"—the Saarinens' home and studio in Finland, a center of high culture and serious environmental thought in the heartland of the United States, including as it did the Cranbrook Boys School, the Cranbrook Academy of Art, Kingswood, and the Cranbrook Institute

Figure 1. John Deere & Company Headquarters, Moline, Illinois, 1957–1963. Courtesy of W. Miller.

329

Figure 2. Dulles International Airport, Washington, D.C., 1958–1962. Courtesy of W. Miller.

of Science. The entire family's creative powers were brought to bear on these projects, and Eero joined the Cranbrook Architectural Office over the summer of 1928 and on graduating from high school in 1929. While work at Cranbrook continued through the Great Depression, Eero left for Paris in the fall of 1929 to study sculpture at the Académie de la Grande Chaumière through the spring of 1930. He continued to study sculpture at Cranbrook on his return. In 1931, he was contracted to do design work for a range of furniture pieces at Kingswood School. These exhibit a diversity of stylistic resonances appropriate to diverse uses, a trait that was to inform his later career in architecture.

Eero Saarinen did not attend college, but in the fall of 1931 he enrolled in the graduate School of Fine Arts at Yale University, completing a 4-year program in 3 years. The traditional courses were guided by the structure of the Beaux Arts Institute of Design, and Saarinen's consistently high placement exhibited an ability to work well within a limiting framework. Known as "Second Medal Saarinen" for his record of awards, he also graduated in 1934 as the Charles Arthur and Margaret Ormrod Matcham Fellow. During a brief stay in New York, where he worked with several classmates from Yale, Saarinen submitted an entry to the Central Post Office and Telegraph Competition in Helsinki on a site adjacent to the famous train station designed by Eliel Saarinen; he placed third. In the late fall of 1934, Eero went to Italy; he spent much of 1935 traveling in Europe and the Near East before returning to Finland. It was here that he joined the office of Jarl Eklund, who was completing work on an extension and renovations to the Swedish Theater, a job Eliel Saarinen had secured in a 1916 competition but relinquished after undertaking the work at Cranbrook.

In Scandinavia Eero came into more direct contact with the international style. Interested in modernism, and ultimately convinced of the progressive trends of technological innovation, he began his personal synthesis through observations of both historical architecture in his travels and the new architecture then emerging in Europe. In Helsinki, he became familiar with Alvar Aalto's work, which was a form of modernism independent of ideologic content. A series of competition projects executed during this period, some with the help of Yale classmates who came to visit at Hviatträsk, exhibited the features of the international style, while at the same time the reworking of the Swedish Theater illustrated his ability to accommodate the context of an existing classical vocabulary.

On his return to America in 1936, Eero entered into a partnership with his father independent of Cranbrook work, as well as maintaining a separate identity of his own through additional designs and collaborations. The firm of Eliel Saarinen and Eero Saarinen produced a small Community House in Fenton, Michigan, in 1937 that combined the stylistic features of Eliel with a greater formal simplification from Eero's dispositions. Eero also was employed as design architect during this period by the Flint Institute of Research and Planning and was hired as a designer for the office of Norman Bel Geddes in early 1938 during the development of the General Motors Futurama building for the New York World's Fair the following year. While in New York at the Bel Geddes office, Eero submitted an independent entry to the 1938 Wheaton College Art Center Competition and placed fifth.

On his return to Cranbrook in the summer of 1938, Eero and Eliel placed second in a national competition for a campus plan and college library at Goucher College. The Saarinens were beginning to be recognized as progressive modernist designers whose work was acceptable because of its stylistic independence from the radical international style. They developed a practice separate from the close association with Cranbrook. The first major commissions were as design architects for the Kleinhans Music Hall in Buffalo, New York, of 1938–1940, with Kidd and Kidd and the Crow Island School in Winnetka, Illinois, of the same period (the latter associated with Perkins, Wheeler and Will of Chicago).

They also drew on a unique wealth of design talent from the graduate program at the Academy of Art, which

Figure 3. Jefferson Westward Expansion Memorial, St. Louis, Missouri, 1948–1964. Courtesy of W. Miller.

Figure 4. Chapel, Massachusetts Institute of Technology, Cambridge, Massachusetts, 1953–1957. Courtesy of W. Miller.

had been initiated by Eliel Saarinen in 1931. By the mid-1930s, Charles Eames was the head of design; Harry Bertoia ran the metal workshop; Eliel was the head of architecture, which emphasized urban design; and Eero officially joined the faculty as Assistant to his father from 1939 to 1941. Eero entered the competition for a National Theater at the College of William and Mary in 1939 with Cranbrook students Frederic James and Ralph Rapson, winning first prize. The same year, the office achieved major recognition by winning the national competition for the Smithsonian Gallery of Art, a modernist building planned to be located on the Mall in Washington, D.C.; this project also included J. Robert F. Swanson as an associate. Perhaps the most famous commission of this period was the First Christian Church in Columbus, Indiana, of 1939–1940, which Charles Eames worked on. Eames and Eero began their lifelong friendship during this period,

collaborating on an innovative exhibit at Cranbrook using a lightweight tensile system and development of furniture designs using molded plywood techniques (the "potato-chip" concept), which won first prize in the Organic Design in Home Furnishings Competition sponsored by the Museum of Modern Art in New York in 1941. Before the outbreak of World War II, Eero demonstrated his modernist inclination in two house designs, a project for Sam Bell in New Hope, Pennsylvania, and a completed house for A. C. Wermuth (who had been the contractor for Cranbrook and the First Christian Church). During this period, Eero married Lilian Swann, who had arrived at the Academy of Art in 1938 to study sculpture with Carl Milles, and they spent their wedding trip in Europe on the eve of war.

The outbreak of war brought an initial flurry of activity followed by a virtual suspension of construction. The need for defense housing for workers at Detroit area plants resulted in several developments, among them Center Line (Kramer Homes), where Eero personally worked on the design of several experimental units, and Willow Run near Ypsilanti, which began as a comprehensive town-planning project and resulted in the construction of Willow Lodge dormitories.

In late 1941, George Booth informed Eero Saarinen that he could not continue at Cranbrook, and the office relocated to Birmingham, Michigan, first becoming Eliel Saarinen and Eero Saarinen/J. Robert F. Swanson Architects (1942–1943) and then Saarinen and Swanson (1943–1946). In early 1943, Eero was retained as a civilian consultant to the Office of Strategic Services and was appointed Chief of the Special Exhibits Section, recommended by several Yale classmates who were already in the OSS. It is perhaps here that Eero became aware of the intricacies of coordinating large projects, a management technique that was to serve him later.

Saarinen and Swanson also maintained a small office in Washington, which Eero ran in the design of Lincoln Heights Housing for the National Capital Housing Authority. In this office were several young architects who went on to their own distinguished careers, and Eero himself joined with OSS colleague Oliver Lundquist in producing the first prize entry for the Designs for Postwar Living Competition sponsored by *California Arts and Architecture*. Their entry, called the PAC (Pre-Assembled Component) System, was one of several projects that manifested Saarinen's commitment to industrial production and technology. In 1940, Eero designed the Opera–Concert Hall at Tanglewood employing a roof supported by tensile rods in turn hung from a series of bow-shaped laminated wood arches; a project sponsored by the United States Gypsum Company in late 1941 for a "Community House" proposed a roof carried on tensile rods from a central mast support. The enclosure was a modular facade system, suggesting both flexibility and indeterminacy. The PAC System continued this theme, as it combined a series of packaged service cores with housing types that could be arranged in several configurations. The ultimate statements included an "Unfolding-House" made of modular trailer units and the "Serving Suzy" restaurant, where food service was decentralized by mobile carts. This work represented interests different from that of his father Eliel, who produced the more traditional Cranbrook Museum and Library at the same time. If the approaches might be qualified on the basis of style, then separate entries by Eliel and Eero for a Legislative Palace in Quito, Ecuador, of 1944 exhibit the real artistic distance between father and son.

With the end of the war, a variety of circumstances and the high profile achieved by the Saarinen office through consistent publication of their work over the previous decade led to an expanding practice. A national interest in planning reinforced Eliel's reputation as a planner, which had been enhanced not only by a generation of Cranbrook students in responsible positions but also by means of wartime activity in establishing the Architects Civic Design Group in Detroit and a number of planning commissions. A resurgence of building activity, particularly in the Midwest, brought new work. Campus plans for Antioch College (Yellow Springs, Ohio), Drake University (Des Moines, Iowa), and Stephens College (Columbia, Missouri), and, by 1949, Brandeis University (Waltham, Massachusetts) and Yale University (New Haven, Connecticut) all led to actual buildings. Institutional work followed with projects and completed buildings for the Des Moines Art Center (Des Moines, Iowa), the Fort Wayne Art School and Museum (Fort Wayne, Indiana), and a variety of planning and building feasibility studies. In 1946, the firm name was changed to Saarinen, Swanson, and Saarinen, but in the fall of 1947 the family practice divided into Saarinen and Saarinen Associates and Swanson Associates.

Perhaps the most potentially significant project that came to the practice after the end of the war was the General Motors Technical Center. Certainly the Saarinen name was the best known in Detroit architectural circles, but the initial scheme combines some familiar Eliel Saarinen motifs such as the formal interplay between a horizontal space (a manmade lake) and the vertical accent of a water tower. The design imagery, however, reflected

Eero Saarinen's transitional attempt at defining a new modern architecture; its imagery was at once associated with the previous decade's "streamlining," but metaphorically as postwar automobiles reflected in their styling. The original project had been budgeted at $20 million for a 350-acre site. The project lapsed for 3 years, during which time a number of smaller works occupied the office, among them new work on the Detroit Civic Center Plan (1947–1951).

During the time that the partnership was being restructured, both Eliel and Eero Saarinen made submissions to the Jefferson National Expansion Memorial Competition in St. Louis, Missouri. The notice at the end of the first phase was inadvertently sent to Eliel, when in fact it was Eero's concept of a great stainless steel arch that made him one of the five finalists; he was eventually selected as the winner in February 1948. No more clear proof could have been made to distinguish son from father.

At about the same time, postwar sales of automobiles encouraged General Motors to reactivate the Tech Center, and the scope was enlarged to a $100 million project on a 900-acre site in Warren, Michigan. Eero had by this time come into direct contact with Mies van der Rohe's work at the campus of the Illinois Institute of Technology, and in 1948 a new scheme for the GMTC was proposed, which developed over the next half decade as sections were gradually completed. Part of the critical decision to proceed was due to the national fame Saarinen had achieved, but also as the result of partner Joseph N. Lacy (who had arrived in 1945 from Louis I. Kahn's office) having been successful in engaging the large Detroit firm of Smith, Hinchman and Grylls to assume delivery of full professional services. The design firm changed its name after the death of Eliel Saarinen to Eero Saarinen and Associates, and its staff rose from 10 to 50 and finally to 90 during the course of the GMTC construction. Joining the firm in the early phases of design were John Dinkeloo from Skidmore, Owings, and Merrill, Chicago, and Kevin Roche, who had been briefly a graduate student of Mies at IIT and worked for the United Nations architects.

Saarinen retained some touches of Eliel's disposition at GMTC, such as a fascia detail not unlike a molding that made a shadow and color-glazed brick end walls evoking a crafts content. However, a standard module was used for all buildings, and he metaphorically embraced technology, basing the design on steel, the metal of the automobile. Technical innovations included development of a thin, porcelain-faced "sandwich" panel serving as both exterior skin and interior finish, an extremely thin-shell dome for the Styling Auditorium, and the use of neoprene "zipper gaskets" for all window glazing, modeled on the system used for installation of automobile windshields.

Although to a great degree the General Motors commission carried the office financially, a number of innovative corporate and institutional buildings were completed, including the first all-glass bank for the Irwin Union Trust Company in Columbus, Indiana (1950–1955); a house for J. Irwin Miller in Lake Muskoka, Canada, with Alexander Girard (1950–1952); the MIT Chapel (Fig. 4); and master plans for the University of Michigan North Campus in Ann Arbor (1951–1957) and the University of

Chicago (1954–1961). Many buildings involved development of a curtain-wall aesthetic, such as Noyes House at Vassar College, Poughkeepsie, New York (1955–1958), the Law School of the University of Chicago (1955–1961), the IBM Manufacturing Plant at Rochester, Minnesota (1956–1959), and the IBM Thomas J. Watson Research Center in Yorktown Heights, New York (1956–1961). However these projects may have been related to the use of thin-skin technologically produced enclosure, the purest "endless" use was in the Rochester plant, whereas the others had particular variations in overall form: Noyes House was a concave curve to complete a campus oval, the Law School's faceted profile evoked surrounding Gothic revival buildings, and the Watson Center's convex curve both eliminated endless corridors and comfortably captured the crest of its hill site.

The Kresge Auditorium and interdenominational chapel at Massachusetts Institute of Technology (1950–1955) were buildings with contrasting images of architectural technique. The auditorium was a shallow, thin, one-eighth dome with a triangular plan form supported at each point, whereas the chapel was a circular masonry cylinder. Saarinen thwarted those who would place him in the Mies aesthetic by further isolating the auditorium on a circular brick platform and the chapel in a circular sunken moat, then contending that they were more Miesian than were the surface resemblances at the GMTC because of "a consistent structure and a forthright expression of that structure" (1) exploring the principle of universal space in the auditorium and the precise definition of pure form in both.

It was during this period that Saarinen's marriage to Lily Swann Saarinen ended in divorce in late 1953; he subsequently married *The New York Times* art critic Aline Bernstein Loucheim. Aline Loucheim had fanned the intensity of Saarinen's emerging fame with an article in the *Times* Sunday Magazine entitled "And Now, Saarinen the Son" (2). Her own lifestyle and personal interests reinforced his career direction, and Aline Bernstein Saarinen took an active role in guiding the professional notice of Eero Saarinen and Associates while maintaining her own career as a writer and critic.

Never directly committed to the international style, Saarinen remained free in his conceptions and his talent for formal invention and exploration left him with little interest in a universal vocabulary. His systematic, almost engineer-like, insistence on analyzing the nature of a project suggested the possibility of an autonomous architecture for each building, a concept of "the Style for the Job." Saarinen sought to direct a contemporary technology in a diverse architectural expression within the tradition of the early modern masters. He was committed to the advancement of the symbolic and environmental content of that tradition through the exploration of special architectural vernaculars for each project. Critic Reyner Banham observed, "It was not a style he had to offer . . . since no two functional problems are alike, no stylistically consistent approach could either serve or survive" (3).

Saarinen once observed that design was word-poor and that he was attempting to "enlarge its alphabet beyond ABC." Whereas many of his contemporaries were engaged in the development and promotion of identifiable personal styles, the only "signature" Eero Saarinen left was consistent inconsistency, what Walter McQuade characterized as "Unity in Diversity" (4). The work ranged from the most reductionist and abstract, such as the IBM Rochester plant or the Bell Telephone Laboratories Development Center in Holmdel, New Jersey (1957–1962), to the evocative expressionism of the Trans World Airlines Flight Center at Idlewild (now Kennedy) Airport (1956–1962). His method included the spirit of the program, an aim beyond simple pragmatism, which embodied an updated concept of *architecture parlante*, an associative formal language of allusion to arouse emotions and affect sentiments.

For Concordia Lutheran Senior College in Fort Wayne, Indiana (1953–1954), community was suggested in the evocation of a village image, whereas the David S. Ingalls Hockey Rink at Yale University (1956–1959) was both a dynamic diagram for preferred seating and a fluid form dramatizing the movement of the sport. The TWA building's complex curvilinear forms suggested a hovering bird and "the excitement of the trip." The Women's Dormitories at the University of Pennsylvania (1957–1961) negated the internal–external continuities of modernism and frankly engaged in allusion; figuratively a castle approached by a metaphorical drawbridge, it presented a tough, contextual image to its dark red-brick Philadelphia neighborhood, while its interior was bright, delicate, white, and in an extension of meanings, feminine. The Ezra Stiles and Samuel F.B. Morse Colleges at Yale (1958–1962) evoked a range of associations, most strongly the image of a medieval community of scholars, and the conjunction of the two colleges suggested a townlike quality of urban spaces. His only tall building was the Columbia Broadcasting System Headquarters in New York City (1960–1964), the last design in his career, which proposed, in its solid, dominantly masonry cladding, a departure from the modernist glass box based on the context of the traditional city.

Saarinen's inventiveness not only influenced mainstream architectural practice through his clients and commissions but also through a string of technical accomplishments that had extensive use in the late 1960s and throughout the 1970s. In addition to the continuing use of structure as a formgiver, such as in the eventual realization of the St. Louis Arch for the Jefferson National Expansion Memorial (1957–1968) or the integrative inclusion of support in his Pedestal Furniture series (1958), he evolved thin-skin technology and reduced the curtain wall through the neoprene gasket technique and sandwich panels, as mentioned at GMTC and ultimately refined in the IBM Rochester plant. Reflective mirror glass was given its first major application at the Bell Laboratories, and self-rusting Cor-Ten steel was employed as structure, scale-giving ornament, and exterior finish in the John Deere and Company Administrative Center in Moline, Illinois (1956–1963). The precise use of concrete was developed for the Vivian Beaumont Repertory Theater at Lincoln Center in New York City (1958–1964), the Athens Airport (1960–1964), and Washington Dulles International Airport (1958–1962). At Dulles, Saarinen displayed his conception of architecture at the larger order of environment, acknowledging that he had learned from Eliel to "design for the next larger thing." Dulles, being the first all-jet airport, was conceived at a scale beyond the object limits of architecture: the perception of arrival through the orchestration of movement, the clarity of the all-encompassing order of the terminal, and ultimately the provocative solution of the "mobile lounge" to free the problem from strictly limits of a building.

Eero Saarinen's death in Ann Arbor, Michigan, on September 1, 1961, was sudden, within 2 weeks of the first symptom and on the eve of relocation from Bloomfield Hills, Michigan, to Hamden, Connecticut. Ten major design projects were in various stages of construction, documentation, or design development at that time. Saarinen did not live to see final completion and occupancy of his own major works. Because his will explicitly dictated that no project would bear his name that he had not worked on directly, his partners completed relocation and execution of the remaining projects as Eero Saarinen and Associates, but re-formed their partnership in 1966 as Kevin Roche John Dinkeloo and Associates.

Perhaps an even greater legacy is the list of individuals who were associated with Saarinen, for many were by the late 1970s the leading practitioners in America's professional architectural mainstream.

BIBLIOGRAPHY

1. A. Temko, *Eero Saarinen (Makers of Contemporary Architecture* series) Braziller, New York, 1962.
2. A. Loucheim, "And Now, Saarinen the Son," *The New York Times* Sunday Magazine (April 26, 1953).
3. R. Banham, "The Fear of Eero's Mana," *Arts Magazine,* 70, 73 (Feb. 1962)
4. W. McQuade, "Eero Saarinen, A Complete Architect," *Architectural Forum,* 102–119 (April 1962).

General References

"Eero Saarinen," *Architecture + Urbanism (A+U)* (April 1984).
W. McQuade, "Eero Saarinen, A Complete Architect," *Architectural Forum,* 102–119 (April 1962).
P. C. Papademetriou, "Coming of Age: Eero Saarinen and Modern American Architecture," *Perspecta 21,* 116–141 (1985).
"Recent Work of Eero Saarinen," *Zodiac* (4), 30–67 (1959).
A. Saarinen, ed., *Eero Saarinen on His Work,* Yale University Press, New Haven, 1962.
R. Spade and Y. Futagawa, *Eero Saarinen (Masters of Modern Architecture* series), Simon & Schuster, New York, 1968.
A. Temko, *Eero Saarinen (Makers of Contemporary Architecture* series), Braziller, New York, 1962.
A. Temko, "Eero Saarinen: '. . . something between earth and sky . . . ,'" *Horizon* 76–83, 123 (July 1960).

PETER C. PAPADEMETRIOU, AIA
Rice University
Houston, Texas

SAARINEN, ELIEL

The 50-year career of Eliel Saarinen (1873–1950) can be divided into two parts. Practicing in Finland for 25 years, he first established an international reputation based on his "National Romantic" and *Jugendstil*-inspired architecture. The second phase of Saarinen's career began when he emigrated to the United States in 1923, after placing second in the 1922 Chicago Tribune Tower competition. While practicing in the United States, he also assumed the role of educator, first at the University of Michigan and then at the Cranbrook Academy of Art. Saarinen not only designed the Cranbrook complex but, under his stewardship, it became one of the most influential design schools in the nation.

Gottlieb Eliel Saarinen was born in Rantisalmi, Finland, in 1873. A portion of Saarinen's childhood was spent in the Russian region of Ingermanland near St. Petersburg, a result of his father being in the clergy. The proximity of St. Petersburg provided the young Saarinen with an urban experience unequaled in more provincial Finland and also gave him access to The Hermitage. He initially intended to be a painter, a desire that he acknowledged was stimulated by visits to the museum. After graduating from high school in 1893, he enrolled in the Department of Architecture at the Technical Institute in Helsinki, simultaneously taking drawing courses at Helsinki University. While at the Institute, he formed friendships with Herman Gesellius and Armas Lindgren; the three formed an architectural partnership in 1896, a year before Saarinen graduated. The Gesellius, Lindgren and Saarinen office lasted until 1905, when Lindgren left the partnership; Gesellius and Saarinen continued to practice together for two additional years. Saarinen married Gesellius's sister Louise (Loja) in 1904 (his second marriage); they had two children, a daughter Eva-Lisa (Pipsan) and a son Eero.

When the Gesellius, Lindgren, and Saarinen partnership was formed, Finland was undergoing a period of national self-awareness, a nationalism founded on the desire to search out and understand traditional Finnish cultural origins. This interest in Finland's origins was stimulated when Elias Lönnrot published the first edition of the national folk epic, the *Kalevala*. The powerful, poetic imagery of the *Kalevala*, coupled with the interest in developing a national form of artistic expression, provided a profound source of inspiration for Finnish artists that resulted in a style known as national romanticism. National romantic architecture was an adventurous, eclectic admixture of sources that included Finnish vernacular and medieval architecture, continental art nouveau imagery, and the Romanesque-inspired work of American architect H. H. Richardson. Although the first commission given the firm was the Tallberg Apartments in Helsinki (1897), the Pohjola Insurance Company in Helsinki (1899–1901) was their first truly national romantic work. The Finnish Pavilion for the Paris Exhibition of 1900 established their international reputation. As the firm's reputation increased, so did the commissions, villas, apartment complexes, and major public works. These works were characterizcd by picturesque plan compositions, irregular building massings, tactile material vocabulary, and the incorporation of motifs and images from Finnish architectural history. Public buildings, such as the Pohjola Insurance Company and the National Museum in Helsinki (1901–1911, Fig. 1), are of granite construction with decorative ornamentation derived from Finnish nature or folktales and included specific references to Finnish medieval churches and castles as well as to Richardson's work. Apartment complexes in Helsinki, such as Tallberg, Olofsborg (1900–1902), Fabianinkatu 17 (1900–1901), and EOL (1901–1903), were rendered in painted stucco, with stone appointments and tile roofs and were accented by bay windows and towers.

The villas, Hvitträsk (1902–1904, Fig. 2) and Suur-Merijoki (1901–1903), represent the English arts-and-crafts concept of a totally integrated work of art. Hvitträsk, the studio house of Gesellius, Lindgren, and Saarinen, is an excellent example of Finnish national romantic architecture. Located on a steep hillside outside Helsinki, the compound is ordered about a courtyard within a series of terraced gardens. Presented as a reinterpretation of Finland's vernacular past, the picturesque massing of the complex is articulated with a rustic stone

base and stuccoed or shingled walls, has upper stories of log construction, and is capped by a tiled roof. The interior spaces of the Saarinen house contain a variety of images and detail qualities: the great hall alludes to vernacular farmhouses and a sitting area incorporates motifs from medieval churches; inglenooks and sleeping rooms are executed in the arts-and-crafts style. These spaces are furnished with appointments designed by either the Saarinens or their artist friends. Suur-Merijoki, a splendid country house located near Viipuri, contains the best-developed Saarinen interiors of his early career. Moreover, these interiors demonstrate a realized total artistic conception facilitated by the close working relationship between architect, artist, and artisan.

After his association with both Lindgren and Gesellius ended, Saarinen expanded his practice to engage in city planning projects as well as building design. By 1906, having the stylistic limitations of national romanticism, a more classical and monumental spirit emerged in his work as exemplified by the Helsinki Railroad Station (1904–1914). Saarinen's original competition entry was a rusticated, medieval-referenced national romantic design, whereas the completed work is a balanced, *Jugendstil*-inspired composition incorporating delicate concrete-

Figure 1. National Museum (with Gesellius and Lindgren), Helsinki, Finland, 1901–1911. Courtesy of the Museum of Finnish Architecture.

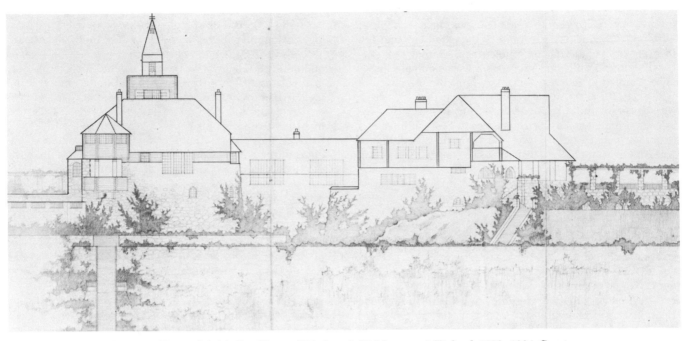

Figure 2. *Hvitträsk* (with Gesellius and Lindgren), Kirkkonummi, Finland, 1902–1904. Courtesy of the Museum of Finnish Architecture.

vaulted interior spaces. This transformation was fostered by the negative criticism Saarinen's entry received from the more progressive architects of the period; Gustaf Strengell and Sigurd Frosterus launched a vigorous press attack on what they considered to be the backward-looking stylistic qualities of the design. In moving away from national romanticism, Saarinen's final design, influenced by Frosterus's competition entry, also included suggestions for the urban development surrounding the station.

Symmetrical planning combined with pyramidal volumetric massing articulated by strong vertical accents, which often included a dominant tower element, characterized Saarinen's work before World War I. Saarinen's competition entries for the Palace of Peace in the Hague (1906) and the Finnish Parliament House (1908), as well as his designs for the town halls in Lappeenranta (1906), Joensuu (1909–1911), Lahti (1911), and Turku (1911), are representative of the classical sensibility informing his architecture at this time. The *Kalevala* House designed for Helsinki (1921), although never built, is among his most successful monumental designs. Saarinen was twice commissioned during this period to design Finland's currency, first in 1909 while it was still a Russian Grand Duchy, and again in 1918–1919 after it became an independent nation.

As a town planner, Saarinen was as concerned with political and social issues as with artistic and technical ones. While the English utopian socialists John Ruskin, William Morris, and Raymond Unwin influenced Saarinen's social consciousness, it was the work of the Austrian Camillo Sitte that gave physical substance to his planning concepts. Based on Sitte's work, Saarinen was able to combine medieval and baroque organizational notions into fully developed spatial ensembles that had

uniquely urban qualities. Of all of his planning proposals, which included the Budapest Master Plan Report (1911), the Canberra City Plan competition (1911), and the Greater Tallinn Master Plan (1911–1913), two projects for Helsinki demonstrate his ability best, the Munkkiniemi-Haaga plan (1910–1915) and the "Pro Helsingfors" plan (1917–1918). The Munkkiniemi-Haaga plan, in particular, with its axial order, residential squares, use of large apartment blocks, and the reconciliation of the automobile to the human scale of the pedestrian, presents a coherent urban and architectural totality. With the exception of portions of the Munkkiniemi-Haaga design, none of Saarinen's planning proposals were realized.

In 1923 the Saarinen family emigrated to the United States where his career would focus on education as well as architectural practice. Although his placing second in the Chicago Tribune Tower competition (1922, Fig. 3) is often cited as the reason for his immigration to the United States, the economic conditions in Finland prompted his departure. In 1917 Finland declared its autonomy from Russia; in 1919 it became an independent nation after a year-and-a-half of civil war. These events resulted in an economic collapse, and construction slowed; it was for this reason Saarinen entered the Tribune competition. After spending a brief period in Evanston, Illinois, Saarinen was invited to join the architecture faculty at the University of Michigan in 1924. In that same year one of his students at Michigan, Harry S. Booth, introduced Saarinen to his father, George Gough Booth, from whom he received the commission to design the Cranbrook complex in Bloomfield Hills, Michigan.

Cranbrook, in particular the Academy of Art, was the manifestation of George Booth's vision of a Midwestern institution that would facilitate the integration of the arts atmosphere found in the earlier Hvitträst atelier. Saarinen personally directed the graduate program in architecture, which focused city planning concerns. The studies done in the graduate studio became the structure for Saarinen's book *The City* (1), his definitive statement on urbanism.

At Cranbrook, between 1925 and 1945, Saarinen executed the School for Boys, the Kingswood Schools for Girls, the Academy of Art, the Institute of Science, the museum and library, faculty housing, and the resident artist's studios. These works ranged in style from the picturesque Boys Schools, to the Frank Lloyd Wright-inspired Kingswood School, to the more austerely classical Museum and Library complex (Fig. 4). Within this stylistic diversity, the Cranbrook designs exhibit Saarinen's arts-and-crafts desire for totally integrated environmental works, realized through their excellent siting, exquisite masonry detailing, interior surface treatments, and attendant furnishings and weaving. However, Cranbrook is more than an enclave of Saarinen buildings; it is a resonant environment incorporating sculptures, artwork, furnishings, and decorative appointments designed and produced by the Academy's faculty and students, as well as by the Saarinen family.

Saarinen took few outside commissions in the 1920s, although he produced a design for the Christian Science Church in Minneapolis (project, 1925) and entered the League of Nations competition in Geneva (1927). In the 1930s and 1940s, as Saarinen's practice expanded, he was involved in partnerships with his son Eero and J. Robert F. Swanson, a former student at Michigan (Saarinen and Saarinen, 1936–1942; Saarinen and Swanson, 1943–1946; Saarinen, Swanson, Saarinen, 1946–1947; and Saarinen and Saarinen, 1947–1950). Representative works of this period include Goucher College Plan and Library competition (second prize, 1938, with Eero); Kleinhans Music Hall in Buffalo (1938–1940, with Eero); Crow Island School in Winnetka, Illinois (1939–1940, with Eero and Perkins, Wheeler, and Will, associated architects); First Christian Church in Columbus, Indiana (1939–1942, with Eero); Smithsonian Art Gallery competition in Washington, D.C. (first prize, 1939, with Eero); and Wayne University Campus Plan competition (second place, 1942, with Swanson). In designs involving Eero's participation, a more modernist posture emerges. Although these buildings and projects often include reflecting pools, towers, and excellent masonry detailing—hallmarks of Eliel's hand—their simplified cubic volumes, elemental plan compositions, and incorporation of horizontal strip windows indicate Eero's influence. At the time of Eliel's death, in July 1950, the Saarinens were engaged in the design of the General Motors Technical Center in Warren, Michigan, a work eventually completed under Eero's direction.

Although the elder Saarinen was tied to the romanticism of nineteenth-century arts-and-crafts ideas, and he was unable to incorporate modernism's machine aesthetic into his work successfully, he remains an important and influential twentieth-century architect. The sensitivity of his architecture and the perceptiveness of his town plan-

Figure 3. Chicago Tribune Tower competition entry, Chicago, Illinois, 1922. Courtesy of the Museum of Finnish Architecture.

and crafts into contemporary culture. Under Saarinen's direction as president of the Academy and program head of architecture, Cranbrook became a nationally recognized school of design. The faculty included Carl Milles, Maija Grotell, and Marianne Strengell, in addition to the Saarinen family, while Charles and Ray Eames, Florence Knoll, Harry Bertoia, Harry Weese, Edmund Bacon, and Jack Lenor Larsen are among its more noteworthy students. At Cranbrook, individuality and freedom were stressed and the sense of community was much like the

Figure 4. Museum and Library, Cranbrook Academy of Art, Bloomfield Hills, Michigan, 1940–1943. Courtesy of The Museum of Finnish Architecture.

ning ideas still provide excellent examples of how to make humane and memorable environments.

BIBLIOGRAPHY

1. E. Saarinen, *The City: Its Growth, Its Decay, Its Future,* Reinhold Publishing, New York, 1943; republished by the MIT Press, Cambridge, Mass. 1965.

General References

A. Christ-Janer, *Eliel Saarinen: Finnish-American Architect and Educator,* The University of Chicago Press, Chicago, 1948, Rev. ed., 1979. Foreword by Alvar Aalto.

R. J. Clark, et al, *Design in America: the Cranbrook Vision 1925–1950,* Harry Abrams, New York, 1983.

S. Fayens, "Baukunst und Volk," *Moderne Bauformen* 8(8), 337–353 (1909).

"Gesellius, Lindgren, und Saarinen," *Moderne Bauformen,* **6**(4), 137–162 (1907).

M. Hausen, "Gesellius-Lindgren-Saarinen," *Arkkitehti,* **64**(9) 6–12 (1967).

M. Saarinen, *Munkkiniemi-Haaga ja Suur-Helsinki,* Osakeyhtio M. G. Stenius, Helsinki, 1915.

E. Saarinen, *The Search for Form: A Fundamental Approach to Art,* Reinhold Publishing, New York, 1948; republished as *The Search for Form in Art and Architecture,* Dover Publications, New York, 1985.

Saarinen in Finland: 1896–1923, The Museum of Finnish Architecture, Helsinki, 1984.

Saarinen's Interior Designs: 1896–1923, The Finnish Museum of Applied Arts and The Museum of Finnish Architecture, Helsinki, 1984.

J. S. Sirén (ed.), *Eliel Saarinen, Muisonayttely,* J. Simeliusen Perillisten Kirjapaino Oy, Helsinki, 1955.

WILLIAM C. MILLER, AIA
Kansas State University
Manhattan, Kansas

SAFDIE, MOSHE

Moshe Safdie was born in Haifa, Israel, in 1938. He did his early schooling in Israel and in 1953 moved with his family to Montreal, Canada. Safdie received his degree in architecture from McGill University at age 22. His thesis, a three-dimensional modular building system, was published by Aldo van Eyck in the Dutch journal *Forum.* Safdie apprenticed with van Eyck's partner, H. P. D. van Ginkel, focusing on large-scale urban designs. He continued his apprenticeship in Philadelphia with Louis I. Kahn, where he worked on the Mikveh Israel Synagogue in Philadelphia and the Institute of Management at Ahmedabad, India.

In Philadelphia, in collaboration with Anne Tyng and David Rinehart, Safdie was introduced to the work of D'Arcy Thompson, the British morphologist, whose work had a profound impact on Safdie's thinking of the origins and evolution of form in architecture. Thompson's morphological theories were related to Rudofsky's reinterpretation of vernacular architecture, ideas that were later expressed in Safdie's *Form and Purpose* (1).

In 1963, Safdie returned to Montreal to join the Canadian Corporation for the 1967 World Exhibition. He played a major role in the design of the Expo master plan and developed a proposal for a major permanent theme exhibit: an adaptation of his McGill thesis, which became known as Habitat '67 (Fig. 1). Habitat pioneered large-scale prefabrication techniques in a structure where dwelling units were accessed off a "street in the air," and possessed a garden positioned on the roof of the unit below.

With Habitat's approval by the Canadian cabinet in 1964, Safdie resigned his position at Expo to open his private practice, devoted initially to the realization of Habitat. After Habitat's completion in 1967, Safdie was engaged in a number of commissions aimed at applying the concept of Habitat on a larger commercial scale. These included projects in New York, Puerto Rico, the Virgin Islands, and Israel. Collaborations were undertaken with industry (Polymer Corporation Canada), developers, leading engineers in the field (T. Y. Lin, Conrad Engineers), and governmental housing agencies (U.S. HUD, Israel). A major proposal for the U.S. project "Breakthrough" was submitted jointly with a developer based in Puerto Rico.

In the Habitat and post-Habitat projects, Safdie was preoccupied with the reconciliation between technology's inclination to standardized and repetitive production of components and the desire for creating diversity and variety in the spatial configurations of buildings. Thus, the idea of a larger three-dimensional industrialized compo-

nent (a concept of production) is manipulated in an exploration of discovering the many permutations and combinations possible and their meaning at the environmental level. In Habitat and the subsequent projects, this is always coupled with the notion that the spatial reconfiguration of tall buildings can create levels of amenities heretofore unknown: the idea of the garden for everyone, the street in the air, and of three-dimensionally reconfiguring the various urban activities (living, work, retail, and entertainment).

The post-Habitat projects culminated in Coldspring New Town, the only project to be realized. Here, Safdie abandoned the notion of large-scale fabricated closed systems for off-the-shelf, open, small-scale prefabrication of masonry construction and precast concrete. The emphasis was in achieving high densities in a nonelevator environment and the reconciliation between vast parking spaces and the provision for open public space.

In 1967, Safdie was selected in an international search by the student body of San Francisco State College to design the Student Union, his first nonresidential building. In this project, the theme of creating diverse public spaces with a limited set of building elements is taken to new limits. It is combined with the idea of "a building as topography," its surfaces forming a continuation of the ground plane, enabling circulation. The design was re-

Figure 1. Habitat '67, Cite du Havre, Montreal, Canada. Photograph by Graetz Photography.

Figure 2. Yeshivat Porat, Joseph Rabbinical College, Old City, Jerusalem, Israel. Photograph by Moshe Safdie.

jected by the trustees as excessively radical and resulted in the 1968 campus uprising. This theme later recurred in a submission in 1972 for the Place Centre Pompidou competition in Paris (in collaboration with his Yale students) and was awarded second prize; it was finally realized in the Quebec Museum of Civilization.

In 1970, Safdie was commissioned to undertake a number of projects in Jerusalem, including the restoration of a major part of the Jewish quarter in the Old City and the design of the Yeshivat Porat Joseph Rabbinical College (Fig. 2), also in the Old City. He opened his Jerusalem office that year for the purpose of executing this work. Shortly thereafter, he was commissioned to design Jerusalem's business district, Mamilla, bridging the old and new cities, and to develop a plan for the Western Wall precinct. The Mamilla project received final approval in 1987, following extensive public review, and is scheduled for construction in 1989. In 1976, Safdie commenced work on the Hebrew Union College campus, one of the acclaimed Jerusalem works that was substantially completed in 1987.

In these projects, particularly the new buildings in the walled city of Jerusalem, the idea of a modular construction system evolved to include the cohabitation of traditional and contemporary technologies in the same project. In Porat Joseph, the traditional load-bearing stone construction is juxtaposed with prefabricated precast structures. This notion was further developed and refined in the Hebrew Union College campus designed in 1976.

The Jerusalem work focused on the issue of the harmonious relationship between the contemporary building and a city of strong architectural heritage. The search was for buildings that were generated by contemporary, programmatic, and technological concerns, yet harmonious with their setting. Safdie's position is that there is sufficient flexibility in contemporary processes of construction to affirmatively respond to a building's formal setting. This is more vividly demonstrated in the formal variations of the Quebec Museum of Civilization (Fig. 3) and the National Gallery of Canada (Fig. 4) with their respective physical settings.

In the design for the Western Wall precinct, Safdie explored transformations as manifested in Bach's fugal music and in the works of painter M. C. Escher. The pre-

cinct's generative geometry is a transforming grid of geometric progressions of spiraling structures that attempts to deal with both gradual scale changes and the thematic overlaying of ancient and contemporary geometries on the site.

In the 1970s, Safdie became increasingly involved with housing and urban development in the Third World. Master plans for Frobisher Bay in the Northwest Territories of Canada and for housing for Inuit families were developed, followed by a master plan for a new city with a population

Figure 3. Musée de la Civilisation, Quebec City, Canada. Photograph by Pierre Soulard, Quebec Museum of Civilization.

Figure 4. National Gallery of Canada, Ottawa, Ontario. Photograph by Fiona Spalding-Smith.

of 100,000, Keur Farah Pahlavi in Senegal. A housing complex was also proposed in Iran, and a series of medical clinics were designed for the Ivory Coast. Safdie collaborated with a Singapore shipbuilder to develop plans for both prefabricated and conventionally built housing, Ardmore, a 25-story twin tower complex, which was completed in downtown Singapore in 1985. Also for the same client, Safdie developed a master plan for a 4000-acre new town, Robina, in the Gold Coast, Queensland, Australia, which included housing design and a proposal for a major casino tourist complex.

In the large-scale urban forms, the Expo '67 master plan, Keur Farah Pahlavi, and Robina, Safdie explored the city as a linear form: the focus is on the issue of hierarchal structure and the growth patterns of cities. Gnomotic growth (ie, additive growth that is nondestructive to the original fabric) is explored in the overall structure.

In 1978, Safdie joined the faculty of Harvard University as director of the Urban Design Program. He served in the post of director until 1982 and continued teaching there as the Ian Woodner Studio Professor of Architecture and Urban Design. At that time, a head office was established in Boston. Boston commissions included master plans for the North Station area of Boston; the Harvard Business School in Cambridge; Cambridge Centre, a 1,500,000-ft² mixed-use complex, completed in 1987; and the Esplanade, a terraced housing complex located on the Charles River in Cambridge.

In 1985, Safdie commenced work in collaboration with Boston Properties on the 3 million-ft² mixed-use Columbus Center project in New York (winner of a developer–architect competition), which was to accommodate the headquarters of Salomon Brothers. The project was sus-

pended following Salomon Brothers withdrawal in late 1987 (after the Wall Street crash).

Safdie's activities in Canada resumed in 1980 when he won the limited competition for the Quebec Museum of Civilization in Quebec City, completed in 1987 (with Belzile Brassard Gallienne Lavoie, Sungur Incesulu, and Desnoyers Mercure). This was followed by the National Gallery of Canada (completed in 1988), the Montreal Museum of Fine Arts (projected completion in 1991), the Toronto Ballet Opera House (Fig. 5) (an international competition, projected completion in 1992), and the Ottawa City Hall (a national competition, projected completion in 1991). Other public buildings were pursued elsewhere: the Hebrew Union College Cultural Center for American Jewish Life and Skirball Museum in Los Angeles (projected completion in 1991), and the Holocaust Memorial for Children in Jerusalem (completed in 1987).

In a paper given at Harvard in 1981, "Monumentality and the City," Safdie explored the structuring and orienting devices of ancient cities, the design of public processional routes and the main public monuments, as differentiated from the general fabric of the city. He proposed the relevant lessons in the National Gallery in Ottawa, in the design for the Supreme Court of Israel, in the Ballet Opera House in Toronto, and in the Ottawa City Hall. All of these buildings were conceived as components of the primary spine of the city, their public rooms forming extensions and important symbolic nodes.

Safdie has had an ongoing commitment to architectural education. He taught at McGill University, followed by the Davenport Professorship of Architecture at Yale (1972–1973). He served as director of the Desert Research and Environment Department at Ben Gurion University,

Figure 5. Toronto Ballet Opera House, Toronto, Ontario. Photograph by Steve Rosenthal.

Beersheva, Israel, and from 1978 to the present, he has been on the Harvard faculty as director of Urban Design and now as an Ian Woodner professor. He has also lectured to academic and lay groups throughout the world.

Safdie has been honored in Canada with the Order of Canada, honorary doctorates from both McGill and Laval universities, Massey Medal for Architecture, Lieutenant Governor's Gold Medal, the Canadian Architect Award for Excellence, the Mt. Scopus Award of the Montreal Chapter of the Friends of Hebrew University, and the Prize for Excellence in Architecture of the Quebec Order of Architects. His honors in Israel include the Rechter Prize for Architecture. In the United States, his awards include the Gold Star Award from the Philadelphia College of Art, the Synergy Award, the Urban Design Concept Award by the U.S. Department of Housing and Urban Development, the International Design Award in Urban Design by the American Society of Interior Designers, a Merit Award from the Pennsylvania–Delaware Chapter of the American Society of Landscape Architects, and the Tau Sigma Delta Gold Medal for Distinction in Design. His current practice and residence are in Boston and Cambridge, respectively, with offices in Jerusalem, Toronto, and Montreal.

BIBLIOGRAPHY

1. M. Safdie, *Form and Purpose,* Houghton Mifflin Co., New York, 1982.

General References

M. Safdie, *Beyond Habitat,* MIT Press–Tundra Books, Cambridge, Mass., 1970

M. Safdie, *For Everyone a Garden,* MIT Press, Cambridge, Mass., 1974.

M. Safdie, *Habitat Bill of Rights,* Ministry of Housing, Imperial Government of Iran, 1976.

M. Safdie, *The Harvard Jerusalem Studio,* MIT Press, Cambridge, Mass., 1986.

M. Safdie, *Beyond Habitat by Twenty Years,* Tundra Books, Montreal, Canada, 1987.

M. Safdie, *Jerusalem: The Future of the Past,* Houghton Mifflin Co., Boston–Optimum Press, Montreal, Canada, 1989.

M. Safdie, "Moshe Safdie: Building in Context," No. *Process Architecture,* 56 (Feb. 1985).

M. Safdie, "Private Jokes in Public Places," *Atlantic Monthly,* Vol. 248 No. 6 (Dec. 1981).

MOSHE SAFDIE AND
ASSOCIATES INC. ARCHITECT
Somerville, Massachusetts

SALVADORI, MARIO

Mario Salvadori, engineer, educator, and author was born in Rome, Italy, on March 19, 1907. Educated in Italy, he received his civil engineering doctoral degree from the University of Rome in 1930 and a degree in pure mathematics in 1933. As a student he became a life member of the Italian Alpine Club (1932).

Some time after finishing school, Salvadori emigrated to the United States. He was a consultant to the Manhattan Project from 1942 to 1944. In 1948, he received the Moisseieff Award of the American Society of Civil Engineers, and in 1953, he received the Wason medal of the American Concrete Institute. He was a member of the faculty of both the architectural and civil engineering programs at Columbia University. He has also taught at the University of Rome, in both architecture and engineering, and at the Princeton University School of Architecture. In 1954, he was named Honorary Professor at the University of Minas Gerais in Brazil. He is the James Renwick Professor Emeritus of Civil Engineering at Columbia University, and he received an honorary Doctor of Science from the university in 1978.

Salvadori has developed courses on why buildings stand up and taught teachers and students from kindergarten through high school in the public schools of New York City since 1972. His methodology has been featured in newspapers, on radio, and on television, and has been adopted by schools all over the United States and abroad.

In addition to teaching, he is the author of many books in applied mathematics, eight books on structures and architecture, and *Building from Caves to Skyscrapers* (1). His writing has been translated into many foreign languages. In addition to the books, Salvadori has published over 150 technical papers in several countries. He is also known for his translation of the poems of Emily Dickinson into Italian.

As an engineer, he has been involved in many projects, and was chairman of the board of the engineering consulting firm Weidlinger Associates in New York City. He is a fellow of the American Society of Mechanical Engineers, New York Academy of Sciences, and the American Concrete Institute.

Salvadori is a popular speaker and has lectured extensively on engineering, architectural, and mathematical subjects as well as on technology and society, on creativity in art and science, and on the Italian underground movement of World War II.

BIBLIOGRAPHY

1. M. Salvadori, *Building from Caves to Skyscrapers*, Macmillan, New York, 1985.

General References

M. Salvadori, *Structure in Architecture*, 3rd ed., Prentice Hall, Englewood Cliffs, N.J., 1986.

M. Salvadori, *Why Buildings Stand Up*, W. W. Norton, New York, 1980.

See also WEIDLINGER, PAUL

DAVID GUISE
New York, New York

SANT'ELIA, ANTONIO

The Italian architect Antonio Sant'Elia was born in 1888 in Como, and studied in Milan and in Bologna at the Scuola de Belli Arti. Although he was killed in action during World War I at Monfalcone in 1916, he is remembered for his proposals for a new architecture recorded in his work from 1912 to 1914. He was identified with the futurist movement in Italy, and his work shows the influence of the Viennese work of that time. He shared the antihistoric quality and the search for new directions that inspired the international art nouveau architects at the turn of the century.

Italy began its industrial development after 1900. The futurist movement was an attempt to relate the arts to the developing industrial world. The first futurist manifesto written by Filippo Tommaso Marintetti (1876–1944) in 1909 appealed to painters and sculptors in Italy. In 1910, five young Italian artists published their *Technical Manifesto of Futurist Painting* in Milan. The work of Umberto Boccioni, Giacomo Balla, and Gino Severini are the most typical of the futurist artists of movement and action. Exhibiting in Paris, they were not treated kindly by the art critics. The future belonged to cubism as exemplified in the prewar work of Pablo Picasso (1881–1973) and Georges Braque (1882–1963).

In 1914, Sant'Elia and Mario Chiattone published their *Futurist Manifesto of Architecture,* which took issue with the influence of the architects of other countries on the Italian "Liberty" architects, and called for a new futurist architecture. The language of the manifesto was stirring. "Get hold of picks, axes, hammers, and demolish, demolish without pity the venerated cities." The new city would rise in "concrete, glass and iron, without painting and without sculpture, enriched solely by the innate beauty of its lines and projections, extremely 'ugly' in its mechanical simplicity" (1).

However, the evidence of Sant'Elia's work shows his understanding of German and Austrian theories. Comparison may be made between Sant'Elia's work and that of Erich Mendelsohn (1887–1953) of that period. The futurist proposals recorded in Sant'Elia's 1912–1914 "Citta Nuova" drawings suggested a future direction for urban architecture. Because of his death at age 28, his drawings were little studied until the 1930s. The archives of his work in the Museo Civico at Como ensure his fame because of his vision of the industrial and commercial cities of the future. Skyscrapers with setbacks, traffic on multiple levels, and curved buildings for commercial and industrial use were prophetic. The studies for various building types and urban forms were recorded in drawings of high quality. These drawings have assured Sant'Elia a place in the history of architecture and urban planning.

His inability to actually build in his short life left an image of great talent and almost science-fiction architecture. Speculation on what he might have achieved if he had lived is recorded by Robert Hughes. He guesses that Sant'Elia might have become Mussolini's favorite architect (2).

The futurist movement was not a dominant movement in European art. Despite their many manifestos, the Italian artists were not the leaders of new art. Some feel they were rejected because their propaganda was not altogether fulfilled in their work. Rather, the cubist artists in France and such architects as Le Corbusier became the leaders of the early twentieth century. The rise of fascism in Italy caused a decline of interest in Italian art of the twentieth century until after World War II. Now futurist work is valued for its commitment and willingness to grapple with contemporary subjects. Futurist art is now exhibited in museums, and Sant'Elia's reputation seems secure.

BIBLIOGRAPHY

1. A. Sant'Elia and M. Chiatonne, *Futurist Manifesto of Architecture,* Milan, 1914. See U. Apollonio, ed., *The Futurist Manafestos,* Viking, New York, 1973.
2. R. Hughes, *The Shock of the New,* Alfred A. Knopf, New York, 1981, p. 170.

General References

S. Giedion, *Space, Time and Architecture,* Harvard University Press, Cambridge, Mass. 1941, and later editions.
S. Kostoff, *A History of Architecture: Settings and Rituals,* Oxford University Press, New York, 1985.

ROBERT T. PACKARD, AIA
Reston, Virginia

SASAKI, HIDEO

Hideo Sasaki (b. 1919) is an American-born landscape architect of Japanese descent. He became a very influential teacher during his long career in landscape architecture. His approach to design integrated the disciplines of planning, landscape architecture, and architecture. His work is recognized by strong geometric forms articulated by the rich application of plant material. Pavilions and/or sculptural fountains are often present in his designs. In Sasaki's corporate, campus, and resort-community plans the intention is always to establish a coherent network of designed landscaped spaces.

Sasaki's aesthetic is based on a heritage of Japanese landscape design. A reverence for the void is apparent in his work and was well suited to the aesthetic of the modern movement. The desire to preserve honesty in the medium led Sasaki to an approach that idealized the natural condition of the land. The statement of this condition in the development of his landscape design schemes set up a natural tension between the site and the buildings, which were superimposed onto the landform. This condition of tension strengthens the unity that is established between the building, structure, and landscape. Sasaki is recognized by his attention to scale, his concern for site and contextual issues, and his ability to create a very human condition in his designs.

Sasaki believes in developing a strong conceptual base for his design. The concept originates from a clear realization of the full potential of the site. In order to execute his conceptual notions, Sasaki exercises to its fullest the potential of the site. He then reinforces his conceptual statement through the careful placement and location of introduced design elements, such as fountains, sculpture, and

natural elements. The composition as a whole is meant to imply a conceptual thought process that ultimately creates a reality.

Hideo Sasaki was born in Reedley, California, a small town 20 miles south of Fresno, on November 25, 1919. He received his primary and secondary school education in California. At the age of about 19 he enrolled at the University of California at Los Angeles to study architecture. He later transferred to Berkeley. He was a student at Berkeley during the declaration of war with Japan. This was a very difficult time for Japanese Americans, particularly those living in California.

Sasaki ended his studies at Berkeley in 1941. In 1943 he continued his education at the Central YMCA College in Chicago. He finally received his Bachelor of Fine Arts degree in landscape architecture from the University of Illinois in 1946, graduating with highest honors. In 1948 he received his Master's degree in landscape architecture from Harvard University.

In 1948 he returned to the University of Illinois to accept a position on the landscape architecture faculty. From 1950 to 1952 he taught at the Harvard Graduate School of Design. On December 23, 1951 Hideo Sasaki married Kisa Noguch. The Sasakis have raised two children. In 1952 he returned to the University of Illinois. In 1953 Harvard University offered Sasaki the position of Chairman of the Landscape Architecture Program. He accepted the offer and remained in the position of Chairman until 1970. During this time he also served as a member of the United States Commission of Fine Arts and on the Advisory Committee for Arts and Architecture, John F. Kennedy Memorial Library.

Sasaki's professional career began with his partnership in Sasaki, Walker Associates (1952–1966). His professional practice continued under the name Sasaki, Dawson, Demay Associates from 1966 to 1978. From 1978 to the present, he has practiced under the firm name of Sasaki Associates, with his main office in Watertown, Massachusetts. In addition, he has maintained associated offices in Toronto and San Francisco.

Throughout his professional career Sasaki has been involved in a wide variety of projects. He has worked on small- and large-scale building and grounds renovations and restorations, urban design developments, building design and siting problems, and open civic space. The diversity of his work can be demonstrated in three of his most significant works: The John Deere Administrative Center in Moline, Illinois, 1959–1980; Copley Square Development Plan, Boston, Massachusetts, 1966–1970; and Greenacre Park, New York, New York, 1972 (Fig. 1).

In the John Deere Administrative Center, Sasaki developed the site plan in collaboration with building architects, Eero Saarinen and Associates. The site was carefully selected, with a high priority set on its inherent natural beauty. Sasaki was acting on the philosophy that the landscape and the architecture should at the same time be in tension and a part of one another when he sited the main administrative building. The building acts as both a dam and bridge that traverses a depression in the site. The building's placement creates a large lake to the east, providing natural views out over the lake from all

Figure 1. Greenacre Park, New York City, 1972. Photograph by Darrell Meyer.

the offices on the eastern elevation. From the interior the perception of vehicular site circulation and parking is kept to a minimum. All of the roadways and parking areas are obscured by the landform and vegetation. During the initial site development, more than 1000 trees were planted. For 20 years, Sasaki visited the site annually to consult on additions and adjustments to the landscape. New site features, including a Henry Moore sculpture and Japanese garden, have been added with the intention of complementing and enriching the existing character of the site. The John Deere Administrative Center is considered to be a classic landscape design. It set the standard for its type and is referred to by landscape architects as the model for corporate park development.

In the late 1960s, the Boston Redevelopment Agency sponsored a national design competition to reorganize and renovate the Copley Square area in Boston. Out of 650 entries, the Sasaki, Dawson and Demay submission was selected as the winning solution.

Copley Square is surrounded by a number of significant architectural edifices: H. H. Richardson's Trinity Church, McKim, Mead and White's Public Library, The Copley Plaza Hotel, and the New Old South Church. Sasaki, Dawson and Demay's solution unified the grandeur of the buildings. It created an uncluttered open space to act as an important pedestrian link and public gathering space. The plaza was sunken to protect it from the visual impact and noise of the surrounding streets. A fountain, pool, planted embankment, and trees were introduced to the site to provide a restful oasis in a rapidly growing urban environment.

Greenacre Park, which is located on Manhattan's East Side, was developed as a "vest-pocket park" in a very dense urban environment. The park, no larger than a tennis court, provides seating areas at several levels. The central seating area is elevated above the adjacent street. A small sculptural fountain is located near the street entrance to the park to serve as an invitation to enter and to mask the noise of the surrounding vehicular traffic. The site design centers on a relief sculpture executed in granite on an interior end wall. A waterfall washes over its surface and produces a strong visual focus. Trellises covered with honey locust provide a protective canopy from

the sun and screen the view of the surrounding buildings. The design was developed to accommodate year-round pedestrian use.

Hideo Sasaki has had an important impact on the landscape profession both as an educator and practitioner, and a profound influence on U.S. landscape in the second half of the twentieth century.

BIBLIOGRAPHY

General References

"Back Bays Sedate Square," *Architectural Forum* **133**(3), 60–63 (1970).

"Deere and Company Administrative Center," *Landscape Architecture* (9), 606–607 (1981).

H. Sasaki, "Thought on Education in Landscape Architecture," *Landscape Architecture* **40**(4), 158–160 (1950).

See also LANDSCAPE ARCHITECTURE

CLARK LUNDELL
Auburn University
Auburn, Alabama

SCARPA, CARLO

At the time of his death in 1978 at the age of 72, Carlo Scarpa was at the height of his fame and influence. His buildings and projects were being studied by architects and students throughout the world, and his decorative style had become a model for architects wishing to revive craft and luscious materials in the contemporary manner. Yet Scarpa remains an enigmatic character in the history of modern architecture and design. His work does not submit easily to explanation and analysis, despite attempts by numerous architects and historians, nor is it particularly photogenic.

Scarpa was born in Venice on June 2, 1906, the son of an elementary school teacher. When he was 2 years old the family moved to Vicenza where he attended the Technical High School. In 1919, after the death of his mother, the Scarpa family returned to Venice, where Carlo attended the Royal Academy of Fine Arts. After receiving his diploma in 1926, Scarpa began teaching architectural drawing at the Academy. He never completed a full-scale architectural eduction and was never recognized as an architect (he was once accused, but was exonerated, of practicing architecture without a license).

During the late 1920s and 1930s Scarpa became acquainted with a number of influential intellectual figures in Italy and abroad. Massimo Bontempelli, Carlo Carrà, and Arturi Martini became his friends. It was during this time that he also began a relationship with the Venini Glass Works in Venice, for whom he created many designs. He painted avidly during this period in a *novecento* style reminiscent of Mario Sironi and Carrà. Also during the late 1920s, Scarpa began his career as an interior designer and industrial designer.

His first important commission was the 1935 restoration and renovation of the School of Economics at the University of Venice, in the Cà Foscari. This project was a portent of the future, with elegant glass, metal, and wood details subtly integrated into the architecture of medieval Venice. Various commissions for renovations followed, along with many installations of exhibitions in galleries and museums. In the 1930s, Scarpa's reputation remained local; he enjoyed none of the national recognition of many of the Milanese and Roman architects such as Albini, Libera, Pagano, and Terragni.

It was after World War II that Scarpa's reputation grew to international proportions. His works after the war began to show the increasing influence of the work of Frank Lloyd Wright, as well as that of Josef Hoffmann, whom Scarpa had met in the middle 1930s. In 1951 the awarding of an honorary degree to Wright by the University of Venice enabled Scarpa to meet the American architect, whom he idolized. (It is said that he prostrated himself before Wright on their first meeting). Scarpa was influential in gaining Wright the (ill-fated) commission for the Masieri Foundation building, which was to have been built along the Grand Canal in Venice.

The first important commission of this period was the renovation of the Accademia Museum in Venice, located in an old convent. This project was the first of Scarpa's museum renovations to exhibit a "minimalist" style within historic buildings, a style that allows the existing context to pass beneath and behind the new work without being disturbed. The extraordinary care in the execution of handrails, floor patterns, benches, door pulls, and the like set Scarpa's work apart from others of his generation. It was not the invention of spatial themes with which he was involved, but rather the manipulation of materials in relation to the human body. His work greatly influenced that of other Italian interior designers, most notably Franco Albini.

He remained a teacher at the University of Venice throughout the early postwar period, but began to receive commissions that would become his masterpieces. The most important are the Canova Plaster Cast Gallery in Possagno (Treviso) (1955–1957); the Castelvecchio Museum in Verona (1956 onward) perhaps his most significant masterpiece; the Olivetti showroom in Piazza S. Marco, Venice (1957–1958); the Querini-Stampalia Foundation in Venice (1961–1963); the Brion Tomb in San Vito d'Altivole (Treviso) (1969); and the Banca Popolare di Verona in Verona, begun by Scarpa in 1973 and finished after his death by Arrigo Rudi.

In the Querini-Stampalia Scarpa began by redesigning the traditional Venetian footbridge. Here the bridge is a kind of leaf-spring of steel carrying a plank floor, with black steel supports holding a lacquered wooden handrail. The interior of the ground floor of the renovation contains channels that control and divert the water (the so-called *aqua alta*) that periodically floods Venetian houses. A carefully considered and elegant play of rough concrete and more precious materials raises the concrete to the level of a more aulic material.

It is in the Castelvecchio Museum in Verona that Scarpa's delicate handling of ancient buildings comes to its highest achievement. Here floor patterns and materials interact to form a tactile play of pliant versus hard surfaces. The new is held apart from the old by reveal-joints and spatial slots that function as miniature conceptual "moats," and each work of art is lovingly held up to view by a stand or a bracket that is almost human in its anthropomorphic configuration.

Scarpa resisted the postmodern and neorationalist influences of the 1970s, preferring to elaborate a decorative system derived from the materials of modern architecture used in a craft tradition. He was in constant touch with his artisans, and his drawings were revised almost daily to reflect a preindustrial attention to old methods of construction.

Like many Renaissance architects, Scarpa rarely got to build an entire building. The exception of this is the Brion Tomb complex in the cemetery at San Vito d'Altivole (Treviso), considered by some to be his most fecund and important work. It is a complex and difficult work, filled with symbolic gestures and a myriad of interlocking forms. The major elements are an arched bridge that shades the tombs of the Brion spouses, a family tomb, and a chapel. Scarpa's emblematic step motif and interlocking circular windows are the dominant leitmotifs of the details in this project, along with a typical use of concrete with more precious materials.

The Brion cemetery was the culmination of Scarpa's career, and he is appropriately buried there. He fell to his death accidentally in Japan in 1978.

BIBLIOGRAPHY

General References

"Carlo Scarpa," *Architecture and Urbanism,* extra ed. (Oct. 1985).

M. A. Crippa, *Carlo Scarpa, Theory, Design, Projects,* MIT Press, Cambridge, Mass., 1986.

F. Dal Co and G. Mazzariol, *Carlo Scarpa, the Complete Works,* Electa/Rizzoli, New York, 1984.

V. Gregotti and coworkers, "Carlo Scarpa, Frammenti, 1926–1978," *Rassegna* (July 1981).

THOMAS L. SCHUMACHER
University of Maryland
College Park, Maryland

SCHAROUN, HANS

Hans Scharoun, architect and town planner, was born in 1893 in Bremen, in what is today the Federal Republic of Germany. He was the second of three sons in the family of a businessman. In the first year of his life, his family settled in Bremerhaven, Bremen's satellite on the North Sea, which at the time was developing into an international port. In 1912 he moved to Berlin, then Germany's capital, to study architecture at the Technische Hochschule Berlin–Charlottenburg, today Technische Universität Berlin. In 1914 he interrupted his studies to volunteer for service in World War I. Both his brothers died in the war. He was assigned to a military building bureau in East Prussia as an assistant of Paul Kruchen, who had been his teacher in Berlin, and for whom he had been working there occasionally since 1913.

After the war, Scharoun did not return to Berlin to finish his studies, but remained in East Prussia. In 1919, he opened a private office in the city of Insterburg (today called Tschernjachowsk and in the boundaries of the USSR). In 1925, he was appointed a professor at the Staatliche Akademie für Kunst und Kunstgewerbe (State Academy of Fine and Applied Arts) in Breslau (today the Polish city of Wroclaw) and moved there subsequently. This school was closed in 1932. From 1926 to 1932, he was in partnership with Alfons Rading, with offices in Berlin. During this period, he belonged to a select group of German avant garde architects, artists, and intellectuals, and he was an active member of their associations. With the rise of Nazism, he decided to retire from public life. In 1932, he opened an office of his own in Berlin. There he survived the Third Reich almost without work.

After World War II, Scharoun continued his work as an independent architect and town planner from his Berlin office until his death in 1972. In addition, he held a number of public offices and honorary posts. He was Stadtrat (a city council member); director of the Abteilung Bau- und Wohnungswesen (Department of Building and Housing) of the city of Berlin, and member of the Planungskollektiv (a planning group), 1945–1946; professor of town planning at the Technische Universität Berlin, 1946–1958; director of the Institut für Bauwesen of the Deutsche Akademie der Wissenschaften (Institute of Architecture of the German Academy of Sciences), East Berlin, 1947–1950; and president of the Akademie der Künste (Arts Academy), West Berlin, 1955–1968.

Scharoun is a leading figure of the German architectural scene of the twentieth century and of the international modern movement. He is best known to a wider public only for his later works, such as his Concert Hall for the Berlin Philharmonic Orchestra in West Berlin (1956–1963). It is also only in the last decades, since the reevaluation of German organic architecture as a fundamental tendency within the modern movement, that he has received adequate recognition by the critics. The study of his work has only begun, and some aspects, such as his projects as a town planner, have not even been considered at all until now.

The evaluation of the German organic tendency has not yet been brought to a satisfactory conclusion. It is still extremely polarized, as it was from the beginning in the effervescent days of the Weimar Republic between the World Wars. In that period, its opposite, the rationalist tendency within the modern movement, was more successful.

In the years after World War I the protagonists of the discussion were the German avant garde architects, those who later were to become some of the major figures of the international scene. They were then united in associations such as the Novembergruppe, an artistically radical group founded in 1918; the Arbeitsrat für Kunst, a political group associated with the revolutionary Arbeiter- und Soldatenräte, which emerged in 1918 from the crisis of the war; the Gläserne Kette, founded in 1919, a "glass chain" of expressionists with the aim of exchanging ideas through circulars; and Der Ring, the largest of all, an interest and pressure group of modern architects, which existed from 1926 to 1933, that succeeded in its struggle against the established conservative circles for public appointments and commissions.

In these groups such disparate architects as Otto Bartning, Walter Gropius, Hugo Häring, Erich Mendelsohn, and Ludwig Mies van der Rohe, all of them born in the 1880s, met with some elder colleagues and a few younger architects born in the 1890s, such as Scharoun, as well as some artists and critics. What united them was a common feeling for the historical situation and of the need to overcome what they perceived as a bourgeois preindustrial society and its culture and to build up a new art and architecture, akin to the social and economic conditions of modern times. There was, in addition, the necessity of joint action because of the weakness inherent in intellectuals acting individually.

The total standstill of construction after 1918 condemned the architects to a long period of search without the prospect of realization. This was the time of the expressionists, whose media were texts, drawings, sketches, sculptures, and very few buildings. Building activity notably increased after 1924. The opportunity to build now brought the feasibility of realization to the foreground of the design; it became the time of the rationalists. Between 1924 and 1930, most of the buildings today considered typical of the early modern movement in Germany were realized, and most of these were by members of Der Ring. These buildings, together with similar ones from other countries, were soon consecrated as the "international style" and widely publicized by Siegfried Giedion, Henry Russell Hitchcock, and others.

The declaration of modern architecture as a degenerated art by the Nazis, the prosecution of every kind of progressive elements, and the closing of many architectural schools and associations resulted in the retreat of modern architects from public life in Germany. The most prominent figures emigrated, mostly to the United States, where they soon acquired positions in accordance with their international renown. The younger and less famous architects had fewer problems with staying. Scharoun was one of the few prominent architects who opted for "internal emigration," ie, for staying in Germany and holding out in the background.

After World War II, Scharoun was the most important prewar architect in Germany who had neither left nor cooperated with the Nazis. And he was, in 1945, already 52 years old. Thus he was treated with honor. However, he had no opportunities to build until the mid-1950s. In the first years after the war, the reconstruction of the cities demanded cheap ways of building. Scharoun's architecture was either considered unbuildable or too expensive to build. Thus he had to wait until the beginning of the country's "economic miracle" to finally get the chance to demonstrate the contrary. Then, from the mid-1950s onward, he realized the language of organic architecture as he had developed it in the previous decades.

Scharoun's development as an architect had begun

early. He participated in competitions even as a school-boy. The models he preferred then came from nonacademic central and northern European regional architecture of medieval character and from the *Jugendstil*. His drawings of the time already show his preference for strong and expressive forms, and his typical sense for dramatic articulation of masses, with lower, subordinated elements added irregularly around a tall and massive dominant body.

As an architectural student he soon acquired the recognition of older architects and participated in their activities. His sketches from the years following 1918 show him inspired by expressionists such as Mendelsohn, with the same way of handling masses as in the early drawings, but now with strongly polychrome crystalline bodies. His competition projects were more controlled and show him trying functional approaches, shaping his floor plans according to the flow of the circulation, to the specific form of the different rooms, and to crystalline elements that he favored for the main halls.

In the 1920s, Scharoun's projects were influenced by the rationalists, specifically by Gropius and Mies van der Rohe, the leading figures of the time. From them he adopted their sense for an economic construction based on the use of simple orthogonal grids in the plans and sections. While doing so, he did not aim at the same cool, geometrically reduced, and repetitive aesthetics. On the contrary, he maintained his preference for a differentiated design, in accordance with the flexibility of the artisanlike ways of building common at the time, wherever this did not seem to complicate the structural system. Thus he earned the rationalists' criticism; they considered him to be lacking in determination and consistency.

The first of Scharoun's mature buildings date from these years. He acquired his main commissions because of his connections with Der Ring. These were the house for the 1927 Werkbund exposition at the Weissenhof in Stuttgart, FRG; the apartment house at the Kaiserdamm in West Berlin from 1929; the hostel at the 1929 Werkbund exposition in Breslau (Wroclaw); the general plan and the housing project at Siemensstadt in West Berlin from 1930; and the Schminke house in Löbau, GDR, from 1933.

In the Siemensstadt his three buildings were the only irregular ones in the whole complex: one formed a circle's segment; the one at the Jungfernheideweg was composed of staggered blocks; and the third, the only almost straight body—Scharoun lived in it himself for several decades—lay forming a sharp angle to the Jungfernheideweg. All of the buildings were of standardized, economical construction, but the facades show a diversity of window openings, balconies, and parapets, corresponding to the functional diversity behind the facades which Scharoun intended to accentuate. The expressiveness is evident, despite the relative geometric simplicity of the blocks and the uniformity of the white plastered facade surfaces (Fig. 1).

The rationalists' criticism of Scharoun's architecture was a symptom of profound ideological divergences. Indeed, their aesthetic approaches corresponded to completely antagonistic philosophical positions, and the one cannot be understood from the position of the other.

The aesthetics of the rationalists were based on formal canons, on the laws of proportions and on the geometric bodies considered to be perfect; the sphere, cube, cylinder, prism, and pyramid. Le Corbusier explicitly recommended the use of these canons in order to achieve beauty in architecture. Design thus consisted in reducing the functional and constructive requirements to such ideal forms. Such a method implied the faith in the universal validity of laws preexisting the material world. This marked the rationalists as typical idealists, in the philosophical sense.

In opposition to this, Scharoun's interest did not lie in reducing functional complexity, but in expressing it. He accepted geometry only where it seemed to be indispensable and part of the essence of his task. In fact, he did not believe in any formal recipes and considered the confrontation with function and construction to be the only possible way to discover something formally essential. Such a

Figure 1. Siemensstadt housing-estate, block Jungfernheideweg, West Berlin, 1929–1932. Courtesy of Manuel Cuadra.

belief in the material world as the only point of departure shows Scharoun to have been a basically materialistically thinking artist.

Thus the differences between rationalism and what was to become the organic tendency were those of two worlds existing parallel to one another. Seen this way, neither is better then the other, and Scharoun's Breslau exposition building and his Schminke house are, as important examples, to early organic architecture what the Bauhaus building and the Villa Savoye are to rationalism. All of these buildings are brilliant realizations of the early modern movement.

Other materialistically thinking architects were Hannes Meyer and Hugo Häring. Meyer considered construction and Häring function in an extended sense to be the points of departure. Scharoun soon discovered his affinity to Häring, whom he had known since their Der Ring meetings. Scharoun's development was, from the 1930s onward, marked by Häring's theories. In fact, in a way Scharoun's architecture of the next decades can be considered as an architectural complement to the theoretical work of Häring, who did not build much himself.

Häring saw himself clearly as an opponent of the rationalists, and Le Corbusier was his main adversary. He recognized the absolute incompatibility of his ideas with those of the rationalists. He invented a new vocabulary to better differentiate his thinking from that of the rationalists. He spoke of architecture as part of the past and of his *Neues Bauen* (new building) as its contemporary substitute. He rejected any formal canon and saw his *Neues Bauen* as based exclusively on the empiric comprehension of the task. He dismissed any idea of design as giving a building form and insisted on the necessity of a *Gestaltfindung*, of the finding of a Gestalt as the unity of content and form inherent to every building task. He did not consider beauty as a goal for architecture, but the finding of the essence of the task, in all its material and spiritual dimensions. In a first phase he defined the *Leistungsform*, form in accordance to function, as his goal. Then he extended his idea of functionalism, finally substituting for it the idea of organicism, and putting the comprehension of genetic processes at the basis of his theory. Buildings had to become organs in order to correspond to the organic essence of humans as parts of nature.

These theories of Häring were part of a larger philosophy, which convinced Scharoun, stimulating him to go further in developing what *Neues Bauen* could be. From the 1930s onward his projects show a growing complexity, spatially, formally, and constructively. Simultaneously, they avoided any pretentiousness or perfection. In this phase he built his main works: the Baensch house in West Berlin, 1935; the Romeo and Juliet apartment houses in Stuttgart, 1954–1959; the Geschwister-Scholl-Gymnasium in Lünen, FRG, a school built from 1956 to 1962; and the Concert Hall for the Berlin Philharmonic Orchestra in West Berlin, built from 1956 to 1963.

A comparison of his housing project in the Siemensstadt with the Romeo and Juliet apartment houses illustrate both the different historical situation and Scharoun's development. Romeo and Juliet, two tall buildings, are part of an ensemble. Romeo is a 19-story compact tower; Juliet is a lower, U-shaped terraced buildings. Shops and garages unite them on the ground floor. Juliet in particular has an extremely irregular appearance, although it consists of apartments with typical floor plans and facade-detail solutions. Scharoun searched here simultaneously for a repetitive economic construction and an individualization of the apartments in the small scale and an expressive form in the large scale. For the building as a whole, he developed the idea of a tall building as a tree to live in. He saw in such towers the chance of new landmarks for modern cities. Scharoun was successful in demonstrating both that his projects could be realized at normal prices and that his language was formally convincing for a broader public tired by the sterility of widespread uniform housing towers (Fig. 2).

The Concert Hall for the Berlin Philharmonic Orchestra—the Philharmonie—perhaps Scharoun's most complex and ambitious realization, best represents his understanding of architecture as an answer to the spiritual and material dimensions of the building task. In such a concept the fulfillment of functional and constructive requirements was merely a rudimentary point of departure.

The central ideas of his design came from the understanding of the event taking place: of the individuals coming to the building, searching and finding the entrance, entering it, going into the concert hall, gathering there and forming groups, constituting a community of spectators in front of the community of musicians, communicating with these and among themselves, sharing the musical performance, being moved each person in his or her own right and all together. Considering this, the Philharmonie appears completely congruent, with the closed appearance of the concert hall from the outside, the small entrances, the intricate passages around the hall, the spaciousness of the concert hall itself, the organization of the public in terraces around the orchestra, the slightly shifted orientation of these terraces.

With great sensitivity, Scharoun recreated the personal and social situations that he had identified as being inherent parts of the event to take place. His architecture became an expression of the community and gave, at the

Figure 2. "Romeo and Juliet" apartment houses, Stuttgart, FRG, 1954–1959. Courtesy of Manuel Cuadra.

same time, each person his own place. Simultaneously, Scharoun's work profoundly corresponded to his personal sense for architectural form, as already mentioned in relation to his early drawings. The Philharmonie showed how profoundly personal and social architecture can take shape in one, thus constituting an excellent materialization of the ideals of the organic movement (Fig. 3).

In the years following the completion of the Philharmonie, Scharoun worked in association with Edgar Wisniewski and designed many additional buildings, including the Staatsbibliothek der Stiftung Preussischer Kulturbesitz in West Berlin, 1967–1978, a large library in front of the Philharmonie; the Deutsches Schiffahrtsmuseum in Bremerhaven, 1970–1975, a ship museum; and the Musikinstrumentenmuseum, 1971–1984, and the Kammermusiksaal, 1971–1988, an instruments museum and chamber music hall, respectively, both in West Berlin and around the Philharmonie.

The Staatsbibliothek, in particular, possesses a character somehow diverging from Scharoun's earlier buildings. It is an impressive building of grandiose inner spaces. Although corresponding to Scharoun's language, it shows a tendency toward monumentality and a material perfection in the detail solutions unusual to him and in disaccord with his principles. An explanation for this is the growing influence of Wisniewski, owing to Scharoun's age and to the fact that it was Wisniewski who finished most of the buildings after Scharoun's death in 1972. Despite this, the high quality of this building is as indisputable as the fact that it presents a realization on the lines established by Scharoun himself (Figs. 4 and 5).

Figure 3. Philharmonie, Concert Hall for the Berlin Philharmonic Orchestra, main entrance, West Berlin, 1956–1963. Courtesy of Manuel Cuadra.

Figure 4. Staatsbibliothek der Stiftung Preussischer Kulturbesitz (National Library of the Prussian Heritage Foundation), main entrance, West Berlin, 1964–1978. Courtesy of Manuel Cuadra.

Figure 5. Staatsbibliothek der Stiftung Preussischer Kulturbesitz (National Library of the Prussian Heritage Foundation), main reading room, West Berlin, 1964–1978. Courtesy of Manuel Cuadra.

BIBLIOGRAPHY

General References

J. C. Bürkle, *Hans Scharoun und die Moderne: Ideen, Projekte, Theaterbau*, Campus, Frankfurt am Main, FRG, 1986.

E. Janofske, *Architektur-Räume: Idee und Gestalt bei Hans Scharoun*, Vieweg, Braunschweig and Wiesbaden, FRG, 1984.

P. B. Jones, *Hans Scharoun*, The Gordon Fraser Gallery, London, 1978.

H. Lauterbach and J. Joedicke, eds., *Hugo Häring: Schriften, Entwürfe, Bauten*, Karl Krämer, Stuttgart, 1965.

P. Pfankuch, ed., *Hans Scharoun: Bauten, Entwürfe, Texte*, Schriftenreihe der Akademie der Künste 10, Gebrüder Mann, West Berlin, 1974.

H. Scharoun, "Struktur in Raum und Zeit" in *Handbuch moderner Architektur*, Safari, West Berlin, 1957, pp. 11–21.

MANUEL CUADRA
Technische Hochschule
Darmstadt
Federal Republic of Germany

SCHINDLER, RUDOLPH M.

Rudolph Michael Schindler's significance as one of the pioneers in the development of modern architecture in the United States has only recently been generally recognized. As with fellow Austrian émigré Richard Neutra, Schindler established his architectural practice on the West Coast, yet his achievements never received the public or professional acclamation given Neutra's work. An avid proponent of modernism, he was opposed to the precepts of functional determinism and favored a more independent position as an architect-as-artist. For Schindler, modern architecture was not a question of creating new types or styles, but one of developing " 'space forms' as a new medium for human expression" (1). His work tended to avoid the stereotyped architectural vocabulary of the international style and exhibited more idiosyncratic explorations in modernist vocabulary and syntax.

Schindler was born in Vienna in 1887 and was educated both as an engineer and an architect, receiving degrees from the Technische Hochschule of Vienna (1911) and the Vienna Akademie der bildenden Künste (1913). While studying at the academy, he worked as an architectural draftsman in the office of Hans Mayr and Theodor Mayer in Vienna. As a young student he was firmly committed to the progressive architectural ideas being advocated by Otto Wagner and Adolf Loos, and their theories and buildings had a lasting influence on his later work. In 1912, Schindler wrote *A Manifesto* in which he argued against the structural and functional origins of architectural styles and in support of an architecture that concerned itself with " 'space' as its raw material and with the articulated room as its product"(2). Loos's enthusiastic response to contemporary architectural development in the United States, along with the publication of Frank Lloyd Wright's highly influential *Ausgefuhrte Bauten und Entwurfe* in 1910 and 1911 (the Wasmuth Folios), led Schindler to leave Vienna for the United States in 1914. After working for the Chicago firm of Ottenheimer, Stern and Reichart, he joined Wright's office in 1917. Schindler's engineering expertise assisted Wright in completing the drawings for the Imperial Hotel in Tokyo, and in time he was called on to supervise the construction of Wright's Hollyhock House for Aline Barnsdall in Los Angeles (1917–1920). His working relationship with Wright was one of mutual respect, and he went on to design two additional residences at the Barnsdall complex while in Wright's employ.

Schindler's experience with Wright's work in California led him to settle on the West Coast and establish his own architectural practice. His house at Kings Road in Los Angeles, designed as a double residence for himself and Clyde Chase, an engineer, was completed in 1922 and served as his home and office until his death in 1953. A highly original and experimental work, Schindler's design was based on each inhabitant having a private retreat directly related to an outdoor living space (Fig. 1). Bedrooms in the form of sleeping porches placed on the roof, a common kitchen, and outdoor fireplaces in the two major patio areas contributed to an unconventional, relaxed living environment for the two married couples that inhabited its unique spaces. With its 4-ft.-wide concrete tilt-slab wall sections separated by 3-in. glass strips, thin internal wood walls, and sliding canvas doors opening onto adjacent outdoor spaces, the R. M. Schindler House was "a marriage between the solid, permanent cave and the open, lightweight tent"(3). His subsequent designs of the early and mid-1920s displayed Wrightian and expressionist in-

Figure 1. Kings Road House, Hollywood, California, 1922.

fluences as he sought to establish his own architectural aesthetic. He continued to experiment with concrete construction during this period, and he frequently combined wood roof framing systems with poured-in-place concrete walls. In his Pueblo Ribera Court, a 12-unit court housing project built in La Jolla (1923), he incorporated a "slab-cast" concrete wall system that utilized a slip-form casting technique similar to one developed earlier by Lloyd Wright in California. Schindler's detailing of the formwork itself resulted in a series of pronounced horizontal joints that gave both scale and texture to the monolithic concrete walls. The site plan for Pueblo Ribera Court had its antecedents in the California bungalow court concept, and Schindler's design, which featured paired L-shaped units, private patios, and generous roof terraces, remains one of the most unique multiunit housing schemes of the period. A system of redwood trellises hovered above each roof terrace to support canvas screens used for shade or privacy, the whole again reflecting Schindler's fascination with the tent–cave analogy in the design of contemporary dwellings.

A reluctance to fully accept the standard balloon frame and stucco sheathing system that dominated residential construction in California sustained Schindler's efforts to explore alternative building technologies. In the John C. Packard House in South Pasadena (1924), he experimented with Gunite construction and produced 1-in.-thick concrete walls with integral concrete wall studs. In the three-level hillside house for James Howe in Los Angeles (1925), he combined a slab-cast system for the lower, earthbound level with a light wooden upper structure. Continuous horizontal joints in the concrete base, along with wide redwood boards separated by specially milled battens, produced a decidedly horizontal articulation that

contrasted with the building's sloped site. The design maintained a uniform scale by the use of "unit lines" both in plan and elevation. Such a unit system, in addition to the pronounced horizontality of the wide board siding, were to become constituent parts of Wright's later Usonian houses of the 1930s, and the Howe House thus stands as a signficant precursor to this entire series of later Wright houses.

The Lovell Beach House at Newport Beach (1925–1926) (Fig. 2) is Schindler's best-known and most-celebrated work. As Schindler's biographer David Gebhard has noted, this extraordinary residence deserves to be ranked with Walter Gropius's Bauhaus at Dessau (1925–1926), Mies van der Rohe's German Pavilion at Barcelona (1929), Neutra's Lovell House in Los Angeles (1929), and Le Corbusier's Villa Savoye at Poissy (1929–1930) as "a key work of twentieth-century architecture" (4). Designed for Dr. Phillip Lovell, who was later to commission Neutra to design his landmark house in Los Angeles (1929), this vacation house fully embraced the ideals of the international style as promulgated by Henry-Russell Hitchcock and Philip Johnson in their "Modern Architecture: International Exhibition" held in 1932 at the Museum of Modern Art in New York. Schindler's design incorporated 5 three-story high, freestanding cast-in-place reinforced concrete frames and a secondary system of wood-framed floors, roofs, and balconies. Prefabricated wood and glass wall units were inserted within the exposed concrete primary structural frame, emphasizing the independence of support and enclosure. In raising the house above the ground with an open lower level, Schindler achieved greater privacy, optimum ocean views, and an explicit expression of the main structural supports. The two-story living room volume was clearly revealed on the building's

Figure 2. Lovell Beach House, Newport Beach, California, 1926.

exterior, and upper level balconies and sleeping porches with smooth, stuccoed parapets wove through and across the concrete frames in a de Stijl-like composition of advancing and receding planes. Despite its conceptual relatedness to international style precepts, however, the Lovell Beach House did not adhere to the orthodox stylistic formula espoused by Hitchcock and Johnson, and it was not included in their seminal exhibition of 1932.

With Schindler's assistance, compatriot Richard Neutra emigrated to the United States in 1923 and eventually moved to California in 1925, after a brief period at Wright's office at Taliesin. Like Schindler, Neutra had been attracted to the United States because of Wright's astonishingly fresh and innovative work. Schindler and Neutra began to collaborate on a number of projects, and they soon formed the Architectural Group for Industry and Commerce (AGIC), a professional organization that ultimately produced a series of interesting but mostly unrealized projects between 1925 and 1931. Their joint entry for the international League of Nations Competition (1926) exhibited constructivist tendencies in its massing and form articulation, and it was included in a traveling exhibition of noteworthy entries. By the end of the 1920s, Schindler's work had moved away from his earlier experiments in concrete and the use of textured surfaces. His designs now incorporated the building industry's more conventional balloon frame and stuccoed surface, along with massing strategies based on intersecting, rather than resolutely singular, volumes. As a result, his buildings displayed a sculptural interlocking of planes and volumes akin to the work of the de Stijl architects Theo van Doesburg and Gerrit Reitveld. The volumetric interdependence of many of Schindler's internal organizations had their origins in Loos's *Raumplan,* or "plan of volumes," concept and interior spaces were often interrelated by means of split-levels (C. H. Wolfe House, Catalina Island, 1928) or double-height primary volumes (R. F. Elliot House, Los Angeles, 1930). In describing the concept for the Wolfe House, he referred to the house as a composition of "space units" floating above the hill, indicating his tendency to avoid a direct merger of dwelling and hillside site.

Unlike Neutra, who was five years younger, Schindler had failed to achieve international recognition by the early 1930s and his exclusion from the important Museum of Modern Art exhibition was a great personal disappointment. In an article titled "Space Architecture," he lambasted the functionalists (whom he accused of totally dismissing architecture as an art). "To make matters worse, and public attention more concentrated, a group of functionalists have given their breed a name: international style. . . . The classical code of set forms for columns, architraves and cornices, is replaced by a stereotyped vocabulary of steel columns, horizontal parapets, and corner windows, all to be used equally both in the jungles and on the glaciers" (5). A number of residential commissions during the 1930s illustrates the restive nature of his architecture in this period. The W. E. Oliver House in Los Angeles (1933) appeared as a flat-roofed, eroded rectangular prism from the street, and yet its garden-side elevation revealed a gabled and shed roof system as well as a roof terrace. One of his most contradictory designs, the Oliver House demonstrated the conceptual ease and compositional skill with which he could juxtapose overtly disparate elements in a "collaged" whole. The John Buck House in Los Angeles (1934) and the W. Delahoyde House, projected for a site in Los Angeles (1935), incorporated ribbon windows and smooth, unadorned surfaces in planar compositions that strongly resembled Neutra's more disciplined residential work of the same period.

But it was in his highly sculptural, complexly profiled compositions that Schindler's design virtuosity was most fluent. His designs for a prototype service station for the Union Oil Company (Los Angeles, 1933), the Victoria McAlmon House (Los Angeles, 1935), and the C. C. Fitzpatrick House (Los Angeles, 1936) all featured interlocking wall planes and roof slabs in complex assemblages of interpenetrating interior and exterior volumes. In keeping with the underlying spatial concepts of his houses, Schindler preferred to design built-in furniture for his interiors, and he developed a "unit furniture" system that enabled him to devise varied combinations of interdependent tables, seating areas, and storage–shelf units. Despite his professed distaste for the international style, his H. Rodakiewicz House in Los Angeles (1937) outwardly shared many of the style's aesthetic attributes. A large, three-story hillside dwelling, the house was a more prismatic composition of unadorned, rectilinear volumes and large window walls with polished metal mullions, but its interior spaces still revealed Schindler's penchant for complexly profiled volumes and varying spatial zones. Designs for several apartment complexes demonstrated Schindler's ability to transpose his developed architectural vocabulary to multiunit housing complexes. The orthogonal interplay of projecting flat roof slabs and recessed wall planes of his apartment building for A. Bubeshko (Los Angeles, 1938 and 1941), for example, was characteristically "Schindleresque," while his projected apartment building for Mrs. S. T. Falk (Los Angeles, 1942), which featured obliquely oriented rooms to achieve optimum views, clearly illustrated his finesse with skewed geometries and shifted volumetric relationships.

Throughout the 1940s and into the 1950s, Schindler's work lacked the architectural control and stylistic consistency of his earlier practice. Recognizing the popularity of a more regional architectural idiom being developed in southern California by a number of architects, he now turned to a greater use of wood, stone, and pitched roofs in his residential work. In his A. V. Dekker House in Canga Park (1940), a series of copper-covered gable and shed roofs, exposed rafters, and interior fieldstone walls reflected a more "woodsy," informal and natural California residential style. His design for the S. Rodriquez House in Glendale (1941) featured varying flat roofs, fieldstone walls, and an overall composition strongly resembling Wright's Usonian houses of the same period. In the Bethlehem Baptist Church in Los Angeles (1944), his only church commission, he utilized a series of stepped, stuccoed wall segments to create an abstract pattern that possessed aesthetic overtones of his work of the late 1920s. By the early 1950s, his buildings were more aggressively discordant. Strains of his earlier spatial and formal investigations were apparent in some of the work of this period (W. Tucker House, Hollywood, 1950), but his architectural inventiveness frequently produced outwardly *ad hoc* assemblages (E. Janson House, Hollywood, 1949).

Schindler's predominantly residential practice, which continued in Los Angeles until his death in 1953, produced two of modern architecture's pioneering works (R. M. Schindler House and Lovell Beach House) along with many projects that made a substantial contribution to the development of contemporary architecture on the West Coast. His architecture had always remained outside the hallowed orthodoxy of the international style (for many, the absolute paragon of modernism), and his independent position was continually sustained by his fervent belief in the fundamentally expressive power of architecture. For Schindler, the functionalists had forgotten that "architecture as an art may have the much more important meaning of serving as a cultural agent—stimulating and fulfilling the urge for growth and extension of our own selves" (1).

BIBLIOGRAPHY

1. D. Gebhard, *Schindler,* Viking Press, New York, 1972, p. 195.
2. Ref. 1, p. 191.
3. Ref. 1, p. 51.
4. Ref. 1, p. 80.
5. Ref. 1, p. 194.

General References

D. Gebhard, *Schindler,* Viking Press, New York, 1972. Includes a complete chronological list of buildings and projects by Schindler as well as a full bibliography.

E. McCoy, "R. M. Schindler," in *Five California Architects,* Praeger, New York, 1975, pp. 149–192.

E. McCoy, *Vienna to Los Angeles: Two Journeys,* Arts & Architecture Press, Santa Monica, Calif., 1979. Includes letters between Schindler and R. Neutra and L. Sullivan.

See also LE CORBUSIER (CHARLES-EDOUARD JEANNERET); NEUTRA, RICHARD; WRIGHT, FRANK LLOYD

GREGORY K. HUNT
Virginia Polytechnic Institute
and State University
Blacksburg, Virginia

SCIENCE CENTERS. See SUPPLEMENT.

SEALANTS

The considerations in sealant selection, application, and joint design are quite numerous; high performance sealants of an elastomeric nature will specifically be treated here. Building sealants are designed for a single purpose: becoming a barrier, that is, preventing the passage of water, air, noise, and dirt. The right sealant for a particular

sealing application is the one that has the necessary adhesive and cohesive characteristics to become the proper seal.

Sealants (1) and adhesives are often grouped together by design professionals because of their shared characteristics. However, adhesives are usually used to hold two or more surfaces together. Sealants are chosen for both strength and adhesion and are more accurately thought of as flexible materials with adhesive capabilities.

Nearly every concrete structure and high-rise building has joints that must be sealed to ensure integrity and serviceability. Satisfactory sealing is not always achieved. The sealant used or its poor installation usually receives the blame for failure observed in the field, whereas there are often deficiencies in the location and design of the joint that make it impossible for any sealant to have done a good job. By combining the right sealant with the proper joint design for a particular application and then carefully installing it, there is every prospect of successfully sealing the joint and keeping it sealed.

Without specific knowledge of the structure, its design, service use, environment, and how much can be spent, it is impossible to prescribe a best joint design or a best sealant. The information and experience contained in this discussion is based on current practices and experience. The correct choice of a suitable joint-sealing system is one that is properly detailed, specified, installed, and maintained.

There are several ways to clarify sealants for comparative purposes. This article specifically categorizes them as rigid or flexible hardening types and nonhardening types, as well as those of a very high performance nature.

Several sealants may be qualified for a specific application after factors involved in selecting a sealant are evaluated. These factors include type of preparation, joint design, service temperature range, durability requirements, cohesive strength, weatherability, abrasion and chemical resistance, flammability, and the consequence of joint failure. Consideration must also be given to the performance and physical properties of the eligible sealants to further narrow the selection (1) (Table 1).

REASONS FOR USE

In order to have a thorough understanding of sealant materials, knowledge of the various types of joint that can be encountered should be described (2). There is movement in all structures, regardless of depth, height, and width. To accommodate or cushion this structural movement there is a need for elastic joints at strategic locations; consideration should also be given to potential torsional, seismic, or vibrational stresses. The dimension and location of joints are directly related to the tolerances of thermal movement characteristics of the various types of substrate that make up the walls and floors.

Concrete Structures

Abnormal volume change, usually permanent expansion, may occur in concrete due to operative time reactions in alkali from the cements, certain additives, and other causes. In glass, expansion and contraction are principally

Table 1. Representative Properties of Sealants[a]

Test Method Sealant Base	Tensile Strength, ASTM D412, psi	Elongation, ASTM D412, %	Durometer, ASTM 676 Shore A	Abrasion Resistance	Operating Temperature, °F	Shrinkage, %
Polysulfide	50–125	150–500	15–60	Fair to good	−60 to 250	0–3.0
Polymercaptan	50–125	150–500	15–50	Good to excellent	−65 to 250	0–3.0
Polyurethane	55–300	250–950	10–50	Excellent	−65 to 200	Nil
Silicone	400–600	250–1000+	10–55	Fair to good	−60 to 550	0–5.0
Neoprene	1000–1500	250–350	30–80	Excellent	−45 to 300	0–10.0
Epoxy, modified	1200–3500	10–20	40–60 Shore D	Good to excellent	−50 to 300	0–3.0
Acrylic	50–400	100–270	5–50	Fair to good	−10 to 300	5.0–15.0
Butyls, mastic type		5–150	5–70	Poor	0 to 200	15–40
Polybutene		5–20	20–40	Poor	−20 to 250	0–3.0

[a] Ref. 1.

cyclical due to expansion and contraction of the glass. The result of these changes are movements, both permanent and transient, of the extremities of the concrete structural unit. If for any reason the contractural movements are excessive or excessively restrained, then cracking may occur within the unit. The restraint of expansion movements may result in distortion and cracking within the units, crushing of their ends, and the transmission of unanticipated forces to abutting units. In most concrete structures, these effects are objectionable from a structural and aesthetic viewpoint. One of the means of minimizing them is to provide joints at which movement can be accommodated without the loss of integrity of the structure.

In many buildings, the concrete serves to support the frame as well as support or frame curtain walls, cladding, doors, windows, partitions, and mechanical and other surfaces. To prevent development of distress in these areas, it is often necessary for them to move to a limited extent independently of overall expansion, contraction, and deflection occurring in the concrete. Joints may also be required to facilitate construction without serving any structural purpose. Creating joint openings, which usually must be sealed in order to prevent passage of gases, liquids, or other unwanted substances into the building, is a severe problem.

Other Issues

Foreign solid matter, including ice, must be prevented from collecting in the open joints; otherwise, the joints cannot close freely and high stress may be generated, damaging the joint. In industrial applications, where there are concrete or tile floor or walls, joint edges often need the protection of a filler-up sealant, often between armored faces to prevent damage from impact of concentrated loads such as steel wheel traffic and women's heels.

The specific function of a sealant is to prevent intrusion of liquids, solids, and gases and to protect the joint from damage. In some applications, secondary functions are thermal and acoustical insulation, dampening vibration,

and prevention of unwanted matter collecting in the crevices. They must often perform their prime function while subject to repeated contraction or expansion as the joint opens and closes and while exposed to heat, moisture, and sunlight as well as unwanted airborne chemicals. The functioning of the sealant depends on the movement to be accommodated at the joint, on the shape of the joint, and on the physical properties of the sealant. Experience in trying to keep joints sealed indicates that joint movement may vary widely from theoretical prediction.

TYPES OF JOINT

Construction Joints

Construction joints (2,3) are created as a matter of "breaking up" lengthy expanses of concrete or other masonry surfaces. The precise location of these joints is predetermined by the architect or design engineer. Construction joints are appropriate only when the net result of the contraction and any subsequent expansion during service is such that the abutting units are always shorter than they were at the time the material was placed. They are frequently used to divide large, relatively thin structural units such as pavements, floors, and retaining and other walls into smaller panels. Construction joints in structures are often called control joints because they are intended to control the crack location. In addition, construction joints may run horizontally and vertically depending on the placing sequence prescribed by the design of that particular structure.

Expansion or Isolation Joints

Expansion or isolation joints (2,3) prevent crushing distortion, including displacement, buckling, and warping of the structure slab, which can be caused by expansion or settlement. They are used primarily to isolate walls from floors or roofs, columns from floors or pavements, and slabs and decks from abutments of various sources.

Contraction Joints

Contraction joints (2,3) are used to control cracking that might occur from the contraction of the various members of the building. Principally placed in concrete slabs, they are used frequently to divide large, relatively thin structural units such as pavements, floors, and retaining walls into smaller panels (Fig. 1).

Movement Joints

Joints (2,3) are generally described according to their function. Movement joint refers to a joint that will expand and contract with a change in temperature. This generally is called a working joint or dymeric joint. Movement joints perform as butt joints or lap joints. Butt joints are designed in the structural unit being formed where they abut each other. Lap or shear joints are used where the surfaces being formed override each other. This generally occurs with metal construction. Any relative movement is one of sliding (Fig. 2).

JOINT CONFIGURATION

In the various schematic joint details for various types of concrete structure shown in Figures 3 and 4, two basic configurations occur from the standpoint of the functioning of the sealant. These are known as butt and lap joints.

First, there are open surface joints, as in pavements and buildings in which the sealant is exposed to outside environmental conditions on at least one face. Second, there are joints, as in containers, dams, and pipelines, in which the primary line of defense against the passage of water is a sealant such as a waterstop or gasket buried deeper in the joint. The functioning, suitability of sealant material, and method of installation are affected by these considerations.

As a joint opens or closes, the sealant must deform in response to the movement without any other change that would adversely affect its ability to maintain the seal. The sealant (2) material behaves in a composite and plastic manner. Which type of action predominates at any time depends on the following:

1. The type and shape of the joint.
2. The movement and rate of movement occurring.
3. Installation and service temperatures.
4. The physical properties of the sealant.

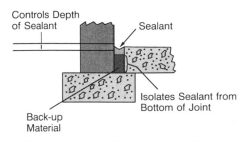

Figure 1. Contraction joint (3). Courtesy of Sealant & Waterproofers Institute.

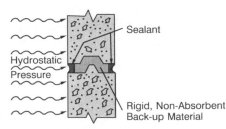

Figure 2. Butt joint—below grade or underwater (3). Courtesy of Sealant & Waterproofers Institute.

Sealants may be classified into two main groups, liquid field-applied and preformed into the required shape within the mold provided at the joint opening. The other preformed sealants are functionally preshaped by the manufacturer, so that only a minimum of site fabrication is necessary for installation. Of concern here are the liquid- or mastic-type consistency sealant.

As a sealed butt joint opens and closes, one of the three functional conditions can exist (Fig. 5).

1. The sealant is always in tension.
2. The sealant is always in compression.
3. The sealant is cyclically in tension and compression.

Where secondary movements occur in either or both of the directions or at right angles to the main movement, including impact at joints under traffic, shear forces occur across the sealant. Except where the secondary movements are relatively large, shear is not a governing criterion for butt joint sealants. The depth (and length) of the sealant required to accommodate the primary movement can more than provide any shear resistance required.

Effect of Installation and Service Temperatures

Changes in temperature between that at installation and the maximum and minimum experiences in service influence sealant behavior. The service range of temperature is not the same as the ambient range. It is the actual temperatures of the slab or other structural mass being joined that govern the magnitude of joint movements and sealant performance. By absorption and transfer of heat from

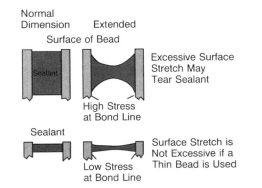

Figure 3. Butt joint. Courtesy of Sealant & Water-Proofers Institute.

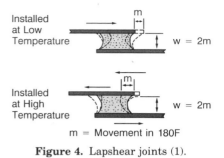

Figure 4. Lapshear joints (1).

the sun and loss due to radiation, etc, depending on the location, exposure, and materials being joined, the difference can be considerable.

Condition 1 above presupposes that the sealant is installed when the joint is in its fully closed position so that thereafter, as the joint opens and closes, the sealant is always extended. Liquid field-applied sealants cannot be used this way and would likely fail as the joint opened in service. Most sealing systems used in open surface joints are, therefore, designed to function under either conditions 2 or 3 to take best advantage of the properties of the available sealant materials.

Malfunctioning of a sealant, intended to function cyclically in tension or compression, may develop with repetitive cycles of stress reversal or under sustained stress, a constant deformation. It must be remembered that while selection of shape factor is essentially based on accommodating cohesive stresses in the sealant, at the same time an adequate area must be provided at the joint face to accommodate adhesive (bond) stress.

JOINT MOVEMENT

The movement potential of a joint is difficult to determine accurately. The estimates of movement in a given number of joints are based on the theoretical approach to structural movement and the job site tolerances of various substrates that affect joint movement and dimension. When it has been decided how much movement is to take place at the prescribed number of joints, a minimum theoretical joint width can be calculated for a particular sealant de-

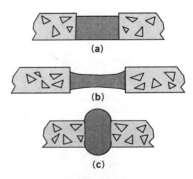

Figure 5. Effect of joint volume change on a sealant (4). (**a**) simple butt joint; (**b**) increase in joint extends sealant; (**c**) decrease extrudes sealant. Courtesy of McGraw-Hill, Inc.

pending on the sealant's movement or stretch capability. The capability of the sealant to adhere to the sides of a joint as movement occurs will be a determining factor in the selection of an appropriate sealant for a specific project, and its ability to withstand extreme movement before cohesive failure is yet another measure of the caliber of sealant. Table 2 offers coefficients of linear expansion of common building materials; expansion is more readily calculable by plotting the coefficients of linear expansion to the graph in Figure 6. For this reason, experience indicates in certain applications, such as in concrete pavement, a minimum 3:2 (depth over width) shape factor

Table 2. Coefficients of Linear Expansion[a]

Construction Material	in./in./°F × 10^6
Clay masonry	
Brick, clay or shale	3.6
Brick, fire clay	3.1
Tile, clay, or shale	3.3
Tile, fire clay	2.5
Concrete	
Gravel aggregate	6.0
Lightweight structural	4.5
Concrete masonry	
Cinder aggregate	3.1
Dense aggregate	5.2
Expanded shale aggregate	4.3
Expanded slag aggregate	4.6
Volcanic pumice and aggregate	4.1
Metals	
Aluminum	
Brass, red 230	13.0
Bronze, arch 385	10.4
Copper, 11C	11.6
Iron	
Cast gray	9.8
Wrought	5.9
Lead, common	7.4
Monel	16.3
Stainless steel	7.8
Type 302	9.6
Type 304	9.6
Structural steel	6.7
Zinc	19.3
Glass	
Plate	5.1
Plaster	
Gypsum aggregate	7.6
Perlite	5.2
Vermiculite aggregate	5.9
Plastics	
Acrylics	40–50
Lexan	37.5
Phenolics	25–66
Plexiglas	39
Polyesters, glass reinforced	10–14
PVC	33
Vinyls	24–40
Stone	
Granite	6.2
Limestone	3.5
Marble	7.3

[a] Ref. 3.

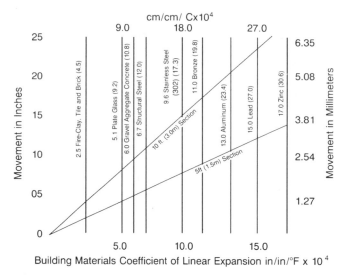

Figure 6. Joint movement for sections of various building materials at T = 130°F (72°C) (3). Courtesy of Sealant & Waterproofers Institute.

rather than the theoretically more desirable ratio of 1:1 or 1:2 in order to achieve a better service performance (Fig. 7).

Because of the prime necessity of accommodating significant amounts of movement in joints, it is this class of sealants that is used far more extensively than any others in large expanses of concrete, glass, and other substrates used for high-rise construction. Each generic type in the class of 1:1 depth over width may have its own characteristics and may also have certain relative merits or limitations. The particular manufacturer should be consulted for specifics.

EVALUATION OF SEALANT CHARACTERISTICS

There are various standard laboratory methods for measuring and evaluating the most essential properties and characteristics of sealants, and these are incorporated in many of the sealant specifications. Laboratory testing cannot be expected to predict accurately the in-use performance of a given sealant. The reasons for this are quite obvious. Laboratory tests are necessarily conducted on small specimens and under ideal conditions of cleanliness, with careful attention to procedure and workmanship. It is seldom possible to provide such conditions at the job site.

Adhesion and Cohesion

The critical properties of medium and high performance sealants are generally measured in two ways: (1) by the "durability," or adhesion–cohesion tests required in the federal specifications for elastomeric compounds and in ANSI 116.6, and (2) by the adhesion-in-peel type of test. In essence, the durability test involves the casting of 1/2 × 1/2 × 2-in. joint sections between plates of concrete or other combinations of substrates and then after curing, subjecting these joint specimens to lateral stress at various temperatures. Both federal specification and ASTM Test Method C719 require first, a seven-day immersion of the specimen in water, then seven day's heat aging under compression, followed by cycled compression and extension at room temperature and at alternating high and low temperatures (Fig. 8).

The adhesion-in-peel test is also required in most specifications. It involves embedding a strip of strong fabric in a bed of sealant, allowing the sealant to cure, and then measuring the force required to peel the fabric from the sealant by pulling at an angle of 180° on an appropriate instrument.

Hardness

Hardness is the ability to resist surface penetration by a blunt probe. It is determined by using a durometer, which measures the extent of the probe's penetration into the sealant. The term "Shore A" denotes a specific type of durometer made by the Shore Instrument Co. and equipped with a scale of hardness measurement, A, ranging from 0 (no penetration resistance) to 100 (complete resistance). The Rex durometer is also used.

Sealant hardness may be important at two stages: (1) immediately after application and (2) after aging. The effect of long-term exposure on sealant hardness is of the utmost importance, as a significant change can radically affect the sealant's ability to function. Hardness may be changed by ultraviolet degradation of the plasticizers or the base polymer, by heat from another source, by a faulty curing mechanism, or by a combination of other factors.

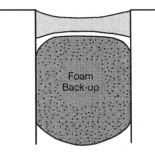

Sealant Depth Approximately
1/2 Joint Width Min 1/4" x 1/4"

Figure 7. Joint shape (1).

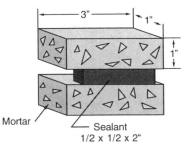

Figure 8. Adhesion in tension— specimen (1).

Elastic Recovery

Elastic recovery is the ability of the cross-linked sealant to recover from a constant external deformation load. The elastic recovery is a measure of the cross-linking or chemical cure that will result in a better fatigue modulus and superior performance of the sealant. The elastic recovery is lost completely at the brittle point of the sealant. This elastomeric property is expressed as percent recovery or the ratio of recovered length to original length.

Permanent Set

Permanent set occurs when a sealant is stretched, released, and does not return to its original length but remains longer. The increase in length, expressed as percent of the original length, is called permanent set. It depends principally on the amount and time of deformation, the state of cure, and the degree and type of loading.

Compression Set (Cold Flow)

Compression set occurs when a sealant is subject to a compression load for some time and does not return to its original dimension when the load is removed. A high compression set is undesirable in a sealant, because it reduces the extension capabilities and may cause further degradation of performance as the sealant ages.

Effects of Ultraviolet Exposure

It is essential that sealants have high resistance to the effects of ultraviolet (uv) exposure. The degrading effects of uv exposure must be considered. This is especially true with sealants used in glazing application.

Other Properties

In recent years there has been active development of many types of "elastomeric" sealant that are largely elastic rather than plastic and that are flexible rather than rigid at normal service temperatures. Elastomeric materials are available as field-applied sealants. Although initially more expensive, they may be cheaper in the long run because they usually have a longer service life.

Furthermore, as will be seen, they can seal joints that could not possibly be sealed with traditional materials because of the occurrence of considerable movement. This has opened up new engineering and architectural possibilities to the designer of concrete and unusual substrates.

For satisfactory performance, a construction sealant must conform to the following specifications:

1. Be an impermeable material.
2. Deform to accommodate the movement and rate of movement occurring at the joint.
3. Have the elastomeric characteristics to recover to its original properties and shape if subjected to cyclical deformations.
4. Adhere to all construction substrates. This means that, for all sealants that exert a force against these surfaces, the sealant must bond to the substrate and not fail in adhesion or peel at corners or other local areas of stress concentration.
5. Not internally rupture (that is, fail in cohesion).
6. Resist flow due to gravity or fluid pressure or unacceptable softening at higher service temperatures.
7. Not harden or become unacceptably brittle at lower service temperatures.
8. Not be adversely affected by aging, weathering, or other service factors for a reasonable service life under the range of temperatures and other environmental conditions that occur.

In addition, depending on the specific service conditions, the sealant may be required to resist one or more of the following: intrusion of foreign material, wear, indentation, pickup, or attack by chemicals present. Further requirements may be that the sealant have a specific color, resist change of color, or be nonstaining.

BUTT JOINT WIDTHS FOR FIELD-APPLIED SEALANTS

The selection of the width (and depth) for field-applied sealants to accommodate the computed movement in a joint is based on the maximum strain allowable in a sealant (Fig. 9). The part of the total movement that extends the sealant is that which increases the width of the joint at the time the sealant is installed to the width of the joint at its maximum opening. The temperature difference between that at installation and that at maximum opening is the main contribution to the extension of the sealant, but any residual drying shrinkage of the concrete that has yet to occur and shrinkage in the sealant as it sets or cures will impose additional extension on the sealant.

JOINT DETAILS

Figures 10 through 13 illustrate the application of joint sealants to a wide variety of situations that occur in various types of construction. The details shown are representative of current practice and cover most possibilities, although every possible variation in use cannot be shown. The details are presented in outline form, omitting for the sake of clarity structural details such as reinforcing steel, dowel, etc, not directly relevant to the problem of sealing the joint. The location of a joint is indicated only where this is significant to appreciation of the type of joint and sealant that may be suitable. As stated earlier, the location and spacing of joints for particular applications are beyond the scope of this discussion. Similarly, sealant reservoirs and expansion or contraction gaps are not dimensioned as to width or depth because sealants have different performance capabilities and should be determined as outlined in manufacturers' recommendations.

INSTALLATION

The practical aspects of constructing a joint and sealing it must be kept in mind when its details are being drawn up. It must be remembered that a joint detail that makes it

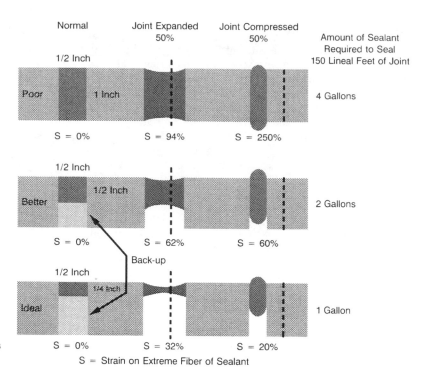

Figure 9. Butt joints—various depth to width ratios (5).

S = Strain on Extreme Fiber of Sealant

unnecessarily difficult to install the sealant properly is one that is likely to lead to premature failure.

The most appropriate technique for applying a joint sealant depends on the material, the width, shape, inclination, and accessibility of the joint as well as whether it is a small or large job. Each step in the construction and preparation of the joint to receive the sealant and for its installation requires careful workmanship and thorough inspection to avoid defects that may be costly and time-consuming to correct.

The specification for the work should state how the selected sealant is to be installed and any special features required in the construction or preparation of the joint to receive it. Before the containers of sealant are opened, their labels should be checked to make sure the right one has been supplied and that there is no essential conflict between the specification and the manufacturer's instructions for installation. Any discrepancy should be referred to the architect, engineer, or designer before work commences.

The most auspicious time for installing liquid-applied sealants, if the construction schedule permits, is on dry days when the temperature is close to the annual mean. However, a satisfactory job can and usually must be done in less than ideal conditions provided their effects are taken into consideration.

JOINT CONSTRUCTION WITH SEALING IN MIND

Some of the defects resulting from improper concrete joint construction can be avoided by the following:

1. Saw or form the joint to the required (and uniform) depth, width, and location shown on the plans.
2. Align the joint with any connecting joints to avoid blockage to free movement.

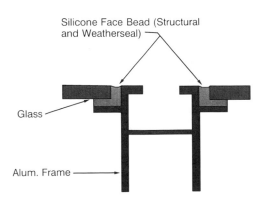

Figure 10. Structural and weatherseal joint (6).

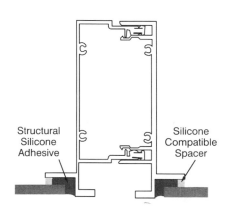

Figure 11. Curtainwall adhesive/sealant structural glazing application (7). Courtesy of Dow Corning Corporation.

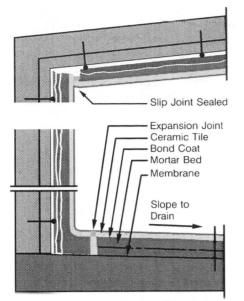

Figure 12. Expansion joint in tile mass (8).

3. Judge the time of sawing to avoid edge spalling.
4. Correct and position dowels and other joint hardware, fillers, waterstops, and bulkheads and rigidly support them to avoid displacement during concreting.
5. Remove any temporary material or filler used to form the sealant reservoir by raking out or rotary cutting to the specified depth.
6. Keep curing compound and other materials from contaminating joint faces.

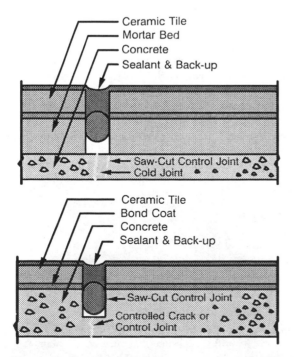

Figure 13. Expansion joint tile mass and concrete (8).

PREPARATION OF JOINT SURFACES

Joint surfaces must be clean and free of defects that would impair bonds with liquid-applied sealants. Removal of contaminants may require washing out of debris left by sawing, wire brushing, routing, or sand blasting. Although sand blasting is more expensive, it is more likely to succeed and therefore is warranted where relatively expensive, chemical-curing, thermosetting sealants are used. Solvents intended to remove oil, etc, usually have the opposite effect and carry the contaminants further into the pores of the concrete. Solvents are, however, distinctly useful in cleaning nonporous surfaces such as glass, ceramic tile, and metal frames. Final cleanup to remove dust is usually required. This is essential where a good bond must be developed with chemically-curing, thermosetting sealants. Final cleanup can be done by brush, but the use of oil-free compressed air or a vacuum cleaner is more likely to be successful.

As a general rule, joint faces must also be dry, because the sealant must bond with a particular substrate of the structure. Exceptions are claimed by some sealant manufacturers. Notwithstanding, better results will be achieved if sealant installation is done under dry conditions.

Bond Breakers and Backup Materials

Bond breakers and backup materials are used (Fig. 14) to achieve the desired shape factor in field-applied sealants. The principal material requirement is that the sealant should not adhere to the bond breaker. Secondary benefits of using a backup material are that it supports the sealant for tooling, helps resist indentation and sag, and allows the sealant to take advantage of maximum extension. These may often be important considerations when selecting the appropriate type and shape of preformed backup material. The material must also be compressible without extruding the sealant and must recover to maintain contact with the joint faces when the joint is open (Fig. 15).

Fillers in Expansion Joints

Fillers are used in expansion joints to assist in making the joint and to produce room for the inward movement of the abutting concrete units as they expand. Additionally, they

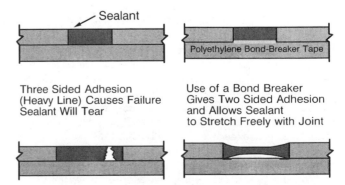

Figure 14. Polyethylene bond breaker tape (9).

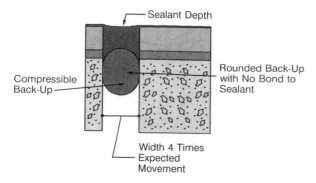

Figure 15. Expansion joint with backer rod (8).

may be required to provide support for the sealant or limit its depth in the same manner that backup materials do. These requirements are usually met by preformed materials that can be compressed without significant extrusion and preferably recover their original width when compression ceases. Stiffness to maintain alignment during concreting and resistance to deterioration due to moisture and other service conditions are also usually required (Table 3).

Primers

Laboratory and field experience indicate that priming joint faces is essential for certain field-applied sealants and can generally improve bonds and enhance extensionability of other sealants, especially at low temperatures and conditions of water immersion. Improvement in adhesion may depend on the type of sealant and condition of joint interface.

As a general rule, priming is required for all porous surfaces such as concrete, tile, and possibly plastics if chemical-curing, thermosetting sealants are to adhere satisfactorily. Where priming is required with the selected sealant, the recommended primer is usually supplied with the sealant and can be applied by brush or spray. Brushing can be tedious; unless excess material is properly brushed out to insure a uniform film over the whole joint face, adhesion failures may result. For horizontal joints on larger jobs, spray applications may be more appropriate. Most primers require time to dry before the sealant is installed. Failure to permit this may lead to adhesion failure or exudation of the primer.

INSTALLATION OF LIQUID-APPLIED SEALANTS

Except for extremely short joints or in touch-up work, sealants are usually extruded under pressure from a nozzle whose orifice may be sized and shaped to mold the required bead of sealant to fill the joint opening. The simplest piece of equipment for this purpose is either supplied prepackaged in cartridges to suit the gun or the chamber of cartridges are loaded on the job from bulk containers as required; in the case of two-component sealants, they are filled with the compound after mixing. Depending on the size of the job, more sophisticated pressure-application equipment is available, including models where two-com-

ponent materials are brought by individual lines to the nozzle where they are intimately and continuously mixed in a chamber immediately prior to extrusion.

With two-component sealants, full and intimate mixing is essential if the material is to cure out with uniform properties. Little can be done with patches of sealant that do not harden except to remove and replace them with properly mixed material. For small batches, hand-held electric drills with paddle blades or jiffy-type mixers can be used. Large batches, usually from 55 gal drum kits, require a specific type of meter–mix machine.

Application of the sealant to fill the joint reservoir is a skilled operation. The gun nozzle must be controlled at an angle (about 45°) and moved steadily along the joint so that a uniform bead is applied without dragging, tearing, or leaving unfilled spaces. A skilled applicator will push the bead rather than draw it with the gun leading. In large joints, several runs may be needed, building up the sealant in roughly triangular wedges at each run.

For nonsagging sealants, when the joint has been filled with the required amount of material it must be tooled to insure contact with the joint faces, to remove any trapped air or voids, to consolidate the material, and to provide a neat, uniform appearance. At the joint faces, the exposed face of the sealant should usually match the level of the edge of the concrete. An exception is in areas subject to traffic where self-leveling sealants are used. In that case, the sealant should be left slightly lower than the plane of the floor (Fig. 16).

It must be remembered that two-component sealants in particular have a limited working (pot) life, especially on hot days. Once the accelerator is mixed in, the curing reaction starts. The batch size should be limited to what can be used within the pot life (which depends on the material and its temperature).

Neatness and Cleanup

Nothing looks worse on a new joint than a ragged job of joint sealing in which the sealant is uneven or is adhering to everything except the joint faces. Careful workmanship, such as uniform depth of installation, proper tooling, and lack of spilled or excess material on surfaces adjacent to the joint, are all signs of a good job.

Proper cleaning of equipment and tools immediately after their use ceases, for even a short period, will avoid contamination of the work or delays due to hardened sealant. The instructions on the container of cold-liquid-applied sealants usually list suitable solvents for this purpose.

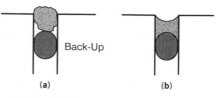

Figure 16. (a) Untooled joint: poor adhesion contact; (b) Properly tooled joint: full adhesion (3). Courtesy of Sealant & Waterproofers Institute.

Table 3. Preformed Materials Used for Fillers and Backup[a]

Composition and Type	Uses and Governing Properties	Installation

Natural rubber
  Sponge
  Solid
	Expansion joint filler—readily compressible and good recovery, closed cell, nonabsorptive, solid rubber may function as filler but primarily intend as gasket	High pliability may cause installation problems; weight of plastic concrete may compress it; in construction joints attach to first placement with adhesive

Neoprene or butyl sponge tubes	Backup—where resilience required in large joints; check for compatibility with sealant as to staining	Compressed into joint with hand tools
Neoprene or butyl sponge rods	Backup—used in narrower joints, eg, contraction joints in canal linings and cover slabs and pavements; check for compatibility with sealant as to staining	Compressed into joint with hand tools or roller
Expanded polyethylene, polyurethane, and polyvinyl chloride polypropylene flexible foams	Expansion joint filler—readily compressible, good recovery, nonabsorptive Backup—compatible with most sealants	Must be rigidly supported for full length during concreting Compressed into joint with hand tools
Expanded polyethylene, polyurethane, and polystyrene rigid foams	Expansion joint filler—useful to form a gap; but after significant compression will not recover	Support in place during concreting; in construction joints attach to first placement; sometimes removed after concreting where no longer needed
Bituminous or resin-impregnated corkboard	Expansion joint filler—readily compressible and resilient; not compatible and must be isolated from most nonasphaltic sealants	Support in place during concreting or attach to preceding placement boards; easily damaged by careless handling
Bentonite or dehydrated cork	Filler with self-sealing properties—absorption of water after installation causes material to swell; cork can be compressed; bentonite incompressible	Cork available in moisture-proof liners that require removal before installation; bentonite in powder form, loose or within cardboard liners
Wood: cedar, redwood, pine, chipboard, untreated fiberboard	Expansion joint filler—has been widely used in the past; swells when water is absorbed; not as compressible as other fillers and less recovery; natural woods should be knot free	Rigid and easily held in alignment during concreting
Bituminous-impregnated fiberboard	Expansion joint filler—widely used, resilient cane fiber used, has moderate recovery after compression, should not be compressed more than 50% or bitumen extruded, which may damage sealant	Reasonably rigid to hold alignment during concreting or placed against preceding placement
Metal or plastic	Expansion joint filler—hollow, compressible, thin-gauge box, used only in special applications Backup—foil, inert to sealants, but shape irregular	Installed as for wood or fiberboard material Crumple and place in joint
Glass fiber, mineral wool	Expansion joint filler—made in board form by impregnating with bitumen or resins, easily compressed Backup—inert without impregnation so as not to damage sealant	Installed as for wood or fiberboard material In mat form or packed loose material or yarn
Oakum, jute, Manila yarn and rope, and piping upholstery cord	Traditional material for packing joints before installing sealant; where used as backup should be untreated with oils, etc	Packed in joint to require depth
Portland cement grout or mortar	Used at joints in precast units and pipes to fill the remaining gap when no movement is expected and sometimes behind waterspots	Bed (mortar); inject (grout)

[a] Ref. 2.

SEALANT MATERIALS

Because of space limitations of this article, only those sealants that can be categorized as high performance and meeting specification criteria will be discussed. More complete reviews of sealants have been published (10,11).

In service, environmental conditions often dictate additional performance requirements beyond those needed to accommodate movements alone. Selection of the most appropriate materials for a particular application is not a simple matter in view of all the variables involved. Once an understanding is gained of basic properties of materials required, then available materials can be classified and related to their suitability in various types of joint.

Finally, sealants must not deteriorate when stored for a reasonable time prior to use, must be relatively easy to handle and install, and must be free of substances harmful to the user and concrete or other material that may abut. In some locations, regulations may restrict the use of sealants that may contain solvents deemed to be pollutants.

Classification of Joint Sealants

The high performance thermosetting sealant and caulk have predicted cyclic dynamic joint movement capability of ± 12.5% to ± 25% throughout their useful service life. Those with the lower movement capability are designated as Class B in Federal Specifications TT–S–00227, TT–S–0023, and TT–S–001542 and as Class 12 1/2 in ASTM C920. The higher capability sealants are designated Class A in federal specifications and Class 25 in ASTM. There are now available neutral-cure silicone sealants that have movement capability of ± 50%. Note that there is no classification for ± 50% capability in either federal or ASTM specification. Sealants in this class are either one- or two-component systems that cure by chemical reaction to a solid state from the liquid form in which they were applied.

The generic types of sealant included in this high performance category include acrylics, polymercaptans, polythioethers, polysulfides, polyurethanes, silicones, and hybrid combinations of polymers. The properties that make them suitable as sealants are their resistance to weathering and ozone, flexibility and resilience at both high and low temperatures, and inertness to a wide range of chemicals, solvents, and fuels.

The most critical concern in evaluating sealants of this range is their ability to perform satisfactorily under dynamic joint movement. As previously mentioned, it is no single characteristic, but a proper balance of several essential properties, that determines sealant performance. The sealant will perform only as long as this balance is maintained.

Butyl

Butyl rubber (4) resulted from research on a method of obtaining synthetic rubber from petrochemicals. It is a copolymer of 98% isobutylene and 2% isoprene. The butyl molecule is long, closely knit, and tightly packed and is close to chemical saturation, being 98% saturated. A high degree of saturation (or very low degree of unsaturation) is the primary reason for the stability and superior aging quality of butyl plus its many natural resistance properties. Natural rubber is 100% unsaturated. This high degree of unsaturation is the principal reason why natural as well as many synthetic rubbers deteriorate quickly when exposed to weather, sunlight, moisture, and gases.

Sealants based on this system or combinations are generally compounded in a single package of ready-to-use material that requires no additional mixing or on-the-job preparation. Attempts have been made to introduce two-component, low molecular weight butyls that are semi-liquid and cure at room temperature. Those new polymers require p-quionedioxime plus an oxidizer for cure and generally can be adjusted depending on application. These systems have been used as insulating glass sealants and as roof coatings. The nondrying or noncuring type of polyisobutylene sealant is permanently tacky and remains flexible and is recommended for internal or nonexposed applications; it cannot be classified as a high performance sealant due to its lack of overall strength.

Butyl sealants are used for joint and panel sealing application as well as for general glazing. Many times they are compounded into tapes for glazing applications. They possess good package stability and are relatively low in cost, easy to apply, and relatively odor free. Typical properties are shown in Table 4. A comparison of advantages and disadvantages is shown in Table 5.

LP Polymers—High Sulfur

The first synthetic rubber was manufactured in the United States in 1929 (4) and was known as polysulfide. The most interesting property of this new polymer was the unusual inertness to solvents and hydrocarbon fuels in contrast to the easy swelling of natural rubbers. In early 1942, work began that led to the invention by J. C. Patrick and H. R. Ferguson of a process of reductively cleaning, to a predetermined degree, a portion of polymeric polysulfide groups to a curable file (—SH polymer chain terminals). Subsequently, these studies led to a wide range of liquid polymers, ranging from below 1000 molecular weight to viscous liquids of about 5000 molecular weight. LP is the trademark for liquid polymer. Polysulfides are polymers of bis (ethylene oxy) methane containing disulfide linkages. The reactive terminal groups used for curing are mercaptans (—SH general structure is HS) (13,14).

$$(C_2H_4O—CH_2O—C_2—H_4SS)_xC_4—O—CH_2—O—C_2—H_4SH$$

Curing of the liquid polysulfide polymers to high molecular weight elastomers is normally accomplished by oxidizing the thio SH terminals to disulfide—S—S bonds.

$$2—RSH + (0) \rightarrow — RSSR — +H_2O$$

$$2 \text{ⵜ} RSH + P_bO_2 \rightarrow \text{ⵜ} RSR \text{ⵜ} + P_bO_2 + H_2O$$

The curing agents (13,14) most commonly used as oxygen-donating materials such as lead dioxide, manganese dioxide, calcium peroxide, cumine peroxide, and T-quinone dioxime. Lower valence metallic oxides, other organic per-

Table 4. Typical Properties of a Butyl-based Sealant[a]

	Tests Performed	Required by TT–S–001657	Typical Values
3.2	Stability	12 mo not exceeding 80°F	Pass
3.4.1	Color	5 d air exposure with no change	Pass
3.4.2	Bubble formation		
	Aluminum	Not to exceed 25% of surface	Pass
	Concrete		
3.4.3	Tenacity	Bent over 1/4 in. mandrel; no cracking, separation, delamination, or adhesion loss	Pass
3.4.4	Shrinkage	25% maximum shrinkage	23%
3.4.5	Slump	0.15 in. maximum	0.05 in.
3.4.6	Extrudability	9 s/mL, maximum	1s/mL
3.4.7	Stain	Stain index maximum 2.50	Pass
3.4.8	Tack-free time	3 d maximum	2 d
3.4.9	Adhesion loss, cracking, and discoloration after aging	None allowed	Pass
3.4.10	Bond-cohesion		
	Mortar	Loss of bond or cohesion not to exceed 1.5 in.^{2}	0 in.^{2}
	Glass		
	Aluminum		

[a] Ref. 1. Courtesy of Bostik Construction Products.

oxides, metallic paint dryers, and aldehydes can also function as curatives. The most widely used are lead peroxide, manganese dioxide, and selected dicromates (protected by U.S. Patents 2,787,608 and 2,964,503).

As with most sealant compounds, the selection of the ingredients such as filler, pigments, and plasticizers is governed by the end use. This also holds true with curing mechanisms (4). Polysulfides, as compared with other elastomeric sealants, have some of the most extensive history in regard to their use as a sealant. Polysulfide sealants were introduced into the construction marketplace in the early 1950s. They enjoyed increasing popularity for the next 10 years and then began sharing the market with solvent-based acrylics and urethanes through the 1970s. The early versions of polysulfides were of a two-component nature.

Approximately 10 years later, the now popular single-component system was introduced. Based on extensive laboratory evaluation and over 20 years of actual field experience, it is now a fact that one- and two-part polysulfide sealants can be used interchangeably. A wide variety of formulations are available for the end uses, and typical properties can be listed. Data presented in Tables 6 and 7 are based on the type of cure mechanism used.

Over the years, polysulfide sealants have been used extensively in such applications as potting and molding of electrical connectors, glazing of windows, bonding of sealed insulating glass units, and sealing of automobile windshields. With modifiers such as asphalt and cold tar, polysulfides have been used as sealants for roadways, bridges, and airport runways, giving the specific properties required in that type of application. Table 8 lists a few of the advantages and disadvantages of one- and two-component polysulfides.

Silicones

The earliest work on silicones (11) probably dates back to the Swedish chemist Berzelius in the early 1800s. In the 1930s, General Electric Co. and Corning Glass began work on developing high temperature insulation materials. It was then that Corning Glass and Dow Chemical

Table 5. Advantages and Disadvantages of Butyl Caulks[a]

Advantages	Disadvantages
1. Reasonable cost	1. Very slow cure
2. Availability	2. High shrinkage
3. Good flexibility	3. High compression set
4. Good adhesion to most substrates	4. Limited to joints with ± 7.5% joint movement
5. One-component	5. Not recommended for expansion joints
6. Little surface preparation	
7. Good water resistance	
8. Good color stability	
9. Four colors available	
10. Only material for capping neoprene gaskets	

[a] Ref. 11.

Table 6. Two-component Building Sealant Metallic Oxide Cure[a]

Nonvolatile content	95% minimum
Application life at 75°F, 50% rh	3 h minimum
Tack-free time at 75°F, 50% rh	36 h
Cure time at 75°F, 50% rh	72 h maximum
Hardness, Shore A (5 s reading)	20–35
Shrinkage	Negligible
Sag	1/16 in. maximum
Adhesion-in-peel	5 lb/in. minimum
Durability, area failure under cycling	0 in.^{2}

[a] Ref. 15. Courtesy of Bostik Construction Products.

Table 7. Single-component Building Sealant, Calcium Peroxide Cure Complex[a]

Stability	12 mo
Sag	1/16 in. minimum
Initial hardness, Shore A	30
Tack-free time at 75°F 50% rh	48–72 h
Stain and color change	None
Shrinkage	Negligible
Adhesion-in-peel	10 lb/in. minimum
Durability, area failure under cycling	0 in.^{2}

[a] Ref. 16. Courtesy of Bostik Construction Products.

formed the Dow Corning Corp. to carry out their developments and expand the Grignard process of the early production of silicones.

Two major suppliers in the United States are General Electric and Dow Corning who are at present manufacturers of finished goods. Rhodia, part of Rhone-Poulenc of France, also manufactures finished goods in the United States and does not supply raw materials. Suppliers of raw materials are companies such as Mobay of the United States, Beyer of the FGR, Wacker of the Federal Republic of Germany, and ICI of the UK.

Table 8. Advantages and Disadvantages of One- and Two-component Polysulfides[a]

Advantages	Disadvantages
One-component Polysulfides	
One-component sealant	Requires moderate temperature for faster cure
Broad color range	
Good durability	Requires high humidity for faster cure
Good adhesion	
Can meet TT–S–00230C	Slow cure at low temperatures
Can meet ASTM C920	
	Poorer recovery
	Limited package stability
	Not recommended for pedestrian traffic areas
	Not recommended for sidewalks
	Slight odor
Two-component Polysulfides	
Overall better physical characteristics: recovery, adhesion-in-peel, and tensile-adhesion	Requires mixing, but easily mixed
	Slower cure below 40°F
Fast through cure	Light colors a problem
Better uv resistance	Limited pot life
Better water resistance	Very short pot life at 100°F
Life expectancy over 20 yr	Slight odor
Nonstaining to masonry	Poorer uv resistance compared to urethane and silicone sealants
Can meet TT–S–00227E	
Can meet ASTM C920	
Cost slightly lower than one-component, because tubing and labor are expensive	Poorer recovery compared to urethane and silicone sealants
	Primers needed for porous substrates

[a] Ref. 11.

Silicone sealants used in construction today are generally one-part materials that cure by reacting with atmospheric moisture. They are available in three basic types—low, medium, and high modulus with a range of properties. All use the same basic polymers but different cure mechanisms that control the modulus of the cured material. Typical reactions of silicones follow (11):

$$Cl-\underset{\underset{CH_3}{|}}{\overset{\overset{CH_3}{|}}{Si}}-Cl + H_2O \rightarrow HO-\underset{\underset{CH_3}{|}}{\overset{\overset{CH_3}{|}}{Si}}-\left[O-\underset{\underset{CH_3}{|}}{\overset{\overset{CH_3}{|}}{Si}}-\right]_n-OH$$

Intermediate A

$$CH_3-\underset{}{Si}-(O\overset{\overset{O}{\|}}{C}CH_3)_3 + \text{Intermediate A} \rightarrow$$
Reactant A

$$\left[HO-\underset{\underset{CH_3}{|}}{\overset{\overset{CH_3}{|}}{Si}}-\left[O-\underset{\underset{CH_3}{|}}{\overset{\overset{CH_3}{|}}{Si}}-\right]_n O-\underset{}{\overset{\overset{CH_3}{|}}{Si}}-(O\overset{\overset{O}{\|}}{C}CH_3)_2\right] + \text{acetic acid}$$

Intermediate B

Intermediate A is dimethyl polysiloxane and Intermediate B is the base polymer that reacts with moisture in air to give the curved polymer and acetic acid. Generally, silicones have the highest performance characteristics of all in comparison to acrylics, polysulfides, polymercaptans, and other high performance sealants, and they will generally outperform all other materials. They can be applied over a wider temperature range than other materials, from −35 to 140°F. They also have a wider service temperature range, from −65 to +350°F, and the recovery from joint movement or deformation is superior, approximately 95–100%. Weatherability is superior, because all silicones are not affected by ultraviolet radiation or by other oxidation conditions. When compared with polysulfides, for example, after 100 hours in a weatherometer, polysulfides will develop surface crazing and harden, whereas silicones exposed to the same conditions after 6000 hours show no increase in hardness or surface crazing. Statistics show that building sealants represent only 0.1% of the total building costs, yet sealant failures can cause 10% of the new building problems. It is known that silicones are more expensive; however, with the exceptional service life, these sealants are cost effective and offer state-of-the-art design flexibility. Tables 9 through 11 illustrate the properties of both one- and two-part sealants used for glazing and structural glazing types of application in addition to secondary insulating glass edge seal application.

Because of the unique weathering characteristics of silicones, they meet the needs of the architect to withstand the movements encountered in glass structures while maintaining weatherproofing qualities. Figures 17 and 18 illustrate the typical details of silicone sealants used in structural-glazed applications.

An area that must be discussed when talking about silicone sealants pertains principally to fire stops, fire

Table 9. Single-component Building Sealant Acetoxy Cure[a,b]

Property	Value	Test Method
Hardness, (Shore A scale)	35	ASTM D2240–68
Ultimate tensile strength, at maximum elongation	450 psi (31.7 kgf/cm^2)	ASTM D412–68
Peel strength, glass	20 lb/in. (3.57 kg/cm)	TT–S–001543A (COM–NBS) CGSB 19–GP–9
Specific gravity	1.07	
Staining	None	TT–S–001543A (COM–NBS)
Weathering, after 10,000 h in Atlas weatherometer	No change	ASTM C793–75
uv resistance	Excellent	ASTM C793–75
Ozone resistance	Excellent	ASTM D1149–64
Dynamic movement capability	± 25%	TT–S–001543A (COM–NBS)
Tear strength, die B	45 lb/in. (8 kg/cm)	ASTM D624–73
Tack-free time	1 h	TT–S–001543A (COM–NBS)
Curing time	5–7 d at 75°F (25°C), in 1/4 in. (6.4 mm) section	
Storage life, below 80°F (27°C)	2 y	
Sag; slump	None	TT–S–001543A (COM–NBS)

[a] Ref. 21.
[b] After 7 d at 77°F (25°C) and 50% rh. Courtesy of Dow Corning Corp.

wall, and penetration seals. Building codes require that where fire- or smoke-rated walls or fire-rated floors are penetrated they must be restored to their original integrity using approved fire-stopping methods. Failure to do so may allow destructive heat, smoke, and toxic fumes to spread throughout a building, threatening life, property, and operations. Public opinion and complex liability issues may soon force new more stringent fire and building codes.

Generally, fire stop systems (23) are two products: a silicone foam and silicone sealant. Foams are generally two-part silicone elastomers that expand when mixed to fill complex penetrations such as multiple cable tray pass through with tight compressive seals. This product can be mixed by hand or by automated mixing and dispensing equipment.

The single-component sealant is a ready-to-apply elastomer that is gunned into a simple wall to floor penetration, such as basic wiring or plumbing. This is very similar to standard sealants used for expansion–contraction joint applications.

Tests show that some silicone fire stop foams and sealants will last up to 20 years when applied properly. Most of the fire stop materials today are supplied by Dow Corning, General Electric, and 3M and do have UL classified ratings from one to three hours of fire-rated penetration seal designs. Typical values for foam materials, such as fire penetration sealants, are shown in Tables 12 and 13.

Table 10. Single-component Building Sealant Neutral Cure[a,b]

Property	Value	Test Method
Color	Limestone, gray, white, black, bronze	
Tack-free time, 50% rh, h	3	MIL–S–8802
Curing time, 50% rh, d at 77°F (25°C)	7–14	MIL–S–8802
Full adhesion, d	14–21	
Flow, sag, or slump, in.	0.1	MIL–S–8802
Working time, min.	20–30	
Durometer hardness, Shore A	30	ASTM D2240
Tensile at 150% elongation, psi	80	ASTM S412
Ultimate tensile strength (maximum elongation), psi	170	ASTM D412
Peel strength, lbs/in. (milled aluminum, glass, and concrete)	32	MIL–S–8802
Staining	None	ASTM C510
Tear strength, die B, ppi	27	ASTM D624
Ozone resistance	Good	ASTM D1149
Weathering, after 1500 h in Atlas weatherometer	Remains elastomeric	ASTM D1149
Joint movement capability, after 14-d cure, %	± 50	

[a] Refs. 21.
[b] After 7 d at 77°F (25°C) and 50% rh. Courtesy of Dow Corning Corp.

Table 11. Two-component Silicone–curtain wall adhesive–sealant[a,b]

Property	Value	Test Method
Base		
Color	White	
Specific gravity	1.40	
Storage life, mo	12	
Curing agent		
Color	Black	
Specific gravity	1.03	
Flammability	Nonflammable	
Storage life, mo	12	
As catalyzed		
Color	Black	
Specific gravity	1.36	
Working time, min	20–25	
Corrosiveness	Noncorrosive	
Consistency	Nonslumping	
Snap time at 75°F (25°C), min	36	
Handling time, h maximum	3	
As cured, 7 d at room temperature		
Tensile strength, psi (MPa)	275 (1.9)	ASTM D412
Elongation, %	200	ASTM D412
Durometer hardness, Shore A	45	ASTM D676
Tear strength, die B, ppi (N/m)	56 (9.8×10^3)	ASTM D624
Lap shear adhesion, psi (MPa)		
aluminum	205 (1.4)	
glass	205 (1.4)	
Tensile adhesion, psi (MPa)	140 (1.0)	
Cold flow, creep	Negligible	
Heat resistance, °F (°C)	300 (190)	

[a] Ref. 21. Courtesy of Dow Corning Corp.

[b] Mixed by weight at 12:1 or by volume at 8.8:1 base to curing agent ratio.

Table 14 is a summary of the advantages and disadvantages of silicones.

Polythioethers

A family of novel polymers trademarked Permapols (24) has been developed by Products and Chemical Corp. to meet the exacting demands required in structural materials for high performance sealants and adhesives that can adhere to a variety of substrates used in the building trades. Formulated sealants exhibit adhesion to a wide variety of difficult substrates as well as having excellent hydrolytic stability and other physical properties. These compositions show additional desirable properties of high temperature, hydrocarbon fuel and chemical resistance, and bond durabilities after exposure to boiling water for 100 hours. Early attempts to introduce polymercaptans

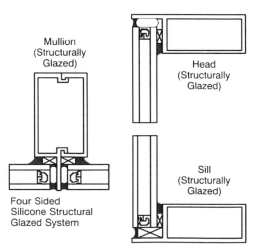

Figure 17. Four-sided structural glazed system (22).

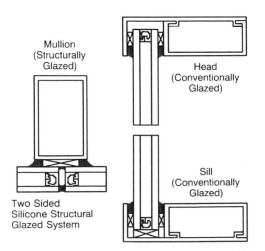

Figure 18. Two-sided structural glazed system (22).

Table 12. Single-component Penetration Seal[a,b]

Property	Value
Color	Black
Consistency	Soft, spreadable paste
Specific gravity	1.23
Solids content	Contains no solvent
Application rate, gm/min (3.2 mm orfice at 6.3 kg/cm²)	
(0.125 in orfice at 90 psi)	500
Tack-free time, h at 25°C (77°F, 50% rh)	3
Shelf life, (from shipment)	6 mo at 77°F (25°C)
Mechanical	
Hardness, Shore A	40
Tensile strength, kg/cm² (lb/in.²)	25 (350)
Elongation, %	280
Shear strength, kg/cm² (lb/in.²)	14 (200)
Peel strength, kg/lcm (lb/in.)	7 (14)
Flammability (UL94), 3.4 mm (0.133 in.) thick	94-V-0
Thermal:	
Brittle point, °C (°F)	below −60°C (−75°F)
Thermal conductivity, cal/s, cm² °C/(Btu/lh, ft², °F/ft)	0.0005
	(0.12)
Coefficient of thermal expansion, cm/cm, °C (in./in., °F)	27×10^5 ($15^3 \times 10^5$)
Test Data	
Flame spread, ASTM E84	13
Smoke development, ASTM E84	118
3-h ASTM E119 floor test and hose stream	Passes as part of system

[a] Ref. 23. Courtesy of General Electric Co.
[b] This numerical flame spread rating is not intended to reflect hazards presented by this or any other material under actual fire conditions.

Table 13. Two-component Foam Silicone Penetration Seal[a]

Property	Value
Part A Base as Applied	
Appearance	Black liquid
Specific gravity	1.22
Consistency	Pourable
Viscosity	80 poise
Shelf life	12 mo
Part B Curing Agent as Supplied	
Appearance	Off-white liquid
Specific gravity	1.22
Consistency	Pourable
Viscosity	80 poise
Shelf life	12 mo

Cured Properties—Equal Parts A and B as Cured 12 h at 25°C (77°F)

Work life (after mix)	Maximum 120 s 25°C (77°F)

Silicone foam has been incorporated into systems that meet the 2-h endurance criteria of ASTM E119 (fire tests of building construction and materials).

Appearance	Black RTV foam
Density	16–20 lb/ft³
Specific gravity	0.29
Predominantly closed cell	
Oxygen index	28

[a] Ref. 25. Courtesy of Dow Corning Corp.

were made by Diamond Alkalai in the late 1960s and 1970s. These had a backbone of polyoxyalkylene and were more sensitive to water immersion, obviously making poor candidates for sealants in the building trade. Patents for these products were sold at a later date to Thiokol. All promotion had been stopped at that time by Diamond Alkalai.

In mid-1970, Hooker Chemical also introduced a polymercaptan (11) that had a greater amount of sulfur than the Thiokol polysulfide polymer, approximately 55% compared to 37%. Generally, the properties were about the same and adhesion was somewhat poorer. The principal complaint was strong odors. Many compounders of sealants were sampled; however, little interest was generated and the project was abandoned by Hooker.

Permapol P2 is one family of mercaptan-terminated polymers available in a range of molecular weights and functionalities. Structure of these polymers allows a number of valuable characteristics to be incorporated into sealant or adhesive combinations based on these polymers. Due to the greater compatibility of the Permapol, base systems can tolerate large amounts of plasticizers and fillers, which gives these systems economic advantages without sacrificing their physical properties. Tables 15 and 16 show typical properties of formulations for single-component building sealants and two-component building sealants.

Table 14. Advantages and Disadvantages of Silicone Sealants[a]

Advantages	Disadvantages
One-component sealant	Slightly more expensive
Colors available	Limited color range
Color stable	Critical surface preparation
High temperature resistance	Possible concrete adhesion problems
Low temperature gunnability	Dirt pickup
Excellent uv resistance	Poor tear resistance with high modulus
Excellent ozone resistance	Slight odor problem
Nonstaining	Aluminum surfaces a problem with some
High movement capability	sealants
Very high recovery	Short tooling time
No shrinkage	Primer selection needed for various surfaces
No hardness increase with time	
Improved tear resistance with low modulus sealants	
Various moduli available	
Medium to high movement capability from ±25 to ±50%	
Long durability over 20 yr	

[a] Ref. 11.

Permapol P3 polymer is a family of liquid polymers of polythioether, with a backbone structure containing about 30% polymer. These polymers exhibit hydrocarbon fuel and solvent resistant hydrolytic stability and excellent elastic properties over a wide range of temperature when cured. They also possess high ultraviolet and thermal resistance. The Permapol P3 structure has a similar backbone to that of polysulfide (24).

$$\left[\left(O-\underset{\underset{CH_3}{|}}{C}-CH_2-S-CH_2-CH_2 \right)_m \left(-O-CH_2-CH_2-S-CH_2-CH_2 \right)_n \right]$$

Table 15. Single-component Polythioether "Polymer P" Building Sealant[a,b,c]

Property	Value
Rheological properties	
Vertical at 122°F	3/32 in.
Vertical at 40°F	3/32 in.
Horizontal at 122°F	None
Horizontal at 40°F	None
Extrusion rate	2 s
Hardness at standard condition	22 s
Weight loss, cracking and chalking after heat aging	2.5% weight loss No cracking or chalking
Tack-free time	12 h
Stain and color change	Conforms
Durability	
glass	Conforms
aluminum	Conforms
mortar (primed)	Conforms
Adhesion-in-peel	
Glass	14 pli
aluminum	No adhesive loss 15 pli No adhesive loss
mortar (primed)[c]	12 pli No adhesive loss

[a] Ref. 24. Courtesy of Products Research & Chemical Corp.
[b] As curing condition 18 d at 75°F, 50% rh, followed by 3 d at 158°F were used. The sealant meets or exceeds the requirements of Federal Specification TT–S–230–C, Type II, Class A and the requirements of ASTM C920–79, Grade NS, Class 25, use NT, A, and O.
[c] On mortar, primer #57 was used.

Table 16. Two-component Polythioether "Polymer P" Based Building Sealant[a,b]

Property	Value
Rheological properties	
Vertical at 122°F	1/16 in.
Vertical at 40°F	1/16 in.
Horizontal at 122°F	None
Horizontal at 40°F	None
Application life	3 s
Hardness at standard condition	32
Hardness after heat aging	35
Weight loss, cracking and chalking after heat aging	6% weight loss No cracking or chalking
Tack-free time	20 h
Stain and color change	Conforms
Durability	
Glass	Conforms
Aluminum	Conforms
Mortar (primed)	Conforms
Adhesion-in-peel	
Glass	12 pli No adhesive loss
Aluminum	12 pli No adhesive loss
Mortar (primed)	10 pli No adhesive loss

[a] Ref. 24. Courtesy of Products Research & Chemical Corp.
[b] The sealant meets or exceeds the requirements of Federal Specification TT–S–227E, Type III, Class A and the requirements of ASTM C920–79, Type M, Grade NS, Class 25, use NT, A, and O.

Table 17. Two-component Polyurethane Construction Sealant[a,b]

	Property	Requirements		Typical Chem-Calk 500 Results
3.4.22	Type 2 nonsag	3/16 in maximum sag		0.0 in.
3.4.3	Application life	3 h minimum		3 h minimum
3.4.4.1	Initial hardness, Shore A	15–50		20–30
4.3.4.1	Hardness, heat-aged	50 maximum		25–35
4.3.5	Weight loss after heat aging	10% maximum		7%
4.3.6	Tack-free time	72 h maximum		Pass
4.3.7	Stain and color change	None		None
4.3.9	Durability: area failure under cycling	Glass Aluminum Concrete	Combined area 1½ in.² maximum	0.0 in.
4.3.10	Adhesion–in–peel	Glass	5 lb in minimum	22 lb in minimum
		Aluminum	5 lb in minimum	22 lb in minimum
		Concrete	5 lb in minimum	22 lb in minimum

[a] Ref. 4. Courtesy of McGraw-Hill, Inc.
[b] Interim Federal Specification TT S 00227E, Type 2, Class A.

Polyurethanes

Having first been released in the United States construction market in the 1970s, polyurethanes have come to represent a popular and most versatile classification of building sealants. Polyurethanes are available in a wide range of formulations, compounded as one-component or two-component materials. Depending on the intended application, a variety of modifications can be compounded into these polymers.

There are two main systems of polyurethanes (4): the one-shot and the prepolymer. With the one-shot system, the complete reaction between the diisocyanate and other reactants, such as polyester or polyether, is carried out by the user. In the prepolymer system, the diisocyanate and the other reactants are partially reacted before being supplied to the user. The one-shot system involves handling raw diisocyanates, which are quite toxic. The prepolymer system does not have this disadvantage.

Isocyanate Components. Several major diisocyanates are used in urethane sealants or at least are recommended as good candidates for the preparation of isocyanate or hydroxyl-terminated prepolymers:

1,5-Naphthalene diisocyanate (NDI).

4,4-Diphenylmethane diisocyanate (MDI).

Polymethylene polyphenyl isocyanate (PAPI).

2,4/2,6-Isomers, 80/20 blend of tolylene diisocyanate (TDI).

A two-component sealant for glazing, caulking, and sealing of building, flashing, precast tilt-up panels, curtain walls, and other areas where a watertight seal and severe structural movement is required is shown in Table 17. Properties of a one-component thixotropic-type sealant is shown in Table 18.

Table 18. Single-component Polyurethane Building Sealant[a,b]

	Property	Requirements		Typical Chem-Calk 500 Results
3.4.22	Type 2 nonsag	3/16 in maximum sag		0 in.
3.4.3	Application life	3 h minimum		3 h minimum
3.4.4.1	Initial hardness, Shore A	15–50		20–30
4.3.4.1	Hardness, heat-aged	50 maximum		25–35
4.3.5	Weight loss after heat aging	10% maximum		7%
4.3.6	Tack-free time	72 h maximum		Pass
4.3.7	Stain and color change	None		None
4.3.9	Durability: area failure under cycling	Glass Aluminum Concrete	Combined area 1½ in.² maximum	0 in.
4.3.10	Adhesion-in-peel	Glass	5 lb in minimum	22 lb in minimum
		Aluminum	5 lb in minimum	22 lb in minimum
		Concrete	5 lb in minimum	22 lb in minimum

[a] Refs. 20.
[b] Interim Federal Specification TT–00230C, Type II, Class A. Courtesy of Bostik Construction Products.

Table 19. Advantages and Disadvantages of Urethane Sealants[a]

Advantages	Disadvantages
Can be used in joints up to 6 in.	Light colors can disorder
± 25% movement capability	Poor water immersion resistance
Excellent recovery	
Excellent uv resistance	Not recommended for wet joints
Excellent ozone resistance	
Fast cure for multicomponents	May require more priming
Long work life for multicomponents	Limited package stability for one-component
Negligible shrinkage	
Excellent tear resistance	One-component requires more cure time
Excellent chemical resistance	
Excellent durability (20–30 yr)	Multicomponent requires mixing
Can meet ASTM C920 for all systems	
Much better than polysulfides	One-component not recommended for traffic areas
	Not recommended for stopless glazing

[a] Ref. 11.

Over the past 20 years or so, polyurethanes (28) have replaced both polysulfides and silicones in many electrical cable splicing and potting applications. Due to the experience gained, where flexibility, good weather resistance, and high tensile strength is required, this type of chemistry has found its way into the construction and insulating glass industries. Other important properties required by the architectural industry are impact strength and a broad range of temperature limits. Polyurethanes have been used as cryogenic sealants.

Over the past several years, primers were generally required for most urethanes, regardless of intended application, in order to obtain satisfactory adhesion to a given substrate. For the most part, polyurethanes are not recommended for glasses; however, within the past five years they have become prominent as edge sealants for both single and dual systems in insulating glass units. Table 19 compares the many advantage (11) and disadvantages of polyurethanes.

Acrylics

Acrylic chemistry dates back to 1843, with the commercial development of polymers beginning in the late 1920s. $CH{=}CH{-}COOH$ is the basic acrylic acid (4) building block required. It was not until the late 1950s that the first acrylic sealant for the building industry was devel-

oped. One of the single biggest advantages was a single-component product that requires no primers.

Although the acrylic solvent-based sealants are more recent new product entries, they have nevertheless been employed in both architectural and industrial sealant applications for a number of years. These sealants are based on high solids, acrylic-solution polymers that offer the characteristic acrylic polymer advantages of excellent adhesion and superior exterior durability.

If performance properties of the sealants that existed some years ago are examined, the market entry of the acrylic type is not at all surprising. At that time, there were many application areas in which the butyl caulks could not be employed because of certain performance shortcomings such as high shrinkage and poor elongation and recovery properties. This left a sealant performance gap because it was economically undesirable to employ the more expensive elastomeric-type sealants in these areas where elastomeric-type properties were not really required. The introduction of the acrylic solvent-based sealants filled this performance gap, because they possessed many properties intermediate in nature between the butyls and the truly elastomeric-type sealants. To an extent, this is still true today, and acrylics continue to be specified in many intermediate performance-type applications where butyls do not qualify and the elastomers are unnecessary. Of course, the acrylic sealants have also enlarged on both ends of their originally intended performance range and have replaced the butyls and elastomerics in many application areas (Table 20).

Aqueous or water-base sealants (4), more commonly known as latex–acrylic caulks, are very recent entries and are still a rather new and unique product concept. Aqueous caulks, as the term denotes, are those in which the solvent or dispersing medium is water. Their cure is therefore a result of water rather than organic solvent evaporation. The acrylic-emulsion polymers received attention for caulk and sealant applications because it was felt that their use might eliminate some of the problems of the polyvinyl acrylic (PVA) sytems as well as allow an aqueous caulk to be employed in exterior applications. Aqueous acrylic caulks have now been developed that offer substantial improvements over the earlier water-based products. Because these caulks are formulated with acrylic emulsions similar to those employed in exterior latex–acrylic paints, the caulks are expected to display the same excellent exterior durablity properties. On the basis of accelerated laboratory tests, these aqueous caulks

Table 20. Single-component Cross-linked Solvent Acrylic Sealant[a]

Property	Test Method	Value
Viscosity, poise, 75°F		10,000
Density lb/gal		12.4
Hardness, Shore A	TT–S–00230	45
Sag	TT–S–00230	No sag
Tack-free time		Less than 3 d
Adhesion-in-peel	TT–S–00230	7.0 lb/in.
Bond durability	TT–S–00230	65 psi
Elongation	Cure 3 wk at 150°F	280%
Chalking	Cure 3 wk at 150°F	None

[a] Ref. 19. Courtesy of Bostik Construction Products.

appear completely suitable for exterior applications (Table 21). Table 22 offers some of the advantages and disadvantages of both latex and solvent-containing acrylics.

REFERENCE STANDARDS

The construction, building, and industrial markets utilize many standards for specifications involved in waterproofing, caulking, glazing, etc. Table 23 contains a comprehensive list of specifications and standards that govern generic materials.

Table 21. Single-component Latex–Acrylic Caulking Compound[a]

Property	Value
Tack-free time	20–40 min
Extrudability	Excellent
Weight loss	15%
Sag	Negligible
Staining	None
Adhesion-in-peel	8.2 lb/in.
Adhesion-in-peel after uv exposure	10.0 lb/in.
Freeze–thaw stability	5 Cycles
Package (tube) stability	1 yr

[a] Refs. 18–19.

Table 22. Advantages and Disadvantages of Latex and Solvent-containing Acrylics

Advantages	Disadvantages
Excellent color stability	Long tack-free time
Low shrinkage	Poor water resistance
Single-component with low stability	Slow cure
Superior adhesion to most building surfaces	Low extensibility
	Strong odor

Table 23. Sealant Specifications and Standards

Specification (Date)	Description
	Construction
Federal Specifications	
TT–S–00227E (11/4/69)	Sealing compound elastomeric type, multicomponent (for caulking, sealing, and glazing buildings and other structures)
TT–S–00230C (10/9/70)	Sealing compound elastomeric type, single-component (for caulking, sealing, and glazing buildings and other structures)
TT–S–01543A (6/9/71)	Sealing compound, silicone rubber base (for caulking, sealing, and glazing buildings and other structures)
TT–S–001657	Sealing compound, single-component, butyl rubber based, solvent-release type (for buildings and other types of construction)
ASTM Specifications	
ANSI/ASTM C920–79 Standard specification for elastomeric joint sealants	
Canadian Specifications	
19–GP–5M (4/83)	Sealing compound, one-component, acrylic base, solvent curing
19–GP–9Ma, Type 1/2 (9/82)	Sealing compound, one-component, silicone base, chemical curing
19–GP–13M (9/82)	Sealing compound, one-component, polysulfide base, chemical curing
19–GP–14M (6/83)	Sealing compound, one-component, butyl–polyisobutylene polymer base, solvent curing
19–GP–16M, Type 1/2 (2/82)	Sealing compound, one-component, polyurethane base, chemical curing
9–GP–17M (9/82)	Sealing compound, one-component, acrylic-emulsion base
CAN2–19.24–M80, Type 1/2, class 2/B (9/82)	Sealing compound, multicomponent, chemical curing
CAN–19.24–M80 (9/82)	Sealing compound, multicomponent, chemical curing, nonsag, nonglazing
	Insulating Glass
ASTM Specifications	
ASTM E774–81	Standard specification for sealed insulating glass units
Canadian Specifications	
CAN–2–12.8–M76	Insulating glass units

GLOSSARY

Following is a concise glossary of terms used in the seal-ant, adhesive, and building industries (2,3,29,30).

Abrasion. The wearing away of a material surface by friction. Particles become detached by a combined cutting, shearing, and tearing action. Important factor in tire treads, soles, and conveyor belts.

Accelerated Aging. Any set of conditions designed to introduce in a short time the result obtained under nor-mal conditions of aging. In accelerated-aging tests the usual factors considered are heat, light, and oxygen, ei-ther separately or combined. Sometimes called acceler-ated life. Most often accomplished by heating samples in an atmosphere of oxygen at 300 psi pressure and 70°C (Bierer–Davis), or by heating them in an oven provided with circulating air, maintained at 70–100°C (Geer).

Accelerated Weathering. Machine-made means of du-plicating or reproducing weather conditions. Such tests are particularly useful in comparing a series of products at the same time. No real correlation between test data and actual service is known for many resins and rubbers used in many products.

Accelerator of Vulcanization. Any substance that has-tens the vulcanization of rubber causing it to take place in shorter time or at a lower temperature. In earlier days, basic oxides such as lime, litharge, and magnesia were recognized as having this function. Nowadays, the impor-tant accelerators are organic substances containing either nitrogen or sulfur or both. According to potency or speed of action accelerators are sometimes classified as slow, me-dium, rapid, semiultra, and ultra-accelerators. Most accel-erators enhance tensile properties, and many improve age resistance.

Acrylic. A group of thermosplastic resins formed by po-lymerizing the esters of acrylic acid.

Activator. A substance that, by chemical interaction, promotes a specific chemical action of a second substance. Most accelerators require activators to bring out their full effect in vulcanization (eg, zinc oxide or other metallic oxides); some accelerators require a fat acid, especially with zinc oxide.

Adhesion. The clinging or sticking of two material sur-faces to one another. In rubber parlance, the strength of the bond or union between two rubber surfaces or plies, cured or uncured. The bond between a cured rubber sur-face and a nonrubber surface, eg, glass, metal, or wood fabric. (Note: The word *adhere* is an intransitive verb and should never be used as a transitive verb.)

Adhesive Failure. (*1*) The separation of the two surfaces with a force less than specified. (*2*) The separation of the two adjoining surfaces due to service conditions.

Backfill. Placing material into the opening between glass and glazing stops.

Blowing. Porosity or sponginess occurring during cure. In latex goods, a permanent deformation caused when the deposit leaves the form during curing or drying.

Bond Strength. The force per unit area or strength nec-essary to rupture a bond.

Butyl Rubber. A copolymer of about 98% isobutylene and 2% isoprene. It has the poorest resistance to petro-leum oils and gasolines of any rubber. Excellent resis-tance to vegetable and mineral oils; to solvents such as acetone, alcohol, phenol, and ethylene glycol; and to ester and gas absorption. Heat resistance is above average. Sunlight resistance is excellent. Its abrasion resistance is not as good as natural rubber. Usually low permeability to gases.

Catalyst. Substance that markedly speeds up the cure of an adhesive when added to minor quantity as compared to the amounts of primary reactants.

Caulking. The process of sealing a joint or the materials used. Most often refers to linseed oil and lead compounds and to cotton or oakum strands used in the back of seams rather than to the more recently developed sealing mate-rials.

Centipoise. $1/100$ of a poise, which is a value for viscos-ity. The viscosity of water at 20°C is approximately 1 cen-tipoise. (1 millipoise equals $1/1000$ poise.)

Chalking. Formation of a powdery surface condition caused by disintegration or surface binder or elastomer due to weathering or other destructive environments.

Channel Depth. The measurement from the bottom of the channel to the top of the stop, or measurement from sight line to base of channel.

Channel Glazing. The sealing of the joints around light or panels set in a U-shaped channel employing removable stops.

Coefficient of Expansion. The coefficient of linear ex-pansion is the ratio of the change in volume per degree to the length at 0°C. The coefficient of volume expansion (for solids) is three times the linear coefficient. The coefficient of volume expansion for liquids is the ratio of the change in volume per degree of the volume at 9°C.

Cold Flow. The permanent deformation under constant stress. Also defined as the continuing dimensional change under static load that follows initial instantaneous defor-mation. If subjected to pressure long enough, no organic material will return exactly to its original shape. Com-pression set is the amount by which a small cylinder fails to return.

Compression Set. The residual decrease in thickness of a test specimen measured 30 min after removal from a suitable loading device in which the specimen had been subjected for a definite time to compressive deformation under specified conditions of load application and temper-ature. Method A measures compression set of vulcanized rubber under constant load. Method B employs constant deflection. (See ASTM method D395.)

Cure. To change the properties of a material by a chemical reaction such as condensation, polymerization, or vulcanization. Usually accomplished by the action of heat and catalysts, alone or in combination, with or with-out pressure.

Cure Time. The time required to produce vulcanization at a given temperature. The cure time varies widely, de-pending on the type of compounding used, the thickness of the product, etc.

Curing Agent. Generally the second of a two-part sys-tem that, when added to the base material, cures or solidi-fies the base material by a chemical reaction.

Density. The ratio of the mass of a body to its volume or

the mass per unit volume of the substance. When GGS units are used, the density of a substance is numerically equal to the specific gravity of the substance referred to water at 4°C, the maximum density (1000) of water. For ordinary practical purposes, density and specific gravity may be regarded as equivalent.

Durometer. An instrument for determining the hardness of rubber by measuring its resistance to the penetration (without puncturing) of a blunt indentor point impressed on the rubber surface against the action of a spring. A special scale indicates the resistance to penetration or "hardness." The scale reads from 0 to 100, 0 being very soft and 100 being very hard.

Elasticity. The property of matter by virtue of which it tends to return to its original shape after deformation such as stretching, compression, and torsion. It is the opposite of plasticity. It is often loosely employed to signify the "stretchiness" of rubber. As applied to rubber, it usually refers to the phenomenal distance to which vulcanized rubber can be stretched without losing its ability to return very nearly to its original shape; in this respect, rubber is the most elastic substance known.

Elongation. Increase in length expressed numerically as a fraction or percentage of initial length.

Face Glazing. On rabbeted sash without stops, the triangular bead of compound applied with glazing knife after bedding, setting, and clipping the light in place.

Filler. Relatively nonadhesive substance added to an adhesive to improve its working properties, permanence, strength, or other qualities.

Glazing. The securing of glass in prepared openings in windows, door panels, screens, partitions, etc.

Hardness. Property or extent of being hard. Measured by extent of failure of the indentor point of any one of a number of standard hardness testing instruments to penetrate the product.

Interface. The common boundary surface between two substrates. Sometimes described as two surfaces with no space between them (for example, where the air contacts this paper is the air–paper interface).

Joint. The location at which two adherends are held together by an adhesive. (See also Starved Joint.)

Lap Joint. A joint made by overlapping adjacent edge areas of two adherends to provide facing surfaces that can be joined with an adhesive.

Low Temperature Flexibility. The ability of a rubber product to be flexed, bent, or bowed at low temperatures.

Mastic. An adhesive of such a consistency that it must be applied by notched trowel, gob, or buttering methods.

Modulus. In the physical testing of rubber, the ratio stress to strain, ie, the load in pounds per square inch or kilos, per square centimeter of initial cross-sectional area necessary to produce a stated percentage elongation. It is a measure of stiffness and is influenced in pigmentation, state of cure, quality of rubber, and other factors.

MVTR (Moisture Vapor Transmission Rate). Rate at which moisture passes from atmosphere into sealed space between sealed unit lites.

Permeability. The quality or condition of allowing passage of liquids or gasses through a rubber layer.

Polysulfide Elastomer. A synthetic rubberlike elastomer practically insoluble in oils and solvents, prepared from ethylene chloride and sodium tetrasulfide commonly called Thiokol. It was the first commercial synthetic elastomer (1930). Other dichlorides used are di-(2-chloroethyl) ether and di-(2-chloroethyl) formal. These are not vulcanized with sulfur but by heating with zinc oxide.

Polyurethane. A family of polymers ranging from rubbery to brittle. Usually formed by the reaction of di-ioscyanate with a hydroxyl.

Primer. Special coating designed to provide adequate adhesion of a coating system to new surface. In the case of new wood, it is used to allow for the exceptional absorption of the medium. Metal priming coatings for steel work contain special anticorrosive pigments or inhibitors, such as red lead, white lead, zinc powder, zinc chromate, etc.

Rabbet. A two-sided, L-shaped recess in sash or frame to receive light or panels. When no stop or molding is added, such rabbets are faced glazed. Addition of a removable stop produces a three-sided, U-shaped channel.

Reversion. (1) The change that occurs in vulcanized rubber as the result of aging or overcuring in the presence of air or oxygen, usually resulting in a semiplastic mass. (2) It is the basis of rubber reclaiming processes and is aided by the use of swelling solvents, chemical plasticizers, and mechanical disintegration to obtain a workable mass.

Rex Hardness. The hardness of a "soft" vulcanized rubber or other similar elastic material as measured by Rex Hardness Gauge.

Sealant. (1) A continuous film to prevent the passage of liquids and gaseous media; a high bodied adhesive generally of low cohesive strength to fill voids of various sizes to prevent passage of liquid and gaseous media. (2) A coating used to seal the sand-scratched surface of a primer in order to obtain a smooth uniform paint base over rough metal. Sealants are products of low pigmentation.

Shear. The progressive relative displacement of adjacent layers because of strain or a lateral motion.

Shelf Life. The period of time a packaged adhesive or sealer can be stored under specific temperature conditions and remain suitable for use.

Shrinkage. The percent loss of volume of material when put through a particular process as, for example, the washing and drying of crude rubber. The percent diminution in area or volume of a piece of processed unvulcanized rubber compound on cooling. Also, the contraction of molded vulcanized rubber on cooling.

Silicone Rubber. A rubber prepared by the action of moisture on dichlor-dimethyl-silicone. These rubbers withstand temperature from 120 to 500°F and are vulcanized with benzol peroxide.

Specific Gravity. Specific gravity equals weight of substance. It is a ratio of the weight of any volume of a substance to the weight of an equal volume of a standard substance at stated temperatures. For solids or liquids the standard substance is usually water, and for gases the standard is air or hydrogen.

Starved Joint. A joint that has an insufficient amount of adhesive to produce a satisfactory bond.

Surface Preparation. The procedure required with respect to a foundation surface or the materials to be adhered that will promote optimum performances of an adhesive, coating, or sealer. For example, if higher bond strength is required, abrading or acid etching the surfactants can be the means of improving the adhesion of the bonding material to the mating surfaces. Common methods of surface preparation are solvent washing, sandblasting, and vapor degreasing.

Tensile Strength. The capacity of a material to resist a force tending to stretch it. Ordinarily the term is used to denote the force required to stretch a material to rupture and is known variously as breaking load, or ultimate tensile strength. In rubber testing, it is the load in pounds per square inch or kilos per square centimeter of original cross-sectional area supported at the moment of rupture by a piece of rubber on being elongated at a constant rate.

Thixotropic. A term used to describe certain colloidal dispersions that, when at rest, assume a gel-like condition but that, when agitated, stirred, or subjected to pressure or other mechanical action at ordinary temperatures, are transformed into a liquid condition. The action is reversible and can be repeated at will. Thixotropic colloids occur in nature, the best known example being bentonite, a colloidal American clay. Rubber dispersions are not thixotropic colloids.

Tooling. Operation of pressing in and striking a compound in a joint in order to press compound against the sides of a joint and secure good adhesion. Also, the finishing off of the surface of a compound in a joint so that it is flush with the surface. A narrow, blunt bladed tool is used for this purpose.

Toxicity. A term referring to the physiological effect of absorbing a poisonous substance into the system through the skin, mucous membranes, or respiratory system. When describing their toxic effect, solvents are usually classified as having high, medium, or low toxic effect, depending on whether a solvent vapor concentration of less than 100, 100 to 400, or over 400 parts per million, respectively, is the maximum amount permissible in the air for safe or healthful working conditions.

Ultimate Elongation. The elongation at the moment of rupture.

Water Resistance. The ability to withstand swelling by water for a specified time and temperature, usually 48 h at 100°C, expressed as percentage swelling or volume increase of the specimen.

Working Life. Period of time during which an adhesive, sealer, or coating, after mixing with catalyst, solvent, or other compounding ingredients, remains suitable for use.

CONCLUSION

Over the past several years, polyurethanes have become one of the mainstays for building joints. Silicones have captured the imagination with their success in structural glazing application due to their favorable performance in weathering, particularly uv resistance, and polysulfides have been losing ground. In addition, these three generic materials plus polymercaptans have the capability of meeting a variety of standards relative to the ± 12.5% to ± 25% extension range, and some silicones perform at

higher ranges. All are priced competitively. Butyls and acrylics still have their place and appear to remain static in growth because of limited performance properties, even though pricing is lower in general.

Much experience of poor sealant performance and resulting damage to a wide variety of structure exists. Concern with such problems spurred the development and introduction in the last decade of higher class sealants. Failures have continued to occur, however, often within days or weeks rather than months or years, for five specific reasons:

1. The joint as designed was of an impossible width, shape, or potential movement to seal successfully, yet the joint was constructed and sealed.
2. Unanticipated service conditions have resulted in greater joint movements than those allowed for when the joint design and type of sealant were determined.
3. The wrong type of sealant for a particular condition was selected, often on the false grounds of economy in first cost.
4. New sealants have sometimes been initially overpromoted and used before their limitations were tested and realized.
5. Poor workmanship occurred when constructing the joint, in preparing it to receive the sealant, or during sealant installation.

BIBLIOGRAPHY

1. J. S. Amstock and G. J. Bouchey, "The Right Sealant," in *U.S. Glass, Metal & Glazing* (July 1986).
2. *ACI 504 R-77 Guide to Joint Sealants for Concrete Structures,* American Concrete Institute, Detroit, Mich., 1977.
3. *Sealants: The Professional Guide,* Sealant and Waterproofers Institute, Kansas City, Kans., 1984.
4. J. S. Amstock, *Handbook of Adhesive Bonding,* McGraw-Hill Inc., New York, 1982, Chapt. 7.
5. *The Construction Specifier* (Dec. 1985).
6. *Architectural Technology,* 65 (May/June 1986). No additional data available.
7. *Silicone,* Technical Service Bulletin 983, Dow Corning Corp., Midland, Mich., 1986
8. *Installation Handbook,* Tile Council of America, Princeton, N.J., 1986.
9. *Sealant Facts,* Bostik Construction Products, Huntingdon Valley, Pa.
10. A. Damusis, *Sealants,* Reinhold Publishing Corp., New York, 1967.
11. J. P. Cook and J. R. Panek, *Construction Sealants and Adhesives,* 2nd ed., John Wiley & Sons, Inc., New York, 1984.
12. *Chem-Calk 300,* Technical Bulletin, Bostik Construction Products, Huntingdon Valley, Pa., 1987.
13. E. R. Bertozzi, "Chemistry and Technology of Elastomeric Polysulfide Polymers," in *Rubber Chemistry Technology,* (1) (Feb. 1968).
14. U. S. Pat. 2,466,963 J. D. Patrick and H. R. Ferguson, Thiokol Chemical Corp.

15. *Chem-Calk 250,* Technical Bulletin, Bostik Construction Products, Huntingdon Valley, Pa., 1987.
16. *Chem-Calk 100,* Technical Bulletin, Bostik Construction Products, Huntingdon Valley, Pa., 1987.
17. *Chem-Calk 500,* Technical Bulletin, Bostik Construction Products, Huntingdon Valley, Pa., 1987.
18. *Chem-Calk 600,* Technical Bulletin, Bostik Construction Products, Huntingdon Valley, Pa., 1987.
19. *Chem-Calk 800,* Technical Bulletin, Bostik Construction Products, Huntingdon Valley, Pa., 1987.
20. *Chem-Calk 900,* Technical Bulletin, Bostik Construction Products, Huntingdon Valley, Pa., 1987.
21. *Silicone Construction Sealants,* Dow Corning Corp., Midland, Mich., 1986.
22. *Exteriors Magazine,* 950–951 (Summer 1986).
23. *Pensil (TM), Silicone Penetration Sealant,* Technical Bulletin, General Electric Co., Waterford, N.Y., 1983.
24. H. Singh, *Permapol (R) P-3 Polymers,* Products Research and Chemical Corp., Glendale. Calif.
25. Technical Bulletin 975, Dow Corning Corp., Midland, Mich.
26. Technical Bulletin 982, Dow Corning Corp., Midland, Mich.
27. *Fire Stop System 7.11/Do,* Dow Corning Corp., Midland, Mich.
28. D. Corhill, *Missile Sealants,* Products Research and Chemical Corp., Glendale, Calif, 1968.
29. *Publication 1006,* Building Research Institute, Washington, D.C., 1963.
30. *Flat Glass Marketing Association Sealant Manual,* Flat Glass Marketing Association, Topeka, Kans., 1983.

See also ACRYLICS; ADHESIVES; BRICK MASONRY; CONCRETE MASONRY; ENVELOPES; BUILDING; PLASTICS; SILICONES

JOSEPH S. AMSTOCK
Bostik Construction Products
Huntingdon Valley,
Pennsylvania

SECONDARY SCHOOLS

School design is one of the most important and meaningful challenges found in the discipline of architecture. In determining the character and quality of a society, schools are almost as influential as the institutions of home and family.

The secondary, or high school, provides a social and educational link between childhood and adulthood. For teenage youth, the school is a primary force in educational development and social adjustment; for people of all ages, the school is often the center of community interaction. Everyone, from students and parents to members of the community, is influenced by the school at some time in his or her life. All must share in its financial support.

Beyond the basic task of providing education for youth, the school provides opportunities for adult education, library services, cultural and artistic activities, indoor and outdoor sports and recreation, and social gathering space. In addition, the high school is often an aesthetically landscaped space that serves as an architectural focal point for the entire community.

The planning and design of such facilities are inseparable from the broader concerns inherent in community planning. For example, while the design of a school is heavily influenced by its surrounding context, it can directly affect the character of the neighborhood streets and communities it supports.

It is necessary to reexamine these institutions, because architecture for education is a task that is worthy of society's best efforts. From years of experience in designing school buildings, architects have learned an important lesson: good communities require good schools.

A BRIEF HISTORY

The concept of the U.S. public high school evolved in New England in the nineteenth century. By the 1880s, a few thousand high schools throughout the country were serving hundreds of thousands of students. Educators saw the high school as part of a continuous spectrum of learning, creating a transition between elementary school and college. Some school buildings from this era still exist. They are compact, multifloor masonry buildings with historic details. Some of the surviving school buildings are good candidates for historic landmark designation.

For years, educators have debated whether high schools should be primarily for college preparation or whether vocational education should also be an important part of the curriculum. During the early twentieth century, vocational education became increasingly important. Other major developments during that century included the creation of separate junior high schools and the increasing impact of progressive education.

Some of the largest and finest secondary school buildings were built in the early part of the twentieth century. Chicago architect Dwight Perkins designed many outstanding high schools in the midwest including Evanston Township High School, Evanston, Ill, whose subdivided "school-within-a-school" design has been expanded through the years to serve more than 6000 students (Fig. 1).

Following World War II, thousands of new high schools were constructed in response to national geographic shifts and increases in population. Many of these schools were built well and incorporated new architectural concepts. In Texas, Caudill Rowlett and Scott were innovative architects in the secondary school field as were many other architects throughout the country. For example, in designing Hillsdale High School, Hillsdale, Calif., designers John Lyon Reid and Partners emphasized adaptability to future changes in space requirements through the use of nonload-bearing movable partitions. In sharp contrast to these innovative approaches, many schools were built poorly, spurred by a short-term goal of economy.

After the 1957 launching of *Sputnik,* the federal government began to provide renewed financial support for the construction of schools, especially those with science facilities and active science programs. These programs, and the new methods of "open plan" and team teaching that emerged at this time, began to significantly alter the ways in which schools were being designed.

Figure 1. Evanston Township High School, Evanston, Ill.; Dwight Perkins, architect. The Collegiate Gothic building has served the community well for over 60 years.

In the 1950s and 1960s, school design was influenced by the research and publications of The Educational Facilities Laboratories, Inc., with funding from the Ford Foundation. The 1960s saw the design and construction of a record number of new high schools, as the baby boomers were growing up and out of their elementary schools. In suburban areas of the country, schools such as New Trier West High School, Northfield, Ill., designed by Perkins & Will and The Architects Collaborative, looked more like college campuses than high schools (Fig. 2). Cities were also constructing new secondary schools, including "magnet schools," which attracted students from all parts of the city to specialized programs in science, business, the arts, and other areas.

By the 1970s, school construction began to fall sharply as demographics changed and school districts found themselves saddled with too many classrooms. The once filled-to-capacity New Trier West high School was now deemed "surplus school space" (Fig. 3).

In the late 1980s, with some signs that enrollments are rising, school design has once again become an important topic. In the south, west, and northeast, new schools are being planned to replace obsolete and long neglected buildings, with some cities expecting to spend billions of dollars in new construction.

CURRENT TRENDS IN HIGH SCHOOL DESIGN

Community Schools

Tomorrow's schools will be different in a number of fundamental ways. Most important, they will be "community schools," serving the needs of all citizens through recognition of the fact that learning is a lifelong process in which everyone has a stake. The concept has been championed for the last 50 years by the Mott Foundation and by the National Community Education Association.

The community school will function as an activity center for the entire community, in addition to serving the needs of traditional high school students. The school will be open past regular class hours, so it can serve as a center for educational, cultural, and recreational activities for

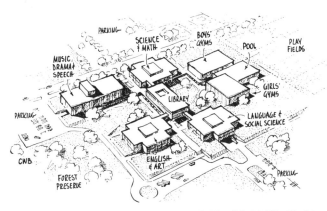

Figure 2. New Trier West High School, Northfield, Ill.; Perkins & Will and TAC, architects. A half-dozen building units are linked to create a collegelike campus.

Figure 3. New Trier West High School, Northfield, Ill.; Perkins & Will and TAC, architects. With enrollment decline in the 1970s, the school building became available for adaptive use.

the entire community. It will be a community center (with media and social rooms), a cultural center (with theater, music, and art facilities), a recreation center (with gymnasium, courts, and a pool for both high school physical education and community fitness, recreation, and lifetime sports). Because a community school involves people from the entire community and not only students, it is more likely to be supported, both financially and developmentally, than a regular high school.

VARIOUS EDUCATIONAL PROGRAMS

All high schools in a large district need not be identical. In fact, there are distinct advantages to having a variety of high school programs accessible to students, whether under one roof or at different locations. Different schools-within-a-school are possible, where each small school offers a special kind of program.

Some schools may provide a standard comprehensive program, others might emphasize the basics, and still others might base their curricula on independent study and individual scheduling. A district-wide career education center can offer specialized vocational and technical courses, especially those requiring equipment that is often too costly to duplicate at every school. For example, a student might go to the career center on Tuesday and Thursday afternoons, but would attend classes at the home-base high school most of the time. Schools such as these are becoming increasingly common and signify a trend away from imposing the same educational system on all students without regard to their individual differences.

EDUCATION CAN BE MULTILOCATIONAL

In relation to the various kinds of schools noted above, there is another new idea evolving in school design: having a student attend a different school each day. In this system, students are assigned to a "home-base" high school where they spend the majority of their time, but on certain days, they report to locations other than the high school, such as a cultural arts school, a business school, an art museum, or a concert hall. This system extends education into the working world, giving students the opportunity to make contacts with adults, to be exposed to career choices, and to become more involved in their community.

It is important to recognize that this type of outreach program still requires a home base, a new kind of community center and high school. Fragments of this idea can be found in some schools, but the full implications of such a system have not yet been fully tested. School design will be a concurrent challenge; new kinds of spaces and new kinds of buildings will be needed.

NEW TECHNIQUES FOR TEACHING AND LEARNING

The most conspicuous change in learning has come about through the increasing use of computers, television, and other new media. Although computer-assisted instruction has been predicted and promoted for years, the principal places and methods of instruction continue to be the classroom lecture, individual discussions with teachers, and books, which are read in the classroom, the library, at home, or under a tree.

Will the computer and television ever partially or completely replace the classroom and the classroom teacher? Will information retrieved from computer storage partially or completely replace books? Will students continue to go to school or will they learn at home, in which case the school would take on a new form as a center for social, cultural, physical, large group, and educational activities? From the standpoint of architecture, the message is not crystal clear, but it is loud enough to be heard and cannot be ignored.

The secondary school, being a long-term investment, should be designed to accommodate both traditional educational programs that are based on classroom instruction, with class size ranging from 20 to 30 students, and educational programs that rely on new teaching and learning techniques, including extensive use of computers, television, and other new media. The traditional classroom, which was challenged in the 1960s, has survived for hundreds of years, and it is unlikely that it will ever be completely eliminated; however, it is likely that it will be challenged again.

The ideals of independent learning (education tailored to the unique needs of each individual) and the ideals of individual scheduling (learning at each student's own pace) are stable components of educational philosophy in the U.S. Only a few good examples of individual study can be found today, but perhaps it is an idea whose time has come. If so, secondary school design will change. Rather than placing classrooms along corridors, open space, as is found in office buildings, will be accepted as more appropriate.

Each student will need his or her own study space for reading, writing, drawing, artwork, computer use, storage, and discussions with teachers and other students. From this space, the student will go to lecture rooms, laboratories, studios, the library, the gymnasium, the dining room, and out into the community, but will have the home base to return to when desired (Fig. 4).

ADAPTABILITY

One of the proudest accomplishments of architects in recent decades has been the achievement of higher levels of flexibility in the design of spaces, with the modern office building being the best example of this concept. When an office building is designed, the architects are generally unaware of who the tenants will be, so space must be flexible enough to accommodate both large and small firms. Structural, mechanical, and electrical systems have evolved that permit future users of space to arrange it to suit their individual needs using a broad variety of equipment.

Secondary schools can benefit from this type of adaptability. Like businesses, educational programs experience change through the years; as space requirements alter and new equipment is implemented, the school's structural, mechanical, and electrical systems must be able to support such equipment and the people who use it. In old bearing-wall buildings, these changes can be difficult and expensive. Well-designed new schools, which provide a high level of flexibility, have the distinct advantage of being able to conveniently and economically satisfy new space requirements.

GREAT SPACES

The flexible spaces discussed above imply one possible disadvantage: they can be boring, whether arranged as identical classrooms or open space. Thoughtful design will provide a wide array of spaces that vary in size, height, shape, materials, color, lighting, views, etc. To achieve the needed spatial variety, the architect should be alert to opportunities for great spaces in the program of space requirements.

A secondary school program includes large spaces that

Figure 4. Space for individual learning; sketch by C. William Brubaker. In tomorrow's school, each student may have a home base workplace.

Figure 5. Robert Morgan Vocational–Technical Institute, Dade County, Fla.; Perkins & Will, architects. Air-conditioned shops and laboratories flank a shaded open-air student mall.

require special design considerations: gymnasiums, a pool, an auditorium, a theater, a music room, a dining room, commons areas, a library, and major circulation spaces. These areas can become great spaces, some quiet and serene (the library), some noisy and challenging (the gymnasium), and some busy and exciting (the student "main street" through the school). Circulation space is an especially interesting design challenge. Instead of having only long corridors lined with classrooms and lockers, a school should have some special nodes, or focal points, for informal associations, social encounters, exhibitions, and notices. A two- or three-story galleria for circulation can also provide visual linkage between the floors. In areas where the climate is rigorous, an atrium can serve as the heart of the school, while in more temperate climates where outdoor circulation is possible, courtyards, plazas, porches, porticoes, stoas, alamedas, and ramadas are often desirable (Fig. 5).

DESIGN FOR ENERGY CONSERVATION

Energy-efficient architecture is a prime consideration for all schools, in light of the millions of dollars worth of energy that a school can consume in a 5–10 yr period and the scrutinized spending by public agencies for energy efficiency. Many of the schools built in the booming 1960s were energy hogs, flat roofed, thin walled, and poorly insulated, with little thought given to orientation or mechanical systems. Because these buildings use an extensive amount of energy for heating and cooling, efficiency is often a major factor in determining schools that warrant replacement.

There are both old and new buildings that get high marks for energy efficiency. Basic passive design is the most important consideration in achieving reasonable energy use per square foot. Some states mandate energy-efficient performance, but because every school board is concerned about operating costs, there is no reason that a high level of energy efficiency should fail to be achieved.

South-facing windows make economic sense and are most effective when equipped with an overhang that provides shade from the high summer sun while allowing the low winter sun to enter and create a greenhouse effect. Insulated north and east windows are acceptable for daylight and views, but west-facing windows should be avoided because the low summer sun can make a classroom's temperature uncomfortable.

The payback from well-insulated roofs and walls is easy to calculate, but the efficiency of mechanical and electrical systems is not so easy. The architect, who generally relies on his or her energy consultant for design details and specifications, should make very clear the energy goals of the project.

As energy costs continue to rise, architects will be forced to explore the possibilities of active solar energy systems as they did in the 1970s. Most of the active systems installed during that period were experimental in nature, and most of them are no longer in use. Regardless of this, when energy prices soar, designers and owners will be highly motivated to again explore new ideas. The stakes will be high, and design for energy conservation will be a widespread goal.

Innovative Structures

Nearly all new schools are built using conventional structures of steel, concrete or, where allowed, wood. Significant innovations are rare, probably because classrooms, laboratories, and offices do not often inspire such unusual structural systems as tent- or air-supported fabric structures, thin shells of concrete, or exotic space frames of steel or aluminum. Regardless of this structural conservatism, exploration of new concepts is most appropriate.

Structural systems should be integrated with other systems. For example, structural units may use their necessary depth to include mechanical and electrical systems, factory-made, truck-width hollow boxes that provide not just the structural floor, but also the finished ceiling, conditioned air, lighting, and communications systems.

Meanwhile, modular "portable" classrooms are used throughout the country to satisfy short-term space needs. They also need the attention of architects. When thoughtfully clustered together and landscaped, these facilities can be agreeable. The questions for future study include durability and flexibility.

Additions and Renovations

Nearly every school is expanded eventually to include one or more additions, whether planned or unplanned, and some old school buildings are worthy of quality renovation and continued use. In both cases, good design is the key to success.

In addition to regular maintenance, school buildings, like buildings in general, need periodic renewal when certain components wear out or when program changes require existing spaces be upgraded. Additions are often necessary when enrollments increase or when specialized spaces, such as a swimming pool or an auditorium, are needed that the existing building cannot accommodate.

Few existing schools enjoy the firm guidance for future growth that can be obtained from a master plan, prepared by the original architect. Too often, for lack of a long-range plan, later generations are forced to make *ad hoc* additions. To provide for future expansion, new schools clearly need a master plan that demonstrates the ways in which a building can grow and that illustrates land available for such expansion.

The initial design concept should include consideration of various phases for growth, including a plan for the ultimate development of the property. By preparing such a plan, mechanical and electrical systems can be designed to logically adapt and serve future additions. Access and exiting become increasingly important as a school grows, and the campus benefits from a unified design concept that guides long-term growth. In most instances, it is unreasonable to assume that a high school will not grow and change during its development.

As colleges and universities have discovered, alumni often hold old buildings, especially "Old Main," in high esteem. They demand that their alma maters be preserved, restored, and occupied, and are generally willing to support such endeavors with gifts of cash. Most college campuses have splendid examples of historic preservation, restoration and reuse.

Many school districts now have the opportunity for this same type of experience. Through the efforts of concerned school alumni members, many high school buildings, which a generation ago would have been demolished, are being restored. In the past, many fine, older high schools were demolished to make way for new school buildings, but some of the surviving schools from the late nineteenth and early twentieth centuries are well built, thick walled, and richly detailed and are fine candidates for restoration.

Surplus School Space

Due to changing demographics, some existing schools are no longer needed for education. Available for adaptive use, these "surplus schools" have been successfully recycled to create rental office space, corporate headquarters, shopping centers, art centers, cultural centers, town halls, and apartments.

Location is a key factor in these adaptive uses. If the surplus school is located in a commercial area, commercial reuse is appropriate; if it is in a residential neighborhood, apartments are considered more acceptable to most residents. A typical classroom of 850 ft^2 can provide space for a generous one-bedroom apartment. The best examples of such conversions are found in New England, where citizens enjoy living in converted schools that are a part of the community's history. In some instances, additional apartments have been constructed in new buildings on the site to more intensely utilize space.

In Norwalk, Conn., Perkins & Will served as architect for the conversion of a 1920s high school into the Norwalk City Hall. The project included recycling of the existing 100,000 ft^2, E-shaped school building and the addition of 40,000 ft^2 on three floors (Fig. 6). Successful conversions of this type raise a question, and possibly an emerging trend, in new school design: should a school be planned with future adaptive use in mind?

Finally, another idea for surplus school space must be considered. If the schools of a district are thought of not only as traditional schools, created to serve students of a particular age, but also as community schools, designed to serve all citizens, then the community may not have surplus school space at all; instead, the citizens are blessed with busy and valued centers for community education and life.

PROGRAMMING AND CONCEPT PLANNING

Office building design is quite different from school design in that the architect does not generally know who the end user of the building will be during its planning. The shell and core of an office building are established during the design phase, but the partition plans, equipment, and furnishings are left to future tenants. Only flexible, unfinished space is provided on the building's completion, leaving tenants to lay out the space, build walls where desired, and add equipment and furnishings.

School design is different. The architects work with users of the school building, determining (programming) the space requirements in detail and designing the building to satisfy these complex space needs. Obviously, this is a much more complex task than designing for an office building and, therefore, the professional services required are more costly.

Programming and determining how spaces relate are the most critical phases in the initial design of a high school. During these phases, the architect works with owners and users of the proposed building to gain an understanding of their needs. During programming and concept planning, or schematic design, the architect explores alternative concepts for the building, using the knowledge and understanding gained from meeting with the owners and users to provide a firm foundation for design decisions.

Different concepts are usually considered that involve a variety of space relationships, degrees of compactness,

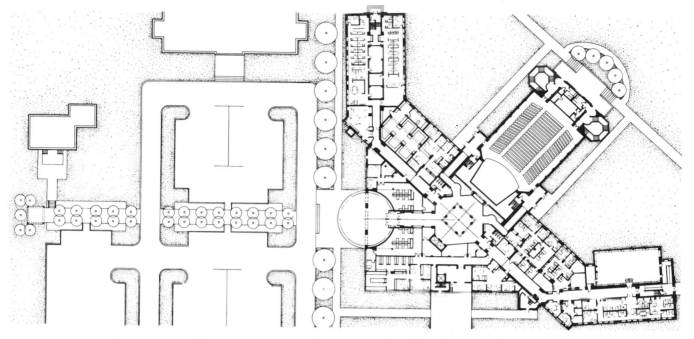

Figure 6. Norwalk City Hall, Norwalk, Conn. Perkins & Will, architects. A classic high school has been converted into a new city hall.

numbers of stories, various circulation systems, and an array of building forms. Bubble diagrams may be helpful in organizing and conveying alternatives. For example, the architect and the owner–user may determine that one promising concept places the school library at the heart of the school with four houses, or small schools, clustered around it. Shared arts and physical education facilities are placed at opposite ends of the complex. The resulting bubble diagram records that concept while other alternatives are considered (Fig. 7).

Secondary school designs range from one extremely compact building on a small site, to a number of widely spaced buildings arranged on a campus. The former is most likely to be encountered in a city with a rigorous climate; the latter is generally found in a suburban or rural location with a more benign climate.

The compact building might consist of one large single floor, possibly relieved by courtyards, but implying acceptance of some windowless space. (If too many or all of the spaces are windowless, students and teachers might object.) On the other hand, the compact building might be a multistory facility in the form of a cube, providing class-

rooms with views but relying on elevators or escalators for vertical circulation. Where property values are high, this is an option that should be considered.

The campus plan, in contrast, is appropriate where the climate permits outdoor circulation, recreation, assembly, and dining. Good examples of this plan can be found in California, where climate, state standards, and general economics suggest the use of a half-dozen or more separate buildings featuring outdoor circulation (Fig. 8).

A third concept falls between the compact and campus plans. Separate building units can be linked to form a complex that functions as one building, but that has the advantages of a number of separate building units that serve and express different functions. The building units may include a different number of floors, may utilize separate structural systems for economy, and may provide an array of options for daylight, natural ventilation, view, etc. One-, two- or three-story buildings can be linked with second- or third-story pedestrian bridges, keeping the ground floor open while creating continuous spaces at the second or third levels (Fig. 9).

Obviously, concepts are limitless. Every school has a unique site, a unique relationship to its community, an appropriate size, and a program that is tailored to the needs of the community. Therefore, every school has in its own program and site the primary design generators. A successful design concept will evolve from these fundamental facts of need and location.

NET USABLE AREAS, GROSS AREAS AND THE COSTS OF SCHOOLS

During the programming phase, the many components of the high school are identified and sized. Typical class-

Figure 7. House plan bubble diagram. Space relationships are recorded for various alternative schemes using diagrams.

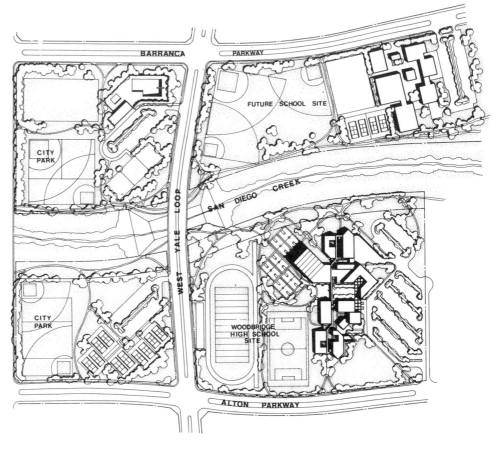

Figure 8. Woodbridge High School, Irvine, Calif.; Perkins & Will, architects. California's climate suggests use of the campus plan with outdoor circulation.

Figure 9. Warsaw High School, Warsaw, Ind.; The Odle Group and Perkins & Will, architects. For a 2000-student high school, building units are linked around a central quadrangle.

rooms may contain 850 ft² each, so if 10 English classrooms are required, the net usable area for those 10 classrooms will be 8,500 ft². Faculty office space, storage space, and a workroom may add another 1,500 ft², bringing the total net usable area for the English department to 10,000 ft².

When all of the net usable space requirements have been determined, the total net usable area is translated into gross area to allow for lobbies, walls, circulation, mechanical spaces, etc. Depending on local custom, budget, and design aspirations, and strongly influenced by whether circulation is indoors or outdoors, the total net usable area is multiplied by a factor (1.65, for example) to arrive at the total gross area. If the total net usable area, as programmed, is 180,000 ft², this figure is multiplied by an appropriate factor, such as 1.65, to give a total gross area of 297,000 ft².

Secondary schools vary widely in their size-per-student ratio. In southern and western climates, where outdoor circulation, recreation, assembly, and dining are possible, a high school for 1600 students could be as small as 144,000 ft², or 90 ft² per student (gross area). In communities, where indoor circulation is common, a 1600-student high school could be 200,000 ft², or 125 ft² per student. In affluent communities, when the program includes extensive physical education and arts facilities, a 1600-student high school could be 280,000 ft², or 175 ft² per student. The contrast in size makes an important point: differences in climate, culture, and economics largely influence school design and help to generate broad differences in the size, and therefore the costs, of schools.

Not only does area per student vary widely, but cost per square foot of construction can also be vastly different. A rural southern school may cost only $60.00/ft² while a northern urban school may cost $120.00/ft². When the differences in area per student and the differences in cost per square foot are combined, it is not unusual to see high schools, on a cost-per-student basis, costing four times as much in some areas as in others. The calculations (simplified for discussion) are as follows:

School A: 1600 students × 90 ft²/student
$$\times \, \$60.00/\text{ft}^2 = \$ \ 8,640,000$$

School B: 1600 students × 175 ft²/student
$$\times \, \$120.00/\text{ft}^2 = \$33,600,000$$

This extreme and simplified example serves as a reminder of the dangers in comparing school construction costs.

Finally, considering capital costs alone is a mistake. Operating and maintenance costs must also be evaluated if meaningful cost comparisons are to be made. A poorly designed school with inadequate insulation and inefficient mechanical and electrical systems can be an energy hog, consuming costly energy year after year and making the "low cost school" truly uneconomical. High quality design and construction are often the keys to long-term economy.

SITE PLANNING

Site planning should begin concurrently with programming and concept planning. School sites vary greatly from block-long city sites to 60- and 80-acre rural and suburban sites. The architect can be helpful in site selection.

Different sites should be tested by performing preliminary site studies to determine the advantages and disadvantages of alternative sites and to examine access, orientation, soil conditions, neighbors, traffic, etc. Depending on the state and community, the size of the site is determined by a number of factors:

1. The state may recommend or mandate school sizes.
2. Local government may influence site size via urban planning.
3. Local developers may plan school sites as part of their master plans for development.
4. Availability: if the recommended high school size is 60 acres, but if a well-located 50-acre site is available, the architect should seek ways to plan more compact school development for the smaller site.
5. Program requirements: a fresh analysis of need is the best way to establish site size. For example, the building zone may require 8 acres; bus loading, 2 acres; parking for 900 cars, 9 acres; entrance area and drives, 6 acres; landscaped zone around the perimeter, 9 acres; and playfields (football, soccer, track, practice, baseball, softball, and tennis), 26 acres. These requirements total 60 acres. If only a smaller site is available, some of the site areas can be reduced.

If most students arrive by bus, the bus loading area is the front door for the high school; however, some students drive to school, so entrances from the parking lots are also important. For public activities, especially in the evening, separate entrances are desirable for athletic events and recreation; cultural events in the theater and auditorium; and access to classrooms, laboratories, and shops. Schools tend to be used for more evening activities, so lighting for parking lots, walkways, and entrances is important (Fig. 10).

Pedestrian access from locker rooms and gymnasiums to outdoor playfields should be direct, without interference from automobile and truck traffic. Proper orientation affects the placement of football, baseball, softball, and tennis facilities. It is important to consider multipurpose possibilities for playfields, as soccer fields and softball outfields often overlap. Tennis courts are popular community resources, used early, late, and on weekends, so parking should be convenient.

With quality landscaping, the high school can be a parklike asset for the community. The open space it provides can be enhanced by trees and other landscaping materials. A landscape concept is important; a master plan for the site should guide future development if all of the desired features cannot be achieved during the initial construction period. Future areas for building expansion

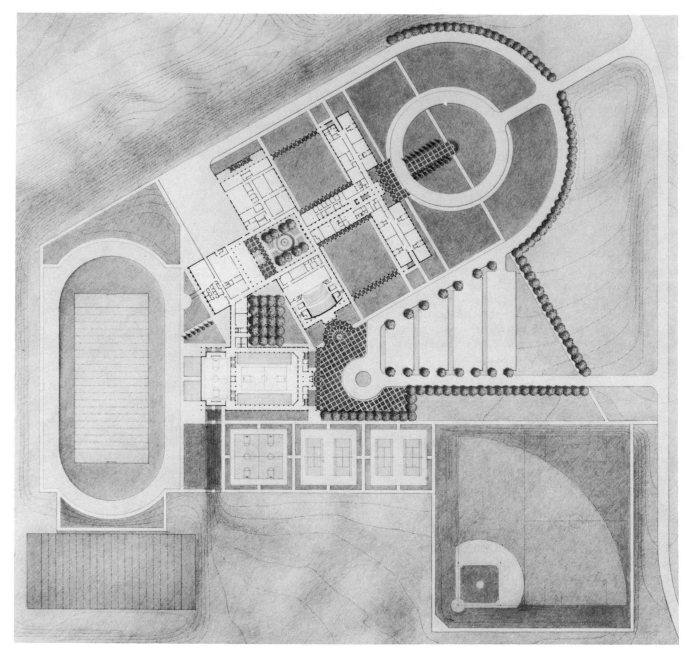

Figure 10. Capital High School, Santa Fe, N.M.; Mimbres, Inc. and Perkins & Will, architects. Bus loading is on the big circular drive, while public access to the gym and theater is off the small circle.

should be identified, and the site development plan should recognize these future building areas. Almost all high schools are eventually expanded, but unfortunately, not many high schools are initially prepared for these additions.

REGIONALISM RESPONDING TO LOCAL CLIMATE, CULTURE, AND CUSTOM

In every era, many schools tend to look alike, regardless of their location or the regional climate. The two- and three-story, brick- and stone-trimmed schools of the 1910s and the 1920s, whether collegiate Gothic, Romanesque, or Colonial, were often similar with their symmetrical, E-shaped plans and pitched roofs. In contrast, the schools of the 1950s and 1960s were austere, flat-roofed modern boxes with continuous, sometimes excessive, windows and spandrel panels of blue porcelain enameled steel.

Today, many schools embrace similar current design clichés, entrapped by the wiles of fashion. This is unfortunate, because good design is influenced by local climate, culture, custom, materials, and building methods. Good design is regional design, architecture that is particularly

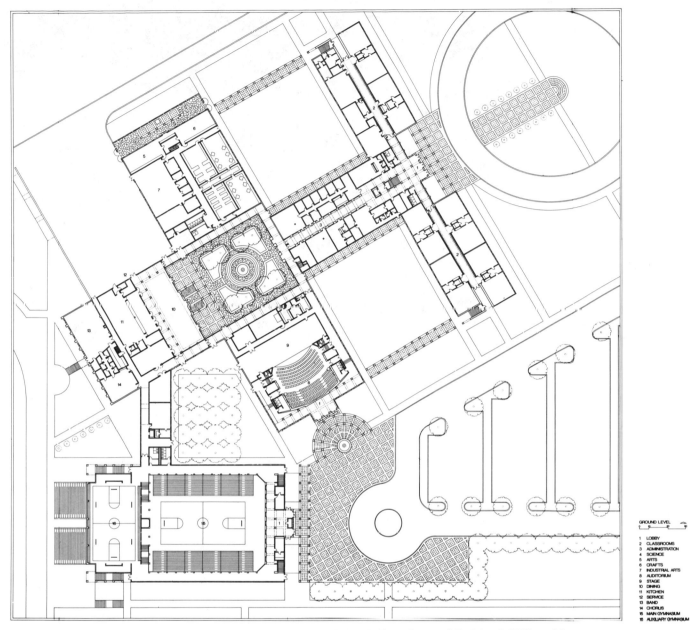

GROUND LEVEL

1 LOBBY
2 CLASSROOMS
3 ADMINISTRATION
4 SCIENCE
5 ARTS
6 CRAFTS
7 INDUSTRIAL ARTS
8 AUDITORIUM
9 STAGE
10 DINING
11 KITCHEN
12 SERVICE
13 BAND
14 CHORUS
15 MAIN GYMNASIUM
16 AUXILIARY GYMNASIUM

Figure 11. Capital High School, Santa Fe, N.M.; Mimbres, Inc., and Perkins & Will, architects. The heart of the school is a central plaza enclosed by four buildings.

appropriate to a special time and place. A great high school is tailored to its own place, its own region, and its own neighborhood. Regionalism helps to generate appropriate design and keep schools in different parts of the country from looking the same (Fig. 11).

Good examples of regionalism exist and offer valuable lessons. The campus-plan high schools of southern California are logically designed for that type of climate. The use of wood in the Pacific Northwest gives schools in Oregon and Washington a special character.

Some Arizona schools have appropriate desert features such as ramadas (shaded walks for circulation) as in the Desert View High School in Tucson, designed by TMP Associates. A high school on a small urban site in Chi-

cago, Ill., uses escalators to serve its eight stories. In a northeastern city of redbrick buildings, a new redbrick high school is welcomed, but in Florida, where concrete is commonly used, a redbrick school would be out of place. In the San Francisco Bay area, high schools are generally not air-conditioned, with balconies, natural ventilation, and narrow buildings making it unnecessary; however, in Houston, Texas, air-conditioning in a school is a major design generator.

Capital High School, in Sante Fe, N.M., is designed in the local "territorial style," using materials, colors, spaces, and details characteristic of the area (Fig. 12). The design is appropriate for Sante Fe, but would not be correct in Pittsburgh or Philadelphia, Pa. Architects should

Figure 12. Capital High School, Santa Fe, N.M.; Mimbres, Inc., and Perkins & Will, architects. Local materials, colors, spaces and details, identified as the "Territorial Style," are incorporated into the design concept.

Figure 13. Capital High School, Santa Fe, N.M.; Mimbres, Inc., and Perkins & Will, architects. Regional character should be encouraged in school design.

welcome opportunities to design local schools in the regional manner, shaping a building's character in response to local climate, culture, and custom and not on national or worldwide fashion, which can too easily be a substitute for creativity (Fig. 13).

BIBLIOGRAPHY

General References

CEFPI Journal, Council of Educational Facilities Planners, International, Columbus, Ohio.

Guide for Planning Educational Facilities, Council of Educational Facilities Planners, Columbus, Ohio, 1985.

S. Leggett, C. W. Brubaker, A. Chodes, and A. Shapiro *Planning Flexible Learning Places,* McGraw-Hill Inc., New York, 1977.

R. Propst, *High School—The Process and the Place,* Educational Facilities Laboratories, Inc., New York, 1972.

"Study #657—Schools," *Architectural Record,* (Sept. 1988).

See also ADAPTIVE USE; CAMPUS PLANNING; ELEMENTARY SCHOOLS; SOLAR AND ENERGY EFFICIENT DESIGN; VOCATIONAL EDUCATION

C. WILLIAM BRUBAKER, FAIA
Perkins & Will Partnership
Chicago, Illinois

SECURITY SYSTEMS

The concept of security for a site or facility have advanced over the centuries from slaves assigned to night watch in the courtyards of ancient Greek homes, to strolling peacocks in Persian palace grounds, to geese in Roman villas, to fences around American prairie land and brands on cattle, to fully integrated systems of electronic sensors and automated alarm annunciators, controlled and monitored by single and dual computers.

The architectural design drawings for the residence of Claudia Octavia in Rome show an apartment for the guardian with a clear access route to the master's private quarters for a quick response in emergencies. Japanese castles had a form of early warning intrusion detection built into their wood-planked "nightingale" floors. Purposefully designed to "sing" or squeak under the pressure of intruders' footsteps, the effective detection system alerted the armed night shift of Samurai to the defense of their sleeping lord.

Architects and engineers have long been charged with designing security into sites and buildings. Many of the most imaginative and challenging uses of natural materials and forces were designed into castles and forts and their entryways. The moats and drawbridges of European castles in the Middle Ages were efficient forms of access control. The heavily magnetic loadstones that the ancient Chinese used to build the footbridges to their walled compounds were effective weapons detection and automatic detention systems. As sword and dagger-bearing steel-armor-clad invaders charged onto the footbridge, the magnetic field of the loadstone held the warriors motionless. The design of trapdoors incorporated an understanding of the engineering principles of balancing distributed weight above with the tension of pulleys and counterweights below so that the owner could step knowingly across a rug and plunge a pursuer or companion to death below. Whether a volunteer group of citizens or a paid individual kept a night watch, there was dependence on human sensing abilities. As the nose could smell smoke and the ears could react to unusual sounds, the eyes could observe and inspect throughout neighborhoods along docks, and in camps, warehouses, banks, or estates.

The age of electricity and signal transmission over telegraph and telephone lines brought change-of-state, normally open or normally closed mechanisms or devices called detectors, and the ability to send alarm signals to manned remote monitoring facilities. Commercial facilities such as warehouses, banks, and shops protected their properties and contents, often at the insistence of lenders or insurers, with monitored alarm systems. The burglar alarm industry provided detectors to sense door, safe, and window intrusion or interior human motion with local on–off controls and provided remote monitoring at a commercial central station or at a manned policy agency. Installation of sensors, cabling, and connectors was completed after general construction was finished. The exposed conductors, surface-mounted detectors, and external telephone line connections were state of the art and satisfactory to insurance underwriters, but subject to attempted compromise by thieves. Unless a manned proprietary facility was installed at the protected site, all signal transmission was over telephone lines, and in many communities, these lines were strung from pole to pole along public thoroughfares.

The development of the transistor and miniaturization of electronic circuitry enabled the production of more sensitive sensors and wider variety of detecting devices, as well as signal-gathering transponder–multiplexers and full duplex communication capabilities.

In the post-World War II period, equally rapid radical changes took place in the construction industry. Scratch, rough, and finish coats of hand-applied plaster on wood lath, supported by 2 × 4-in. wood studs a true 16 in. apart on center were replaced by paper-covered gypsum 4 × 8-ft panels and cartridge-gun-driven threaded screw nails secured to hollow three-sided metal studs. The expanding range of building materials available to the design architect required means and methods of construction and protection systems installation. These provided for the integration of low-voltage power conductors, alarm signal conductors, dedicated raceways of conduit, junction boxes, and device or detector backboxes into the fabric of the architect's walls, ceilings, floors, and surrounding space. The age of design by the burglar alarm salesperson or technician was shortened by the architect, who demanded protection systems integrated into condominiums, corporate headquarters, museums, libraries, research facilities, etc, so that the vocabulary of design features was not punctuated by disproportionately dimensioned, surface-mounted, unaesthetically placed detectors, cameras, annunciators, and cover plates. Equipment manufacturers responded with a large range of recess-mountable magnetic contact door switches and miniature motion detectors employing ultrasonic and microwave frequencies, active and passive infrared energy, piezoelectric sensors and wire, microswitches, and pressure-change-responsive sensors. Time-and frequency-divided signal multiplexing transmitters; microprocessor-controlled automated monitoring systems; radio frequency electronic article surveillance systems; and barium ferrite insert, swipe, and proximity access control card readers also became available. Full duplex voice, data, and image transmission over coaxial cable equipped with signal annenuators, cable taps, and splitters was soon followed by miniature microwave dishes capable of transmitting video and audio without dedicated cable. Time-lapse transmission of digitized video images over telephone lines of fiber optic cables permitted monitoring of far distant alarms and remote visual inspection of the alarm area, as well as the recording of events virtually simultaneously with their occurrence.

The successful employment of the numerous noninteractive and nondependent components of contemporary technology in detectors, sensors, and the other elements of a security system requires an integration of design experiences. The successful designer of security systems must understand the responsibility of all other members of the design team. The site of the facility and any regional, local, or immediate constraints on the design must be examined, as well as threats or hazards. The site may be in the path of an unseen microwave dish transmitting a field of energy with telephone conversations, TV images, and high-speed data. The frequency of lightning strikes or electrical storms, earth tremors, utility failures, and natural disasters must be known so the systems designer can develop a network of components appropriate to threats beyond an intruder.

As a consultant to the design members, the security systems engineer must review the designs in progress and work with each team member. Before commencing the design of the electronics system that will constitute the network of detectors, sensors, and alarm transmitters and receivers, the security systems designer must review the work of the electrical consulting engineer to have a full understanding of any exposures that may exist in the location of the incoming electrical service as well as in the locations of distribution panels, breaker panels, and high- and low-voltage circuitry providing power, lighting, motor-starting and other electrical service to the building. This awareness is critical to the success of the security system design, installation, and operation. Although access to these critical distribution points must be controlled and intrusion detected, the operating characteristics of 110- or 220-V-power must be thoroughly understood. Such knowledge ensures that the security system cabling will not be incorrectly designed or inadvertently installed in proximity to the power cable. Normal operation of the facilities requires motors to switch on and off frequently during the day. The electromechanical interference to which low-voltage alarm signal conductors are prone must be designed out so that false alarms are not generated during the use of the electrical system. A thorough knowledge of the National Electrical Code, national and local standards for installation of electrical conductors and conduit, restrictions on the placement of panels housing the connections, and the signal multiplexing capabilities of the security system and their adjacency to power panels within electrical closets must be documented for the design of the security system. Similarly, the efforts of the lighting designer must be reviewed while those designs are in progress, as the video monitoring requirements appropriate to security and alarm investigation may require light levels appropriate for TV cameras as well as control of that lighting when the building is unoccupied or at night. Although the levels of illumination

necessary for public safety are commonly known, the physical locations of light fixtures may be beneficial or detrimental to the use of TV cameras. Such fixtures must illuminate the scene the camera views and not create a "bloom" effect if aimed directly at the lens of the camera. The location of outdoor and internal lighting, or the illumination of scenes for which panning and tilting cameras with zoom lenses are used, is equally critical to the success of the video system.

As the consulting mechanical engineer preliminarily lays out the fresh air intakes, air-handling units, chillers, condensers, motor control units, and distribution and return ductwork, the security system designer must review those drawings. The fresh air intakes represent areas where entrance can be gained from the exterior, and ductwork is often of a size adequate to permit internal passage from a less sensitive area to a critical vault, computer room, storage area, or other internal facility where either products or data may be stored. Grilles on the air intake openings should be adequate to withstand cutting and torch attacks, but motion detection equipment located within the air intake and throughout the internal ductwork is also required to detect attempted and successful intrusion. The access panels required for manually resetting code-required fire dampers need protection with magnetic contact switches mounted on the interior side of the access panel. The locations of the air-handling units, filter banks, and water treatment equipment must be reviewed, and such sensitive equipment provided with means of controlling access as well as detecting attempted intrusion and equipment tampering.

The design concepts of the landscape architect or designer require review by the individual responsible for security design to prevent the development of attractive hideouts or concealed areas where an intruder could prey on nighttime workers, service personnel, or visitors.

Landscaping should not preclude visual observation of the exterior of the facility patrolling law enforcement officers or television cameras, and the security systems designer may elect to use outdoor long-range microwave energy motion detectors, buried coaxial cable, or seismic detectors for early warning of attempts at intrusion or unauthorized movement toward the building.

In working closely with the design architect, the security systems designer must identify the anticipated methods of construction; wall, ceiling, and floor finishes; as well as all internal locations of furniture, electrical operating equipment, window and door types, and hardware schedules. A security system design truly integrated into the architectural fabric of the facility requires an awareness that microwave energy motion detectors can see through perimeter glass and sense movement of shrubbery and falling foliage, as well as authorized outdoor vehicle and personnel movement, and thereby cause unnecessary alarms. Similarly, this physical characteristic can be employed to discreetly hide microwave energy motion detectors behind gypsum board panels, above acoustical ceilings, and behind nonmetallic thread curtains, thus achieving successful detection without intruding into the environment. The operating characteristics of ultrasonic frequency motion detectors and active or passive infrared energy motion detectors should be reviewed with the design architect to avoid specifying a detector type that will cause false alarms in an environment hostile to its manner of operation.

The range of detection coverage or the pattern of each type of motion detector requires similar review, as each detector type is designed to fill a specific role in security system applications. These operating characteristics dictate the height above the finish floor at which a detector of any type may be mounted. A unit that can be ceiling-mounted may have a different detection coverage or pattern in such an application. Knowledge of the furniture placement as well as the interior finishes enables the security systems designer to specify types and models capable of functioning correctly in each environment. Ultrasonic frequency transmitter–receiver units detect human movement by sensing the disturbance of the returned frequency. Some items of modern operating equipment, including many ringing telephones, generate a frequency sufficiently close to the one being transmitted and monitored that false alarms occur. Air movement generated by fan-driven air-conditioning supply diffusers can also generate a change in air mass within a space protected by an ultrasonic frequency motion detector so that unnecessary alarms occur, requiring replacement or relocation of the unit. Detectors of human motion that employ passive infrared energy detectors report alarms on sensing infrared energy emitted by direct or reflected natural or artificial light. The fact that infrared energy can be sensed through glass requires that passive infrared motion detectors be located to preclude unwanted alarms.

Systems of access control using the wide variety of card readers require knowledge and experience of the operating characteristics of each type of card and each type of card reader, its associated control and signal transmission panels, and the cabling in between. Proximity-type card readers or sensors must be sufficiently isolated from adjacent metal door frames, metal studs, other forms of metals, and radio frequency emitting or receiving elements of the building. A wide range of electronic article surveillance systems is available to lending libraries and to retail and other commercial premises for the automatic detection of attempts at removing protected volumes, products, or garments without the cashier or cash register clerk having received payment and deactivated the transmitter affixed to the item. Successful application of such detection equipment in a security system requires knowledge of the operating characteristics of both the sensing equipment and the tag, thread, or other type of signal transmitter placed on the protected item. Certain of these units detect innocent shoppers carrying company-issued proximity access control cards on their persons and generate unwarranted alarms.

There is an ever-increasing range of magnetic switch pairs available for surface or recess mounting on perimeter and interior doors, operable windows, roof hatches, access panels, etc. The switch pair must be individually selected and specified to ensure successful fitting in each type of door, window, frame, etc, reflected in the architect's door and window schedules. The recessed mounting of the magnetic contact switch pairs protects the components from attempted tampering and precludes avoidance of the alarm by a partially opened door or window. The frame and door or window cutouts provided by the door, hollow metal, or window supplier must conform to the template provided by the magnetic contact switch pair manufacturer specified by the security systems designer. Allowances must be made in advance for any door that requires gasketing, weather stripping, and automatic door closers or openers, or a hold-open device to ensure compatibility of the devices specified by the architectural hardware consultant, the architect, and the security systems designer.

The application of metallic foil to glass continues to be appropriate in certain environments. The breaking of the glass causes a break in the continuous loop of the internally applied foil, causing a change of state in the milliamperage of the electrical current flowing through it and setting off the alarm. In aesthetically sensitive fenestration where such foil is not desired, or where the window is exposed to extremes of sunlight and frequent window washing, which eventually deteriorate the continuity of the foil, there is an opportunity for internal application of shock sensors to the window frames or mullions or, more internally, of audio break-glass detectors. The latter units serve basically as microphones set to the frequencies generated by disintegrating glass or repeated pounding. Another type of internally located detector, called an infrasonic detector, is capable of detecting any change of environment or atmosphere when a door, hatch, window, or other entrance is opened and permits entrance of air or alien atmospheric particles, and automatically generates an alarm.

Although the variety of detecting and alarm initiating devices is extensive and continually expanding, the concern for the physical environment in which both the detectors and the central monitoring equipment are placed is a constant in every project.

The integrity of the site or structure must be a primary design consideration. Sensitive sites can be protected by detecting intrusion through the use of buried cable systems or above-grade long-range microwave or radar transmitter and receiver links. TV cameras equipped or with infrared light sources or with "starlight" lenses exist for remote inspection of areas in alarm. In all applications of detecting devices, the environment must be designed so that the structural elements of the site or building constitute the intitial sphere of protection. Site security detecting devices are appropriately employed only in support of a fence, wall, or other physical barrier defining the perimeter of the land area. Fences can be equipped with strain-gauge sensing cable to detect attempts at scaling or cutting. Walls can be equipped with vibration shock sensors, and internal cable or above-ground detecting links can confirm actual intrusion. The lack of physical barriers at a site perimeter contributes to the frequency of false alarms and postponed or negated responses due to the presence of animals or innocent intruders.

The structure in which the detecting devices composing the security system are placed should be capable of withstanding attack and either preventing, or seriously delaying, intrusion. Although the role of sensing devices is to detect and report attempts at actual intrusion, the integrity of the structure must be at a level that the detecting equipment complements. Selection of construction material, as well as exterior and interior wall partitions, doors, windows, etc, must be part of the overall application of security to any structure.

The design of the integrity of the site and the structure is a primary concern for those responsible for providing a secure environment. The role of the detecting devices is to determine the success or failure at withstanding attack and intrusion of the primary system. Proprietary alarm reporting and monitoring systems today depend largely on automated equipment operating on minicomputers or redundant computers with a software database intended to identify immediately the point of alarm and to provide a textual description of the alarm and text detailing the response appropriate to that alarm at that location and that time of day. Map displays or graphic annunciators are frequently employed to supplement the text data. As computers, even hardened military-grade computers, are susceptible to surges and dips in electrical power, all power to the disk drives, central processing units, and terminals and printers must be protected against ground faults and utility power surges and dips. Similarly, as this equipment is highly susceptible to stray radio frequencies, the control room where the equipment is located should be protected with a continuous-lap copper screen shield grounded to a triangular configuration of copper rods embedded in the soil. Room environmental considerations require air-handling equipment to dissipate the heat load generated by operating computers, terminals, TV monitors, and other equipment, as well as by the human occupants. The design of lighting levels must take into consideration glare from TV monitors and terminals, as well as distracting reflectants of background scenes.

Sound-absorbing materials with high noise reduction coefficient values are appropriate to an environment where stress in emergency situations can detract from the efficiency of the designed systems.

The standards promulgated by insurance rating organizations and industry boards govern the installation and maintenance of systems intended to provide physical protection and detect intrusion. Some systems are automated to the extent that reaction by robots is virtually instantaneous. However, the security systems designer must develop design documents, operations, and procedures dependent on human contributors for installation, database development, intelligent responses, periodic tests, and evaluation.

BIBLIOGRAPHY

General References

S. L. Gulick, *The Evolution of the Japanese,* Fleming H. Revell Co., London, 1903.

R. J. Healy, *Design For Security,* John Wiley & Sons, Inc., New York, 1968.

C. R. Jeffrey, *Crime Prevention Through Environmental Design,* Sage Publications, Beverly Hills, Calif., 1971.

C. Heimsath, *Behavioral Architecture,* McGraw-Hill Inc., New York, 1977.

J. G. Miller, *Living Systems,* McGraw-Hill Inc., New York, 1978.

W. Horn and E. Born, *The Plan of St. Gall,* University of California Press, Berkeley, Calif., 1979.

"Standards for Safety," #1076, 3rd ed., Underwriters Laboratories, Inc., Northbrook, Ill., Mar. 15, 1982.

J. C. Wyss, W. J. Anderson, and R. D. Orr, *Building Penetration Project,* National Bureau of Standards, U.S. Department of Commerce, Washington, D.C., 1984.

B. R. Inman, *Report of The Secretary of State's Advisory Panel on Overseas Security,* U.S. Department of State, Washington, D.C., 1985.

"Standards for Safety," #464, 5th ed., Underwriters Laboratories, Inc., Northbrook, Ill., Dec. 20, 1985.

"Standards for Safety," #1638, 1st ed., Underwriters Laboratories, Inc., Northbrook, Ill., May 21, 1987.

R. L. Barnard, *Intrusion Detection Systems,* Butterworths, Stoneham, Mass., 1988.

"Standards for Safety," #1037, 2nd ed., Underwriters Laboratories, Inc., Northbrook, Ill., Apr. 10, 1988.

"Standards for Safety," #365, 2nd ed., Underwriters Laboratories, Inc., Northbrook, Ill., May 17, 1988.

"Standards for Safety," #609, 9th ed., Underwriters Laboratories, Inc., Northbrook, Ill., May 20, 1988.

"Standards for Safety," #636, 9th ed., Underwriters Laboratories, Inc., Northbrook, Ill., May 23, 1988.

"Standards for Safety," #1023, 4th ed., Underwriters Laboratories, Inc., Northbrook, Ill., May 25, 1988.

"Standards for Safety," #1610, 1st ed., Underwriters Laboratories, Inc., Northbrook, Ill., May 25, 1988.

"Standards for Safety," #1635, 1st ed., Underwriters Laboratories, Inc., Northbrook, Ill., May 26, 1988.

"Standards for Safety," #611, 12th ed. Underwriters Laboratories, Inc., Northbrook, Ill., July 22, 1988.

"Standards for Safety," #681, 10th ed., Underwriters Laboratories, Inc., Northbrook, Ill., Sept. 12, 1988.

See also AIRPORTS; BANKS; ELECTRICAL EQUIPMENT; ELECTRICAL PRINCIPLES; ELECTRICAL SYSTEMS; EMBASSIES.

JOSEPH M. CHAPMAN
Joseph M. Chapman, Inc.
Wilton, Connecticut

SEISMIC DESIGN

THE LOCATION OF EARTHQUAKES

Earthquakes are a global phenomenon. The earthquake-free areas are largely uninhabited: Greenland, Siberia, Northern Canada, most of Australia, the Amazon basin, the Sahara, and Antarctica. Inhabited areas that have no seismicity are limited to northern Europe and parts of the southeastern United States. Table 1 shows the average incidence of earthquakes per year in the world compared with that for California, the area of the United States with the most seismicity.

Table 1. Average Number of Earthquakes in the World and California[a]

Magnitude	Average Earthquakes per Year, World	Average Earthquakes per Year, California
8.0–8.9	1	0.01 ($^{1}/_{100}$ yr)
7.0–7.9	15	0.12 ($^{12}/_{100}$ yr)
6.0–6.9	140	0.80 ($^{80}/_{100}$ yr)
5.0–5.9	900	4.00 ($^{400}/_{100}$ yr)
4.0–4.9	8000	20.0 ($^{2000}/_{100}$ yr)

[a] Ref. 1.

THE CAUSES AND NATURE OF EARTHQUAKES

Ground motion refers to the vibration of the ground caused by earthquake waves both within the earth and on its surface. Almost all earthquake damage is caused by ground motion, and seismic design aims to enable a building to withstand ground-motion effects.

According to the now generally accepted theory of plate tectonics, the earth's crust is divided into several major plates, some 50 mi (80 km) thick, that move slowly and continuously over the interior of the earth. Earthquakes are initiated when a geological fault on or near a plate boundary slips abruptly due to slowly accumulating pressure or strain, which results in vibrations that radiate from the line of fracture. The resulting vibration of the earth is transferred to the building, causing it to vibrate in a complex manner, and induces forces within the building that are determined by the nature of the ground motion and the construction characteristics of the building.

The point where the fault first slips is termed the "focus" or "hypocenter." The point on the earth's surface directly above the focus is termed the "epicenter" (Fig. 1). The initial break in the fault moves rapidly along the line of the fault, and the distance of this movement largely determines the extent of the ground shaking. Thus, the 1906 San Francisco earthquake ruptured along some 250 mi (400 km) of the San Andreas Fault.

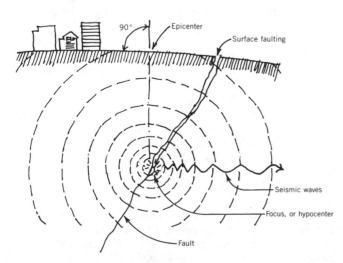

Figure 1. Earthquake initiation.

Ground motion travels in the form of four clearly defined waves away from the fault rupture. First to arrive at a site are the P (or primary) waves, which travel at about 18,000 mph. These waves alternately push and pull at the ground, like the action of extending and compressing a spring. The next waves are the S (or secondary) waves that have a sideways motion to the forward direction of travel.

The two other waves are surface waves. The Love waves move from side to side with no vertical motion; the Rayleigh waves move the material both vertically and horizontally. Although the constituent parts of ground motion can be distinguished by instruments, and even by an experienced observer, their interaction creates motion at the site that appears random, complex, and unpredictable. For this reason, for design purposes, earthquake motion is assumed to come from any direction and to have both vertical and horizontal components.

However, because vertical ground motion is generally somewhat less severe than horizontal motion and buildings are usually designed with a large factor of safety to resist vertical loads, the design problem in seismic engineering is predominantly that of dealing with dynamic horizontal forces.

EARTHQUAKE-INDUCED HAZARDS

While earthquake damage is primarily a result of ground shaking, four other earthquake-induced effects have caused significant damage and casualties in historic earthquakes. These are ground surface fault rupture, liquefaction, landslides, and tsunamis.

Ground Surface Fault Rupture

As noted above, earthquakes are a result of the rupture of a fault, which may occur at or near the earth's surface, in which case the break in the fault may be visible on the earth's surface. If the fault slips at some distance below the surface, the break may not reach the surface and no visible sign of faulting will appear.

If a fault rupture breaks the surface, it will normally do so in close proximity to an existing fault line. Earthquakes have caused fault displacements ranging from a fraction of an inch to more than 20 ft (mm to approximately 6 m) of differential horizontal movement. Similar ranges of vertical movement have been observed. Fault rupture may result in a horizontal offset on either side of the break, a vertical offset, a horizontal gap, or some combination of these.

Buildings are not designed to protect against fault rupture, but in areas where fault lines are well mapped land-use regulation sometimes is used to restrict development. In California, the Alquist-Priolo Act limits development directly over mapped faults.

Liquefaction

Liquefaction is a process that sometimes takes place during earthquakes. In such cases, the ground temporarily loses its strength and behaves as a viscous fluid, akin to quicksand, rather than a solid. The phenomenon is restricted to specific geologic and hydrologic environments, mainly areas where sands and silts were deposited in the last 10,000 years and where ground water is within 30 ft of the surface. While special foundation systems or subsoil treatment are sometimes used in areas of suspected liquefaction, restriction of development on such areas is the only reliable way of dealing with the problem.

Landslides

Landslides are sometimes earthquake induced. The most common landslides of this type are rock falls and slides of rock fragments on steep slopes. In past earthquakes, landslides have been abundant in areas having intensities of ground shaking as low as VI on the Modified Mercalli scale.

Land-use planning is the only effective way of reducing the risk from landslides. For protection against rock slides, especially in areas adjoining highways, steel netting is sometimes used, particularly in Japan.

Tsunamis

Tsunamis are sea waves produced by an undersea earthquake. These sea waves may travel thousands of miles from the initial event that triggered them and can devastate coastal cities and low-lying coastal areas with high waves and subsequent flooding. In deep water, tsunamis may travel at over 400 mph, but the wave height would be small. As tsunamis reach shallow water, the height of the wave may reach 80 ft.

This hazard is very site specific and is considered to be a potential threat along the immediate west coast of the United States and along coastal areas in the states of Hawaii and Alaska. Protection against tsunamis is best achieved by control of waterfront development. In Japan, considerable lengths of coast have been protected by specially shaped reinforced concrete barriers, which also protect against conventional storms.

THE NATURE AND MEASUREMENT OF GROUND MOTION

The nature of ground motion can be conceptually summarized as follows. Waves of vibration emanate from a line of fault rupture and approach a building from a given direction. However, the complex interactions of wave motions produce motion at any site on the ground that is essentially random: predominantly horizontal, but sometimes with considerable vertical action and often with an overall directional emphasis. The actual horizontal ground movement is small, generally measured in fractions of an inch, but in severe earthquakes it can reach as much as a foot. These small vibrational displacements should not be confused with those of surface fault rupture, which may be very large.

Ground motion is recorded and measured by a seismograph, which records over time the motion of a freely suspended pendulum by use of an ink trace on a revolving drum. In modern seismographs the pendulum motion is converted into electronic signals on tape. Strong-motion seismographs are called accelerometers and produce a record referred to as an accelerogram.

Instruments are placed in buildings and on or under the ground ("free-field"), and they are normally located so as to measure along the two horizontal axes (north–south and east–west) and vertically. The accelerometer measures the size of the ground motion wave, and by relating this to time, acceleration can be calculated. In addition, two other measures can be mathematically derived: velocity and displacement, or the distance the instrument moves in space from its resting position. The instrument also records the duration of significant shaking.

Acceleration, which is a critical measure for establishing earthquakes forces, is measured in g, the acceleration of a free-falling body due to gravitation (this is approximately 32 ft/s/s, or 980 cm/s/s, or 980 gals in international terminology, or 1.0 g. Velocity is measured in inches or centimeters per second, and displacement is measured in inches or centimeters.

A level of acceleration of 0.10 g (or 10% g) is that which begins to cause damage to weak construction. A ground acceleration of 0.5 g is high, although earthquake-induced accelerations of over 1.5 g have been recorded, but only for fractions of a second. These are not damaging due to their short duration. Besides acceleration, the parameters of motion that determine the extent of damage are primarily duration and the frequency, or period, of the waves (period is the reciprocal of frequency). Period will be discussed later in considering ground motion effects on buildings.

THE MEASUREMENT OF EARTHQUAKES

Two main types of comparative measure for earthquakes are in common use. Earthquake magnitude is expressed internationally as Richter magnitude, based on the scale devised by Professor Charles Richter at the California Institute of Technology in 1935. The Richter scale is based on the maximum amplitude of the seismic wave as recorded by a standard seismograph located at a distance of 100 k from the epicenter.

The graphic range of wave amplitude is recorded on a logarithmic scale to base 10, so each unit of magnitude indicates a 10 times increase in wave amplitude. But the energy increase represented by each unit is approximately 35 times. Thus, the amplitude of an 8.0 magnitude earthquake is 10,000 times that of a 4.0 magnitude event, and its energy release is approximately 1,000,000 times greater. The Richter scale has no fixed maximum, but an earthquake of magnitude 2 is the smallest normally felt by humans, a magnitude 7 event or above is a major event, and the greatest ever recorded is about magnitude 9.

Intensity scales provide a measurement of building damage. They are developed by the subjective assessment of building damage in relation to a standardized verbal description of damage. In the United States, the most commonly used scale is the Modified Mercalli (MM), originally developed in Europe in 1902 and modified in 1931 to fit construction conditions then prevalent in California and the United States in general.

As a result, the MM scale is somewhat outdated, with no reference to common modern construction systems. The MM scale is a 12-point scale, I–XII. The descriptors for MM I are (in abbreviated form) "Not felt. Marginal and long-period effects of large earthquakes." For MM XII, the descriptor reads, "Damage nearly total. Large rock masses displaced. Lines of sight and level distorted. Objects thrown into the air." Because earthquake effects will vary depending on distance from the epicenter, nature of the ground etc, an earthquake will have several MM values.

BUILDING REACTION TO GROUND MOTION

Inertial Forces

Ground motion damages buildings as a result of inertial forces generated by vibration of the building mass. Inertial forces are the product of mass and acceleration (Newton's $F = ma$). Hence the significance of values for acceleration, derived from seismic instruments, and the building mass, which is represented by weight, and assumed to act at the geometrical center of the building components under consideration. A secondary detrimental aspect of mass is that of failure of vertical members, such as columns and walls, often occurs by buckling, due to lateral shaking; when this happens, the building mass pushes vertically downward and collapse is likely. This phenomenon is known as the P-(Δ), or P-e, effect, in which P is the force and e is the eccentricity of action of the vertical force (Fig. 2).

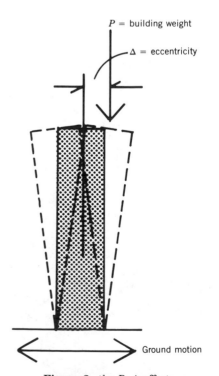

P = building weight

Δ = eccentricity

Ground motion

Figure 2. the P–Δ effect.

Although earthquakes often have large vertical force components, buildings generally have large reserves of vertical strength due to safety factors. As a result, the vertical earthquake forces seldom represent a problem.

Period

The relationship between the period (or frequency) of the ground motion and the period of the building are of great importance. Buildings have fundamental periods of between about 0.05 s (for a one-story building) to 1–2 s for buildings in the 10–20 story range. Period increases with height, but the proportions and materials of the buildings also affect it.

Ground generally vibrates at a period of between 0.2 and 4.0 s. If the period of the ground vibration and the natural period of the building coincide, the building may approach resonance, and building responses, including acceleration, become greatly amplified. Amplification of more than fivefold is not uncommon. In the Mexico City earthquake of 1985, the maximum acceleration at the ground was approximately 0.16 g, but it exceeded 1 g at the top of high-rise buildings.

Damping

Buildings are relatively inefficient vibrators because they are damped and tend to return to rest quickly. Damping is dependent on the building mass, its shape, its connections, its materials, and the extent of nonstructural elements such as partitions and exterior cladding. Damping is measured as a percentage of critical damping, or that damping that will cause the building to return to the center when vibrated, with no further vibration. Tall frame buildings, particularly moment-resisting steel frames, may have relative little damping and will continue swaying for several minutes after the ground motion has ceased.

Even if resonance is avoided and the building is well damped, in a severe earthquake a building will still be subject to forces that are much higher than those provided for in the building codes. To design for maximum forces would result in a very uneconomic design, and the size and placement of resisting elements would pose planning and architectural problems.

Ductility

The gap between design capacity and possible actual forces is largely dealt with by relying on the material property of "ductility." This is the property of certain materials, steel in particular, that will fail only after considerable inelastic, or permanent, deformation has taken place. This deformation dissipates the energy of the earthquake.

Brittle materials, such as unreinforced masonry, or inadequately reinforced concrete, fail suddenly, usually with a minimum of distortion. The crushing of nonstructural materials, such as partitions, also provides some reserve capacity for the structure as a whole. To achieve good ductility also requires special, and sometimes expensive, detailing of joints.

Duration

An aspect of earthquake motion that tests all the building's structural attributes is that of duration. Strong motion in earthquakes generally lasts from a few seconds to as much as 90 s. The strong motion in the San Fernando earthquake of 1971 lasted for about 10 s; in 1906 in San Francisco, the shaking lasted for about 45 s; in the Alaska earthquake of 1964, the duration was over 2 min. In the Mexico City earthquake of 1985, the shaking lasted for about 60 s, which, combined with the unusually long vibration period of about 2 s, did tremendous damage to buildings in the 5–20 story range, but had little effect on buildings that were lower or higher.

Torsion and Symmetry

The resultant force due to the horizontal acceleration of a building floor acts through the center of mass, or center of gravity, of the floor. If the resultant of resistance, provided by walls or frames, also acts through this point, the translational balance is maintained, and there is no tendency for horizontal rotation, or torsion, to occur (Fig. 3). Hence, in a building in which the mass is approximately evenly distributed in plan, which would be typical of a symmetrical plan with uniform floor, wall, and column masses, the ideal arrangement is for the resisting elements to be correspondingly symmetrically located. Then whichever direction the lateral forces operate, the resisting elements respond with a balanced resistance, and there is no tendency for torsion to occur.

Torsion is very undesirable because it causes stress concentrations. The effect of torsional forces is difficult to calculate, resulting in great uncertainty. Hence, the general rule is that symmetry is a valuable configuration characteristic. In practice, this rule is somewhat simplistic. Mere geometrical symmetry does not guarantee freedom from torsion, and a careful design can provide balanced resistance, which is the important issue, even if geometrical symmetry does not exist.

Strength and Stiffness

In lateral force design, the stiffness of the structure is of great importance. Here, stiffness is distinguished from strength; strength is a measure of the ability of a material to resist loads without exceeding a specified stress, while the measure of stiffness is the extent to which the structure moves horizontally out of alignment, or drifts. Drift is a horizontal analogy to vertical deflection.

The relative rigidity, or stiffness, of resisting members is of great significance in seismic design because seismic forces are distributed to the vertical elements (columns, walls, etc) in a structure in proportion to their individual stiffnesses. This is reflected in seismic codes by requiring stiff elements to be designed for greater forces. One of the results of this is to place a premium on flexibility, because the design forces are reduced. Hence, many buildings are designed to be flexible, with capacity for relatively large deflections. Although such buildings may be structurally safe, such design may result in extensive nonstructural and contents damage caused by differential movement between the structure and attached elements such as ceilings, partitions, exterior walls, and glazing.

Another important issue is that of inadvertent stiffness. Frequently, later building remodeling results in the addition of stiff nonstructural infill walls that then "attract" a disproportionate share of the seismic forces to a member that was not designed for such forces.

Resistant Systems

There is a small vocabulary of components that can be combined to resist seismic forces. In the vertical plane, there are three kinds of component: shear walls, braced frames, or moment-resisting frames (sometimes called rigid frames). In the horizontal plane, diaphragms are used, usually consisting of floor or roof components, although horizontal bracing can also be used for the same purpose. These components are also basic architectural elements of the building (Fig. 4).

Because the vertical components have somewhat different attributes, particularly as to comparative stiffness, buildings generally use one or another system consistently. It is undesirable to mix shear walls and moment-resisting frames, for example. An exception is the occasional use of an additional system as backup: a moment-resisting frame might back up a shear wall system to provide additional safety if the walls should fail. Such a system would be expensive, but might be appropriate for an important building such as a hospital.

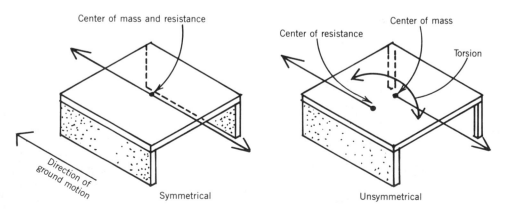

Figure 3. Torsion occurs when the centers of mass and resistance do not coincide.

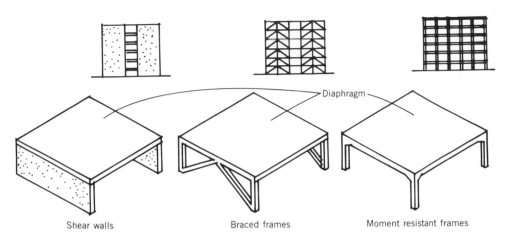

Figure 4. Types of lateral force resistant systems.

Shear walls   Braced frames   Moment resistant frames

Diaphragm

Shear Walls

Shear walls are vertical elements that resist lateral forces in the direction of the plane of the wall. They are designed to receive lateral forces from the diaphragms and transmit the forces to the foundation. Hence such walls should run uninterrupted from roof to foundation. They should be approximately equal in length in all the building directions and, to resist torsion, are most effective when located toward the building perimeter.

If the building requires solid walls for architectural reasons, a shear wall building is very economical. The system results in a very stiff building, which tends to reduce nonstructural damage. If sufficient walls are provided, the unit stress in the wall can be quite low so that elaborate and expensive reinforcing is not necessary. Collapse of a reinforced concrete shear wall building is very rare, and even if the walls are severely cracked, they often can be effectively repaired with epoxy cement. The use of plywood on wood frame walls results in an economical and effective shear wall for these types of structure.

Braced Frames

Braced frames act to resist lateral forces in a way similar to shear walls, although they tend to be more flexible and of lower resistance. The use of steel braced frames in a steel structure results in a very economical structure. Because the braced frame acts as a stiff section of the building, the detailed design of the bracing and its location in the building is very critical. In particular, the bracing must be sufficiently strong to resist both tension and compression as the loads reverse under successive cycles of shaking.

Braced frames are used less commonly in reinforced concrete structures. They are often used in wood, or mixed wood and steel frame structures, where the design does not permit the use of plywood shear walls.

Moment-resisting Frames

In moment-resisting frames, the lateral forces are resisted at the joints, which must be specially detailed in either steel or concrete, because the joints become highly stressed. Large lateral forces are resisted by ductile be-

havior at or near the joints, and the deformation of the material acts to dissipate the earthquake energy.

A common form of moment-resisting design, both for steel and reinforced concrete construction, is the use of a perimeter moment frame, with the interior frame designed only to resist vertical loads. Because of the need for strength in the joints, moment-resisting frames are difficult to design in wood or precast concrete.

The use of moment frames is of considerable architectural significance. Because no walls are required to provide resistance, the building interior can be completely open; this is particularly attractive for buildings subject to frequent internal rearrangement, such as rental office buildings. The specialized detailing and necessary inspection to ensure correct construction results, however, in an expensive structure. In addition, as noted previously, such structures are flexible and may result in extensive nonstructural earthquake damage.

THE ARCHITECTURE OF SEISMIC DESIGN

Architectural decisions have a significant effect on building seismic performance. The important decisions are those that determine the configuration of the building.

Configuration is defined as building size and shape, and the size, nature, and location of both structural elements and nonstructural elements that may affect seismic performance (2). These include elements such as walls, columns, floors, service cores, and staircases as well as the quantity, location, and type of interior partitions and the ways in which the exterior skin is left opaque or open.

Configuration influences, and sometimes determines, the kind of seismic resistance systems that can be used and the extent to which they will be effective. Furthermore, many failures of engineering detailing that result in severe damage or collapse originate as configuration failures. The building configuration is such, either as a whole or in some detail, that seismic forces place intolerable stress on a member, or connection, and it fails. The set of configurations that present problems are generally agreed on, based on experience in earthquakes and analysis. In general, they are referred to as "irregular" designs, which implies some deviation, either in vertical or hori-

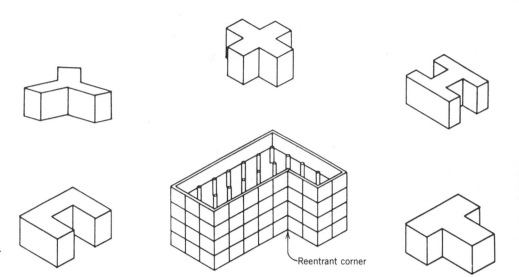

Figure 5. Building forms with re-entrant corners.

Reentrant corner

zontal layout, from a symmetrical, rectangular form, in which floor heights are approximately equal and the disposition of perimeter elements results in balanced resistance, approximately equal from any direction.

The four most serious configuration issues are described below.

1. *Reentrant Corners in Plan.* This refers to buildings, often residential, that are L-, T-, U-shaped, and the like in plan; their common characteristic is the use of reentrant corners (Fig. 5). The seismic problem is that the corner forms a stiff element and consequently attracts a concentration of forces. In addition, such forms are very prone to torsion, which is highly undesirable.

2. *Soft Stories.* This refers to buildings in which one story, generally the first, is significantly lower in strength or stiffness than adjoining floors. This condition can occur in several ways. The use of taller columns in the first floor results in a more flexible structure and less stiffness at this level. The use of a heavy exterior cladding above an open first floor results in a discrepancy of stiffness. The use of a small number of supports at the first floor, which amounts to omitting vertical supports at the floor

that will experience the greatest forces, results in a relatively weak floor (Figs. 6 and 7). A particular case of the soft first floor, which has resulted in serious damage, is that of the discontinuous shear wall, in which shear walls are omitted at the first floor, generally to achieve planning flexibility at this location (Fig. 8). The effect of all these designs is to concentrate stress at the second floor column-floor connections, due to the exaggerated deflection of the weaker or more flexible first floor.

3. *Variations in Perimeter Strength and Stiffness.* This condition generally occurs as a result of varying functional requirements around the perimeter of the building. This results in facades that vary in an unbalanced fashion from solid to open. A characteristic condition is that of a corner storefront building, which may have two adjacent open sides, and two adjacent heavy party walls (Fig. 9). This condition creates unbalanced resistance, caused by lack of symmetry in the location of resistance elements (even though the plan may be rectangular and symmetrical), and consequent severe torsion.

4. *Abrupt Variation in Support Stiffness: Short Columns.* This condition occurs when the vertical resistance consists of elements that vary greatly in

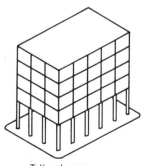

Tall columns

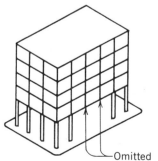

Omitted
Omission of vertical support

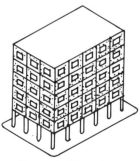

Heavy cladding above
open first floor

Figure 6. Types of soft first story.

Figure 7. Open stores at base of office building in Mexico City in the 1985 earthquake create soft first story and cause dangerous collapse.

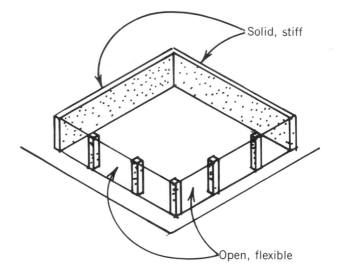

Figure 9. Unbalanced lateral resistance in a corner building.

stiffness. The forces will be attracted to the stiffer elements, which will be called on to carry a disproportionate share of the loads. A particular case of this is referred to as the short column condition, in which columns occur that are significantly shorter than those on adjoining floors or even the same floor and, because of their additional stiffness, may become overstressed. This condition is frequently caused by remodeling during building occupancy, in which heavy infill, nonstructural walls are added that seriously modify the designed structural behavior (Fig. 10).

5. *Other Architectural Issues.* In addition to the four major configuration problems above, other architectural decisions may have seismic consequences. Designs that are set back in elevation need careful structural design to prevent stress concentrations. Stairs and elevator cores may represent local areas

of stiffness, so their location is important to reduce torsion. Design considerations may also affect column and wall location, or even the effective location of reinforcing in concrete.

There are solutions to these conditions, which are dependent on early coordination between architect and structural engineer. The importance of the configuration issue is that it represents architectural decisions made at the inception of the design process that prove to be critical to later structural design conditions. Furthermore, while solutions to these conditions may be possible, they may be very expensive in engineering design time and construction.

EXISTING HAZARDOUS BUILDINGS

New construction adds only approximately 2% to the nation's building stock every year. Hence, earthquakes occurring for a number of years into the future will predominantly affect existing buildings. A number of common structural types in the United States have consistently performed inadequately during past earthquakes. This is not to suggest that a given building of one of these types is certain to fail in an earthquake, but only that experience

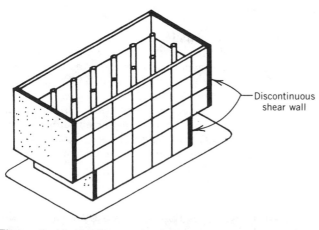

Figure 8. A special case of soft first story, the discontinuous shear wall.

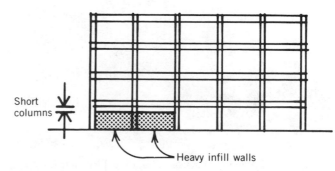

Figure 10. Heavy infill walls cause short column condition.

has shown that these types should receive special investigation, particularly if they are heavily occupied or house essential or hazardous activities, equipment, or materials. Three structural types that are currently considered seismically suspect follow.

Unreinforced Masonry Bearing Wall Buildings

These are often referred to as UMB or URM buildings. Structures of this type have exterior and sometimes interior load-bearing walls constructed of brick, stone, adobe, or concrete block, without steel reinforcing (Fig. 11). Buildings of this type were constructed in California only prior to 1933, because in that year the Long Beach earthquake occurred that seriously damaged a number of schools. As a consequence, legislation was introduced (the Field Act, regulating public school construction, and the Riley Act, affecting most other buildings) that effectively mandated reinforcing for masonry buildings. In other parts of the country, unreinforced masonry buildings are still constructed.

Modifications that may be necessary to improve the earthquake resistance of these buildings include strengthening floors and roofs, securely anchoring floors and roofs to walls, strengthening the existing walls, and constructing additional concrete walls or adding steel bracing. The Los Angeles Ordinance of 1981 (3) requires the owners of URM buildings to strengthen or demolish them within varying time frames depending on the occupancy of the building. Some 8000 buildings are affected. Similar ordinances exist in Long Beach and Santa Rosa, California. Recent legislation in California requires all towns and cities to identify their URM buildings.

Nonductile Reinforced Concrete Frame Buildings

The need for extensive ductility in concrete was not fully understood until after the failure of a number of reinforced concrete buildings in the San Fernando earthquake of 1971. As a result, such buildings constructed in California prior to about 1973 (when the code was changed), may be suspect. This problem particularly applies to frame buildings, in which the structure does not include solid

Figure 12. Severe damage to nonductile reinforced concrete frame building in the 1985 Mexico City earthquake.

walls to provide lateral resistance. The severe damage in the 1985 Mexico City earthquake occurred mostly to this type of building, which is particularly prevalent in Latin America because of its economy (Fig. 12).

Strengthening of these buildings can be done, but is expensive, and in general consists of adding walls and possibly increasing column size and reinforcing. Outside of California nonductile concrete buildings are commonly built today, because the method is safe for resisting vertical forces.

Precast Concrete Tilt-up Buildings

This type of building consists of concrete walls that are precast on site and tilted vertically into position during construction. The walls are commonly one story, but occasionally two or three stories are built. The floors and roofs may be constructed of timber: generally glulam beams, wood joists, and plywood diaphragms, but are sometimes constructed of steel members and steel deck.

The lack of earthquake resistance in these structures stems from the inadequacy of the panel-to-panel connections of the tilt-up elements and from weak connections between walls and upper floor and roof diaphragms. Their perimeter walls act as shear walls and may transmit large forces.

Many of these buildings failed in the 1971 San Fernando earthquake, after which the building code in California was changed to remedy observed deficiencies. In the Whittier Narrows earthquake of 1987 a number of tilt-up buildings experienced partial roof collapse and other minor damage, but the post-1971 buildings performed significantly better than earlier buildings. Remedial measures consist primarily in improving roof-to-wall connections, but may also consist of strengthening panel-to-panel connections.

Other Suspect Building Types

Other structural types that are regarded as seismically suspect include certain types of steel structure with inadequate braced frames, long-span precast and prestressed

Figure 11. Unreinforced masonry building damage in Coalinga, California, in 1983 earthquake.

beam and plate structures, older reinforced concrete frame structures with masonry or tile infill, and buildings with irregular configurations.

SEISMIC BUILDING CODES

The first quantitative seismic code was developed in Italy following the 1908 Messina-Reggio earthquake. This code required buildings to be designed to withstand a lateral acceleration of 8% g. Following the 1923 earthquake in Tokyo, Japan, the Home Office of Japan adopted a seismic coefficient of 10% g for all important structures and limited building height to 100 ft, a limitation that remained until the 1960s.

The 1906 earthquake in San Francisco resulted in a wind load code, as a disguised form of earthquake code. Not until 1927, following the 1925 Santa Barbara earthquake, was a set of seismic design requirements published in the United States, but a code was not enforced until 1933, when in California a design coefficient of 2% g was established (Riley Act), with 10% g for public schools (Field Act).

The earthquake provisions of the Uniform Building Code (UBC) (4), the model code used in California, are based on recommendations of the Structural Engineers Association of California (5). The California seismic provisions have been very influential in other states and other countries.

Seismic codes are still predominantly concerned with establishing minimum design force levels, expressed as a percentage of building weight, although prescriptive requirements relating to building materials, details, and connections, are also stated. Earthquake forces are expressed as a horizontal base shear, or equivalent lateral force, which represents the complex dynamic multidimensional earthquake forces by a single (maximum) force applied at the base of the building.

The base shear is derived, in the Uniform Building Code, from the formula $V = ZIKCSW$, where V = total base shear; Z = numerical coefficient depending on seismic zone; I = importance factor, relating to building function; K = factor relating to type of structural system; S = coefficient relating to site; and W = dead weight of building. If the maximum values are used for the coefficients in the formula, $V_{max} = 0.28W$, or 28% g.

In 1988 the formula was changed to $V = ZICW/Rw$, in which C incorporates S, Rw incorporates K in the old formula.

An important parallel development, since 1978, has been the development of the NEHRP (National Earthquake Hazards Reduction Program) Recommended Provisions (6). This document is part of a program to develop and update a source document for seismic code development that reflects the latest knowledge on seismic design and construction, with emphasis on national applicability. Changes in the 1988 UBC reflect the methodology used in the NEHRP Provisions.

While previous UBC codes dealt with building configuration issues in a nonnumerical advisory way, quantitative values are given in the 1988 revisions for definition of irregular buildings. Classification of a building as irregular results in a requirement for the use of a more complex and expensive force analysis procedure, and the equivalent lateral force method is no longer applicable.

Modern building codes also include requirements for the connection and anchoring of nonstructural components such as ceilings; exterior cladding; storage units; mechanical, electrical, and plumbing systems; and elevators. All these components have suffered considerable damage in recent earthquakes, even in buildings in which the structure has performed as anticipated.

INNOVATIONS IN SEISMIC DESIGN

In recent years, some innovative approaches to seismic design have been developed. A modification to the steel braced, frame-resistant system is that of the eccentric-braced frame. In this system, diagonal bracing is located in such a way as to leave a short horizontal link between the beam–column connection and the point at which the diagonal brace is attached to the beam (Fig. 13).

The system is designed in such a way that, in the event of severe lateral forces, nonlinear behavior and distortion are concentrated at the link, dissipating energy and protecting the connection and the column. Thus the point of failure is controlled. Eccentric braced frame systems are now in use and have proved to have many of the benefits of ductile moment-resisting frames at much less cost.

Base isolation systems are now in use. In the most common form, the building superstructure is isolated from the ground by the use of rubber bearings. This has the effect of considerably changing the building period so that it responds to ground motion with much reduced accelerations. The building may deflect laterally several inches at the bearings, and space must be left around the building for this to occur, but motion in the superstructure is greatly reduced (Fig. 14). The system is particularly effective in controlling damage to nonstructural components and contents.

Base isolation requires additional cost in the foundation system, but reduced forces in the superstructure result in compensating economies. Base isolation is effective for buildings between about 3 and 15 stories; it is not suitable for slender buildings (because of possible overturning problems), and it is most effective for buildings located in rock or other relatively short period material.

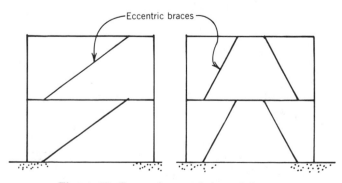

Figure 13. Types of eccentric braced frame.

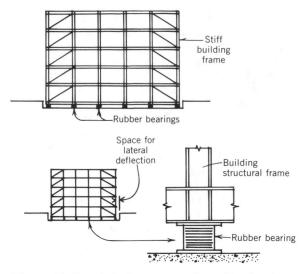

Figure 14. Base isolation system using rubber bearings.

Other innovations include the use of devices to improve the building's damping characteristics. These generally involve the dissipation of energy by bending or twisting metal. All these innovations are based on dissipating energy in controlled ways or reducing the transmission of forces to the building. They contrast strongly with traditional seismic design approaches that seek to connect the building very strongly to the ground and then to design a very strong building.

BIBLIOGRAPHY

1. J. M. Gere and H. C. Shah, *Terra Non Firma,* Stanford Alumni Association, Stanford, Calif., 1984.
2. C. Arnold and R. Reitherman, *Building Configuration and Seismic Design,* John Wiley & Sons, Inc., New York, 1982.
3. *Earthquake Hazard Reduction in Existing Buildings,* Division 88, Los Angeles City Municipal Code, February 13, 1981.
4. *Uniform Building Code,* International Conference of Building Officials, Whittier, Calif., 1988.
5. *Recommended Lateral Force Requirements and Commentary,* Structural Engineers Association of California, San Francisco, Calif., 1988.
6. *NEHRP Recommended Provisions for the Development of Seismic Regulations for New Buildings: Part 1, Provisions: Part 2, Commentary,* Building Seismic Safety Council, Washington, D.C., 1988.

General References

D. J. Dorwick, *Earthquake Resistant Design,* 2nd ed., John Wiley & Sons, Inc., New York, 1988.

J. L. Stratta, *Manual of Seismic Design,* Prentice-Hall Inc., Englewood Cliffs, N.J., 1987.

C. Arnold, "In Earthquakes, Failure Can Follow Form, *AIA Journal* **69**(6), 33–40 (June 1980).

C. Arnold, "Quake Codes," *Architectural Technology* **2**(1), 27–33 (Spring 1984).

D. B. Ward, "The Coming Changes in Earthquake Codes," *Architecture* **76**(7), 86–87 (June 1987).

C. Arnold, "Rolling with the Punch of Earthquakes," *Architecture* **72**(9), 64–66 (Sept. 1983).

See also CONCRETE—GENERAL PRINCIPLES; FOUNDATION SYSTEMS; OFFICE BUILDINGS; STEEL IN CONSTRUCTION; STRUCTURAL STEEL—GENERAL PRINCIPLES

CHRISTOPHER ARNOLD, AIA
Building Systems Development Inc.
San Mateo, California

SERT, JOSÉ LUIS

José Luis Sert's professional contribution in architecture spanned a half century and along the course earned for him such accolades as Father of City Planning, Dean of Architects, Collaborative Arts Advocate, and Architect of the People. His architectural legacy reveals him to be the consummate blend of all of these diverse titles.

Sert was born in Barcelona, Spain, in 1902. He emigrated to the United States during the Spanish Civil War, but his proud Mediterranean heritage remained a pervasive influence in his life's work. Sert's early development was closely linked with the arts. A member of his family was among Antoni Gaudi's supporters, and Sert, later in life, paid published tribute to Gaudi's work. Sert's uncle, José Maria Sert, was a well-known painter. He executed the mural for the lobby of New York City's Rockefeller Center. Sert's association with artists was further expanded after his graduation from his formal studies in 1929, from Barcelona's Escuela Superior de Arquitectura, when he moved to Paris to join the atelier of Le Corbusier. In Paris, his circle of companions included the artists Pablo Picasso, Fernand Léger, Joan Miró, and Alexander Calder; his association with them remained lifelong. After having spent 2 years in Paris, he returned to Spain and opened his own architectural office in Barcelona.

It was during these years that Sert began to make his imprint on architectural history. In 1929, he organized the first group of architects in Barcelona affiliated with the International Congress for Modern Architecture (CIAM). The CIAM organization encouraged and practiced teamwork and emphasized the role of the architect in the replanning of cities. Sert was actively involved in CIAM throughout its 10 Congresses and thereafter. In 1942, he authored a book on the collected work of the CIAM Congresses, focusing on urban problems. His book, entitled *Can Our Cities Survive?*, brought him international recognition for this timely presentation on the urban condition and its directives for urban planning.

In 1938, because of the turmoil of the Civil War, Sert left Spain and returned to Paris for 2 years before coming to the United States. During his stay in France, Sert designed the Pavilion for the Republic of Spain at the Paris

World's Fair. It was here that Sert, in the spirit of his established beliefs in artistic collaboration, coupled with his diplomatic ability to "get those highly individual, prima donnas to agree on things . . ." (1), brought forth a notable union of the arts. For Sert's Pavilion building in Spain, Picasso painted his masterpiece, *Guernica,* on one of the building walls. A mercury fountain by Calder graced the ground-floor center, and a large painting by Miró, *Catalan Peasant in Revolt,* was positioned over the stairs.

In 1939, when Sert came to the United States, he settled first in New York State. Concentrating his professional work on city planning and urban design, he founded the firm of Town Planning Associates along with Paul Lester Wiener and Paul Schulz. During the 10 years that followed, he worked on several projects for South American cities, including the new towns of Cidade dos Motores, near Rio de Janeiro, and Chimbote, Peru, and the master plan for Bogotá, Colombia. He also developed a master plan for the city of Havana, Cuba, which, although it was never implemented, remains a worthy study for urban planners and administrators.

Concurrent with these professional activities, he served as Professor of City Planning at Yale University in 1944 and held the office of President of CIAM from 1947 to 1956. In 1953, he accepted appointment as Dean of the Faculty of the Graduate School of Design and Professor of Architecture at Harvard University.

His role as an educator provided him with the opportunity to share his experiences and thoughts about art, humanism, and urbanism. He was instrumental in strengthening and expanding Harvard's undergraduate studies department into the widely respected Department of Visual and Environmental Studies. He brought such notable artists as Mirko Basaldella and Constantino Nivola to teach and participate in the program.

Another major credit to him and benefit to the arts program was his active role in bringing forth the sole Le Corbusier building in the United States, The Carpenter Center for the Visual Arts, which houses the Harvard Arts Program. And it was Sert, the urbanist visionary, who created the nation's first degree program in urban design, at Harvard's Graduate School of Design. It was a move that many university-based architectural programs have since followed.

In 1955, concurrent with serving in his academic post as Dean, he opened his own architectural office in Cambridge, Massachusetts. Two years later, it became the partnership of Sert, Jackson and Gourley, and since 1963, it has operated under the name of Sert, Jackson and Associates. It was during this period that Sert became involved in the design and construction of larger structures. Harvard University, having embarked on an expansion program, commissioned Sert to design three major building projects: the Peabody Terrace Married Student Housing Project (Fig. 1); Holyoke Center, a multiuse urban-center project; and Harvard's Undergraduate Science Center. His design firm received numerous awards and citations for these projects.

With projects of variable scale on both local and international sites, Sert produced many other buildings of distinction, among them the U.S. Embassy in Baghdad; the Charles River Campus of Boston University; Harvard University's Center for the Study of World Religions; and undergraduate dormitory housing on the Massachusetts Institute of Technology campus. In Europe, his buildings include the Museum of Contemporary Art for the Foundation Maeght in Saint-Paul-de-Vence, France; the Joan Miró Studio in Palma, Majorca; the Miró Foundation in Barcelona; and in Ibiza, Spain, a residential development, Urbanización de Punta Martinet, and his own residence.

For these and numerous other architectural works, Sert and his firm attained a position of preeminence in architecture. In 1977, the American Institute of Architects awarded his office the Architectural Firm Award, and in 1981, Sert was recipient of the U.S.'s highest honor in architecture, the AIA Gold Medal from the American Institute of Architects.

Figure 1. Peabody Terrace Married Student Housing, Harvard University, Cambridge, Mass.

In placing the architectural language of José Luis Sert among the modern mannerists, Bruno Zevi writes (2):

> There are two versions of this modern Mannerism: one . . . confines itself to discoursing on the forms of the masters; the other is open, generous, productive, ready to consider new ideas and with a firm belief in content. Sert belongs to the latter faction. . . . He has explored, enriched, and articulated the language of Le Corbusier, transmitting it to Catalonia, taking it back to Paris, extending it to town planning projects in South America, then to Cambridge, Massachusetts and to Boston, and more recently back to Europe again, in work done in France and Spain. He has constructed his own personality slowly, without any impatience or prima donna attitudinizing. . . . And the result is that he stands out today as an unmistakable individual figure against the contemporary international horizon.

José Luis Sert's work, beyond its modern mannerist expression, is additionally reflective of a pervasive humanistic spirit. In the urban setting, Sert consciously maintained a humanistic concern for establishing a proper balance between people and automobiles, people, buildings and open space, and people and landscape. His extensive work in housing also addresses a dominant reference to the human individual, allowing for a carefully weighted emphasis of privacy and community and providing variability in dwelling sizes and plan layouts accommodating multivariate personal needs and lifestyles.

In this same vein, Sert's work faithfully adhered to Le Corbusier's *Le Modulor* dimensioning system that is based on human proportions, further evidencing his belief that building massing, interior spaces, fenestration, scale, color and texture are all to be determined from a human point of reference (3). Ultimately, Sert's concern for the human condition carried through as the instructive premise underlying all his professional contributions, whether "teaching, cultural organization, or architectural coherence (4)."

BIBLIOGRAPHY

1. "Sert Named AIA's 42nd Gold Medalist," *AIA Journal,* 13–25 (January 1981).
2. B. Zevi, *Sert's Architecture in the Miro Foundation,* Ediciones Poligrafa, Barcelona, Spain, 1976, pp. 26–29.
3. Le Corbusier, *Le Modulor,* The MIT Press, Cambridge, Mass., 1968.
4. Ref. 2, p. 27.

General References

K. Bastlund, *José Luis Sert,* Praeger, New York, 1967.

M. L. Borras, *Sert: Mediterranean Architecture,* New York Graphic Society, Boston, Mass., 1975.

R. Campbell, "Urban Daring," *The Boston Globe Magazine,* 13–19 (May 24, 1981).

R. R. Isaacs, "José Luis Sert" in *Macmillan Encyclopedia of Architects,* The Free Press, New York, 1982, pp. 40–41.

M. Schmertz, "José Luis Sert" in *Contemporary Architects,* St. Martins Press, New York, 1980, pp. 740–742.

J. L. Sert, *Can Our Cities Survive?,* Harvard University Press, Cambridge, Mass., 1942.

Karen J. Dominguez
Pennsylvania State University
State College, Pennsylvania

SEWAGE TREATMENT.   See Wastewater Management.

SEWERS.   See Site Utilities.

SHEET METALS.   See Supplement.

SHEPLEY BULFINCH RICHARDSON AND ABBOTT

Shepley, Rutan, and Coolidge inherited the practice of the famous American architect Henry Hobson Richardson who died in 1886 at the early age of 47. At that time, George Foster Shepley was 26, the engineer Charles H. Rutan was 35 years old, and Charles Allerton Coolidge was 28. They completed several of Richardson's projects, including the Allegheny County Courthouse in Pittsburgh, the Marshall Field Wholesale Store in Chicago, the Cincinnati Chamber of Commerce, the Glessner House in Chicago, and the New London Northern Railroad Stations. The firm prospered from the start with a large number of new commissions.

Over the years, the firm underwent a number of name changes, simplified by the intermarriages within the firm. George Shepley married Richardson's daughter Julia, and Charles Coolidge married Shepley's sister. The firm name of Shepley Rutan and Coolidge was used until Rutan's death in 1915. From 1915 to 1924, the firm was Coolidge and Shattuck. From then until 1952, the name was Coolidge Shepley Bulfinch and Abbott, since then Shepley Bulfinch Richardson and Abbott.

Although initially involved with the Richardsonian style, they later were known for their classically inspired work as promoted by the Chicago Fair of 1893. A discussion of their role in the architectural design community of the late nineteenth century is included in Henry Russell Hitchcock's book on Richardson (1). It was not until recent times that the firm has been known for its successful contemporary designs, which have achieved a number of design awards.

The large number of major projects in the past century includes the Chicago Public Library (1893) and the Chicago Art Institute (begun 1892). The firm opened an office in Chicago, which by 1916 had become a separate firm under the name Coolidge and Hodgson.

One of the most famous projects of the early years was the design of Stanford University in Palo Alto, California (started in 1888). The strong design of arcaded buildings of yellow limestone and red tile roofs proved successful. Other new campuses were planned for the University of Oklahoma at Norman, the University of Nebraska at Lincoln, and Southern Methodist University in Dallas. From

Figure 1. Arthur M. Sackler Gallery, Washington, D.C., designed by Jean Paul Carlhian. Courtesy of Robert C. Lautman.

1900 to 1916, the firm built more than a dozen buildings at the University of Chicago. Later work has included buildings on the campuses of Northeastern University, Vassar and Wellesley Colleges, and the Groton School.

The firm's work at Harvard, beginning with Richardson's Sever Hall of 1878, included the Medical School (1903) and many other buildings on the campus. Their design of medical schools, laboratories, and hospitals in many parts of the United States and abroad is a major area of practice. A few of their projects of the 1920s and 1930s in this area include several buildings for the Rockefeller Institute and the New York Hospital and Cornell Medical Center in New York (1934).

Other areas of practice have been in transportation, commercial offices, libraries, college residential halls, and government projects. Some of the more recent projects have included Quincy House, Harvard University 1960; Carl S. Ell Student Center, Northeastern University, Boston, 1965; Leverett House Library, Harvard University, 1961; Wellesley College Library 1910–1959; Bio-Medical Center, Brown University, 1970; Continuing Care Unit, Hartford Hospital, 1967; Graduate Center, Brown University 1969; Mather House, Harvard University, 1971; the Tramway Terminal, Squaw Valley, 1970; and the addition to the Walters Art Gallery in Baltimore. The Vassar College Center project, an addition to the original Vassar College building, won an AIA Honor Award in 1977. Other published work includes the Penobscot Bay Medical Center in Rockport, Maine; the addition to the Andover, Massachusetts Savings Bank; and the Sherman Fairchild Physical Sciences Center at Dartmouth College, Hanover, New Hampshire. The AIA awarded Shepley Bullfinch Richardson & Abbott the 1973 Firm Award.

A current project of the firm completed in 1987 is the two new museums added to the Smithsonian Institution on the Mall in Washington, D.C. The National Museum of African Art and the Arthur M. Sackler Gallery were designed by Jean Paul Carlhian, a principal of the firm. Earlier, the site had been identified for an underground structure, preserving open space for what is now the Enid Haupt Garden. Entrance to the new museums is from carefully designed pavilions flanking the garden. These pavilions give access to three levels below grade. The gardens, pools, and fountains are designed to differentiate between the two museums. The Sackler Gallery (Fig. 1), next to the Freer Gallery to which its collections relate, is covered with gray granite facing, and is identified by its group of pyramid roofs. The African museum's pavilion is in pink granite, with clustered dome roofs. A separate domed entrance in the garden gives access to the lowest floor where an auditorium may be used in the evening when the museums are closed. Daylight is introduced through skylights to the mall on the lowest level. The architect has expressed reservations about changes to the buildings by the curatorial staff for the opening exhibitions (2,3).

BIBLIOGRAPHY

1. H. R. Hitchcock, *The Architecture of H. H. Richardson and His Times,* The MIT Press, 1966; originally published by the Museum of Modern Art, 1936, Chap. 14.

2. M. Schmertz, "Underneath a Garden," *Architectural Record* **175**(10), 112–121 (1987).

3. H. Dudar, "New Treasures on the Mall," *Smithsonian* **18**(6), 44–63 (1987).

See also RICHARDSON, HENRY H.

ROBERT T. PACKARD, AIA
Reston, Virginia

SHOPPING CENTERS

The marketplace is as old as the city itself, forming an essential core where people meet for the exchange of goods. It is here that much of urban life—the social contacts, ideas, conversation, eyeing of others, news, gossip—has traditionally taken place. The shopping center, a wholly modern building type, draws on this tradition, differing primarily and substantially in being wholly owned, planned, and controlled, and catering primarily to the use of the private car. Largely a development of the last 40 years as an outgrowth of suburbanization, it has proved to be not only an important concept in retailing, exerting a profound impact on the economy of the nation, but also an important part of everyday life, playing a major social role in today's communities. Disdained by traditional architects and long ignored by architectural historians because of its single-minded commercial intent, the shopping center has also proved to be a formidable factor in urban planning, exerting a powerful influence on the life, health, and vitality of the modern city.

Although the concept arose in the 1920s in the United States, where its primary development took place, it was not until the 1950s that the building type or complex was officially codified. It was then defined as a group of commercial establishments planned, developed, and operated under a single ownership as a single unit, with off-street parking provided and related in location, size, and type of store to the trade area it serves. Wholly planned and controlled, it differs thus from the traditional marketplace, the ordinary retail district or street, where independently owned stores and services have simply concentrated. Three major types have been distinguished on the basis of size and function. The neighborhood shopping center serves 10,000–20,000 people on a 5–10-acre lot, with 10–15 stores clustered around a drugstore or supermarket and offers convenience goods and services to families in the immediate neighborhood. The community shopping center serves 20,000–100,000 people, on 20–25 acres, with 20–40 stores anchored by a junior department store and provides a somewhat broader coverage of merchandise including hardware and apparel. The large-scale regional shopping center serves a population of 100,000 or more, on 35 or more acres, with 50–100 or more stores including at least one major department store and offers a full range of stores and services comparable to those in the retailing district of the downtown. In common usage, the term mall is often used interchangeably with center; strictly speaking, however, a mall is a pedestrian walkway or street, usually paved, sometimes covered, and typically lined with shops and stores on both sides.

The design of the shopping center is fundamentally a problem in planning (1). Enormously complex, it demands the careful coordination of specialists in real estate investment, development, economics, market analysis, engineering, city planning, traffic engineering, merchandising, shopping center management and operation, community relations, and promotion. The more the principal architect or project director knows about each of these fields, the better equipped he or she is to make critical decisions in design and planning. A basic understanding of all of them has proved to be essential at the very outset of the planning process.

The roots of the institution can be traced back to the earliest accounts of the city, where people met for the buying and selling of essential goods. Forming a core of trade in the center of the city and connected to it by a circulation system uniting it with other civic districts, the tradition of the downtown marketplace remained basically unchanged until the twentieth century. The agora, center of a broad base of urban activity in the classical Greek city, was such a communal center. It was basically an informal, irregularly shaped open space or public plaza surrounded by public buildings with continuous colonnaded porticoes at the base facing onto the street, behind which were aligned permanently built shops. Typically located in the middle of town, with the major arterial streets leading into it, the agora was arranged to allow freedom of movement of people and traffic in the central open space, with trade confined to the periphery; streets generally terminated in the agora rather than crossed it, again in the interest of safe, convenient pedestrian as well as vehicular circulation.

This tradition was later formalized in the Roman forum, where small speciality shops were grouped in specially built market buildings. Each individual shop opened onto the street, with sales counter in front and space behind for storage. In the Orient, trading typically took place in bazaars, where rows of independent shops or stalls were informally clustered, offering a wide variety of staples and specialty goods.

In the Middle Ages, throughout Europe and elsewhere, formalized retailing declined, and as permanent quarters fell into disrepair, their place was taken by itinerant merchants and seasonal fairs. In time, simple market halls, often only temporary pavilions, served as the town marketplace, where merchants brought their goods, laying them out in temporary stalls or simply on the ground, to display and sell. These were typically located in centralized squares or places, usually fronting a church or cathedral. Town and guild halls were located nearby, attracting trade and concentrating civic activities. Roads radiated out from the plaza or market square, with secondary roadways connected to them, so that the marketplace was easily accessible from all parts of town. As travel and trade throughout the world increased in the later Middle Ages and cities increased in size, they grew more densely structured; by the seventeenth century, permanent stores and shops were once again built, typically small spaces facing out onto the street, on the ground floor of residential or commercial buildings. Small narrow streets or arcades lined with miscellaneous small specialty shops, where normal vehicular traffic was prohibited, appeared and served as local or neighborhood trade centers.

As the production of glass increased in the nineteenth century, often these passages with their rows of small independently rented shops were glazed, like the narrow Passage Choiseul of 1827 in Paris, or later the broad, boulevard-scaled grand Galleria Vittorio Emanuele in the 1860s in Milan (2) (Figs. 1 and 2). These offered customers the convenience of shopping in inclement weather, as well as encouraging the increasingly popular custom of win-

Figure 1. Passage Choiseul, Paris, 1827 (2). Courtesy of Roger-Viollet, Paris.

dow shopping. The critical difference between these older forms of concentrated retailing and the modern shopping center, apart from their downtown locale, is that in the latter everything is planned, controlled, and coordinated by a single organizing body, so that nothing—selection of tenants, their location in the center, access, operating hours, signage, parking facilities—is left to chance.

With the industrial revolution, the rise of large cities; the development of mass means of production, railroad and other forms of mass transportation; the higher standard of living; and the increase in population of the nineteenth century, retailing procedures changed. This led, in the 1860s, to the rise of the modern department store, where a wide range of mass-produced, moderately priced goods was sold in semi-independent departments under a single management and under a single roof. Basically, the pattern remained the same, with a concentration of retailing facilities in the core of the city, near major sources of public transportation, until the first decade of the twentieth century.

The suburbanization process begun in the latter part of the nineteenth century gradually intensified in the United States, especially after the introduction of the mass-produced car in 1913, setting the stage for a fundamental change in these traditional retail patterns. Cities began decentralizing in the 1920s, a process that continued in the 1930s and accelerated rapidly after World War II. As the population dispersed, mobilized by the private car, so too did retailing. In 1907, the Roland Park-Shop Center opened in a Baltimore neighborhood 5 mi north of

the town center; catering to a residential community that had developed around 1891, it consisted of six stores, one of which was a drugstore. Its most distinctive feature was its off-street parking.

Less than a decade later, in 1916, the real estate developer J. C. Nichols advertised a plan for a 1000-acre country club residential community outside Kansas City that included a small local shopping center; this was the kernel of the much-celebrated Country Club Plaza, opening in 1923, later recognized as a major landmark in shopping center design (3,4) (Fig. 3). Planned from the outset to cater to a small, affluent, suburban community, it consisted of a carefully chosen collection of small, locally owned stores housed in an architecturally unified complex of buildings, all managed under a single body, and located on the outskirts of town, with off-street parking provided. Its main attraction, in addition to its free parking, was its claim to offer its newly motorized suburbanites all of the stores and services needed in daily life without the inconvenience of the downtown. The Country Club Plaza was heralded as the first of its kind to be situated away from a major mass transit hub, catering primarily to customers equipped with their own private cars. By the time the center opened in 1923, the Nichols real estate company plan had grown into a 5000-acre residential district that

Figure 2. Galleria Vittorio Emanuele, Milan, 1867 (2). Courtesy of Roger-Viollet, Paris.

Figure 3. Country Club Plaza, Kansas City, Missouri, 1923 (5). Courtesy of J. C. Nichols Co.

provided the new shopping center a built-in, walk-in trade of some 40,000 people, and the center had expanded to include 142 retail stores and other services. It also included several double- and triple-deck parking structures as well as ground-level parking lots.

In the later 1920s, other small neighborhood centers appeared, conforming to the same basic type. Most of them were "strip" centers, with stores aligned along the street front and parking in the rear, or were grouped in an L- or U-shape form, with parking in the middle, and typically were part of a housing development or community, many of which were then being planned. Following the pattern of suburbanization throughout the nation, the new retailing institution spread more rapidly in the West, where there was both the room to expand and more cars *per capita,* than in the East.

In the meantime, a related retailing change took place. As cities became increasingly congested and parking more difficult with increasing use of the private car, first specialty shops, then chains and department stores began following their motorized customers, opening individual branch stores on the fringes of the city. I. Magnin's of San Francisco opened branches in Santa Barbara and Pasadena in 1912 and 1913; a decade later Filene's of Boston began branching, then in 1925 Lytton's of Chicago and Harris & Frank in Los Angeles followed suit. Sears Roebuck and Company was one of the first to recognize the full significance of the automobile revolution. Early in the 1920s, as it was changing over from a mail-order house to an over-the-counter retailer. Sears Roebuck established a series of large freestanding stores catering specifically to a motorized suburban clientele, with on-site parking behind or on the roof, and a location well outside the central downtown business district. Department stores in the Midwest soon followed. In the Chicago area, Marshall Fields and Company opened a branch in Lake Forest in 1928 and in Evanston and Oak Park in 1929. Bullock's led the pack in the West, opening a branch on Wilshire Boulevard, with an expansive parking lot in the rear, in 1929; Broadway followed suit with a store in Hollywood the fol-

lowing year. Strawbridge and Clothier of Philadelphia and B. Altman and Company of New York spearheaded the movement in the East in 1930, with branches in Ardmore and White Plains, New York, respectively.

These were individual branch stores, however, not shopping centers. In the 1930s, the number of small neighborhood centers began to increase, appearing on the outskirts of most major cities throughout the country. In 1931, Highland Park Village, Dallas opened, a small neighborhood shopping center on 10 acres of land, with stores turned away from the street and grouped around a central court; parking was provided for 600 cars. Farmers' Market in Los Angeles (Fig. 4), a tight cluster of stores and open stalls grouped in the center of a large lot surrounded by parking on all sides, opened at about the same time. The Big Bear Shop Center, publicized as an "automobile shopping center" and part of an eastern train of self-service department stores specializing mainly in groceries, opened two units in 1934, in Paterson, New Jersey and Jersey City, both well outside traditional shopping areas. They offered a limited range of food, dry goods, household furnishings, auto accessories, hardware, apparel, wine, and liquor, plus free parking for 500–1000 cars. And in 1938, Northwood, a center of 12 stores on a planned street, with parking in the middle and six stores on each side, opened in suburban Baltimore (6).

This slow, steady process of retail decentralization, carried out largely by specialty stores, chains, and department stores, with an occasional small neighborhood or community shopping center often developed by a real estate firm as part of a planned neighborhood or community housing development, continued throughout the 1930s. As the depression deepened, and the pressure for low-cost, large-scale housing developments increased, so too did the need for local shopping facilities. The community center in Greenbelt, Maryland, serving a residential area of 885 families and located 12.5 mi from the center of Washington, D.C., was typical. The first of three towns built by the Resettlement Administration (later assumed by the Farm Security Administration), it was begun in 1935 and fin-

Figure 4. Farmer's Market, Los Angeles, California, 1934 (5). Courtesy of Dick Whittington Collection, CSULB.

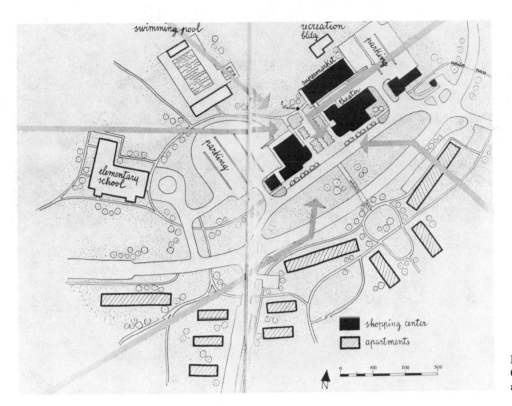

Figure 5. Greenbelt, Maryland (5). Courtesy of G. Baker and B. Funaro and Reinhold Publishing Co.

ished in 1938, and included a shopping center consisting of four buildings clustered around a pedestrian mall or paved, landscaped central courtyard, with seven stores including a supermarket, theater, bus terminal, post office, and communal hall; other community facilities included a park, school, and swimming pool (Fig. 5). Another was the Interlocken development in Eastchester, New York, located 16 mi from the heart of New York City, and planned eventually to serve 3500 family units.

Invariably these new suburban centers were designed around principal use of the private car. As the demand continued to rise in the late 1930s and into the 1940s, centers began increasing in size. Often these were in conjunction with new government-sponsored, large-scale housing projects, following the national trend in the home building industry, with an increasing number of speculative houses built in large groups rather than individually custom designed. Hecht Department Store opened a branch in Silver Spring, Maryland, which in little over a decade grew to a center of some 200 stores. Others similarly expanded as the demand rose, especially after the war. Cameron Village, Raleigh, North Carolina, was another well-known shopping center that started small in the 1940s and simply grew. Typically these centers either conformed to the downtown pattern of stores, lined up flush with the street and with limited free parking in the rear, or were indented, set back from street in an L- or U-shape form and with stores grouped around parking in the center. Increasingly, new centers bore evidence of extensive predevelopment planning and the analysis of factors such as population shifts, available transit facilities, automobile use, neighborhood values, and existing retail facilities.

River Oaks Center, part of a planned neighborhood of 5000 units in Houston, developed in 1940 by Hugh Potter, president of the Urban Land Institute, was a well-known, prewar example with a semicircular layout, providing off-street access to all stores and parking in both front and back. In an article on the development, the *Architectural Forum* pointed out the increasing need for careful planning, with market analyses to determine the size and nature of the particular community (7); a neighborhood of only 30–2000 families needed only a few basic stores, the article maintained, whereas a center for a larger community of up to 10,000 families should include at least six markets, drugstores, and stationery shops; four bakeries and delicatessens; three liquor stores; two hardware stores, banks, and theaters; and a department store, bowling alley, post office, telephone office, and public library. The aim was to provide all the basic daily supplies and services a growing community might need—everything for one-stop shopping.

An important trend-setter, proposed in 1940 by Morris Ketchum, was that of a multistory office block set back on its site, with parking on the rooftop of a low single-story building, which filled the remainder of the lot (Fig. 6). Most likely influenced in basic conception by the recently opened Rockefeller Center, the Ketchum proposal also prefigured the Lever House plan of a decade later. Ketchum's main concern, in addition to the free parking, was for maximum flexibility in store design. The buildings were to consist of flat slabs on regularly spaced columns, with shops below and parking above. This allowed complete flexibility in the partitioning of space so that it could be changed as store size and requirements changed. The multistoried office building located on one edge of the lot

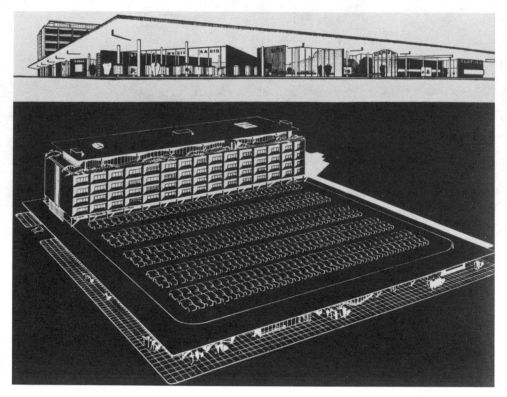

Figure 6. Ketchum Proposal, shopping center, 1940 (8). Morris Ketchum, architect. Courtesy of *Architectural Forum*.

would provide walk-in trade for the center, in addition to that from the local community; storage space was in the basement, with direct access under the buildings for delivery services. Another set of ramps would lead to the roof, where there was parking for 342 cars; additional parking was available in an adjacent lot. All stores would be visible from the street, with large plate glass storefronts protected by a continuous marquee. Escalators were the primary means of vertical transportation from the parking to the main shopping level, with elevators in the office building. A restaurant and day-care center, plus a garden on the roof of the multistoried building were additional amenities. Ketchum eventually envisioned the main street blocked off for pedestrian use only, with all vehicular traffic diverted to the side. The proposal was for a universal model, a generalized type Ketchum believed adaptable to any city of reasonable size.

Shopping center construction all but ceased in the early 1940s, when restrictions were placed on nonwar-related building. While hampering the development of retail design, it offered architects a good opportunity to study new experiments in shopping center design carried out as part of large-scale, war-related housing developments, as well as the uses of new industrial products such as stainless steel, aluminum, synthetic lumber, and plastics, and new structural systems, such as the steel-truss roofing system and laminated wood arch.

On the other hand, wartime shopping facilities were urgently needed (9). New shopping centers, construction of which had lagged behind war housing by as much as two years, were recognized as a vital part of these new planned communities; without them, workers and their families were forced to walk sometimes 2–3 mi for daily

supplies. These wartime centers, typically reduced to the barest minimum of facilities and services and built with only the humblest of means, represented a major contribution of architects to the war effort, taxing their ingenuity because of the restrictions on space and materials.

Orchard Heights in Vancouver, Washington, designed by Pietro Belluschi of A. E. Doyle Associates as part of a planned community for 4500 families of shipyard workers, was one of the first of the new federally financed shopping centers for defense housing to reach the construction stage. The design for the new center, begun before the war broke out, consisted of shopping facilities plus a 1000-seat theater, bowling alley, beer parlor, and other recreational structures; gradually it was pared down as heightened restrictions limited resources to only the barest essentials. Groceries, variety store, apparel, and other related retailing were grouped in one wing; services such as shoe repair, barber, telephone office, and dry cleaners, in another. Construction was simple: wood frame, with exteriors of tongue-and-groove pine, rough side exposed, treated only with pigmented oil. A covered walkway, deemed necessary in the rainy climate of western Washington, connected the building units and architecturally unified the complex. Vehicular and pedestrian traffic were separated, with service traffic routed to the back of the center in the interest of both efficiency and public safety. Ample space for parking was provided.

Linda Vista was one of eight public defense housing projects that were conceived as completely new, planned communities, sponsored by the Public Buildings Administration to provide housing for aircraft workers and their families in the San Diego area (10). It was planned early on when defense housing standards were still at peacetime levels, but by the time the project was actually built, funds for the retail center were no longer available. Residents were thus forced to walk some 2 mi to the center of town to buy supplies, calling national attention to the critical need for accessible commercial facilities. Thirteen acres of the 1200-acre development were originally set aside in 1942 for the shopping center; by the time it was built in 1944, however, the development had expanded from 3000 to 4800 housing units. Occupying only a portion of the original 13-acre shopping center site, with the remainder set aside for future commercial development, buildings included a 5 & 10, grocery, and junior department store, and were grouped around a pedestrian-only park, pursuing a "Grass on Main Street" idea originally proposed by Ketchum in *Forum* of Oct 1940. Parking and merchandise delivery were confined to the periphery. A flexible structural system was used throughout, conforming to a 14-ft modular grid that allowed a variety of building dimensions to accommodate different merchandising requirements. Construction was again simple, timber post-and-beam with concrete floors, uniform board-and-batten exteriors of gray-green painted redwood, and show windows of varying sizes to meet individual tenants' needs. Uniform graphics were used throughout.

The *Architecture Forum* article, addressing the problem of an increasingly congested downtown, had suggested alleviating the situation by diverting vehicular traffic around rather than through the downtown retail district, providing parking on land off the principal shopping street where it was actually cheaper. The main street, the article proposed, could then be converted into a pedestrian-only, landscaped park. This was in response to a eries of articles that had appeared earlier pointing out the increasing problem of parking in major cities. Already by 1941, the parking problem had become acute and was seriously threatening the economic viability of business establishments in affected areas. Twenty years earlier it had been predicted that if steps were not taken to improve the situation, retailing would decentralize. These steps had not been taken, and as a result, retail establishments in congested areas had lost business and the land values of property owners in the area dropped, resulting in tax losses to the local city government.

These losses were particularly dramatic in the West. In Los Angeles, census data showed that while in 1930 34% of retailing was transacted in the central business district, by 1935, that had dropped to only 25%. A number of major cities, among them Detroit, Philadelphia, Boston, and San Francisco, were attempting to stem the tide by erecting parking structures, such as the underground parking garage in Union Square (11); but even then, these were recognized as stopgap techniques only, not long-range solutions. Cities everywhere were facing the same problem. A typical report was that from Seattle. "Downtown property owners of retail stores, theaters, and other establishments are now in the position of the Mississippi river bottom farmer standing knee-deep in the flood and watching the waters carry away his land wealth. Thousands of automobiles cruising around downtown blocks, backing in and out . . . constitute a menace to the very prosperity of the city." And after the war, when wartime restrictions were

finally lifted, central city traffic problems returned with a vengeance. By 1946, 90% of the people in the United States traveled by car (12).

Meanwhile, store design changed. Earlier shopping centers, such as the Kansas City Country Club Plaza of 1923, had become history, typically cast in traditional styles that fit the character of the local community. By the 1940s, the modern or functional style dominated. Clean lines, rational forms, absence of ornament, broadly glazed fronts with large panes of plate glass, new sleek graphics, and what was described as a "styleless architecture" based on a simple direct expression of both program and structure was the order of the day. The open treatment was advocated for storefronts, as it was seen as more appealing, better suited to displays, and allowing a closer coordination of displaying and selling. During the day, it provided ample natural daylight; at night, appropriately lit, it acted as a stage set for the merchandise on display. Capitalizing on much of the new technology developed during the war, store architects increasingly experimented with new structural systems to make space more useful; increasingly, completely open, wide-span universal spaces were used, with intermediary partition walls replacing load-bearing walls or column-supported structures in the interest of maximum floor area and flexibility.

As the production of glass improved dramatically in the decade of the 1930s, glass block, doors, and plate glass had considerable impact on store design; panes became larger and less expensive, and the use of window walls increased, opening up store interiors to make them appear larger and providing more space. Meanwhile, fluorescent lighting, developed in the 1930s, led to an increasing interest in the manipulation of artificial lighting and the use of new features such as the circular tube fluorescent lamp, introduced into store design in 1945 (13).

In the years immediately following the end of the war, several trends affecting shopping center development emerged. The absence of a recognized body of professionally trained planners had aroused considerable concern over city and regional planning on the part of the architectural community; this is evident in articles in the *Journal of the A.I.A.*, especially in the first half of the 1940s. This concern intensified in the postwar period. Clearly recognized as an essential aspect was the planning of retail trade. A second trend was the increasing technical knowledge among architects. Prior to the war, there had been little interest among practicing architects in the use of new methods and materials. The war spurred their investigation; this was reflected in the professional journals, with the incorporation of new technical sections devoted specifically to the use of new materials and technology. A third trend was toward a greater collaboration among architects, engineers, builders, and clients as the scale of postwar projects proved increasingly to be beyond the expertise of a single individual. This was especially true in shopping center design.

Housing was the nation's number one priority in the postwar period. Confronted with an extraordinary demand, entrepreneurial developers recognized the tremendous potential, providing large privately financed housing developments. This was the era of the merchant builder.

Before 1939, speculative housing was spotty, accounting for only about half the number of houses built; by 1949, fully 80% of the year's production was provided by the large-scale developer. Most of this building took place in the suburbs, and with it, the demand for more convenient shopping facilities rose. This, plus the postwar affluence and flourishing economy, resulted in one of the greatest store-building eras in U.S. history, with a huge flood of consumer goods destined for a rich, hungry market making up for wartime restrictions. In 1947, $618 million were spent on store construction alone (14,15).

Most of this construction was in the suburbs, as already experts were predicting the demise of the large central city downtown store. Prewar difficulties with downtown parking and traffic had in the postwar era swollen to virtually impossible conditions. Cities retrenched, with downtown stores modernizing and renovating in the hope of drawing back their trade. But this hardly sufficed. Customers wanted convenience, not show; as a result, the main center of building activity remained in the suburbs.

Rye, by this time an affluent, "silk stocking," bedroom community outside New York City, was rapidly losing its formerly prosperous retailing trade because of downtown congestion. The city council used the lull during the war to study the situation, seeking the expertise of Homer Hoyd, an associate professor of urban land economics, and Frederick Adams, professor of city planning at M.I.T. The results of their analysis of the business district were alarming: because of its inadequate traffic and parking facilities, by 1944, fully a third of Rye's customary retail trade was going to stores outside the city limits. A new town plan drawn up by Morris Ketchum and Vincent Furno called for diverting all vehicular traffic from the main shopping district to the periphery, remodeling storefronts so they faced both front and rear, and converting the main shopping street into a pedestrian-only landscaped mall. Brought to Rye citizens for their approval in the fall of 1946, the plan was defeated. Nonetheless, because it was well publicized, it served as an important model for subsequent shopping center development.

Bellevue, a small but steadily growing, affluent community outside Seattle, Washington, fared better. Described as a brand new business center out in the suburbs addressing the needs of the explosive housing movement, Bellevue Square opened in early 1947 (Fig. 7). Located on 15 acres of land just off a main highway about 10 mi east of Seattle's downtown, in an already developed community whose existing retail facilities were noticeably inadequate, the new suburban shopping center was big enough to be economically self-sufficient. Anchored by a newly opened branch of a major department store, it included a supermarket, two drugstores, variety store, barber shop and beauty salon, restaurant, theater, and medical building; major stores were grouped in the center, with smaller stores and recreation facilities on the periphery, and parking in between. All stores in the complex were thus assured of easily accessible parking. Two square feet of parking for every square foot of store area was provided, following the standard formula of the day. All sidewalks were protected by an 8-ft cantilevered overhang; exteriors were of brick and concrete block, with large expanses of plate glass display windows, distinctively handled in a contemporary, nonhistorical style.

By this time, the traditional concentration of retail facilities around a core of department stores in one centralized area of the downtown had reached the saturation point; henceforth, downtown department store building declined dramatically. Traffic and parking were the major hurdles, as consumers now equipped with their own cars, were free to shop in more convenient locales. New department store construction was almost entirely in the suburbs, typically clustered with other decentralized retail businesses in neighborhood or community shopping centers now geared specifically to patrons using the private car.

1950 marked the emergence of the large-scale regional center, and with it, a major surge of activity in suburban shopping center development. U.S. Census Bureau statistics indicate what was happening: suburban retail sales in 1948 were up 226% over 1939, as compared to only 177%

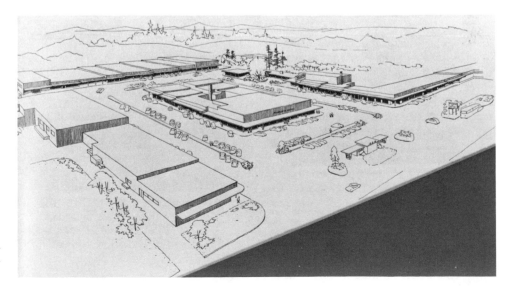

Figure 7. Bellevue Square, Bellevue, Washington, 1947 (16). Photograph by Dearborn-Masser.

for stores in the downtown. As a result, department stores everywhere were capitulating to the suburban trend.

The new regional shopping center, gargantuan in scale, differed not only in size but also in concept from its predecessors (1). Initially referred to as a "suburban retail district" to distinguish it from the traditional, local suburban shopping center, it was conceived of as a transplanted downtown shopping complex, going well beyond the local shopping center, which had limited merchandise geared only to daily needs, by offering a full range of goods and services equivalent to the downtown. At least two of every type of store or facility ensured a healthy competition and provided ample opportunity for comparison shopping; this also provided additional cumulative pull. Extensive enough to answer the shopping needs of an entire region and involving multimillion dollar investments, these huge centers demanded meticulous predevelopment planning, with the full services of a wide-ranging team of specialists, from traffic engineers to publicity experts. Extensive marketing analyses were used to determine buying power of the pegged trade areas; to survey the competition, determining the location of existing stores and marketing potential of new ones; and to establish the appropriate size of the center, given the size and income level of the particular trade area and its accessibility by car. Careful, skilled site planning was vitally important, with the safe, convenient circulation of pedestrian shoppers, customer traffic, and service trucks constituting a critical design factor. Parking was equally crucial, not just the number of parking spaces provided, but their location and proximity to each store in the complex, because it was this, plus the center's traffic-free accessibility by car, that gave the center its primary competitive edge over the downtown.

Several of these new regional centers were being planned simultaneously in different parts of the country at this time. The market was ripe and astute developers knew it, racing against time to be the first to open. One of the best publicized was that being developed by the Conant Real Estate Trust, a group of Boston investors who enlisted the assistance of William Wurster, dean of architecture and planning at M.I.T. and one of the nation's foremost planners; Frederick Adams, city planner; Kenneth Welch, architect and economic adviser; and Ketchum, Gina & Sharp, architects. They advised thinking in terms of a vast planned retail district on a regional scale, broad enough in its coverage to satisfy all of the shopping needs of an entire regional area. Publicized as early as 1947, by 1949 plans were already underway for the first of the chain. This was the huge North Shore Center, a $6 million investment on 62 acres of land near Beverly, Massachusetts, initially planned with some 30 retail stores, "unlimited" parking, and a pedestrian mall (Fig. 8). A second in the proposed chain of completely integrated retail, service, and entertainment facilities, modeled on the same plan as North Shore, was the $5 million Middlesex Center, later known as Shoppers' World in Framingham, Massachusetts, with 60 stores plus theater and restaurants at one end of the mall, a circular department store at the other, plus peripheral parking for 6000 cars. The construction of other centers in Pleasantville,

New York, and Paramus, New Jersey, was scheduled to start soon. Each was to be built around a broad, landscaped pedestrian-only mall 150–200-ft wide flanked on either side by two levels of stores and services, and anchored at the one end by a major branch department store. Complications arose with the planning of these colossal centers, however, delaying construction.

Meanwhile, on the other side of the continent, the Northgate Regional Shopping Center opened in April 1950, in Seattle, Washington. Northgate was the first of the fully matured, completely integrated regional shopping centers, with a single coordinating body responsible for planning, development, ownership, management, and promotion. Conceived by Rex Allison, ambitious new young president of one of Seattle's major department stores, and masterminded by architect John Graham, Jr., it was recognized immediately as a paradigm (1).

Northgate consisted of a $12 million retail center, occupying 60 acres of a wholly owned 150-acre site of what was then still undeveloped farmland 7 mi north of Seattle, in a rapidly growing community of mostly new, young, moderately affluent families. The center was located just off a major highway, with easy access to the surrounding neighborhood. It contained 80 stores, at least two of each kind offering comparison shopping comparable to the downtown; 800,000 ft^2 of retailing area; a major branch of the Bon Marche department store with a second department store planned; and parking for 5000 cars. Northgate proved an immediate financial success, far exceeding expectations. The plan was compact, though the scale was huge, with a narrow centralized pedestrian mall 48 × 1500 ft, flanked by stores and services on either side, with the principal department store in the middle. The second department store was to face the first on the opposite side of the mall, and a one-way underground service tunnel ran the length of the mall, completely separating all merchandise deliveries and refuse pickups from customer traffic. Surrounding the complex on all sides was a vast sea of parking. The architecture was simple: modern, straightforward, and practical. Parking and the site plan were the architect's main priorities, not distinctive architectural design.

Recognized immediately by planners and developers, if not by architects, as an important landmark in regional shopping centers, Northgate broke the ice and served as the prototype. It was followed by Shoppers' World, which opened in October 1951 on a 70-acre site 18 mi west of Boston. This center had 40 stores providing 500,000 ft^2 of retailing area, about 250,000 ft^2 of which was occupied by the Jordan Marsh department store, its principal anchor; parking was available for 6000 cars. Another regional center, the Lakewood Center in Los Angeles, opened at about the same time. These were followed by Stonestown Center in San Francisco in 1953, the Northland Regional Shopping Center outside Detroit, Hillsdale in San Mateo, California, and Panorama City in Los Angeles in 1954.

The Northland Regional Shopping Center, developed by the J. L. Hudson Company, with Victor Gruen, architect, proved another milestone. Occupying a portion of the wholly owned 250-acre site 12 mi northwest of Detroit when it opened in 1954, it was the largest suburban shop-

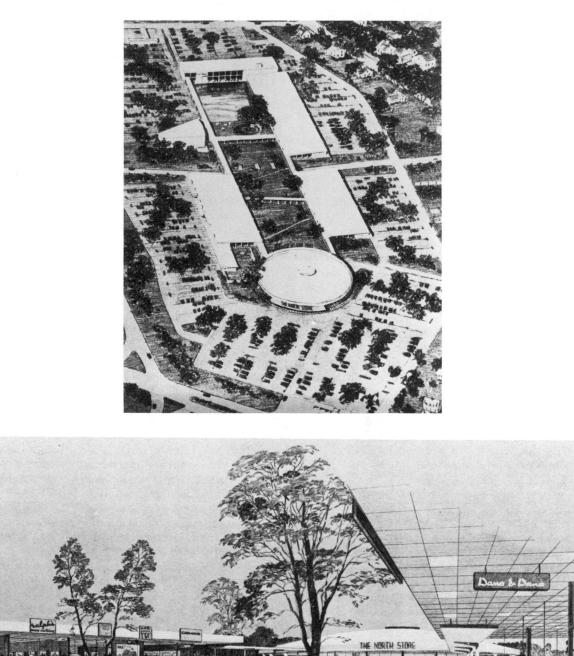

Figure 8. North Shore, Beverly, Massachusetts (17). **(a)** Aerial view; **(b)** architectural rendering. Courtesy of de Bartolo Corporation.

ping center in the nation. Stores were grouped around a single centralized department store rather than aligned along a mall, the first of the so-called cluster type. Parking was on the periphery to minimize distances shoppers would have to walk from stores to their cars. Fully air-conditioned as well as centrally heated, it marked a major

advance in the architectural design of the shopping center as well, as investors facing fierce competition began to acknowledge the importance of an attractive appearance, with amenities such as extensive landscaping in addition to high quality architecture.

1956 was a vintage year in suburban shopping center

development. Eight regionals opened that year, four of them by Allied Stores with the John Graham architectural firm alone. This was also the year Victor Gruen's Southdale Center, Minneapolis, opened on 84 acres of a full 462-acre site, the first fully enclosed, air-conditioned and heated regional shopping mall in the nation (Fig. 9). Between 1956 and 1959 at least six more of these huge centers, each on sites of anywhere from 60 to 120 acres, and with more than 700,000 ft² of retailing space, opened, among them Bergen Center, Paramus, New Jersey, 1957, and North Shore, Peabody, Massachusetts, 1958, again both by Allied, which by now was one of the major shopping center developers in the nation. Scores of smaller regionals and community-sized centers were also built during these years. In 1958, 60% of all new apparel shops, 70% of all new variety stores, 50% of all new supermarkets, and 77% of all new drugstores opened in suburban shopping centers (19).

The Southdale Center in Minneapolis ushered in the era of the big mall. Its high, spacious, glass-covered, landscaped interiors surrounded by several levels of store-lined open galleries harked back to an important historic predecessor, the Galleria Vittorio Emanuele in Milan. A second completely enclosed, air-conditioned type, modeled after a very different historical type, the Oriental bazaar, was introduced by Ketchum, Gina & Sharp at Parker Square, Witchita Falls, Texas. On 41 acres of a 53-acre site, it was far more compact in scale, with a pattern of small, low, covered shop-lined "streets" opening onto a series of plazas or "wells" of natural light. Parker Square raised the prediction of this kind of smaller-seeming, more-compact shopping center in the future. The reign of the gargantuan, sprawling center continued, however, with new centers such as Eastland Plaza, Detroit, opening in 1957. A $15 million project on a 103-acre site located 9 mi outside the center of town, again sponsored by J. L. Hudson with Victor Gruen, it had a full assembly of stores arranged in a spacious oval, with parking both in the center and on the periphery. To keep walking distances from car to stores down to a reasonable level, a split parking scheme was used, with additional rooftop parking planned for the Hudson store. Stores were sited with the Hudson department store at one end, theater at the other, with all major stores in between receiving double frontage, and display windows facing both inside and outside

parking areas; deliveries and service traffic were segregated from customer traffic by means of an underground road on the periphery.

Gruen was by this time conceiving of the regional shopping center as more than just a place to buy (20). Although he saw it as the result of a conscious effort of a group of commercial entrepreneurs focused on a single aim, a profit in retailing, the regional center as Gruen envisioned it could serve as a civic, cultural, and social center for the region as well. An amenable gathering place, wholly planned and coordinated for the mutual benefit of all, patrons, merchants, and investors alike, and comparable to the traditional urban marketplace but now geared fully to the private car, he saw it as complementing, rather than competing with, the downtown.

It did compete. The 1950s was the golden age of suburban shopping center development. Not all succeeded, as the catastrophic failure and subsequent bankruptcy in 1956 of Shoppers' World made clear. Although it was bought the following year by Allied Stores who, aided by the John Graham architectural firm, turned its fate around, enabling it to reopen in 1957, the lesson was clear: shopping center development was still experimental, with enormous risks. Princeton Center in New Jersey was another notable debacle; there were others, as an article in *Barron's*, June 1960, pointed out, having to sell out at distress prices (21).

Despite the occasional failure, however, far more centers were successful. Although developers were exercising new caution, no longer the hit-or-miss approach of earlier times, many were urging compact, multilevel centers rather than sprawling, land-consuming malls. The Mondawmin Regional Shopping Center, Baltimore, Maryland, the first of the real estate developer, James Rouse and Company, with Welch, Belluschi, and Kiley, architects and planners, 3 mi from the downtown on 46 acres of land, with 47 stores and parking space for 4500 cars, was conceived of as a rambling, informal, intimate market town, with a two-level plan creating the effect of a small European village that was to disguise the center's huge scale. Aimed at beguiling the customer with the scale and charm of old shopping streets of Europe rather than overwhelming him or her with the impression of vast size, designers shunned monumentality. Investors had also by now learned that costly amenities such as enclosed malls,

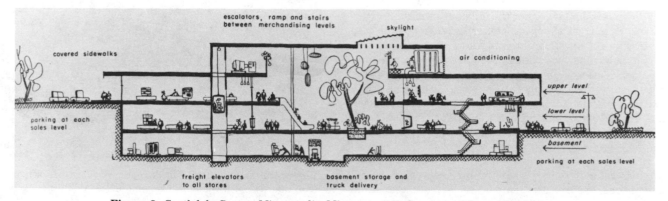

Figure 9. Southdale Center, Minneapolis, Minnesota (18). Courtesy of Gruen Associates.

air-conditioning, well-planned circulation, and quality designed buildings paid off.

Significantly enough, it was at this time, 1960, that Victor Gruen, creator of some of the largest regional shopping centers in the world, published one of the first major books devoted to the planning of shopping centers. In this book, he refers to the shopping center not as a retail district but as a shopping town, discussing its development as an aspect of city planning, not architectural design (22).

By the 1960s, hit by development on this scale, downtowns throughout the country reeled, their retailing centers declining dramatically under the impact. Lathrop Douglas, a prominent shopping center architect, was one of many who saw the preservation and revitalization of the downtown as a serious challenge. Gruen himself predicted two trends resulting from the growing competition from regional shopping centers throughout the decade: revitalized downtown cores, with improved facilities for both public and private transportation, and "new town" development, in the outlying areas of metropolitan regions, planned and developed to duplicate, on a smaller scale, the downtown retailing center. Valencia Center in California was his proposal for a new compact multilevel shopping center, planned as part of a large, all-purpose, integrated urban city in a new town development, concentrating 1,200,000 ft^2 of retail area on 1,080,000 ft^2 of land, with deck parking. As he envisioned it, the single-purpose sprawling suburban shopping center would give way to integrated, multifunction urban subcenters, where the shopping center *per se* would be but one unit in a larger whole, comprising residential units, office buildings, cultural and educational facilities, hotels, amusements, churches, and other community and civic functions. All of these urban functions would be so integrated with retailing facilities as to make the car both unnecessary and impossible within the urban complex. Gruen's notion of a compact, multilevel retailing structure, if not the idea of expanded functions, had been anticipated several years earlier in Queens, New York, where increasing costs and scarcity of suitable land had led to the design of Rego Park, a compact multilevel parking facility, with a department store above serving as a core, surrounded by several stories of small shops on the perimeter.

Faced with the increasing high cost and dwindling supply of suitable land, soaring energy prices, slowed population growth, and uncertain economy in the late 1960s, downtown retailers were not the only ones weighing alternatives. Suburban shopping center developers were also reassessing the situation, seeking new options to the traditional suburban type. One approach was the remodeling or adaptive use of existing buildings in the downtown. Influenced by the growing awareness of the nation's architectural heritage, and spurred by the preservation movement of the 1960s, centers such as Old Town in Los Gatos, California, 50 mi south of San Francisco, were being developed. The Old Town Center, opening in 1969, was an old 1923 Mission-style schoolhouse just off the main street that was converted into a community center, with specialty shops, restaurants, cafés, and a main communal

hall used for conferences, art exhibitions, and musical events. A major aim was to create a viable retailing center that was consistent with the scale and character of the small town.

This trend accelerated in the 1970s, with the remodeling of existing downtown structures for use as commercial centers, rather than erecting new centers on raw, undeveloped suburban land. Among these was Faneuil Hall Marketplace in Boston. Faneuil Hall, one of the nation's oldest extant civic landmarks dating back to the 1700s, was by the 1970s vacant. The traditional farmers' market, Quincy Market, had for a long time functioned successfully adjacent to it, but by the 1970s it too had become dilapidated, and both buildings were in need of repair. Developer James Rouse with Benjamin Thompson, architect, bought and renovated the complex, modernizing it by extending protective high-tech glass and metal shelters over the open plaza for a lively array of shops and stores (Fig. 10). Transformed into a thriving new marketplace, it served as a catalyst in revitalizing the whole once-moribund area, offering the hope that similar revitalized downtown marketplaces could become viable commercial centers by drawing trade back into the center of the city. Although a number of objections have since been raised over the "Rousification" of the U.S. landscape, with the transformation of historic landmarks and authentic farmers' markets into chic, sanitized, fast-food and trendy

Figure 10. Faneuil Hall Marketplace, Boston, Massachusetts (23). Courtesy of Benjamin Thompson and Associates.

merchandise shopping complexes, nonetheless the financial success of Faneuil Hall Marketplace and other Rouse–Thompson commercial centers have established an undeniable precedent.

Another approach to adaptive use, remodeling obsolete but historically significant buildings into thriving commercial centers that avoided the pitfalls of Rousification, was the rehabilitation of existing downtown marketplaces. Pike Place Market in Seattle was begun in 1906 as a sheltered market where farmers from outlying areas of the city trucked their meat and produce into the center of town to sell. It had become increasingly dilapidated over the years, especially as traffic congestion and parking problems in the 1940s drained it of business, and by the 1950s, city planners talked of tearing it down and replacing it with a new modern structure. As the pressure for large-scale urban renewal mounted in the 1960s, a group of local preservationists in 1971 launched a campaign to save it. A 7-acre historic district was created and rehabilitated, with funds from the federal government as well as local investment. Opening in 1974 and receiving an average of 7,000,000 visitors a year, tourists and local citizens alike, the newly revived Pike Place Market provided a major impetus for the economic redevelopment of downtown Seattle, establishing an important model for other federally aided rehabilitation projects throughout the country.

A second trend of the 1970s marking a decline in traditional suburban shopping center development was the new town idea. Seen as a source of much-needed urbanity, the suburban shopping center, which had borrowed some of the best characteristics of the central city, now served as a model for the creation of new towns. The separation of vehicular and pedestrian traffic, extensive use of moving sidewalks, ramps, and stairs to transport large numbers of people; multilevel arcaded spaces at once compact and enclosed; and amenities such as glazed interiors, sparkling fountains, landscaped plazas, and trees integrated with heavily used pedestrian areas, were some of the principles or techniques that had been successfully employed in suburban shopping centers and were now regarded closely by downtown urban planners. Two major shopping centers in the 1970s, broadening their concepts of the shopping center and encouraging the coordinated development of other nonretailing city activities to bring in a concentration of people, were Columbia Mall, Columbia, Maryland, and Eastridge Regional Mall, in San José, California. The Columbia Mall, another Rouse Company development that opened in 1971, was an expansive 2,000,000 ft² shopping district, with centralized two-level enclosed mall, and multilevel parking garage on the periphery, nearby garden apartment and townhouse development for immediate walk-in trade, a bank, Rouse Company headquarters, hotel, two movie theaters, and two department stores with three more expected. Heralded as a model of urbanity, it was seen as encouraging the kind of activity people ordinarily associate with the downtown. Seeking an urbanistic, city-of-the-future image, its principal architectural feature was its futuristic, high-tech space frame, used as roofing over all portions of the mall. Glazed with tinted sheet plastic set in gasketed aluminum supports,

with lush foliage, flowing water, and dramatic lighting, it aimed at creating an aura of innercity excitement.

A second more compact, but equally glamorous, new commercial center was Eastridge, in San Jose (Fig. 11). Billed in 1973 as the second largest shopping center in the United States, with 1,750,000 ft² of retail area and four major pullers, designed for maximum density with three levels of retailing in the large central court, it was lauded as a commendable step toward greater compactness. Its major drawing card was its huge glazed central court at the intersection of the center's two major malls, 400 ft across at its widest point, ringed by three levels of shops interconnected by a series of stairs, ramps, and escalators,

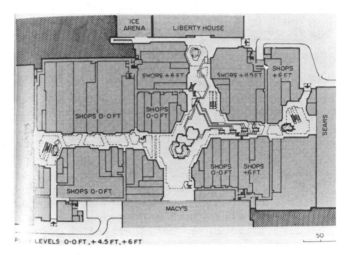

(a)

(b)

Figure 11. Eastridge, San Jose, California (24), (a) plan; (b) view. Courtesy of Eastridge Shopping Center.

with pools of water spilling from one to another down the gently graded, stepped ground-floor level. Natural sky-lighting was supplemented with specially placed lighting fixtures to ensure an even level of brightness even on cloudy days, following a by now customary precedure.

However, both of these gargantuan new centers, despite the talk of new town planning, lacked housing, office space, and civic buildings as part of the overall concept, and perhaps most important, lacked the actual connection with a thriving city, hence were basically suburban shopping centers on a larger scale. Paralleling this new concern for urbanity in shopping center design, perhaps indeed catalyzing it, was the return to the downtown (25). As prices continued to rise in the 1970s, energy costs soared, land became increasingly scarce, and competition became keener. A number of older, smaller, obsolete centers, originally located out in semirural suburbs but by this time surrounded by city development, were revamped, remodeled into what were called new urban centers. Typically this meant increasing the number of stores, adding more department stores and deck parking,

and remodeling or enclosing the mall. Northpark, which was cited as one of the country's most successful regionals when it opened in 1966 in a suburb of Dallas, was renovated and expanded in 1976, with a two-level enclosed mall and new multilevel parking structures added on the perimeter. The Stanford Shopping Center owned by Stanford University, originally opening in 1955, was remodeled in 1977, giving its mall a new theatrical look, a festive atmosphere created by a sequence of spaces protected by a glazed metal-framed loggia, sweeping arches, outdoor display areas, new graphics, benches, fountains, and lush landscaping. The whole mall complex was unified by its overhead protective glazed framework of white bent piping. Another was the Cleveland Arcade, a renovation of the old nineteenth century glazed arcade built by architects Eisenmann and Smith in 1888 (Fig. 12).

Perhaps the most striking evidence of a rejection of the suburban ideal is the rise of new, multiple-purpose, vertical shopping complexes, located in the heart of the downtown (27–29). Pioneering real estate ventures, involving convention hotels, office buildings, and residential units,

Figure 12. Cleveland Arcade, Cleveland, Ohio, 1889; remodeled 1980 (26). Photograph by W. Chin. Courtesy of Kaplan, McLaughlin, Diaz, Architect.

as well as shopping facilities, these vast new multistoried complexes are currently considered the shopping centers of the future. Broadway Plaza in Los Angeles was one of first of these new urban retailing complexes. A $85 million project planned and designed by Charles Luckman Associates representing a joint venture of Ogden Development Corporation, Broadway-Hale Stores, Inc., and Urban Centers Associates, it opened in 1973, on a 4.5-acre site in downtown Los Angeles. Recognized as a laudable effort on the part of private developers to renovate or reinvigorate downtown Los Angeles, it marked the erection of the first downtown department store in the city in 50 years and the first new downtown hotel in 20. Designed specifically to lure the suburban shopper back to the downtown, it comprises a fully enclosed two-level shopping gallery, which is roofed by a glazed tubular steel space frame, 500-room hotel, and a 32-story office building, all in a single multileveled structure. The expectation was that with the gasoline shortage in the 1970s, there would be a turnaround in shoppers' transportation habits, with an increasing use of public transportation facilities, and that this new type of downtown office–hotel–shopping mall complex would serve as a catalyst for city revitalization and the ultimate demise of the suburban shopping center type.

Two new retailing centers that continue these trends in the 1980s are Harborplace, Baltimore, by architects Benjamin Thompson and Associates, and developer James Rouse, and Plaza Pasadena, in Pasadena, California. Unlike the Faneuil Hall center, which started with a long-vacant historic building, Harborplace (Fig. 13) is a wholly

new marketplace development designed to recapture some of the vitality of the old Baltimore harbor district. Two new glass and steel rod, shedlike pavilions facing the waterfront directly recall, without imitating, the old wharf buildings that originally occupied the site, providing 250,000 ft^2 of sheltered quarters for stores, restaurants, and cafés. Comprising the shopping center proper, these two buildings are only one part of an extensive waterfront redevelopment that includes a national aquarium, new world trade center, hotels, office buildings, and an extensive landscaped park. Despite problems with service access, Harborplace has thus far proved to be another urbanistically as well as commercially successful example of a privately developed urban marketplace, revitalizing a once-moribund downtown area.

The Plaza Pasadena, another all-new urban shopping mall, has been likened to the Galleria Vittorio Emanuele in its exemplary compatibility with the existing city fabric (Fig. 14). Assuming Garfield Avenue linking the old beaux arts civic center with the civic auditorium at the far end as their point of departure, architects Charles Kober Associates working in collaboration with the Pasadena Redevelopment Agency, oriented the shopping mall at right angles to the street, thus acknowledging its formal axis. The mall entrance faces directly onto the boulevard, echoing in its design the traditional, familiar, low-sweeping segmental arch of the barrel-vaulted tunnels along the Pasadena–Los Angeles freeway. It also reinforces the original retailing activity of the street by incorporating display windows along Garfield, rather than turning its back on the street, as is traditional in shopping center

Figure 13. Harborplace, Baltimore, Maryland (30). Photograph by Steve Rosenthal.

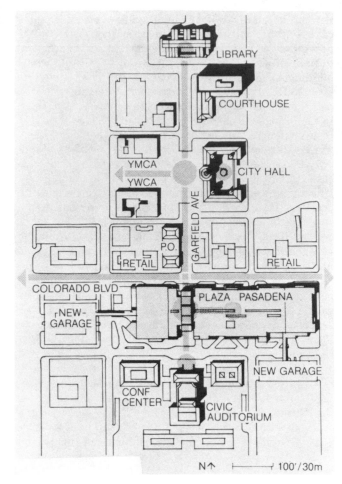

Figure 14. Plaza Pasadena, Pasadena, California (31). Courtesy of Charles Kober, Architect.

design. Seen as a landmark in urban sensitivity for centers of such scale, it already has proved to be a significant model for other retailing developments (32).

The shopping center, in its traditional sense a wholly owned, planned, and controlled suburban retail development catering primarily to the private car, has now taken on a new meaning. When the concept first emerged in the 1920s, it was seen as a suburban phenomenon, part of the decentralization pattern that emerged as city dwellers increasingly equipped with their own means of transportation began moving to the outskirts of the city. It consisted then of a cluster of stores owned and managed by a single administrative body, with off-street parking provided, and located well outside the by-then traffic-congested center of town. The term itself was not officially defined until the early 1950s, when the emergence of the regional shopping center and beginning of the first major wave of suburban shopping center design prompted a distinction among types. During the next two decades, as the suburbanization process sped up under the influence of postwar housing developments, downtown retailers abandoned the city, following their customers to the hinterlands. Suburban shopping center development boomed, aided by plentiful inexpensive land, cheap energy, a growing population,

and a flourishing economy. By the mid 1950s about 1000 centers had been built in the United States. Development continued to flourish in the 1960s and early 1970s, then declined in the later 1970s with the energy crisis, dwindling land, slowed population growth, and uncertain economy. A sudden rebound and unexpected proliferation of enclosed malls in 1980 defied all predictions. By 1980, a year in which 1850 new centers opened alone, the nation's total, according to the International Council of Shopping Centers, was well over 20,000. Today the major trend appears to be toward utilizing existing sites, either revitalizing obsolete suburban shopping centers or developing new sites in the downtown, typically mixed-use multilevel complexes integrated with the existing fabric and activities of the city itself.

A fourth type has emerged within recent years: the urban shopping center, or "urban retail complex," that, rather than divorcing retailing from other aspects of the city as did its suburban prototype, reintegrates the traditional marketplace with the circulation system and other activities of the downtown. Whether this new urban shopping center can in fact solve the problems of the downtown remains to be seen.

BIBLIOGRAPHY

1. M. L. Clausen, "Northgate Shopping Center—Paradigm from the Provinces," *Journal of the Society of Architectural Historians*, 144–161 (May 1984).

2. J. F. Geist, *The History of a Building Type*, Vol XLIII, MIT Press, Cambridge, Mass., 1983

3. J. C. Nichols, *The Country Club District*, Kansas City, Mo., 1916.

4. *Forum*, 114 (1949).

5. G. Baker and B. Funaro, *Shopping Centers—Design and Operation*, New York, 1951.

6. B. S. Gruzen, "Automobile Shopping Centers," *Architectural Record*, 43–48 (1934).

7. R. W. Dowling, "Neighborhood Shopping Centers," *Architectural Forum*, 76–77 (1943).

8. *Architectural Forum*, 294 (Oct. 1940).

9. "Commercial Facilities for 4,500 Families," *Architectural Record*, 68 (1942).

10. "Grass on Main Street Becomes a Reality," *Architectural Forum*, 82–92 Sept. (1944).

11. "Forum of Events—Parking Garage," *Architectural Forum*, 14 (1941).

12. "Parking Jam," *Architectural Forum*, 9 (1946).

13. "U.S. Architecture 1900–1950," *Progressive Architecture*, 90–103 (1950).

14. "40 Stores," *Architectural Forum*, 93 (1948).

15. "The Builder's House 1949," *Architectural Forum*, 81 (1949).

16. *Forum*, 77 (April 1947).

17. *Forum*, 86, 91 (June 1947).

18. *Forum*, 129 (March 1953).

19. "Building Types Study—Shopping Centers," *Architectural Record*, 205–219 (1957).

20. V. Gruen and L. P. Smith, "Shopping Centers: The New Building Type," *Progressive Architecture*, 66–109 (1952).

21. L. A. Armour, "Prosperity Restored," *Barron's*, 3 (1960).

22. V. Gruen and L. Smith, *Shopping Towns USA: The Planning of Shopping Centers*, New York, 1960.

23. *Progressive Architecture*, 61 (Jan. 1975).

24. *Architectural Record*, 126, 127 (March 1972).

25. "Shopping Centers: Downtown is the Next Target," *Architectural Record* **146**, 95, (Oct. 1969)

26. *Architectural Record*, 91 (Oct. 1980).

27. M. Schmertz, "Building Types Study: New Directions for Downtown and Surburban Shopping Centers," *Architectural Forum*, 137 (1974).

28. "Shopping Malls in the Center City," *Architectural Record*, 117 (1978).

29. "Introversion and the Urban Context," *Architectural Record*, 49 (1978).

30. *Architectural Record* 100, 101 (Oct. (1980).

31. *Progressive Architecture*, 96 (July 1981).

32. "Shopping Goes to Town—Urban Shopping Centers," *Progressive Architecture*, 81–98 (1981).

General References

Refs. 1, 3, 20, 22, and 27 are good general references.

"Community Shopping Centers," *Architectural Record*, 100 (June 1940).

"Big Stores Vote for Downtown Again," *Business Week*, 38, 40 (Sept. 20, 1976).

"Evolution of the Shopping Center," *Community Builders Handbook*, Urban Land Institute, Washington, D.C., 1954.

"Shopping Center for Suburban Boston," *Architectural Forum*, 84–93 (June 1947).

"Markets in the Meadows," *Architectural Forum*, 114–124 (March 1949).

"New Enclosed Mall Shopping Center is Designed as Small Commercial City," *Architectural Record*, 142–143 (March 1967).

"Sears-Roebuck Stores—Five Retail Stores Planned for a Motor Age," *Architectural Record*, 31–40 (Sept. 1940).

"Shopping Facilities in Wartime," *Architectural Record*, 63 (Oct. 1942).

"Suburban Malls Go Downtown," *Business Week*, 90–94 (Nov. 10, 1973).

"Suburban Retail Districts," *Architectural Forum*, 106–121 (Aug. 1950).

"Roundtable on Rouse," *Progressive Architecture*, 100–106 (July 1981).

"Planning the Urban Marketplace," *Architectural Record*, 90–94 (Oct. 1980).

"Three-level Centers, Next Step in Malls?" *Chain Store Age* **47**, 34–35, 37, 41 (May 1971).

G. Baker and B. Funaro, *Shopping Centers Design and Operation*, Reinhold Publishing Corp., New York, 1951.

I. Barmash, "Lean Times for Shopping Centers," *The New York Times*, March 16, 1975, sect. 3, pp. 1, 4.

P. Belluschi, "Shopping Centers," in T. Hamlin, ed., *Forms and Functions of Twentieth Century Architecture*, Vol. IV, Columbia University Press, New York, 1952, pp. 114–139.

G. Brechkenfeld, "Jim Rouse Shows How to Give Downtown Retailing New Life," *Fortune*, **97**, 84–91 (April 10, 1978).

H. Carpenter, Jr., *Shopping Center Management*, International Council of Shopping Centers, New York, 1978.

Directory of Shopping Centers in the United States and Canada, 16th ed., National Research Bureau, Washington, D.C., 1975.

J. B. Douglas, "The Enclosed Mall and Other Development Trends in the Shopping Center Business," *Urban Land*, 3–5 (Sept. 1962).

L. Douglas, "Revitalizing Downtown Shopping Centers," *Architectural Record*, 136–137 (July 1969).

The Editors of the Fortune, *The Exploding Metropolis*, Doubleday and Co., New York, 1958.

J. F. Geist, *Arcades—The History of a Building Type,* MIT Press, Cambridge, Mass. (1983).

R. Gratz, "Downtown Devitalized," *Progressive Architecture*, 82 (July 1981).

V. Gruen, "From Shopping Center to the Planned City," *Stores*, 14–16 (March 1966).

V. Gruen, "A New Look at Past, Present, and Future Shopping Centers," *Architectural Record*, 168–171 (April 1969).

J. S. Harris, "The Design of Shopping Centers," *Town Planning Institute Journal*, 245–251 (Sept. 10, 1961).

J. S. Hornbeck, *Stores and Shopping Centers*, McGraw-Hill Book Company, New York, 1962.

M. Ketchum, *Shops and Stores*, Reinhold Publishing Co., New York, 1948.

W. S. Kowinski, *The Malling of America. An Inside Look at the Great Consumer Paradise*, William Morrow & Company, Inc, New York, 1985.

E. Lion, *Shopping Centers—Planning, Development, and Administration*, John Wiley & Sons, Inc., New York, 1976.

C. Kober, "Regrowth for Existing Shopping Centers," *Urban Land*, **36**, 3–9 (1977).

C. T. Jonassen, *The Shopping Center Versus Downtown: A Motivational Research on Shopping Habits and Attitudes in Three Cities*, Bureau of Business Research, Columbus, Ohio, 1955.

T. D. MacGregor, "The Shopping Center—Logical Adjunct of Group Housing in Suburban Areas," *Engineering News Record*, 16–17 (Aug 12, 1984).

J. R. McKeever, N. M. Griffin, and F. H. Spink, *Shopping Center Development Handbook*, Urban Land Institute, Washington D.C., 1977.

J. F. Orr, *Malls, Pedestrian Malls, and Shopping Centers*, Vance Bibliography, Montecello, Ill., 1979.

L. G. Redstone, *New Directions in Shopping Centers and Stores*, McGraw-Hill, New York, 1973.

C. S. Stein and C. Bauer, "Store Buildings and Neighborhood Shopping Centers," *Architectural Record*, 175–187 (Feb. 1934).

M. Villanueva, *Planning Neighborhood Shopping Centers*, National Committee on Housing, New York, 1945.

K. C. Welch, "Regional Shopping Centers," *American Institute of Planners Journal*, 4–9 (Fall 1948).

Meredith L. Clausen
University of Washington
Seattle, Washington

See also Department Stores

SHORING AND UNDERPINNING.   See Foundations Systems.

SHRUBS AND TREES

The primary usefulness of trees and shrubs compared to smaller plant forms is structural, as opposed to decorative. Trees and shrubs can be used to create, reinforce, and modify three-dimensional space. It is within this broader definition of their architectural usefulness that these plants are considered here. As living building materials, plants have special advantages, limitations, and maintenance requirements. The cultivation requirements of trees and shrubs are described in a general context. Specific cultivation requirements for a particular plant species and locality may be found in the accompanying references.

This article is organized in three sections based on the way designers pursue their work: aesthetic criteria (Design), characteristics of individual plant types (Materials), and technical knowledge needed to use plants in design (Construction). Trees and shrubs are treated separately because of the extent to which tree use differs functionally from shrub use in design.

Emphasis is placed on urban use of trees and shrubs because of the more rigorous constraints on urban sites for planting. Planting over structure (eg, roof gardens) engenders different technical constraints from at-grade planting.

Interior planting has completely different environmental criteria, materials, and construction techniques from outdoor planting; therefore it is treated separately. No distinction will be made in the first section (Design) because aesthetic criteria are essentially the same.

DESIGN

Design Use of Trees

The scale-modifying function of trees is the most important aspect of their use in design. Trees are divided into two categories by size for the purpose of exposition.

1. *Large Trees.* 50 ft (15 m) or more in height at maturity with crown width at least one-third of height dimension.
2. *Small Trees.* At least 16 ft (5 m) but not over 50 ft (15 m) in height at maturity.

Woody plants less than 16 ft (5 m) in height at maturity will be classified in this article as shrubs for the purpose of design discussion.

Large trees define space horizontally by surrounding an area to create an outdoor room. They can also define effective spaces vertically by creating a ceiling or canopy of branches where the lowest branches are more than 2 m above the ground. Because of the visual permeability of most deciduous-type tree crowns and their nonregular patterns, spaces defined by trees are dramatically different in light quality and visual character from spaces made by most architectural materials. As used here, "deciduous type" includes some broad leaf trees in the warmer climates that are evergreen but have the form and character of deciduous trees in leaf. Evergreen trees can function

the same way but are generally more dense and do not change character seasonally. As used here, "evergreen trees" refers to coniferous-type, narrow-leaved evergreens, which can generally be found in northern states. Clipped trees can define spaces, giving a more architectural character, and sometimes make a more urban spatial transition. Trees are most effective in horizontally defining space at eye level where the dimensions of the space do not exceed four times the tree height. Small trees are inappropriate for most streets and public spaces where they can hamper pedestrian circulation and tend to screen rather than frame views.

The use of trees to articulate and to link spaces is best illustrated by the use of street trees that give unity and continuity to the streetscape where a single large species of deciduous tree is used. Where trees are used for visual buffering or screening, coniferous evergreen trees are often advantageous because of their density, low branching, and winter foliage. As a noise buffer, trees are not very effective because they lack the density to achieve effective diminution of sound in a narrow space. A strip of evergreen trees narrower than 200 ft (61 m) is less effective in buffering urban noise than a masonry wall or earth berm. Deciduous trees can be very useful in creating transitions between outdoor spaces because of their semitransparency. This translucent quality of a tree crown is one reason why large deciduous trees can link spaces in the city without closing off views or obscuring the architectural richness of the buildings seen through the branches. The enhancement of urban spaces with large deciduous trees results from

1. A rich textural background and modified quality of light filtered through the crown.
2. Expression and amplification of the natural cycles, notably the seasons, by changes in form, color, texture, and density.
3. Enframement of views and facades.
4. Visual harmony and rhythm in the spacing and arrangement of the trunks.

The spacing of trees in landscape design is largely an aesthetic and functional question because trees will grow well at any spacing if other cultural conditions of the environment are acceptable. Trees, spaced far enough apart so that each individual tree canopy is distinguished from the next, become sculptural objects in space rather than space-defining bands or living colonnades. The minimum practical spacing for trees is limited by the size of the root ball at transplanting and hence by the size of trees being installed. Where close spacing is required of the design, less than 8 ft (2.5 ms) on center, it may be necessary to plant younger, hence smaller, trees than are usually desirable on an urban site in order to allow the roots and branches to adjust to the spacing as the trees grow.

The desire for tree spacing substantially closer together than the mature branch spread often results from the need to produce a solid tree canopy sooner than it takes the trees to reach their full size. To the person standing on the ground, the significant difference between a planting of young and mature trees is the spread of the branches (Fig. 1). If the trees are planted closer together and increased in quantity, the branches will touch sooner even though they are not as tall. In many instances the resulting cost increase is acceptable to produce a more immediate closed canopy when seen from the ground.

Similarly, there is no practical limit to the maximum spacing between trees. Usually functional questions such as circulation, and visual demands such as continuity, relation to surroundings, and the desired crown form, determine how far apart to plant trees. There is a pronounced difference in the tree crown form and the continuity of the tree canopy between closely spaced shade trees and widely

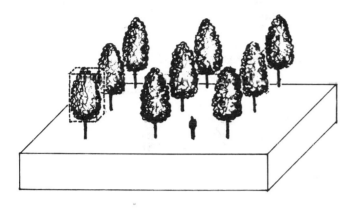

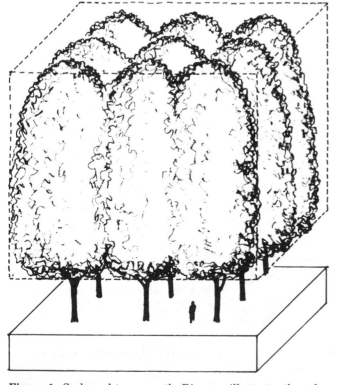

Figure 1. Scale and tree growth. Diagram illustrates the volumetric difference between trees when they are planted and 40 years later. The visual impact of trees is largely dependent on the mass or volume of the crowns but from eye level it depends mostly on the branch spread (1). Courtesy of Van Nostrand Reinhold.

spaced shade trees. Trees planted in a forest pattern with trunks closer together than the mature crown dimension for an open-grown specimen will be more upright, higher branched, and less dense in crown and leaf structure than an open-grown tree of the same species. Open-grown trees develop with a more dense, symmetrical, and lower branched crown. In general, where a continuous canopy and high branches are desirable, street tree spacing for large deciduous trees between 16 ft (5 m) and 26 ft (8 m) promotes this canopy form.

Design Use of Shrubs

Shrubs are broadly defined for the purposes of this article as woody plants that reach less than 16 ft (5 m) in height at maturity. The usefulness in design has both visual and functional considerations. Shrubs are used in multiple arrangements to define, reinforce, and articulate space at and below eye level. Tall shrubs can be used as a foil or screen to control views; lower shrubs can visually define edges without blocking views beyond. Used in masses, lines, or repetitively, they can enhance scale, continuity, and coherence. Shrubs enrich open spaces with their colors, textures, and seasonally changing qualities. Functionally, shrubs are useful as circulation barriers, as ground covers to protect the soil, as camouflage for undesirable views, and for orientation as in lining paths. Their functional usefulness is directly related to size and form, which is easily manipulated with some types by pruning. Sizes of shrubs and their most common functions follow.

1. *Dwarf or Prostrate.* up to 16 in. (400 mm): low ground covers, edge planters.
2. *Low.* 16–27 in. (400–700 mm): ground covers, barriers, hedges.
3. *Medium.* 27–54 in. (700–1400 mm): hedges, barriers, mass planting.
4. *Tall.* over 54 in. (1400 mm): hedges, screens, backdrops.

There is a great diversity in form, density, and texture among the many species of both evergreen and deciduous shrubs that grow in the United States. They vary in density from very open and irregular (*Pyracantha*) to very solid (*Buxus*). Textures range from coarse with very large leaves (*Viburnum*) to very fine with small leaves (*Cotoneaster*).

Frequent pruning and clipping are often standard practice with shrubs so that their form, density, and size can be modified. The type of pruning is referred to as follows.

1. *Natural.* Unpruned or pruned by selective branch removal (thinning).
2. *Pruned.* Kept within specific size limits by pruning; not severely shaped or manicured.
3. *Clipped.* Uniformly cut to a regular geometric form.
4. *Espaliered.* Trained by selectively clipping to produce a flat pattern that emphasizes and displays the branch structure; attached to a wall or fence.
5. *Topiary.* Clipped into geometric solid or other imitative form such as an animal, sculpture, or a tree.

The spacing of shrubs, as with trees, is an aesthetic question. As shrubs can be grown at any practical spacing, the distance apart is determined by the intended purpose (eg, a hedge) and the immediacy of effect. Shrubs are planted closer together than their mature spread to make a hedge or mass and further apart when the individual shrub form is to remain distinct.

MATERIALS

Plants

Nomenclature. Plants are given botanical names that, to assure precision, are used in the nursery trade and in design. Most plants are known by a common name, which may vary with locality. Therefore, botanical names are used here for accuracy. The botanical name consists of two or three parts: a genus, a species, and sometimes a variety or cultivar. The genus name is capitalized and the species name is begun with a lower case letter. Variety names may or may not be capitalized. For example, the common name Green Mountain Sugar Maple has the botanical name *Acer saccharum* "Green Mountain."

Criteria for Selection. Aesthetic selection criteria deal with the physical features of plants and include scale, structure, and details of foliage such as density and color. Cultural selection criteria for plants deal with biological suitability for the location. Aesthetic and cultural criteria are discrete for trees and shrubs and are discussed separately. The operational selection criteria, which usually take precedence over design considerations, are the practical limitations. These constraints may be set by the project owner or potential suppliers of plants and include, for example, cost and availability. Operational criteria are discrete for each project and will not be discussed further. In seeking data on plant form and growth requirements, there is wide variation from source to source. A plant growing in an urban location has a very different form from the same species growing in a less restricted nonurban environment. The literature on plants does not illustrate the typical urban form. Therefore direct observation must be relied on for information on the urban growth requirements and form of trees and shrubs growing in similar conditions and locations.

Tree Species Aesthetic Selection Criteria
1. *Scale and Growth Rate.* Both height and crown volume are critical.
2. *Context.* Relationship to surroundings, especially proximate trees.
3. *Density and Structure of Crown.* Transparency vs dense shade.
4. *Seasonal Attributes.* Spring, summer, and fall color; winter sunlight and shadow patterns.
5. *Other Visual Characteristics.* Crown texture and bark color.

Tree Species Cultural Selection Criteria
1. *Site Tolerance.* Ability to withstand urban conditions, for example. Note that all nursery grown trees, even swamp species, require good drainage and will not grow when transplanted into poorly drained soil. There are not significant enough differences in shade tolerance among species of large trees to merit making a distinction.
2. *Hardiness.* Adaptability to local climate and microclimates (Fig. 2).
3. *Transplanting Tolerance.* Ability to survive loss of roots in moving.
4. *Maintenance Requirements.* Ability to remain healthy with the proposed level of maintenance.
5. *Resistance to Pests.* Insect and disease tolerance.
6. *Salt Tolerance.* Depends on local snow-melting practices or proximity to saline conditions, eg, seashore, highways.

Tables, 1–3, present characteristics of some common shade trees. These describe major selection criteria for a limited sample of commonly used trees that grow in each region. Local authorities and sources such as state university horticulture department publications, botanical gardens, and state agricultural experiment stations should be consulted for more localized and more complete lists of recommended species including trees for the southeast that are too variable to typify in a table.

Shrubs

Shrub Species Aesthetic Selection Criteria.

1. *Form.* Prostrate, spreading, intermediate, upright, columnar, fastigiate.
2. *Height.* Dwarf, low medium, tall (see Design Use of Shrubs).
3. *Texture–Color.* Factors affecting the general appearance.
4. *Seasonal Attributes.* Changes in color and texture; evergreen, deciduous.
5. *Adaptability to Clipping.* Where precise form is needed.
6. *Structure.* Sculptural, stiff, soft, regular, irregular.

Shrub Species Cultural Selection Criteria.

1. *Hardiness.* Adaptability to local climate and microclimate (Fig. 2).
2. *Shade Tolerance.* Full sun, partial sun, shade.
3. *Resistance to Pests.* Insect and disease tolerance.
4. *Soil Compatibility.* Conflicting pH and watering requirements for different plants growing in close proximity.
5. *Salt tolerance.* Proximity to saline conditions, eg, seashore, highways.

Because of the extensive numbers of shrubs that will grow under urban conditions, consult horticultural books, local botanic gardens, and sources such as state university horticulture department publications and state agricul-

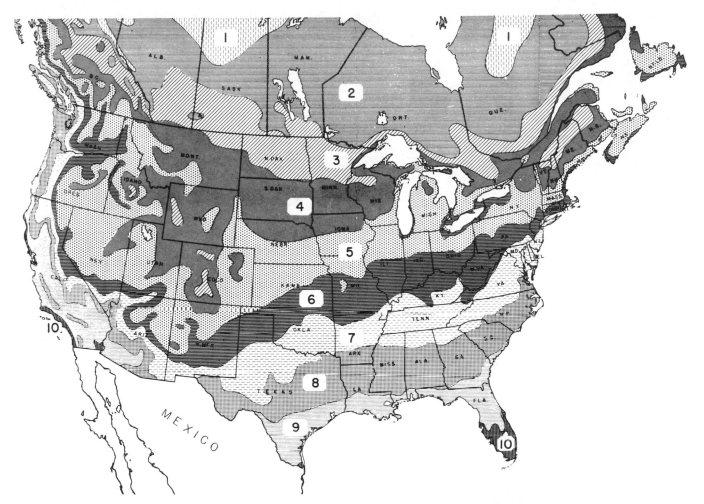

Figure 2. Plant hardiness zone map (2). Approximate range of average annual minimum temperatures for each zone: Zone 1, below −50°F; Zone 2, −50 to −40°F; Zone 3, −40 to −30°F; Zone 4, −30 to −20°F; Zone 5, −20 to −10°F; Zone 6, −10 to 0°F; Zone 7, 0 to 10°F; Zone 8, 10 to 20°F; Zone 9, 20 to 30°F; Zone 10, 30 to 40°F.

tural experiment stations for lists of shrubs suitable for use in a given locality.

Handling

Tagging Plants. Most plant material is purchased from existing nurseries. If time and budget allow, plants can be contract grown according to specifications, in which case quantities and quality can be controlled. Sometimes plants are transplanted from fields where they are growing naturally. These field-collected plants are usually more difficult to transplant and are lower in quality than nursery-grown plants. Plants are usually specified and handled following standards set by the American Association of Nurserymen. These standards govern height to caliper ratio, crown configuration, branching form, and height of branches above the ground. The designer selects and tags plants in the field prior to digging because of the great variations in quality and character occurring within a single species in a single size range.

Method of Handling Plants. Trees and shrubs are transplanted using one of three methods for handling the root system. These methods are "bare root," "balled and burlapped," and "container grown." Each has the following advantages and limitations.

1. *Bare Root.* Plants are dug with soil carefully removed from around the roots. During handling, the roots are protected with mulch and kept constantly moist. Only dormant deciduous shrubs and trees up to 3 in. in caliper are handled this way. Bare root is less expensive and is often the most practical way to transplant large quantities of ground cover shrubs or hedge plants and occasionally small trees.

2. *Balled and Burlapped.* Plants are dug with a ball of earth surrounding the roots. The ball is wrapped with burlap and tightly laced to hold the soil. The disadvantage compared to bare root planting is the weight of soil that must be handled. However, any

Table 1. Characteristics of Broadleaf Shade Trees—Northeast and Midwest States

Botanical Name[a]	Common Name	Scale[b] Height, m	Scale[b] Maximum Spread, m	Crown Trans-parency[c]	Crown Structure[d]	Growth Rate[e]	Seasonal Attribute[f]	Hardiness Zone[g]	City Tolerances[h]
Acer platanoides	Norway maple	14–17	13	Opaque	Symmetrical; dense	M	2	3	Good
Acer rubrum	Red maple	15–18	11	Intermediate	Irregular; open	M	3	3	Moderate
Acer saccharum	Sugar maple	18–21	14	Opaque	Symmetrical; open	M	4	3	Moderate
Cladrastis lutea	Yellowwood	9–14	8	Intermediate	Irregular; open	S	3	4	Moderate
Fagus grandifolia	American beech	18–21	17	Opaque	Symmetrical; dense	S	3	4	Poor
Ginkgo biloba	Maidenhair tree	15–18	13	Intermediate	Irregular; open	S	3	4	Good
Gleditsia triacanthos inermis	Thornless honeylocust	15–18	12	Translucent	Irregular; open	F	2	4	Good
Gymnocladus dioicus	Kentucky coffee tree	21–24	15	Intermediate	Irregular; open	F	1	4	Good
Liquidambar styraciflua	Sweet gum	15–18	12	Opaque	Symmetrical; dense	M	3	5	Moderate
Liriodendron tulipifera	Tulip tree	23–27	12	Opaque	Symmetrical; dense	M	2	4	Poor
Phellodendron amurense	Amur cork	11–14	10	Intermediate	Irregular; open	M	2	3	Good
Platanus acerifolia	London plane tree	21–24	18	Intermediate	Irregular; open	F	3	5	Good
Prunus sargentii	Sargent cherry	12–15	10	Opaque	Symmetrical; open	M	5	4	Moderate
Quercus alba	White oak	21–24	20	Opaque	Symmetrical; dense	S	4	4	Moderate
Quercus borealis	Red oak	21–24	18	Opaque	Symmetrical; dense	M	3	3	Good
Sophora japonica	Japanese pagoda tree	15–18	18	Intermediate	Irregular; open	M	4	4	Good
Tilia cordata	Littleleaf linden	12–18	12	Opaque	Symmetrical; dense	M	2	3	Good
Ulmus alata	Winged elm	15–18	13	Translucent	Irregular; open	F	2	4	Good
Zelkova serrata	Japanese zelkova	15–18	15	Opaque	Symmetrical; dense	F	2	6	Good

[a] A representative selection of trees for urban conditions suitable for street use, varieties or cultivars not listed. However, there are important differences among horticultural varieties and cultivars that must be taken into account in evaluating species.
[b] Estimated mature dimensions attained in 25–30 years allowing for urban constraints on plant growth. To convert to ft, multiply by 3.3.
[c] Applies to mature trees in leaf.
[d] Applies to mature tree-branching form.
[e] Estimated relative rates of growth under urban growth constraints: S = slow; M = medium; F = fast.
[f] Rated from 1, least change during one year, to 5, greatest change during one year.
[g] Refers to plant hardiness zone map (Fig. 2).
[h] Based on observations of trees growing on urban sites with constricted root space and compacted soil.

size tree or shrub can be moved over a longer planting season and there is generally a higher rate of survival than for bare root transplanting. A variation on balled and burlapped handling of trees is the "boxed" tree method used extensively for larger trees in the southwestern states. See Table 4 for digging standards.

3. *Container Grown.* Evergreen and deciduous plants are grown from smaller plants or seedlings in metal or plastic nursery containers. Although economical only for shrubs and trees up to 3-in. caliper, it has the highest plant survival rate of the three methods of handling nursery stock.

Growing Media

The growing medium requirements for any particular project depend on many variables including local soil analysis, plant species, and local economic considerations. The medium must have both good drainage and the ability to retain air, nutrients, and water. The retention of air in the soil is as critical as retention of water for plant growth and survival.

Growing media prototypes for different conditions follow.

1. *Nonurban Sites.* Existing loam topsoil and fertilizer or existing topsoil and fertilizer with organic matter and coarse sand added to improve porosity and drainage.

2. *Average Urban Site.* Prepared soil mixture: loam topsoil, 3 parts by volume; compost or peat moss, 1 part by volume; sand, 1 part by volume; fertilizer, as indicated by topsoil analysis.

3. *Planter over Structure.* Prepared soil mixture: loam topsoil (with less than 15% clay), 1 part by volume;

Table 2. Characteristics of Broadleaf Shade Trees—Northwest and Rockies

Botanical Name[a]	Common Name	Scale[b] Height, m	Scale[b] Maximum Spread, m	Crown Trans-parency[c]	Crown Structure[d]	Growth Rate[e]	Seasonal Attribute[f]	Hardiness Zone[g]	City Tolerance[h]
Acer platanoides	Norway maple	14–17	13	Opaque	Symmetrical; dense	M	2	3	Good
Acer rubrum	Red maple	15–18	11	Intermediate	Irregular; open	M	3	3	Moderate
Acer saccharum	Sugar maple	18–21	14	Opaque	Symmetrical; open	M	4	3	Moderate
Aesculus carnea	Red horse chestnut	12–18	12	Opaque	Symmetrical; dense	S	4	4	Good
Alnus rhombifolia	White alder	15–23	12	Intermediate	Symmetrical; open	F	3	5	Moderate
Carpinus betulus	European hornbeam	10–12	10	Opaque	Symmetrical; dense	M	2	5	Good
Cladrastis lutea	Yellowwood	9–14	8	Intermediate	Irregular; open	S	3	4	Moderate
Fagus sylvatica	European beech	15–18	15	Opaque	Symmetrical; dense	S	3	5	Poor
Fraxinus latifolia	Oregon ash	12–24	10	Opaque	Symmetrical; open	F	2	5	Good
Fraxinus pennsylvanicum	Green ash	18–24	15	Opaque	Symmetrical; dense	F	3	2	Good
Ginkgo biloba	Maidenhair tree	15–18	13	Intermediate	Irregular; open	S	3	4	Good
Gleditsia triacanthos inermis	Thornless honeylocust	15–18	12	Translucent	Irregular; open	F	?	4	Good
Liquidambar styraciflua	Sweet gum	15–18	12	Opaque	Symmetrical; dense	M	3	5	Moderate
Liriodendron tulipifera	Tulip tree	23–27	12	Opaque	Symmetrical; dense	M	2	4	Poor
Platanus acerifolia	London plane tree	21–24	18	Intermediate	Irregular; open	F	3	5	Good
Populus tremuloides	Quaking aspen	12–15	5	Translucent	Symmetrical; open	F	5	2	Poor
Quercus alba	White oak	21–24	20	Intermediate	Symmetrical; dense	M	5	4	Moderate
Quercus borealis	Red oak	21–24	18	Opaque	Symmetrical; dense	M	3	3	Good
Quercus coccinea	Scarlet oak	18–22	15	Intermediate	Symmetrical; open	M	4	5	Moderate
Tilia cordata	Littleleaf linden	12–18	12	Opaque	Symmetrical; dense	M	2	3	Good
Zelkova serrata	Japanese zelkova	15–18	15	Opaque	Symmetrical; dense	F	2	6	Good

[a] A representative selection of trees for urban conditions suitable for street use, varieties or cultivars not listed. However, there are important differences among horticultural varieties and cultivars that must be taken into account in evaluating species.

[b] Estimated mature dimensions attained in 25–30 years allowing for urban constraints on plant growth. To convert to ft, multiply by 3.3.

[c] Applies to mature trees in leaf.

[d] Applies to mature tree-branching form.

[e] Estimated relative rates of growth under urban growth constraints: S = slow; M = medium; F = fast.

[f] Rated from 1, least change during one year, to 5, greatest change during one year.

[g] Refers to plant hardiness zone map (Fig. 2).

[h] Based on observations of trees growing on urban sites with constricted root space and compacted soil.

masonry sand, 1 part by volume; peat moss or shredded compost, 1 part by volume; fertilizer, as indicated by topsoil analysis.

Specially designed lightweight soil with weight reduced by 30–40% can be used where structural cost reduction is significant. Such lightweight soils offer less support to trees and do not retain nutrients as well as soils with a clay content.

Subsurface Drainage Material

Soil Separator. A soil separator is a woven or sometimes nonwoven fabric made of strong plastic or fiberglass that is used as a filter between soil and drainage layer to prevent soil particles from clogging the porous drainage layer while permitting the percolation of water.

Drainage Layer. A drainage layer is a layer of porous material placed in the bottom of a tree pit or planter to absorb and convey water from the soil above to a drain line or outlet. The thickness of the drainage layer varies in relation to the bottom slope of planters from 1 to 10 in. (25 to 250 mm). In tree pits, it is usually 6 in. (150 mm) thick. Material may be a graded stone aggregate, sheets of permeable plastic board, a three-dimensional plastic wire mat, or other manufactured matrix material that permits unrestricted flow of water. The advantages of the manufactured semirigid matrix materials are that they require less space, are lighter weight, and are easier to install than a stone aggregate layer.

Protection Board. A layer of rigid plastic, fiber composition, or other material placed over the waterproof membrane to prevent puncturing during construction and

Table 3. Characteristics of Broadleaf Shade Trees—Southwest

Botanical Name[a]	Common Name	Scale[b] Height, m	Maximum Spread, m	Crown Trans-parency[c]	Structure[d]	Growth Rate[e]	Seasonal Attribute[f]	Hardiness Zone[g]	City Tolerance[h]
Ceratonia siliqua	Carob tree	9–12	11	Opaque	Symmetrical; dense	M	1	10	Good
Cinnamomum camphora	Camphor tree	9–12	14	Opaque	Symmetrical; dense	S	3	9	Good
Erythrina caffra	Coral tree	8–12	18	Opaque	Irregular; dense	S	5	10	Good
Eucalyptus camaldulensis	Red gum	18–21	9	Intermediate	Irregular; open	F	1	9	Good
Eucalyptus ficifolia	Red-flowering gum	9–15	11	Opaque	Irregular; dense	F	3	10	Good
Eucalyptus polyanthemos	Silver-dollar gum	6–18	5	Intermediate	Irregular; open	F	3	10	Good
Eucalyptus sideroxylon 'Rosea'	Pink ironbark	6–24	10	Intermediate	Irregular; dense	F	2	9	Good
Fraxinus velutina	Arizona ash	6–14	9	Intermediate	Symmetrical; open	M	2	5	Good
Gleditsia triacanthos inermis	Thornless honeylocust	15–18	12	Translucent	Irregular; open	F	2	4	Good
Harpephyllum caffrum	Kaffir plum	9–11	8	Opaque	Symmetrical; dense	F	2	10	Moderate
Jacaranda acutifolia	Jacaranda	8–12	9	Translucent	Irregular; open	M	4	10	Moderate
Liquidambar styraciflua	Sweetgum	15–18	12	Opaque	Symmetrical; dense	M	3	5	Moderate
Melaleuca quinquenervia	Cajeput tree	6–12	10	Intermediate	Irregular; open	F	3	10	Good
Pistacia chinensis	Chinese pistache	12–18	15	Opaque	Symmetrical; dense	M	4	9	Good
Pittosporum undulatum	Victorian box	9–12	12	Opaque	Irregular; dense	M	2	10	Good
Platanus acerifolia	London plane tree	21–24	18	Intermediate	Irregular; open	F	3	5	Good
Podocarpus gracilior	Fern pine	12–18	9	Intermediate	Irregular; dense	S	1	7	Good
Quercus ilex	Holly oak	12–21	18	Opaque	Irregular; dense	M	1	9	Good
Tristania conferta	Brisbane box	9–18	10	Opaque	Symmetrical; dense	M	2	10	Good

[a] A representative selection of trees for urban conditions suitable for street use, varieties or cultivars not listed. However, there are important differences among horticultural varieties and cultivars that must be taken into account in evaluating species.
[b] Estimated mature dimensions attained in 25–30 years allowing for urban constraints on plant growth. To convert to ft, multiply by 3.3.
[c] Applies to mature trees in leaf.
[d] Applies to mature tree-branching form.
[e] Estimated relative rates of growth under urban growth constraints: S = slow; M = medium; F = fast.
[f] Rated from 1, least change during one year, to 5, greatest change during one year.
[g] Refers to plant hardiness zone map (Fig. 2).
[h] Based on observations of trees growing on urban sites with constricted root space and compacted soil.

Table 4. Root Ball Size Standards for Trees and Shrubs

Ball Diameter	mm	Ball Depth	mm	Plant Size	mm	Estimated Weight, lbs[a]	kg
10 in.	255	10 in.	255	19–24 in.	482–610	35	77
12 in.	305	12 in.	305	2–3 ft	610–915	50	110
13 in.	330	12 in.	305	3–4 ft	915–1220	70	154
15 in.	380	13 in.	330	4–5 ft	1220–1525	90	198
16 in.	405	14 in.	355	5–6 ft	1525–1830	125	276
18 in.	455	14 in.	355	6–8 ft	1830–2440	180	396
21 in.	535	15 in.	380	8–10 ft	2440–3050	260	573
22 in.	560	16 in.	405	1–1.5 in. caliper	25–40	300	662
24 in.	610	16 in.	405	2 in. caliper	50	375	827
26 in.	660	17 in.	430	2.25 in. caliper	55	550	1,213
28 in.	710	18 in.	455	2.5 in. caliper	65	775	1,709
32 in.	815	20 in.	510	3 in. caliper	75	1,000	2,205
36 in.	915	24 in.	610	3.5 in. caliper	90	1,400	3,086
40 in.	1015	25 in.	635	4 in. caliper	100	1,900	4,189
4 ft	1220	2 ft 6 in.	760	4–5 in. caliper	100–125	2,880	6,349
5 ft	1525	2 ft 9 in.	840	5–6 in. caliper	125–150	5,950	13,117
6 ft	1830	2 ft 9 in.	840	6–7 in. caliper	150–175	8,950	19,731
7 ft	2135	3 ft	915	7–8 in. caliper	175–205	13,000	28,660
8 ft	2440	3 ft	915	8–9 in. caliper	205–230	16,600	36,596
9 ft	2745	3 ft 3 in.	990	9–10 in. caliper	230–255	22,800	50,264
10 ft	3050	3 ft 6 in.	1070	10–12 in. caliper	255–305	32,000	70,547
12 ft	3655	3 ft 6 in.	1070	12–14 in. caliper	305–355	42,500	93,695

[a] Weights are slightly high and include weight of plant.

maintenance operations is referred to as a protection board.

Drain Lines. Perforated pipes (a variety of materials is available) are used in drainage fields or trenches to provide subsurface drainage. The pipes intercept excess water and convey it to an outfall or storm-drain system.

Tree Area Pavement

The area beneath tree canopies where pedestrian traffic is expected should be paved with pervious, semiporous material. Stabilized crushed stone is appropriate in areas of light traffic, but in areas of intensive use, unit pavers such as brick, stone, or concrete blocks with open joints may be used. This pavement acts as a mulch, allowing the infiltration of air and water needed by tree roots. In general, the smaller unit pavers 4 × 4 in. (100 × 100 mm) or 4 × 8 in. (100 × 200 mm) and 3–4 in. (75–100 mm) thick provide the best permeability, settle with less abrupt changes in the paving surface, and bind together better than larger unit pavers or slabs.

Mulch

Areas around trees where pedestrian traffic is not intended and areas around shrubs are surfaced with a pervious material to retard moisture loss from the soil, insulate the root zone from extreme fluctuations in temperature, and create an acceptable appearance that includes preventing weed growth. The best mulch materials to achieve all three objectives are coarse and medium-size granular inorganic materials such as crushed stone. Organic mulches (shredded bark, wood chips, etc) are less successful because of chemical interaction with soil and disintegration over time. These can deplete the soil of nitrogen, an important plant nutrient. Lawn, flowers, or ground cover plants do not act as a good mulch because they compete with tree roots for soil, air, and water. In general, organic mulch materials should not exceed 3 in. (75 mm) in depth to avoid conditions such as rotting of roots and nesting habitats for insects and rodents.

Interior Plants

Most durable plants for interior spaces are foliage plants without spectacular flowers. The combined constraints of low light, low humidity, and constant temperature limit the available dependable species to those most frequently listed in tropical plant nursery catalogs. The horticultural requirements and methods of handling interior plants differ in many respects from those of trees and shrubs used outdoors. Five basic considerations affecting interior plant growth are light, water, drainage, growing media, and climate.

Light. For interior planting, light poses the most severe limitation on what can be grown. Most trees and shrubs grow in natural illumination that averages several thousand footcandles continuously over a 12-h day. Where interior illumination is less than 1000 footcandles for at least 12 h each day, most trees and shrubs must be accli-

matized to the lower level of light before moving into the interior space.

Water. Controlling the amount of water in the planting soil is critical to interior plant survival. Most interior plants benefit from ample water followed by a period of drying out before watering again.

Drainage. All interior plant containers must be provided with a drainage system to correct overwatering and ensure that roots will receive adequate air.

Growing Media. There are many variations of growing media. Typical growing mixtures for trees in pots contain a coarse organic material such as pine-bark chips mixed with a fine organic material such as peat moss. Typical growing mixtures for large, built-in planters contain sand or coarse lightweight aggregate in addition to organic materials to provide support for the plants as well as hold nutrients. Soils with clay are avoided in most interior plant growing media to prevent clogging the drainage layer. Horticultural references should be consulted for design of growing media to suit the needs of particular plant types.

Climate. Most interior plants are tropical types thriving at temperatures in the range of 15–30°C and preferring a temperature about 5°C cooler at night than during the day. Temperatures at or below 0°C will kill most indoor plants. A relative humidity range between 40 and 80% best suits most indoor plants and below 30% can produce severe stress on many of the tropical plant types used indoors.

CONSTRUCTION

Transplanting

Deciduous trees and shrubs are transplanted during their dormant period. Evergreens are transplanted during any season when water is available and the ground is not frozen. Spring and fall are best seasons for transplanting in most localities. Consult plant references and local guides for plants that have special requirements. Transplanting trees and shrubs involves three distinct operations: root preparation, delivery, and installation.

1. *Root Preparation.* Most trees and shrubs are balled and burlapped to protect the roots in transplanting. Hand-dug root balls are more satisfactory for balled and burlapped trees than machine-dug root balls. Refer to Table 4 for minimum root ball and container sizes. Shrubs are sometimes moved with bare roots when there are large quantities being installed at a single site. The most common and soundest practice is to transplant shrubs with a balled and burlapped or a container-grown root system.
2. *Delivery.* Roots of trees and shrubs are protected from drying during transportation to the site by covering to retard evaporation. Excessive heat or freez-

ing are prevented during delivery by use of climate-controlled vans.

3. *Installation.* Typically, in the street environment of cities, trees grow poorly. Most large cities in the United States witness an average street tree life span of less than 20 years. Different sources vary widely on the correct street tree mortality figure. The two most quoted extremes are 7 years for New York City and 32 years for cities at large. Of arborists and city tree managers polled, the lower figure seems more plausible for large city centers and the higher figures for lower intensity urban streets. This is not long enough for a large tree type to reach its mature size. However, suitable species of shade trees can grow to a mature size in an urban environment if adequate planting standards are followed. In urban locations, the most critical need in transplanting is provision of an adequate zone for root growth. This entails a sufficient volume of prepared soil mixture to allow development of a large tree, providing good subsoil drainage and assuring a pervious surface over the entire root zone area. Tree roots typically grow in a very shallow and wide-spreading configuration (3) (Fig. 3). It is essential to provide a subsurface drainage system at a depth of 30–48 in. (800–1200 mm) wherever rapid percolation of subsoil under trees is not assured (Figs. 4–6). Prepared soil mixture with at least 35% pore space when compacted is essential in the root zone to provide air and water to roots (4). A surface of mulch or pervious paving 170 ft² (16 m²) in area is a minimum requirement for each large tree to allow penetration of air and water to the roots. The shape of the pervious surface area and the corresponding

root zone may vary. Roots will grow in whatever configuration allows them to obtain the best water, air, and nutrients. The ideal shape would be circular because this results in the greatest stability in anchoring the tree. Where the pervious area is not symmetrical around a tree, as in many sidewalk locations where the length is two or three times the width, the minimum width should be 2 m (6 ft). Table 5 summarizes the soil requirements for urban trees and shrubs.

Ground Surface Treatment

Mulch. Mulch is placed 1.5–3 in. (40–80 mm) deep on tree pits and shrub beds immediately after installation. Temporary mulch is used around trees until ground has settled enough to lay unit pavers (Figs. 4 and 7).

Paving Around Trees. Where trees are planted in paved areas, the required area of pervious material over the root zone may consist of open-jointed unit pavers, stabilized crushed stone, or a perforated paving material. The use of standard metal tree grates as commonly practiced is generally unsatisfactory because the pervious surface area is too small for a root zone adequate to support a large tree. Also, because of their size, weight, and monolithic quality, tree grates need support at the edges, thereby limiting the extension of the tree root zone beyond the grate area. The most common acceptable method is the use of open-jointed unit pavers. This requires adequate tamping of backfill in 6-in. (150-mm) layers, allowing 2–4 weeks for settling and then laying open weave reinforcing fabric over compacted planting soil. The pavers are set over the fabric on a sand setting bed 40 mm deep with close unsealed joints (Figs. 5

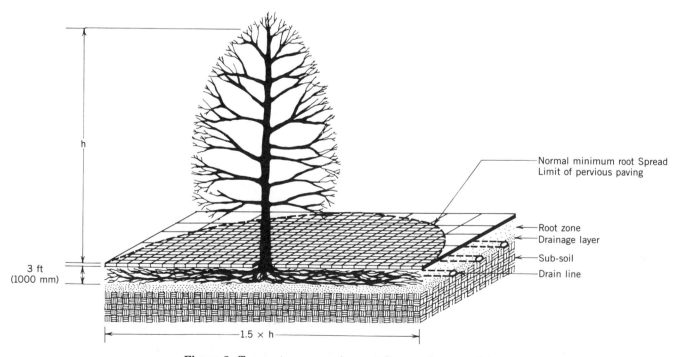

Figure 3. Tree root space requirement diagram (not to scale).

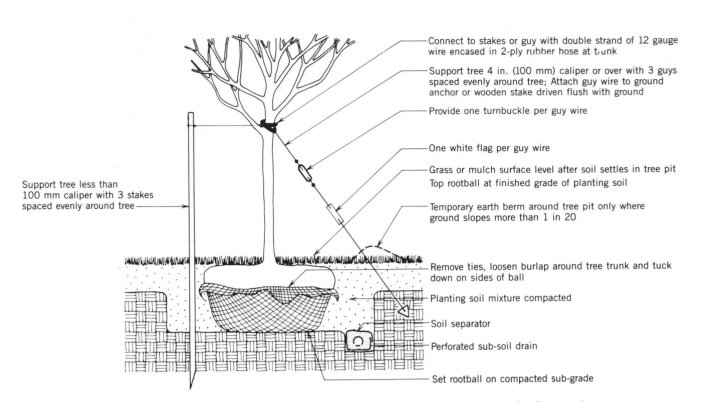

Connect to stakes or guy with double strand of 12 gauge wire encased in 2-ply rubber hose at trunk

Support tree 4 in. (100 mm) caliper or over with 3 guys spaced evenly around tree; Attach guy wire to ground anchor or wooden stake driven flush with ground

Provide one turnbuckle per guy wire

One white flag per guy wire

Grass or mulch surface level after soil settles in tree pit
Top rootball at finished grade of planting soil

Temporary earth berm around tree pit only where ground slopes more than 1 in 20

Remove ties, loosen burlap around tree trunk and tuck down on sides of ball

Planting soil mixture compacted

Soil separator

Perforated sub-soil drain

Set rootball on compacted sub-grade

Support tree less than 100 mm caliper with 3 stakes spaced evenly around tree

Figure 4. Typical section tree planting at grade in lawn or planting bed (not to scale). Prune only after planting by thinning to remove enough whole branches (not just ends) to reduce foliage by ⅓; retain normal crown size and shape.

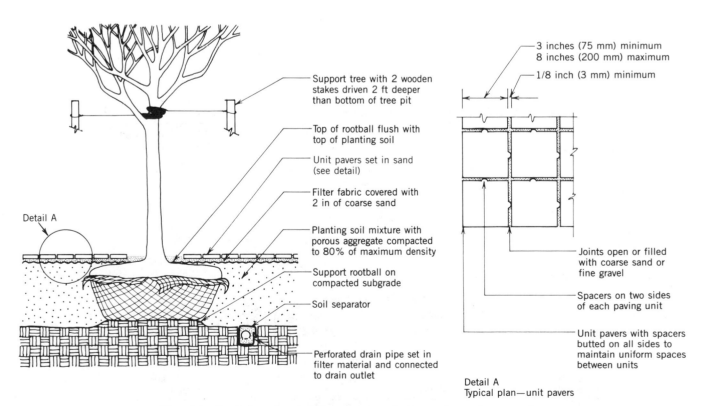

Support tree with 2 wooden stakes driven 2 ft deeper than bottom of tree pit

Top of rootball flush with top of planting soil

Unit pavers set in sand (see detail)

Filter fabric covered with 2 in of coarse sand

Planting soil mixture with porous aggregate compacted to 80% of maximum density

Support rootball on compacted subgrade

Soil separator

Perforated drain pipe set in filter material and connected to drain outlet

Detail A

3 inches (75 mm) minimum
8 inches (200 mm) maximum

1/8 inch (3 mm) minimum

Joints open or filled with coarse sand or fine gravel

Spacers on two sides of each paving unit

Unit pavers with spacers butted on all sides to maintain uniform spaces between units

Detail A
Typical plan—unit pavers

Figure 5. Typical section tree planting at grade in paved area (not to scale).

431

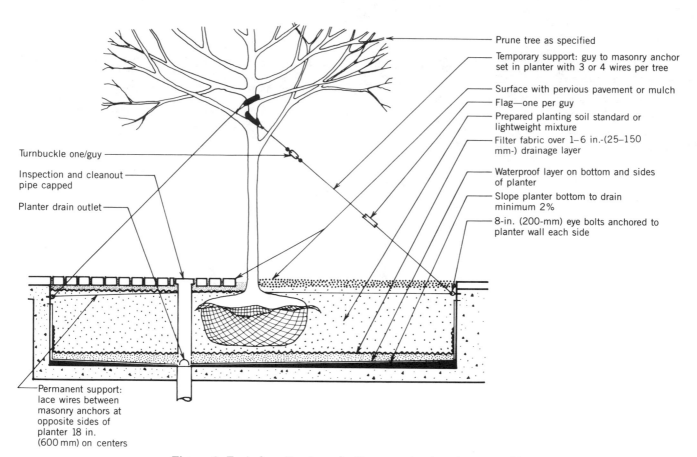

Turnbuckle one/guy

Inspection and cleanout pipe capped

Planter drain outlet

Permanent support: lace wires between masonry anchors at opposite sides of planter 18 in. (600 mm) on centers

Prune tree as specified

Temporary support: guy to masonry anchor set in planter with 3 or 4 wires per tree

Surface with pervious pavement or mulch

Flag—one per guy

Prepared planting soil standard or lightweight mixture

Filter fabric over 1–6 in.-(25–150 mm-) drainage layer

Waterproof layer on bottom and sides of planter

Slope planter bottom to drain minimum 2%

8-in. (200-mm) eye bolts anchored to planter wall each side

Figure 6. Typical section tree planting over structure (not to scale).

Tree Planter Size Guidelines

	Minimum dimension, mm					
	Depth		Width		Length	
	ft.	mm	ft.	mm	ft.	mm
Large tree	3	900	10	4000	10	4000
Small tree	2.5	750	8	2400	8	2400

See Table 5 for planting soil volume requirements.

Table 5. Minimum Area and Volume Requirements for Plant Root Zone

	Minimum Depth, ft(m)	Minimum Pervious Surface Area, ft² (m²)	Minimum Prepared Soil Volume, ft³ (m³)
Large Tree			
At grade	2–2.5 (0.6–0.8)	170 (16)	450 (13.0)
Over structure	3–4 (0.9–1.2)	170 (16)	680 (19.0)
Small Tree			
At grade	1.5 (0.5)	100 (9)	150 (4.5)
Over structure	2.5 (0.8)	100 (9)	250 (7.2)
Large Shrub			
At grade	1.2 (0.4)	Not critical	70 (2.0)
Over structure	1.5 (0.5)	Not critical	90 (2.5)
Small Shrub			
At grade	1.0 (0.3)	Not critical	16 (0.5)
Over structure	1.2 (0.4)	Not critical	28 (0.8)

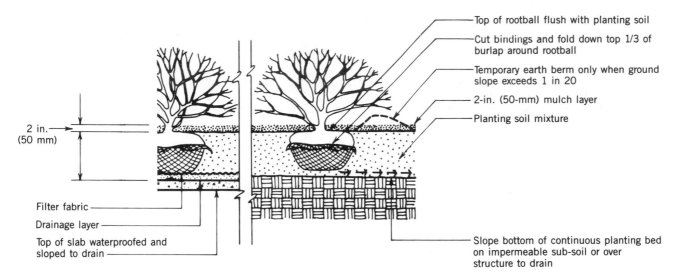

Figure 7. Typical section shrub planting (not to scale).

and 6). The use of a planting soil mixture with 50% porous aggregate allows compaction of mixture without limiting air and water movement through the root zone and reduces settling of pavers.

Protecting Trees

Guying and Staking. Trees up to 4-in. (100-mm) caliper are supported by temporary staking. Trees larger than 4 in. (100 mm) are temporarily guyed, leaving supports in place for one or two growing seasons (Figs. 4–6). Permanent buried cable supports in planters are recommended over structures where weight of soil mass may not hold tree upright in strong wind (Fig. 6).

Wrapping Trees. Tree wraps are applied only when specially required for the tree species being installed. Tree wrapping is of doubtful benefit for most species. Painting trunks up to the height of the first branches with white latex paint is an acceptable alternative where trunk protection is considered beneficial.

Shrubs. These have cultural requirements similar to trees for transplanting, but the much smaller root systems are more easily handled. The shallower root zone, though requiring drainage, usually does not need an elaborate piped drainage system except when in planters over structure. Shrubs are commonly installed in mass plantings in beds rather than individual plant pits. When used for hedges, shrubs are installed in shallow trenches. Table 5 shows the minimum depth of prepared soil mixture for plantings (Fig. 7).

Interior Plant Installation

Successful installation of interior plants depends as much on the design of the building space as on the actual plant installation methods. To successfully accommodate interior trees, a building space must address the following concerns.

Lighting. Daylight is highly desirable as a primary light source for interior plants. It must be designed and calculated in relation to the building design taking into account latitude, building orientation, season, and weather. Both a high level of ambient light and shading from extensive periods of direct sunlight are critical considerations in the design of a building for natural plant illumination. Where high levels of natural light for long periods of each day are not available, the use of supplemental artificial light directed down onto the leaves may be necessary. The quality, intensity, duration, and direction of artificial light determine its effectiveness. Standard cool white fluorescent lamps, HID deluxe white mercury, and phosphor-coated, metal halide lamps are effective sources with good color rendition. A light level of 250 fc for 12 h/day is generally the minimum amount of illumination that will sustain healthy low light level tree types, such as *Ficus*, once they are acclimated to this environment. Light directed at the upper surface of leaves is three or four times as effective in promoting photosynthesis as light from below.

There are several species of low growing plants or vines such as *Scindapsus* that will tolerate light levels between 50 and 100 footcandles over a 10-h day. Such low light levels cannot be relied on unless other growing requirements such as water, drainage, and humidity are near optimum levels.

Planters. Planter accommodation in the building design permits recessed planters with trees growing from the floor level, allowing people to circulate under the branches. The common alternative of raised pots inhibits circulation and visually interrupts the space. The size and presence of large freestanding tree containers constitute a visual problem in the design of interior spaces (5,6).

Plant installation requirements vary depending on the building configuration, type and size of planter, species of plant, and planned methods of maintenance. Interior plantings are of two types: those installed in permanent planters and trees in movable planters, usually large, freestanding pots. In most cases, the latter type function as stationary planters because of their weight; however, they have different technical requirements from built-in planters for plant installation. References on interior planting, landscape architects, and plant growers should be consulted in planning the layout, installation, and support systems for interior plants.

Water and Drainage. Watering by automatic irrigation systems cannot be relied on for interior plantings. Building design should recognize the need for convenient hose bibs, moisture resistant floor surfaces, and other appurtenances that aid manual plant watering. Most interior plants grow best when the soil or growing medium is allowed to dry out between waterings. This allows the roots to obtain air that would not be available in saturated soil.

Drainage of planters is a key element in planning for interior planting. Planters must have provision for removal of gravitational water to allow sufficient drying to promote plant growth. Failure to provide for this plant growth requirement at the building design stage can result in plant maintenance that is too expensive to support the planting design intent.

Atmospheric Conditions. Temperature for the types of tropical plants that are best adapted to interior use should be maintained at between 70 and 75°F (21 and 24°C) during the day. At night a 10°F (6°C) drop in temperature is desirable. Extremes of temperature are deleterious. For example, temperatures below 40°F (4.5°C) or above 85°F (29°C) can be harmful to many indoor plants.

Relative humidity for tropical interior foliage plants in natural habitats is over 60%. Because most cool climate winter interiors are maintained at between 35 and 50% relative humidity, there is some stress on the plants' systems. This is critical only when the relative humidity drops below 35%, a condition that is not common where adequate human contact levels are maintained. Providing relative humidity at the higher end of the normal range, either through the air-conditioning system operation or frequent misting of plants, is beneficial and will help to compensate for other stressful environmental conditions inherent in the typical interior plant space.

Ventilation. Slow air movement is necessary to assure the replenishment of CO_2 and prevent heat buildup around the foliage that can occur because of the "greenhouse effect." Another purpose of ventilation is to remove air pollutants such as volatile cleaning chemicals, varnish or paint fumes, chlorine gas (from swimming pools), and cigarette smoke. Interior plants can be severely damaged by direct placement in the airstream from air-conditioning supply ducts. This is an often overlooked planning consideration when buildings are designed to include interior plantings.

BIBLIOGRAPHY

1. H. F. Arnold, *Trees in Urban Design*, Van Nostrand Reinhold Co., Inc., New York, 1980.
2. USDA Agricultural Research Service, *Miscellaneous Publication No. 814*, United States Department of Agriculture, Washington, D.C., 1960.
3. T. O. Perry, "The Ecology of Tree Roots and the Practical Significance Thereof," *Journal of Arboriculture* 8(8), 197–221 (1982).
4. J. C. Patterson, "Soil Compaction and its Effects upon Urban Vegetation," *USDA Forest Service General Technical Report NE–22* Northeast Forest Experiment Station, Upper Darby, Pa., 1976.
5. R. Saxon, *Atrium Buildings, Development and Design*, Van Nostrand Reinhold Co., Inc., New York, 1983.
6. R. L. Gaines, *Interior Plantscaping: Building Design for Interior Foliage Plants*, Architectural Record Books, New York, 1977.

General References

USA Standard for Nursery Stock, American Association of Nurserymen, Washington, D.C., 1969.

Associated Landscape Contractors of America, Interior Landscape Division, *A Guide To Interior Landscaping*, 3rd ed., ALCA McLean, Va., 1982.

Grades and Standards, Part I and Part II, Florida Association of Nurserymen, Department of Agriculture, Gainsville, Fla., 1963.

B. Cloustan, ed., *Landscape Design with Plants*, Van Nostrand Reinhold Co., Inc., New York, 1984.

B. Colvin, *Land and Landscape*, John Murray, London, 1970.

H. L. Flint, *Landscape Plants for Eastern North America*, John Wiley & Sons, Inc., New York, 1983.

M. Gothein, *A History of Garden Art*, 2nd ed., J. M. Dent, N.Y. 1928.

A. B. Graf, *Exotia II*, 2nd ed., Roehrs Co., East Rutherford, N. J., 1959.

R. G. Halfacre and A. R. Shawcroft, *Landscape Plants of the Southeast*, Sparks Press, Raleigh, N.C., 1979.

R. S. Hoyt, *Check List for Ornamental Plants of Subtropical Regions*, Livingston Press, Los Angeles, Calif., 1958.

G. Jellico and S. Jellico, *The Landscape of Man*, The Viking Press, Inc., New York, 1975.

P. O. Pirone, *Tree Maintenance*, 4th ed., Oxford University Press, Inc., New York, 1976.

A. Rehder, *Manual of Cultivated Trees and Shrubs*, 2nd ed., rev., Macmillan Co., New York, 1940.

The editors of *Sunset Magazine*, *Sunset Western Garden Book*, 3rd ed., Lane Magazine & Book Co., Menlo Park, Calif., 1971.

B. F. Wilson, *The Growing Tree*, University of Massachusetts Press, Amherst, Mass., 1970.

D. Wyman, *Shrubs and Vines for American Gardens*, Macmillan Co., Collier–Macmillan Canada Ltd., Toronto, 1969.

D. Wyman, *Trees for American Gardens*, Macmillan Co., New York, 1970.

See also ENVIRONMENT—PLANNING WITH THE NATURAL ENVIRONMENT; LANDSCAPE ARCHITECTURE

HENRY ARNOLD
Arnold Associates
Princeton, New Jersey

SIGNING—ENVIRONMENTAL GRAPHICS

Lettering on buildings, conceived as an integral aspect of their architecture, flourished first and chiefly in Roman times, then in the Renaissance and beaux-arts periods.

Until comparatively recently, Roman lettering carved over entrance portals or into cornerstones was the chief graphic element of most buildings, if frescoes and pure decoration are discounted from this category.

Today, signing, more broadly described as environmental graphics, plays an important part in the majority of building programs. Whether or not the name of the building is prominently displayed over its main entrance in permanent carved or incised lettering, the complexity of modern life usually demands a correspondingly complex array of directional, regulatory, and identifying signs within and without. The graphic and architectural resolution of such signing systems has come to be generally recognized as a specialized design discipline, whether carried out by independent consultants or by dedicated individuals or departments within architectural or interior design firms. The Society of Environmental Graphic Designers, gaining increasing support and exposure in the United States, reinforces this specialized professional status.

Ideally, the development of the signing system should form part of the architectural and planning process, with the graphic designer a key member of the design team from the inception of the project. In practice, graphic design is too often treated as an afterthought or cuttable budget extra, with the graphic designer brought in late in the project to impose visual order on a confusing plan, to clarify a change of use or program alteration, or to add a human dimension to an impersonal environment.

Although it is freed from some of the functional criteria governing architectural design (and indeed such characteristics as wit, whimsicality, or exaggeration may be deliberately built into the program), in terms of style graphic design usually follows broad architectural trends. In the heyday of the modern movement, with Bauhaus traditions dominant and taboos against ornament, Swiss-influenced graphic design all but mandated a lean and clean appearance; adherence to a strict, organizing grid; the use of Helvetica or related sans serif typeface; discreet white on white signs complementing pure white geometric architectural forms; or clear, strong primary colors used in geometric configurations. Later, the use of strong primary-color coding systems to identify floors, departments, or sections within a building complex was often exaggerated to "supergraphic" scale, with whole walls painted in vivid affirmation of the essential organizing theme.

With the retrospective and derivative preoccupations of postmodernism, environmental graphics have embraced with gusto the many freedoms allowed (Fig. 1): the breaking down of accepted rules of typography to create the "new wave" or the funky; the return of the serif; the extravagant use of neon; the encompassing of entire building facades within trompe l'oeil murals; and the move away from primary colors to dayglow or pastel shades.

With all of this, modernist principles have not been completely abandoned. Helvetica has continued to be a popular typeface, and some of the most respected and influential graphic design firms still adopt a minimalist approach to much of their work. In every environmental graphics award program, at least one understated corpo-

Figure 1. Hanging signs in the "Pic-Nic" section of Baltimore's White Marsh Mall Shopping Center demonstrate how Old World themes can be used with modern panache in a pluralist design atmosphere. Courtesy of RTKL Associates, Inc. and Dave Whitecomb.

rate signing program is sure to make its appearance among the winning schemes (1).

Environmental graphics programs obviously vary considerably in scale and complexity, but it may be helpful here to enumerate some of the key elements of a typical assignment. Site signing will include traffic regulatory and directional signs, as well as signs identifying main and subsidiary or departmental entrances and parking areas (Figs. 2–5). Sizes, content, placement, and lighting of some of these signs are controlled by code. It may be necessary to distinguish different destinations or kinds of traffic at the outset by means of color coding or related device (Figs. 6–8). Airports use colors and identifying letters to differentiate terminals; zoos may devise animal-based logotypes for the different species and trails; and the architects of one award-winning corporate complex in

Figure 2. Jan Lorenc's signing program for the Wildwood Office Park near Atlanta, Georgia, responds to a beautiful site and includes a sculptural, monolithic entrance sign. Courtesy of Jan Lorenc Design Inc.

Figure 4. Wildwood garage entrance bar and typography are as low key as possible. Courtesy of Jan Lorenc Design Inc.

California color-coded whole exterior walls of the building and then continued the same colors inside as an aid to orientation.

Many corporate complexes are set in attractive rural or parklike surroundings, where the graphic designer is faced with the challenge of providing signing that harmonizes with the natural setting, without compromising visibility or legibility. Lighting standards and fixtures, seats, trash cans, and so on are often the responsibility of the environmental graphics team, as are kiosks of various kinds. Parking lots, and especially multilevel parking structures, also call for special graphic treatment to help people remember where they left their cars and to lend some flavor of humanity to a characteristically bleak and faceless building type. This often results in superscale let-

ters or numbers rendered in different colors for the different floors.

Inside the building the information desk and reception area usually need special treatment, possibly involving lighted signs, to identify them immediately and distinguish them from general office areas. Usually, a building directory, today often electronic, will fall within the scope of the environmental graphics program. Public amenities and spaces such as elevators and restrooms may require pictographs as well as signs, whereas egress and safety signing is regulated by code. In many cases, the graphic designer is faced with a difficult task in integrating the signing with the building's architecture, specifying the appropriate hardware, and deciding whether and how to attach signs to the architectural surfaces. In some cases, an incremental vocabulary must be established and a manual drawn up to allow the building owners or tenants to add to or alter the signs as business expands or functions, departments, and personnel change.

In addition to rendering a building intelligible to its users, the graphic designer may be called on to create graphic murals or other kinds of decorative effect to enliven such rooms as cafeterias, health clubs, lounges, or

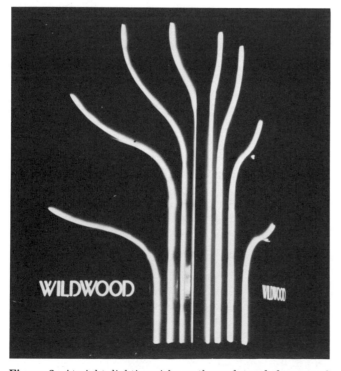

Figure 3. At night, lighting picks up the sculptural elements of the main Wildwood sign. Courtesy of Jan Lorenc Design Inc.

Figure 5. Traffic regulatory signs at Wildwood are easy to read but not too obtrusive in the landscape. Courtesy of Jan Lorenc Design Inc.

Figure 6. Color coding in word and deed identifies parking in the Ft. Lauderdale Galleria, Florida. Courtesy of The Bugdal Group.

Figure 8. Ft. Lauderdale Galleria curbside directional signs are color coded to relate to major stores and contain removable message strips that can be changed without use of exposed screws or fastenings. Courtesy of the Bugdal Group.

meeting rooms, which may be used by the general public as well as by employees and which require a recognizable change of pace. In some buildings, the lobby areas will contain coffee shops, restaurants, stationers, and other concessions, whose signs must be coordinated within the general graphic framework (Figs. 9 and 10).

To achieve some visual order in a complex program of

this kind, it is important for the graphic designer to maintain a responsive dialogue with both architect and client and to establish as early as possible a hierarchy of type styles and sizes and a rational vocabulary of materials and colors that inform the user while complementing the architecture.

The complexities of the graphic designer's mission can hardly be overemphasized, particularly when the graphic design team is confronted by an environment where many of the graphic elements are outside its control. The building may be a vehicle for advertising or other kinds of visual propaganda, or it may contain safety or traffic-control signs, whose colors, type sizes, placement, and lighting are mandated by government regulation. The designer may have to work within an already established

Figure 7. Lampost-mounted plaza parking signs at the Ft. Lauderdale Galleria consolidate a considerable amount of information in neatly designed panel construction with concealed mounting hardware. Courtesy of the Bugdal Group.

Figure 9. Restaurant sign in elegantly coordinated graphic system for the 650-room Le Centre Sheraton Hotel, Montreal. Courtesy of GSM Design.

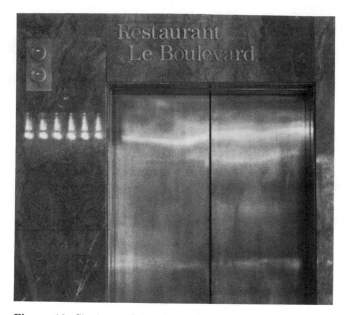

Figure 10. Signing and interior architecture complement each other at Le Centre Sheraton. Courtesy of GSM Design.

corporate logo and type style. Then the graphic designer must anticipate maintenance problems that may obscure the message, or the potential misuse of "do-it-yourself" components. (There are dangers as well as advantages in a flexible signing system.) The graphic designer must also consider the perspectives of different types of user and of vehicular and pedestrian traffic. It may well be necessary to define in a distinct yet visually integrated manner a number of clear paths through a complex for incompatible types of traffic.

For many users, the graphic component of a building may be the most important. Being able to find one's way in an unfamiliar setting without having to ask for help greatly enhances confidence and thus enjoyment of a building. This is especially true if language or cultural differences or physical handicap place the individual user at a disadvantage or in a vulnerable situation. Where very broad cultural differences exist among the users of a building or environment, in airports or aircraft, for example, even the established conventional pictographs may be confusing and may have to be restudied (2).

Environmental graphics in the latter half of the twentieth century has steadily increased in importance, has expanded its visibility, has penetrated every building type, and with the use of pictographs and international symbols, is approaching a universal language. Indeed, the complexities of modern society now often cast the graphic designer in a frankly problem-solving role in various environmental and social contexts. In the mid-1970s, the city of Seattle used a graphic redesign of its manhole covers to improve surface safety, to act as an orientation guide to downtown, and to demonstrate the value of design input into every aspect of the cityscape. At about the same time, the New York City Municipal Arts Society collaborated with private industry in the sponsorship of a program testing what graphic design could do to improve the ambience and even the safety of selected subway stations. Hos-

pitals have been one of the prime users of environmental graphics, not only as an aid to orientation, but also to bring warmth, color, life, and human scale to an inevitably stressful, sometimes threatening, environment.

The lines between environmental graphics, fine art, industrial design, interior design, and even planning and architecture are sometimes hard to draw. For a graphics program can involve the creation of a mural, the specification of upholstery colors to reinforce a color-coded orientation system, the design of street furniture or transportation maps, the drawing up of design guidelines to control the development of individual storefronts and concessions within a shopping mall, or even the creation of entire temporary environments such as the one created for the 1984 Los Angeles Olympic Games (3).

The organizational element, at the hub of the environmental graphics program, is a key determinant of its success or failure. For if, despite exuberant banners, playful murals, or human-scale typography, one still ends up in the airport gift shop instead of the departure lounge, the signing system can be said to have failed, causing intense user anxiety along the way.

BIBLIOGRAPHY

1. "The Best in Environmental Graphics," *Print Casebooks,* RC Publications, Bethesda, Md., 1975–1988 (and continuing biannually).
2. S. Braybrooke, "Flight Signs," *Print Magazine,* 76–81 (March/April 1988).
3. Ref. 1, *Print Casebook 7,* 1987–1988, pp. 64–73.

SUSAN BRAYBROOKE
London, United Kingdom

SILICONES.   See SUPPLEMENT.

SINGLE-FAMILY RESIDENCES

Single-family detached housing has its origins in remote antiquity, where each family often found its own cave in which to live, coming together with others primarily for the purposes of mutual protection and other cooperative needs. Then, as now, adults spend at least half their day in the home—sleeping, eating, relaxing, etc; children are usually there a much greater percentage of the time. In prehistoric times, there were few other available living alternatives, but present-day single-family detached homes are found desirable by those who believe this provides an optimum environment in which to raise children.

In recent years, more than 60% of all year-round housing units (and of new housing starts) are attributed to structures with one residential unit. Other single-family housing can be classified as attached rather than detached. Units can be joined in groups of two (zero lot line), three (triplexes), four (quadriplexes), and more (town houses). These have in common the aspect of direct ground-level access without substantial change in elevation from interior floor to exterior surface, irrespective of type of tenancy: rental, condominium, cooperative, fee-simple ownership (about 65% of all households), etc.

These units can be tenanted by a variety of using groups beyond the typical married couple with children. These include singles, mingles (unrelated adults sharing a house), marrieds without children, and extended families.

Certainly, adults profit by living in this type of housing with its associated status, privacy, and spatial flexibility for gardening, recreation, garaging of automobiles, etc. (The median-size new house in the late 1970s was about 1700 ft².) But they are also encumbered with the need for lawn mowing, leaf raking, swimming-pool maintenance, snow shoveling, and other routine chores and larger expenses for energy and repairs as compared with multifamily housing types. Most people in the U.S. believe the advantages outweigh the costs and opt for the best and largest single-family detached home they can afford.

THE PRESIDENT'S CONFERENCE

The popularity of single-family housing was evident from the time of the earliest settlements in the New World, accelerated during the westward expansion of the nineteenth century, inspired an early manufactured-housing industry in the early years of the twentieth century, and was institutionalized by the governmental developments of the early 1930s, which were stimulated by the 3700-member President's Conference on Homebuilding and Homeownership in 1931. Convened by President Herbert Hoover in the waning days of his administration, this meeting of builders, bankers, brokers, and buyers helped shape the legislation later passed under President Franklin Roosevelt, which began the significant federal support of the housing industry in succeeding decades.

The principal Conference findings can be summarized:

- Development in communities of building programs meeting local needs, with *single-family houses as the most desirable*.
- Improved planning and zoning.
- Better homes at lower costs through improved technological processes.
- Broadening of home ownership.
- Adequate system of home credit for better protection of home owners and lending institutions.
- Rehabilitation of old homes.
- Facilitation of large-scale housing operations.
- Relief of homes from excessive taxation.
- Modernization and standardization of local building regulations.

These findings have proved to be prototypical, as many later inquiries have found similar objectives. However, owing to the resulting legislation, their magnitude is much less in most cases, and (with less than 3% of all units lacking complete plumbing facilities and less than

5% having more than 1.01 persons per room) the United States currently has the best overall housing stock in the world.

HOUSING FINANCE INSTITUTIONS

The Conference recommended the proposal of President Hoover for a system of home-loan discount banks, resulting in establishment of the now prevalent savings and loan associations under a 1932 act. The Federal National Mortgage Association (FNMA) was chartered in 1938 to establish a secondary market for home mortgages. In 1968, FNMA became a private corporation and the Government National Mortgage Association (GNMA) was created to operate special financial-assistance functions for subsidized programs.

FEDERAL HOUSING ADMINISTRATION

The Federal Housing Administration (FHA), also recommended by the Conference, was founded in 1934 as a mortgage insurance agency. Under this important legislation, homebuyers were able to purchase sound single-family homes with low down payments, paying a fee for insurance to protect the local lending institution from any foreclosure losses. This occasioned the development of operating regulations, including an *Underwriting Manual* and *Minimum Property Standards* (MPS). The latter defined sound insurable Section 203 single-family housing in terms of planning and architectural and engineering criteria that promoted, among other things, high resale values.

In subsequent years, the FHA legislation was expanded to include other building types—multifamily rental housing, senior citizens' housing, nursing homes, hospitals—and below-market interest-rate financing concepts, including the major programs known by their legislative Sections of the National Housing Act: 221(d)(3), 235, and 236. Also, most single-family MPS requirements have been superseded by the succeeding enactment of more sophisticated local development regulations.

Farm-housing programs were initiated under the Bankhead–Jones Farm Tenant Act of 1937. As they expanded, the Farmers Home Administration (FmHA) was created in the Department of Agriculture in 1946.

In 1942, President Franklin Roosevelt placed FHA and FNMA, and the Public Housing Administration (PHA) created in 1937 to supply low-rent housing, under one administrative head in the National Housing Agency, renamed the Housing and Home Finance Agency (HHFA) in 1947. In the Housing Act of 1949, Congress declared a national goal of a "decent home, in a suitable living environment, for every American family." FHA and PHA were principal ingredients of the Department of Housing and Urban Development (HUD), established under President Lyndon Johnson in 1965. The new housing goal was first quantified under the HUD Act of 1968: 26-million new units in 10 years, 23% of which were to be for low- and moderate-income families.

HOUSING PRODUCTION

The housing production industry is composed of millions of business enterprises, small and specialized, that fiercely compete through a four-phase process:

1. *Preparation.* Developable land is identified and planned.
2. *Production.* Financing is arranged, the site is improved and the house is designed and constructed.
3. *Distribution.* The house is marketed, a repetitive task throughout the life of the building, given significant population mobility.
4. *Servicing.* The house is maintained and repaired, an activity continuing throughout its life.

The housing industry can be characterized as localized, fragmented, small-scale, and dependent on outsiders. It is localized because it is largely tied to land and locally regulated. Only a few home builders, home manufacturers, or housing consultants (including architects and engineers) look for national markets for their work. Zoning in some communities requires that no two single-family houses appear identical. The resulting variety of product has led to fragmentation of the industry into an elaborate complex of interlocking production elements, few of which can afford significant research and development efforts or marketing strategies.

Most firms are small, owing to the above, as well as seasonality in construction and cyclic variations in the supply of mortgage credit. Housing developers, builders, and contractors are often dependent on larger enterprises whose primary business is not housing. Financial institutions are the most important aggregation of private-sector power in the industry.

EMERGING INDUSTRIALIZATION

Factory-built housing has its origins in the early provision of precut components for houses, which were then to be site-assembled. Several major companies offered these mail-order homes, of which the most prominent was Sears, Roebuck & Co. They provided a variety of sizes and styles to their customers and promised substantial time and cost savings under the relatively permissive levels of local building codes prevalent early in this century.

In 1921, a Division of Building and Housing was created in the National Bureau of Standards (NBS), which is now known as the Center for Building Technology in the National Institute of Standards and Technology (NIST). This organization began to develop and test national criteria and building-code recommendations for building materials to add performance-oriented background to the several emerging national organizations of building officials that produce "model" code documents for local government adoption.

Following this and the popularity of the automobile, some manufacturers began to develop the concept of a house trailer that could be moved from site to site behind a car. Popularity of the mobile home concept was, and is,

significant in times of financial hardship, as it avoids many local building regulations and offers lower initial costs and a promise of mobility to new employment centers, although some aspects of planning, design, and construction quality may be compromised.

After World War II, HHFA performed significant work in institutionalizing dimensional coordination of building materials, as a means of facilitating increased construction to serve the needs of returning veterans.

However, housing has lagged behind other sectors of the economy in incorporating new technology, as serving a mass market is required if the cost savings and quality increases associated with industrialization are to be realized. This is difficult because of the fragmentation of the industry. Thus housing producers cater to the most traditional views of consumers or attitudes shaped by the makers of other products in order to sell their homes.

Also, in contrast to regulation for most consumer products, housing regulation—covenants, trade-union rules, building codes, subdivision regulations, development review ordinances, community plans, transportation rules, health laws, etc—is substantially a matter of state and local control. Not only is it nearly impossible to market a competitive regional or national model home approved by all authorities, but gaining nationwide acceptance of even a significant new material, component, or method requires a substantial investment in money and time.

OPERATION BREAKTHROUGH

The major federal research effort to address these issues and stimulate technological development of the housing industry was called Operation Breakthrough. Begun in 1969 by then HUD Secretary George Romney, a former automotive industry executive, it involved more than 600 proposals from industry for assistance with their design and development work. Many of these were from organizations not previously involved in housing. A selection was made and construction began of prototype models on prototype sites across the country. Criteria for testing the prototype models were carefully developed by NIST (then NBS) on a performance-oriented basis, so that the tested products would find optimum levels of code and market acceptance.

Market aggregation in Operation Breakthrough depended substantially on the availability of unit allocations under HUD's subsidized housing programs. When these programs were suspended or reduced in the early 1970s based on matters unrelated to industrialization, the research effort was fatally weakened. All in all, mitigation of some of the constraints previously identified was greatly accelerated.

MANUFACTURED HOUSING

Growing from an annual production rate of 1300 units in 1930, top fabrication of manufactured housing reached more than 575,000 units in 1972: nearly one fourth of all dwelling units produced in the peak year of U.S. housing production. The Manufactured Housing Institute now defines such a unit as:

> . . .a structure, transportable in one or more sections, which, in the traveling mode, is 8 body feet or more in width or 40 body feet or more in length, or, when erected on site, is 320 or more square feet in floor area.

Built on a permanent chassis and designed to be used as a dwelling with or without a permanent foundation when connected to the required utilities, most units produced since 1976 have conformed to the then-initiated HUD standards for FHA insurability purposes.

About half these homes are placed on individually owned sites, generally in rural or small-town locations, with the others in mobile or manufactured home communities of 150–175 units. A principal physical problem is aesthetics. A much smaller percentage of new manufactured units can stand on their own as objects of beauty compared with site-built homes. Landscaping may have to be relied on to develop a satisfactory community appearance: in many such communities landscaping has been completed in a degree and quality not found in subdivisions of site-built housing.

SITE-PLANNING ISSUES

Organization of the single-family residential community, project, or site cannot be called planned if it merely imposes or conforms to some abstract geometry without social rationale. Planning should include a concern for civil rights and needs implications, adequacy of recreational and food facilities for the targeted market, accessibility (a particularly important issue for the rapidly growing elderly population, as transit equipment may not be fully accessible or conveniently available), crime mitigation through territoriality concepts, etc.

In Section 4 of the Housing and Urban Development Act of 1968, the U.S. Congress wisely declared:

> . . .that in the administration of housing programs which assist in the provision of housing for low and moderate income families, emphasis should be given to encouraging good design as an essential component of such housing and to developing housing which will be of such quality as to reflect its important relationship to the neighborhood and community in which it is situated, consistent with prudent budgeting.

FUTURE DEVELOPMENTS

Future U.S. housing will have to consider the wants, needs, and desires of an increasingly older population. It should also deal with expanded leisure time due substantially to early retirement potentials as well as the recovery of commuting time through the increasing presence of the home office linked electronically to employment/business center(s). The smart house, one that is fully equipped with electronic and other technological aids to family well-being, using solar energy and satellite communications, etc, will increasingly appear and may optimally develop exciting new prototypical single-family housing forms for a mature, decentralizing society.

BIBLIOGRAPHY

General References

R. Bauchum, *Cluster Housing . . . An Annotated Bibliography,* Vance Bibliographies, Monticello, Ill., 1982.

D. J. Berg, *Country Patterns,* rev. 2nd ed., The Main Street Press, Pittstown, N.J., 1986.

S. L. Best, *Housing Rehabilitation,* Vance Bibliographies, Monticello, Ill., 1985.

Bureau of the Census, U.S. Department of Commerce, *County and City Data Book, 1983,* U.S. Government Printing Office, Washington, D.C., 1983.

Center for Residential Security Design, *Improving Residential Security,* U.S. Government Printing Office, Washington, D.C., 1973.

C. E. Clark, *The American Family Home, 1800–1960,* The University of North Carolina Press, Chapel Hill, N.C., 1980.

Community Builders Handbook Series—Residential Development Handbook, Urban Land Institute, Washington, D.C., 1980.

J. DeChiara, ed., *Time-Saver Standards for Residential Development,* McGraw-Hill Inc., New York, 1984.

D. Dickinson, *The Small House,* McGraw-Hill Inc., New York, 1986.

L. Doumato, *The American Home: A Historical Background of General Works,* Vance Bibliographies, Monticello, Ill., 1985.

A. Gowans, *The Comfortable House,* The MIT Press, Cambridge, Mass., 1986.

L. Grow, *More Classic Old House Plans,* The Main Street Press, Pittstown, N.J., 1986.

R. Gutman, *The Design of American Housing,* Publishing Center for Cultural Resources, New York, 1985.

R. Gutman, ed., *People and Buildings,* Basic Books, Inc., New York, 1972.

D. Hayden, *Redesigning the American Dream,* W. W. Norton & Company, New York, 1984.

Housing and Urban Development Act of 1968, Public Law 448, 90th Congress, August 1, 1968.

R. Korman, "Marching Toward the Promised Land," *Engineering News Record,* (November 10, 1988).

J. B. Lansing, R. W. Marans, and R. B. Fechner, *Planned Residential Development,* Braun-Brumfeld, Inc., Ann Arbor, Mich., 1970.

C. Leider, "Planning for Housing" in F. So and J. Getzels, *The Practice of Local Government Planning,* 2nd ed., International City Management Association, Washington, D.C., 1988, p. 363.

M. Lipske, *Artists' Housing,* Publishing Center for Cultural Resources, New York, 1987.

V. McAlester and L. McAlester, *A Field Guide to American Houses,* Alfred A. Knopf, Inc., New York, 1984.

C. Moore, G. Allen, and D. Lyndon, *The Place of Houses,* Holt, Rinehart & Winston, New York, 1979.

National Housing Act, Public Law 479, 73rd Congress, June 27, 1934.

R. M. Nixon, *Statement by the President on Federal Policies Relative to Equal Housing Opportunity,* June 11, 1971.

Office of General Counsel, Housing and Home Finance Agency,

Chronology of Major Federal Actions Affecting Housing and Community Development, U.S. Government Printing Office, Washington, D.C., 1963.

P. Oliver, *Dwellings,* University of Texas Press, Austin, Tex., 1987.

Planning Environment International, *Interim Guide for Environmental Assessment,* U.S. Government Printing Office, Washington, D.C., 1975.

B. B. Raschko, *Housing Interiors for the Disabled and Elderly,* Van Nostrand Reinhold Co., Inc., New York, 1982.

Real Estate Research Corporation, *The Costs of Sprawl,* U.S. Government Printing Office, Washington, D.C., 1974.

W. Rybczynski, *Home,* Viking Penguin Inc., New York, 1986.

W. Sanders, *Regulating Manufactured Housing,* Planning Advisory Service Report Number 398, American Planning Association, Chicago, Ill., 1986.

W. Sanders, *The Cluster Subdivision: A Cost-Effective Approach,* Planning Advisory Service Report Number 356, American Planning Association, Chicago, Ill., 1980.

W. Sanders, J. Getzels, D. Mosena, and J. Butler, *Affordable Single-Family Housing,* Planning Advisory Service Report Number 385, American Planning Association, Chicago, Ill., 1984.

W. Sanders and D. Mosena, *Changing Development Standards for Affordable Housing,* Planning Advisory Service Report Number 371, American Planning Association, Chicago, Ill., 1982.

N. Schoenauer, *6,000 Years of Housing,* Garland Publishing, Inc., New York, 1981.

R. L. Smith, *Smart House,* GP Publishing, Inc., Columbia, Md., 1987.

G. Sternlieb and J. W. Hughes, "Demographics and Housing in America, *Population Bulletin* **41**(1) (January 1986).

K. C. Stevenson and H. W. Jandl, *Houses by Mail,* The Preservation Press, Washington, D.C., 1986.

M. Sumichrast and S. A. Frankel, *Profile of the Builder and His Industry,* National Association of Home Builders, Washington, D.C., 1970.

The Staff of the Bibliographic Research Library, *The Courtyard House as a Spanish Legacy in California Domestic Architecture,* Vance Bibliographies, Monticello, Ill., 1984.

M. Vance, *Country Homes: Monographs,* Vance Bibliographies, Monticello, Ill., 1984.

M. Vance, *Housing Policy: A Bibliography,* Vance Bibliographies, Monticello, Ill., 1983.

M. Vance, *Low Cost Housing: A Bibliography,* Vance Bibliographies, Monticello, Ill., 1983.

F. T. Ventre, "Innovation in Residential Construction," *Technology Review* (November 1979).

R. Warburton, "Design for Individuality," in *Challenge,* U.S. Government Printing Office, Washington, D.C., November-December 1969.

R. Warburton, "Housing," *Urban Planning Guide,* American Society of Civil Engineers, New York, 1986.

R. Warburton, ". . .Housing Design. . . .," *Journal of the American Institute of Architects,* (April 1968). Reprinted in *Congressional Record,* U.S. Government Printing Office, Washington, D.C., Vol. 114, No. 66, 1968.

R. Warburton, ed., *Housing Systems Proposals for Operation Breakthrough,* U.S. Government Printing Office, Washington, D.C., 1970; reprinted 1972.

S. Woodbridge, ed., *Bay Area Houses,* Peregrine Smith Books, Salt Lake City, Utah, 1976; new edition, 1988.

G. Wright, *Moralism and the Model Home,* The University of Chicago Press, Chicago, Ill., 1980.

See also Cluster Development And Land Subdivision; Multifamily Housing; Planned Communities; Residential Buildings; Review Boards

Ralph Warburton, FAIA,
F.ASCE, AICP
University of Miami
Coral Gables, Florida

SINGLE-PARENT HOUSING

One striking demographic trend of the 1970s and 1980s is the increased proportion of single-parent families among American households. In 1985 approximately 6.8 million family households with children were headed by female single parents, and 600,000 were headed by male single parents; together these figures represent 21% of all family households with dependent children. From 1970 to 1980, family households headed by women grew at a rate 10 times faster than that for two-parent families (1).

The characteristics of these households and their subsequent housing needs differ from those of the general population in several ways. The most striking characteristic is poverty. In 1984 the median income for a female single-parent family with children was $7,608; for a male single-parent family with children, $20,024; and for a family with both parents and children, $29,730 (2). Nearly 40% of families headed by women remain below poverty levels compared to 7% of families headed by men (3).

But poverty and low incomes are not the only problems many of these households face. Even single parents who are economically well off and who live in decent, standard housing, may express problems with housing (4). Most city zoning ordinances do not allow alternative housing arrangements (such as home sharing or accessory apartments), limiting the housing options of households seeking to share space in order to reduce costs and maintenance (5). Housing discrimination may also compound the housing situation. One national survey (6) indicated that landlords feel single parents are an undesirable tenant group because there is no one at home during the day to watch over the children. Coupled with housing discrimination against families with children—76% of rental apartment units in this country place some type of restriction on renting to families with children (7)—finding a suitable home remains a sizable obstacle for many single parents.

To address such concerns, planners, architects, and some government agencies have begun to focus on new housing forms for single-parent households. These include temporary shelters for battered women and their children, as well as transitional and permanent housing for single parents and their children. Many of these innovations have occurred outside the United States, particularly in Holland, Britain, and the Scandinavian countries where the proportion of single parents is as high as in the United States but where government intervention and support is more forthcoming. Among these housing developments designed for single-parent families are some common characteristics: (1) affordable housing oriented toward low-income residents; (2) location near public transit and community services; (3) design features that enhance on-site security; and (4) shared common spaces with other residents, to enhance the pooling of services and social support. The provision of space for social services and shared living spaces is a distinctive feature of much transitional housing for single-parent families.

DEVELOPMENTS IN EUROPE

The Mother's Home in Amsterdam, designed by Aldo van Eyck, was completed in 1980 (8,9). Sponsored by the Hubertusvereniging Foundation, this development houses families who are in cultural transition, have irregular working hours, or who are pregnant teenagers, infants awaiting adoption, temporarily homeless, or single parents. Once a family becomes a tenant, there is no deadline to leave.

The project was commissioned in 1973 and involved renovating an urban nineteenth-century building and designing a new wing to the renovated building. There are accommodations for 16 mothers and their children as well as a 24-hour-service shelter for as many as 90 people.

This development follows the form of the Israeli kibbutzim of separate living quarters for parents and children. The children's wing contains five apartments, each with space for five children. They live and sleep on the lower level of these quarters and play on the upper level. Mothers have their own sleeping quarters in the renovated building but share sitting areas and baths with other residents (Fig. 1).

Common areas shared among residents include a kitchen and snack bar, dining room, and counseling room. The kitchen and snack bar are accessible to anyone, although there is a kitchen staff, cleaning crew, linen person, maintenance staff, and housing director.

Housing for single parents also exists in Great Britain, where Nina West has pioneered numerous developments (10). Many of these homes started as conversions of small buildings to multiunit housing with day-care centers. West believed on-site day care to be a critical component of the housing development so that parents are able to work during the day. In 1972 she hired Sylvester Bone to design Fiona House in London. Besides the private household units, Fiona House also has a day-care center and intercoms between apartments. The interior corridors are carpeted and have windows looking out from the apartment units onto the corridors (Fig. 2) through which parents can watch their children playing. Fiona House and the other housing complexes Nina West developed are typically transitional housing, with residents leaving a year or two after moving in.

DEVELOPMENTS IN NORTH AMERICA

Questions abound about whether housing developments with shared services and spaces can be successfully trans-

lated to the United States. A recent survey of 6000 women respondents (47% married, 36% single parents; more than half earning more than $20,000 a year) indicates that a surprising number seem willing to share housing resources, amenities, and space (11). Although single and low-income residents were most amenable to such sharing, 26% of the total respondents said they would be willing to share a kitchen or living room, 21% would share a garden, and 19% said they would share a bathroom.

Transitional housing with shared living spaces has been developed in the United States. Warren Village is the first and currently the largest housing development for single parents in North America. The first stage was completed in 1974 in Denver, and the second stage at another site in Denver in 1984. It was originally operated by the Methodist Church, but it currently advertises itself as a nonsectarian, nonprofit organization. Prospective tenants must meet several eligibility requirements: the parent must be at least 18 years of age; the oldest child cannot be more than 11 years old at the time of enrollment; the parent must be a single parent; there may be no more than four children per household; there must be a source of income to pay rent (this can be a government subsidy such as those available from the Section 8 federal assistance program); children must live with parents; and residents must express a strong need and desire to reach personal development and financial goals.

A primary focus of Warren Village is to have residents set tangible goals for themselves when they move in (eg, improve budgetary, parenting, occupational, domestic, or child-care skills) and to use their residency time to meet these goals. This objective is supported by the facility with on-site counseling, job training, and educational services.

Warren Village is transitional housing, with residents typically staying 2 years. There are units for more than 200 families on the two sites, as well as on-site child care for children between the ages of 6 weeks and 12 years, who may live at Warren Village or in the community. The child-care facilities are licensed for 197 children.

The apartments consist of one-, two-, and three-bedroom units ranging from 520 to 965 ft². Six units are handicapped-accessible apartments. In Warren Village II, there are commercial spaces and space for training programs (eg, classrooms with computers for computer classes).

ABT Associates in Boston conducted a survey of residents at the time of their enrollment and after leaving Warren Village. Whereas 47% of residents were employed at the time of entrance, 94% were employed 2 years after they left Warren Village. Even more striking is the finding that whereas 65% were receiving public assistance at the time of enrollment, only 6% were doing so 2 years after leaving the program (12). Although no evidence is provided that these striking changes are the result of living in Warren Village, it is likely that residency, along with the eligibility requirements, contribute to these trends.

Another housing development for single parents is Constance Hamilton House in Toronto, Canada, designed by Joan Simon in 1982 (13). It is a 31-unit town-house complex, occupied by both single women and single par-

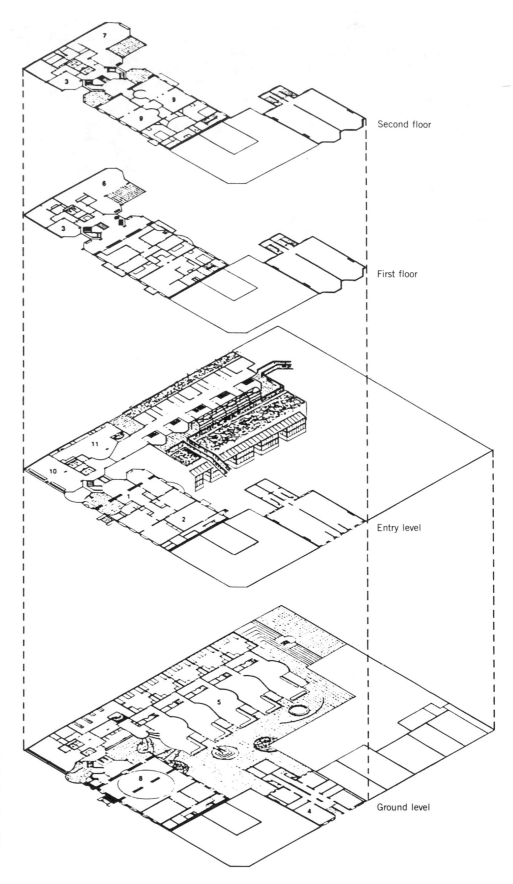

Second floor

First floor

Entry level

Ground level

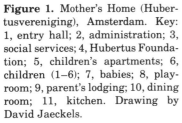

Figure 1. Mother's Home (Hubertusvereniging), Amsterdam. Key: 1, entry hall; 2, administration; 3, social services; 4, Hubertus Foundation; 5, children's apartments; 6, children (1–6); 7, babies; 8, playroom; 9, parent's lodging; 10, dining room; 11, kitchen. Drawing by David Jaeckels.

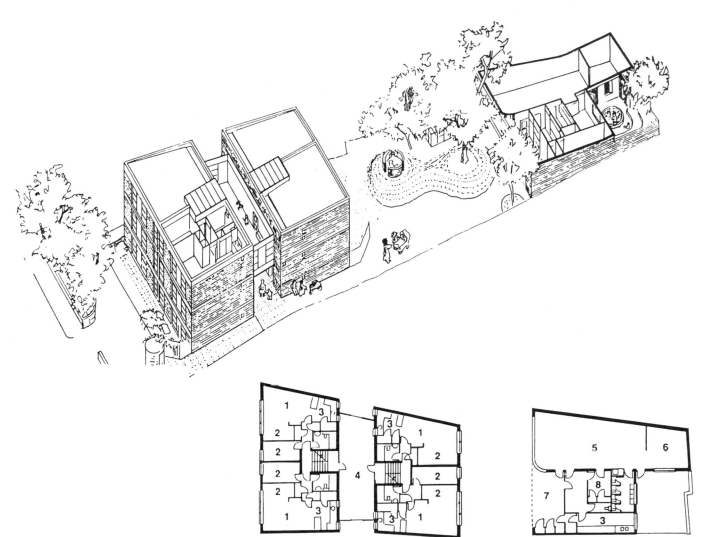

Figure 2. Fiona House, London. Key: 1, living room; 2, bedroom; 3, kitchen; 4, playroom; 5, nursery; 6, quiet room; 7, veranda; 8, office. Drawing by David Jaeckels.

ents with children. As a female-run cooperative sponsored by the Canadian government, each household must be headed by a woman.

At Constance Hamilton, units range in size from one to three bedrooms, and there is a six-bedroom hostel for women in need of second-stage crisis housing, whose stay is typically between 6 months and 1 year. Because of budgetary cuts by the Canadian Mortgage Housing Corporation, common areas such as day care, a tearoom, a cooperative shop, and a meeting room were eliminated in the final design.

Sparksway Common in Hayward, California, was designed by architects Mui Ho and Sandy Hirschen and sponsored by Eden Housing, Inc. It is a series of two-story town houses with a total of 45 units, ranging from one to four bedrooms, with connections between kitchen and eating areas of households. Units are clustered in groups around courtyards to encourage neighboring and informal observation of children. On-site day care, laundry facilities, offices, and board meeting rooms are housed in a

central building. Residents, many of whom are single parents, maintain cooperative ownership in the development.

Passage Community is exclusively for single-parent families. It is located in an inner-city neighborhood in Minneapolis, Minnesota. The building is an extensively renovated apartment building, completed in 1986, and designed by architect Mary Vogel-Heffernon. It consists of 17 units, a child-care center, community rooms, staff offices, laundry facilities, and indoor and outdoor play spaces (Fig. 3). The units range in size from one bedroom to three. The architect and Board of Directors developed a set of design guidelines expressly for the housing of single parents and their children (14).

Passage Community, developed by the Women's Community Housing Corporation in the Twin Cities area, is transitional housing where residents stay from 6 months to 2 years or more. Residents are encouraged to define goals and move toward them during their residency there, similar to the philosophy of Warren Village. In addition, residents are expected to take an active part in support groups, resident meetings, and workshops. Also similar to Warren Village is the restriction on initial residency of teenagers living in the development. Both developments believe that teenagers require special programming, space, and supervision, resulting in prohibitive costs.

TRENDS

The descriptions of developments above include only a few of those housing developments designed expressly for and occupied mostly by single-parent families (for others, see Refs. 15 and 16). Others include the more than 10 developments in the northeastern United States developed by the Women's Development Corporation; Discovery House in Calgary; and Monroe House in Vancouver. The Women's Institute for Housing and Economic Development, Inc., of Boston has been a significant force in development services for low-income women and their families.

More developments are currently under construction. These include two in Boston: Elizabeth Stone House, designed by comunitas and developed by Elizabeth Stone House, a women's group in Boston; and the Tree of Life,

initiated by the City of Boston and designed and developed by the Boston Redevelopment Authority, the Pavilion Partnership, and South Park Partnership, based on a program developed by the Women's Institute for Housing and Economic Development, Inc. of Boston (17).

Dayton Court in St. Paul, Minnesota is the result of the winning design of Troy West and Jacqueline Leavitt for the New American House Competition sponsored by the National Endowment for the Arts and the Minneapolis College of Art and Design in 1984 (18). Although this development is not exclusively devoted to single-parent families, the architects conceived the design as responsive to the needs of single-parent families.

Willowbrook Green in Los Angeles, designed by Ena Dubnoff, will be a housing development of 48 units with child-care facilities for 60 children. The majority of tenants are expected to be single-parent families with some elderly, singles, and couples with children. Sponsored by the Drew Economic Development Corporation and the Los Angeles Community Development Commission, this development incorporates the central features of most precedent housing developments for single parents: on-site child-care facilities; spaces and services for counseling

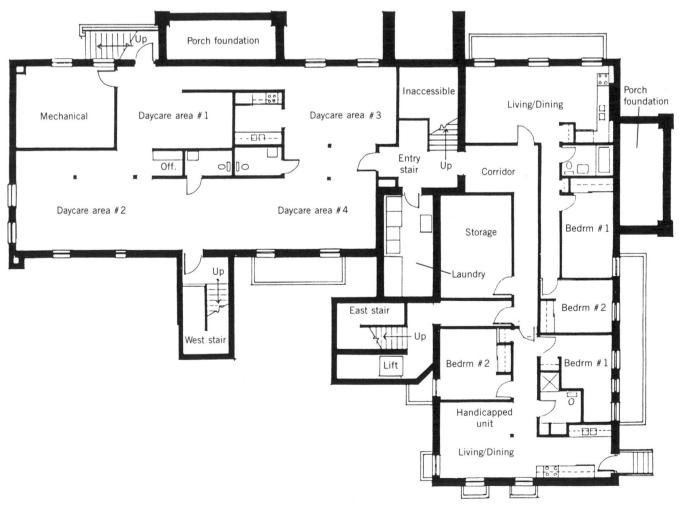

(a)

and job training; location near public transportation and commercial facilities; community building with community rooms, offices, and laundry; and design addressed to security concerns of adults and children at play.

One questions whether single-parent families should live exclusively among other single-parent families or with a mixture of household types. Many single parents do not want to live exclusively with other single parents (19). As such, many of the housing developments described here have a mixture of household types as occupants. However, all of the designers and sponsors of these projects intentionally addressed the housing needs of single-parent families in their developments.

Estimates of the number of housing complexes in the United States developed for single-parent families range between 30 and 60 (these do not include crisis shelters). Certainly these developments are few compared to the numbers of conventional multifamily housing complexes. Yet they respond to the contemporary changes in the nature of U.S. families and their housing needs.

BIBLIOGRAPHY

1. United States Bureau of the Census, "Money Income and Poverty Status of Families and Persons in the United States: 1984," *Current Population Reports,* Series P-60, no. 149, U.S. Government Printing Office, Washington, D.C., 1985.

2. D. J. Besharov and A. J. Quin, "Not All Female-Headed Families are Created Equal," *Public Interest* **80,** 48 (1987).

3. K. Hapgood and J. Getzels, *Planning, Women and Change,* American Society of Planning Officials, Chicago, Ill., 1974.

4. J. Leavitt, "Two Prototypical Designs for Single Parents: The Congregate House and the New American House" in K. A. Franck and S. Ahrentzen, eds., *New Households, New Housing,* Van Nostrand Reinhold, New York, 1989.

5. M. Ritzdorf, "Women in the City: Land Use and Zoning Issues," *Urban Resources* **3** (2), 23 (1986).

6. United States Department of Housing Urban Development, *Housing Our Families,* U.S. Government Printing Office, Washington, D.C., 1980.

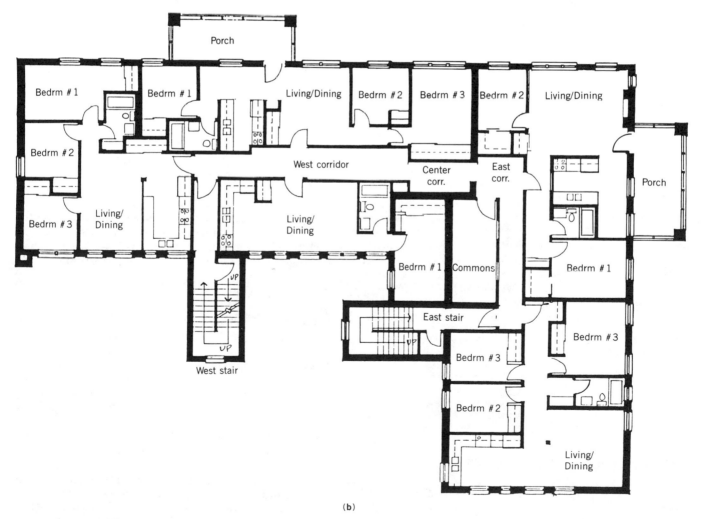

(b)

Figure 3. Passage-Community. (**a**) Ground floor plan; (**b**) second floor plan. Courtesy of Christine C. Cook.

7. R. W. Marans, M. E. Colten, R. M. Groves, and B. Thomas, *Measuring Restrictive Rental Policies Affecting Families with Children: A National Survey,* Office of Policy Development and Research, Department of Housing and Urban Development, Washington, D.C., 1980.

8. I. France, "Hubertusvereniging: A Transition Point for Single Parents," *Women and Environments* **7**(1), 20 (1985).

9. H. Hertzberger, A. van Roijen-Wortmann, and F. Strauven, eds., *Aldo van Eyck,* Stichting Wonen, Amsterdam, 1986.

10. S. Strong, "Nina West Homes," *Architectural Design,* **497** (1975).

11. L. Van Gelder, "Special Ms. Poll: Dream Houses," *Ms.* **4**, 34–40, 88 (1986).

12. "Communities for One-Parent Families," Brochure distributed by Warren Village, Denver, Col.

13. G. Wekerle and S. Novac, "Developing Two Women's Housing Cooperatives" in K. A. Franck and S. Ahrentzen, eds., *New Households, New Housing,* Van Nostrand Reinhold, New York, 1989.

14. C. Cook, "Passage Community: Second-Stage Housing for Single Parents" in K. A. Franck and S. Ahrentzen, eds., *New Households, New Housing,* Van Nostrand Reinhold, New York, 1989.

15. *A Manual on Transitional Housing,* Women's Institute for Housing and Economic Development, Inc., Boston, Mass., 1986.

16. *Housing the Single-Parent Family: A Resource and Action Handbook,* State of New Jersey, Department of Community Affairs, Trenton, N.J., Mar. 1987.

17. J. F. Sprague, "Two Cases of Transitional Housing in Boston" in K. A. Franck and S. Ahrentzen, eds., *New Households, New Housing,* Van Nostrand Reinhold, New York, 1989.

18. J. Leavitt, "Two Prototypical Designs for Single Parents: The Congregate House and the New American House" in K. A. Franck and S. Ahrentzen, eds., *New Households, New Housing,* Van Nostrand Reinhold, New York, 1989.

19. S. Anderson-Khlief, "Housing Needs of Single-Parent Mothers" in S. Keller, ed., *Building for Women,* Lexington, Toronto, 1981, pp. 21–37.

General References

Ref. 4 is a good general reference.

K. Anthony and C. L. Cornfield, *Single Parent Families and Housing: A Bibliography,* Public Administration Series P2280, Vance Bibliographies, Monticello, Ill., Nov. 1987.

E. L. Birch, ed., *The Unsheltered Woman: Women and Housing in the 80's,* Center for Urban Policy Research, New Brunswick, N.J., 1985.

SHERRY AHRENTZEN
University of
Wisconsin-Milwaukee
Milwaukee, Wisconsin

SKIDMORE, OWINGS AND MERRILL

Skidmore, Owings and Merrill (SOM) is a large partnership that provides complete professional multidisciplinary services in architecture, engineering, and planning. On January 1, 1936, the firm of Skidmore and Owings was founded by Louis Skidmore and Nathaniel Owings in Chicago, Illinois, with the name changing to Skidmore, Owings and Merrill with the addition of John Merrill, Sr. to the partnership in 1939.

By then, the firm had established its New York City office, led by Skidmore. A large number of extensive government contracts were handled by the firm during World War II. The San Francisco, California, office was established in 1946. The Portland, Oregon, office was organized in 1951 upon the decision of Pietro Belluschi to move to the position of Dean of the School of Architecture and Planning at the Massachusetts Institute of Technology (MIT), Cambridge, Massachusetts. Thus, the Portland office, closed in 1987, was known initially for five years as Pietro Belluschi and Skidmore, Owings and Merrill.

In 1950, the New York Museum of Modern Art accorded SOM an exhibition, the first ever devoted to a firm rather than to an individual. The first Architectural Firm Award given by the American Institute of Architects (AIA) was received by SOM in 1962, recognizing the achievements of the firm as a group of professionals working together as a team. By 1964, the firm had 18 general partners and 750 employees in its 4 principal offices. The Washington, D.C., office was established in 1967, followed by offices in Los Angeles, California, and London. By 1980, the firm had 29 partners, 9 offices, and a staff of over 1700 and was consistently placed at or near the top of lists of architectural engineering firms ranked by estimated volume of work by such publications as *Building Design and Construction* and *Engineering News Record.* In the former publication's July 1988 issue, SOM was estimated to receive the most architectural/engineering revenues, with 70% of its work in commercial construction and 20% in institutional facilities. It has undertaken projects in more than 40 foreign countries in addition to its extensive work in the United States.

The SOM partnership uses a type of matrix management in which each project is assigned both an administrative partner and a design partner, who are supported, respectively, by a project manager and a senior studio architect. This team provides complete service to the project from start to finish, establishing and maintaining its quality.

SOM typically hires over 400 professionals per year, and has one of the oldest affirmative action programs in the profession. For example, minorities and women represented nearly half of the staff of the Chicago office in 1986. Most of the current partners have advanced through the ranks and have been with the firm for over 15 years.

The offices vary somewhat in practice directions because of local market, staffing, and construction industry factors. The New York office has taken a lead in interiors, where significant capacity exists. The Chicago office has staffed a full complement of engineering disciplines and has served as the center for firm-wide management execution.

SOM has been a pioneer in the use of computers in architectural/engineering firms since the early 1960s, with this in-house activity centered in Chicago. Computers are used comprehensively for all aspects of the practice, including planning, graphics, design development, engineering calculations, working drawings and specifications, etc. In mid-1988, the firm announced the development of an Architecture and Engineering Series of software for International Business Machines, for the IBM RT/PC. Encompassing graphics, rendering, structure, energy, heating, ventilation, air conditioning, power, lighting, and piping, it will be available to the industry.

In his Introduction to *Architecture of Skidmore, Owings and Merrill, 1963–1973*, Arthur Drexler said:

> [f]or more than 35 years . . . the firm has tested the validity of the modern movement.

> The firm's commissions range from the exotic—a Presidential Library, for example— to such more or less routine matters as industrial or transportation facilities . . . all of these buildings receive an attention to detail vital to the philosophy and ethics of modern architecture.

More than 200 of the firm's projects have received over 500 design awards in its over 50 years of existence, as documented by Figures. The following paragraphs provide some background information on the founding Partners, and later key Partners, listed alphabetically.

EDWARD CHARLES BASSETT

Following service in the U.S. Army, Pacific Theater (1943–1946), and receipt of his Bachelor of Architecture degree from The University of Michigan, Ann Arbor, Michigan, in 1949, he worked with Eero Saarinen and studied at the Cranbrook Academy of Art, Bloomfield Hills, Michigan, obtaining its Master of Architecture degree in 1951. Joining SOM in 1955, he received the Brunner Award in Architecture from the National Institute of Arts and Letters in 1963 and is a Fellow of the AIA.

His most important building designs include the John Hancock Mutual Life Insurance Co. (San Francisco, 1960), the Weyerhaeuser Co. (Tacoma, Washington, 1971), and the Southeast Financial Center (Miami, Florida, 1983).

GORDON BUNSHAFT

Born in Buffalo, New York, in 1909, he was educated at MIT, where he received Bachelor of Architecture (1933) and Master of Architecture (1935) degrees. He received the Rotch and MIT Traveling Fellowships for study in Europe and North Africa (1935–1937). He served as Chief Designer for SOM from 1937 to 1942 and, after service as a U.S. Army Corps of Engineer Major in World War II, was a General Partner from 1949 to 1979 and the principal design partner in the New York office.

Bunshaft's most important building designs include the Lever House (New York, 1952) (Fig. 1) (recipient of the AIA's 25 Year Award and many others), Manufacturers Hanover Trust (New York, 1955) (Fig. 2), the Connecticut General Life Insurance Co. (Bloomfield Hills, Connecticut, 1957) (Fig. 3), the PepsiCo World Headquarters

Figure 1. Lever House, New York 1952. Courtesy of SOM, photograph by ESTO.

(New York, 1960) (Fig. 4), the Union Carbide Co. (New York, 1962) (Fig. 5), the Chase Manhattan Bank (New York, 1962) (Fig. 6), the Beinecke Rare Book and Manuscript Library, Yale University (New Haven, Connecticut, 1965), Banque Lambert (Brussels, Belgium, 1965) (Fig. 7),

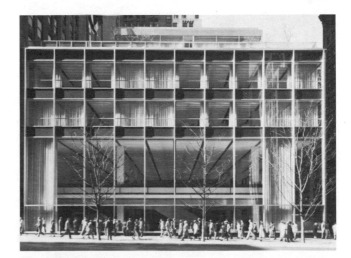

Figure 2. Manufacturers Hanover Trust Company Bank and Office Building, 510 Fifth Avenue, New York, 1954. Courtesy of SOM, photograph by Ezra Stoller.

Figure 3. Connecticut General Life Insurance Company Office Building, Bloomfield Hills, CT, 1957. Courtesy of SOM, photograph by Ezra Stoller.

Figure 4. Pepsico, Inc. World Headquarters, New York, 1959. Courtesy of SOM, photography by Ezra Stoller, Esto.

Figure 5. Union Carbide Corporation Headquarters Office Building, New York, 1961. Courtesy of SOM, photo by Ezra Stoller, ESTO.

Lincoln Center Library and Museum, and Beaumont Theatre (with Eero Saarinen) (New York, 1965), the L. B. Johnson Library, University of Texas (Austin, Texas, 1971) (Fig. 8), the Hirshhorn Museum and Sculpture Garden (Washington, D.C., 1974) (Fig. 9), and the National Commercial Bank (Jeddah, Saudi Arabia, 1981) (Fig. 10).

Among his activities in support of design education, he served on the Visiting Committees of the MIT School of Architecture (1940–1942), the Harvard University Graduate School of Design (1954–1960), and the Yale University School of Art and Architecture (1959–1962). He is a former Trustee of New York's Museum of Modern Art and of Carnegie Mellon University, was appointed by the President as a member of the Washington, D.C., Commission on Fine Arts (1963–1972), and received an honorary Doctor of Fine Arts degree from the University of Buffalo in 1962.

Among his other honors are the Brunner Award (1955) and Gold Medal (1984) of the National Institute of Arts and Letters. He received the Medal of Honor of the New York Chapter of the AIA in 1961 and the Chancellor's Medal from the University of Buffalo in 1969. An Honor-

Figure 6. Chase Manhattan Bank Headquarters, New York, 1961. Courtesy of SOM.

ary Member of the Buffalo Fine Arts Academy, he is a Fellow of the AIA and an Academician of the National Academy of Design. In 1988, he was joint recipient of the Pritzker Prize in Architecture. The citation read:

> Bunshaft has created a rich inventory of projects that set a timeless standard for buildings in the urban/corporate world. In a career that has spanned forty years of accomplishment, he has demonstrated an understanding of contemporary technology and materials in the making of great architecture that is unsurpassed.

MYRON GOLDSMITH

Born in Chicago in 1918, he received a B.S. degree in architecture from Armour Institute of Technology, Chicago, in 1939 and his M.S. in architecture in 1952 from its

successor, the Illinois Institute of Technology (IIT). After several early positions as a structural engineer, including service with the U.S. military, he joined the office of Mies van der Rohe in 1946 as an architect and structural engineer. He studied with Pier Luigi Nervi on a Fulbright Fellowship at the University of Rome from 1953 to 1955, after which he joined SOM in its San Francisco office as Chief Structural Engineer. He served as an Associate Partner and senior designer in the Chicago office from 1958 to 1967, after which he became a General Partner. He has served as a Professor of Architecture at IIT since 1961. He is a Fellow of the AIA.

His most important designs include the Solar Telescope (Kitt Peak, Arizona, 1962), Keating Hall, IIT (Chicago, 1968), Chicago Transit Authority stations (1970), and the Republic Newspaper Plant (Columbus, Indiana, 1971) (Fig. 11).

BRUCE J. GRAHAM

Born in La Cumbre, Bogota, Columbia, in 1925 of U.S. parents, he served in the U.S. Navy, Pacific Theater, and received Bachelor of Fine Arts and Bachelor of Architecture degrees from the University of Pennsylvania, Philadelphia, Pennsylvania, in 1949. He then worked in the Chicago office of Holabird, Root and Burgee until 1951, after which he joined SOM's Chicago office, where he became a design General Partner in 1960.

He was named an Honorary Professor by the University Nacional Federico Villareal, Peru, in 1980, served as the Eliot Noyes Visiting Professor of Architecture at Harvard University, Cambridge, Massachusetts, in the fall of 1986, was appointed a Trustee of the University of Pennsylvania (and Chairman of the Board of Overseers of its Graduate School of Fine Arts) in 1981, and was a member of the Board of the Temple Hoyne Buell Center at Columbia University, New York, in 1984. He is an Honorary Member of the Institute of Urbanism and Planning of Peru.

His most important building designs include the Equitable Life Insurance Society (Chicago, 1965) (Fig. 12), the John Hancock Center (Chicago, 1971) (Fig. 13), the Hartford Fire Insurance Co. (Chicago, 1971) (Fig. 14), One Shell Plaza, (Houston, 1971), and the Sears Tower (Chicago, 1974) (Fig. 15), currently the world's tallest building.

Figure 7. Banque Lambert, Brussels, Belgium, 1965. Courtesy of SOM, photograph by Ezra Stoller, ESTO.

Figure 8. Lyndon Baines Johnson Library and Sid W. Richardson Hall, University of Texas, Austin, Texas, 1971; in association with Brooks, Barr, Graeber & White. Courtesy of SOM, photograph by Ezra Stoller, ESTO Photographics Inc.

He has served as President of the Chicago Central Area Committee, and as a Director of the Chicago Council on Foreign Relations and the Urban Land Research Foundation. He is a member of the Royal Institute of British Architects and the Royal Architectural Institute of Canada and is a Fellow of the AIA.

WILLIAM E. HARTMANN

Born in 1916 in Springfield, New Jersey, he received the Bachelor of Architecture degree in 1938 from MIT. He was awarded the Rotch Traveling Fellowship in 1939 for study in Europe and Asia. He served with the U.S. Army Corps of Engineers (1941–1945), ending as a Lieutenant Colonel. Joining SOM in 1945, he served for many decades as managing General Partner of the Chicago office.

Among his many contributions to the development of this prolific and comprehensive office and to the profession was his successful recruitment and persuasion of Pablo Picasso, on behalf of Mayor Richard Daley and business leaders in Chicago, to create in the 1960s the large contemporary steel sculpture for the city's Civic Center, spearheading an international environmental art movement.

He has served as Executive Director of the Graham Foundation for Advanced Studies in the Fine Arts in Chicago (1959–1960); as a Trustee of the Committee on Economic Development in Chicago, IIT, and the Art Institute of Chicago; and as a member of the Corporation of MIT. He is a member of Lamda Alpha, an honorary land economics society, is a Fellow of the AIA, and received an honorary doctorate from Lake Forest College in Illinois in 1968.

Figure 9. Hirshhorn Museum and Sculpture Garden, Washington, D.C., 1974. Courtesy of SOM, photograph by Ezra Stoller, ESTO.

Figure 10. National Commercial Bank, Jeddah, Saudia Arabia, 1983. Courtesy of SOM, photograph by Wolfgang Hoyt, ESTO.

Figure 11. *The Republic* Newspaper Plant and Offices, Columbus, Indiana, 1971. Courtesy of SOM, photograph by Ezra Stoller, ESTO.

FAZLUR RAHMAN KHAN

Born in 1929 in Dacca, East Pakistan (now Bangladesh), Khan received a Bachelor of Engineering degree from Bengal Engineering College, Calcutta, India, in 1950 (graduating first in his class) and served as a faculty member at the University of Dacca (1951–1952). He received Fulbright and Pakistani scholarships for U.S. study, and earned three degrees from the University of Illinois at Champaign-Urbana: the Master of Science in structural

Figure 12. Equitable Life Assurance Society Office Building, Chicago, Ill., 1965. Courtesy of SOM, photograph by Hedrich-Blessing.

Figure 13. John Hancock Center, Chicago, Ill., 1970. Courtesy of SOM, photograph by Ezra Stoller, ESTO.

engineering (1952), the Master of Science in theoretical and applied mechanics, and the Ph.D. in structural engineering (1955). He joined SOM in 1955, remaining with the firm except for his return to Pakistan (1957–1960).

He designed the structure for the 714-ft tall One Shell Plaza building in Houston (the world's tallest building in lightweight concrete), the 100-story John Hancock Center in Chicago (the world's tallest multiuse building), the 110-story Sears Tower in Chicago (the world's tallest building), and in 1982, the Haj Terminal in Jeddah, Saudi Arabia (utilizing an innovative large fabric-covered roof system) (Fig. 16). The 52-story One Shell Square building in New Orleans, Louisiana, utilized his new composite system for tall buildings, combining the advantages of steel and reinforced concrete construction.

He was Vice-chairman of the Steering Group of the Council on Tall Buildings and Urban Habitat, sponsored

454 SKIDMORE, OWINGS AND MERRILL

Figure 14. Hartford Fire Insurance Company, Chicago, Ill., 1961. Courtesy of SOM, photograph by Ezra Stoller, ESTO.

by six professional societies (International Association for Bridge and Structural Engineering, American Society of Civil Engineers, AIA, American Institute of Planners, International Federation for Housing and Planning, and International Union of Architects), which produced the important five-volume, state-of-the-art *Monograph on the Planning and Design of Tall Buildings* in 1978.

A Partner in the firm and its Chief Structural Engineer at the time of his death in 1982, he was a Fellow of the American Society of Civil Engineers and received, posthumously, the 1983 Institute Honors Medal of the AIA.

JOHN O. MERRILL, SR.

Born in St. Paul, Minnesota, in 1896, John O. Merrill, Sr. received a Bachelor of Architectural Engineering degree from MIT in 1921, following service as a Captain, Artillery, from 1917 to 1919. He later was Chief Architect for the Federal Housing Administration in Chicago (1934–1939), which he left to become a partner in SOM. An architect and engineer, he directed the revision of the Chicago Building Code (1947–1950). He retired from the firm in 1959 after participating in work on the town of Oak Ridge, Tennessee, permanent installations for the U.S. Army and Air Force on several Pacific islands, and the U.S. Air Force Academy. He was a Fellow of the AIA.

WALTER NETSCH

Born in Chicago in 1920, he received a Bachelor of Architecture degree in 1943 from MIT and entered the U.S. Army Corps of Engineers for service until 1946. After brief work for L. Morgan Yost, he joined SOM in 1947, becoming a General Partner for design in 1955. During this period, he also worked in the firm's offices in Oak Ridge, San Francisco, and Tokyo.

His most important designs include the Chapel for the U.S. Air Force Academy (Colorado Springs, Colorado, 1963) (Fig. 17), the University of Illinois at Chicago Circle (1966), and the Regenstein Library, University of Chicago (1970) (Fig. 18).

Active in educational projects and endeavors, he has served as a trustee of the Rhode Island School of Design and a member of the Art Committee of MIT, the Advisory Committee of Educational Facilities Laboratories, Inc., the Advancement of Architectural Education Committee of the Association of Collegiate Schools of Architecture, and the Advisory Committee of the School of Architecture at the University of Illinois.

He has served as Chairman of the Chicago Park District, is a member of the Society of American Military Engineers, and is a Fellow of the AIA. Netsch has received

Figure 15. Sears Tower, Chicago, Ill., 1974. Courtesy of SOM, photograph by Timothy Hursley.

Figure 16. Haj Terminal, King Abdul Aziz International Airport, Jeddah, Saudi-Arabia, 1982; associated with Airways Engineering Corporation. Courtesy of SOM, photography by Owens-Corning.

an honorary Doctor of Fine Arts degree from Lawrence University, and he retired from the firm in 1979.

NATHANIEL A. OWINGS

Born in Indianapolis, Indiana, in 1903, "Nat" Owings won a Rotary Club trip to Europe and began his architectural education in France with visits to Chartres, Mont Saint Michel, and Notre Dame. He entered the Architecture School at the University of Illinois, and finished at Cornell University, Ithaca, New York, in 1927. Later that year, he worked for York and Sawyer in New York City, and he recalled that Bertram Grosvenor Goodhue was his hero. In 1929, he met Louis Skidmore, later became interested in the Century of Progress Exposition in Chicago, and in 1936 formed the partnership that was to become SOM. He later established its San Francisco office and remained with the firm until his retirement in 1979.

He was a member of the Advisory Board of the Cornell University School of Architecture and the Cornell University Council, the Advisory Committee of the Department of Architecture at IIT and the Citizen's Board of the University of Chicago, and was a Trustee of the American Academy in Rome. He has supported an Owings Professorship in Architecture at Cornell University, and the California Council of the AIA presents the annual Nathaniel A. Owings Award for the preservation of nature in the built environment.

Owings served as Chairman of the Chicago Plan Commission from 1948 to 1951 and from the early 1960s to 1978 was the principal leader in the rejuvenation of Pennsylvania Avenue in Washington, D.C., through his initial appointment by President Kennedy as Chairman of the Advisory Council on Pennsylvania Avenue. In 1965, he became a Chairman of the Pennsylvania Avenue Commission, newly formed to implement his recommendations to President Lyndon Johnson the previous year, and he served as a board member of its successor, the Pennsylvania Avenue Development Commission. Through his successful leadership efforts in developing SOM as well as his public sector endeavors, he was much more a goal setter than a designer, creating in the words of partner Bruce Graham, ". . . opportunities for architecture from almost nothing."

A Fellow of the AIA and a past president of its Chicago

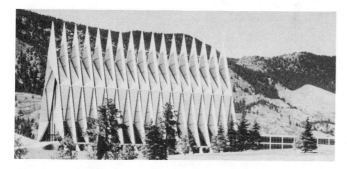

Figure 17. Chapel, United States Air Force Academy, Colorado Springs, CO, 1962. Courtesy of SOM, photograph by Williams and Meyer Co.

Figure 18. Regenstein Library, University of Chicago, Chicago, Ill., 1970. Courtesy of SOM, photograph by Ezra Stoller, ESTO.

Chapter, his 1983 Gold Medal Citation from the AIA stated that "[h]is drive, imagination and sense of mission inspired many of America's most brilliant designers . . ."

In his Gold Medal acceptance speech, he said that "[a]n abyss has been created between . . . the recognized environmentalist movements and the public enterprises which often are unwisely blind to anything but the dollar. This abyss must be bridged. And it can best be bridged through the leadership of a trained architect-planner."

LOUIS SKIDMORE

Born in 1897 in Lawrenceberg, Indiana, he was educated at Bradley University, Peoria, Illinois, prior to service with the U.S. Army Air Corps in the United Kingdom during World War I. He then attended the MIT School of Architecture and worked for Boston architect Charles D. Maginnis. He spent three years in Europe, including a year at the American Academy in Rome, following winning the Rotch Traveling Scholarship in 1926. Returning to the United States in 1929, he became Chief of Design for the successful 1933 Century of Progress Exposition in Chicago, assisted by Nathaniel Owings, whose sister he married. After the beginning of SOM in 1936, he led its development until his retirement in 1956.

A member of the Society of American Military Engineers, he received an honorary Doctor of Laws degree from Bradley University, served as Chairman of the Advisory Council to the Princeton University School of Architecture (1953–1955), and was a member of the Visiting Committee of the MIT School of Architecture. He was President of the New York Building Congress (1949–1952) and received the Medal of Honor of the New York Chapter of the AIA in 1949. A Fellow of the AIA, he received its Gold Medal in 1957, prior to his death in 1962. The citation read

> Architect in a new technology pioneering new paths in a profession depending hitherto largely upon individual service. You have built an organization with the name of Skidmore, Owings and Merrill, in which you have united with singleness of purpose the manifold skills, imagination and judgment fitted to serve, with marked distinction, a wider and more diverse clientele than had been thought possible. In giving architectural service to the needs of an era of vast building activity, you and your collaborators have won for the profession a wider understanding and appreciation.

SOM SENIOR PERSONNEL

Clearly, the above highlighted individuals could not alone have produced the quantity of quality teamwork mentioned herein. Other exceptionally contributing Partners, Fellows of the AIA, are listed herewith in alphabetical order: Roy O. Allen, David M. Childs, Walter A. Costa, Robert W. Cutler, James R. DeStefano, Robert Diamant, Thomas J. Eyerman, Marc E. Goldstein, Peter Hopkinson, Richard Keating, Michael McCarthy, John O. Merrill, Jr.,

David A. Pugh, Roger Seitz, J. Walter Severinghaus, Adrian D. Smith, John R. Weese, and Gordon Wildermuth. Similarly, important AIA Fellows at the Associate Partner and Associate level are John L. Fisher and Thomas P. Houha.

Many noted architects have served the firm, contributing for some time to its work. These include some Fellows of the AIA who formerly occupied positions at the Associate level or above in SOM, listed in alphabetical order: Natalie DeBlois, Tallie B. Maule, Edward Petrazio, Walter A. Rutes, John Schruben, Jack D. Train, Ralph Warburton, and Ralph Youngren.

There are in addition those prominent architects who served for a time in the great SOM "postgraduate school" and moved on, also achieving recognition as Fellows of the AIA. This alumni group includes John Dinkeloo, John M. Johansen, Stephen Kliment, Fumihiko Maki, Richard Meier, Gyo Obata, Ambrose Richardson, Stanley Tigerman, and Harry Weese.

SOM has been associated with other firms on large projects where their geographic presence or special skill warranted this relationship. These firms have included A. Epstein and Associates, Chicago; C. F. Murphy Associates, Chicago; Hertzka and Knowles, San Francisco; and Wilson, Morris, Crain and Anderson, Houston.

ANCILLARY CONTRIBUTIONS

The firm supported for many years the Skidmore, Owings and Merrill Traveling Fellowship at MIT, and the SOM Foundation was established in 1980. In addition to support of several traveling fellowships, the Foundation began an institute for research on architecture and urbanism in 1986 and has given grants to such architectural organizations as The Chicago Architectural Foundation and the National Building Museum. An architectural educator fellowship is supported, and three principals in the Chicago office sponsored a series of Boston-oriented design studios at the Harvard University Graduate School of Design beginning in 1988.

BIBLIOGRAPHY

General References

Skidmore, Owings and Merrill, Skidmore, Owings, and Merrill, Chicago, Ill., 1958.

A. Temko, "Goldsmith: Chicago's New Structural Poet," *Architectural Forum*, (May 1962).

Architecture of Skidmore, Owings and Merrill, 1950–1962, Frederick A. Praeger, Inc., New York, 1963. With an introduction by H. R. Hitchcock, text by E. Danz.

Skidmore, Owings and Merrill, Skidmore, Owings, and Merrill, Chicago, Ill., 1964.

R. Warburton, "Central Area Lakefront Development Plan," *Inland Architect* (Oct. 1966).

W. Netsch, "Center City Aerial Distribution for Pittsburgh," *Journal of the Franklin Institute* **286**(5), 463 (Nov. 1968).

Skidmore, Owings, and Merrill, Simon and Schuster, New York, 1970. With an introduction and notes by C. Woodward.

J. Gane, ed., *American Architects Directory*, R. R. Bowker Co., New York, 1970.

N. Owings, *The Spaces In Between*, Houghton Mifflin Co., Boston, Mass., 1973.

Architecture of Skidmore, Owings and Merrill, 1963–1973, Architectural Book Publishing Co., Inc., New York, 1974. With an introduction by A. Drexler and commentaries by A. Menges.

L. S. Beedle, ed., *Monograph on the Planning and Design of Tall Buildings*, American Society of Civil Engineers, New York, 1978, 5 vols.

P. W. Goetz, ed., *The New Encyclopedia Britannica*, Encyclopedia Britannica, Inc., Chicago, Ill., 1980, Vol. IX, p. 256.

L. Doumato, *Nathaniel Owings of Skidmore, Owings and Merrill*, Vance Bibliographies, Monticello, Ill., 1980.

Skidmore, Owings and Merrill 1936–1980, Skidmore, Owings and Merrill, Chicago, Ill., 1980.

S. Stephens, "SOM at Midlife," *Progressive Architecture*, 138–149 (May 1981).

Chicago Architects Design, Art Institute of Chicago, Chicago, Ill., and Rizzoli International Publications, Inc., New York, 1982.

S. Strauss, "Skidmore, Owings and Merrill," in A. Placzek, ed., *Macmillan Encyclopedia of Architects*, Vol. 4, The Free Press, New York, 1982, pp. 77–80.

Skidmore, Owings and Merrill, *Skidmore, Owings and Merrill Architecture and Urbanism 1973–1983*, Van Nostrand Reinhold Co., Inc., New York, 1983. With an introduction and regional prefaces by A. Bush-Brown.

R. G. Wilson, *The AIA Gold Medal*, McGraw-Hill Inc., New York, 1984.

F. C. Gretes, *Skidmore, Owings & Merrill, 1936–1983*, Vance Bibliographies, Monticello, Ill., 1984.

L. Craig, "Walter Netsch," in C. Ware, *Plan*, School of Architecture and Planning, Massachusetts Institute of Technology, Cambridge, Mass., Nov. 1986.

O. W. Grube, "Skidmore, Owings and Merrill," In V. M. Lampugnani, ed., *Encyclopedia of 20th Century Architecture*, Thames and Hudson, Ltd., London, and Harry N. Abrams, Inc., New York, 1986.

W. Blaser, ed., *Myron Goldsmith, Buildings and Concepts*, Rizzoli International Publications, Inc., New York, 1987. With an essay by A. Temko.

D. Billington and M. Goldsmith, eds., *Technique and Aesthetics in the Design of Tall Buildings*, (Fazlur Rahman Khan Memorial Session, American Society of Civil Engineers, Houston, Tex., 1983), Lehigh University, Bethlehem, Pa., 1988.

P. Goldberger, "What Pritzker Winners Tell Us About the Prize," *New York Times* (May 29, 1988).

Who's Who in America, 45th ed., Macmillan Directory Division, Marquis Who's Who, Wilmette, Ill., 1988.

C. Krinsky, *Gordon Bunshaft of Skidmore, Owings & Merrill*, The Architectural History Foundation, New York, and The MIT Press, Cambridge, Mass. and London, 1988. With a foreword by S. Anderson.

A. Dean, "Profile: SOM, a Legend in Transition," *Architecture* **78**, 2 (Feb. 1989).

Ralph Warburton, FAIA,
F.ASCE, AICP
University of Miami
Coral Gables, Florida

SKYSCRAPERS.   See Apartment Buildings—High Rise; Office Buildings.

SLOPING SITES.   See Site Development.

SOANE, SIR JOHN

John Soane, (1753–1837) one of the UK's most original and idiosyncratic architects, left an encyclopedic record of his life, architecture and taste in his famous London house at 13 Lincoln's Inn Fields. The extraordinary Soane Museum (Fig. 1), a pilgrimage site for contemporary architects, has come to represent this complex and difficult figure to the modern world. Yet Soane's long career created over 200 buildings, produced significant writings, published designs, left major collections of drawings and objects, and advanced the profession of architecture in ways that are only recently being uncovered. The man whose style John Summerson has called "one of the curiosities of European architecture" (1), has remained elusive in his

Figure 1. Photograph of the Soane Museum at 13 Lincoln's Inn Fields, London.

greatness. Was he classical or anticlassical, a man ahead of his time or centuries behind it?

Soane was born in 1753 at Goring-on-Thames, on the Oxfordshire–Berkshire border. The seventh child of the bricklayer John Soan, the young man determined to better his humble lot by becoming an architect, and throughout his life was driven by a fierce ambition. He was articled at 15 to George Dance, who would become not only a mentor but a kind of surrogate partner during Soane's formative years. After four years with Dance, he entered the Royal Academy, won the Gold Medal, and worked briefly for Henry Holland, before embarking for Italy on the Royal Academy Travelling Student fellowship in March of 1778. His two years on the grand tour, partially under the patronage of the Bishop of Derry, were marked by an intense absorption of the classical language of architecture and a sophisticated study of current neoclassical theory. Soane returned to Great Britain with a cache of travel sketches, a list of potential patrons met abroad, books such as Laugier's *Essai sur l'architecture* (1753) (2), and a group of designs made for academic *concours*. Moreover, the monuments of antiquity left an indelible impression on his consciousness, leading eventually to his substantial personal collection of architectural fragments. Soane owned 11 copies of the Abbé Laugier's famous book and was heavily influenced by its primitivism and call for a return to the first principles of trabeation (3).

Back in London, Soane had a difficult time getting started in practice. Without the immediate patronage of aristocrats, which such predecessors as Adam had achieved, he was forced to become a solid businessman, taking whatever small work he could find. Even the publication of two books of his designs, in 1778 and 1788 (4,5), and entry into such competitions as that for the Howardian prison in 1781 did not immediately establish his name as an architect. Only after 10 years of small residential jobs did he receive his first important commissions, the alterations for the third Earl of Hardwicke at Wimpole Hall, Cambridgeshire (1791–1794) and appointment as architect to the Bank of England for work in 1788 on the Bank Stock Office, which began construction in 1791.

These two works of the "middle period" mark Soane's first use of the spatial and decorative elements that would characterize his mature style, an almost revolutionary reinterpretation of classical vaulting and ornamental motifs. In the yellow drawing room at Wimpole, the architect experimented with a floating, illuminated vault, crowned by a great lantern. Surface decoration, in the manner of Holland and Dance, was in low relief, combining classical elements with little regard for traditional syntax. At the Stock Office, Soane made first use of the "pendentive dome," a continuously curved surface formed by four segmental arches over a square plan, again punctured by a lantern. He dispensed completely with overtly classical ornament, incising the plaster surface with minimal linear and plastic motifs, so as to emphasize the light, fabriclike quality of the vaulting. Although indebted to Dance, these breakthroughs had no real precedent in European design.

Soane's most fertile creative period, from 1792 to 1825, produced country houses, churches, and public works

marked by his distinctive distillation of the spatial, monumental, primitive, and decorative ideals of classicism. Tendering Hall, Suffolk (1784), and Tyringham, Buckinghamshire (1792), were his most elaborate essays in the villa-type country house. Each employed a rectangular two-story block, with bow-curved central sections, and utilized extraordinary manipulations in section for dramatic expression on the interior. He rebuilt Pitzhanger Manor, at Ealing near London, for his family in 1800, giving it the same museumlike quality that he put into the three Lincoln's Inn houses (1808, 1812, 1823), which he gradually recomposed into the building known today. His London "Commissioner's" churches, St. Peter's Walworth (1822), St. John's Bethnal Green (1826), and Holy Trinity Marylebone (1820) are all rather dry in comparison to his best works. Notwithstanding his continuing work on the bank offices, Soane was frustrated by his failure to build major public buildings—he designed elaborate projects for the Houses of Parliament (1824) and New Law Courts (1821) at Westminster. The former was shelved and the latter built to a revised Gothic design, which Soane disowned. His service as a government architect is today recalled by the rooms he remodeled at No. 10 Downing Street (1824–1826).

Soane's greatest building, the 3-acre Bank of England offices in the heart of the City of London at Threadneedle Street, took some 45 years of his career and cost an estimated £860,000 (6). Evoking the vaulted splendors of Roman baths, the various offices and courts Soane designed summed up his formal and ornamental innovations in the classical tradition. While the orders were used in key places, the arches and vaults comprised the major theme. The stark Rotunda (1794–1796) was a modern Pantheon, Lothbury Court (1797) was a reinterpretation of the Arch of Titus with a new composite order derived from the Temple of Vesta at Tivoli, and the Consuls Offices (1797) was a variation on vaulting themes established at the Stock Offices with a stunning series of floating caryatids ringing the lantern. Soane drew from many classical sources in the decoration, but always made ornament subservient to surface and volume. His strong alliance with antiquity was aptly conveyed by the fact that he portrayed his finished building as a ruin in a famous painting by J. M. Gandy in 1830. A century later, in one of London's most tragic losses, his monumental work was largely demolished to make way for Sir Herbert Baker's larger, taller building.

Another masterpiece, left in rubble by the blitz, but rebuilt after the war, Soane's Dulwich Picture Gallery (1811–1814) (Fig. 2) represents the architect in his purest and most abstract vein. This rather austere brick structure was built as hybrid of almshouses, a mausoleum, and a private museum to house 360 paintings from a royal collection. Using a linear, five-part plan, Soane created a series of top-lit, complex spaces that, while not strictly vaulted, were related to his experiments at the bank. Forced by costs to work only with volume and light, Soane created a building with the abstract force of a modern design, and one with a substantial legacy in this century.

As a teacher, collector, and leader in his profession, Soane's achievements were also considerable. He was

Figure 2. Dulwich Picture Gallery.

elected to the Royal Academy in 1802, and in 1806 became Professor of Architecture, giving a series of controversial lectures that established his theory (7). He served London and the crown as Surveyor to Westminster and Whitehall in the 1820s. His famous museum collection is crowned by such treasures as the Egyptian sarcophagus of Seti I, purchased for £2000 when the British Museum refused it in 1824, a vast trove of architectural fragments, drawings from sources as diverse as Robert Adam and the Renaissance Codex Coner, and the famous Hogarth paintings series, the "Rake's Progress," housed in a special room (8). Yet, despite his professional and monetary success, Soane was bitter and dour in his later years, having endured family strife occasioned by his wife's early death and a strained relationship with his two sons. He died at his home in London on January 20, 1837 and is buried under a pendentive dome, in the tomb he designed for himself and his wife in St. Pancras Gardens.

BIBLIOGRAPHY

1. J. Summerson, "Soane: The Man and the Style," in D. Dunster, ed., *John Soane*, Architectural Monographs Series, Academy Editions, London, 1983, p. 9.
2. M. A. Laugier, *Essai sur l'architecture*, Paris, 1755.
3. D. Watkin, "Soane and His Contemporaries," in Ref. 1, pp. 40–59.
4. J. Soane, *Designs in Architecture, Consisting of Plans, Elevations and Sections for Temples, Baths, Casinos, Pavilions, Garden-Seats, Obelisks, and Other Buildings*, J. Taylor & S. Gosnell, London, 1778.
5. J. Soane, *Plans, Elevations and Sections of Buildings Erected in the Counties of Norfolk, Suffolk, etc.*, Taylor, London, 1788.
6. H. R. Steele and F. R. Yerbury, *The Old Bank of England*, Ernest Benn Ltd., London, 1930.
7. A. T. Bolton, ed., *Lectures on Architecture by Sir John Soane, R.A.*, Jordan-Gaskell, London, 1929.
8. J. Summerson, *A New Description of Sir John Soane's Museum*, Trustees of Sir John Soane's Museum, London, 1955.

General References

Ref. 1 is a good general reference.
A. T. Bolton, *The Works of Sir John Soane, R.A.*, Trustees of Sir John Soane's Museum, London, 1924.
A. T. Bolton, *The Portrait of Sir John Soane, R.A. (1753–1837) Set Forth in Letters from His Friends (1775–1837)*, Butler & Tanner, London, 1927.
M. A. Laugier, *Observations sur l'architecture*, 1765.
P. du Prey, *John Soane: The Making of an Architect*, University of Chicago Press, Chicago, 1982.
J. Soane, *Designs for Public and Private Buildings, by John Soane*, Priestley, London, 1828.
D. Stroud, *Sir John Soane, Architect*, Faber & Faber, London, 1984.
J. Summerson, *Sir John Soane*, Art & Technics, London, 1952.

MARK HEWITT
Columbia University
New York, New York

SOILS ENGINEERING

SOIL CLASSIFICATION

For civil-engineering purposes, soil is defined as the residual or transported product of rock decay. Soil may be excavated without blasting and is penetrated in borings by ordinary soil-sampling equipment. Soil deposits are usually described in general terms according to the geological process involved in their formation. On this basis there are four principal categories plus secondary types whose characteristics are summarized in Table 1.

SOIL IDENTIFICATION

A complete engineering soil identification includes (1) the classification of constituents, (2) the description of appearance and structural characteristics, and (3) the determination of compactness or hardness in situ.

Field Classification. Constituent materials are identified visually by their gradation or plasticity characteristics.

1. *Coarse-grained Soils.* Coarse-grained soils, those with sand, gravel, or cobbles predominating, are classified according to grain size.
2. *Fine-grained Soils.* Fine-grained soils cannot be divided between silt and clay by visual identification of grain size, but are distinguishable by plasticity characteristics.

   • *Clays.* Clays exhibit a high degree of dry strength in a small cube allowed to dry, high toughness in a

Table 1. Soil Types and their Properties[a,b]

Division	Letter	Color	Soil Description	Value as a Foundation Material	Frost Action	Drainage
Gravel and gravelly soils	GW	Red	Well graded gravel, or gravel–sand mixture, little or no fines	Excellent	None	Excellent
	GP	Red	Poorly graded gravel, or gravel-sand mixtures, little or no fines	Good	None	Excellent
	GM	Yellow	Silty gravels, gravel-sand-silt mixtures	Good	Slight	Poor
	GC	Yellow	Clayey-gravels, gravel-clay-sand mixtures	Good	Slight	Poor
Sand and sandy soils	SW	Red	Well-graded sands, or gravelly sands, little or no fines	Good	None	Excellent
	SP	Red	Poorly graded sands, or gravelly sands, little or no fines	Fair	None	Excellent
	SM	Yellow	Silty sands, sand-silt mixtures	Fair	Slight	Fair
	SC	Yellow	Clayey sands, sand-clay mixtures	Fair	Medium	Poor
Silts and clays LL <50[c]	ML	Green	Inorganic silts, rock flour, silty or clayey fine sands, or clayey silts with slight plasticity	Fair	Very high	Poor
	CL	Green	Inorganic clays of low to medium plasticity, gravelly clays, silty clays, lean clays	Fair	Medium	Impervious
	OL	Green	Organic slit-clays of low plasticity	Poor	High	Impervious
Silts and clays LL >50[c]	MH	Blue	Inorganic silts, micaceous or diatomaceous fine sandy or silty soils, elastic silts	Poor	Very high	Poor
	CH	Blue	Inorganic clays of high plasticity, fat clays	Very poor	Medium	Impervious
	OH	Blue	Organic clays of medium to high plasticity, organic silts	Very poor	Medium	Impervious
Highly organic soils	Pt	Orange	Peat and other highly organic soils	Not suitable	Slight	Poor

[a] Ref. 1.
[b] Consult soil engineers and local building codes for allowable soil bearing capacities.
[c] LL indicates liquid limit.

thread rolled out at plastic limit, and exude little or no water from a small pat shaken in the hand.

- *Silts.* Silts have a low degree of dry strength and toughness and dilate rapidly on shaking so that water appears on the sample surface.

3. *Organic Soils.* Organic soils are characterized by dark colors, order of decomposition, spongy or fibrous texture, and visible particles of vegetal matter.

Appearance and Structure. Appearance and structure are best evaluated at the time of sampling. Frequently, however, it is not possible to give a detailed description of undisturbed samples in the field. Secondary structure in particular may not be recognized until an undisturbed sample has been examined and tested in the laboratory. On visual inspection, the following items should be noted:

1. Ordinary appearance, such as color; moisture conditions, whether dry, moist, or saturated; and visible presence of organic material.
2. Arrangement of constituent materials, whether

stratified, varved, or heterogenous; and typical dip and thickness of lenses or varves.

3. Secondary structure, such as fractures, fissures, slickensides, large voids, cementation, or precipitates in fissures or openings.
4. Condition of individual grains in coarse-grained soils, such as their angularity, cementation, surface coating, and hardness of particles.

Compactness or Hardness. Consistency in situ is estimated by measuring resistance to penetration of a selected penetrometer or sampling device. Ordinarily, this is the number of blows of a 140-lb hammer falling 30 in. required to drive a 2-in.-OD, 1-3/8-in.-ID split spoon sample 1 ft into undisturbed soil in a boring. The number of blows per foot thus obtained is known as the standard penetration resistance.

1. *Descriptive Terms.* Penetration resistance of coarse grained soils depends on both density and overburden pressure acting at depth samples so that terms of compactness rather than density are appropriate.
2. *Fine-grained Soils.* A pocket penetrometer calibrated to unconfined compressive strength is used to check the hardness of fine-grained soils.

3. *Routine Methods.* These methods do not provide precise values of soil consistency in situ, but they should be made routine in exploration work.

Unified Soil Classification System

Soils are classified in accordance with the Unified System and include the appropriate group symbol in soil descriptions. A soil is placed in one of 15 categories or as a borderline material combining two of these categories. Laboratory tests may be required for positive identification.

Sands and Gravels. Sands are divided from gravels on the No. 4 sieve size, gravels from cobbles on the 3-in. size. The division between fine and medium sands is at the No. 40 sieve, between medium and coarse sand at the No. 10 sieve.

Silts and Clays. Fine-grained soils are identified according to plasticity characteristics determined in Atterberg limit tests.

Organic Soils. Materials containing vegetal matter are characterized by relatively low specific gravity, high water content, high ignition loss, and high gas content. A decrease in liquid limit after oven-drying to a value less than three quarters of the original liquid limit is a definite indication of an organic soil.

EXPLORATION AND SAMPLING

Exploration Programs

Subsurface investigation has three phases; reconnaissance, preliminary exploration, and detailed exploration.

Reconnaissance. Reconnaissance includes a review of available topographic and geologic information, aerial photographs, data from previous investigations, and site examination. Geophysical methods are applicable in special cases. Reconnaissance establishes the number and locations or preliminary borings.

Preliminary Exploration. Preliminary exploration includes borings to recover samples suitable for identification tests only. Even if a more detailed program will follow, obtain samples and boring logs of such quality that results may be incorporated with the data from the final investigation.

Detailed Exploration. Based on the results of previous phases, detailed exploration generally includes recovery of undisturbed samples for structural properties tests and, in some cases, field tests and observations.

Test Borings

Selection of Boring Method. Choice of boring method depends on (1) the efficiency of the boring procedure in prospective materials, (2) ability to determine strata changes and material type, and (3) possible disturbance of materials to be sampled.

Specific Procedures

1. *Boring without Sampling.* When only depth to rock or existence of cavities are to be determined, borings may be made without sampling; the utility of boring for sampling is not important.
2. *Auger Borings.* These borings are used primarily for shallow exploration above groundwater. Although materials recovered are disturbed, auger borings furnish continuous samples of soils encountered.
3. *Wash Borings.* These borings are used for recovery of either disturbed dry samples or undisturbed samples. Ordinarily, this is the type most suitable for locations with difficult access.
4. *Rotary and Percussion Borings.* These borings are used for deep exploration or for penetration of hard soils or strata containing boulders and rock seams.
5. *Rotary Core Drilling.* This procedure is followed in bedrock to recover continuous core or to pass obstructions in overburden.

Requirements for Exploration Program

Layout of Test Borings. Rules for preliminary and final borings are presented here as general guides to planning and do not cover all the details necessary for specific sites or structures. Requirements for spacing of test borings are given below.

Preliminary Borings. For large sites, preliminary borings are located to furnish an overall subsoil survey rather than to follow a rigid geometric pattern.

Final Borings. Final borings are arranged so geological sections may be determined at the most useful orientations. Borings in slide areas should establish geological sections necessary for stability analyses. To ensure that exploration is adequate in its final form, boring logs are evaluated as received to develop a picture of subsoil conditions. Final borings are planned for a certain sequence; exploration contracts should be open-ended so intermediate borings may be added in areas that prove to be critical.

Spacing Requirements

1. *Uniform Conditions.* On large sites where subsurface conditions are relatively uniform, preliminary borings should be spaced 100–500 ft apart. Spacing is decreased in detailed exploration by intermediate borings as required to define variations in subsoil profile. Final spacing of 25 ft usually suffices for even erratic conditions.
2. *Cavities and Fractures.* Where factors such as cavities in limestone or fractures and joint zones in bedrock are being investigated, wash or rotary borings (without sample recovery) or soundings and probings are spaced as close as 10 ft center-to-center.
3. *Critical Strata.* Where detailed settlement, stability, or seepage analyses are required, a minimum of one boring should be included to obtain undisturbed samples of critical strata. Sufficient preliminary dry-sample borings should be provided to determine

the most representative location for undisturbed sample borings.

4. *Subsurface Irregularities.* Inclined borings are required in special cases when surface obstructions prevent use of vertical holes, or subsurface irregularities such as buried channels, cavities, or fault zones are to be investigated.

Depths of Test Borings. Required depths depend to some extent on sizes and types of proposed structures. They are controlled to a greater degree by the characteristics and sequence of subsurface strata.

Types of Strata. The depth of borings depends on the type of underlying strata.

1. *Unsuitable Foundation Strata.* All borings should be extended through unsuitable foundation strata, such as unconsolidated fill; peat; highly organic materials; soft, fine-grained soils; and loose, coarse-grained soils, to reach hard or compact materials of suitable bearing capacity.

2. *Fine-grained Strata.* Borings in potentially compressible fine-grained strata of great thickness should be extended to a depth where stress from superposed load is so small that corresponding consolidation will not significantly influence surface settlements.

3. *Compact Soils.* Where stiff or compact soils are encountered at shallow depths, boring(s) should be extended through this material to a depth where the presence of an underlying weaker strata cannot affect stability or settlement.

4. *Bedrock Surface.* If bedrock surface is to be determined and character and general location of rock are known, borings should be extended 5 ft into sound, unweathered rock. Where the character of the rock is unknown, or where boulders or irregularly weathered material overlie bedrock, you must core 10 ft into sound rock and include 20 ft of coring in one or two selected borings. In cavitated limestone, borings should be extended through strata suspected of containing solution channels.

Check Borings. During final exploration, at least one boring should extend well below the zone involved in the apparent stability, settlement, or seepage problem to make sure no unusual conditions exist at greater depth.

Securing Borings. Borings made in foundation areas that eventually will be excavated below groundwater, or where artesian pressures are encountered, must be plugged or grouted unless used for continuing water-level observations. In boreholes for groundwater observations, the casing should be placed in tight contact with the walls of the hole.

LABORATORY TESTS AND TEST PROCEDURES

Test Selection for Design

Index Properties Tests. Index properties are used to classify soils, to group soils in major strata, and to extra-polate results from a restricted number of structural properties tests to determine properties of other similar materials. Procedures for most index tests are standardized. Either representative dry samples or undisturbed samples are used. Tests are assigned after review of boring data and visual identification of samples recovered.

Structural Properties Tests. These tests must be planned for particular design problems. Rigid standardization of test procedures is inappropriate. Tests should be performed only on undisturbed samples obtained as specified in the section on Exploration and Sampling or on compacted specimens prepared by standard procedures. In certain cases, completely remolded samples are used to estimate the effect of disturbance. Tests should be planned to determine typical properties of major strata rather than arbitrarily distributing tests in proportion to the number of undisturbed samples obtained. A limited number of high quality tests on carefully selected undisturbed samples is preferred to many mediocre tests on specimens selected at random.

Compacted Sample Tests. In prospecting for borrow materials, index tests or tests specifically for compacted samples may be required in a number proportional to the volume of borrow involved or the number of samples obtained. Structural properties tests are assigned after borrow materials have been grouped in major categories. Samples for test should be selected that represent the main soil groups and probable compacted condition.

Typical Test Properties. Various correlations between index and structural properties are available, showing the probable range of test values and relation of parameters. In testing for structural properties, correlations should be investigated to extend results to similar soils for which index values only are available. Correlations are of varying quality, expressed by standard deviation, which is the range above and below the average trend, within which about two thirds of all values occur. These relationships are useful in preliminary analyses, but they must not supplant careful tests of structural properties. The relationships should never be applied in final analyses without verification by tests of the particular material concerned.

FIELD TESTS AND MEASUREMENTS

Utilization

Observations include measurement of vertical or horizontal movement, groundwater, or soil pressures for these purposes: to determine conditions existing at the start of construction for use in design, to control construction procedures or rate of construction, and to predict the performance of the completed structure.

Vertical Movement

Observations of surface and subsurface settlement must be made.

Surface Settlement. Observation points must be protected against damage from construction activities or from frost heave. Reference bench marks must be provided on materials known to be incompressible, on rigidly supported structures, or on pile or pipe driven to refusal.

1. *Observation Points.* Suitable settlement observation points within structures must be provided. These points should be established as soon as practicable during construction.
2. *Measuring Elevations.* In most cases, measurement of elevations to 0.01 ft is sufficiently accurate.

Subsurface Settlement. Measurements are made of the settlement at the base of fill or at points within compressible strata. These observations are used in construction of earth dams, for fills over sand drains, or to evaluate heave of foundation excavation.

1. *Settlement Plate.* A settlement plate should be placed with the riser pipe attached at the base of fill.
2. *Probes.* Probes should be driven into the subsoil to measure foundation movement or the probe should be pushed below the bottom of the test boring.
3. *Crossbars.* For important earth dams, a string of telescoping pipes with crossbars attached at vertical intervals in the fill should be placed as it is constructed. Movement of crossbars should be measured by a special torpedo device lowered into the pipe. The procedure in Ref. 2 should be used.

Horizontal Movement

Measurements of horizontal movement are made in connection with stability problems.

Soft Foundations. To control the rate of filling on soft foundations, T-stakes are placed near the embankment toe and horizontal movement is observed.

Slide Areas. A slope indicator should be installed in active or potential slide areas to determine failure plane location and speed of shear. Shear strain observed in failure zone is compared with shear strain in a laboratory triaxial test to estimate strength mobilized in situ.

Earth Dams. For important earth dams, vertical plates in the fill should be connected with the telescoping pipe system to observe horizontal strains. The procedure in Ref. 3 should be used.

TOTAL PRESSURES

Total measurements are made to determine total pressures.

Pressure Cells. Combined earth and water pressures are measured with pancake cells having strain gages attached to an interior flexible diaphragm. Their installation and operation involves technical problems requiring specialized assistance. See Ref. 4 for a description of pressure cells and interpretation of observations.

Indirect Measurements. Pressures on flexible wall are determined indirectly by measuring strain in sheeting or bracing system. Devices used include electrical strain gauges and accurate mechanical gauges. Their use involves technical problems requiring specialized assistance.

Ground Water Pressures

Pressures may be encountered in the following conditions: (1) hydrostatic state with insignificant seepage, (2) a flow field of steep gradients, possibly with perched or depressed water levels, and (3) as hydrostatic excess pore pressures built up in materials of low permeability by volume change under load.

Hydrostatic Conditions. Few refinements are required in measuring techniques for hydrostatic conditions. Water levels in test borings are observed to allow sufficient time for water to reach an equilibrium position. In material of low permeability, the equilibrium level is determined by raising or lowering water in the borehole until no tendency for movement to equilibrium is observed.

Seepage Conditions. Where piezometric head varies greatly on a vertical line because of seepage, ordinary open borings or observation wells uncased for their entire length may be unsuitable for measurement. Water pressures in the stratum of greatest permeability, which delivers the largest flow to the hole, will dominate the observations. Porous tube or well-point piezometers should be used. For materials and installation of porous tube piezometers, see Ref. 5. The intake point of the piezometer must be sealed from contact with upper water levels to isolate observation to a specific point in the flow field.

Hydrostatic Excess Pressures. For rapid response to pore pressure changes, the required flow of water into the piezometer is minimized by providing a large intake point and small diameter standpipe. Porous tube piezometers are sensitive enough to follow pressure changes in many clays with insignificant time lag.

1. *High Pore Pressure.* To observe high pore pressure, a Bourdon gauge is attached near the top of the standpipe with a vent for bleeding air or gas above gauge.
2. *Measurements.* To avoid inaccurate measurements caused by gas pressures on inorganic soil, piezometer seamless and jointless plastic standpipe with ID no less than 3/8 in is used. Metals should not be used in the piezometer point. The water level in the borehole or in the piezometer must not fall below pore pressures in soil surrounding the piezometer point.
3. *Special Installations.* For special piezometer installations within high earth dams, see Ref. 6.

SETTLEMENT ANALYSIS

Settlement analysis concerns (1) settlement produced by volume change during consolidation, (2) criteria for tolerable settlement, and (3) methods of reducing or accelerating consolidation. Procedures described apply to compressible fine-grained strata subjected to leads of wide extent.

For foundations on clay and silt, it is essential to make a reliable estimate of the probable differential settlement to determine if the design contemplated is satisfactory. If differential settlement will be excessive, alter the proposed foundation type or take measures to reduce settlements.

Superposed loads develop pore pressures in compressible strata exceeding the original hydrostatic pressures. As pore-pressure gradients force water from a compressible stratum its volume decreases, causing settlement.

Analysis of Stress Conditions

Preconsolidation. Stresses exceeding the present effective vertical pressure of overburden produce preconsolidation (1) by the weight of material that existed above the present ground surface and that has been removed by erosion or excavation, (2) by capillary stresses from desiccation, and (3) by lower groundwater levels at some time in the past.

Underconsolidation. Compressible strata may be incompletely consolidated under existing loads as a result of recent lowering of groundwater or recent addition of fills or structural loads. Residual hydrostatic excess pore pressure existing in the compressible stratum will dissipate with time, causing future settlements.

Evaluation of Existing Conditions. Consolidation condition at the start of construction is determined by the following steps:

1. Review the data available on site history and geology to estimate probable preconsolidation or underconsolidation.
2. Compare the profile of preconsolidation stress determined from laboratory consolidation tests with the profile of effective overburden pressures.
3. Estimate preconsolidation from the S/Pc ratio using laboratory shear strength, and check by the approximate relationship with the liquidity index.
4. If underconsolidation is indicated, install piezometers to measure the magnitude of hydrostatic excess pore water pressures.

Computation of Added Stresses. In general, the elastic solutions are used to determine the vertical stress increment from applied loads. On vertical lines beneath selected points in the loaded area, profiles of estimated preconsolidation, effective overburden stress, and the increment of applied stress are plotted. For rigid boxes, piers, or silos, formulas for stress distribution beneath rigid structures are applied. Lowering of groundwater during construction or regional drawdown reduces water pressures at the boundaries of the compressible stratum and initiates consolidation. Stress applied by drawdown equals the reduction in buoyancy of overburden corresponding to decrease in boundary water pressure. In developed locations, settlement of surrounding areas from

drawdown must be carefully evaluated before undertaking dewatering or well pumping.

Settlement Computation

Total Settlement. If preconsolidation stress is determined reliably, total settlement may be predicted with reasonable accuracy. The percentage error is greatest for settlement from recompression only. In this case, an overestimate of several hundred percent may result unless high quality, undisturbed samples are used for consolidation tests.

Typical Loading Cycle. Foundation excavation causes swell. Application of a structural load recompresses subsoil and may extend consolidation into a virgin compression range. Stress changes are plotted on a semilogarithmic pressure-void ratio e-p curve.

Pressure-Void Ratio Diagram. The appropriate e-p curve to represent average properties of compressible stratum from consolidation tests must be determined. The e-p curve is drawn to conform to these straight lines. Depending on variability of material, more than one e-p curve representing different sections of the stratum may be required.

Settlement Magnitude. The settlement magnitude is computed from the change in void ratio corresponding to the change in stress from initial to final conditions, obtained from the e-p curve. A laboratory e-p curve includes an amount of secondary compression that depends on duration of test loads. Secondary compression continues exponentially with time without definite termination. Thus, total or ultimate settlement includes secondary compression to a specific time following completion of primary consolidation.

Differential Settlement. For an important structure, total settlement must be computed at a sufficient number of points to establish the overall settlement pattern. From this pattern, the maximum slope of the settlement profile or the greatest difference in settlement between adjacent foundation units is determined.

Effect of Structure Rigidity. Computed differential settlement is less accurate than computed total or average settlement because of the influence of the structure rigidity in redistributing loads on the foundation. A rigorous analysis of the effect of rigidity on settlement is generally not practicable. The rigidity of an ordinary multistory building frame reduces center settlement by about 6–12% of the computed value for flexible loading and increases edge settlement by about 4–8% of the computed flexible value.

Tolerable Settlement of Structures. Except where a structure is connected to a supported utility or adjacent building, differential settlement within the structure, rather than total settlement, causes damage.

Structural Criteria. Where maximum differential settlements are expected to approach tolerable values, the designer should consider their effect on stresses in the structural frame.

Reduction of Differential Settlement Effects. For methods of reducing or accelerating consolidation settlements, see Methods of Reducing or Accelerating Settlements. Settlement that can be completed during the early stages of construction, before placing sensitive finishes, generally will not contribute to structural distress. In buildings with light frames where large differential settlements will not harm the frame, special provisions should be made to avoid damage to utilities or operating equipment. Sensitive equipment, such as motor-generator sets within the structure, should be isolated on separate rigidly supported foundations. Flexible couplings should be provided for utility lines at critical locations.

Time Rate of Settlement

Applications. Settlement time rate must be determined for foundation treatment involving acceleration of either consolidation or preconsolidation before placing the final structure. Knowledge of settlement rate or percent consolidation completed at a particular time is important in planning remedial measures on a structure damaged by settlement.

Primary Consolidation. Where pore water drainage is essentially vertical, the ordinary theory of consolidation defines time rate of settlement. Using the coefficient of consolidation, cv, percent consolidation completed at specific elapsed times by time factor Tv curves is computed.

Secondary Compression. *Settlement Computation.* Settlement is computed from secondary compression following primary consolidation as follows:

$$\Delta \, Hsec = Cx \, (Ht) \log \frac{tsec}{tp}$$

where   Hsec = settlement from secondary compression
Cx = coefficient of secondary compression
Ht = initial thickness of compressible stratum
tsec = useful life of structure or time for which settlement is significant.
tp = time to completion of primary consolidation

Combining Secondary and Primary Consolidation. If secondary compression is important, compute the settlement from primary consolidation separately, using an e-p curve that includes only compression from primary consolidation. A semilogarithmic straight line for the time-rate of secondary compression is made tangent to the final portion of the time curve for primary consolidation.

Methods of Reducing or Accelerating Settlements

Methods of minimizing consolidation settlements include two general procedures: (1) removal or displacement of compressible material and (2) preconsolidation in advance of final construction.

STABILITY ANALYSES

Overstressing a slope or foundation stratum may cause sudden failure with rapid displacement or gradual shear strain damaging structures or improvements. The possibility of movement is evaluated by comparing forces resisting failure to those causing failure. This ratio is the safety factor. Stability is also considered in determination of wall pressures where the triangular active wedge in the backfill is subject to failure.

Varieties of Failure

Form of Movement. Principal modes of failure are rotation on curved surface approximated by a circular arc, translation on a planar surface whose length is large compared to depth below ground, and displacement of wedge-shaped mass adjacent to yielding vertical surface.

Causes of Movement. Failure follows changes in shear stress or shear strength that lead to unbalanced driving forces.
Natural Slopes. Unbalance of forces may be caused by a change in slope profile that adds driving weight at the top of a slide or decreases resisting force at its base; an increase of groundwater pressure, resulting in a decrease of friction resistance in cohesionless soil or swell in cohesive material; or time-conditioned decrease in shear strength due to weathering, leaching, mineralogic changes, opening and softening of fissures, or continuing gradual shear strain.
Foundations for Embankments or Structures. Failure may be caused by an increase in applied load without a comparable increase in foundation shear strength or a decrease in foundation shear strength by rise of piezometric levels, opening of fissures, or continuing shear strain.

Effect of Soil Type. Differences in stability of coarse- and fine-grained soils are caused primarily by the influence of pore pressure on strength. Shear strength cannot increase under load application unless effective stresses in the grain skeleton increase. This stress transfer occurs rapidly in previous coarse-grained soils but may be long delayed in impervious clays.

Analysis Methods

Effective Stress Method. Strength parameters c' and Φ' determined from effective stress-test envelope or c and Φ from CU tests are used. Pore pressures resulting from seepage and consolidation should be estimated and applied as boundary pressures normal to potential failure surface. Effective stress analysis is used in the following situations:

1. For long-term stability and drawdown in pervious, incompressible, coarse-grained soils, use Φ', usually neglecting c'. Apply pore pressures from groundwater or seepage only.
2. For dense, moderately compressible soil, such as an earth dam embankment, use c' and Φ'. Apply only seepage or drawdown or consolidation pore pressures if piezometers are installed to confirm pore pressures assumed in design.
3. For compressible soils where some drainage occurs during load application, use c and Φ from CU tests.

Apply groundwater plus consolidation pore pressures, including an allowance for dissipation of hydrostatic excess pressures.

Total Stress Method. Shear strength determined from undrained laboratory tests or from vane shear tests should be used. Φ is taken equal to zero. These strengths represent initial conditions without considering drainage of pore water during stress changes. Total stress analysis is used for the following applications:

1. Failures in slopes of normally consolidated or slightly preconsolidated clays, where little dissipation of hydrostatic excess pore pressures occurs before critical stability conditions.
2. Analysis of embankment or structure load applied rapidly on a clay stratum where no provision is made to drain pore water.

Procedures.

Rotational Failure, General Method. For details of slip-circle analysis with movement on a surface approximately by a circular arc, use procedures described in Ref. 7.

Embankments on Soft Clay. The probable form of failure is determined from the relationship of berm and embankment widths and foundation thickness.

Required Safety Factor. The following values should be provided for reasonable assurance of stability:

1. Safety factor no less than 1.5 for permanent or sustained loading conditions.
2. For foundations of structures, a safety factor exceeding 2.0 is desirable to limit movements necessary for strength mobilization or local plastic strains at foundation edge.
3. For temporary loading conditions or where stability reaches a minimum during construction, safety factors may be reduced to 1.3 or 1.25 if controls are maintained on load application.
4. For transient loads, such as earthquake, safety factors as low as 1.2 or 1.15 may be tolerated.

BIBLIOGRAPHY

1. R. T. Packard, *Ramsey/Sleeper Architectural Graphic Standards,* John Wiley & Sons, New York, 1982, p.126.
2. *Earth Manual,* USBR, Method E-29.
3. Ref. 1, Method E-30.
4. D. W. Taylor, *Pressure Distribution Studies on Soils,* Soil Mechanics Fact Finding Study Progress Report, Department of the Army, Corps of Engineers, Waterways Experiment Station, Vicksburg, Miss.
5. Ref. 1, Method E-28.
6. Ref. 1, Method E-27.
7. K. Terzaghi and R. B. Peck, *Soil Mechanics in Engineering Practice,* 2nd ed., John Wiley & Sons, New York, 1967.

General References

D. D. Barkan, *Dynamics of Bases and Foundations* (transl. from Russian), McGraw-Hill, New York, 1962.

D. M. Burmister, *Stress and Displacement Characteristics of a Two-Layer Rigid Base Soil System: Influence Diagrams and Practical Applications,* Proceedings, Highway Research Board, 1956, Highway Research Board, Washington, D. C.

Foundations Subject to Vibratory Loads, U.S. Army Office Chief of Engineers, EM 1110-345-310.

Handbook of Drainage and Construction Products, Armco Drainage and Metal Products, Inc., Middletown, Ohio.

M. Hetenyi, *Beams on Elastic Foundation,* University of Michigan Press, Ann Arbor, Mich.

M. J. Hvorslev, *Subsurface Exploration and Sampling of Soils for Civil Engineering Purposes,* Department of the Army, Corps of Engineers, Waterways Experiment Station, Vicksburg, Miss.

J. C. Jaeger and N.G.W. Cook, *Fundamentals of Rock Mechanics,* Methuen, London, 1969.

M. S. Ketchum, *The Design of Walls, Bins and Grain Elevators,* Engineering News Publishing Co., New York.

M. R. Mehta and A. S. Veletsos, *Stresses and Displacements in Layered Systems,* Structural Research Series No. 178, University of Illinois, Urbana.

L. Obert, W. I. Duvall, and R. H. Merrill, *Design of Underground Openings in Competent Rock,* Bulletin 587, U.S. Bureau of Mines.

Soil Mechanics Design, Seepage Control, Engineering Manual, Civil Works Construction, Department of the Army, Corps of Engineers chapt. 1, Part CXIX.

K. G. Stagg, and O. C. Zienkiewicz, *Rock Mechanics in Engineering Practice,* John Wiley & Sons Ltd., London, 1968.

D. W. Taylor, *Pressure Distribution Studies on Soils,* Soil Mechanics Fact Finding Study Progress Report, Department of the Army, Corps of Engineers, Waterways Experiment Station, Vicksburg, Miss.

K. Terzaghi, *Theoretical Soil Mechanics,* John Wiley & Sons, Inc., New York, 1943.

K. Terzaghi, *Rock Defects and Loads on Tunnel Supports, Section 1 of Rock Tunnelling with Steel Supports,* The Commercial Shearing and Stamping Co., Youngstown, Ohio.

C. Van der Veen and L. Boersma, *The Bearing Capacity of a Pile Pre-Determined by a Cone Penetration Test,* Proceedings, Fourth International Conference on Soil Mechanics and Foundation Engineering, Butterworths Scientific Publications, London.

HARCHARAN S. GILL
Trow Dames & Moore
Brampton, Ontario, Canada

SOLAR AND ENERGY EFFICIENT DESIGN

We must begin by taking note of the countries and climates in which homes are to be built if our designs for them are to be correct. One type of house seems appropriate for Egypt, another for Spain . . . and so on with lands and countries of varying characteristics. This is because one part of the Earth is directly under the sun's course, another is far away from it, while another lies midway between these two. . . . It is obvious that designs for homes ought to conform to diversities of climate.

The principles of solar and energy-efficient buildings begin with this observation by Vitruvius (1). In response to the context of climate and sun, such buildings provide comfort and shelter with minimal reliance on fossil fuels and electrical energy. Solar designs rely on the energy provided by the sun for space heating, hot water, or photovoltaic electrical generation. Energy-efficient designs are those that use a wide range of design strategies to provide comfort with minimal use of fossil fuel energy. Energy is saved by a building design in two ways: by requiring less conventional energy to operate than a similar nonenergy-efficient design or by using renewable, site-available energy sources. Design strategies to achieve these goals vary from location to location as latitude, climate, and site characteristics vary. Appropriate strategies will also vary significantly between building types. Buildings that are thermally impacted by the outside climate are termed "skin load dominated." Little heat is generated inside such buildings and the building skin or envelope therefore acts as a mediator between the climate and the building occupants. Design strategies for skin load dominated buildings include site scale decisions such as location and orientation as well as thermal mediation by building form, massing, envelope, and component design. "Internally load dominated" buildings tend to be larger buildings thermally dominated by the heat generated inside the building rather than the climate outside the building skin. Design strategies for energy efficiency emphasize reduction of internal heat sources, such as lighting, and efficient mechanical systems.

Nonenergy-efficient, nonsolar building designs can, at a cost, provide comfort to building occupants while denying or ignoring the basic relationship between location, shelter, and occupant. The cost of this approach is manifested most directly in high energy bills throughout the life of the building. The buildings sector in the United States consumes approximately 40% of the total energy used, amounting to $176 billion in energy costs in 1985, or 4.4% of the GNP (2). Energy used in building operation also carries significant indirect costs for both the occupant and society at large. Supplying the required fossil fuels and electricity can produce serious environmental degradation in the form of strip mining, acid rain, radioactive waste, offshore oil spills, and potential climatic changes from the "greenhouse effect." These costs are borne by society as a whole rather than by the building developer or occupant. In addition, the design that denies the relationship of occupant and building to location and climate will also ignore qualities of habitation related to thermal experience. Ralph Knowles points out that "rhythm is recognized in all natural processes . . . when we cannot feel natural tempos, we lose contact with a basis of our perceptions" (3). Solar and energy-efficient designs can, by virtue of responding to the natural thermal environment, connect the occupant to the rhythms of the environment. Rather than producing a thermally neutral world, solar and energy-efficient designs have the potential to create thermal environments that play profound roles in the lives of the building occupants, providing rhythm, sensuality, and cultural and symbolic expressions.

ENERGY USE IN BUILDINGS

Solar and energy-efficient designs, by definition, address the quantity of energy consumed by buildings. This is an issue that appears and disappears from public debate, depending on the current and perceived costs of fossil fuels and nuclear energy. However, the decisions made by the architect at one point in time will affect the cost of building operation through many cycles of energy demand, availability, and cost. During the period of inexpensive energy in the 1950s and 1960s, energy use in U.S. buildings increased more than 5% per year, tripling building sector energy use in the United States between 1950 and 1973 (4). These buildings will still exist into the next century and continue to require energy in complete disregard of the costs or availability of fuel and electricity. In addition, it is estimated that 80% of the U.S. buildings occupied in 1980 will still be in use in the year 2000. The United States will be paying the price of design decisions made today through the life of the buildings, for the next 50–100 years. In industrial countries, energy use by buildings is approximately one-third of the total energy use. In 1978, for example, building sector energy consumption varied from 21% of the total energy use in Japan to 39% of the total in the FRG (5). Developing countries still spend less than 10% of their total energy on buildings, but the provision of better living conditions coupled with an increase in western-style buildings will begin to shift this percentage. In the United States alone, solar and energy-efficient designs could reduce this demand for energy in the building sector by $50–100 billion per year (2).

How Buildings Use Energy

Buildings consume energy in all phases of their existence: construction, operation, and demolition. Energy used in building construction is approximately 5% of total U.S. energy consumption, with most of the construction energy in the manufacture of building materials and components. This "embodied energy" varies with building type; construction of office buildings, hospitals, laboratories, and libraries requires two to three times the embodied energy required for residential single-family and multifamily buildings. The remaining energy in building construction, approximately 30%, is used in transportation of materials and machinery, administration, and direct fuel purchases for construction processes (6). Energy consumed in building operation provides thermal comfort to occupants via space conditioning, supplies, hot water, lighting, refrigeration, and electricity to run machines and appliances. The energy required for these tasks depends on the building design and climate, as well as on the comfort standards of the occupants, the efficiency of the lighting and mechanical systems, machines and appliances, and the cost of energy determined by governmental policies and the international economy. Demands for energy in building operation therefore vary significantly from country to country. For example, in 1978 the building sector in Japan used one-quarter of the per capita energy consumed in the U.S. building sector (5). Energy consumed in building demolition is, again, less than that required by building operation. However, because 70% of the energy in building construction is embodied in the materials of the building, design for reuse of the building without demolition or recycling of materials offers potential energy conservation.

Types of Energy Used in Building Operation

The true impact of building energy consumption is not revealed by the Btus or the watts of energy consumed during the life of the building. Energy can be characterized by "quality" related to the terminal process temperatures. Low grade energy demands are those that require low temperature energy sources (such as space heating) that can be provided by a large range of energy sources (solar radiation, wood, coal, gas, oil, etc). Electricity is a very high grade energy source that is generally produced through the use of a large quantity of lower grade fuel. Approximately two-thirds of the lower grade energy used to produce electricity is lost in waste heat, making electricity an energy-intensive source for building operation. In spite of this, demand for electricity is expected to rise twice as fast as demand for other energy sources. Designers of solar and energy-efficient buildings need to look carefully at the issue of the quality of energy source related to the end use. The more closely matched the task and the source, and the less energy lost in production and delivery, the more energy conserving the building design. Strategies to reduce electrical consumption are an important addition to solar and energy-efficient designs. Approximately 20% of all electricity produced in the United States is used to provide lighting in buildings. The use of daylight for illumination, the use of nonelectric fuels for low grade tasks such as space heating and water heating, and the use of natural ventilation to replace air-conditioning during transitional seasons will reduce electrical demands in building operation.

HISTORY OF SOLAR AND ENERGY-EFFICIENT DESIGN

The desire for shelter from thermal stresses has contributed to building designs that modify climate for thermal comfort. Extremes of arid heat and cold have been met with thermal enclaves such as the igloo, the underground houses of Tunisia, and the thick adobe pueblos of the southwest United States. In contrast, loosely woven thatch and bamboo have exposed the inhabitants of the tropics to whatever breezes may be available in the humid heat. Pace of life, daily schedules, and social rituals have aided the architecture in mediating climate. Occupants of temperate climates in particular have faced the annual cycles of cold winters and hot summers. In the Mediterranean, houses were designed to admit the sun and block cold winds in the winter months while providing shade and cross-ventilation in the summer, accommodating the stresses of both seasons in one design. In contrast, the Japanese have traditionally chosen to accommodate the heat of the summer with lightweight, open buildings that remain cold and drafty in the bitter winter months. Rather than heating the building, the culture has chosen to heat only the person with hot baths and the *kotatsu*, a portable burner of coals. The development of solar and energy-efficient buildings has rested most importantly on

cultural, political, and economic contexts as well as on development of relevant technologies and building materials.

Solar Heating

The Greek cities of Olynthus and Priene were planned so that each house was made comfortable by a courtyard facing south to catch the winter sun. This is one of the earliest documented solar designs, developed at a civic scale to benefit occupants of individual buildings. Somewhat later, the Romans developed the technology of hypocast floor heating systems, which enabled them to build without reference to the sun for heat. In a situation that presaged the events of the late twentieth century, these systems were remarkably energy intensive and could consume more than two cords of wood per day in heating one house. Rome's fuels supplies were soon depleted. Turning to the precedent of the Greek courtyard designs, the Romans substituted available solar radiation for wood to heat their homes. The expansion of the Roman empire developed these early solar designs for a range of climates, applied the technology to public buildings as well as residences, and used solar energy in agricultural greenhouses. In the second century A.D. a building's access to solar radiation was ruled inviolate and this ruling was codified in the Justinian Code of Law in the sixth century A.D. The Roman technology of solar heating and the legal status of solar rights were lost during the Middle Ages. In particular, solar greenhouses were denounced by the church, which saw in the act of growing plants out of season a "demonic tampering with the divine plan" (7). As empirical science challenged the control of the church in the sixteenth century, solar technology was rediscovered. Scientific applications of solar design techniques took place in the field of horticulture rather than architecture through the eighteenth century.

Comfort via Machines

In the west, the concept of comfort in buildings grew within the scientific paradigm of the Enlightenment and addressed medical issues more readily than issues of comfort. By the nineteenth century, the gas lighting and air pollution of the industrial revolution produced conditions within buildings that were acknowledged to be extremely unhealthy. Fresh air became an issue not only of comfort but of health. In the effort to provide ventilation to the building interior, the building was for the first time understood as a bubble of warmed air. Health and associated personal comfort became something achievable with machines and technology. Once machinery and science were understood to provide thermal comfort, the development of heating systems, air-conditioning, fluorescent lighting, and the like followed as quickly as the technical problems could be overcome. The paradigm of the building as a container of conditioned air was perfectly matched to the availability of cheap energy and the trust in technological solutions that characterized the twentieth century in the industrialized world. The exterior climate, available daylight, the building skin as climatic mediator, and even the specific task to be illuminated or conditioned became issues largely irrelevant to architectural design. Corbusier's "house as a machine for living" was, in fact, a building separated from thermal responsibilities by a dependence on hidden machines and off-site energies. "Machines to maintain our thermal comfort were conceived of as mechanical servants, providing for our every need while, like an English butler, remaining as unobtrusive as possible" (8).

The last 200 years in architecture have been characterized as a movement from local, renewable energy sources to imported, nonrenewable sources; from labor-intensive to energy-intensive practices within buildings; and from energy awareness to unconscious energy use, which was largely complete in the industrialized world by the late 1960s. The 1973 oil embargo by the Organization of Petroleum Exporting Countries (OPEC) forced a review of this paradigm of building technology. More efficient machines for heating, cooling, and lighting buildings were called for and were developed. More important, the design of the "container" itself was also questioned. Earlier work on European community planning for solar access in the 1920s, George Keck's solar houses of the 1930s, and the *House Beautiful* articles of the 1940s all identified many solar strategies for residential designs. Because many homes were heated with fuel oil, the dramatic increase in oil prices prompted a concentration of building research in residential solar heating and conservation. Residential cooling and reduced energy consumption in nonresidential buildings are technically more complicated and less directly impacted by oil prices. These issues were addressed by researchers, architects, engineers, and builders primarily in the 1980s after much work in solar heating had been completed.

Codes and Standards

Worldwide, technical knowledge and design abilities have grown substantially since the mid-1970s. Much of the current understanding has developed from experimentation with actual building designs as well as from the increasing ability to simulate building thermal behavior with tests cells and computer software. Following the lead of builders and researchers, building codes and standards on the national, state, and local levels have consolidated and codified the new methods of designing energy-efficient buildings. In most countries these codes and standards follow the available information with a significant lag time, subject to the vicissitudes of national politics, fuel prices, and trade balances. Most energy standards of the 1980s are not significantly more rigorous than standard good building practice and do not deliver the energy savings proved to be attainable with good energy-efficient design.

United States Standards. In the United States, the federal government has been looking at national energy standards for a number of years. Late in 1979, the U.S. Department of Energy proposed Building Energy Performance Standards (BEPS), whole building energy budgets for 16 building types in 78 metropolitan areas. The American Society of Heating, Refrigerating, and Air-Conditioning Engineers (ASHRAE) Standard 90 is the other recognized national building energy standard. Since the early 1980s, work on BEPS has largely been folded into this ASHRAE Standard; the newest ASHRAE Standard 90.1P

has incorporated the performance-based approach of BEPS as one of three different methods of demonstrating energy compliance. The standard allows an architect to follow a prescriptive set of building components, meet a prescribed set of system performance criteria, or demonstrate that the annual whole building energy cost is less than or equal to that of a reference building. As design flexibility increases from the prescribed components method to the annual energy cost calculation, so does the complexity of analysis required of the architect or engineer. In accommodating energy design strategies such as daylighting, thermal storage, and passive cooling, the annual energy cost analysis requires the use of computer software that can simulate the performance of these design options. ASHRAE 90 has been adopted by the Building Officials and Code Administrators International (BOCA) and is therefore used by many states and municipalities in the United States. Many states and municipalities also have adopted energy codes written specifically for their regional climate conditions and construction practices, which take precedence over national standards.

Solar access and daylight access codes are another approach to developing more energy-efficient neighborhoods and cities. Zoning codes that protect a property owner's access to solar radiation have been adopted by individual communities throughout the United States since 1973. These codes protect an individual's investment in a house design or solar equipment that depends on receiving solar radiation to heat the house or provide hot water. They will also protect access to the sun for photovoltaics, which convert solar radiation to electrical energy. Daylight access codes have been adopted by the city of New York for midtown Manhattan and by the city of San Francisco. Such codes require new high-rise buildings to allow sun into the streets and parks and to maintain the access to daylight shared by surrounding buildings (Fig. 1).

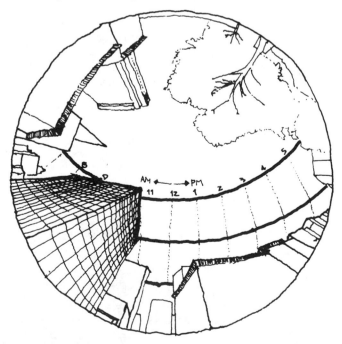

Figure 1. Illustration of Portsmouth Square in San Francisco showing the impact of a proposed building on solar access (9). Courtesy of Peter Bosselman.

DESIGN STRATEGIES FOR SOLAR AND ENERGY-EFFICIENT BUILDINGS

Buildings do not necessarily save energy because the architect and engineer are well intentioned. The last 80 years of architecture demonstrate a profound schism between formal and technical concerns, a loss of the intuitive understanding and traditional ways of building that connected the building with the thermal environment. Since 1973, work in energy and buildings has attempted to rebuild design capabilities through analysis of thermal behavior and whole building performance. The information made available to architects, engineers, and builders is in the form of analysis and evaluation techniques, design guidelines, and case studies of whole buildings. These need to be understood within a conceptual framework of the building, the occupant, and thermal behavior.

One model of the relationship between the building and energy describes the buildings as a shell that intercedes between a person and the exterior environment. Occupants have specific requirements for thermal and luminous conditions related to building use. In addition, both occupants and equipment generate heat that impacts the thermal environment of the building interior. Outside the building, the climate is a dynamic thermal environment, changing from day to night as well as seasonally. To minimize the use of energy within any building, the energy resources in this system should be matched with the energy requirements of the occupants. To do so, the designer must understand the characteristics of both the interior and exterior thermal conditions unique to that program and site.

The Exterior Climate

Climatic factors that affect thermal behavior of buildings are temperature, relative humidity, solar radiation, air movement, and availability of daylight. Much of this information is available for major cities worldwide. Many countries have published detailed data from their own meteorological stations. In the United States, the National Oceanic and Atmosphere Administration (NOAA)

publishes climatological data for many cities and the National Bureau of Standards (NBS) publishes solar radiation data. Designers looking for information will also find relevant climate data published in many of the standard solar design sources in the bibliography.

To design a building in response to a table of annual temperatures or a chart of sun angles is virtually impossible. Analysis of the climate data that reveals patterns of thermal comfort and site energy sources is critical. Plotting annual climate data on a bioclimatic or psychrometric chart will identify diurnal and seasonal periods of comfort (Fig. 2). Sun and shade patterns as well as monthly wind flows on the site provide critical information for locating and orienting the building. Patterns of sky cover and daylight availability are crucial for determining the potential of solar heating and daylighting as energy-conserving strategies. Most of these techniques allow the designer to evaluate the climate without requiring actual on-site measurements.

The Program and Building Occupants

"The only reason buildings use energy is that people use buildings. In order to understand how buildings use energy we must understand how people use buildings, since no one ever designed and built a building *just* to save energy" (10). The ways people occupy buildings will determine requirements for thermal comfort and appropriate lighting. Energy, either on site or fossil fuel, is generally relied on to meet these requirements. The number of people within a space, the use of electric lights, and equipment such as restaurant stoves or computers generate heat that may reduce the heating load, increase the cooling load, or both over the course of the year.

Analyzing the building program to identify and quantify comfort requirements and internal heat sources, like the analysis of the exterior conditions, is a critical step in designing an energy-conserving building. From this analysis, the designer can discover opportunities for establishing zones of spaces with similar thermal or lighting requirements. Those activities that require access to the building skin for light, wind, or sun can be identified and

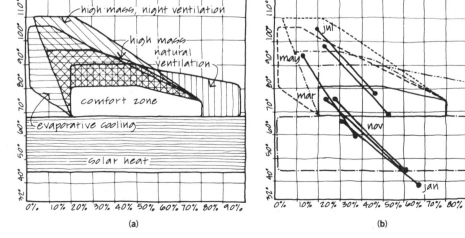

Figure 2. (a) Bioclimatic chart indicating design strategies for thermal comfort; **(b)** annual climatic data for Phoenix, Arizona plotted on the bioclimatic chart indicates solar heating as a winter comfort strategy. Natural ventilation, high mass and evaporative cooling are appropriate design strategies for summer comfort (11).

can suggest plan and sectional organizational strategies to take advantage of these site energies. Thermal opportunities in occupancy schedules and the possibility of seasonally expandable building areas can also be explored. Analysis of the program from an energy standpoint can reveal the direction most profitable for minimizing energy use prior to evaluation of a specific design proposal and can often provide a sophisticated and rich set of design ideas that would not arise if energy issues were ignored.

The Building as a Mediator

The siting, form, organization, and materials of the building act between the exterior climate and the internal program. In general, mediation of climate conditions at the site scale (for example, shading during hot months) will free the designer from these concerns at the building or component scale, so it is important to consider energy-conserving design strategies at all scales. In a similar way, if the occupant behavior or the building–site design can provide thermal and luminous comfort with available site conditions, the necessity of using machines and fossil fuels is reduced or alleviated.

An understanding of building mediation of climate and program on three levels—by location, form, and metabolism—has been proposed (3). A building design can use location, in either dynamic or static aspects, to provide thermal comfort to occupants. The traditional use of location for thermal comfort is migration, both within a building and to other locations. The static response involves issues of building orientation to the sun and wind, the juxtaposition of one building relative to others (for example to allow solar access or to provide shade), and the relation of a building to the natural topography. Building form, as the second level of mediation, may also adapt dynamically, for example, with the opening and closing of shutters. Usually hidden within the static design are other thermal responses: the size of the buildings, the amount of building envelope and the volume it encloses, and the thermal characteristics of the building structure and envelope. The choice of building materials and their assembly will determine the thermal mass, the heat transfer through the building envelope, and the amount of light and sun that are allowed into the building. The third level of mediation is metabolism: the chemical and mechanical processes that provide energy to the building, including the heat produced by occupants and the energy brought from off site such as electricity or gas. Developing an energy-efficient building design requires the architect to address potential responses in all three areas of design.

Formal Considerations. Early work in solar and energy-efficient design often prominently displayed the solar technology chosen, such as the Trombe wall, or allowed technical concerns to supplant those of space, experience, order, and symbol, which are necessary for a rich architectural design. By the time some architects had begun to master the spatial implications as well as the technology of solar and energy-efficient designs, the perceived energy crisis had passed and energy-conserving designs remained in the popular consciousness as awkward and extreme

building types. Two writers in particular have brought clarity of thought to this issue of aesthetics, form, and energy design. In the 1984 article "Formal Speculations on Thermal Diagrams" (12), Harrison Fraker demonstrates spatial and ordering implications relative to thermal and luminous design aspects in 23 solar and energy-efficient buildings. In "Model, Metaphor and Paradigm" (13), also from 1984, Donald Watson challenges architects to use both the "habit of imagination" as an artist and the "habit of truth" as a scientist to generate and to evaluate energy-efficient designs. Watson states that metaphors of energy efficiency and models by which to test performance are both necessary, joined by an ethical sensibility that brings questions of value to the design work.

THE COMPLEX WHOLE: FIVE ENERGY-CONSERVING BUILDINGS

Published guidelines for the design of solar and energy-conserving buildings generally separate appropriate design strategies into "primary" and "secondary," suggesting that the design responds to the predominant thermal problem such as keeping a building warm in Minnesota. There are many times, however, that the secondary thermal problem, such as staying cool in Minnesota's hot, humid summers, is also important if the building is occupied throughout the year. The dynamic character of the climate as a context poses the greatest challenge to a designer and also is that which offers the greatest opportunity for a rich design solution. Most solar and energy-efficient buildings are occupied year-round and do respond to the annual climatic cycle. Real building examples are able to demonstrate the way in which multiple-design strategies are combined in a single-design solution to perform over the course of the diurnal and annual cycles of climate and occupancy. Discussions of five solar and energy-efficient buildings follow. The buildings, which range from a house addition to a 64,000 ft^2 (5946 m^2) school are listed with relevant climate information in Table 1.

Pfister Residence Retrofit

The vast majority of the houses now occupied in the United States were built prior to 1973 and are neither solar heated nor very energy efficient. Most of these houses as well as those being designed and built now will be occupied for many years into the future. Strategies for retrofit are therefore of prime importance in any discussion of the energy future in the building sector. In the 1980 Pfister residence retrofit (Fig. 3), the back wall of a typical 1920 frame house was opened to the winter sun and summer breezes.

Climate and Program. Minneapolis has a continental climate of bitter cold winters and relatively hot, humid summers. The winter winds come from Siberia across Canada and the summer winds bring heat and humidity up the Mississippi River valley from the Gulf of Mexico. Spring and fall act as transition seasons, with many days comfortable with only the sun or the wind. As a skin load

Table 1. Climate Data for Building Examples[a]

Building	Closest City for Climate Data	Latitude	January Dry Bulb Temperature		HDD[b]	July Dry Bulb Temperature		CDD[b]
			High, °F(°C)	Low, °F(°C)		High, °F(°C)	Low, °F(°C)	
Pfister retrofit	Minneapolis, Minn.	45°N	20(−7)	2(−17)	8007	83(28)	63(17)	662
Security State Bank	Minneapolis, Minn.	45°N	20(−7)	2(−17)	8007	83(28)	63(17)	662
Kelbaugh house	Princeton, N.J.	41°N	38(3)	24(−4)	4972	86(30)	68(20)	1091
Cottage Restaurant	Cottage Grove, Oreg.	44°N	46(8)	34(1)	4799	83(28)	51(11)	261
Florida A&M University School of Architecture	Tallahassee, Fla.	30°N	63(17)	40(4)	1652	91(33)	71(22)	2492

[a]Ref. 14.
[b]Heating degree days (HDD) and cooling degree days (CDD) base 65°F.

dominated building, a house in this climate needs to provide a heated enclosure in the winter and then varying degrees of buffered spaces open to the sun or the wind as the seasons progress. The programmatic basis of the Pfister retrofit is a change of focus within the house from the street on the north to the garden on the south. A strong visual connection of the interior rooms with the backyard was achieved with the addition of 200 ft² (18.5 m²) to the 1830-ft² (170-m²) house, making a solarium for the kitchen and upstairs study (Fig. 3a and b).

Design Strategies. Heating is the predominant energy cost in operation of a house in Minnesota. A direct gain passive-heating approach was chosen, which involves (1) admitting solar radiation, (2) storing the heat from the sun, (3) retaining the heat within the building envelope, and (4) distributing the heat throughout the house. To admit solar radiation, the house form was modified to include two primary solar gain areas: a two-story solarium, 9 × 12 ft. (2.75 × 3.7 m), and a window bay at the stairway landing, increasing the south-facing glass from 50 ft² (4.5 m²) to 200 ft² (20.5 m²) total (Fig. 3c). The large tree to the south of the deck is deciduous and drops its leaves to allow sun to reach the house during the winter and spring months when heat is needed. Quarry tile over a 10-in. (25.5-cm) concrete slab in the kitchen and a bank of phase change thermal storage rods installed behind the stair window store the heat during the day and release it late in the evening. An exterior reflector is used to increase the solar radiation received through the stair window bay.

To keep the heat from escaping, the frame walls were insulated with polystyrene beads to R15 and the attic was insulated with batt insulation to R40. Motorized insulating shades cover the solarium windows and a motorized roll-down insulation is installed at the stair window. These shades are operated by a thermostat to close at night and on overcast winter days. Weather-stripping and caulking of windows and doors cuts infiltration of cold air into the house. Distribution of hot air is achieved by heat rising to the second floor from the kitchen through a metal grate ceiling. Heat also rises up the stairwell from the phase change rods. From there, a fan recirculates the warm air to the living room and dining room on the north side of the house. The back-up heating system is a gas-fired, hot-water system with radiators in each room. A direct gain design for heating requires shading during summer months. This is achieved with shade from the lawn trees that leaf out on a schedule consistent with the months of hot weather. Cross-ventilation occurs when the windows are open on the north and south.

Performance. The passive solar system, including insulation and weatherization, reduced the cost of heating this house by 65%, while creating higher levels of occupant comfort with the warm kitchen floor mass. In addition, the openings of the south wall allowed improved cross-ventilation and increased use of the shady backyard areas in the spring, summer, and fall. Moreover, the openness, the connection to the garden, and the additional light in the house substantially improved the quality of space and the enjoyment of the occupants in the patterns of seasonal change (15–18).

The Kelbaugh House

In choosing to use a Trombe wall in his 1975 passively heated house, Doug Kelbaugh has posed a design in contradiction to the open south wall of the Pfister retrofit (Fig. 4). Behind the all-glass south wall of the Kelbaugh house is a 800-ft² (74-m²) concrete wall, painted black toward the glass. All rooms face onto the concrete wall and receive heat indirectly through the wall. View of the private south yard and large deciduous trees is through "windows" cut in the 15-in. (38-cm) wall (Fig. 4b). Sited on a street of nineteenth-century, two-story houses, this well-publicized solar house was designed by Kelbaugh after he lived in an eighteenth-century farmhouse built of 2-ft (60-cm) thick stone walls. The Trombe wall, developed by Felix Trombe in Odeillo, France, provides a similar sense of enclosure, but with sophisticated mechanisms for both heating and cooling.

Climate and Program. Princeton, N.J. is warmer than Minneapolis, but still provides the dynamic of cold, snowy winters, hot summers, and comfortable transitional seasons found throughout much of the United States and Europe. With approximately 50% possible sunshine in the winter, the house must accommodate cloudy days as well as clear. The design of this house was intended to maximize the private south-facing yard while saving the existing silver maple. In addition to three bedrooms, there is a greenhouse for an ornamental horticultural business. The postindustrial vocabulary is used with modesty and a "Yankee economy" in this house of 1900 ft² (176 m²) with an attached greenhouse of 200 ft² (18.6 m²).

(a)

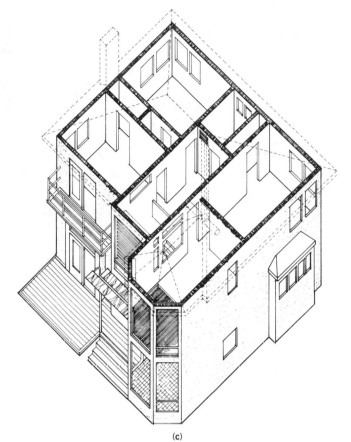

(c)

(b)

Figure 3. (a) Pfister Residence Retrofit, south elevation showing the solarium, stairwell window with reflector and rear deck with shade tree. Clients: Peter and Darlene Pfister. Architect: Peter Pfister and The Architectural Alliance. Structural/Mechanical: Martin R. Lund. Owner built with the assistance of friends and Rocon Construction Co. **(b)** Interior of kitchen and solarium showing the quarry tile floor and the metal grate ceiling. **(c)** Axonometric of the passive solar systems in the Pfister Residence. (Courtesy of Peter Pfister. Photographs by Franz C. Hall.

(a)

(b)

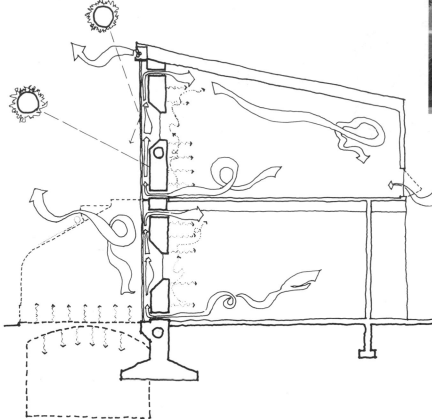

Figure 4. (a) Kelbaugh house south elevation with the Trombe wall and attached greenhouse. Windows show as white where the shades are down. Four eave vents are visible at the top of the elevation. Clients: Doug and Meg Kelbaugh. Architect: Doug Kelbaugh. (b) Interior of house looking through a window in the concrete Trombe wall. Vents for convection are visible at top and bottom of photo. (c) Section through the Kelbaugh house with thermal strategies for heating and cooling described in the text. Courtesy of Doug Kelbaugh.

Design Strategies. A Trombe wall (Fig. 4c) provides solar heat indirectly to occupied space through convection of hot air from the space between the wall and south glass into the rooms during the day. By evening, the wall is warmed and heat radiates to the rooms. The low winter sun strikes the south wall directly, and the double-pane glass traps approximately two-thirds of the heat for distribution. In the summer, the same convection of heated air up through the space between the wall and the glass exhausts the hot air through a vent, pulling cool air into the rooms from the shaded north side of the house. The more oblique summer sun angle helps to avoid overheating. The concrete is cooled down by venting at night. The greenhouse and cellar share heat stored in the greenhouse floor during the winter. Eave vents and shades in the greenhouse provide summer cooling. The nonsouth walls are wood frame with an average R18 from cellulosic fiber and the roof is insulated to R40. The back-up system is a gas-fired, hot-air furnace with ducts in the concrete wall.

Performance. The literature on the Kelbaugh house is especially interesting because the architect monitored auxiliary space heating, domestic hot water, cooking, and electrical consumption for eight years and continually reported on the "fine tuning" of the design for comfort and energy performance. Back-up heating during the early 1980s cost approximately $100 per year, 20% of the $500 typical annual heating bill in New Jersey. To increase winter comfort, movable insulation and storm windows were added to the east, north, and west windows. A damper to prevent reverse flow of air through the Trombe vents and a thermal curtain separating the greenhouse and living room were added in the first two years of occupancy. The greenhouse was double glazed, which halved the heat loss, and eight drums of water were added to even out the temperature swings in the greenhouse. The furnace runs on winter mornings and during the day if the sky is cloudy. Average winter temperatures inside are 60°F (17°C) downstairs and 66°F (19°C) upstairs. Warm room surfaces add another 2–3°F (1.5–2°C) of apparent air temperature for comfort. Summer comfort was improved with the addition of small operable skylights to the bedrooms because the eave vents in the Trombe wall were never quite large enough for cross-ventilation. The Kelbaugh house is a refined and disciplined design that reveals the experiential and spatial power of an architecturally understood thermal design. Kelbaugh's willingness to publish the fine tuning of the design allows other designers to learn the importance of common sense in a successful solar design (19–22).

The Cottage Restaurant and Lane Energy Center

Completed in 1981, this commercial building by Equinox Design, Inc. houses a restaurant and small energy store on a commercial strip in Cottage Grove, Oreg. (Fig. 5). At 2000 ft² (185 m²), this building is the size of many passive solar houses. The design intentions and energy strategies respond to programmatic and site concerns different from most solar houses. Beyond the direct gain passive-heating system and night-flushing cooling systems, this building is designed to take maximum advantage of seasonal change by expanding and contracting spatial layers of varied thermal conditioning to the south. The building is a rare example of a design that minimizes energy use in construction and demolition as well as operation. Materials and systems, such as the scored concrete floor, were chosen and designed so they could be reused in another building after this one is demolished.

Climate and Program. Temperatures in Cottage Grove, Ore., 20 mi (32 km) south of Eugene, are influenced by maritime air from the Pacific Ocean, forming cool, wet winters of high humidity and hot, dry summers. Although the latitude is comparable to Minneapolis, long periods of very hot weather and severely cold winters are mediated by proximity to the ocean. This relatively temperate annual cycle provides real opportunities for outdoor rooms that are buffered to extend use through spring, summer, and fall. The Cottage Restaurant was initially designed to house the Lane Energy Center in 1000 ft² (93 m²) to model the energy products sold by the clients. The remaining space was to be leased for retail. By the time of occupancy, the restaurant had claimed the entire building and a small western addition accommodates the store. The restaurant generates more heat than the store would have, which has reduced dependence on back-up heating systems during the winter and initially caused some overheating problems in the summer.

Design Strategies. A shift in building geometry immediately identifies the difference between the city grid and true solar orientation. The building mass is situated perpendicular to the highway with a clerestory facing southeast, while the wall below is skewed 25° so the windows face due south. This wall is developed to include several layers of outside space modified for seasonal comfort (Fig. 5a). The interior zone is completely indoors and kept comfortable with passive heating and cooling. The next zone is sheltered from sun and rain by louvers and corrugated fiberglass. An arbor extends beyond with grape vines providing shade in the summer and filtered sun in spring and fall. The north, east, and west walls are thermally unbroken.

A direct gain system is used for winter heating. Sun is admitted through the clerestory and the south windows (Fig. 5b). Heat is stored in both the 6-in. (15-cm) concrete floor and in barrels of water mounted on the north wall and behind the south windows near the floor. Because the collection and storage systems are distributed through the space, no separate system is required to distribute the heat evenly. The heat is held inside the building at night with insulated shutters on the clerestory and motorized thermal shades on the south windows. The walls and roof are wood frame with corrugated metal siding, insulated to R19 and to R30, respectively. The kitchen zone is heated with internal gains from the cooking equipment.

In the dry summer, the clerestory is shaded with exterior bamboo shades and the louvers and grape vines shade the south windows below. Insulated swing walls closed in the winter open up to allow breezes and access to outdoor dining. Five vents with wind turbine ventilators in the north roof exhaust hot air. The cool nights are used to flush out heat stored in the slabs and the barrels with air supplied through an 18-in. (46-cm) steel culvert. For some days each summer cross-ventilation is insufficient for comfort and the building is closed to outside air. Then night chilling of the mass is coupled with an auxiliary swamp cooler to provide a cool interior.

Performance. The Cottage Restaurant provides thermal comfort to the staff and clients both winter and summer. In the winter, the back-up wood stove operates in the morning and early evening (Fig. 5c). The stove uses ap-

(a)

(b)

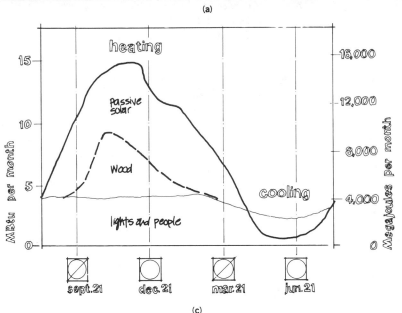

(c)

Figure 5. (a) Southeast view of The Cottage Restaurant showing the layered south wall, clerestory wind gravity turbines. Clients: Doug and Hanna Still. Architects: Equinox Design, Inc. with G. Z. Brown, John S. Reynolds and R. Kellett. Structural: Paul Weir. Contractor: Archie Wynn. Photograph by G. Z. Brown. (b) Interior view showing concrete floor and water barrels for thermal mass. Insulating shutters on the clerestory are drawn open. Photographs by G. Z. Brown. (c) Annual energy balance indicates the contribution of internal gains, wood and solar energy to heating the restaurant from late August to April and the cooling load from May to August. Courtesy of Equinox Design, Inc.

proximately four cords of wood during the heating season, which cost $160–200 per year in the mid-1980s. This building, like the Kelbaugh house, has been fine tuned since it was occupied in 1981. Occasional summer overheating, in particular, has been addressed by installing fans in the earth tube to increase night flushing of the thermal mass. The multiplicity of means to accommodate the building to the exterior climate allows this building to function well throughout the spring and fall, as well as days of extreme and variable weather (23–25).

Security State Bank

The owners of the Security State Bank in Wells, Minn. (Fig. 6), were interested in passive solar design to reduce

heating bills. At 11,012 ft^2 (1,023 m^2) the bank is larger than the houses or restaurant discussed above, yet the building still proves to be skin load dominated—thermally impacted by the cold winters and hot summers of southern Minnesota. Unlike the houses and restaurant, however, the building is occupied exclusively during the day and requires high levels of illumination for the visual tasks associated with a bank. These particular circumstances led the solar designer, John Weidt Associates, to design a building that could provide both solar heating and daylighting to reduce energy consumption in the new bank.

Climate and Program. Wells, Minn., a town of 2800, is approximately 100 mi (160 km) south of Minneapolis and

(a)

St. Paul and offers a climate very similar to that described for the Pfister retrofit. The winters are severe enough to require heating in most commercial buildings as well as residential. High winds blow off the prairie on hot summer days. The previous bank had only one window, located in the door, and the clients were very interested in a light, open character in the new design. A full-service community bank, the Security State Bank is designed for a maximum of 30 employees. Operating hours occur during weekdays from 8 A.M. to 4:30 P.M.

Design Strategies. Occupancy during daytime working hours led the designers to an emphasis on heavy insulation and tight construction. With these, the building will behave like a thermos bottle. The bank heats ups quickly in the morning once the sun enters south-facing glass in a direct gain passive-heating system. Heavy thermal mass for storage of heat, used in the Pfister retrofit, the Kelbaugh house, and the Cottage Restaurant to retain heat through the night, was not used because the bank remains unoccupied at night and is allowed to drop to 50°F (10°C). The building is not completely lightweight, with both the vault area and the floor slab providing mass not exposed to direct solar radiation. This mass helps to keep the building stable in temperature over 24 hours. The south-facing clerestory and the southeast walls contain 2240 ft^2 (208 m^2) of glass (20% of total floor area), while the north, east, and west walls are insulated to R33 and have no windows. The roof is insulated to R46.

The south clerestory was carefully modeled to provide high quality illumination to the banking areas. Direct sun is allowed into the lobby for visual delight. Areas with more demanding visual tasks, however, require diffused lighting with no direct sun that might cause glare (Fig. 6b). Box beams 3 × 5 ft (0.9 × 1.5 m) were constructed to baffle the sun entering through the clerestory, diffusing the daylight over the areas below. These beams also carry the HVAC ducts and the back-up fluorescent lighting. Photocells turn the electric lights off when sufficient illumination is provided by the clerestory and double-glazed windows. Glass areas that act as winter sun collectors can cause serious heat gain problems during summer months. Both the clerestory and lower window areas are shaded with retractable awnings operated by solar cell controls. Override switches for the awnings are operated manually, but also by a wind sensor to prevent damage during periods of high wind.

Performance. This building was extensively monitored in 1982–1983 and in 1984 as part of the Passive Solar Commercial Buildings Program of the U.S. Department of Energy. The owners report that their utility bills have dropped by 60–70% and their business has grown by 25%, well beyond expectations. The building uses only 10% of the lighting energy used by comparable bank buildings in the state. Monitoring of the building, however, has shown that energy savings were not necessarily as predicted and were improved by fine tuning of the HVAC controls and with education for the occupants on the passive systems. In the first year of occupancy the electric lighting system used twice the energy predicted. Some additional nonday-lit space had been occupied in the basement and hours of

(b)

Figure 6. (a) Southwest view of the Security State Bank. Awnings are retracted on the clerestory for ambient light while awnings on the lower windows provide shade for employees. Clients: Security State Bank. Architect: Eugene E. Hickey and Associates. Solar Designer: John Weidt Associates. **(b)** Interior of bank shows direct sun from clerestory diffused by the white ceiling and baffles for even ambient lighting over work stations. Photographs by John Weidt.

operation had increased from the original by 20%. Both of these changes increased the use of electric lights. A larger factor was that one employee arriving early would switch on the electric lights so that the automatic switching was not in effect. Even in periods of sufficient daylight, the electric lights would be on, drawing energy unnecessarily.

Security State Bank is cooled mechanically with two systems: a conventional multizone air conditioner and an economizer fan with a high velocity duct system. The high velocity system is used to keep the hottest air up near the ceiling at the clerestory windows during mechanical cooling. This fan also can supply sufficient outside air so that ventilation rather than refrigeration can be used up to 65°F (18°C), shortening the refrigeration season substantially. Controls for the high velocity fan, as well as controls for the heating system, have both required some reprogramming and fine tuning, including occupant education on thermostat setbacks and fan operation. Unlike conventional buildings, good operation is dependent on fine tuning more than simply the mechanical system. Occupants and building components are also major contributors to the energy savings of the bank (26–28).

Florida A&M University School of Architecture

Occupied in January 1985, the School of Architecture building (Fig. 7) at Florida A&M University in Tallahassee, Fla., was the result of a design competition for a demonstration of state-of-the-art techniques in passive heating, cooling, ventilation, and lighting systems. Although the students and faculty are pleased with the new building, it is not a total success in providing thermal comfort with minimal energy consumption. The problems faced by the architects, engineers, and occupants are revealing to anyone working with solar or energy-efficient designs because they are not unique to this building program, design solution, or construction process.

Climate and Program. Tallahassee is approximately 30 mi (48 km) north of the Gulf of Mexico coast in the Florida panhandle. Winters are mild, although cool enough to require heating in buildings. Clear days tend to be colder than overcast days throughout the winter months. Spring and fall are quick transitional seasons between winter and the long, hot and humid summer months. The School of Architecture operates year-round and it is expected that 400 students and 35 faculty will occupy the building. The 64,000 ft² (5946-m²) building includes faculty offices, design studios, seminar and lecture rooms, a gallery, computer laboratory, library, and building science laboratories.

Design Strategies. Two thermal design strategies were chosen for the school. First, varying degrees of thermal conditioning required by program activities were identified and a building massing was developed with five separately zoned building pieces. The eastern spine containing the computer laboratory, gallery, library and lecture rooms is pushed into a hill for earth sheltering and is 100% mechanically conditioned. The administration–faculty areas and the design studios each form a wing of the

(a)

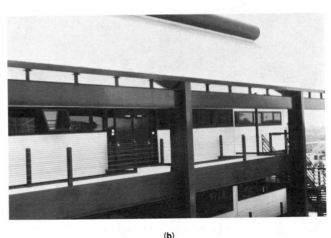

(b)

Figure 7. (a) Florida A&M School of Architecture. Southwest view of the studio and administrative wings. Solar chimneys on the south wall and roof exhaust air through the large ridge vent. (b) North side of the studio wing shows the translucent roof and the exterior circulation. Small windows in the studios open for natural ventilation. Photographs by Susan Ubbelohde.

building perpendicular to the east spine oriented for passive heating and natural ventilation (Fig. 7a). These are also mechanically heated and air-conditioned when so required. The third wing is composed of laboratories that are naturally ventilated and either passively or mechanically heated. The fourth wing is an open construction shed with unit space heaters. Exterior circulation requires no conditioning. Approximately 42,000 ft², or 66% of the building, can be mechanically conditioned.

The second thermal strategy was the use of thermal or solar chimneys on the south wall and roof area of the administrative offices, studio, and laboratory. The chimneys contain a 2-ft (60-cm) cavity between the glazing and red-painted metal. Air in the cavity is heated by the sun year-round. In the winter, this warmed air rises, is collected by a duct, and is circulated through the regular mechanical system in each wing. Electrically heated hot air supplements the heat from the chimney as necessary. In the summer, the warm air rises and is exhausted through the ridge ventilator, pulling cool air from the courtyards through open windows in the north wall of each wing (Fig. 7**b**). During hot summer periods the building is closed and mechanical conditioning is used. A controller connected to sensors both in and outside of the building determines the proper state of operation for the building.

Performance. Thermal comfort and energy efficiency of the building have not achieved those predicted for a variety of reasons. In the value engineering stage of design review, the hot air collection ducts were removed from the administrative and laboratory wings to reduce cost, thereby rendering the passive heating system useless in these two wings. The duct was left in the studio wing, which is, therefore, heated by the solar chimney. The building was designed with few if any thermal breaks between the concrete slab floors and the exterior, causing a very low floor surface temperature in uncarpeted spaces during the winter, even though the air temperature is maintained at a comfortable level. Electric space heaters and area rugs are used by the students to minimize the discomfort.

In the summer months, the heat from the chimney radiates through to the rooms behind, causing discomfort although the air in the rooms is mechanically cooled. During the spring and summer months, it was discovered that the high humidity makes it very difficult to cycle between mechanical refrigeration during the day and natural ventilation at night. If the building is opened up at night for ventilation, the chillers must work for hours the following day to remove the humidity, canceling out any benefit in terms of energy efficiency. The controls system has been reprogrammed to make the best use of the systems in the building in connection with exterior conditions.

The final performance issue, related to the success of the Security State Bank, is that of lighting. The School of Architecture is a building that houses visually demanding tasks in an envelope with a great deal of surface area. The interiors, however, are quite dark unless the fluorescent lights are on, even during a clear bright day. The south wall is essentially opaque, due to the solar chimneys. The north-facing roof has been glazed with translucent fiber-

glass, allowing light down to the north walls. However, the exterior circulation blocks much of this light. More important, the small window areas in these north walls are glazed with 30% transmission glass, blocking 70% of the daylight that does make it to the window.

The thermal and energy problems described here do not keep the students and faculty from enjoying and being proud of the building. Both fine tuning and occupant adaptation have overcome many of the problems. Those inherent in the design, such as the lack of daylighting, are tolerated. The performance of this building, as in the performance and fine tuning of the other buildings discussed, makes clear the necessity of understanding the thermal design as a whole, from site to construction details, from glass specifications to false "cost-cutting" decisions. One or two visible energy moves in a design do not necessarily guarantee energy savings or occupant comfort. The detailing, the controls, and the occupants will all impact the performance of an energy-efficient design (29–31).

Other Design Approaches

Although the five buildings discussed above introduced many of the design strategies appropriate for solar and energy-conserving buildings, there are other equally valid design approaches not utilized by these designs. Many variations on solar collection and thermal storage strategies can be found in the books and articles listed in the bibliography, but the fundamentals remain the same as in the Pfister retrofit or the Kelbaugh house. Different in approach, however, are the use of earth sheltering, superinsulation, and some commercial building strategies.

Earth-sheltered Designs. Earth-sheltered designs, or underground buildings, minimize the amount of building envelope exposed to the extremes and cycles of the exterior climate. The earth remains at a relatively stable temperature throughout the year, providing a nonstressful thermal environment for the building and its occupants. Williamson Hall at the University of Minnesota (Fig. 8) illustrates the design requirements associated with earth sheltering; lighting and ventilation become extremely important if the building envelope is not exposed to light and air. This building design uses a large light well with sloped glazing and interior atria to light the public circulation areas of the building. The offices and bookstore, however, rely heavily on the electric lighting system. Ventilation, heating, and cooling in this building are all mechanical. Earth-sheltered houses, with smaller inter-

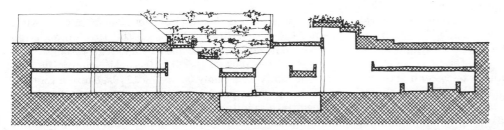

Figure 8. Section through Williamson Hall in Minneapolis, Minnesota illustrates the light court for the office floors underground (11).

nal heat gains and less demanding visual tasks, are easier to passively heat, cool, and ventilate.

Superinsulated Designs. Superinsulation refers to the "thermos bottle" design approach for residential scale buildings. This strategy is not based on using solar energy or daylighting, but rather on minimizing thermal transfer through the building skin. Superinsulation as a design strategy is most applicable in very cold overcast climates where there is little solar energy to collect and in high latitudes with only a few hours of daylight or sun during the cold winter months. Canada, Denmark, Sweden, Austria, and the FRG have all been active in developing superinsulated design technology.

Superinsulation implies the use of very heavily insulated building components. Walls are generally insulated between R19 and R30, roofs between R38 and R60, and exterior foundations at R10. Window areas are kept to a minimum and are generally triple glazed. The building is very tightly constructed, with extreme care in making a continuous vapor barrier and weather stripping. The ventilation is controlled at 0.5 air charges per hour and heat exchangers that can reach 70% efficiency are installed to prevent heat loss when fresh air is brought into the house.

Superinsulated designs are appropriate for some climates and building programs. The thermos bottle approach, however, trades many qualitative aspects of architectural experience and connection to the exterior environment in order to "heat a house with a light bulb." In addition, concern with health effects from materials outgassing and radon exposure is increased in extremely tight houses. As with earth-sheltered buildings, excluding the exterior environment in such an extreme way creates performance and quality of life questions that must be addressed by the designer.

Commercial Building Strategies. Nonresidential buildings are generally larger and contain more sources of internally generated heat than most houses. Lighting and cooling are major energy uses in most commercial buildings and energy costs are often tied to the time of day electricity is used ("peak" or "demand" charges by the utilities). Design strategies to reduce both energy consumption and costs in these buildings often focus on daylighting to reduce electrical demand during peak afternoon periods and daily or annual storage of heat.

Lockheed Missiles and Space Building 157 in Sunnyvale, Calif., designed by the office of Leo A. Daly, is a preeminent example of commercial daylighting design in the United States (Fig. 9). The office floors receive daylight from the exterior building skin and two interior atria. The exterior windows are designed to provide diffuse, even light over the work space, using light shelves and high ceilings. Lighting controls maintain the required level of illumination by operating the electrical lighting system in response to the levels of daylight in the building.

Thermal storage to take advantage of cooler nights and winters or lower demand charges for electricity is another commercial strategy. In Princeton Professional Park (Fig. 10), designed by Harrison Fraker, Short & Ford and

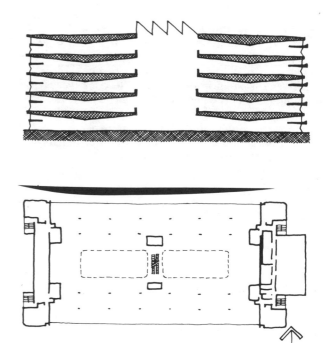

Figure 9. Section and plan through Lockheed Building 157 shows the center atrium and exterior light shelves for the offices (11).

Princeton Energy Group, both daylighting and diurnal storage work to reduce energy demands. Heat for winter nights is collected in the atria and drawn through rock beds below the office floors. The heat stored in the rocks then radiates through the floors into the offices during the night. In the summer, the roof is sprayed with water during the day to reduce roof surface temperatures. At night, the spray of water and the night sky cool the metal roof. Air is circulated past this cooled roof to be drawn down and through the rock bed, to cool it. The rock bed then becomes a source of cool air for operation the following day or, on hot days, a source of precooled air for the mechanical system.

Large absorption–refrigeration systems which provide air conditioning in commercial buildings require an input of heat at one point in the cycle in order to regenerate the salt solution used in the process. In an energy conserving design, this heat for regeneration may be supplied by waste heat high-temperature processes within the building or from solar energy provided by rooftop solar collectors.

DIRECTIONS FOR THE FUTURE

Interest in solar and energy-efficient design has decreased since the period directly following the 1973 oil embargo. Two conditions in future decades may cause renewed interest on the part of the architectural community. Economic motivations may, as in the 1970s, cause a renewed interest and investment in this approach to architectural design. In addition, the continuing development and affordability of new materials and building technologies

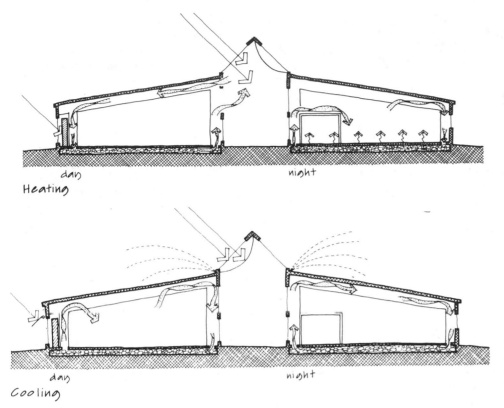

day   night
Heating

day   night
Cooling

Figure 10. Sections through Princeton Professional Park illustrate the diurnal storage cycles for both heating and cooling of the offices (11).

will assist designers in providing greater energy efficiency with fewer design limitations.

Economic Incentives

Architects are likely to face new economic motivations for designing solar and energy-efficient designs. These may stem from artificially raised fuel prices, as in 1973, or from the true environmental costs of fossil fuel and nuclear energy sources. The world of international politics is fluid and volatile. Many analysts believe it is just a matter of time before energy resources are again priced very high, causing a return to conservation and renewable, site-available resources in the building sector. As public concern grows about the degradation of the ozone layer, the greenhouse effect, acid rain, and toxic waste, governmental actions are recognizing the real costs of energy use. Paying for the environmental consequences of burning fossil fuels and generating electricity for buildings will provide great incentive to care about the energy consumed by both existing and future buildings. As an example, local and state governments in the United States are now working with the utilities to look at conservation as an economic alternative to the construction of new power-generating plants.

New Technologies

Continuing research in photovoltaics, mechanical systems, control systems, and building materials will have a strong impact on energy consumption in the building sector. Recently announced breakthroughs on the manufacturing of photovoltaics brings this technology closer to use in residential and commercial buildings. Economically feasible photovoltaics that allow buildings to generate electricity directly from solar radiation will completely change the relationship between design and energy resources. Research and development in glazing also has the potential to make a large impact on building design and energy consumption. Advances in photochromic and electrochromic glass will enable window and skylights to have controlled light and heat transmission characteristics. Insulating glass technologies such as aerogels promise to combine variable insulation characteristics with good light transmission. Low E glass with R values of nearly 5 was only dreamed of in the 1970s. This glass has been adopted throughout the United States to reduce window heat loss and heat gain. In developing countries that face an extreme hot humid climate, research has focused on the use of desiccants for dehumidification. Chemical desiccants which absorb humidity from the air are found in small bags packaged with cameras, vitamins, and other consumer products. Research in the application of these chemicals to room-size dehumidification is concentrating on the use of solar energy to regenerate the desiccants once saturated with water vapor removed from the inhabited rooms.

Integrated Systems

Ultimately, the issues of energy efficiency will join with new technologies and environmental issues and buildings will be viewed as integrated systems, inhabiting a planet that is also a completely integrated system. Such an approach was used by designer Michael Jantzen in the 1970s

Figure 11. The Autonomous Dwelling Vehicle designed by Michael Jantzen, Ted Blakewell III, and Ellen Jantzen produces electricity with photovoltaics and uses both active and passive solar systems for space heating. Rain water is captured, used and filtered for reuse in washing and bathing. Minimum use of resources is coupled with minimum impact on the surrounding ecology. Photograph by Michael Jantzen.

with a series of experimental designs considered at the time to be extreme and odd. What is becoming clear since that time is that the understanding, if not the forms, of Jantzen's autonomous dwelling vehicle (Fig. 11) will continue to be of importance for building designers. In the late twentieth century, the words of the Greek playwright Aeschylus do not lose their accuracy: "Though they had eyes to see, they saw to no avail; they had ears, but understood not. But like shapes in dreams throughout their time, without purpose they wrought all things in confusion. They lacked knowledge of houses . . . turned to face the sun" (32).

BIBLIOGRAPHY

1. Vitruvius, *On Architecture,* VI.i.1, Quoted in K. Butti and J. Perlin, *A Golden Thread,* Cheshire Books, Palo Alto, Calif. 1980, p. 15.

2. A. H. Rosenfield and D. Hafemeister, *Scientific American* **258,** 78 (Apr. 1988).

3. R. Knowles, *Sun Rhythm Form,* MIT Press, Cambridge, Mass., 1981, p. 9.

4. C. Flavin, *Energy and Architecture: The Solar and Conservation Potential,* Worldwatch Paper 40, Worldwatch Institute, Washington, D.C., Nov. 1980, p. 5.

5. Ibid., p. 12.

6. B. Stein, J. S. Reynolds, and M. J. McGuinness, *Mechanical and Electrical Equipment for Buildings,* 7th ed., John Wiley & Sons, Inc., New York, 1986, pp. 22–23.

7. Ref. 1, p. 41.

8. L. Heschong, *Thermal Delight in Architecture,* MIT Press, Cambridge, Mass., 1979, p. 55.

9. P. Bosselmann, J. Flores, and T. O'Hara, *Sun and Light for Downtown San Francisco,* IURD Monograph No. 34, Berkeley California College of Environmental Design, 1983.

10. M. Kantrowitz, *Progressive Architecture* **LXVII,** 118 (Apr. 1986).

11. G. Z. Brown, *Sun, Wind, and Light: Architectural Design Strategies,* John Wiley & Sons, Inc., New York, 1985.

12. H. Fraker, "Formal Speculations on Thermal Diagrams," *Progressive Architecture* **LXV,** 104 (Apr. 1984).

13. D. Watson, "Model, Metaphor and Paradigm," *Journal of Architectural Education* **37**(3/4), 4 (Spring–Summer 1984).

14. "Normals Means and Extremes" for Minneapolis–St. Paul, Minn., Newark, N.J., Eugene, Oreg., and Tallahassee, Fla.," in *Local Climatological Data,* National Oceanographic and Atmospheric Administration (NOAA), Asheville, N.C., 1984.

15. Interview with Peter Pfister, architect. Minneapolis, Minn. Dec. 10, 1987.

16. J. Cook, *Award Winning Passive Solar Designs,* McGraw-Hill Inc., New York, 1984, pp. 127–131.

17. D. Wright and D. Andrejko, *Passive Solar Architecture: Logic and Beauty,* Van Nostrand Reinhold Co., Inc., New York, 1982, pp. 147–151.

18. *Solar Age* **5,** 17 (May 1980).

19. Interview with Doug Kelbaugh, Dec. 12, 1987.

20. D. Kelbaugh, *Solar Age* **1,** 18–23 (July 1976).

21. *Solar Age* **9,** 36–37 (Apr. 1984).

22. D. Kelbaugh, *Passive Solar State of the Art,* American Section of the International Solar Energy Society, Newark, Delaware, 1978, pp. 69–75.

23. Interviews with G. Z. Brown and J. S. Reynolds of Equinox Design, Inc., Dec. 5, 1987.

24. J. Germer, *Solar Age* **9,** 32–37 (Aug. 1984).

25. *The Construction Specifier,* 44–49 (June 1982).

26. Interviews with John Weidt, The Weidt Group (formerly John Weidt Associates), Chaska, Minn., Dec. 2, 1987.

27. Burt Hill Kosar Rittleman Associates and Min Kantrowitz Associates, *Commercial Building Design: Integrating Climate Comfort and Cost,* Van Nostrand Reinhold Co., Inc., New York, 1987, pp. 137–152.

28. M. Kantrowitz, "Energy Past and Energy Future," *Progressive Architecture* **XLVII,** 118–123 (Apr. 1986).

29. T. Fisher, *Progressive Architecture* **XLVI,** 74–77 (Apr. 1985).

30. J. Wineman and C Zimmring, *Progressive Architecture* **XLVII,** 114–117 (Apr. 1986).

31. M. S. Ubbelohde, "The New School of Architecture at Florida A&M University," *Proceedings of the 11th National Passive Solar Conference,* American Solar Energy Society, Newark, Del., 1986, pp. 38–41.

32. Ref. 1, p. 13.

General References

Ref. 11 is a good general reference.

Proceedings of the National Passive Solar Conferences, American Solar Energy Society, Newark, Del., Vol. 1, 1975 to the present. The best source of technical research.

Solar Energy Research Institute, *The Design of Energy-Responsive Commercial Buildings,* John Wiley & Sons, Inc., New York, 1985. Good introduction to energy issues in commercial building design.

E. Mazria, *The Passive Solar Energy Book,* Rodale Press, Inc., Emmaus, Pa., 1979. The classic book for designing a solar house.

P. Niles and K. Haggard, *Passive Solar Handbook,* California Energy Commission, Sacramento, Calif., 1980. Excellent explanation of passive systems with construction details provided.

V. Olgyay, *Design With Climate,* Princeton University Press,

Princeton, N.J., 1963. The seminal research on climate and architectural design.

R. Stein, *Architecture and Energy*, Anchor Press–Doubleday, Garden City, N.Y., 1977. The best source on embodied energy and lighting energy costs.

D. Watson and K. Labs, *Climatic Design: Energy-Efficient Building Principles and Practices*, McGraw-Hill Inc., New York, 1983. Thorough technical introduction and design strategy compilation. Extensive bibliography.

See also ENVELOPES, BUILDING; LIGHTING—DAYLIGHTING; LIGHTING—ELECTRIC; MECHANICAL SYSTEMS; POWER GENERATION—FOSSIL FUELS; POWER GENERATION—GEOTHERMAL; POWER GENERATION—NUCLEAR; POWER GENERATION—WIND, TIDAL

M. SUSAN UBBELOHDE
University of Minnesota
Minneapolis, Minnesota

SOLERI, PAOLO

Italian architect Paolo Soleri is one of the best-known utopian planners of the twentieth century. His elaborate sociological philosophies and city plans, bearing the unmistakable evidence of a highly creative mind, depict the ideal self-sufficient societies that have always been the stuff of visionary dreams. His controversial megaplans and experimental communities are poetic manifestos of the type of world that is possible once man decides to live in harmony with nature.

Paolo Soleri was born in Turin, Italy in 1919. After receiving a doctorate with highest honors from the Polytechnic University of Torino, 1946, he moved to the United States where he was apprenticed to Frank Lloyd Wright at Taliesin West from 1947 to 1949. Wright's philosophies, particularly the twin theories of plasticity and continuity, had a profound effect on Soleri's later work. In 1950 he returned to Italy where he designed and built a uniquely sculptural ceramics factory on the Amalfi Coast, south of Naples. Although the factory at Vietri sul Mare is decidedly influenced by Gaudi's Sagrada Familia, it is a remarkably original work. Bulging, thin-shelled walls enhance rather than disturb the natural curves of the cliffside setting. Another important project from Soleri's early years was the tubular bridge designed in the late 1940s. This ingenious reinforced concrete bridge unfolds where structural stresses are small, then closes back into tubular shapes at midspan. Although the project was never built, it is possibly the first innovative concept in bridge design since Maillart.

In 1955, Soleri moved to Paradise Valley, a small desert outside of Phoenix, Arizona, where he built his own "earth house" (1956–1958), just a few miles from Taliesin West. The earth house, one of two related structures, explores natural forms and building techniques. Here again are traces of Gaudi's work and suggestions of Wright's philosophies. Built with the help of an apprentice system similar to Wright's, the partially subterranean complex, later named Cosanti, incorporated residences, ceramics studios, and apprentice quarters. Based on passive solar principles, the structures are cool in the hot desert days and warm in the cold desert nights. Cosanti is 25 × 35 ft, 6 ft below the level of the desert floor, and is covered by a 3-in.-thick curved and ribbed shell roof that touches the desert floor on two long sides of the plan. The ends of the house open onto excavated patios designed with collection pits for rainwater that supports a planting system that will eventually cover the entire roof. The technology is innovative. Soleri first built a huge mold from hardened desert sand. This was scored with crisscrossed indentations from end to end and covered with reinforcing rods and mesh. Concrete was then poured and sprayed over the mold. Once the shell was completely cured, the sand mold was excavated with a bulldozer.

Soleri eventually moved 70 mi north of Cosanti to escape the encroaching suburban sprawl of Phoenix. This was chosen as the building site for Arcosanti, a minicity capable of supporting 3000 people on 10 acres of land surrounded by a greenbelt. Ultimately designed to be 20 stories high, the prototype city supports a study center for experimental workshops and performing arts. Its builders are typically students under contractual agreement in which they promise both fees and labor for the privilege of being a part of Soleri's community. Apprentice quarters are 12-ft concrete cubes with porthole windows.

Arcosanti was a prototype "arcology," an idea developed by Soleri in the 1960s. Arcology, which conceptually addresses the interrelationship between architecture and ecology, was conceived by Soleri as a vital process as well as an end product. Arcologies ultimately provide alternatives to horizontal growth that characterizes most American cities and their resulting suburbs. By contrast, arcologies are self-contained, vertically layered megabuildings that combine living, working, and natural environments into condensed superorganisms. Although unconventional in form, the underlying assumptions are intensely urbanistic in that they support a complex philosophical position that relates megacities to the entire process of evolution. Soleri makes a scientific analogy between the compactness in nature and the density, or critical mass, essential to urban societies. Because the degree of liveliness, energy, and efficiency is directly proportional to density, the city must be predicated on compactness: lack of density is synonymous with inefficiency.

Arcosanti is only a small test model in comparison to Soleri's ultimate vision. He compiled 30 other arcologies in the 1969 publication, *Arcology: The City in the Image of Man*. Included in the selection are Veladiga, supporting 15,000 people on a site near a dam, and Babelnoah, a community accommodating six million people on a site ideally located near a coastal swamp. Soleri has also experimented with arcologies that turn with the sun and incorporate bases of economic activities including timbering and mining. All of these concentrated cities can be traversed by foot or bicycle. Cars are not allowed, thus eliminating vehicular circulation as a determining factor of form as in other modern city planning. Soleri has a deep dislike for cars and suburbs and the flat, amorphous dispersal of community that they produce. The stated objectives in all of his plans include the development of an extended list of environmental variations and possibilities; the illustration of benefits to be garnered from concentration and high densities in cities; the expansion of conceptions of inner space and volume; the development of alternatives to vehicular traffic; the exploration of the varieties of economies made possible by automation, standardization, and density; the conversion of leisure activities into useful contributions to the city; and the reinterpretation of the artist's role in society.

The second planned arcology is the dreamlike "City on a Mesa," which Soleri designed and drew in meticulous detail on dozens of rolls of butcher paper, each several hundred feet long. Mesa City will support more than two million people on approximately 55,000 acres of land, 13.5 mi long and 6 mi wide. Thirty-four villages will be grouped around civic buildings and shopping centers in clusters of five. This city plan begins with the conviction that the city is the most relevant aesthetic phenomenon on the earth. Mesa City is to be located in the western United States or a similar region. The land is internationalized under a world government authority. Located on a semiarid plateau and surrounded by grounds for agricultural activities, the ecology is closely controlled by a complex system of watersheds, dams, and canals. Providing the backbone of the society are a man-made park, a center for advanced study, and a theological complex.

Soleri believes that in this world of ever-changing beauty and splendor, architecture offers a path for man to equal the power and grace of nature: he is searching for that path. Of all the demands inherent in the act of architectural design, he sees the creation of an environment harmonizing with nature as the most urgent.

BARBARA WADKINS
Chula Vista, California

SOUND CONTROL.   See ACOUSTICS—GENERAL PRINCIPLES.

SOUND MEASUREMENT.   See ACOUSTICS—GENERAL PRINCIPLES.

SOUND REINFORCEMENT SYSTEMS

Most sources of natural sound, such as human voice or musical instruments, produce sound levels that are adequate for listening at relatively short distances in rooms with small volume. It is generally accepted that acoustically well-designed auditoriums with a volume in excess of 1500 m^3, where the voice must travel more than 15 m, will require a sound reinforcement system to provide adequate loudness and uniform distribution of sound. Even in smaller rooms, such as meeting rooms with a seating capacity for 100 people or more, where strong-voiced speakers can be heard clearly, the weaker voices must be reinforced. Often, there is the need to reproduce a program from a disk, tape, or motion picture sound track. Outdoors,

sound reinforcement may be required for a talker whose audience is at a distance of more than 7 m. In rooms with long reverberation, which is not favorable for speech, the intelligibility can be improved with a sound reinforcement system, which increases the amount of direct sound at the listener's position. For satisfactory intelligibility, in order to avoid masking, the voice should be at least 25 dB above the level of ambient noise. In many instances, this will require reinforcing of the useful sounds. In theaters and opera houses, sound reinforcement systems are needed to amplify the voices of the performers so that they will not be overpowered by the sounds of the orchestra.

The issue of sound reinforcement in opera is a subject of musical concern, because many people prefer to hear the performance without artificial amplification. This is not always possible, especially with singers who have less than perfectly trained voices. The need for amplification has become more pronounced in recent times, when reasons of profitability led to the construction of lyric theaters with seating capacities larger than before. In other instances, loudspeakers are used for reproduction of organ sound in halls not equipped with this instrument. In the Barbican Theatre in London, a sound system is used to feed into the hall the sounds of an orchestra playing in another room.

The human voice has a sound power spectrum with a maximum between 500 and 600 Hz, and the sound power decreases above 1000 Hz at a rate of about 8 dB per octave. The vowel sounds are not as critical to the speech intelligibility as the consonant sounds. The consonant sounds are relatively weak and therefore easily masked by noise. Most of the sound energy in consonants is in the high frequency range. At high frequencies voice is directional and the intelligibility of speech drops off rapidly when the speaker turns away from the listeners. This poses problems during conferences and theatrical plays, when the speaker or the actors do not always face the audience. The intelligibility of speech can be restored through the amplification of speech sounds at frequencies above 500 Hz. However, reinforced speech, with the bandwidth limited to high frequencies, does not sound natural. For that reason high quality sound reinforcement systems include frequencies starting at approximately 125 Hz to ensure a pleasant and natural quality of speech.

Sound systems intended for the reinforcement or reproduction of music must cover a wider frequency range. The fundamental frequency of organ pipes starts at 16 Hz and that of the bass drums starts between 16 and 20 Hz. Few sound systems are capable of reproducing such low frequencies. A normal frequency range for high quality reinforcement systems extends from 40 to 12,000 Hz.

Sound reinforcement systems must be designed to produce adequate sound pressure levels without distortion or other signs of overload. Typically, the systems intended for reinforcement of speech should be capable of delivering sound levels of between 85 and 90 dB. Systems for reinforcement or reproduction of concert music should be designed to deliver sound pressure levels of between 100 and 105 dB. Sound reinforcement systems used by rock bands can develop sound levels of 110 dB or more. The exposure to such high sound levels for extended periods of time can lead to hearing damage.

The localization of a sound source by the listener occurs with the arrival of the first sound impulse from that source. Successive repetitions of the same signal, either in the form of natural sound reflections from hard surfaces in the room or in the form of sound impulses from loudspeakers, are not registered by the listener as separate sounds until the delay reaches relatively large values of more than 50 ms. The suppression of echoes arriving with short delays is called the Haas effect, after the discoverer of this phenomenon. Such repeated impulses contribute to the loudness of the primary signal, and under some circumstances increase the intelligibility. The Haas effect is widely used in the design of sound systems when the directional realism in reinforcement must be preserved. This requires placement of the loudspeakers in such a way that the reinforced sound arrives at the listener's ears with a slight delay following the sound from the natural source. In this arrangement, the listener will localize the sound as arriving from the direction of the source, not from the loudspeaker. The largest increase in the intelligibility of speech due to the operation of a sound system will occur if most of the sound from the loudspeakers reaches the listeners directly, without reflections from the walls or from the ceiling. This requires that the loudspeakers either be placed close to the listeners, or that they radiate the sound in a highly directional way, or both.

The size of the room in which a sound system operates has an effect on the performance of the system and will influence the choice of loudspeakers most suitable in a given situation. In small rooms, for example, such as domestic living rooms, all sound reflections from the room boundaries arrive at the listener in very quick succession, following the direct sound within a few thousandths of a second, and are easily integrated with the direct sound. In small rooms, therefore, loudspeakers with wide dispersion of sound will perform satisfactorily, and there is no need to use highly directional loudspeakers. In very large rooms, sound reflections from the walls arrive following the direct sound with very long delays, sometimes in tens or hundreds of milliseconds. Such long-delayed reflections do not integrate with the direct sound and are generally harmful to the intelligibility and clarity of sound. Therefore, in large rooms, better results are generally obtained through use of loudspeakers that radiate sound within a narrow angle and are pointed toward the audience. Their directivity tends to reduce the amount of harmful sound reflections from the walls.

In rooms with small volume, intended for private listening, background noise can be maintained at very low levels. Consequently, the efficiency of the employed loudspeaker systems is of little consequence and they are being selected primarily from the standpoint of delivering the sound with highest possible fidelity over the widest possible frequency range. In very large spaces, such as sports arenas, where the background noise due to the presence of audience cannot be effectively controlled, the ability of a loudspeaker system to deliver sound at a very

high output with very high efficiency is of great importance.

LOUDSPEAKER SYSTEMS

There are two basic types of loudspeaker arrangement used in sound reinforcement systems: the central and the distributed loudspeaker systems. In a central system, the loudspeakers are normally located above the source of live sound. In medium or large size auditoriums, a central loudspeaker system is the preferred type in most situations, because it preserves the directional realism in sound reinforcement. In instances when the arrangement of the audience areas is such that the distance from the central loudspeaker system to the nearest listeners is much shorter than the distance to the most remote seats, it may not be possible to obtain a satisfactorily uniform coverage of the audience area with the sound from a single source, without the use of supplemental loudspeaker systems. Typically, supplemental loudspeakers may provide the coverage for listeners in deep balcony or under-balcony areas, or for the listeners sitting in the first rows of auditoriums that are wide in the front. Supplemental loudspeakers must operate with properly delayed signals, so that the sound from different loudspeakers is received in a close sequence to preserve the directional realism and to avoid artificial echoes. A section through an auditorium with a central loudspeaker system and with supplemental loudspeakers is shown in Figure 1. In supplemental or distributed systems that use directional loudspeakers operating with delayed sound, the loudspeakers must be oriented away from the source of the non-delayed sound in order to avoid artificial echoes.

The other basic arrangement of loudspeakers in a room is a distributed system that uses a large number of loudspeakers distributed uniformly over the audience area. An example of such a loudspeaker arrangement is shown in Figure 2. Usually, the loudspeakers in distributed systems are recessed in the ceiling. However, in rooms with a fixed seating, they can be installed in the backs of the seats or, in church sound systems, in the backs of the pews. With the loudspeakers located near the audience, each listener receives the sound primarily from the closest loudspeakers. Although the directional realism in reinforcement using a distributed system cannot be main-

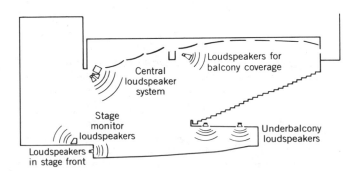

Figure 1. Auditorium with central loudspeaker system and supplemental loudspeakers.

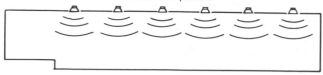

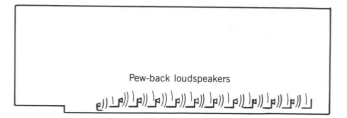

Figure 2. Distributed loudspeaker systems.

tained, the clarity and intelligibility of sound is usually very good. Distributed systems are used in situations where a low ceiling does not allow for a central system or where not all the listeners can have unobstructed lines of sight to a central system. The distributed systems are also used in large meeting, convention, or exhibition rooms, which must have a flexible arrangement of seats or require the reinforcement of sound from any position in the room, or when the room is divisible by movable partitions. The distributed loudspeaker systems with loudspeakers mounted in the ceiling should not be used in rooms where the ceiling is very high.

A well-designed, carefully installed, and properly operated sound system will provide a pleasant, natural quality of sound without distortion or coloration. The distortion of sound occurs when the system, for one reason or another, is not capable of delivering at its output an acoustical signal that has the same shape as the signal at the input of the system. Common causes of distortion are an improper selection of components, which are undersized for the required output; an incorrect gain structure, with a resulting overload of intermediate stages of amplification; or an input overload, when a signal of excessive amplitude is applied to the input of the system. Undersized components are largely a matter of an incorrect design and cannot be easily corrected at a later stage. The incorrect gain structure may be a matter of an incorrect design or incorrect adjustments; the first may not be easy to rectify, the second can be easily readjusted by instruments and tests. An input overload is always a matter of the incorrect operation, easy to avoid and correct. The sound coloration is a state in which the sound system loses the naturalness of sound reproduction and acquires an unpleasant, ringing quality. This may be caused by a nonuniform frequency response, when certain frequencies are amplified more than others, or it may be the result of operating the system with an excessive gain, near the point of an acoustic feedback or howling. Both conditions can be corrected, although the corrections of the overall frequency response may require changes in the equipment, in its adjustments, or in the system design.

EQUIPMENT

Microphones

Microphones are electroacoustic transducers that convert acoustic energy into electric energy. They convert sound waves into electric signals, which are further amplified, transmitted, or processed as required in a sound system installation. The microphones most commonly used in sound systems are the electrodynamic transducers. An electrodynamic microphone is based on the principle of the sound pressure acting on an electrical conductor, either a specially folded metal ribbon (ribbon microphones) or a coil (moving coil microphones), causing it to move in a magnetic field and to have current induced in it, at a frequency corresponding to the fluctuations of the sound wave. The moving coil microphone is currently the most popular type. Its advantages are an excellent quality of reproduction; rugged construction; directional sensitivity, which can be varied through simple means; and the fact that it needs no supply of power.

From the standpoint of directivity, microphones can be omnidirectional, used mostly for recording or for close pickup in sound reinforcement, and directional, with maximum pickup from the direction of their main axis. Directional microphones, with cardioid or supercardioid pickup characteristics, are most widely used in sound systems because they help reduce the acoustic interaction between the loudspeaker and the microphone that causes the acoustic feedback, the interference caused by reverberation, and the effect of ambient noise. In order to use all of these advantages, the directional microphone should be placed close to the source of sound, pointing away from the loudspeakers. A variety of microphones used in sound reinforcement systems is shown in Figure 3.

In addition to the conventional microphones, hand-held or on stands, there are miniature (lavaliere) microphones, which can be worn to allow more freedom of movement. Other special microphone types include the ultradirectional, narrow beam, "shot-gun" microphones, used for a distant pickup in theatrical reinforcement. The condenser, also called capacitor; microphones are less rugged than the electrodynamic microphones and require a power supply. They are used in sound systems for their very small size and exceptionally smooth frequency response. Microphones of any type can be used with small, wireless transmitters to allow full freedom of motion of the speaker. The wireless microphones are especially useful in the reinforcement of theatrical plays.

Preamplifiers

The function of a preamplifier is to reinforce the signal from the microphone to a level suitable for further processing and feeding other components of the sound system. In addition to the inputs for microphones, the preamplifiers may have inputs especially designed to accept signals from phono cartridges, tape, film, or other signal sources. Preamplifiers are normally provided with several inputs allowing the mixing (combining) of signals from several sources. Preamplifiers may be equipped with tone controls, allowing tonal corrections to the signal. A mixer

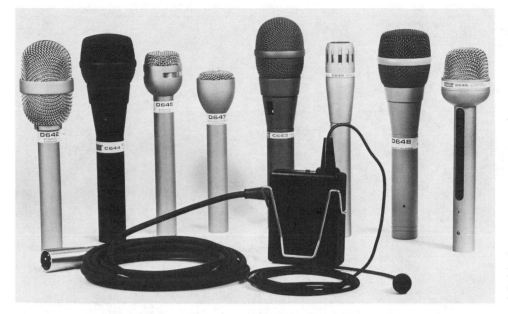

Figure 3. Microphones used in sound reinforcement systems. Courtesy of Altec Lansing Corp.

preamplifier used in small sound reinforcement systems is shown in Figure 4.

Control Consoles

The control consoles fulfill the same role as the preamplifiers, except that they are much more complex and offer more flexibility in signal processing. Typical control consoles have 12, 16, 24, 32, or 40 inputs and two or four main outputs, depending on the requirements. Control consoles often include elaborate frequency equalization in each channel, allowing the introduction of peaks or dips at selected frequency bands. Some consoles include matrix circuitry at the outputs, which allow the delivery of separate and different mixtures of sound (mixes) as needed for simultaneous sound reinforcement, recording, broadcasting, and monitoring on the stage. A mixing console with 12 input channels, used in small to medium size theater and auditorium sound systems, is shown in Figure 5.

Signal Processing Equipment

There is a large variety of signal processing equipment that is used in sound reinforcement systems. Equalizers are used to alter the frequency response of the system. In their simplest form, they act as tone controls; in a more elaborate version, they are used to increase or decrease the gain in the individual frequency bands with an octave or ⅓ octave bandwidth. The purpose of an equalizer is to introduce corrections in the electrical frequency response of the system to compensate for irregularities in the frequency response of transducers (microphones and loudspeakers) combined with the effects of room acoustics. The detailed equalization of a sound system for a smooth overall frequency response is invaluable for obtaining a natural quality of sound and for increasing the gain of the system before feedback. A graphic ⅓ octave band equalizer with low pass and high pass filters used to equalize sound systems is shown in Figure 6.

Limiters restrict the level of the signal that can be applied to the inputs of the electronic equipment, thus protecting the amplifiers and loudspeakers from an overload. Limiters are particularly useful in sound systems serving large arenas or outdoor stadiums, where the components, in order to deliver the high sound pressure levels required, are likely to operate near their power handling capacity.

Electronic delays are used to retard the signal to the amplifiers serving the supplemental loudspeakers located closer to the listeners than the main loudspeaker system. The purpose of the delay is to compensate for the difference in time it takes the sound to travel from the main loudspeaker system and from the supplemental loudspeakers. Electronic delays typically employ digital delay lines; they have one input and one or more outputs, each with a different delay, as required.

Figure 4. Mixer preamplifier. Courtesy of Altec Lansing Corp.

Figure 5. Mixing console. Courtesy of Rupert Neve, Inc.

Electronic delays may also be used with distributed loudspeaker systems to compensate for the difference in time required for sound to travel from the live source and nearby loudspeakers. A typical application is for distributed systems with loudspeakers in pew backs in churches. Caution is needed when this approach is used in large, acoustically live halls, especially when the installation involves loudspeakers mounted in the ceiling and operated with relatively high sound levels, so that the sound from the loudspeakers in the rear of the hall can be heard in the front. Under such circumstances, delaying the sound to the rear loudspeakers may adversely affect hearing conditions near the live source located in the front of the hall. The delay in hearing the sound from distant loudspeakers, added to the electronic delay, may create conditions of artificially increased reverberation.

Feedback suppressors are used in systems that must operate with weak-voiced speakers or with a long-range

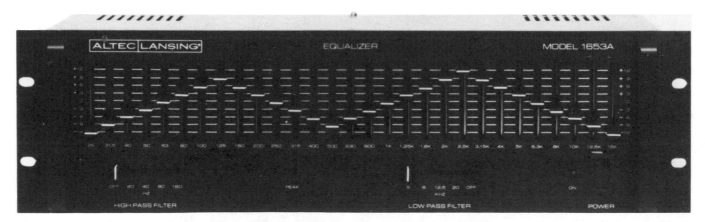

Figure 6. ⅓ Octave band equalizer. Courtesy of Altec Lansing Corp.

microphone pickup, such as in theatrical reinforcement. Some feedback suppressors automatically reduce the gain in the system when the threshold of howling is reached. The preferred type of feedback suppressor employs the method of frequency shifting. This method consists of shifting by a few cycles per second the frequency of sound radiated from the loudspeaker with respect to the frequency picked up by the microphone. Consequently, the peaks in the point-to-point acoustical frequency response in the room are shifted into the valleys of the response, allowing an increase of the gain before feedback by several decibels.

Distribution amplifiers are used in large sound systems consisting of several independent amplification tracks, where it is necessary to feed a number of signal lines from one source without affecting that source through an interaction from the lines or from the increased load. This is best accomplished through the use of distribution amplifiers, which provide the division of signals while maintaining the isolation between the source and the receivers.

Power Amplifiers

Power amplifiers are designed to provide a signal output with sufficient power (voltage and electric current output) to feed the loudspeakers connected to the system. Typically, in a large sound system, in order to reduce the losses due to the resistance in the loudspeaker lines, the distribution of loudspeaker power is via 70- or 100-V lines. The size of the power amplifiers is selected to allow connecting the loudspeaker loads provided in the design plus at least 10% reserve capacity. Typically, power amplifiers are sized in 3 dB increments of power, delivering output at 50, 100 or 200 watts.

Loudspeakers

Electromagnetic, direct-radiator loudspeakers are the most commonly used in sound reinforcement. The task of a loudspeaker is to convert the electric signal supplied from the power amplifier into an air vibration that the ear perceives as sound. An electromagnetic loudspeaker consists of a magnet with a round air gap and a voice coil, which moves inside the gap. The voice coil is attached to a paper cone or diaphragm, which is designed to radiate the vibration. The cone-type loudspeakers vary in size from less than 7 cm in diameter, for loudspeakers intended for reproduction of high frequencies, to over 45 cm in diameter for low frequency loudspeakers. Direct-radiator loudspeakers must be housed in enclosures to cancel the effect of radiation from the back of the cone. Small diameter loudspeakers are not as efficient as large diameter ones in radiation of low frequencies. The efficiency of conversion of the electric energy into the acoustic energy is relatively low for the direct-radiator loudspeakers. The typical efficiency of such loudspeakers is between 1 and 4%.

One of the shortcomings of a simple, direct-radiator loudspeaker is its directional characteristic, which tends to focus the high frequency sounds into a narrow beam. An improved radiation characteristic, with a wider radiation angle at high frequencies, is possible with a coaxial design, in which the radiation of low frequencies originates from a large diameter diaphragm, and the radiation of high frequencies originates from a separate, small radiator, installed concentrically inside the large unit. Coaxial loudspeakers show a uniform dispersion angle of at least 60° up to a frequency of 4 KHz. They are the preferred loudspeaker type in installations that use distributed loudspeakers.

The efficiency of radiation of loudspeakers can be dramatically improved when an electromagnetic driver is coupled to the outside atmosphere via a horn. The horn acts in this arrangement as an impedance transformer, decreasing the losses due to the impedance mismatch between the driver diaphragm and the air. In the middle and high frequency ranges, horn-type loudspeakers with compression drivers can have radiation efficiencies of up to 50%, making them the most efficient loudspeaker systems currently available. A high frequency, horn-type loudspeaker with constant directivity radiation over a wide range of frequencies is shown in Figure 7. The nominal coverage angle of this loudspeaker is 90° in the horizontal plane and 40° in the vertical plane. Figure 8 shows a compression-type, high frequency reproducer used with the high frequency horn shown in Figure 7.

Due to physical limitations, it is not possible to produce a simple loudspeaker capable of satisfactory reproduction of the entire audio-frequency range from one unit. The accepted method is to divide the audio-frequency range into two, three, or four frequency bands, assigned for reproduction by separate loudspeakers. The performance of the individual units is optimized from the standpoint of directivity, frequency response, efficiency, and the power-handling capacity in their respective frequency bands. Large sound reinforcement systems frequently use two- or three-way loudspeaker systems with the audio-frequency range divided at 500 or 800 Hz and 6000 Hz crossover frequencies. A two-way loudspeaker system used behind the screen in large motion picture theaters is shown in Figure 9. A large low frequency loudspeaker used in the loudspeaker system shown in Figure 9 is shown in Figure 10.

Sound Control

No sound reinforcement system will operate satisfactorily unless it is properly controlled. The optimum location for a sound control room or position is in the rear of the auditorium, in an arrangement in which the operator can directly hear the sound he or she is controlling and can follow the activity. The sound control position should be either fully open to the volume of the auditorium, which is practical only for small systems, not involving much control equipment, or it should be located in a special sound control room provided with a large, operable sound control window. Controlling the sound during the reinforcement of live events while listening to a monitor loudspeaker, or from a control room located remotely, without lines of sight to the activity being reinforced, will invariably lead to unsatisfactory results.

Many performing arts sound reinforcement systems now use control facilities located entirely within the audience area. These may be dedicated locations where all

Figure 7. High frequency constant directivity horn. Courtesy of Electro-Voice, Inc.

Figure 8. High frequency reproducer. Courtesy of Electro-Voice, Inc.

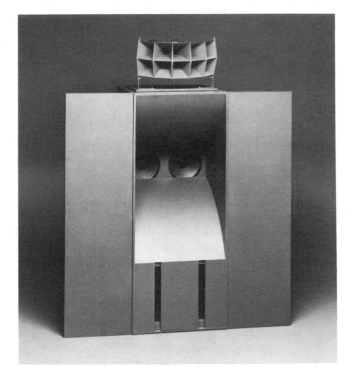

Figure 9. "Voice of the Theatre" loudspeaker system. Courtesy of Altec Lansing Corp.

Figure 10. Low frequency loudspeaker. Courtesy of Altec Lansing Corp.

control equipment and all activity occurs, or auxiliary locations intended only for events during which their use is feasible. A block diagram of a sound reinforcement system is shown in Figure 11.

EXAMPLES OF SOUND REINFORCEMENT AND REPRODUCTION SYSTEMS

There is an almost infinite number of variations in the design of sound systems that are applicable to rooms of various uses. It is essential that many aspects concerning sound systems be considered in early phases of facility planning. These include a clear understanding of the functions that the sound system must perform, the size and the placement of loudspeakers, the location of a sound control

position, and the provision of adequate space and ventilation for the signal processing and the amplification equipment. Electrical conduit of adequate capacity must be provided in the structure a long time before the sound system equipment can be installed. All of these factors require careful coordination with the architects and engineers.

Laying out of conventional distributed loudspeaker systems may be simple and may require only coordination of the loudspeaker placement on reflected ceiling plans, with the locations of lights, sprinklers, and air-handling system diffusers taken into consideration. Design of central loudspeaker systems often involves application of large loudspeakers, which require a design of suitable architectural enclosures and adequate supports. To give an idea of the size of various loudspeaker system components, a typical small, high frequency horn loudspeaker is roughly 45 cm wide, 35 cm high, and 50 cm long. A typical full-size, high frequency horn is approximately 75 cm wide, 85 cm high, and 100 cm long. While a typical vented-box, low frequency enclosure may be 100 cm high, 60 cm wide, and 45 cm deep and have an internal volume of 270 L, a large horn-loaded, bass-reflex, low frequency loudspeaker system may be 85 cm high, 200 cm wide, and 75 cm deep and have a gross volume of roughly 1275 L.

The design of larger sound systems is a complex task that requires knowledge of several areas of acoustics including room acoustics, psychoacoustics, and electroacoustics. In many instances, therefore, the design requires services of an expert who, in addition to a thorough understanding of the field, has sufficient experience in practical applications. Many specialists who design sound systems can be found among members of the National Council of Acoustical Consultants; some others operate independently. Before engaging a consultant, it is recommended to check his or her performance on projects completed in the past.

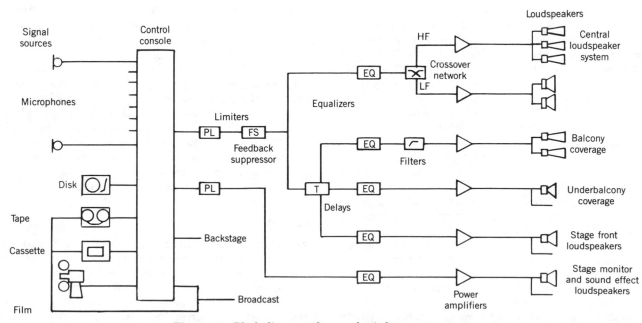

Figure 11. Block diagram of a sound reinforcement system.

It should be emphasized that even properly designed sound systems that use the best components may not perform satisfactorily if they have been installed in spaces with unsuitable acoustics. Factors of room acoustics, such as reverberation, distribution of sound-reflecting and sound-absorbing surfaces, and a level of ambient noise from interior and exterior sources, must be considered together in connection with the sound system, for they will influence the overall results.

Theaters and Opera Houses

The critical needs of theatrical reinforcement, where the directional realism plays an important role, require the sound systems in theaters and opera houses to use central loudspeaker systems located at the proscenium. Depending on the shape of the hall, the system may include supplemental loudspeakers.

Receptacles for microphones are provided at the stage front for use with microphones located at the footlights. Additional microphone receptacles are normally available in the stage wings. If the acting area is deep, microphone pickup from the footlight locations becomes unsatisfactory due to the large distance from the actors. Because the use of microphones suspended overhead generally does not provide a usable pickup and they often interfere with the movements of stage equipment and scenery, the best recourse is to use wireless systems with miniature microphone capsules concealed in the costumes of the performers.

Signal pickup for recording or broadcasting of live performances with audience is normally accomplished by means of microphones suspended in front of the proscenium. Halls designed for opera or for musical comedy are equipped with orchestra pits with one or more floor platforms on lifts. Microphone receptacles are provided in the pit floor because a performance of ballet frequently requires amplification of the orchestra sound from the pit onto the stage.

Sound effects during theatrical plays are reproduced by means of portable loudspeakers located offstage or in the scenery. There are large collections of prerecorded sound effects available. For use in stage productions, these effects are dubbed from disk to tape and provided with identification cues marked on the inserts of leader tape. The playback of sound effects is performed from the sound control room or from the stage wing, following visual or aural cue signals.

Halls that are designed for multipurpose uses, including performances of popular music with vocalists, require more microphones than those restricted to the performances of opera or drama. Microphones used by popular music groups are connected via multipair microphone cables called "snakes," the use of which reduces the equipment clutter on the stage floor. Performances of popular music also require the use of a multitude of loudspeakers on the stage for monitoring of sound by the performers. Full-size monitoring systems are independent from the sound reinforcement systems serving the house and employ separate sound control consoles, equalizers, power amplifiers, etc; this equipment is normally located in one of the stage wings.

The transmission of information to the cast offstage is accomplished by means of a program monitoring and stage manager's paging system covering the backstage areas. The loudspeakers in this system are distributed in the dressing rooms, waiting areas, and access corridors. The house sound, as heard by the audience, is derived from the sound reinforcement system during amplified events, or during events without amplification, from a house sound pickup microphone suspended in the hall. The loudspeaker circuits in the dressing rooms normally include individual volume controls. The equipment allows defeating the settings of the local controls to ensure the priority of the stage manager's announcements. The program monitoring and stage manager's paging system is independent from the sound reinforcement system serving the house proper, and its equipment is normally located in one of the stage wings, near the stage manager's position, where it can be used without the help of a sound system operator during events not requiring amplification.

The staff positions are interlinked by a production communications system. This is an intercom system of special design that allows a hands-free operation and voice communication in environments with high levels of ambient noise. The production intercom system normally includes a master station located at the stage manager's position and a number of fixed and portable remote stations. These are located in the light and sound control rooms, projection rooms, at follow spot locations, on lighting catwalks, etc. The fixed stations can be equipped with loudspeakers or with handsets. Portable remote stations are constructed in form of beltpacks connected to outlets through extension cables. Remote stations with wireless transmission provide the utmost mobility. The stations allow the use of single- or double-muff headsets with boom microphones. The production communication systems typically have at least two independent channels; one used by the lighting staff and one used by the sound crew, for example. More elaborate systems have four or eight channels. Even more flexibility in communications can be provided with a matrix arrangement for connecting the channel outputs with the lines to the remote intercom stations. The system allows listening to the house sound program. All channels are accessible for announcements by the stage manager. Outlets for production intercom are provided at the play director's and lighting director's positions in the audience area for use during rehearsals and setting up of the performance. During rehearsals, the play director makes announcements to the actors and to the conductor through a separate system with fixed loudspeakers at the proscenium and portable loudspeaker extensions that can be placed where required.

Concert Halls

Although the performances of classical music and vocal and instrumental recitals are normally not amplified, modern concert halls are equipped with high quality, full-range sound reinforcement systems. These systems are needed to meet the requirements of multipurpose uses of the concert halls, for announcements, the reinforcement of speech during concerts with narration, and for use by an increasing number of vocalists and instrumentalists who use reinforced sound as an integral part of their performances. The challenge in designing sound systems for concert halls is in reinforcing speech with high intelligibility in spaces that have long reverberation. Typically, concert halls use central loudspeaker systems with high directivity, similar to the systems in theaters and opera houses. Due to the lack of a proscenium wall, those systems are often suspended in free space or integrated architecturally with sound reflectors or canopies used above the orchestral platform. Many concert halls are used for mixed theatrical and concert productions, ballet, etc, and have orchestra pits. Receptacles for microphones are provided in the front of the orchestra platform, in the orchestra pit, and at the ceiling for suspended microphones. If the concert hall is used for performances of popular music, the sound system will include, in addition to the central loudspeaker system, loudspeakers for reinforcement directly from the stage, and stage monitor loudspeakers. Concert halls require systems for performance monitoring and paging backstage, as well as production intercom systems.

Auditoriums and Lecture Halls

Most auditoriums and lecture halls are equipped with central loudspeaker systems for full-range reinforcement of speech and reproduction of motion picture sound. Microphone receptacles are provided in the front of the platform and in locations designated for portable lecterns. For economy of space, the sound, projection, and lighting control are frequently located in one room. A desirable feature is the provision, at the lecturer's position, of remote controls for projection, volume control of sound, and dimming of the lights.

Meeting and Conference Rooms

Meeting and conference rooms often have systems of distributed loudspeakers recessed in the ceiling. Audio facilities may include microphone preamplifiers designed for automatic operation and mixing of sound. Depending on the requirements, these rooms may include specialized equipment for teleconferencing and equipment for projection of images from slides, film, videotape recorders, or television. Front projection is used when a complete blackout of the room is possible; it is not advisable for functions where note taking is essential. Rear projection provides satisfactory results in rooms that must remain partially lit during the event.

Motion Picture Theaters

The loudspeakers for playback of motion picture sound are located in the front of the room, behind a perforated screen. The high frequency loudspeakers in the system are placed approximately ⅓ of the screen height below its top. The number of independent sound channels may vary from one, for films with single-channel sound tracks, to four, for Cinema Scope sound reproduction, with three loudspeaker systems serving the main channels, located behind the screen, and the sound effects loudspeakers serving the fourth channel, distributed on the walls of the hall in a surround fashion. Figure 12 shows two-way loud-

Figure 12. Loudspeakers used in motion picture theaters. Courtesy of Altec Lansing Corp.

speaker systems used in medium size motion picture theaters. The unit on the right is a compact loudspeaker with shallow depth, used for reproduction of sound effects in surround fashion. Motion picture films that rely heavily on the use of sound effects may require the installation of special sound systems including ultralow frequency loudspeakers called subwoofers, used to simulate spectacular events, such as earth tremors, explosions, and the like. Many sound systems in motion picture theaters have inputs for playback of music during intermissions and for use with microphones for announcements, or during events when the hall is used as an auditorium.

Office Spaces

Except for meeting and conference rooms, the functions of the sound systems covering offices are limited to announcements or to the playback of background music. Open plan offices are frequently equipped with systems emitting a low level, bland noise, which helps to mask speech sounds intruding from adjacent work stations and improves the speech privacy. Such systems can combine both the masking noise and the distribution of announcements. Offices, as a rule, employ systems of distributed loudspeakers either recessed in the ceiling or concealed in the ceiling plenum behind sound-transparent ceiling panels. Depending on the building code requirements, the high-rise office towers may include sound systems designed for life safety announcements and for the transmission of warning signals. Such systems are normally separate from other systems and use fire-resistant equipment, wiring, and installation materials.

Houses of Worship

Houses of worship generally require acoustics suitable for music, that is, conditions with long reverberation. The problems facing the designer of sound systems for houses of worship are similar to those with concert halls, except that the requirement of the high intelligibility of speech is of primary importance, with the requirement of directional realism in reinforcement playing a lesser role. Under these conditions, distributed systems with loudspeakers in the backs of the pews are sometimes a solution. The use of wireless microphones for mobility and of automatic microphone mixers for simplicity of operation are common in the present-day installations in houses of worship.

Exhibition Halls

Sound reinforcement systems in exhibition halls are designed for reproduction of announcements and of background music. If an exhibition hall includes a permanent or demountable platform allowing some form of stage presentations, the design normally includes a central loudspeaker system located above the front of the platform to provide sound reinforcement with directional realism.

Hotel Ballrooms and Banquet Halls

Hotel ballrooms and banquet halls are often divisible spaces with microphone pickup required from any location on the floor. Like exhibition halls, hotel ballrooms and banquet halls use distributed systems of overhead loudspeakers. If a stage platform or a motion picture screen is provided, the design includes a central loudspeaker system. Hotel ballrooms and banquet halls often feature such functions as floor shows and fashion shows, in many respects resembling theatrical performances. For this reason, production communications facilities serving lighting, projection, and sound control are often essential.

Assembly Halls

Sound reinforcement systems for assembly halls may use either central or distributed loudspeaker systems, depending on the configuration of the space and the requirements of the users. Microphone arrangements may vary from simple to the most complex, when the participation of the audience or of the delegates from the floor is required. Assembly halls for multinational conferences must be equipped with systems for simultaneous translation.

Sports Facilities

Typically, indoor arenas, designed strictly for sports events, with seating capacities of up to 15,000 spectators have directional loudspeaker systems located in the center of the arena. Often, arenas are also used for other types of performance staged in the center or at the end of the floor. In such instances, more loudspeaker systems are required, one for each performing platform location. In multipurpose arenas, the provision of performance monitoring and paging systems in dressing rooms and locker rooms and the provision of production intercom system for stage management, lighting, and sound is required. In extremely large indoor arenas, such as the Houston Astrodome or the Louisiana Superdome, it is not possible to provide the sound coverage with adequate sound level and with a sufficient ratio of direct to reflected sound employing only one central loudspeaker system. These huge spaces have sound systems using many powerful, directional loudspeaker arrays distributed above the audience areas.

In such large systems, as well as in other distributed systems, the loudspeaker arrays or loudspeaker groups should be provided with cut-off switches to limit sound coverage to the occupied areas. This measure helps reduce reverberation. In cases when the microphones are located in the areas covered by loudspeakers, muting certain loudspeakers can reduce the danger of feedback.

Some large arenas, in order to save construction cost, use acoustical treatments that have depth insufficient to control reverberation at low frequencies. The low frequency reverberation time in such spaces may be several times longer than the reverberation time at higher frequencies. Operation in such spaces of a full-range sound system causes almost uninterrupted persistence of a low frequency sound, which is harmful to the clarity and intelligibility of speech. Because the reproduction of low frequencies is not essential for maintaining intelligibility, this situation can be remedied by limiting the bandwidth of the transmitted sound to higher frequencies only. Typically, the low frequency roll-off is selected at 200 or 300 Hz. Higher roll-off frequencies will impair the naturalness of speech.

The selection of the configuration of a sound system for an outdoor stadium depends entirely on the stadium uses, the seating configuration, and the availability of supporting structures for the loudspeakers. A major problem in many outdoor stadium sites is echo from large, hard surfaces such as scoreboards, unoccupied bleachers, nearby housing structures, etc.

Sound systems in natatoriums are designed primarily for announcements to the spectators. The loudspeaker coverage is normally restricted to the bleachers, using systems of distributed, directional loudspeakers. In some instances, underwater sound is provided for swimming instruction and coaching of the swimmers.

SPECIAL SOUND SYSTEM INSTALLATIONS

Paging and Voice-alarm Systems for Power Plants and Other Industrial Facilities

Power plants and large manufacturing facilities create difficult conditions for voice communications through public address systems that use loudspeakers. This is due to high levels of ambient noise normally present in such facilities and to their typically long reverberation time caused by large volume of rooms and by scarcity of sound-absorbing materials. Both high background noise and long reverberation time are harmful to speech intelligibility.

Intelligibility decreases rapidly if the average levels of reproduced speech are less than 20 dB above the A-weighted levels of ambient noise. Because listening to public address announcements at speech levels of more than 95 to 100 dB creates discomfort, industrial plants in which the average ambient noise levels exceed 75 to 80 dB_A are generally not suitable for use of public address systems. Another aspect is that a provision in large industrial plants of public address systems capable of delivering a uniform coverage with very high sound levels requires application of large quantities of loudspeakers and amplification equipment, the cost of which may be prohibitive. In plants with high noise levels, it may be necessary to use lights or sirens to communicate simple messages. If reliable transmission of voice messages to selected individuals is indispensable, it can be, in case of high ambient noise, accomplished through headsets equipped with effective earmuffs.

"Hard-of-hearing" Systems

Systems for people with hearing impediments are required in many public auditoriums. Often, the hard-of-hearing stations are provided at selected seats in the auditorium. Each such station is equipped with an outlet jack for headsets and with an individual volume control. A typical location for a jack and a volume control is under the armrest of an auditorium chair. If the coverage of all audience areas with a hard-of-hearing system is required, a wireless system is used with the transmission via an induction loop or frequency-modulated infrared radiation.

Simultaneous Interpretation Systems

Auditoriums designed for international conferences are equipped with multilanguage simultaneous translation systems. In such systems, the signal from the speaker's microphone (floor language) is distributed to the interpreters' booths. The interpreters listen to the floor language via headsets and translate the speech into other languages. The translated language signals are reinforced and distributed to the delegates' seats in the hall. The delegates listen to the translation via headsets, having selected the language channel with a switch. Each listening station is provided with an individual volume control. Another method of distribution of translated speech is via wireless transmission using radio waves, induction loops, or frequency-modulated infrared radiation. In a wireless transmission system, each delegate carries his own receiver and headset and is not restricted by a connecting cord in his freedom of movement. Wireless systems are required in halls with movable seats and flexible seating arrangements. The interpreters' booths must have satisfactory sound isolation between each other and must be located and oriented so that the interpreters see the lips of the person whose language they translate. Each booth must accommodate two interpreters sitting side by side.

BIBLIOGRAPHY

General References

AES Recommended Practice Specification of Loudspeaker Components Used in Professional Audio and Sound Reinforcement, AES2–1984 (ANSI S4.26–1984). Special Publications Office, Audio Engineering Society, Inc., New York.

G. M. Ballou, *Handbooks for Sound Engineers, the New Audio Cyclopedia,* Howard Sams Publishing Company, Indianapolis Ind., 1987.

M. C. Sprinkle, "Environmental Control—Sound Systems," in J. H. Callender, ed., *Time Saver Standards for Architectural Design Data,* 5th ed., McGraw-Hill Inc., New York, 1974, Chapt. 4, p. 1013.

L. L. Doelle, *Environmental Acoustics,* McGraw-Hill Inc., New York, 1972.

J. J. Figwer, "The Louisiana Superdome Sound System," *J.A.E.S.* **24**(7), 554 (Sept. 1976).

C. M. Harris, "Sound and Sound Levels," in C. M. Harris, ed., *Handbook of Noise Control,* 2nd ed., McGraw-Hill Inc., New York, 1979, Chapt. 2.

Also selected papers in the *Journal of the Audio Engineering Society.*

D. L. Klepper, ed., *Sound Reinforcement (Anthology of Papers),* Audio Engineering Society, Inc., New York, 1978.

H. Kuttruff, "Electroacoustic Installations in Rooms," in *Room Acoustics,* 2nd ed., Applied Science Publishers Ltd., London, 1979, Chapt. 10.

M. Rettinger, *Practical Electroacoustics,* Chemical Publishing Company, Inc., New York, 1955.

M. R. Schroeder, "Improvement of Acoustic Feedback Stability by Frequency Shifting," *J.A.S.A.* **36**, 1718 (Sept. 1964).

J. C. Webster, "Effects of Noise on Speech," in C. M. Harris, ed., *Handbook of Noise Control,* 2nd ed., McGraw-Hill Inc., New York, 1979, Chapt. 14.

See also ACOUSTICAL DESIGN—PLACES OF ASSEMBLY; ACOUSTICAL INSULATION AND MATERIALS; ACOUSTICS—GENERAL PRINCIPLES; MUSIC HALLS; THEATERS AND OPERA HOUSES

J. JACEK FIGWER, PhD
Jacek Figwer Associates, Inc.
Concord, Massachusetts

SOUTHEAST ASIAN ARCHITECTURE

HONG KONG

The history of Hong Kong is part of the Chinese civilization, which is one of the oldest in the world in terms of a continuous tradition (1–8). The Book of Changes, *I Ching,* articulated very early a universal harmony between humanity and the cosmos. Only recently have philosophical attempts again integrated the old concepts of the *yin* and *yang* as well as the concept of *Feng Shui* into contemporary building after a long period in which they were considered only obscurantic and irrelevant. *Feng Shui,* a principle of mutual energies in the human body and in the cosmos, was fully developed in the tenth century AD; it literally means "wind water" (9,10).

The area of Hong Kong was settled in neolithic times, and recently, the tomb of Lei Cheng Uk from the seventh-century Han Dynasty was discovered in Kowloon. The oldest existing villages of the Tang clan in the new territories date back to the eleventh century AD. The specific history of the Hong Kong area was determined by the first foreign settlements, which occurred in 1557 in nearby Macao, a Portuguese colony. The British came to Hong Kong, then a small fishing village, in 1841 when Captain Elliott founded the colony and made land allotments "pending Her Majesty's further pleasure." These first settlements were located between today's Ice House Street and Western market. By 1854, the site expanded to Bonham Road and Caine Road, and by 1861 to Robinson Road. From the outset, Hong Kong was surprisingly unplanned, based on improvisation and haphazard decision making, which continues up to the present day. Many fires and epidemics contributed to a basic sense of discontinuity and uncertainty. A fire in 1851 destroyed large parts of the settled areas. In 1853, the population consisted of 491 Europeans and 2416 Chinese. In 1860, the colonial administration took over the lease of Kowloon Peninsula, and the expansion that was already in progress continued until it reached Kowloon. The population reached 119,000 in 1861. Kennedy Town was laid out on reclaimed land along the northern shore of the island in 1866, as were many subsequent developments such as the Praya Reclamation (1890–1904). In 1894, bubonic plague killed 2,500 people in Hong Kong, and more than 80,000 left the colony (11). The early twentieth century saw large-scale planning expansions continued by the Kai Tak Land Company in Kowloon in 1919 and in the Kowloon Tong Garden City in 1922.

Architectural activities were manifested in a wide range of styles and idioms. St. John's Cathedral, which has been the cathedral of the Anglican bishops in Hong Kong since 1850, introduced Gothic revival architecture in Hong Kong. St. Mary's Church in the eastern district of Causeway Bay, built in 1936–1937, has a rare combination of neo-Chinese elements and monumental features characteristic of the 1930s. The White Pagoda, along with other structures in the Tiger Balm Garden (1935) in the Causeway Bay district, is a large environment conceived by the immigrant Aw Boon Haw from Rangoon, who had made a fortune from "tiger balm." His private garden with its terraces, caves, and pavilions was opened to the public after his death.

In programmatic contrast to these and numerous other alternatives, the concept of modernism was introduced to Hong Kong by British architects, among them Palmer and Turner, who was 23 years old when the most prominent banking institution in Hong Kong, the Hong Kong and Shanghai Banking Corporation, entrusted them with the design of its new headquarters on One Queen's Road Central in 1936. The 12-story air-conditioned building, which dominated the skyline, was then the most modern achievement in the colony. It was only recently demolished and replaced by the new bank headquarters designed by Norman Foster. The war between Japan and China in 1937 created serious changes for the colony, eventually leading to the Japanese occupation from 1941 to 1945.

Following the reestablishment of the British administration in 1946, planning and building activities in Hong Kong took on a new concept. The rapid growth in population was further increased after the establishment of the Communist regime in Beijing. In 1946, the population had reached 1 million, in 1959 it was 3 million, and in 1984 it was 5.5 million, a growth rate unprecedented in any urban conglomeration. In 1990, a population of 8 million is expected.

The urban planning strategies, of immediate necessity because of the rapid growth, remained improvisational; long-term planning was utopian. The government ap-

pointed the British planner Sir Patrick Abercrombie, who completed a report in 1948 proposing a limitation of the population to a maximum of 2 million, a concept that was immediately proven unrealistic. Refugee colonies in the new territories and in Kowloon became necessary improvisational solutions that had little to do with the Abercrombie plan, as did squatter colonies that existed before World War II and house boats (12).

After 1949, severe and extensive administrative measures were taken to resolve the increasingly catastrophic population explosion, epidemics, and sanitary problems. In 1949–1950, while approximately 750,000 new immigrants from China were continuously being absorbed, large fires destroyed whole slum neighborhoods. In January 1950, about 20,000 people were forced out of their shelters by one fire alone in Kowloon. Government action included slum zoning, dividing land into "approved areas" with one-story buildings for the refugees and "tolerated areas" in which wooden cabins for the poorest could be erected. Of course, these measures did not resolve the problems, and further actions became necessary (13).

When in 1953, on Christmas Day, again 53,000 squatters of Shep Kip Mei were left homeless by a large fire, the Public Works Department took action and created the Resettlement program. In the mid-1950s, large housing estates consisting of concrete blocks built in a seven-story H-shape were designed as emergency housing. According to the plan, a family of four or five adults was allocated 36 m² of living space, with lavatories and washing and bathing facilities on each floor. The ground floor usually contained commercial functions, stores, and workshops; the first floor contained professional offices, including illegal doctors; and the upper floors contained apartments. The roofs were often turned into schools or playgrounds, run by religious or charity organizations (14). The small spaces between the blocks were used for markets. The people adjusted the plan of the government to suit their needs. The user proved to be more significant than the planners and architects (15):

> The transformation of these resettlement blocks into self-contained socioeconomic structures was not planned. This process was dictated by the needs of the people. As a result, a whole new life pattern with a new set of socioeconomic values was created among the residents of early resettlement blocks.

The architectural development of postwar Hong Kong was dominated by British architects, and the leading firm was Palmer and Turner, whose later developments included educational buildings (Hong Kong Polytechnic, 1973–1979), hotel buildings, office buildings (the shipping offices and warehouse at North Point, 1960), and residential buildings. In 1980, the firm designed the Jingling Hotel in Nanking, mainland China.

The Town Hall of Hong Kong, built in 1962 at the waterfront of Hong Kong Harbor, was designed by the Housing Department. It is a modern 12-story high-rise that contains a library, a museum, a concert hall, and recreational facilities. At the time of its erection, the building manifested the state of architecture in the international context. Among British architects located in

Hong Kong is Eric Cumine, who, although predominantly engaged in housing schemes, has also designed hotels, offices, police stations, and a sports stadium.

A large number of British firms have extended commissions in Hong Kong, transplanting the expertise of British architecture to the colony. Llewelyn-Davies Weeks and Ove Arup were in charge of the 700-bed Queen Mary Hospital. Rosenberg, Yorke and Mardall, often in collaboration with Arup, designed the Prince Philip Central Teaching Hospital and the Carlsberg Brewery, the latter with Anders Helsterd as partner. In collaboration with Prescott and Partners, Arup built the Members Clubhouse for the Royal Hong Kong Jockey Club in Shatin (1983–1985). Arup, with his firm in collaboration with Gordon Wu and Associates, planned the Hopewell Centre, a circular high-rise office tower, which has become a landmark of the city. The firm Ove Arup and Partners also had large-scale commissions for the Mass Transit Railway (Luk Yeung Sun Chuen Development) as well as the Tsuen Wan Depot, the latter in collaboration with Tao Ho. Most of these buildings reflect contemporary British architecture applied to a specific regional situation that has parallel examples in other parts of the world.

Among the numerous Chinese architects working in Hong Kong, some have established their distinct individuality and have made contributions that help to define the identity of the country. The firm Wong, Tung and Partners, established in 1961, planned and built large-scale housing developments in Hong Kong. Among them is Mei Foo Sun Chuen Development, a city within a city for 70,000–90,000 people, built in several phases between 1963 and 1976. The total complex, on a very limited site, comprises 99 20-story apartment blocks, which in their arrangement are rather rigid and inflexible. Commercial areas as well as schools, playgrounds, and a large number of art works are part of the neighborhood, which can be evaluated only in terms of the necessitated emergency, not with regard to solutions to the architectural aspects of the problem.

The problem was again faced, with similar results in large-scale developments such as the Taikoo Shing (1972) and the Chi Fu Fa Yuen Condominiums (1976) (Fig. 1). As part of Taikoo Shing, a center for entertainment and leisure, named City Plaza, was added in collaboration with Ove Arup and Partners as structural engineers. Most large-scale housing in Hong Kong, like these settlements, addresses only immediate necessities. Other realizations, by the firm Wong, Tung and Partners, such as the tower for the First National Bank on Queen's Road Central (1974), buildings for the University of Hong Kong (phase 1), and smaller recreational buildings, among them the Discovery Bay Golf Clubhouse and the Silverview Lodge, demonstrate adjustments to the given task and solutions that are in harmony with the environment.

One of the Chinese architects of the younger generation is Tao Ho. Born in 1936 in Shanghai, he studied in the United States under Walter Gropius and returned to Hong Kong in 1964. Since his studies he has been involved not only in architecture, but also in painting, sculpture, and art history. Among his early works are the Hong Kong International School (completed in 1975) in collaboration with Wong and Ouyang, the Hua Hsia Building (1975–1977), and the Shouson Hill residential development (1979) in collaboration with Eric K. C. Lye.

Ho's most important work is the Hong Kong Arts Centre (1974–1977), in which a synthesis of old and new as

Figure 1. Chi Fu Fa Yuen Condominiums, Hong Kong (1976). Architects Wong, Tung and Partners. Courtesy of Wong, Tung and Partners, Hong Kong.

Figure 2. Bowen Road Apartments, Hong Kong (1984). Architect: Tao Ho. Courtesy of U. Kultermann.

and Turner, Australian architect Harry Seidler designed the new Hong Kong Club in 1981, replacing the old and distinguished landmark from the nineteenth century. Facing Cenotaph Square to the west and with extensive views of the harbor to the north as well to the peak in the south the location is one of the most prominent in the city. The 20-story building contains a main hall, restaurants, bars, a garden lounge, a bowling alley, and health club facilities.

Another landmark is the New Coliseum of Hong Kong, built by the Public Works Department of Hong Kong. Completed in 1982, this multipurpose structure is located over the Hung Hom Railway Terminus overlooking the bay. Shaped in the form of an inverted pyramid, it contains facilities for basketball, table tennis, badminton, and skating as well as for concerts, ballets, circuses, and parades (17).

The Lowland and Headland Ocean Park, located on a peninsula jutting into the South China Sea, was designed by architects Leigh and Orange. Completed in 1977, it constitutes a fascinating environmental ensemble. Divided into two areas, the lowland and the headland, it offers the world's largest oceanarium. The main attraction of the complex is the Atoll Reef with a 2 million-L aquarium for the study and exposition of underwater marine

Figure 3. Hong Kong Club, Hong Kong (1981). Architect: Harry Seidler. Courtesy of Harry Seidler, Sydney.

well as of art and architecture was achieved. With its prominent site on the waterfront of Hong Kong, the 19-story building contains 2 theaters, studios, a concert hall, exhibition spaces, clubs, and offices, all encompassed in a system based on triangulation in plan and elevation as in old Chinese buildings.

A recent large complex by Ho is the Bowen Road Apartments (1984), a 12-story luxury apartment with two penthouses and a swimming pool. Following the local Hong Kong tradition of improvisation and order in chaos, Ho organized and structured the units without sacrificing the individual and without giving the whole the illusion of uniformity (16):

> The life activity inside an apartment block is random, chaotic, not uniform and monotonous. Then why should the architecture be uniform? My building expresses the variety of life-activity inside.

Hong Kong's architectural environment is further distinguished by a large number of individual buildings by foreign and local architects. In association with Palmer life. A recent project for an equally ambitious environmental landscape is Kowloon Park by Buero Happold (engineers) and Derek Walker Associates (architects and landscape architects) to be completed in 1989.

Among the U.S. architects contributing to the new architecture in Hong Kong are I. M. Pei, Paul Rudolph, and William Turnbull. In 1980, Rudolph designed a project for 10 bungalows, and in 1988, he completed the Bond Centre, a private office development partly owned by Australian entrepreneur Alan Bond. In 1987, William Turnbull Associates completed the American Club in Hong Kong on a cliff overlooking the bay. It was the winning design of a competition to which 35 entries were submitted (18).

The year 1983 was important for the history of architecture in Hong Kong. A competition for a private club located on the peak of Hong Kong Island resulted in 539 entries from countries all over the world. The jury, consisting of John Andrews, Arata Isozaki, Gabriel Formosa, Ronald Poon, and promoter Alfred Siu, awarded the first prize to Iraqi architect Zaha Hadid, a decision that caused international attention. A revolutionary design was catapulted into fame by an architect who had no architectural experience, but had the potential to articulate a completely new concept. Zaha Hadid defined the project as a "suprematist geology" in which "the architecture appears as a knife cutting through butter, devastating the traditional principles and establishing new ones. Defying nature but not destroying it" (19).

In a dynamic constellation of spatial systems, this horizontal skyscraper was projected for the highest point of Hong Kong Island. The program called for a private club including 15 studio apartments, 20 apartments, and 4 penthouse apartments and club facilities with a swimming pool, restaurants, a sauna, and a health club, all connected by roof gardens, ramps, foyers, and terraces in order to achieve a balanced dynamic environment containing natural and artificial elements in a new relationship. This project, which is one of the most innovative designs of the 1980s, has had an impact beyond the architectural scene of Hong Kong. Among the numerous entries, two by Chinese architects deserve special attention, one by Ho and the other by Rocco S. K. Yim; neither was awarded a prize.

The present reality of contemporary architecture in Hong Kong and the changing of the physical and symbolic skyline is articulated by two bank buildings of recent years, both representing the present and future power constellation in Hong Kong. The Hong Kong and Shanghai Banking Corporation by Foster Associates (1979–1985) is one of the most discussed and published buildings internationally. Housing the old banking institution that financed the trade of the British colony for nearly a century, it replaced the old landmark building by Palmer and Turner of 1936 at One Queen's Road Central. The work is the paradigmatic articulation of an architecture based on both innovative technology and Chinese traditions. The shape of the 35-story building is differentiated by its various approaches. The large enclosed plaza continues to the pedestrian area of Statue Square. Ove Arup and Partners were the engineers of the suspended structure, which constitutes a combination of bridge technology and lightweight construction in an innovative form allowing for the utmost flexibility in terms of the erection of the structure: ". . .the building can quite literally build itself" (20). Prefabrication was developed to an extent unknown in most other contemporary buildings, involving a net-

Figure 4. Statue Square and Hong Kong and Shanghai Banking Corporation, Hong Kong (1979–1985). Architect: Foster Associates. Courtesy of Foster Associates, London.

work of factories on three continents. The building was also designed in harmony with the old principles of the Japanese *Shoji* and the Chinese *Feng Shui* (21):

> The use of energy in the building cannot be separated from observations about people, umbrellas, and sunshine in a hot climate. . . . We tried to learn some lessons from the past in protest against the banality, the repetition, the institutionalized wastage, the poor performance, the miserable appearance of office towers the world over.

The second important building, which is taller than Foster's bank, is the new Bank of China at 2A Des Voeus Road Central by the Chinese-U.S. architect I. M. Pei in collaboration with Wong/Kung and Lee Associates, expected to be completed in 1990. The building was commissioned by the government in Beijing, which will be in charge of the administration of Hong Kong after 1997. The site of the new Bank of China is very close to that of the Hong Kong and Shanghai Bank. Its 70-story crystalline structure will be the dominating landmark of the total urban environment. The building is a combination of the most recent international technology and Chinese iconography. Four triangular shafts of glass and steel rise from a square two-story granite base surrounded by water fountains and gardens. Its triangulation, as before in the Hong Kong Arts Centre, is in harmony with the Chinese tradition and design philosophy, specifically with the symbol of bamboo, which is expressed in the thin skin sections of the soaring structure, metaphorically gaining strength by the growth of its sectioned trunk. Bamboo as a metaphor of the building articulates the symbol of growth and strength in old Chinese thinking.

Further large-scale structures are in the design phase or under construction, all signs of an enormous building boom that continues to characterize the present situation. Three of them are the Bond Centre by Rudolph, the Exchange Square by P. + T. Architects and Engineers, in collaboration with Arup, and Pei's Sunning Plaza at 1 Hysan Avenue. There is also the new Hong Kong Convention and Exhibition Centre by Ng Chun Yon Assoc. and Rocco Design, which is to be completed in 1989. Located in Wanchai and destined to be Asia's dominating center for exhibitions and conferences, it contains large halls for exhibition purposes, conferences, and conventions; a large hall with a maximum capacity of 2600 people; auditoria; a 33-story commercial tower; and two hotels.

The present reality of architecture in Hong Kong is a hybrid situation that contains elements from various phases of architecture over the last decades and unites them with improvisational skills (22). The lack of a general plan or the nonobservance of existing plans can be seen as a symbol of the architecture of Hong Kong. This combination of vulnerability and flexibility and a general laissez-faire attitude nevertheless has great potential. Uncertainty has been accepted as a basic condition. Both tradition and modern technology are part of this reality, and steps towards their unification can be recognized. Hong Kong is evidence that a Third World country can be in the center of international developments in architec-

ture, offering solutions that appropriately define its own identity.

INDONESIA

Architecture in Indonesia is determined by a mixture of regional and foreign elements, which over several centuries merged into a new identity. From the earliest times, the local population, mostly Malay and Papuan, was confronted with influences from outside, such as Hinduism and Buddhism from India, Islam from Arabia, and other cultural and religious influences from China and Europe, the latter predominantly Portuguese and Dutch. Dutch colonial rule lasted nearly 350 years, from 1596 until 1945, manifesting itself in buildings that are a blend of Dutch architectural language and Indonesian vernacular, often in harmony with the dominant climatic conditions (23). Among the outstanding older structures are the Batavia City Hall (1707–1710) by W. J. Van de Velde and Jan Kemmer and the Batavia Government Center (ca 1770) by Johannes Rach, which included a harbor, a church, a library, and barracks in an axial urban plan. Two outstanding examples of early twentieth-century architecture are the old campus of the Institute of Technology in Bandung (ITB) by Dutch architect McLaine Pont and the old colonial government center in Bandung by architect J. Gerber, to which new administration wings have recently been added by the architect Sudibyo Pr.

After long and often heroic struggles, the country became independent in 1945, facing new problems of unprecedented dimensions. In his address in 1956 at Gadjah Mada University in Jakarta, Mohammad Hatta, one of the Indonesia's founding fathers, said, with a strong sense of self-criticism, "I am not straying too far from the truth when I say that as long as we were under colonial domination we did not lack ideals, but that these ideals have become rather shapeless since we gained our independence" (24).

Architecture in Indonesia today is part of the general problem of constituting the identity of a modern country with linkages to its own past. Architects face the challenge of finding an articulation for the country's new tasks and at the same time regaining access to a rich local tradition.

Most leading architects work for the large firms; for example, Atelier 6, founded in 1969 by six graduates of the Bandung Institute of Technology, is associated with Darmavan Prawirohardjo, Adhi Moersid, Nurrochman Siddharta, and Rugi Sularto Jastrowardaya; Gubahlaras with Suyudi and Aritin Soeradhiningrat; Studio T with Hindro Tjajono Soemarjan; Pembangunan Jaya with Ciputra; and P. T. Kakrea International with Iman Sunario.

As in all other countries, the question of cultural identity is crucial in Indonesia, and it is neither theoretically nor practically easy to solve. Indonesian architect Yuswadi Saliya, head of the school of architecture at the ITB, questioned the term in general. Saliya claimed that cultural identity can only be something that follows someone's actions, that it should not be seen as a goal or an end in itself (25).

In his approach to tradition, Moersid combined the continuation of architecture of the past with the creation of symbols: "Traditional architecture tried basically to reconstruct a series of components with symbolic content" (26). The old Indonesian symbolism of heaven, humanity, and earth, as well as relevant settlement patterns, seen in the Kampung Naga Village with its distinct organization of individual residences, village hall, and ceremonial center, should be further investigated not only for their historical relevance, but also for their significance for the essence of a new contemporary architecture in harmony with the past. One of the most important tasks of contemporary architects in Indonesia and elsewhere is regaining the cultural consciousness of the country and creatively exploiting it for present-day needs.

Many buildings of the firm Atelier 6, of which Moersid is one of the directors, are indicative of the general attempt to encompass traditional elements in contemporary buildings. However, the degrees to which this is done can differ intensively according to the problem in question. With regard to hotel buildings, recreational facilities, and housing, a traditional approach is evident. The Nusa Dua Beach Hotel (1980–1983) on Bali is a prominent example. The 450-room resort hotel by Prawirohardjo programmatically incorporates elements from the Balinese tradition, most significantly old Balinese roof forms, which are brought into harmony with the requirements of a three-story modern hotel complex.

In religious buildings, such as modern mosques, the symbolic element of tradition is even more evident. Hariyanto Sudikontoro's mosque Said Naum in Kebon Kacang, Jakarta, takes from the old *Joglo,* a Javanese type of house, with its characteristic roof form. Sudikontoro, who is a member of Atelier 6, is concerned with elements of local tradition through which, in the opinion of the architect, qualities of religious content can be communicated, even in this case, where a residential element is used in a religious building. The old Javanese tradition followed the idea that "the higher the god, the more roofs there are," reflecting the interconnections of building details and the symbolic beliefs of tradition (27).

Herman S. Sudijono's Headquarters for Family Planning at Jalan M. T. Haryono in Jakarta has been interpreted as one of the most significant prototypes of a contemporary use of traditional building elements for a different and complete new building function. Not only is the type of social institution innovative as a first articulation of its kind in Indonesia, it also exploits its traditional content in a new manner; past and present here establish an architecturally significant solution.

Traditional aspects of contemporary Indonesian architecture find their most radical articulation in Wija Wawo Runtu's Tandjung Sari Hotel in Bali, built in intervals between the years 1961 and 1978. As both architect and client of the beach hotel, Runtu created an intimate atmosphere of a village-type settlement that directly continues in plan and detail the Balinese tradition (28).

In opposition to tendencies in Indonesian architecture to attempt programmatically to continue to reconstruct traditional architectural forms are those that look for solutions in the spirit of international architecture. The architect Han Awal, who graduated from the University of Delft in the Netherlands, promotes an architecture that has little to do with old Indonesian architectural traditions; instead, his buildings adjust to forms that exploit modern concepts. Several examples are his Katholic University Atmajaya in Jakarta, his high school in Panguchi Luhur in Jakarta, and other works in recent years in Serpong and Jawa Barat. His recent work rejects contextual configurations of the Indonesian past and instead establishes an architectural language that, in principle, could be built in other countries as well.

Several other new buildings in Indonesia follow the same line of thought. The Datascript Building on Jalan Angkasa in Jakarta Pusat (1979) by Siddharta, within the firm Atelier 6, is a contemporary office environment that only remotely relates to traditional Indonesian building forms. Prawirohardjo's Lipi Headquarters Building in Jakarta (1980–1983), for the same firm, Atelier 6, advocates a solution on the basis of a contemporary language. Here a structure of 10 stories in an oval-shaped plan serves modern office functions without any kind of integrating element of the local or regional past. The building was originally designed as part of a larger ensemble in which a tower was to be the dominating form. Yuswadi Saliya's Hilton Executive Club in Jakarta (1973–1975) finally achieved the desired unity that is necessary to bring old and new into harmony. By using pyramidal units that meet in a central terraced core, and by expanding the complex by means of gardens and pools, the tradition of Indonesian old architecture here has found a contemporary equivalent.

In works by the architect Tony Candrawinata, who was educated at the University of New South Wales in Syd-

Figure 5. Lipi Headquarters, Jakarta (1982). Architect: Pt. Atelier 6. Courtesy of Pt. Atelier 6, Jakarta.

ney, Australia, still another form of articulating the contemporary scene is visible. Candrawinata built the Rinjani Court Housing in Semarang (1977), in which Australian architectural patterns were imported to Indonesia. His work marks a transplantation of a building typology from another part of the world (29).

The work of Moersid exploits two possibilities of present-day Indonesian architecture, one traditional and the other modern, and both can be found side by side in different buildings. In his mosque in Jakarta (1979–1980), he adapted traditional roof structures of the Indonesian past in order to give shape to a contemporary religious building type. On the other hand, his Nurtanio airplane factory complex in Bandung is the competent solution of an industrial program in which tradition is transcended.

The work of perhaps the most important Indonesian architect, Suyudi, shows the full harmony between traditional and contemporary elements. Suyudi achieved the most convincing articulation to date of a contemporary Indonesian architecture. As the most important architect of his generation, he was given the commissions for the most prominent buildings the new country had to offer; thus the country's representational image has been shaped by its most significant architect. Suyudi studied at the School of Architecture in Bandung and thereafter continued his studies in Paris, Delft, and Berlin, achieving the most universal education possible. After his return to Indonesia, he worked for the firm Gubahlaras in Jakarta and soon was given the opportunity to design a series of buildings that today stand as landmarks: the National Parliament Building, the Ministry of Forestry, and the French Embassy, all in Jakarta, as well as buildings outside the country, such as the Indonesian Embassies in Belgrade, Yugoslavia, and Kuala Lumpur, Malaysia, the last completed in 1975.

Suyudi's architecture is the elaborate integration of elements of contemporary architectural form shaped in such a manner that functional requirements communicate elements of tradition in a rearticulated manner. The overhanging sunscreens covering the horizontally structured windows in the Indonesian Embassy in Kuala Lumpur are one of the most spectacular examples in this regard and can be seen as a personal touch of the architect. Tradition here is fully incorporated into a contemporary architectural identity rooted in the past, distinctly Indonesian and personally Suyudian. In his Main Conference Hall in the Parliament Building Complex in Jakarta, Suyudi created a monumental image by juxtaposing the two cantilevered shells of the symmetrical structure into an imposing representational symbol.

The most recent tendencies of Indonesian architecture are best signified in the works of Robi Sularto Sastrowardoyo, who was born in 1938 and lives and works in Bali. Since 1965, he has been a member of Atelier 6, engaging in commissions in Bali for the preservation of old temples as well as for contemporary constructions. Sularto has also been involved in building outside Indonesia, for example, in the Indonesian Pavilion at Expo' 70 in Osaka, Japan, and more recently, in the pavilion for the 1986 World Exposition in Vancouver, Canada.

In Sularto's work, such as his own residence in Bali and a bank building in Denpasar, Bali, a synthesis of traditional elements derived from the careful study of local conditions and the contemporary needs of a functional building at this time has been achieved. For Sularto, this is not the copying of forms of buildings or architectural details from the past, but rather understanding their essence in a spiritual presence. Architecture for him is the congenial continuation of a great past, even though the results may differ considerably in formal appearance and in the use of materials.

It is a sign of great hope that important commissions for buildings in Indonesia were given to local architects and that only a small percentage of buildings, mostly hotels, were commissioned to foreigners. This is not so in neighboring countries like Malaysia and Singapore, where foreign ideas have much more strongly influenced the local architectural scene. Among the foreign contributions to contemporary Indonesian architecture are designs by U.S. architects Bruce Graham for Skidmore, Owings and Merrill (Hyatt International Hotel in Surabaya,

Figure 6. Main Conference Hall, National Parliament, Jakarta (ca 1970). Architect: Suyudi. Courtesy of Suyudi, Jakarta.

Figure 7. Bank in Denpasar, Bali (1984). Architect: Robi Sularto Sastrowardoyo. Courtesy of U. Kultermann.

1978) and Anthony Lumsden (Bank Bumi Daya in Jakarta, 1972–1976, the commercial complex Gujah Mada in Jakarta, 1977, as well as Harapan Plaza in Jakarta, 1977) as well as projects and buildings by the Australian architect Peter Muller (Kayu Aya Hotel in Bali) and the Chinese architect Ho (extension to the Orchid Palace Hotel in Jakarta, 1978, and interior renovation of the Orchid Plaza Hotel in Jakarta, 1979).

There are fundamental differences between buildings by the most important Indonesian architects, such as Suyudi and Sularto, and foreign firms. The foreign firms rely on the touristic and surface application of traditional motifs, whereas the Indonesians produce a more genuinely contemporary Indonesian architecture.

Another important fact has to be taken into consideration. Contemporary Indonesian architecture cannot develop without the appropriate recognition of one of its most important challenges: housing for the masses, which, unfortunately, is the least solved area of building in the country. Several recent low-cost housing complexes in the central urban area of Jakarta lack both the values that exist in rural settlements as well as a new social imagination.

At the other end of the spectrum are government-assisted programs in the slums to improve squatter settlements. Surprisingly, these programs stand a much better chance of seriously dealing with the contemporary living conditions of the poor population. One of the programs, the Jakarta Kumpung Improvement Programme, was awarded an Aga Khan Award for Architecture in 1980 for a solution recognized internationally as one of the realistic alternatives to other government-sponsored housing systems.

In comparison with other countries of the Third World and Southeast Asia, Indonesia can feel proud and confident to be in the position of solving many of its largest problems without foreign help. How much of its self-reliance is justified is open to debate. As elsewhere in the world, balance and harmony between traditional values of the region and the needs and unprecedented demands of a new age have yet to be achieved. What counts now is to set new priorities, different from those established after 1945, which leaned toward monumental representation. The new priorities have to tend toward social responsibility and cultural values. The opportunities are there, and the resources are in place for a creative and exciting development that could, in the years to come, bring forth appropriate results.

SINGAPORE

The history of Singapore dates back to an old Chinese chronicle of the third century AD in which Pu-luo-chung is described as an island at the end of a peninsula. In the seventh century, present-day Singapore was known as Temasek, or "sea city," and was part of the Srivajaya Empire based in Sumatra. The Prince of Palembang of Sumatra, ang Nila Utama, who claimed to be a descendant of Alexander the Great, visited the island at the end of the thirteenth century and had an encounter with a strange animal, which in old chronicles is referred to as a lion. The name *Singapura* means in Sanskrit "lion city."

A new phase in the history of Singapore began in 1819 when Thomas Stamford Raffles, an agent from the East India company, arrived and signed a treaty with the Temenggong of Johor. The city as it is known today began taking shape in the decades after 1819 and especially after the arrival of the Irish architect George Drumgoolde Coleman. Regulated planning prescribed not only different residential quarters for the Chinese, Indians, Muslims, and Europeans, but also buildings for government, trade, and education. Within a short time, the population grew to about 5000. The residence Coleman built for John Argyle Maxwell in 1826–1827 was first used as a courthouse and later as the Parliament House. In 1875, it was expanded to accommodate the new and much larger government functions of Singapore, which then was part of the British Commonwealth. Two other still-existing buildings by Coleman are the America Church (1835) and the Caldwell House (1840). The city continued to develop rapidly, and around 1900, architects Swan and MacLaren were the most successful in Singapore. Their works include the University of Malaya and the Raffles Hotel (1896), as well as several residences.

The recent history of Singapore was determined by the Japanese occupation in 1942, its return to the British Empire in 1945, the foundation of the Federation of Malaysia

Figure 8. Kayu Aya Hotel, Bali (ca 1975). Architect: Peter Muller. Courtesy of Peter Muller, Sydney.

with Singapore as a member in 1963, and finally, its withdrawal from the Federation of Malaysia in 1965, which created the Republic of Singapore, as it exists today.

Because of the high percentage of their population in Singapore, Chinese architects dominate the architectural scene. This began with the work of Ng Keng Siang, who, following his studies in the United Kingdom, had a strong impact in Singapore after World War II with several of his works, such as the Asia Insurance Building (1954), with its now dwarfed but significant silhouette. His buildings, along with many others by British architectural firms in the first years after independence, continued to be influenced by the international style, or a combination of superficial elements of local vernacular and modern requirements as found in most parts of the southern hemisphere.

Today, among the prominent firms dominated by Chinese architects in Singapore are Team 3 International (Lim Chong Keat), the Regional Development Consortium (RDC Architects), Akitek Tenggara, Paul Tsakok and Associates, the Alfred Wong Partnership, and Design Partnership (DP) Architects PTe (William Lim). Together with various government agencies, such as HDBURA, and firms from outside of Singapore (Kenzo Tange, Pei, Moshe Safdie, John Portman, International Project Consultants with Geoffrey T. Malone and Phillip Conn) have created a hybrid architectural and urbanistic development in Singapore.

The firm Team 3 International is active beyond the borders of Singapore, with a large number of realized commissions in Malaysia (under the firm name Jurubena Bertiga), Hong Kong, and Indonesia. The founder and Chief Designer of the firm is Lim Chong Keat, who was born in 1930 and studied at Manchester University and the Massachusetts Institute of Technology in Cambridge, Mass. Lim's interests transcend the field of architecture. He has had an inspiring impact on the art and culture of Southeast Asia, and his collection of peasant paintings from Bali is one of the finest in the world. Lim is Project Director of the Southeast Asian Cultural Research Programme, which is concerned with the documentation of the traditional architecture of the region. In what appears to be a contrast, but in fact is not, Lim supports the principles of synergetics of his friend, the late Richard Buckminster Fuller, which has proven to be of great significance to the countries of the Third World.

Lim's importance for early architectural development in Singapore can hardly be overestimated. In 1961, with Chen Voon Fee and William Lim, he founded the Malayan Architects Co-Partnership, forming a link between architectural practice in the United States and Southeast Asia. Between 1966 and 1969, he was President of the Singapore Institute of Architects. In 1967, the present firm Team 3 International was founded. His principal works are the Conference Hall and Trade Union House (1961), the Malaysia Singapore Airlines Building (1967), the Overseas Bank Headquarters (1971–1974), and the highrise apartment towers of the Ardmore Park Project (1978). His most outstanding work is the Jurong Town Hall (the architect in charge was Raymond Woo), designed for a competition in 1969 and built between 1971 and 1974. It became the landmark for a new town development 15 km west of the center of Singapore.

Figure 9. Jurong Town Hall, Singapore (1971–1974). Architect: Jurubena Bertiga. Courtesy of Jurubena Bertiga, Singapore.

RDC Architects was founded in 1974 and is specifically concerned with the large-scale development of commercial and residential buildings. The present heads of the firm are Chan Fook Pong and Kenneth Chen. Among their many realizations are the Rich East Gardens Condominiums (1983), which contain 40 units of 2-story maisonettes in an arrangement with private gardens on the ground level as well as on all the upper floors. The principle is similar to that of Safdie's Habitat, built in Singapore in 1984–1985 in collaboration with RDC Architects.

The work of the firm Akitek Tenggara is devoted to residential, commercial, and religious architecture. The senior designer-architect Tay Kheng Soon graduated from the Singapore Polytechnic in 1964. One of the important recent buildings of the firm is the Chee Tong Temple in Singapore, completed in 1987. Derived from a student project by Ho Kwancjan in 1983 and in collaboration with Patrick Chia and Soon, the final design and its realization articulated a new approach to a religious contemporary architecture. The efforts invested in the work were described by Tay Kheng Soon in this way: "Throughout the design the artistic problem was how to maintain a balance and an aesthetic integrity without inclining towards the traditional iconography nor falling back on functional expressionism and industrial forms" (30).

The work of architect Paul Tsakok is predominantly dedicated to restoration. Tsakok, who was born in Hong Kong in 1941, studied in London at the Architectural Association, and after his return to Singapore worked for two years with DP Architects. In 1976, he began his own practice. His greatest achievements are the restorations of old houses in the Emerald Hill area in Singapore, for example, Numbers 20 and 26 Saunders Road, which were completed in 1982. He received the Honorary Award of the Singapore Institute of Architects in 1984 for this work. In his restoration of the Number 23 Emerald Hill Road House for client Wan Ai Fung, he introduced modern materials such as steel and glass in a consequently integrated ensemble without losing the character of the old environment.

The architectural firm of Alfred Wong Partnership extends its work to Hong Kong, Malaysia, Indonesia, and Australia in addition to its contribution of several significant structures that shape the skyline of Singapore. The principles of Wong, who was educated in the United Kingdom and Australia, are toward comprehensive planning rather than isolated buildings. One of his first commissions was the National Theatre at the corner of Clemenceau Avenue and River Valley Road. Built in 1963, it symbolizes the freedom and independence of Singapore with its cantilevered roof form. Another early work of Wong is the Marco Polo Hotel (1962) on Tanglin Road, originally called Hotel Malaysia. Many of his early works show the influence of his foreign education, as seen in a 1968 house on a hillside in Singapore. His Catholic Junior College (1977) on Whitley Road continues to reflect the architectural traditions of the United Kingdom and Australia. The Singapore Polytechnic, which has an enrollment of 8000 students, was completed in 1979 and marks a change in direction in the development of the architect. Here, he achieved a vivid sculptural language of vertical and horizontal elements integrated into a comprehensive whole. The plan, which is in two parallel blocks, achieves an orientation based on natural ventilation. The two most recent works by Wong are the Furama Singapore Hotel and the Scotts Residential and Shopping Complex (1984); both show significant points of design that initiate a new visual and urbanistic character. This is especially evident in the 24-story Scotts Complex with its shops, offices, and 177 apartments.

Among the architects in Singapore, William Lim is the most important with regard to the architecture of the region. Comparable only with Lim Chong Keat, with whom he collaborated in the early years of the Malayan Architects Co-Partnership between 1960 and 1967, his impact is felt in Singapore and the neighboring countries, and his comprehensive activity in research, planning, lecturing, and building has no rival in Southeast Asia today. William Lim was born in Hong Kong in 1932, studied in London and at Harvard University, and returned to Singapore in 1957. After working in the firm Malayan

Architects Co-Partnership, he became, with Soon and Koh Seow Chuan, a leading partner of DP Architects and after this firm was dissolved in 1975, he became Chairman and Principal Partner of DP Architects (PTe). In 1981, he resigned from DP Architects and went into private practice under the firm name William Lim Associates.

The early work of William Lim concentrated on large building types for the commercial urban environment of Singapore. The two largest commissions were the People's Park Complex (1972) and the Woh Hup Complex (1974), also called the Golden Mile Shopping Centre. The architectural articulation of the Golden Mile Shopping Centre is a unique terrace-shaped urban form containing a large shopping mall, offices, and apartments; it was a type of mixed-use complex, which has since become a model for several other developments. With the planning and construction of St Andrew's Junior College in 1978 and its later additions, Lim entered a new phase of his development. The shift was from a basically commercial public form to a new type of educational complex with a language that exploited geometric elements along with the meaningful use of color. The Southeast Asian adaptation of elements of international modern architecture found a prominent articulation and was a precursor to later developments in the work of the architect.

The development of William Lim opened innovative dimensions of type and form: the Crittal Factory (1979) continued the emphasis on color in technological construction; the Yeo Hiap Seng Factory (1981–1982) developed barrel-vaulted shaped elements for a large industrial complex; the house for Mr. Thai achieved a complex and intriguing synthesis of earlier-anticipated experiments. Mr. Thai's house is the culmination of a series of residences, among them those built for the Gan, Rahim, and Chao families. The most advanced and convincing realization of the architect is a group of condominiums on Holland Road

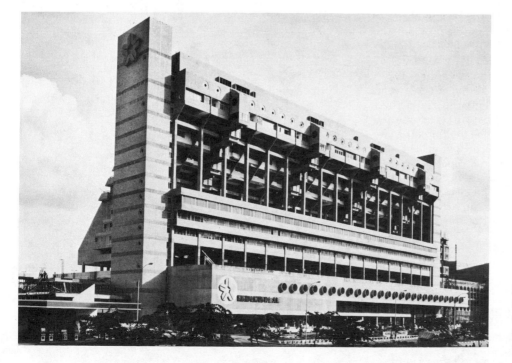

Figure 10. Golden Mile Shopping Center, Singapore (1969–1973). Architects: William S. W. Lim and DP Architects. Courtesy of William Lim, Singapore.

Unit 8 (1984), combining eight luxury apartments and recreational facilities. It is a synthesis of the architect's earlier isolated design achievements and a masterpiece of contemporary architecture in Singapore.

In spite of the spectacular prominence of many buildings by foreign architects, their impact on the urban environment of Singapore was for a long time not as significant as that of the works by local architects. Only in recent years, and mainly because of the contributions of Japanese architect Kenzo Tange, has the situation changed. Most of the works by foreign architects remain isolated from the fabric of the city and carry on the traditions of other parts of the world. The British firm of Palmer and Turner, for example, established a type of architecture in Singapore that was within the framework of colonial architecture familiar in many parts of the southern hemisphere. Its old Odeon Cinema on North Road (1953), the Macdonald House on Orchard Road (1948–1949), and the China Bank Building on Battery Road are perfect examples. With its seven stories, the Macdonald House was the first tall building in Singapore after World War II. The China Bank Building, with its octagonal tower, resembles U.S. bank buildings of the 1920s.

The involvement of Tange in Singapore began with his consultancy in the design of the National Stadium in Kalland in 1973. Only after 1980 did his contribution to the architecture of Singapore take on enormous dimensions. Among his works are the Overseas Union Bank Centre (1980), the Telecommunication Centre (1980), the G. B. Building (1981), the Nanyang Technological Institute (1981–1986), the International Petroleum Centre (1982), and the King's Centre (1982). The new campus of Nan Yang Technological Institute at the west end of the city accommodates 6000 students. Centered around an academic spine 400 m in length, bridges connect wings to both sides, which contain offices, laboratories, and classrooms.

In addition to these works by Tange, there are many large-scale commissions that are in the design phase or under construction: the United Overseas Plaza (1983), the urban design for Marina South (1983), the OCBC Condominiums (1983), the MRT Raffles Place Station (1983), the New World Park (1984) Singapore Indoor Stadium (1985), and the Military Academy (1984). Many of these complexes dominate the urban scene and give spatial connections to each other by coordinating existing structures and new additions into an urban unity. The height of the two bank buildings (OUB and UOB) will be 280 m. The skyline of Singapore will be given a new metropolitan character. Tange's project for Marina South is a vast reclamation area south of the present center of the city and is scheduled to be used as the eventual site for an extension of the city center.

In comparison with the extensive work of Tange, the works by other foreign architects have mostly been isolated commissions or design projects that have yet to be built. Rudolph, for example, has worked out plans for a commercial center, and Harry Seidler a housing scheme for Bushy Park that contains 450 apartments in a serpentine plan. Portman built the Pavilion Intercontinental, transplanting one of his hotel schemes to the environment

of Singapore and, in addition, has recently designed three more hotels for Marina Square.

The works of Pei in Singapore have a special significance, among them his Oversea Chinese Bank and his scheme for Raffles City. The Oversea Chinese Bank, built in 1976, is a carefully detailed high-rise slab with office space suspended in huge transverse girders between curved twin cores. It was a challenge to the local construction industry and has become a landmark, enhanced by its placement behind the Singapore River. A third project by Pei is the Gateway Project on Beach Road (1986).

Among the foreign firms building in Singapore, besides Tange and Pei, two architects stand out: Safdie from the United States and Geoffrey Malone from Australia. Safdie's Ardmore Luxury Condominiums were executed in collaboration with RDC Architects in 1984–1985. Two 17-story towers contain alternating apartments and maisonettes with roof terraces as an extension of the living area. A second project by Safdie is the Tampines Condominium Development, designed in 1985. It is a cluster of 5- to 12-story apartments around a large quarry situated in the area near the second airport of Singapore. This type of a continuous development introduces new alternatives to the already multiple housing reality in Singapore and one day may be assimilated into the predominantly Chinese tradition.

The second firm that adds new possibilities to the architectural scene in Singapore is International Project Consultants with Malone and Phillips Conn as the senior partners. Malone's Crystal Court of 1984 as well as several terrace housing schemes, such as the Palisades Condominium (1984), have made him a serious contributor to the future of architecture in Singapore. The Crystal Court on River Valley Road continues the old Chinese tradition

Figure 11. Ardmore Condominiums, Singapore (1984). Architect: Moshe Safdie. Courtesy of Moshe Safdie, Boston.

Figure 12. Crystal Court Building, Singapore (1984). Architects: International Project Consultants (Geoffrey Malone). Courtesy of Geoffrey Malone, Singapore.

of shop houses in a radical contemporary form. It serves as head office and showroom for Crystal Court Lighting, with apartments on top and the residence of the owner in the penthouse. Born in 1943 in Sydney, where he also studied, Malone became a partner in International Project Consultants in Singapore in 1980. The work of the firm extends today to the United Kingdom, Indonesia, Malaysia, and New Guinea. Among the specific characteristics architects like Malone and Conn have added to the existing tradition in Singapore is the fundamentally important integration of landscape into architecture and a new sense of color, which reminded a local critic in Singapore of the work of Michael Graves.

The architectural and urbanistic situation in Singapore is rich and full of potential. What is crucially needed is the merging of the various traditions into one regional form of architectural identity, an identity which cannot be achieved by isolated landmarks and high-rise buildings alone, but in the constitution of the urban fabric as a continuous architecture. The unification of tradition and present needs, buildings and open spaces, as well as the different articulations of the multiple elements in the population has to remain in the center and possibly will help to establish Singapore as one of the centers of international architecture in the future.

THAILAND

The development of architecture in Thailand since the establishment of Bangkok as the capital in the late eighteenth century is a typical blend of Western styles and old

Thai architecture, often resulting in bizarre mixes of East and West and old and new. Some examples can be seen in buildings by British architect John Chinitz (Throne Hall in the Grand Palace, 1876–1882), French architect Charles Bequelin (Krom Phra Chan Palace for Queen Sirikit, ca 1926), German architect Karl Doering (Bang Khun Prom Palace in Bangkok, ca 1920), and in more recent times, by British architects Robert Matthew and Johnson-Marshall and Partners (Asian Institute of Technology in Bangkok), U.S. architect John Carl Warnecke (U.S. Embassy in Bangkok), and Japanese architect Kisho Kurokawa (The Japanese Studies Institute at Thammasat University in Rangsit).

The Throne Hall by Chinitz is still one of the landmarks of Bangkok and interconnects the historical part with rival forms of the twentieth century. The book *Old Homes of Bangkok* by Michael Broman, published in Bangkok in 1984, gives a picture of the rich treasure of colonial architecture paralleling that in other countries. The distinct difference is that in Thailand the majority of the clients were Thai, and the choice of the architectural language was their own independent expression. They preempted Western colonization by colonizing their own country.

A fascinating recent project is the Building Together Housing in Bangkok by architects S. Angel, P. Channiern, and Bruce Etherington. Designed in 1979, the first phase of 121 units was completed in 1982, and the second phase was completed in 1983. This synthesis of Thai and Western traditional low-income housing was built without government funding (31).

Thailand's continuing tradition of openness to Western culture is also evident in the two most important architects practicing in the country today, Sumet Jumsai and Satrabandhu Ongard, who, after studying in Europe and the United States, returned to their homeland and successfully established architectural practices. Both present individual and personal articulations of a contemporary architecture expressing a regional identity that, although being unmistakably Thai, is neither underdeveloped nor provincial.

The work and philosophy of Jumsai especially repre-

Figure 13. Throne Hall of the Grand Palace, Bangkok (1876–1882). Architect: John Chinitz. Courtesy of U. Kultermann.

sents the present situation of architecture in Thailand, as it shows the difficult middle road of merging Western and local traditions. Born in Bangkok in 1939, Jumsai studied in the United Kingdom and France, eventually establishing his own office in Bangkok in 1969. Early in his career, he received commissions for important architectural works, among them the planning of a satellite town for 100,000 people in Nava Nakorn (1969), the School for the Blind in Bangkok (1971), a Guest House in Pattaya (1973), and the Science Museum in Bangkok (1977). In his residential and commercial buildings, Jumsai developed a system of prefabrication specifically tailored for Third World countries that combines economic efficiency with the limited resources of technology and labor in Thailand.

Jumsai's position on architecture in Thailand was made clear in a statement in which he refers to the survival of equatorial Pacific and Southwest Asia's history of 2.5 million years (32): "This culture, which is instinctive and spontaneous, as against intellectual, is a link to the longest human experience and possibly a key to humanity's next test in survivability." He concludes by applying this to his own architectural work: "I am now gradually unlearning what I have learned in architecture, and if my work reflects this unlearning approach, then perhaps I shall be contributing something useful to the future of humanity."

Jumsai's architectural philosophy thus incorporates two divergent elements: (1) the advanced concepts of Le Corbusier and Fuller from the West and (2) the old symbolic traditions of Southeast Asia articulated in *Angkor Thom* and *Ayutya*. Examples of this philosophy can be found in two illuminating articles by Jumsai (33,34). The most recent results of Jumsai's research were published in 1988 (35).

Jumsai's recent architectural works demonstrate his ability to adapt Western technology to Thai tradition using an upscaled method. His Energy Technology Complex at the Asian Institute of Technology (AIT) (1981–1983) explores new means of solar air conditioning; his Condominium Village at Ban Saray Seaside Resort (1982) created a new shape for vacation architecture with imaginatively shaped walls and the enclosure of outside spaces; his Bank of Asia New Head Office Building in Bangkok (1987) is a powerful homage to contemporary technology; and his plan for the new campus of Thammasat University at Rangsit, begun in 1984, shows the merging of traditional planning schemes and modern ideas.

Preservation also programmatically enters the work of Jumsai. The restoration work on two Bangkok landmarks, the Old Clock Tower and the Old Drum Tower in 1982–1984 demonstrates his ability to transform respected old structures into viable elements of the contemporary urban fabric. The reconstructed Drum Tower once again stands in front of Wat Po, where it had stood since its construction in the second half of the nineteenth century, interconnecting original and eclectic phases of the architectural tradition in Bangkok with the present time. Jumsai's work encompasses many layers of architectural attitudes, and he continues to grow in several new directions.

Another architect of equal importance in Thailand is Ongard, who was born in 1943 in Bangkok and studied architecture in the United States at Cornell and Yale Universities. Among his U.S. teachers were Werner Seligman, Stanley Tigerman, Serge Chermayeff, and Charles Moore; the last had an especially strong impact on the young Thai architect. After his return to Bangkok in 1969, Ongard opened his own architectural office, which has since been extremely successful in the development and construction of commercial buildings, residential architecture, and a large number of renovations of existing buildings combining past and present into a new whole. Among his early works are classrooms and dormitories for the Panabhandu (1969–1970) and the Administration and Sales Center for the Summakorn Housing Complex in Bangkok (1972–1973).

A new phase in his development is marked by the design of a group of houses in which old and new are combined in a sophisticated manner. The client of the Suriyasat Residence (1976–1978) envisioned a brick house with formal and informal elements, an eloquent interrelationship of brick and glass, and an extensive spatial organization of the interior. The residence for Khun V. Ed (1982–1983) presented a completely different problem, which was solved accordingly. The client, a collector of Thai and European antiquities, wanted to use three existing houses on a site southeast of the center of Bangkok to which a fourth part would be added in a more European style. Ongard successfully connected all four parts, forming an architectural collage in which Thai and Western architectural elements are united.

The culmination of this merging of Western and Eastern elements is demonstrated in the residence of Khun R. Sirichai. In an elaborate and extremely complex solution

Figure 14. Energy Technology Complex, Bangkok (1980–1981). Architect: Sumet Jumsai. Courtesy of Sumet Jumsai, Bangkok.

designed in 1982–1983 and completed in 1985, Ongard remodeled a residence he had originally built for the same client. On a large and ambitious scale, this house combined elements from European architecture of the sixteenth century in an extensive symbolic and formal reuse for a wealthy Thai importer of marble. Once again, a merging of purpose and content was successfully accomplished.

In his last two completed works, Ongard imaginatively continued the use of Western and Eastern traditions, combining them into new unifications. The Mah Boonkrong Marble Showroom in Bangkok (1982–1983) is a building located on a corner site of a recently developed commercial center in the city, designed as a showcase to exhibit Thai and imported marble. Ongard therefore had to come up with a solution that would work as a display area for marble as well as a building in which marble would be the primary material. The architectural form not only had to be in harmony with the material, but also had to demonstrate the opportunities for marble to be used in the context of modern design. The curved entrance facade with its glass-covered portico especially reflects traditions that already existed in the eclectic Thai architecture of the past. Ongard's work thus refers to a multiple set of traditional roots; it includes old Thai architecture, Western architecture, and the mix of both as it existed in the late nineteenth and early twentieth centuries in Bangkok.

Ongard's most recent commission continues these complex and highly sophisticated mergings of cultural traditions, this time for a Japanese client, in the Thai Toshiba Headquarter/Service Building on Viphavadi Rangsit Road in Bangkok. Designed in 1983–1984 and completed in 1985, it is a functional mix of housing, offices, and service facilities articulated in a parallel mix of materials such as brick veneer over steel frame, glass-reinforced concrete, and Thai marble. The front portion of the building refers to models of European traditions of architecture rearticulated in a hybrid manner. An architectural language using elements from divergent roots in an eclectic manner has emerged here and is reminiscent of and transcends the work of Moore and Arata Isozaki.

Ongard's last realizations have to be seen in the same international context as those of Moore and Isozaki. His buildings are reflections of a phase of Thai architecture

Figure 16. Xavier Hall Chapel, Bangkok (1972). Architects: CASA Co., Ltd. Courtesy of U. Kultermann.

that has found its own distinct form equivalent to architectural forms in other countries that have also found their own regional roots.

The scope of contemporary architecture in Thailand goes beyond the work of these two leading architects and encompasses traditions that directly continue other types of Thai architecture, ranging from old wooden houses to a direct application of Western models. The Xavier Hall Chapel in Bangkok (1972) by the firm CASA Co., Ltd., the restoration of the Riverside House in Chiang Mai (1980) by architect Chulathat Kitbutr (today housing the Ethnological Museum), and the Guest House on a boat garage in Phukat (1981) by architect Nitt Chaurorn are examples of the use of divergent roots and polarities.

The fist two rely predominantly on the use of traditional materials and building types, whereas the third relies predominantly on the Western prototype of vacation architecture and the formalistic architectural solutions related to it. Nevertheless, they are all solutions in the context of a contemporary architecture in Thailand, reflecting the country's possibilities. The house of architects Boonyawat and Pussadee Tiptus in Bangkok (1982) is still another example of how the alternatives of Western or Thai traditions can be transcended in a contemporary synthesis.

Among the numerous other works of contemporary architecture in Thailand, the buildings by the firms Plan Architect Co., Ltd. and CASA, Co., Ltd. should be singled out. One of the most prominent realizations by Plan Architect Co., Ltd. is the Sithakarn Condominium at Chidlom Road in the Patumwan district of Bangkok. This 18-story complex with residential units, a squash court, a sauna, a swimming pool, a cafeteria, and a terrace was built in 1982–1984. It can be compared with high-rise buildings in other countries and is a demonstration of the international standards in Thailand.

The new Bangkok Airport-Hotel by CASA, Co., Ltd. is also modeled after the Western recreational type of building, but equally fits into the heterogeneous tradition of Southeast Asia. Both of these complexes reflect an accep-

Figure 15. Marble Showroom, Bangkok (1982). Architect: Satrabandhu Ongard. Courtesy of Satrabandhu Ongard, Bangkok.

tance of modern building types that are Western in character yet harmonious in the contemporary context of Thailand.

Some of Jumsai's and Ongard's solutions also accomplish this on a different level, and their individual personalities give their works a fresh and unique identity. The most prominent foreign contribution to the architecture in Thailand is Kurokawa's Japanese Studies Institute of Thammasat University in Rangsit (1985), in which the traditional interconnections between old Japanese and old Thai principles are in the center of the design attitude. Kurokawa wrote the following about the complex (36): "Based upon the layout in ancient Buddhist architecture (*Garan-haichi*) and aristocratic palace architecture (*Shin-den-Zukuri*) of Japan, four main buildings, each with different functions, are located along each side of the inner courtyard, while behind the west building a Japanese garden with a tea ceremony house is located."

Contemporary architecture in Thailand has its own and complex identity that is in line with its independent traditional roots. The fact that these regional expressions are on the same sophisticated level as solutions in other parts of the world indicates the need to take a second look at architecture in general. After a long phase of accepting the illusion of an international style, architecture in all parts of the world is once again, as in the past, the expression of many divergent societies that relate to each other on the level of cultural equality. In this regard, international understanding and cultural exchange between different countries are possible when they are based on mutual respect and equality.

BIBLIOGRAPHY

1. G. B. Endacott, *A Biographical Sketchbook of Early Hong Kong,* Singapore, 1962.
2. R. Hughes, *Hong Kong. Borrowed Place–Borrowed Time,* New York, 1968.
3. I. C. Jarvie, ed., *Hong Kong. A Society in Transition,* London, 1969.
4. F. M. Rea, *Hong Kong,* Menlo Park, Calif., 1969.
5. T. Wiltshire, *Hong Kong. An Impossible Journey Through History,* Hong Kong, 1971.
6. R. Elegant, *Hong Kong,* Amsterdam, the Netherlands, 1977.
7. P. Geddes, *In the Mouth of the Dragon,* London, 1982.
8. Special Issue of *Third World Planning Review* **6** (Feb. 1984).
9. A. Chang Ih Tiao, *The Existence of Intangible Content in Architectonic Form Based upon the Practicability of Laotzu's Philosophy,* Publisher, Princeton, N.J., 1956.
10. T. T. Yong, "Fengshui: Its Application in Contemporary Architecture," *Mimar* **27** (1988).
11. R. Bristow, *Land-use Planning in Hong Kong,* publisher, Hong Kong, 1984.
12. K. H. Tang, "High Density Housing in Hong Kong," *I.T.C.C. Review* **5**(3) (July 1976).
13. S. Williams, "Hong Kong. Packing 'em in," *RIBA Journal* (July 1980).
14. M. Huerlimann, *Hong Kong,* London, 1962.
15. T. Ho, "Hong Kong: A City Prospers Without a Plan," *Process Architecture* **20,** 84 (1980).
16. T. Ho, *Vision* **13,** 25 (1984).
17. *Mimar* **21,** 35, 38 (1986).
18. *Architecture* **133,** 134 (May 1988).
19. *Vision* **4,** 29 (1983).
20. D. Lasdun, *Architecture in an Age of Scepticism,* publisher, New York, 1984, p. 120.
21. Ref. 20, p. 125.
22. A. Gar-On Yeh, "Planning for Uncertainty: Hong Kong's Urban Development in the 1990's," *Built Environment* **II**(4) (1985).
23. V. I. van de Wall, *Oude Hollandsche Bouwkunst in Indonesia,* Antwerp, Belgium, 1942.
24. M. Hatta, "Past and Future," address at Gadjah Mada University, Jakarta, Indonesia, 1956.
25. Y. Saliya, "Notes on Architectural Identity in the Cultural Context," *Mimar* **19** (1986).
26. "Arsitekture Dengan Sentuhan Tradisional," *Eksekutif,* 5 (Sept.) 1984.
27. F. A. Wagner, *Indonesia. The Art of an Island Group,* publisher, New York, 1959, p. 191.
28. *Mimar* **11,** 34–39 (1984).
29. U. Kultermann, *Architekten der Dritten Welt,* publisher, Cologne, FRG, 1980, pp. 134–138.
30. T. K. Soon, *Mimar* **27,** 49 (Mar. 1988).
31. *Mimar* **17** (1985).
32. S. Jumsai, *Contemporary Architects,* London, 1980.
33. S. Jumsai, "Water and Mountain: How Cities Strive for Harmony by Being Macrocosmically Planned," *Ekistiks* (Sept. 1975).
34. S. Jumsai, "The World of Buckminster Fuller," *The Nation* (Mar. 19, 1978).
35. S. Jumsai, *Naga Cultural Origins in Siam and the West Pacific,* Oxford University Press, New York, 1988.
36. K. Kurokawa, *Japan Architect,* 30 (Jan. 1986).

UDO KULTERMANN
Washington University
St. Louis, Missouri

SOVIET UNION ARCHITECTURE.   See SUPPLEMENT.

SPACE FRAMES

DEFINITION

Z. S. Makowski, a pioneer in the design of space frames, defines space frames as a plane grid framework, "as a two-dimensional structure consisting of two or more sets of beams or lattice girders, intersecting each other at right or oblique angles. The beams are interconnected at all intersections and are loaded by forces perpendicular to the plane of the grid or by moments whose vectors lie in the plane of the grid (1)."

John Borrego (2) adopts Makowski's definition "space structures" as "space grids" and says they are

> Flat skeletal double-layer grids; a three dimensional development of the grid. Grids are made up of two parallel-plane grids interconnected by vertical and inclined web members in which external loads are spread omnidirectionally among many bars in three or more directions in space. Axially loaded members have an even stress distribution on their cross-sectional area because of the elimination of bending moments. Because they are highly indeterminate structures with the ability to distribute concentrated loads evenly throughout the rest of the grid, the buckling of a member under a concentrated load does not lead to the collapse of the entire structure.

In summary, space frames are three-dimensional structural systems that transfer loads applied at the nodes through a network of interconnected members. They are light and admirably suited to mass production and computer calculation.

SPACE FRAMES TODAY

Tens of thousands of space frames have been constructed throughout the world. The simple, flat structures of a decade ago have developed complex geometries. There have been international conferences, research, and publications. Space-frame construction and research have been encouraged by NASA and was used by the military during World War II for radar domes.

The use of repetitive members and joints for a large variety of structures of different shapes and areas has led to the development of standardized proprietary systems. Most of these provide a complete "kit" of members and nodal joints, and many accommodate changes in both member and nodal joint sizes, depending on the grid dimension and depth selected. These are fairly low weight per unit of surface area.

Individually designed systems are usually constructed of rolled steel shapes with fabricated steel joints often used for large grid structures. The design revolves around node design. Nodes determine the geometry of the framing system selected. Large modules are generally preferred because the frame members are selected from standard sizes. The number of members framing into a node is held to a minimum, and overall geometry is kept as simple as possible.

Weight is not the most important cost factor. Nodes account for from one to three quarters of cost. Connection is a major part of fabrication and erection. The actual weight of the truss can be of secondary importance. In general, the finer the grid, the less weight. The penalty paid for a finer grid is more joints.

An economically designed joint used repetitively permits more joints, a finer grid, and reduced costs. Joint design makes proprietary systems competitive. Generally, proprietary systems weigh 25–30% less than unique designed systems. Use of space structures generally will increase—not only space frames, but fabric structures and other ingenious devices as well, in the opinion of Peter Pearce, president of Pearce Structures: "Space structures are not so much an idea whose time has come as an idea that the times have finally begun to catch up with."

The energy crisis made natural light in the center of the building popular as a means of conserving fuel consumption. A sensitivity to the earth–sun relation of the building geometry developed as a means of heating and cooling buildings. Tools for analyzing buildings, first in sophisticated hand calculators and then in personal computers and inexpensive software for personal computers, became available. The Department of Energy encouraged research, funded projects, and publicized the results.

COMPUTERS

With the introduction of high speed, low cost computers, there has been a widespread use of space-frame computer programs. Manufacturers of proprietary space frames have developed computer-aided design (CAD) programs that integrate design, load analysis, and cost estimation with automatic generation of component lists, assembly drawings, and fabrication instructions for computer-controlled milling machines. Theoretically, connected to automated factory production, space frames could be designed at the computer screen and arrive packaged and ready to erect on the site untouched by human hand. Proprietary systems are available to designers with a variety of choices for projects ranging from atriums, canopies, sloped glazing walls, clear-span spaces, towers, and pyramids.

Space-frame prices have steadily declined during the past 20 years. There are almost unlimited possibilities of geometric shapes, configurations, modular dimensions, support locations, material finish, and price.

Space frames are a structural means of spanning long distances and large spaces with light elements. They are elegant, complex solutions expressing contemporary manufacturing technology and electronic calculation. Most space frames in the 1950s and 1960s were flat planes. The Gyraton and Fuller's dome at Expo 67 in Montreal were notable exceptions.

The architects Skidmore Owings and Merrill's Interfirst building in Dallas, Texas, completed in 1981 has the geometry of the space truss matching the half-pyramid of the building. The Javits Convention Center in New York City, completed by architects I. M. Pei and Partners in 1987, with its complex changes of elevation would have been difficult, impossible, or prohibitively expensive to calculate without present computer analysis techniques.

Space frames such as those used in stores, shopping centers, and office complexes with spans of 30–100 ft can use "off-the-shelf" manufacturer's calculations. Longer spans for stadium roofs and airplane hangars require engineering analysis and review. If a proprietary system is used, the firm supplying the frame should inspect design, fabrication, and erection. Many fabricators supply these services.

Standard connections make attachment of space frames to other forms of construction relatively simple. Roof-deck and glazing-equipment manufacturers are equipped to match their systems to most proprietary space-frame systems.

SPACE-FRAME GEOMETRY

Viewed at a distance of 400 ft, the overall geometry and color of the space frame will dominate. At 40 ft, the outstanding visual characteristics are shape and size of members, finish, and perhaps node design; at 4-ft, the connection details can be studied. During the past few years space frames have tended to use smaller elements with finer textures.

The majority of space-frame designs are based on square modules, although triangular, rectangular, and other geometric configurations are possible. For planning purposes, a grid is visualized. For example, modular dimensions of 4, 5, 7, and 10 ft are possible choices for an 80- × 80-ft roof opening. The choice of grid dimensions may be determined by cost, interface, and span. In general, the larger the module of a given area, the lower the space-frame unit cost. Joint, node, or connection cost is relatively fixed, with fewer connections as modules increase in size.

The unit dimensions of the space frame are dictated by the following considerations. The height and width of the space-frame module, the shape of the space-frame member (round, square, T section, etc), building planning module in relation to the space-frame module, joint cost (the larger the tributary feet to the joint, the more economical because joints are more expensive than frame members), ratio of bending stress to direct stress, and ratio of the horizontal spacing to the depth of the structure.

Geometrically, the space grid can be visualized as a three-dimensional development of a flat, two-dimensional grid.

- Direct grids are two parallel grids similar in design, with one layer directly over the top of the other; thus both grids are directionally the same. Upper and lower grids are interconnected by bracing (Fig. 1).
- Offset grids are two parallel grids similar in design, with one grid offset from the other (in plan) but remaining directionally the same. The upper and lower grids are interconnected by bracing (Fig. 2).
- Differential grids are two parallel grids that may be of different design and are therefore directionally different but are chosen to coordinate and form a regular pattern. Upper and lower grids are interconnected by bracing.
- Lattice grids have their upper and lower members braced to form a girder before erection; they generally are factory-fabricated assemblies. The upper and lower members are placed close together and, when joined by bracing, may be considered as a stiffened single-layer grid. In all other respects, lattice grids are similar in appearance to direct grids.

Geodesic domes are space frames in the round. Their structure is formed by chords of a grid system of approximate great circle arcs on the surface of a sphere. As portions of spheres, they enclose the greatest volume with the least surface area and do not rely on internal structure.

The tetrahedron, the simplest polyhedron, encloses the

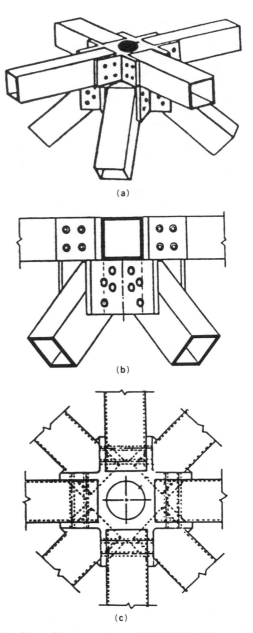

Figure 1. Space-frame systems—GEO*HUB, Starnet Structures. **(a)** Patent pending perspective Type A; **(b)** elevation; **(c)** plan.

least volume with the greatest surface area. The sphere is the strongest shape against internal and radial pressure; the tetrahedron against external and tangential pressure.

The grid for a geodesic dome is developed from a basic grid of spherical polyhedrons (polyhedrons projected onto a sphere). Regular polyhedrons are ideal for grids because of their symmetry and regularity. Regular polyhedrons are formed when all face angles are equal, all edges are equal, all vertices are the same, all faces the same, and all dihedral angles are equal. A grid with polyhedrons composed of triangles works best because a triangle is the simplest polygon—the simplest subdivision of surface. An equilateral triangle is the simplest triangle, with all edges and angles equal; it is the only triangle regular enough to be a face of a regular polyhedron.

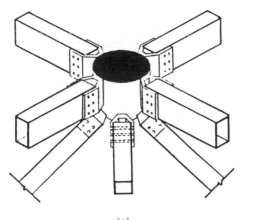

(a)

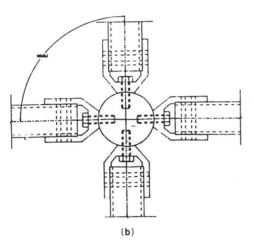

(b)

(c)

Figure 2. Space-frame systems—GEO*HUB, Starnet Structures. (a) Perspective Type B (b) plan (c) actual.

HISTORY

There are more space frames planned for terrestrial and outer space use today than during the heyday of modernism or the frantic conquest of space following the launching of Sputnik in 1957. Many of today's inventors and marketers are ingenious adventurers and imaginative

dreamers: architects, engineers, industrial designers. In the late 1960s and 1970s, the leading advocates of space structures were the best-educated and most affluent cultural dropouts the world had ever known. The commune builders of California, New Mexico, and Colorado dotted the countryside with ingenious arrays of inventive domes in weird configurations and unlikely materials. It was, some said, the expression of a truly American architecture worthy of the traditions of the New England house, balloon frame, grain silo, and steel-framed skyscraper.

The fascination with space structures has always transcended vocation and profession. One of the first and most successful of generally acknowledged and admired space structures was the work of Sir Joseph Paxton, a builder of greenhouses, who designed and built the great Crystal Palace in Hyde Park, London, for the Great Exhibition of 1851.

Alexander Graham Bell, the inventor of the telephone, flew space-frame kites and built a 40-ft-high space-viewing tower to amuse his friends. Konrad Wachsmann designed space frames to span 320 ft in the 1950s. Buckminster Fuller invented geodesics, and the counterculture living in communes in California, Arizona, New Mexico, and Nevada circulated published do-it-yourself books on geodesics. The most widely circulated were *Domebook One* and *Domebook Two*.

In the early 1970s, high-school students, bearded physicists, and motorcycle-gang members used NASA computer printouts to establish chord factors to erect domes as solar Casbahs on the rolling hills of California, the deserts of New Mexico, and the high plains of Nevada.

Space-frames addicts, dropouts, and scientists have always been somewhat eccentric. But, as the hippies of the 1960s and 1970s metamorphose into today's yuppies, space structures have become upwardly mobile. Instead of rounded domes for a tribal commune, Marine Corps barracks, or Arctic radar, space structures now top urban atriums, casinos, jet airplanes, and gas digester tanks.

SPACE FRAMES ARE BORN

Many space-frame designers today were inspired by the space-frame structures at Expo 67 in Montreal. But space frames are an expression of the continuity of the iron structures of the 19th century. Bell may be the "father" of space structures, but it is interesting that following Bell's work the subject did not evoke much interest in the building arts during the first half of the 20th century.

However, the design of air-frame structures relied heavily on the principles of space-frame systems according to P. Pearce. A little later, the space frame found its way into high performance European sports and racing cars. Many of these vehicles had sophisticated space-frame chassis. These included cars like the Jaguar, Ferrari, Maserati, Lotus, Mercedes Benz, and Porsche in the 1950s. These vehicles were performance-oriented structures. The high strength-to-weight ratios characteristic of space frames, along with their potential for enormous torsional stiffness, were a substantial advantage.

Buckminster Fuller worked on the evolution of an "energetic and synergetic geometry," from which evolved a series of "geodesic/tensegrity" structures. Fuller was searching for the maximal advantage in environmental-control structures through effective energy use. He used the term "energetic" to refer to separated and individual working parts of a system and "synergy" to define the way a whole system acts as more than the simple sum of its parts.

Fuller saw energy in structural systems polarized into push and pull, compression and tension. Historically, humankind's structures were dominated by great compressive strengths, mainly stone piled up in great mass. The tensile strength in natural fiber cords was used only in ships' rigging and guy ropes. In 1927, Fuller sought to separate compression and tension energy into their most advantageous forms. He designed relatively short compressive members and combined these with long cable-and-rod tensions. He discovered the principle of discontinuous compression combined with continuous tension, employing each at maximal operational strength in his space structures.

The space frame symbolized "optimization." It required less material than linear systems, because, in a two-dimensional structure, all the elements lie in the same plane, whereas the parts of a space structure form a three-dimensional assembly. A roof truss or a portal frame resists loads in one plane. A dome—a typical space structure—cannot be analyzed as a plane system. It resists loads from any direction applied at any point.

FROM THEORY TO MARKET

Architect Charles Attwood, who founded Unistrut Systems in 1942, began to practice about the same time Fuller was conducting his early housing experiments. Attwood saw the problem of modern architecture, practically, as one of getting more building for the client's dollar. More complex functions were being demanded of buildings; their uses were changing. If a building did not adapt, it would become obsolete.

Buildings, therefore, should be constructed to be easily transformed with changeable parts that would be salvageable, Attwood believed. Demountable building systems were an answer. Because all building materials must be handled, their weight affects the cost of building. A demountable structure, easily changed, offers savings over the entire life of the building. When the building is discarded, the structure is easily disassembled for the parts to be reused. This makes it cheaper to use strong, durable, high quality materials.

Attwood's system has often been described as an overgrown "Meccano" set because the parts can be so easily put together, taken down, and reassembled in a seemingly endless variety of combinations. The system was first used to support numerous kinds of electrical and mechanical equipment and for shelves and storage racks in factories, warehouses, and supermarkets.

Unistrut entered the space-frame market in 1951. Its system was the Model T of space frames, but, unlike the car, the Unistrut system continues to be the most popular system for short-span solutions.

It is a system of but four basic parts: a standard strut, a standard plate connector, and a nut and a bolt. The strut is used interchangeably on the upper and lower planes and in the diagonal web of the roof trusses. Holes in the ends fit over lugs in the plate connectors. Erectors attach a single bolt and nut at each connection, nuts are identical and functions self-evident. Roof-space trusses are put together in the field without measuring tapes, squares, plumb bobs, or levels.

Attwood had very little technical information available concerning the space-frame stress distribution. Tests that he had conducted at the University of Michigan in 1952 confirmed that the space frame was unusually strong in proportion to its weight and that the entire structure acted as a single three-dimensional unit. A more extensive test of his theories came in 1957. At the request of the U.S. Department of Commerce, crates were packed with aluminum struts, steel connectors, and assorted other materials, including colored Plexiglas, aluminum-faced plywood, prewired fluorescent lighting fixtures, and translucent plastic ceiling panels. The whole package was shipped to Utrecht in the Netherlands, where local workers erected a pavilion in 4½ days. The pavilion was used as an exhibition for 9 days and then dismantled in 2½ days and shipped to Spain. Parts were added, and a larger pavilion was erected in Barcelona. This building was used for about a month and then dismantled. Some of its parts were shipped to Salonika, Greece, for a trade fair and the remainder to Tunis, Tunisia, to be used as a television studio, a feature of the U.S. exhibit at the Tunisian Fair.

In the 1960s the space frame was an exotic experiment. The builders of the U.S. Pavilion at Montreal's Expo 67 were pioneers, although Buckminster Fuller had conceived the principles 40 years earlier. Today, space frames are commonplace—no longer experiments designed in hopes of solving world housing needs, now they are covers for offshore oil rigs, ships' radars, and NASA's proposed docking armatures in outer space.

STRUCTURAL BEHAVIOR

Space frames today differ from those of 20 years ago in that architects understand them better. Computer programs make space-frame design easier says Matthys Levy, structural engineer with Weidlinger Associates, New York City.

> The computer's virtue is that it makes it much easier to work with indeterminate structures. You do not have to use approximation, and that's a plus. The tendency is to optimize the structure by computer. On the minus side is that you can only optimize for one set of loads, and there might be a set of conditions at the site that you did not consider. When doing space frame calculations by hand, you tend to be more conservative, and the design therefore has more built-in safety factors.

Because the space frame is a highly indeterminate structure with the ability to distribute concentrated loads evenly throughout the rest of the space grid, the buckling of a member under a concentrated load does not lead to the collapse of the entire structure.

A space grid may behave as a grillage or as a slab.

Offset and differential space grids, which behave as slabs, provide stiffness as pin-jointed systems, whose members can be axially loaded with little bending, just as in a planar truss. The behavior of the space grid can be compared to that of a reinforced concrete slab, except that in the space grid the forces must follow the path provided by the members, instead of spreading as they would in a slab.

Offset and differential grid space frames can resist torsion or twisting movements through axial member loading alone; they are stiffer than the grillage-type of space frame. Lattice and direct space grids function like grillages with top chords and bottom chords, with vertical and inclined web members contained in a plane normal to the flat roof or floor system.

No matter how many directions there are in such vertical trusses, the result is still a grillage of planar trusses and must be analyzed and designed accordingly. The actual force distribution of either type, slab or grillage, depends primarily on the nature of the supports.

Space-frame supports must be located at nodal points, either at the top (roof) or at the lower (ceiling) plane. Support locations may be randomly placed to suit the design of a layout. Support locations significantly affect the structural efficiency of the space grid, so that those systems with symmetry about two or three axes are preferred. Systems with cantilevers have less chord material and less overall material, but they do not change the size of web members. The transfer of loads from the space grid to the supporting structure can be achieved by making the structure continuous with the space grid or by placing a pin connection at the junction between the space grid and the vertical support. It is usually not necessary to make supports continuous with the space grid for the purpose of reducing deflections, because space grids are deep and many times stiffer than their vertical supports. The lateral loads can be resisted by vertical supports with fixed bases. The problem of support perimeter can be solved, regardless of continuity, by using shear-head-type connectors at the junction of the vertical support and the space grid.

CONNECTIONS

Sun Chien Hsiao, an architect, engineer, and head of Unistrut Systems' space structure division, has described the various methods of forming the space frame nodal connections and has grouped them under seven general types:

- Connector plate—flat, dished, or bent plate with holes that match the adjoining members.
- Hollow section—spherical, hexagonal, or square box with holes that match the adjoining members.
- Hollow ring section—circular, hexagonal, or square ring section with holes that accept the adjoining members.
- Solid section—spherical or cubical section with tapped holes for bolted connection to the adjoining members.
- Extruded section—round section with slots or square section with tags to receive adjoining members.

- Members with ears, tags, or other devices for connection to adjoining members.
- Welded, gusseted fittings—fittings with holes that match adjoining members.

Space-frame connectors and nodes are made from hot rolled-steel sections, hot forging, cast steel, aluminum alloys, etc. Space-frame members are made from steel or aluminum materials but, in theory, can be fabricated from any material that can meet the structural requirements. The joint fabrication, to be economical, must consider the type and size of the members, their geometric relationships, desired appearance, and connecting techniques (bolting, welding, or special connectors). Tubular members, structural tees, angles, and wide-flange members each imply a special connection discipline. For instance, the advantage of the welding connection is that it eliminates extra connection material and connection devices. On the other hand, bolted connections require joint material or assemblies that extend out of the members, increasing the cost of the connection.

SPACE ENCLOSED BY SPACE FRAMES

Not only are space frames different today from what they were 20 years ago, they enclose different space configurations. Most of the discussion in the past concerned the possibilities of horizontal spanning. Today, space frames often top off vertical atrium space in tall buildings.

Atria have become increasingly important. From 1959 to 1984, buildings containing atria won national American Institute of Architects (AIA) honor awards in 18 of the 25 years. As to why atrium buildings and their space-frame crowns have been so universally accepted, Robert Halverson, chief structural engineer of Skidmore, Owings and Merrill, New York City proposes:

> An automobile magazine wrote an equation for beauty. It said types of cars that had a great deal of complexity but could be understood in a short period of time were found to be the most beautiful. Cars that were complex but people could not understand or those that were very simple and easily understood were not considered as attractive. People thought things were beautiful when they were complex and repeated many times, and they could begin to understand them. I think that's also true about space frames.

In addition, space frames of today offer greater design flexibility. "The first Unistrut system, now marketed as System No. 1, is the 'Model T'" of space frames, Hsiao says. "It would only span 30 or 40 feet and had a limited geometry. To make it do more things, more parts had to be added. But by then the 'Model T' no longer was economical, so one might as well buy a Camaro." Figure 3 is an example of the use of the Unistrut system, and a winner of the Most Unique Application Unistrut Space-Frame Award.

Space frames have a good building safety record John Loss says:

> We [Architecture and Engineering Performance Information Center, AEPIC] have found no special problems with space frames in relation to building failures. However, an area of

Figure 3. Most unique application, Unistrut Space-Frame Award. Monkey Island Project, Cleveland Metroparks Zoo.

reservations is multistory atria and the issue of fire. We presume that if we wash water down the glass it will dissipate the heat generated by the fire. But there are structural elements that are, perhaps, not considered. We have not yet seen major fires in multistory atria.

Levy adds, "Space frames do not usually fail because they are so highly indeterminate. A joint may yield or a strut may crush, but there is a tremendous amount of redundancy." Levy also believes that space frames will continue to have a "big building" image: "Space frame applications most recently in the headlines were the Crystal Cathedral and Javits Center—generally the most visible space frames spanning the largest spaces. They create architectural images." Space frames have not been adopted to housing because they are not an inexpensive way of building.

Space-frame roofs are not the least expensive means of building a roof. Roof trusses and one-way joists would have been a lot more economical for a building such as the Javit's Center in New York City (Fig. 4), which is one of the most well-known space-frame structures of the 1980s. But the space frame solves other problems as well as structuring space—the image is very appropriate. When a space frame provides both structure and architectural image it becomes economically competitive. But considered as structure alone, it is an expensive building system. Future developments in space frames will be in the joints, predicts Levy. The cost is in the joints; if this is reduced, space frames will become more economically competitive.

SPACE FRAMES IN OUTER SPACE

Some space-frame manufacturers are designing "high-tech" outer-space projects. NASA has developed space-frame hubs based on a hand-operated latch system designed by Langley Research Center engineers. The system eliminates the need for tools, which are difficult to handle at zero gravity. The system was tested at the McDonnell

Figure 4. Javits Convention Center, New York City.

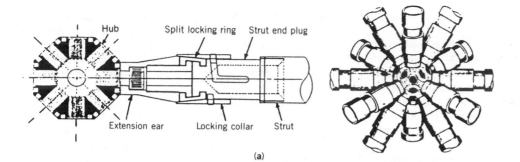

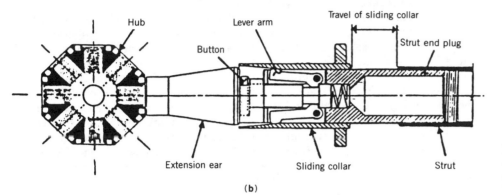

Figure 5. Space-frame systems—STAR★BAY fasteners, Starnet Structures. (a) STAR★BAY 1; (b) STAR★BAY 2.

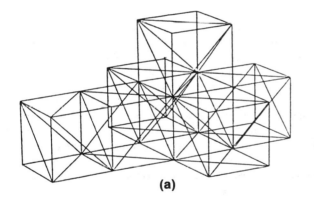

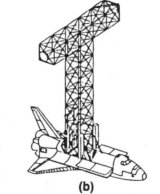

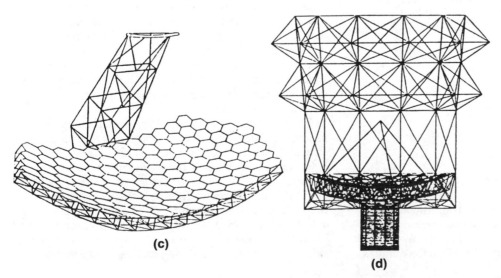

Figure 6. Space-frame systems—global space structure system design drivers, Starnet Structures. A geometrically viable system (a) seven bays of the space station; (b) space station 5M × 5M × 5M spacetruss (c) reflector spacetruss (d) reflector telescope.

Douglas underwater neutral buoyancy test facility in 1987 and found to be satisfactory.

Two full-sized 15- × 15-ft bay modules were assembled in the neutral buoyancy tank at the rate of approximately one strut per minute. Struts were removed and replaced twice to illustrate the modularity and repairability of the system. Extrapolations of test data collected indicate that the entire 728 strut main truss of the space station could be assembled in one space-shuttle trip (Fig. 5).

Space frames of lightweight composites rather than the present steel and aluminum are a possibility because major research is being carried out today in composite materials. Robotic assembly techniques are particularly applicable to space frames because of the repetitive motion of assembly inherent in their erection. It is estimated that the deployment of human labor would cost $50,000 an hour (1986) including the cost of labor transportation. The space-station's design (1986) called for a 450-ft hub-and-strut spine to which radar, telescopes, solar cells, and crew's quarters can be attached. It is scheduled for construction in the mid 1990s (Fig. 6).

BIBLIOGRAPHY

1. Z. S. Makowski, "Modern Grid Structures," *Architectural Science Review* **3,** 52 (July 1960).

2. J. Borrego, Space Grid Structures, MIT Press, Cambridge, Mass., 1968, p. 3; Z. S. Makowski, "Double-layer Grid Structures, *Architectural Association Journal,* p. 218 (March 1961).

See also ARCHITECTURAL AND ENGINEERING PERFORMANCE INFORMATION CENTER (AEPIC); ATRIUM BUILDINGS; FULLER, R. BUCKMINSTER; GEODESIC DOMES; MEMBRANE STRUCTURES; SUSPENSION CABLE STRUCTURES

FORREST WILSON, PhD, FRSA
College Park, Maryland

SPECIAL CONDITIONS.   See CONSTRUCTION DOCUMENTS.

SPECIALTY LIGHTING

THE ARCHITECT AND THE LIGHTING CONSULTANT

The use of light should be inseparable from the architectural conception. Yet, it is only the architect who can visualize how the finished structure should appear. Today, special consultants are often required to solve the complex problems of a lighting system design. For proper collaboration, clear communication in mutually understood terms is essential.

The first meeting between the architect and the lighting consultant should establish those lines of communication by fully exploring the original architectural design concept, often known as the "parti," and the project program. The consultant is presented with a full set of drawings for a complete understanding of the scope of the project. If the project involves a new building, a model is often presented for inspection; in the case of a renovation, a site visit is appropriate.

These initial discussions should also clearly establish the role that light will play in the finished space. Light can take a dominant role in the design scheme as an obvious, theatrical application, or it can take a more subtle, subordinate role in illuminating architectural surfaces and forms. Light can create an ambient condition and a direct focus as well as provide decorative enhancements. In all cases, the way light is integrated with the architecture affects perceptions of space, orientation, and surface texture while influencing psychological reactions. Lighting must be considered as an essential component of the architectural concept.

THE DESIGN PROCESS: SCHEMATIC DESIGN

A common mistake when providing light is to select the lighting equipment first, thinking of the hardware as objects in the design. The importance is not in what produces light, but rather where the light lands. After the initial architect–consultant meeting, the first step a lighting design consultant takes is to establish an appropriate emotional environment for the activity that will occur in the space. Light can have a strengthening or reinforcing effect in the creation of a suitable psychological setting, similar to that provided by background music. Light can affect impressions of spaciousness, relaxation, privacy, intimacy, and pleasantness. It can evoke a festive atmosphere or encourage quiet contemplation. It can create a cold, impersonal public space or, as in the case of a dining room, a desired atmosphere of a warm, intimate, private space. After mood has been considered, the next step is to determine where light is needed. The consultant must decide which surfaces and objects will receive light and which should be left in shadow. Only in this play between light and dark can the designer influence spatial perception and emotional response.

The formal dining room (Fig. 1) points up this approach. In this project, the program calls for a large, oval, central dark wood table and rose-colored marble floor, fireplace, and mantel across the room from a buffet beneath the windows. Glass doors lead to an exterior terrace at one end and to an interior hall at the other. Plaster walls and ceiling are painted off-white. Trim and wainscoting are oak. Paintings are hung above the mantel, on the wall between the doors leading to the terrace, and on either side of the door to the hall. Given this room arrangement,

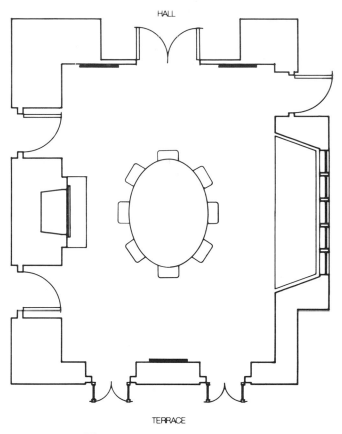

Figure 1. Dining room floor plan.

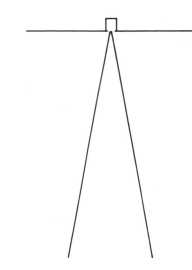

Figure 2. Downward concentrating distribution.

the lighting consultant can begin to develop an appropriate design. The surfaces and objects chosen to receive light here are the table, the fireplace and the painting above it, the buffet, the painting between the terrace doors, and the paintings on the opposite wall. This selection establishes a visual hierarchy that must precede the design. Attention is immediately drawn on entry to the table and to the painting beyond. Light on surfaces along the sides and on the entry wall visually balance the room.

This selection of surfaces and objects to be lighted establishes patterns of brightness within the space, emphasizing some areas and leaving others more subdued. These brightness patterns produce a much more interesting, dynamic space than one that is illuminated by indiscriminate lighting from overhead. The arrangement of patterns determines the emotional response to lighted space. When horizontal surfaces are illuminated, people and activities become the dominant features. The increased consciousness of movement and nearby detail encourage a gregarious attitude in the room's occupants. If the lighting emphasis shifts to the architecture, activity becomes subordinate to surrounding forms, causing introspection. Often, the best solution is a combination of horizontal (downlight) and vertical (wall wash) illumination. In the dining room, the convivial atmosphere is encouraged by brightness on the table. Vertical illumination on paintings on the surrounding walls serves to reduce the exces-

sive contrast that would exist if the perimeter were in darkness, creating a relaxed, intimate atmosphere.

Decisions then are made on direction and distribution of light, distribution referring to the way in which a luminaire emits light. Concentrated distribution focuses light in a narrow cone (Fig. 2); diffuse distribution scatters light in a wide pattern (Fig. 3). These distributions affect the degree of contrast, the gradient difference between light and dark, perceived on objects and surfaces. Lighting fixtures are designed to produce downward, upward, or multidirectional light output with either concentrated or diffuse distribution (Fig. 4). The combined characteristics of direction and distribution induce subjective responses. Downward concentrated light tends to emphasize horizontal surfaces, limiting light on vertical surfaces, thus creating an impression of low general brightness but with high brightness accents. A luminaire providing diffuse down-

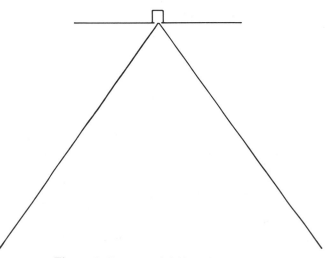

Figure 3. Downward diffuse distribution.

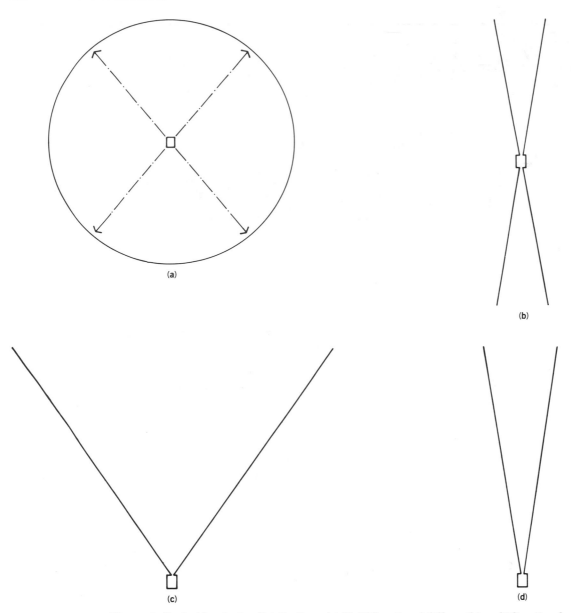

Figure 4. Typical luminaire distributions. **(a)** Multidirectional diffuse; **(b)** multidirectional concentrating; **(c)** upward diffuse; **(d)** upward concentrating.

light yields lower contrast. Upward diffuse lighting, such as indirect uplighting of ceilings, is often used to emphasize architectural detail, and provides low contrast, general lighting. Luminaires with multidirectional distributions combine both upward and downward components and are often used to provide diffuse ambient lighting as well as direct task lighting. In the dining room example, narrow concentrated distributions of light are chosen to illuminate only the surfaces designated to receive light (Fig. 5). Diffuse lighting could be specified but would result in a less dramatic, more casual atmosphere because all surfaces, including the floor and walls, would receive equal light, diluting the intended effect (Fig. 6).

Surface finishes play an important role in the control and redirection of light. Light-colored, reflective surfaces

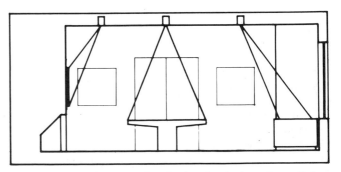

Figure 5. Concentrating distribution luminaires for a dining room.

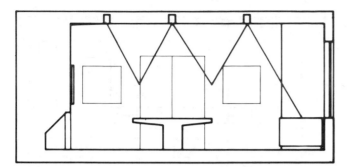

Figure 6. Diffuse distribution luminaires for a dining room.

Figure 8. Masonry/concrete grazing illumination.

tend to bounce light around the room, contributing to a bright, diffuse lighting condition. Dark-colored, absorptive surface treatments reduce reflectivity, imparting the impression of a darker, high contrast lighting condition, regardless of the amount of the illumination directed onto them. In the dining room, the dark tabletop limits reflections, while the off-white walls reflect a larger proportion of the light.

The consultant then considers the effect of light on the surfaces and forms that define the space. The observer sees three-dimensional form as a relationship between highlights and shadows. Lighting can enhance perception

of texture. Grazing light, from luminaires located near a surface, reveals the relief in a stone or masonry wall, but exaggerates imperfections in plaster or gypsum board (Figs. 7 and 8). Diffuse wall washing eliminates undesired highlighting, creating an impression of smoothness (Figs. 9 and 10). Direct, high contrast lighting on objects contributes to a dramatic effect, but may affect viewer ability to discern detail. Also, the angle at which light strikes an object evokes particular responses. Psychologically, light emanating from at least 45° above horizontal is perceived

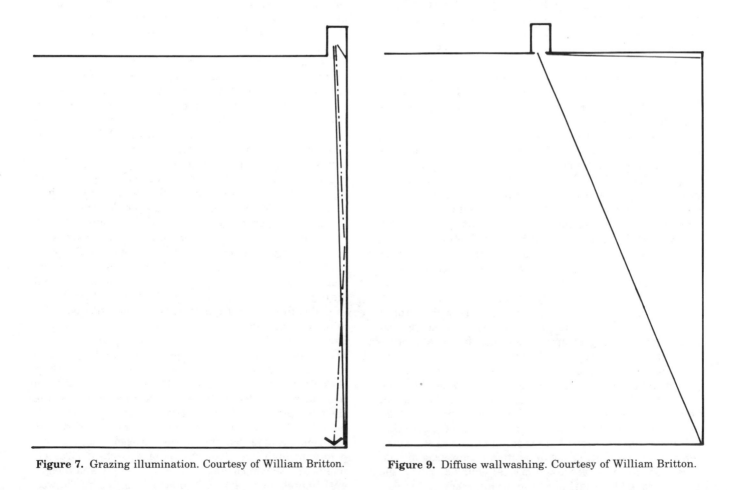

Figure 7. Grazing illumination. Courtesy of William Britton.

Figure 9. Diffuse wallwashing. Courtesy of William Britton.

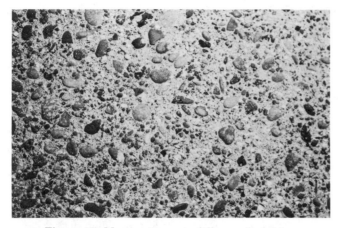

Figure 10. Masonry/concrete diffuse wallwashing.

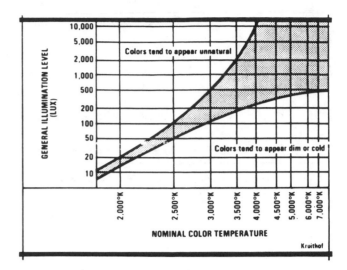

Figure 11. Color "whiteness" amenity curve (1).

as normal because it replicates daylight. Light coming from the side, from behind, or below an object can induce a sense of mystery or uncertainty. In the dining room, light is directed onto the table from directly above, maintaining familiar shadows on guests and the centerpiece. Objects on the mantel and buffet will receive light from 30° back from vertical to provide a natural-looking effect.

Color and color rendition are also important considerations. Incandescent lamps produce what is called warm light; they are the electric light source that is considered most pleasing because illuminated objects and complexions look familiar. Although the color-rendering ability of incandescent lamps is by no means perfect, it is a familiar source of light. As such, an arbitrary 100-point scale known as the Color-Rendering Index (CRI) holds the incandescent source as the standard against which other electric sources are compared. Tungsten–halogen lamps produce light of a slightly higher color temperature, thus appearing cooler. Fluorescent sources are available in a range of color temperatures and color-rendering capabilities, depending on the phosphor content of the glass tube. In general, warmer color temperatures of light make surfaces and objects appear closer, while cooler colors seem to recede. Psychological reactions are also influenced by the quantity of light. At low levels of light, people prefer warm-toned lighting, while at high levels, the preference is for cooler color temperatures (Fig. 11). In the dining room, an incandescent source was selected because of its ability to pleasingly render both food and complexions and to complement the relatively low brightness levels.

Next, the lighting consultant considers the control of brightness. Visual comfort is a concern in selecting and positioning lighting equipment so that glare is at a minimum. Indirect lighting, by definition, conceals the source from view. However, care must be taken with direct lighting fixtures so that lamps are properly shielded from the occupants' field of view. Controlled glare from small points of light, such as clear low wattage lamps, contributes as a source of "sparkle." Sparkle is "good glare" that is produced by very small areas of high brightness, having the effect of enhancing the appetite and encouraging conversation. For that reason, a crystal chandelier over the table is added for sparkle in the dining room.

The actual quantity of light to be provided is also a factor. The Illuminating Engineering Society publishes recommended light levels for specific seeing tasks. These are intended as guides to average levels of light required for performing tasks, but are never used as a starting point. In any commercial, industrial, or office setting in which task-lighting ratios are an important consideration, qualitative concerns are as important as quantitative illumination levels.

Based on these parameters, suitable light sources (called lamps) must be chosen. Point sources, such as incandescent and tungsten–halogen lamps, are able to be directed in specific dispersion patterns and also provide excellent color rendering. Linear fluorescent sources are more energy efficient, but they are inherently diffuse in nature and have a fair to very good CRI. High efficiency mercury, metal-halide, and high and low pressure sodium lamps are point sources of light with poor to good color-rendering abilities. The control needed to precisely spotlight an object is possible only with a point source of light. In the dining room, it has already been determined that warm incandescent light is required. To produce the narrow concentration called for previously, incandescent PAR-38 lamps are recommended for lighting the paintings. Low voltage PAR-36 lamps, providing a narrower, more concentrated beam, are chosen for the table and buffet to eliminate "stray" light on adjacent surfaces.

Only after all these qualitative and quantitative determinations have been made, can the selection of lighting fixtures begin. At this point in the schematic design phase, the consultant selects generic types of equipment, ie, recessed wall washer or recessed downlight, dictated by the design. Whatever the decision, the lighting equipment must be coordinated with the architecture. In some cases, the appropriate lighting solution may be incorporated as part of the architectural detailing. In other cases, surface- and pendant-mounted luminaires are used. These visually dominant lighting elements become architectural elements and are important to design harmony and the general impression of space. A proper relationship between

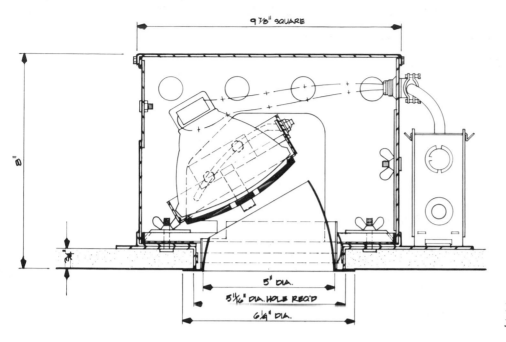

Figure 12. Recessed adjustable object light.

lighting units and materials produces a coordinated architectural result. In a well-integrated space, a casual observer should even be unaware of the lighting and the mechanics of light production. For the dining room, recessed adjustable object lights are chosen to perform the principal lighting tasks (Fig. 12). Recessed lighting fixtures arranged in a grid pattern become an integrated, and therefore unnoticed, component of the ceiling system and are ignored (Fig. 13). The regular pattern eliminates

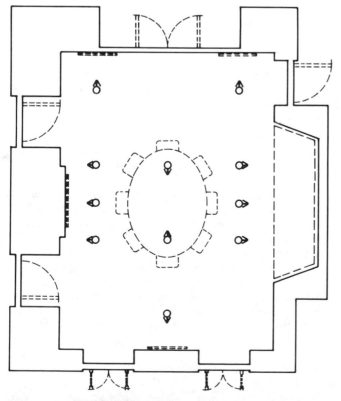

Figure 13. Luminaire grid pattern.

the distraction created when recessed fixtures are indiscriminately placed. The pendant-mounted chandelier establishes a source of illumination and interest at "people level."

SCHEMATIC DESIGN PRESENTATION

The lighting consultant now presents a schematic layout of the design for discussion with and approval by the architect. The submitted documents include a reflected ceiling plan, as seen in Figure 13, indicating the proposed arrangement and distribution of generic lighting units. The reflected ceiling plan follows the outline of the floor plan supplied by the architect, but is drawn as if a mirror were placed on the floor to reflect the ceiling and the lighting fixtures. Symbols corresponding to the type and precise location of the fixtures are placed on the plan. A lighting equipment schedule, without specific manufacturer recommendations, accompanies the plan. This schedule is a detailed key to the symbols denoting generic fixture types. Drawings of lighting fixture possibilities are also included for review. Installation detail sketches, such as coves and other architectural features, are also submitted. An estimated budget and expectations of equipment availability are provided.

DESIGN DEVELOPMENT PHASE

Once the lighting concept has been accepted, the consultant develops the design into a plan that can be built. The architect's reactions are incorporated, mock-ups of architectural details are built, illumination calculations are performed, switching and dimming plans are devised, and luminaires are evaluated. Appropriate lighting fixture selections are made based on performance evaluation and research of manufacturers' specifications. Photometric data are consulted to ensure proper performance of the

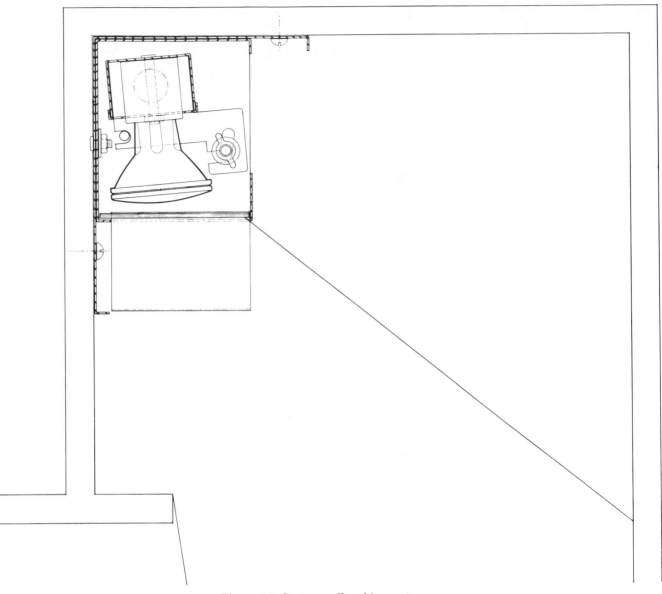

Figure 14. Custom wallwashing system.

lighting plan. Equipment is selected to integrate with the other building systems.

If no luminaires are found on the market to fulfill the design, the consultant will develop a custom fixture. When lighting is integrated into an architectural detail, such as a cove, or a custom fixture is required, physical verification of design ideas must be mocked up at full size using finishes similar to those called for in the design. That is the only way the designer can judge the effectiveness of the special application. The consultant diagrams the architectural feature in detail (Fig. 14), taking into account construction methods, materials, building and electrical codes, and maintenance as well as lighting effectiveness. These details are provided as part of the design document packages to the architect, client, and contractor.

During the design development phase, the consultant also calculates illumination levels to be achieved by the lighting system. Using the manufacturers' photometric information, the consultant is able to check lighting distributions and predict light levels to verify the expected effectiveness of the design.

The conclusion of the design development phase is a presentation of the design to the architect. This package includes a dimensioned reflected ceiling plan, a lighting fixture schedule with complete equipment information, luminaire drawings, installation detail drawings, and transformer recommendations for low voltage equipment. A switching plan that lists switch and dimmer recommendations is also included. A revised budget estimate is submitted. The architect is then able to issue approval to the consultant, who then proceeds to develop contract documents.

CONTRACT DOCUMENTS PHASE

In contract documents, a reflected ceiling plan with locations and mounting heights of all equipment dimensioned

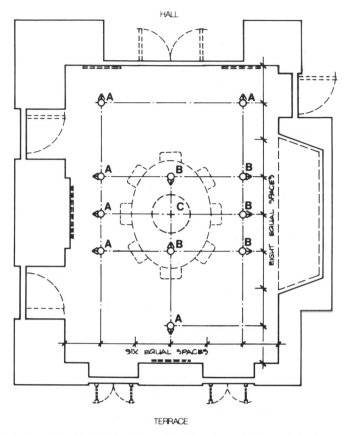

Figure 15. Reflected ceiling plan. Courtesy of Edison Price Inc.

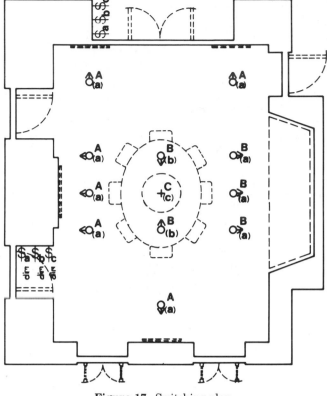

Figure 17. Switching plan.

is accompanied by a lighting fixture schedule that lists fixture type, lamps designation, manufacturer and catalog number, and total connected wattage for the equipment indicated on the plan (Figs. 15 and 16). Switching and dimming circuiting is drawn on a separate plan (Fig. 17). The contract document package includes fixture details that fully indicate how the unit is to be installed and operated. A written description of the specified lighting system is included to clarify the recommendations. Fixture circuiting schedules are included to describe how a switching or dimming system is to be used for precise control of the lighting.

BIDDING AND CONSTRUCTION PHASE

The approved contract documents are transmitted to the architect for integration into the construction process of the building. The lighting consultant works with the contractor to resolve design problems. During the bidding phase, the consultant may be called on to assist or to negotiate on behalf of the client with equipment suppliers. Although the consultant never operates as the contractor, the experience and expertise of the designer may be needed to resolve certain problems. Site visits are required for supervision of the lighting installation, especially when the design calls for equipment unfamiliar to the contractor.

The finale of the lighting design is the actual focusing of the installed equipment. Focusing involves checking for proper lamping and correct orientation of sources and reflectors. These procedures ensure that the equipment performs as intended. Adjustable object lighting fixtures require particular attention to direction and focal variables, as well as locking the focus firmly in place. Focus supervision allows the consultant to assure the architect that the lighting is being used as designed.

Symbol	Type	Description	Lamp Code	Manufacturer and Catalog No	Total Watts
⭕→	A	Recessed incandescent adjustable object light	75PAR38/3FL	Lighting Company 1001	150
⭕→	B	Recessed incandescent adjustable object light	50PAR36NSP	Lighting Company 2001	150
⊕	C	Pendant mtd incandescent decorative chandelier	(5) 40CAC/L	Chandelier Company 3001	200

Figure 16. Lighting equipment schedule.

APPLICATIONS

Art Museum and Gallery

The relationship of artwork to the surrounding architecture is the first lighting consideration of the architect and lighting designer. Art can be featured dramatically by focusing light on individual works while leaving the surround in relative darkness, allowing the art to achieve prominence over the architecture (Fig. 18). Alternatively, entire vertical surfaces can be washed in light without creating a hierarchy, letting viewers select their own focus (Fig. 19). In either case, the lighting system must provide high color rendering for the proper appreciation of art and also take into account the potential harm that lighting levels will cause.

In museums or galleries that undergo frequent exhibit changes, a flexible lighting system is an appropriate consideration. Track lighting is often selected, not only because lighting fixtures may be located and aimed as needed, but the track itself serves as the wireway providing a simple method of power distribution. If track lighting is to be used, the consultant must specify adequately durable equipment in a system that is flexible enough to provide for a variety of sources, lenses, filters, and brightness controls. Track fixtures must provide proper shielding for brightness control and prevention of glare. Devices such as cross baffles are preferred to cube cell louvers, which block almost 50% of the light output. Framing projectors require attention and adjustment and are impractical to maintain.

Paintings must be carefully considered as to the medium, surface texture, frame, and whether a glass or Plexiglas enclosure is used. Usually, the best angle for lighting a painting is from 30° back from vertical (Fig. 20). That is the best compromise between preventing shadows from being cast by the frame and eliminating reflected glare from a glossy surface in the observer's field of view.

The way sculpture is lighted affects the viewer's per-

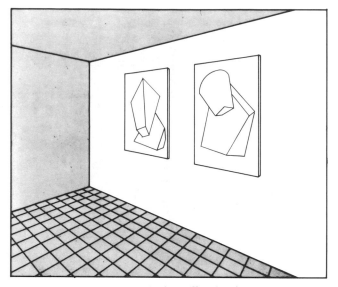

Figure 19. Uniform illumination.

ception of the art. Concentrated beams create higher contrast, deepening shadows, and emphasizing form and texture. Diffuse lighting lessens contrast. Typically, frontal lighting from 30 to 45° of horizontal and 30 to 45° of vertical is recommended for modeling that best replicates the effect of sunlight. However, the designer can choose to disturb a naturalistic effect by lighting sculpture from a less traditional angle. Uplighting can create an ominous impression. Backlighting throws an object into silhouette. Sidelighting provides a dramatic "lift" to three-dimensional forms.

Conservation of materials is always of primary concern. Great care must be exercised when lighting materials susceptible to degradation from heat and light. Pig-

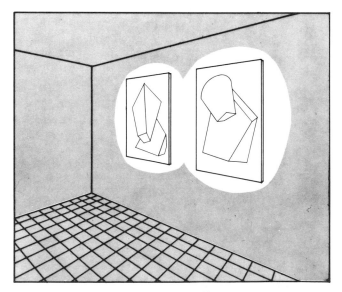

Figure 18. Nonuniform illumination.

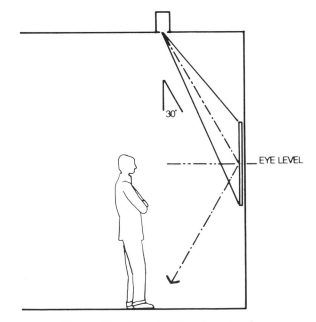

Figure 20. Proper lighting for artwork.

ments can fade and media can dry and crack if not properly protected. Daylighting introduces an enormous amount of ultraviolet (uv) radiation that must be shielded and filtered to prevent harm to these works. The best uv filters are acrylic and other plastic sheetings formulated to eliminate the transmission of harmful radiation. Special varnishes may be used to glaze windows to similarly protect artwork. Electric lighting, to a lesser degree, also produces uv energy that requires attention. The uv emissions from incandescent sources typically used in museums are generally insignificant compared to daylight, but all fluorescent sources require some type of uv shielding. Plastic sheets of uv absorption material are commercially available from manufacturers of color filters. Often, curators limit light levels on sensitive materials to a range of 5–15 footcandles, which challenges the consultant to not only properly light the object, but also create an appropriate ambient lighting condition that allows the viewer to adjust to low levels of light and still be able to distinguish and appreciate details.

Exterior

Until the advent of electric lighting, architectural forms and materials were chosen partly in response to prevailing daylighting. Historically, the architect completely controlled the exterior appearance of a building. In a sense, it was a sculpture that could only be perceived in the daytime. However, in the twentieth century, electric lighting presents the opportunity for structures to assume a nighttime identity as well. In daylight, structural detail that distinguishes a building is readily discernible. However, its nighttime prominence depends entirely on the lighting. The decision as to how to light an exterior is predicated on the building's design and purpose.

An exterior may be lighted in a manner that mimics daylighting, making a building immediately recognizable at night, or another treatment may be employed to create a separate nighttime identity (Figs. 21 and 22). The decision as how to treat an exterior is part of the architect's and lighting designer's initial thinking. A broad, indiscriminate wash of light creates an impression of solidity, emphasizing the mass of the structure. Exterior screening can be frontally lighted to create a definite perimeter or rear illuminated for a silhouetting effect. Selectively focused lighting can direct attention to particular features and outline distinctive details (Fig. 23). Interior luminance can be used to create a glow from within, using the silhouette to highlight structural rhythms (Fig. 24).

The relationship between interior and exterior brightness can either extend or confine a viewer's perception of the exterior. The ability to visually penetrate the clear glass plane separating interior and exterior depends on the balance of brightness between the two. That balance enables a viewer to see outside when the exterior brightness is higher or to see into a building or shop window when there is greater interior brightness. Greater brightness within a building reveals the interior, placing relative importance on the activities that take place inside. From within, greater brightness on the exterior places the

Figure 21. Empire State Building, New York City. Courtesy of The Douglas Leigh Organization.

emphasis on the landscape, allowing one's limits of space to extend beyond the glass enclosure to the exterior.

There are three basic types of exterior lighting equipment. Lighting fixtures can be integrated in the interior scheme specifically for nighttime use, which often creates a silhouette of the structure or the impression of a self-luminous glow. The advantage to this approach is in the access to equipment for maintenance. Structurally integrated equipment mounted on the exterior can also give a building the appearance of being self-luminous. Lighting fixtures mounted away from the building and focused onto it can provide a wash of light or highlight features sculpturally. In all cases, equipment is selected for design in-

Figure 22. One Liberty Place, Philadelphia. Flack + Kurtz Lighting design. Photograph by John McGrail.

tent. As with interior lighting design, the selection of lighting equipment is dictated by direction, distribution, color, and quantity of light needed. Sources must be chosen for appropriate color temperature, intensity, and life expectancy. The color of light produced by incandescent sources is appropriate for good rendering of flowers, while that produced by mercury sources is complementary to green foliage. Frequently, HID sources are specified for energy efficiency and long lamp life.

Figure 23. U.S. Capitol, Washington, D.C. Courtesy of View-Master International Group.

Figure 24. Jefferson Memorial, Washington, D.C. Courtesy of View-Master International Group.

Landscape

As with interior lighting design, patterns of brightness and color influence perceptions of the exterior environment. Landscape elements such as trees and shrubbery become points of visual focus, delineating the limits of exterior space. Whether used to imitate moonlight or to create dramatic highlights, landscape lighting should be designed to enhance appreciation of outdoor elements and activities.

Trees can be used as major brightness elements to develop a sense of scale, direction, or limit the definition of space. Uplighting a tree's foliage canopy can be used to create a closure or ceiling effect (Fig. 25). Directional

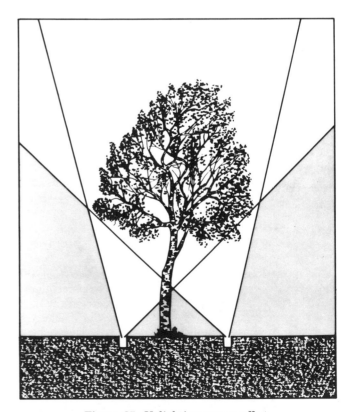

Figure 25. Uplighting canopy effect.

lighting of tree trunks and foliage produces dramatic highlighting. An effect of moonlighting can be approximated by directing lighting onto foliage from above (Fig. 26). Trees and shrubs can be frontally lighted to establish a vertical delineation of the space (Fig. 27). Exterior screens and walls can function in the same way as clustered shrubbery, reflecting light that defines the landscape border. Water is very effective in outdoor lighting. Still water acts as a mirror or a clear transmitting surface. When agitated, it imparts a sense of sparkle and motion in the light it reflects. The foam and spray of a fountain or waterfall makes an excellent diffuse reflector (Fig. 28).

The color of outdoor lighting sources should be chosen to complement foliage colors. Mercury vapor is especially good for rendering green leaves. Incandescent and tungsten–halogen sources enhance flowers and flowering trees. Lighting fixtures for landscape applications are almost as varied as those for interiors. Proper shielding is particularly important because glare from unshielded sources can be disabling. Categories of exterior lighting fixtures include below-grade, buried uplighting (Fig. 29), ground-mounted uplighting and adjustable object lighting (Fig. 30), and bollards and diffuse spread lighting for path and area lighting (Fig. 31). Pole-mounted lighting units can be used to wash the landscape in imitation of moonlight.

Office

Many lighting systems are designed solely to allow performance of or participation in an activity. By increasing the

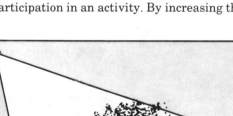

Figure 26. Moonlighting.

Figure 27. Directional lighting from front.

general brightness level and filling in shadows, these systems reduce or eliminate contrast, producing a diffuse environment. These systems are intended to permit casual circulation and informal congregation. This line of thought led to development of the distraction-free work-

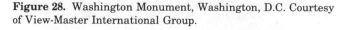

Figure 28. Washington Monument, Washington, D.C. Courtesy of View-Master International Group.

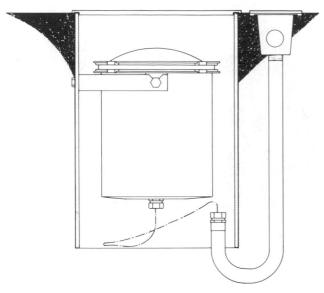

Figure 29. Below-grade exterior uplight.

ing environment: an area suitable for difficult and sustained visual tasks. Lighting systems that indiscriminately flood a space with general overhead illumination, however, have little influence on an individual's impressions or behavior. The diffusion and uniformity of light create a bland psychological effect, reminiscent of a cloudy, overcast day. The lighting consultant must design a system that not only introduces a base level of illumination and satisfactory task lighting, but lighting that provides visual interest as well.

Office lighting should encourage the performance of a task, not simply permit it. The Illuminating Engineering

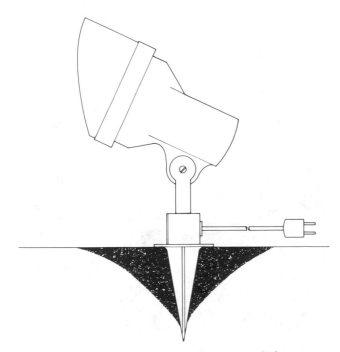

Figure 30. Ground mounted exterior uplight.

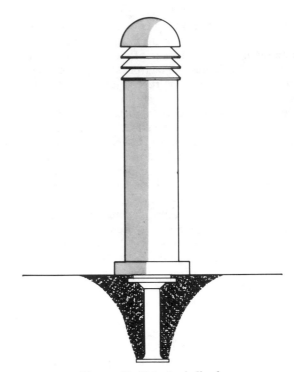

Figure 31. Exterior bollard.

Society publishes recommended light levels for an extensive list of tasks, which the consultant takes into account when designing office lighting. However, good visibility is not simply a matter of putting light onto a surface. The human eye constantly adapts to accommodate changing lighting conditions. To reduce the physical fatigue caused by the eye having to constantly adapt to varying levels of brightness, those levels must be balanced. Although horizontal tasks require a high quantity of illumination on that surface, the worker should be provided with vertical background brightness to reduce extreme contrast. For example, a lighted wall surface provides background brightness that mitigates the tension that would be created by a brightly lighted task and a dark surround (Fig. 32).

Visual comfort also depends on the control of glare, excessive uncontrolled brightness in the field of view. Lighting equipment must be positioned in a way that does not cast direct glare into a worker's eyes. Properly shielded luminaires that reduce surface brightness, such as fluorescent fixtures with parabolic louvers instead of prismatic diffuser lenses, prevent distracting patterns of brightness across the ceiling plane. Those patterns are particularly disruptive for work with computer monitors; reduced contrast on the ceiling helps eliminate computer screen glare. Indirect lighting systems are frequently employed for this reason, but it must be noted that higher initial levels of light must be produced to provide proper ambient levels and ceilings must be high enough to allow for pendant-mounted equipment. Proper lighting-fixture location is crucial in controlling reflected glare from the task itself. Luminaires placed so that light is directed from either side of the desk fills in shadows cast by both sources and reflects light away from the worker's eyes (Fig. 33).

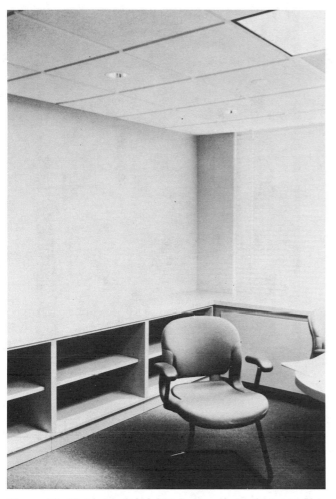

Figure 32. Lighted wall provides background brightness. Gary Gordon Architectural Lighting, Michael Andaloro Associates, interior design. Photograph by Richard Lee.

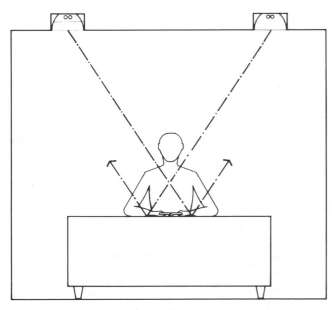

Figure 33. Proper desk lighting.

Figure 34. Lighting reinforces circulation patterns. Gary Gordon Architectural Lighting design. Photograph by Richard Lee.

Public Lobby

Public spaces and lobbies often establish the identity and importance of the occupying entity, as well as serving as an introduction to the building. Light can be used to create a visual hierarchy among the objects and surfaces in a lobby. By doing so, the lighting designer affects perception and emotional response to the space. Light also helps delineate circulation patterns that guide visitors logically through the space (Fig. 34).

Vertical surfaces require special attention. These are the first surfaces seen on entering space; therefore, they define the space. As a display for signage, works of art, or written information, walls play a major part in setting the mood and creating an atmosphere. Therefore, the impression imparted by the vertical surfaces determines, to a great extent, the overall impact of a design.

Lighting that emphasizes vertical surfaces rather than horizontal ones therefore reinforces the viewer's subjective impressions of spaciousness, visual clarity, relaxation, intimacy, or pleasantness. During the 1970s, research by John E. Flynn at The Pennsylvania State University demonstrated that wall lighting creates favorable attitudes about interior space. His research compared overhead and peripheral wall lighting systems. He found that changes in wall lighting induce predictable reactions to the space. Uniform wall lighting strengthens feelings of spaciousness and visual clarity (Fig. 35). Nonuniform wall lighting, especially when provided by warm-toned sources, reinforces feelings of relaxation, intimacy, and pleasantness (Fig. 36). A change in the lighting condition can render the same space cold and impersonal or warm and inviting.

Lighting also influences the perception of the interior as enclosed (Fig. 37) or spacious (Fig. 38). A cool-toned, wall-grazing lighting system will cause the perimeter to recede, seeming to enlarge the lobby space (Fig. 39). Sculptural objects receive warm-toned direct illumination from incandescent PAR lamps to give them prominence (Fig. 40). The lighting has been designed to display interior materials to their best advantage, imparting to the

Figure 35. Uniform lighting reinforces feelings of spaciousness. Courtesy of Linda Segretto.

Figure 36. Nonuniform lighting reinforces feelings of relaxation and intimacy.

Figure 37. Enclosed. Courtesy of Gregory Hansen.

Figure 38. Spacious. Courtesy of Gregory Hansen.

visitor visual clues to the corporate identity. Interreflections have been controlled to eliminate glare by grazing the mirrorlike marble walls, but still provide satisfactory ambient levels from redirected light. Circulation patterns are clearly reinforced with patterns of brightness that direct attention through the lobby to the elevators.

Residential

The feel of a residence is strongly influenced by its lighting system. As with all lighting designs, determinations are made regarding how the lighting will best integrate with the architectural intent. However, each room presents conditions that can be enhanced by an understanding of the direction and quantity of the lighting, as well as choices of sources and luminaires. Whether incandescent or fluorescent sources are chosen, it must be noted that lighting effectiveness is far more important than efficiency. Its aesthetic potential outweighs concerns for energy conservation. In the home, the best energy control for lighting is the judicious use of the switch.

A living room lends itself to the soft ambient light produced by indirect systems, such as lighting concealed behind architectural coves, or by recessed fixtures (Fig. 41). Comfortable lighting can be produced by traditional table lamps with translucent white or off-white shades (Fig. 42). Opaque shades create distracting silhouettes, while colored shades produce colored lighting that might not

Figure 39. Cool-toned wall grazing systems. Gary Gordon Architectural Lighting design. Photograph by Peter L. Goodman, Edison Price Inc.

Figure 41. Recessed wallwash luminaires. Gary Gordon Architectural Lighting design. Photograph by Peter L. Goodman, Edison Price Inc.

flatter complexions. Decorative wall sconces and floor lamps or torchères are also useful. Niche and shelf lighting provide perimeter highlights and direct attention to displayed objects.

The objective of lighting for the dining room is to provide a greater amount of light on the dining table and a lesser amount around the perimeter to reduce extreme contrasts. Psychological research indicates that light between people tends to draw them together, improving communication, while light behind people tends to pull them apart, increasing feelings of anonymity and separa-

tion. An element of sparkle, in particular, will stimulate conversation and enhance the appetite. This sparkle is easily achieved by a decorative chandelier or by candles placed on the table. Psychological reactions are also involved in changes of light levels: high intensity illumination contributes to a sense of increased activity while low intensity lighting creates an attitude of relaxation. A simple wall-box dimmer provides an important ingredient of control over lighting intensity that is especially useful in the dining room.

A working kitchen requires good, shadow-free lighting. There are many ways to achieve this, with either recessed or decorative surface-mounted lighting fixtures. These must be carefully located to produce a general, overall level of illumination. Direct lighting over the sink and stove is advisable. Undercabinet lighting, located above counters, puts light directly onto the work where it is needed while also providing an element of warmth and decorative interest (Fig. 43). Incandescent sources are preferable to fluorescent, because good color rendering is critical to food preparation and presentation.

Figure 40. Warm-toned focused illumination. Gary Gordon Architectural Lighting design. Photograph by Peter L. Goodman, Edison Price Inc.

Figure 42. Traditional lamps. Gary Gordon Architectural design. Photograph by Peter L. Goodman, Edison Price Inc.

Figure 43. Proper kitchen lighting. Gary Gordon Architectural Lighting design. Photograph by Peter L. Goodman, Edison Price Inc.

The bathroom also requires shadow-free lighting of a relatively high intensity for proper visibility for shaving or applying makeup. A light source that makes one's complexion appear natural and healthy is important and provides a welcome ego boost. Correctly positioned incandescent or fluorescent luminaires that light the person and not the mirror accomplish the task quite well (Fig. 44).

The bedroom is another area where table and floor lamps are appropriate. A single lighting unit in the center of the ceiling that throws light indiscriminately around the room is seldom the correct lighting solution. Reading lights on the bedside nightstand, bracket-mounted to the wall, or recessed in the ceiling direct light where it is needed. A switch located next to the bed is a simple, but thoughtful convenience. Another important feature is a lighting fixture in the closet that is turned on when the door is opened. A child's bedroom is one of the few places in the home where track lighting is suitable. Children derive satisfaction from being able to control the light in their own room, and as they grow older they will have the ability to direct the lighting as desired.

The home office or studio requires critical attention to the lighting. This room needs an even, shadow-free general level of illumination over the entire space, as well as light directed onto the work surface. For proper ambient lighting, luminaires must be placed so that light from one fills in the shadows created by another (Fig. 45). Fluorescent lighting is frequently appropriate because of its relative high efficiency, provided a correct color rendering is achieved. Task lighting should be directed onto the work surface to provide the higher level of illumination required, but without creating harsh and distracting shadows.

Figure 44. Proper bathroom lighting. Gary Gordon Architectural Lighting design. Photograph by Peter L. Goodman, Edison Price Inc.

Restaurant

The lighting of restaurants comes in three types. An ambient, diffuse lighting condition is appropriate in the fast food or cafeteria setting. High level, indiscriminate brightness contributes to the anonymous, bustling environment conveyed by this kind of establishment. Opposite

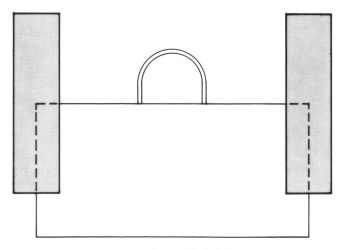

Figure 45. Proper desk lighting.

Figure 46. Horizontal illumination. Courtesy of GE Slide Library.

Figure 47. Vertical illumination. Courtesy of GE Slide Library.

to this approach, high contrast, focused lighting is well suited to the modern, dramatic restaurant. Low voltage pinspots directed onto tabletops or candles flickering in the center of tables set the scene for a more serious dining experience. A third theory, adding to the comfortable homeyness of the traditional dining room, calls for lower level, lower contrast illumination. Chandeliers and decorative sconces help create a relaxed, familiar setting. In all cases, there must be a lighting element at the table for faces and focal attention. Peripheral lighting is necessary to reduce excessive contrast.

High brightness contrasts can make a restaurant setting magical. A lighting system designed to illuminate horizontal surfaces, such as tabletops, de-emphasizes the architecture, making people and activities the dominant feature. This kind of lighting condition increases awareness of nearby detail, people, and movement and encourages gregariousness among the patrons. The architecture becomes a subordinate (Fig. 46). The architectural environment, however, is perceived by the lighting of vertical and overhead surfaces. When lighting emphasizes peripheral surfaces, such as walls, objects and people in the central area fall into silhouette. Activity becomes visually subordinate to the general space, inducing a more intimate atmosphere in which individuals feel a sense of privacy or anonymity (Fig. 47). All restaurant settings benefit from a combination of both horizontal and vertical surface illumination.

Psychological reactions are also involved in these changes. High intensities contribute to a sense of increased activity and efficiency (Fig. 48). Low intensities induce an attitude of relaxation (Fig. 49). The impression of relaxation can be further reinforced by nonuniform wall lighting. Uniform illumination can increase the visual perception of a space, but a nonuniform play of light and shadow establishes a sense of privacy or intimacy.

An important counterpart of shadows is the presence of sparkle or glitter. Relatively small areas of high intensity brightness are points of sparkle and highlight that give a sense of vitality to an environment. Just as highlights on a sunny day can be emotionally stimulating, brightness

Figure 48. High intensity illumination. Courtesy of Hank Forrest.

Figure 49. Low intensity illumination. Courtesy of Hank Forrest.

Figure 50. Ambient and focal lighting. Photograph by Eliot Brown.

Figure 51. Customer traffic patterns can be controlled by ambient lighting system. Photograph by Eliot Brown.

accents can add visual interest to an interior. The presence or absence of sparkle and highlight are the visual attributes that make sunny days interesting and stimulating and cloudy, overcast days flat and dull. Sparkle can be introduced indoors by low intensity light sources, such as Christmas tree lights or clear filament lamps in conjunction with crystal glass, as in a chandelier. Candles, with dancing shadows cast by their flickering points of flame, can add a sense of enchantment to an environment, stimulating conversation and enhancing the appetite.

Color rendering of food and complexions is a critical component of any restaurant lighting scheme. Incandescent lighting is generally the preferred source, possessing the advantages of an inviting "warmth" at low brightness levels and familiar color-rendering capabilities. Where fluorescent lighting is appropriate, good color-rendering, triphosphor lamps should be used.

Retail

Lighting directly influences buying. Proper lighting is necessary for all consumer target levels, from budget to luxury, and must be tailored to the particular application. No matter what is for sale, the lighting must make the merchandise appealing while creating an appropriate ambience. Two different types of lighting system are required in all retail spaces: ambient and focal (Fig. 50).

Ambient lighting creates the overall lighting condition that sets the tone for the store. It is the background "glow" against which the displays are featured. The lighting designer integrates the ambient lighting system with the architectural intent, taking into account horizontal and vertical arrangements of display systems. By doing so, attention can be directed and customer traffic patterns controlled (Fig. 51).

Focal lighting directs attention to the merchandise. It can be washed evenly, highlighted in adjustable focused light, or illuminated in a combination of the two. The merchandise must always have prominence and be viewed under high color-rendering illumination so that it appears to its greatest advantage. Contrast must be maintained at

a level that makes details easily perceived but still distinguishes the merchandise. Focused lighting requires brightness control to divert unpleasant glare from customers' eyes. Frequently, special display and niche lighting is required to illuminate recessed displays satisfactorily. Again, this equipment must be properly shielded so that glare does not distract from the appreciation of the merchandise (Fig. 52).

Consistency in the selection of direction, distribution, color, and quantity of the lighting ensures that the merchandise maintains its appeal from the display to the fitting room to the cashier. High color-rendering incandescent, halogen, and triphosphor fluorescent sources are preferable, despite relative inefficiency and expense. The dividend of attractively presented merchandise outweighs arguments for less pleasing, though more economic, lighting schemes. Thus, dressing and fitting areas must make customers see themselves in flattering angles, tones, and levels of light.

Figure 52. Special display and niche lighting to illuminate recessed displays. Photograph by Eliot Brown.

BIBLIOGRAPHY

General References

J. B. deBoer and D. Fischer, *Interior Lighting,* Philips Technical Library, Deventer, 1981.

P. R. Boyce, *Human Factors in Lighting,* Macmillan Publishing Co., New York, 1981.

D. M. Egan, *Concepts in Lighting for Architecture,* McGraw-Hill Inc., New York, 1983.

B. Evans, *Daylight in Architecture,* McGraw-Hill Inc., New York, 1982.

J. E. Flynn and S. M. Mills, *Architectural Lighting Graphics,* Reinhold Publishing Corp., New York, 1962.

J. E. Flynn and A. W. Segil, *Architectural Interior Systems,* Van Nostrand Reinhold Co., Inc., New York, 1970.

J. E. Flynn, "A Study of Subjective Responses to Low Energy and Nonuniform Lighting Systems," *Lighting Design & Application* 7(2), 6–14 (Feb. 1977).

R. G. Hopkinson and J. D. Kay, *The Lighting of Buildings,* Faber & Faber, Winchester, Mass., 1972.

L. C. Kalff, *Creative Light,* Krieger Publishing Co., Melbourne, Fla., 1971.

J. E. Kaufman and J. F. Christensen, eds., *IES Lighting Handbooks,* 7th ed., Illuminating Engineering Society, New York, 1984, 1987.

W. M. C. Lam, *Perception and Lighting as Formgivers for Architecture,* McGraw-Hill Inc., New York, 1977.

L. Larson, *Lighting and Its Design,* Whitney Library of Design, New York, 1964.

J. L. Nuckolls, *Interior Lighting for Environmental Designers,* 2nd ed., John Wiley & Sons, Inc., New York, 1983.

D. Phillips, *Lighting in Architectural Design,* McGraw-Hill Inc., New York, 1964.

G. Thomson, *The Museum Environment,* Butterworth & Co. (Publishers) Ltd., Kent, UK, 1978.

See also LIGHTING—DAYLIGHTING; LIGHTING—ELECTRIC

GARY GORDON
MARK LOEFFLER
Gary Gordon Architectural
Lighting
New York, New York

Drawings by Gregory F. Day

SPECIFICATIONS

DEFINITION

For construction purposes, architects communicate their concepts to others by a set of documents containing both words and graphics. Although words and graphics are combined in the drawings, words predominate in the bidding requirements, conditions of the contract, and specifications. Of these three, the one most closely related to the drawings is the last.

Words serve essentially different purposes in the drawings and specifications. In the former, words primarily function as broad, generic identifiers of materials or assemblies; in the latter, words describe in detail the qualities of products and installations illustrated and identified on the drawings. The two are intended to represent a coordinated and complementary set of documents.

On the drawings, the symbols, conventions, dimensions, and words are combined with two-dimensional graphic representations in the form of plans, elevations, sections, and details to inform about quantities, locations, relationships, sizes, and shapes of building components.

In the specifications, qualitative requirements are defined in words for products, as related to materials, assemblies, equipment, fabrication, and finishing, and for execution of the work, as related to the installation, application, and erection of products. Included are administrative and other procedures needed for quality control during construction. Information in the specifications, when combined with that on the drawings and other contract documents, enables bidders to develop proposals for submission to the owner. After the construction contract is awarded, the specifications provide the measure of quality by which the work is performed and judged.

Traditionally, drawings for building construction are thought of as being reproduced on sheets several times larger than the pages bound in books. Conversely, specifications are always thought of as normal book-sized publications. Although there are exceptions to both of these generalizations, the project manual concept, which is discussed later in this article, is based on combining other written documents with the specifications for issuance in book-sized volumes.

No matter what general rules are offered for where and how information should be provided, the choice of methods, locations, and forms should combine efficiency of document preparation with clarity of understanding for those responsible for interpretation.

EXPLANATION OF THE PROJECT MANUAL

The project manual title and concept were originated by The American Institute of Architects (AIA) in the early 1960s to identify and organize the various written documents required for the bidding and construction phases of building construction. Before this time and until this new concept became generally accepted by the building design professions and the construction industry, the title "Specifications" was assigned to the volume containing these documents.

The project manual is divided into two principal parts: the bidding requirements and the contract documents. The first part contains information related to the procedures and requirements for preparation and submission of bids for construction, which occur before the execution of the agreement between the owner and contractor. Although normally bound into the project manual for the convenience of the bidders, the bidding requirements are normally not part of the contract documents. The second part includes the various contract documents either by reference or by direct binding into the volume or volumes composing the project manual.

The bidding requirements are grouped under the following four principal headings:

1. Invitation to bid.
2. Instructions to bidders.
3. Information available to bidders.
4. Bid forms.

The contract documents consist of the following principal elements:

1. Agreement between owner and contractor.
2. The conditions of the contract, composed of the general conditions and supplementary conditions.
3. The drawings, which are bound separately, but joined to the project manual by inclusion of a schedule of drawings or other reference.
4. The specifications.
5. Addenda and modifications.

To identify the project manual and to facilitate access to its contents, it is customary to include the following in the order listed:

1. A cover imprinted with the name of the document (project manual), the volume number (if more than one), the project name, the owner's name, the architect's name, the date, and for work involving multiple prime contracts with separate project manuals for each, a brief contract description.
2. A title page imprinted with the same information as the cover, but supplemented by the addresses and telephone numbers of the owner, architect, and principal consultants plus, where required by law, the certification, signature, seal, and registration number of the architect (as an option the latter information can be included on a separate page where law does not require it on the title page).
3. A table of contents.

The number of volumes required for the project manual is dictated not only by the number of pages that can be practicably bound into a single volume, but also by convenience of use in the field and office and convenience of distribution to the various parties performing the work.

Addenda and modifications are written instruments of change to the contract documents that are normally part of the project manual. Addenda refer to changes made, usually during the bidding or negotiating stage, before the contract for construction has been awarded, and modifications refer to those made after its award. Although either can include changes to the drawings as well as to other contract documents, it is customary to document changes to drawings as written items in an addenda or modification even if the changes are made either by revising and reissuing the originals, with appropriate notation, or by supplementary drawings prepared for this purpose.

ORGANIZATION OF SPECIFICATIONS INTO DIVISIONS AND SECTIONS

The fundamental organizing element of the specifications is the section, which is analogous to a chapter in a book. Each section is limited to a single subject or closely related subjects. These subjects can correspond to a discrete unit of work of defined scope that is performed by the contractor singly or in combination with one or more subcontractors; they can also include a set of related requirements that affect the work generally.

Prior to publication by the Construction Specifications Institute (CSI) in 1964 of *The CSI Format for Building Specifications,* sections were numbered and arranged in an order corresponding to the time sequence in which the work described in each section was to be performed. Because the sequence of work was often difficult to establish and often varied between projects, the need became evident for establishing a consistent method for organizing specifications capable of adapting to variations in practice, project scope, and construction practices. The result was *The CSI Format for Building Specifications,* which organized the specifications into 16 basic groupings, called divisions. Each division was assigned a fixed number and name. Division names were selected to identify in the broadest and most recognizable sense the various kinds of work specified in the sections that related to one another and thereby belonged within a particular division.

The division numbers and their current names, which only appear as such in the table of contents for the specifications, are as follows:

Division 1. General Requirements.
Division 2. Sitework.
Division 3. Concrete.
Division 4. Masonry.
Division 5. Metals.
Division 6. Wood and Plastics.
Division 7. Thermal and Moisture Protection.
Division 8. Doors and Windows.
Division 9. Finishes.
Division 10. Specialties.
Division 11. Equipment.
Division 12. Furnishings.
Division 13. Special Construction.
Division 14. Conveying Systems.
Division 15. Mechanical.
Division 16. Electrical.

The 1964 CSI format became the basis for two subsequent joint industry publications: *The Uniform System for Construction Specifications, Data Filing and Cost Accounting; Title 1—Buildings,* published in 1966, and the *Uniform Construction Index—A System of Formats for Specifications, Data Filing, Cost Analysis and Project Filing* (UCI), published in 1972. In these publications, each division was assigned a recommended section title representing a unit of work or set of general requirements that fit within the generic description assigned to the division's name, but no numbers or other alphanumeric notations were assigned to individual sections. Instead, the choice of notation system for identifying sections was left to individual preference. However, in the 1966 publication, two notation systems were suggested: an alphanumeric designation, where the division number formed the prefix, ie, 9A, 9B, etc, or a four-digit system included with "Part 3—Cost Accounting Guide" of *The Uniform System,* where the first two digits were reserved for the division number, ie, 0901, 0926, etc. The number of digits was later increased to five in the *Uniform Construction Index.* It was also suggested that sections be placed and numbered in a sequence corresponding to that proposed within each division grouping.

Both *The Uniform System* and the *Uniform Construction Index* also included a separate part for organizing and classifying product data in a consistent and standardized way for purposes of simplifying storage and retrieval. In this part, titled "The Filing System" in *The Uniform System* and "Data Filing Format" in the *Uniform Construction Index,* the various headings and subheadings, which sometimes corresponded to titles assigned to specification sections, were arranged alphabetically to allow for the future insertion of additional headings to cover new materials and techniques without disrupting a fixed sequence or numerical designation system. These systems recognized that the most effective way to file data requires the establishment of one correct place for each subject, unlike specifications where products may be included in more than one section. They also accommodated subjects other than those associated only with specifications. Another feature introduced in the *Uniform Construction Index* was a guide for project filing.

Throughout the evolution of these joint industry documents, CSI continued its efforts to improve *The CSI Format.* In 1978, as a continued extension of the *Uniform Construction Index* and in recognition of the growing acceptance of the five-digit numbering system, CSI and Construction Specifications Canada jointly published *MASTERFORMAT.* This publication differed from the two preceding it by abandoning the use of separate formats for data filing, construction cost accounting, and project filing. The five-digit section numbering system recommended in the *Uniform Construction Index* was expanded and revised, and its use recommended for section numbering and titling, for product technical data filing and retrieval, and for project cost classification.

Although not published as a joint effort of the previous participants in the *Uniform Construction Index, MASTERFORMAT* gained rapid acceptance in both the United States and Canada and effectively replaced the *Uniform Construction Index,* which soon went out of print. A second edition of *MASTERFORMAT* appeared in 1983 and included a rearrangement of numbering and section locations to allow for expansion, revision of selected section titles, and introduction of special headings primarily intended for data filing purposes. Further revisions are included in the third edition of *MASTERFORMAT* published in 1988.

A new level of sections was introduced at this time to solve a problem that had developed. In the 1978 edition, sections were classified as either broad-scope or narrow-scope titles, and both were assigned numbers. Broad-scope sections were defined as those encompassing the greatest practicable number of products and procedures that could be considered a unit of work, as opposed to narrow-scope sections, which did the opposite. An example of a broad-scope section title is "Unit Masonry," and "Concrete Unit Masonry" is a narrow-scope section that would fall under it.

Because the five-digit numbering system did not provide an adequate number of slots under certain broad-scope headings to include all the narrow-scope titles considered desirable, an intermediate level of titles was introduced as medium-scope sections. Medium-scope sections now represented the lowest level of sections assigned fixed numbers, and the numbering of narrow-scope titles was left to the discretion of the user. This revision not only effectively unblocked those parts of the system where insufficient numbers were available to assign to revised current narrow-scope titles, but also allowed for future expansion of listings.

The decision to prepare narrow-, medium-, or broad-scope sections for various parts of the work depends to some extent on the complexity of each item of work involved and the amount of detail needed to specify it. It also depends on the degree to which the work must be divided up into smaller units to provide greater clarity in organizing the entire specification and to assist the contractor in controlling the work and assigning subcontracts. Concerning the latter, it is important to realize that the sole responsibility for dividing the work into subcontracts must remain with the contractor regardless of how the specifications are divided into sections. This is a standard provision in AIA document A201, "General Conditions of the Contract for Construction."

One of the principal benefits of *MASTERFORMAT*'s section numbering system, when compared with the more discretionary systems preceding it, is that sections can be inserted or withdrawn from the specifications during the production process without any concern for disrupting the numbering system or the sequence of sections.

CONTENTS OF SPECIFICATIONS SECTIONS

In the preceding explanation, it was noted that each section is limited to either a subject corresponding to a discrete unit of work of defined scope or a set of related requirements affecting the work generally. If the contents of a section fit the first definition, it belongs in Divisions 2–16; if the second, Division 1.

Division 1 sections are also distinguishable from sections in the other divisions by their broader and different effect on the other contract documents (Fig. 1). Unit-of-work sections basically complement the other contract documents, whereas Division 1 sections also supplement them.

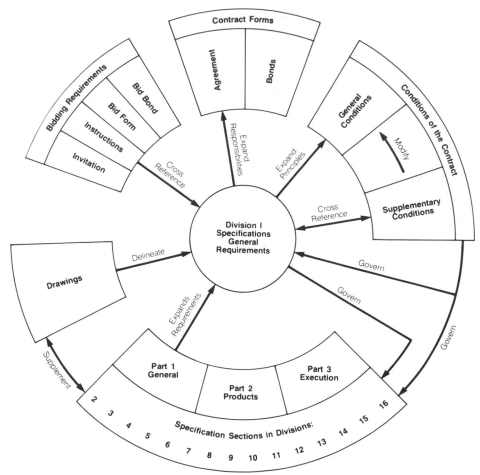

Figure 1. Diagram showing relationship of Division 1 to other documents (1). Courtesy of the Construction Specifications Institute, Inc.

In relation to sections in Divisions 2–16, Division 1 sections consolidate and coordinate those procedural and administrative requirements applicable to more than one section and eliminate the need to repeat the requirements in each section where they apply. An example of this is the requirement for submittal of product data, shop drawings, samples, etc, for architect's review, which is applicable to all sections where such submittals are indicated. This results in having to include information about submittals only in each section that supplements the general procedures incorporated in Division 1 and "General Conditions." The same would be true of requirements for quality assurance; project conditions; delivery, storage, and handling; and, where applicable, allowances and alternatives.

Certain Division 1 sections function as extensions of those provisions remaining in the "Conditions of the Contract," which are also covered in Division 1. Examples of such provisions include those for submittals, progress schedules, cutting and patching, allowances, cleaning, work performed by owner or under separate contract, and procedures for project closeout. Where provisions of this kind occur in the "General Conditions" and require modification or deletion to avoid conflicts with Division 1 requirements, these modifications or deletions should occur in the "Supplementary Conditions."

Another important function of Division 1 sections is their coverage of requirements that are particularly im-

portant during the bidding period but remain in effect during construction or that elaborate on provisions included in the agreement between owner and contractor that affect others involved in the work.

ORGANIZATION OF SPECIFICATION SECTIONS

If the primary and secondary organizing elements of the specifications are the divisions and sections, then the corresponding elements of the section are its parts and articles. CSI developed the three-part section format for reasons similar to those applicable to *The CSI Format for Construction Specifications,* but at a lower order of classification. The parts, and to a somewhat lesser degree the articles under each part, offer the specifier a method of organizing information within each section that is consistent throughout the specifications regardless of differences in the units of work specified in each. This results in the specifier as well as the user knowing where like information is supposed to occur from section to section.

The three section parts are "Part 1—General," "Part 2—Products," "Part 3—Execution." "Part 1—General," as its name suggests, includes those administrative and technical requirements that are specific to the unit of work covered in the section and apply to both of the other parts. They should neither duplicate nor conflict with the requirements that are included in Division 1 sections, which are meant to apply to more than one section.

"Part 2—Products" is where requirements are located for basic materials, finished products, equipment, and prefabricated assemblies that are associated with a manufacturing or fabrication process that takes place either away from the project site or prior to installation.

"Part 3—Execution" is where the installation of products and associated requirements are covered.

In certain Division 1 sections where only administrative or procedural requirements are specified, Parts 2 and 3 are not used, but should still be included with a note of explanation, eg, Part 2—Products: Not used.

Unlike the titles of the three parts ("General," "Products," and "Execution"), which always stay the same, the article titles listed in CSI document MP-2-2, "Section Format," may be supplemented, deleted, or modified to fit the needs of the unit of work covered in each section, but their order of appearance within each part should always remain the same. It is also important to note that articles subdivide each part and thereby represent a lower rank of titles. However, the part titles are exempted from being a part of a hierarchical series of titles and text-containing elements in terms of their positioning on the page. This is done so that the articles that follow them need not be indented to signify subordination. This practice is dictated by the need to conserve page space for text and not waste it on wide left-hand margins created by unnecessary indentation. In turn, the articles are normally subdivided into paragraphs, but sometimes subarticle titles are introduced where the length of any article needs further division of its contents to make subordination and relationships of requirements clearer to the user.

For most specifications, the first text-containing element is the paragraph. Depending on the complexity of the information involved, the paragraph may be further subdivided into one or more subparagraphs, but subordination beyond the first subparagraph level often indicates that the scope of requirements being expressed is too broad to contain under one paragraph.

PAGE LAYOUT AND DESIGNATION OF SECTION ELEMENTS

Certain conventions have developed for arranging and designating titles and text on individual pages of the "Specifications" section to satisfy the following needs:

1. To arrange titles and text that, by indentation, line spacing, or use of upper-case letters for article titles and other devices, are clearly subordinate and group related topics. This helps the reader to locate information quickly and then to progress in an orderly manner from general headings to detailed requirements.

2. To designate titles and text in a manner that enables effective and precise reference to, or finding of, words, lines, paragraphs, articles, etc, of the text in oral and written communications.

3. To fill each page with as much text as possible without making it so crowded that it becomes unreadable.

4. To fit the capabilities of the personnel and equipment available for preparation, production, and printing of the specifications.

Subordination of section elements is shown essentially by the following methods, which are illustrated in the sample sections:

1. Capitalization of all letters forming part and article titles.

2. Indentation and line spacing between elements of text and titles.

3. Underlining of titles and introductory key words of subparagraphs where no article and paragraph designations are used. There are many who object to underlining on the grounds that any advantages gained from it are more than offset by the wasted motion caused by underlining during manual or automated typing as well as by its potential for producing errors when editing computer-generated text.

Of the various methods adopted to facilitate written and oral communication when referencing selected portions of the text within each section part, two predominate: a system of alphanumeric designations addressing each rank of text and line numbering of the text.

The alphanumeric designation system recommended by CSI for addressing articles, paragraphs, and subparagraphs is diagrammed below. It also represents CSI's suggested page format for indentation, line spacing between elements of different ranking, and use of upper- and lower-case letters:

PART 1—GENERAL

1.01 ARTICLE:

    A. Paragraph.
      1. Subparagraph.

    B. Paragraph.
      1. Subparagraph.

    C. Paragraph.
      1. Subparagraph.
        a. Subparagraph.
        b. Subparagraph.
      2. Subparagraph.

PART 2—PRODUCTS

2.01 ARTICLE:

A. Paragraph.
   1. Subparagraph.

B. Paragraph.
   1. Subparagraph.

PART 3—EXECUTION

3.01 ARTICLE:

A. Paragraph.
   1. Subparagraph.

B. Paragraph.
   1. Subparagraph.

Line numbering accomplished by one of the methods described below represents an alternative system, which may be less familiar to those who have no experience with output from computers produced either by dedicated word processing systems or word processing programs written for minicomputers and larger systems:

1. Computer-printed line numbers arranged to be consecutive on a page-by-page basis or from the beginning to the end of a section, with or without numbers assigned to blank lines. Where text is right-hand justified, numbers are typically located in a column in the right-hand margin. Integrated line-numbering capability was formerly available only with word processing software for minicomputers and larger systems. It is now available with several popular word processing programs for microcomputers.

2. Manually keyboarded line numbers. If text is right-hand justified, then placement of line numbers in right-hand margins is still feasible; otherwise, they may have to be shifted to left-hand margins.

3. Prenumbered sheets of paper placed in a typewriter or printer. The disadvantage of this method is the misalignment between lines of text and line numbers, which often occurs. A solution to this, which seems awkward but works, is to refer to both line numbers that bracket the line being referenced or, if there are multiple lines, those of the first and last lines enclosing text.

4. Imprinting line numbers during the reproduction process, which is accomplished by placing either a prenumbered strip or a transparent template in the photocopier to superimpose the line numbers on the face of originals as they pass before the camera during the copying process. This too can result in the line numbers being out of register with the lines they mark.

With line numbering, underlining is often introduced, as the example below shows, to complement other devices such as upper- and lower-case letters and blank line spaces between various elements to facilitate quicker recognition of key elements and specific subject matters when searching the text for information.

<u>PART 1</u>—<u>GENERAL</u>	1
	2
	3
<u>ARTICLE</u>:	4
	5
<u>Title-</u> or <u>keyword-introduced</u> paragraph.	6
	7
<u>Title-</u> or <u>keyword-introduced</u> subparagraph.	8

A third system, which is a variation of the alphanumeric method described above, is the use of an all-number system such as that depicted below, with decimals introduced to show ranking.

1 General

1.1 ARTICLE

   .1 Paragraph.

Although all three systems work, and each has its strong adherents, the system chosen should be the one that combines efficiency of preparation and reproduction with ease of retrieval and precision of reference, rather than one that is based on traditional ways of presenting specification information, ways existing prior to the development of automated production methods and master specifications systems.

Other aspects of page layout that must be considered are the margins and information contained in page headings and footings. The method selected for binding the project manual determines the width required for the binding margin, which must be large enough not to obscure the printed portions of an open page. Typically, each page contains footings and sometimes headings other than those on the first page. These include the name and number of the project, the date of the project manual, the section title, and the page number.

CSI recommends in its *Manual of Practice* that only the first page of a section have a heading and that it consist of two lines, with the word "Section" followed by the applicable five-digit number on the first and the section title on the second, with both centered. CSI also recommends that each page's footing contain in the center the section's five-digit number followed by a hyphen and the sequential section page number. If required, the footing line should also contain the project identification next to the unbound edge and the date of the project manual next to the bound edge. It is also recommended that the words "end of section" be centered two lines below the last line of text.

An alternative arrangement is to have a header line on each page, containing the project name and number next to the bound edge and the date next to the unbound edge. In the page footing, the section title is centered, and the section number, combined by a hyphen with the section page number, is placed next to the unbound edge.

Before leaving the subject of page layout, there is one other consideration deserving discussion, and that is treatment of fragmented text at the beginning or end of a page. The recommended practice is to avoid interrupting a paragraph such that its last line ends up on the succeeding page or having a title for a part or article occur on the last line of a page. This is feasible when text is keyboarded on a typewriter or for the first time on a microcomputer. However, some word processing software does not cause this reformatting to happen automatically when text is revised, and it must be done manually, in which case the benefits gained in readability may not be worth the labor cost involved.

SPECIFICATION WRITING PRACTICES

Effective practices in specification writing are those that convey information clearly and concisely. Achieving these qualities requires observing certain conventions for expository and descriptive usage that have become associated with specifications. These conventions relate to syntax; vocabulary; spelling; use of abbreviations, symbols, and numerals; capitalization; punctuation; and style.

Two sets of verb forms are used to communicate requirements to the contractor in specification sentences: the imperative and the indicative moods. Although both are equally effective in clearly expressing requirements, the imperative mood often involves the use of fewer words than the indicative to achieve the same result, as the following examples indicate:

1. *Imperative mood.* Lay tile with grain running in one direction.
2. *Indicative mood.* Tile shall be laid with grain running in one direction.

Although statements made in either mood are understood to be addressed to the contractor, an explanation of these and similar conventions adopted for expressing specification requirements that are not common to other forms of writing should be defined in the project manual. An appropriate location for these definitions is either in a Division 1 section entitled "Definitions and Standards" or in the "Supplementary Conditions."

Another device commonly used in writing specifications is streamlining. This term refers to elliptical construction, where the words omitted are clearly understood. Its obvious purpose is to shorten text, and it is most frequently used for specifying products and referencing standards. In the examples below, the omitted words are enclosed within parentheses:

Fine Aggregate: (Furnish material complying with) ASTM C 144.

Ultimate Strength: Entire access floor system (shall be) capable of sustaining twice the concentrated panel loading indicated.

Where acts of the owner or architect require explanation because they affect the work of the contractor, the indicative mood is used, but with the verb "will" substituted for "shall" and the party responsible for performing the act named to emphasize the difference. This practice is followed in AIA document A201, "General Conditions of the Contract for Construction."

The meanings of words selected for specifications should precisely and consistently relate throughout the documents to the items they describe. This is particularly important in establishing relationships between requirements in the specifications and the items on the drawings to which they refer. Either the same generic terms or abbreviations representing them must be consistently and precisely used for drawing notes if ambiguity is to be avoided.

Although various attempts have been made to compile terms that are especially associated with specifications, no dictionary or glossary currently exists that has achieved wide distribution or formal acceptance in the construction industry. Until one is available, the best rule to observe is to choose technical terms that are well defined in either acknowledged national standards or other publications that are known by, and accessible to, those responsible for performing the work. For definitions of nontechnical terms, a good general dictionary should be referenced.

Spelling should be consistent and conform to preferred spellings in the dictionary cited or adopted for reference. Technical terms not included in the standard dictionaries should conform, where possible, to the spelling adopted in the referenced standard in which the accepted meaning of the word occurs. In certain instances, compound terms may have to be invented in the specifications to establish labels for drawing notations.

Capitalization in specifications follows certain conventions in giving special recognition to selected nouns besides those representing proper names. Capitalization is used for the first letter of words representing specific parties defined in the agreement and general conditions, such as the owner, architect, or contractor, and of the names of the various contract documents as well as the work, when it represents work of the contract.

Abbreviations and acronyms should generally be avoided, except for those representing names of associations and organizations whose standards or other publications are referenced in the specifications. The only other abbreviations that can be included are those considered well enough known to be instantly recognizable to anyone involved in the construction process without having to refer to a dictionary or a list of abbreviations included in a Division 1 section. However, it is essential to list in the appropriate Division 1 section the names of associations and organizations, along with their addresses and telephone numbers, that are represented in the specifications by abbreviations and acronyms. Any other abbreviations included in the specifications, no matter how well known, should also be explained in the same Division 1 section. Abbreviations on drawings are a different matter since there is often inadequate sheet space to enter nonabbreviated terms. However, for them to be effective there must be included on the drawings a list that explains abbreviations in terms correlated with the specifications.

Symbols, like abbreviations, should be readily recognizable for them to be acceptable in the specifications. A further limitation on their use often depends on the capability of the typewriters or computer systems involved to print them. With typewriters it may be that the symbol is missing from the keyboard and type bar or printing element. With computer systems, either the word processing software or the printer, or both, might not reproduce the symbol. Often, it is the printer that is incapable either of recognizing the command characters for symbols generated by the software program or of printing the symbols because they are missing from print wheels or changeable printing elements. Also to be avoided are small symbols that bleed together when printed and become unreadable. Symbols commonly used in specifications are those for feet ('), inches ("), and by ($\times$).

In summation, the language in specifications should conform to the same rules for grammar, sentence structure, punctuation, etc, that apply to technical writing in general. This means avoiding overly long or convoluted sentences, particularly where missing punctuation or misplaced words could result in misinterpretation of meaning. It also implies a need to select terms that are intelligible to those who perform the work and to compose them in a way that expresses the intent exactly and concisely.

SPECIFYING METHODS

Four methods of specifying exist: descriptive, performance, proprietary, and reference standard. Essentially, the descriptive method involves explaining in detail the means for achieving unstated results related to either products or execution, and the performance method defines the results required without identifying the means. The proprietary method involves naming specific products or manufacturers. The reference standard refers to specifying products or processes to comply with established standards incorporated by reference only; the standard itself may be a descriptive or performance specification, or both.

The descriptive method results in a nonrestrictive specification if requirements are described broadly enough to allow several products to comply. The same result can be achieved by naming acceptable products or manufacturers, provided these names are furnished for informational purposes only, ie, to establish a level of quality that must be matched or exceeded by unnamed manufacturers or products.

However, if the selection is restricted to one or several named products or products of named manufacturers, it becomes a proprietary specification; sometimes the distinction between naming one and several is made by referring to the latter method as semiproprietary. Proprietary specifying methods can be structured either to limit the contractor to furnishing the product or products named or to serve as the basis for judging substitutions that the contractor may propose during bidding or after award of the contract. Where no substitutions whatever are allowed before or after the contract award, it is termed a closed proprietary specification.

Where one or more named products are listed as accept-

able in the specifications, but other, unnamed, products may be permitted during the bidding phase, subject to acceptance of the architect or owner or both prior to submission of bids, the result is an open proprietary specification.

The terms "or approval equal" or, preferably, "accepted substitute" are used to describe specifications where substitutions must be either submitted and accepted prior to the contract award or submitted and accepted afterwards. Proprietary methods combined with descriptive or performance methods provide specifications where not only brand names of products or names of manufacturers are listed, but also, respectively, descriptive or performance requirements are included.

In proprietary specifications, the acceptability of a substitute is judged by comparison with the qualities of the named product or products; in proprietary specifications combined with other methods, acceptability is judged on the basis of compliance with the most restrictive requirements.

The rules for accepting substitutes must be established in either the "Instructions to Bidders," if substitutions are allowed only during the bidding period, or the appropriate Division 1 section that covers substitutions, if allowable after contract award.

Where a name or names of products or manufacturers are included for informational purposes only, the specification no longer qualifies as a proprietary or semiproprietary specification and effectively becomes a nonproprietary specification.

Descriptive specifying of products involves explaining the characteristics and properties of materials or equipment, including procedures for their fabrication, assembly or mixing, and finishing, where applicable. Specifying execution requires indicating the manner for installing products, including procedures to be followed on the job site before and after installation. This method can be limited to describing just those outward characteristics of a product that are sufficient to distinguish it from similar but unacceptable items, or it can be expanded to include the most detailed aspects and properties. Often, the simpler descriptive form is inadequate in itself to prevent substitution of an unacceptable product where the item involved can easily be modified to resemble superficially the product desired. It is a method more likely to succeed for standard, mass-produced products, where it would be economically infeasible for manufacturers to lower the quality of their products just to gain a competitive edge for a particular project. Writing a detailed descriptive specification may avoid these problems, but it is a lengthy process and could involve extensive research.

Specifying by referencing standards for products or execution instead of by full descriptive or performance methods is a common practice that serves to shorten specifications and save specifying effort. A standard may be a performance or descriptive specification or a combination of both. It is never a proprietary specification. Reference standards such as those produced by the American Society for Testing and Materials (ASTM) or the American National Standards Institute (ANSI) are specifications, test methods, or recommended practices that have been developed through a consensus process involving representatives of manufacturers, consumers, government, and other interested groups. Other reference standards may be developed by associations in which participation is limited to all or selected manufacturers in one industry and that have decided that publication of standards adds credibility to their products.

A good reference standard is one that truly represents products and practices that are recognized and followed by the majority of manufacturers and the mechanics of a given trade. An excellent reference standard is one that also reflects the different qualities of products available rather than just compliance with minimum requirements. Unfortunately, the majority of standards only define minimum requirements. This is because the consensus process tends to seek the lowest common denominator in quality rather than the highest. Without standards to adopt by reference, nonrestrictive specifications not only would be difficult to write, but would be extremely voluminous, and for projects commissioned by governments at all levels, the use of nonrestrictive specifications is normally mandated.

Referencing standards is often combined with proprietary specifications, particularly those that are open, as a backup to establish minimum requirements for judging the quality of a product or installation should a problem develop during or after construction. Although it may be possible to hold manufacturers responsible for the compliance of their products with their advertised claims for properties and performance, changes in formulations or product composition can occur between the time the specifications are written and work begins, which can result in the product no longer being suitable for the intended use. Under these or similar circumstances, the added existence of a referenced standard or other set of requirements simplifies dispute resolution.

Many reference standards include several choices of grade or quality level as elective requirements that must be specified along with the reference to the standard itself. The better standards clearly identify these choices, which may relate to different properties or characteristics of products and their suitability for different applications. Others sometimes bury this information in the text so that it is overlooked. Further compounding this problem is the typical practice of many manufacturers of claiming compliance of their products with such standards, but not with specific grades or quality levels.

The sheer number of standards commonly referenced in specifications and building codes, combined with the diverse organizations and associations that must be contacted to obtain them, tends to discourage many offices from acquiring and maintaining an up-to-date and comprehensive office library of standards. This is because of the costs associated with their purchase, as well as with their handling, filing, updating, and storage.

Performance specifications theoretically offer the contractor total freedom in the selection of materials and methods for fabrication and installation, unlike proprietary specifications. However, it is rare to find sections, much less entire specifications, written completely by the performance method. This is because it is difficult to identify all the results that a given item of work must achieve, and even harder to verify actual performance, particularly where durability must be predicted.

One of the benefits of performance specifying is that it encourages the use of new technology, both in product development and in methods of installation. However, because the cost of developing new products is high, it can rarely be justified by manufacturers in a competitive environment, unless they have a reasonable expectation of recovering their investment from future sales of the new product on other projects. Unlike the automobile and similar mass-production industries, building construction rarely offers the opportunity for thorough testing of full-scale prototypes of major new building components or assemblies before they are incorporated in the actual project.

Because of these limitations, performance specifying for the average project is generally limited to establishing criteria for the physical performance of the component products or assemblies where there also exist laboratory or field tests that provide a reasonable means of predicting how a product will actually perform in service. Such specifications are a particularly appropriate choice for selected sections in nonrestrictive specifications, where it is possible to identify the minimum levels of laboratory- and field-tested performance needed to ensure satisfactory results with the installed product and where it is known that more than one available product will qualify.

Concrete is an example of a material that can be specified to comply with performance requirements for the cement, aggregates, and admixtures by referencing material standards, which are performance based, and also for the mixed product by calling for laboratory tests to verify the specified structural performance and other physical properties.

The use of cash allowances offers a means for selecting products where the owner or architect wishes to postpone decisions regarding appearance characteristics or wants to exercise more direct control over the selection of a materials supplier. An example of the first situation is a cash allowance for face brick or fine wood veneers, and an example of the second is an allowance for finish hardware or elevator cabs. In either case, it is important to include information in the specifications and on the drawings that is adequate for the contractor to estimate installation costs. It is a method that should be reserved for items that cannot be selected or easily specified until the project is underway and the names of related products, whose appearance affects the selection of the allowance item, have been submitted by the contractor and approved by the architect.

Combining specifying methods can be appropriate, provided conflicts are not created. As noted above, reference standards are often combined with proprietary and semiproprietary specifications. Since reference standards can be either descriptive or performance oriented, this implies the feasibility of combining either of these methods with the naming of products or manufacturers to establish added quality control. What must be guarded against is the creation of a set of requirements by one method that makes fulfillment of a second set by another method impossible, or that causes confusion.

An example of such a situation would be to specify that dimension lumber for structural framing comply not only with one set of descriptive requirements for species and grade, but also with another set of performance requirements for minimum stress values that exceed the capabilities of the particular grade and species.

Many considerations enter into the choice of methods for specifying products. For most projects, no one method is suitable for all sections in the specifications. Obviously, it is impossible to use the proprietary method to specify site grading, excavating, and backfilling for buildings and similar work where manufactured products are either not involved or involved in a very minor way. In other instances, where appearance is not involved and the level of quality for construction can be achieved just as well and more economically by the use of nonproprietary methods, it serves no useful purpose to specify products by name or manufacturer. In some cases the choice may be dictated by the owner because of policy, regulation, or economic necessity. Where the decision is the architect's alone or is based on the architect's recommendation, an analysis must be made of how each method will affect the following:

1. Construction costs, by either encouraging or discouraging competition. Obviously, the more restrictive a specification becomes, the more likely costs will be higher, and vice versa, assuming the same degree of quality is required.

2. The cost of the architect's services during the design, bidding, and construction phases by determining which method results in the most efficient allocation of the architect's time. As an example, it may be less costly to develop a specification that reduces or eliminates the time needed to review substitutions during bidding and construction than one that increases this time, assuming in either case that the same degree of control over construction cost and quality is intended. This could be influenced by whether the architect's services extend into the construction administration phase or whether staff resources are adequate to investigate and accept substitutions in a timely manner.

3. Construction quality control either by limiting or increasing opportunities for the contractor to substitute inferior products or to provide substandard work, or both. Methods that limit choices or provide effective means during construction to evaluate and verify the performance levels specified are more successful in this regard.

4. Construction time by simplifying the product evaluation process and thereby shortening the time required to order and deliver products to the project. Obviously, allowing the contractor fewer choices in either making substitutions or performing tests to prove compliance with performance requirements reduces this time, particularly for products needed in the early phases of the project or involving long delivery times.

PREWRITTEN SPECIFICATION FORMS

The two opposites in prewritten specification forms are master specification systems and guide specification systems. The ultimate in master specification systems is a comprehensive compilation of known requirements, methods, and formats for specifying building construction that is organized for selective editing to produce specifications for any project and for integrated updating. At the other extreme are guide specification systems providing only the barest framework of requirements, methods, and formats and that involve extensive filling in of information, deletions, and additions to make them complete.

Although the computer theoretically makes possible the achievement of the ultimate specification system, it is probably safe to assume that no such system yet exists. This includes both systems developed and maintained by individual offices and government agencies strictly for their own use and those developed by offices, associations, or government agencies primarily for use by others. Instead, existing systems represent a compromise between the two extremes by including not only requirements that can be retained with little or no modification, but also those that serve as examples or require completion by filling in the blanks.

Master specification systems can serve the following purposes:

1. To provide a centralized resource of specification text that can be drawn on to prepare specifications for individual projects, selected from a broad range of requirements arranged in a variety of formats and specifying methods to suit specific conditions relating to bidding and contracting procedures.

2. To act as a repository for new specification text and formats as they are developed in the continuing preparation of project specifications.

3. To function as a source of technical information for general, product, and execution requirements that can be reviewed in checklist fashion to assist in the production and specifications that are complete and coordinated.

4. To reduce the time and cost involved in preparation and production of specifications by eliminating repetitive work that would otherwise be required of the professional and administrative staff. The repetitive preparatory work could involve either rewriting specifications for each project or assembling the text by copying and modifying requirements extracted from one or more project manuals from previous jobs. Production time and costs can be reduced only where automated techniques are employed that avoid rekeyboarding of the entire text, whether it duplicates exactly the requirements copied from previous specifications or is a combination of existing, revised, or partially new subject matter.

5. To release technical and administrative personnel to perform other, more productive and interesting tasks.

6. To standardize office practices and specification language for purposes of improving the quality of per-

formance for design and production, estimating construction costs, and administering construction.

7. To open up the specifying process to other members of the professional staff and thereby give them a greater understanding of, and involvement in, the whole decision-making process. Like purpose 6 above, this can improve the overall quality of professional performance. It can also result in the project manager or another experienced member of a project team becoming directly responsible for project specifications, rather than having to depend entirely on staff or consultants to prepare them. It can also be a disadvantage when project managers cannot keep up to date on changes in, or knowledge of, products or be as efficient in production.

8. To establish clear, unambiguous specifications whose intent can be easily interpreted during the bidding and construction phases to produce projects of a predictable quality and cost.

9. To enable the architect to demonstrate to owners and others the decision-making process. This can be done during the preparation of contract documents by submitting marked-up drafts of master specification sections for review by owners or their professional staff, who then have an opportunity to understand and compare the requirements selected with those deleted or modified. It can also occur during or after construction, if the architect is required to justify judgments made.

As indicated before, master specifications may be developed and maintained by an office or government agency for preparing specifications for projects designed by its own professional staff with or without the services of consultants. For an office master specification system to function effectively, it must be tailored to the needs of the office's practices as they relate to the following:

1. The kinds and sizes of projects undertaken.
2. Owner limitations on bidding requirements and contracting procedures as they affect the choice of one or more specification methods and formats.
3. The organization and capabilities of the professional staff as they relate to the assignment of responsibilities for preparing specifications and the role of principals, project managers, designers, consultants, and others in the process.
4. In-office quality control as it relates to supervising the professional staff and providing for feedback based on experiences gained from current and past work.
5. The organization and capabilities of the administrative staff as they relate to preparing and maintaining the master specification text and related technical data needed to support it.
6. The availability of office equipment, including computer hardware and software needed to create, edit, correct, check, print, organize, update, store, retrieve, and access master specification text.
7. Printing capabilities inside or outside the office not

only for production of specification originals on computer-connected printers, but also for reproduction of multiple copies either for review purposes or for distribution to bidders and contractors.

The importance of knowing the organization and capabilities of the professional staff maintained in an office cannot be overemphasized. For example, in an office where it is established policy to have on staff one or more full-time specification writers who not only maintain the master specification system, but also prepare the project manuals, there is less need to include information either as part of the master specification text itself or in supplementary form to explain the editing process or the kinds of decisions to be made. Although this has the disadvantage of not involving other important players in the decision-making process, it does simplify the work needed to develop and maintain the text. However, if the project architect or another experienced member of the project team is made responsible for the preparation of the specifications as just one of several assignments, then providing guidance for decision making and editing becomes very important.

The most typical process for working with a master specification system is outlined below:

1. In the early stages of design, but no later than the beginning of the working drawings, the sections required for a specific project should be determined by comparing currently available information with the table of contents for the master specification system. This not only indicates existing sections, but also reveals how many new sections must be specially developed for this project and added to the master.
2. Decisions should be elicited from the architect and owner when the foregoing analysis has indicated a need to obtain more detailed information before a final determination of the exact sections required can be made. This may require the owner or architect to make certain decisions that otherwise would be delayed, to the detriment of the project in terms of production efficiency or control of construction costs. One step that might assist this process is the development during the design development phase of a checklist or outline specification that identifies each section required and the principal products and installation conditions then under consideration.
3. Sections from the master system and other sources should be assembled as required to begin the editing and specification writing process. Those sections should be distributed to consultants whose input is required to complete the specifications.
4. Specification requirements applicable to the project should be investigated, based on an analysis of programmatic requirements, information on drawings, contents of sections assembled from the master specification system and other sources, product data from manufacturers, building codes, industry standards, and other data developed through research. This research could involve conferring with owners, consultants, manufacturers, and other outside

sources to determine more specifically how to satisfy architects' and owners' expectations relative to performance, durability, etc, when the expertise needed is not available in the office.

5. Applicable sections of the master specification system should be edited by methodically and comprehensively reviewing their entire contents and deleting those requirements that do not fit project conditions, modifying others that can be adapted effectively and efficiently, and inserting new text that is not included but is needed to make the section complete.

6. The master specification system should be updated by incorporating new sections just written as well as significant new or modified requirements affecting existing sections so that they are retrievable for writing future project specifications.

It is often more efficient to have another way of initially processing the text to eliminate contents that are not relevant to specific projects, in addition to reviewing the entire contents of sections selected from master specification text. Possibilities include the following techniques and practices, some of which are still under development:

1. Developing criteria based on project types, owner requirements, geographical location, contracting and bidding methods, and similar considerations that permit extraction of only those portions of the master specification system that are needed.

2. Extracting applicable data from the master by completing a computerized checklist broadly identifying the choices of products, equipment, assemblies, systems, etc, that must be considered in designing and producing construction documents for a project. This process can be undertaken by either the specification writer or by members of the project team.

3. Incorporating in the program for a computer-aided design and drafting system the capability of generating automatically those specification requirements applicable to a particular project from the way products are indicated on the drawings. Depending on the degree of sophistication of the program, this process can identify either a broad range of specification choices available or narrow them down to the exact set of requirements that fit the criteria entered on the drawings.

The exact choice of method depends on the sophistication of the master specification system and the capabilities of the professional staff and computer software directly involved in the specification process to analyze and interpret technical data effectively as they relate to specification language, formats, and methods. It is also affected by the level of automation available and how the professional personnel can be used in the most cost-effective way, consistent with the level of quality an office wishes to achieve in overall performance.

Master specification systems that are offered for sale or on a subscription basis to architects must be adaptable to a variety of office practices to be successful. Unlike an office master specification system, which generally continues to grow in size, commercial master specification systems are generally restricted to those sections that cover the kinds of work and general requirements that are most frequently required in general office practice from project to project. The number of sections is purposely kept within certain limits, rather than allowed to constantly expand, to balance the expenses of development, updating, publishing, distributing, and marketing against the income received from subscriptions or sales. To meet costs or attain a profit, the subscription or sales fee must be perceived in the marketplace as affordable in relation to the value received. Although larger architectural firms might be able to justify paying for a system with a greater number of sections, the smaller firms, which represent the majority of practices, are less likely to do so.

Despite the immense progress made during the last 20 years in standardizing specification practices and in the field of automation as it relates to text editing, there remain great differences of opinion among architects and specifiers about how a master specification system should be organized and written and what it should contain. As automation capabilities evolve, master specification systems of the commercial variety become more adaptable to the diverse needs of architectural practice.

The two nationally marketed master specification systems that are most widely known are *MASTERSPEC* and *SPECTEXT*. The *MASTERSPEC* system is produced by the Professional Systems Division of the AIA, and *SPECTEXT* by the Construction Sciences Research Foundation (CSRF), an affiliate of CSI.

MASTERSPEC, which was originated by the AIA in 1969, is marketed as a master specification system. Although *MASTERSPEC* may not fully qualify as a master specification system in the ultimate sense, its approach, wherever possible, is to provide the editor with a wide choice of specification requirements to suit a variety of construction conditions and specifying methods. The text is organized and presented to permit simple deletion, which is the primary editing function. *SPECTEXT* includes blanks for filling in product names and selecting related characteristics of the named products.

Editor's notes are interspersed throughout each *MASTERSPEC* and *SPECTEXT* section to explain where alternative choices have to be made or a need exists for the editor to refer to other information before deciding on a course of action.

SPECTEXT was originally developed by CSRF for the benefit of the more experienced specifier. The sections are designed to permit editing by deletion of inapplicable requirements and completion of selection of applicable data from choices offered in brackets within the text.

MASTERSPEC and *SPECTEXT* are both furnished in printed or hard copy form and, as an add-on service, on magnetic media for automated editing on word processing and microcomputer systems. The hard copy form is furnished in loose-leaf binders with vinyl covers and clear plastic pockets on the spines to hold labels furnished to identify contents.

Master specification systems offered on a subscription

basis are used by offices in a variety of ways. Although they are designed to be edited directly without substantial rewording or reorganization, they often serve as just one source of specification and technical information among many to which an office's professional staff refers in developing or maintaining its own master system. Sometimes offices incorporate selected parts of the commercial master into their own office masters to suit the specialized needs of their practices. In effect, this becomes the first step in removing inapplicable text from consideration and reducing future production costs by simplifying and shortening the editing process required to develop each new project specification.

A master specification system must be carefully edited to eliminate requirements that are inapplicable or too restrictive. To do otherwise risks increasing construction costs unnecessarily. There is sometimes a mistaken belief that retaining superfluous provisions not only does no harm, but may actually reduce professional liability exposure and improve quality control. In fact, it may have the opposite effect by revealing that the architect does not understand the actual scope of the work indicated in the bidding documents. It is also likely to result in the contractors increasing their prices to cover work that cannot be found on the drawings, but which they fear has been overlooked in the typical last-minute rush of putting final proposals together.

In addition to the master specification systems described in detail above, there are several guide specification systems developed and maintained by federal agencies, including the U.S. Army Corps of Engineers and the U.S. Naval Facilities Engineering Command. Architects engaged by these agencies are required to prepare specifications based on the applicable guides furnished to them. Other forms of guide specifications are those prepared by manufacturers to encourage the use of their products.

SPECIFICATION PRODUCTION METHODS

The continuing evolution since 1980 of microcomputer hardware and software into affordable systems with ever-increasing memory and word-processing capabilities has finally given small and medium-sized architectural offices the same opportunities for in-office automated production of specifications that were available only to large practices that could justify owning a minicomputer or larger system. Before this time, batch processing from a time-sharing organization was the only automated method that a small or medium-sized office could even consider as a cost-effective alternative to manual typing of specifications.

The increasing sophistication of computers and packaged computer programs has finally caught up with master specification technology and has passed present techniques for distribution and analysis of technical data needed to make specification-related decisions. In the late 1960s, when the *MASTERSPEC* program was first conceived by the AIA and developed by AIA-owned and -created Production Systems for Architects and Engineers (PSAE), it was expected that a substantial number of sub-

scribers would employ automated techniques by sending their edited text for batch processing to a time-sharing organization licensed by PSAE. It soon became evident that manual production of text would continue to be the most economical choice for the majority of existing and potential subscribers to *MASTERSPEC*. It also became evident that a system originated for computer processing was too complex and costly for the small to medium-sized general practice firms that represented the majority. This led to restructuring the system into separate packages. CSRF had similar experience with *COMSPEC*, its text manipulative time-share program, which led to the development of *SPECTEXT*.

Advances in computer technology will undoubtedly have a pronounced effect not only on the methods of production, but also on how specifications are organized, structured, edited, and generated. The next development will be a menu-driven system in which the editor generates the actual text by answering a series of questions without ever seeing the original contents of the entire master specification database. Included as part of the system will be help files that can be accessed on the computer screen during the editing process to provide the backup data needed to answer questions. The future will probably bring integrated systems in which analysis and selection of specification requirements will occur by combining information shown graphically with attributes for building performance entered into the computer. Such programs will include the capability to coordinate and correlate automatically related provisions that are dispersed throughout one section or throughout the entire contract document.

From the foregoing discussion, it is obvious that non-automated preparation and production techniques will gradually fade. Many offices will soon find that the old techniques of drafting new text on yellow pads or manually assembling it by cut-and-paste methods from older specifications or master specification systems are more expensive and less reliable than automated methods. The only manual process that is likely to persist is the mark-up editing of hard-copy text, which is then given to word processing operators for keyboarding. Eventually, even this step may be eliminated, as the editor of the specification will operate the computer directly and use software being developed to check spelling, reformat text, and perform other word processing and proofreading operations automatically.

Preparers of specifications can range from a single individual who specializes exclusively in this area, either as a full-time employee of the architectural firm or as a specifications consultant, to several members of a project team in which one coordinates the overall effort. Between these extremes is a principal, or an experienced member of the firm, who is assigned specification writing or coordination as just one of several important responsibilities. Large firms may have a specification department, which either writes all project specifications or just maintains the office master specification system while performing technical research for specific projects and checking project specifications prepared at the team or studio level.

Once the specifications are ready for reproduction and

distribution, a choice must be made that takes into account not only printing costs and handling, but also the needs of the contractor in issuing bidding and contract documents to subcontractors and materials suppliers. For the average competitively bid, or even negotiated, project, the large number of copies required generally dictates that they be printed outside the office, which is more economical, unless the firm is large enough to support its own printing department. Where the project manual includes many pages, consideration should be given to printing on both sides of each page to reduce thickness and save paper. Another means of achieving this result is to place the original text on larger-than-normal size sheets and then reduce them photographically. The two reproduction processes most frequently chosen are photocopying and offset printing. Generally, the greater the number of copies required, the more likely that offset printing will result in the lowest cost.

Binding methods include loose-leaf binding, where either metal or plastic strap fasteners, brads, or screw posts serve to hold pages together. Another method that allows the pages to be opened flat is the use of plastic multiring spines. Loose-leaf methods allow individual sections to be pulled out and distributed to subcontractors and vendors. This practice should be discouraged because the reader of only selected portions of a project manual will be unaware of other requirements that affect the reader's work and responsibilities.

SPECIFICATION REFERENCES

As noted above under specifying methods, standards developed by industry, independent agencies, or the federal government that by reference are made a part of the specification represent a valuable and efficient means of establishing requirements for products, practices, and test methods. Good industry standards serve as a guide to acceptable practice for a given area of work since they are usually prepared by a consensus process involving a broad cross section of the principal manufacturers of the products involved plus others brought in to provide the viewpoints of the user and designer. Standards have two principal disadvantages: they represent all too often the lowest common denominator of product performance rather than the various quality levels available, and they often take too long to develop and update and thus do not relate to current technology. This is particularly true of standard specifications developed by the federal government, which are gradually being phased out where they can be replaced by industry consensus standards.

The most recognized consensus standards are those of ASTM and ANSI, but of the two, ASTM standards predominate in number as they relate to building products and practices. ASTM standards are much more accessible to the specifier than ANSI standards. There also are many standards developed by associations representing groups of manufacturers that compete with one another. Sometimes this is the result of the recognition that it helps rather than hinders the manufacturers individually as well as a group to develop mutually acceptable quality standards. In other cases, it is just an attempt to restrict competition.

The principal source of product information is manufacturers' literature. The first place an architect looks for product data is *Sweets Catalog Files* published by McGraw-Hill. Currently, this represents the best and most convenient compilation of volumes containing product catalogs. It has been further enhanced by the addition of a volume that provides selection data for a variety of products and assemblies. Because the cost of this catalog is borne primarily by the manufacturers, the recipients paying only a nominal price to defray costs of distribution, it is generally restricted to major national manufacturers, which can afford to participate. Another source of product information is CSI's *SPEC-DATA* sheets, which are prepared by manufacturers to conform to a uniform editorial style. Participation in this program is again limited to manufacturers that market their products nationally.

Building codes, technical periodicals, CSI's TAS, *Spec-GUIDES*, and other association documents plus books on technical subjects represent the other major sources of data about products as well as specification writing practices and related subjects.

The largest obstacle to efficient and effective product selection is the lack of a comprehensive and well-maintained database that is affordable and accessible to the majority of design professionals and that allows information on given subjects to be quickly found, analyzed, and then returned to storage. Past and present efforts have concentrated on gathering data in the form of either paper copy or microfilm and indexing them with systems such as the *Uniform Construction Index* or CSI's *MASTERFOR-MAT*. The capability to collect, update, and organize technical information from a wide variety of sources, to distribute it in photocopy or original form to one or more staff members, and to retrieve originals and refile them in the proper location requires an investment in personnel, publications, and equipment that may be out of reach of all but the larger firms.

Although microfilm libraries can represent an alternative to a full-blown technical library, they are only a partial solution, are not inexpensive, and have been somewhat limited by the lack of computerized support for indexing and retrieving data. Even where a microform database is combined with automated indexing to allow either direct on-line access of the index on the mainframe computer by a remote terminal or indirect access through a computer operator, the information retrieved is not the data, but only the frame or frames of the microfiche or microform roll where the data are located. Then, the roll or microfiche must be found by manual search and manually placed in either a microform reader for direct viewing or a microform reader–printer for reproduction and distribution in paper form.

Obviously, a computerized data base that allows direct access to the data on a terminal or computer screen at each professional work station is needed. Although computerized text display is perfectly readable, graphic information digitized from photographs or finally detailed drawings is not. The other inhibiting factor is the immense amount of memory required to store the vast amounts of text required for a comprehensive computerized data base containing not only text, but also illustrative matter in color. At present, the only solution is on-line telephone access of data stored in a centralized mainframe computer on a time-sharing basis. This can result in considerable expense for computer time and line charges.

There is some indication that the solution to this problem may be the distribution to users of laser disks that not only can accommodate both graphics and text, but also can store considerably more data than floppy disks. In this way, the data are accessed directly, without the need for telecommunications. Updating is accomplished by replacing old disks with new ones.

The ultimate solution will be an interactive, automated data base that is accessible to all who want it and that provides data in a form that permits quick analysis and selection of products and installation methods that satisfy project requirements in all respects, including prediction of life cycle costs.

BIBLIOGRAPHY

1. *Manual of Practice*, Construction Specifications Institute, Inc., Alexandria, Va., 1985 ed., fig. 1-8-1.

General References

Reference 1 is a good general reference.

D. W. Gale, *Specifying Building Construction*, Reinhold Publishing Corp., New York, 1961.

The CSI Format for Building Specifications, Construction Specifications Institute, Inc., Alexandria, Va., 1963 and 1964.

Uniform System for Construction, Specifications, Data Filing and Cost Accounting; Title 1–Buildings, American Institute of Architects, Washington, D.C.; Associated General Contractors of America, Inc., Washington, D.C.; Construction Specifications Institute, Inc., Alexandria, Va.; and Council of Mechanical Specialty Contracting Industries, Inc., Washington, D.C., 1966.

Uniform Construction Index, American Institute of Architects, Washington, D.C.; Associated General Contractors of America, Inc., Washington, D.C.; Construction Specifications Institute, Inc., Washington, D.C.; Consulting Engineers Council of the United States, Alexandria, Va.; Council of Mechanical Specialty Contracting Industries, Inc. (now American Consulting Engineer Council), Washington, D.C.; Professional Engineers in Private Practice/National Society of Professional Engineers, Washington, D.C.; The Producers' Council, Inc.; and Specification Writers Association of Canada, 1972.

MASTERFORMAT, Construction Specifications Institute, Inc., and Construction Specifications Canada, 1978 and 1983.

H. J. Rosen, *Construction Specifications Writing Principles and Procedures*, 2nd ed., John Wiley & Sons, Inc., New York, 1981.

Architect's Handbook of Professional Practice, American Institute of Architects, Washington, D.C., 1985.

C. R. Carroll, Jr., "The Product Selection Barrier—How Far Have We Come?" *The Construction Specifier*, 21–23 (Feb. 1985).

H. L. Simmons, *The Specifications Writer's Handbook*, John Wiley & Sons, Inc., New York, 1985.

W. Rosenfeld, "Changing Influences in Product Selection," *The Construction Specifier*, 34–39 (Feb. 1986).

See also CONSTRUCTION DOCUMENTS; SWEET'S CATALOG FILES

ROSCOE REEVES, JR., AIA
The American Institute of
Architects
Washington, D.C.

SPENCE, SIR BASIL

Born in Bombay, India, in 1907 of British parents, Basil Spence received most of his education in Edinburgh at George Watson's College and subsequently at the Heriot-Watt University Architectural School. Having developed his exceptional gift for drawing there, he completed his architectural education at the Bartlett School of Architecture, University College London. Subsequently, he entered the office of Sir Edwin Lutyens, where he worked on the designs of the government buildings for New Delhi in India. His association with Lutyens was a key formative period, and it is from Lutyens that Spence seemed to have acquired his sense of monumental design as well as his perception of architecture as a "great and personal art" (1).

In the early 1930s he left Lutyens's office to begin private practice, designing large country houses in the tradition of his mentor. The then-current ideology of the modern movement had no major impact on him, for he was never involved in the work of such organizations as the MARS group and did not share the international style idealism of his contemporaries. However, he did adopt the forms of his continental contemporaries, and his ICI pavilion at the Empire exhibition, Glasgow (1937), was rather modern. In fact, his was the first Scottish firm to show any interest in the international style.

After service in World War II as a major, Spence returned to a practice that was largely concerned with the design of exhibitions, particularly those for the British Industries Fair, including Britain Can Make It (1946), Enterprise Scotland (1947), and the Scottish Industries Exhibition (1949). These were followed by a major role in the festival of Britain Exhibition (1951), in which he designed the heavy industries exhibition and the Sea and Ships Pavilion, the latter of which was thought to be the most exciting display at the Festival. At the same time he continued his pursuit of the domestic vernacular style in several housing projects, including his award-winning design of fishermens' cottages in Dunbar, East Lothian, Scotland (1950).

His successful design for the Coventry Cathedral Competition (1951) represents a confluence of his design approaches. His almost baroque sense of monumentality coupled with a sensitivity for craftsmanship and his comprehension of spatial design, modern materials, and techniques were synthesized into his own idiomatic vision of a modern cathedral. On first impression the general public, whose expectation was for a pure Gothic cathedral, hated it, but soon the powerful image of the war-wracked ruins of the cathedral placed at right angles to the original building, serving as antechamber to the Spence design, made him the best-known architect in Britain since Christopher Wren. Traditional architects condemned its modernity and dismissed its lighting as exhibition design theatrics. Modernists decried the stylized, nonload bearing vaulting. Liturgical modernists further criticized the longitudinal plan as too traditional. Further, very much in the manner of the Scandinavian modernists of an earlier period, it was Spence's desire that the Cathedral be an example of modern *Gesamtkunstwerk* devoted to the glory of God. As a result, Graham Sutherland designed the tapestry, John Piper and Lawrence Lee the stained glass, and Jacob Epstein the sculpture.

After a short period during which he was considered merely a church architect, commissions began to pour into Spence's London and Edinburgh offices: universities, schools, town halls, power stations, and embassies—far too many for Spence to devote adequate time to. His assistants were often left to interpret only a broad conception, quickly laid out. Some of the commissions involved difficult structural and or social problems that Spence was not well-equipped to solve. His flamboyant presentation style and free hand with design led to more formal excesses, making his entire oeuvre very uneven.

It was only when he limited his architectural vocabulary and maintained an almost classical system of design that Spence was the most successful. In Sussex University (1962–1970), for example, through the use of a simple repertory of forms consisting of brick walls and low concrete vaults and arches, all loosely based on Le Corbusier's Maisons Jaoul, he created a cohesive and distinct image that is known for its subtle external spaces whose forms create a unique relationship with the undulating local landscape. The idiom of flat arches and vaulting was again successfully used at his Glasgow airport (1966), but in the Household Cavalry Barracks, Knightsbridge (1970), he exploded them into a heavy-handed composition.

The Edinburgh University Library and the British Embassy in Rome were further examples of the success of his work when he designed within a disciplined framework of limited architectural forms. In fact, the British Embassy was, after Coventry Cathedral, Spence's most important building. Roman art critic Bruno Zevi described its simple architectural forms as "Ambiguous enough to be both fascinating and repellent, which is perhaps the highest achievement an architect can hope to attain today" (2).

Spence's later major works were embroiled with controversy, in part abetted by his own frequent rush to print to defend his work. His further belief that the beauty of his works transcended their context only served to create more problems, as in the Household Cavalry Barracks, whose tower looms over Hyde Park. His reaction to the criticism of his Queen Anne's Mansions office development (1976) on similar grounds of excessive massing and heavy decoration with an unresolved silhouette only served to turn popular and critical opinion against his work. It was a clear demonstration of the merits and fail-

ures of his work, namely his ability to assemble the elements of modern design in vigorous eclecticism, but his lack of real discipline generated a decline in public interest in his work. Spence died in 1976.

The profession did recognize his occasional genius, making Spence a fellow in the RIBA in 1947 and a Royal Academician in 1960. He received a bronze medal from the RIBA in 1962. As President of the RIBA from 1958 to 1960, he injected a renewed interest in architecture as an art rather than a social service. He was then knighted in 1960 and received the Order of Merit in 1962.

Spence's enthusiasm for architecture was unending, and he possessed an unparalleled skill as a communicator, easily transmitting this passion for the profession to all who would listen. He wanted his country to understand that architecture was important. As an individual figure in the architectural world he may have been one of the last heroic types of the twentieth century.

BIBLIOGRAPHY

1. F. Gibberd, "Sir Basil Spence: 1907–1976," *Architectural Review* **161,** 254 (April 1977).
2. B. Zevi, "Foggy Colloquy," *Architectural Review* **150,** 153 (September 1971).

General References

B. Spence, *Phoenix at Coventry*, Bles, London 1962.
B. Spence, *The Idea of a New University*, Bles, London 1964.
"Sir Basil Spence," *The Architects' Journal* **164,** 972 (Nov. 1976).

STEVEN BEDFORD
Middlebury, Connecticut

SPORTS STADIA

The sports stadium enjoys a tradition that dates to ancient times. The stadium of today, however, is a phenomenon of the twentieth century and more particularly of the period since the early 1960s. From a simple grandstand or a bowl for viewing of events, the modern stadium has rapidly evolved to a complex entity distinguished by its size, its complicated economics, and its varied physical functions.

This evolution has been stimulated by several factors. The expanding influence of television has helped foster comparable growth in the popularity of sports as entertainment. New sophistication in marketing and leisure, innovations in stadium engineering and design, and new financing techniques have impacted stadium development. The successful planning of a sports stadium now requires solving an equation that includes these factors along with an unusual combination of design requirements.

"Stadium": Definition and Use

The term *stadium* is appropriately reserved for structures built for the viewing of sporting events with seating capacities in the range of 40,000 or more. Originally an open, outdoor structure, the stadium today may be either open or domed. *Arenas* built for indoor sports differ significantly from stadia in both scale and function. Characteristically designed for basketball or ice hockey in North America, arena capacities are normally in the range of 12,000–20,000 seats. Smaller outdoor facilities such as a minor league baseball park may be referred to as "stadia," but they entail a different and much simpler set of functional requirements as compared with a major sports stadium.

North American stadia are developed for major league baseball, for college or professional football, or to serve both baseball and football. A capacity of 40,000–60,000 is found appropriate and economical for major league baseball. Professional football stadia are most often built with capacities of 60,000–80,000. Major stadia are built internationally for soccer and for Olympic track and field events. Stadia are also increasingly built to accommodate a variety of secondary uses, from rodeos to trade conventions.

Etymologically, the word *stadium* has passed to English via Latin from the Greek *stadion*. The Greek word originally referred to a fixed measure of length; later it was applied to the tracks and seating structures developed for footraces and other outdoor games. Two alternative plurals, "stadia" and "stadiums," are both correct in modern English.

Scope of Article

The remainder of this article is developed in four parts:

1. An historical overview of sports stadia from ancient times to current trends in design and development.
2. A brief summary of major objectives and initial design decisions in planning the modern stadium.
3. Design requirements and typical solutions for structural and functional program elements of the sports stadium.
4. A survey of stadium domes and roofs including structural solutions, design issues, and feasible roof systems.

A BRIEF HISTORY OF SPORTS STADIA

The Greek Stadium and Hippodrome

The origin of sports stadia lies in the Classic Period of ancient Greece. Greek stadia were designed for footraces and field sports and acquired permanent form in the fifth century B.C.. They were built by hollowing out a slope and constructing rows of seats in the form of an extended U-shape, open at one end and semicircular at the other. A length of about 600 ft was typically provided for the track and games surface. The stadium at Athens, begun in 331 B.C. and reconstructed in 160 A.D., accommodated 50,000 spectators and was restored for the Olympic Games of 1906 (Fig. 1).

Paralleling the development of the Greek stadium was

Figure 1. The Stadium, Athens, reconstructed c A.D. 160 and restored in 1896 (1). Courtesy of Charles Scribner's Sons.

the theater, built for the presentation of public rites and plays. Like stadia, theaters were built into a convenient slope, but with the seating forming a circular arc around a central orchestra. Theaters were found in every Greek town of consequence. The hippodrome was a later Greek evolution, developed for horse and chariot racing. It was similar to the stadium in shape and construction, differing chiefly in its greater length.

The Roman Circus and Amphitheater

The hippodrome was the direct prototype of the Roman *circus,* which retained the traditional extended U-shape and was similarly used for horse and chariot races. Roman engineering, however, brought a larger scale and new construction methods. In the building of both circuses and amphitheaters, the Romans dispensed with the scooped-out hillside and built large, self-supporting and sometimes monumentally sized structures. These new building techniques were made possible by the use of concrete and depended on a multitude of vaults, which formed the foundations of successive tiers of seats. In prominent structures, these tiers led to a crowning colonnade.

The Circus Maximus of Rome is considered to have been the largest stadium ever constructed. The building underwent many stages of improvement; its major phase of construction began in 46 B.C. The structure, which has long since vanished, was 2000 ft long by 650 ft wide and held 250,000 spectators. Smaller stadia for viewing of footraces were most often built as part of Roman *thermae,* the often palatial "entertainment complexes" that also included baths and pools, gymnasiums, gardens, and apartments.

Paralleling the Roman development of the circus was the amphitheater, a type of building unknown to the Greeks. The Colosseum of Rome is foremost in this class; it measures 620 × 513 ft and provided seating for 50,000 (Fig. 2). Amphitheaters were primarily used for displays of mortal combat involving man and beast and were found in every important Roman settlement. The typical form was an ellipse with rising tiers of seats surrounding an oval arena floor.

Figure 2. The Roman Colosseum (reconstructed) (1). Courtesy of Charles Scribner's Sons.

Historic Parallels and Discontinuity

Similarities between ancient and modern stadia exist for inherent reasons of usage, size, and the solution of common functional and engineering problems, rather than because of a continuous tradition. In both Roman and modern times, the stadium has been a characteristically urban phenomenon. Churches and theaters have offered places of public assembly in both cities and small communities. The large stadium, however, stands apart as a facility serving mass assemblages of people and requiring a city or well-populated region with adequate transportation for its support.

Among stadia of all eras, there are common patterns in general configuration, function, and seating arrangements. These result from the solution of problems related to crowd movement, sight lines, and viewing distances. Parallels in social significance can also be observed. The prominent charioteers of ancient Rome were richly paid popular idols. The four leading stables of the city competed for popularity in an analogy to modern sports franchises. The use of modern stadia for conventions and demolition derbies recalls the multipurpose nature of the Roman amphitheater. Some were built with water-piping systems to permit flooding of the arena floor for use in the presentation of naval displays.

With the decline of cities, organized trade, and transport in the Middle Ages, a long hiatus ensued during which large stadia were not constructed in the Western world. The single exception is the bull-fighting arena, which has descended from the Roman amphitheater in a continuous tradition to its widespread present use in areas of Spanish and Portuguese cultural inheritance. The modern stadium began to appear only at the end of the nineteenth century and is, for practical purposes, a new invention.

Evolution of the Modern Stadium

The widespread popularity of sports as a spectator activity is also a relatively recent phenomenon. Soccer, baseball, and U.S. football were born as organized sports in the mid-1800s and grew to popularity in later decades of that century. The first facilities to incorporate spectator seating were called fields and provided only rudimentary, often temporary grandstands beside the playing area. The term *parks* was used as the facilities became larger and more permanent. Still, little was provided beyond wooden bleachers and a circumferential fence reflecting the growing role of income production from ticket sales.

The first large-scale stadia were constructed around the turn of the century. The modern Olympics were inaugurated in the 1890s; this led to construction of track and field stadia in London (1908) and Stockholm (1912), along with restoration of the ancient stadium of Athens.

Many of the prominent early stadia were built between World War I and II. Several of these famous stadia are still in use, including soccer fields in Wembley, UK (Fig. 3) and in Florence and Turin, Italy; Soldier Field in Chicago, Yankee Stadium in New York (Fig. 4) and the Los Angeles Memorial Coliseum. Many have been subsequently enlarged and improved; Comiskey Park in Chi-

Figure 3. Wembley Stadium, Wembley, UK. Courtesy of The Sports Council.

cago has undergone four phases of expansion. The world's largest stadium is Rio de Janeiro's Municipal Stadium. It has a seating capacity of 155,000, but has accommodated up to 200,000 soccer spectators through the use of standing terraces.

The early stadia lacked many amenities. The dispensing of food, beverages, and souvenirs was generally left to the outside private vendor; today it is a major source of revenue. With increasing age, these early stadia have suffered from deterioration or fires, and many have vanished. Among the older European soccer facilities, serious incidents of structural collapse have occurred, caused by riots or sudden movements of excited crowds and leading to casualties and loss of life. Several of the better-constructed early stadia still prosper and will continue to do so. A growing number are now being considered for replacement.

The 1960s and 1970s: Modernization and Growth in Stadium Design

The period of 1960–1977 saw an important new phase of growth as 30 major professional stadia were built and opened in the United States. Prior to the 1960s, U.S. stadia were designed either for professional baseball or college football. Professional football games were played in baseball stadia, eg, the New York Giants in Yankee Stadium and the Chicago Bears in Wrigley Field. These facilities were limited in capacity and the baseball seating arrangement was often not conducive to football viewing.

The 1960s saw a rapid increase in the popularity of professional football, due in large part to the exposure of television. There was an expansion in the number of teams, while the baseball leagues expanded as well. The architectural response of the 1960s, in cities with newfound teams was the first attempt at a multipurpose stadium. These facilities were circular in plan and, therefore, still limited in capacity because of sight-line distances. Examples are the Oakland Coliseum, Shea Stadium in New York, and Busch Stadium in St. Louis. The first domed stadium was the Houston Astrodome, which opened in 1966 (Fig. 5). The Louisiana Superdome and Seattle Kingdome followed, opening in 1975 and 1976. These stadia had rigid roofs of steel or concrete construction. The Pontiac Silverdome opened in 1976 and was the first stadium with an air-supported fabric dome.

The intent of the multipurpose stadium was to achieve a compromise whereby both sports were treated equally. This was often the case, because frequently neither sport was adequately accommodated. The limited seating for football and the sometimes extreme viewing distances created hardships for both sports. While some of these stadia have been successful, their limitations are now recognized and several teams have chosen to leave these facilities.

Problems with the circular multipurpose design led to

Figure 4. Yankee Stadium, Bronx, New York. Photograph taken in 1932 before later additions. Courtesy of the New York Yankees.

Figure 5. The Astrodome, Houston, Texas. Courtesy of Leisure Management.

renewed interest in the single-purpose stadium. In the 1970s, stadia began to be built specifically for professional football. The nation's first dual stadium complex opened in Kansas City in 1972, including the 78,000-seat Arrowhead Stadium for football and 42,000-seat Royals Stadium for baseball (Fig. 6). The gap between these appropriate size capacities illustrates the inherent difficulties in a multipurpose stadium.

The 1980s: Current Trends

The 1980s have witnessed a slowing of the rate of stadium development in the United States. Those stadia that have been built and those currently under development, however, show continued change and innovation. Much change results from efforts to generate the revenue levels necessary to amortize the formidable and growing investments required for development. Continuing attention is being focused on flexibility and increase in utilization. It

is difficult to consider supporting a stadium by playing football 10 or 12 times per year. The Pontiac Silverdome, built primarily for football, provides a turf surface that can be rolled up in 30 min to ready the facility for a variety of other events (Fig. 7).

Because of the high cost of rigid roofs, air-supported fabric domes have become the standard method of roof design since 1976. These have their own limitations, requiring extensive means to limit the escape of air as well as being susceptible to weather conditions. New systems that draw from the positive aspects of previous methods are now being developed. In St. Petersburg, Florida, a rigidly supported fabric dome is being constructed, which eliminates the undesirable characteristics of an air-supported roof cover (Fig. 8). There has also been recent interest in openable roof structures, and an openable steel roof is under construction in Toronto, Canada. However, the added cost of such structures is very substantial.

Systems providing movable seating sections are gain-

Figure 6. Truman Sports Complex, Kansas City, Missouri. Courtesy of Architectural Fotographics. Photograph by T. A. Sanders.

Figure 7. The Silverdome, Pontiac, Michigan. Courtesy of Pontiac Silverdome.

ing increasing use in stadia. These increase the flexibility for secondary sports and events. Movable seating can also be a key factor to create acceptable sight lines and spectator distance for both football and baseball within a single stadium.

Financing and sponsorship arrangements have also evolved. Historically, most stadia have been publicly financed. As costs have increased and priorities have changed, private ventures and public–private participation plans have been carried out.

Economic analysis aimed at increasing profitability has led to other functional and design innovations. A major growth component has been concessions development and, in particular, the club level and luxury or lounge suites. Typical of this new direction is Joe Robbie Stadium, recently completed north of Miami, Florida (Fig. 9). Instead of a single stadium club, which is difficult for spectators to reach in a large stadium, the facility's club level provides a series of clubs at intervals around the stadium, each with lounge seating, large television screens, and a high level of bar, grill, and food service. Revenue projections now include analysis of the full per capita expenditure of those in attendance.

An additional tendency in stadium development is toward closer integration with other economic development activities. In some cases, this has meant the selection of urban sites. The stadium may be the centerpiece of a downtown revitalization program. Locational decisions will continue to be made on a case-by-case basis. In other instances, lower land costs in suburban locations with ample space for parking, a revenue producer in itself, may continue to be an overriding factor.

Figure 8. Florida Suncoast Dome, with cable-supported roof, St. Petersburg, Florida. Courtesy of Architectural Fotographics.

The Hubert H. Humphrey Metrodome in Minneapolis, British Columbia Place Stadium in Vancouver, British Columbia, and the Indianapolis Hoosier Dome illustrate the urban site option. The Hoosier Dome's downtown location relies on parking, road, and transit infrastructures that were largely in place. The facility can be fairly considered as an 80,000-ft^2 expansion of an existing 120,000-ft^2 convention center. Here and elsewhere, a public partnership in the development is considered justified by the impact on economic development.

At this point in the evolution of stadium design, advances in major component systems are merging to permit a new generation of stadia that may be substantially more workable on a multipurpose basis than previous efforts. These approaches can also permit significantly enhanced revenues. If they prove economically successful, the result could be an increase in stadium development in both the United States and other countries.

Outside of the United States and Canada, only a few major stadia have been constructed since World War II. Notable examples are stadia built for the Rome Olympics in 1960 and the Munich Olympics in 1972, a major soccer stadium in Saudia Arabia in 1985, the 1988 Seoul Olympic facilities (Fig. 10), and a domed baseball stadium in Tokyo in 1988. Interest in stadium development is now increasing in many countries, however, accompanying the growing international popularity of sports. As a "cathedral of modern times," the stadium will continue to hold an attraction for image-conscious communities. The future is likely to see more construction of Olympic track and field facilities, baseball stadia in Japan, and new soccer stadia on a worldwide basis.

INITIAL PLANNING OBJECTIVES AND DESIGN DECISIONS

The ultimate form of any sports stadium will be influenced and constrained by its location, development budget, and projected uses and revenues. At an early stage of the planning process, priorities should be selected within this framework, which will determine many of the larger aspects of the stadium. These decisions deal with several major areas including:

- Event capabilities.
- Building size and capacity.
- Building shape and field and seating configurations.
- Dome or roof covering.
- Site planning, parking, transportation, and urban design relationships.

The choices made in these areas will tend to establish the requirements and the options available in the detailed design work that follows. It is during the early planning stage that major compromises and trade-offs must be made between competing objectives. For example, a larger capacity will normally increase spectator distance and reduce sight-line quality. Expensive extras such as a roof cover or movable seats will compete against other pro-

Figure 9. Joe Robbie Stadium, Dade County, Florida. Courtesy of Hellmuth, Obata & Kassabaum, (HOK) Architects, Inc. Photograph by William Mathis.

posed cost components. Cost savings may be achieved initially by limiting material and systems quality, but the result may be higher long-term operating and maintenance costs.

Event Capabilities

In planning for event capabilities, the first step is to determine the primary emphasis in major sports. In North America, this means choosing either football or baseball,

Figure 10. Seoul Olympic Stadium, Seoul, Korea. Courtesy of Geiger Engineers.

or else accepting the compromises and requirements for flexibility that can serve both. Regardless of the choice of major sport, versatility will be a key objective. Publicly funded facilities of the past were under less pressure to show a profit; their operating deficits were often subsidized on the basis of the stadium's larger economic contribution to the locality.

It is now considered essential to maximize event days. This means building in the capability for secondary programs ranging from an NBA All-Star game to concerts, rodeos, tractor pulls, conventions, trade shows, or whatever events the local community will support and needs a venue for. Arena sports, including basketball, ice hockey, and tennis matches, are not appropriate as primary programs for a stadium facility. They may, however, be scheduled in the case of major events attracting large attendance.

Provision of a dome or roof cover is a major design decision; one of the chief advantages is in the enhancement of flexible stadium use. Where the stadium operator is required to guarantee that an event will be held, protection from the elements can become critical. Secondary uses must be analyzed and planned from the outset. Special installations, such as inserts for the anchoring of circus rigging, will be expensive to add at a later date. Possible secondary uses should be prioritized and selected on the basis of their expected frequency, revenue contribution, and the degree of modification and accompanying expense required of the facility.

Building Shape and Capacity

The decision on maximum seating capacity is determined by several factors. Chief among these are the primary sports program and the size of the market area. Stadium size is also strongly influenced by the development budget and the specific aims of the sponsors, owners, and public institutions backing the development.

The basic form or shape of the stadium has important impacts. It affects the types of roof available, the quality of sightlines for various events, and the appearance of the facility. Sightlines and spectator distance are primary determinants of design. The spectator distance from the sidelines and end zone for football and from the infield for baseball are two of the most important design decisions.

With the use of movable seating sections, the combined baseball and football stadium has now become a viable solution. There remain inherent limitations in this compromise solution, however, including the different desired capacities for the sports and the requirements for operations and scheduling of two major tenants. The geometries of the two fields are also distinctive. Football is viewed primarily from two opposite sides of a rectangle, whereas baseball is viewed primarily from two adjoining sides of an approximate square. Figures 11 and 12 indicate the size, proportions, and orientation for baseball and football stadia.

In competition with other public and entertainment activities, the stadium is itself a key element in the marketing of sporting events. An understanding of the ingredients of enjoyment in the experience is essential for successful planning. Besides seating and sightlines, internal configurations now pay close attention to concession areas and luxury suites or lounge facilities. The design of these areas has evolved rapidly, accompanying the realization of their contribution to net income.

Urban Design Relationships

The external relationship of the building to its location can also have a large significance, especially in an urban location. Parking, transportation, and the relation to other adjacent public or convention facilities may help to determine the larger shape and design of the stadium.

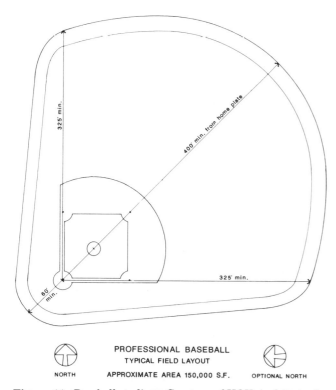

Figure 11. Baseball stadium. Courtesy of HOK Architects, Inc.

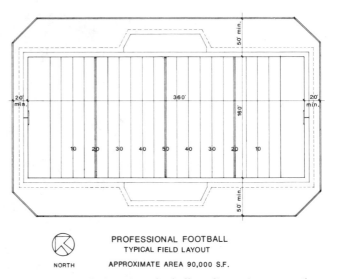

Figure 12. North American football stadium: size, proportions, and orientation. Courtesy of HOK Architects, Inc.

The decision to include a dome or roof cover should be dictated first by climate, budget, and the impact on event opportunities and revenue. To a greater extent than in the past, the public expects the stadium to make an architectural statement. Pilot Field, in Buffalo, New York, was designed for compatibility with an adjacent National Register Historic District (Fig. 13). Where there is a public cosponsorship or funding contribution, the appearance of the stadium may be viewed as an element of civic image and a rallying symbol for community economic progress.

Initial planning decisions establish the parameters within which specific components of the stadium are to be designed. The requirements are extensive and must provide for the activities of spectators, sports teams, media, and support operations. In effect, the facility must be able to move, care for, and entertain a small city's population.

DESIGN REQUIREMENTS AND SOLUTIONS FOR STADIUM PROGRAM ELEMENTS

Once the major objectives of stadium design have been determined, the next step in the design process is to establish criteria and requirements for specific program elements. These requirements are then fulfilled in the final, detailed design. The program elements should include

1. Site development and orientation.
2. Spectator facilities.
3. Playing field.
4. Team facilities.
5. Media and communications facilities.
6. Stadium administration, operations, and maintenance.
7. Lighting.
8. Acoustics and sound systems.
9. Construction materials.

Figure 13. Pilot Field, Buffalo, New York. The stadium was designed for compatibility with an adjacent National Register Historic District. Courtesy of HOK Architects, Inc. Photograph by Patricia Layman Bazelon.

Domes and roof cover systems are discussed later in this article. The following discussion summarizes major design requirements and typical solutions for each of the above program elements, based on current standards for major stadia with capacities of 40,000 or more. These descriptions are oriented toward current design practice for North American baseball and football stadia. While many variations are possible and do occur, these stadia incorporate the latest advances in stadium evolution. They frequently establish standards that are reflected in stadium design for other sports and in other countries.

Site Development and Orientation

Apart from the stadium structure, development of the site, in most cases, also includes parking areas and an extensive vehicular and pedestrian movement system.

Transit Modes and Parking. In many cases, an urban site will offer little potential for facility-only parking. These sites normally depend on nearby available parking facilities and the use of public transit. A minimum urban site requires approximately 15 acres without consideration of any parking areas.

For sites that permit on-site parking, such as a suburban location, the appropriate total site acreage will vary depending on the overall scale of the project. The amount of land actually available may impose a practical constraint on the parking provided and on other site developments. A parking consultant is normally retained to study parking needs and availability and to define the potential for other modes of transportation to an event such as bus, train, or light rail. There are no simple formulas for determining the number of parking spaces required. Calculations may employ the assumption of up to three or four persons per automobile. Special parking areas should be

provided as appropriate for the handicapped, media, sports teams, VIP use, and stadium operations.

Vehicular and Pedestrian Circulation. A major determinant of site acceptability is a location adjacent to suitable off-site road systems and providing adequate access and egress. Entrance roads to site parking must allow for the stacking of vehicles. Design of the site should provide for ease of vehicle movement and access to assigned parking areas. The movement patterns for vehicular, parking, and pedestrian circulation need to be strongly delineated, easily understandable, and focused on the stadium. The circulation patterns should be reinforced with continuous street planting and lighting along the roads. Appropriate graphics, safety and control devices, and equipment are required to aid vehicular and pedestrian movement.

Pedestrian walks leading to the stadium should offer efficient movement and maximum flexibility and freedom of choice of entrances at the perimeter of the stadium itself. It is sometimes desirable to plant rows of trees along the walkways to help orient pedestrians and reduce the apparent size of the parking lots. The maximum walking distance from any parked vehicle to the stadium should not exceed 0.5 mi.

Orientation of the Stadium. The directional orientation of the stadium must take into account the sport to be played, the time of the year the sport is played, and the predominant time of day the sport is played. It is a common belief that stadia are given a basic north–south orientation. This is rarely the case. For example, in orienting a U.S. football stadium it is assumed that the bulk of games will be played from September through January, between approximately 1:00 P.M. and 4:30 P.M. An analysis of sun locations at the beginning, middle, and end of the season indicates that the stadium's best orientation is approximately 45° off the north–south axis. A similar analysis for baseball indicates that the optimum orientation when facing from home plate to third base would be approximately due north. A second orientation would be facing due east (Figs. 11 and 12).

Spectator Facilities

Spectator facilities must provide for the movement, comfort, entertainment, and safety of large numbers of people during relatively compressed time periods. The average level of amenity and comfort has increased steadily during the last two decades, and fans' expectations have grown proportionately. Today's spectators expect easy movement in accessing and leaving the stadium, an unobstructed view from all seats, and convenient restrooms and concessions. They may be willing to pay for expanded food and beverage service, the comfort of air-conditioned suites, or the service of a club or lounge. Stadium planners must meet these expectations if the stadium venture is to be successful.

Seating Arrangements and Sight Lines. Most large stadia are built with two or three levels of seating. These are referred to as the field level, club level, and upper level. Each level extends partially over the level or levels below, thus reducing the sight-line distance for spectators at the upper levels. Figure 14 shows a section of Joe Robbie Stadium in Dade County, Florida. The club level is smaller in total depth and height than the others and is designed to offer superior and specialized amenities and services. Each level should be served by concession stands, toilets, vendor commissaries, and other necessary facilities.

For capacities of up to 40,000 a single-level stadium can be a workable solution, although this approach has

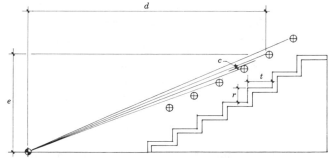

FOCAL POINT

Figure 15. Illustration of formula for the design of seating with optimal sight-line and distance characteristics.

become increasingly uncommon. A single-level stadium would not be feasible for major league baseball but can be applicable for college football, soccer, or track and field.

The seating arrangement should be designed to provide optimal sight lines and viewing unobstructed by the structure. Throughout all levels, the floors are stepped so that each row of seats is mounted on a tread that is elevated above the row in front of it. The following is a basic formula providing for the most efficient arrangement with optimal overall sight lines (Fig. 15).

$$\frac{d}{t} = \frac{e}{r + c}$$

where d is the distance from spectator's eye to focal point on field, t the tread depth, r the riser height, e the elevation of spectator's eye above focal point, and c the vertical distance between the sight line and the eye of the spectator in the preceding row. This equation is normally solved

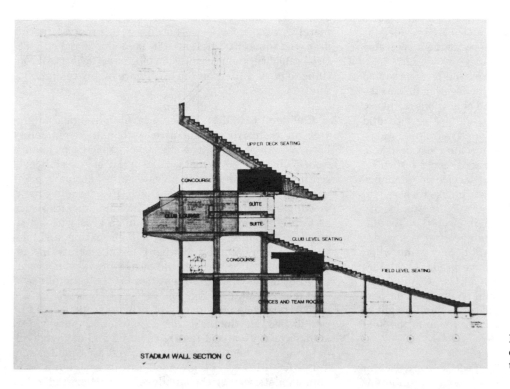

STADIUM WALL SECTION C

Figure 14. Section, Joe Robbie Stadium, Dade County, Florida. Courtesy of HOK Architects, Inc.

for *r*, to determine the distance by which each tread should be elevated over the preceding tread. The formula dictates that riser height will increase incrementally with greater distance from the focal point. This results in a parabolic, bowl-shaped, upward curve for each level of the stadium. The formula is simple, but its application requires judgment and consideration of many special factors resulting from construction requirements and the unique aspects of each stadium design problem.

Seating. The quality and type of seating may range from bench seats to self-rising armchair seats. Seat width and the depth of the seating area also affect spectator comfort. Current standards for seat width are a minimum of 18 in. from center to center. A minimum of 30-in. tread depth is required. Decisions on type and spacing of seats will be a function of cost, budget, and appropriateness to the use of the stadium and its different areas. In North American professional stadia, current standards normally indicate self-rising armchair seats for the majority of seating areas. At the club level, wider chairs and more frequent aisle spacing are often provided. Bench seating may be appropriate for the more distant, lower priced ticket areas of the stadium.

Handrails and guardrails must be provided in seating areas and at aisles to comply with applicable safety and building codes and so as not to obstruct sight lines. Provision for handicapped individuals must also be established to comply with local and national statutes.

Circulation. At the seating levels, circulation is provided by horizontal and vertical aisles. In determining the frequency and width of aisles, the requirements of local and national codes should be followed. These standards are also applicable to other critical aspects of circulation including concourses, stairways, ramps, and exits. The appropriate aisle frequency is also affected by cost factors and by the anticipated usage. More aisles are provided for baseball than football because of more frequent spectator movement.

Concourses, located behind the seating levels, provide horizontal circulation and are also the location for concessions, toilets, and other spectator and operations facilities. Vertical circulation for spectators and for service and maintenance personnel can be provided by ramps, stairs, escalators, and elevators. Ramps are the most desirable method of moving very large numbers of people vertically. They can also be used by vehicles to service maintenance and concession operations. Stairs can be used where site limitations dictate or where additional exit-only capacity is required and ramps are not a feasible solution. Escalators should be provided as a convenience in cases where vertical travel distances are great. This may result when a facility is constructed entirely above grade. Escalators are also valuable for persons with physical limitations and for the elderly. Elevators should be provided for passenger service to VIP areas, for food service and freight to all levels, and for media personnel service from the field level directly to the press box.

Movable Seating. Movable seating sections are used in order to allow varied seating arrangements for different

Figure 16. Florida Suncoast Dome, St. Petersburg, Florida, illustrating movable seating sections. Courtesy of HOK Architects, Inc.

sports and events. Systems available from manufacturers include seating sections mounted on tracks or wheels or using an air or water cushion to lift and slide the seating structure. The appropriate amount of movable seating depends on the types of event to be held. More extensive use of movable seating is made in domed stadia, which serve a wider range of events. Figure 16 shows a plan of the Florida Suncoast Dome in St. Petersburg, Florida. The primary use is baseball, but movable seating adds substantial flexibility for secondary events.

With the use of movable seating, it is possible for a stadium to achieve acceptable quality viewing for both football and baseball. Such a stadium may, in general terms, provide good but not excellent service for both sports. Alternatively, it can be excellent for one sport and merely average for the other. Despite progress in this area, the inherent differences in field shape and size, desired capacity, and presentation of the two sports will continue to place a limit on the excellence of any compromise solution.

Club-level Facilities. The club level is designed to provide an exclusive seating area with a higher amenity level. Where provided, the club-level capacity may range from 5,000 to 12,000 seats. Part or all of the club-level seating may be provided in private suites, normally offering from 10 to 40 viewing seats each. Besides a fixed-seat viewing area, private suites may include amenities such as a fully finished and carpeted lounge area with a bar, sink, undercounter refrigerator, lounge seating, and television monitors. These and other types of amenity, including bar and grill service, should also be provided in larger, adjacent lounge facilities identified for the general use of club-level spectators (Fig. 17).

The number and capacity of private suites should be established on the basis of a marketing survey. All lounges and private suites are enclosed and have individual control of heating, ventilation, and air-conditioning. Toilet facilities can be provided within each suite or in public toilets serving the club level. In earlier stadia that

Figure 17. Denver Broncos' Suite, Mile High Stadium, Denver, Colorado. Courtesy of HOK Architects, Inc. Photograph by William Mathis.

were built with club levels, a single "stadium club" was often provided. The current approach is to locate these services at intervals throughout the club level, in order to reduce travel distance and increase utilization.

Club-level seating has also emerged as a vehicle for generating early stadium funding. For Joe Robbie Stadium in Miami, 10,000 club-level seats were preleased as part of the financing package. The stadium plan also included 222 suites accommodating 10–38 seats each (Fig. 18).

Public Toilets. Public toilets for men and women are provided at every concourse level. These are equipped with general lighting and exhaust and with cold-water service only, except at the club level. An attendant closet with service sink and storage is required for each toilet room. Appropriately designed facilities should be provided for disabled spectators. The number and spacing of toilet fixtures on each level requires an analysis of the seating areas served and expected utilization. Stadia have traditionally provided greater numbers of men's toilets, but the current trend is toward an equal ratio.

Figure 18. Stadium lounge, Joe Robbie Stadium, Dade County, Florida. Courtesy of HOK Architects, Inc. Photographs by William Mathis.

Concessions. Concession stands for food and beverage service are located at intervals on each concourse level. Recently designed stadia also include permanent novelty stands at appropriate locations throughout the facility. These improvements may be a part of the base stadium construction or they may be provided by one or more concessionaires who have rights to operate within the stadium.

Concession facilities must be attractive, convenient, and able to serve a high total volume efficiently. At a minimum, concession stands consist of shell space with utility service. A food service design consultant should be utilized to design these spaces. Concession operations also require a central office, commissary, and other suitable enclosed spaces for efficient food handling, preparation, and storage.

Graphics. Environmental and directional graphics must be planned for the entire stadium and its site. Environmental graphics include banners, symbols, or color elements enhancing the appearance of the facility. Directional graphics are also coordinated for the entire complex. These include signage for identification of site entrances and parking areas; trailblazer signage directing traffic to the stadium; identification of pedestrian gates as well as directions to concourse levels, seating sections, aisles, rows, and seat numbers; identification of toilet rooms, first aid, exits, concession and novelty stands, and other public facilities; and a format for advertising.

Spectator Safety and Security. One or more first-aid facilities for emergency medical treatment should be provided within the stadium. This facility should contain office space for a physician and nurse, cot room, waiting room, and toilet and storage rooms. Office space is also required for the permanent stadium security force. Other security facilities should include a command post for game-day security personnel and a detention room for arrest or restraint of individuals.

Fire protection equipment, such as sprinklers and standpipes, should be provided in accordance with applicable building and safety codes. Stadium design should offer security against illegal entry to the stadium or improper access to areas within the stadium through the use of fencing, walls, gates, and doors.

Other Spectator Facilities. Ticket booths are provided for event ticket sales with handrails for crowd guidance and queuing. These are distributed at major entrances to the stadium. Separate ticket windows are provided for advance sale of tickets for other events. These are a part of the main stadium ticket office and should be conveniently located and accessible from within the stadium.

Turnstiles and space for ticket takers are provided at all points of spectator access. Turnstiles are portable, reversible, and registering. The turnstile area is covered to provide protection from precipitation, and railings are used for crowd guidance. Storage space is required for checking items or for confiscated items not permitted in the stadium. One exit turnstile is required at each major entrance.

Frost-proof drinking fountains are provided at all concourse levels; these are normally nonrefrigerated. Refrigerated drinking fountains are required for the team locker rooms as well as press and administrative areas. Space and conduit for public telephones are provided at all concourse levels.

The Playing Field

The playing field proper and its surrounding surface area require approximately 90,000 ft² for football or 150,000 ft² for baseball. Both natural and synthetic turf systems are used for playing fields.

Synthetic, or artificial, turf was developed and introduced to serve the first domed stadia. To date, the ability to grow natural turf suitable for athletics in domed stadia has not been achieved. Synthetic turfs have gained increasing use in both domed and open stadia over the past 20 years. They have also evolved substantially and continue to improve in playability, drainage, longevity, and capability of removal for other events. Manufacturers use a variety of synthetic material including nylon and polypropylene for the turf and underlying pad.

Systems for growing natural turf are also becoming more efficient and sophisticated. Irrigation and drainage systems have been devised that allow for the construction of a level playing surface. This eliminates the need for a crown for drainage purposes. Natural turf has traditionally been irrigated with pop-up sprinklers or with spray units at the edge of the field. A newly developed system allows for irrigation from below along with precise regulation of nutrients and weed and pest control (Fig. 19). This involves the use of plastic membranes approximately 30 cm deep, within which layers of soil and sand are laid over a piping system.

Both athletes and team managements currently express a general preference for natural turf. The chief advantages of synthetic turf are in the ability to stage other events and in making possible the use of domed or roofed stadia. Regardless of the turf system employed, adequate drainage and storm sewer or run-off systems must serve not only the field, but other portions of the stadium and site as well.

For baseball stadia, a warning track is provided at the field wall. The preferred width of the warning track for professional stadia is 20 ft in the outfield portion and 15 ft for the infield portion of the track. An entry through the

field-level seating or wall is required to provide access to the playing field. This must be adequate for large trucks, with minimum 4.5 m clearance. The opening is secured with an overhead door or grille and an adjacent pedestrian door is provided. Other requirements related to use of the field are noted in relation to team equipment storage and stadium and field maintenance facilities.

Team Facilities

The stadium must furnish a variety of facilities to serve the needs of athletes and sports teams. Many of these facilities are for the exclusive use of a home sports team, which will be the stadium's major tenant. In the case of a combined baseball–football stadium there are two home-team organizations, each requiring separate facilities. Team management should participate in establishing design requirements for these facilities, which are leased on a long-term basis.

Team Locker Rooms. Locker-room complexes are provided for each major tenant. In addition, two locker facilities are provided for visiting teams so that games can be held between two nontenant teams. Each locker-room facility includes provision of a locker area; shower, toilet room, and drying areas; training room; head coach's office and dressing room; assistant coach's locker, shower, and toilet; team equipment storage; and a waiting room for players' relatives equipped with toilet facilities. Other team facilities may include laundry, weight, and exercise rooms; player lounge; hydrotherapy room; rehab room; trainers' and doctors' offices; and meeting rooms (Fig. 20).

Team facilities are located at the field level and have direct access to the playing field. An exception to this is the team administrative office that may be at an upper level. Passenger elevators offer direct access from team facilities to the press box and to the team administrative office. A service drive provides access by truck or bus to the team locker facilities.

Other Team- and Game-support Facilities. A player interview room is required for media interviews, which should be convenient to the home and visitor locker rooms. The interview room must meet appropriate electrical requirements and provide open-tray conduit for television cables. Also adjacent to team facilities is an x-ray room for examination of injuries, used by both teams during games and by the home team at all other times. Separate locker rooms with toilet and shower facilities are provided for game officials and umpires. A field toilet with refrigerated drinking fountain is located adjacent to the field.

Additional provisions for baseball include dugouts with team access directly from locker rooms, batting and pitching practice tunnels, and bull pens. In cases where a football team will hold its daily practices at the stadium, additional strength and conditioning facilities will be needed as well as practice fields outside of the stadium.

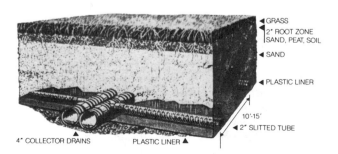

◀ GRASS
2" ROOT ZONE
SAND, PEAT, SOIL
◀ SAND
◀ PLASTIC LINER
10'-15'
◀ 2" SLITTED TUBE
▲ 4" COLLECTOR DRAINS   PLASTIC LINER ▲

Figure 19. Prescription Athletic Turf System. PAT is a patented system. Courtesy of Dr. W. H. Daniels, Turfgrass Services Company.

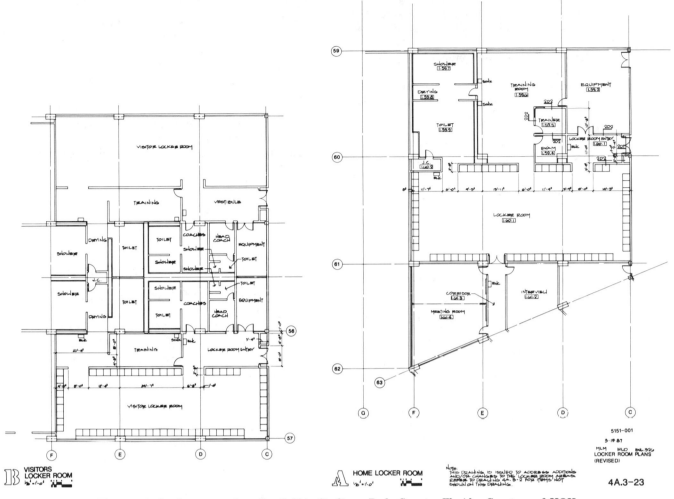

Figure 20. Locker room plan, Joe Robbie Stadium, Dade County, Florida. Courtesy of HOK Architects, Inc.

Media and Communications Facilities

Stadia must be designed to efficiently support the work of news and communications media. Sporting events compete for attention in print and electronic media. A stadium that provides optimum facilities and working environment for press and media coverage will compete more effectively for televised events. This in turn enhances the revenue and overall image of the facility. The stadium also contains internal communications including the scoreboard and public-address systems.

Press and Broadcast Areas. The press box facilities should provide working space for media personnel including writers' stations, broadcasting booths, and support facilities. The press box area is positioned to provide excellent field-viewing conditions, normally at the club level of the stadium. The press box facilities are normally air-conditioned and equipped with operable sash windows. Television monitors are provided and are wired for closed-circuit viewing.

Writers' stations for the working press should contain built-in writing counters, seating, electrical and tele-

phone outlets, and sound system. Broadcasting booths are equipped in similar fashion and also have acoustical treatment on walls and ceiling. Open-tray conduit is installed for television cables leading to television van parking locations. Three to five broadcasting booths are normally provided, depending on the number of television and radio organizations that may need to be served.

Other support for media operations includes an adjacent workroom offering space for statisticians, document reproduction, and telefax equipment. A standby room for equipment repairmen is located adjacent to the broadcasting booths. A press-club room serves the media personnel and is furnished with dining room seating. Game observation and working stations are also provided for home and visiting team coaches. These are usually located near the press box facilities and are equipped with television monitors, built-in writing desks, and telephone connections to player benches.

Camera Stations. Television camera platforms for a football facility should be located at the 50 and 25 yard lines on one side of the field, at each end zone and at the opposite 50 yard line. For baseball, camera platforms include high and low locations for home plate and for the first and third base paths, plus other key locations as appropriate.

At the field level, space for a minimum of 10 photographers is required. One or more darkrooms should be located at the playing-field level with counter and sink for developing film. Camera platforms are also required for team photographers. For football, these are located at the 50 yard line and the end zone.

The television networks should be consulted on all aspects of broadcasting including camera position, booth, platform, conduit, and electrical requirements. Parking for television vans should be provided in or adjacent to the stadium, with convenient access to the press box facilities. Enclosed space directly accessible to the van parking is required for electrical and telephone equipment service and operation.

Scoreboard and Public Address. Current standards of stadium design require a scoreboard that is illuminated and electrically operated by remote control. The majority provide instant replay capability for reproducing video transmissions. The video board shown in Figure 21 is horizontally lengthened to allow side-by-side video and message–graphic displays. As in this example, sound speakers may also be installed within the scoreboard. The complete scoreboard system includes the scoreboard itself and supporting structure, remote control equipment, and control wiring and conduit. A working space for the scoreboard operators should be provided in the press box area, equipped with controls and built-in writing counter.

Like scoreboard systems, public-address systems are designed and installed by contracting specialist manufacturers. This system includes the announcer's equipment and controls, wiring, amplification, and loudspeaker equipment. (Placement of loudspeakers is discussed below in connection with stadium acoustics.) The public-address announcer's booth is located in the press box area. It is soundproof and equipped with built-in counter and all necessary controls for operation of the entire public-address system.

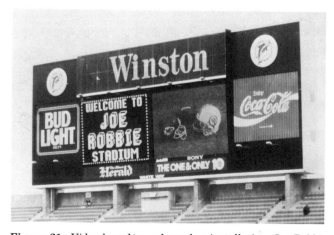

Figure 21. Video board/sound speaker installation, Joe Robbie Stadium, Dade County, Florida. Courtesy of HOK Architects, Inc. Photographs by William Mathis.

Stadium Administration, Operations, and Maintenance

Office space within the stadium is required for stadium administrative offices and a stadium ticket office. Space requirements for administrative offices can vary greatly, depending on the nature and functions of the ownership or management organization. Home-team administrative offices may also be located at the stadium. This is especially common in the case of baseball teams. Football teams often have separate practice and administrative facilities located apart from the stadium.

The stadium design must also provide personnel and locker facilities, maintenance facilities, and storage and transportation of equipment and supplies. Separate locker facilities are needed for different personnel crews including those serving concessions, field and stadium maintenance, security staff, ushers and other stadium personnel, and band members and cheerleaders for football games. Locker rooms should furnish adequate toilet facilities, space for dressing, and locker storage for uniforms.

To provide for stadium maintenance operations, a management office is required plus an enclosed shop area and adequate storage facilities for materials and equipment. Hose connections for maintenance and cleaning of concourses and seating areas are provided throughout the stadium. A separate operation for field maintenance is normally provided. This includes a management office and storage space for game equipment and field maintenance equipment.

A truck loading dock serves all stadium operations. This is typically a two-position dock with manual dock levelers. Its location should provide direct access to concessions and maintenance facilities. It also supports the refuse removal operation, which should include provision of a mechanical self-loading trash compactor located near the dock.

Lighting

Appropriate lighting must be provided for all areas of the stadium. An emergency lighting system, powered by an emergency generator, is provided for selected fixtures and egress areas in case of an electrical power outage.

The levels and color temperature of field lighting are dictated by the requirements of television. The lighting levels needed for television have recently been reduced, but still exceed those of normal viewing. Field-lighting lamps are generally metal halide, which is compatible with television. In the past, field lights required warm-up times of 10–15 min. Recent developments have produced instant restrike lamps, which allow flexibility in darkening and raising the field lights.

Baseball field lighting systems are subject to the approval of Major League Baseball. Required levels of illumination vary across the playing area. These differ for the infield versus the outfield. Lighting manufacturers that act as stadium subcontractors are conversant with applicable requirements. In designing a system of field lights, computers are used to calibrate illumination levels for a grid of aiming points across the field area.

Acoustics and Sound Systems

Although a sports stadium may host concerts or musical events, acoustical excellence is not its primary function. The consideration of serving large crowds will dominate planning decisions. The challenge of acoustical design is, therefore, to meet the public's expectations and to avoid uncomfortable acoustical effects. Domed stadia can present special problems of excess reverberation. With any large facility, the intelligibility and fidelity of announcements is an important feature of the presentation. Achieving acceptable acoustical quality depends on the characteristics of both the building space and the sound-amplification and loudspeaker system.

In the case of an open-air stadium, acoustics cannot be analyzed by traditional methods because true reverberant conditions rarely exist. Nevertheless, the size of the structure and overhanging seating levels can result in echoes and sound buildup, especially for listeners seated under overhangs or in corners of a rectangular-plan stadium. Virtually all of the sound-causing acoustical problems originate from either the stadium's permanent public-address system or from temporary concert sound systems. Any analysis must consider the nature and location of these systems. Prevention or control of problems can also be achieved by the geometry of the stadium and the shaping of individual elements. More complex shapes typically result in better performance.

Enclosing a large stadium presents a different set of acoustical problems, chiefly resulting from excess reverberation and building mechanical systems. Excess reverberation in these buildings has led to baseball players wearing earplugs.

With proper acoustical control, it is not necessary for an indoor stadium to be an acoustically uncomfortable environment. For domed stadia, it is almost always necessary to employ a sound absorptive ceiling roof treatment. Fabric domes are usually constructed of two fabric layers for weather insulation. In this case, the space in between should be filled with sound absorbing material. Absorptive material can be suspended from the ceiling as another option.

Loudspeaker Systems. In stadia of all types, the acoustical design cannot be separated from the design of the sound-reinforcement or public-address system. The configuration of the loudspeaker system strongly affects acoustical performance. In practice, there are three primary system arrangements: central cluster, distributed satellite clusters, and a highly distributed system.

The central cluster places the loudspeakers in a single location, typically in the outfield or at one end of the stadium. (The video board–sound speaker installation shown in Figure 21 incorporates central clustered speakers.) This approach may work well if there is no seating near the cluster. Otherwise, the surrounding seats may be subject to very high and uncomfortable sound levels. This can be avoided if the cluster is center-hung over the playing field. In the case of domed stadia, however, it is preferable to consider design approaches other than the central cluster, in order to minimize exciting of the space's reverberant nature.

The satellite cluster design breaks up the central cluster and moves loudspeakers closer to the spectators. This is the approach most commonly used in domed stadia. The third basic configuration is to distribute the loudspeakers at a high level, supporting them from stadium and lighting structures or poles. This approach minimizes environmental noise problems, allows easier video display synchronization and provides high quality sound. Highly distributed systems may not provide good sound projection to the playing field. They also tend to be expensive in comparison with other configurations. To date, these systems have been used most often for stadium renovation projects.

Construction Materials

The selection and appropriate integration of construction materials for a sports stadium in many ways parallels the process as it applies to other types of public building. The stadium also has certain unusual characteristics calling for specialized priorities and solutions. In particular, large portions of a stadium facility are exposed to the elements, often while also being subject to very high levels of public use. Durability and maintenance factors must be given a high priority. At the same time, the stadium must project and maintain a positive public image.

Structural Materials. As compared with other buildings, the structure of the stadium comprises a larger percentage of construction costs and requires specialized attention for this reason alone. Stadium structures are built of either steel or reinforced concrete. This choice is influenced by soil conditions and building weight as well as the relative costs of construction in a given locality. A concrete structure typically offers greater ease of maintenance. The structural elements themselves are frequently exposed to the weather. As a result, consideration of longevity, climate, thermal expansion, maintenance, and protection from deterioration is necessary in the selection of structural materials.

The treads and risers that form the floor of the seating areas are generally built of precast concrete where they are elevated on a structural frame. The majority of stadia are at least partially sunk into the ground. This provides a savings in construction costs and also reduces the vertical travel distances required of spectators. Where seating areas are at or below grade level, treads and risers are poured concrete slabs-on-grade.

Building Envelope and Walls. The building envelope is responsive to environmental as well as aesthetic factors. Public circulation areas of the stadium may be either partially or wholly enclosed. This is determined primarily by consideration of weather and climate. Concourses and ramps are frequently covered but not enclosed. The architectural design of the envelope and general exterior is most often an expression of the structural system, which is usually evident if not actually exposed. Design elements may provide emphasis of the entry gates, to create recognition and accentuate the public nature of the facility. As with other areas of the building, the level of finish of the envelope will be strongly influenced by budget and cost considerations.

The wall surface areas of the exterior envelope, concourses, ramps, public areas, and specific enclosures such as offices are generally visible to the public and subject to high levels of use and traffic, as well as occasional vandalism. Many of these surfaces are also exposed to the weather. High use areas such as concourses must be capable of thorough and efficient cleaning, often during the several hours available between events.

It is important for the facility not only to project a positive visual image, but to maintain this image consistently without continual and excessive repair requirements. Finishes or surfaces that can withstand severe use and repetitive cleaning are therefore of great importance. The most common solutions involve concrete surfaces with a sealant applied. Concrete masonry units offer durability and resistance to vandalism combined with reasonable construction costs.

STADIUM ROOF STRUCTURES

The major technical considerations in covering a stadium are structural. The cost and ultimate feasibility of covering the facility depends on the structural efficiency of the roof design and the ease of its implementation. The critical structural problem is the span of the roof. All of the enclosed multipurpose stadia built to date have roof structures that clear span the field and seating areas without internal columns or supports, providing unobstructed views of the field. Coupled with the size of the stadium, this requires roof spans that have no equivalent in other types of building. Unique structural and construction process solutions are therefore required.

Considering professional stadia seating 45,000 for baseball and 65,000 for football, the clear-span area of the roof structure will need to be between 350,000 and 400,000 ft^2 (8–9 acres), requiring a minimum clear span in excess of 600 ft. The length-to-width ratio will probably not be in excess of 1.5–1.0 (1.5 aspect ratio). The roof structure is normally supported at the perimeter of the seating structure, as much as 100 ft above the field level. The minimum rise or height of the roof structure above its lowest perimeter support will be about 80 ft for baseball. For football, such clearance is not required, thus permitting, in principle, the use of a planar structural system such as a space truss.

Long-span Roofs: The Structural Problem

In the design of long-span roofs, there are inherent issues that need to be considered. As a general rule, the dead load or self-weight will be kept as low as possible to reduce the work the structure must do to resist its own weight. The system typically carries loads as much as possible by means of axial force in the structural elements, as opposed to resisting load by bending in either beam or plate action. This increases efficiency, requiring less material to resist the same load conditions.

One-way, Two-way, and Space Structures. It is convenient to separate long-span roof systems into three categories based on how they resist applied load: one-way, two-way, and space structures. These types are inherently different in their structural efficiencies, one-way structures being the least efficient and space structures being the most efficient.

The one-way system is composed of a series of parallel elements such as trusses, ribs, girders, cables, or arches that span across the width of the space covered. Loads are carried in only one direction to the supports, which are only required along two opposite edges of the structure.

A two-way structural system may be a grid of trusses or other elements distributing applied loads primarily in two directions. Supports must be distributed around the perimeter of the structure. The two-way distribution is practical when the aspect ratio of the structure is less than 2.0.

Space structures are distinguished by their ability to distribute applied loads throughout the structure to the supports. They are typically nonplanar and include doubly curved shells, such as domes. The supports for space structures are distributed around the perimeter of the structure. All of the existing covered stadia for professional sports utilize this type of system for their roof structures.

Space systems are more efficient than one-way or two-way systems because they exploit the continuity of their three-dimensional form to advantage. However, this efficiency is highly dependent on specific geometry. Domes, shells, and membrane structures are continuous in several or all directions, Discontinuities or changes in shape, curvature, and geometry aimed at suiting either aesthetic or functional requirements could effectively destroy the efficiency of the system.

In many space systems no part of the structure is self-supporting until the structure is complete. Even when this is not the case, the integrity of the final structure may depend on the sequence of erection, as detrimental stresses can be locked into the system. Furthermore, systems composed of large numbers of small prefabricated elements can easily be subject to accumulative assembly errors.

Open and Closed Systems. Another useful means of classification of long-span systems is by open and closed structural systems. A closed system requires only vertical support at the perimeter of the roof structure to resist vertically applied loads, whereas an open structural system requires both vertical and horizontal supports. As an example, consider a dome composed of a radial arrangement of arches. As an open system, this dome requires supports or buttresses able to resist the horizontal component of the arch thrust at the base of the dome. If this dome has a circular plan, then a circular tension ring will equilibrate all the horizontal base thrusts in axial tension, at least for symmetrically distributed loads. If the plan is not circular, then the ring would have to resist horizontal thrust by a combination of beam action or bending and axial tension. The use of the tension ring can eliminate the need for buttresses at the base of the dome.

This is particularly relevant to the application of covered stadia. It is highly advantageous to support the roof structure at the perimeter of the seating structure, which may be as much as 100 ft above grade. The alternative would be to span entirely across the seating superstructure from grade, which would greatly increase the required total span. In springing the roof from the seating structure, however, the support conditions required by the roof system significantly impact the required design of the supporting superstructure. If the roof system develops large horizontal thrusts, it could be prohibitively expensive for the superstructure to provide adequate resistance high above grade.

Structural Applications. Because of the considerations described, closed structural systems are preferred for covering stadia. The nine multipurpose covered facilities listed in Table 1 all employ closed structural space systems springing from an elevation high above grade at the perimeter of the seating. The roof structures of the Louisiana Superdome, the Kingdome (Fig. 22), and the Astrodome (Fig. 23) all have circular plan configurations, exploiting an efficient tension ring as closed systems.

Air-supported, low profile roofs utilized for a number of stadia also illustrate the considerations of geometric efficiency in a closed system. Included are B.C. Place Stadium (Fig. 24), the Hoosier Dome in Indianapolis (Fig. 25), and the Hubert H. Humphrey Metrodome in Minneapolis (Fig. 26). The plan configuration for this type of system is nominally a rectangle with curved corners, adopted for both functional and structural reasons. The primary load-carrying elements are cables that span the roof in a two-way grid, laid out parallel to the diagonals of the rectangle. The longer cable span along the diagonal direction results in a much more cost-effective perimeter ring beam required to close the structure.

Closed, long-span space systems have a number of common physical characteristics. They are typically symmetrical, as a direct consequence of their closed nature. Often

Figure 23. Astrodome, Houston, Texas. Courtesy of Geiger Engineers.

the symmetry is quite marked, as with spherical or radial systems. The geometry may be complex, as with most air-supported or other membrane systems, but it is never arbitrary. Any symmetry is helpful in reducing costs, because it reduces the number of unique components that must be fabricated.

The sensitivity of space structure systems to nonuniform or unbalanced loading conditions can be significantly

Figure 22. Kingdome, Seattle, Washington. Courtesy of Geiger Engineers.

Figure 24. B.C. Place, Vancouver, British Columbia, Canada. Courtesy of Geiger Engineers.

Table 1. North American Coed Sports Stadia Facilities for Professional Baseball or Football with Seating Capacities in excess of 40,000 Seats

| | General | | | Roof Data | | |
Facility and Location	Maximum Number of Seats	Year Completed	Type[a]	Plan Shape	Clear-span[b] Plan Area, ft^2	Maximum (Minimum) Clear Span, ft
Astrodome Houston, Tex.	53,000	1965	F, T	Circular	324,000	642
Louisiana Superdome New Orleans, La.	75,600	1975	F, O	Circular	332,000	680
Kingdome Seattle, Wash.	65,000	1976	F, O	Circular	343,000	661
Silverdome Pontiac, Mich.	80,000	1976	F, T	Superelliptical	371,000	722(553)
Hubert H. Humphrey Metrodome Minneapolis, Minn.	63,000	1982	F, T	Superelliptical	378,000	706(592)
B.C. Place Stadium Vancouver, B.C.	60,000	1983	F, T	Superelliptical	388,000	736(601)
Hoosier Dome Indianapolis, Ind.	60,000	1984	F, T	Superelliptical	317,000	660(528)
Skydome Toronto, Ont.	56,000	1989	R, O	Rectangular with semi-circular ends	339,000	NA(675)
Florida Suncoast Dome St. Petersburg, Fla.	40,000	1989	F, T	Circular	372,000	688

[a] F = fixed, R = retractable, O = opaque, T = translucent.
[b] Area is the face of innermost supports and does not include area under the ring beams. In some stadia, there is seating in this area, outside the innermost supports.
[c] N = not insulated, Y = insulated.
[d] N = not provided, Y = provided.

magnified in closed systems. This issue can be addressed by adopting a roof shape and aerodynamic profile that do not attract highly nonuniform snow or wind loads. Two-way, space-and-shell structures are also sensitive to displacement of their supports, whether by settlement of their foundations or by elastic deformation (deflection) of their supporting structural members.

Implications for Retractable Structures. The objective of achieving a truly retractable roof system greatly complicates the long-span roof problem. For the sake of discussion, a truly retractable structure is one in which the pri-

Figure 25. Hoosierdome, Indianapolis, Indiana. Courtesy of Geiger Engineers.

Figure 26. Hubert H. Humphrey Metrodome, Minneapolis, Minn. Courtesy of Geiger Engineers.

Structural System	Insulation[c] (R-value)	Weather Membrane	Acoustic Provisions[d]	Approximate Roof Cost		Dollars per ft² Clear-span Area, 1988
				Total Original[e]	Total 1988[e]	
Steel Kewitt dome	N	Hypalon on tectum board	N	4.5[f]	20.5	63
Steel Kewitt dome	Y	Hypalon on urethane	N	10.7[f]	25	69
Reinforced concrete radial rib	Y	Elastomeric on foam	Y	9.3[f]	21.5	63
Air-supported, cable-restrained, fabric roof	N (R-2)	Teflon-coated fiber glass	Y	5.1[g]	12.3	33
Air-supported, cable-restrained, fabric roof	N (R-2)	Teflon-coated fiber glass	Y	8.7[g]	13.0	43
Air-supported, cable-restrained, fabric roof	N (R-2)	Teflon-coated fiber glass	Y	9.7[g]	12.1	32
Air-supported, cable-restrained, fabric roof	N (R-2)	Teflon-coated fiber glass	Y	8.0[g]	10.5	33
Segmented one-way steel arch–truss panels	Y (R-12)	Single-ply PVC	Y	76[g]	80	236
Circular cable dome with fabric	N (R-2)	Teflon-coated fiber glass	Y	15.6	16.7	45

[e] Roof cost, in millions of dollars, includes all components of the roof system, including ring beam when appropriate, but not the supporting structures.

[f] These costs are estimated, because cost breakouts for the roof system were not available.

[g] It is important to note that costs for these roof systems do not include items indirectly related to the roof such as sealing and mechanical equipment for air-supported roofs ($1–2 million) and the track and buttresses for the retractable roof on the Skydome (unknown costs).

mary structure is moved. The problem is twofold: either the structure is moved as a unit so that its continuity can be maintained or the structure is split, or otherwise made discontinuous, in order to make an opening. The first option probably results in the loss of the well-distributed support around the perimeter, at least while moving the roof. The second option destroys the beneficial efficiency achieved by a continuous space structure.

Problems of support displacement become exacerbated in the case of a movable roof structure, because varying loads will occur during roof operation. This type of system may require great structural rigidity in its supporting structure to limit deflections and prevent the roof system itself from seeing continuously varying support conditions as it moves along its track or tracks. Alternatively, the roof system can be designed to be sufficiently flexible to adapt to these support movements. The specific consequences of retractable system design are further discussed in the concluding segment of this study. Several options are considered, including lift-off, roll-off, and multiunit retractable systems and partially openable roof systems.

Assessment and Reduction of Risk Factors

In order to reduce the risk of roof system problems or failure, the system that is adopted should be a reasonable extension of known and demonstrable technology. This applies to both the structure and any mechanical systems employed. Many systems have been used to cover arenas and other facilities of similar size, and these can be consid-

ered to be small-scale prototypes. The basic erection sequences and processes are known for these systems and can be used to establish the feasibility of much larger structures.

By their nature, operable roof systems will have a greater risk of failure of some component as compared with fixed or static systems. An operable system is one that requires mechanical or human control to perform its intended function. This includes any type of retractable roof as well as air-supported and air-inflated roof systems.

The air-supported roof system demonstrates many aspects of risk assessment and reduction. The system is dependent on mechanical systems to maintain its structural integrity, either manually or automatically. The more highly automated the control systems are the more expensive they will be. The consequence of failure of an air-supported roof is deflation. The significance and the life safety consequences of this event are orders of magnitude less severe than, say, the collapse of a rigid roof structure. In a deflated state, the roof structure is designed to hang 20 ft clear of all the seating and occupiable space. Significant warning is also given by the distortions of the roof that result from any system problem. Thus, the acceptable probability of a deflation event will be significantly greater than that for a typical roof collapse.

The potential for deflation may be reduced substantially, but cannot be totally eliminated with an air-supported roof. This system is particularly vulnerable to snow loads, because it is neither desirable nor cost effective to pressurize the building adequately to carry all snow loads under normal operating conditions. Where the potential for snow exists, the roof system should include a snow-melting system. The melting system reduces risk in a critical snow event, but requires properly timed human response to function effectively.

The design of Korakuen Stadium, the "big egg," in Tokyo, Japan, incorporates an unusual degree of risk-reduction features. Roof support systems are fully automated and computer controlled. The building includes a snow-melting system and can, if necessary, also produce internal pressure adequate to carry the full design snow load. This high pressure level is not to be maintained during normal operations due to the undesirable effects on building access; thus, the requirement for snow-melting capability.

As with all other types of risk, the lower the target level of acceptable risk the greater the cost that must be expended to reach it. The air-supported roofs illustrate well the kinds of assessments involved with operable systems. In the case of air-supported roofs, a number of potential undesirable events and the factors that contribute to their likelihood of occurrence are known historically.

As larger steps are taken in technological development, the potential for problems is proportionally greater. This must be weighed in the consideration of movable or retractable roofs. The retractable systems that are most likely to be economical may not be so if they are required to resist all of the potential environmental loads while in transitory or open state. However, the planned use must also be considered. If the roof is not operated in the winter months and never when the potential for snow is present, it may be reasonable to design a system that is not capable of resisting the snow load when open or in transit. The same questions arise relative to wind loads, but the answers here are even less clear cut. Relatively high winds can occur without being preceded by warning. Thus the roof should be designed to resist significant wind loads in all potential positions. The specific potential consequences of exposure of the system to wind loads must also be considered.

A reasonable balance between potential for risk and both capital and operational costs must be established for all operable systems. In practice this is achievable, but with some difficulty. A major means of reducing risk is by assembling a design team of qualified design professionals with specifically relevant experience. All affected parties must be involved in determining the proper balance, including building officials, architect, engineer, operator, owner, and insurer. Ultimately this will result in the establishment of appropriate design criteria for the system.

Building Code Requirements. A stadium is typically required by applicable codes to be the equivalent of Type 1 construction, (BOCA designation), due to the facility's great size and its use as a place of assembly. This entails specified fire-rated assemblies for building components and combustibility requirements for materials. Type 1 construction is required to be noncombustible, meaning that the basic building materials will not contribute fuel to a fire or result in significant smoke generation.

The Type 1 roof requirements limit the roof construction to noncombustible materials, with the exception of fire-retardant–treated wood complying with provisions. The required rating varies depending on the clear height to the lowest member in the roof system. Roof construction 20 ft or more above the highest balcony, seating area, gallery, or floor can be unrated. Codes provisions also apply to the fire performance of roof coverings. Stadium roofs typically require a minimum of a Class C roof covering. Teflon-coated fiber glass fabric, the material typically used in permanent membrane structures, satisfies the noncombustibility and Class C roof-covering requirements.

Design Issues

There are three overriding considerations that dictate to a large extent the design of the roof system, namely openness, cost, and geometric configuration.

Openness of the Stadium. The history of the development of covered sports stadia in North America illustrates a continuing concern with maintaining the outdoor character of the stadium while also creating an enclosed environment with its inherent advantages. This desire for openness, which may be ultimately realized with a retractable roof, stems from the fact that the primary sports originated as outdoor activities. Thus the first covered stadium, the Astrodome, was designed with a transparent roof. The steel structure, however, was so visually dense that much of the effect was lost. Moreover, it was exceedingly difficult for baseball players to visually track baseballs against the bright openings in the dark matrix of the steel structure. This problem was mitigated by painting a significant portion of the roof white, creating a translucent roof and reducing glare.

Both the Kingdome and the Louisiana Superdome, built in the 1970s, made no concessions to this issue, using opaque materials. This led to less than satisfactory results, and since then, every covered professional stadium has made some concession toward the goal of openness. The Silverdome in Pontiac, Michigan, was the first to employ a translucent, cable-restrained, air-supported, fabric roof, a system that has been repeated in other cities (Table 1).

The designs of two stadia presently being constructed have also addressed this issue. The design for the Florida Suncoast Dome in St. Petersburg, Florida, features a cable-supported, translucent fabric dome. (Fig. 8). This system provides a significant improvement over existing air-supported translucent roof structures, in that with a penalty of a slight increase in the visual mass of the structure, the roof does not require any mechanical or human assistance to maintain its structural integrity.

The Skydome in Toronto, Ontario, is the first stadium to feature a fully retractable roof, so that as many of the seats as possible are exposed to the sun when the roof is in the open position. (Fig. 27). The intent was to create a multi-purpose facility with the openness of an outdoor ballpark. This achievement required consideration of more than just the roof structure. The constraints of an extremely tight site and the larger Canadian football field

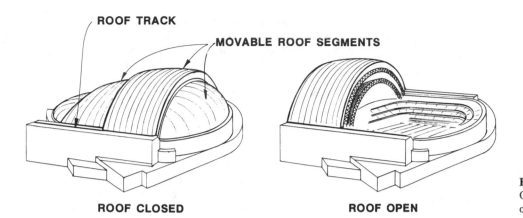

ROOF CLOSED   **ROOF OPEN**

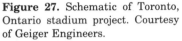

Figure 27. Schematic of Toronto, Ontario stadium project. Courtesy of Geiger Engineers.

have dictated that the seating be arranged in as many as four tiers. The result is that an estimated 15% of the seats do not have a view of the sky. Thus, the perception of openness in a facility may be governed by the seating layout as well as by the roof structure.

Cost Factors. The cost of a roof system, which includes the weather proofing, insulation, ceiling finish, and the roof structure, is a major element in the capital budget for an enclosed stadium. Historically, the capital cost of a complete roof system has averaged about 13% of total facility capital cost, excluding land acquisition. As much as 90% of the roof system is for the roof structure. There are other capital costs associated with the roof system that are not easily broken out of the total facility costs, such as the additional cost of the structure and foundations that support the roof system. The costs of retractable roof systems are substantially greater than those for fixed systems. For the Skydome, the roof system costs are about 30% of a total facility capital cost, which is much higher than average for covered sports stadia (Table 1).

Operation and maintenance costs for the facility will be directly impacted by the roof system. The operational costs impacted are chiefly the energy costs associated with heating and air-conditioning the facility and to a lesser degree the lighting costs.

The major maintenance cost issue for a fixed roof is the durability of the roof weather proofing and finishes. Many roof-covering systems are available and the capital costs may range from approximately $7.00 to $15.00 per square foot installed, in 1988 prices. For rigid structural domes, the covering with least maintenance would be standing seam copper or stainless steel sheet metal. A less expensive and more likely choice would be a high quality single-ply membrane system. Materials for fabric structures meeting roof-covering fire code requirements will have a life of 20 years or more. Ideally, the roofing material should be colorfast and not retain visually objectionable layers of dirt or other contaminants.

In the case of a retractable roof, the programmed operation of the system will impact capital, operating, and maintenance costs in direct and indirect ways. The impact on the cost of heating and cooling systems can be significant. If the roof is envisaged as seasonally retractable, then there may be no need to provide cooling to the main seating area. However, if the roof is opened and closed frequently during either the heating or cooling season, a substantially larger heating or cooling capacity system may be required than would be needed for the same facility with a fixed roof.

This situation results from the extremely large volume of air in an enclosed stadium as well as the building's large thermal mass. The time and cost required to change the internal environment from that of the ambient environment can be very substantial. This would occur, for example, if an air-conditioned event is scheduled following a hot summer day, or in the changeover from a fall football game to a heated concert facility. If the heating and air-conditioning system is limited in its ability to accomplish these changes, this may in turn impact the ability to schedule roof-open to roof-closed events back to back. The tendency in operating the facility will be to make this change as few times as possible in order to conserve energy.

Retractable systems may also result in the interior surface being exposed to the outdoor environment for extensive periods, affecting the maintenance requirements for the ceiling and major roof structural elements. Thus the finishes and corrosion protection of these elements must be suitable for this exposure condition and will require more ongoing maintenance. Finally, the energy cost of operation of the actual retraction process must be considered.

Geometric Configuration. The geometric form of the roof system configuration is primarily dictated by functional requirements of the seating and field layout. The earliest domed, multiuse stadia employed circular plans. However, the sacrifice in spectator sight lines and distances from a circular seating plan is now considered excessive and not necessary. The plan configuration of the roof system should mimic that of the seating plan as much as possible to minimize the spans required. Structural roof systems with circular plans are not precluded from consideration, but they are at a cost disadvantage. It is possible to cover any layout of the facility with a circular roof, but only at the expense of increasing the clear span beyond the area needing to be covered.

Stadium Roof Construction Systems

The final section of this study describes and evaluates 12 different dome and roof construction systems. These systems and their advantages, disadvantages, and potential costs are summarized in Tables 2 and 3.

While many systems are technically possible and can produce excellent results, the considerations of economic feasibility is a prime factor in determining which systems are actually adopted for a particular project. The growth in development of stadia with air-supported roofs during the 1980s has occurred because that system has been judged cost effective in generating revenue to amortize its relatively reasonable capital cost. Municipalities and public institutions will at times choose to invest in more elaborate, higher image systems with less attention given to budget factors. In most cases, however, the application of technological advances, including retractable roofs, will occur when cost and feasibility considerations are judged to be satisfied.

Saddle Roofs. The term *saddle* is generally used to describe a roof type where a series of parallel cables or other tension members ("sagging" members) hang from an arch or ring beam that completely encircles the roof; parallel tension members ("hogging" members) curve in a perpendicular direction with the effect of pulling the first set of tension members down. All applied loads are resisted by tension in these members. There are several well-known examples of saddle roofs on arena-size structures. To date there have not been any stadium-size saddle roof systems constructed.

Air-supported Roofs. The majority of the covered stadia built to date have air-supported fabric roofs. The structural system typically comprises a structural membrane, restraining cables, and a perimeter ring beam. There is one built example of a metal, air-supported roof utilizing a stainless steel sheet roof membrane that has sufficient strength to preclude the necessity of restraining cables. The distinguishing feature in all of the systems is reliance on air pressure developed within the occupiable space below the roof to support the structure.

A two-way cable net, coupled with internal pressure, provides the structural resistance to wind uplift. All applied loads, including snow load in the deflated condition, are resisted primarily by pure tension in the membrane and cables and by compression with some secondary bending in the perimeter ring beam.

Air-supported roof structures have relatively low profiles allowing for good aerodynamic performance as well as preventing the roof from engaging the floor or seats when deflated. The latter attribute has recently been adopted as a code requirement in the BOCA and other model codes for air-supported structures covering large assembly buildings. The ratios of rise to span for air-supported roofs range between 1:20 and 1:8.

In general, operators of stadia with air-supported roofs are satisfied with their facilities, but wish that the roofs were easier to operate. The preferred plan configuration and roof shape are well suited for stadium applications. The major advantages of air-supported roofs are its relatively low and predictable capital cost and, with the fabric structures, the unsurpassed translucency of the system. The major disadvantages are the risk of deflation and the need for continuous and proper management to prevent deflation and to minimize problems. Air-supported roofs and related structures are further discussed elsewhere in this *Encyclopedia*.

Rigid Domes. Long-span, rigid roof structures may encompass a range of systems and materials including vaults, trusses, and a variety of domes. Neither vaults nor trusses, however, are likely to be feasible applications for major professional sports stadia. A truss system, however, can potentially be used for spanning a football stadium.

The discussion here is limited to rigid, integrated spatial dome systems that may include lamella domes, Schwedler domes, Kewitt domes, and various dome-ribbing systems. Loads are resisted primarily through compression and some secondary bending of the structural elements. The system can be supported on buttresses ei-

Table 2. Capital Costs for Stadium Roof Systems

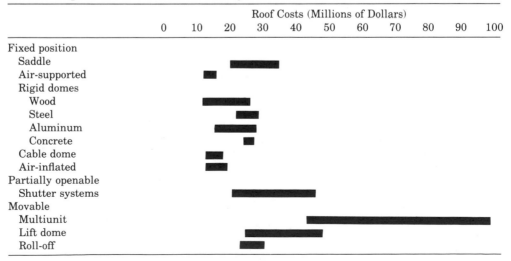

Table 3. Characteristics of Stadium Roof Systems[a]

	Cost Primary	Secondary	Adding Openness	Estimate Reliability	Openness Degree of Openness	Ease of Movement	Risk Experience with System	Complexity	Operator Error	Code and Safety Fire Resistance	Strength	Collapse Resistance	Functional Acoustic	Shadow and Glare	Energy	Maintenance and Operations
Fixed Position																
Saddle	−	−	0	−	−	NR	0	+	++	+	+	+	+	0	0	+
Air-supported	+	−	−	+	0	NR	++	+	−−	+	0	+	0	+	0	−
Rigid domes																
Wood	+	0	0	0	−	NR	+	+	++	+	+	0	0	0	+	+
Steel	−	0	0	0	−	NR	++	+	++	+	+	0	0	0	0	+
Aluminum	+	0	0	0	−	NR	0	+	++	+	+	0	0	0	0	+
Concrete	−	−	0	−	−	NR	+	+	++	+	+	0	0	0	0	+
Cable dome	+	0	0	+	0	NR	+	+	++	+	+	+	+	+	0	+
Air inflated	+	−	0	0	0	NR	−	+	0	+	0	+	+	+	0	0
Partially openable																
Shutter systems	+	−	NR	−	+	+	−	−	−	+	+	0	0	−	−	−
Movable																
Multiunit	−	0	NR	−	++	+	−−	−−	0	+	+	NR	0	+	−	−−
Lift dome	−	−	NR	−	+	−	−−	−−	−	+	+	NR	0	−	−	−−
Roll-off	+	0	NR	0	++	0	−−	−	−	+	+	NR	0	+	−	−

[a] + = the system addresses the issue, ++ = a very good solution; 0 = the system has no particular advantage or disadvantage in this regard; − = the system does not address the issue at all or the issue constitutes a negative point for the system, −− = a strong negative point; NR = a rating is not appropriate or not enough is known about the system to comment.

ther on grade or more likely at a suitable elevation above grade. With the addition of a perimeter tension ring element, the dome system can be employed as a closed structural system. Typical to most compression dome systems, the structural efficiency is best when the rise of the dome is between 1:4 to 1:6 of the span. Flatter profiles can be achieved at a significant cost penalty.

Structural materials for rigid dome systems include steel, aluminum, wood, and steel-reinforced concrete. The majority of long-span fixed roof structures built to date are steel. The two existing steel domes covering professional sports stadia are spherical domes of the Kewitt design (Fig. 23).

Aluminum dome systems have been employed in a significant number of buildings of various sizes. The largest aluminum dome built to date is a spherical shell dome with a circular plan spanning 415 ft.

Wood structures employ glue-laminated wood purlins and heavy timber deck, creating an integral space structure. This is classified by code as Type 4 construction and has excellent fire-resistance characteristics. If pressure treated with an appropriate fire retardant, this type of wooden structure will be considered to be Type 1 noncombustible construction. There are a number of existing wooden domes with spans ranging from 200 to 400 ft. The largest wooden dome built to date is the Tacoma Dome with a span of 525 ft. A wooden dome proprietary system may possibly be the lowest cost rigid, opaque, long-span roof system. The system is relatively cost sensitive to plan

configuration and support conditions, but in a circular configuration may prove to be most economical.

The discussion of concrete domes is limited here to compression domes that carry load by virtue of shell action, primarily in compression and secondary bending. Concrete domes are the heaviest of the various dome types considered. Consequently, a concrete system will have the greatest impact on the supporting superstructure and foundations. Preferred plan configuration of the structure is circular (Fig. 22).

Cable Domes. The cable dome is a proprietary structural framing system utilizing continuous radial and circumferential tension cables and discontinuous struts, prestressed against a perimeter compression ring (Fig. 8). The system may be clad with either translucent tensioned fabric or more conventional metal deck supported by steel joists.

The primary framing elements are radial ridge-and-valley cables emanating from a central, structural steel, tension ring and terminating at a perimeter compression ring beam. The ridge cables are supported by concentric rings of "floating" steel compression struts. A typical strut is supported by a diagonal cable attached at its base and connected to the top of the next strut radially toward the perimeter. The horizontal reaction of the diagonal cable at the base of each strut is resisted by a continuous tension "hoop" that interconnects the bases of all the struts in a ring. The tension hoops are thus concentrically arranged at increasing elevations toward the center of the structure. The net effect is similar to a spatial structure consisting of radial cable trusses in which concentric tension rings have been substituted for the bottom truss cords.

In contrast with other nonair-supported systems, the cable dome is most efficient in a low profile configuration. The optimum rise-to-span ratio is between 1:15 to 1:8 or less. The cost-preferred configurations are either circular or superelliptical. The fire resistance of a fabric-clad cable dome system is roughly equivalent to that of a rigid steel dome. The major exception is that the life-safety consequences of a fire-related or other structural failure is significantly less severe.

Although the development of the cable dome system is relatively new, there is adequate experience to substantiate costs and erection schemes. A fixed, fabric-clad cable dome is the lowest cost, fully translucent, nonair-supported roof system. The erection method and connection details have been worked out and are suitable for very long spans. The basic structural system is also suitable for two different retractable options by virtue of its extremely low weight and the low density and minimal size of the primary framing elements.

Air-inflated Roof Systems. An air-inflated structure differs from an air-supported structure in that the space that is pressurized to maintain the structural stability of the roof membrane is completely contained in the roof system. Similar to the air-supported structure, applied loads are resisted by pure tension in the membrane and reinforcing members. The simplest type of air-inflated roof structure is a pressurized lens. This system consists of two membranes, either sheet steel or cable-restrained fabric nominally identical to an air-supported roof membrane. The space between these two membranes is pressurized to create a lens-shaped inflated structure. The outer membrane

is convex creating a domelike exterior appearance, while the lower ceiling membrane is concave with its low point at the center of the roof.

Partially Openable Systems: Retractable-cladding or Shutter System. A shutter or retractable-cladding system leaves the primary structure in place while opening a portion of the cladding. This retractable concept can be based on any of the structural systems described above. It favors systems that have the minimum visual structural mass and density (Figs. 28 and 29).

Fully Retractable Roofs: Multiunit Systems. The category of multiunit retractable roof systems is potentially broad. The distinguishing characteristic is that the roof system is composed of two or more structural units that are moved to open the roof so that the roof structure is not continuous over the covered area. This sacrifices the efficiency of a continuous space structure. The design of the Skydome in Toronto achieves retractability by employing a structure composed of segmented, one-way, steel arch-truss panels. The concept for a fan dome provides full retraction while allowing a translucent roof in the closed position (Fig. 30).

Lift Dome Openable Roof. For a closed system, the method of moving the roof structure with the least structural consequence to itself would be to lift it straight up without changing its support points. By raising the structure as a unit, the continuity of the system is preserved. The structure would be elevated mechanically on large perimeter towers to create a clerestory at the perimeter of the roof. Mechanical considerations aside, this is probably the least costly structural method for obtaining a movable roof, provided it does not have to be lifted to a great height. The system can be most economically realized with very light roof structures such as the cable dome, the

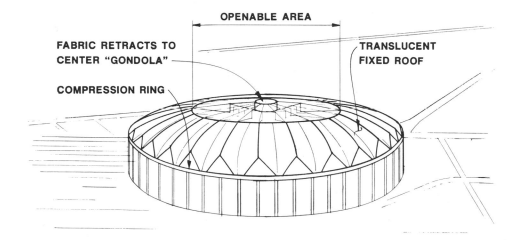

Figure 28. Schematic of center retracting cable dome. Courtesy of Geiger Engineers.

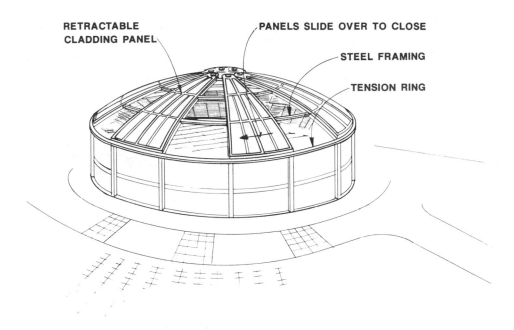

RETRACTABLE
CLADDING PANEL

PANELS SLIDE OVER TO CLOSE

STEEL FRAMING

TENSION RING

Figure 29. "Rolladome" shutter roof in open position. Courtesy of Geiger Engineers.

air-inflated lens, or possibly an aluminum dome. Whether this system accomplishes the desire of opening the facility may be questionable, as the roof structure might have to be lifted quite far before it would be perceived as retracted.

Figure 30. Fan-Dome as proposed for Chicago White Sox. Courtesy of HOK Architects, Inc.

Single-unit Translating (Roll-off) Roof. A retracting roof system can be translated to one side of the facility by rolling or sliding it as a single unit. The advantage of this concept is that the roof's structural continuity does not have to be compromised to accomplish the desired removal. This concept does require a significantly larger site area for the facility than other retractable systems. Ignoring site acquisition costs, the roll-off roof has the potential to be the lowest cost, truly retractable roof system.

The translating structure is fully supported around its perimeter in the closed and open positions. (This would not be necessary if a one-way structural system were used, but the cost associated with long-span, one-way systems probably would preclude their use.) Two sides of the roof structure are supported on parallel tracks that extend outside the superstructure of the facility. In order to utilize the simplest type of rolling mechanical equipment, the roof structure should be a closed structural system, requiring only vertical support at the track.

During the transition, the roof structure will be required to span one way. The inherenet structural advantage of a two-way, or spatial system, therefore, cannot be exploited if the roof must resist a large self-weight in a condition where full support is not available. As a result, the use of a low weight structural system is required, which also will reduce the rolling weight that must be carried by the mechanical equipment.

Two structural systems are potentially well suited to the concept: a superelliptical, air-inflated lens roof or a superelliptical, fabric-clad cable dome (Fig. 31). The superelliptical plan shape is necessary in order to create two nominally parallel sides to accommodate retraction. Utilizing structural steel instead of the more common precast concrete for the perimeter compression ring beam results in either of the structural systems having a total unit weight between 8 and 10 lb/ft^2. By comparison, the retractable roof system for the Skydome in Toronto has an estimated unit weight of 50 lb/ft^2.

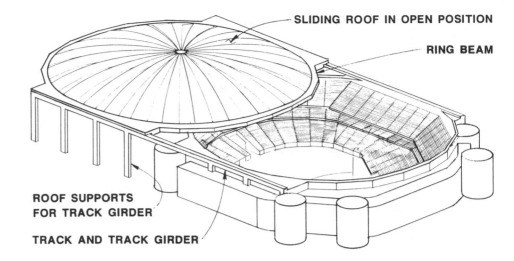

SLIDING ROOF IN OPEN POSITION

RING BEAM

ROOF SUPPORTS
FOR TRACK GIRDER

TRACK AND TRACK GIRDER

Figure 31. Single-unit translating ("roll-off") roof. Courtesy of Geiger Engineers.

Comparison of Dome Systems. Tables 2 and 3 illustrate comparative costs and features of the stadium roof systems described here. In Table 2, probable cost ranges are shown. These are all for a stadium roof of about 375,000 ft^2 in plan area, with 1988 construction costs. The cost ranges in some cases reflect varying possible arrangements or options for each system. In other cases, the ranges reflect the uncertainty of costs or the disparity between proponents' claims and available historical data. The primary roof costs generally include the full roof structure (not including columns), roof decking, ring beam, roof covering, flashing, insulation, and acoustic treatment or other basic ceiling finish.

BIBLIOGRAPHY

1. B. Fletcher, *History of Architecture on the Comparative Method,* 17th ed., rev. by R. A. Cordingley, Charles Scribner's Sons, New York, 1967.

General References

R. T. Packard, ed., *Architectural Graphic Standards,* 7th ed., John Wiley & Sons, Inc., New York, 1981.

R. L. Knapp, "Sports Arenas," *Time Saver Standards for Architectural Design Data,* 2nd ed., McGraw-Hill, New York, 1980, p. 1176. This article provides an overview of planning requirements for indoor sports arenas generally having a capacity of up to 20,000 seats, which may serve as a useful comparison to the present article. "Olympic Domes First of Their Kind," *Engineering News Record,* (Mar. 6, 1986). This article discusses the cable dome or cable net system for construction of stadium roofs.

"The Hybrid Arena," *Engineered Design and Construction,* (Mar. 1985). This article discusses the cable dome or cable net system for construction of stadium roofs.

"Enclosed Stadiums Sprout under Air-Supported Roofs," *Building Design & Construction,* (Jan. 1981). This article describes applications of air-supported roof systems.

See also MEMBRANE STRUCTURES; RECREATIONAL FACILITIES; SPACE FRAMES; SWIMMING POOLS

RONALD J. LABINSKI, AIA
Hellmuth, Obata Kassabaum
    Architects
Kansas City, Missouri

DOUG KINGSBURY
Kingsbury & Associates
Kansas City, Missouri

SPRINKLERS AND OTHER FIRE CONTROL METHODS

FIRE ALARM, DETECTION, AND COMMUNICATION SYSTEMS

Building fire alarm, detection, and communication systems are primarily intended to provide life safety for occupants, so that occupants have sufficient time to safely exit. Alarms may be initiated manually by a person detecting a fire or automatically by equipment designed to detect the presence of fire. At a minimum, a fire alarm system is designed to notify building occupants of emergency conditions for evacuation purposes. They may also be used to

1. Alert organized assistance within the building (trained staff), at a site (fire brigade), or outside a site (municipal fire department).
2. Detect *specific* stages of a fire—incipient, growing, or fully developed.
3. Activate suppression systems and other active and passive fire protection measures, eg, activate smoke-control systems or close fire doors.
4. Supervise fire protection systems for trouble that might render the system inoperative.

The basic concept for fire alarm system design may be envisioned by a simple system familiar to most persons, a school building fire alarm system. An initiating device, such as a manual fire alarm pull station, is activated by a person who detects a fire. A signal is transmitted via a control path (in this case hard wiring) to a processing point (main fire alarm control panel). By a predetermined design, the input signal results in a specific output signal transmitted to indicating devices, such as alarm bells. Electric current in a supervised system may flow continually in a closed-circuit design so that interruption, via a ground fault or short, results in a trouble alarm. The building zone where a device is activated is shown graphically at a central location on an annunciator panel. These basic concepts are shown schematically in Figure 1. Many building fire alarm systems are essentially this simple, and advances in technology have not dramatically changed these simple systems, which are used in small office, mercantile, and commercial buildings. In single-family residences or dwelling units, single-station smoke detectors form the entire detector/processor/alerting "system."

Until the late 1960s and early 1970s, even large buildings to a great extent used relatively simple fire alarm systems based on manual fire alarm pull stations and alarm bells. More sophisticated emergency alarm systems, using prerecorded voice messages and integrating other fire safety features such as elevator recall and smoke control, were developed in response to a series of significant and highly publicized fires in high-rise buildings. The U.S. General Services Administration (GSA) focused attention on the development of integrated fire alarm systems and is largely responsible for initiating the development of the high-rise fire alarm/voice communication system as it is used today (1). GSA developed a guide specification for fire alarm systems (2) which provides a good blueprint for the design of integrated fire alarm systems. These integrated fire alarm/voice communication systems are not limited in application to high-rise buildings but may be found in large convention hall, public assembly, mercantile/shopping mall, health-care, and multiuse facilities. The development of integrated fire

alarm/voice communication systems, together with improvements in smoke-detector technology driven by the residential smoke-detector market and computer-controlled signal processing, have advanced the design and capability of fire alarm systems.

Fire Signatures and Types of Detectors

Fires produce a variety of environmental changes or "signatures" that can be detected by available hardware (3). Fire signatures that can be detected are heat, aerosol (smoke particulate), and light radiation. Heat is an energy-release signature that is readily detected. Convected thermal energy causes an increase in the air temperature of the surrounding environment. The time required for release of sufficient energy to produce significant heat varies, depending on fire growth, but it can be measured in minutes or even hours. Heat detectors are the oldest type of automatic detection device. Fixed-temperature-type heat detectors alarm when a specified temperature is reached. Rate-of-rise heat detectors alarm when the rate of temperature change of the environment exceeds a predetermined value, typically 15°F (8.3°C) per minute. Compensation features are built in to eliminate false alarms from normal changes in ambient temperature. Combination heat detectors combine the features of fixed temperature and rate-of-rise detectors. Heat detectors are best suited for fire detection in small, confined spaces where relatively large, rapidly growing fires are likely to occur (eg, where flammable liquids are stored). They are particularly suited for property-protection applications. Because of their relatively long activation time, they are generally not suited for life-safety applications.

Aerosol signatures in a fire environment result from the release of solid and liquid particulate. These particulates may range in size from 5×10^{-4} to 10 μm. Small particles, having diameters less than 0.3 μm, do not scatter light efficiently and are classified as invisible. Ionization smoke detectors are most effective in measuring invisible particulate, which is more common in high energy, open-flaming conditions. Larger particulate, particles having diameters greater than 0.3 μm, scatter light and are classified as visible. Photoelectric smoke detectors are most effective in measuring visible smoke, which is common in smoldering fires. Smoke detectors provide considerably faster detection time than heat detectors and are appropriate for life-safety and high property-value applications. Detection time is usually measured in seconds. Smoke detectors are also used in locations for specific functional applications. They are located in HVAC system ductwork to shut down supply and recirculation fans in the presence of smoke. They are located in elevator lobbies to activate controls to prevent elevators from opening onto smoke-filled spaces and at doors to activate closure devices in smoke/fire partitions.

The earliest energy signatures detectable with standard hardware are infrared (ir) and ultraviolet (uv) radiation. Ir and uv sensors detect radiation given off by flames or glowing embers. Detection times are very rapid and can be measured in seconds or milliseconds. These detectors

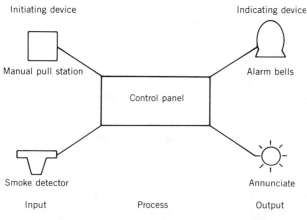

Initiating device | Indicating device

Manual pull station | Alarm bells

Control panel

Smoke detector | Annunciate

Input | Process | Output

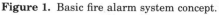

Figure 1. Basic fire alarm system concept.

Table 1. Detector Application and Occupancy Considerations

Detector	Relative Response Time	Relative False Alarm Rate	Application and Occupancies
Heat	Slow	Low	Confined spaces; well suited for property protection and process controls; flammable liquid storage areas, conveyor belts, power plants
Smoke	Fast	Medium	Life safety and high value property protection; residential sleeping areas, corridors, and elevator lobbies of commercial, mercantile, and business occupancies; health care, including smoke partition door closure; area protection for computer rooms; HVAC ducts for fan shutdown; residential sleeping areas
Flame	Very fast	High	Flammable material storage and processing; aircraft hangars; offshore oil and gas platforms; hyperbaric chambers; fuel loading platforms

are typically used in high hazard areas where hazardous atmospheres or very rapidly growing fires may occur. Table 1 summarizes detector application considerations and typical occupancy applications.

The application of codes and standards for fire detection, alarm, and communication systems is outlined in the *Fire Alarm Signaling Systems Handbook* (4). Codes specify when detection and alarm systems are required. Examples are the NFPA Life Safety Code (5), and model building codes, such as the BOCA National Building Code (6). Installation standards provide details on how the specified protection is to be achieved. An example is the Protective Signaling System and Detection Device Standards of the NFPA, eg, the 72 series. Performance standards specify the capabilities and functions required of the hardware. Nationally recognized testing laboratories, such as Underwriters Laboratories (UL) and Factory Mutual (FM) have developed performance standards. There is overlap in the codes and standards in terms of these categories. Protection standards often contain requirements for both installation and performance. The same holds true for installation standards.

Basic System Design

Fire detection, alarm, and communication systems must meet applicable codes and standards as mandated by local jurisdictions (the "authority having jurisdiction"). A high-rise fire alarm and voice communication system can be used to frame basic design considerations. The system should be capable of:

1. Directing occupants of the fire zone to the outside or to an area of refuge.

2. Notifying the central control center or off-site central station of the existence and location of a fire.

3. Delaying transmission of alarms outside the immediate fire area until an authority in charge considers the sounding of alarms to other areas appropriate.

4. Operating in a simple and reliable manner.

5. Providing indication of trouble on all necessary equipment.

The audible fire-alarm signal to the occupants of the fire zone should include continuous sounding devices and/or voice direction that momentarily silences the continuous-sounding devices. There is a difference of opinion on the desirability of continuous-sounding devices. Some maintain that such devices are needed to get the undivided attention of the occupant, whereas others contend that noise makers only add to the confusion. Typically, a message is sent to the fire area, floor above the fire area, and floor below the fire area. However, there are some notable exceptions to this approach. The capability should be provided at the main control panel to manually activate voice and sounding-device alarms in any combination of zones. The voice system should be capable of transmitting to all zones simultaneously. In many jurisdictions, the emergency voice system is prohibited from being part of the same system as the building music/paging systems.

The control center should be located adjacent to the primary fire-department arrival point. If the control center is integrated with other building systems (ie, security, energy management controls) and is remote from the fire-department response point, a separate annunciator panel should be provided at the primary fire-department response point. In larger buildings, additional annunciators may be necessary at secondary fire-department response points.

A fire-alarm voice-communication system typically includes several components:

1. Main fire alarm panel.
2. Primary annunciator panel.
3. Remote annunciators.
4. Fire department two-way telephone systems.
5. Remote sounding devices.
6. Input devices.
7. Peripheral equipment and controls.

A conceptual example of this type of system is shown in Figure 2.

Testing and Maintenance

Fire-alarm and detection-system reliability is dependent on testing and maintenance. This is the responsibility of the owner and the designated building manager. Many owners elect to contract the testing and maintenance services to specialists, typically vendors of the equipment. Reliability decreases as maintenance requirements are ignored. Systems malfunction or fail because of faulty design, poor installation, inadequate installation testing, vandalism, and lack of maintenance. Every fire alarm system should be completely tested after installation to assure that the system functions as designed. All input and output devices, control functions, and supervisory systems should be tested. Tests should include a check of all conductors and an operational check of all initiating- and indicating-device circuits and equipment. Detector sensitivity and restoration should be checked, and auxiliary power tests should be conducted. Complete records and

documentation of all tests should be maintained. Applicable codes and standards provide specific requirements for system testing. Reference 7 provides information for performing installation wiring and operational acceptance tests.

Technical Advancements

Multiplexing is a signaling method characterized by simultaneous and/or sequential transmission of multiple signals on a communication channel. Modern multiplexing systems use microprocessors or computers. Often, only initiating-device circuits are multiplexed to remote data-gathering points (transponders), whereas indicating-device circuits remain hard wired.

Addressable fire alarm systems are similar to multiplex systems except that transponders are located in the initiating devices themselves. Advantages include wiring reductions and the ability to locate alarms and trouble conditions specifically.

Intelligent systems are an extension of addressable systems where detectors send analog information to the control panel, which makes the alarm "decision." Intelligent systems improve detector reliability in terms of better filtering of false fire signatures, reducing false alarms, and increasing discrimination. Individual detectors are fully identifiable and tests can be performed at the control panel. Expanding communication technologies, including fiber optics, should increase the extent of building management systems. These systems incorporate security and energy management systems.

Engineering advances in fire-alarm-system design include improved techniques for calculating the audibility of signaling devices such as horns, bells, and speakers in different areas of a building. Response time of detectors, particularly heat sensors, can be estimated. These esti-

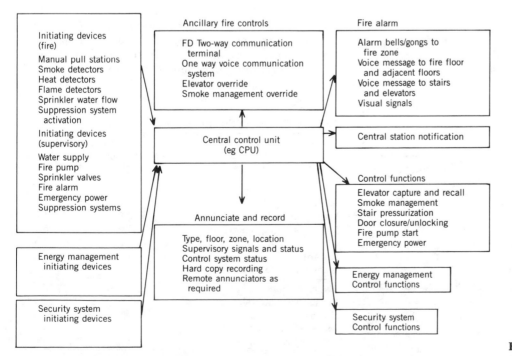

Figure 2. Example of an integrated system.

mating techniques address factors such as ceiling height and design, ventilation flow, and fire signature variables and provide an improved basis for detector spacing and location.

AUTOMATIC SPRINKLER SYSTEMS

Sprinkler systems were first installed in textile mills in the 1850s (8). Technical advancements since these early years have primarily focused on the fire-control effectiveness of the sprinkler head itself. Although sprinkler heads were first introduced around 1878, the first major technical advancement was the development of the standard sprinkler by Factory Mutual in the 1950s (9). The standard sprinkler and subsequent sprinkler head models have been designed to discharge water in a downward direction, with a uniform and more effective spray pattern than their predecessors (Fig. 3).

Modern sprinkler systems are designed to respond to a fire during its incipiency, discharging water in sufficient quantities to control or extinguish the fire before excessive damage or injuries and loss of life occur. The early systems installed in textile mills were designed to prevent destruction of the entire building or complex; current systems can contain fires to a portion of a building or floor, or even to part of a single room. The design and installation of modern sprinkler systems require consideration of (1)

building design and construction, (2) occupancy hazards, and (3) available water supplies.

The performance history of sprinkler systems is outstanding. Fire loss surveys estimate that sprinklers have performed satisfactorily in more than 96% of the cases recorded (11). Records kept by the National Fire Protection Association (NFPA) reveal that no multiple life loss fires have occurred in fully sprinklered buildings. Factory Mutual (FM) estimates property losses to be 10 or more times higher in unsprinklered industrial and commercial facilities (12).

Nearly three fourths of all sprinkler system failures are the result of preventible causes such as water to the system shut off or partial rather than complete sprinkler coverage (Table 2). Misconceptions are frequently expressed about the performance of sprinkler systems. For instance, concern that water sprays may cause panic among building occupants, preventing or delaying escape, cannot be documented in NFPA records of more than 10,000 fires in sprinklered buildings (13). A concern that all sprinkler heads discharge water in a fire, causing excessive water damage, is not true. Normally, each sprinkler head opens independently when heated to its activation temperature. Typically, only the number of sprinklers necessary to control or extinguish the fire are activated. As illustrated in Figure 4, records for wet-pipe sprinkler systems indicate that more than half of the fires were controlled by two or less sprinklers, and in 90% of the fires control was achieved with 10 or less sprinklers (14). Although accidental water discharge can occur from a sprinkler system because of mechanical failure, freezing, overheating, or corrosion effects, this is a rare occurrence. Rigorous installation requirements, component testing, and maintenance substantially reduce the potential for such failures.

The principal design standard for automatic sprinkler systems is NFPA 13, Installation of Sprinkler Systems. NFPA 13 provides detailed guidance on water supplies, system components, spacing and location of sprinklers, and system performance requirements for a wide range of system types and applications. Compliance with NFPA 13

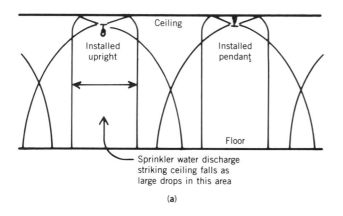

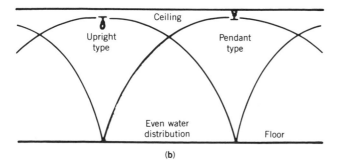

Figure 3. (a) Distribution pattern of water from old style sprinklers (previous to 1953); (b) Distribution pattern of water from standard sprinklers (in use since 1953) (10). Courtesy of the National Fire Protection Association.

Table 2. Causes of Sprinkler System Failures[a]

| | Percent of Failures | |
	NFPA Data	New York Data
Preventable Causes		
Water to sprinklers shut off	27.7	56.6
Partial protection	8.1	6.1
Inadequate water supply	9.9	1.5
Faulty building construction	5.9	5.1
Obstruction to spray distribution	8.2	0.5
Hazard of occupancy	7.7	
Inadequate maintenance	8.4	
Unpreventable Causes		
Premature water shut off	7.8	
Explosion	5.9	13.8
External exposures		4.1
Other/miscellaneous	1.9	5.6

[a] After Ref. 11.

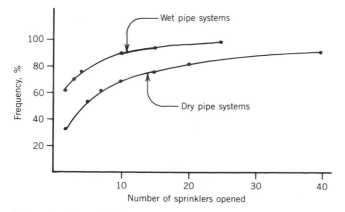

Figure 4. Record of frequency and number of sprinklers opened in actual fire incidents (14).

is customarily required by code/enforcement authorities. Nationally recognized building codes reference NFPA 13 as the design standard for automatic sprinkler systems. Several other NFPA standards have been adopted for automatic sprinkler protection of high-piled storage in warehouses. These special hazards [eg, solid piled storage greater than 15 ft (4.6 m) high or palletized or rack storage greater than 12 ft (3.7 m)] high are outside the intended scope of NFPA 13 and are covered by NFPA 231, Indoor General Storage; NFPA 231C, Rack Storage of Materials; and NFPA 231D, Storage of Rubber Tires. NFPA 13D, Sprinkler Systems for One and Two Family Dwellings and Mobile Homes, has been adopted to address sprinkler system design regulations for residential applications.

Sprinkler system components such as sprinkler heads, pipe and fittings, valves, and pumps are listed for use in sprinkler systems by testing laboratories such as Underwriters Laboratories (UL) or FM. For example, sprinkler heads are listed by UL in accordance with UL 199, Automatic Sprinklers for Fire Protection Service.

Operating Principles and Basic System Design

A sprinkler system consists of several components, including (1) one or more water supplies, (2) a network of piping, (3) geometrically spaced sprinkler heads, (4) valves, pumps, and other associated hardware, and (5) alarms. The systems are activated by heating of the sprinkler heads near the fire until a predetermined operating temperature is exceeded, opening the sprinkler head and discharging a uniform water spray.

There are several types of automatic sprinkler systems, including (1) wet pipe, (2) dry pipe, (3) preaction, (4) deluge, (5) combined, and (6) special. All six types include sprinkler heads and piping network. However, the design and accompanying hardware (eg, valves, supervision, pumps, alarms) can vary considerably.

Wet-pipe Type. These systems are the least complex in terms of required components. The piping network contains pressurized water. When a fire occurs, activation of a sprinkler head results in immediate application of water

in the fire area. These systems provide a highly valuable means of fire control and usually result in minimal water damage. However, such systems should not be used in areas subject to freezing without special considerations, eg, the use of antifreeze solutions. Because of cost and maintenance demands, antifreeze solutions are usually only used in small, unheated areas.

Dry-pipe Type. These systems are used in unheated areas of buildings where freezing and thawing are potential problems. The pipe network usually contains air or nitrogen, under pressure. When a sprinkler activates, the pressure in the system is reduced, opening a dry-pipe valve to the water supply. The water is then forced under pressure through the system to the "open" sprinkler(s). The response time to actually spray water into the fire area is slower than for a wet-pipe system, frequently resulting in activation of additional sprinklers (Fig. 4). Special considerations include (1) the capability to rapidly repressurize the system, (2) total system drainage after operation, and (3) heated areas for the dry valve and auxiliary equipment.

Preaction Type. In these systems the piping network is filled with air. The system may or may not be pressurized. A heat-sensitive detector is used to sound an alarm and open a control valve, filling the pipe network with water in the event of a fire. The system then behaves as a wet-pipe system, water being discharged from opened sprinkler heads. However, the alarm provides an opportunity for occupants to extinguish the fire manually before water discharge from the sprinkler system. This feature is particularly attractive in areas such as computer facilities or control rooms where accidental water discharge and delayed detection are both undesirable.

Deluge Type. In this type of system, all sprinkler heads are "open." The system is activated by a heat-sensing detector that opens a deluge valve, discharging water from all sprinkler heads in the area or zone. These systems are commonly employed in areas such as industrial-processing plants or aircraft hangars where initiating fires can be expected to grow rapidly (eg, flammable liquids fires). Where such systems are employed, large water demands and unusual ceiling configurations require careful analysis during the system design stage.

Combined Dry-pipe and Preaction Systems. In these systems the basic features of dry pipe and preaction systems are combined. On detecting fire, a heat-sensing detector opens a water control valve and an air exhauster at the end of the unheated pipe network. The piping network, initially pressurized with air, is filled with water and operates as a wet-pipe system. In addition, if the heat detector fails to detect the fire, the system will behave as a dry-pipe system.

Special Types. Special systems typically do not comply fully with the requirements in NFPA 13. They generally involve limited-capacity water supplies, reduced pipe sizes, partial coverage, and nonstandard sprinkler heads and auxiliary hardware. These systems are used where conditions make it advisable to install sprinklers, but it is not feasible to meet the requirements of NFPA 13. They employ such features as small-capacity pressure tanks, substandard water supplies, and partial coverage and address special property or life-safety problems. The reliability and performance of such systems to achieve the desired level of protection must be carefully addressed.

Water-supply Requirements

Acceptable sources of water include public street mains, gravity tanks, reservoirs, fire pumps, pressure tanks, rivers, lakes, and wells. The preferred primary supply is a reliable public water supply of adequate pressure and capacity to meet the sprinkler system and associated fire department demands. All sprinkler systems must have at least one adequate "automatic" water supply, eg, a source of water that is not dependent on manual operations to actually supply the water to the system. Frequently, multiple sources of water supply are necessary, depending on the capacity, pressure, and reliability of the primary source, the size and occupancy type of the building, and the relative importance of the facility and its operations. A typical water supply design for a sprinkler system is illustrated in Figure 5.

Several factors influence the actual water supply requirements for a particular application. Included are the hazards of the occupancy, potential obstructions to water spray, ceiling height, unprotected vertical openings, size of individual areas, exposure hazards, the type of sprinkler system (eg, wet or dry), and the building's height and hydraulic friction losses in the piping network. Frequently, pressure losses require that the available pressure be supplemented by pumps or pressure tanks, eg, in high-rise buildings.

Hazard Classification and Pipe Sizing

The primary consideration in determining the water-supply demand and subsequent pipe sizes necessary to deliver the demand to the sprinkler heads is the relative hazard of

Table 3. Examples of Occupancy Classifications

Light Hazard Occupancies
Churches
Clubs
Educational Institutions
Hospitals
Museums
Offices
Restaurant seating areas

Ordinary Hazard Occupancies (Group 1)	*Ordinary Hazard Occupancies (Group 2)*	*Ordinary Hazard Occupancies (Group 3)*
Parking garages	Cereal mills	Feed mills
Canneries	Cold storage	Paper and pulp mills
Electronic plants	Libraries	Repair garages
Restaurant service areas	Machine shops	Warehouses (moderate to high combustibility)
	Mercantile	

Extra Hazard Occupancies (Group 1)	*Extra Hazard Occupancies (Group 2)*
Combustible hydraulic fluid areas	Asphalt saturating
Metal extruding	Flammable liquids
Plywood manufacturing	Spraying
Rubber reclaiming	Mobile home assembly plants
Plastic foam upholstering	Solvent cleaning
	Varnish and paint dipping

the occupancy. NFPA 13 has adopted three basic hazard classes: light, ordinary, and extra. There are three subcategories in the ordinary hazard class and two in the extra hazard class. Typical examples for each hazard classification are provided in Table 3. Minimum water supply requirements (eg, pressure, flow rate, and duration) have been established for each hazard class.

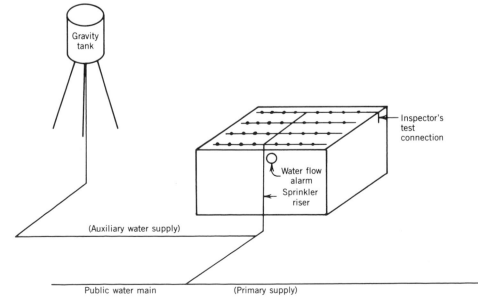

Figure 5. Typical water supplies for automatic sprinkler systems.

Table 4. Guide to Water Supply Requirements for Pipe-schedule Sprinkler Systems[a]

Occupancy Classification	Residual Pressure Required[b]	Acceptable Flow at Base of Riser[c]	Duration in Minutes[d]
Light hazard	15 psi[e]	500–750 gpm[f]	30–60
Ordinary hazard Group 1	15 psi or higher	700–1000 gpm	60–90
Group 2	15 psi or higher	850–1500 gpm	60–90
Group 3	Pressure and flow requirements for sprinklers and hose streams to be determined by authority having jurisdiction.		60–120
High-piled storage	Pressure and flow requirements for sprinklers and hose streams to be determined by authority having jurisdiction. See Chapter 7 of NFPA 13 and NFPA 231 and NFPA 231C.		
High-rise buildings	Pressure and flow requirements for sprinklers and hose streams to be determined by authority having jurisdiction. See Chapter 8 of NFPA 13.		
Extra hazard	Pressure and flow requirements for sprinklers and hose streams to be determined by authority having jurisdiction.		

[a] Ref. 15. Courtesy of the National Fire Protection Association. This reprinted materials is not the complete and official position of the NFPA on the referenced subject, which is represented only by the standard in its entirety.
[b] The pressure required at the base of the sprinkler riser(s) is defined as the residual pressure required at the elevation of the highest sprinkler plus the pressure required to reach this elevation.
[c] The lower figure is the minimum flow, including hose streams ordinarily acceptable for pipe-schedule sprinkler systems. The higher flow should normally suffice for all cases under each group.
[d] The lower duration figure is ordinarily acceptable where remote-station water-flow alarm service or equivalent is provided. The higher duration figure should normally suffice for all cases under each group.
[e] 1 psi = 0.0689 bar.
[f] 1 gpm = 3.785 L/min.

Pipe sizes may be determined by one of two methods: pipe schedule or hydraulic calculations. When using pipe-schedule methods for sizing pipe, the total water supply required for the sprinkler system can be determined from Table 4. Included in this table is an estimate of fire-department hose-stream demand. However, the hose-stream demand should be carefully addressed for each sprinkler system design to assure that the estimation is reasonable for the conditions.

A hydraulically designed sprinkler system uses the Hazen–Williams pressure-loss calculation method for sizing pipe. It is based on providing a minimum water-spray density [gpm/ft² (L/min/m²)] over a specified area of sprinkler operation, and is expressed as

$$p = \frac{4.52}{C^{1.85}\, d^{4.87}} \times Q^{1.85}$$

where

p = friction loss/ft of pipe (psi)
d = internal pipe diameter (in.)
Q = flow (gpm)
C = Hazen–Williams coefficient

In SI units:

$$p = 6.05 \times \frac{Q^{1.85}}{c^{1.85}\, d^{4.87}} \times 10^5$$

where

p = bars/m of pipe
Q = L/min
d = mm

Values for the C coefficient, a measure of the smoothness of a pipe lining, range from 100 to 150 for common sprinkler piping (see Table 5). The C value is one of several approximations and varies as a function of the life of the pipe and water quality.

The required water density, area of coverage, and total water supply are based on the occupancy classifications. Table 6 lists the combined sprinkler and hose stream flow rates and duration for hydraulically based designs. The area–density requirements are given in Figure 6. Systems must only be calculated to satisfy a single point on the appropriate design curve, providing the designer with flexibility relative to available water supplies.

Table 5. Hazen–Williams C Values[a]

Pipe or Tube	C Value[b]
Unlined cast or ductile iron	100
Black steel (dry systems including preaction)	100
Black steel (wet systems including deluge)	120
Galvanized (all)	120
Plastic (listed)—all	150
Cement-lined cast or ductile iron	140
Copper tube or stainless steel	150

[a] Ref. 16. Courtesy of the National Fire Protection Association. This reprinted materials is not the complete and official position of the NFPA on the referenced subject which is represented only by the standard in its entirety.
[b] The authority having jurisdiction may recommend other C values.

Hand calculation of friction losses by the use of the Hazen–Williams formula is very tedious for other than small systems. Several computer programs are available that can be used to perform these calculations. A detailed review of selection programs is presented in reference (18).

Sprinkler Heads

Automatic sprinkler heads are thermosensitive devices that "open" at a predetermined temperature. The heat-sensitive operating element may be a fusible metal alloy, an organic softening material, or an expanding liquid contained in a glass bulb (Fig. 7). Modern sprinkler heads are classified according to the size of the discharge opening (Table 7) and the temperature rating of the operating element (Table 8).

The discharge opening and the deflector are designed to provide specific spray characteristics. The different temperature ratings are used to assure that sprinklers do not inadvertently open due to ambient temperature conditions. For example ordinary rated sprinklers [135–170°F (57–77°C)] are used in office buildings, but in a warehouse where ambient conditions can be expected to vary significantly an intermediate or high temperature sprinkler may be required.

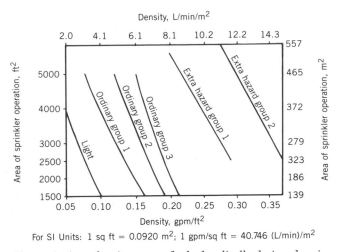

Figure 6. Area-density curves for hydraulically designed sprinkler systems (17). Courtesy of the National Fire Protection Association.

Sprinkler heads are evaluated and "listed" for specific applications by UL and FM. Listed sprinklers are tested to evaluate a wide range of performance parameters in order to assure dependable performance under actual fire conditions. Table 9 lists typical performance tests used to evaluate sprinkler heads. Listed sprinklers are marked (Fig. 7) to provide information on year and manufacturer, temperature rating (including color coding in accordance with Table 7), and general type.

System Supervision and Alarm

Electrical supervision is required for system components such as valves and pumps as well as for water-flow detection and water supply system monitoring. Typically, supervisory systems consist of detection devices and electrical monitoring systems, signal transmission circuits, and supervisory signals (eg, alarms) at designated locations. Such systems detect water flow due to an open sprinkler, leakage, or an accidental valve trip. They also detect other

Table 6. Table and Design Curves for Determining Density, Area of Sprinkler Operation and Minimum Water-supply Requirements for Hydraulically Designed Sprinkler Systems[a]

Hazard Classification	Sprinklers Only, gpm[b]	Inside Hose, gpm	Total Combined Inside and Outside Hose, gpm	Duration, min
Light	See 2-2.1.2.1[c]	0, 50, or 100	100	30
Ordinary group 1	See 2-2.1.2.1	0, 50, or 100	250	60–90
Ordinary group 2	See 2-2.1.2.1	0, 50, or 100	250	60–90
Ordinary group 3	See 2-2.1.2.1	0, 50, or 100	500	60–120
Extra hazard group 1	See 2-2.1.2.1	0, 50, or 100	500	90–120
Extra hazard group 2	See 2-2.1.2.1	0, 50, or 100	1000	120

[a] Ref. 17. Courtesy of the National Fire Protection Association. This reprinted materials is not the complete and official position of the NFPA on the referenced subject which is represented only by the standard in its entirety.
[b] 1 gpm = 3.785 L/min.
[c] NFPA 13.

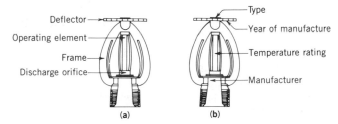

Figure 7. Typical sprinkler head design. (**a**) Components; (**b**) identification markings.

operating problems such as inadvertently closed valves and water supply failure. There are various types of supervisory systems that can (1) notify building emergency personnel, (2) alert building occupants, and (3) signal the local fire department. Also, a water-motor-powered alarm is located on the outside of the building to provide an outside alarm in the event of water flow somewhere in the system.

Testing, Approval, and Maintenance

Four general types of acceptance tests are required for sprinkler systems:

1. Flushing of underground connections
2. Hydrostatic testing
3. Testing of dry-pipe system components
4. Tests of drainage facilities

Table 7. Orifice Size and Temperature Ratings of Automatic Sprinkler Heads[a]

| Orifice Type | Nominal Orifice Size | | Discharge Coefficient |
	in.	mm	K
Small orifice	1/4	6.4	1.3–1.5
Small orifice	5/16	7.9	1.8–2.0
Small orifice	3/8	9.5	2.5–2.9
Small orifice	7/16	11.1	4.0–4.4
Standard orifice	1/2	12.7	5.3–5.8
Large orifice	17/32	13.5	7.4–8.2

[a] From UL 199, standard for Automatic Sprinkler Systems for Fire Protection Service. Courtesy of the Underwriters Laboratories Inc. Copyright 1986.

Table 9. Examples of Sprinkler Head Performance Tests

Leakage
Corrosion
Water hammer
Cold soldering
Flame strength
High temperature
Flow calibration
Spray distribution
Pressure operation
Hydrostatic strength
Short-term/long-term leak testing
Load and strength of operating element

Typically, the sprinkler system installer is responsible for approval testing of the system and completion of appropriate reports and documentation. Approval is granted by the local authority having jurisdiction.

Wet-pipe sprinkler systems require very little maintenance. However, other types, such as dry-pipe or deluge systems, require periodic maintenance of associated hardware such as dry-pipe valves and accompanying detection devices. Although maintenance requirements are modest, sprinkler systems should be inspected routinely (as frequently as weekly), and critical components should be periodically tested. Inspections are necessary to ensure that control valves are properly positioned, that fire pumps will deliver the necessary water flow, that storage tanks are adequately filled, and that the sprinkler heads and piping have not been damaged or blocked in a manner that could cause poor system performance. Detailed requirements for sprinkler-system maintenance are contained in NFPA 13A, Sprinkler Maintenance.

Technical Advancements

Recent advancements in sprinkler technology include development of several new special-purpose sprinkler heads. Two prominent examples are the residential head and the early suppression fast response (ESFR) head. Both sprinklers are characterized by a more sensitive operating element and unique water spray characteristics.

The residential sprinkler resembles a standard sprinkler. Typically, it has a 165°F (74°C) temperature rating

Table 8. Temperature Ratings and Color Codes for Automatic Sprinklers[a]

| Temperature Rating | Operating Temperature | | Color | Maximum Ceiling Temperature | |
	°F	°C		°F	°C
Ordinary	135–170	57.2–76.7	Uncolored[b]	100	38
Intermediate	175–225	79.4–107	White	150	66
High	250–300	121–149	Blue	225	107
Extra high	325–375	163–191	Red	300	149
Very extra high	400–475	204–246	Green	375	191
Ultra high	500–575	260–302	Orange	475	246

[a] Sprinklers with an operating temperature of 135°F (57.2°C) may be colored black.
[b] From UL 199, standard for Automatic Sprinkler Systems for Fire Protection Service. Courtesy of Underwriters Laboratories, Inc. Copyright 1986.

and a ½-in. nominal discharge opening. However, it will respond much earlier in a fire and has spray characteristics that permit substantially lower water supplies [18–26 gpm (68–98 L/min)]. The scope of application of residential sprinkler systems is limited by requirements in NFPA 13 and NFPA 13D.

The ESFR sprinkler head was developed to protect palletized, solid-piled, and rack storage of common materials stored up to 25 ft (7.6 m) high in warehouses and similar occupancies having ceiling heights up to 30 ft (9.1 m). FM has developed installation guidelines and a "listing" or approval standard for such devices. The ESFR sprinkler has response characteristics similar to residential sprinklers, but the 0.7-in. (17.8-mm) discharge orifice is considerably larger than those in residential or standard sprinklers. However, although each sprinkler requires a relatively higher flow rate than typically needed for conventional system designs, it is only necessary to design the system to supply a total of 12 sprinklers at an operating pressure of 50 psi (3.45 bars or 345 kPa). The intent of the ESFR design is to provide rapid and full extinguishment of fires in high challenge, expensive commodities while the fire is confined to a small area.

SPECIAL HAZARDS FIRE-SUPPRESSION SYSTEMS

Special hazards such as flammable liquid processes and storage, electrically energized equipment, and hazards susceptible to water damage are frequently not protected by automatic sprinklers because of the poor suppression effectiveness of water or the potential for collateral damage. Halon, carbon dioxide, and dry chemical systems are commonly used to protect these special hazards. Such systems can be total-flooding or local-application types. Total-flooding systems discharge agent throughout the entire enclosure, whereas local-application systems protect specific process areas or equipment. Basically, any of these suppression systems is comprised of three components: (1) agent storage (tanks, cylinders), (2) actuation and control devices (manual switches, automatic detectors, and control panels), and (3) a distribution system (piping, valves, nozzles).

Total-flooding Halon 1301

Halogenated suppression agents are used in areas such as computer rooms, aircraft engines, telephone exchanges, and switch gear rooms because of their relative effectiveness and their low impact on non-fire-related damage. Although there are several types of halogenated suppression agents, Halon 1301 (bromotrifluoromethane) is most commonly used in total–flooding systems. Halon 1301 rapidly suppresses fires by cooling the flame reaction zone and interrupting the combustion reaction. The basic concepts used in the design of these systems include (1) early detection and alarm, (2) rapid agent discharge (less than 10 sec), and (3) maintenance of a uniform, well-mixed concentration of the agent for a specified time.

Although the toxicity of Halon 1301 to humans appears minimal at low concentrations (< 5–7%) and short exposure periods (< 10 min), unnecessary exposure should be avoided. NFPA 12A, Standard on Halon 1301 Fire Extinguishing Systems, provides detailed guidance on alarm and evacuation requirements, depending on system design concentrations. NFPA 12A is the basic design and installation standard for total-flooding Halon 1301 systems. Individual system components are listed by UL in accordance with UL Standard 1058.

A basic design approach incorporates several critical steps, including:

1. Hazard determination and design concentrations.
2. Detection, actuation, and alarm-system design.
3. Selection of nozzle locations for coverage and mixing.
4. Piping design to ensure adequate flow.
5. Enclosure leakage evaluation.
6. Incorporation of purging equipment for postdischarge removal of agent.
7. Testing and evaluation of installed system.

Systems are tested and approved in accordance with NFPA 12A. Testing is essential in order to assure adequate system performance.

Total-flooding Carbon Dioxide Systems

Carbon dioxide (CO_2) is a colorless, odorless gas that suppresses fires by reducing the oxygen concentration and cooling the flame reaction zone, without causing collateral damage. However, the required concentrations (greater than 34%) for total-flooding systems pose a serious hazard to occupants because of oxygen depletion. Therefore, it is not appropriate for occupied areas that cannot be quickly evacuated. It is also inappropriate to use CO_2 for protection of materials containing oxidizing agents or for reactive metals.

Total-flooding CO_2 systems are designed in accordance with NFPA 12, Standard on Carbon Dioxide Extinguishing Systems, and must meet specific design concentrations and discharge times, depending on the hazard. High pressure CO_2 storage systems store CO_2 at its normal vapor pressure at ambient temperature, between 800 and 1800 psi (5516 and 12,411 kPa). Low pressure systems, typically used where large quantities of CO_2 are needed, require refrigeration systems to store the agent below ambient temperature [approximately 0°F (-18°C)] and therefore at a lower vapor pressure [325 psi (2240 kPa)].

Critical elements in system design include:

1. Pipe size and flow calculations.
2. Piping configuration and materials.
3. Nozzle location.
4. Detection, actuation, and alarm-system design.
5. Excess discharge pressure venting.
6. Testing and maintenance.

Dry-chemical Extinguishing Systems

The most common dry chemical agent is sodium bicarbonate (or ordinary dry chemical). Potassium bicarbonate (PKP or Purple K) is a dry chemical agent that is more effective than sodium bicarbonate on hydrocarbon fuel fires. Both sodium bicarbonate and potassium bicarbonate agents are effective on flammable liquid fires and are safe to use on fires in energized electrical equipment. Multipurpose or "ABC" dry chemical can be used on fires involving ordinary combustibles in addition to flammable liquid fuels and electric hazards. A major advantage of dry chemical systems is their excellent effectiveness in extinguishing flammable liquid and combustible gas fires. However, collateral damage can be extensive, requiring considerable postfire cleanup.

Dry chemical systems are usually categorized as preengineered or engineered systems. Preengineered systems are prepackaged and designed to protect against a specific hazard. The size of the system, required quantity of agent, piping configuration, fittings, and nozzles are predetermined by fire tests. A common type of preengineered dry chemical system is a kitchen range and hood protection system found in most restaurants. Preengineered systems are also used for mining, agricultural, construction, and forestry vehicles.

Engineered dry chemical systems are designed on an individual basis, depending on the hazard. Large systems are used to protect hazard areas such as refinery process equipment, gasoline loading racks, offshore platforms, flammable liquid storage spaces, and natural gas equipment. These systems will often incorporate hand-held hose lines as well as fixed nozzles. General guidance for system design, components, and so forth are included in NFPA 17, Standard for Dry Chemical Extinguishing Systems.

Dry chemical agent residues are hygroscopic, and in some cases corrosive. Therefore, they are not appropriate for electronic data-processing protection or use where highly polished metal surfaces might be exposed to the agent, such as precision tools and dies. The design of the piping system is critical because the fluidized powder does not have the hydraulic characteristics of a liquid or gas. Agent application rate and quantity should be based on specific test data for the hazard. As with any fire protection system, it is unwise to mix agent and hardware from one manufacturer with that of another unless specifically approved by the manufacturers or an independent testing laboratory.

SMOKE-CONTROL SYSTEMS

Smoke-control systems are intended to protect building occupants and property from smoke and toxic gases. They use walls, ceilings, floors, and other barriers in conjunction with air flows and pressure differences to restrict the movement of smoke in a building. This is accomplished by confinement of the smoke to the area of fire origin, or the maintenance of smoke-free escape paths and/or areas of refuge. Regardless of the basic approach, several factors must be considered in the initial design, including system flexibility, energy conservation, and other fire protection systems.

Although such systems can be effective in protecting building spaces outside the fire area, they will not significantly reduce the hazard in the fire zone itself. In addition, it is inappropriate to assume that a state-of-the-art smoke control system can provide a smoke-free environment or significant smoke venting in large volumes such as atriums. Although current practice includes the design of atrium smoke-control systems, research is ongoing to provide improved guidelines, and an NFPA recommended practice should be available in the near future that will contain detailed design criteria for atria and shopping malls.

There are no nationally recognized standards for the design and installation of smoke-control systems. Several building codes specify criteria for such systems, but there is no consensus as to their appropriateness. To provide a common technical basis for smoke-control design, the American Society of Heating, Refrigeration, and Air Conditioning Engineers (ASHRAE) and the National Institute of Standards and Technology (NIST) (formerly the National Bureau of Standards) jointly published a comprehensive handbook on building smoke-control design (19). In addition, in 1987 the NFPA adopted NFPA 92A, Recommended Practice for Smoke Control. This guideline provides basic technical information on smoke control fundamentals, system design and criteria, equipment and controls, and testing.

Basic Principles and System Design

Several forces affect the movement of smoke in buildings. Stack effect is caused by temperature differences between the inside and outside air. Under summer conditions, where the outside air is warmer than the inside air, the prevailing flow is downward through the building's vertical shafts (Fig. 8). The opposite occurs under winter conditions. The neutral plane is the height in the building where the pressure difference due to temperature conditions is zero. The fire itself results in a buoyancy force due to heated gases that are less dense than gases at ambient conditions elsewhere in the building. As the gases migrate away from the fire, the temperature approaches ambient, decreasing the buoyancy effect. The fire also introduces gas expansion, which can increase the volume of the smoke by several factors. Wind can have a pronounced effect on smoke movement. It provides uniform pressure on the outside of the building, influencing air movement in the building by infiltration. And finally, the HVAC system can play a dominant role in smoke transport as well as supplying air to the fire.

The design of modern smoke-control systems is based on analysis of these factors for the particular building

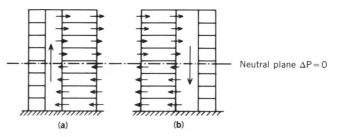

Figure 8. Air movement due to stack effect (19). (**a**) Winter; (**b**) summer. Note: arrows indicate direction of air movement.

Table 10. Suggested Minimum Design Pressure Difference Across Smoke Barriers (NFPA 92A)[a]

Building Type	Ceiling Height, ft	Design Pressure Difference, in. of water gauge
Sprinklered	Any	0.05
Nonsprinklered	9	0.10
Nonsprinklered	15	0.14
Nonsprinklered	21	0.18

[a] Courtesy of National Fire Protection Association. Copyright 1987.

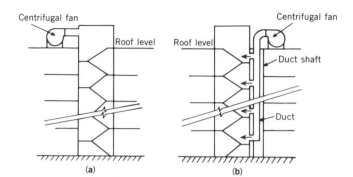

Figure 9. Examples of (**a**) single point top injection and (**b**) multiple injection systems (19).

under consideration. Air flow and pressure difference requirements, door-opening forces, and interaction of the smoke-control system with other building systems (eg, detection and alarm systems, automatic sprinklers, HVAC, elevators) should be considered. Often, the smoke-control system is integrated into the HVAC system, using common air-flow paths and control systems. NFPA 92A provides recommended criteria such as minimum pressure differences for sprinklered or unsprinklered buildings (Table 10) and maximum pressure differences across stairwell doors (Table 11).

Currently there are two basic types of smoke control systems, stairwell pressurization and zoned. Pressurized stairwells are intended to provide a smoke-free escape route. This requires an adequate pressure difference across the stairwell door on the fire floor to minimize smoke infiltration. This pressure difference must be maintained, even with several doors open to the stairwell, without resulting in such high pressure differences that stairwell doors cannot be opened by building occupants. Several techniques, including single- and multiple-point injection, are used to maintain pressure differences (Fig. 9). In tall buildings the inability of a single-point injection system to maintain uniform pressure differences necessitates the use of multiple-point injection systems. A detailed method of analysis for pressurized stairwells is provided in the ASHRAE Handbook (19).

Zoned smoke-control systems are designed to confine the smoke to some portion of a building. Several examples of zoned smoke control are illustrated in Figure 10, all of which depend on pressure differences and smoke dampers to confine the smoke to a single zone. These systems can incorporate exterior venting, interior smoke shafts, and mechanical exhaust.

Table 11. Maximum Pressure Differences Across Doors (In. of Water Gauge) (NFPA 92A)[a]

Door Closer Force, lbf[b]	Door Width, in.				
	32	36	40	44	48
6	0.45	0.40	0.37	0.34	0.31
8	0.41	0.37	0.34	0.31	0.28
10	0.37	0.34	0.30	0.28	0.26
12	0.34	0.30	0.27	0.25	0.23
14	0.30	0.27	0.24	0.22	0.21

[a] Courtesy of National Fire Protection Association. Copyright 1987.
[b] Assumes total door opening force of 30 lbf; door height = 7 ft.

Testing and Approval

Building codes generally require that smoke-control systems be tested in accordance with the requirements of the "authority having jurisdiction" (AHJ). A particular code may specify certain performance parameters (eg, minimum stairwell pressurization or number of air changes for an atrium). However, approval rests with the AHJ, and the designer must have a clear understanding of the AHJ's expectations and any special requirements.

Common types of smoke control system tests are chemical-smoke tests, tracer-gas tests, and pressure-difference tests. The use of chemical smoke has the advantage of being visible. However, although its visibility imparts

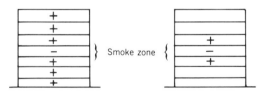

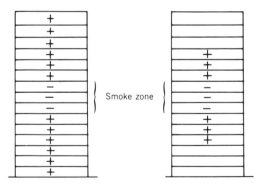

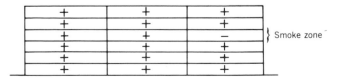

Figure 10. Typical smoke control zones (19). −, Indicates smoke zone; +, indicates pressurized spaces.

some sense of similarity to a real fire, it does not behave in the same manner as hot smoke. Therefore, observations may be misleading. Tracer gases such as sulfur hexafluoride have the advantage of being invisible and nontoxic, permitting use while the building is occupied. These gases can be heated to simulate hot gases from fires, but measurement techniques only permit testing of concentrations. The leakage paths cannot be determined. The third method, pressure-difference testing, uses pressure and flow-measurement devices to measure pressure differences and air velocities across any barriers of interest. This method permits quantification of pressure differences and leakage rates under differing building conditions, which would allow a designer to test various scenarios without significant interference with building operations.

NFPA STANDARDS AND RECOMMENDED PRACTICES

NFPA 12	Standard on Carbon Dioxide Extinguishing Systems
NFPA 12A	Standard on Halon 1301 Fire Extinguishing Systems
NFPA 13	Installation of Sprinkler Systems
NFPA 13A	Sprinkler Maintenance
NFPA 13D	Sprinkler Systems, Dwellings
NFPA 17	Standard for Dry Chemical Extinguishing Systems
NFPA 72A	Standard for the Installation, Maintenance and Use of Local Protective Signaling Systems for Guard's Tower, Fire Alarm and Supervisory Service
NFPA 72B	Standard for the Installation, Maintenance and Use of Auxiliary Protective Signaling Systems for Fire Alarm Service
NFPA 72C	Standard for the Installation, Maintenance and Use of Remote Station Protective Signaling Systems
NFPA 72D	Standard for the Installation, Maintenance and Use of Proprietary Protective Signaling Systems
NFPA 72E	Standard for Automatic Fire Detectors
NFPA 72F	Standard for the Installation, Maintenance and Use of Emergency Voice/Alarm Communication Systems
NFPA 72G	Guide for the Installation, Maintenance and Use of Notification Appliances for Protective Signaling Systems
NFPA 72H	Guide for the Testing Procedures for Local, Auxiliary, Remote Station, and Proprietary Protective Signaling Systems
NFPA 74	Standard for the Installation, Maintenance and Use of Household Fire Warning Equipment
NFPA 90A	Standard for the Installation of Air Conditioning and Ventilating Systems
NFPA 92A	Recommended Practice for Smoke Control
NFPA 231	General Storage of Materials (Sprinkler Systems)
NFPA 231C	Rack Storage of Materials (Sprinkler Systems)
NFPA 231D	Storage of Rubber Tires (Sprinkler Systems)

FM STANDARDS

FM 3210	Thermostats for Automatic Fire Detection
FM 3230–50	Smoke-Actuated Detectors for Automatic Fire Alarm Signaling
FM 3260	Flame Radiation Detectors for Automatic Fire Alarm Signaling
FM 3820	Electrical Utilization Equipment for Fire Alarm Control Equipment

UL STANDARDS

UL 199	Automatic Sprinkler Systems for Fire Protection Service
UL 217	Standard for Single and Multiple Station Smoke Detectors
UL 268	Standard for Smoke Detectors for Fire Protective Signaling Systems
UL 268A	Standard for Smoke Detectors for Duct Application
UL 464	Standard for Audible Signal Appliances
UL 521	Standard for Heat Detectors for Fire Protective Signaling Systems
UL 864	Standard for Control Units for Fire Protective Signaling Systems
UL 985	Standard for Household Fire Warning System Units
UL 1058	Halogenated Agent Extinguishing System Units
UL 1480	Standard for Speakers and Amplifiers for Fire Protective Signaling Systems
UL 1481	Standard for Power Supplies for Fire Protective Signaling Systems
UL 1638	Standard for Visual Signaling Appliances
UL 1730	Standard for Smoke Detector Monitors and Accessories for Individual Living Units of Multi-Family Residences and Hotel/Motel Rooms

BIBLIOGRAPHY

1. *International Conference on Firesafety in High Rise Buildings, April 12–16, Airlie House,* General Services Administration, Washington, D.C., May 1971.
2. *Public Buildings Service Tentative Guide Specification—Fire Alarm System,* PBS 16723T, General Services Administration, Washington, D.C., October 1978.
3. R. L. P. Custer and R. G. Bright, *Fire Detection: State of the Art,* NBS Technical Note 839, National Bureau of Standards, Washington, D.C., June 1974.

4. R. W. Bukowski, R. J. O'Laughlin, and C. E. Zimmerman, *Fire Alarm Signaling Systems Handbook,* National Fire Protection Association, Quincy, Mass., 1987.

5. *Code for the Safety of Life from Fire in Buildings and Structures,* NFPA 101, 1988 ed., National Fire Protection Association, Quincy, Mass., 1988.

6. *The BOCA National Building Code/1987,* 10th ed., Building Officials and Code Administrators International, Inc., Country Club Hills, Ill., 1987.

7. *Guide for Testing Procedures for Local, Auxiliary, Remote Station and Proprietary Protective Signaling Systems,* NFPA 72H, 1985 ed., National Fire Protection Association, Quincy, Mass., 1988.

8. E. Budnick, *Estimating the Effectiveness of State-of-the-Art Detectors and Automatic Sprinklers on Life Safety in Residential Occupancies,* NBSIR 84-2819, National Bureau of Standards, Washington, D.C., 1984, p. 7.

9. J. L. Bryan, *Automatic Sprinklers and Standpipe Systems,* National Fire Protection Association, Quincy, Mass., 1980, pp. 166–168.

10. A. Cote, ed., *Fire Protection Handbook,* 16th ed., National Fire Protection Association, Quincy, Mass., 1986, pp. 18-1–18-95.

11. J. K. Richardson, *An Assessment of the Performance of Automatic Sprinkler Systems,* SFPE TR 84-2, Society of Fire Protection Engineers, Boston, Mass., 1984, p. 8.

12. *Report of Congress on Fire Protection Systems: Detectors, Remote Alarm Systems, and Sprinklers,* prepared by the Federal Emergency Management Agency, Washington, D.C., 1981, p. 274.

13. G. P. McKinnon, ed., *Fire Protection Handbook,* 14th ed., National Fire Protection Association, Quincy, Mass., 1976, p. 14-3.

14. R. Jensen, ed., *Fire Protection for the Design Professional,* Cahners Publishing Company, Boston, Mass., 1975, p. 60.

15. J. Bouchard, ed., *Automatic Sprinkler Systems Handbook,* 3rd ed., National Fire Protection Association, Quincy, Mass., 1987, p. 39.

16. *Ibid.,* p. 314.

17. *Ibid.,* p. 40.

18. B. W. Melly, *Comparison of Several Computer Hydraulics Programs for the IBM PC and Compatibles,* SFPE TR-87-1, Society of Fire Protection Engineers, Boston, Mass., 1987, pp. 1–15.

19. J. Klote and J. Fothergill, Jr., *Design of Smoke Control Systems for Buildings,* American Society of Heating, Refrigeration, and Air Conditioning Engineers, Atlanta, Ga., 1983.

General References

Ref. 3 is a good reference for the design and operation of detection devices.

Ref. 4 is the most comprehensive, up-to-date reference on the subject, particularly in regard to design practices and application of codes and standards.

Ref. 9 is a comprehensive review of the history and current design concepts for automatic sprinkler systems.

Ref. 10 pp. 18-1–18-95, provides a detailed discussion of sprinkler system design, water supply, supervision and alarm, and maintenance.

Ref. 15 is a detailed guide to the use and intent of NFPA 13, Installation of Sprinkler Systems, 1987 edition.

R. W. Bukowski and G. W. Mulholand, *Smoke Detector Design and Smoke Properties,* National Bureau of Standards, Washington, D.C., November 1978.

R. W. Bukowski and R. L. P. Custer, and R. G. Bright, *Fire Alarm and Communication Systems,* National Bureau of Standards, Washington, D.C., April 1978.

J. L. Bryan, *Fire Suppression and Detection Systems,* 2nd ed., Glencoe Press, Beverly Hills, Calif., 1982.

D. D. Evans and D. W. Stroup, *Methods to Calculate the Response Time of Heat and Smoke Detectors Installed Below Large Unobstructed Ceilings,* National Bureau of Standards, Washington, D.C., 1985.

H. Wass, Jr., *Sprinkler Hydraulics,* IRM Insurance, White Plains, N.Y., 1983. A reference for hydraulic design of automatic sprinkler systems.

E. Butcher and A. Parnell, *Smoke Control in Fire Safety Design,* William Clowes and Sons, London, 1979.

J. Fothergill, "The Atrium as a Fresh Air Channel—A Different Concept in Smoke Control," *ASHRAE Transactions* **86,** Part 1, 624–635 (1980).

J. Klote, "Stairwell Pressurization," *ASHRAE Transactions,* **86,** Part 1, 636–673 (1980).

J. McGuire and G. Tamura, "Simple Analysis of Smoke Flow Problems in High Buildings," *Fire Technology* **11**(1), 15–17 (1975).

W. Schmidt, "Smoke Control System Testing," *Heating/Piping/Air Conditioning* **54**(4), 77–80 (Apr. 1982).

G. Tamura, J. McGuire, and A. Wilson, "Air-Handling Systems for Control of Smoke Movement," *Proceedings of Symposium on Fire Hazards in Buildings, ASHRAE Semi-Annual Meeting, January 1970,* San Francisco, Cal., 1971, pp. 14–19.

See also: FIRE SAFETY-LIFE SAFETY; FIRE RESISTANCE; STAIRS AND RAMPS-SAFETY ASPECTS; ZONING CODES AND BUILDING REGULATIONS.

EDWARD K. BUDNICK, PE
P. J. DiNENNO, PE
J. L. SCHEFFEY, PE
Hughes Associates, Inc.
Wheaton, Maryland

STAINLESS STEEL

CLASSIFICATION AND TYPE

In many architectural construction documents, reference has been made, and is still made, to stainless steel in the singular sense, as if it were one material. Actually, there are more than 57 stainless steels recognized by the American Iron and Steel Institute (AISI) as standard alloys. In addition, many proprietary alloys are produced by the different stainless steel producers. Stainless steels are a family of corrosion- and heat-resisting iron-base alloys containing a minimum of 10.5% chromium. Both corrosion-resistance and fabrication characteristics are further improved through modification with nickel and other elements.

Stainless steels are broadly divided into three groups

according to composition and metallurgical characteristics: austenitic, ferritic, and martensitic. They are further standardized and classified by numbering systems. In North America, both the AISI numbering system and the new unified numbering system (UNS) are being used. Numbering systems used in other countries are listed in the *Handbook of Stainless Steels* (1).

Austenitic Stainless Steels

Austenitic stainless steels (Table 1) containing chromium and nickel are identified as AISI 300 series types. Alloys containing chromium, nickel, and manganese are identified as AISI 200 series types. These steels are normally nonmagnetic. They cannot be hardened by heat treatment, but their tensile strength can be increased materially by cold working.

The austenitic stainless steels are characterized by a combination of properties that are especially suitable for architectural metal applications. These include excellent corrosion resistance, high strength, and ease of fabrication. They account for about 70% of stainless steels produced and comprise a much greater percentage of those used in building construction. Type 304 (frequently referred to as 18-8 stainless) is the most widely used alloy of

Table 1. Austenitic Stainless Steels[a]

AISI Type	Equivalent UNS
201	S20100
202	S20200
205	S20500
301	S30100
302	S30200
302B	S30215
303	S30300
303Se	S30323
304	S30400
304L	S30403
	S30430
304N	S30451
305	S30500
308	S30800
309	S30900
309S	S30908
310	S31000
310S	S31008
314	S31400
316	S31600
316L	S31603
316F	S31620
316N	S31651
317	S31700
317L	S31703
321	S32100
329	S32900
330	NO8330
347	S34700
348	S34800
384	S38400

[a] Courtesy of The American Iron and Steel Institute.

Table 2. Ferritic Stainless Steels[a]

AISI Type	Equivalent UNS
405	S40500
409	S40900
429	S42900
430	S43000
430F	S43020
430FSe	S43023
434	S43400
436	S43600
442	S44200
446	S44600

[a] Courtesy of the American Iron and Steel Institute.

the austenitic group. It has a nominal composition of 18% chromium and 8% nickel.

Ferritic Stainless Steels

Ferritic stainless steels (Table 2) are straight-chromium AISI 400 series types that cannot be hardened by heat treatment and they can be only moderately hardened by cold working. They are readily fabricated, but do not retain as much ductility as the austenitic grades after cold working. They are magnetic, have good ductility, and have fair resistance to corrosion. Type 430 is the general-purpose stainless of the ferritic group.

Martensitic Stainless Steels

Martensitic stainless steels (Table 3) are straight-chromium AISI 400 series types that can be hardened by heat treatment. They resist corrosion in mild environments. They are magnetic. They have fairly good ductility, and some can be heat-treated to tensile strengths exceeding 1,379 MPa (200,000 psi).

The stainless steels most commonly used in architectural applications are AISI types 301, 302, 304, 304L, 303, 305, 316, 316L, and 430, with type 304 in North America and type 316 in Europe having the largest usage. Representative physical and mechanical properties of these steels are summarized in Table 4.

Table 3. Martensitic Stainless Steels[a]

AISI Type	Equivalent UNS
403	S40300
410	S41000
414	S41400
416	S41600
416Se	S41623
420	S42000
420F	S42020
422	S422000
431	S43100
440A	S44002
440B	S44003
440C	S44004

[a] Courtesy of the American Iron and Steel Institute.

Table 4. Representative Properties of Alloys Commonly Used in Architectural Work[a]

Type	Description	Chemical Analysis, %[b]								Tensile Strength		Yield Strength (0.2% offset)		Elongation in 2 in. (30.80 mm), %	Rockwell Hardness	Product Form
		C	Mn	P	S	Si	Cr	Ni	Mo	ksi	MPa	ksi	MPa			
301	A variation of 302. Can be rolled to high tensile strength for special and structural applications.	0.15	2	0.045	0.03	1	16–18	6–8		110	758	40	276	60	B85	
302	Original basic Cr–Ni stainless T304 now used instead on most end uses.	0.15	2	0.045	0.03	1	17–19	8–10		90	612	40	276	50	B85	
303	Good machinability for nuts, bolts, etc	0.15	2	0.2	0.15	1	17–19	8–10	0.60[c]	90	621	35	241	50		Bar
304	Most commonly used. Readily available in many forms. Good weldability.	0.08	2	0.045	0.03	1	18–20	8–10		84	579	42	290	55	B80	
304L	Low-carbon variation of T304 for welding heavy-gauge sections	0.03	2	0.045	0.03	1	18–20	8–12		81	558	39	269	55	B79	
305	A cold-heading variation stainless for screws, bolts, nails, etc.	0.12	2	0.045	0.03	1	17–19	10–13		85	586	38	262	50	B80	
316	Even better corrosion resistance through addition of molybdenum. Suitable for seacoast atmosphere.	0.08	2	0.045	0.03	1	16–18	10–14	2–3	84	579	42	290	50	B79	
316L	Better-welding (heavy-gauge) variation of T316.	0.03	2	0.045	0.03	1	16–18	10–14	2–3	81	558	42	290	50	B79	
430	Ferritic stainless steel. Lower corrosion resistance than 300 series. Can be used for interior applications.	0.12	1	0.04	0.03	1	16–18			75	517	50	345	25	B85	

[a] Courtesy of the American Iron and Steel Institute.
[b] Maximum unless otherwise noted.
[c] May be added at manufacturer's option.

USE OF TYPE 304 (T302) AND TYPE 316

Types 302 and 304 stainless steels have a record of highly satisfactory performance in industrialized cities in North America. The corrosion resistance of these basic types of stainless steel is well demonstrated by the Chrysler Building in New York City, where type 302 stainless steel sheathing of the roof and large ornamental gargoyles have withstood the effects of weather for a period of some 60 years. Resistance to severe exposure conditions can be increased by the addition of special alloying elements. For example, molybdenum, when added to the base 18% chromium and 12% nickel combination of type 316 stainless steel, effectively increases its corrosion resistance to atmospheric chlorides. For this reason, type 316 is preferred for use in coastal environments, especially where there are frequent fogs and heavy dews and extended periods between rains, which provide a natural washing action. It is also suitable for installation near chemical plants or pulp and paper mills. The addition of molybdenum also improves the resistance of nickel stainless steel to the damp sulfurous atmospheres that result from the burning of high-sulfur fuels in localities where the relative humidity is high. The atmospheric conditions that make type 316 the preferred alloy over type 304 are probably the reasons that type 316 is used more commonly in the UK and Western Europe than in North America.

STAINLESS STEELS IN COMBINATION WITH OTHER MATERIALS

In addition to having excellent corrosion resistance themselves, stainless steels are the least active metals in accelerating galvanically the corrosion of other architectural metals such as aluminum and steel, which is why stainless steel fasteners are usually chosen for joining aluminum sections. Stainless steels have the advantage over copper and high-copper-content alloys of not releasing corrosion products that cause accelerated attack on aluminum or zinc surfaces with which they come in contact by drainage. This feature is also important in avoiding unsightly staining of marble, granite, or other masonry located below or adjacent to the metal in a structure. Because stainless steels are also resistant to masonry alkalinity, they are especially suitable for stone and masonry anchors and accessories.

RESISTANCE TO CORROSION

All stainless steels contain sufficient amounts of chromium to give them corrosion-resistant properties. Proper alloy selection for resistance to atmospheric corrosion conditions is simple for the architect, and the main choice of T304 and/or T316 was described earlier.

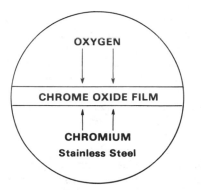

Figure 1. Formation of chrome oxide film.

Chromium and, for the austenitic grades, nickel and additional elements are added at the melting stage so that stainless steels are stainless throughout. They do not require painting or other surface treatments to improve or maintain their corrosion-resistant properties. Ordinary steel, when exposed to the natural environment, oxidizes, and powdery rust or iron oxide forms on the surface. If left unchecked, the rusting continues until the steel is eaten away. Stainless steels also oxidize, but instead of common rust (iron oxide), a thin, impervious chrome oxide film forms on the surface as an armor against corrosion attack. When this film is removed, it reforms instantly by combining with oxygen from the atmosphere (Fig. 1).

Corrosion: Cause and Cure

There are five main corrosion hazards to the successful use of stainless steel.

1. Intergranular corrosion.
2. Galvanic corrosion.
3. Contact corrosion.
4. Pinhole or pitting corrosion.
5. Stress corrosion.

Many failures can be prevented simply by recognizing the hazard and taking the necessary steps to avoid it. In addition, with a few exceptions, the architect or builder is not affected by these hazards.

Intergranular Corrosion. Improper heat-treatment and some welding procedures can introduce susceptibility to carbide precipitation and intergranular corrosion. The solution is to specify L grades if heavy-gauge austenitic stainless steels are to be welded. Few failures occur from this cause.

Galvanic Corrosion. This is one potential hazard the designer should recognize when the detail calls for dissimilar metals (any metals) to be in contact with each other.

In a corrosive medium, the dissimilar metals form short-circuited electrodes, which establish an electrochemical cell. This action results in the dissolution of the anodic electrode, whereas the cathode remains unattacked. The potential varies with the position of the metals and alloys on the galvanic series chart presented in Table 5. The closer to the bottom of the list a metal is, the more anodic it is, and it will suffer accelerated corrosion when coupled with a metal listed above it. The farther apart the metals are on this list, the greater the corrosive action on the anode metal.

The relative mass of each metal must also be considered. A large mass of the less noble metal weakens the potential for galvanic action. For instance, stainless steel in contact with a structural steel system does not appreciably affect the structural steel in terms of galvanic corrosion.

No problems occur when stainless steel screws are used to assemble an aluminum window. Aluminum screws in a stainless steel window can cause serious corrosion problems with the screws. This occurs when the dissimilar metals are in contact with each other. An insulator between the two solves the problem.

Contact Corrosion. A small piece of carbon steel, scale, copper, or foreign material lodged on stainless steel may be sufficient to destroy passivity at the point of contact and cause pitting. Contact corrosion can easily be prevented by ensuring that stainless building components are clean and free from scale, small particles of metal, etc.

Pitting and Pinhole Corrosion. Pitting and pinhole corrosion are generally not problems in building construction with stainless steel. They can be prevented simply by eliminating cracks, crevices, and stagnant pockets from designs. Good clean surfaces afford the best resistance to pitting.

Stress Corrosion. This can occur when highly stressed stainless steel is used in a warm, moist, chloride-containing atmosphere ie, structural hangers in an indoor swimming pool. This potential problem can be prevented by proper alloy selection; a corrosion expert should be consulted. Stress corrosion is not normally a potential problem for the architect or builder.

Table 5. Galvanic Series of Metals and Alloys in Seawater[a,b]

Gold	Cast iron
Monel	Alloy steel
Stainless type 316	Low steel
Stainless type 304	Aluminum 5052
Stainless type 430	Aluminum 6063
Silver	Aluminum 6061
Aluminum bronze	Aluminum 3003
Copper	Alclad 3003
Red brass	Zinc
Yellow brass	Magnesium
Muntz metal	

[a] Ref. 2.
[b] The series proceeds from more noble cathodic to less noble anodic metals and alloys.

SHAPES, SIZES, AND FINISHES

Figure 2 shows mill processes for making various stainless steel products. Because alloy compositions must be carefully controlled, various refining steps (not shown in this illustration) are used in conjunction with electric furnace or vacuum furnace melting. During such remelting steps, the alloy content is adjusted closely, and impurities are reduced to absolute minimum levels. During the final stages of producing basic mill forms (sheet, strip, plate, and bar) and bringing these forms to specific sizes and tolerances, the materials are subjected to hot and cold rolling operations, annealing, cleaning, etc. Also, further steps are required to produce other mill forms such as wire and tubing. Table 6 shows how the mill forms are classified by size.

Finishes are produced by three basic methods:

1. Rolling between polished or textured rolls.
2. Polishing and/or buffing with abrasive wheels, belts, or pads.
3. Blasting with abrasive grit or glass beads.

Plate may be specified in the standard hot-rolled, annealed, and pickled condition. Plates are also available with improved surfaces, such as cold-rolled or skin-passed. Some fabricators also grind and polish plate surfaces with results similar to polished sheet surfaces.

For sheet, a numbered descriptive system of standard mill finishes established by the AISI is generally recognized and used (Table 7).

Samples. Since standard finishes may vary slightly on different products and because of the many nonstandard finishes available, the architect may wish to consult producers or fabricators and examine samples before making important finish specifications.

Finish Availability. Sheet products are available in all of the AISI standard mechanical finishes. However, No. 2B cold-rolled finish, usually subsequently refinished by the fabricator, and No. 4 polished finish are the most commonly used in architecture and are generally available in stocked sheet. Sheets in some nonstandard proprietary polished finishes are stocked by steel service centers, and others are available from mills only.

Patterned finishes are made by rolling by means similar to those for the mill-rolled standard finishes, and are available in a wide variety of sculptural and functional designs and textures. These are proprietary in nature, as are the proprietary polished and buffed finishes, and are generally produced by rerollers and metal finishers.

Bar Products. Bar products are designated by finishing method. Hot-finished bar products supplied for architectural applications are hot-rolled, forged or extruded, and then annealed and pickled or blast-cleaned to remove scale. Rounds may be descaled by rough turning or grinding.

Cold-finished bar products are produced by the same methods as hot-finished products, but are subsequently finished by one of several methods to provide closer dimensional tolerances and smoother surfaces. For ornamental purposes, bars can be polished and/or buffed.

Tubing and Pipe. The only product used regularly for architectural end users in this product category is welded tubing. Pipe and seamless tubing are not normally used in architectural applications. Stainless tubing is available in round, square, rectangular, hexagonal, and oval shapes. The ornamental tubing normally used in architecture is the most economical because it is not pressure-tested. It can be furnished with the outside surface polished or buffed to a satin or mirrorlike finish.

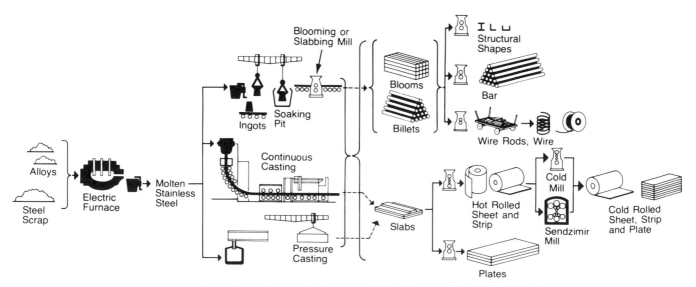

Figure 2. The making of stainless steel. Courtesy of The American Iron & Steel Institute.

Table 6. Classification of Stainless Steel Product Forms[a]

Item	Description	Dimensions		
		Thickness	Width	Diameter or Size
Sheet	Coils and cut lengths			
	mill finishes Nos. 1, 2D, and 2B	Under 3/16 in. (4.76 mm)	24 in. (609.6 mm) and over	
	polished finishes Nos. 3, 4, 6, 7, & 8	Under 3/16 in. (4.76 mm)	All widths	
Strip	Cold-finished coils or cut lengths	Under 3/16 in. (4.76 mm)	Under 24 in. (609.6 mm)	
Plates	Flat-rolled or forged	3/16 in. (4.76 mm) and over	Over 10 in. (254 mm)	
Bars	Hot-finished rounds, squares, octagons, and hexagons			1/4 in. (6.35 mm) and over
	Hot-finished flats	1/8 in. (3.18 mm) and over	1/4–10 in. (6.35–254 mm), inclusive	
	Cold-finished rounds, squares, octagons, and hexagons			Over 1/2 in. (12.7 mm)
	Cold-finished flats		3/8 in. and over (9.53 mm)	
Wire	Cold finished only: round, square, octagon, hexagon, and flat wire	0.01 in. (0.254 mm) to under 3/16 in. (4.76 mm)	1/16 in. (1.59 mm) to under 3/8 in. (9.53 mm)	1/2 in. (12.7 mm) and under
Pipe and tubing	Several different classifications, with differing specifications, are available. For information on standard sizes consult stainless steel producers.			
Extrusions	Not considered standard shapes, but of some interest. Currently limited in size to approximately 6½-in. (165.1-mm) diameter circle or structurals to 5-in. (127-mm) diameter.			

[a] Courtesy of the American Iron and Steel Institute.

Table 7. AISI Standard Stainless Steel Sheet Finishes

Finish	Description
Unpolished finishes	
No. 1	A rough, dull surface produced by hot rolling to the specified thickness, followed by annealing and descaling.
No. 2D (for widths under 24 in., referred to as No. 1 strip finish)	A dull finish produced by cold rolling, followed by annealing and descaling and sometimes by a final light roll pass on dull rolls.
No. 2B (for widths under 24 in., referred to as No. 2 strip finish)	A bright cold-rolled finish commonly produced in the same way as No. 2D finish, except that the annealed and descaled sheet receives a final light, cold roll pass on polished rolls. This is the general-purpose cold-rolled finish.
No. 2B (bright annealed)	A bright, cold-rolled, highly reflective finish is retained in final annealing by a controlled atmospheric furnace.
Polished finishes	
No. 3	An intermediate polished surface obtained by finishing with a 100 grit abrasive. Generally used where a semi-finished polished surface is required. It may or may not be additionally polished during fabrication.
No. 4	A polished surface obtained by finishing with approximately a 150 mesh abrasive or finer, following initial grinding with coarser abrasives.
No. 6	A dull satin finish having lower reflectivity than No. 4 finish. It is produced by Tampico brushing the No. 4 finish in a medium of abrasive and oil.
No. 7	A high degree of reflectivity, which is obtained by buffing finely ground surfaces, but not to the extent of completely removing the grit lines. It is used chiefly for architectural and ornamental purposes.

Finish	Description
No. 8	The most reflective surface, which is obtained by polishing with successively finer abrasives and buffing extensively until all grit lines from preliminary grinding operations are removed. It is used for applications such as mirrors and reflectors.

Hot-rolled and Extruded Structurals. Hot-rolled and extruded structurals are available only in annealed and pickled conditions. Cold-rolled shapes are produced by bending cold-rolled sheet or strip. Their smooth, rolled finish is suitable for polishing and/or buffing. More detailed information on finishes can be found in "Finishes for Stainless Steel" (3).

FABRICATING ARCHITECTURAL STAINLESS STEEL

Because of stainless steel's high corrosion resistance and high strength, light gauges are more frequently used than when using other architectural metals. Hollow, formed sections rather than solid ones provide ample strength and stiffness with minimum weight and cost. Therefore, the common methods of cutting, forming, assembling, fastening, welding, and soldering sheet, strip, and light plate are of chief concern to the architect. All operations are accomplished largely with the same equipment and methods used for mild carbon steel.

Cutting

When stainless steel sheet or strip is used in the form of coils, it is slit to width in the mill or by rerollers. In all other cases, straight cutting sheet, strip, and light plate and cutting to length from coil are done by shearing.

Blanking, perforating, and nibbling are used to cut notches or opening of any shape out of stainless steel stock. Tubing and formed sections are cut by sawing or by abrasive wheels, and thick plate is often cut with torches.

The cutting methods for stainless steels are the same as for mild steel. However, a few special considerations must be kept in mind. For instance, for shearing operations, the equipment capacity in relation to the thickness of the material is from 30 to 50% greater because of the toughness of stainless steel(s). When sawing, riding the teeth over the cut can cause work-hardening, which slows down the cutting rate. When using abrasive cutting, proper coolant should be used to avoid any possible heat damage to the stainless steel.

Brake Forming and Roll Forming

Although for softer metals, such as aluminum or bronze, extruding is the most often used method for forming structural and ornamental architectural sections, brake and roll forming are the more commonly used methods for such sections and profiles in stainless steel. Press brakes are the means most commonly used to produce various bend configurations for architectural applications. Almost any shape can be formed, provided it is rectilinear. Linear shapes, such as for mullions, column covers, door framing, ribbed siding panels, etc, can be easily and economically fabricated on a press brake. Although some fabricators have large brakes that can produce sections up to 40 ft (12 m) in length, most fabricating shops have power-operated press brakes with a capacity to bend stainless steel up to ⅛ in. (3.175 mm) thick in lengths up to 12 ft (3.65 m).

Press brakes are especially economical for forming bends in components for small jobs inasmuch as they can use low-cost or general-purpose dies. For larger productions, press brakes may also be economical if the components do not require too many handling and forming operations to produce the required shape. Some typical brake-formed shapes and die designs are shown in Figure 3.

The minimum bend radii for austenitic (type 300) stainless steels are as follows, where T = metal thickness:

Annealed	0*–1.5T
One-quarter	1–2T
One-half	2.5–4T
Full-hard	4–6T

Bends of 90° in annealed austenitic stainless steel in very light gauges such as 0.019 in. (0.482 mm) and 0.024 in. (0.609 mm) require a zero inside radius. From 0.030-in. (0.762-mm) to 0.047-in. (1.194-mm) thicknesses, a minimum inside radius of 0.010 in. (0.25 mm) is required. For 0.059 in. (1.5 mm) and heavier, one-half the thickness of the sheet forms the minimum inside radius.

Although brake forming is the method most commonly used for producing linear architectural shapes from sheet stock, roll forming offers a number of advantages that can result in substantial savings in cost. Although tooling costs are generally expensive, rapid production rates and

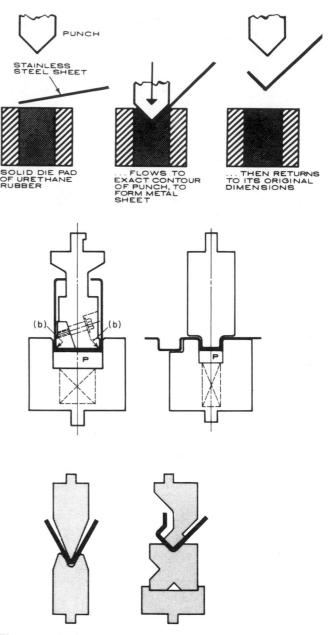

Figure 3. Brake forming stainless steel sheet. Courtesy of Nickel Development Institute.

the use of more economical coil stock offer significant advantages for forming either simple or complex shapes in large quantities. Long lengths of 20–40 ft (6–12 m), which often present problems for press brake operations, pose no difficulties on roll-forming equipment.

Roll forming is a continuous process for cold forming coiled sheet or strip into linear shapes having a wide variety of cross-sectional profiles. The metal is fed from a coil through a series of pairs of matched forming rolls mounted in tandem at successive stations. Each pair is profiled differently to produce successive changes in the shape of the metal. The number of pairs or "stands" of rolls used in the line may vary from 3 or 4 for simple sections to as many as 36 for complex ones. Minimum economical runs vary from approximately 3,500 to 10,000 ft (1050 to 3050 m), depending on size, gauge, and complexity of shape.

Complex shapes as shown in Figure 4 can be produced on roll-forming machines with other operations synchronized with the forming operations. These include seam and spot welding, notching, perforating, and cutting to length.

Other forming and bending methods used for architectural fabrication include press forming for the production of pan shapes: simple draws for shallow architectural panels and deep draws requiring multiple strokes for items such as kitchen sinks. Roll and tube bending operations are used to bend stainless plate and tubing, respectively.

Modern extruding techniques for stainless steel using molten glass for lubrication and insulation have made it possible to produce some profiles suitable for architectural applications (thresholds, angles, I beams, channels, and tees). However, generally speaking, the high temperatures and large mechanical forces required in the extrusion of stainless steels establish die design limitations that generally require the use of sections heavier and correspondingly higher in cost than comparable brake-formed or roll-formed profiles. Since new techniques are being developed continually, the designer should consult the extruder to obtain the latest capabilities, tolerances, and limitations.

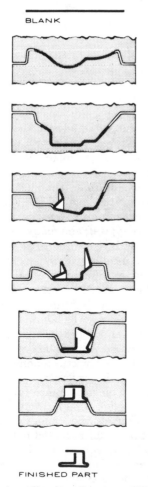

Figure 4. Progressive roller dies. Courtesy of The American Iron & Steel Institute.

Joining Stainless Steels

Mechanical fastening is possible because a full selection of austenitic stainless steel screws, bolts, clips, and other fastening hardware is available. Stainless fasteners are used for fastening stainless to stainless and stainless to other metals and materials as well as for fastening aluminum parts. Carbon steel fasteners should not be used for joining stainless steel parts, even when the fasteners are coated and/or concealed. This precaution prevents the possibility of rust streaks appearing at the joints.

For architectural component details, welded stainless steel studs have gained increased acceptance. Studs, which may be threaded or tapped, are welded to one part to provide a means of mechanical fastening to another part, thus avoiding exposed welds, which would require costly refinishing procedures. Two systems are employed: the arc welding type and the capacitor discharge (CD) type. Arc stud welding is used where the design calls for a parent metal thickness greater than 0.078 in. (1.88 mm) and where backside marking is not a critical factor. These studs are used in diameters of 1/4–1 1/4 in. (6.5–31.75 mm). For complete freedom of backside marking, a minimum sheet thickness of 0.119 in. (3 mm) is recommended with the smallest-diameter stud possible. It is preferred to increase the number of studs rather than use fewer studs of larger diameter. CD stud welding is used to fasten small-diameter (1/2 in. (12.7 mm) or smaller) studs to stainless steel. Stainless steel blind rivets are used regularly in attaching joints between sections in industrial and/or sandwich wall installations.

Welding

Metal parts that are to be assembled rigidly and permanently usually are joined best by welding, and austenitic stainless steel is welded easily by all common methods. The most frequently used methods include welding with covered electrodes and submerged arc, metal inert gas, tungsten inert gas, and resistance welding. Such factors as gauge, size, configuration of the parts to be welded, and number of assemblies to be produced determine the preferred method. Compared with carbon steels, stainless steels have lower thermal conductivity and somewhat higher thermal expansion, resulting in a greater tendency to distort during welding.

Proper techniques, such as the use of chill bars, can prevent such distortion. Since less heat is used in resistance welding, stainless steels are particularly well suited for this method. Good design practice dictates that, as much as possible, welds, particularly fusion welds, be placed in concealed locations wherever possible to avoid the expense of refinishing. At times, however, exposed outside corners or butt welds are unavoidable. In such cases, the excess weld metal is removed during the finishing process by grinding, and the joint is then polished until the weld zone completely blends with the polished finish of the base metal. This blending of welds is common practice in the fabrication of custom architectural components and is possible only on mechanically polished finishes of the base metal. Mill finishes cannot be blended. Therefore, when those finishes are used, any welding must be located in areas that are aesthetically unimportant.

Soldering

Sheet metal soldering today is practically a lost art and has been largely replaced by welding. The reason is that soldered joints have relatively low strength. However, it is still used to seal light-gauge steel metal joints, particularly in roofing and ductwork, as well as in some plumbing applications.

The brighter stainless steel finishes are more difficult to solder than the duller and mechanically polished ones, such as Nos. 3 and 4.

In specifying soldered joints, the architect must insist on careful precleaning and proper flux selection. Commercial acid-type fluxes containing chlorides, such as hydrochloric acid or ammonium chloride, can be used only with extreme care and should not be used if immediate and thorough neutralizing and flushing after soldering are impractical. These fluxes often cause pitting of stainless steel. The preferred fluxes are those with a phosphoric acid base because the phosphoric acid is active only at soldering temperatures. Commonly used tin—lead solder alloys are 50–50 or 60–40. Some prefer 70–30. The higher the tin mix, the better the color match with the base metal.

ARCHITECTURAL END USES

In architecture, as in any other industry, stainless steels are used in applications where function and economics combine to make them a logical choice. Clear examples in buildings that reflect purely functional and economical factors in the selection of stainless steel as the main construction material are kitchen sinks, commercial kitchens, hospital and laboratory equipment, residential chimney flue liners, bank vaults, etc. In most architectural applications, however, appearance, prestige, and quality image combine with functional considerations such as high strength; impact, abrasion, and corrosion resistance; and durability.

Because of the quality image and aesthetic importance of the building components made with stainless steels, proper care in steel mill production, component fabrication and erection, and, on the part of the designer, good detail design are of great importance. Minor faults in appearance or function that an architect might accept when other materials or metals are used are considered unacceptable when stainless steel is used. Stainless steel is expected to be without even minor flaws in material and workmanship when corporate headquarters, major bank buildings, or similar prestigious projects are involved.

The four principal areas where stainless steel is often used in architectural metal work are

1. Miscellaneous ornamental metal.
2. Building entrances and storefronts.
3. Building facades.
4. Roofing, siding, and ductwork (generally called sheet metal work).

Miscellaneous and Ornamental

Mechanically polished and buffed mirrorlike finishes are generally used in this type of end use, where visual attractiveness with a sense of strength and permanence are required. Elevator lobbies, escalators, wall and ceiling paneling, partitions, railings, ornamental stairs, and column covers are some of the building components often finished in stainless steel.

Most of these installations are subject to close contact and observation by the building occupant, and stainless is specified not only for appearance, but also because only simple and minimal maintenance is required. Components subject to abrasion, impact, and, generally, direct contact from the public are best specified in polished or buffed finishes, which are easily cleaned and which can be easily repaired if scratched or abraded. Mill-rolled finishes should only be used in areas that are out of reach, whereas some functional and ornamental textured patterns are often used in areas such as elevator cabs, which have to withstand even heavier wear. Unlike for structural steel, there are virtually no generally accepted standard connections for architectural metalwork in stainless steel. The designer aims to achieve simplicity, structural efficiency, and economy.

Joints and attachments that take into consideration economy in both fabrication and erection can permit the use of stainless steel even when budgets are limited. Precisely fitted joints may be more easily and less expensively fabricated under shop conditions where close supervision, good working conditions, and special equipment are available. Aligning fixtures, power-operated clamps, accurate working surfaces, and stationary welding equipment all contribute to accuracy in shop joining. Field joining should be held to a minimum and kept as simple as possible when it is required. Some suggested typical joints for wall paneling or column covers are shown in Figure 5. These details are typical, and many variations of the ones shown are used for both laminated and unbacked stainless steel panels and column covers. For good visual flatness of flat paneling for interior application, particularly when brightly polished or buffed finishes are used, it is recommended that relatively light-gauge sheet (0.059 or 0.049 in. (1.5 or 1.24 mm) thick) be laminated to a core material of good dimensional stability. This core material can be ¾-in. sanded plywood, cement—asbestos board, or another hardboard. The use of structural adhesives, time-cured in stationary presses, is preferred over contact adhesives pressed in place by means of pinch rollers. A requirement or performance specification confining the work to qualified laminators avoids the danger of inadequate detail specifications calling for outdated laminating techniques or improper adhesive selection.

In miscellaneous and ornamental metalwork, exposed welds often cannot be avoided. If this is the case, it must be kept in mind that only welds in polished, scratch-rolled, or buffed finishes can be blended to match the origi-

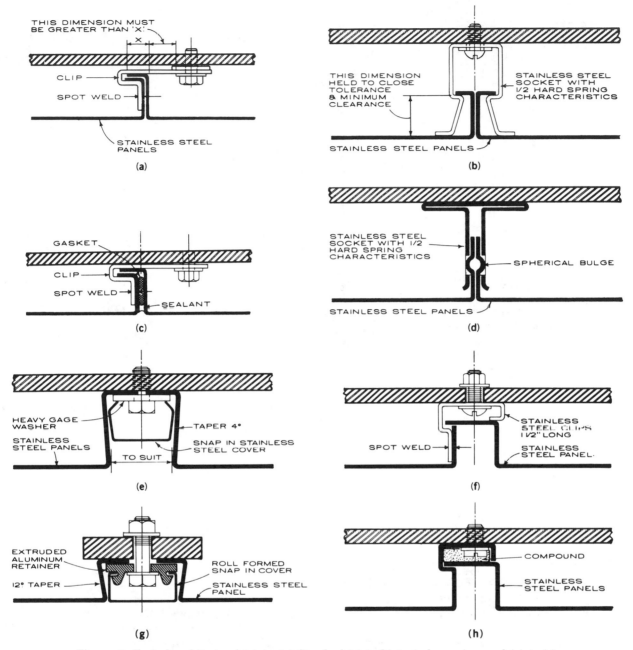

Figure 5. Typical architectural joints. (**a**) Standard joint; (**b**) typical snap-in panel joint; (**c**) interlocking flanged joints; (**d**) typical removable snap-in panel joint; (**e**) recessed panel joint; (**f**) interlocking recessed panel joint; (**g**) recessed panel joint with flush snap-in cover; (**h**) interlocking recessed panel joint with sealant.

nal overall finish. Fabricators often offer their own finishes to avoid blending to a standard finish. These finishes do not necessarily match the standard mill finishes. Thus, the designer should request samples from the fabricator.

A number of proprietary finishes specifically designed for easy blending are now available from mills and specialized metal finishers. Hand-held wheels and cloths that quickly reproduce the original finish are available.

Building Entrances and Storefronts

Almost all stainless steel installations of these high-impact and abrasion building components are specified in polished or buffed finishes. Ease of cleaning and refinishing are the main reasons for the selection of these finishes. Although many variations in design exist, particularly in storefronts, the two basic components are mullions that must accommodate large glass areas and doors that allow easy access and egress under high-demand conditions.

There are three basic approaches to the design of this type of stainless steel mullion. The mullion may have a thin nonstructural veneer of stainless steel over a structural steel core (Fig. 6a). The stainless steel cladding may be structural and work in conjunction with a carbon steel inner structure (Fig. 6b), or the stainless steel section may be designed with sufficient thickness and size to meet

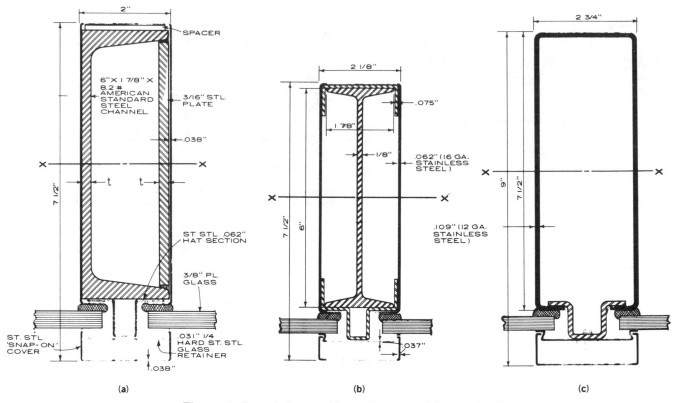

Figure 6. Ground floor mullions. Courtesy of International Nickel Company.

Part	(a)		(b)		(c)	
	lb/ft	Ixx	lb/ft	Ixx	lb/ft	Ixx
Steel	11.8	15.6	6.6	11.3	1.3	
Stainless steel	3.5		4.3	5.0	8.2	
Total	*15.3*	*15.6*	*10.9*	*16.3*	*9.5*	*16.5*

structural requirements (Fig. 6c). The method in 6b seems to be the one most frequently used.

All types of doors (hinged, pivoting, balanced, double-acting, revolving, and sliding) are available as standard packages complete with framing from several companies. At the same time, semi-custom-made variations with standard components can be produced to special requirements specified by the architect. Details from different manufacturers vary from roll- or brake-formed stainless steel profiles for stiles, rails, and framing to lighter-gauge stainless steel drawn or rolled tightly on aluminum extrusions. Because of the welding procedures often used in the joining of stiles to rails and because of high-impact and -abrasion conditions requiring occasional repair or refinishing, the stainless steel is always finished with mechanical polishing and/or buffing. Doors and framing made entirely out of stainless steel should have a material thickness of no less than 0.062 in. (1.5 mm) to allow for proper welding and refinishing operations. Lighter gauges can be used (0.034-in. (0.75-mm) minimum) when stainless steel is tightly drawn on aluminum or hardwood cores.

Building Facades

Stainless steels, because of their high strength and high resistance to corrosion, have been used in a great variety of end uses, with each different end use having specific requirements, ie, weldability, formability, even higher corrosion resistance, tolerance for high temperatures, etc. The stainless steels quite often are specially tailored to suit those varied end uses by means of special tolerances, properties, or chemical compositions. In the case of the building construction industry, special architectural finishes varying from mirror finishes to various matte and textured finishes are produced. In addition, sheet or coil made to special physical tolerances regarding size, gauge, shape, and flatness can be supplied on demand. It is important that the architect recognize this and specify such special finishes and tolerances carefully for those curtain walls (or other building components) that require extra care. They are, of course, unneeded for purely functional items such as a stone anchor supporting thin granite wall covering, but are essential for large flat spandrel panels.

In order to use stainless steel most effectively and thus obtain the best results and best value, it is necessary to recognize the limitations as well as the advantages of stainless steel as a curtain wall material. Cold-formed light-gauge sections are better than heavier wall extrusions. Stainless steel facing the weather should be used with aluminum extrusions for the backup grid. Exposed welds that might require expensive refinishing should be avoided, and all stainless steel members should be designed to take full advantage of the properties of the metal, using no more material than necessary.

The cost of stainless steel for curtain wall construction is such that in initial capital outlay it is generally competitive with other quality architectural materials. These include the high-quality aluminum alloys and finishes as well as bronze, copper, and natural stone such as marble or granite. Because of its minimal maintenance cost and virtually unlimited durability, stainless steel is even more competitive when life-cycle costs are considered. Repairs and replacement costs are virtually nil over the life span of a building.

Stainless steel building exteriors can be bright and shiny if the design requirements demand such a feeling or more solid and structural in feeling if that is the designer's preference. The more reflective finishes often assume the color of their environment. On the facade of the Royal Bank Building in Toronto, Ontario, Canada, (Fig. 7), the stainless steel mullions and panels reflect the gold color of the glass; and often, stainless steel, like the glass of the

Figure 7. Royal Bank Building Toronto, Ontario. Architect: The Webb Zerafa Menkes, Houston partnership, Toronto, Ontario.

curtain wall, appears blue or silver because of the color of the sky. When a combination with other materials is used, stainless steel can either blend with the color of the other material or provide contrast and delineation.

Stainless steels combine well with other materials. One potential problem of galvanic corrosion that may exist when stainless steel is coupled with other metals can be prevented, as explained before. It is resistant to masonry alkalinity, making it particularly suited for stone and masonry anchors. Stainless does not release corrosion products that could cause accelerated attack on aluminum or zinc surfaces and does not stain marble or other masonry located below. However, stainless steel can be affected adversely by staining from other materials such as carbon steel rust or copper oxide.

As described in the earlier discussion on forming and cutting methods, stainless steel is sufficiently ductile to allow it to be formed into an almost infinite variety of shapes and profiles for curtain wall components.

The ability of stainless steel to be optically flat on large flat panels has been a source of complaints in the past. This problem can be solved by simply recognizing the causes of "oil canning," by detailing and specifying the right fabrication and detail design, and by choosing the right finish. There are two principal factors contributing to oil canning: failure to provide adequate stiffness in the component, particularly in large spandrel panels, and failure to accommodate movement within a component, between components, or between components and the building. Stiffness is affected by the thickness of the material and the design of the panel, each having a direct relationship to the other. Large surfaces can be stiffened by forming grooves, flutes, or ribs and, generally, by giving them brake- or press-formed sculptured effects. Another excellent method of avoiding oil canning is to curve the panel. Figure 8 shows an example where very bright, finished stainless steel in curved shapes shows no oil canning. However, if no surface deformation is possible, stiffeners must be attached to the back of the face sheet.

Materials of good dimensional stability, such as sanded plywood, cement asbestos, or honeycomb, act as a core with stainless steel sheet laminated to the face and an aluminum, stainless steel, or galvanized light-gauge balance sheet to the back of the panel. Alternatively, top-hat sections or channels can be attached to the back as stiffeners. Care must be taken that such attachments themselves do not cause unnecessary strain. Teflon washers and sufficiently large slotted holes for mounting fasteners such as welded studs allow for proper movement caused by thermal expansion and contraction. Movement or distortion of the structure caused by positive and negative wind loads should also be considered in design to avoid stressing panels and subsequent oil canning, particularly in high-rise structures. The designer should, in addition to the above-mentioned considerations, specify tension- or stretcher-leveled sheets, select wherever possible the appropriate finish, and make certain that proper fabrication techniques are used.

An excellent example of good stiffener design and finish selection can be seen on the large flat panels shown in Figure 9. Laminating techniques were used on the span-

Figure 8. Price Waterhouse Building Vancouver, B.C. Architect: Toby Russell Buckwell & Partners, Vancouver, B.C.

drel panels of the building shown in Figure 10. It is difficult to give a rule of thumb for the specification of flatness tolerances since they depend on the gauge and reflectivity of the stainless steel. The permissible slope of the waviness of the face sheet should be closely defined, and a general method and suggested tolerance are shown in Figure 11.

Roofing, Siding, and Ductwork

For standard North American sheet metal roofing methods such as standing seam, batten seam, and flashing detail, a "dead soft," fully annealed stainless sheet with a dull or lightly textured finish is being produced on a regular basis. Standard methods and the same equipment used for other metals are used when working stainless steels.

The suggested thickness of the stainless steel for this end use is 0.015 in. (0.38 mm). When comparing the cost of stainless with that of copper roofing, it must be kept in mind that this means a weight savings of materials of 35%.

For industrial siding and load-bearing roofs, roll-forming techniques are similar to those for other metals, and an excellent variety of standard profiles is available to the designer. Because large unbroken areas are often encoun-

tered in this type of construction, it is important that a good color match exist in the profiles formed from different coils. To ensure good uniformity of color, all coils used on the building should be purchased from the same mill, and the steel mill should produce all the coils in one continuous production sequence, particularly in the annealing and pickling operations.

CLEANING AND MAINTENANCE AT THE CONSTRUCTION SITE

Often, absorptive wrappings such as interleaving paper, cardboard, and other materials are used to protect stainless steel during on-site storage. Such material should not be allowed to become wet because water-soaked paper may discolor stainless steel. Tarpaulins or plastic sheeting must be used to protect the stainless steel. This is particularly important on construction jobs where dirt, dust, carbon steel particles from grinding or welding, etc, in the presence of moisture may cause discoloration. Indoor storage is preferred.

Any drainage from concrete or mortar containing chlorides should be immediately removed. This is particularly true when cleaning masonry with strong acid cleaners. Protective coatings such as adhesive paper or plastic when stripped from the stainless steel can leave small amounts or a very thin coat of adhesive on the metal surface. This facilitates the adherence of airborne dirt particles, and the removal of the adhesive residue is important to maintain good overall appearance. A thorough initial cleaning is therefore required. The recommended practice is as follows:

1. The surface is precleaned using a slow evaporating solvent system that is compatible with water and that exhibits low toxicity. It is wiped or brushed using a long-fibered nylon brush and light strokes. It is advisable to work on one reasonably small area at a time, ie, 4×4 ft (1×1 m).
2. The surface is cleaned with detergent by wiping or brushing as in step 1.
3. It is rinsed with clean ambient-temperature water until all detergent residue is removed.
4. It is dried in ambient air; the use of a squeegee is recommended.

This initial cleaning is to be followed at regular intervals (on curtain walls when the glass is washed) by normal cleaning:

1. The surface is rinsed with water to remove as much soil as possible.
2. Soap or liquid detergent or 5% ammonia solution in water is applied.
3. It is rinsed well with water.
4. Water is removed, ensuring that all strokes are in the same direction, preferably top to bottom and overlapping, and the surface is then allowed to dry.

All architectural stainless steel materials are supplied in a passivated corrosion-resistant condition. They re-

(a)

(b)

Figure 9. (a)–(c) Commerce Court West, Toronto, Ontario. Architects: I. M. Pei, New York, N.Y. and Page & Steele, Toronto, Ontario.

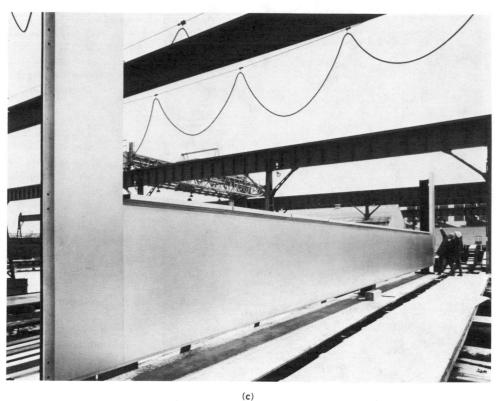

Figure 9. *Continued.*

(c)

Figure 10. University Place, Toronto, Ontario. Architect: Parkin Partnership, Toronto, Ontario.

quire periodic cleaning just as other materials do when in service. Exterior components, for example, are subjected to road salt spray at ground level and deposits from polluted urban air at higher levels. Finger marks, deposits from tobacco smoke, and other stains can detract from the original appearance of interior stainless steel applications. Since each architectural project is unique, it is difficult to generalize cleaning procedures adequate for each specific project or environmental condition. The recommended practices given serve as a basis. For situations not responsive to these guidelines, the stainless steel supplier should be contacted. The use of qualified competent specialists for this type of work is strongly recommended. Another source for cleaning recommendations for specific conditions is the suppliers of cleaning materials and products.

The architect can be the most important contributor to a building's low-cost maintenance by careful attention to some basic design considerations.

- The architect should minimize horizontal components that can collect dirt. This dirt, when washed off by rain, causes uneven streaking of the areas below.
- Designs that concentrate or directionalize the flow of rainwater should be avoided. An overhang can be projected beyond any lower one to avoid splatter or concentration of dirt-carrying water.
- Sheltered areas, such as canopies or soffits, should be designed so they can be readily cleaned, particularly in low, streetside locations.

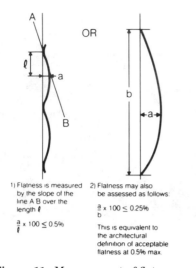

1) Flatness is measured by the slope of the line A B over the length ℓ

$$\frac{a}{\ell} \times 100 \leq 0.5\%$$

2) Flatness may also be assessed as follows:

$$\frac{a}{b} \times 100 \leq 0.25\%$$

This is equivalent to the architectural definition of acceptable flatness at 0.5% max.

Figure 11. Measurement of flatness.

- Joints that minimize dirt accumulation should be designed.
- The possibility of staining of the stainless steel by runoff from other materials, ie, rust from carbon steel clips or fasteners, should be avoided.
- Grooves, recesses, and excessively complex contours, which hamper the regular easy cleaning associated with stainless steel, should be avoided.

BIBLIOGRAPHY

1. D. Peckner and I. M. Bernstein, *Handbook of Stainless Steels,* McGraw-Hill Inc., New York, 1977, appendix I.
2. *Corrosion in Action,* International Nickel Co., Inc., New York.
3. "Finishes for Stainless Steel," AISI #9012, Committee of Stainless Steel Producers, American Iron and Steel Institute, Washington, D.C., June 1983. Available from Nickel Development Institute, Toronto, Ont., Canada.

General References

Architects' Stainless Steel Library—Design Manual, 2nd ed., The International Nickel Co. of Canada Ltd., Toronto, Ont., Canada, 1970.

Steel Products Manual Stainless and Heat Resisting Steel, American Iron and Steel Institute, Washington, D.C., December 1974.

Stainless Steel for Building Exteriors, Nickel Development Institute, Toronto, Ont., Canada, and American Iron and Steel Institute, Washington, D.C., June 1984.

B. A. Smits, *Architecture—A Demanding Market for Stainless Steel,* Nickel Development Institute, Toronto, Ont., Canada, Aug. 1986.

The Designers' Handbook Series, Design Guidelines for the Selection and Use of Stainless Steel, Nickel Development Institute, Toronto, Ont., Canada, and Committee of Stainless Steel Producers, American Iron and Steel Institute, Washington, D.C.

See also CORROSION; ENVELOPES, BUILDING; KITCHENS, RESIDENTIAL; RESTAURANT AND SERVICE KITCHENS; STRUCTURAL STEEL—GENERAL PRINCIPLES

NICKEL DEVELOPMENT
INSTITUTE
Toronto, Ontario, Canada

STAINS. See PAINTS AND COATINGS.

STAIRS AND RAMPS—SAFETY DESIGN ASPECTS

According to the National Safety Council, more than 12,000 Americans die each year in falls, which is the nation's cause of accidental deaths second only to motor vehicle accidents. For people over 75 years old, falls are the leading cause of accidental deaths. Of the total number of fatal falls, about 3800 people die on stairs. The Consumer Product Safety Commission's National Electronic Injury Surveillance System (NEISS) substantiates that falls on stairs alone result in more than 800,000 injuries each year involving hospital treatment. The NEISS is a computerized data base compiled from records in selected hospitals across the United States. In addition to reporting that falls are the second leading cause of accidental deaths in the United States, the National Safety Council also reports that a majority of falls arise from accidents in the home. (From this data it is inexplicable that the One and Two Family Dwelling Code has more relaxed stair safety criteria for residences than the national model code.) It has also been estimated that there are more than 2.5 million falls on stairs that result in minor or temporary disability not involving professional medical attention.

Various statistical studies estimate that the annual cost of stair fall injuries alone (in terms of medical expenses, lost earnings, and liability claims) exceeds the annual construction costs of new stairs in the United States, more than $2 billion (1). Of course, it is not possible to quantify the toll in human pain, suffering, and degradation in life quality resulting from fall injuries.

Because the incorporation of safe design criteria for stairs and ramps adds little to either design or construction costs, it can be seen that safety engineering of facilities before construction is extremely cost efficient. Therefore, professional architects or engineers should pay particular attention to safety and human factors in their professional role because of the U.S. accident record regarding falls, the tendency toward an increasingly litigious society, and a heightened awareness of professional liabilities.

TRADITIONAL APPROACHES

Traditionally, building/facility designers have tended to rely on compliance with statutory codes and, to a lesser extent, on consensus standards as safe design criteria.

However, there are important reasons why that approach is inadequate; these include the following:

- Codes and standards are normally developed by consensus. That is, various factions, usually having a variety of conflicts of interest, meet and agree on criteria. This sort of "least common denominator" approach is neither the most effective nor the "right stuff." A recent example of a code conflict of interest is illustrated by a 1988 U.S. Supreme Court ruling that upheld a jury verdict against Allied Tube & Conduit Corp. for its role in defeating a 1981 version of the National Fire Protection Association's model building code. The change would have allowed the use of Poly(vinyl chloride) electrical conduit (not manufactured by Allied) as an alternative to steel conduit (made by Allied). Allied blocked the change by paying the NFPA memberships of 150 people whose votes helped to defeat the code change. Consensus standards are, therefore, considered by code compliance officials to be minimum requirements, and codes can represent inadequate safety guidelines.
- Good architectural design for stairs and ramps requires the combination of scientific and engineering principles with aesthetic regard. Considerable judgment is required; no code can anticipate every possible combination of field conditions.
- Codes can contain technical errors (including typos) and grammatical errors, and they are silent on many technical issues. Codes are only a partial guide, are limited in scope, and have dubious technical origins for some of their requirements (2).

Therefore, because it is readily apparent that fall accidents are foreseeable, the architect, engineer, public facility manager, property owner, and municipal authority should exercise reasonable care and professional judgment in the layout, design, construction, and maintenance of stairways and ramps. The trend in case law is that mere compliance with a code or standard is not, by itself, a defense against negligence per se.

Because code and standard development has been a committee effort with inadequate stair safety engineering representation, statutory guidelines incorporating only minimum safety measures have been promulgated and some hazardous stair and ramp design features have been legitimized. In all major codes, certain stair safety aspects have been addressed by "silence." Examples of the latter are the lack of code provisions barring the presence of visual distractions in commercial occupancies at the very top or bottom of stairs and the lack of a definition of the term "slip-resistant." With regard to hazardous design there has been a particular problem in connection with accessibility requirements. The ANSI A117.1 committee and the compilers of many municipal, regional, and county codes have been engrossed with safe access for the handicapped; as a result, insufficient regard for the safety of the able-bodied majority has resulted. Strict compliance with the ANSI code can still permit some serious hazards

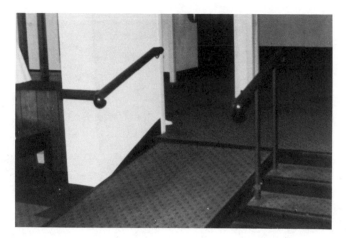

Figure 1. Unsafe ramp imposed over existing stair.

if practical judgment is not exercised (3). Actually, there is no code that pays adequate attention to safe design criteria for the ambulatory, and some of the recommended design features to accommodate the handicapped cause accidents to the population at large. The concerns of two population segments are not mutually exclusive, and a better effort is needed to accommodate everyone. Figure 1 shows an incompatible mixing of an existing stair and a handicap access ramp. In this situation, the handrail is not the length of the ramp and the ramp also projects out such that it is a tripping hazard to crosswise pedestrian traffic in the room.

Safety criteria that should be considered in designing stairs and ramps (paying particular attention to the needs of the people who will be expected to use the facilities being designed) follow.

STAIR AND RAMP DESIGN

A safe ramp and stairway system (including existing stairs that have one, two, or three steps) should have the following characteristics for both commercial/residential occupancies including one and two family dwellings:

1. Reachable, continuously graspable, and structurally stable handrails on both sides, with intermediate handrails as required.
2. Risers and treads properly proportioned (geometry) having minimal tolerances.
3. Slip-resistant tread, tread nosing, and ramp surfaces.
4. Adequate lighting, appropriately located and controlled.
5. Good maintenance.
6. Guardrails (and toeboards on steps if open on the side).
7. Absence of environmentally triggered factors.
8. General compliance with an up-to-date major building code, or, preferably, the NFPA Life Safety Code.
9. Stairs with at least three steps (except those exist-

ing "stairs" with one or two steps, which should be replaced by a ramp or modified, as discussed in the section on short flights).

Handrails

It could well be argued that the single most important safety element of stair (and ramp) safety is the handrail, because even on an otherwise safe stair, an accidental fall can occur for unknown reasons. A handrail certainly is, at least, one of the most important elements, and it is inexpensive to implement or retrofit. All major U.S. building codes and standards require handrails to be installed for stairs and ramps. Some codes qualify certain stairs as required for egress/ingress, and some architects have argued that stairs in excess of the "minimum required" or only having one or two steps do not need handrails. This is erroneous logic for two reasons. First, major codes have issued formal interpretations to the contrary and, second omitting handrails from any stairway or a short flight of steps is against common sense and is not compatible with the spirit of codes to enhance public safety. Finally, because of the large number of falls in homes, residential stairs and or steps should have handrails, contrary to the relaxed attitude expressed in the One and Two Family Dwelling Code.

Handrails serve three fundamental purposes:

- A visual signal to the approaching pedestrian of the change in elevation.
- A support to the stair user, especially children, the elderly, and others who may be motor impaired, to avoid the occurrence of fall accidents.
- A last chance that a fall victim might arrest the fall by grasping the handrail and creating braking forces or moments that may reorient the pedestrian to reduce injury severity.

Because one primary function of a handrail is visual (especially in short flights of one, two, or three steps), it is important that it be obvious, preferably of high contrast with its background. Of course, it is important that the handrail parallel the pitch of the steps to provide a reliable visual cue to the slope of descent as well as to assure that it is within the convenient range of reach for most users.

Because handrails must also serve as support to those who are fearful of falling and those who have begun to fall, careful consideration should be given to their graspability. Human factors engineers have known for many years that the optimum diameter of a tool handle for long-term gripping is 1.25 in. Stair safety researchers have found that the best shape for handrails is round and that for most people the best diameter for gripping is between 1.375 and 1.75 in. It has been pointed out that this shape and size is one of the least expensive in either wood or metal (4). In order to facilitate emergency use, handrails should be 1.5 in. away from a wall or other obstruction. In addition, any handrail should be structurally strong enough to adequately support the weight of a falling per-

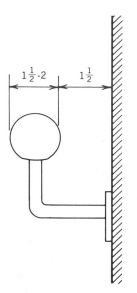

$1\frac{1}{2}$-2 $1\frac{1}{2}$

Figure 2. Handrail with optimal shape, dimensions, and proper spacing from wall.

son. The ability to support a 200 lb load applied in any direction is a common minimal code strength requirement (Figs. 2–4).

One stair-safety researcher, Jake Pauls, has suggested what he calls "The Acid Test of Graspability." Because the purpose of a handrail is to provide a secure grip for people who may be taking urgent and desperate action to prevent an accident that could lead to disability (if not death), Pauls has suggested that designers of handrails be required to hang from two sections of their proposed handrails, one grasped with each hand, and maintain that

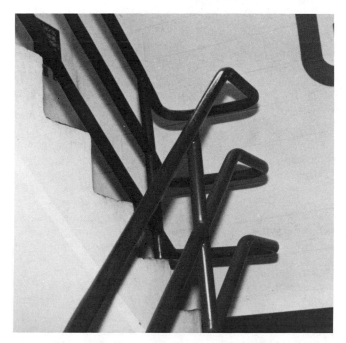

Figure 3. Example of continuous, structurally stable, and graspable handrail.

(a)

(b)

Figure 4. (a) An ungraspable handrail; (b) Handrail portion rendered unusable because of a lack of clearance.

grasp while hanging over a vat of acid (4). If his proposal were invoked, there would certainly be fewer handrails constructed of 2 × 4s, 2 × 6s, 2 × 8s, and large diameter pipes that are absolutely ungraspable by human beings. To be functional, handrails must be graspable, which means that one can curl the fingers and thumb around and underneath the handrail. Based on hundreds of fall-down accidents investigated by the author, the proper design of handrails has, evidently, been beyond the mental grasp of many designers.

The National Fire Protection Association publishes Standard No. 101, which is the Life Safety Code (LSC). The LSC contains extensive architectural/engineering criteria relative to the safe design of stairs and ramps. The 1988 LSC handily summarizes handrail graspability as follows (5):

Handrails should be designed so that they can be grasped firmly with a comfortable grip and so that the hand can slide along the rail without encountering obstructions. The profile of the rail should comfortably match the hand grips. For example, a round profile such as is provided by the simplest round tubing or pipe having an outside diameter of 1-½ to 2 in. (3.8 to 5 cm) provides good graspability for adults. Factors such as the use of a handrail by small children and the wall fixing details should be taken into account in assessing handrail graspability. The most functional as well as the most preferred handrail shape and size is circular with a 1.5 in. (3.8 cm) outside diameter (according to research with adults). Handrails used predominately by children should be designed at the lower end of the permitted dimensional range. It should be noted that handrails are one of the most important components of a stair; therefore, design excesses such as oversized wood handrail sections should be avoided unless there is a readily perceived and easily grasped handhold provided. At all times in handrail design it is useful to remember the effectiveness of a simple round profile that permits some locking action by fingers as they curl around the handrail.

The lack of any handrail or an oversized one represents a very unsafe condition. Graspable handrails can prevent or reduce the severity of a pedestrian fall regardless of the causation, existing defect(s), or environmentally triggered factor.

Steven Rosen, in *The Slip and Fall Handbook*, which is aimed at an attorney readership, states the following in his discussion of handrails (6):

A handrail . . . can aid a stair fall victim to avoid serious injuries. . . . A very important human factors aspect of handrails is that the handrail is a visual cue as to the presence of a stair system. . . . There is usually a duty on the defendant to provide at least one handrail. . . . A plaintiff may have a good case where . . . no handrails were present even though it cannot be determined what in-fact caused the person to fall. . . . Where handrails were lacking. . . the plaintiff's case is strongest.

Finally, handrails must be reachable by pedestrians; to help accomplish this end, a recent major model code change addresses this aspect by requiring handrails to be reachable within 30 in. (76 cm) of all portions of stairs (7). Figures 5–8 show additional handrail designs.

Step Geometry and Tolerance

How People Walk. As a pedestrian approaches a stair, the normal method of negotiation is to look down and deliberately position the leading foot on the first tread. After the second step is taken, the human "computer" subconsciously calculates the rise and run of the steps and subconsciously controls the locomotion of the body according to this initial computation. Stairs are normally ascended and descended via a mental process that is below the level of conscious thought (8). This mental process depends on uniformity of step geometry, however. Research has found that it is common for subjects' feet to clear the step nosings by as little as ¼ in., so that variations in riser height or tread depth predictably lead to missteps. Therefore, most building codes allow for tolerances in dimensions of no more than 3/16 in. (5 mm) be-

Figure 5. Attractive and graspable handrail.

Figure 7. Continuous, graspable handrail that runs full length of stair.

tween adjacent risers and treads, with the largest variance between any risers and treads in any flight of stairs being 3/8 in. (10 mm).

Because of the aforementioned, in investigating fall accidents on stopped escalators, it has been determined that stopped escalators are a serious safety hazard, especially in the descent mode. A stationary escalator has several risers at the top and bottom with widely varying height dimensions. To compound this, escalator treads give a visual illusion to some pedestrians and a fall can results in contact with very hard, sharp edges that easily produce injuries. Therefore, escalators should not be re-

lied on as a stationary stair, which is the practice of some mass transit systems during the rush hour.

The size of the person as well as the size of his or her feet are also significant parameters. Various modern experiments have established the importance of having treads wide enough to permit pedestrians to descend stairs without having to twist the feet to one side in a "crabwise" gait. Increasing tread depth was found to have more effect on stair safety than reducing riser heights. A study of the dimension of stairs found that the fewest missteps on experimental stairs occurred with tread

Figure 6. Improper shape, size, and slippery handrail.

Figure 8. Residential handrail that fails to protect full length of stair by a length greater than a clarinet.

depths of at least 12.3 in. (313 mm) and risers of 4.6 to 7.3 in. (117 to 183 mm). It also found that minimum energy was expended by pedestrians when climbing stairs with a pitch of about 33° (8).

Riser and Tread Geometry for Stairs. Obviously, there are many combinations of riser and tread dimensions and ratios; however, not all of them are safe. For more than 300 years architects have known the importance of step geometry, starting with the 1672 publication of experimental investigations by Francois Blondel of the Royal Academy of Architecture in Paris. His findings that humans required uniformity of geometry and a relationship of riser height to tread depth led to the development of what is known today as the universal formula for step geometry. The formula is

$$2R + T = 24\text{--}25 \text{ in.}$$
$$\text{Where } R = \text{riser height}$$
$$T = \text{tread depth}$$

Two other rule-of-thumb formulas are:

$$\text{Riser} + \text{tread} = 17\text{--}17.5 \text{ in.}$$

and,

$$\text{Riser} \times \text{tread} = 70\text{--}75 \text{ in.}^2$$

Recent scientific investigations in laboratories and observations of people using public stairs have gone far beyond Blondel's findings, however. Major model building codes have recently deleted the use of or reference to these formulas. Although these formulas are far from perfect and would exclude certain safe geometries, Rosen states in his *Slip and Fall Handbook* that ". . . ninety percent (90%) of forward fall accidents are on stair systems which do not meet this (Blondel) formula (9)." It is also known that a layperson cannot sense improper step geometry, and it is not visually apparent either. Riser and tread relationships cannot be expressed by a linear relationship.

To conclude the subject of risers and treads, it is important to note that, based on a review of the literature, the ideal riser height is 7 in. and the tread should be at least 11 in. deep exclusive of tread nosing projections (a 7–11 step). Recent building codes and the LSC minimum for riser height, however, is set at 4 in. There is no research data on the maximum allowable tread width, but the Lincoln Center Stairway in New York has deep treads and it has been the scene of numerous stumbles (8). Excessively deep treads force the pedestrian into an unusual gait and hence should be avoided. It is also interesting to note, in contrast to that allowed by code, that riser heights less than 6.25 in. have correlated to increased missteps in ascent (10). Finally, Section A-5.2.2.2.3 of the 1988 NFPA Life Safety Code gives good guidelines and illustrations of how to measure the dimensions of treads and risers.

Slip-Resistant Tread and Ramp Surface

Coefficient of Friction. Often in a court of law involving a fall-down case, a plaintiff's claim is made that the stair tread or ramp surface was slippery and that it caused the fall. Although most slips and falls occur on icy or wet surfaces, slips can and do occur when clean and dry. Some stair researchers believe that it is more likely that slips will occur on level flooring than steps, given the same surface. As a general rule, however slip-resistant floor covering is suitable for use on stairs and ramps. On the other hand, slips on stairs were found by J. Templer and coworkers, to account for more than twice as many falls as any other cause, and slips in descent were more severe than in ascent. In descent the critical area is at the tread nosing, the place at which first contact is made while the foot still has forward motion. If the tread is slick at this point, then a slip is likely (10).

The coefficient of friction (static or dynamic) is a unitless number that is used to account for the fact that tengential forces (friction) will develop if one surface moves over another, eg, shoe sole on tread. The type of friction of interest here would be under dry conditions, ie, Coulomb friction. To illustrate and better understand this concept, Figure 9 shows a block of weight W resting (static) on a flat surface with a small horizontal force (P) applied.

For the block to remain stationary, the force F opposing force P must balance it. Force F is the static friction force. Force F is created by the summation of smaller forces created by the irregular (texture) in the contact area between the block and resting plane. Research has shown that the maximum force F is equal to μN. The μ is the coefficient of friction and depends on the nature of the surfaces in contact and not on the total area. Example values of μ are listed below:

Rubber on concrete, 0.60–0.90
Metal on metal, 0.15–0.60
Metal on leather, 0.30–0.60
Wood on wood, 0.25–0.50

Should force P be increased, then there is a point reached when the block will start to slide and, hence, overcome force F. As soon as the block slides, then the force P required to keep it moving drops to a lower value. This is

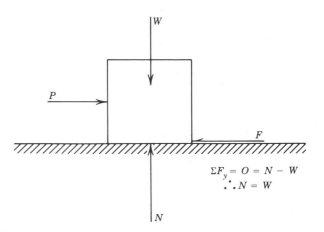

Figure 9. Diagram of the forces acting on a block on a flat surface with a small horizontal force applied. W = weight; P = applied force; F = static friction force.

the reason one senses that it is easier to keep a heavy object sliding once in motion. Therefore, from the above, intuitive insight as to how a slip or fall progresses faster once the static friction force is overcome can be generated. Static coefficient of friction (COF) is a discrete number, but the dynamic COF will vary with velocity.

Much has been written about the static and dynamic coefficient of friction and its influence as a factor in slip-and-fall accidents. Almost all fall accident investigators agree with the body of case law that a minimum COF of 0.50 is required for a safe walking surface under most conditions. There is less agreement about whether the COF should be static or dynamic or what method should be used to measure it. Increasing the COF of a surface will reduce the chance for slippage; however, achieving this is not easy because of cleaning considerations (rough surfaces harbor dirt). The challenge is to strike a balance between surface texture, cleanability, durability, appearance, and cost (13).

A recent report prepared for OSHA points out that after 50 years of research it is still not possible to define the term "slip-resistant" quantitatively. The vast majority of U.S. stair researchers and fall safety investigators think that the static COF is the index of relevance. This is because the dynamics of foot placement were observed at the National Bureau of Standards in the 1940s by the use of motion pictures and it was revealed that no slippage occurred between the floor and the shoe during normal walking (12). Others (especially European researchers) aver that dynamic COF is of more interest, because most slips or falls occur while people are in motion. By far the most widely used COF testers (the Brungraber NBS tester and the various horizontal pull slip-meters) measure static COF. The British Portable Skid Tester and the more recently developed TORTUS meter purport to measure dynamic COF.

Another part of the problem of measuring COF is that research by various laboratories shows that COF meter readings among the various types of meters are not consistently comparable for either dynamic or static measurements. Even when one holds the type of COF meter constant, meter results are not repeatable when variables such as shoe material and floor contaminants are introduced. Unfortunately, neither laboratory experts nor lawyers have come up with practical, repeatable, and precise methods for measuring slip-resistance (11).

Neither OSHA, NBS, nor any other federal organization has been able to produce an objective index measurement for the performance standard for measuring slipperiness. There are a number of ASTM standards that cover various aspects of COF testing, and these are under the jurisdiction of ASTM Committees F-13, F-15, C-21, and D-21. There are many variables, and usually some variant such as surface wear, shoe construction, or the presence of some contaminant on the floor or shoe can be found as a contributing factor in a slip accident. Figure 10 is a chart prepared by the U.S. National Bureau of Standards that shows the variation of COF indications among four kinds of static COF testing meters.

All of that is not to say that COF meter readings are totally irrelevant or useless. A clean, dry surface with a

Brungraber indication of 0.34 using leather is probably a more hazardous floor than one with a 0.78 measurement on a BPST. Meters can produce some approximation of COF that can be helpful in a laboratory environment, but COF laboratory tests alone are insufficient evaluation of walkway materials and finishes. Many safety investigators do not test for COF in the field.

Material Selection. Variables in the determination of the slipperiness or slip-resistance of any surface make it difficult to state specifically what type of floor is "safe." For example, within a shipment of floor tile of a certain specification there may be variations of COF and wear-resistance because of manufacturing tolerances. Another problem is specifying conditions, eg, clean and dry, clean and wet, that the COF should be tested under. The problem is further complicated by the type of floor dressing as well as what cleaning methods and materials will be used and there are similar variables for almost any floor material that might be specified. General categories of materials have been demonstrated to have varying degrees of safety or hazard in various environments, as determined by both accident experience and case law. Some walkway materials listed by Rosen in *The Slip and Fall Handbook* as "very dangerous" and "high risk" are terrazzo, marble, ceramic tile, quarry tile, asbestos and vinyl tile, and paint (9).

Of course, most hard surfaces can be made slippery by improper polishing or waxing. Various institutions, eg, Marble Institute of America, can be contacted for their recommendations on finishes. Be aware that floor finish materials listed by UL as being nonslip are not a complete solution because floor finish materials are seldom used as tested by UL. Furthermore, UL Subject 410 is only a tentative guide and subject to limitations (13). The architect should pass this information on to the owner when the building is turned over, and the prospective walkway surface finish should be evaluated as built. There has been an unfortunate increase in the use of ceramic (especially glazed) tiles on walkway surfaces. Most of these products belong on the wall and *not on the floor, ramp, or tread surface*. The recent trend in case law to hold the tile manufacturer responsible for accidents will soon help reverse this trend.

Carpet is a relatively safe covering material for both floors and steps, if it is short pile, lightly padded, and well secured to the substrate. Concrete can be made extremely slippery by overfinishing or use of a steel trowel during placement. For exterior surfaces, brushed concrete provides a high COF, but in high-traffic areas, it can wear smooth; on steps, slip-resistant nosings should be cast into the concrete. See Figures 11 and 12.

Factors such as durability of surface finish and variation in manufacturing tolerances should also be considered. Despite the COF measurement problems and such uncontrollable factors as pedestrian shoe selection, some effort must be made by the architect to specify a degree of slip-resistance into any stair or ramp walking surface. The architect should avoid specifying known slippery walkway surfaces, eg, ceramic tiles or polished marble, and, also, should provide the owner with a recommended

CONDITIONS EVALUATED

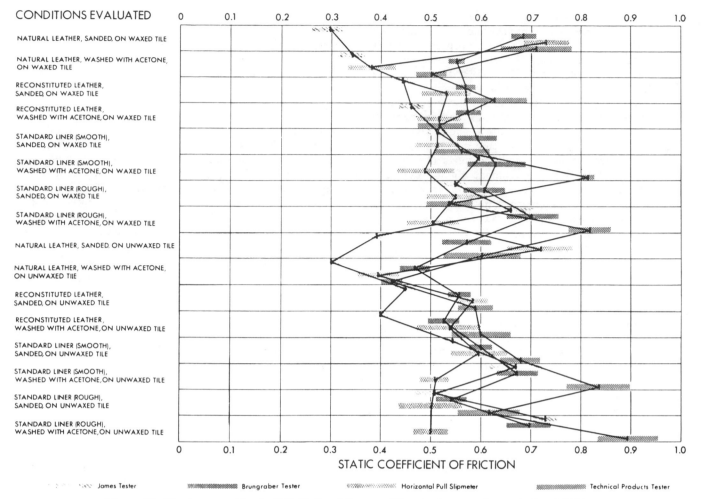

STATIC COEFFICIENT OF FRICTION

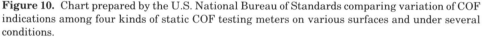

James Tester   Brungraber Tester   Horizontal Pull Slipmeter   Technical Products Tester

Figure 10. Chart prepared by the U.S. National Bureau of Standards comparing variation of COF indications among four kinds of static COF testing meters on various surfaces and under several conditions.

Figure 11. Steel pan stairs with smooth nosings should not be used. Not only is the tile too smooth, but the missing pieces create a perfect tripping hazard for a pedestrian in descent. This approach to provide a tread surface should be avoided because it cannot withstand the test of wear and tear.

system approach for maintaining the walkway surface. See Figures 13–15 for additional illustrations pertaining to slip-resistance.

Illumination of Stairs and Ramps

The subject of illumination is more complex than it appears from reviewing the requirements of building codes. First, the code compilers tend to be more expert in means of evacuating buildings during fires and other emergencies, and, second, all human factors cannot be quantified.

For example, the design of a short flight of two risers in a fancy restaurant or a furniture showroom becomes an exercise in how to highlight the steps so that they will be obvious to every pedestrian, many of whom would tend to be distracted by displays or activities the owner had provided as means of attracting customers. In such cases, handrails and spot illumination on the steps two or three times brighter than the surrounding area would be appropriate. Also, consideration should be given to who will be expected to use the stairs and under what conditions, for example, the degree of dark-adaptation. Illumination on stairs would have to be brighter if an invitee is entering a darkened room from outside at noon on a sunny summer

Figure 12. Flush slip-resistant nosings can be cast into concrete stairs. Courtesy of William English.

Figure 14. Example of stair with slip-resistant treads and nosings. Also, handrails and step geometry are correct.

day than might be otherwise required at night. Stairs used by older people might require brighter illumination than those used exclusively by elementary school students. The problem of glare must be considered along with indicated light levels. These aspects are not addressed by the building codes.

Minimum illumination levels allowed by most codes are scarcely adequate for general populations. For comparison purposes, building code illumination values are presented below:

Minimum Lighting Levels Specified by Major Codes

BOCA, 1 fc	SBC, 2 fc
UBC, 1.5 fc	LSC, 1 fc

On the other hand, the minimum illumination level recommended by the National Safety Council for stairs is 20

fc. Hence, a wide variation of recommended illuminances is in evidence. Of equal importance is that no single bulb failure should cause an area to be in total darkness.

Other considerations regarding illumination include emergency illumination performance duration, power sources, and single-failure criteria. Emergency illumination performance should be sufficient for continuous operation for 1–1.5 hours and be available for either the loss of primary power or for emergency egress. Illumination power sources should have a highly reliable source such as a public utility service as their primary power source. Emergency lighting can be powered by battery, and the emergency illumination may decline to 0.6 fc at the end of the emergency time duration. Given the failure of the primary power source, the failure of a single lighting unit should not allow any area to be in total darkness, and the

Figure 13. An upside-down floor. Because of many slips and falls on its ceramic tile foyer, the Athletic Express wisely decided to replace it. An architect specified something worse, however: highly-polished granite tile. This error was caught just before installation and it was decided to simply turn the tiles over. The tiles were sealed and a beautiful, textured floor resulted that was slip-resistant even when wet. Courtesy of Athletic Express Health Club, Gaithersburg, Md.

Figure 15. Hard rubber treads usually fail the test of wear and tear. This is a typical failure that occurs right at the nosing, which is a critical area. Also, even without the crack this tread design is unsafe because the nosing area is not slip-resistant.

emergency lighting should automatically actuate on loss of primary power.

Guards and Toeboards

Besides the support required for adult stair users, some safety engineers recommend a secondary rail at a lower level to facilitate support of small children, a high risk population on stairs. Also, any open-sided stair and ramp should be guarded so as to make it impossible for children to climb through the railing and fall below. Many codes require guards to be at least 42–44 in. high, although some permit them to be only 36 in. high (especially residential occupancies). Open guards require railing or ornamental patterns so as not to allow a 6-in. diameter sphere to pass through. See Figures 16–19 for illustrations of guard rail installations.

Another consideration is the need for toeboards to prevent objects from sliding or rolling off the edges of stairs and landings and falling to lower levels. OSHA requires 4-in. toeboards.

Absence of Environmentally Triggered Factors

Besides riser:tread proportions, dimensional tolerances, and slope, other significant safety factors are changes in direction of the stairway, low headroom, "orientation edges," and other distractions while traversing stairs or ramps.

To the extent possible, changes in direction should be avoided. For stairs, tapered treads or "winders" are very confusing to the stair user and are so hazardous as to be prohibited under the OSHA regulations. If a change in direction is required, a landing should be used as an intersection.

Figure 17. No guards needed here; one side of stair has lower handrails available.

Research by the National Bureau of Standards supports the findings of many researchers that inadequate headroom can cause stair and ramp accidents. Striking of the head on obstructions can cause serious head injury from impact, and such incidents can also lead to secondary fall accidents. Various investigators have recommended minimum headroom ranging from 7 ft 4 in. to 6 ft 6 ½ in., depending on the height range of the expected exposed population. The widely used architectural convention of 6

Figure 16. Well-guarded stair in a school. Note placement of lower handrail.

Figure 18. Good example of solid guard; however, no handrails have been provided although it is a good speculation that the top of the guard was being passed off by the architect as a handrail.

Figure 19. Open guard with inadequate protection. Accident scene where a small child stepped through the guard and fell 30 ft to his death.

ft 8 in. minimum head clearance is better for public facilities, because expected invitees of 6 ft 5 in. or taller are not rare. When an inch or so of shoe height is added along with a little margin for normal locomotion locus, the traditional 6 ft 8 in. clearance is a prudent minimum and is required by some codes. In general, the issue of headroom has been well treated by the codes.

A clear path of travel on stairs and ramps is important. The NBS and NFPA recommend that doors not swing out into stairs. In cases where that is necessary (as in fire exits), the door should open onto a landing that is configured so that opening the door does not disrupt pedestrian traffic. A glass panel compatible with the fire rating of such doors also helps to reduce the chance of a pedestrian on the stairs being surprised by a door opening into the path of travel.

Any condition that could divert the user's attention from the task of negotiating the stairs should be avoided. Such distraction would include a blast from a ventilation register discharging into the face of the pedestrian, the dripping of moisture from condensate or plumbing leaks, retail sales displays, or sharp contrasts in lighting (glare).

Projections into the path of travel can cause both accidents and injuries. Careful consideration should be given to the design of handrail hardware, decorations, and the physical features of the stair environment to minimize the chance of injury resulting from forceful contact with hard or sharp objects.

Glass panels in stairways (such as windows, mirrors, or lighting fixtures) should be protected against accidental breakage by barrier, by the use of safety glazing materials, or both. Besides the cut hazard from broken glass, it may also be possible for a pedestrian to fall through the glass to a lower elevation.

In residential occupancies and environments where stairs may not be continuously lighted, light switches should be located at landings where the stairway is en-

tered so that lighting can be readily turned on. In commercial or retail facilities, special care is required to prevent the placement of retail sales displays near the top or bottom of steps. It is suggested that architectural drawings be marked to serve as a follow-on reminder to interior designers not to place sales displays or other visual distractions within about 8 ft of the top or bottom of stairs.

Short Flights

Steps between small changes in elevation are inherently hazardous because the steps are not readily apparent. In fact, flights of one or two risers are undesirable, so much so that the major building codes and the National Fire Protection Association's Life Safety Code committees in the past have attempted to prohibit their use, requiring the substitution of ramps for stairs with less than three risers or in connecting changes of elevations less that 21 in.

The primary reason short flights are so dangerous is that the difference in elevation is so slight that visual clues are poor. The result is that many people do not see the steps until they have already begun to fall. Also, most stairway fall accidents occur on the first or second step ascending or descending, so if the flight only has two steps, it can be seen that they will always be in the higher hazard zone in either direction of travel. The NFPA Life Safety Code recommends now and in the past the avoidance of short flights, but in the 1988 edition it states that if steps are used in a short flight, then the tread should be a minimum of 13 in. (33 cm) and that each step location be readily visible. The reader is also well advised to read section A-5-1.6.2 of the 1988 NFPA LSC Standard No. 101.

The most elegant remedy for safeguarding short flights is to leave them out (Figs. 20–23). Most small changes in

Figure 20. A perfect example of where single steps should have been omitted.

Figure 21. Apartment complex steps that have no lighting and no handrails. Grading during construction could have eliminated all steps and afforded handicap access. Scene of a fall fatality.

elevation are for cosmetic reasons alone. Before designing multileveled rooms for the sake of ambience enhancement, the architect should investigate whether the benefits of the expected increase in business adequately offsets the additional costs of construction and accidents over the life of the facility.

If the client insists on having short flights, there are several treatments that can significantly reduce the incidence of falls to guests. Because the primary problem is one of perception, care should be taken to design in all possible visual cues to the presence of steps. This would include the following:

Figure 22. Residential step with no handrail. The existing wood guard could have been tied to an attractive wood handrail.

Figure 23. Without the arrow it is impossible to know where the step down is located. Scene of a fall.

- Use highly visible handrails sloping downward with the same pitch as the stairs. For example, polished brass against a dark background can provide the kind of visual contrast needed.
- Use textured and colored wall finishes that run parallel to the floor and steps to highlight the change in elevation further.
- If there is a parapet or low-level wall separating floor levels, it should slope downward at the steps, along with the railing, as an additional visual cue.
- Do not use a "busy" geometric carpet print on steps that can camouflage their presence. Greens and blues are said to be less visible than warmer color patterns.
- Highlight the steps with relatively intense lighting. A spotlight directly above the top step is a big help. Another approach is to provide small spotlights just below the handrails on both sides focused on the steps.
- Step nosings with illuminated strips embedded in their top surface are available for use in dim environments.
- If the room has a ceiling that is near the normal height of 8 ft., sloping it downward over the steps parallel to the pitch of descent will help.
- Tactile cues can be added to the visual. Using hardwood treads on all steps (including the top landing) can alert a pedestrian approaching from above of an impending change underfoot. The sensation of stepping from padded carpet to a hard surface tends to cause one to look down to see what the change is.
- As a last resort, signs on each side of the steps with arrows pointing downward can help attract a pedestrian's attention to the walking surface.

Proper treatment of short flights is a special challenge to the architect as well as the interior designer, but success in this area of vital concern goes a long way toward reducing fall accidents (Figs. 24 and 25). When existing short flights are inherited, the architect should insist on modifying them according to the above criteria.

Orientation Edges. Perhaps the most subtle hazard confronting the stair designer is the phenomenon known

Figure 24. A short flight with proper architectural treatment that includes graspable handrails on both sides, sidewall treatment, and increased lighting. Photograph by William English, PE.

among safety investigators as "orientation edge" distraction. This refers to activities, architectural vistas, or particularly "rich" views that might distract the attention of pedestrians. The challenge is intensified perhaps by a conflict between the interests of safety and profitability. Some of the dramatic presentations that might be most attractive to prospective buyers would be distractions from the task of negotiating stairs safely. An effort should be made to coordinate the two interests as delicately as possible.

RAMPS

Before the Vietnam era, most paraplegics were victims of polio or some other illness, and many of them tended to be so weak and frail as to often require assistance in getting around. The Vietnam War has given the United States a new generation of wheelchair navigators with the upper body strength sufficient to permit them to function autonomously in most situations.

The resulting pressures from veteran's groups and other handicap lobbies has forcefully brought to attention the need to remove unnecessary architectural barriers. It

is a professional challenge for the architect to design facilities that accommodate the handicapped population without discriminating against the vast majority of ambulatory guests by presenting tripping hazards to them.

The design and construction of safe ramps is as sophisticated a discipline as designing stairs. Contrary to conventional wisdom, ramps are not safer or easier to walk on than steps, unless they are very carefully designed and constructed. Visibility is even more of a problem on ramps than on stairs, because they are inherently less obvious and more difficult to highlight. The most common types of accidents on ramps result from people tripping over the edges or slipping because they are too steep and too slippery.

General Principles of Ramp Design

Several general principles contribute to ramp safety:

- Often, no ramp or steps may be required if forethought is given to configuration of the walking surface and the normal traffic flow. If architectural barriers are not built in, no means of traversing them need be provided.
- If a ramp is required, it is usually possible to position it slightly to one side of the main pedestrian traffic flow so that most people do not walk on it, and positioning handicap parking to the side of the entrance opposite the main traffic flow also helps.
- A depressed curb is almost always less hazardous than a ramp extending from the curb out into the parking lot (Figs. 26 and 27).
- Where a ramp extends into a parking lot, it is best to make it of white concrete against the black background of asphalt pavement. Ramps should not normally be painted for contrast. Yellow does not contrast very sharply with white concrete, and unless slip-resistant paint is used, the surface is likely to be slippery when wet. Painted walking surfaces also require the continual maintenance expense of frequent repainting.
- Open-sided ramps present a tripping hazard to pedestrians, frequently requiring a railing along the open side.

Figure 25. A short flight with ungraspable handrails. Photograph by William English, PE.

Figure 26. Extended ramp into parking lot offers tripping hazards over its edges.

Figure 27. A well-designed ramp using a depressed curb approach.

- Ramps should have roughened or highly slip-resistant surfaces.
- The slope of a ramp should be no greater than 1:10 and, preferably, 1:12, especially for those intended primarily for the handicapped.
- An exterior ramp should have a level platform connecting it to the doorway.
- There should be at least 6 ft of level straightaway at the top and bottom of a ramp.

One leading source of ramp problems is workmanship. Often when a safe ramp configuration is shown on construction drawings, a well-intentioned mason will "improve" it by dishing the surface or raising a curb on the open side, or he or she may apply a steel trowel finish rather than the brushed finish specified. Compliance with drawings is another field problem that can be reduced by showing adequate detail and adding cautionary notes.

OSHA

It is well known that OSHA "general industry" standards (CFR 1910) apply only to employees, and some designers tend to disregard these federal requirements in facilities intended primarily for use by the public, but there are two very good reasons why the OSHA standards should be complied with: (1) nearly every business dealing with the public has employees who are exposed to all parts of the facility, thereby invoking OSHA's jurisdiction; and (2) the OSHA requirements are well known in the courts as minimum safety precautions.

CASE HISTORIES OF SELECTED FALLS THAT ILLUSTRATE UNSAFE ARCHITECTURAL DESIGN

The cases presented here are hybrids of actual cases the author has investigated. The basic facts, engineering analyses, and findings have been modified, so any resemblance to specific loss situations is purely coincidental. The case synopses are presented to help make the reality connection between unsafe stairs and ramps and their correlation to actual pedestrian fall accidents. The author has inspected or investigated hundreds of stair and ramp systems; the cases selected are typical in terms of injury, monetary award, and/or design defect.

Fall on a Stair in a Retail Setting. The plaintiff was shopping at the defendant's premises and proceeded down a long interior stairway to the basement level. She reached the stairway landing near the bottom, turned left, and descended a flight of three steps. On reaching the last step, the plaintiff slipped on the tread nosing, fell forward, and landed on the floor. The most serious injury sustained was a fractured knee, which was the knee that struck a jagged edge depression in the floor located about 2 ft away from the last step.

The stairway in question was surfaced with a heavy-duty black rubber tread with a diamond crosshatch pattern on the horizontal surface to render it slip-resistant. However, the tread-nosing portion was smooth. The rubber tread mat was attached onto the 4 ft 9 in wide tread nosing by only two tacks—one at each end. There was no evidence of an adhesive used to secure the tread nosing along the step proper. The riser height was 7 in. and the tread depth was 12 in. (Fig. 28). At trial, the following defects were pointed out and accepted by the court:

1. The wooden "handrail" was a guardrail because it was not graspable; therefore no handrail existed.
2. The tread nosing was curved and very smooth; therefore, a slip-resistant surface was not provided for the pedestrian in the direction of descent.
3. The bottom steps were a short flight and a ramp would have been preferred or the total stair system should have been divided with a midpoint landing.
4. A retail sales shelf was contiguous to the top of the short flight and created a visual distraction.

The case was settled after the plaintiff's expert testimony, and during the trial process when the above defects were brought out and received by the jury. The stair design deficiencies were reinforced by the judge's comments made to the jury and were violations of the state-adopted building code (BOCA). This created significant pressure on the defense to settle. The plaintiff was permanently injured by the accident because of the severity of the knee fracture. The monetary award was $125,000.

Fall on a Stair with a Bad Step Design and No Handrail. This case involved a fall, on the descent, on an exterior stairway at a hotel. The plaintiff fell on a short flight of steps that connected an exterior corridor on grade to a lower level on grade. The vertical difference in elevation was about 28 in. Figure 29 illustrates the general arrangement.

An investigation was performed, and a report was produced that identified the following deficiencies:

1. No handrail was provided.
2. The riser heights were excessive.
3. The tolerance variations exceeded 3/16 in.
4. The top step had a projected lip of 1 3/4 in., which was excessive. It reduced the effective width of the

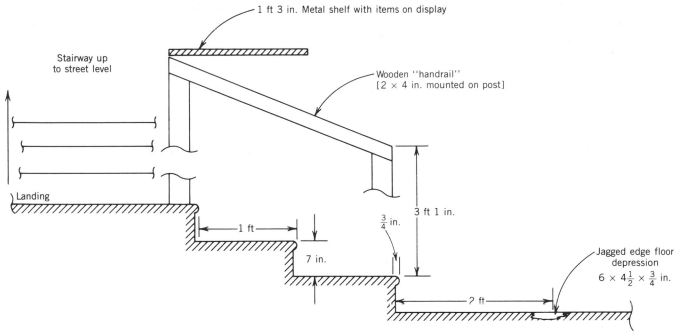
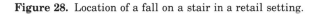

Figure 28. Location of a fall on a stair in a retail setting.

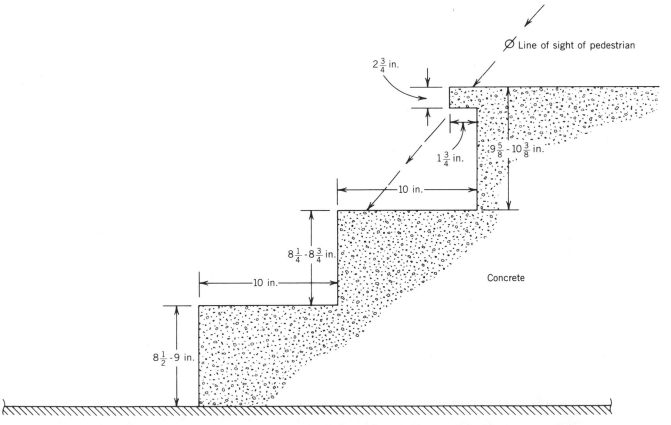

Figure 29. Location of a fall on a stair with a bad step design and no handrail.

second tread, and, more importantly, as one approached from the higher level, it disrupted the line of sight to a sufficient degree to hide the existence of the second step.

This case was settled out of court for $175,000, but the plaintiff, who was elderly, was left with a permanent disability.

Fall on an Interior Stair with Retail Sales Display Distraction and No Handrail. The plaintiff entered an upscale shopping mall store and proceeded to an elevated deck in the back via an open, interior stairway. At the top and within 2 ft of the top step of the stair a retail sales display was positioned. While examining this merchandise, the plaintiff stepped backward for a better view and fell off the top step. She reached frantically for a handrail but none was provided. Her injuries were serious, including crushed vertebrae in the neck region that subsequently required a bone-fusion operation. This injury was permanent. A lawsuit was filed citing the obvious building-code deficiencies and the other unsafe condition involving the retail sales display. The primary safety defects explained to the jury included: (1) the lack of a handrail and a guardrail; and (2) the positioning of a sales display near the top step.

It was pointed out in court that the architectural plans reviewed during the fall investigation did not specify either a handrail or a guardrail. Also, these same drawings indicated the future position of sales displays (which distracted the plaintiff) at the very top of the stairs.

This case went to trial and the jury found for the plaintiff. In addition to the use of expert witnesses, plaintiff's council brought in county inspectors who also stated that the subject stair did violate the building code regarding the absence of handrails and guardrails. The plaintiff was awarded $350,000.

Wheelchair Accident on a Ramp. After a reception at a country club, an invitee who was confined to a wheelchair was leaving via a ramp that led from the top of the front-door steps to the driveway. Figure 30 is a side view of the ramp and step arrangement. The ramp was installed over

existing steps. The control of the wheelchair was lost, and, when the wheelchair reached the bottom, the ramp slope was sufficiently steep so as to cause the wheels to hit and stop at the intersection of the ramp with the driveway. The wheelchair occupant was thrown out of the wheelchair and landed on the driveway, sustaining significant injuries.

An investigative report revealed the following deficiencies:

1. The ramp slope was excessive.
2. The ramp should have had a 6-ft level landing at the top and bottom of the ramp.
3. A ramp located outside of a doorway must be separated from the doorway by a level platform; this ramp was connected to the front door by a separate smaller ramp.
4. The wheelchair accident was primarily caused by the excessive slope of the main (second) ramp.

This case was settled out of court for an undisclosed sum of money.

CONCLUSION

Because of the unfavorable accident record in the U.S. regarding fall-related deaths and injuries, safe stair and ramp design demands serious attention by the architect, engineer, and all others responsible for design, construction, modification, layout, and maintenance. Although major building codes and the NFPA LSC contain much helpful stair and ramp criteria (especially the latest editions), they do have limitations that require in-depth, detailed, and independent professional input. In other words, a "cookbook" approach is insufficient. The retention and use of a safety engineer specializing in fall prevention may be necessary, especially for facilities having many or unusual stairs or ramps. Falls on stairs and ramps have complicated causes, so the safe design of stairs and ramps can easily go beyond a local code or consensus standard.

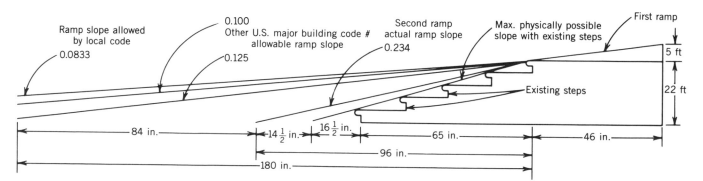

Figure 30. Location of a wheelchair accident on a ramp. Note: (1) the ramp is composed of two separate sections; (2) the larger ramp traverses five steps, and the other section is over a small landing located directly at the front door; and (3) the primary ramp has an incline (slope) of 0.234, whereas the smaller ramp over the landing has an incline of 0.109.

Fall prevention on stairs and ramps is a very worthwhile endeavor simply because of the magnitude of the public safety problem. Safe stair and ramp engineering is the practical application of "engineering common sense" and specialized safety knowledge. This is best acquired by the use and understanding of human-factors engineering, codes and standards, and the investigation of the many types of fall accidents involving stairs and ramps.

BIBLIOGRAPHY

1. J. Pauls, "What Can We Do To Improve Stair Safety?," *The Building Official and Code Administrator,* Part I, 9 (May/June 1984).

2. J. Pauls, "Stair Safety: Review of Research," *Proceedings of the 1984 International Conference on Occupational Ergonomics,* Ottawa, Canada, 1984.

3. W. English, "Deciding on Proper Fall Protection May Depend on Design of Industry," *Occupational Safety and Health* 47, 48 (Aug. 1985).

4. J. Pauls, "What Can We Do To Improve Stair Safety?," *The Building Official and Code Administrator,* Part II, 16 (July/Aug. 1984).

5. *Life Safety Code Standard No. 101,* National Fire Protection Assn., Quincy, Mass., 1988, Section A-5.2.2.6.5(c).

6. S. Rosen, *The Slip and Fall Handbook,* Hanrow Press, Columbia, Md., 1983.

7. Ref. 5, p. 8.

8. J. Templer and coworkers, "The Dimensions of Stairs," *Scientific American* (Oct. 1974).

9. Ref. 6, pp. 9, 82, 84.

10. J. Templer and coworkers, *An Analysis of the Behavior of Stair Users,* National Bureau of Standards, Washington, D.C., Nov. 1978, pp. 30, 34.

11. W. English, "What Floor Tile is Safest?," *National Safety News* 64 (Dec. 1984).

12. R. Brungraber, *A New Portable Tester for the Evaluation of the Slip-Resistance of Walkway Surfaces,* National Bureau of Standards, Washington, D.C., July 1977, p. 4.

13. *Outline of the Proposed Investigation for Determining the Slip-Resistance of Floor Treatment Materials,* UL Subject 410, Underwriters Laboratories, Chicago, Ill., Jan. 1974.

General References

Accident Prevention Manual for Industrial Operations—Engineering and Technology, 9th ed., National Safety Council, Chicago, Ill., 1988.

A Design Guide for Home Safety, U.S. Department of Housing and Urban Development, Washington, D.C., Jan. 1972.

S. Adler and coworkers, *A History of Walkway Slip-Resistance Research at the National Bureau of Standards,* National Bureau of Standards, Washington, D.C., 1979.

American National Standard for Buildings and Facilities, ANSI A117-1, American National Standards Institute, New York, 1986.

T. Cohn, "Escalators: The Visual Illusion," *ITS Review* 7(4), 4 (Aug. 1984).

W. English, "Don't Fall Down on the Job," *National Safety News* (Feb. 1976).

N. Ellis, *Introduction to Fall Protection,* American Society of Safety Engineers, Country Club Hills, Ill., 1988.

W. English, "Maintain a Fall-Free Environment," *Safety & Health,* 39 (July 1988).

W. English, *Why People Fall Down,* Hanrow Press, Columbia, Md., in press.

J. Fruin, "Pedestrian Falling Accidents in Transit Terminals," *Proceedings of the Human Factors Society—28th Annual Meeting,* San Antonio, Tex., 1984.

B. Maki, *Influence of Handrail Height and Stairway Slope on the Ability of Young and Elderly Users to Generate Stabilizing Forces and Moments,* National Research Council, Toronto, Ontario, March 1984.

J. Miller and coworkers, *Work Surface Friction: Definitions, Laboratory and Field Measurements, and a Comprehensive Bibliography,* Occupational Safety and Health Administration, Washington, D.C., 1983.

Accident Facts, National Safety Council, Chicago, Ill., 1985.

J. Pauls, "Are Functional Handrails Within our Grasp?," *Proceedings of the Environmental Design Research Association—18th Annual Conference,* Ottawa, Canada, 1987.

J. Pauls, *Means of Egress and Stair Design,* synopsis of a presentation, National Fire Protections Assn. Fall Meeting, Atlanta, Ga., Nov. 1986.

J. Pauls, "The Movement of People in Buildings and Design Solutions for Means of Egress," *Fire Technology* **20**(1), 27 (Feb. 1984).

J. Pauls, *Recommendations for Improving the Safety of Stairs,* Building Practice Note, National Research Council of Canada, Ottawa, June 1982.

M. Redfern, "Preventing Slip and Fall Injuries Requires Environmental Controls," *Occupational Safety and Health,* 34 (Sept. 1987).

J. Templer, "The Forgiving Stair," *Proceedings of the Human Factors Society—28th Annual Meeting,* San Antonio, Tex., 1984.

See also Fire Safety—Life Safety; Handicapped Access Laws And Codes; Movement Of People; Physical And Mental Disability, Designing For; Zoning And Building Regulations

Gregory A. Harrison, PE
Gaithersburg, Maryland

The author thanks William English, PE, and Elizabeth Murphy for their help in preparation of this article.

STANDARDS, BUILDING.   See Zoning And Building Regulations.

STEEL IN CONSTRUCTION

Steel, because of its great tensile and compressive strength in relation to weight, is a major structural material in building construction and the structural material of choice for very tall buildings and long-span structures. The ability to produce steel with differing chemical and thus structural properties, to transform these steels into structurally efficient shapes during manufacture and during both off- and on-site fabrication, and then to fasten the resulting shapes together to create supporting structures of an even wider variety of configurations, makes it a truly remarkable material.

Apart from its use in building as the primary structural material, steel also is used for beams, joists, columns, and fasteners in predominantly timber or masonry structures, as reinforcement for concrete and unit masonry, and in composite construction. As a consequence, there are many facets to structural design in steel. Space limitations, however, necessitate giving attention here primarily to the more basic principles and applications.

LOADS

Regardless of the material(s) used, structural design of buildings begins with a determination of the forces that must be resisted. These are divided into dead loads, live loads, and environmental loads. Dead loads are those produced by the dead weight of the structural support system itself and by the permanent supported materials and equipment. Generally, these loads are expressed in pounds per square foot (psf) or pounds per lineal foot (plf) or as a point (concentrated) load in pounds (lb). Live loads are those produced by what are essentially occupancy loads—eg, people, movable furniture, equipment and partitions, and stored materials. They generally are expressed in psf of surface over which they are applied. Environmental loads include those produced by wind, snow, rain, soil and hydrostatic pressure, and earthquakes. With the exception of earthquake forces, these loads also generally are expressed in psf. Earthquake loads generally are expressed in terms of an equivalent lateral load—ie, building weights are assumed to be collected at the roof and each floor level and then converted to equivalent horizontal loads. There also are special loads such as those produced by impact and isolated, temporary concentrations such as can occur when a very heavy object or piece of equipment is placed over or suspended from a structural member (both of which are considered as part of the live load), and overpressures and self-straining forces such as those caused by temperature- and moisture-induced movement.

Much of the process of structural analysis and design involves tracing the various loads from point of first impingement—eg, on a floor, exterior wall, or roof—through the structure and ultimately to the foundations. In the case of dead loads that result from the weight of materials, including the structural elements and assemblies themselves, there is the added problem of being unable to accurately determine their magnitude until the structure has been designed and the various elements have been selected. This means that the process of design must be one of successive approximations; ie, weights are assumed, members and assemblies are designed, actual weights are calculated, and the calculated weights are compared to those assumed. If the latter are substantially different from those assumed at the outset, the process is repeated. Actually, with increased design experience, starting assumptions become quite good and recalculation is minimized. Live loads also have a unique aspect in that they can vary over time—eg, different space utilization—therefore, the approach to live-load calculation generally involves drawing on experience for the establishment of

acceptable minimums for various types of occupancy and then stipulating occupancy limitations to avoid those that could materially differ from those assumed for design. For example, 40 psf is considered normal for dwellings and school classrooms, 50–80 psf for offices, and 75–100 psf for retail stores. In the case of environmental loads, the approach again is to rely heavily on accumulated experience—wind loads, for example, being derived from historical records of wind velocities and frequency of extreme occurrences, snow loads from historical records of snow accumulations, and earthquake loads from both historical and geological data.

Finally, it is necessary to determine what combination of the various loads are likely to produce the most unfavorable effect in the structural element being considered. This may occur when one or more of the contributing loads is "not" acting. The basic combinations for what is known as "allowable stress design," as recommended in the ASCE/ANSI *Minimum Design Loads for Buildings and Other Structures* (1), are

$$D$$
$$D + L + (L_r \text{ or } S \text{ or } R)$$
$$D + (W \text{ or } E)$$
$$D + L + (L_r \text{ or } S \text{ or } R) + (W \text{ or } E)$$

In the above formulas, D = dead loads, L = live loads, L_r = roof live loads, S = snow loads, R = rain loads, W = wind load, and E = earthquake load.

Although the most unfavorable effects from both wind and earthquake loads must be considered, they need not be assumed to act at the same time. Also, under certain circumstances there are permissible reductions in live loads, eg, for members having an area of influence of 400 ft^2 or more.

There also are provisions for loads produced by fluids (F), the aforementioned loads due to soil and water in soil (H), loads due to ponding of water on roofs (P), and loads due to the noted self-staining forces (T).

Where life safety is concerned, however, the actual building code in force, many of which are based on the ASCE/ANSI Standard (past or present) will govern what actual unit loads are to be used in design and how they are to be determined and applied. Actual load determinations will be introduced as they become necessary to the analysis and design processes.

TERMINOLOGY

Many analytical methods, terms, and symbols used in structural analysis and design are generic in the sense that one will find them in use regardless of the basic structural material used—eg, steel, timber, concrete, unit masonry, or composites. However, the reverse also is the case, either because of unique material properties or simply the fact that design procedures have grown up around the material itself. As a result, there are, unfortunately, more than a few instances of overlap, ie, where the same terms and symbols are used to designate quite different things. It is important, therefore, that care be taken not to assume that a term or symbol used for one material means the same thing for another. For this reason, a glossary of terms and symbols for use with steel has been provided at the end of this article. The use of this glossary can readily begin with a discussion of working stresses, a logical starting point in the analysis of material response to applied forces.

WORKING STRESSES

The term working stress is a carryover from early design procedures and can be loosely defined as the unit stress to which steel will be subjected in actual use (based on the elastic performance of the structure). The allowable working stress is considerably less than the breaking strength of the steel. Building codes—at least the model codes and those actual codes that are up-to-date—are in reasonably good agreement on allowable working stresses for steel. This is largely due to the work that has been done by technical societies and industry associations, most notably the American Institute of Steel Construction (AISC), ASTM, the American Iron and Steel Institute (AISI), and the Steel Joint Institute (SJI).

The allowable working stresses for steel are listed in the 1978 AISC *Specification for the Design, Fabrication, and Erection of Structural Steel for Buildings,* which is incorporated in the eighth edition of the AISC *Manual of Steel Construction* (2). (Both these documents will be referred to frequently here because they are relied on so heavily as guides to and aids in the design of steel buildings.) Working stresses are given as a percentage of the yield stress, which varies with each type and grade of steel. Because the yield stress is closely associated with that point where permanent deformation takes place, it is a basic and important physical property of the material and a guide to its strength. Furthermore, the allowable working stress depends on the type of stress under consideration, ie, axial tension, bending, shear, and such. For example, except in the case of plates more than 8-in. thick, a steel with the designation A36 has a yield point of 36,000 psi and, under certain circumstances, would have an allowable working stress in bending that is 60% of 36,000 or 21,600 psi, which is rounded off to 22,000 psi or 22 ksi (kips per square inch, where a kip is 1000 lb). It should be noted that the tensile breaking strength of this same steel is between 58 and 80 ksi. The design of light-gauge steel members will not be treated here; for information on working stresses for these steels refer to Refs. 3 and 4.

Again, it should be borne in mind that any given building code will not necessarily reflect the latest AISC, AISI, and SJI specifications nor even the model codes; therefore, the actual code in effect where the design is to be implemented should always be consulted on allowable working stresses as well as other pertinent design and construction requirements.

FACTOR OF SAFETY

No structural member is ever designed to carry a load that will develop its full ultimate strength under normal ser-

vice conditions. There are too many uncertainties in determining loads and in the quality of materials and construction to attempt to take structural materials to their performance limits. As a result, some margin of safety must be provided; this is done by setting allowable working stresses at values that are well below the ultimate strength. The ratio between ultimate strength and working stress is often referred to as the factor of safety. However, this is not a wholly adequate definition, because failure of a structural member in a building actually begins when the stress exceeds the yield point or, more precisely, the elastic limit. This is due to the fact that deformations resulting from stresses above this value are permanent and thus change the shape of the structure even though there may be no danger of collapse. The relationships between ultimate strength, elastic limit, yield point, and deformation under stress are better left to a text on strength of materials.

TYPES

The types of structural steels available are discussed in the article on Structural Steel and need not be repeated here. The assigned designations are those given by ASTM. A7 Steel, which is no longer produced, may still be encountered in rehabilitation work; however, the standard structural steel for buildings today is A36, and where higher strength is desired, the choice likely will be A572. The strength of A36, A572, and other steels used in building construction are shown in Table 1.

The higher strength steels understandably cost more, but this does not mean that the overall cost of a structure will necessarily be greater where these steels are used. Because steel prices are based on weight, the use of higher strength steels can reduce average weight and thus overall cost even though the steel itself may cost more per pound. Also, the higher strength steels often can help resolve architectural problems by reducing the dimensions of members or enabling one to maintain consistent member measurements even when loads increase; eg, in the case of lower-story columns that would otherwise be larger than those above because of the increased weight they must support.

ARCHITECTURAL CONSIDERATIONS

Although the structural frame for any given building will be developed from the standpoints of structural adequacy and economy, column locations and spacing will usually be determined by architectural considerations arising from anticipated as well as immediate occupancy requirements. It is important to recognize that just as there generally is more than one architectural scheme that will satisfy occupancy requirements, so too there will be several satisfactory structural solutions. Obviously, the architectural and structural schemes should be compatible; ie, they should "build" well without resorting to unduly complex or extravagant structural arrangements. The same can be said for mechanical/electrical and communications schemes.

Table 1. Structural Steels for Buildings[a]

ASTM Designation[b]	Strength		Available Forms (ASTM Rolled Shape Groups[d] and Plates)[e]	
	Minimum Yield Stress, ksi	Tensile Stress,[c] ksi		
A36	36	58–80[f]	All shapes, plates, bars	
A441	40	60	No shapes	Plates over 4 to 8
	42	63	Shape groups 4, 5	Plates over 1½ to 4
	46	67	Shape group 3	Plates over ¾ to 1½
	50	70	Shape groups 1, 2	Plates to ¾
A242	42	63	Shape groups 4, 5	Plates over 1½ to 4
	46	67	Shape group 3	Plates over ¾ to 1½
	50	70	Shape groups 1, 2	Plates to ¾
A588	42	63	No shapes	Plates over 5 to 8
	46	67	No shapes	Plates over 4 to 5
	50	70	All shapes	Plates to 4
	42	60	All shapes	Plates over ½ to 6
A572[g]	50	65	All shapes	Plates to 2
	60	75	Shape groups 1, 2	Plates to 1¼
A514	90	100–130	No shapes	Plates over 2½ to 6
	100	110–130	No shapes	Plates to 2½

Corrosion-resistant steel: A242, A588

[a] Ref 5.
[b] It should be noted that A440 steel, which was not recommended for welding, is no longer produced.
[c] Minimum unless range is given.
[d] Shape groups are in accordance with ASTM A6.
[e] All thickness are in inches.
[f] Minimum 58 ksi for shapes over 426 lb per ft.
[g] Also available in stress grade.

In multistory buildings of skeleton-frame construction, the most economical center-to-center column spacing for average loads is on the order of 22 to 28 ft. Spacings of less than 20 ft are seldom economical from a structural standpoint, and those greater than 30 ft, even in one direction, can usually be justified only when occupancy considerations call for the greater unobstructed floor area that such spans provide. These guidelines do not, however, apply to tall buildings, which frequently pose unique structural problems. The principles that are presented herein are generally applicable to all types of steel-frame buildings; however, emphasis has been placed on the more common types of low- and medium-rise buildings such as low- to medium-rise commercial and industrial buildings, schools, apartment houses, and hospitals.

DESIGN PROCEDURE

The general arrangement of floor framing, and especially the location of columns, should be borne in mind during development of the architectural scheme. Preliminary framing plans (Fig. 1) should be made and column dimensions approximated before a final scheme is adopted. This is necessary because the size of columns and the clearances required, especially in the lower stories, may materially affect the architectural layout. As soon as the floor-framing arrangement has been established, beams (or joists), and girders can be designed, followed by the final

design of columns and foundations. Note that the beams (or joists) are designed first because they are the first to receive the loads from the flooring. They deliver the floor loads, plus the weight of the floor and the beams themselves, to the girders, which in turn carry the loads to the columns. Throughout development of the structural design, the architectural, structural, and mechanical/electrical plans must be constantly checked against one another to ensure adequacy and efficiency of the design, its constructibility, and its ultimate operation as a finished building.

Although for small buildings the structural framing is sometimes shown directly on the architectural drawings, this is not a recommended practice. For projects of any appreciable size, a separate set of framing plans is essential if the location, size, and joining of structural members are to be recorded and made readable without confusion with other information.

BEAM DESIGN

Apart from exterior cladding and deck, and interior flooring, the structural member usually given initial design attention is the beam (or its equivalent, the joist, or in roof construction, the purlin). The complete design of beams requires an analysis of bending, shear and deflection, and lateral and local buckling. Deflection and buckling, which are associated with beam sections not having adequate

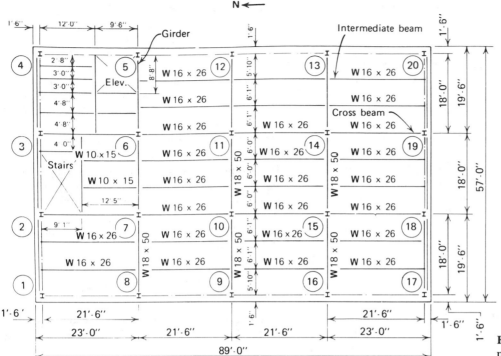

Figure 1. Typical floor-framing plan (5).

lateral support (not restrained from lateral movement), must be investigated because they could affect the maximum allowable fiber stress to be used in the design.

THE BEAM BENDING FORMULA

The expression for resisting moment is the beam or flexure formula and takes the form

$$M = \frac{F_b I}{c}, \quad f_b = \frac{Mc}{I}, \quad \text{or} \quad \frac{I}{c} = \frac{M}{F_b}$$

where F_b is the maximum allowable fiber stress for the material, M is the maximum bending moment the beam can resist, and the expression I/c (moment of inertia divided by the distance c) is the section modulus (S) of the beam shape. By letting $I/c = S$, these formulas become $M = F_b S$, $f_b = M/S$, and $S = M/F_b$. In the first case, when the dimensions of the beam shape are known and thus the section modulus (I/c or S) is known, solving for M gives the maximum bending moment the beam can resist. In the second, when the maximum bending moment due to the loading and the shape dimensions are known, solving for f_b gives the developed bending stress in the extreme fiber. And when the bending moment and the allowable extreme fiber stress are known, solving for S gives the required beam shape section modulus. The last-named form is the one most often used in design; ie, solving for S and then selecting a beam section that will provide a section modulus equal to or greater than this value.

As noted earlier, the basic allowable bending stress (F_b) is taken as 60% of F_y. (It should be noted, however, that there are circumstances—not important to this discussion—under which this value can be increased to 66%

of F_y and in others decreased to 20 or 30% of F_y.) F_b and F_y are expressed in psi, c in in., S in in.[3], I in in.[4], and M in in.-lb (inch-pounds). If the computed value of M from reactions and loads is in ft-lb, as is generally the case, it must be multiplied by 12 before use in the above formulas. For A36 Steel, when $F_y = 36$ ksi, $F_b = 0.6(36) = 21.60$, which is rounded to 22 ksi; and when $F_y = 42$ ksi (eg, A572 steel), $F_b = 0.6(42) = 25.20$; or 25 ksi.

SHEAR RESISTANCE

Once a beam has been designed for bending, it should be checked for resistance to shear. Where the span is short and/or the beam is heavily loaded or must support large, concentrated loads near its supports, shear failure is a possibility. The shear formula is $f_v = V/A_w$, where V is the maximum permissible web shear, A_w is the beam web thickness (actual depth of the beam times its web thickness), and f_v is the average unit shearing stress. The allowable shear stress is $F_r = 0.45 F_y$.

DEFLECTION

Establishing a deflection limit is difficult because with the exception of ponding of water on a roof, safety seldom will be affected by the deflection of a beam that is adequate in other respects. Beam deflections can have other unwanted effects, however. For example, there may be a need to control deflection to a specific amount under dead load to maintain construction clearance. Under live load, if allowed to deflect too much, a beam can affect materials and constructions abutting or attached to it, eg, door frames, windows, and plastered ceilings. In the absence of a need to control deflection to a specific dimension, it is customary to set a live load limit of 1/360 of the span when plaster or other frangible materials are attached and a total load limit of 1/240 otherwise. Indeed, for psychological reasons, if the deflection will be visible or will result in a perceptively "springy" floor, it would be well to control it by imposing one of these limitations.

The AISC Manual (2) provides similar deflection-limiting guides; eg, for large, open floor areas, free of partitions that can dampen the effects of repeated live loads such as can be produced by foot traffic, a minimum beam depth equal to 1/20 of the span is suggested. For fully stressed beams and girders supporting floors, a depth guide in the form of the ratio $F_y/800$ is provided; for roof purlins, the value is $F_y/1000$. In the case of an A36 floor beam over a simple span of 30 ft, for example, the minimum depth would be

$$\frac{36}{800}(30)12 \simeq 16 \text{ in.}$$

Beam diagrams with deflection formulas for the most frequently encountered loading conditions can be found in the AISC Manual (2) and other reference works (5). It is not feasible to develop deflection formulas for every conceivable combination of beam support and loading; indeed, in some instances the problem of determining deflection may be so complex that the use of a computer program may be the only feasible solution. The symbols I (moment of inertia) and $\triangle$ (deflection) can be reversed so as to compute the required moment of inertia rather than the actual deflection. An effective beam-design procedure is to establish the needed section characteristics and then select a section and test the choice made. If a beam is subjected to both distributed and concentrated loads, the total deflection at any point is the sum of the deflections calculated separately at the same point.

BEAM-DESIGN PROCEDURE

The usual beam-design procedure is as follows:

1. Construct the beam loading (or space) diagram.
2. Assume a beam depth and a beam weight.
3. Construct shear and moment diagrams and determine maximum values of M and V (or use appropriate formulas).
4. Solve for S required (M actual/F_b allowable) and select a trial beam section from the AISC Allowable Stress Design Selection Table (2) or Dimensions and Properties Table (2). The value of F_b must be assumed to be some percentage of F_y and either verified or refined, based on the trial section selected. (As noted earlier, both deflection and beam buckling could affect the value of F_b.)
5. Compare the actual beam weight with that assumed. If the assumed weight is significantly more or less than the actual, repeat steps 3 through 5 until there is reasonable agreement.

6. Check for shear resistance:

$$f_v \text{ actual} = \frac{V_{\text{actual}}}{A_{w\text{ actual}}} \leqslant F_{v\text{ allowable}}$$

If f_v is greater than the allowable, return to step 4 and select another trial section having a greater web area (A_w). Then, repeat steps 3 through 6 until the trial section meets requirements for both bending and shear. (With standard rolled sections, resistance to shear will seldom be a problem.)

7. Determine the desired allowable deflection ($\triangle$) inches and calculate the maximum deflection. (A standard formula can be used if available.)

For example, for a floor beam supporting a uniform load on a simple span, the formula is

$$\triangle_{\text{actual}} = \frac{5wL^4}{384EI} \leqslant \triangle_{\text{allowable}}$$

and if it supports a single concentrated load at its center, the added deflection would be calculated using the formula

$$\triangle_{\text{actual}} = \frac{PL^3}{48EI} \leqslant \triangle_{\text{allowable}}$$

In the case of a typical floor girder where a simple span girder accepts third-point or quarter-point loads from the beams, the formulas are

$$\triangle_{\text{actual}} = \frac{23PL^3}{648EI} \text{ for third-point loads}$$

and

$$\triangle_{\text{actual}} = \frac{19PL^3}{384EI} \text{ for quarter-point loads}$$

In this case, the girder also would support a uniform load—its own weight—so the $5wL^4/384EI$ formula for uniform load also would be needed.

If the $\triangle_{\text{actual}}$ exceeds the $\triangle_{\text{allowable}}$, return to step 4 and select another trial section having a larger moment of inertia (I). Then, repeat steps 3 through 7 until the trial section meets requirements for bending, shear, and deflection.

The AISC Manual (2) provides many charts and tables that aid in the selection of the most economical and appropriate sections and thus in carrying out the design procedure. Only those necessary to augment this presentation are, with the courtesy of AISC, included herein.

APPLICATION OF DESIGN PROCEDURE

The following examples illustrate the total design procedure for bending, shear, and deflection, but without consideration of buckling. (The numbering of steps will differ from that of the general procedure outlined above.)

Example 1

Design the lightest weight section that will support a uniform load of 750 plf over its entire simple span of 24 ft (Fig. 2). Use A36 Steel with $F_b = 0.66F_y$ and $E = 29,000,000$ psi. Limit maximum total load deflection to 1/240 of the span.

1. Assume a beam weight of 25 plf, or $w = 775$ plf If $L/24$ is used as a guide for the depth, $d_1 = 12$ in. If $F_y/800$ is used as a guide for the depth.

$$d_2 = \frac{36}{800}(24)12 = 13.0 \text{ in.}$$

The beam load reactions are

$$R_L = R_R = V = \frac{775(24)}{2} = 9300 \text{ lb}$$

$$V_{max} = 9300 \text{ lb}$$

2. The maximum bending moment at midspan is

$$M = \frac{wL^2}{8}$$

$$= \frac{775(24)^2}{8}$$

$$= 55,800 \text{ ft-lb}$$

$$M = 55,800(12)$$

$$= 669,600 \text{ in.-lb}$$

3. Compute the required section modulus, assuming the depth will be adequate to use $F_b = 0.66(36) = 24$ ksi

$$S = \frac{M}{F_b} = \frac{669,600}{24,000} = 27.9 \text{ in.}^3$$

4. Select the lightest weight beam that will provide the required section modulus. Referring to Table 2, select W 14 × 22.

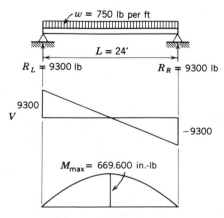

Figure 2. Beam diagram.

$$S = 29.0 \text{ in.}^3 > 27.9 \text{ in.}^3 \text{ required}$$

The 14-in. depth > 13.0, as determined in step 1; therefore, $F_b = 24$ ksi is verified.

5. Check the W 14 × 22 for shear; $F_v = 14,500$ psi; $A_w = t_w$ (thickness of web) × d (depth of section).

$$f_v = \frac{V}{td} = \frac{9300}{0.230(13.74)} = 2,943 < 14,500 \text{ psi}$$

6. Check the maximum deflection at midspan. From Figure 3, the moment of inertia (I) for the W14 × 22 is 199 in.⁴, and the allowable deflection is

$$\triangle_{allowable} = \frac{\text{span}}{240} = \frac{24(12)}{240} = 1.20 \text{ in.}$$

and

$$\triangle = \frac{5wL^4}{384EI} = \frac{5(775)(24)^4(12)^3}{384(29,000,000)199}$$

$$= 1.00 < 1.20 \text{ in.}$$

Because the actual deflection does not exceed the allowable, the beam is satisfactory in deflection.

The W 14 × 22 satisfies all three requirements (for bending moment, shear, and deflection) and is adequate. The assumed beam weight of 25 plf is slightly greater than the actual, however, not enough greater to justify a recalculation in the hope of being able to use a lighter section. This can be checked by computing $\triangle$ based on a 772-plf load. Had the assumed weight been considerably less than the actual, a decision would be necessary, ie, whether the difference would have sufficient effect of justify a recalculation to see if a heavier section is needed.

Example 2

The problem of Example 1 also may be handled beyond step 6 by solving the deflection equation for the moment of inertia required. Steps 1 through 6 are the same.

7. Determine required moment of inertia to limit deflection to the 1.20 in. specified.

$$I = \frac{5wL^4}{384E\triangle} = \frac{5(775)(24)^4(12^3)}{384(29,000,000)1.20} = 166 \text{ in.}^4$$

8. Select the lightest weight section furnishing an $I \geq 166$ in.⁴ and an $S \geq 27.9$ in.³ Referring to Table 2, make a trial selection based on section modulus only. This is W 14 × 22. Next, refer to Table 3. From the table, it will be seen that the lightest weight section having an $I \geq 166$ is the same W 14 × 22. As seen from step 5, shear is not critical, and the actual weight is close enough to the assumed weight to consider the selection adequate.

Table 2. Typical Allowable Stress Design Selection Table S_x (For Shapes Used as Beams)[a]

$F_y = 50$ ksi								$F_y = 36$ ksi		
L_c, ft	L_u, ft	M_R, kip-ft	S_x, in³	Shape	Depth d, in.	F_y' ksi		L_c, ft	L_u, ft	M_R, kip-ft
4.1	4.7	80	29.0	W 14 × 22	13¾			5.3	5.6	58
5.2	8.2	77	27.9	W 10 × 26	10⅜			6.1	11.4	56
7.2	14.5	76	27.5	W 8 × 31	8	50.0		8.4	20.1	55
3.6	4.6	70	25.4	W 12 × 22	12¼			4.3	6.4	51
5.9	12.6	67	24.3	W 8 × 28	8			6.9	17.5	49
5.2	6.8	64	23.2	W 10 × 22	10⅛			6.1	9.4	46
3.6	3.8	59	21.3	W 12 × 19	12⅛			4.2	5.3	43
2.6	3.4	58	21.1	M 14 × 18	14			3.6	4.0	42
5.8	10.9	57	20.9	W 8 × 24	7⅞	64.1		6.9	15.2	42
3.6	5.2	52	18.8	W 10 × 19	10¼			4.2	7.2	38
4.7	8.5	50	18.2	W 8 × 21	8¼			5.6	11.8	36
2.9	3.6	47	17.1	W 12 × 16	12			4.1	4.3	34
5.4	14.4	46	16.7	W 6 × 25	6⅜			6.4	20.0	33
3.6	4.4	45	16.2	W 10 × 17	10⅛			4.2	6.1	32
4.7	7.1	42	15.2	W 8 × 18	8⅛			5.5	9.9	30
2.5	3.6	41	14.9	W 12 × 14	11⅞	54.3		3.5	4.2	30
3.6	3.7	38	13.8	W 10 × 15	10			4.2	5.0	28
5.4	11.8	37	13.4	W 6 × 20	6¼	62.1		6.4	16.4	27
5.3	12.5	36	13.0	M 6 × 20	6			6.3	17.4	26
1.9	2.6	33	12.0	M 12 × 11.8	12			2.7	3.0	24
3.6	5.2	32	11.8	W 8 × 15	8⅛			4.2	7.2	24
2.8	3.6	30	10.9	W 10 × 12	9⅞	47.5		3.9	4.3	22
3.6	8.7	28	10.2	W 6 × 16	6¼			4.3	12.0	20
4.5	14.0	28	10.2	W 5 × 19	5⅛			5.3	19.5	20
3.6	4.3	27	9.91	W 8 × 13	8			4.2	5.9	20
5.4	8.7	25	9.72	W 6 × 15	6	31.8		6.3	12.0	19
4.5	13.9	26	9.63	M 5 × 18.9	5			5.3	19.3	19
4.5	12.0	23	8.51	W 5 × 16	5			5.3	16.7	17
3.4	3.7	21	7.81	W 8 × 10	7⅞	45.8		4.2	4.7	16
1.9	2.3	21	7.76	M 10 × 9	10			2.6	2.7	16
3.6	6.2	20	7.31	W 6 × 12	6			4.2	8.6	15
3.5	4.8	15	5.56	W 6 × 9	5⅞	50.3		4.2	6.7	11
3.6	11.2	15	5.46	W 4 × 13	4⅛			4.3	15.6	11
3.5	12.2	14	5.24	M 4 × 13	4			4.2	16.9	10
1.8	2.0	13	4.62	M 8 × 6.5	8			2.4	2.5	9
1.7	1.8	7	2.40	M 6 × 4.4	6			1.9	2.4	5

[a] Ref. 6. Courtesy of the American Institute of Steel Construction.

LATERAL BUCKLING

A beam subjected to bending is in tension at one flange and in compression at the other. It is the compression flange that tends to buckle, and this tendency increases as the stress increases. If buckling occurs, it will be in the direction of least resistance. As the web firmly holds both flanges vertically, this direction is sideways or laterally and is nearly always accompanied by some twisting. Figure 3 illustrates the hypothetical buckled position of a simply supported beam. The vertical displacement shown is normal deflection and is not due to buckling.

The shape of a beam also affects its tendency to buckle. An economical beam usually has a large moment of inertia about its x-x axis and a relatively small moment of inertia about its y-y axis. The tendency to buckle increases as the ratio $Ix\text{-}x/Iy\text{-}y$ increases. Therefore, the deeper and narrower the section, the more susceptible it is to buckling.

Table 3. Typical Moment of Inertia Selection Table I_x (For W and M Shapes)[a]

Shape	I_x, in⁴	Shape	I_x, in⁴	Shape	I_x, in⁴	Shape	I_x, in⁴
W 36 × 300	**20,300**	**W 30 × 99**	**3,990**	**W 24 × 55**	**1,350**	**W 16 × 26**	**301**
		W 14 × 283	3,840	W 21 × 62	1,330	W 14 × 30	291
W 36 × 280	**18,900**	W 21 × 147	3,630	W 18 × 76	1,330	W 12 × 35	285
		W 27 × 102	3,620	W 16 × 89	1,300	W 10 × 49	272
W 36 × 260	**17,300**	W 12 × 305	3,550	W 14 × 109	1,240	W 8 × 67	272
		W 24 × 117	3,540	W 12 × 136	1,240	W 10 × 45	248
W 36 × 245	**16,100**	W 14 × 257	3,400	W 21 × 57	1,170		
				W 18 × 71	1,170	**W 14 × 26**	**245**
W 36 × 230	**15,000**			W 16 × 77	1,110	W 12 × 30	238
W 14 × 730	14,300			W 14 × 99	1,110	W 8 × 58	228
W 33 × 241	14,200			W 18 × 65	1,070	W 10 × 39	209
				W 12 × 120	1,070		
W 36 × 210	**13,200**	**W 27 × 94**	**3,270**	W 14 × 90	999	**W 12 × 26**	**204**
W 33 × 221	12,800	W 21 × 132	3,220				
W 14 × 665	12,400	W 12 × 279	3,110	**W 21 × 50**	**984**	**W 14 × 22**	**199**
		W 24 × 104	3,100	W 18 × 60	984	W 8 × 48	184
W 36 × 194	**12,100**	W 14 × 233	3,010	W 16 × 67	954	W 10 × 30	170
W 33 × 201	11,500	W 21 × 122	2,960	W 12 × 106	933	W 10 × 33	170
				W 18 × 55	890		
W 36 × 182	**11,300**	**W 27 × 84**	**2,850**	W 14 × 82	882	**W 12 × 22**	**156**
W 14 × 605	10,800	W 12 × 252	2,720				
		W 24 × 94	2,700	**W 21 × 44**	**843**	**M 14 × 18**	**148**
W 36 × 170	**10,500**	W 21 × 111	2,670	W 12 × 96	833	W 8 × 40	146
W 30 × 211	10,300	W 14 × 211	2,660	W 18 × 50	800	W 10 × 26	144
		W 21 × 101	2,420	W 14 × 74	796	W 12 × 19	130
W 36 × 160	**9,750**	W 12 × 230	2,420	W 16 × 57	758	W 8 × 35	127
W 14 × 550	9,430	W 14 × 193	2,400	W 12 × 87	740	W 10 × 22	118
W 30 × 191	9,170			W 14 × 68	723	W 8 × 31	110
				W 10 × 112	716		
W 36 × 150	**9,040**	**W 24 × 84**	**2,370**	W 18 × 46	712	**W 12 × 16**	**103**
W 14 × 500	8,210	W 18 × 119	2,190	W 12 × 79	662	W 8 × 28	98.0
W 30 × 173	8,200	W 14 × 176	2,140	W 16 × 50	659	W 10 × 19	96.3
W 33 × 152	8,160	W 12 × 210	2,140	W 14 × 61	640		
				W 10 × 100	623	**W 12 × 14**	**88.6**
W 36 × 135	**7,800**					W 8 × 24	82.8
W 33 × 141	7,450			**W 18 × 40**	**612**	W 10 × 17	81.9
W 14 × 455	7,190			W 12 × 72	597	W 8 × 21	75.3
W 27 × 178	6,990	**W 24 × 76**	**2,100**	W 16 × 45	586		
		W 21 × 93	2,070	W 14 × 53	541	**M 12 × 11.8**	**71.9**
W 33 × 130	**6,710**	W 18 × 106	1,910	W 10 × 88	534	W 10 × 15	68.9
W 14 × 426	6,600	W 14 × 159	1,900	W 12 × 65	533	W 8 × 18	61.9
W 27 × 161	6,280	W 12 × 190	1,890			W 10 × 12	53.8
W 14 × 398	6,000			**W 16 × 40**	**518**	W 6 × 25	53.4
						W 8 × 15	48.0
W 33 × 118	**5,900**	**W 24 × 68**	**1,830**	**W 18 × 35**	**510**	W 6 × 20	41.4
W 30 × 132	5,770	W 21 × 83	1,830	W 14 × 48	485	W 8 × 13	39.6
W 27 × 146	5,630	W 18 × 97	1,750	W 12 × 58	475	M 6 × 20	39.0
W 14 × 370	5,440	W 14 × 145	1,710	W 10 × 77	455		
W 30 × 124	5,360	W 12 × 170	1,650	W 16 × 36	448	**M 10 × 9**	**38.8**
W 24 × 162	5,170	W 21 × 73	1,600	W 14 × 43	428	W 6 × 16	32.1
				W 12 × 53	425	W 8 × 10	30.8
W 30 × 116	**4,930**			W 12 × 50	394	W 6 × 15	29.1
W 14 × 342	4,900			W 10 × 68	394	W 5 × 19	26.2
W 24 × 146	4,580	**W 24 × 62**	**1,550**	W 14 × 38	385	M 5 × 18.9	24.1
		W 18 × 86	1,530			W 6 × 12	22.1
W 30 × 108	**4,470**	W 14 × 132	1,530	**W 16 × 31**	**375**	W 5 × 16	21.3
W 14 × 311	4,330	W 16 × 100	1,490	W 12 × 45	350		
W 27 × 114	4,090	W 21 × 68	1,480	W 10 × 60	341	**M 8 × 6.5**	**18.5**
W 12 × 336	4,060	W 12 × 152	1,430	W 14 × 34	340	W 6 × 9	16.4
W 24 × 131	4,020	W 14 × 120	1,380	W 12 × 40	310	W 4 × 13	11.3
				W 10 × 54	303	M 4 × 13	10.5
						M 6 × 4.4	7.20

[a] Ref. 7. Courtesy of the American Institute of Steel Construction.

Plan of top flange

Section at
mid-span

Figure 3. Beam lateral buckling (5).

Obviously, no beam could buckle if the surrounding construction prevented it. When a beam is thus prevented from lateral movement, it is classified as laterally supported. The task of deciding when a beam is laterally supported, however, is not always a simple one. When in doubt, the beam should be designed as laterally unsupported, as this is the more critical assumption. Figure 4 shows several types of construction that are generally recognized as providing adequate complete lateral support of the top flange. Precast floor systems held in place by clips, for example, are not generally considered sufficiently rigid to provide lateral support, nor is a beam embedded in

a conventional masonry wall necessarily provided lateral support by the the wall alone.

Special or regular intermediate members also may be introduced at predetermined points along the length of a beam to provide needed lateral support. However, connections must be carefully detailed to assure this support and even then can buckle between points of lateral support if the distances are too great. The general rule, therefore, is that the shorter the laterally unsupported length, the greater the resistance to buckling. It should be noted too that because it is the compression flange that may buckle, this will be the bottom rather than the top flange over

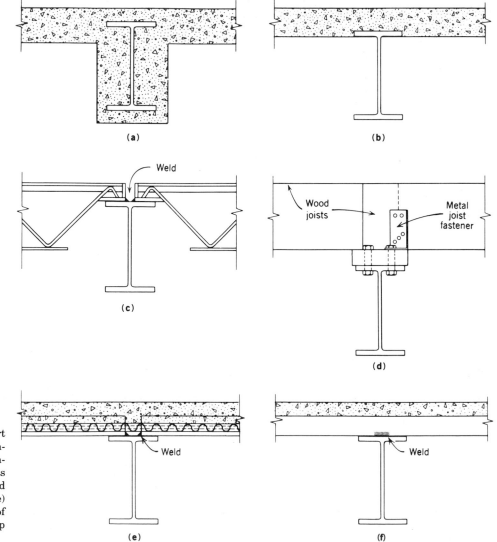

Figure 4. Complete lateral support of top flange (5): (a) beam fully encased in concrete; (b) beam flange encased in concrete; (c) bar joists welded to top flange of beam; (d) wood nailer bolted to top flange of beam; (e) bulb tees welded to top flange of beam; (f) metal deck welded to top flange of beam.

portions of any beam having negative bending moment such as at overhangs. It is necessary to establish early in the design process whether a beam should be classified as one having adequate lateral support or as one that is laterally unsupported. The proper classification depends on the proportions of the beam, and as a general rule, these proportions cannot be determined until the design process has begun and a trial selection has been made. When this is the case, a successive approximation procedure is necessary; ie, assume a condition to exist, then modify it as subsequent calculations indicate the need.

BEAMS: LATERALLY SUPPORTED

Two principal factors must be considered: conditions that constitute adequate lateral support, and those that dictate the allowable stress (F_b) for beams having adequate lateral support. Under the conditions shown in Figure 4, any beam, regardless of its proportions, can automatically be classified as having adequate lateral support, provided the beam is subjected to positive bending only (ie, compression on the top flange). Other constructions do not provide continuous lateral support but do furnish support at specific points along the length of the beam. If the distance from one point of lateral support to another is excessive, then, as earlier noted, the compression flange could buckle between these points (Fig. 5).

When beams have adequate lateral support, the allowable bending stress varies between $0.6F_y$ and $0.66F_y$. The higher value ($0.66F_y$) can be used only if the beam is classified as compact and its unbraced length (L_b) does not exceed a special L_c length for each flanged beam. Most rolled beam shapes are compact (particularly if made from A36 steel).

Because each flanged beam will have an identifiable beam width, depth, and flange area for a specific grade of steel, each will have a unique length for the limits of its bracing points if it is to be classified as laterally supported. There are two formulas for calculating the L_c length of a given beam. According to the AISC specification (2), both conditions must be met in order to use the higher allowable stress ($0.66F_y$). The first formula, based on lateral buckling, is

$$L_c = \frac{76b_f}{\sqrt{F_y}} \quad \text{and controls when } d/t_f \leq \frac{263}{\sqrt{F_y}}$$

The second formula, based on torsional twisting, is

$$L_c = \frac{20,000}{(d/A_f)F_y}$$

and controls when

$$d/t_s > \frac{263}{\sqrt{F_y}}$$

Both values for L_c can be calculated, and then the smaller of the two can be used for comparing with L_b; alternatively, the limiting formula can be established first by observing its proportions (d/t_f) and comparing this value with $263/\sqrt{F_y}$. The term d/A_f in the twisting formula is the depth of the section divided by the area of the compression flange; the value of d/A_f for each rolled beam is listed along with its other properties in the AISC Manual (2). All other terms in the formulas are identifed in Figure 6. The controlling value of L_c for each rolled section is listed in the AISC Manual along with other design values in both the Allowable Stress Design Selection Table and the table of Uniform Load Constants (2).

When the actual buckling length L_b exceeds L_c, $0.66F_y$ cannot be used for the allowable bending stress. Under these conditions, the stress drops the $0.6F_y$ or less. There is a unique length L_u for each flanged beam associated with to $0.6F_y$ allowable stress. When the actual buckling length L_b exceeds the L_c but does not exceed its L_u, it is still classified as having adequate lateral support, but the allowable stress is equal to $0.6F_y$. When L_u is exceeded, the beam is considered laterally unsupported.

The complete explanation of L_u includes two additional factors. In resisting buckling, an important property of a shape is its radius of gyration. The symbol is "r" and can be calculated from the formula $r = \sqrt{I/A}$. Here the proportions of the compression flange when referenced to the y axis of the beam (Fig. 7), which includes one third of the area of the compression part of the web, are of importance. This specific radius of gyration is referred to as r_T, and the value for each rolled section, together with its other dimensions and properties, is listed in the AISC Manual (2).

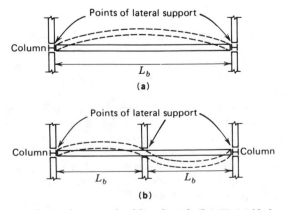

Figure 5. Lateral support buckling length (L_b) (5). (**a**) No lateral support (planview); (**b**) lateral support at midspan (planview).

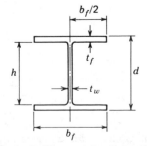

Figure 6. Beam proportions (5).

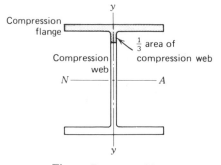

Figure 7. r_T area (5).

The use of r_T in determining L_u is shown in the formulas that follow.

The other feature influencing buckling length is the moment gradient multiplier. Its symbol is C_b, and its value ranges from 1 to 2.3. It can be applied only if the beam is loaded in the plane of its web, and is bent about its major axis and the rectangular compression flange has an area not less than that of the tension flange.

The value of C_b is frequently taken as unity (1.0) and, therefore, could constitute a conservative assumption—ie, when $C_b = 1.0$, the assumption can be made that the compressive bending stress will remain constant between braced points or that its maximum value will be located somewhere between the braced points and not at the ends. If less critical conditions are known to exist, there will be a lesser tendency to buckle. The value of C_b depends on the variation in bending moment throughout the length of the beam in relation to the location of the bracing points.

The 1978 AISC specification (2) provides the following formula for calculating C_b

$$C_b = 1.75 + 1.05 \left(\frac{M_1}{M_2}\right) + 0.3\left(\frac{M_1}{M_2}\right)^2 \leq 2.3$$

where M_1 is the smaller and M_2 the larger bending moment at the ends of the unbraced length, taken about the strong axis of the member, and where the ratio of the end moments (M_1/M_1) is positive for reverse curvature bending and negative for single curvature bending. When bending at any point within an unbraced length is larger than at both ends of this length, the value of C_b is taken as 1.0

For a further explanation of C_b, refer to the beam shown in Figure 8. Bracing points are located at the reac-

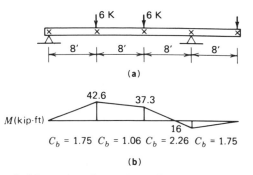

Figure 8. Moment gradient (5). (**a**) Beam loading; (**b**) moment diagram.

tions and at each applied concentrated load (denoted by the symbol "x"). The cantilever length is

$$C_b = 1.75 + 1.05 \left(-\frac{0}{16}\right) + 0.3\left(-\frac{0}{16}\right)^2 = 1.75$$

The length between the right reaction and the first 6-kip load is

$$C_b = 1.75 + 1.05 \left(+\frac{16}{37.3}\right) + 0.3$$

$$\left(+\frac{16}{37.3}\right)^2 = 1.75 + 0.45 + 0.06 = 2.26$$

The length between the two concentrated loads is

$$C_b = 1.75 + 1.05 \left(-\frac{37.3}{42.6}\right) + 0.3$$

$$\left(-\frac{37.3}{42.6}\right)^2 = 1.75 - 0.92 + 0.23 = 1.06$$

Two formulas are used to establish L_u, the length that cannot be exceeded if $0.6F_y$ is to be used as the allowable bending stress. The formula based on twisting is

$$L_u = \left[\frac{20,000}{(d/A_f)F_y}\right]C_b$$

and controls when $(r_T)\dfrac{d}{A_f} \leq \dfrac{62.62\sqrt{C_b}}{\sqrt{F_y}}$

The formula based on buckling is

$$L_u = \left[r_T \sqrt{\frac{102,000}{F_y}}\right]\sqrt{C_b}$$

and controls when $(r_T)\dfrac{d}{A_f} > \dfrac{62.62\sqrt{C_b}}{\sqrt{F_y}}$

Both values of L_u can be calculated and then the larger of the two used for comparing with L_b, or the governing formula can be established first by comparing the product of r_T and d/A_f with $62.62 \sqrt{C_b}/\sqrt{F_y}$.

When $C_b = 1$, the twisting formula for L_u is the same as for L_c. The controlling value of L_u for each rolled section when $C_b = 1$ is listed in the AISC Manual, together with other design values in both the Allowable Stress Design Selection Table and the table of Uniform Load Constants (2).

Although not explicitly described in the AISC Specification, the listed value of L_u, if based on the twisting formula, can be multiplied by C_b and the resulting product used for comparison with L_b. However, when the buckling formula controls, the listed value should be multiplied by $\sqrt{C_b}$. Expressed in equation form, a beam has adequate lateral support for a stress of $0.6F_y$ if

$$L_b \leq L_u C_b, \quad \text{when twisting controls}$$

or

$$L_b \leq L_u\sqrt{C_b}, \quad \text{when buckling controls}$$

The eighth edition of the AISC Manual (2) lists a total of 226 shapes commonly used as beams: W, those having essentially parallel flange surfaces; S, American Standard beams, which have a slope on their inner flange surface; and M, shapes that cannot be classified as W, HP (bearing pile), or S shapes.

As an example, consider a W 10 × 30 beam of A36 steel. It has a depth-to-flange thickness ratio of 10.47/0.510 = 20.53 < 263/$\sqrt{36}$ = 43.83, so buckling controls the L_c length. Therefore,

$$L_c = \frac{76b_f}{\sqrt{F_y}} = \frac{76(5.81)}{\sqrt{36}(12)} = 6.13 \text{ ft}$$

Checking the product of r_T and d/A_f, 1.55(3.53) = 5.47 < 62.62/$\sqrt{36}$ = 10.44. Consequently, the twisting formula controls the L_u value. Taking $C_b = 1$,

$$L_u = \frac{20,000}{(d/A_f)F_y} = \frac{20,000}{3.53(12)36} = 13.1 \text{ ft}$$

The beam is considered to have adequate lateral support if the actual unbraced length L_b is $\leq$ 13.1 ft. However, should the moment gradient C_b be equal to 1.25, the unbraced length could be increased to 1.25(13.1) = 16.4 ft. Once it is established that a beam has adequate lateral support, the allowable bending stress (F_b) will range between $0.6F_y$ and $0.66F_y$, the exact value depending on L_c and the degree of compactness of the particular section. Exceptions to this are beams of A514 steel, some built-up box beams, and built-up beams of two different grades of steel (hybrids).

Compact beams are defined as those sections (Fig. 6) meeting the following width-thickness ratios:

$$\frac{b_f/2}{t_f} \leq \frac{65}{\sqrt{F_y}} \qquad \frac{d}{t_w} \leq \frac{257}{\sqrt{F_y}}$$

the latter of which assumes an axial as well as a bending stress, which is not always the case.

Compact sections are braced so that $L_b \leq L_c$ may have a higher allowable bending stress, ie, $F_b = 0.66F_y$. Most rolled beam sections meet the requirement for compactness when the yield stress is relatively low. The AISC Manual *Dimensions and Properties* tables (2) list, for each section, values of $F_y{}'$ and $F_y{}'''$, which is the theoretical yield stress at which the section ceases to be compact. $F_y{}'$ pertains to the flange and $F_y{}'''$ to the web. (See Symbols at the end of this article for more detailed definitions.)

Beams that are braced so that $L_b \leq L_c$, but that are not fully compact, have F_b values ranging between $0.6F_y$ and $0.66F_y$ and are established by the blending formula

$$F_b = F_y\left[0.79 - 0.002\left(\frac{b_f}{2t_f}\right)\sqrt{F_y}\right]$$

Note that when $b_f/2t_f$ becomes $95/\sqrt{F_y}$, the quantity within the bracket becomes 0.6.

Summarizing, the allowable bending-stress formulas for beams that are laterally supported are:

When $L_b \leq L_c$, $L_b \leq L_u$, and the beam is compact,

$$F_b = 0.66F_y$$

When $L_b \leq L_c$, $L_b \leq L_u$, and the beam is not compact,

$$F_b = F_y\left[0.79 - 0.002\left(\frac{b_f}{2t_f}\right)\sqrt{F_y}\right]$$

When $L_b > L_c$, but $L_b \leq L_u$

$$F_b = 0.6F_y \quad \text{(compactness not a consideration)}$$

When $L_b > L_c$ and L_u, the beam is not adequately laterally supported and

$$F_b < 0.6\,F_y$$

Example: Design of a Roof System

A plan showing beams and girders of a 24 by 30 ft interior bay is shown in Figure 9. The beams, girders, and columns will be attached with flexible connections; therefore, only simple reactions are generated. The deck is of 20 ga. metal, topped with 2-in. reinforced-stone concrete—ie, a one-way deck transferring all its load directly to the beams. The top flange of the beams is 1 in. above the top flange of the girders; therefore, the deck does not come in contact with the girders. The deck is spot-welded (with welding washers) to the beam, providing the latter with complete lateral support (similar to Fig. 4f).

One inch of rigid insulation and a 5-ply built-up roof is applied to the deck, and a metal lath and gypsum plaster ceiling is hung from the deck. The combined live and environmental load is 30 psf. Using A36 steel, the beam and girder are designed and checked for roof ponding.

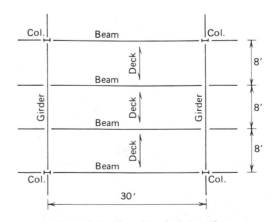

Figure 9. Interior bay framing plan.

1. Loads

The dead load is

5-ply built-up roof	6.0 psf
1-in. rigid insulation	1.5 psf
2-in. reinforced-stone concrete deck	25.0 psf
20-gauge metal decking	2.5 psf
Metal lath and gypsum plaster hung ceiling	10.0 psf
	Total = 45.0 psf

The total beam loading (shown in Fig. 10a) a maximum moment and shear are as follows:

Live and environmental load	30(8) = 240 plf
Dead load	45(8) = 360 plf
Assumed beam weight	= 30 plf
	Total = 630 plf

then

$$M_{max} = \frac{0.63(30)^2}{8} = 70.9 \text{ ft-kips}$$

$$V_{max} = R = \frac{0.63(30)}{2} = 9.45 \text{ kips}$$

2. Estimate the beam depth and allowable bending stress, using a span-depth guide of 1/24.

$$d_{min} = \frac{30(12)}{24} = 15 \text{ in.}$$

Because the beam's compression flange (top) has complete lateral support, and the selected beam will likely be compact, the stress can be assumed to be

$$F_b = 0.66(36) \approx 24 \text{ ksi}$$

3. Determine required moment of inertia (I). From step 1, the combined live and environmental load $w = 240$ plf. The maximum allowable live load deflection for a plastered ceiling is

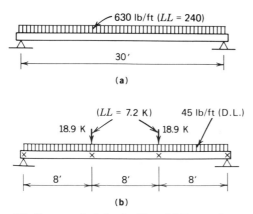

630 lb/ft (LL = 240)

30′

(a)

(LL = 7.2 K)   45 lb/ft (D.L.)

18.9 K   18.9 K

8′   8′   8′

(b)

Figure 10. Beam and girder loading. (a) Beam; (b) girder.

$$\triangle_{max} = \frac{30(12)}{360} = 1.00 \text{ in.}$$

and

$$I_{req} = \frac{5}{384} \left(\frac{0.24(30)^4(12)^3}{29,000(1.00)} \right) = 151 \text{ in.}^4$$

4. Calculate the required section modulus and select a trial section.

$$S_{req} = \frac{M}{F_b} = \frac{70.9(12)}{24} = 35.5 \text{ in.}^3$$

Because there are no 15-in. deep W shapes, refer to Table 4 for the 16-in. deep beam group. The lightest weight section having an $S \geq 35.5$ in.^{3} and an $I \geq 151$ in.^{4} is W 16×26 ($S = 38.4$ in.^{3} and $I = 301$ in.^{4}).

5. Check to see if the W 16×26 is compact. Flange maximum width-thickness ratio

$$\frac{65}{\sqrt{36}} = 10.8$$

Actual ratio

$$\frac{5.500}{2(0.345)} = 7.97 \quad \text{OK}$$

The section is compact, and $F_b = 24$ ksi; the assumed beam weight (30 lb/ft) is satisfactory. No changes are necessary.

6. Check shear

$$f_r = \frac{V}{A_{web}} = \frac{9.45}{15.69(0.250)} = 2.41 \text{ ksi}$$

because

$$2.41 < 14.5 \text{ allowable,} \quad \text{OK}$$

7. Calculate and sketch girder loading and determine maximum moment and shear (Fig. 10b).

The girder supports an area of $30(24) = 720$ ft^2. As noted earlier, in some instances codes permit a live load reduction for roofs as well as floors; however, appropriateness depends greatly on the exposure and nature of the live load expected. None will be taken here. Because a beam frames into the girder from each side

girder point live load = 0.24(30) =	7.2 kips
girder point dead load = 0.39(30) =	11.7 kips
	Total = 18.9 kips

Assume a girder weight of 45 plf. Then, referring again to Figure 10b

$$M_{\text{max}} = \frac{18.9(24)}{3} + \frac{0.045(24)^2}{8}$$

$$= 151 + 3 = 154 \text{ ft-kips}$$

$$V_{\text{max}} = 18.9 + 0.045\left(\frac{24}{2}\right) = 19.4 \text{ kips}$$

8. Estimate the girder depth and allowable bending stress using a depth-span ratio of 1/24

$$\text{depth}_{\text{min}} = \frac{24(12)}{24} = 12 \text{ in.}$$

Beams provide point lateral support at 8-ft intervals, therefore, $L_b = 8$ ft. If the girder selected has an $L_c \geq 8$ ft and is compact, $F_b = 0.66F_y$. If the girder selected has an $L_c > 8$ ft $< L_u$, $b = 0.66(36) = 24$ ksi.

9. Determine the required moment of inertia. The maximum live and environmental load deflection is $24(12)/360 = 0.8$ in.

$$I = \left(\frac{23}{648}\right)\frac{7.2(24)^3(12)^3}{29,000(0.8)} = 263 \text{ in.}^4$$

10. Calculate the required section modulus and select a trial section.

$$S_{\text{req}} = \frac{154(12)}{24} = 77 \text{ in.}^3$$

Referring to the AISC Manual "Allowable Stress Design Selection Table" (similar to that of Table 2) and Table 3, the W 21 × 44 in Table 3 having an $S = 81.6$ in.^{3} and $I = 843$ in.^{4} is selected as a trial section.

11. Verify the assumptions and modify the selection if required.

From the Allowable Stress Design Selection Table for A36 steel (2), the W 21 × 44 has L_c and L_u values (6.6 ft and 7 ft, respectively) that are less than $L_b = 8$ ft. Also, $C_b = 1.0$ because the center 8 ft has a maximum moment between braced points. Therefore, this first trial section does not have adequate lateral support and $F_b < 0.6F_y$. Although this section might still be found to be satisfactory if it were analyzed as a beam without adequate lateral support, as examined here, it does not verify the assumptions made in step 8. Therefore, select a W 18 × 50, which is 6 lb more in weight but 2.67 in. less in depth.

From the AISC Manual (2) for the W 18 × 50, it will be found that $I = 800$ in.^{4}, $S = 88.9$ in.^{3}, $L_c = 7.9$ ft, and $L_u = 11.0$ ft.

Because $L_b = 8$ ft > 7.9 ft but < 11.0 ft, F_b is not equal to the 0.66 F_b assumed and is therefore $0.6F_y$. Then, $F_b = 0.6(36) \simeq 22$ ksi and

$$f_b = \frac{154(12)}{88.9} = 20.8 \text{ ksi}$$

Because $20.8 < 22$, the bending stress is acceptable.

12. Check shear.

$$f_v = \frac{19.4}{17.99(0.355)} = 3.04 \text{ ksi} \qquad \text{OK}$$

13. Check for roof ponding.

The AISC Specification provides that unless a roof surface is provided with sufficient free drainage, it must be analyzed to assure safety under ponding conditions. The system is considered safe if

$$C_p + 0.9C_s \leq 0.25$$

and

$$I_d \geq 25S^4/10^6$$

where

$$C_p = \frac{32L_sL_p^{\,4}}{10^7I_p}$$

and

$$C_s = \frac{32SL_s^{\,4}}{10^7I_s}$$

In the above formulas

L_p = column spacing in the direction of the girder, in ft (length of primary members)

L_s = column spacing perpendicular to the direction of the girder, in ft (length of secondary members)

S = spacing of secondary members in ft

I_p = moment of inertia of primary members in in.^{4}

I_s = moment of inertia of secondary members in in.^{4}

I_d = moment of inertia of the steel deck supported as secondary members in in.^{4} per ft

Then

$$C_p = \frac{32L_sL_p^{\,4}}{10^7I_p} = \frac{32(30)(24)^4}{10^7(800)} = 0.040$$

$$C_s = \frac{32SL_s^{\,4}}{10^7I_s} = \frac{32(8)(24)^4}{10^7(263)} = 0.0323$$

$$0.040 + 0.9(0.0323) = 0.069 < 0.25 \quad \text{Satisfactory}$$

The I_d does not have to be checked because the structural deck is of reinforced concrete. The system is safe from ponding.

Table 4. Typical W Shape Dimensions and Properties Table[a]

				Web			Flange				Distance		
		Depth		Thickness			Width		Thickness				
Designation	Area A, in.^{2}	d, in.		t_w, in.		$\frac{t_w}{2}$, in.	b_f, in.		t_f, in.		T, in.	k, in.	k_1, in.
W 18 × 119	35.1	18.97	19	0.655	5/8	5/16	11.265	11¼	1.060	1 1/16	15½	1¾	15/16
× 106	31.1	18.73	18¾	0.590	9/16	5/16	11.200	11¼	0.940	15/16	15½	1 5/8	15/16
× 97	28.5	18.59	18 5/8	0.535	9/16	5/16	11.145	11 1/8	0.870	7/8	15½	1 9/16	7/8
× 86	25.3	18.39	18 3/8	0.480	½	¼	11.090	11 1/8	0.770	¾	15½	1 7/16	7/8
× 76	22.3	18.21	18¼	0.425	7/16	¼	11.035	11	0.680	11/16	15½	1 3/8	13/16
W 18 × 71	20.8	18.47	18½	0.495	½	¼	7.635	7 5/8	0.810	13/16	15½	1½	7/8
× 65	19.1	18.35	18 3/8	0.450	7/16	¼	7.590	7 5/8	0.750	¾	15½	1 7/16	7/8
× 60	17.6	18.24	18¼	0.415	7/16	¼	7.555	7½	0.695	11/16	15½	1 3/8	13/16
× 55	16.2	18.11	18 1/8	0.390	3/8	3/16	7.530	7½	0.630	5/8	15½	1 5/16	13/16
× 50	14.7	17.99	18	0.355	3/8	3/16	7.495	7½	0.570	9/16	15½	1¼	13/16
W 18 × 46	13.5	18.06	18	0.360	3/8	3/16	6.060	6	0.605	5/8	15½	1¼	13/16
× 40	11.8	17.90	17 7/8	0.315	5/16	3/16	6.015	6	0.525	½	15½	1 3/16	13/16
× 35	10.3	17.70	17¾	0.300	5/16	3/16	6.000	6	0.425	7/16	15½	1 1/8	¾
W 16 × 100	29.4	16.97	17	0.585	9/16	5/16	10.425	10 3/8	0.985	1	13 5/8	1 11/16	15/16
× 89	26.2	16.75	16¾	0.525	½	¼	10.365	10 3/8	0.875	7/8	13 5/8	1 9/16	7/8
× 77	22.6	16.52	16½	0.455	7/16	¼	10.295	10¼	0.760	¾	13 5/8	1 7/16	7/8
× 67	19.7	16.33	16 3/8	0.395	3/8	3/16	10.235	10¼	0.665	11/16	13 5/8	1 3/8	13/16
W 16 × 57	16.8	16.43	16 3/8	0.430	7/16	¼	7.120	7 1/8	0.715	11/16	13 5/8	1 3/8	7/8
× 50	14.7	16.26	16¼	0.380	3/8	3/16	7.070	7 1/8	0.630	5/8	13 5/8	1 5/16	13/16
× 45	13.3	16.13	16 1/8	0.345	3/8	3/16	7.035	7	0.565	9/16	13 5/8	1¼	13/16
× 40	11.8	16.01	16	0.305	5/16	3/16	6.995	7	0.505	½	13 5/8	1 3/16	13/16
× 36	10.6	15.86	15 7/8	0.295	5/16	3/16	6.985	7	0.430	7/16	13 5/8	1 1/8	¾
W 16 × 31	9.12	15.88	15 7/8	0.275	¼	1/8	5.525	5½	0.440	7/16	13 5/8	1 1/8	¾
× 26	7.68	15.69	15¾	0.250	¼	1/8	5.500	5½	0.345	3/8	13 5/8	1 1/16	¾

[a] Ref. 8. Courtesy of the American Institute of Steel Construction.

The girder is 5 plf heavier than the 45 plf assumed; however, this is not great enough to require a recalculation.

BEAMS: LATERALLY UNSUPPORTED

As earlier noted, a laterally unsupported beam is one having lateral support of its compression flange at points a greater distance apart (L_b) than the unique L_u value for that beam. In determining the value of L_u, as well as the accompanying value of the allowable bending stress (F_b), the term C_b either can be taken conservatively as 1.0 or calculated more accurately. When $L_b > C_b L_u$ (or $\sqrt{C_b} L_u$ when buckling controls), the value of F_b will always be less than $0.6F_y$; whether the beam is compact or not is irrelevant. The procedure used to determine F_b for laterally unsupported beams is different than for beams having adequate lateral support.

When determining the value of F_b for a given section for a laterally unsupported condition, the procedure is direct. However, when designing beams that are known to be laterally unsupported, the procedure is indirect and likely will require a number of assumptions and trial sections. This is particularly true if design aids, such as the charts and tables furnished in the AISC Manual (2), are not available. To select the lightest weight section as well as one that is structurally adequate, may necessitate making even more trial selections.

The procedure for the design of laterally unsupported beams is, however, beyond the scope of this article and the reader is referred to steel design texts (5).

LOCAL BUCKLING

Whenever thin plates, such as webs and flanges, are subjected to a large compressive force, there is a tendency to buckle. When local buckling does occur, two major events are likely to occur: the loss of load-carrying capacity in the buckled plate itself; and, more important, shortly thereafter (sometimes even before a noticeable buckle develops), redistribution of stress to other parts of the beam, which, by subjecting these parts to forces for which they were not designed, could lead to subsequent failure.

Because the principal functions of a beam web are to separate the flanges so as to gain maximum benefit from beam depth and to resist nearly all generally small shear stresses, there is a tendency to make webs as thin as possible and the distance (depth) between flanges as large as

	Properties													
	Compact Section Criteria						Elastic Properties					Torsional Constant	Plastic Modulus	
Nominal Wt per ft, lb					r_T, in.	$\dfrac{d}{A_f}$	Axis X-X			Axis Y-Y				
	$\dfrac{b_f}{2t_f}$	F'_y, ksi	$\dfrac{d}{2t_w}$	F'''_y, ksi			I, in.⁴	S, in.³	r, in.	I, in.⁴	S, in.³	r, in.	J, in.⁴	Z_x, in.³
119	5.3		29.0		3.02	1.59	2190	231	7.90	253	44.9	2.69	10.6	261 69.1
106	6.0		31.7		3.00	1.78	1910	204	7.84	220	39.4	2.66	7.48	230 60.5
97	6.4		34.7	54.7	2.99	1.92	1750	188	7.82	201	36.1	2.65	5.86	211 55.3
86	7.2		38.3	45.0	2.97	2.15	1530	166	7.77	175	31.6	2.63	4.10	186 48.4
76	8.1	64.2	42.8	36.0	2.95	2.43	1330	146	7.73	152	27.6	2.61	2.83	163 42.2
71	4.7		37.3	47.4	1.98	2.99	1170	127	7.50	60.3	15.8	1.70	3.48	145 24.7
65	5.1		40.8	39.7	1.97	3.22	1070	117	7.49	54.8	14.4	1.69	2.73	133 22.5
60	5.4		44.0	34.2	1.96	3.47	984	108	7.47	50.1	13.3	1.69	2.17	123 20.6
55	6.0		46.4	30.6	1.95	3.82	890	98.3	7.41	44.9	11.9	1.67	1.66	112 18.5
50	6.6		50.7	25.7	1.94	4.21	800	88.9	7.38	40.1	10.7	1.65	1.24	101 16.6
46	5.0		50.2	26.2	1.54	4.93	712	78.8	7.25	22.5	7.43	1.29	1.22	90.7 11.7
40	5.7		56.8	20.5	1.52	5.67	612	68.4	7.21	19.1	6.35	1.27	0.81	78.4 9.95
35	7.1		59.0	19.0	1.49	6.94	510	57.6	7.04	15.3	5.12	1.22	0.51	66.5 8.06
100	5.3		29.0		2.81	1.65	1490	175	7.10	186	35.7	2.51	7.73	198 54.9
89	5.9		31.9	64.9	2.79	1.85	1300	155	7.05	163	31.4	2.49	5.45	175 48.1
77	6.8		36.3	50.1	2.77	2.11	1110	134	7.00	138	26.9	2.47	3.57	150 41.1
67	7.7		41.3	38.6	2.75	2.40	954	117	6.96	119	23.2	2.46	2.39	130 35.5
57	5.0		38.2	45.2	1.86	3.23	758	92.2	6.72	43.1	12.1	1.60	2.22	105 18.9
50	5.6		42.8	36.1	1.84	3.65	659	81.0	6.68	37.2	10.5	1.59	1.52	92.0 16.3
45	6.2		46.8	30.2	1.83	4.06	586	72.7	6.65	32.8	9.34	1.57	1.11	82.3 14.5
40	6.9		52.5	24.0	1.82	4.53	518	64.7	6.63	28.9	8.25	1.57	0.79	72.9 12.7
36	8.1	64.0	53.8	22.9	1.79	5.28	448	56.5	6.51	24.5	7.00	1.52	0.54	64.0 10.8
31	6.3		57.7	19.8	1.39	6.53	375	47.2	6.41	12.4	4.49	1.17	0.46	54.0 7.03
26	8.0		62.8	16.8	1.36	8.27	301	38.4	6.26	9.59	3.49	1.12	0.26	44.2 5.48

possible, with the result that the web plate could be weak in the vicinity of concentrated loads (Fig. 11).

In Figure 11, four types of vertical web buckling are shown. Which one will occur depends on the kind of support the top flange receives from the surrounding con-

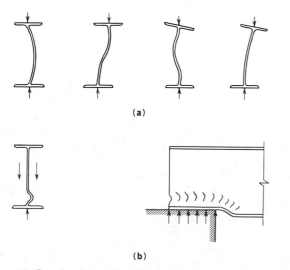

(a)

(b)

Figure 11. Local web buckling (5). (a) Vertical buckling; (b) web crippling.

struction. The possibility of beam failure due to vertical buckling exists only in the vicinity of large concentrated loads—ie, at reactions where the beam rests on its support or at points where columns or other beams rest on the top flange of the beam. At the same points, there also is the possibility of another type of web failure known as web crippling (Fig. 11). Experience indicates that a standard rolled beam that is safe from web crippling is also safe from vertical buckling; therefore, it is crippling that is investigated with such shapes.

It is assumed for purposes of design [AISC Specification (2)] that the web acts as a column, with cross-sectional dimensions equal to $(N + k)$ times the thickness of the web t at reactions (Fig. 12a) and $(N + 2k)$ times t at interior loads (Fig. 12d). The distance N is equal to the length of bearing. The AISC procedure, permitting a value slightly greater than N (ie, k or $2k$) assumes that the portion of the web directly over or under N does not act as a free column. Instead, because of its continuity with the rest of the web and the flanges, it distributes a part of the load to the adjacent web material. The distance k is equivalent to the distance from the outside face of the flange to the web toe of the fillet (Fig. 12b). Values of k for the various rolled sections are given in the AISC Manual tables under Dimensions and Properties (2).

At end supports, the actual unit compressive stress de-

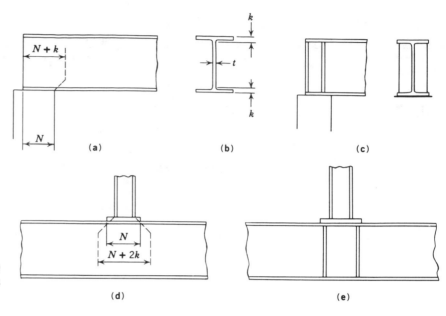

Figure 12. Local buckling dimensions (5). (**a**) End reaction; (**b**) section; (**c**) bearing stiffeners; (**d**) intermediate load; (**e**) bearing stiffeners.

veloped on the cross section of the assumed column is equal to the beam reaction R divided by the effective column area, or

$$\text{Stress} = \frac{R}{t(N + k)}$$

The allowable maximum unit stress from the AISC Specification (2) is 0.75 times the yield point, or 27,000 psi for A36 steel. Therefore, the required minimum length of bearing for any given reaction is

$$N_{(\min)} = \frac{P}{0.75F_y t} - k$$

At an interior point where a heavy concentrated load P is applied to the top flange, the minimum length of bearing (Fig. 12**d**) is

$$N_{(\min)} = \frac{P}{0.75F_y t} - 2k$$

Where the needed length of bearing cannot be provided, either a beam with a thicker web is necessary or the web of the chosen section must be reinforced by vertical stiffener plates, generally placed on both sides as in Figures 12**c** and **e**.

Example

The end reaction of an A36 steel W 12 × 26 is 28 kips. Determine the minimum required length of bearing at the support to prevent web crippling.

1. From the AISC Manual (2), $t = 0.230$ in. and $k = 7/8$ in. $= 0.875 \simeq 0.88$ in.
2. Solving for N

$$N = \frac{R}{0.75F_y t} - k = \frac{28}{0.75(36)0.230} - 0.88 = 3.63 \text{ in.}$$

WEB DIAGONAL BUCKLING

Diagonal buckling is yet another possible mode of failure in the web of a steel beam. Such failure would be due to a combination of stresses resulting from shear and flexure. The deeper the section and thinner the web, the more susceptible the beam is to diagonal buckling. However, precise analysis of principal stress and its tendency to produce diagonal buckling is unwarranted in the majority of cases encountered in practice.

BEAM DESIGN TABLES

The AISC Manual (2) provides tables of uniform load constants for laterally supported simple beams with no overhangs. Such tables are very helpful in design as long as their advantages and limitations are understood. Once the required constant is determined, the beam is selected directly from these tables.

BEAM CHARTS

The AISC Manual also provides charts for the selection of W and M shapes having different unbraced lengths. Two separate sets of charts are used: one for A36 steel and the other for $F_y = 50$ ksi steels. A typical chart for A36 steel is shown in Figure 13. It can be seen that the allowable resisting moment for most W and M rolled shapes is plotted vertically for corresponding values of L_b, plotted horizontally. Some heavy W 14 shapes are not shown because their principal use is for columns.

These charts also are important design aids because they illustrate the resisting-moment profile for many shapes over long ranges of unsupported lengths and many sections can be seen at one time. The unbraced lengths in feet are for the compression flange. In all cases, C_b has the conservative value of 1.0.

ALLOWABLE MOMENTS IN BEAMS ($C_b = 1$, $F_y = 36$ ksi)

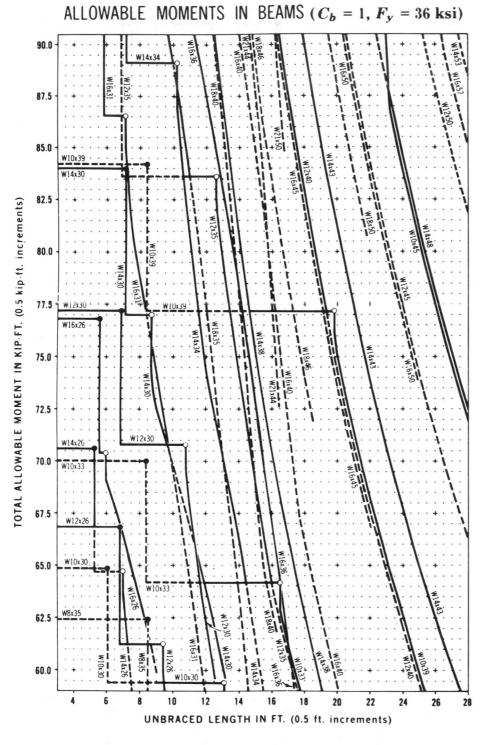

Figure 13. Typical beam chart (9). Courtesy of the American Institute of Steel Construction.

TRUSSED BEAMS

Open-web and long-span steel joists, often referred to as bar joists or trussed beams, are illustrated in Figures 4c and 14. The former are used extensively in low- to medium-rise building construction to carry floor and roof loads to beams or girders (Fig. 6c). Often, light-gauge metal decking, frequently with a concrete topping, is used to span between the joists (Fig. 15). If the decking is shal-

low or not used in combination with concrete, the joists must be spaced quite closely, as little as 18 in. apart. However, depending on the loads, adequacy of the deck, and depth of the joist, spacing can be as much as 8 ft. Joist depths for the regular series run from 8 to 30 in. and can span up to 60 ft. There also are the long-span and deep long-span joists that can span up to 96 ft and 144 ft, respectively.

Most joist manufacturers as well as the Steel Joist In-

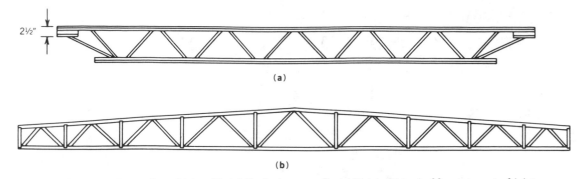

Figure 14. Typical steel joists (5). (a) Typical open-web steel joist; (b) typical long-span steel joist.

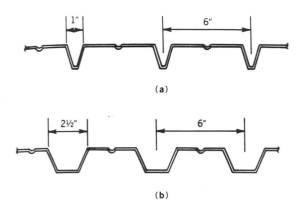

Figure 15. Light-gauge metal decking (5). (a) Narrow rib; (b) wide rib.

stitute (3) provide safe load tables as aids to the designer. The joists generally are designed as simply supported, uniformly loaded trussed beams. If not otherwise laterally restrained, bridging at intervals—attached continuously to the top and bottom chords and diagonally between the lines of bridging at the chords—is required to prevent twisting and buckling. Load limits for control of deflection also are provided in the tables, and a shear check is necessary to be sure that the reaction limit is not exceeded.

PLATE GIRDERS

It is generally the case that the heavier W shapes or trussed beams will prove adequate for most building applications; however, where unusually heavy loads over long spans are encountered, a plate girder may prove to be an appropriate solution. For example, in order to achieve a large unobstructed floor area at the lobby level in a multistory building, it may be necessary to land one or more columns on a horizontal spanning member supporting the floor above, and this member could well be a plate girder. Figure 16 shows several cross sections and a side view of both riveted (or bolted) and welded plate girders. The stiffeners are used to help prevent buckling of the relatively thin web plate.

COLUMNS

The term column is usually applied to relatively heavy vertical members, whereas the lighter vertical and inclined members, such as braces and the compression members of roof trusses, are called struts. By definition, columns and struts are lineal compression members having a length substantially greater than their least lateral dimension.

COLUMN SHAPES

Because of a column's tendency to buckle, its strength depends on its cross-sectional area and shape and the grade of steel of which it is made. Unbraced columns tend to buckle in a direction perpendicular to the axis about which the moment of inertia is least. Therefore, the ideal cross section is one having the same moment of inertia about any axis through its center of gravity. This obviously is a circle. Because material near the center of gravity of a section contributes little to the moment of inertia, the most efficient column is one having as small an amount of material as possible placed near the axis. A hollow circular section (pipe) approaches this ideal: however, pipe columns are used selectively in buildings. One obvious reason is the difficulty in making effective beam connections.

A rolled W-shape column is shown in Figure 17a, and the same section, reinforced with flange plates, in b. Figure 17c shows a structural tee cut from a W shape for use as a column (WT). There also are tee shapes cut from S shapes (ST) and tees cut from M shapes (MT). Columns built-up of angles, plates, and channels are shown in d and e, which may be welded, bolted, or riveted. Angle sections used as struts are shown in f, g, and h; they may be equal length tee angles back-to-back, or unequal length leg angles with either short or long legs back-to-back.

Structural tubing is available in square, round, or rectangular shapes, and in a variety of wall thicknesses and overall dimensions. The AISC Manual (2) includes data on the more frequently used square and rectangular shapes.

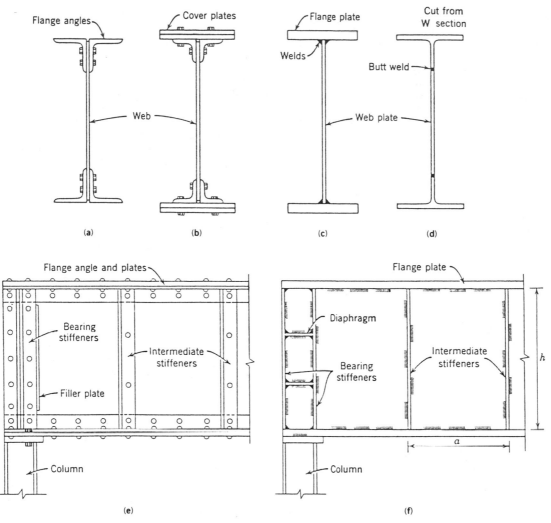

Figure 16. Plate girders.

Most steel pipe is of ASTM A53, grade B steel ($F_y = 35$ ksi) and tubing, of ASTM A500, grade B steel ($F_y = 46$ ksi).

For structural shapes such as those shown in Figure 17, the least lateral dimension is not an accurate measure of the tendency of a column to buckle. Therefore, the radius of gyration, which is a better measure of the stiffness of column sections, is used in column design formulas.

Two other factors affect buckling tendency—actual length and end-conditions. These combine to produce what is termed effective buckling length—ie, the distance between points of contraflexure (between points where there is a change in curvature). For a pin-ended column (Fig. 18), points of contraflexure occur at the column ends where lateral movement (translation) is prevented. As may be seen from Figure 18, the effective length may be quite different for various end conditions.

End conditions are accounted for in design through use of an effective length factor, ie, a dimensionless number (K-value) that, when multiplied by the actual length of the column, gives the effective length for buckling. The ratio of effective length to least radius of gyration (KL/r) is called the slenderness ratio. It is the absolute measure-

ment of the column's tendency to buckle. L and r are both expressed in inches.

A great deal of judgment must be used in selecting the appropriate K-value. Figure 18 illustrates the six most common theoretical end conditions and the recommended K-values for each. The difference between theoretical and recommended values is largely because joint fixity or truly pinned ends are seldom realized in actual construction. Case **d** is the condition found most frequently.

The proper value of k is derived from an analysis of the degree of restraint imparted to the column end by other structural members framing into that end. The commentary on the AISC Specification (2) furnishes an alignment chart to aid in determining proper K-values. For a more thorough discussion of this topic, refer to the Commentary on the AISC Specification in Part 5 of the 1980 AISC Manual (2).

COLUMN FORMULAS

The average unit stress in a column at the time of failure is less than the yield strength of the material by an

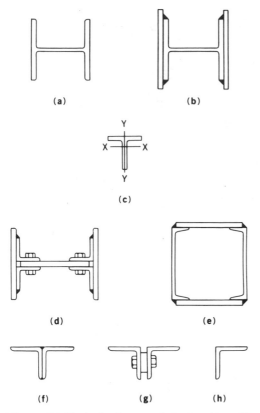

Figure 17. Typical column and strut sections (5).

amount dependent on its buckling tendency. Therefore, the allowable average stress to be used in design is influenced as well, and depends on the slenderness ratio as well as the compressive strength of the material. Using an average factor to safety of 1.67 and A36 steel, the maximum permissible column design stress would be

$$\frac{36,000}{1.67} = 21,600 \text{ psi}$$

It is this quantity that must be reduced to allow for buckling stresses.

All columns are classified in one of two categories: those that would fail owing to "elastic buckling"—ie, those having very large slenderness ratios—and those that would fail due to "inelastic buckling."

The basic Euler formula for the ultimate load of a long, slender, pinned-end column is

$$P_u = \frac{\pi^2 EI}{L^2}$$

To establish the relationship between this formula and the 1978 AISC Specification (2), divide both sides by the column area (A), ie,

$$\frac{P_u}{A} = \frac{\pi^2 EI}{L^2 A}$$

where P_u/A is the average unit stress at failure, or F_a. Substituting this and the relationship $I/A = r^2$ in the above formula,

$$F_a = \frac{\pi^2 E}{(L/r)^2}$$

The end-condition factor K has been omitted because it was initially defined as unity (Fig. 17, case **d**).

It is estimated that the upper limit of elastic buckling failure will likely occur when the average column stress is equal to one half the yield stress; therefore,

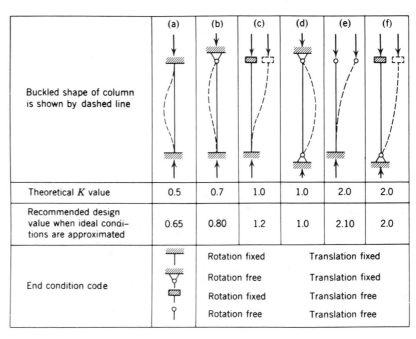

Figure 18. Effect of end conditions (10). Courtesy of the American Institute of Steel Construction.

$$\frac{F_y}{2} = \frac{\pi^2 E}{(L/r)^2}$$

and, solving for L/r,

$$\frac{L}{r} = \sqrt{\frac{2\pi^2 E}{F_y}}$$

This is the formula that establishes the slenderness ratio that distinguishes elastic from inelastic buckling. It will vary with the yield point of the steel, and the symbol for this value of L/r is C_c. Therefore,

$$C_c = \sqrt{\frac{2\pi^2 E}{F_y}}$$

For the various steels, this value is given in the Appendix to the AISC Specification (Part 5 of the AISC Manual) (2). For example, the value for A36 steel is 126.1, and for steels with a 50-ksi yield point, 107.0. Summarizing, if the actual slenderness ratio $KL/r \geq C_c$, elastic buckling would be the assumed mode of failure. If, on the other hand, $KL/r < C_c$, inelastic buckling would best describe the mode of failure. The AISC Specification (2) provides a special reduction formula for F_a in each case.

INELASTIC BUCKLING

The maximum average unit stress should not exceed

$$F_a = \frac{\left[1 - \frac{(KL/r)^2}{2C_c^2} F_y\right]}{\text{FS}}$$

where FS is the factor of safety.

This factor of safety reflects the inconsistencies in column performance under test. The recommended formula for factor of safety is

$$\text{FS} = \frac{5}{3} + \frac{3(KL/r)}{8C_c} - \frac{(KL/r)^3}{8C_c^3}$$

Note that when $KL/r = 0$, FS = 1.67, and when $KL/r = C_c$, FS = 23/12 = 1.92.

ELASTIC BUCKLING

The maximum average unit stress should not exceed that resulting from the Euler formula when a constant factor of safety of 23/12 is used. Therefore,

$$F_a = \frac{\pi^2 E}{(KL/r)^2 \text{FS}} = \frac{12\pi^2 E}{23(KL/r)^2}$$

This formula does not include a factor representing the stress grade of steel because E does not vary appreciably with F_y and controls buckling. Thus, the same limiting stress applies to all grades of steel.

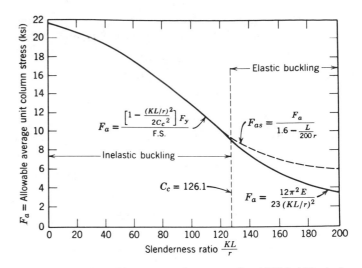

Figure 19. Allowable compressive stress for ASTM A36 steel (original source: Column Research Council).

STRUTS

Many structural elements are classified as secondary members, and as such the AISC Specification (2) allows slightly higher stresses than for columns when the slenderness ratio is greater than 120. In determining the slenderness ratio, K is always taken as unity.

The increased allowable stress F_{as} is determined by dividing the applicable maximum average unit stress F_a (for elastic or inelastic buckling) by $1.6 - L/200r$, ie,

$$F_{as} = \frac{F_a}{1.6 - \frac{L}{200r}}$$

The three limiting stress formulas for A36 steel are plotted in Figure 19, the upper limit of the slenderness ratio being 200, which is the maximum permitted by the AISC Specification (2).

INVESTIGATION OF COLUMNS

To determine the safe axial load that a column can carry according to any particular specification, first compute the slenderness ratio and compare it to C_c for the specified grade of steel. In so doing, the column is placed in one of the two categories—inelastic buckling if $KL/r < C_c$, or elastic buckling if $KL/r \geq C_c$. The appropriate column formula is then selected, and the slenderness ratio is substituted in that formula to determine the allowable average stress F_a. The safe load on the column will be equal to the allowable average stress times the area of the column section.

Example

Determine the total safe axial load on a W 12 × 79 column with an unbraced height of 14 ft. Assume pinned column ends braced against translation. Use A36 steel.

1. From the AISC Manual tables *Dimensions and Properties* (2), the area and radii of gyration of this section are

$$A = 23.3 \text{ in.}^2$$
$$r_x = 5.34 \text{ in.}$$
$$r_y = 3.05 \text{ in.}$$

2. A36 steel has a yield point $F_y = 36,000$ psi; therefore

$$C_c = \sqrt{\frac{2\pi^2 E}{F_y}} = \sqrt{\frac{2\pi^2(29,000)}{36}} = 126.1$$

3. The maximum slenderness ratio is

$$\frac{KL}{r} = \frac{1(14)12}{3.05} = 55.1$$

4. Because $55.1 < 126.1$, the column would fail due to inelastic buckling. From the AISC Specification, the factor of safety is

$$\text{FS} = \frac{5}{3} + \frac{3(KL/r)}{8(C_c)} - \frac{(KL/r)^3}{8(C_c)^3} =$$
$$\frac{5}{3} + \frac{3(55.1)}{8(126.1)} - \frac{(55.1)^3}{8(126.1)^3} = 1.82$$

and the average allowable stress is

$$F_a = \frac{\left[1 - \frac{(KL/r)^2}{2C_c^2}\right] F_y}{\text{FS}} =$$
$$\frac{\left[1 - \frac{(55.1)^2}{2(126.1)^2}\right] 36,000}{1.82} \approx 17,900 \text{ psi}$$

5. The allowable axial load on the column, including its own weight, is

$$P = F_a A = 17,900(23.2) = 415,300 \text{ lb} \approx 415 \text{ kips}$$

BUILT-UP SECTIONS

There are times when ordinary rolled sections must be reinforced with plates as shown in Figure 17**b** and **d**, and it may even be necessary or desirable to "build-up" a column section using plates and angles or other standard shapes. The strength of built-up sections is determined in the same general manner as for regular sections. Properties of the most widely used built-up sections, such as area and radii of gyration, also can be found in steel handbooks. When this is not the case, the moment of inertia of the built-up section must be determined.

UNBRACED HEIGHT

In multistory steel-frame buildings, the unbraced height of a column is usually taken as the floor-to-floor distance. There are occasions, however, when there is need to brace

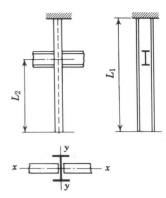

Figure 20. Unbraced heights (5).

a column against buckling at closer intervals in at least one direction. It has been noted that the slenderness ratio (KL/r) is determined by using the least radius of gyration. This is valid only when the column has equal unbraced heights for both axes, and end conditions are the same for both axes. When the unbraced height is different for each axis, the column buckling tendency is greatest for that axis having the largest slenderness ratio. In Figure 20, the proper slenderness ratio for design would be KL_1/r_x or KL_2/r_y, whichever is greater. It is obvious that whenever intermediate supports are possible, it would be desirable to orient the column so that the axis having the smallest radius of gyration is the one braced.

COLUMN DESIGN

The design of columns is not a direct process. Generally, the column length and load to be applied are known, but the rolled shape or built-up section in which the average (actual) stress does not exceed the allowable stress must be selected. The two unknowns are A and r, and the value of one cannot be computed without knowing the other. Design, therefore, is a trial-and-error process. A trial section is selected and investigated. If either the load-carrying capacity of the trial section is found to be less than required or is so much greater than necessary that the section would be uneconomical, another trial section is chosen using the first as a guide. This process is repeated until a satisfactory section is found. Steel handbooks contain tables of safe loads for different column sections and lengths that can aid in this process.

To summarize, the steps essential to the design of a column, when safe-load tables are not used, are

1. Assume a trial section based on the known applied load, unbraced heights, and end conditions for each axis.
2. Find the area and radii of gyration of the trial section from tables of properties for designing.
3. Compute the maximum slenderness ratio (KL/r).
4. Compute the allowable average stress by the appropriate formula.
5. Compute the allowable load on the column by multi-

plying the stress found in step 4 by the area of the section.

6. Compare the allowable load found in step 5 with the applied load plus the column weight. If the actual load exceeds the allowable, repeat the process until a satisfactory section is found.

DESIGN AND INVESTIGATION OF STRUTS

Struts, including the lighter compression members of roof trusses, are designed in the same manner as columns. The more common strut cross sections, as noted earlier, are illustrated in Figure 16f, **g**, and **h**. In f, two angles are shown in contact and connected by welds. In **g**, the same angles are shown separated, the separation being accomplished by ring-fillers and bolts or rivets. A single angle strut is shown in **h**.

If the slenderness ratio exceeds 120, the 1978 AISC Specification (2) permits an increased allowable average stress over that used for main members. Under such conditions, the recommended minimum K-value is 1.0

Example

A 9-ft strut of A36 steel is composed of two $5 \times 3 \times 1/2$-in. angles with the 5-in. legs back-to-back. The angles are spaced 3/8 in. apart; $K = 1.0$. Find the allowable load on the strut.

1. From the AISC double-angle strut tables, for two unequal angles, long legs back-to-back, it will be found that

$$A = 7.5 \text{ in.}^2$$
$$r_x = 1.59 \text{ in.}$$
$$r_y = 1.25 \text{ in.}$$

If tables are not available or do not include the particular combination of angles and spacing selected, r_x must be computed.

2. The slenderness ratio is

$$\frac{KL}{r} = \frac{1(9)12}{1.25} = 86.4$$

3. The allowable average stress is

$$F_a = \frac{\left[1 - \frac{(86.4)^2}{2(126.1)^2}\right] 36,000}{\frac{5}{3} + \frac{3(86.4)}{8(126.1)} - \frac{(86.4)^3}{8(126.1)^3}} = 14,600 \text{ psi}$$

4. The allowable load on the strut is equal to the average stress times the area, or

$$P = F_a A = 14,600(8.0) = 109,500 \approx 110 \text{ kips}$$

Note that when designing a single-angle strut, the least radius of gyration is about a diagonal $(Z-Z)$ axis. [See properties tables for angles in Part 1 of the AISC Manual (2)].

The design of struts composed of two angles is made easier by safe-load tables.

SAFE-LOAD TABLES—COLUMNS AND STRUTS

The AISC manual provides tables that give the total axial load that columns and struts can safely carry for various effective unbraced heights. Once the total axial load to be carried has been determined, and the effective unbraced length established, the column or strut is selected directly from the tables.

Column safe-load tables of the type presented in the AISC Manual (2) include W-, M-, S-shapes and double angles, of 36- and 50-ksi yield point grade steels, structural tubing of 46-ksi yield point grade steel, and steel pipe of 36-ksi grade only. Table 5 is a typical column safe-load table. It will be noted that this particular table is for 10-in. W-shapes of A36 and $F_y = 50$ ksi steels, and that allowable axial (concentric) loads are given in kips. These tables can be used directly only when buckling takes place about the y-axis.

COLUMNS WITH ECCENTRIC LOADS

To this point, column loads have been assumed to be concentric, ie, applied along the axis of the column. This assumption is valid when the load is applied uniformly over the top of the column, or when beams having equal reactions frame into the column opposite each other as would be the case in Figure 20a if beams A and B had the same reactions and beams C and D had the same reactions. However, if beam B was omitted, as shown in Figure 20b, or if the reaction of beam B was considerably less than that of A in Figure 21a, the loads on the column no longer would be symmetrical and the left column flange would be subjected to a greater unit stress than the right. This eccentric loading condition occurs frequently in exterior wall columns, where a floor beam is supported on the interior face without a corresponding load on the exterior face.

It is generally true in buildings that columns carry a direct axial load in addition to any eccentric loads that may exist. Where such is the case, a formula for calculating the unit stress at the edge of the section is

$$f = \frac{P}{A} + \frac{P'ec}{I}$$

in which P is the total vertical load including the eccentric load, P' is the eccentric load alone, e is the eccentricity, and c is the distance from the axis to the extreme fiber.

For the sake of this discussion, stresses resulting from buckling of the column will be neglected.

Example

A W 10×68 column, 12 ft long, supports the loads shown in Figure 22. The point of application of the 50,000-lb load is assumed to be 8 in. from the axis of the column. Neglect the weight of the column, and assuming the effect of buck-

Table 5. Typical Column Load Table: W Shapes, Allowable Axial Loads in kips[a]

Designation of F_y wt/ft[b]	W10									
	112		100		88		77		68	
	36	50	36	50	36	50	36	50	36	50
0	711	987	635	882	559	777	488	678	432	600
6	663	906	592	808	521	712	454	620	402	548
7	653	888	583	792	513	697	447	607	395	537
8	642	869	573	775	504	682	439	593	388	525
9	631	848	562	756	495	665	431	579	381	512
10	619	827	551	737	485	648	422	564	373	498
11	606	805	540	717	475	630	413	548	365	484
12	593	782	528	696	464	611	404	531	357	469
13	579	757	516	674	453	591	394	513	348	454
14	565	732	503	651	442	571	384	495	339	437
15	550	706	489	627	430	550	373	476	330	421
16	535	679	476	602	417	528	362	457	320	403
17	519	651	461	577	405	505	351	437	310	385
18	503	622	446	550	392	481	339	416	299	366
19	486	591	431	523	378	457	327	394	289	347
20	469	560	416	494	364	432	315	371	278	327
22	433	495	383	435	335	379	289	324	255	285
24	395	425	348	372	304	323	261	275	230	242
26	355	362	312	317	271	275	232	234	204	206
28	313	313	273	273	237	237	202	202	177	177
30	272	272	238	238	206	206	176	176	155	155
32	239	239	209	209	181	181	155	155	136	136
34	212	212	185	185	161	161	137	137	120	120
36	189	189	165	165	143	143	122	122	107	107
38	170	170	148	148	129	129	110	110	96	96
40	153	153	134	134	116	116	99	99	87	87
Properties										
U	2.45	2.45	2.46	2.46	2.49	2.49	2.51	2.51	2.52	2.52
P_{wo} (kips)	255	354	214	298	177	246	143	199	116	162
P_{wi} (kips)	27	38	24	34	22	30	19	27	17	24
P_{wb} (kips)	1388	1636	1014	1196	714	842	480	566	335	395
P_{fb} (kips)	352	488	282	392	221	306	170	237	133	185
L_e (ft)	11.0	9.3	10.9	9.3	10.8	9.2	10.8	9.1	10.7	9.1
L_u (ft)	53.2	38.3	48.2	34.7	43.3	31.2	38.6	27.8	34.8	25.1
A (in.²)	32.9		29.4		25.9		22.6		20.0	
I_x (in.⁴)	716		623		534		455		394	
I_y (in.⁴)	236		207		179		154		134	
r_y (in.)	2.68		2.65		2.63		2.60		2.59	
Ratio r_x/r_y	1.74		1.74		1.73		1.73		1.71	
B_x ⎫ Bending	0.261		0.263		0.263		0.263		0.264	
B_y ⎭ factors	0.726		0.735		0.744		0.751		0.758	
a_x ⎫	106.5		92.7		79.5		67.9		58.7	
a_y ⎭ c	35.2		30.8		26.7		22.8		20.0	

[a] Ref. 11. Courtesy of the American Institute of Steel Construction.
[b] Effective length in ft. KL with respect to least radius of gyration r_y.
c Tabulated values of a_x and a_y must be multiplied by 10^6.

ling and lateral deflection to be negligible, the maximum unit compressive stress can be determined.

1. The total vertical load P = 134,000 + 20,000 + 20,000 + 50,000 = 224,000 lb. The eccentric load P' = 50,000 lb.
2. The following properties of the W 10 × 68 section are found from the AISC Manual (2):

$I_x = 394$ in.⁴ $r_x = 4.44$ in.
$I_y = 134$ in.⁴ $r_y = 2.59$ in.
$A = 20.0$ in.² $d = 10.40$ in.
$c = 5.20$ in.

3. The maximum value of the unit compressive stress is

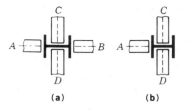

Figure 21. Column loads (5). (**a**) concentric load; (**b**) eccentric load.

$$f = \frac{P}{A} + \frac{P'ec}{I} = \frac{224{,}000}{20.0} + \frac{50{,}000(8)5.20}{394}$$

$$= 11{,}200 + 5280 = 16{,}480 \text{ psi}$$

This investigation will not, however, reveal whether the column is safe unless there is a known allowable stress for this condition of loading, with which the 16,480 psi can be compared. The design of columns for combined axial and eccentric loadings is beyond the scope of this article.

CONNECTIONS

Types of Connector

Rivets are little used in building construction today. The two most common types of steel structure connector are bolts and welds, and the former is only one in a family of mechanical fasteners that are referred to in the AISC Manual as "Bolts, Threaded Parts, and Rivets" (2).

Bolts. Bolts are easily installed, reasonable in cost, and can be visually checked for imperfections and damaged material. The 1978 AISC Specification (2) lists four basic types of steel for use in the manufacture of bolts for structural connections. Type A307 of standard rod stock is seldom used.

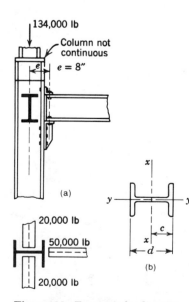

Figure 22. Eccentric loading (5).

The 1978 AISC Specification lists three types of material for the type of high-strength that are most frequently specified for steel buildings—A325, A490, and A449. For general purposes, the A325 bolt, with approximately 85-ksi yield-point stress, is the most common. A325 bolts also are available in three subtypes: Type 1 of medium carbon steel, Type 2 of low carbon steel, and Type 3 of corrosion-resistant, weathering steel. Type 1 is usually supplied unless otherwise specified. The stronger A490 high-strength bolt (approximately 120-ksi yield) may be more suitable when a higher strength material is to be connected.

Bolts frequently are installed by use of a pneumatic or similar impact wrench that can be adjusted to the degree of stress to be put on the bolt and threads.

Welded Studs. Threaded fasteners, with one end welded to a steel member or plate, are being used more frequently because of their unique characteristics. The weld is made automatically; one end of a threaded stud is inserted into an electrified hand tool and the other end is brought into contact with the base metal at the desired position. When contact is made and the tool (or gun) triggered, the stud is immediately fused to the base metal. Welding guns, materials, types of stud, etc, vary with different manufacturers. Typically, manufacturers use a stud material having a 50-ksi yield point and a corresponding design shear-stress capacity of 24 ksi.

Rivets. Having stated that rivets are seldom used today in building construction, it is nevertheless true that some fabricating shops continue to use them on a limited basis. The 1978 AISC Specification (2) lists two basic types of steel for rivets, A502, Grade 1, and A502, Grade 2. Their respective yield points are approximately 28 and 38 ksi. For general purposes, Grade 1 (carbon steel) usually is specified, and when a higher strength steel is desired, Grade 2 (carbon manganese steel).

Welds. The fourth type of connector is the weld. There are numerous welding procedures, but the only procedure acceptable in structural work is fusion welding by the electric arc process. There are basically four different processes by which the fusion arc weld can be achieved.

Shielded arc electrodes are available in a variety of structural steel grades. The ultimate tensile strength of a properly placed weld varies from 60 to 110 ksi, and the design shear strength from 18 to 33 ksi. The common E70XX electrode, for example, has a design shear strength of 21 ksi and is used with A36 steel. The E80XX electrode is used with A572 Grade 65 steel and has a design shear strength of 24 ksi.

With large-size welds and/or with the higher strength steels, a minimum preheat temperature of the parent steel is required, so that the mass of the parent metal will not dissipate the heat from the arc so rapidly that proper fusion will not occur. Also, shrinking accompanies the cooling process and usually results in residual stresses in the weld and parent metal; therefore, sufficient strength must be provided to compensate for these stresses.

Combinations of these various connectors (rivets, bolts, and welds) may be used in making structural connections.

For example, one end of a connecting piece might be welded to a structural member in the fabricating shop and then be bolted to another structural member on the building site. This is generally referred to as "shop-welded and field-bolted construction." Also, members often are temporarily bolted into position and then field welded.

The two most common types of steel construction are

Type 1, designated as "rigid-frame" (continuous frame), in which beam-to-column connections have sufficient rigidity to hold the original angles between intersecting members virtually unchanged.

Type 2, called "simple" framing (unrestrained, free-ended), in which, insofar as gravity loading is concerned, the ends of the beams and girders are connected for shear only and are free to rotate under gravity load.

Type 1 construction is unconditionally permitted by the AISC Specification (2). When Type 1 construction is used, the building frame is statically indeterminate. It is necessary that a careful stress analysis be made and that the normal unit working stress values allowed by the specification not be exceeded in the design of members and connections. Design entails elastic theory and the design of continuous beams and frames, subjects that are beyond the scope of this article. The 1978 AISC Specification (2) also permits an analysis based on plastic design for Type 1 construction.

Type 2 construction is permitted if some structural system is used to develop the lateral forces on the frame, such as can result from wind and earthquake loading. One such system is known as a "wind bent," in which a limited number of specific beam-to-column connections are selected and designed for moment resistance. In this kind of Type 2 construction, care must be taken to ensure that flexible connections have adequate inelastic rotation capacity to avoid overstress of the connectors under combined gravity and wind loading.

Common Connections

The different types of connections dealt with in practice are too numerous to list here. Each type of connector—rivet, bolt, or weld—has its own peculiar advantages and disadvantages, and each type of connection will be detailed differently, depending on the type of connector used.

Following are several examples of connections most frequently used in steel buildings, with the type of connector (bolt or weld) intermixed. The connections shown in Figures 23–25 permit enough end rotation so that beams may be assumed to be simply supported and thus suitable for Type 2 construction. A moment-resisting connection, suitable for Type 1 construction is shown in Figure 26.

Lap or Butt. Lap or butt joints are generally the simplest to use when two members are in essentially the same plane and arranged so that they will or will not require additional pieces of metal to complete the connection. The lap connection or splice may be in tension or compression.

Framing Angles. Structural members framing perpendicular to one another usually require the use of an angle to effect a connection. Bolts or welds may be used. Once the members are positioned, they can be temporarily held in place with drift pins, bolts, or tack welds until the permanent connection can be made.

Shear Plates. A shear plate welded to the end of a beam may be used in place of the paired angles used as framing angles. Bolts are then used to connect the plate to the supporting member. Shear-plate connections require much closer fabricating tolerances for the beam, assuming that ends are cut parallel and to exact length.

Beam Seats. Beam seats provide a ledge or shelf for the beam to rest on while the permanent connection is made. The clip angle at the top of the beam provides lateral support at this point only and is assumed to carry no load.

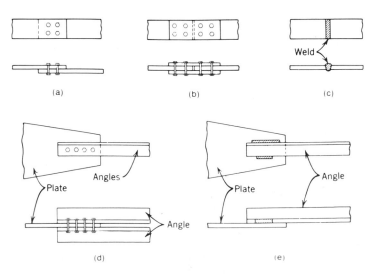

Figure 23. Lap and butt connections (5).

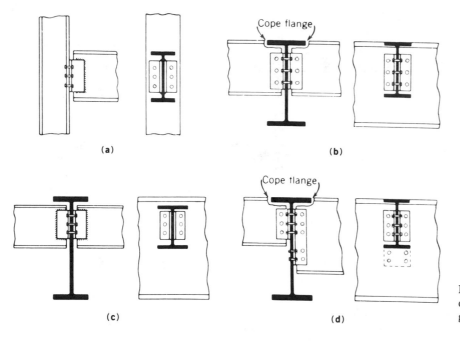

Figure 24. Framing angles (5). (**a**) Beam-to-column; (**b**) beam-to-girder; (**c**) beam-to-girder; (**d**) beam-to-girder.

Flexible beam seats are the simplest and most desirable. Because the thickness of the seat angle provides the only resistance against bending in the outstanding leg, the outstanding leg must be stiffened when the load becomes too large.

Direct Web Connections. For beam-to-column connections it is sometimes possible to secure the beam web directly to the column flange. The shelf angle is used to facilitate erection only and is assumed to carry no load. Welds may be used, as well as rivets or bolts.

Bracketed Connections. The bracketed type of connection is necessary when two members to be fastened do not intersect. It is not a desirable type of connection structurally because a significant eccentricity is introduced both in the connection and in one of the members to be joined.

Moment-resisting Connections. Either bolts or welds can be used in moment-resisting connections. Any one of the previously discussed shear connections can be used to develop the vertical force. In addition, some means of developing the horizontal force at the beam flanges is required. These connections prevent rotation of one member with respect to the other; however, there may be some rotation of the entire joint, depending on the relative stiffnesses of the members.

TYPES OF FASTENER LOADS

Most connections are detailed and constructed so that the fastener itself is under a load perpendicular to its shank. Such fasteners are designated as "shear type" (Figs. 22–24). This designation will be used herein even though in some cases the shank itself is not in shear. Also, there are times when a fastener is actually in tension (eg, hanger-type connections). Only rivets or high-strength bolts in friction-type connections are recommended for developing this kind of load. In the bolted, moment-resisting connection of Figure 25, the bolts attaching the structural tee to the flange of the column are loaded in tension; the other bolts in the connection are in shear.

The third kind of load is a combination of shear and tension. Brackets and stiffened beam seats load the fasteners in combined tension and shear.

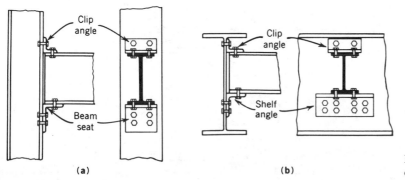

Figure 25. Flexible beam seats (5). (**a**) Beam-to-column; (**b**) beam-to-girder.

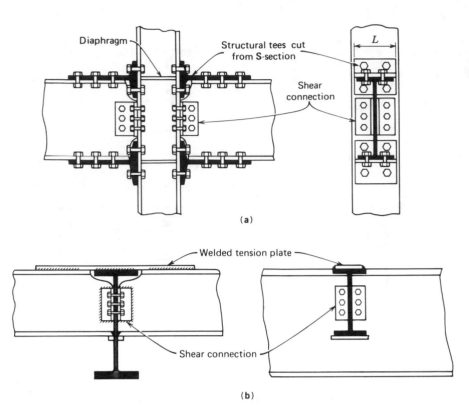

(a)

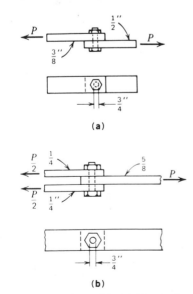

Welded tension plate

Shear connection

Figure 26. Moment-resisting connection (5). (**a**) Beam-to-column (bolted); (**b**) beam-to-girder (welded).

(b)

HOLES FOR FASTENERS

Determining the size, type, and arrangement of holes for fasteners is an important part of the design procedure. Holes are usually made by punching, using standard dies. However, if the material is too thick (eg, larger than the diameter of the fastener to be used) the holes must be drilled or subpunched and reamed. Slotted holes require additional labor.

Figure 27 shows the standard or most frequently used type of hole. Unless another type of hole is specified, this standard (STD) hole is assumed. It is round and 1/16 in. larger than the fastener, allowing reasonable tolerance for fabrication. Four other types of hole are allowed by the 1978 AISC Specification (2), and reference to this Specification should be made for diameters larger than 7/8 in.

BEARING-TYPE FASTENERS

A good example of a bearing-type fastener is the standard A307 bolt in a simple lap joint, as shown in Figure 28a.

The hole is slightly larger than the bolt shank so that initially the fit is loose. Even though the nut is well tightened, the small amount of friction is easily overcome with the application of the load (P) and the pieces "slip into bearing." When using A307 bolts, they must always be designed as bearing-type fasteners. The same is true for rivets. High-strength bolts (A325 or A490) may be used as bearing-type or as friction-type fasteners. The high-strength bolt in a bearing-type connection is strongest and is more economical than a friction-type. Therefore, it is the most widely used of fastener connections.

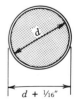

(a) STD.

Figure 27. Standard fastener hole (5).

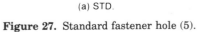

(a)

(b)

Figure 28. Fasteners in shear (5). (**a**) Single shear; (**b**) double shear.

STRENGTH OF A FASTENER IN SHEAR

The joint shown in Figure 28**a** is constructed so that the fastener tends to shear in one plane. In this case, the fastener is said to be in single shear and transfers the load (P) from one plate to the other. The joint shown in Figure 28**b** has two shearing planes; therefore, the fastener is in double shear and transfers the load (P) to the two outside plates.

The shear resistance of a fastener depends on the cross-sectional area of the shank and the allowable unit shearing stress of the fastener. The 1978 AISC Specification (2) establishes allowable shearing stresses for all fasteners except welded studs.

The symbol BV (bolt value) is used to designate the strength capacity of a single bolt. For shear, this is determined by the product of the allowable shear stress and the area, ie,

$$BV_s = F_v A_v$$

in which

BV_s = bolt value in shear (kips)

F_v = allowable unit shearing stress (ksi)

A_v = the nominal cross-sectional area ($\pi d^2/4$) of the shaft or shank (in.^{2}).

The strength of a fastener in double shear is, of course, twice the single shear value.

Example

Find the shear bolt value for an A307 bolt, ¾ in. in diameter, in standard (STD) bolt holes and in single shear.

1. Area of the bolt = $\pi d^2/4$

$$A_v = \frac{3.14(0.75)^2}{4} = 0.4418 \text{ in.}^2$$

2. The allowable shear stress (F_v) for an A307 bolt, bearing type, is 10 ksi and

$$BV_s \text{ (single shear)} = F_v A_v$$

$$BV_s = 10(0.4418) = 4.42 \text{ kips}$$

The three standard fastener sizes most often used in steel buildings are ¾, ⅞, and 1 in. Also, Part 4 of the AISC Manual (2) contains tables listing load values in kips for all rivets and threaded fasteners (excluding welded studs) in sizes from ⅝ through 1-½ in.

STRENGTH OF A FASTENER IN BEARING AND END SHEAR-OUT

The bearing on a fastener is assumed to be the force exerted on that fastener by the steel through which it passes. The bearing area is the projected area of the surface—ie, the area of a rectangle with the fastener diameter and the holed metal thickness, using the nominal diameter of the fastener, as the dimensions. Expressed in equation form, the bearing area is

$$A_b = dt$$

If two plates of different thickness are fastened together, the bearing capacity will be determined by the thickness of the thinner plate.

The strength of a fastener in bearing is equal to the allowable bearing stress (F_p) times the bearing area, or

$$BV_b = F_p A_b$$

The upper limit of bearing strength is $1.5F_u$, where F_u is the specified minimum tensile strength of the connected part. A table listing values of F_u for different grades of steel is furnished in Appendix A of the 1978 AISC specification (2). For example, A36 steel may have an F_u varying from 58 ksi to 80 ksi, whereas A588 steel, Grade-50, has an F_u = 70 ksi.

Assuming the plates of the connection in Figure 28**a** are of A36 steel with a minimum specified tensile strength of 58 ksi, the maximum bearing stress is

$$F_b = 1.5(58) = 87 \text{ ksi}$$

and the capacity of the fastener in bearing is

$$BV_b = 87(0.281) = 24.4 \text{ kips}$$

In the joint in Figure 28**b**, the thickness of the thinnest plate is ¼ in., but the two ¼-in. plates act in the same direction; therefore, the load (P) must be divided between them. Assuming ¾-in. fasteners, the bearing area acting to the left of this joint is

$$A_b = (0.25 + 0.25)0.75 = 0.375 \text{ in.}^2$$

The bearing area of the ⅝-in. plate on the right is

$$A_b = 0.625(0.75) = 0.469 \text{ in.}^2$$

The maximum allowable bearing strength ($F_p = 1.5F_u$) can be used only if the spacing of the fasteners and end distance (in the direction of the stress) meet limiting specifications; otherwise F_p must be reduced. Figure 29 shows three fasteners in a line parallel to the direction of the stress. The fastener spacing is center-to-center of fasteners, and the end distance is from the center of the fastener to the end of the member, parallel to the direction of the stress. The distance L_e is the length from the center of one fastener to the nearest side of the next hole in the direction parallel to the stress. Edge distance is measured from the center of a fastener to the edge of the material, perpendicular to the direction of the stress. To prevent gaps and bulging of the material near its edge, a minimum edge distance is specified. This minimum edge distance also is the minimum end distance. The 1978 AISC Specification (2) provides values for these minimum distances,

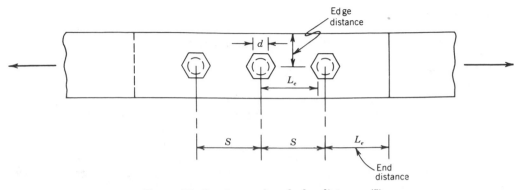

Figure 29. Spacing, end, and edge distances (5).

the variables being the diameter of the fastener and the edge condition of the material.

The variables controlling allowable bearing stress are the tensile strength of the part, the diameter of the fastener, and the spacing (L_e). The usual fastener spacing is 3. in., which is adequate for a bearing stress of $1.5F_u$ for fastener sizes up to and including ¾ in. The 1978 AISC Specification (2) establishes a minimum preferred spacing of $3d$ and an absolute minimum of $2\text{-}^2\!/_3d$. The bearing values for ¾-, ⅞-, and 1-in. fasteners for various spacings and end distances are given in Part 4 of the eighth edition of the AISC Manual (2).

The limiting value for the capacity of any given fastener is the smallest value calculated for shear and bearing as described herein.

Example

Referring to Figure 28b, if the parent metal is A36 steel, the bolts are ¾ in. and of A325N steel, and standard (STD) holes and end distances for maximum bearing stress are assumed, the limiting bolt value (BV) is determined as follows. The connection is a bearing type with threads in the shear plane, therefore:

1. Determine the bolt value in shear. The bolt shank is in double shear and the area of a ¾-in. bolt is 0.442 in.²

$$F_v = 21 \text{ ksi}$$

$$BV_s\text{(double shear)} = 2F_vA_v = 2(21)0.442$$
$$= 18.6 \text{ kips}$$

2. Determine the bolt value in bearing. The combined thickness of the two ¼-in. plates is ½ in., which is less than the ⅝-in. plate and thus controlling. The area in bearing is

$$0.5(0.75) = 0.375 \text{ in.}^2$$

and

$$F_p = 1.5F_u = 1.5(58) = 87 \text{ ksi}$$

therefore

$$BV_b\text{(bearing)} = F_pA_b = 87(0.375) = 32.6 \text{ kips}$$

3. Establish the limiting value. The limiting value will be the smaller of the capacities determined on the basis of shear and bearing, or

$$BV = 18.6 \text{ kips}$$

GROSS AND NET SECTION

The unit stress in tension members is considered to be uniform throughout the entire cross section. Expressed in equation form,

$$f_t = \frac{P_t}{A}$$

where:

> f_t = unit tensile stress (psi)
> P_t = total force (1b)
> A = total area resisting stress

The presence of fastener holes punched or reamed to full size reduces the effective area available to resist stress. This is referred to as "net section." As previously noted, fastener holes are punched ¹/₁₆ in. larger in diameter than the fastener. Punching holes in steel damages a small amount of the metal around the hole; therefore, in computing net section, the holes should be assumed ¹/₁₆ in. larger in diameter than their punched dimension, or ⅛ in. larger than the nominal fastener diameter.

Where one hole is involved —ie, a single row of fasteners along the line of stress—the net section A is determined by multiplying the thickness of the member by its net width (width of member minus the hole diameter). For example, in Figure 30a, the net section is

$$A_{net} = t(W - d)$$

When more than one row of holes is involved and holes are not staggered (Fig. 30b), the net section is

$$A_{net} = t(W - nd)$$

where n is the number of holes across the section (in Fig. 30b, $n = 2$).

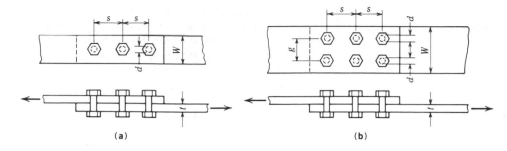

Figure 30. Net section (5). (**a**) One row of bolts; (**b**) two rows of bolts.

The AISC Specification (2) also requires that the net section through a hole be no more than 85% of the corresponding gross section.

Fasteners may be placed in a variety of patterns, depending on the available area and the shape of the members to be connected. Savings in material can be achieved by keeping the fasteners in as tight a group as possible. However, a lesser spacing can reduce the bearing capacity. Fastener pitch is a term indicating the center-to-center spacing of fasteners in a row. The symbol s is used to indicate pitch. Fastener gauge (g) is another term indicating a dimension, this time measured perpendicular to the line of stress in the joint. In a lap joint, the gauge would be the center-to-center distance between rows of fasteners.

Fasteners also can be placed in staggered rows or in a zigzag pattern. The AISC Specification (2) provides an empirical formula for determining net sections with staggered rows of fasteners and applied to all possible paths of tension failure.

$$A_{net} = t \left[W - nd + \Sigma \frac{s^2}{4g} \right]$$

where:

A = net area
s = pitch
g = gauge
d = diameter of hole
Σ = sum of values of $s^2/4g$, for each diagonal path of possible failure

Using this formula, the least area is the net area on which the strength of such a tension member could be based. However, this net section area (A_{net}), applicable to splice and gusset plates only, cannot be greater than 85% of the gross area. If 85% of the gross area is less than the actual net area, then the former becomes the net area that must be used. Further, refinements are required when a structural shape is connected by only one part—eg, one leg of an angle.

FRAMING ANGLES—FASTENER CONNECTED

The type of connection shown in Figure 24 is the one most frequently used to connect floor beams to other beams or to girders and columns. The angles generally are in pairs, and the legs straddling the web of the member being sup-

ported are called connected legs because they usually are attached to the member in the fabricating shop before the assembly is transported to the building site. The other legs are called outstanding legs.

When the connected legs of framing angles are attached only to the beam web, enough end rotation is permitted to enable the connection to be classified as "flexible" and thus appropriate for Type 2 construction (ie, beams can be assumed to be simply supported). Furthermore, unless the framing angles are welded, any eccentricity is ignored, meaning that the beam reaction is treated as though it was concentric with the row(s) of fasteners that transfer the load from the web to the framing angles. The beam reaction also is treated as though it was concentric with the row(s) of fasteners transferring the load from the angles to the supporting member. The thickness of framing angles purposely is kept small to assure necessary flexibility.

The stresses that must be considered are shear in the fastener; bearing on the beam webs, column flange, and framing angle; and gross shear on the vertical section through the beam web and framing angles. The limiting fastener value is established as follows:

1. Connected leg
   • Double shear for fasteners through the beam web.
   • Bearing on the web.
2. Outstanding leg
   • Single shear for fasteners through the girder web or column flange.
   • Bearing on the girder web, column flange, or angle thickness.

In the past, there were three standard sizes of framing angles: 4 × 3½-in., 4 × 6 in., and 6 × 6 in. They were considered to be most suitable for use with standard ¾-in. rivets in one or two vertical rows, providing adequate driving clearances and standard gauge dimensions. With high-strength bolts, however, use of other sizes often is required to allow for nut, washer, bolt projection, and impact wrench clearances.

The thickness of framing angles generally is so selected that bearing on the angle legs will not control the fastener load value. The thickness of the angles also can be determined by limiting the allowable shear to 0.40 F_y on the gross area of the vertical section through the connecting angles. The angle sizes and fastener spacings shown in Figure 31 are recommended unless further investigation indicates that increased clearances are required. It is cus-

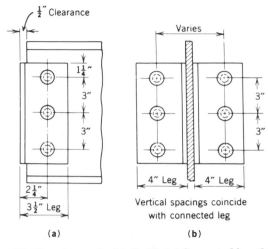

Figure 31. Framing angle details (5). (**a**) Connected leg; (**b**) outstanding leg.

tomary to arrange fasteners symmetrically in beam connections, even though this may necessitate more fasteners than are required to resist the total stress. When the top flange is coped at the end of the member, an investigation of web tear-out (referred to as "block shear") is required.

Example

Design the framing angle connection for a W 16 × 40 girder framing to the flange of a W 10 × 33 column, both of A36 steel. The end reaction is 42 kips. Use ¾-in., A325N bolts in a bearing-type connection with threads in the shear plane and standard holes.

1. Determine the limiting bolt value for the connected leg.

$$BV_s = 2(21)0.442 = 18.6 \text{ kips}$$

$$BV_b = 1.5(58)0.75(0.305) = 19.9 \text{ kips}$$

The limiting bolt value is 18.6 kips, and the minimum angle thickness is 0.5(0.305) = 0.153 in.; use ¼ in.

2. Calculate the number of bolts required in the connected leg.

$$n = \frac{42}{18.6} = 2.26; \quad 4 \text{ bolts are needed}$$

3. Determine the limiting bolt value for the outstanding leg.

$$BV_s = 21(0.442) = 9.28 \text{ kips}$$

$$BV_b = 1.5(58)0.75(0.25) = 16.31 \text{ kips}$$

The limiting bolt value is 9.28 kips.

4. Calculate the number of bolts required in the outstanding legs.

$$n = \frac{42}{9.28} = 4.53; \quad 5 \text{ bolts are needed,} \\ \text{but use 6 for symmetry.}$$

5. Select an arrangement for the bolts and detail the joint (see Fig. 31). The W 16 × 40 has a "T" depth of 13-⅝ in.; therefore, the length of angle is limited to 13-⅝ in., which is adequate for three fasteners in one row and an angle length of 8-½ in.

6. Check shear on the gross area of the angles.

$$F_v = 0.4(36) = 14.4 \text{ ksi}$$

With two angles, each 8-½ in. long, the thickness required for shear is

$$t = \frac{42}{14.5(2)8.5} = 0.17 \text{ in.}$$

The ¼-in. angle thickness is adequate.

The AISC Manual (2) lists standard framed-beam connections and their respective allowable loads for various beam sizes, number and type of fasteners, size of fastener, and thickness of framing angle. Part 4 of the AISC Manual (2) lists standard, framed-beam connections using one row of fasteners in each leg. Separate procedures are needed for eccentrically loaded fastener connections.

WELDED CONNECTIONS

This presentation on welding design is applicable to members and joints of ordinary building frames in which the loads to be carried are essentially static in nature—ie, not subject to dynamic loads such as those produced by moving loads as discussed earlier herein. In the case of impact loads on building members, increasing the assumed total load to be carried in accordance with the AISC Specification (2) usually will suffice. However, a thorough understanding of the behavior of materials under fatigue conditions is essential to the intelligent design of structures subjected to dynamic loadings, which cause many repetitions of maximum design stress.

Lamellar tearing, which can occur when very thick welds are used in attaching large members, is another danger. It can be described as the failure of steel in its through-thickness dimension (Z-direction), if the x and y axes are oriented in the plane of rolling. Failure occurs in the parent metal and not the weld deposit. It is best to avoid welds more than 1-½-in. thick. As a general rule, this is not difficult to do in building design. With welded connections, it is sometimes possible to attach one member directly to another without the use of any additional connecting parts, such as are necessary when using fasteners. Welded connections, therefore, are customary in rigid construction where the intent is to develop full member strength. Where this is not the intent, as in Type 2 construction, it is difficult to achieve a connection allowing free rotation without use of connecting parts such as angles and plates to transmit loads. Consequently, welded connections between beam and girder and beam and column in such construction are in many respects similar to fastener connections except that welds replace the fasteners.

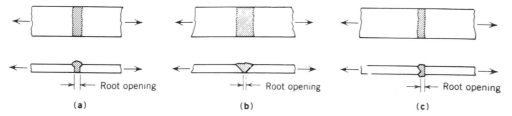

Figure 32. Groove welds (5). (**a**) Square butt; (**b**) single vee butt; (**c**) double vee butt.

TYPES AND STRENGTHS OF WELDS

Most welds used to join structural elements in buildings are of two general types: groove and fillet.

Groove Welds

Groove welds are used in joints between two abutting parts lying in approximately the same plane (Fig. 32). They are classified according to the method of grooving or preparing the base metal before weld metal is deposited. The square butt weld (Fig. 32a) requires no preparation; however, for complete penetration, it is limited to plates not more than ¼ in. thick. For greater thicknesses, it is necessary to weld from both sides (or use a back-up bar on one side) and/or to groove the parts that are to be welded. There are nine recognized forms of groove weld.

Complete penetration butt welds have an effective thickness or throat dimension equal to the thickness of the thinner member joined. Therefore, when the full width of the member is welded, the full strength of the member is developed in the weld. It is important that the "matching" steels and electrodes (Table 6) meet the AISC Specification (2).

When the weld is made from both sides, the root of the initial layer of weld metal (or bead) must be thoroughly chipped out on the reverse side before welding is started on that side. This removal of slag also is required when making more than one pass to build up the size of weld.

Fillet Welds

Fillet welds are shown in Figure 33. They have a cross section that is approximately triangular. The weld size is designated D, in Figures 33b, c, and d. This type of weld generally is used to join two surfaces at right angles to each other and is the most common in making structural connections. Unless specifically noted otherwise, such welds are assumed to have equal legs (45° faces) and the throat dimension is the size multiplied by sine 45°. When an unequal-leg fillet weld is necessary for a special design condition, the design throat dimension is the least dimension from the root to the face.

Because the strength of a fillet weld is determined by its throat dimension; small welds are most economical. This is true because the throat dimension is proportional to the leg size, whereas the amount of weld metal varies approximately as the square of the leg size. Fillet welds of ⅛-, 3/16-, ¼-, and 5/16-in. size can be made in one pass of the electrode along the axis of the weld. Larger welds are made in several passes. As with groove welds, the surface of each weld must be thoroughly chipped and wire-brushed to remove all slag before the next pass.

Fillet welds may be loaded in two ways. Figure 33c shows two fillet welds, each having its axis parallel to the direction of stress in the members. Each weld transfers stress from one member to the other by means of shear parallel to its axis. The shearing stress is assumed to be uniformly distributed over the length of the weld. Figure

Table 6. Electrodes[a,b]

Manual Shielded Metal Arc	Submerged Arc	Gas Metal Arc	Flux-Cored Arc	Allowable F_v for Deposited Weld Metal, ksi	ASTM Designation for AISC and AWS "Matching Base" Metals
E60XX or E70XX	F6X-EXXX or F7X-EXXX	E70S-X or E70U-1	E60T-X	18.0 or 21.0	A36,A53 Grade B, A500,A501,A529, A570 Grades D and E, A709 Grade 36
E70XX	F7X-EXXX	E70S-X or E70U-1	E70T-X	21.0	A242,A441,A572 Grades 42–55; A588; and A709 Grades 50 and 50W
E80XX	F8X-EXXX	Grade E80S	Grade E80T	24.0	A572 Grades 60 and 65
E100XX	F10X-EXXX	Grade E100S	Grade E100T	30.0	A514,over 2½ in. thick
E110XX	F11X-EXXX	Grade E110S	Grade E110T	33.0	A514, 2 ½ in. thick and under

[a] Ref. 5.

[b] Key: E, electrode; F, flux; S, bare solid electrode; U, coated solid electrode; T, flux-cored electrode; 60, 70, 80, 100, 110 min. tensile strength; X, design specification numbers.

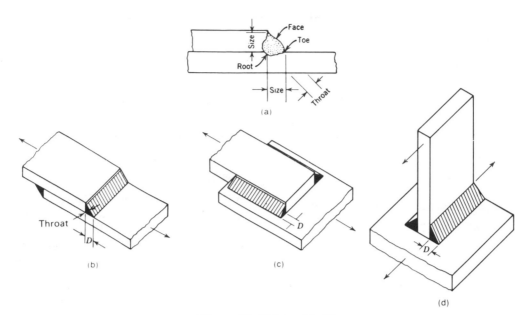

Figure 33. Fillet welds (5).

33**b** shows two fillet welds, each having its axis perpendicular to the direction of stress in the members. Welds of this type fail through the throat as a result of the combined effect of shear and tension (or compression). Because the strength of such welds in tension or compression are greater than that for shear, it is reasonable to limit the strength to that controlled by shear alone.

For design purposes, then, it is generally assumed that the strength per linear inch of fillet weld is the shearing strength, regardless of the direction of load on the weld. The allowable shearing stress for various fillet welds is shown in Table 6. Because the critical section is through the throat of the fillet, the strength per lineal inch (F) is equal to the leg size times sine 45° multiplied by the allowable shear stress; for example, for the 18,000 psi-strength weld,

$$F = D \text{ (sine 45°) } 18,000 = 12,700D \text{ per lineal in. (pli)}$$

and for the 21,000 psi-strength weld,

$$F = 14,800D \text{ pli}$$

Shear strength also can be calculated on the basis of the "per $\frac{1}{16}$-in. of fillet weld size." Using this method strengths are

For the 18,000 psi-strength weld,
  $F = 800$ pli per $\frac{1}{16}$ in. of D

For the 21,000 psi-strength weld,
  $F = 930$ pli per $\frac{1}{16}$ in. of D

To compensate for irregularities in weld deposit and the tapered shape at the ends of fillet weld passes caused by starting and stopping the weld, the actual length should always be $2D$ greater than the computed length. However, the length shown on detailed drawings is always the net or computed length.

The ends of fillet welds sustain greater than average shears. Therefore, where possible, fillet welds should be continued around corners a short distance. This is referred to as a return and is usually equal to $2D$. Returns are not generally shown on detail drawings but are executed by the welder wherever feasible.

There are a number of limitations on the maximum and minimum size of welds. Generally speaking, it can be said that it is as unsatisfactory to use a weld that is too small for thick parts as it is to use one too large for thin parts. And, when the connected member is not symmetrical and significant eccentricity is thus introduced, welds should be proportioned whenever possible.

Example

Figure 34 shows an angle strut with a total stress of 40 kips welded to a $\frac{1}{2}$-in. gusset plate. The action line of the load coincides with the gravity axis of the angle, which is

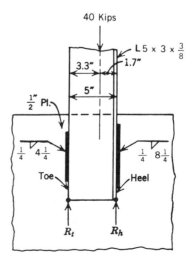

Figure 34. Truss member-to-gusset connection.

1.7 in. from the back of the 5-in. connected leg. By taking moments about a point on the weld action line (R_h), the amount of weld resistance (R_t) along the toe can be determined.

$$R_t(5) - 40,000(1.7) = 0$$

$$R_t = \frac{40,000(1.7)}{5} = 13,600 \text{ lb}$$

As the total resistance of both welds must be equal, the applied load is

$$R_h = 40,000 - 13,600 = 26,400 \text{ lb}$$

The angle must be connected for at least 13,600 lb along the toe and 26,400 lb along the heel. The maximum size of weld along the toe of the angle is $\frac{3}{8} - \frac{1}{16} = \frac{5}{16}$ in.; use a ¼-in. weld. For a ¼-in. weld, produced from E60 electrodes (Table 6), the length required is

$$\frac{13,600}{4(800)} = 4.25; \text{ use } 4\frac{1}{4} \text{ in.}$$

The length of ¼-in. weld required along the heel of the angle is

$$\frac{26,400}{4(800)} = 8.25; \text{ use } 8\frac{1}{4} \text{ in.}$$

The 1978 AISC Code (2) no longer requires proportioning of welds, so the total length ($4\frac{1}{4} + 8\frac{1}{4} = 12\frac{1}{2}$ in.) actually could be divided equally between heel and toe (ie, $6\frac{1}{4}$ in. along the heel and $6\frac{1}{4}$ in. along the toe).

WELDED MOMENT-RESISTING CONNECTIONS

As noted earlier, the principal reason for using moment-resisting connections in buildings is to resist the effect of lateral forces such as wind and earthquake. Consequently, they are used most frequently between main beams and columns, creating a "rigid frame." However,

even though they are used principally to resist lateral loads, the vertical gravity load will develop negative bending moments at the ends of the beams.

A bolted, beam-to-column, moment-resisting connection was shown in Figure 26. The structural tees could be replaced by rectangular plates, field-welded to the flanges of both beams and column (Fig. 35a). It also is possible to omit tees and plates altogether and field-weld flange to flange directly, as shown in Figure 35b. However, this procedure requires exactness in fabrication (allowing only a ¼-in. clearance) that may become too costly.

TRUSSES

The truss as a structural element has been in use for many years. It is an effective means of carrying loads over relatively long spans. Figure 36 shows several of the more common configurations. The truss is composed of top and bottom chords and web members in various configurations between the chords. Although it is most often the case that the truss is seen as a roof-support element, it also can be used to support floors and other types of building elements and loads. The top chord in roof applications generally is sloped, with the bottom chord horizontal; however, trusses can be inverted for flat roofs, and the normally horizontal bottom chord can be cambered to provide greater head room.

Trusses can rest on concrete, unit masonry, or wood frame walls or can be part of a steel frame. For low-rise structures, this combination often takes the form of a bent (Fig. 37), and several bents, with bracing or portals between the bents, can be used to create a building (Fig. 38). The design of bents and portals is beyond the scope of this article; however, more needs to be said about trusses.

It is difficult to generalize about economical truss spans and spacings; however, for spans of some 70 ft, a 15–20 ft spacing is generally adequate for normal roof loads. Spacing between top chord panel points (Fig. 36) is generally in the order of 8 ft. Purlins span between trusses, usually, but not always, at the panel points to avoid subjecting the top truss chord to bending between panel points. The roof decking then spans between purlins.

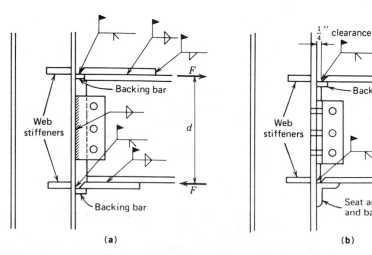

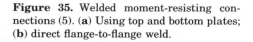

Figure 35. Welded moment-resisting connections (5). (**a**) Using top and bottom plates; (**b**) direct flange-to-flange weld.

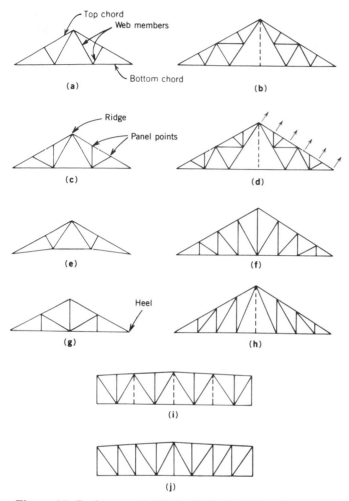

Figure 36. Roof trusses. (**a**) Fink; (**b**) Fink; (**c**) fan; (**d**) Fan; (**e**) cambered Fink; (**f**) Howe; (**g**) king-post; (**h**) Pratt; (**i**) flat Warren; (**j**) flat Pratt.

Loads on roof trusses are those transmitted by the purlins, the purlins themselves, and the truss itself. The purlins carry the weight of the roof deck and covering, the environmental loads, and often a live load allowance as well, eg, load due to maintenance if not occupant traffic. As noted at the outset of this article, the most frequently encountered environmental loads are wind, snow and ice, and rain, the last-named being a concern when ponding is possible and when it combines with snow or forms ice.

Obviously, the wind load is a function of geographic location and exposure. Wind is considered to be horizontal and is translated into a force perpendicular to the roof surface. This force can be either positive or negative, depending on whether pressure or suction is created both

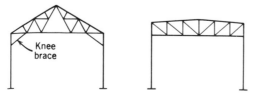

Figure 37. Bents (5).

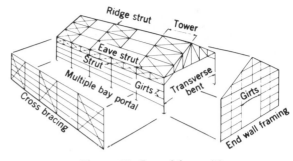

Figure 38. Braced frame (5).

externally and internally. Figure 39 shows the application of typical dead, snow, and wind loads to the panel points of a truss. The procedure for designing a truss roof system involves most if not all of the elements thus far discussed. The steps are as follows:

1. Select the most appropriate truss configuration for the span, loads, and overall design.
2. Calculate the weight of the roof covering and deck in psf and calculate the plf to be supported by each purlin—ie, psf load times the truss spacing (½ this amount for heel and ridge purlins), plus an allowance for the weight of the purlin itself.
3. Given the allowable or estimated psf live load, calculate the load psf in terms of psf of horizontal projection of the roof surface and multiply by the truss spacing as in step 2 and convert to a plf load on the purlin.
4. Similar to step 3, calculate the balanced snow and/or rain load and convert to plf load on the purlin.
5. Determine the psf wind loads (transverse and longitudinal) acting normal to the roof surfaces (pressure or suction) and convert to plf load on the purlin.
6. Determine the most unfavorable combination of loads. (See load combinations under this article heading on loads.)
7. Design the purlins for the most unfavorable load combination. Note that if the truss has sloping top chords, the purlins will in all likelihood have their y axes perpendicular to the roof surface at the panel points. In most instances, the roof deck will provide lateral support to the purlin, and, if not, tie rods between purlins can be provided as needed along the purlin span from heel to ridge (and across the ridge if double purlins are used). In this event the purlin need be designed for only that component of the load normal to the roof surface.
8. Estimate the weight of the truss and add to the above calculated panel point loads. It is customary to assume a trial weight of 2 to 5 psf of supported area.
9. Determine panel point loads due to balanced and unbalanced snow loads.
10. Determine panel point load due to wind using the data developed in step 5.
11. Calculate the stresses in each member of the truss for the various loads and prepare a stress analysis

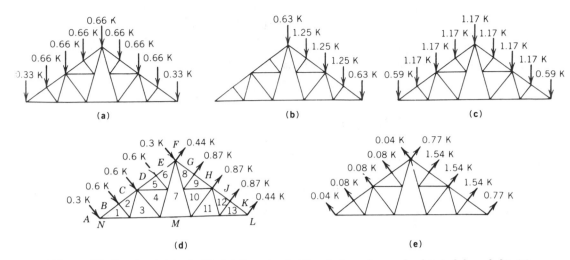

Figure 39. Panel point loads (5). (**a**) Snow load; (**b**) unbalanced snow load (wind from left); (**c**) dead load; (**d**) wind load. External forces plus internal suction (wind from left): (**e**) wind load. External forces plus internal pressure (wind from left).

diagram; ie, determine the compressive or tensile stress on each truss member, noting if a stress reversal is possible, and record the totals.

12. Determine the critical stress(es) for each member based on the most unfavorable load combination for that member.
13. Select the truss members (compression and tension).
14. Design the joints.
15. Design the end bearing and anchorage.
16. Design bracing.
17. Prepare a design drawing to facilitate fabrication.

Figure 40 illustrates a typical welded truss resting on a masonry wall, with a 70-ft span and 12-ft 6-in. rise. As

earlier noted, if such a truss is married to columns at the heel and a knee brace is provided (Fig. 37), the result is a bent; and, if further combined with portals or bracing between bents, the result is a framed structure.

CONTINUITY

Throughout this article there has been frequent reference to indeterminate structural elements and frames with use of such terms as fixed, rigid, continuous, and moment-resisting. Although beyond the scope of this article, no discussion of steel design would be complete without mention of the concept of indeterminacy.

Structural systems are intended to enclose three-dimensional space. This can be done in a variety of ways, perhaps the simplest being with longitudinal load-bearing

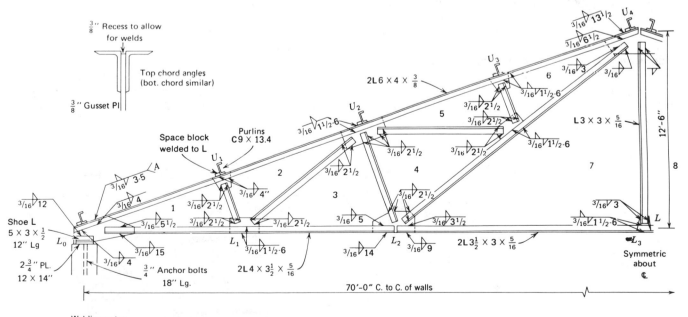

Figure 40. Typical welded truss (5).

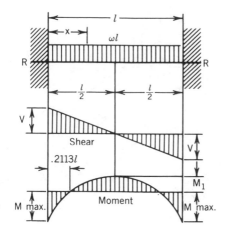

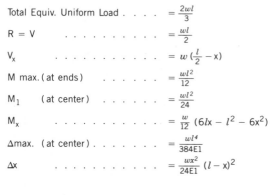

Total Equiv. Uniform Load	$= \frac{2wl}{3}$
$R = V$	$= \frac{wl}{2}$
V_x	$= w\left(\frac{l}{2} - x\right)$
M max. (at ends)	$= \frac{wl^2}{12}$
M_1 (at center)	$= \frac{wl^2}{24}$
M_x	$= \frac{w}{12}(6lx - l^2 - 6x^2)$
Δmax. (at center)	$= \frac{wl^4}{384EI}$
Δx	$= \frac{wx^2}{24EI}(l - x)^2$

Figure 41. Uniformly loaded fixed-end beam.

exterior walls and beams or joists spanning between the walls to form a roof. If the span between walls is too large for beams and joists, trusses can be used. For even larger spans between exterior walls, interior longitudinal load-bearing walls or columns can be introduced, and, of course exterior load-bearing walls can be replaced by columns. In either event, there is the need to prevent racking of the structure due to uneven or lateral loads. This can be done by introducing cross walls, or in the case of a structure with exterior columns, with bracing both transverse and longitudinal. These configurations refer primarily to "flexible" or Type 2 construction, ie, construction in which the various elements can rotate with respect to each other. However, it also is possible to create a stable structure by making the structure "rigid," ie, by introducing moment-resisting connections.

Returning to the beam as a basic element, Figure 41 shows a single-span beam fixed at its ends and supporting a uniform load. It will be seen that the maximum moment $(wl^2/12)$ occurs at the ends rather than the center, as with a beam identically loaded but free to rotate at supports $(wl^2/8)$, and that there also is a moment at the center of the span $(wl^2/24)$. When beams are continued over one or more interior supports (Fig. 42), a reversal of stress will occur at the interior supports because the beam is not free to deflect between its end supports.

Finally, several indeterminate frames are shown in Figure 43, and the comparable frames in a determinate mode in Figure 44, to illustrate the difference between the

two—the freedom or lack of freedom of members to rotate at joints. To ascertain the magnitude of the moments in determinate members, the laws of statics are sufficient; ie, only two of the three equations $\Sigma H = 0$, $\Sigma V = 0$, $\Sigma M = 0$ are needed. However, with indeterminate structures, the unknowns are too many and other means, such as the method of consistent deformation, are necessary. Therefore, although indeterminate structures are beyond the scope of this article, they are nevertheless a major component of steel building design.

LONG-SPAN STRUCTURE

Where it is necessary to frame spans of 100–150 ft and more, modifications of the forms thus far discussed are needed. The three-hinged arch (Fig. 45), composed of hinged, trussed elements has been in use for many years for buildings such as exhibition halls and gymnasia. Steel rib arches and ridged frames can be fabricated to span these larger distances as well.

COMPOSITES AND LRFD

Finally, there is need to touch on two other developments in steel building design: composite (steel and concrete) construction and load and resistance factor design (LRFD).

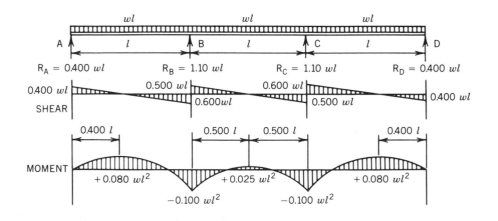

Figure 42. Uniformly loaded continuous beam.

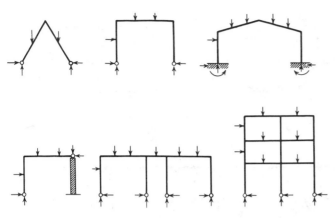

Figure 43. Indeterminate frames (5).

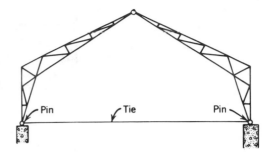

Figure 45. Three-hinged arch (5).

Composite Construction

Noted earlier was steel decking with or without a concrete topping to restrain the top flange of steel beams from lateral movement (Fig. 4f). In the case shown, the deck is tack-welded to the top flange of the beam. However, if an adequate number of steel studs are placed in the concrete and welded through the deck (or a hole in the deck) to the top flange of the beam (Fig. 46), the concrete can be considered to provide compressive resistance to bending as well as providing lateral support. Compressive bending resistance is added to that of the top chord of the steel beam; and this also is true for steel beams with welded studs at the top flange that extend into concrete slabs whether or not the top flange of the steel beam is actually imbedded in the concrete and for steel beams that are fully encased in concrete (2 in. or more on the sides and bottom, and 1½ in. on the top—Fig. 4a), thus creating a natural bond between the two elements. Unless adequately shored and laterally braced, the steel beam in composite construction must be capable of supporting all loads imposed prior to hardening of the concrete, and the effective width of the concrete slab that can be considered as contributing to the strength of the beam must not exceed either (13):

⅛ the beam span, center-to-center of supports

½ the distance to the centerline of adjacent beams, or

the distance to the edge of the slab

Columns also can be made composite by encasing them in reinforced concrete, or, in the case of pipes and tubes, filling them with concrete (Fig. 47).

Although composite construction is suitable for any loading, it is most efficient where there are heavy loads, relatively long spans, and beams spaced to the maximum allowable.

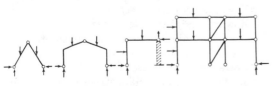

Figure 44. Determinate frames (5).

Load and Resistance Factor Design

The American Institute of Steel Construction has introduced a new design procedure, specification, and Manual (6) for what is termed load and resistance factor design (LRFD), one that it believes will lead to an improved approach to the design of steel buildings. Involved is the concepts of both load and resistance. A discussion of LRFD is beyond the scope of this article; however, refer to Ref. 13. In the future, LRFD will certainly supplement if not replace the allowable stress design (ASD) approach in current use. As the AISC states (13):

> . . . the new LRFD method [should not] give designs radically different from the older methods, since it was tuned, or "calibrated," to typical representative designs of the earlier methods. The principal new ingredient is the use of a probabilistic mathematical model in the development of the load and resistance factors, which made it possible to give proper weight to the degree of accuracy with which the various loads and resistances can be determined.

CONCLUSION

Of necessity, only the basics of steel building design have been treated herein, and although an effort has been made to familiarize the reader with steel design, it should not be assumed that sufficient information has been provided to permit the execution of a satisfactory analysis and design even for relatively simple members, assemblies, and structures. For this purpose, refer to the texts on structural analysis and design and the specifications and design guides referenced.

SYMBOLS

A Cross-sectional area (in.²); Gross area of an axially loaded compression member (in.²).

A_e Effective net area of an axially loaded tension member (in.²).

A_f Area of compression flange (in.²).

A_w Area of girder web (in.²).

C_b Bending coefficient dependent on moment gradient
$$= 1.75 + 1.05 \left(\frac{M_1}{M_2}\right) + 0.3 \left(\frac{M_1}{M_2}\right)^2.$$

E Modulus of elasticity of steel (29,000 ksi).

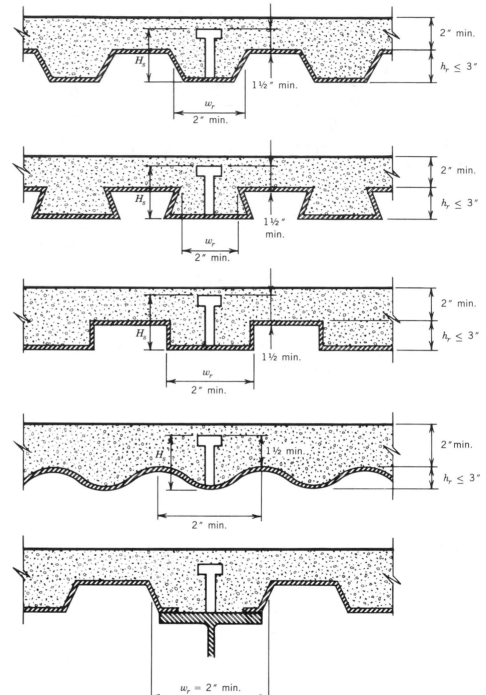

Figure 46. Composite beams and girders with formed steel deck (12). Courtesy of the American Institute of Steel Construction.

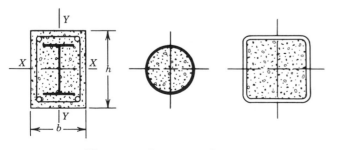

Figure 47. Composite columns.

F_a	Axial compressive stress permitted in a prismatic member in the absence of bending moment (ksi).
F_b	Bending stress permitted in a prismatic member in the absence of axial force (ksi).
F_p	Allowable bearing stress (ksi).
F_t	Allowable axial tensile stress (ksi).
F_u	Specified minimum tensile strength of the type of steel or fastener being used (ksi).
F_v	Allowable shear stress (ksi).
F_y	Specified minimum yield stress of the type of steel being used (ksi). As used in the AISC Manual,

"yield stress" denotes either the specified minimum yield point (for those steels that have yield point) or specified minimum yield strength (for those steels that do not have a yield point).

F_y' The theoretical maximum yield stress (ksi) based on the width–thickness ratio of one half the unstiffened compression flange, beyond which a particular shape is not "compact." See AISC Specification Section 1.5.1.4.1.2.

$$F_y' = \left(\frac{65}{b_f/2t_f}\right)^2$$

F_y''' The theoretical maximum yield stress (ksi) based on the depth–thickness ratio of the web below which a particular shape may be considered "compact" for any condition of combined bending and axial stresses. See AISC Specification Section 1.5.1.4.1.4.

$$= \left(\frac{257}{d/t_w}\right)^2$$

I Moment of inertia of a section (in.^{4}).

I_x Moment of inertia of a section about the X–X axis (in.^{4}).

I_y Moment of inertia of a section about the Y–Y axis (in.^{4}).

L Span length (ft); Length of connection angles (in.).

L_b Actual unbraced length of the compression flange.

L_c Maximum unbraced length of the compression flange at which the allowable bending stress may be taken at $0.66F_y$ or as determined by AISC Specification Formula 1.5-5a or Formula 1.5-5b, when applicable (ft).

L_u Maximum unbraced length of the compression flange at which the allowable bending stress may be taken at $0.6F_y$ (ft).

M Moment (kip-ft); Factored bending moment (kip-ft).

M_1 Smaller moment at end of unbraced length of beam-column.

M_2 Larger moment at end of unbraced length of beam-column.

N Length of bearing plate (in.).

P Applied load (kips); Force transmitted by a fastener (kips); Factored axial load (kips).

R Maximum end reaction for 3½ in. of bearing (kips); Reaction or concentrated load applied to beam or girder (kips); Radius (in.).

S Elastic section modulus (in.^{3}).

V Maximum permissible web shear (kips); statical shear in beam (kips).

Z Plastic section modulus (in.^{3}).

b Actual width of stiffened and unstiffened compression elements (in.); Dimension normal to the direction of stress (in.); Fastener spacing vertically (in.); Distance from the bolt center line to the face of tee stem or angle leg in determining prying action (in.).

b_f Flange width of rolled beam or plate girder (in.).

d Depth of column, beam, or girder (in.); Nominal diameter of a fastener (in.).

d_c Column web depth clear of fillets (in.).

f Axial compression stress on member based on effective area, Section C3 (ksi).

f_a Computed axial stress (ksi).

f_b Computed bending stress (ksi).

f_p Actual bearing pressure on support (ksi).

f_t Computed tensile stress (ksi).

f_v Computed shear stress (ksi).

g Transverse spacing locating fastener gauge lines (in.).

h Clear distance between flanges of a beam or girder at the section under investigation (in.).

in. Inches.

l_h Distance from center line of fastener hole to end of beam web (in.).

l_v Distance from center line of fastener hole to free edge of part in the direction of the force (in.).

lb Pounds.

n Number of fasteners in one vertical row.

r Governing radius of gyration (in.).

r_T Radius of gyration of a section comprising the compression flange plus ⅓ of the compression web area, taken about an axis in the plane of the web (in.).

r_x Radius of gyration with respect to the X–X axis (in.).

r_y Radius of gyration with respect to the Y–Y axis (in.).

s Longitudinal center-to-center spacing (pitch) of any two consecutive holes (in.).

t Girder, beam, or column web thickness (in.); Thickness of a connected part (in.); Wall thickness of a tubular member (in.); Angle thickness (in.).

t_b Thickness of beam flange or moment connection plate at rigid beam-to-column connection (in.).

t_f Flange thickness (in.).

t_w Web thickness (in.).

x Subscript relating symbol to strong axis bending.

y Subscript relating symbol to weak axis bending.

Δ Beam deflection (in.); Displacement of the neutral axis of a loaded member from its position when the member is not loaded (in.).

kip 1000 pounds.

ksi Expression of stress in kips per square inch.

BIBLIOGRAPHY

1. Standard ASCE/ANSI 1-88 (Formerly ANSI A58.1), American Society of Civil Engineers, Minimum Design Loads for Buildings and Other Structures.

2. *Manual of Steel Construction*, 8th ed., American Institute of Steel Construction, Chicago, 1979.

3. *Standard Specifications for Open Web Steel Joists*, Steel Joist Institute, 1986.

4. *Formed Steel Structural Members and Specification for Design of Light Gage Cold-formed Stainless Steel Structural Members*, American Iron and Steel Institute.

5. S. W. Crawley, and R. M. Dillon, *Steel Buildings: Analysis and Design,* 3rd ed., John Wiley & Sons, New York, 1977.

6. Ref. 2, p. 2-9.

7. Ref, 2, p. 2-18.

8. Ref. 2, pp. 1-18, 1-19.

9. Ref. 2, p. 2-62.

10. Ref. 2, p. 5-124.

11. Ref. 2, p. 3-26.

12. Ref. 2, p. 5-137.

13. *Manual of Steel Construction: Load and Resistance Factor Design,* American Institute of Steel Construction, Chicago, 1986.

General References

H. Parker and J. Ambrose, *Simplified Design of Structural Steel,* 5th ed., John Wiley & Sons, New York, 1983.

See also OFFICE BUILDINGS; SPACE FRAMES; STAINLESS STEELS; STRUCTURAL STEEL

ROBERT M. DILLON, AIA
Silver Spring, Maryland

STANLEY W. CRAWLEY, P.E.
University of Utah
Salt Lake City, Utah

STERN, ROBERT A. M.

Robert A. M. Stern, a practicing architect, teacher, and writer, is principal in the firm of Robert A. M. Stern Architects. New York born, Stern has stated that he became an architect because he loved the architecture of his native city (1):

> When I was growing up, the skyscrapers of Manhattan seemed to me the peaks of an astonishing man-made mountain range: fabulous buildings—the Woolworth, the Chrysler, the Empire State—seemed part of an Emerald City. They were my personal Oz—a great movie set through which I could wander freely. . . . I always wanted to be an architect, to make buildings like those I saw in the Manhattan skyline, soaring towers filled with dreams of modern power married to ancient form.

Stern was educated at Columbia University (B.A., 1960) and Yale University (M. Architecture, 1965). On his graduation from Yale, Stern served as program director of the Architectural League of New York where he conceived and organized "40 under 40," an exhibition of work by forty architects under the age of forty. He subsequently worked with the New York City Housing and Development Administration for three years. In 1969, he formed an architectural partnership with John S. Hagmann and in 1977, he became the principal of his own firm.

In his design work, Stern has striven to break with the modernism of the 1950s and 1960s that he found conventionalized and pessimistic in its hyperemphasis on material and programmatic functionalism over symbolic content. Breaking with the prevailing architectural culture, which tended to disregard the buildings of the past in the design process, Stern sought to develop an approach to design rooted in contextually meaningful tradition. Rejecting the idea that modern technology inevitably gives rise to a universal international style, Stern believes that (2):

> Architecture is a dialogue with the past carried on in the present with an eye cast toward the future. . . . Believing as I do in the continuity of tradition . . . I try to create order out of the chaotic present by entering into a dialogue with the past, with tradition. The depth of that dialogue is, I believe, the essence of architecture and, in fact, of all culture. I do not believe that the past offers a cure for the ills of the present; I do believe it offers standards for evaluation.

Stern initially expressed the link with the past through the use of traditional building materials while largely rejecting historical forms in favor of modern ones. Over the course of his career, Stern has increasingly mined architectural history, exploring the multiple meanings of the past in building designs that demonstrate the depth and scope of the new–old approach, which he has called modern traditionalism.

Since 1980, Stern, widely known as an architect of houses distinguished by a sensitivity to local architectural traditions and a commitment to the highest standards of craftsmanship, has further developed his ideas in a wide variety of building types. Recent projects have included office buildings in Massachusetts (Fig. 1) and California; a dormitory and dining hall at the University of Virginia; and the headquarters of Mexx International, Inc. in the Netherlands. Currently underway are the resort town of Grand Harbor in Vero Beach, Florida; an art gallery and dance building for the University of California at Irvine; the Center for Jewish Life at Princeton University; a library for the St. Paul's School in Concord, New Hampshire; the Norman Rockwell Museum at Stockbridge, Massachusetts; and the Bancho House office building in Tokyo, Japan. The firm, which presently employs more than 65 architects, has received numerous design awards including the Distinguished Architecture Award of the New York Chapter of the American Institute of Architects in 1982, 1984, and 1985. Additionally, Stern, a Fellow of the AIA, received the Medal of Honor of its New York chapter in 1984.

Professor and first Director of the Temple Hoyne Buell Center for the Study of American Architecture at Columbia University, Stern has lectured extensively in the United States and abroad. While still a student at Yale, he edited a special issue of *Perspecta,* the school's architectural journal, that included a prepublication excerpt of Robert Venturi's *Complexity and Contradiction in Architecture.* Stern is the author or coauthor of numerous books including *New Directions in American Architecture* (3), *George Howe: Toward a Modern American Architecture* (4), *East Hampton's Heritage: An Illustrated Architectural Record* (5), *New York 1900: Metropolitan Architecture and Urbanism 1890–1915* (6), *New York 1930: Architecture and Urbanism Between the Two World Wars* (7), and *Modern Classicism* (8).

Stern is also the author of *Pride of Place: Building the American Dream,* the companion book to his eight-part

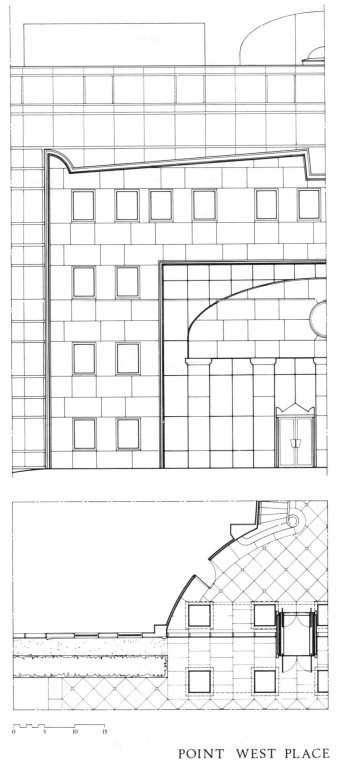

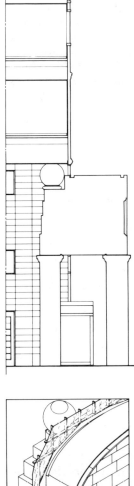

POINT WEST PLACE

FRAMINGHAM   MASSACHUSETTS

Figure 1. Point West Place, Framingham, Massachusetts. Courtesy of Robert A. M. Stern Architects.

documentary television series on U.S. architecture, aired nationally in the spring of 1986 on public television. The controversial and widely watched series was filmed throughout the nation at more than 100 locations. Examining a variety of building and planning types, including the campus, the dream house, the suburb, and the sky-

scraper, in their historical and cultural contexts, Stern explored what he considered to be the genius of U.S. architects: "to interpret the past in its fullest complexity in order to turn the assemblage of bricks and mortar into art, to lift mere building into the realm of architecture" (8).

Three books about Stern's work have been published:

Robert Stern (9), *Robert A. M. Stern: Buildings and Projects 1965–1980* (10), and *Robert A. M. Stern: Buildings and Projects 1981–1986* (2). Stern's work has been exhibited at numerous galleries and universities as well as the Museum of Modern Art, the Metropolitan Museum of Art, the Drawing Center, the Cooper-Hewitt and Whitney museums in New York, the Walker Art Center in Minneapolis, and the Art Institute of Chicago. In 1982, Stern was the subject of a one-man exhibition at the Neuberger Museum of the State University of New York at Purchase. In 1980, he designed the section devoted to the 1970s in the Forum Design Exhibition held in Linz, Austria. In 1976 and 1980, he was among the architects selected to represent the United States at the Venice Biennale.

BIBLIOGRAPHY

1. R. A. M. Stern, with T. Mellins, and R. Gastil, *Pride of Place: Building the American Dream,* Houghton Mifflin, Boston; American Heritage, New York, 1986, pp. 1–2.

2. R. A. M. Stern, "Introduction: Modern Traditionalism," in L. Rueda, ed., *Robert A. M. Stern: Buildings and Projects 1981–1986,* Rizzoli International Publications, New York, 1986, p. 6.

3. R. A. M. Stern, *New Directions in American Architecture,* Braziller, New York, 1969; rev. ed., 1977.

4. R. A. M. Stern, *George Howe: Toward a Modern American Architecture,* Yale University Press, New Haven, 1975.

5. R. A. M. Stern, C. Lancaster, and R. Hefner, *East Hampton's Heritage: An Illustrated Architectural Record,* W. W. Norton, New York, 1982.

6. R. A. M. Stern, G. Gilmartin, and J. M. Massengale, *New York 1900: Metropolitan Architecture and Urbanism 1890–1915,* Rizzoli, New York, 1983.

7. R. A. M. Stern, G. Gilmartin, and T. Mellins, *New York 1930: Architecture and Urbanism between the Two World Wars,* Rizzoli, New York, 1987.

8. R. A. M. Stern with Raymond W. Gastil, *Modern Classicism,* Rizzoli, New York, 1988.

9. Ref. 1, p. 9.

10. D. Dunster, ed., *Robert Stern,* Academy Editions, London, 1981.

11. P. Arnell and T. Bickford, eds., *Robert A. M. Stern: Buildings and Projects 1965–1980,* Rizzoli, New York, 1981.

General References

C. Moore, "Lang Residence: Where Are We Now, Vincent Scully?" *Progressive Architecture,* 78–83 (April 1975).

P. Goldberger, "Allusions of Grandeur," *The New York Times Magazine,* 66–67, 72 (June 8, 1975).

"The Work of Robert A. M. Stern and John S. Hagmann," *Architecture and Urbanism,* special feature, 85–150 (Oct. 1975).

P. Goldberger, "Robert A. M. Stern's Two Houses," *Architecture and Urbanism,* 81–92 (Sept. 1977).

C. Jencks, *Post Modern Classicism,* Academy Editions, London, 1980, pp. 11, 35–42.

C. Jencks, "Stern and Post-Modern Space," *Architectural Design News Supplement,* 1, 6–7 (July 1981).

V. Scully, "Robert Stern: Perspecta to Post Modernism," *Architectural Design,* 98–99 (Dec. 1981).

P. Portoghesi, *After Modern Architecture,* Rizzoli International Publications, New York, 1982, pp. 7–13.

P. Goldberger, "The Maturing of Robert Stern," *The New York Times,* sect. D, 31, 34 (Apr. 4, 1982).

C. Jencks, "On the Edge of Content: Charles Jencks Reviews Robert Stern's Oeuvre," *Skyline,* 28–29 (June 1982).

S. Tigerman, "The Kaleidoscopically Wonderful R. A. M. S.," *The Residential Works of Robert A. M. Stern, Architecture and Urbanism,* extra ed., 149–151 (July 1982).

A. Greenberg, "Recent Houses by Robert Stern," *The Residential Works of Robert A. M. Stern, Architecture and Urbanism,* extra ed., 155–156 (July 1982).

T. S. Hines, "Citizen Stern: A Portrait of the Architect as Entrepreneur," *The Residential Works of Robert A. M. Stern, Architecture and Urbanism,* extra ed., 227–231 (July 1982).

P. Jodidio, "La decoration n'est pas un crime," *Connaissance des arts,* 74–81 (May 1983).

P. Goldberger, "Shingle Style Again," *House and Garden,* 168–177, 211 (June 1984).

V. Scully, "Architecture: Robert A. M. Stern," *Architectural Digest,* 136–141, 164, 166 (June 1984); reprinted Japanese ed., 64–69 (Sept. 1984).

G. Macrae-Gibson, "Scenography and the Picturesque," *The Secret Life of Buildings: An American Mythology for Modern Architecture,* MIT Press, Cambridge, Mass., 1985, pp. 98–117.

C. Vogel, "The Trend-Setting Traditionalism of Architect Robert A. M. Stern," *The New York Times Magazine,* 40–49 (Jan. 13, 1985).

K. Gustmann, "Great Architects: Robert A. M. Stern," *Hauser,* 59–70 (March 1985).

P. Portoghesi, "Il Progetto," *Eupalino,* 6–11 (April 1985).

R. Campbell, "Shingle Style Reinvented: Residence at Chilmark: Robert A. M. Stern," *Architecture,* 262–267 (May 1985); reprinted in *Architecture Quarterly,* 18–23 (Fall 1985).

H. Newell Jacobsen, "Architecture: Robert A. M. Stern," *Architectural Digest,* 210–219 (May 1985).

G. Macrae-Gibson, "Robert A. M. Stern and the Tradition of the Picturesque," *Architecture and Urbanism,* 83–90 (Aug. 1985).

S. Tigerman, "Villa with a View: Melding Traditions on Oyster Bay," *Architectural Digest,* 132–341 (1985).

Other Books by Robert A. M. Stern

R. A. M. Stern, *40 under 40: Young Talent in Architecture,* exhibition catalog American Federation of Arts, New York, 1966.

R. A. M. Stern, guest ed., "White and Gray," *Architecture and Urbanism,* special feature, 25–180 (April 1975).

R. A. M. Stern, guest ed., "40 under 40 + 10," *Architecture and Urbanism,* special feature, 17–142 (January 1977).

R. A. M. Stern, Commentary, *Philip Johnson: Collected Writings,* Oxford University Press, New York, 1979.

R. A. M. Stern and D. Nevins, *The Architect's Eye: American Architectural Drawings from 1799–1978,* Pantheon, New York, 1979.

R. A. M. Stern and J. M. Massengale, *The Anglo-American Suburb,* Academy Editions, London, 1981.

R. A. M. Stern, guest ed., "American Architecture after Modernism," *Architecture and Urbanism,* special issue (March 1981).

R. A. M. Stern with T. P. Catalano, *Raymond M. Hood,* Rizzoli International Publications, New York, 1982.

R. A. M. Stern, ed., *International Design Yearbook 1985/86*, Abbeville Press, New York, 1985.

THOMAS MELLINS
Robert A. M. Stern Architects
New York, New York

STIRLING, JAMES

The British architect, James Stirling, was born in Glasgow, Scotland in 1926. He received his architectural degree from the University of Liverpool School of Architecture in 1950. He undertook postgraduate study at the School of Town Planning and Regional Research, London, 1950–1952. Early experience was obtained in the firm of Lyons, Israel and Ellis, where James Stirling was Senior Assistant (1953–1956).

In 1956, James Stirling entered into a partnership with James Gowan based on a commission for development of private flats at Ham Common, on the outskirts of London. The design of this project was based on Stirling's close study of Le Corbusier's Jaoul houses in Paris (1954–1956). The firm of James Stirling and James Gowan lasted until 1963, after which James Stirling practiced alone (1964–1970). In 1971, James Stirling formed a partnership with Michael Wilford. The firm is currently James Stirling, Michael Wilford and Associates.

Although not free of controversy, James Stirling's work has brought him many awards, including the Gold Medal of the Royal Institute of British Architects (1980) and the Pritzker Prize (1981). James Stirling has written extensively and his work has been widely published. This attention has contributed to his receiving commissions for a large series of important projects outside of the United Kingdom. A number of his projects for unbuilt buildings have also been published, partly because of the high quality of Stirling's presentation drawings. Stirling has taught throughout his career, both in the UK (Architectural Association, London, Regent Street Polytechnic, London, Cambridge University School of Architecture) and abroad. He is the Charles Davenport Visiting Professor at Yale University School of Architecture from 1967, and Guest professor at the Dusseldorf Kunstakademie since 1977.

Stirling's fame is based on the long series of important post-modern buildings. The early buildings were "high tech" and later buildings, particularly additions to older buildings, have shown an interest in reinterpreting the past in a decidedly original manner. The ambiguity inherent in these historic references is a feature of his recent work. A brief description of the more famous buildings follows.

ENGINEERING DEPARTMENT, UNIVERSITY OF LEICESTER (1959–1963)

This project was done with James Gowan. The building has large areas of glazing contrasted with heavy masonry forms. The auditoriums are cantilevered structures of great power. Although all of the materials look made of stock parts, the aesthetic power is striking. The balance of parts creates a memorable image. The building cannot be understood from any one viewpoint, and can be best understood on the basis of an isometric drawing. The Engineering Building was a strong contrast to earlier British post World War II work, and was the origin of his international reputation (Fig. 1).

HISTORY BUILDING, CAMBRIDGE UNIVERSITY (1964–1967)

Selected on the basis of a competition, James Stirling's most controversial work consists of a great double-glazed sloping roof over the reading room contrasted with the multistoried structure containing enclosed spaces, which in turn are stepped to accommodate larger spaces on the lower floors (see Fig. 2). The stair tower is articulated as a separate element. The powerful image caused an ambivalent response from critics and the public. The building design was violently attacked in the British press, although defended by the history faculty. In 1985 consideration was given as to whether the building should be destroyed (1). The building has suffered from lack of maintenance and deterioration, but has since been repaired.

OLIVETTI TRAINING SCHOOL, HASLEMERE, SURREY (1969–1972)

This project pioneered in the use of glass-reinforced polyester panels. The building is in two wings with a much-photographed glass corridor connecting it to the Edwardian country house, which was converted for use as residential space for Olivetti employees. The divisible lecture hall inserted into the plan is used by Stirling to good dramatic effect at the juncture of the glazed link and the lecture rooms. All his work shows this interest in spatial complexity (Fig. 3).

A long period of little building followed this project, until the firm won the competition for the Stuttgart project in 1977.

ART GALLERY ADDITION, STAATSGALERIE, STUTTGART (1977–1983)

This building was an addition to the existing Staatsgalerie. It consisted of a new gallery extension, chamber theater and music school. A feature of the site was a pedestrian walk diagonally across the property to be incorporated in the plan without jeopardizing building security (Fig. 4). The design was not well-received in the German press. It was disturbing because it was not a classically modernist design. As it developed, it was recognized that Stirling had brought off a project which reinterpreted the past in a brilliant new way. It has become a great public success. The complexity of the project, and its references to existing buildings both old and new reward close study. For instance, not far away from the site is the

Figure 1. Engineering Department, University of Leicester. Photograph by Richard Einsig.

Weissenhofsiedlung, with buildings by Mies van der Rohe, Le Corbusier, and J. J. P. Oud. A hint of this may be found in one elevation of the building, at the rear of the chamber theater.

The more obvious source is the reinterpretation of the classical museum such as Shinkel's Altes Museum in Berlin (1824), but in the Stuttgart building, the central domed rotunda is replaced with the open air circular court, a true public space.

Figure 2. History Building, Cambridge University. Photograph by Richard Bryant.

Figure 3. Olivetti Training School. Photograph by Richard Einzig.

Figure 4. Art gallery addition, Staatsgalerie, Stuttgart. Photograph by Richard Bryant.

Figure 5. Clore Gallery, addition to the Tate Gallery. Photograph by Richard Bryant.

THE CLORE GALLERY ADDITION TO THE TATE GALLERY (TURNER MUSEUM) MILLBANK, LONDON (1980–1987)

This project is known as the Clore Gallery in honor of the Clore Foundation that funded the construction 136 years after the Turner bequest (Joseph Mallord William Turner, 1775–1851), and represents the first phase of a planned expansion of the Tate Gallery. This is Stirling's first important project in London. In addition to the Clore Gallery, the firm has prepared a master plan for future enlargement of the Tate Gallery. The main Clore galleries are top-lit by filtered sunlight supplemented with electric lighting (Fig. 5). The reserve galleries are possibly less successful, with the paintings stacked on red walls in the manner of Turner's own studio. From the exterior, the heightened colors and relation to the landscaped areas is a striking but effective contrast with the older 1897 Portland stone Tate buildings.

THE ARTHUR M. SACKLER MUSEUM, HARVARD UNIVERSITY (1979–1985)

An addition to the Fogg Museum, the L-shaped site is directly across the street from the original building. The master plan includes a gallery bridge connector which has not been built. The dramatic feature of the building is the stairway rising through the building, lit from a continuous overhead skylight (Fig. 6). The exterior striped facade of the building is largely closed, in response to the adjoining heavily trafficked streets. The program includes galleries and offices.

This has been another controversial building. The exterior, with its horizontally striped walls and irregularly spaced windows does not reflect the major interior experi-

Figure 6. Arthur M. Sackler Museum, Harvard University stairway. Photograph by Timothy Hursley.

BIBLIOGRAPHY

1. D. Sudjic, *Norman Foster, Richard Rogers, James Stirling; New Directions in British Architecture,* Thames and Hudson, New York, 1987, pp. 69–70.

General References

P. Arnell and T. Bickford, eds., *James Stirling: Buildings and Projects 1950–1980,* with an essay by Colin Rowe, Rizolli, New York, 1984.

R. Banham, "Leicester University Department of Engineering," *Architectural Forum* **121**(2), 118–125 (Aug./Sept. 1964).

"The Clore Gallery, The Tate Gallery, London," *Architectural Record* **175**(8), 104–113 (July 1987).

M. Filler, "Neue Staatsgalerie," *Progressive Architecture* **65**(10), 67–85 (Oct. 1984).

D. Greenway, "Neue Staatsgalerie," *Architecture* **74**(9), 94–101 (Sept. 1985).

C. Jencks, "Olivetti Training Centre, Haslemere," *Architecture Plus* **2**(2), 96–103 (Mar./Apr. 1974).

C. Jencks, "St Andrews' University in Scotland, James Stirling," *Architectural Forum* **133**(2), 50–57 (Sept. 1970).

K. Kikutake, ed., *James Stirling, Leicester University Engineering Department, Leicester, Great Britain. 1959–1963. Cambridge University History Faculty, Cambridge, Great Britain. 1964–1968,* A.D.A. Edita Tokyo, Global Architecture Series, No. 9, 1971.

"Neue Staatsgalerie in Stuttgart," *Architectural Record* **172**(10), 140–149 (Sept. 1984).

"Sackler Museum at Harvard," *Architectural Record* **174**(3), 112–123 (March 1986).

James Stirling, Architectural Design Profile, Academy Editions, London, and St. Martin's Press, New York, 1982.

ROBERT T. PACKARD, AIA
Reston, Virginia

ence, the stairwell rising in a continuous, skylighted run through several stories. Without the bridge connection, which requires community acceptance, the project seems incomplete. The building is not appealing in the ordinary sense, including the monumental entrance with its curious primitive stone form. The collections housed here are oriental, ancient and Islamic art, which may have been the inspiration for the entrance. The galleries greatly increase the exhibition space of the Fogg, adding some 11,000 square feet.

Of equal interest are the designs for projects which have not been built such as the addition to the National Gallery, London, (1985) and the Thyssen Museum at Lugano in Switzerland (1986). James Stirling, Michael Wilford and Associates have won the competition for the Thyssen Museum addition to the existing villa and gallery.

Stirling's work is powerful although criticized. The interest in his recent work relates to his ability to reinterpret the past in new evocative ways—a kind of collage of references. Much of his recent work has been outside of the UK. Stirling sees himself as living in a transitional period of design, more interesting than more settled times.

STONE, EDWARD DURRELL

Born in Fayetteville, Arkansas, Edward Durrell Stone (1902–1978) began his higher education at the University of Arkansas, Fayetteville. Entering in 1920, he remained there until 1923 when he left the South for Boston. There he entered the firm of Strickland, Blodgett and Law and, at the same time, enrolled in the atelier offered by the Boston Architectural Club (now the Boston Architectural Center or BAC) in the evenings. He quickly moved to the firm of Henry R. Shepley, as an apprentice, where he was involved in the restoration of Massachusetts Hall at Harvard University and the construction of one of the new freshman dormitory groups. Stone found Shepley's office "a wonderful place to work" (1) and later praised Shepley as one of the first architects trained in the beaux-arts tradition to "recognize the merit of new ideas in modern design. I know of no architect who has done more to encourage the young modern architect" (1).

After 2 years of days with Shepley and nights at the BAC, Stone entered a competition for special scholarships to Harvard and won, receiving a year's tuition. By the autumn of 1925 Stone was a student at Harvard, but he seemed to find the architectural curriculum there under Jacques Haffner too conservative and transferred to Massachusetts Institute of Technology the next academic year as a fifth, or final, year student. There, under the tutelage of Jacques Carlu, he began to be exposed to more modern design methods or at least the most modern methods that a winner of the Prix de Rome could instill in his charges, namely a decoratively restrained neoclassicism that would become commonplace in the 1930s. In 1927, with a design for an architect's office in a suburb, Stone won the Rotch traveling fellowship and spent the next 2 years in Europe.

While in Europe Stone made it a specific goal to visit the freshly built icons of the modern movement: seeing Dudok's work in Hilversum, Robert Mallet-Stevens and Auguste Perret's work in Paris, Tony Garnier's designs in Lyons, the work of Peter Behrens and Eric Mendelssohn in Germany, as well as Ludwig Mies Van der Rohe's Barcelona Pavilion. By the time of his return, the effect of this immersion in the international style was to create a total convert.

On his arrival in the United States, Stone went to New York where he first entered the firm of Shultze and Weaver, well-known designers of skyscrapers and commercial buildings, before becoming involved with the consortium of architects designing Rockefeller Center. While a member of this latter group as one of Wallace K. Harrison's designers, Stone was assigned his first major architectural work: the interiors of Radio City Music Hall.

Setting off on his own in 1933, Stone began the first of two distinct, and almost diametrically opposed, periods of his architectural career. In this first period his rigidly international style approach to design immediately became manifest. The Mandel House in Mount Kisco, New York, one of his first independent commissions (2), was a concretization of the design principles of the international style, being composed of basic geometric volumes, with strip windows, flat roof, and open plan. The building's ideological statement was completed by the use of all modern materials such as concrete, steel, and glass block. It was, in fact, the first house in the East designed in the international style. In 1936, Stone's commissions, Mepkin Plantation for Henry Luce, and the Albert Koch house, stepped back slightly from this stridently modernist position, but still remained within the idiom of the modern movement.

In Mepkin, for instance, which consists of a series of cubelike volumes united by connecting walkways, the overt modernism was tempered by a more classic treatment of the fenestration. In fact, in 1937, Stone received a gold medal from the somewhat conservative Architectural League of New York for that design (3). In that same year he began the design (with Phillip Goodwin, an architect and trustee of the museum) of one of his most famous commissions, the Museum of Modern Art in New York City.

The Museum of Modern Art stands as a "highly visible and aggressive advocate for the new international style sensibility." (4) Set forward at the limits of the property line, the stark whiteness of the structure defied the ad-

joining brownstones. The rigidity of the facade and its strip windows was successfully countered by the sinuous curvilinear shapes of the entry and information area. The circular skylighted covering of the top-floor terrace softened the harsh image whereas the interior, conceived as a loft space with temporary partitions, emphasized the international style requirement that the plan be open and adaptable for flexible planning of exhibits. Stone claimed that this rooftop garden was one of the first in New York and claimed his design as a prototype for subsequent efforts (2).

His success with the Museum of Modern Art made him one of the premier modern architects of the prewar period and, of course, led to such further international style commissions as the A. Conger Goodyear house (1938) in Old Westbury, Long Island, built for a trustee of the museum. Again Stone used a single space, this time the art gallery, as the primary spatial organizer of the house. All rooms branch off from this space.

Just prior to World War II, Stone's work entered a transitional period in which he rejected the clarity of form of his earlier work and demonstrated a sudden interest in indigenous materials and more natural siting of the structure, particularly in relation to domestic architecture. The Collier's House of Tomorrow of 1940, with its wood finish and vernacular shedlike form, was the harbinger of things to come after the war. The later Robert L. Popper house in White Plains, New York, was typical of Stone's residential work of this period just after the war.

However, his commercial work remained opposed to the softened approach to modernism seen in his residential work. The El Panama Hotel in Panama City (1946) and the Bay Roc in Montego Bay, Jamaica, are strident restatements of the international style.

Throughout the early 1950s Stone slowly evolved an extremely personal architectural style that employed a rather limited repertory of highly decorative forms that were seemingly based on the success of his United States embassy in New Delhi. Its elaborate grillwork and lush courtyard played off against a basic classic symmetry and proportion. Extremely pleased with the results, Stone claimed that Frank Lloyd Wright described the embassy as "one of the finest buildings of the past hundred years" (5).

The building's relative success, along with Stone's demagogic perception of the role of the architect, led to a complete stagnation in his work. The elements developed for New Delhi were repeated with slight variations in a mounting succession of commissions. These included designs for his own townhouse in New York City (1956), the United States Pavilion at the Brussel's World's Fair (1958), the Institute of Nuclear Science and Technology, Islamabad, Pakistan (1961), The State University Campus at Albany, New York (1962), the Huntington Hartford Gallery of Modern Art, New York (1965), and finally culminated in the John F. Kennedy Center for the performing Arts in Washington, D.C. (1969) and the master plan for the Florida State Capitol.

In Stone's high-rise designs a similar stagnation or codification of architectural vocabulary occurred. His General Motors building (with Emery Roth and Sons), with its marble sheathing and dark bay windows, became his own paradigmatic solution to the high rise as seen in his Standard Oil Building in Chicago (with Perkins and Will, 1974).

Stone served as a Professor of Architecture at New York University (1935–1940) and Yale University (1946–1952), as visiting critic at Princeton University, the University of Arkansas, and Cornell University, and on the advisory committees of the Massachusetts Institute of Technology and Columbia University.

BIBLIOGRAPHY

1. E. D. Stone, *The Evolution of an Architect,* Horizon Press, New York, 1962, p. 22.
2. *Ibid.,* p. 34.
3. Ref. 1, p. 36.
4. R. A. M. Stern and coworkers, *New York 1930,* Rizzoli, New York, 1987, p. 144.
5. Ref. 1, p. 139.

STEVEN BEDFORD
Middlebury, Connecticut

STONE, NATURAL BUILDING

Building stone, manufactured by the natural creation of the earth itself, has historically maintained a high-level position in the hierarchy of building materials. From ancient civilizations to the modern age, it has been used in the most prestigious places—palaces and government buildings, temples and corporate headquarters, castles and mansions—making it a material of kings and gods, rulers and the wealthy. Traditionally and contemporarily, stone is an integral part of art and architecture. Many of the great ancient architectural monuments and sculptures as well as the acclaimed artwork and buildings of today are composed of this natural material. Stone is used for both its aesthetic appearance and its durability.

HISTORY OF STONE

Natural stone and dimension stone—a stone product that has been quarried as a block or large piece and then usually cut into a panel, slab, or other shape according to some specified measurements—have been used for several millenia for building, road, and bridge construction (1).

Prior to its recorded use, stone gave its name to an era—The Stone Age. From that period of the very earliest civilization neolithic monuments endure today (2). It was in Imperial Rome that large scale commercial production of marble occurred for the first time in history. Private homes, public statuary and government buildings became more expensive and more numerous as the empire grew. It was during the physical and cultural expansion of the Empire that monumental building was at its height in Rome. Expanding from quarries long worked in the eastern Mediterranean, the Romans opened new ones in northern Africa, the hills of Carrara and the Pyrenees.

In Italy today, Carrara remains the hub of stone activity.

In fact, it is in Rome where the use of marble is first documented, cited by Velleius Patercolus in 1 B.C. for the home of prefect Mamurra on Mount Celio. Marble's use spread tremendously during the Augustan age to temples, forums, villas, basilicas, senate houses, and tombs. Augustus boasted that he had inherited a city of bricks and left behind a city of marble (3). Much of the well-known architecture of Rome is made of stone. The list of famous ancient Roman architecture made of stone includes the Roman Forum, the Colosseum, Circus Maximus, The Arch of Titus, the Arch of Constantine, and the Pantheon.

The spread of stone use throughout other parts of Italy is illustrated by the Tower of Pisa (twelfth century), the green-and-white-marbled cathedral of Florence (1296–1462; 1875) the travertine Arch of Trajan (114 A.D.), and St. Mark's in Venice (twelfth to fifteenth centuries) made of marble, porphyry, and alabaster. Stone's use throughout the world is evidenced by the Acropolis in Athens, Greece (sixth to fifth centuries B.C.), the white marble Taj Mahal in Agra, India (seventeenth century); the Great Pyramids of Giza, Egypt (2570–2500 B.C.), Egypt which were once encased in a smooth limestone skin; the Palace of Westminster in London (begun 1835); the Capitol in Washington, D.C. (begun 1792); and the 1250-ft-tall limestone Empire State building in New York City (1931), once the tallest building in the world. These great works of architecture, among others, illustrate the universality of natural stone.

DEFINITION

Before illustrating the types and methods of building-stone applications, the material must first be defined, and distinction must be made between the various types of natural stone used in architecture such as granite, marble, limestone, sandstone, travertine, slate, and onyx. Their geologic and commercial definitions differ.

Commercially, all calcareous rocks (those containing calcium carbonate, also known as calcite) capable of taking a polish are classified as marble. Defining marble in this way relates to the original meaning of the word marble, derived from Greek, meaning "bright and shining." The commercial definition of marble is determined according to standards set by the American Society for Testing and Materials (ASTM) in the United States, by UNI in Italy, by AFNOR in France, and by similar organizations in other countries.

Geologically, stone falls into three categories—igneous, sedimentary, and metamorphic—that encompass all forms of commercial building stone. Igneous rock was formed when the earth's surface was a viscous liquid that slowly cooled and hardened. Sedimentary rock was formed in two ways: (*1*) from igneous rock that had weathered and deteriorated into deposited soils and that was consolidated with heat and pressure; and (*2*) chemical solutions and biological deposits that were crystallized and hardened. When sedimentary rock is altered with increasing heat and pressure and shear, metamorphic rock is formed (1).

Granite, marble, limestone, sandstone, travertine, and slate are the principal types of dimension stone used in construction. Granite includes all feldspathic crystalline rocks of predominantly interlocking texture and with mineral grains visible to the naked eye. These include igneous and metamorphic rocks. White, gray, black, pink, and red are the common colors for granite, but greens, browns, and other shades are produced in some localities. Limestone includes dolomitic types as well as calcitic. Marble is a recrystallized (metamorphosed) limestone containing grains of calcite or dolomite or both. Sandstone is a sedimentary rock consisting mostly of quartz. Slate is a fine-grained metamorphic rock derived from shale, silt-stone, or claystone (1). Travertine is formed by calcite-saturated water, which evaporates to form layers of calcium crystals. Holes are formed in travertine by escaping gases, and color is added by mineral impurities. Tables 1 and 2 list the properties and characteristics of stones used in architecture.

Table 1. Physical Properties and Characteristics of Granite, Traprock, Limestone, and Sandstone

Characteristics	Granite	Traprock "Black Granite"	Limestone — Low Density	Medium Density	High Density	Sandstone — Sandstone	Quartzitic Sandstone	Quartzite
Geology	Igneous	Igneous	Sedimentary			Sedimentary		
Minerology	Quartz, alkalie, feldspar	Pyroxene, hornblend, biotite	Calcite, dolomite			Quartz, feldspar		
Chemistry (approximate composition)	70% SiO_2, 15% Al_2O_3		50–97% $CaCO_3$, 2–50% $MgCO_0$			$SiO^2NaAlSi^3O_8$ $KAlSi^2O_0CaAlS^3_{13}O_8$		
Geography	NE, NY, GA, WI, MN, MO, OK, TX, CA, SD		NE, NY to AL, IN to MS, IA, KA, MO, OK, AR, TX, WI, CO, SD, WY, CA, MN			Most states		
Colors	Pink, brown, gray, white, blue, black, green, red	Pink, green, blue, black	White, cream, gray, rust, pink, black, buff, tan, ivory, blue, rose			Brown, gray, rose, cream, buff, ivory, pink, tan, yellow, beige, white, red, gold, purple, blue, rust		
Size maximum, ft² ASTM specification	75 C615-80		70 C568-79			C616-80		
Density, lb/ft² Low	ASTM C-97 150		117			135		
Required minimum	160	N.R.	110	136	161	140	150	160
High	190				185			170
Water absorption, % by weight ASTM C121 Low	ASTM C-97 0.02		ASTM C-97 3.6	0.6	2.8	ASTM C-97		
Required maximum	0.40	NR[a]	12	7.5	3	20	3	1
Compressive strength, ksi Required minimum	ASTM C-170 19	NR	ASTM C-170 1.8	4.0	8.0	ASTM C-170 2	10	20
Maximum	52	35		12	32			37
Modulus of elasticity, ksi Low	2		0.6			1		
High	10				1.4			7.5
Modulus of rupture, ksi Required minimum	ASTM C-99 1.5	NR	ASTM C-99 0.4	0.5	1.0	ASTM C-99 0.3	1.0	2
High	5.5			1.6	2.9			
Abrasion resistance ASTM C-241	NA		10	10	10	8	8	8

[a] NR, no requirement.

Table 2. Physical Properties and Characteristics of Marble and Slate

| Characteristics | Marble | | | | Slate | |
| | Calcite | Dolomite | Serpentine | Travertine | Building Stone | |
					Exterior	Interior
Geology	Metamorphic			Sedimentary	Metamorphic	
Minerology	Calcite, dolomite, or serpentine			Calcite, dolomite	Quartz, mica	
Chemistry (approximate composition)	$CaCO_3$, $MgCO_3$				$H_2KAl_3(SiO_4)_3$ $(H_1K)_2(Mg,Fe)_2$ $Al_2(SiO_4)_3$	
Geography	NE, NY to AL, IN to MS, KA, MO, OK, AR, TX, CO, SD, WY, CA, MN, WI				MA to GA, CA, AR	
Colors	White, gray, red, pink, buff, rose, gold, green, yellow, black, brown, tan				Blue, green, black, purple, gray	
Size maximum, ft² ASTM specification	20 C 503-79				C 629-80	
Density, lbs/ft³ Low	(ASTM C-97)			140	173	
Required minimum	162	175	168	144	NR	
High			175	160	179	
Water absorption % by weight ASTM C121 Low	0.65		0.10		ASTM C-121	
					0	0
Required maximum	0.75	0.75	0.75	0.75	0.25	0.45
Compressive strength, ksi Required minimum	ASTM C-170				NR[a]	
	7.5					
Maximum	28.0					
Modulus of elasticity, ksi Low	2.0					
	2.0					
High	15.0					
Modulus of rupture, ksi Required minimum	ASTM C-99				ASTM C-120	
	1.0				7.2 (parallel to grain)	
High	4.0				9.0 (perpendicular)	
Abrasion resistance ASTM C-241	10				8	8

[a] NR, no requirement

TRADE CLASSIFICATIONS OF STONE

The Marble Institute of America (MIA), a trade association formed to encourage the installation of stone, has categorized groups of marble according to soundness (4). The classifications indicate what method of fabrication is necessary. Classification is done by MIA producer and fin-

isher members. A written warranty should be obtained from them before installation.

Group A. Sound marbles and stones with uniform favorable working qualities.

Group B. Marbles and stones similar in character to the preceding group, but with working qualities somewhat less favorable. These may have natural faults. A limited amount of waxing and sticking is necessary.

Group C. Marbles and stones with some variations in working qualities. Geologic flaws, voids, veins, and lines of separation are common. Common practice for repairing these variations is by sticking, waxing, and filling. Liners and other forms of reinforcements are employed when necessary.

Group D. Marbles and stones similar to the preceding group, but containing a larger proportion of natural faults and a maximum variation in working qualities, requiring more of the same methods of finishing. This group comprises many of the highly colored marbles prized for their decorative qualities.

GEOGRAPHIC DISTRIBUTION OF STONE

Stone, in a multitude of types, comes from all parts of the globe. Although Italy is the largest producer of dimension stone among the market-economy countries, there are other significant producers of different kinds of stone. Spain does a great deal of trading in and processing of granite, marble, and travertine and is a major shipper of slate, particularly roofing slate. Portugal is a major shipper of granite, including a number of colored granites and marbles. Finland and Sweden are major shippers of red and dark granites, particularly to European destinations. Brazil is a major shipper of various colors of granite, including pink and red and small amounts of a rare lazulite-containing blue granite. It is also a shipper of various white, pink, and green-white marbles, and small amounts of an exotic riebeckite-containing blue marble (5).

About one half the dimension stone handled in Italy is exported. The large geographic areas of dimension-stone production in Italy are characterized by large, consistent deposits of uniform color that support many quarries. The most important marble-producing area is in the part of Tuscany known as the Apuane Alps. Reserves of white marble are practically unlimited, and this area accounts for about one half of Italy's marble production. The town of Carrara is located in this region. Other major areas of marble production are the Lombardy region in the Po River Valley, Venetia, and Sicily. Travertine, the oldest polishable gneiss, is produced mostly near Domodossola, north of Lake Maggiore, and in Sardinia. Slate production is concentrated near Lavagna and Triora (1).

Spain is a major producer of roofing slate, granite, and marble and also imports sizable amounts of granite and marble for further processing; the final product is often exported. Spanish marble production is centered in the provinces of Alicante and Murcia along the Mediterranean; granite production is mostly located in western Spain toward the Portuguese border. Portugal is a major producer of marble, which is one of its main products. Marble production is centered in Evora and Estremoz, east of Lisbon. Nearly every country in the world produces some dimension stone (1).

Georgia produces almost one-third of the dimension granite quarried in the United States and is the leading state in marble output. Indiana produces two thirds of the country's dimension limestone. Ohio produces about one third of domestic dimension sandstone, and Vermont and Virginia produce about 67% of domestic dimension slate. Leading producer states for granite are Georgia, Vermont, Minnesota, North Carolina, South Dakota, Texas, New Hampshire, and Massachusetts; for limestone, Indiana, Minnesota, Texas, and Wisconsin; for sandstone, Ohio, Pennsylvania, and New York; for marble, Georgia, Vermont, and Idaho; for slate, Pennsylvania, Virginia, and Vermont (1).

APPLICATIONS

The reasons for the universal acclaim of stone are often cited by architects. They mention its heterogeneous colors, veining, and deposits that result in beautiful designs and irregular patterns unmatched by any manufactured material. When uniformity is desired, homogeneity is also available from some forms of stone such as limestones, sandstones, many granites, and even some marbles. Stone is durable, lasting years, as evidenced by the ancient stone architecture that still remains standing. Architects cite these qualities of stone as their reasons for employing it in their designs: permanence, ease of maintenance, durability, opulence, natural beauty, and high-class reputation. Today, stone is specified for all of these reasons, and also because over the years it has developed a reputation for quality.

Because of its desirability and respected reputation, natural building stone is used so widely throughout all areas of the building trade that there is hardly an area of architectural design where it has not or cannot be incorporated. Although possible uses are limited only by the designer's imagination, a finite list follows. On the exterior, where once stone walls were load-bearing, stone is used as a building's skin, combining surface finishes and colors. Decorative uses include columns (Fig. 1), capitals, bases,

Figure 1. Columns of granite. Photo by John Sailer.

Figure 2. Benches of granite. Photo by John Sailer.

canopies, copings, balustrades, cornices, friezes, architraves, arches, moldings, and any other sculpted form. For
roofing, slate is often used. For landscaping, stone is used
for planters, benches (Fig. 2), pavement, fountains, walls,
archways, steps (Fig. 3), and any other decorative element
designed by the landscape architect. "Fountains, planters,
park benches, playground fittings, bases of street lamps
and road signs, pavement curbs, sculptures, etc are components that blend functionality and decorative effects
when made of marble"(3).

In interiors, stone covers walls, floors, and even ceilings. It can be an accent feature as a baseboard, fireplace,
door or window frame, or sill. Many parts of bathrooms
and kitchens are also made of stone, but for these areas
subject to soap, hot water, and steam, it is best to use
stone with a low absorption coefficient and great compactness. In a kitchen, "stone adds a natural element to the
plastic and steel environment of appliances" (3). Almost
anything inside, outside, and around a building can be
made of stone and often is. As a natural material, stone
works well on both a building's interior and its exterior.
Outside, stone makes the building compatible with a natural environment. Stone can also carry nature indoors.

Figure 3. Steps of granite.

It is not only the parts of the actual building that are
made of stone. The design elements that are added after
construction can also be made of stone. More specifically,
furniture in all shapes and sizes is also occasionally made
of stone, which combines structural function with decoration. The designer of stone furniture must consider the
ultimate use of the piece. If it is to be used where alcohol,
coffee, juice, or other acidic substances may be spilled, it
should be a stone that is not susceptible to staining. In the
case of bar tops, dining tops, kitchen counters, and the
like, granite, which is not susceptible to staining from
acids, should be used; alternatively, if alkaline marble is
used, it should be protected with a sealer. If a sealer is
used, it should be one that allows the stone to breathe. It
should also be determined if the sealer used can come into
contact with foods.

Before illustrating the possibilities of interior and exterior design using stone, the structural limitations of marble and granite and other natural stones must first be
defined.

EXTERIOR ATTACHMENT OF STONE

Stone has become almost completely decorative rather
than structural. Previously a load-bearing material, stone
was used in considerable thicknesses or built into masonry as an exterior wall. "With the advancement of structural frame construction (at the beginning of the Twentieth Century), where loads are carried by the frame, not by
the walls, stone was used as ornamental cladding material rather than load-bearing material" (6). Today, non-
load-bearing thin stone veneers create a decorative skin
around skyscrapers. Thin veneers, developed after years
of using thicker slabs to clad buildings, decrease the
weight and therefore the cost of cladding a building with
stone.

"Stone slab veneer is a nonstructural element applied
to a backup supporting structure" (1). Types of methods of
attaching thin stone veneers to building exteriors are as
infinite as the possibilities of architectural design. Anchoring stone slabs to a structure is done by attaching the
anchor, made of noncorrosive and nonstaining metal, to
the back of the slab. The anchor is then attached, leaving
a space between the slabs and the building that allows air
circulation. Anchors used must withstand gravity loads
from the weight of the stone panel and applied loads from
wind or structural movement. The material to which the
anchor-supported stone is attached could be steel, concrete, or masonry, and the type of anchor used depends on
this material. Anchors used to attach stone to a structure
should be made of a corrosion-resistant material. It is
standard trade practice to use anchors of Type 600 grade
extruded aluminum. The stone industry has developed
many accepted connection devices for anchoring stone
slabs to any structure (Fig. 4). Other methods of attaching
stone include framing systems, curtain walls, and precast
concrete (Fig. 5).

Conventional methods require lifting and attaching
each slab individually. Framing systems provide an alternative to attaching each panel of stone individually. A

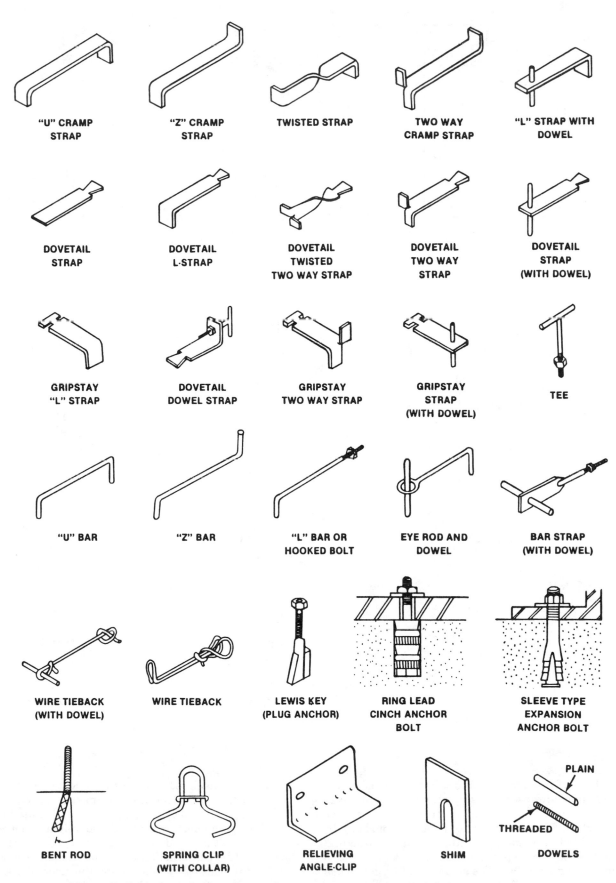

Figure 4. Typical standard anchors and accessories (7). Courtesy of the Masonry Institute of America.

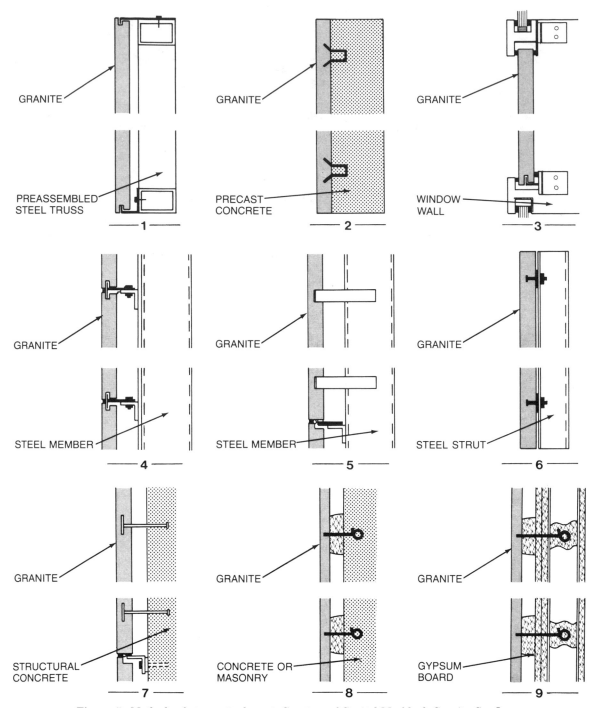

GRANITE

PREASSEMBLED
STEEL TRUSS

— 1 —

GRANITE

PRECAST
CONCRETE

— 2 —

GRANITE

WINDOW
WALL

— 3 —

GRANITE

STEEL MEMBER

— 4 —

GRANITE

STEEL MEMBER

— 5 —

GRANITE

STEEL STRUT

— 6 —

GRANITE

STRUCTURAL
CONCRETE

— 7 —

GRANITE

CONCRETE OR
MASONRY

— 8 —

GRANITE

GYPSUM
BOARD

— 9 —

Figure 5. Methods of stone attachment. Courtesy of Capitol Marble & Granite Co., Inc.

truss is built of tubular steel into which many individual pieces of stone are inserted using aluminum or stainless steel components. The frame is constructed and the stone is attached off site, then the whole panel is brought to the building, lifted into place, and attached to the structural system. Once the frames are installed, they are finished with insulating materials. The actual building design and lifting capacity of available cranes determine the size of the frames. When designing a frame system, the following

should be considered: movements due to temperature, creep, deformation, clearances, shrinkage, deflections, water penetration, and absorption. Anchors to be used with a framing system must resist twice the weight of horizontal loading, or the wind or seismic forces, whichever is greater. The Uniform Building Code requires resisting horizontal loads by the anchor and the stone. For a stone panel, the anchor mechanism must be strong enough to resist twice the weight of the veneer in the horizontal

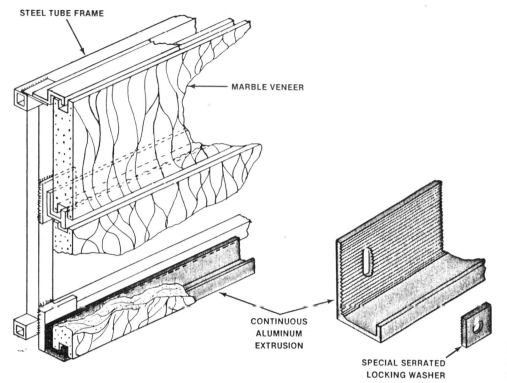

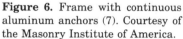

Figure 6. Frame with continuous aluminum anchors (7). Courtesy of the Masonry Institute of America.

direction. This means that the stone, the connection of the anchor to the stone, and the connection of the anchor to its structural backup must be capable of resisting a horizontal force equal to twice the weight of the veneer. A framing specialist should be consulted to ensure proper design. Examples from the large variety of possible approaches to assembling a framing system are shown in Figures 6–9. Methods using precast concrete wall elements are also employed by the stone industry. Concrete panels are faced with stone at the shop, shipped to the site, and erected

onto the building. Precast concrete systems are heavier than framing systems.

Caution must be exercised when selecting stone and a system of attachment for the exterior application of stone. Failures may occur because a particular type of stone is used with the wrong system of attachment or in the wrong environment. One example is the Amoco Building in Chicago, an infamous case where white Carrara marble was used as an exterior cladding material in the Chicago environment. Because of the specific properties of the material

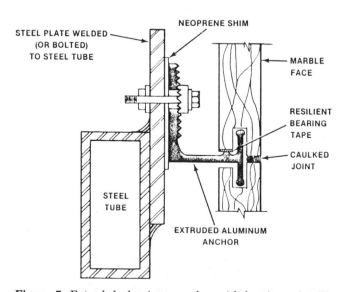

Figure 7. Extruded aluminum anchor with bearing point (7). Courtesy of the Masonry Institute of America.

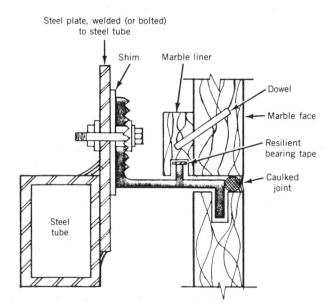

Figure 8. Extruded aluminum offset anchor (7). Courtesy of the Masonry Institute of America.

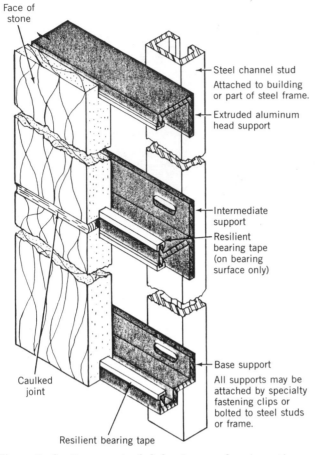

Face of stone

Steel channel stud
Attached to building or part of steel frame.

Extruded aluminum head support

Intermediate support

Resilient bearing tape (on bearing surface only)

Base support
All supports may be attached by specialty fastening clips or bolted to steel studs or frame.

Caulked joint

Resilient bearing tape

Figure 9. Continuous extruded aluminum anchors in continuous slots cut in the stone (7). Courtesy of the Masonry Institute of America.

and their reactions to the thermal environment, the material curved and became structurally insecure. Testing of mock-ups before specification of any stone in any environment is necessary to determine how the material will stand up to many seasons in a particular installation. Because of better resistance to weathering, granite is used more often than marble for exterior installations where weathering is a design consideration.

VENEER DESIGN OF STONE

In all cases of stone attachment, certain elements of design must be considered. Deflection and movement of the structure must be determined by a consulting engineer when designing the suspension system (7).

> The lateral forces due to wind or seismic forces must be calculated so the anchoring system can be safely designed. The attachment system must be designed to resist a horizontal force equal to at least twice the weight of the veneer. A panel or framing system must be designed to resist twice the weight of the entire system, both the frame and stone. Special consideration should be given to all differential building movement. The structural lintels and horizontal supports must not allow deflections greater than 1/500 of the span under the full load of the veneer. Different materials are going to have different

rates of thermal expansion, therefore the maximum differences in thermal expansion must be considered in designing the veneer spacing supports. As a building is constructed, loads increase and elastic deformation occurs in heavily stressed elements. The designer should allow for this expected formation in his details. Delaying application of veneer until late in construction or until after the majority of the deadload elements have been constructed will reduce these problems. For long-term deformation (creep) additional clearances must be provided. When the backup structure is concrete or concrete masonry, there will be shrinkage of the supporting surfaces after initial placement. Again, the designer should allow for possible movement and/or delay application of the cladding until after the majority of the shrinkage has occurred. Two-thirds of the shrinkage takes place within the first three months, and approximately 90 percent during the first year. Allowances must be made for the effects of freezing and thawing on stone cladding. To reduce the possiblity of freezing and thawing damage to the cladding, moisture must be controlled. Proper waterproof caulking of all joints will prevent water from entering from the outside. Waterproofing the back will prevent moisture from migrating through the stone. Proper flashing and weep holes will control the flow of any water that may collect behind the stone and direct this moisture to the outside of the cladding.

Other considerations when designing an exterior system of thin stone veneer attachment include the stone's ability to resist shocks determined by impact tests and the weight and dimensions of each panel. Determining the panel dimensions is important. They must be thick enough to resist bending stresses. Large, thick panels require costly anchors, but if more anchors are used, panel thickness can be reduced. Tolerances of panel joints are determined by the use of either open or closed joints. Open joints allow for greater tolerances of dimension. Installation with open joints is easier, but they require more sealing material. Open joints allow for structural movement. Another method of allowing for structural movement is to use expansion bolts that move with the structure. When designing a system for attaching stone to a building, the properties of the stone to be used must first be determined using tests outlined in the Annual Book of ASTM Standards (8).

DESIGN OF STONE

The designer of stone architecture has a multitude of options available. Colors, surface finishes, dimensions, and other variables can be combined in an infinite number of ways to create an infinite number of designs.

Finishes of Stone

Combinations of different surface finishes or fields of a single texture can be used to create aesthetically pleasing stone patterns and designs. Available surface treatments include polishing, honing, flaming, bush hammering, scoring, sandblasting, and chemical etching.

Polishing produces a flat, glossy finish with mirrorlike qualities. Color and veining is emphasized with this type of finish, and the illusion of depth is created. Porosity is

Figure 10. Lettering etched into the Vietnam Veterans Memorial in Washington, D.C. Photo by John Sailer.

decreased and flexural strength is increased when stone is polished.

Honed finishes are smooth but not glossy. This finish is recommended for areas such as floors subject to heavy traffic, where slip resistance is necessary. Compared to polished surfaces, honed surfaces, which are more porous, are more susceptible to soiling, but they are also more easily refurbished, being capable of withstanding harsher methods of cleaning.

Flaming produces a coarse finish that is recommended for exterior applications and paving. Flamed surfaces are resistant to chemical deterioration due to atmospheric reactions (such as acid rain) and physical wearing due to traffic. Flaming does not work well on granites with high concentrations of iron-rich minerals because the minerals are melted rather than disintegrated, resulting in a smeared appearance.

Bush hammering, one of the oldest finishes, was originally achieved with pointed chisels and is now performed with machines. It is available in many grades of rough-

ness. Scoring produces parallel groves with a machine and results in some desirable aesthetic effects. Alternating depths of the stone's surface with scoring increases the interest of the surface.

Sandblasting produces a matte-textured finish and is recommended for outdoor use. Sandblasting, as well as other techniques, is used to etch letters into stone. For monuments, these lettering techniques are quite advanced and employ computerized machinery. A good example of high-technology lettering is the Vietnam Veterans Memorial in Washington D.C. (Fig. 10). Here, more than 58,000 names were etched into polished granite. Etched lettering is also often used for names on buildings, lobby directories, and other uses.

Smoother finishes require more work, and abrasive finishes require less; therefore, abrasive finishes are more economical. To bring out the qualities of the stone, polished finishes work best. For intricately detailed surfaces, inlays offer the designer the opportunity to "paint" with stone (Fig. 11). To reproduce any picture, artisans choose

Figure 11. Inlaid flooring of differently colored marbles.

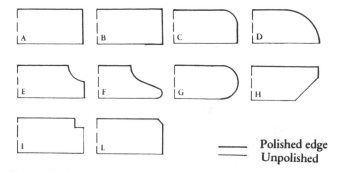

Figure 12. Principal edge treatments of stone. A, straight edge; B, Straight edge with reverse; C, Rounded edge; D, Bird's beak; E, Cove edge; F, O.G. edge; G, Bullnose; H, Quirk mitre (Q.M.); I, Rabbet; L, Beveled edge.

stone in colors to match those in the picture. The pieces are cut and secured together with epoxy resin in whatever form is desired. Another method of stone design is using edge treatments (Fig. 12).

INTERIOR DESIGN OF STONE

For interior designs, stone is as versatile if not more versatile than it is outside a building. "Because of its inherent characteristics, its composition, its grain, its veining, its patterns and its colors and, as a complement to these, the infinite number of ways of working and surface finishing, stone lends itself equally to splendid decoration and to the simplest, most everyday ornamentation"(3).

Standardized thin slabs are generally used on interiors for both floors and walls. Marbles offer the greatest versatility for indoor designs, where their susceptibility to atmospheric conditions is not detrimental as it is on exterior installations and where their veining and color variations create unique patterns and designs. Some designs are based on the way the block is cut. A book-match design matches the veins vertically and horizontally. A diamond-match or quarter-match pattern creates a diamond pattern with the veins of the marble. Finishing adjacent faces of two panels and inverting one over the other creates an end-match pattern. An end-slip pattern is when panels from the same block are placed end to end in sequence to give a repetitive pattern and blended color in the vertical, and a side-slip pattern is when panels are placed side by side to give a repetitive pattern and blended color in the horizontal. The most common pattern is the blend. This is a random design combining panels, in no specified pattern, from different blocks. The blend pattern is also the least expensive, requiring no coding of panels or special packaging. Unless otherwise specified, marble will be installed in a blend pattern (see Fig. 13). Panels to be installed inside a building should be chamfered to remove any deviation from perfect flatness and to prevent chipping at the surface and the sides.

Interior installation employs anchors, similar to those on the exterior, on facings. All joints are closed unless otherwise specified. The joints are pointed with cement dyed to resemble the stone.

Installing marble over wood or concrete subfloors can cause problems. Cracks developing in concrete can be transferred to the marble surface. To prevent this problem, the marble setting bed must be isolated from the subfloor. When installed over wood, movement of tiles and moisture penetration must be controlled. Joint width must be specified to ensure proper setting.

For interior flooring, any type of stone can be used. Many standardized tiles are available in a large variety of colors. With modern tile-making machinery, custom orders of specified stones can be processed into standard tile sizes. This standardization makes for simpler installation, enabling any tile setter to do the job that was previously reserved for a stone masonry setter.

It is important to realize that floors are easily affected by traffic. Polished floors will develop a dulled path at the most heavily traveled areas, ruining the effect of the polished field. Polished marble can also become slippery, so it is not recommended for floors.

In addition to floors installed using the traditional mortar method common for many types of tile installation, a raised-stone method of floor installation may be used. Each stone panel is laid on a metal frame and can be removed using suction cups to gain access to electrical, telephone, and computer cables running under the floor. This type of installation, useful in "intelligent" buildings where access to wiring is important, requires that the stone itself supports the loads.

Stairs offer another opportunity for the interior application of stone. Treads and risers can be made of either solid, sculpted stone or stone veneers. Veneers, which use less stone material, are less expensive. In addition to composing treads and risers, stone can also make up the balustrades of a stairway. A honed finish is recommended to prevent uneven wearing and increase safety. Nonskid materials can also be incorporated into treads to further increase safety.

EXTERIOR DESIGN OF STONE

Exterior stone designs must be more carefully considered than those on the interior due to more severe atmospheric conditions. The selection of stone for the design of exterior paving requires more in-depth analysis than the selection for interior flooring because outdoors stone is exposed to atmospheric agents such as acids in polluted air and freeze/thaw activity. Dense granites with rough surfaces are best for this application. Polished surfaces, which can become slippery, are not recommended for exterior paving. Stone slabs for paving can be set into a bed of plastic portland cement or can be thin-set on a cured bed. Portland cement grout is used to fill joints between the slabs. Open-joint systems can also be employed. These provide for drainage into the subsurface.

Exterior stairs, like paving, should be made of stone with a rough finish for safety. To prevent chipping, the edges of treads and tops of risers must be chamfered. To prevent water seepage through the joint between the tread and the riser, the treads should overlay the risers rather than having the upper edge of the riser exposed.

Before any design can be finalized, whether it be interior or exterior, the architect must consider the environment to ensure that the particular stone selected will

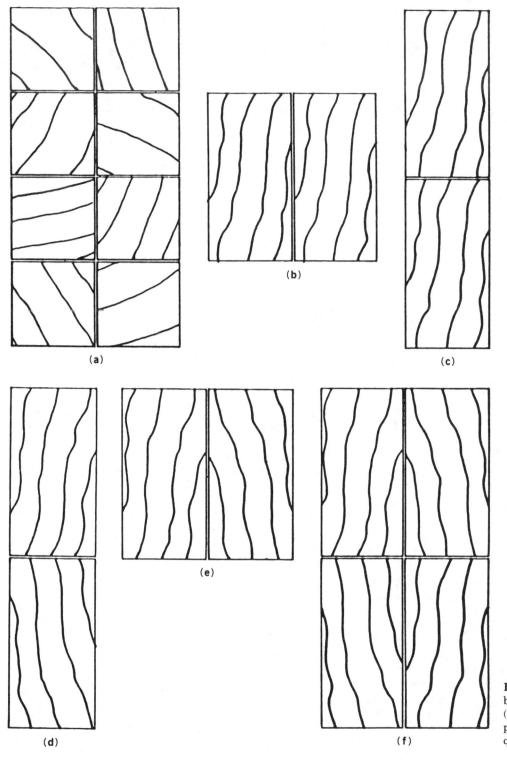

Figure 13. Veneer patterns: (a) blend pattern; (b) side-slip pattern; (c) end-slip pattern; (d) end-match pattern; (e) book-match pattern; (f) quarter or diamond-match pattern.

work in the manner specified by the design. Standardized tests to determine a particular stone's properties and how they may affect design are documented by ASTM (8).

FABRICATION OF STONE

Once a particular stone has been selected according to aesthetic as well as structural considerations, the methods of fabrication must also be watched closely by the

designer to ensure that the design is not altered. Previously an expensive material because of the man-hours necessary for production, stone today is competitive with other building materials yet still retains its durability, its natural beauty, and the high-quality image it has developed over the centuries. The reduction in cost is due primarily to the increase in automation from quarrying through fabrication, resulting in a greater availability of more uniformly dimensioned stone. Diamond-wire saws are used to cut blocks of marble as well as the harder granites. Other methods of removing stone from the ground include the use of explosives and flame throwers. In the plant, computerized machinery saws blocks into slabs, polishes slabs, and cuts stone into specified sizes. Some stone tile plants have computerized the complete operation from block input to tile output, making stone tile as competitively priced as comparable materials.

In a quarry, fracturing, variations in color, and distribution of faults dictate the shape of extracted blocks and therefore also influence finished products manufactured from these blocks. With inhomogeneous colored, variegated, streaked, and breccia marbles there is a presence of unusual characteristics of minerals. This causes the extraction of large-size blocks to be rare, so design must be carefully planned out. The size of the blocks determines the size of the slabs. With these facts in mind, it is obvious that a familiarity with the stone, even before quarrying, will aid the designer. This is evidenced by the somewhat common architectural practice of visiting a quarry before design to determine a stone's strengths and limitations.

Before selection, the designer must determine his or her needs defined by how the stone will be used. The material's compactness is determined using compression tests. On exterior applications, more compact stones (all granites and travertines, and some other stones) will resist deterioration better than less compact stones when exposed to cold and humidity. For interior applications, susceptibility to abrasion should be considered in high traffic areas such as floors and stairs.

Unless they are in standardized sizes, the dimensioned stone pieces to be processed from the blocks taken from the quarry must be fabricated according to the detailed plans and sketches supplied by the designer.

Because a quarry may be exhausted after years of excavation activity, it is beneficial to store a small supply of the stone used on an architectural project in the event that future replacement should become necessary. This is a wise practice that is beneficial even if the quarry is still active at the time replacement is necessary because variations of veining and color can be drastic between stone extracted from different parts of a quarry.

Storing a small supply is useful to ensure maintenance of the design long into the future, which can be expected of stone, which never goes out of style because "Everything that is most noble in man, his admiration of his great fellow men, his remembrance of the dead, his worship of the divinity, the pleasure he takes in beauty and his attempts to give form to this feeling, finds its grandest and most lasting impression in marble"(3).

BIBLIOGRAPHY

1. H. A. Taylor, Jr., *Dimension Stone, Bulletin 675, Mineral Facts and Problems,* Division of Industrial Minerals, Bureau of Mines, U.S. Department of the Interior, Washington, D.C., 1985.
2. C. Rifkind, ed., *Italian Marble Center Newsletter* (Fall 1986).
3. F. Vallardi, *Marmi Italiani,* Italian Trade Commission, New York, 1982.
4. *Dimensional Stone,* vol. 3, Marble Institute of America, Inc., Farmington, Mich., 1986.
5. H. A. Taylor, Jr., *Mineral Industry Surveys, Annual Leading Country Activity, Dimension Stone in 1985,* Division of Industrial Minerals, Bureau of Mines, U.S. Department of the Interior, Washington, D.C., 1986.
6. A. Gere, *Stone World,* 14 (April 1985).
7. J. E. Amrhein, S. E. and M. W. Merrigan, *Marble and Stone Slab Veneer,* Masonry Institute of America, Los Angeles, 1986.
8. American Society for Testing and Materials (ASTM), *Annual Book of ASTM Standards, Volume 04.08, Soil and Rock, Building Stones; Geotextiles,* annual.

See also BRICK MASONRY

JOHN SAILER
Stone World
Oradell, New Jersey

STORES. See DEPARTMENT STORES.

STORM-WATER SYSTEMS

DESIGN STORM FREQUENCY

Each element of the storm drainage system must be designed to handle the peak rate of runoff for a design storm. The frequency of the design storm should be consistent with the ultimate land use of the area to be drained. In urbanized areas this may present problems because neither zoning nor land use plans, if they exist, will necessarily accurately forecast the ultimate land use. Great sensitivity to the rate and pattern of growth are needed to make reasonable assessments on this central design assumption.

In properly designed drainage systems, property damage will only occur when the capacity of the major drainage system is exceeded. Therefore, the value of the property to be protected need be considered only in the major system design. It is recommended that minimum design storm frequency for the major system be 25 years. This minimum is applicable to low-density developments where buildings might incur flooding during events greater than design magnitude but where the contents that might be damaged are not of great value. In residential areas where living quarters would be subject to flooding, a 50-year minimum should be used. For important structures such as major highways, retention basins, and bridges, a 100-year design storm is recommended. Commercial and industrial areas should be judged by the value of the buildings, merchandise, and operations subject to flooding, and storm frequencies may range from 25 to 100 years.

INITIAL DRAINAGE SYSTEM

The storm-water transportation system in an urban area consists of a network of underground pipes and open channels that carry storm water from surface storm inlets in street and paved areas and from the roofs of buildings to its eventual outlet. Storm sewers are generally located within the street right-of-way within a watershed and ordinarily flow by gravity.

Capacities required in the initial drainage system are a matter of convenience. The object is to keep streets, sidewalks, and other frequently used areas clear of storm-water runoff, so that common storms do not disrupt normal activity. It should be noted, however, that activity will not be disrupted as soon as the capacity of the initial system is exceeded. When the sewer becomes overloaded, runoff will be carried by the gutter and then the roadway.

The recommended design storm frequencies for an initial drainage system are

Residential: 5–10 yr
Commercial: 10–15 yr
Industrial: 5–15 yr

As was mentioned before, the local streets serve an important drainage function. Gutter flow in the streets is necessary to transport water to the storm inlets. However, the volume of storm water carried is related to the hydraulic capacity of the road. Local streets with minor traffic volumes are expected to carry a larger portion of storm water than arterial streets, which must permit rapid and relatively unimpeded traffic movement.

On local streets, storm-water inlets are located to intercept gutter flow. These inlets may be located along the roadway slope or at roadway low points. The low point or sump is graded to provide a depth of ponding before water escapes to the next downhill inlet. Wherever possible, storm sewers should be routed to natural waterways or artificial channels designed to store water in transit.

MAJOR DRAINAGE SYSTEM

The major drainage system carries overland flow in excess of flows carried by the initial system. The most stable drainage configuration is the natural one. Alterations in flow paths, velocities, and quantities are likely to cause undesirable changes in stream flow, channel size, and alignment.

The major drainage system then has two functions: to protect the property being drained and to preclude adverse impacts at downstream discharge points. Protecting the drainage area is achieved by providing stable flood paths of sufficient capacity to prevent property damage. Protecting the stream and downstream developments includes control of the peak discharge from the drainage area.

MAJOR DRAINAGE PATHS

During the site-planning phase of development, one of the first investigations should be of the major natural waterways. These natural waterways include stream channels, swales, and gullies.

In planning the development, the major drainage system should be based on these natural paths. The waterways should be left as much as possible in a natural condition. Not only will such paths be more stable than altered or artificial waterways, but they will also provide valuable assets such as open space and recreation areas.

Where natural paths are blocked or diverted, backwater effects and the extent of new flood plains must be determined. Where artificial channels are required, they should be grass-lined and carry subcritical flow. In cases where the water velocity will be greater than the grass can sustain, the channel may be paved.

During a major design storm, such as a 50- or 100-year event, most of the flow in major waterways will be contributed by streets. Streets should empty into streams and channels via safety swales, normally constructed over storm-sewer outfalls, and at other low points adjacent to channels.

In heavily urbanized areas, it may be desirable or necessary to carry major storm flows in underground conduits. Such conduits must be designed to carry the peak flow to be generated by the area drained when full development is reached. Replacing, cleaning, and adding capacity to an underground system is extremely costly and disruptive.

STORM-WATER RETENTION

One of the most effective methods of controlling peak storm-water runoff is the use of short-term storage reservoirs, better known as retention basins. Properly designed, a retention basin can reduce storm-water runoff to any desired rate. Retention basins should be designed to the following criteria:

1. The objective of the retention basin should be the reduction of downstream peak flows.
2. The retention basin should be sized to store the required runoff from a storm of the required frequency.
3. The required storage per unit of time is equal to the rate of inflow minus the rate of outflow.
4. The flow out of the basin is a function of the water surface elevation and the hydraulic control at the outlet.
5. The maximum water surface elevation is reached when the rate of inflow equals the rate of outflow.

Aside from the flood control benefits, retention basins also serve an important function in sediment and debris control.

Storm-water retention basins are normally located at the outlet of the drainage basin area. They may also be constructed with the drainage network. The basins may also be considered to have a multiuse function. If rainfall frequency and soil conditions are appropriate, the basin may have a permanent standing body of water with provisions for flood storage. Many times, natural on-site features make the creation of this type of storage relatively inexpensive.

STRUCTURES

Manholes and catch basins are typical structures that are part of a piped storm-water collection system. Structures normally occur at changes in alignment, slope, diameter, and pipe material. Manhole spacing for piping up to 24-in. diameter is 250± ft, with greater spacing for piping of larger diameter. Manholes should have an inside diameter of 4 ft, with a minimum access of 2 ft. Structures can be constructed of block, but the most common construction is precast concrete.

See also ENGINEERING, CIVIL

MICHAEL WEIN, P.E.
Bellmore, New York

STRUCTURAL STEEL

Steel is essentially an alloyed form of commercial iron. At a density of 490 pcf, it is heavy, it rusts, and loses its strength rapidly at temperatures above 1000°F. However, it is ductile and very strong. It can be rolled or milled into useful, efficient structural shapes, carry enormous loads, and it ultimately can be protected from fire and corrosion.

It is only since the beginning of the twentieth century that architects and engineers have been able to utilize steel framing members to build higher and span farther than had been possible in wood, masonry, concrete, or iron. Today the sight of a high rise steel building being erected is commonplace (Figs. 1 and 2). Many new and bold architectural forms, unique to the capabilities of steel alone, have been developed (Figs. 3 and 4).

Figure 2. Building the World Trade Center Tower, New York City. M. Yamasaki and Associates with E. Roth and Sons, Architects.

Table 1 provides a time line for the development of iron and steel. Incredibly, within the time span of only a quarter of a century, three men changed the world from an iron to a steel age. The most famous of the three was Henry Bessemer (UK) but his process depended on the work of Robert Mushet (UK) who held a prior patent that called for the use of an additive containing manganese, which he called *spiegelsein*. Depending on what source one trusts,

Figure 1. Steel skeleton, IBM Building, New York City. Edward Larrabee Barnes Associates, Architects.

Figure 3. Hong Kong Bank, Norman Foster, Architect. Photograph by Ian Lambot.

Figure 4. Burlington Industries, Inc. Corporate Headquarters, Greensboro, N.C. A. J. Odell & Associates, Architects. Photography courtesy of Burlington Industries, Inc.

Table 1. Time Line for the Development of Iron and Steel

Date	
Prior to 1350 B.C.	Various objects made from pure iron taken from meteorites.
1350 B.C. to 1300 A.D.	Scattered records of iron tools, objects and weapons that were produced directly from ore. Origins of primitive smelting have been attributed to China, India, Assyria, and elsewhere.
1000 B.C.	Tools with hardened steel edges produced in Ceylon.
200 B.C.	Cast-iron utensils in China.
1645	First successful iron works in the United States are constructed at Saugus, Massachusetts.
1740	Benjamin Huntsman (Great Britain) rediscovers lost crucible steel process (cast steel).
1750	Steel furnace constructed at Killingworth, Connecticut, produces cast steel.
1779	Abraham Darby III, builds the Coalbrooksdale Bridge over the Severn River (Great Britain) using cast-iron framing.
1781	An iron frame spanning 15 ft 8 in. is used for a mansard roof in Paris. Built from plans drawn by Jacques-Germain Soufflot.
1817	First iron bars rolled in United States, Uniontown, Pennsylvania, Plumstock works.
1830	U.S. clergyman Frederick Geissenhamer obtains a patent for smelting iron with coal.
1840	First American bridge constructed entirely of cast iron, built over Erie Canal at Frankfort, New York.
1847	William Kelly (United States) develops a process similar to Bessemer's for converting iron into steel.
1847 to 1849	Ferdinand Zores (France) rolls the first iron I-beam.
1854	First U.S. wrought-iron I-beam manufactured (7 in. deep, 81 lb/yd) used for railroad rail; rolled by Peter Cooper at Trenton, New Jersey. James Bogardus is the architect for the first U.S. building to use wrought-iron beams. Harper & Brothers, six-story building in New York City, uses Cooper's I-beams supported by masonry walls.
1855	More iron is smelted using coal as a fuel than charcoal.
1856	Robert Mushet takes out patent on use of *spiegelsein* (manganese additive) in the steel-making process. Bessemer patents his process for producing steel (UK).
1860	First operational Bessemer steelworks; Sheffield, UK.
1861	Kelly converter, for producing steel from iron, built in Johnstown, Pennsylvania.
1863	Steel rail used for Pennsylvania Railroad rails on experimental basis (imported from UK).
1864	First steel using Bessemer process is produced in the United States by William Durfee in Wyandotte, Michigan.
1865	First steel rails made in the United States at North Chicago Rolling Mill from steel produced at Wyandotte mill (used same rollers as they used for producing iron rails).
1870	First successful open-hearth furnace in United States, South Boston. First furnace was in 1868, built by New Jersey Steel & Iron Co. in Trenton.

Table 1. (*Continued*)

1874	First structural use of steel; in a U.S. bridge (Eads bridge) at St. Louis over the Mississippi River. First all-steel bridge built at Glasgow over the Missouri River five years later.
1876	Joseph de Buregue (France) designs rollers for producing a wide-flange beam.
1885	Home Insurance Building in Chicago, a 10-story building designed by William LeBaron Jenney, utilizes a skeleton of iron framing for both the interior and the exterior for the first time. Andrew Carnegie obtained permission to use his steel beams when the structure reached the sixth floor level. This may be the first use of steel framing in a high-rise building.
1886	More hot-rolled steel is produced than iron in the United States.
1887	H. Sack patented a mill that could roll the edges as well as the top and bottom surfaces of a beam. Called a universal mill, it ushers in the era of wide-flange beams.
1890	Rand McNally Building, Chicago, reputed to be first building with an all-steel frame.
1899	First commercial direct-arc electric steel-making furnace, developed in France.
1908	First year during which more U.S. steel was produced by the open-hearth method than by the Bessemer process.
1923	The working stress for designing steel members is set at 18,000 psi by the AISC. This can be compared to the 16,000 psi set in 1889 by the Carnegie mill, and 12,000 psi for wrought iron in 1874. [In 1936 the AISC raised the allowable working stress to 20,000 psi. Today working stresses for bending are set at 66% of the yield stress, or 24,000 psi for A36 steel.]
1960	The current standard A36 carbon steel is approved for building construction.
1963	First use of 100,000 psi steel. Used in angles and plates forming structural columns for the IBM building in Pittsburgh, designed by Curtis and Davis.
1964	Deere and Co. Building, in Moline, Illinois, designed by Eero Saarinen in 1956, is the first major building to use the corrosion-resisting grade steel originally used for railroad cars in 1933.

either Mushet was too poor to pay the three years' stamp duty on his patent, or his lawyer forgot to; in any case it became public property and Bessemer used it. Without Mushet's additive, Bessemer's smelting process could not produce a decent quality of steel. Kelly (the United States) also developed a method of refining pig iron by forcing a great quantity of air onto the molten iron. He was considered crazy at first for trying to use air as a fuel, but the oxygen in the air combines with the carbon in the pig iron to produce great heat. Kelly developed this process eight years before Bessemer and later proved his point in court.

Most of the early steel used in the United States was imported from the UK and called Bessemer steel, because he held the British patent. The name stuck. In 1870 Bessemer was refused an extension on his U.S. patent, on the grounds that he was not entitled to one. Kelly's patent was upheld in the U.S. courts despite serious efforts by the steel industry to thwart him; if they could have done so, there would have been no royalties for them to pay.

It should be noted that the reason Bessemer was working to produce steel was to make a stronger cannon for the French army during the Crimean War. The iron cannons were just not strong enough. The structural use of steel did not come until a half-century later.

Iron has been used by mankind for many centuries. Archaeologists digging in Asia, Africa, and Europe have unearthed decorative objects, primitive tools, weapons, receptacles, and cooking utensils. Iron eventually was used for wagon parts, horseshoes, barrel hoops, and reinforcement for wooden implements such as oar locks and joinery pieces in wood and masonry construction. Ultimately it was the desire to produce a better cannon that led to the development of nineteenth-century processes for producing steel, which is an alloy consisting of approximately 98% iron.

Although iron is the earth's fourth most common element, it does not occur in a natural state except in the form of meteorites and in extremely rare instances as nodules in basalt rock. Mankind has learned to obtain iron by heating an iron-bearing ore in contact with hot carbon in the absence of oxygen. Primitive smelting methods accomplished this by burying the ore under burning charcoal. During the smelting process, the oxygen contained in the iron oxide combines with the carbon, leaving a metallic iron that invariably retains a little carbon and a few impurities, such as sulfates and phosphates. The molten iron could then be poured into molds; hence the term "cast iron." Usually the molten iron produced from the smelting process is cast into blocks (pig iron) for convenience. These blocks could be easily remelted at a later date for pouring into molds for specific shapes.

Cast iron contains roughly 2–6% carbon. It is very hard, but unfortunately also quite brittle and therefore it cannot be hammered, forged, or rolled to change its shape after it has cooled. Cast iron can only be shaped when it is in its molten state, but it can be hardened or tempered by reheating followed by sudden cooling (quenching). This process has been used to produce items such as sword edges. By remelting the cast iron at high temperatures (initially this took days), it became possible to remove more impurities and drive out almost all the carbon that had previously been chemically combined with the iron. The extracted free carbon along with other impurities originally contained in the ore form a slag, some of which inadvertently becomes mixed in with the molten iron. However, the iron itself remains almost pure chemically, containing less than 0.1% carbon and 1–2% mechanically mixed-in slag. When cooled, this purified iron is malleable and capable of being hammered (wrought) into shape.

When iron ore is heated to extremely high temperatures it becomes possible to remove the slag, leaving almost pure iron. Small controlled amounts of carbon (usually a bit less than 1% but not more than 1.7%) are then chemically added back in, in order to harden the wrought iron and produce what is called steel. Most modern steels contain small additive amounts of other metals that are mixed in with the iron in their molten states in order to impart special properties. A molten mixture of metals is called an alloy.

Steel is thus distinguishable from cast iron by having a lower carbon content and by being more malleable. It is distinguishable from wrought iron by containing slightly more chemically combined carbon and is almost free of mechanically mixed-in free carbon and impurities.

Bessemer's (1855) and Kelly's (1847) major contributions to producing a hard malleable iron (steel) was their realization that by blowing air over the molten iron, the oxygen contained in the air could raise the temperature to a sufficient degree to purify the iron without the need of additional fuels. Mushet's *spiegelsein* contained the right amounts of additives needed to make the brew work. This new improved iron alloy, called "steel," could be rolled into structural shapes like wrought iron, but it was stiffer, deflected less, and could span farther than iron.

Structurally, cast iron is only capable of accepting compressive forces and thus is only useful for short columns. Wrought iron possesses tensile capacity but is too "soft" to be used for long span beams without excessive deflection. Today, metallurgists can fine-tune additive alloys to produce steel structural shapes that are capable of withstanding up to 65,000 psi and plates with a 100,000 psi capacity. Architects and engineers can select beam shapes from 3 in. to over 3 ft in depth, and up to 100–120 ft in length.

The Bessemer process for producing steel was supplanted by the open-hearth method just after the turn of the century. Today less than 10% of U.S. steel is produced by open-hearth. Currently, the preponderance of all structural shapes and over 60% of the total amount of steel produced are the product of basic oxygen furnaces, which use oxygen rather than air as fuel. Electric furnaces have become increasingly popular, accounting for just over one-third of the country's steel production. Approximately 10% of the total amount of steel produced in the United States is used for structural shapes and plates.

SHAPE

Structural steel is available in a variety of different shapes (Figs. 5 and 6). These shapes have evolved from the need to distribute material in an efficient manner and to create framing members that can be economically rolled and easily connected to the rest of the structure and building components.

The most prevalent beam section is called a wide flange and resembles the letter **H** turned on its side. This configuration places the bulk of the material at the top and bottom parts of the beam (called flanges), where it is best situated to resist bending. The material contained in the vertical web section is normally sufficient to resist shear stresses. The web also serves to ensure that the top flange, which is normally under a compressive stress, will act in unison with the bottom flange, which is normally under tensile stress. The farther the top and bottom flanges are kept apart, the greater the resisting moment of the beam will be. Therefore, in general, the deeper a beam is, the greater its load-carrying capacity. The inner and outer surfaces of the flanges are parallel, which simplifies the

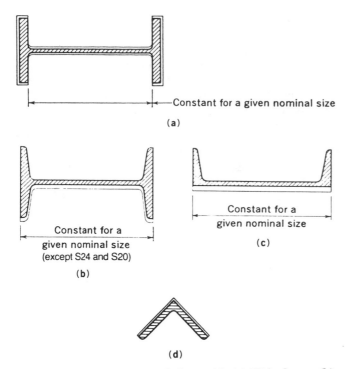

Figure 5. Common structural shapes (1). **(a)** Wide flange; **(b)** American Standard or "I" beam; **(c)** Channel; **(d)** Angle. Courtesy of American Institute of Steel Construction.

methods of connecting other structural members to them, as well as facilitating the connection of clips and supports for securing other parts of the building to the structure.

Beams of different weights are available within each of the commonly available nominal mill depths. This weight differential is due to variations in flange and web thickness. The heavier weight members of a particular depth group of beams may in fact be stronger than the lighter members of the next deeper group. The lightest member contained within each depth group is usually the most economical, because steel is sold on a weight basis. Heavier sections are rolled within a specific depth group to provide the necessary required strength in situations where head room and other considerations make the use of deeper, lighter members infeasible.

Wide-flange beam shapes are proportioned with the depth of their webs being considerably larger than their flange widths. Column shapes are more nearly equal in their depth-to-width ratio, and have much heavier flange and web thicknesses. The largest U.S. rolled wide-flange beam is 37⅜ in. deep, weighs 359 lb/ft and has a 16¾-in. wide flange that is 2 in. thick. The heaviest column shape weighs 730 lb and is 22½ in. deep with 18-in. flanges that are 5 in. thick.

American Standard beams, or I-beams, as they are commonly called, differ from wide-flange shapes in that the inner surfaces of their flanges are not parallel to their outer surfaces, but slope down from the web at an angle of approximately 9° (16⅔%). I-beams are narrower than wide-flange shapes of the same depth and have thicker webs. The wider flange on wide-flange beams make them more efficient in resisting bending (bending resistance is

the most common control for designing beams) than I-beams of the same weight. The I-beam's sloping inner flange may create special connection problems that increase the construction costs. I-beams are used when their proportions and high shear resistance can solve special situations. The largest American-rolled I-beam is 24½ in. deep, 8 in. wide and weighs 121 lb/ft.

Other common structural shapes are channels, angles, and tees. Technically plates are not considered a "shape," but are frequently used to create built-up members and to make connections. Channels are basically one side of an American Standard beam. They are particularly useful for framing around openings such as stairwells and shafts. The omission of flange projections on one side permits a flush finish. Channels are also occasionally used as lintels, roof purlins, and as part of curtain wall support systems. Channels do not usually share the same connecting problems associated with the American Standard beam. The lack of flange projections on one side creates a straight surface that permits simple connections. Structural channels range in size up to 18 in. deep with a 4¼-in. width, and a weight of 58 lb/ft.

Angles are frequently used as lintels, often in combination with other angles, and sometimes in combination with channels and plates when the loads are large. Angles and plates are commonly used as connecting members between other larger structural framing members. Angles are manufactured both with equal and unequal size legs. Their outer corner is a clean, sharp right angle, and their inner and outer leg surfaces are parallel. The maximum size equal leg angle has 8-in. legs and is 1⅛ in. thick. The maximum size unequal leg angle has 9-in. and 4-in. legs and is ⅝ in. thick.

Structural tees are obtained by cutting the web of wide flange or I-beam shapes in half. They are often used as connecting pieces between other framing members, and as (or part of) lintels, hangers, and assemblies for curtain wall attachment. Angles and tees are also used for the chords of trusses, often in combination with plates and sometimes channels.

SYMBOLS AND IDENTIFICATION

The steel producers have developed a uniform standard for designating framing members. In general, the symbol indicates the shape, followed by the nominal depth and the weight per linear foot:

1. W 18 × 40 indicates a wide-flange beam, 18 in. deep, weighing 40 lb/ft.
2. S 12 × 50 indicates an American Standard beam 12 in. deep, weighing 50 lb/ft.
3. C stands for channel.
4. M designates shapes that cannot be classified either W, S, or HP. Most of these miscellaneous beams are very light in weight compared to wide flanges and are usually used only in instances where deflection is not a prime consideration.
5. MC similarly is the designation for miscellaneous channels.

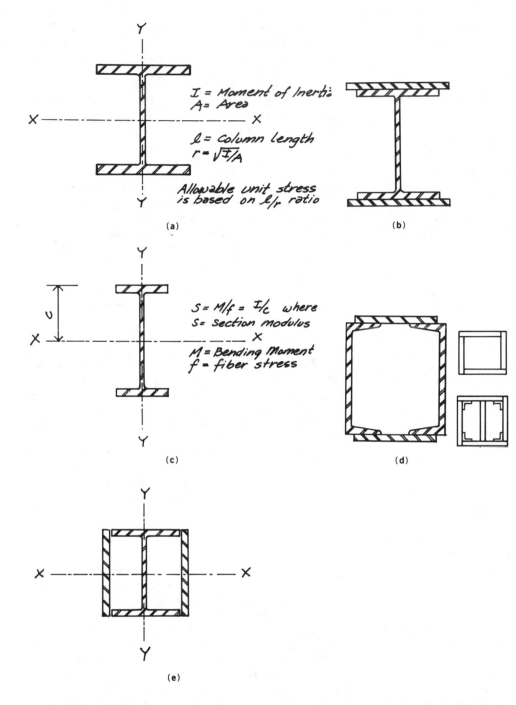

I = Moment of Inertia
A = Area

ℓ = Column length
$r = \sqrt{I/A}$

Allowable unit stress is based on ℓ/r ratio

(a)

(b)

$S = M/f = I/c$ *where*
S = Section modulus
M = Bending Moment
f = fiber stress

(c)

(d)

(e)

Figure 6. The logic of structural shapes (2). **(a)** Column: strength to resist bending in a column comes primarily from how far the column's material is from its vertical axis—the further the more stable; **(b)** Extra stability can be provided in a particular direction when needed, such as when required to resist wind loads; **(c)** Beam: column shapes are heavier in cross-section and more compact than beam shapes. A beam's strength comes primarily from its depth; **(d)** Hollow columns can be fabricated in a variety of different ways; **(e)** Built-up column: the added plates can balance the distribution of a column's cross-sectional area about its X-X and Y-Y axis.

6. HP is the designation for pile shapes, which are similar in appearance to wide-flange shapes. They are available in even-number sizes between 8 and 14 in. in depth. Their depth and flange widths are almost identical, whereas the thickness of their web and flanges are identical.

7. WT, ST, and MT are the designations for tees made by cutting the webs of wide flange, American Standard, and miscellaneous beam shapes.

8. Angles are designated by L followed by the length of their legs and then their thickness. Their weight is not indicated in the standard symbolic notation. Thus L 6 × 4 × ½ indicates an unequal-leg angle with sides 6 and 4 in. long, ½ in. thick.

9. PL is the symbol for plates, which is then followed by the cross-sectional dimension.

Steel framing members do not arrive at the construction site with their size, weight per linear foot, or strength marked on them by the producing mill. General size can be easily checked in the field, but it would not be practical to try, for example, to differentiate between a W 12 × 85 and a W 12 × 92, insofar as their depths differ by only 0.12 in. and their width by 0.05 in., discounting mill tolerances. Different stress grades of steel are usually identified by different colors of paint, which are applied by the steel producer at the mill along with other original identifying marks such as shape, size, and heat number; the marks are placed at the end of the members supplied to the fabricators. These marks are usually lost during the fabrication process. Architects and engineers therefore must rely on the fabricating contractor, who marks numbers and symbols on each piece of structural steel, to permit coordination with the structural drawings.

QUALITY AND STRENGTH CHARACTERISTICS

During the first half of the twentieth century, structural steel availability was basically limited to one stock grade, with its yield strength slowly increasing from 30,000 psi in 1900 to 33,000 psi in the early 1930s, and then to 36,000 psi in 1960. By 1967, A36 steel with a 36,000 psi rating had completely replaced 33,000 psi A7 steel.

The characteristics of steel can be varied by the additions of alloys. A wide range of strength capacities has been developed for structural members, including special corrosion-resisting steels. In general terms, the available structural steels can be classified into four main type-groups: carbon steels; high strength, low alloy steels; weathering high strength, low alloy steels; and quenched-and-tempered steels (Table 2).

Carbon steel is the basic structural steel used for building construction. A36 steel is the primary grade and has a yield point of 36,000 psi. A529 carbon steel has a slightly higher stress value and is available in a limited number of structural shapes. It is seldom used by architects. The A36 steel is suitable for either bolting or welding.

High strength steels have a strength-to-weight advantage over A36 carbon steel, due to the higher permitted stress values they possess. Less high strength steel than A36 carbon steel is necessary to carry a similar load. The currently approximate 10% cost premium for A572 grade 50 is more than overcome by the 15–20% weight savings. The cumulative savings in weight can sometimes be considerable, especially in large, multistory buildings. This can result in cost advantages, especially when savings due to shipping and foundation are included. An important architectural advantage of the high strength steels over carbon steel is the smaller depth required in the case of beams and thinner cross sections for columns, when deflection does not control.

In the case of columns, the slenderness ratio usually limits the allowable design stress so severely as to make the use of high strength steels practical primarily in short, axially loaded columns and where their dead load is a major portion of the total load. When steel is used in tension members, the designer must be careful to allow for the increase in elongation. Due to their smaller cross sections, high strength members are often easier to erect and assemble.

Multimember structural assemblies such as trusses and wind-bracing systems often require the individual pieces of steel within their overall pattern to resist different degrees of stress. By varying the strength of the steel used for particular members (using higher strength steel in the higher stressed members), it is possible to achieve a visually uniform result. It is also possible to use a higher strength steel for the columns supporting the lower floors

in a high-rise building in order to maintain a uniform cross section for the columns on the upper and lower levels. Floor grids can be designed with the girders along the shorter sides of rectangular column bays of higher strength steel than the longer A36 beams framing into them, in order to save weight and maintain maximum headroom for ducts.

The two basic grades of high strength, low alloy steels are A572 and A588. These steels contain small amounts of other metals in addition to iron and carbon. A572 steels are alloys of a vanadium–nitrogen combination in a basic carbon–manganese steel. Both grades are weldable. A572 steel encompasses four grades of steel with yield stresses reaching up to 65,000 psi. These A572 steels are available in a wide range of thicknesses, with the smaller size members available in the higher stress grades. For instance, the 65,000 psi grade is limited to wide-flange shapes no more than 18 in. deep and 17½ in. wide, while the 50,000 psi grade is available in all structural shapes.

Corrosion-resisting steel (which contains between 0.2% and 0.5% copper) was initially used to build railroad cars during the depression. It was produced as far back as 1927 from copper-bearing ore from the Mayari mine in Cuba. At first this new steel was considered for use as corrugated roofing sheets because it possessed a higher strength-to-weight ratio than carbon steel. It was not utilized in serious quantities until 1933, when U.S. Steel started using its brand of copper alloy steel, called COR-TEN, for hopper cars because its higher strength required lesser amounts of steel, and the resulting lower weight permitted greater payloads. It was not until the 1950s that the steel companies fully realized the potential this type of steel offered for longer paint life and that when it was left exposed and unpainted it would form a self-protective oxide coating. Boxcars made from this alloy, in addition to weighing less, need not be painted beyond an identifying logo.

The architect Eero Saarinen took advantage of the weather-resistant quality of this high strength steel and used it for the exposed-steel structure for the Deere and Co. headquarters, which was built in Moline, Illinois, in 1964 (Fig. 7). The rich purple-sepia colored patina of this material has an appeal to many architects. It has been used extensively for bridges, exposed parking structures, and on the exterior of high-rise structures such as U.S. Steel's 64-story tower in Pittsburgh (Fig. 8).

The weathering steels qualify as high strength, low alloy steels and thus have higher permitted stress values than A36 steel, in addition to their corrosion-resisting characteristics. A242 steel has a yield stress range up to 50,000 psi and a corrosion resistance of at least twice that of carbon steel.

The A588 weathering steels have four times the corrosion resistance of carbon steel and are available with yield stress up to 50,000 psi in all shapes, and in plates up to 4 in. thick. Plates up to 8 in. thick are available in a lower (42,000 psi) stress level.

A serious architectural problem associated with the use of weathering steel is that during the first year or two of exposure to the elements, a fair amount of the oxide residue that forms on the steel surfaces washes off, caus-

Table 2. Availability of Shapes, Plates, and Bars According to ASTM Structural Steel Specifications[a,b]

Steel Type	ASTM Designation	F_y Min. Yield Stress ksi	F_u Tensile Stress[c] ksi	Shapes Group per ASTM A6 — 1[d]	2	3	4	5	Plates and Bars — To ½ in. Incl.	Over ½ to ¾ in. Incl.	Over ¾ to 1¼ in. Incl.	Over 1¼ to 1½ in. Incl.	Over 1½ to 2 in. Incl.	Over 2 to 2½ in. Incl.	Over 2½ to 4 in. Incl.	Over 4 to 5 in. Incl.	Over 5 to 6 in. Incl.	Over 6 to 8 in. Incl.	Over 8 in.
Carbon	A36	32	58–80																X
	A36	36	58–80[e]	X	X	X	X	X	X	X	X	X	X	X	X	X	X	X	
	A529	42	60–85	X					X										
High Strength, Low Alloy	A441	40	60													X	X	X	
	A441	42	63				X	X					X	X	X				
	A441	46	67			X					X	X							
	A441	50	70	X	X				X	X									
	A572—Grade 42	42	60	X	X	X	X	X	X	X	X	X	X	X	X	X	X		
	A572—Grade 50	50	65	X	X	X	X	X	X	X	X	X	X						
	A572—Grade 60	60	75	X	X				X	X	X								
	A572—Grade 65	65	80	X					X	X	X								
Corrosion resistant, High Strength, Low Alloy	A242	42	63				X	X					X	X	X				
	A242	46	67			X					X	X							
	A242	50	70	X	X				X	X									
	A588	42	63														X	X	
	A588	46	67													X			
	A588	50	70						X	X	X	X	X	X	X				
Quenched-and-tempered Alloy	A514[f]	90	100–130												X	X	X		
	A514[f]	100	110–130						X	X	X	X	X	X					

Courtesy of the American Institute of Steel Construction

[a] Ref. 3.
[b] X—Available.
[c] Minimum unless a range is shown.
[d] Includes bar-size shapes.
[e] For shapes over 426 lbs/ft, minimum of 58 ksi only applies.
[f] Plates only.

Figure 7. Exposed weathering steel on the Deere and Co. Headquarters, Moline, Ill., Eero Saarinen, Architect. Photograph courtesy of Deere and Co.

Figure 8. U.S. Steel Headquarters. Harrison & Abramowitz and Abbe, Architects. Photograph courtesy of U.S. Steel.

ing undesirable stains on other adjacent materials such as concrete and stone, where they are very difficult, or sometimes impossible, to remove.

A514 steel covers two general types of steel: a carbon steel with grades ranging from 80,000 to 90,000 psi and alloy steels with a 100,000 psi limit. The steel is quenched and tempered to obtain its strength. These superstrong steels are not available in wide-flange shapes. They are available in plates up to 2½ in. thick in the 100,000 psi grade. Structural members can be fabricated by combining plates with other shapes and plates. The first structural use of this grade steel was for the lower three floors of the trussed columns in the IBM building designed by Curtis and Davis and constructed in Pittsburgh in 1963 (Fig. 9).

CONNECTIONS

There are three basic types of connection between structural members: simple, semirigid, and rigid. Simple connections are only capable of transferring by shear connections the accumulated live and dead loads from one framing member to the next. Rigid connections have the capacity to transfer bending stresses as well as the shear stress. The most common example of a simple connection is when a beam is connected to a column or girder by securing it only by its web (Fig. 10), the flanges remaining free to rotate. By also securing the flanges, the connection can be made rigid and capable of transferring bending moments. Rigid connections, in addition to producing a stiffer structure, can also result in the use of somewhat smaller members, due to the increase in the beam's bending moment resistance. If a beam's end rotation is reduced 90% or more by its connection, then it is considered to be rigid. Reductions between 10 and 90% are considered semirigid.

Riveting

Initially, structural steel members were fastened to each other by rivets. A rivet is a round steel shaft with a head at one end. Rivets are heated and driven while still at a minimum of 1000°F through precut holes in the framing members. The protruding end of the rivet's shaft is then hammered into a securing head. When the rivet cools it shrinks, drawing the connected pieces tightly together. Riveting is an efficient securing method, but is costly and an extremely noisy process. Today almost all structural steel is fastened either by bolting or welding.

Bolting

Bolts fall into two main categories: unfinished or machine bolts, designated as A307, and high strength bolts. Building codes limit the conditions under which machine bolts may be used. For example, they may not be used for column splices in buildings over 200 ft in height. A machine bolt having the same diameter as a rivet is not as strong, primarily because bolted connections require a larger working tolerance; therefore, the bolt does not entirely fill the hole in the structural steel. Unfinished bolts can be identified quickly by their square heads. High strength bolts have hexagonal heads. They come in two major strengths, designated as A325 and A490. High strength bolts are made of stronger steel and have heavier heads. The A490 bolts are 50% stronger than the A325 bolts and do not have threads in their shear plane, where they pass through the layers of steel they are joining. High strength bolts can be tightened to the point where the load between the connected members is not transferred by the shear-resisting capacity of the bolt, but by the friction generated between the framing members, which comes from the clamping effect of the high strength bolts. High strength bolt connections can be checked on the job

Figure 9. Building the IBM office structure in Pittsburgh. Truss walls made from a variety of different strength steels.

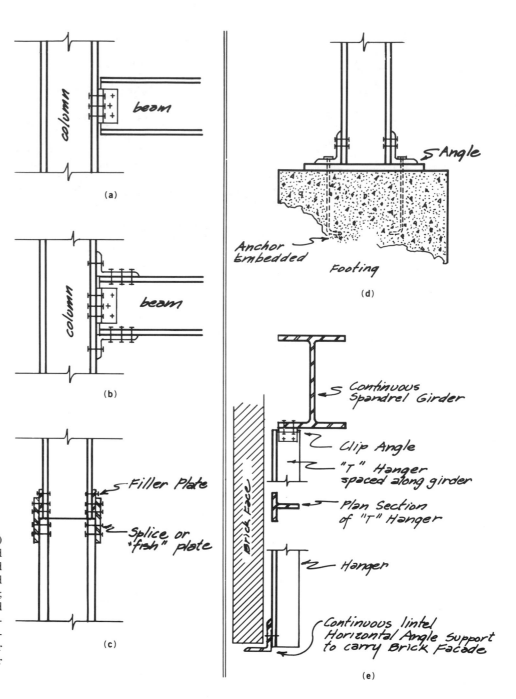

Figure 10. Connections (4). **(a)** Simple connection transfers load only, not bending stress; **(b)** Rigid connection transfers both load and bending stress; **(c)** Column splice; **(d)** Column base: angles, tees, and plates are used to connect one framing member to another. The connections are made either by bolting or by welding; **(e)** Typical support for outer face of building.

either by calibrated torque wrenches, by load-indicating bolts, or by load-indicating washers. Load-indicating washers have several slight protrusions on one surface. When the bolt has been sufficiently tightened, these protrusions become flattened. A metal pick can easily be used to determine whether the gap between the washer and bolt head has been sufficiently reduced by the force of tightening the nut and bolt.

Welding

Welding is a joining method in which the steel is melted at the point where it is to be joined, and a small amount of metal is added as a filler. Welding offers two distinct advantages over bolting. It can accommodate large stress

transfers because it can be continuous, and when the structure is left exposed, it creates a clean uncluttered appearance, which has particular appeal to some architects. It is not uncommon for both welding and bolting to be utilized for different parts of the same connection. For example, an angle, tee, or plate could be welded to a beam end in the fabricating shop, and then bolted to a column in the field. Almost all construction welding is done with an electric arc. There are three basic types of weld: butt welds, plug-and-slot welds (where holes are made in one of the two pieces being connected and then the hole or slot is filled with weld material), and fillet welds (which are used to connect two pieces of material that are at right angles to each other). Certain, mostly discontinued, grades of corrosion-resisting steels cannot be successfully welded.

PROTECTION

Steel has two fundamental drawbacks as an architectural or structural material. It rusts when exposed to air and water, and it quickly loses its structural integrity when exposed to fire.

Oxidation

The deterioration of steel is most noticeable in structures such as bridges or the hulls of ships. Built-in steel framing members cannot be inspected for damage from penetrating moisture or condensation. Exterior steel columns, spandrel beams, and especially elevator sheave beams must all be carefully protected from rusting. Even steel totally embedded in concrete is subjected to eventual deterioration. Parking structures holding cars that drip slush containing snow-melting salts have frequently developed serious problems. The salt accelerates the deterioration of the concrete decking, permitting water to reach the steel reinforcement contained within the concrete. The water reacts with the steel, causing it to oxidize (rust). This process greatly increases the size of the steel reinforcement, and the resulting expansion causes more cracks, which accelerate the entire process.

Structural steel is often given a prime coat of rust-inhibiting paint before being shipped to the job site. This shop coat is sometimes supplemented by another field coat of paint prior to the permanent building in of steel located in positions subject to moisture damage.

In extreme cases, items such as stainless-steel lintels and other structural support for the wall system can be employed. Less drastic situations can call for zinc plating or galvanized steel members. Asphalt coatings have been successfully used, and of course various types and numbers of paint coating.

Additionally, there is the family of corrosion-resisting weathering steels that can be used for exposed structural members not subject to continuous moisture. Architects have also taken carbon steel framing members that have been insulated for fire resistance and then wrapped them in weather-resisting sheet steel in order to simulate or express the structural steel beneath.

Fire Protection

Steel starts to lose strength at approximately 1000°F, well below the temperatures encountered during a building fire. Structural steel can be protected from the ravages of fire by four basically different methods: insulation, cooling, isolation, and shielding. Insulation is by far the most common method. The precise amount of required protection time varies from 4 h to none, depending on how and where a particular framing member is used. For example, in a fully "fireproof" high-rise building, most codes will require the columns to have sufficient protection to prevent their being damaged by fire for a period of 4 h, while the floor beams might require 3h and the roof beams only 2 h with no protection being necessary if the roof beams are located more than 20 ft above the top floor. Not all steel-frame structures require protection. A 10-story parking garage that is accessible to fire-fighting equipment on all sides might not be required to have any of its structure, other than the stairs, fire protected, nor might a low-rise suburban office building. Building codes that are promulgated by different states and communities vary in their standards, but all require protection for people-occupied buildings over a few stories in height.

Insulation. A very long list of materials and combinations of materials can be used to insulate steel. The specific thicknesses required for the particular number of hours necessary for a given situation are spelled out in long charts published by the Fire Underwriters Laboratory and by building codes.

Concrete, plaster, plasterboard, masonry, and spray-on mineral fibers are the most commonly used materials. The choice is often related to the size of the building and to floor and finishing materials used throughout the building. For example, if a poured-in-place concrete floor slab is being used for a small structure, the beams might be protected by encasing them in concrete, while in a larger structure it probably would be more economical to use spray-on insulation. If a metal deck is utilized for the floor system, then the beams can conveniently be protected with the same sprayed-on material used to protect the underside of the metal deck. Similarly, columns could be sprayed or protected with the required amount of the particular material, such as gypsum board or masonry, being used for subdividing the spaces within the building.

Depending on the insulating material selected, various thicknesses are necessary in order to achieve the same required degree of protection. For example, 2 in. of concrete with wire mesh, 1¼ in. of spray-on fiber, and four layers of ⅝-in. thick gypsum board all provide the same 4-h protection. Architects often cover insulated structural members with other finishing material. Sheet metal wrapped around an insulated beam or column has been used to give the appearance of looking at the actual framing member.

Cooling. Sprinklers are by far the most common cooling system. Of course they also provide a method of extinguishing a fire. Unfortunately there is a remote but nagging problem of loss of pressure, whereas insulation, once properly in place, does not need to rely on any further action. Sprinklers have been accepted as the sole fire-protection system for some types of low-rise building and in certain high-rise situations for the protection of floor beams, where the floors are insulated from each other and the columns are also insulated. In most large buildings, sprinklers are relied on to protect the occupants and goods contained within the structure by suppressing the fire until fire fighters can control the situation. Their use usually leads to larger permitted floor areas and longer travel distances to exits, but it does not eliminate fire-rating requirements for protecting the structure or exit stairs and passageways.

Another cooling technique consists of circulating water within hollow framing members. If these members are all connected in loops, then the water contained within them will be free to circulate. When a fire situation occurs, the contained water will protect the steel just as a pot filled with water will not be damaged on a hot stove. The heated water will rise within the loop, causing cool water to circulate to the critical area. These systems have vents to protect them against increases in pressure. The water contains antirust and antifreeze ingredients in a similar manner to a car radiator.

This is an expensive system more easily adopted for protecting columns than beams. One special appeal to architects is that it permits the structural steel to remain visually exposed, unencumbered by any other protection.

Isolation. If structural members can be so located as to render them inaccessible to damage from a fire, then obviously they are not in need of any further protection. This means of achieving safety by isolation, or placing the steel beyond the reach of danger, is commonly seen in roof beams that are located 20 or more ft above the floor level. Occasionally, for special architectural design reasons, spandrel beams of high-rise structures have been left exposed and otherwise unprotected. This is feasible because they have been located a sufficient distance beyond the outside of the curtain wall.

Fire tests on a mock-up of part of the building are usually used to determine what is a safe remote distance. The concept of isolating a member is also related to its size as well as its location. The larger a framing member, the more surface it will have, and thus it will be capable of dissipating heat at a faster rate. Another form of protection, which does not cleanly fall into the categories of either insulation or isolation, occurs when a fire-rated ceiling is placed under an entire pattern of ceiling beams or joists. This is a far more efficient method than insulating each member separately, but creates a problem whenever a duct or light fixture penetrates through the ceiling surface. Because each individual penetration must be protected, this type of application is limited to situations where there are few initial penetrations and little or no expectation of tenant changes in the future.

Flame Shield. If flames can be deflected a sufficient distance away from a framing member, that member can remain structurally sound. Flame shielding incorporates two other concepts. Isolation is involved because the effect of the shield is to deflect the flames in a manner that will isolate the shielded member from the fire. The size of the member will affect the necessary protection distance, because of the heat-dissipating relationship. Flame shielding is applicable for the protection of exterior spandrel beams and columns. As in the case of isolation, a full-scale mock-up of the specific shield is usually subjected to a fire test in order to obtain building department approval.

BIBLIOGRAPHY

1. *Manual of Steel Construction,* 8th ed., American Institute of Steel Construction, Inc., Chicago, 1980.
2. D. Guise, *Design and Technology in Architecture,* John Wiley & Sons, New York, 1985, pp. 43 and 44.
3. Ref. 1, p. 1–5.
4. Ref. 2, p. 16.

General References

U.S. Steel, *Wide Flange Shapes,* ADUSS 27–8587–02, 1985.
J. Swank, *History of the Manufacture of Iron in All Ages,* 2nd ed., American Iron and Steel Association, Philadelphia, 1892.
J. S. Jeans, *Steel, History, Manufacture, Properties and Uses,* E. & F. N. Spon, London and New York, 1880.
D. A. Fisher, *Epic of Steel,* Harper & Row, New York, 1963.
W. A. Starrett, *Skyscrapers and the Men Who Build Them,* Scribner's, New York and London, 1928.
C. Condit, *American Building,* University of Chicago Press, Chicago, 1968.
Historical Record of Beams and Columns, American Institute for Steel Construction, Inc., Chicago, 1953.
H. E. McGannon, ed., *The Making, Shaping and Treating of Steel,* 9th ed., U.S. Steel Corp., Pittsburgh, Pa., 1971.
G. Winter in W. McGuire, *Steel Structures,* Prentice Hall, Englewood Cliffs, N.J., 1968, Chapt. 4.
C. Condit, *The Rise of the Skyscraper,* University of Chicago Press, Chicago, 1952.
E. E. Viollet-le-Duc, *Lectures on Architecture,* trans. by B. Bucknall, Grove Press, New York, 1959.
Modern Steels for Construction—A Selection Guide, Bethlehem Steel, Bethlehem, Pa., 1978.
Steel and America, 1985 Annual Report, American Iron & Steel Institute, Chicago, 1985.
Manual of Steel Construction, 8th ed., American Institute of Steel Construction, Inc., Chicago, 1980.
Steel for Buildings and Bridges, 3748, Bethlehem Steel, Bethlehem, Pa., 1982.

See also CONSTRUCTION SYSTEMS; FIRE RESISTANCE OF MATERIALS; SPRINKLER AND OTHER FIRE CONTROL METHODS; STEEL IN CONSTRUCTION

DAVID GUISE
New York, New York

STRUCTURAL WOOD.   See WOOD, STRUCTURAL PANEL COMPOSITES.

STUBBINS, HUGH

Hugh Asher Stubbins, Jr., born in 1912 in Birmingham, Alabama, the eldest son of Hugh Asher and Lucile Matthews Stubbins, has established an architectural practice that has progressed evenly over 50 years from its regional beginnings in residential and educational architecture to international public commissions and celebrated high-rise structures. Viewing architecture as a social art enhancing everyday life, Stubbins's approach has been that of a pragmatic, problem-solving art, blending the practical with the aesthetic, and subjecting prevailing trends and current design attitudes to a rigid analysis of their suitability to specific program considerations, client needs, and environmental conditions rather than universal solutions. Espousing the principles of modernism in a broad sense, Stubbins has created a body of work synthesizing function with innovative technology, and expressing a sense of people, place, experience, and the spirit of the times.

Stubbins's first professional experience coincided with the emergence of the modern house of the 1930s and 1940s. Having graduated from Georgia Institute of Technology in 1933 and Harvard University's Graduate School of Design in 1935, Stubbins was enlisted into the office of New England architect Royal Barry Wills, whose success in small house design had brought him national recognition. Stubbins helped Wills compete in the field of contemporary design, and enjoyed a mutually supportive association with Wills from 1935 to 1938 that produced six modern houses and several national design competition awards.

The formative experience with Wills was followed by a return to Birmingham to the office of Miller, Martin, and Lewis and a brief partnership in Boston with Marc Peter from 1938 to 1939. Stubbins's early career was in great part supported by "shelter" magazines and competitions that provided a forum and national exposure for his work. In 1940, Walter Gropius invited Stubbins to return to Harvard as his assistant. Declining the offer of Harvard's Wheelwright Traveling Scholarship, Stubbins began teaching at Harvard and established his first design office.

The war years brought a boom in the construction of defense housing and the formation of the Federal Works Agency. Stubbins's low cost Defense Housing Project at Windsor Locks, Connecticut (1941), attracted widespread attention as a model of economy and efficiency with innovative features, including an experimental anthracite stove for heating, cooking, and hot water. For the war effort, Stubbins joined Harvard's Radio Research Laboratory and helped produce a machine later used by the U.S. Air Force to jam enemy radar. He collaborated with Massachusetts Institute of Technology professor John Rule in establishing the Stereographic Company to develop three-dimensional drawing techniques for training naval pilots and gunners, and also worked under Dr. Edwin Land of Polaroid to develop the so-called educated bomb and heat-sensitive homing device.

World War II precipitated an unprecedented demand for housing and, with it, enthusiasm for modern architecture and innovation. Stubbins continued designing houses throughout the 1940s and 1950s. Characterized by flexible plans, visual spaciousness, shed roofs, and regional materials, Stubbins's comfortable houses applied new building techniques using large glass panels and braced frame construction, and reflected the changing, informal U.S. lifestyle. Establishing a strong reputation for the mastery of residential architecture, Stubbins pioneered a northeast regional contemporary style on a domestic scale.

In the late 1940s and early 1950s, Stubbins's gradually expanding practice progressed from single-family houses to schools. The Country School in Weston, Massachusetts (1952), earned Stubbins the Harleston Parker Gold Medal in 1955 and was cited for its sensitivity to human needs and flexibility to accommodate developing educational trends.

Stubbins continued to teach at Harvard for 12 years, becoming chairman of the department in 1953 following Gropius's departure. Stubbins left in 1954 to devote his energies to his emerging practice. During his tenure, many practitioners who later achieved prominence studied in his studio, including Philip Johnson, Paul Rudolph, Ulrich Franzen, and Henry Cobb. In 1949, Stubbins's office was changed in name from Hugh Stubbins, Architect to Hugh Stubbins and Associates and, in 1957, was the first firm to incorporate in the Commonwealth of Massachusetts. The 1940s marked the beginnings of influential professional associations, of which the friendship shared with Alvar Aalto was the most revered and openly acknowledged. The late 1940s also marked Stubbins's involvement with the American Institute of Architects; he later served as vice president.

In 1955, following the U.S. State Department commission to design the United States Consulate in Tangier, Morocco, in 1954, Stubbins was selected to design Congress Hall in West Berlin, FRG (Fig. 1), a major international conference center that served as the expression of goodwill and cooperation from the United States to the

Figure 1. Hugh Stubbins, Congress Hall, West Berlin, Germany, 1957. Photograph by Kessler.

people of postwar FRG. A symbol for freedom in thought and expression, distinguished by its soaring catenary roof, Congress Hall embodied the beliefs in hope and progress in a structure that explored inventive domed and shell structural concepts and contemporary concrete technology.

Opportunities to work on specialty, prototype buildings followed Congress Hall, and included the Loeb Drama Center for Harvard University (1960), the country's first fully automatic and flexible theater; the Francis A. Countway Library of Medicine for Harvard's Medical School (Fig. 2), a model for vertical library planning and interior atrium space; and Philadelphia Veterans Stadium (1971), a multipurpose arena serving both football and baseball based on an "octorad" configuration generated from eight points of radii of two concentric circles.

The 1960s and 1970s witnessed the rapid expansion of college campuses, and Stubbins's office began working at Brandeis, Princeton, the University of Virginia, the University of California at Santa Cruz, Southeastern Massachusetts University, Mount Holyoke College, Bowdoin, Rochester Institute of Technology, Tufts, Oberlin, Hamilton, Teachers College Columbia, and Massachusetts Institute of Technology as well as Harvard. Stubbins's campus architecture of this period embraced the human values of scale, proportion, use, and neighborhood. The considerate siting and use of natural materials such as brick reflected the influence of Alvar Aalto on Stubbins's work. Contemporary in design and construction methods, Stubbins's buildings nevertheless respected the hallowed traditions and character of the campus surroundings. The residential cluster of senior dormitories at the Dana Hall Schools (1965) and the Laboratory Theater at Mount Holyoke College (1966) exemplify these values as two of the most re-

fined and thoughtful achievements of Stubbins's career. This college work was cited as a contributing factor in the receipt of one of the first American Institute of Architects Firm Awards in 1967.

Stubbins is best known for his design of Citicorp Center in New York (Fig. 3), a singular work of power and daring that expressed the aspirations of its age and transformed the vision of the urban environment. Its sloped roof has become a memorable image on Manhattan's skyline and a contrast to the flat-boxed towers of the international style. Recognized for its contribution to the vitality of the pedestrian streetscape, Citicorp Center placed an unprecedented emphasis on its public spaces and the diversity and complexity of activities at its base, including a new structure for St. Peter's Lutheran Church. Collaborating with lifelong friend, structural engineer William LeMessurier, Stubbins synthesized bold aesthetic and technological concepts of skyscraper design by cantilevering the corners of the aluminum tower dramatically above the city block.

Stubbins's Federal Reserve Bank of Boston (Fig. 4) conveyed a similar landmark presence and structural triumph in a dignified and elegant response to its need for secure banking operations. Collaborating again with LeMessurier and using transfer trusses and cantilevered exterior framing, Stubbins achieved a significant opening between the low- and high-rise portions of the building in his most masterful and adventurous union of form and structure.

A succession of successful skyscrapers, mixed-use developments, and corporate commissions followed Citicorp Center and the Federal Reserve Bank, among them, One Cleveland Center, Cleveland, Ohio (1953); Pacwest Center, Portland, Oregon (1984); Metro-Dade Center, Miami, Florida (1984); and the Erie Insurance Group Headquar-

Figure 2. Hugh Stubbins, the Francis A. Countway Library of Medicine, Harvard University, Boston, Massachusetts, 1965. Photograph by Louis Reens.

ters, Erie, Pennsylvania (1984). Stubbins's recent high-rise designs include 150 Federal Center, Boston, Massachusetts, and Fifth Avenue Place, Pittsburgh, Pennsylvania.

In addition to taking a leading role in the business practices and creative accomplishments of his firm that have been cited in over 100 design awards programs, Stubbins has been active in civic and architectural affairs. He is a Fellow of the American Institute of Architects, Fellow of the American Academy of Arts and Sciences, and was awarded the 1980 Thomas Jefferson Medal for Architecture by the University of Virginia. He has served as a member of the Advisory Committee to the State Department of Foreign Buildings, as former vice president of the American Institute of Architects, past president of the Boston Society of Architects, and former chairman of the Design Committee of the Boston Redevelopment Authority, and has chaired and served on numerous architectural committees and juries.

Figure 4. Hugh Stubbins, Federal Reserve Bank of Boston, Boston, Massachusetts, 1978. Photograph by Nick Wheeler.

Figure 3. Hugh Stubbins, Citicorp Center, New York, New York, 1977. Photograph by Edward Jacoby.

BIBLIOGRAPHY

General References

H. Stubbins and S. Braybrooke, eds., *Architecture: The Design Experience,* John Wiley & Sons, Inc., New York, 1976.

K. Ichinowatan "Hugh Stubbins: Architecture in the Spirit of the Times," *Process: Architecture* **10** (1979).

P. Heyer, *Architects on Architecture,* Walker and Company, New York, 1966, pp. 216–223.

DIANNE M. LUDMAN
The Stubbins Associates, Inc.
Cambridge, Massachusetts

STUCCO, SYNTHETIC

Synthetic stucco or *Exterior Insulation and Finish Systems (EIF systems)* are lightweight and economical claddings comprised of insulation (attached to the exterior building wall) and wet-applied finishes. Today, nearly 100 million square feet of EIF systems have been applied in virtually all types of construction in the United States. Architects cite design flexibility, insulation characteristics, price, and prefabrication options as primary reasons for using these cladding systems.

Exterior building envelopes (constructed with masonry, precast concrete, glazing, EIF systems, etc) may be categorized as one of two types; "barrier" or "cavity/rain screen" construction. In "cavity/rain screen" construction, the exterior surface sheds most water, however moisture may penetrate the outermost wall surface into a cavity area. A properly detailed and installed cavity will collect and redirect unwanted water to the building exterior, preventing water penetration further into the building. By contrast, a "barrier-type" exterior surface is designed and constructed to shed all water, thereby preventing any moisture from penetrating past the barrier and into the wall system. EIF systems are designed to perform as "barrier-type" wall systems. Thus, EIF systems must function as skins, excluding water and air infiltration. The EIF system finish must satisfy other functional and aesthetic requirements, as well.

Exterior insulation and finish systems originated in Europe more than 30 years ago, initially as remedial coatings that were combined with rigid insulation. These systems were an outgrowth of the painting and plastering trades. EIF systems were used primarily on retrofit projects. However, it was apparent that EIF system materials could offer advantages in new construction. The development and success of EIF system cladding in Europe is due to its many benefits. Specifically, the exterior application of insulation helps protect the building structure from moisture and thermal changes, thereby saving energy and improving the interior comfort of the building. These systems offer aesthetically pleasing, lightweight, and economical claddings for new or existing facades. By attaching the EIF system boards to the exterior surface, Europeans could insulate their buildings without disrupting the interior living space or reducing existing room sizes. The placement of insulation on the building's exterior reduced the impact of ambient temperature swings, improving building comfort. Finish coatings, applied over the insulation boards, were isolated from movements in the substrate, thereby reducing the potential for cracking. The EIF system allowed the European designer flexibility with many color and finish options, and provided numerous facade variations.

Research on these systems in the Federal Republic of Germany, Switzerland, and France indicates that masonry or tile block are the typical substrates, since most European countries do not use light-frame steel-stud wall construction. Adaptations of original European EIF system are being applied today in the United States. With the on-going demand for low cost, energy-efficient cladding materials, synthetic stucco arrived in North America in the late 1960s. The Dryvit Corporation is credited with importing the EIF system concepts from the FRG and adapting them for construction in the United States. Although the major components of the system remained generically the same, certain modifications were made to accommodate the means and methods of North American construction. The predominant EIF system substrate used in the United States is exterior gypsum wallboard which is secured to light gauge steel-stud framing. This method of construction offers speed in erection, minimal deadweight, stud space for wiring/additional insulation, and framing for attaching interior finish materials. Modifications to the original European system were also made in the application specifications and detailing. In the United States, EIF system materials have been field applied over existing or new construction, prefabricated off-site into panels which are field erected, or a combination of the two. Off-site panel assembly offers many quality control features including protection from inclement weather during application.

In order to help organize the manufacturers in this growing industry and promote the EIF systems overall, the Exterior Insulation Manufacturers Association (EIMA) was established in 1981. This organization includes manufacturers, associate manufacturers, distributors, users, and affiliate members. EIMA plays a major role in the EIF system industry as a communication link between its members, and by promoting specification guidelines, application techniques, testing, quality control, and classification of systems. During the spring of 1988, ASTM (American Society for Testing and Materials) formed a special committee to study the development of specific standards for the performance of EIF systems and their related components.

SYSTEM DESCRIPTION

The EIF system includes the following components: the finish coat, reinforcement embedded in a base coat, the insulator, and the attachment to substrate (adhesive or mechanical). Each EIF system component performs a specific function integral to the overall product performance. The finish coat provides a weathering surface, color, and texture. The base coat supports the finish coat and provides the primary moisture resistance of the system. It also protects the insulation and reinforcing mesh. Reinforcing mesh in the base coat consists of fiber strands, fiber mesh, or metal lath, which provide increased impact resistance and tensile strength for the cladding. Adding polymers to the portland cement in the EIF system base and finish materials, increases strength, flexibility, and moisture resistance of the coatings. Rigid insulation boards provide thermal resistance and isolates the base coat from the substrate. The insulation may be attached to the substrate with mechanical fasteners or adhesives. The substrate supports the EIF system, and is typically concrete, masonry, or sheathing over frame. Accessories provide edge terminations, expansion joints, etc, for various conditions of the system.

CLASSIFICATIONS OF EIF SYSTEMS

EIF systems may be viewed as new technology within the traditional portland cement stucco industry. These systems are classified by the composition of the coatings, and the type of reinforcement used. The materials in the base and finish coats govern application criteria as well as performance characteristics. Various EIF systems have been categorized by EIMA, and are recognized industry-wide (see Figs. 1 and 2 as examples).

> Class "PM"—Polymer Modified, Mineral: Cementitious with polymer modification.
> Class "PB"—Polymer Base: Primarily acrylic polymer.

EIF system reinforcing increases strength, durability, and impact resistance. The reinforcement has been categorized by EIMA as follows:

> Type A—External reinforced. Cloth (woven fiber mesh) Metal lath (expanded, wire woven, wire welded).
> Type B—Internal reinforced. Random fibers.
> Type C—Unreinforced.

Although many combinations are possible, the most widely applied systems are Class PB with Type A reinforcement, Class PM with Type A reinforcement, and Class PM with Type B reinforcement.

EIF SYSTEMS

Class PB

In PB systems, the finish coating is predominantly synthetic polymer. Base coats vary by manufacturer and may be primarily cementitious or synthetic. All PB systems use an external reinforcement of fiber-glass mesh in one or two layers. Expanded polystyrene (EPS) boards are the predominant insulation used in the United States and are typically adhered to the substrate. Many manufacturers offer alternatives allowing a wide specification range.

Polymer-based systems are typically elastic, flexible, and lightweight. Because of their polymer content, PB systems require fewer control joints to resist cracking. As in all EIF systems, control joints are required where the substrate changes. These may occur at window and door openings and at the abutment of dissimilar materials. Control joints and expansion joints must be carefully de-

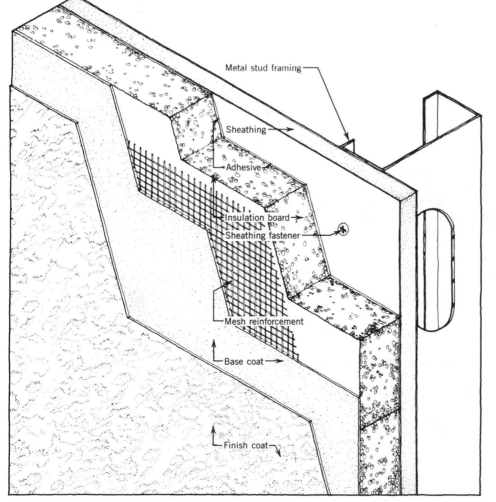

Metal stud framing
Sheathing
Adhesive
Insulation board
Sheathing fastener
Mesh reinforcement
Base coat
Finish coat

Figure 1. Class PB, Type A.

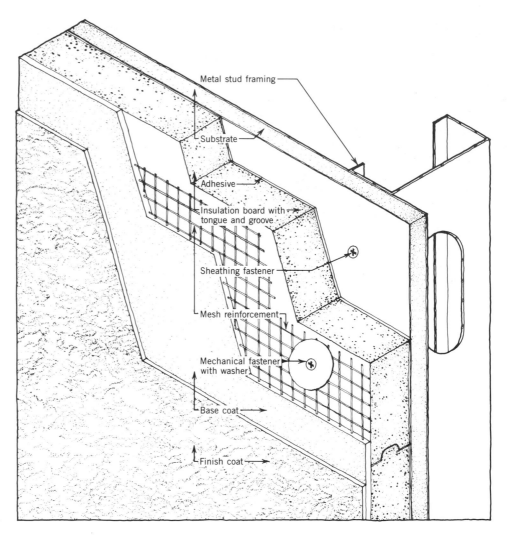

Figure 2. Class PM, Type A.

tailed, adhering strictly to the manufacturer's recommendations.

PB systems are more flexible than PM systems. However, because they are thinner than PM systems, they require extra reinforcement in key areas to prevent damage from punctures, vandalism, and even the errant baseball. Most PB manufacturers offer a heavier mesh to reinforce PB systems in areas of high traffic or places where there is potential for high impact.

As with any adhered system, the condition of the substrate becomes an important factor in the specifications. All substrates must be properly prepared to allow the adhesive to completely bond. Many PB manufacturers offer primers and mechanical fasteners to assure proper bond to marginal substrates. If an existing substrate is questionable, a bond test must be carried out to determine the suitability of the substrate. Gypsum board is the most common substrate used in the United States. Because of the inherent material properties of this type of sheathing, specific attention must be given to detailing and application of EIF systems adhered to gypsum board.

Class PM

PM systems are much thicker than PB systems because of the higher portland cement ratio in their base and finish

coatings. Fiber-glass mesh external reinforcing is common, as well as chopped fiber material reinforcing, and metal lath reinforcement. PM systems are unique as they predominantly incorporate denser insulation (extruded polystyrene) that has been mechanically attached to the substrate.

Many finishes and textures are possible with PM systems, including exposed aggregates. The cement ratio in the base and finish coats provide durable, weather resistant, and impact resistant claddings. Although heavier than PB systems, PM systems are considered lightweight compared to traditional portland cement stucco.

Polymer-modified finishes are less flexible compared to PB systems and require specific attention to the placement and detailing of the control and expansion joints. Typically, panels cannot exceed 150 square feet or be longer than 20 feet in any dimension.

PM systems require mechanical fasteners to attach the extruded foam insulation to the substrate. Accordingly, the condition of the substrate is not as critical to the success of PM cladding as it is to the success of adhesively attached PB cladding. Many types of substrates can be used, whether for new construction or retrofit.

The selection of an exterior insulation and finish system (whether PB or PM) requires an evaluation of the project building program. Consideration must be given to the intended building usage and the type of substrate(s). Specifically, the proposed occupancy, site location, climate, and exposure to impact will influence the selection and specification of the most appropriate EIF system materials. In addition to a general understanding of EIF systems, an understanding of material components is important. Both polymer-base and polymer-modified exterior insulation and finish systems consist of materials with unique properties, which have specific performance characteristics. Understanding these material properties is essential to maximize the best qualities and minimize the weakest aspects of these systems. Given this objective, the following section will examine each component of EIF system, and outline specific material properties. This analysis will begin at the outermost surface, and proceed to the substrate.

COMPONENTS AND PROPERTIES

Finish Coat

The finish coat is the outermost surface of the synthetic stucco system, and therefore provides the final appearance for the completed wall. Although these coatings vary by manufacturer, they typically include polymer, pigment, and fillers.

Many colors are available in the finish coat ranging from light to dark. Many textures are available, however they vary somewhat by applicator. Typical textures include sand finish, patterns, and swirls, all of which are similar to the textures that may be achieved with traditional portland cement stucco. In addition to the large variety of colors and textures, certain manufacturers offer finish coats with exposed aggregate finishes. These finishes emulate the appearance of exposed granite, marble, or building stone.

The finish coat will "telegraph" imperfections of the substrate and base coat. This concern is particularly evident in PB systems, where very fine micro-cracks may develop. When these cracks are linear, they typically are following gaps between the insulation boards. Although minute, such fissures frequently permit water to migrate through the exterior insulation and finish system. Since the finish coat and related components are intended to function as a "barrier-type" wall system, the appearance of micro-cracks indicate a recognizable concern to the overall performance of the wall system.

Typical polymer-based finish coats will soften if exposed to moisture for an extended period, therefore attention must be given to details where the exterior wall terminates. This includes places where the exterior insulation and finish system touches the ground, roof, balconies, windows, or any adjacent construction that may hold moisture.

Expansion joints required in EIF system applications are vulnerable to moisture. Since the typical PB EIF system finish coat will soften if in constant contact with moisture, only closed-cell back-up rods should be used behind sealant joints. Open-cell back-up rods hold moisture, which may accumulate in the rod at breaks in the exterior surface or from condensation that migrates from the building's interior. Regardless of the reason, water that is collected in the back-up rod may cause the finish coat to

lose its cohesion. This is due to the fact that the adhesion between the finish coat and sealant is stronger than the bond between base coat and the aggregates of the finish coat.

The finish coat must be applied with a sufficient thickness to adequately cover the base coat. Depending upon the size of aggregate and desired texture, the actual finish coat thickness will vary. Dark colors tend to fade and chalk over time, and will probably require periodic recoating to maintain the original appearance. Occasionally, small particles of iron are contained within the finish coat materials. These impurities may oxidize and result in rust colored streaks on the facade.

Base Coat

The base coat is the foundation for the finish coat, the mechanism for holding reinforcing mesh in place, and the primary barrier to stop water from penetrating into other wall components. The base coat must be applied with adequate thickness to properly perform its functions. An insufficient application of base coat will result in cracking, reduced impact resistance, and exposure of the reinforcing mesh to moisture. The strength of fiber-glass mesh lessens over time, when exposed to moisture.

The base coat's primary components are polymer, portland cement, and fillers. Typically, the polymer and fillers are combined by the manufacturer and shipped in five-gallon containers. At the site, this material is mixed with portland cement. If the specified proportions of the base coat mix are altered by increasing the amount of cement, or decreasing the polymer, the resultant material will be stiffer and more prone to cracking. Proper proportions in mixing are as important as the correct amount of mixing. Over-mixing or retempering must be strictly avoided. Over-mixing introduces additional air to the formulation, which results in considerable air voids. These voids will permit the passage of moisture through the base coat materials. Similar to the finish, the base coat will "telegraph" gaps in the EPS insulation. This space between the insulation boards will typically fill with base-coat material. The resultant deeper section of base coat is stiffer than the adjacent areas. This difference in material dimensions results in cracking.

Although the base coat of PM systems are less sensitive to the abutment of insulation boards, the application of PM base coats must be limited to 150 square feet sections in a maximum two and one half-to-one (2.5:1) proportion. This requirement is intended to eliminate cold joints in the application, as well as avoid long panel applications. Since the PM systems are thicker by design, and are polymer modified in lieu of polymer based, careful adherence to the square footage and proportion requirements will be necessary in order to minimize cracking.

The base coat must be applied within the temperature and humidity constraints outlined by the manufacturer. If the temperature falls below the prescribed limits before the base coat has fully cured, the reaction between polymers and portland cement will be significantly altered. The effects of low temperature and/or high humidity slows the polymer–portland cement reactions to the point that curing is extended or never completed.

Certain manufacturers offer base coats that are 100% polymer. These ready-mixed non-cementitious base coats provide added flexibility and a high resin/fibers composite protection against weather or impact. This material must also be fully cured prior to the application of the finish coat. Some manufacturers require that a primer be applied over the base coat, prior to installing the finish, to increase weather resistance. In Europe, a key coat (skim coat of base material) is frequently applied prior to application of the finish material. Since the base coat is the primary defense or a system which is designed to shed moisture, the application and detailing of this component is critical.

Reinforcement

Reinforcement is the system component that increases impact resistance in addition to providing tensile strength. Reinforcement may be in the form of metal lath, embedded fiber-glass mesh, or chopped random fibers internally mixed in the base coat. Various types of EIF systems require alternative types of reinforcing. Typically, polymer-base systems incorporate fiber-glass mesh reinforcing fabric. Polymer modified systems frequently include chopped fiber reinforcement within the base coat, with the addition of fabric mesh or metal lath. Most manufacturers of exterior insulation and finish systems offer several types of reinforcing mesh for different applications. Typically in PB Type A systems, the standard grade reinforcing mesh is used for wall areas which have limited exposure to impact. Properly installed, the standard reinforcing mesh can resist minor impact and abrasion. Heavy duty reinforcing mesh should be used wherever impact resistance is required, such as at the base of buildings, around entrance areas, etc. Typically, the edges of the heavy duty mesh are butted together, and the standard reinforcing mesh is applied over the heavy duty mesh.

At edge conditions and returns, most PB Type A systems utilize detail mesh. This reinforcing material readily conforms to, and is easily embedded to the edges of EPS insulation. Proper back-wrapping (extending mesh embedded in base coat materials behind insulation board) and embedment of detail reinforcing mesh at terminations are of critical importance. Design details must provide adequate space for mesh installation. In PM Type A systems, back-wrapping is not as critical, since these systems are applied thicker.

Because reinforcing mesh is critical to the performance of any EIF system, it is imperative that the mesh be fully embedded in the base-coat material.

Rigid Insulation Board

The insulation serves two main functions within the EIF system. It isolates the coating from the substrate (thereby reducing the potential for cracking) and provides thermal insulating qualities. In polymer-based systems, the insulation board is typically expanded polystyrene, semirigid fiber glass, polyisocyanurate boards, or mineral/rock wool (Europe). In polymer-modified systems, the insulation board is typically extruded polystyrene.

Expanded polystyrene (EPS) weighs approximately 0.9 to 1.2 pounds per cubic foot and is vapor permeable. EPS insulation boards can vary significantly in their physical and performance characteristics, depending upon the manufacturers' procedures and quality control standards. The actual density of the board, fusion of beads, and dimensional standards (length, width, thickness, squareness, and planar flatness) will significantly impact the performance and quality of the system. Poor quality EPS board will allow moisture to freely percolate between the beads, lessening the insulation value of the board. EPS boards must be installed without gaps, since the base and finish coat will crack at the voids.

Prior to applying the base coat, the surface of the EPS board must be properly prepared. Site dirt, ultraviolet degradation and unevenness of EPS boards must be corrected by rasping the surface. Without such preparation, delamination of the reinforced base coat from the EPS insulation boards may occur.

Expanded polystyrene offers lower initial cost, lower flame spread rating, and less toxic fumes during construction than extruded polystyrene. However, extruded polystyrene also offers unique material advantages. Extruded polystyrene typically has a higher density (approximately two pounds per cubic foot), greater compressive strength, and is a closed-cell material which is less vapor permeable. These insulation boards are generally manufactured with tighter dimensional tolerances, and include a tongue and groove profile for alignment between boards.

Attachment

Attachment is the means by which the EIF system is held to the building structure of substrate. There are two typical methods of attachment, adhesive and mechanical. Generally, most Class PB systems use adhesive for the attachment, Class PM and Class MB systems use mechanical fasteners. Some manufacturers offer both attachments. In PB type systems, the fasteners are typically counter-sunk and plugged with insulation board to avoid telegraphing the fastener through the base/finish coats. In the typical PM systems, some mechanical fasteners are applied to hold the insulation board in place, and additional fasteners are used to secure the reinforcing mesh.

Adhesive attachment is typically accomplished by placing base-coat material or a special mixture which is 100% synthetic on the insulation and pressing it to the substrate. Two methods are common for applying adhesive to the insulation board. The first places ribbons of adhesive around the perimeter of the insulation board, with dabs of adhesive within. This technique is useful where the substrate is uneven, such as on existing masonry surfaces. The second method covers the entire back of the insulation board with adhesive. The adhesive is applied with notched trowel distributing the proper amount of adhesive.

Before a final decision can be made regarding the method of attachment, consideration must be given to the substrate.

SUBSTRATE

The substrate must be structurally sound for proper attachment of the insulation board. Although EIF systems may be applied virtually over any sound substrate, consideration must be given to proper surface preparation and the means of attachment. New construction offers the designer a selection of substrates to meet structural and building code requirements. Before retrofitting a building facade with an EIF system, the wall integrity must be verified. This examination must include the structural capabilities of the existing wall as well as the surface condition.

Exterior insulation and finish systems should not be installed over questionable substrates, unless they are mechanically attached. If the preferred attachment is adhesive, bond tests are recommended prior to installation. Many of the EIF system applications in the United States incorporate a gypsum board substrate which is fastened to light frame construction. Certain gypsum board manufacturers do not endorse adhesive attachment of exterior insulation and finish systems (or any other product) to gypsum board. This position is based on a concern that the paper face on the sheathing may not remain bonded to the gypsum core if water enters the system. If the paper face delaminates from the gypsum core, the adhesively attached EIF system may not resist positive and negative wind loads acting upon the building facade. The continued presence of moisture within the gypsum sheathing may also lead to deterioration of the stud wall assembly, especially at the fasteners.

It is important to reiterate that the intent of the EIF system is to perform as a barrier. The EIF system moisture barrier is required to prevent damage to the building's interior and to prevent bond failure with the gypsum sheathing substrate.

SPECIFICATIONS AND APPLICATION

It is evident from the component properties that successful performance of EIF systems are directly affected by the quality of manufacture, design and application of materials. Thorough specifications and construction details will be necessary to clarify the materials used, the design intent, and the procedures required for successful application.

Since every building material has specific advantages and limitations, it is important to establish the appropriateness of all materials for a particular project program. Once the project designer/specifier has specified an EIF system for a specific building, consideration must be given to the substrate. Any limitations of the substrate (whether new or existing) should be understood by all parties, including the manufacturer, owner, and specifier.

Good installations typically have thorough detailing in the contract documents. Large scale details are recommended to explain atypical conditions. References to manufacturers' details are sufficient, as long as all parties understand that the intent of these details is to represent standard conditions. Details will be required wherever the EIF system starts, stops, or is penetrated by another building component.

Preconstruction meetings between applicator, manufacturer, specifier, and owner are recommended to clarify all details and their implementation. Applicators should be certified by the manufacturer to assure their knowledge and skill. Further pre-qualification by the project team is also recommended for specific buildings. Complex and large EIF system installations, involving varying profiles, require applicators with expertise in similar kinds of projects.

The specifications should require single source responsibility for the entire exterior insulation and finish system. All components should be approved by one manufacturer, without substitution of materials from alternative systems.

Once the details have been thoroughly reviewed and approved by the manufacturer, written confirmation should be obtained stating that the project details and specifications comply with the manufacturer's requirements. The best manufacturers are assertive about quality control, training, and follow-up to insure that applicators are conforming to their requirements.

EIF systems have introduced new technology into the traditional portland cement stucco industry. Through proper attention to material properties, standards, details and application techniques, the completed EIF system will provide efficient, attractive, and durable cladding.

BIBLIOGRAPHY

1. M. A. Doyle, "Trends in Specifying EIFS," *Building Design & Construction Magazine*, 58–62 (Aug. 1988).
2. G. Wright, "EIFS Offers a Variety of Aesthetic Options," *Building Design & Construction Magazine*, 64–66 (Aug. 1988).
3. *EIMA Guideline Specification for Exterior Wall Insulation & Finish Systems Class PM, Type A*, Exterior Insulation Manufacturers Association, Washington, D.C., April 1987.
4. *EIMA Guideline Specification for Exterior Wall Insulation & Finish Systems Class PB, Type A*, Exterior Insulation Manufacturers Association, Washington, D.C., April 1987.
5. *Classification of Exterior Insulation Systems*, Exterior Insulation Manufacturers Association, Washington, D.C., Aug. 15, 1985.
6. *Recommended Practice for the Installation of Exterior Insulation and Finish Systems*, Association of the Wall and Ceiling Industries-International, Washington, D.C., March 1986.
7. *SpecGUIDE 07240 - Exterior Insulation and Finish Systems*, The Construction Specifications Institute, Aug. 1987.
8. *Special Supplement: Exteriors Magazine*, Exterior Insulation Manufacturers Association, Washington, D.C., 1988.

See also ENVELOPES, BUILDING; WALLBOARD; ACRYLICS; SEALANTS; INSULATION, THERMAL; STYRENE RESINS

MARK WILLIAMS
BARBARA WILLIAMS
Kenney/Williams/Williams,
   Inc., Building Diagnostics
Maple Glen, Pennsylvania

STYRENE RESINS.   See SUPPLEMENT.

SUBWAY SYSTEMS.   See TRANSIT SYSTEMS.

SULLIVAN, LOUIS H.

Louis H. Sullivan was born in Boston, Massachusetts, to immigrant parents on September 3, 1856. His father, Patrick, a dancing master, had migrated to the city alone from his native Ireland in 1847, three years before Louis's mother, Andrienne List, arrived with her family from Switzerland. The second of their two sons, Louis lived with his grandparents and aunt and uncle, as well as with his mother and father until the age of five in a culturally and intellectually rich home environment. Members of the household spoke Gaelic, French, and German; were proficient at dance, drawing, and playing musical instruments; and held religious attitudes ranging from atheism and agnosticism to Baptism and Menonism. In 1862, his grandparents bought a farm in South Reading (now Wakefield), Massachusetts, enabling Louis to spend summers and occasionally entire school years in the country, from which he developed a lifelong love of nature. At the same time, as he and his father regularly explored Boston on foot, he learned to appreciate urban life and architecture. Louis accompanied his parents when they established short-lived dancing academies in Halifax, Nova Scotia, and Newburyport and Gloucester, Massachusetts, so that by the time he was 12 he had lived in a range of physical settings. This array of experiences and exposures made him an exceptionally independent boy. Having decided around age 11 to become an architect, he was willing to stay behind with his grandparents to study in Boston when his family moved to Chicago in 1868.

Commuting 20 mi round trip each day from Wakefield, young Sullivan graduated from the Rice Grammar School in 1870. In his sophomore year at English High he came under the influence of Moses Woolson, a gifted and imaginative teacher, who reinforced and stimulated Louis's intellectual inclinations. Eager to begin his life's work and bored as a junior, Sullivan applied in 1872 for early admission to the Building and Architecture program at the Massachusetts Institute of Technology, the only architecture school in the country at the time. He was accepted as a 16-year-old special student without a high school diploma after passing a rigorous battery of tests. But he found the MIT program, which was modeled on that of the Ecole des Beaux Arts in Paris, to be too traditional and too little concerned with social and architectural theory. So he left college in June 1873 after his first year to take a job with Frank Furness, a boisterous, innovative Philadelphia architect responsible for several major buildings in a kind of Greco–Gothic style and an outstanding ornamentalist after the manner of the Welsh theorist, Owen Jones. Laid off in November during the recession that year, Sullivan followed his parents to Chicago where he found a position with the prominent architect William Le Baron Jenney, a pioneer of metal frame construction in tall buildings. After six fruitful months with Jenney, Sullivan decided to return to school for theoretical grounding, this time to the acknowledged source of architectural wisdom, the Ecole des Beaux Arts. He sailed from New York in July 1874, arrived in Paris in August and, after a period of determined preparation, entered the Ecole in October where he remained for approximately three months. But

he found the Ecole as disappointing as MIT, in large part because of its concentration on Renaissance and classical ideas. After a tour of southern France and northern Italy, where he was staggered by Michelangelo's work, especially at the Sistine Chapel, Sullivan returned to Chicago in June 1875 as a free-lance draftsman.

One of the several architects he worked for during the next six years was Dankmar Adler, who was so impressed with Sullivan's drawing talent and his ability to devise architectural ornament that he made him a junior partner late in 1881 or early in 1882 and then full partner in the new firm of Adler & Sullivan, organized May 1, 1883. From the beginning of their association until July 11, 1895, when Adler temporarily quit architecture because of the national depression, Adler & Sullivan designed approximately 180 buildings. Of these, some 60 or one-third of the total—most commissioned before 1890—were single or multiple residences; 33 (18%) were commercial buildings (generally offices and stores); 27 (15%) were for manufacturing; 17 (9%) were theaters, music halls, and auditoriums; and 11 (6%) were warehouses. The remaining 31 (17%) ran the gamut from stables and mausoleums to railroad stations and libraries.

Adler and Sullivan complemented each other perfectly. Recognized as an outstanding acoustical and structural engineer as well as a reliable architect, Adler nonetheless understood his own limitations as a designer. Though eight years senior to his 26-year-old partner in 1883, Adler turned over to Sullivan full responsibility for facade composition and decorative work. Generally speaking, Adler took care of mechanicals and structurals, Sullivan handled the art, and together they worked out the program. Their mutual talents were first recognized in the theater and concert hall genre. Beginning in 1879, with Sullivan a free-lance assistant on Central Music Hall in Chicago, the partners produced eight reconstructions and one new theater over the next seven years, culminating in their grandest structure, the Chicago Auditorium Building (1886–1890).

The reconstruction of Chicago's Hooley's Theater in 1882 was the first commission to generate praise for Sullivan independent of Adler. He was, said one commentator, "the master spirit directing and shaping the creation" (1) of the new interior. By the time McVicker's Theater was remodeled in 1885, Sullivan's work was "the best" (2) of its kind in Chicago, according to one critic, "superior to anything heretofore seen in any public building in this country" (3), in the eyes of another. Even more impressive to contemporaries than Sullivan's rich enfoliated ornament in a carefully coordinated array of colors, however, was his handling of incandescent light. Adler & Sullivan's theaters did away with flaming chandeliers in favor of electric light fixtures worked into overhead decoration continuing down and around the room sides. The totality, evenness, and clarity of light startled observers accustomed to flickering gas lamps. Together with Adler's impressive acoustics and uninterrupted sight lines, Sullivan's lighting and ornament earned the firm a well-deserved reputation for excellence in theater design.

The same was said of Adler & Sullivan's offices, commercial structures, and factories. In a series of commissions in the 1880s—the 1881 Rothschild, 1882 Jeweler's, 1884 Troescher, and the 1887 Wirt Dexter and Selz, Schwab buildings being the best known—they developed several trademarks. Using isolated footings instead of continuous foundations when possible, Adler widened the spans between masonry-clad columns, thereby increasing fenestration. In his facade compositions, Sullivan projected the comparatively thin columns slightly forward of the building's main mass. The result was his tentative thrust at a system of vertical construction as well as illumination "far greater than is usually obtained by other architects," said a local building magazine. Their alleged motto, "let there be light," this magazine continued, assured them "abounding orders from confiding clients." Their private dwellings were also marked by "originality" and "common sense" (4).

This kind of reputation, but especially their theater successes, landed them the commission for the Auditorium Building on December 22, 1886. At $3,200,000, it was the costliest edifice in the city, and at 8,737,000 ft^3 of volume the largest in the nation. Running from Michigan Boulevard along Congress Street to Wabash Avenue, it was 63,350 ft^2 in plan in 10 stories plus a seven-floor, 40 × 70 ft tower. The program was ultimately arranged as a 400-room hotel on Michigan and partway down Congress, 136 offices and stores on Wabash and in the tower, and a 4200-seat concert hall that, with support facilities, occupied half the total area and one-third the volume of the entire structure, the largest permanent concert hall ever built at the time. The nonsteel building of load-bearing masonry walls weighing 110,000 tons confronted Adler with as many structural challenges as did the acoustics of the vast auditorium. But he solved them as successfully as Sullivan did the aesthetics.

Basing his facade composition loosely on Henry Hobson Richardson's Marshall Field Wholesale Store (1885–1887) in Chicago, Sullivan articulated the granite-and-limestone exterior in a rhythmic and utilitarian manner befitting both the cultural and commercial nature of its interior functions. The lavish auditorium, the main dining room, and the banquet hall were among the finest interior spaces Sullivan ever conceived. Taking his cue from Adler's acoustical requirements, his Auditorium Theater featured four elliptical arches, wider and higher toward the rear, dividing the ceiling into smooth ivory panels of the most delicate lacelike tracery. The arches were not structural, although they appeared to be, and Sullivan made them the basis of his decorative scheme. Chevron moldings divide their faces into hexagons enclosing enfoliated designs that flower into electric lights, into grilled bosses hiding air inlets, and into smaller triangles with additional foliage. The lights run down the arches and across the boxes illuminating the entire room softly and completely. To the rear of the hall where the coved ceiling soars dramatically to provide sight lines for the gallery, Sullivan placed an immense stained-glass skylight. In the great hall, one reviewer wrote, "the sight is one of the most remarkable . . . in the world" (5), an assessment echoing the general sentiment, including that of Montgomery Schuyler, the sober *Architectural Record* critic, who concluded, after considering the pros and cons of the building, that Louis Sullivan was "one of the most striking and interesting individualities among living architects" (6).

The Chicago Auditorium was completed in detail in February 1890. Its enormous success transformed the nature of Adler & Sullivan's practice, bringing in larger commissions from further afield. One new project that year provided Sullivan with the opportunity to tackle a problem that would consume his interest for the rest of the decade. Its solution ensured his place in history.

The problem was the high-rise office building, the skyscraper, as it came to be called in the 1890s. The challenge for Sullivan was not so much structural, for most of the load-bearing and mechanical obstacles to great height had already been solved, as it was the aesthetics of structure. Sullivan was convinced that this historically new building type required a new design treatment, not one based on analogies to other kinds of buildings or one rooted in history, as most architects believed. He saw the skyscraper as a symbol of U.S. business that was the basis of the national culture, and therefore as an opportunity to create a long-anticipated indigenous architectural style. So when Adler and he received a commission in 1890 from St. Louis brewer and real estate promoter Ellis Wainwright for what came to be a 10-story rental structure, Sullivan made the most of it.

His solution to the skyscraper problem did not come easily. Frank Lloyd Wright, his principal assistant at the time, remembered how Sullivan struggled over the facade composition, leaving the office for long walks, throwing away sketch after sketch, until finally he burst into Wright's room and threw a drawing on the table. "I was perfectly aware of what had happened," Wright recalled. "This was Louis Sullivan's greatest moment—his greatest effort. The 'skyscraper' . . . as an entity with . . . beauty all its own, was born" (7) (Fig. 1).

Sullivan outlined his skyscraper theory six years later in his most famous essay, "The Tall Office Building Artistically Considered" (9). By carefully analyzing the program requirements, he decided that skyscrapers had three major clusters of functions, each of which should be expressed separately. The first was public—seen on the one- or two-story base—consisting of entering and leaving, meeting and greeting, waiting, shopping, and locating the entrance from the outside. The second set of functions was private: various kinds of office work. And the third was architectural: the housing of mechanical equipment and storage in an attic that could also serve as an aesthetic device for terminating the facade in a decisive way.

Sullivan had in fact designed the Wainwright Building according to his as yet unwritten theory, with a two-story base treated in an expansive, sumptuous way with an easily identified entrance flanked by broad display windows; a shaft of seven identically articulated floors to indicate the similar nature of work in the various offices; and a richly decorated attic suggesting a crisp termination, and that the functions there were of yet a third and different order.

All this was but one aspect of Sullivan's thinking. It was necessary to differentiate the three principal functions, to be sure, but it was equally important to unite

Figure 1. The Wainwright Building (1890), St. Louis, Missouri (8). Courtesy of *The Architectural Record.*

them harmoniously at the same time, because he believed, as he had written earlier, that every building should reveal "a single, germinal impulse or idea, which shall permeate the mass and its every detail," so that "there shall effuse from the completed structure a single sentiment . . ." (10). What was the skyscraper's single sentiment? Or, as he asked himself in his 1896 essay: "What is the chief characteristic of the tall office building?" He answered in some of his most direct but most memorable prose. "It is lofty. . . . It must be tall, every inch of it tall. . . . It must be every inch a proud and soaring thing, rising in sheer exultation . . . from bottom to top . . . without a single dissenting line" (9). So Sullivan recessed the horizontals, projected forward the structural columns and nonstructural mullions, and took the corner piers all the way from sidewalk to cornice. His "system of vertical construction" was now complete.

But in his 1896 essay he had one more point to make, the most important point of all. Working from the particular to the general, Sullivan advanced his "final, comprehensive formula" for the solution of the skyscraper problem, indeed, of all architectural problems. All things in nature had shapes, forms, and outward appearances "that tell us what they are, that distinguishes them . . . from each other," he asserted. "Unfailingly in nature these shapes express the inner life," and when analyzed reveal that "the essence of things is taking shape in the matter of things." Life seeks form in response to needs, the life and the form being "absolutely one and inseparable." "Where function does not change," he insisted, "form does not change," so it was "the pervading law of all things . . . that form ever follows function. That," Sullivan emphasized, "is the law" (9). With the Wainwright Building and

the assertion of "form follows function," Louis Sullivan's place in architectural history was assured.

Between 1890 and 1895 Adler & Sullivan designed some 13 high-rise projects, only 5 of which were built: the Wainwright and the Union Trust Building (1892) in St. Louis, the Schiller Building (1891) and the Stock Exchange (1893) in Chicago, and the Guaranty Building (1894–1895) in Buffalo. But together with "The Tall Office Building Artistically Considered," they established Sullivan as the premier theorist of skyscraper design with a pioneering style of national importance.

One of the most significant unbuilt skyscraper projects was the 36-story Odd Fellows or Fraternity Temple Building (1891) for Chicago featuring a system of setbacks. Had it been built, the Temple would have been the tallest edifice in the nation. Its impressive scale—450 ft in height occupying an entire 177 × 210 ft block—dramatized certain social problems of which Sullivan was intensely aware, principally those of air and light for tenants and neighbors and of street congestion. In the December 1891 issue of *The Graphic,* a Chicago pictorial review, he proposed an innovative solution. The idea was that above a specified limit—twice the width, or 132 ft on a typical 66-ft thoroughfare, for example—building area should be reduced to 50% of the lot. At twice the limit it should be halved again to 25% and so on indefinitely. To prevent the city from becoming a maze of walled canyons, Sullivan would apply the formula to frontage as well as area, and for corner lots with one narrow and one wide street suggested the distance before setback be the sum of the two (11). Sullivan had already incorporated the principle vertically and horizontally in his 1891 Schiller Building, possibly the first true setback high-rise in the United States. And 25 years later in 1916, New York City's zoning law, which became a model for the nation, incorporated a variation on the theme by dividing central Manhattan into districts with setbacks beginning from one and one-quarter to twice the width of the streets.

By 1895 Sullivan's reputation had crossed the Atlantic. His "Golden Doorway" on the Transportation Building (1891) at the 1893 Chicago World's Fair was awarded a medal the next year by the Union Centrale des Arts Décoratifs in Paris, which exhibited models of his work. The Russian School of Applied Arts in Moscow also asked Sullivan to loan examples of his designs. His skyscrapers, by now even more refined and coherent than the Wainwright Building, were applauded by critics at home, as were his other buildings—tombs, synagogues, hotels, and opera houses conspicuous among them. Much in demand as a speaker and essayist, Sullivan was elected to the Board of Directors of the American Institute of Architects in 1894 and in 1895 to the Board's Executive Committee. A good measure of his standing was Montgomery Schuyler's conclusion in an 1895 issue of *The Architectural Record* that Louis Sullivan "is of the first rank among his contemporaries throughout the world" (12).

Under the surface, however, things had already begun to sour. The economic depression beginning in 1893—the worst in U.S. history to that point—had a devastating effect on architecture. In 1894, Adler & Sullivan received only six new commissions, less than half as many a year as from 1890 to 1893, and four of those were not constructed. With a wife and three children to support, 51-year-old Dankmar Adler terminated the partnership on July 11, 1895, to become architectural consultant and supervising sales manager for the Crane Elevator Company at the enviable salary of $25,000 a year. Although he soon realized he was unsuited to the work, returning to architecture just after the new year, Adler would not resume the partnership, believing that Sullivan had slighted him by claiming sole authorship of the Guaranty Building. For his part, Sullivan could not forgive Adler's disloyalty by leaving a 12-year association for what he took to be selfish reasons. There was no going back for the two proud men. Sullivan carried on alone in the old firm office atop the Auditorium Building Tower while Adler rented a suite several flights down. Although they collaborated briefly on a portion of a Schlesinger & Mayer Department Store project in 1898, their relationship remained strained. Dankmar Adler died suddenly from a stroke on April 16, 1900, at the age of 55.

The remainder of Sullivan's career was a long, sad story of decline, not in design ability or intellectual power, but in his ability to get clients. From 1895 until his last architectural job in 1922, he received some 56 commissions—2 per year on average—of which only 31 were executed. Only 3 were major works: the 1897–1898 Bayard-Condict Building in New York City, a 12-story loft structure, and 2 for the Schlesinger & Mayer Department Store (1898, 1902) in Chicago. The rest were mostly residences, small banks, factories, and shops. When the nation emerged from the depression in 1898 it seemed at first that Sullivan would also recover quite nicely, because between 1896 and 1899 he received 16 commissions, including 7 from Schlesinger & Mayer for alterations and new buildings. However, without that firm he would have had very little work. Never again after 1902 would he get more than 4 jobs in a single year or see to completion more than 2 a year. After 1899 Louis Sullivan slowly sank into grinding poverty.

The many reasons for this are complexly interwoven. Although he was accomplished in structural and mechanical aspects of design—thanks to Adler's tutelage—Sullivan was perceived as an idealistic artist, unsuitable for unrarified jobs; but because he was nonetheless recognized as a commercial architect, few people approached him for houses. He was known for giving clients exactly what they wanted, that is, for providing eminently workable and practical programs, but he was also known for doing things only his way, in his style, no discussion allowed. He was a reasonably good businessman, but not in public relations. Unless he liked people, felt comfortable with them, and respected their cultural sophistication, he was abrupt and condescending, frightening potential customers away. He was also prone to fits of anger, to arrogance, and to conveying the impression of superiority. With very few exceptions, he preferred his own company to that of others. He had also alienated the architectural establishment, specifically the AIA, with a series of intemperate public statements around 1900 condemning not only the "mustiness" of the profession generally but also the "stupidity," indeed, the "criminality" of particular in-

dividuals and groups. When all these factors conspired to drive clients away, he turned to alcohol that, beginning as an effect, soon became a cause of client trepidation. Frustration at his declining status and with the conservatism of the profession combined to make Louis Sullivan a very bitter man.

When he found work after 1900 and was willing to do it—he lost a number of commissions in his last years by provoking fights over totally irrelevant matters—he produced beautiful results. Best known after 1906 was his series of eight executed banks, including one remodeling, scattered across the Midwest in small cities and towns. The National Farmer's Bank (1906) in Owatonna, Minnesota, was a simple cube, 68 ft square by 40 ft high, in tapestry brick, punctuated by 38-ft-diameter semicircular stained-glass windows on two facades. The main banking room, with over 200 tints of color, was ringed by service and officers' areas, suggested on the exterior by small windows at eye level. Soft, diffused light saturated the building that conveyed two important images: a strongbox effect for the securing of valuables and an open, inviting feeling to reassure the agricultural clientele. The bank was such a huge success that the *Architectural Record* reported in 1912 that 25 strangers visited Owatonna each day just to see it.

There followed smaller banks in Cedar Rapids and Grinnell, Iowa; Newark and Sidney, Ohio; Columbus, Wisconsin; Manistique, Michigan; and West Lafayette, Indiana, designed in 1914 for a mere $14,700, an indication of his much-reduced circumstances. All of the banks bore a strong family resemblance, but Sullivan never quite repeated the program, ornament, or form. Each was beautiful, workable, and highly acclaimed by critics; all but one are used today for their original purpose. Paying respect to the scale of the neighborhood, Sullivan nevertheless set new standards for community aesthetics; each one remains a "jewel box" in its prairie surroundings. The banks also addressed their social and philosophical milieu. Sullivan called them "democratic," examples of the indigenous U.S. architecture he had devoted his life to creating. He meant that they were literally and visually accessible to customers. Officers sat in the open, not hidden away in remote sanctuaries. The main entrance was as welcoming as the vault was available, directly in view when customers entered, reassuring them that their valuables were safe. The buildings suggested that farmer and banker might come together easily in business and neighborly dialogue, as their murals in several cases depicted. Sullivan's banks were as important as his skyscrapers in his own work and in his contribution to the national architectural heritage.

In his last years, writing took up more of Sullivan's time than ever. Specific subjects changed, but once he had solidified his thinking in the 1890s his essential message remained the same. He always returned to the importance of architects studying nature to learn the secrets of structure, form, and creativity. He insisted that architecture should be about social life and values in its time and place and not be based on historic styles. Buildings, he argued, were about specific ideas, not about the bare facts of structure alone. He believed that U.S. architecture should be democratic in form and function, that is, it should endorse culturally agreed on customs, ideas, and feelings in familiar materials. Louis Sullivan was probably the first U.S. architect to contend that architecture was fundamentally an expression of social life. His antihistoricism and his cultural interpretation of design were taken up by Frank Lloyd Wright among others of the next generation who gave them permanent place in the mainstream of U.S. design thinking.

As his commissions dwindled away, Sullivan produced the three books for which he is remembered. *Kindergarten Chats* (13) first appeared in 1901–1902 in an obscure Cleveland journal. Constructed as a dialogue between an architectural master and his naive student, the *Chats* comprise some of Sullivan's most penetrating and accessible thinking on design and social issues. His memoirs, *The Autobiography of an Idea* (14), and his monograph, *A System of Architectural Ornament* (15), were published in 1924 at the time of his death. *The Autobiography* is an idiosyncratic example of its genre because it covered Sullivan's life only to 1893. Its real purpose was to chronicle the evolution of his quite private architectural inspiration and emotional development. *A System* is a series of 19 ornament plates with commentary explaining how Sullivan derived his exquisite patterns through geometric manipulation of organic forms. (A fourth book, *Democracy: A Man-Search,* was published posthumously in 1961 (16), as was *Kindergarten Chats* in book form, the first time in 1934 (17).) *The Autobiography* and *A System* were Sullivan's last major works.

The few years before his death were painful ones indeed. Deeply in debt, by 1909 he auctioned off his household goods and most of his architectural library in December. His wife of 10 years, Mary Azona Hattabaugh, left him a few days later. In 1910 he sold the beloved vacation home he had built for himself in 1890 in Ocean Springs, Mississippi. Unable to meet his club and organizational dues, he was dropped from their rolls. By 1918 he could no longer pay his rent, and with his former staff of 50 reduced to 1 or 2 draftsmen, gave up his Auditorium Tower office for much smaller rooms on Chicago's far South Side. Sometimes he had no office at all. Many of his days were spent atop the Fine Arts Building on Michigan Avenue where the Cliff Dwellers Club let him have a writing desk for free.

Sullivan survived his last years largely on the handouts of friends. Architects Sidney K. Adler (Dankmar's son), Max Dunning, George Nimmons, and Frank Lloyd Wright, plus associates at the American and Northwestern Terra Cotta companies, paid his bills, loaned him money, and often bought his meals. When he died on April 14, 1924, of kidney disease and inflammation of the cardiac muscles, they covered his funeral expenses and cleared up his financial obligations. The $189 in his bank account, which had also come from them, was almost all he owned.

Sullivan was buried on April 16, 1924, next to his father, Patrick, and his mother, Andrienne, in Chicago's Graceland Cemetery. In its obituary, *The New York Times* called him the "dean of American architects" (18),

and in short order the pages of the architectural magazines were filled with praise of his greatness. But he had died in poverty, in a cheap South Side hotel room, without an architectural job for his last two years.

Later on he would be remembered as the man who insisted that nature was the best design guide, who preached "progress before precedent," who argued that architecture was basically a social act, who first brought a coherent aesthetic system to the skyscraper, whose ornament was perhaps the finest ever produced in the United States, who built the first modern banks, who trained Frank Lloyd Wright, who influenced generations of progressive architects, and who was the first thoroughgoing innovator in U.S. architectural history.

BIBLIOGRAPHY

1. *The Daily Inter-Ocean,* 13 (August 12, 1882).

2. *The American Architect and Building News* **22,** 299–300 (Dec. 24, 1887).

3. *The Real Estate and Building Journal* **27,** 348 (July 18, 1885).

4. *Ibid.,* p. 348.

5. *The American Architect and Building News* **26,** 299 (Dec. 28, 1889).

6. M. Schuyler, "Architecture in Chicago," *The Architectural Record Great American Architects Series* (2), 48 (Dec. 1895) (Special Issue).

7. F. L. Wright, "Louis H. Sullivan—His Work," *The Architectural Record* **56,** 29 (July 1924).

8. *The Architectural Record* **57,** 290 (April 1925).

9. L. H. Sullivan, "The Tall Office Building Artistically Considered," *Lippincott's* **57,** 403–409 (March 1896).

10. L. H. Sullivan, "What is the Just Subordination, in Architectural Design, of Detail to Mass?" *The Inland Architect and News Record* **9,** 52 (April 1887).

11. L. H. Sullivan, "The High Building Question," *The Graphic* **5,** 405 (Dec. 19, 1891).

12. Ref. 6, p. 24.

13. L. Sullivan, "Kindergarten Chats," *Interstate Architect and Builder* **1–2,** (Feb. 1901–Feb. 1902).

14. L. Sullivan, *The Autobiography of an Idea,* AIA Press, New York, 1924.

15. L. Sullivan, *A System of Architectural Ornament,* AIA Press, New York, 1924.

16. L. Sullivan, *Democracy: A Man-Search,* Wayne State University Press, Detroit, Mich., 1961.

17. L. Sullivan, *Kindergarten Chats,* Scarab Fraternity Press, Lawrence, Kansas, 1934.

18. "Louis Henri Sullivan," *The New York Times,* 23 (April 16, 1924).

ROBERT TWOMBLY
West Nyack, New York

SURVEYING.   See ENGINEERING, CIVIL.

SUSPENSION CABLE STRUCTURES

Today's engineers and architects have at their disposal a rich and growing variety of ways to create light, long-span roofs that utilize cables as their principal load-carrying structural element. Cables are used to support roofs in three basic ways. In cable-supported structures, they are used to support rigid framing members that carry the roof loads. In cable-suspended systems, they serve as the direct load-carrying tension supports for a static roof system. In a cable-tent structure, the roofing membrane is prestressed and is itself in tension. Cables are also used to stabilize and tie down air-supported membrane roofs.

Suspension structures have existed since spiders began spinning webs. Before recorded history, man used vines to swing across, and eventually to span, rivers and gorges. Historical records indicate that iron chain bridges were built in China as early as 65 A.D. One of the earliest documented uses of a suspension roof structure is the sunshade for the Roman Colosseum, completed in 82 A.D. Ropes secured to masts spanned the arena in a radial pattern, supporting a giant removable fabric sunshade. The Incas of ancient Peru constructed the San Luis Rey Bridge over the Aspurimac River, c. 1350. Built of replaceable plaited and twisted ropes, it remained in use for approximately 450 years. A Tibetan monk, Than-Stong rGyal-Po (1385–1465), is credited with building a number of iron chain suspension bridges.

Many Europeans tried to determine the mathematical expression for a flexible inextensible member (ie, chain, rope, cable) hanging freely from two points, called a catenary from the Latin *catena*, for chain. Galileo worked on it in 1638, but came to the wrong conclusion. (He thought it was a parabola.) During the 1670s, many famous men, including Hooke, Wren, and Leibnitz, investigated the catenary. Jacob Bernoulli, in 1690, is generally credited with being the first to determine the equation of the catenary curve. Much of the interest in the catenary was due to the fact that it was realized that if the shape of the catenary's purely tensile curve was used upside down as an arch, it then would be in pure compression, an ideal situation for building with brick or stone, the common materials of the time.

Bronze wire rope was in use as part of a treadmill in 79 A.D., when Mt. Vesuvius erupted. However, wire rope was not manufactured in modern Europe until the 1830s. U.S. machine-made wire rope was first used in 1846. Currently, steel alloy wire rope cables are available in a variety of types and possess ultimate strengths up to 220,000 psi. Prestressing strands, originally developed for stressing concrete, are now being used for cable structures and have ultimate strengths approaching 300,000 psi.

One of the earliest examples of a cable roof was the exhibition pavilion built in 1896 at Nijny-Novgorod, Russia, by the engineer V. G. Shookhov. The Travel and Transport Building at the 1933 Chicago World's Fair was one of the first cable-supported roof structures built in the United States.

The first widely acclaimed permanent cable-suspended roof was not built until 1953, when the Polish architect Nowicki's design for a Livestock Judging Pavilion was erected in Raleigh, North Carolina (Fig. 1). This building is generally credited with starting the interest in, and wide ranging development of, suspended cable roofs. David Geiger's dramatic design for the 393-ft span gymnastic pavilion, built in Seoul, Korea, for the 1988 Olympics, is an exciting example of one of the many new forms that have evolved since the 1950s (Fig. 2).

Cable roof systems are usually considered as possible framing methods when large column-free open spaces, such as sports arenas and exhibition pavilions, need to be enclosed. Sometimes they are selected for the uniqueness of the shapes that can be obtained. Depending on the inherent geometry of the particular system and the creativity of the designers, an almost unlimited variety of architectural shapes can be achieved.

Cable roofs, such as the one designed by Frei Otto for the Munich Olympic Stadium (Fig. 3), can produce almost dreamlike free-form spaces. A surface of interlocking clear plastic panels was attached to a cable-net system, secured in turn from cable-stayed masts and flexible edge cables. Cables that rise (rather than drape) from their anchorage points are utilized as restraining and tie-down members for air-supported membrane roofs such as those over the huge stadia in Pontiac, Michigan (Fig. 4), and Minneapolis, Minnesota.

Figure 1. Livestock Judging Pavilion, Raleigh, N. Carolina.

Figure 2. Olympic Gymnastic Pavilion, Seoul, Korea. Courtesy of David Geiger.

Because cables assume a draped contour between their points of support, they inherently make sense as a system for roofs rather than floors. A cable is too thin and too flexible to be capable of resisting or transmitting any forces other than tensile ones. They are not called on to resist buckling compression or shear (as a beam or truss would be), and thus are very efficient in the amount of material used in relation to their span. For this reason, a cable structural system is more efficient, in the sense that less material is needed to support a given load. It has been calculated that using normal allowable working stresses, a 36-in. wide–flange beam could carry its own weight for a distance of about 220 ft, whereas a suspended steel cable with a 10% sag could carry its own weight for approximately 3.3 mi.

The geodesic dome and the lamella arch were alternative framing methods that until the early 1970s challenged the spanning capability of cable roof systems for constructing arena-type buildings. The Louisiana Superdome is covered with a steel lamella-type dome with a

Figure 3. Munich Olympic Stadium. (**a**) View; (**b**) Cable structure.

Figure 4. Silverdome Stadium, Pontiac, Michigan.

678-ft span. The National Center for Industry, in Paris, is roofed with a 720-ft span, double-layer concrete dome. Modern cable roof systems are far lighter and are currently less costly on a square foot basis than competitive long-span framing methods. While cable systems can ultimately span much greater distances than any other type of support system, as in the case of suspension bridges, buildings (so far at least) have not been required to go nearly so far. The current record for the longest spanning suspension bridge is the 4626 ft of the Humber Estuary Bridge in the UK.

Architecturally, the drape of a cable system will produce entirely different types of interior space underneath it than flat roofs, folded plates, arches, or domes. For this reason, architects will continue to use these alternate framing systems, especially for more modest spans. At extremely large distances, the sag depth could bring the center of a suspended roof down to such a degree as to cause spatial problems that would not be present under a more traditional type of enclosed space. Cable-stayed, air-supported roofs and the recently developed cable dome now offer lightweight, long-span alternatives to the shapes of the traditional compression domes.

There are a variety of interacting decisions involved in the selection of any framing system, and architects must be aware of the ramifications and implications of their choices. Considerations that must be investigated, along with the visual impact of the particular shape being contemplated, are the ramifications of the structural configuration on items such as flutter caused by wind, drainage of rain and snow from any low points, and the integration of air-conditioning ducts and lighting fixtures with the underside of the roof surface. The way these issues are resolved can either enhance or destroy the aesthetic clarity of the space. The manner by which the cables are terminated and secured to an anchorage system and the method used to attach the roof deck to the cable supports are also major considerations, as these items are usually left exposed to view and impact on the overall appearance of the building.

Cable-suspended structures support or carry a roof deck in two basic ways: the deck can be either secured directly to the cables (Fig. 5) or hung below them (Fig. 6). The type of system selected determines the final curve shape. A flexible inextensible cable that is freely draped between two points will, due to its own weight, assume a catenary curve. A suspended cable that supports a roof deck in a manner that transmits the roof load uniformly along the actual cable length will thus approximate a catenary curve (Fig. 7). If a horizontal surface, such as a uniformly loaded roof or bridge deck, is suspended below the supporting cables on a series of vertical hangers spaced an equal distance apart along a horizontal projection, the drape of the supporting cable will approximate a parabolic curve (Fig. 8). However, strictly speaking, it will actually be a funicular polygon, having many small straight sections between each vertical hanger. (To be absolutely precise, each section of the funicular polygon between the vertical hangers will sag a miniscule amount.) The overall shape is usually considered a parabola. From a visual point of view, the parabola and the catenary appear very much alike. From an engineering point of view, however, they behave differently. By the time a cable system has been loaded (and not always symmetrically), stiffened by its roof system, posttensioned, and anchored in place, it is unlikely to have remained a simple mathematical curve.

The use of a suspended cable system to support a flat deck is a logical option for long-span bridges, but from an architectural point of view, the appearance of a suspended flat roof, when seen from below, raises the traditional philosophical question: should the true expression of the

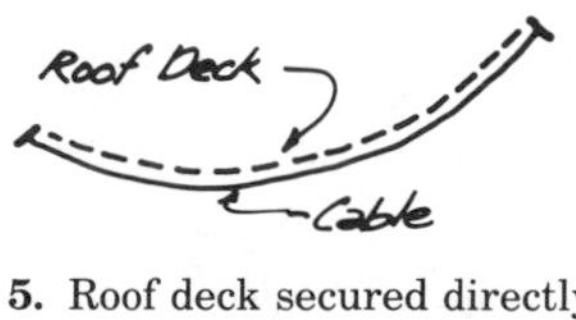

Figure 5. Roof deck secured directly to cables.

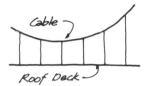

Figure 6. Roof deck suspended below cables. Roof shape is independent of cable configuration.

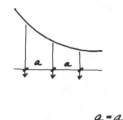

a-a

Figure 8. Parabolic curve.

structural system be discernible? In bridges, both the supporting cables and the flat deck (roadway) are perceived simultaneously; the equivalent phenomenon is not observable from inside a building with an opaque flat roof. Because a roof, unlike a bridge deck or floor, usually does not need to be flat, it can be attached directly to the drape of the structural cables and express the nature of the support system.

Suspended cable roofs can be placed in one of two general categories, open and closed. An open cable system is one in which the horizontal component of the cable's pull has not been resolved and, therefore, will require an anchorage system that can resist both vertical and horizontal forces. A closed system is one that resolves the horizontal forces within it and thus only needs vertical support at the perimeter. An example of an open system would be a series of masts supporting the roof cables. While the unstabilized masts would be capable of carrying the vertical component of the load transmitted to them from the cable, they would tend to tilt inward in response to the cable's pull and thus, in turn, need to be stayed by a cable secured to an anchorage. A system of cables secured to a continuous perimeter compression member would be an example of a closed system. The perimeter of this system could be supported by a series of columns that only need to carry a vertical load.

One of the most common closed-system configurations for cable-suspended roofs is a circular or radial one (Fig. 9). A basic radial system consists of a set of cables spanning between a circumferential compression ring (Fig. 10a) and a central tension ring (Fig. 10b). The tension ring at the hub is necessary to prevent all of the cables from intersecting at a single point, a physically impossible situation. The central ring also provides a means of maintaining a uniform drape as well as simplifying construction. The compression ring can be supported on a series of columns or on a bearing wall. The natural tendency of lightweight roofs to flutter can be controlled by the introduction of a second set of cables, located below the suspen-

sion set and spanning from the central tension ring to anchorages located along the perimeter. The second set of cables can also serve to reduce the sag-to-span ratio of the roof structure or permit greater spans. In a radial system, the outer compression ring acts as a continuous arch and thus is self-stabilizing.

When a series of cables are draped between two parallel supporting systems, a single curve roof is created (Fig. 11). Complicated, undulating shapes can be generated when the opposite lines of support are not parallel. The cable ends must be anchored with a support system that is stable enough to resist the horizontal component of their pull. When cables are secured to masts, as mentioned earlier, the mast must be stayed by other cables.

As in the case of the radial systems, secondary sets of cables can be used to control flutter and decrease the amount of sag (Fig. 12). When a second set of cables having a reverse curvature to those of the suspension cables is introduced in the same plane as the suspension cables and connected to them, a lighter and stiffer system can be achieved. This type of system must be tensioned sufficiently to ensure that both the upper and lower cables remain in tension under any type of loading situation. These types of tensioned systems, referred to as cable beams by engineers, can take a variety of shapes. A con-

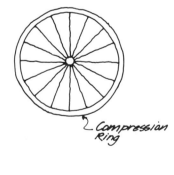

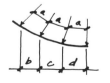

b<c<d

Figure 7. Catenary curve.

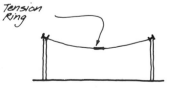

DOUBLE CURVATURE

Figure 9. Radial system.

(a)

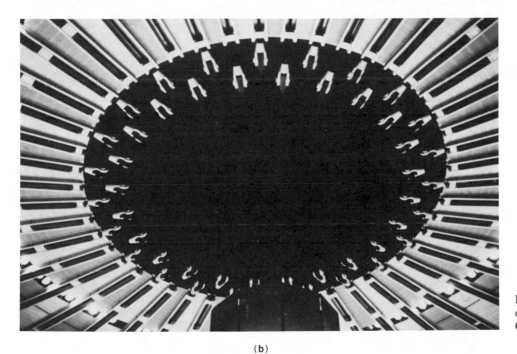

(b)

Figure 10. Madison Square Garden, New York, N.Y. (**a**) View; (**b**) Center tension ring.

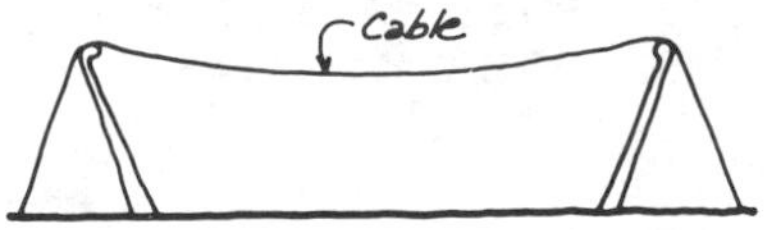

Figure 11. Single curvature roof with one set of cables.

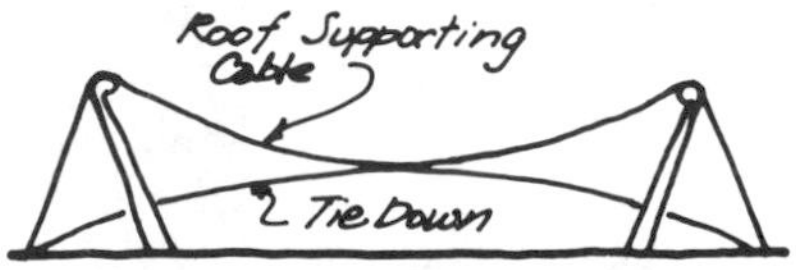

Figure 12. Single curvature roof with double set of cables.

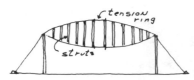

Figure 13. Convex cable beam with separating struts.

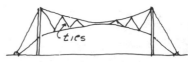

Figure 15. Jawerth cable beam with pretensioned diagonal ties

vex cable beam has vertical compression struts separating the cables (Fig. 13), and a concave cable beam has vertical tension ties securing the cables (Fig. 14). A cable truss system developed by the Swedish engineer David Jawerth resembles a concave cable beam, but has a pattern of diagonal ties connecting the cables in a way that creates a series of pretensioned triangles that make up the truss (Fig. 15).

When a secondary set of tie-down cables is placed at a right or oblique angle to the main set of supporting cables, a double curvature surface is generated. Both the primary and secondary set of cables must be anchored. The necessity of anchoring the secondary set of cables can cause difficult design problems if a building's geometry is complicated. For example, in the Yale hockey rink (Fig. 16), to prevent interference with the architectural form of the openings at the ends of the building, a special set of hidden trusses was introduced within the ceiling in order to provide anchorage for the longitudinal tie-down cables (Fig. 17).

A variety of methods can be employed to secure roof decks to cable systems. Three examples, each using a different material, follow.

The Yale hockey rink (fondly dubbed "the whale" by undergraduates) has a wood plank roof deck covered by a flexible waterproof membrane. Wood blocking was

clamped to the top of the cables with simple U-bolts (Fig. 18). The tongue-and-groove wood decking used to span between the cables was simply nailed to the wood blocking above each cable. The method is neat, simple, and all details are left exposed to view (Fig. 19).

Dulles International Air Terminal in Washington, D.C., has a precast concrete roof deck (Fig. 20). The architect, Eero Saarinen, used the roof cables to support steel reinforcing rods that extended out of each precast concrete roof panel. The space between adjacent panels was then filled with poured-in-place concrete, protecting the protruding rods and support cables and creating a stiff, continuous, monolithic roof deck (Fig. 21).

Madison Square Garden arena in New York City utilizes metal clamps spaced along the support cables. The clamps are connected to a pair of steel channels that straddle each cable. These exposed channels, in turn, support the roof deck (Fig. 22).

There are four basic ways of terminating the ends of cables so they can be secured to their structural supports or anchorage. The two most common methods of securing a cable require the attachment of a fitting to the cable end. These fittings can be either swaged or poured. In a swaged fitting, which is usually used for lighter cables, the fitting is placed around the cable and then squeezed securely in place by a high pressure hydraulic press (Fig. 23). When the fitting is poured, the cable wire ends are splayed and zinc is poured into a socket basket, which surrounds the wires (Fig. 24). Cable fittings are available with a variety of end configurations that can be pinned to, clamped to, or inserted into an anchorage (Fig. 25).

When small diameter cables such as prestressing strands are used, a variety of wedge-type anchors may be used to secure their ends. Wire rope can be looped over a thimble so that it will fold back on itself without kinking, creating a loop eye for attachment. The return leg of the cable is fastened to the live cable with U-bolt clamps. This

Figure 14. Concave cable beam with tension ties.

Figure 16. Yale Hockey Rink, New Haven, Connecticut.

Figure 17. Yale Rink, concealed anchor trusses.

Figure 19. Connection of cables to center concrete arch, Yale Rink.

type of termination is frequently used for temporary connections during construction.

A strand is a symmetrical arrangement of wires wrapped helically around a central wire. A rope is a number of strands wrapped helically around a core, which may be another strand, a wire or some other material. A cable is one or more strands or wire ropes.

Turnbuckles are generally provided along each cable so the entire system can be "tuned" to the required tension. Recently, computer calculations have provided high enough initial accuracy to make this unnecessary for some structures.

When wind forces move across the top of a curved roof surface, they create serious problems of uplift or flutter in the roof deck, similar to those created by wind moving over an airplane wing. This problem is intensified when the roof deck is constructed out of lightweight materials, which is often the condition encountered with cable-suspended structures. This problem is usually solved by one (or a combination) of three approaches: adding additional dead weight to the decking system, introducing a separate set of tie-down cables, or introducing rigidity into the system.

Madison Square Garden is an example of an increased dead weight solution. The mechanical equipment was placed above the cable system in order to dampen it (Fig. 26). The roof of Philip Johnson's New York State Pavilion for the 1964 World's Fair was stabilized with a set of tie-down cables that extended from an inner tension ring to supports along the outer circumference (Fig. 27).

At Dulles International Air Terminal, precast concrete panels were supported on a system of parallel cables. Concrete was poured around each cable (the cables were located in the gap between panels), in effect making a rigid beam out of the combination of cable and concrete (Fig. 21).

Lev Zetlin used two sets of cables to create a "bicycle wheel" for the roof of the Utica, New York, 240-ft-diameter auditorium. The double-layered center tension ring resembles a drum. One set of cables goes from the drum top to the peripheral compression ring while the second set goes from the underside of the drum back to the same

Figure 20. Dulles Air Terminal, Washington, D.C.

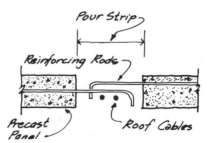

Figure 21. Connection of concrete roof deck to cable system, Dulles.

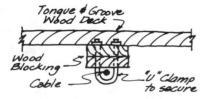

Figure 18. Connection of wood roof deck to cable system, Yale Rink.

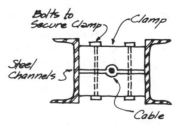

Figure 22. Connection of steel purlins to cable system, Madison Square Garden.

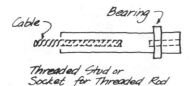

Figure 23. Swaged (clamped on) cable end fitting.

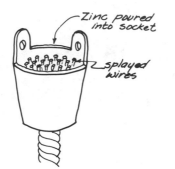

Figure 24. Poured cable end fitting.

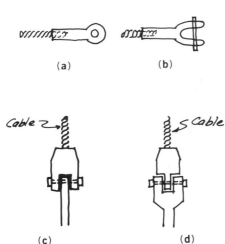

Figure 25. Cable end connections. (a) Eye; (b) Clevis; (c) Open socket; (d) Closed socket.

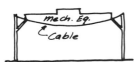

Figure 26. Dead weight of mechanical equipment located above the roof controls flutter, Madison Square Garden.

compression ring (Fig. 28). Vertical struts keep the two cable systems separated. This double-layer system of cables provides a self-damping solution to the flutter problem. Another method of creating rigidity in a roof deck is by posttensioning a set of cables strung through a concrete deck system.

The particular method selected to resolve the issue of flutter has a marked effect on the ultimate appearance of the building, as the shape of the surface created by the underside of the cables dominates the mood of the interior space. The space enclosed between the cable planes in a

double-layer system can be utilized for ducts and lighting fixtures.

The dish shape and undulating curvatures of the various types of suspended roofs create low points that will collect rain and snow. The most straightforward way of removing the water is by roof drains that connect directly to leaders below them. Because the typical cable sag pattern creates a low point at the center of the roof, it means that roof leaders will originate in the middle of the interior space and may create an awkward appearance as they slope over to the periphery, before they can turn and run vertically (Fig. 29). An additional architectural advantage of a double set of cables is that the drainage piping can pitch within the open space between the upper and lower cable layers to a vertical leader located at the circumference of the building (Fig. 30). (A pitch of 1/4 in. per lineal foot is all that is normally needed for storm water drainage.) Occasionally, due to the nature of a building's use, it may be feasible to place a vertical leader directly under the low point of the roof, creating an architectural feature rather than trying to disguise it. Dulles International Air Terminal is a striking case in point (Fig. 31). When used in this manner, however, there is the possibility that the rain leader will be perceived as a structural support.

Water can also be removed from low points with a pump activated by a float valve, as in the case of Edward Stone's Garden State Arts Center (Fig. 32). The water is pumped through pipes or hoses that follow the uphill sweep of the cable curve to the high point. From there, the water can flow by gravity through leaders into the storm water system. Obviously this type of system is expensive and subject to freeze-ups and mechanical failure. Standby

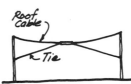

Figure 27. Tie down cables control flutter, New York State Pavilion.

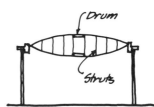

Figure 28. Double cable layer dampens flutter, Utica N.Y. Auditorium.

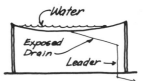

Figure 29. Exposed roof drainage system.

pumps must be provided to prevent overloading the roof with entrapped water. Ponding is always a serious potential problem, especially with lightweight pocketed roof shapes. Even gravity drains can clog, and sufficient redundant drains must be provided to prevent disaster.

The mechanical equipment necessary for heating, ventilating, and air-conditioning (HVAC) the large open spaces created by cable systems can be located on top of the roof (Fig. 26), between the cable sets on a double set system (Fig. 33), or placed entirely outside the roof system (Fig. 34). The latter is often not practical in large structures, because the distribution pattern of ducts tends to become longer, less efficient, and visually awkward to integrate. In smaller structures, it may be possible to obtain adequate environmental comfort levels using only a perimeter HVAC system, and thus avoiding the problem of intergrading a duct pattern with the ceiling design.

Cables share a common problem with all steel framing systems in that they can fail structurally when exposed to fire. The vast majority of cable-suspended roofs are constructed over large arenas, exhibit halls, ice rinks, and other similar structures, which by their very nature place the roof system high above the floor. The combination of two factors, easy access to multiple exits along the perimeter of the building and the isolation of the roof deck and cables by virtue of their being located high above any flammable fuel source, will normally satisfy building code requirements for permitting the use of unprotected or exposed materials for the roof. In situations where the cables and roof deck are within 20 ft of the floor or seating level, they then are usually required to be shielded or insulated to protect them from fire.

Although the image of cables is generally associated

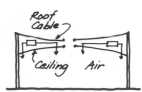

Figure 33. Mechanical equipment located between cable sets.

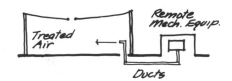

Figure 34. Mechanical equipment placed outside of main structure.

Figure 35. High-rise structures can use cables to support exterior edge of building, freeing plaza area underneath from columns.

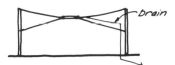

Figure 30. Concealed roof drainage system.

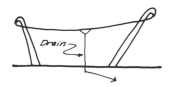

Figure 31. Roof drainage system treated as an architectural feature, Dulles Air Terminal.

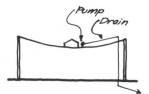

Figure 32. Pumping system removes standing water from roof surface, Garden State Arts Center.

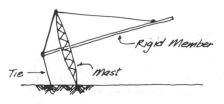

Figure 36. Cable-supported grandstand roof.

Figure 37. Schlumberger Ltd., Cambridge, England.

with bridges and roofs, they have many other structural uses. In the Westcoast Transmission Co. building in Vancouver, B.C. (Fig. 35), the perimeter ends of the floor beams are hung from cables suspended from outriggers at the roof and secured back to the central concrete building core. Pretensioned or posttensioned wires and cables in reinforced concrete construction are common examples of flexible steel in pure tension, as is the use of cables to pretension or posttension steel beams and trusses in order to increase their load-carrying capacity or decrease their depth.

Cable-supported bridge decks are becoming increasingly common, and the same structural principle is used to support rigid long-span girders or cantilevered beams for roofing grandstands (Fig. 36), airplane hangars, arenas, and factories. The support cables can radiate from a single anchor point at the top of a mast to a series of uniformly spaced support points along the bridge deck or roof beam. When the horizontal span of the girder being supported becomes large, the anchorage points on the mast can be stepped to permit those cables going to the more remote support points to have a steeper, and therefore more efficient, angle of support. Undulating roof forms of tensioned fabrics supported by cable-stayed masts and cable networks have created distinctive architectural statements (Fig. 37), entirely different from traditional building forms, yet romantically reminiscent of ships and tents.

Architecturally, there is no one right shape or framing method for covering a particular space, but an array of methods, each with its unique set of advantages and disadvantages. Cable-suspended roofs add a wide set of options that greatly enrich the architectural palette. New forms are constantly being developed. The technologies involved are on the cutting edge of engineering.

BIBLIOGRAPHY

General References

Gotthilf, Goetz, and Schierle, *Lightweight Tension Structures,* University of California Press, Berkeley, Calif., 1986.

Scalzi, Podolny, and Tang, *Design Fundamentals of Cable Roof Structures, ADUSS 55–3580–01,* U.S. Steel Corp., Pittsburgh, Pa., 1969.

J. Szabo, *Structural Design of Cable Suspended Roofs,* Halstead Press, a division of John Wiley & Sons, Inc., New York, 1984.

C. Roland, *Frei Otto: Tension Structures,* Praeger, New York, 1970.

H. Bucholdt, *An Introduction to Cable Roof Structures,* Cambridge University Press, Cambridge, UK, 1985.

P. Krishna, *Cable-Suspended Roofs,* McGraw-Hill Inc., New York, 1978.

H. Irvine, *Cable Structures,* MIT Press, Cambridge, Mass., 1981.

Manual for Structural Applications of Steel Cables for Buildings, American Iron and Steel Institute, Washington, D.C., 1973.

Cable Roof Structures, 2318–A, Bethlehem Steel Corp., Bethlehem, Pa., 1968.

See also MEMBRANE STRUCTURES; SPACE FRAMES

DAVID GUISE
New York, New York

SWEET'S CATALOG FILES

Sweet's Catalog Files, a series of more than 50 hardbound volumes containing individual catalogs from manufacturers of building products, provides a unique marketing system, bringing together buyers and sellers of construction products. Published annually by the Sweet's Division of McGraw-Hill Information Systems Co., *Sweet's Catalog Files* is distributed to design professionals who influence construction specification and purchase. Utilizing the huge computerized data base of individual construction projects from McGraw-Hill's F. W. Dodge Division, Sweet's is able to pinpoint the architectural, engineering, design, and specification offices that do over 90% of the construction planning in the United States. By including their product information in *Sweet's Catalog Files,* manufacturers of building products are assured that their catalogs are distributed to the most active design and specification offices.

Architects, engineers, and other construction specifiers use *Sweet's Catalog Files* daily to compare, evaluate, select, and specify building products and equipment for the buildings they are designing. The individual catalogs do more than just illustrate products: they provide total product information—product descriptions, applications, technical design data, details, specifications, availability, and ordering information—that busy professionals need when specifying building products. Because Sweet's is found in the architectural and design offices doing over 90% of the dollar volume, the files also serve as a standard reference for all building planners to refer to when collaborating on a particular building project.

The files are organized according to an industry-recognized five-digit classification system developed by Sweet's and members of the construction industry, including the American Institute of Architects (AIA), the Construction Specifications Institute (CSI), the Construction Products Manufacturers' Council (CPMC), the Associated General Contractors of America (AGC), and the Consulting Engineers Council (CEC). Using the Sweet's Data Filing Format, product catalogs are classified and subdivided under 16 divisions, making it easier for the design professionals to locate information on a particular type of product.

Sweet's first catalog file was a 760-page, single volume distributed to 7000 architects in 1906 by Clinton W. Sweet. Mr. Sweet was also the owner and publisher of *The Architectural Record*, a quarterly journal covering construction and real estate, and the forerunner of McGraw-Hill's current monthly magazine of the same name. Clinton Sweet and his editor, Henry Desmond, created the catalog file as a solution to the disorganization being caused by the mass of nonstandardized, odd-size product catalogs arriving in architectural offices. This created problems both for the architect, who was not able to retrieve information about products efficiently, as well as for the manufacturer, whose catalog may have been lost or discarded, rendering it ineffective as a sales–marketing tool.

Thomas Nolan, a prominent professor of architecture, described the catalog problem in the introduction to the first edition of *Sweet's Indexed Catalogue of Building Construction* (1):

> For a period of a dozen years, every possible method of collecting, sorting, classifying, filing and indexing all the catalogues and circulars of building materials was conscientiously given a fair trial, and after a thorough test, every method was just as conscientiously abandoned. They were abandoned because they did not work well in the specification room. They were not practicable. Everything was tried, arrangements of shelves, bookcases, pasteboard boxes, filing cases, patent binders, filing cabinets, cases of drawers, indexing schemes and "index-reruns." At first, all the big books were put together in one place and all the little books in another place; and then all the big and little books were mixed up together, and indexed according to subject. Some had four pages, and some had four hundred pages. Barely two were of the same shape or superficies. . . . Then the writer decided, after much time and expense, that the present system of publishing and

distributing catalogues, as far as the architect is concerned, might be rightly termed "The Catalogue Delusion," and that the only solution of the problem must lie in a scientific standard catalogue and index of building materials and construction, gradually developed toward an ideal result by the cooperation of manufacturer and architect.

Eighty years later, in 1986, *Sweet's Catalog Files* had grown to 50 volumes containing nearly 6000 catalogs, a total of nearly one billion pages of product information reaching a million specifiers with ten thousand building products, updated annually.

In addition, Sweet's now distributes catalog files to nine construction markets: *General Building and Renovation*, which covers commercial, institutional, high use residential and public building; *Industrial Construction and Renovation*, added in 1914 to cover construction of manufacturer plants, warehouses, power plants, and utilities; *Homebuilding and Remodeling*, added in 1941, covering single-family and low-rise, multifamily residential construction; *Contract Interiors*, added in 1969 for the commercial interior design market; and three engineering files, *Mechanical Engineering and Retrofit*, added in 1976, *Electrical Engineering and Retrofit*, added in 1978, and *Civil Engineering and Retrofit*, added in 1980. Canadian and International manufacturing firms from all construction disciplines are covered, respectively, in the *Canadian File*, first published in 1966, and the *International File*, published in 1985.

In the early 1920s, two architects joined Sweet's as liaisons between architects and building product manufacturers. These consultants helped manufacturers interpret the informational needs of architects and specifiers and assisted them in preparing their product information from the user's viewpoint. This eventually led to a change, in 1927, with Sweet's placing a new emphasis on individual catalog design for each manufacturer, product advertising being replaced with product information specifically geared to the architect, engineer, or specifier.

As the construction market grew increasingly complicated, with new technology changing the way buildings were being constructed and broadening the choice of building materials and components, Sweet's team of architectural consultants grew in importance. Today Sweet's employs 16 architectural and engineering consultants in offices across the United States, who act as the communication link between manufacturers and users of building products. To improve the effectiveness of a manufacturer's product information, these consultants study building product manufacturer's marketing objectives and analyze their products; recommend catalog content, organized following a standard format (*Sweet's Guide-Lines*); and with in-house designers' assistance, suggest visual form and graphics. Additionally, whenever a manufacturer uses Sweet's catalog printing service, the Sweet's design–production team also transforms the content and format into the final printed form. The result is not only an effective marketing tool for the manufacturer, but a readily accessible specifying medium for the user.

In 1974, as an aid in preparing construction product information and to guide architects in the selection process, Sweet's introduced *Sweet's GuideLines,* a system for determining catalog content as well as its organization, storage, and retrieval; and in 1978, *Sweet's Selection Data,* a volume of generic information about products and materials, was introduced. Sweet's also provides a number of value-added marketing services for building product manufacturers including high volume discounts for printing catalogs, mailing lists of prospective customers, and a toll-free telephone locator service, initiated in 1974 and called Sweet's BuyLine. The BuyLine service puts specifiers of building products in touch with the local sales representative for building products they are considering.

Most importantly, foreseeing the needs of the construction industry, Sweet's, in 1983, along with its sister company, F. W. Dodge, formed the Coordinating Council for Computers in Construction (CCCC). The CCCC now serves as a forum for cooperative development and control of computer uses so all construction participants can benefit. As research conducted by the Council indicated more and more computerization of the architectural, engineering and design professions, Sweet's developed plans to make its catalogs available electronically. In 1985, the company announced its entry into the electronic storage and retrieval of building product information, *Electronic Sweets,* a multimillion dollar project aimed at bringing manufacturers' product information and other construction database services into design offices on their computers.

By 1989, *Sweet's Catalog Files* and the companion product, *Electronic Sweets,* will be delivered as a unit to all qualified professional firms in the construction industry. Both services will be used together, or singly, depending on the depth and complexity of the product search and the needs of the construction professional.

BIBLIOGRAPHY

1. T. Sweet, ed., *Sweet's Indexed Catalogue of Building Construction,* 1906.

General References

K. Longberg-Holm and L. Sutnar, *Catalog Design,* Sweet's Catalog Service, division of F. W. Dodge Corp., New York, 1944.

K. Longberg-Holm and L. Sutnar, *Catalog Design Progress: Advancing Standards in Visual Communication,* Sweet's Catalog Service, division of F. W. Dodge Corp., New York, 1950.

M. Mayer, *The Builders: Houses, People, Neighborhoods, Governments, Money,* W. W. Norton & Co., Inc., New York, 1978, pp. 260–262.

See also Construction Project Report Services; Estimating, Cost; Specifications

Joseph V. Bower
McGraw-Hill Information
Systems Company
New York, New York

SWIMMING POOLS

People have been swimming since before recorded history. In fact, humans probably evolved out of the water. Going in the water and swimming has been done for many reasons: religious, health, exercise and sport, and as a military strategy, as well as the simple objective of cleanliness.

This article deals with the pools and buildings designed and built to accommodate these various activities. It does not deal with pools built for purely decorative purposes, such as fountains and reflecting pools; rather, it concerns those designed for human use. This article is divided along functional headings. In actuality, of course, the same pool may be used for several functions: recreation, competition, health, etc. The article attempts to stress only those requirements that differ to respond to a particular function to avoid repetition. Finally, this is not intended to be a "how to" article. Although specific guidelines of shapes and sizes recommended for pools of different functions are included, codes vary in different countries and locations, and are often being changed. Whole books have been written on construction and mechanical systems. This is a broad outline and points toward areas of concern and importance in the design and construction of swimming pools to help those working on specific projects to get started in the right direction.

HISTORY

The history of pools in many ways is the history of bathing—its styles and its attributes (Table 1). General cleanliness has been the most common reason for going into water throughout history. Swimming or immersion was considered to have both good mental and physical aspects. Early pictographs, bas-reliefs, and sculptures have established that people have been swimming for over 2000 years. From cleansing and swimming came training rituals and finally general bathing and competitive swimming.

Ceremonial purification became another reason for bathing beginning in the thirtieth century B.C. in the Indus Valley. Temples were erected along the Nile and Ganges. Gradually this open and simple form of purification evolved into a more elaborate and private ceremony by priests and followers to include oils and fragrant herbs in private temple spaces. The Mosaic code of the Hebrews also required ritual washing and, in turn, the Muslims incorporated this concept into their ritual. For the Hindus bathing was a religious duty. Bathing for pleasure or comfort is attributed to the Greeks, although baths have been discovered prior to Greek history. The Minoan palace at Knossos had a very sophisticated bathing arrangement with drainage systems and interlocking joints that may indicate they had developed an upward flow of water. Some Egyptian excavations indicate as sophisticated a bathing system as the one on Crete. It is known that priests washed themselves ritually four times a day and it

Table 1. Leading Baths of the Ancients[a]

Century		Baths and Thermae
B.C.	30th	Indus Valley, earliest baths for purification and lustral immersion
	25th	Great bath at Mohenjo-daro in the Indus Valley was made from burnt brick backed by a layer of bitumen, surrounded by a paved walk and eight small baths, all probably served by the same well
		Egyptian swimming bas-reliefs of Nagada
	15th	Minoan bronze age bath systems in Crete at Palaces of Knossos and Phaistos
	14th	Tel el Amarna sacred bathing lakes and Egyptian palaces of Medinet Habu and Malkata
	9th	Assyrian martial swimming bas-reliefs from the reign of Ashurnasirpal II
	5th	Greek luxury bathhouses and gymnasiums included provision for the poor
	4th	Baths of Heracles, attributed as first Greek baths to use heated water
	3rd	Piscina publica, the earliest Roman bath following the construction of Appius Claudius aqueduct
	1st	Stabian and forum, the earliest bathing complexes installed in Pompeii
A.D.	1st	Baths of Nero
		Central baths were under construction when Pompeii was overwhelmed. Titus Baths introduced great statues into bathhouses
		Aquae Sulis, unique Romano–British bathing establishment at Bath, England
	2nd	Trajan Baths, new aqueducts and public buildings commemorating the height of the Empire
		Great Baths of Lepcis Magna
		Hadrian's Baths including a private villa bath at Tivoli
	3rd	Caracalla thermae occupied 33 acres: the main bath 1100×1100 ft catered to 2000 bathers plus seating for 1600 (inspiration for main waiting room of Pennsylvania, New York, railway station and St. George's Hall, Liverpool, UK)
	4th	Diocletian bath, the largest thermae in the world catered to 18,000 at a time. The main bath held 3200 and was twice as large as anything similar: it was built in 305 A.D. by an army of workmen including 40,000 Christian slaves. The Vestibule was eventually converted by Michelangelo into the Church of Santa Maria del Angeli, 1563
		Constantine baths, the last of the great thermae in Rome before the capital was transferred to New Rome (Constantinople)
	5th	Baths in Rome now equaled one establishment for every 1000 citizens. In the city at this time, there were 11 public baths, 856 private baths, and 1352 fountains and cisterns, at the culmination of 13 aqueducts
	6th	Luxury Roman bath design continued in the Eastern Roman Empire for over 1000 years

[a] Ref. 1.

is thought that the Egyptian ruling class bathed regularly. Great waterworks were constructed by the Jews in Palestine during the reigns of David and Solomon arising from religious strictures that enforced cleaning rituals when they had been wandering tribes in the desert.

The Greeks used tubs (forerunners of pools) for bathing and initially only cold water. The Scythians (in the Ukraine) are thought to be the first users of the steam bath. Water was poured over hot rocks inside a tent; a similar arrangement was used by the North American Indians. It is thought the large bathing structures of the Russians and Finns were derived from the Scythians. Like the Romans, they followed their steam (hot) bath with a cold one in either a stream or by jumping into snow. The Greeks initially thought of the bath and swimming as a restorative following vigorous physical exercise such as gymnastics or wrestling. An urn of water was poured over the bather. Soon simple and then elaborate (marble) tubs in which the bather was immersed were developed. In the fifth century B.C., baths were constructed in Athens, although there was some hesitation about their appropriateness in a general Spartan lifestyle. Evidence of the importance of these pools and baths can be seen in Greek paintings of the time.

Roman baths achieved the highest degree of sophistication although, as mentioned earlier, the baths at Knossos were very elaborate. However, the Romans developed a great number of baths, approximately one per 1000 people and extended this concept to their colonies as well as the capital. The remains of Roman baths have been found all over Europe, the United Kingdom, and Africa. The general plan for thermae (baths or pools) consisted of large rooms with pools of varying hot water temperatures and a final room with cold water (Fig. 1). Underground passages were built for servicing the large buildings, gardens, and libraries, and theaters were attached to the buildings. While initially the bath was developed to create a sound body for a sound mind, it became a social gathering center where one spent a day several times a week. The buildings were elaborately constructed of marble with mosaic floors and walls and stucco reliefs. The doors were often constructed of bronze. For ventilation and lighting purposes, the roofs were quite high and the Romans developed buttresses, cross-vaulting, and high galley windows to enhance the beauty and utility of these structures.

Exercise in the athletic halls and ball courts was considered an essential part of the bath followed by rubbings with oils, a succession of immersions in heated water, then a cold bath, and finished with more exercise in a swimming pool. The process was completed with a final rubbing of scented oils. Men and women bathed separately in different establishments or at least at different times. However, there is some record that this was not always the case because Emperors Hadrian and Marcus Aurelius banned mixed bathing (thought to be practiced by courtesans).

Private domestic baths were also built in Roman times and can be seen in great detail at Pompeii. However, because there were so many public baths that were also social centers, the majority of the population used the elaborate public facilities. The ruins of the Baths of Caracalla, Diocletia, and Titus are excavated and open to the public. Now great operatic productions are staged yearly in Rome in the Baths of Caracalla, which covers a space of 33 acres. This bath could hold over 3000 bathers at one time and had a swimming pool almost 300 ft in length.

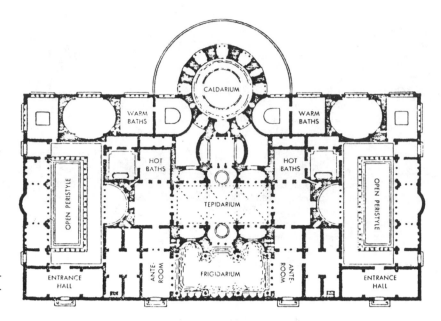

Figure 1. Plan of the Baths of Caracalla (1). Courtesy of John Dawes Publications; Originally published by *Architectural Press*.

The lesser-known Islamic baths combine Eastern and Roman bathing traditions with both Christian and Jewish overtones. The square or rectangular rooms built by the Moors, for example, in the Alhambra and Cordoba, Spain, are in the Roman tradition: warm, hot, and steam rooms followed by a cooling shower or bowl of cold water. The Judaic concept of ritual cleanliness is still a strict part of the Islamic tradition as is the Christian repugnance of luxuries associated with bathing. Islamic laws on personal hygiene achieved a higher standard of cleanliness in the East than medieval Christendom achieved and Muslims were considered the cleanest people in the world. The Turkish bath as it is known today came from this tradition.

Christian influence on pools or baths was extensive. Jews and Christians could not bathe together and the practice of using fragrant oils and cosmetics was considered decadent. Nudity associated with the baths and its traditions was also disallowed. During the Middle Ages, swimming and bathing almost ceased. This was encouraged by the Christian church as a reaction to the Jewish and Muslim traditions of ritual and general cleanliness built into the structure of their religions. It was also thought that outdoor bathing encouraged the spread of disease and the epidemics rampant throughout Europe. A sect of the Christian church preached mortifying the body and an early penance for sins; being dirty was one form of mortification. When the Roman empire came under attack, water supplies to the baths through elaborate aqueducts were interrupted or destroyed; the baths gradually disintegrated or were unusable, thus eliminating some of the tensions around swimming and bathing practices.

The spread of diseases was attributed to public swimming pools even though no scientific proof existed. However, the absence of any disinfectant tends to support this hypothesis. People were not inspired to greater personal hygiene domestically. While a few public bathing facilities existed, private ones were almost nonexistent.

As the Middle Ages receded and the industrial revolu-

tion began, greater attention was given to plumbing. Crowded slums, city factories, and an expanding population focused attention on the unsanitary living conditions and poor personal hygiene of the general population. Public and private groups began building public bathhouses for those without private facilities. These bathhouses were, very simply, places to get clean; no luxurious and social aspects were included. Shower baths and pools were added as athletic activities increased. Dr. Richard Russell's discovery in the mid-1700s of the cleaning action of seawater encouraged the concept of floating baths such as the *Waterloo,* which was moored on the Thames in 1819 (Fig. 2). Floating baths were also very popular on the Seine and lasted much longer than those in the United Kingdom and the United States because of hydraulic water exchangers. Increasing water pollution caused the "people's bath" to fall into disfavor in the United States. (Of late, technological developments have created "floating" vinyl structures easily assembled and dismantled that can be used on lake fronts and rivers during warm seasons where the supply of fresh clean water is closely monitored.) At the same time, municipal baths were reemerging from the dark ages as a social need for the general population; "health spas" for the wealthier classes built on the Roman model (luxurious social gathering places as well as a place for medicinal and cleansing purposes) were growing in popularity throughout Europe.

After the finest example of Roman baths in the United Kingdom was excavated in Bath in 1871, it became a fashionable healing center, using 500,000 gallons of 120°F water a day in the treatment of gout and joint and other diseases. Germany developed over 200 *bad* facilities; Italy and France over 1000 each. These resorts provide medical treatments today as they did in the past in fresh, sea, and mineral waters and solaria (Pliny indulged in "sun" baths and the Assyrians and Egyptians believed in the healing qualities of heliotherapy). Tanning is a relatively recent (early 1900s) benefit of the pool experience.

U.S. public bath establishments have been many, but

Figure 2. The Floating Swimming Bath in the Thames at Charing Cross (1). Courtesy of John Dawes Publications.

one of the more elaborate was constructed in San Francisco by Adolph Sutro (Fig. 3). In the late 1800s, he began construction of the "world's largest aquarium." Originally an outdoor facility, it was changed because of public pressure to the largest indoor baths and swimming pools with vast expanses of glass looking out from the San Francisco cliffs to the Pacific Ocean. It was an incredible engineering feat for its time, requiring the heating of water at different temperatures for each of its five pools, getting the water in and out of the pools, and maintaining different depths for different uses. It was in some respects reminiscent of Roman baths having gardens and statuary, and extensive lawns for family outings and picnics. Contests and band concerts were held and amusements (slides and ferris wheels and swings) were provided for all-day entertainment. The baths officially opened in 1896 and closed

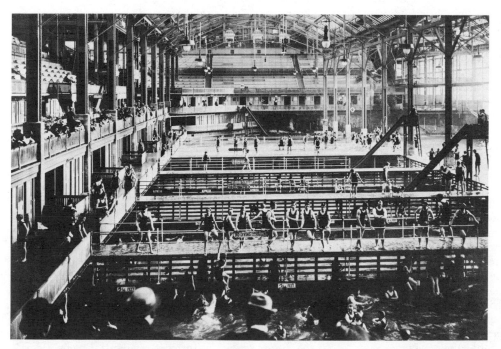

Figure 3. Sutro Baths, San Francisco, Calif., 1900. San Francisco Archives, San Francisco Public Library. Photograph by M. Blaisdell.

in 1952. In the meantime, thousands of San Franciscans learned to swim in this privately owned facility designed for public use. During the Victorian era more and more emphasis was placed on domestic bathing, and interior separate rooms were established for this purpose with often elaborate piping, although these facilities were limited to the upper-middle and wealthier classes.

The pool continued for the most part to be in the public domain until well after the turn of the twentieth century. In the 1930s there was a surge in private residential pool activity but it was a modest one. However, World War II required swimming instruction for all those in military training and this was done by all nations. (12 million U.S. servicemen alone were taught to swim.) After the war, the demand for indoor and outdoor swimming facilities meant a sharp increase in the number of pools. By the 1970s one family in ten in the United States had a private residential pool or access to one in their immediate neighborhood.

The swimming pool again had become fully accessible to the general population. While the luxury and opulence of the Roman baths have not been matched, the concept of general physical fitness and swimming's contribution has been. The pool is, once again, a highly desirable social gathering point.

Japanese Swimming Facilities

The tradition of swimming pools in the Far East, particularly in Japan, developed quite independently from the Western tradition but, in some ways, along similar lines and for similar reasons. Japan is an island country surrounded on all sides by water. It also has many lakes and rivers that provide the opportunity for all Japanese to enjoy water as a friend, food provider, and a place to rest, play, pray, and purify the body. The Japanese have always been involved in keeping their bodies healthy through exercise. Whereas Americans like jogging, the Japanese, young and old, men and women, love to swim. Even young mothers use swimming as exercise during and after pregnancy for their health as well as beauty. They seem to enjoy it as a relaxing sport rather than a competitive sport. Because of the abundance of lakes, rivers, streams, ponds, and of course the ocean, the people feel a need to be prepared for water accidents, floods, tsunami, and big storms. Everyone needs to be able to swim if necessary. Japan has been an agricultural society where water is needed for rice farming. Water also has a great religious significance in the lives of all its people.

Beginning in kindergarten, Japanese children are taught to swim. All elementary schools, junior high schools and high schools have swimming as part of their curriculum. Most schools are equipped with swimming pools and many communities have indoor pool facilities for all seasons. Children as well as adults have relatively easy access to swimming pools throughout the year.

Swimming pools also come in many different sizes and varieties. There are swimming pools with tide-making facilities, swimming pools of enormous sizes with many entertainment facilities built in, swimming pools with salt water, swimming pools with hot spring water, swimming pools used for show business purposes, and even swimming pools built only to train scuba divers. Japan has

become famous throughout the world for its baths, and has developed great teams for the Olympics.

POOLS FOR RECREATION

Probably all swimming pools are used at some time for recreation, but some are almost solely designed for that use. This is particularly true of the small pool on a private lot related to a private residence.

Residential Pools

The twentieth century has seen a tremendous increase in private residential pools. In the United States in 1950, there were 15,000 pools, and in 1975, based on *Swimming Pool Weekly,* the number had increased to 1,455,000 with private residential pools being the leading factor. In the UK, the numbers for the same period increased from 40,000 to 1,100,000. This has come about as a result of the vast expansion of cities into suburban areas, which provide house lots large enough for a private pool and with an economic base able to afford one. No doubt, there has also been the stimulation of greater consciousness of physical fitness, as seen in other activities such as jogging and tennis. As a result of this demand, construction techniques have been developed that bring the residential pool within a reasonable budget.

The first consideration in deciding to build a pool in the backyard is cost. Special factors affecting the construction cost include soil conditions, such as rock, required fill, and water table as well as accessibility of construction equipment. Beyond the cost of the pool itself, there are related costs such as connection to utility and sewer lines and, of course, maintenance over time, particularly in cold climates where pools must be "put away" for the winter. (Simultaneously, checks must be made with the local health and building inspectors to find out about health, safety, and zoning requirements.)

The next decision is where to put the pool. This decision will depend on local factors of climate, and even microclimate. In countries such as much of the United States and northern Europe, consideration should be given to a location that is sheltered from the wind and open to the maximum exposure of the sun. Trees can be an attractive feature and give some shade, but they are best located where their leaves do not get into the pool itself, which causes a maintenance problem. Another consideration is the relation to the house. If it is intended to keep the cost to a minimum, and not provide changing and toilet facilities in a separate structure, it may be desirable to be fairly close to the house, which can provide the facilities. If, on the other hand, a separate structure, such as a cabana, is planned, it becomes a part of the plan and can also be used to provide shelter from the wind, and shade when desired. Pools are also potentially a very attractive element and can be a focus in the planning of a house, for social reasons as well as purely functional. The sizes of private pools vary, but generally range between 20 × 30 ft and 25 × 40 ft. It is important to decide whether to include a diving board, as this affects the depth of the pool. Figure 4 shows required depths as recommended by *Architectural Graphic Standards* (2). In most residential pools a deck-

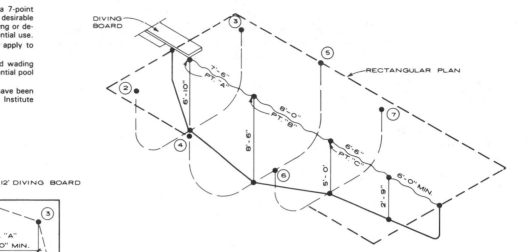

ISOMETRIC OVERLAY VIEW

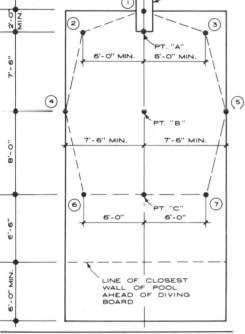

7-POINT GRID DIMENSION PLAN

LONGITUDINAL SECTION AT CENTERLINE

IF BOARD IS 12'-0" PT. "B" MUST BE 8'-6"
IF BOARD IS 10'-0" PT. "B" MUST BE 8'-0"

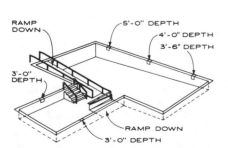

HANDICAPPED POOL ACCESS

PERMITS AND RESTRICTIONS

Required in most areas from building, health, plumbing, and electrical departments and zoning boards. Check for setback restrictions and easements covering power and telephone lines, sewers, and storm drains.

SITE CONSIDERATIONS

Check the site for the following conditions, each of which will considerably increase the cost.

1. Fill that is more than 3 ft below pool deck.
2. Hard rock that requires drilling and blasting.
3. Underground water or springs that necessitate pumping or drains.
4. Accessibility of the site for mechanical equipment, minimum entry 8 ft wide by 7 ft 8 in. high, with a grade easy enough for a truck to reach the site.
5. Place the pool where it will get the most sun during swimming season. If possible, place deep end so a diver dives away from, not into, the afternoon sun. Avoid overhanging tree branches near the pool.
6. The slope of the site should be as level as possible; a steep slope requires retaining walls for the pool.
7. The surface deck around the pool should be of a slip-resistant surface.
8. A surrounding fence is recommended to protect pool area from unwanted visitors and to prevent accidents.

CONSTRUCTION AND SHAPES

Pools may be made of reinforced concrete (poured on the job, precast, or gunite sprayed), concrete block, steel, aluminum, or plastic with or without block backup. Concrete, aluminum, fiberglass, and steel pools are available in any shape—rectangular, square, kidney, oval or free form. Complete plastic installations and plastic pool liners with various backups are available only in manufacturers' standard shapes and sizes.

A rectangular pool is the most practical if site permits, since it gives the longest swimming distance.

POOL CAPACITY

Rule of thumb: 36 sq ft for each swimmer, 100 sq ft for each diver. A pool of 20 x 40 ft accommodates 14 persons at a time, but since not everyone is in the pool at once, pool and surroundings are adequate for 30 to 40 people.

FILTER REQUIREMENTS

Filter, motor, and electrical equipment shall be sheltered and waterproofed.

Figure 4. Recommended depths of pools (2).

level board is adequate if required at all. One problem with diving in a small pool is that there is relatively little length of the pool to make the transition between the deep and the shallow end, and this can be dangerous for beginning swimmers. In many ways, the almost uniformly shallow pool, say varying from 2.5 ft at the shallow end to 4 ft at the deep, can be most satisfactory, and safe for families, but of course this does not allow diving.

Many manufacturing and construction firms have become specialists in various types of pool construction, including poured-in-place concrete, sprayed on concrete using forms on one side only, and steel shells either buried in the ground or totally above grade. The decision on which to use is, of course, partly economic, but also involves aesthetic considerations, particularly if an above-grade pool is considered.

Because an open, unattended pool can be dangerous if a child or someone who cannot swim should fall in, it is important to fence in or otherwise control pools when they are unattended. It is also desirable to have general rules that no one swims alone. During the winter in cold climates, the pool should be covered with a plastic sheet for safety. Solar blankets have been developed that can also be used to reduce heat loss from pools when not in use, as well as providing safety. Sometimes pools are drained, but this can cause frost damage to the pool sides and bottom unless they are on a good gravel base, and there is also the danger of someone falling in.

Although most residential pools are outdoors, indoor pools are also constructed for private use. In some instances an indoor pool is used as a focal point in the design of the house, and can be very attractive. This is obviously much more expensive, and involves many of the structural and mechanical controls covered in the section on indoor competition pools. It is probably desirable to separate the pool from the rest of the house to avoid problems of humidity.

Community Pools

When these are built outdoors, many of the considerations noted under residential pools will apply: proper analysis of initial and operating costs, location on the selected site in relation to sun and wind, and relation to utilities. There are, however, other factors to consider. The selected site should be convenient for the users—if a community pool, at some central location. However, traffic and parking can be a major concern for the neighbors, and this must be worked out in advance. An off-street parking lot is far preferable to merely parking along the street. For public pools the location must be part of an overall master plan that establishes the required number of pools, and how they fit into a total recreational or educational program. The supervision of community pools is particularly important. The following is a summary of the requirements of a community pool set up for about 30 families.

REQUIREMENTS FOR THE USE OF A SMALL COMMUNITY POOL
All Persons Use the Pool at Their Own Risk
Safety

1. No swimming alone for anyone.
2. When the lifeguard is not on duty, a parent or adult member must accompany children under 18. Other than a parent, an accompanying person may not swim at the same time as the children and may not be responsible for more than four children.
3. Children may not use the deep end of the pool unless they have passed the basic swim test given by the lifeguard. Children who have not passed the test must be accompanied by a person over 14 years of age when the lifeguard is on duty.
4. Please, no food within the fenced area. Drinks should not be in glass containers. The common land or the slope outside the fenced area may be used for picnicking.
5. No chewing gum, glass of any kind, or foam objects are allowed in the pool area.
6. Permission must be obtained from the lifeguard for snorkels, scuba equipment, balls, or inflatable toys.
7. Do not hang from the diving board or jump off sideways. Divers should watch for swimmers and swimmers should avoid the diving area while the board is in use. The lifeguard may curtail the diving activities if other swimmers want to do laps. Only one person on the board at a time.
8. No ducking, running, playing ball or tag, throwing, pushing, wrestling, or other undue disturbance around the pool.
9. Anyone swimming in the pool during lifeguard swimming lessons should have someone other than the lifeguard watching them.
10. Children in the wading pool are not the responsibility of the lifeguard. There must be someone in charge of children in the wading pool.

Health

1. Shower before using the pool.
2. No smoking in the pool area.
3. Persons with colds or any contagious disease must not use either pool until symptoms have cleared.
4. No pets allowed inside fenced area or loose around entry.
5. Disposable diapers cannot be worn in the pools. Infants must wear securely fitted pants (training or rubber) or swimsuit.

Although outdoor community pools are often used for competition, their prime use is generally for recreation. For this reason, the shapes of these pools vary substantially. There is no perfect answer for all situations. However, some of the factors to be considered are ratio of deep area to shallow area; diving area, if any; the desirability of being able to use the pool for competition occasionally; and relation to the site and other physical elements. Figure 5 shows a number of shapes and possible arrangements. For very small children it is desirable to have a separate wading pool only a few inches to a foot deep, but even this can be dangerous and must be supervised closely when in use. For public pools, it may be better merely to have a spray pool area.

In outdoor community pools it must be recognized that

GENERAL

Public pools are generally considered to be those that belong to municipalities, schools, country clubs, hotels, motels, apartments, and resorts. Permits for their construction are required in most areas from local and state boards of health as well as the departments of building, plumbing, and electricity.

Community pools should be integrated with existing and projected recreational facilities, such as picnic areas and parks, for maximum usage. Transportation access should be good, and there should be ample parking space. In a hot climate, enough shade should be provided, particularly in the lounging areas, and be so located that it can be easily converted to spectator space by erecting bleachers.

POOL DESIGN

Formerly most public pools were designed to meet competitive swimming requirements. The trend today is to provide for all-around use. The following should be considered:

1. Ratio of shallow water to deep water. Formerly 60% of pool area 5 ft deep and less was considered to be adequate. Now 80% is considered more realistic.

2. Ratio of loungers to bathers. Generally, no more than one-third of people attending a public pool are in the water at one time. Consequently the 6 to 8 ft walks formerly surrounding pools and used for lounging have been enlarged so that lounging area now approximates pool size.

3. For capacity formula see "Public Swimming Pool Capacity" diagram on another page.

RECOMMENDED DIMENSIONS

MAX. BOARD LENGTH	RELATED DIVING EQUIPMENT MAX. HEIGHT OVER WATER	MINIMUM DIMENSIONS								MINIMUM WIDTH OF POOL AT:		
		D_1	D_2	R	L_1	L_2	L_3	L_4	L_5	PT.A	PT.B	PT.C
10′	⅔ m 26″	2.13 m 7′-0″	2.59 m 8′-6″	1.68 m 5′-6″	0.76 m 2′-6″	2.44 m 8′-0″	3.20 m 10′-6″	2.13 m 7′-0″	8.53 m 28′-0″	4.88 m 16′-0″	5.49 m 18′-0″	5.49 m 18′-0″
12′	¾ m 30″	2.29 m 7′-6″	2.74 m 9′-0″	1.83 m 6′-0″	0.91 m 3′-0″	2.74 m 9′-0″	3.66 m 12′-0″	1.22 m 4′-0″	8.53 m 28′-0″	5.49 m 18′-0″	6.10 m 20′-0″	6.10 m 20′-0″
16′	1 m	2.59 m 8′-6″	3.05 m 10′-0″	2.13 m 7′-0″	1.22 m 4′-0″	3.05 m 10′-0″	4.57 m 15′-0″	0.61 m 2′-0″	9.45 m 31′-0″	6.10 m 20′-0″	6.71 m 22′-0″	6.71 m 22′-0″
16′	3 m	3.35 m 11′-0″	3.66 m 12′-0″	2.59 m 8′-6″	1.83 m 6′-0″	3.20 m 10′-6″	6.40 m 21′-0″	0	11.43 m 37′-6″	6.70 m 22′-0″	7.32 m 24′-0″	7.32 m 24′-0″

Data source: National SPA and Swimming Pool Institute.

L_2, L_3, and L_4 combined represent the minimum distance from the tip of board to pool wall opposite diving equipment.

For board heights exceeding 3 m or for platform diving facilities; comply with dimensional requirements of FINA, USS, NCAA, N.F., etc.

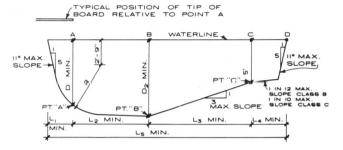

NOTE: Placement of boards shall observe the following minimum dimensions. With multiple board installations minimum pool widths must be increased accordingly.

1 m or deck level board to pool side	9′ (2.74 m)
3 m board to pool side	11′ (3.35 m)
1 m or deck level board to 3 m board	10′ (3.05 m)
1 m or deck level to another 1 m or deck level board	8′ (2.44 m)
3 m to another 3 m board	10′ (3.05 m)

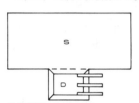

T-SHAPED POOL

Provides large shallow area(s). Diving area off to one side. Water in large part of pool from 3 ft 6 in. to 5 ft deep, adequate for regular competitive events.

L- AND Z-SHAPED POOL

These two shapes generally desired for large 50 m pools.

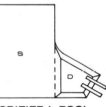

RECTANGULAR POOL

Standard design. Good for competitive swimming and indoor pool design. Shallow area often inadequate.

FAN SHAPED POOL

Successful where there is a high percentage of children. Largest area for shallow depth. Deep area can be roped off or separated by bulkhead.

FREE FORM POOL

Kidney and oval shapes are the most common free forms. Use only where competitive meets are not a consideration.

MODIFIED L POOL

Provides for separate diving area. Shallow area with 4 ft min. depth may be roped off for competitive meets.

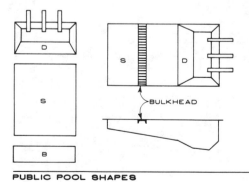

MULTIPLE POOLS

Separate pools for beginners, divers, and swimmers. Ultimate in desirability especially if pool is intended for large numbers of people. Variation at left shows single pool and bulkhead over it with advantage that swimmers are kept out of area reserved for beginners. Both designs may use common filtration system.

WADING POOLS

Generally provided in connection with community and family club pools. Placed away from swimming area to avoid congestion. If near swimming pool, wading area should be fenced off for children's protection. To add play appeal provide spray fittings and small fountains in pool. Also provide seats and benches for adults who accompany children to pool.

PUBLIC POOL SHAPES

NOTE: S = swimming pool, D = diving pool, B = beginners' pool.

Figure 5. Public swimming pools shapes (2).

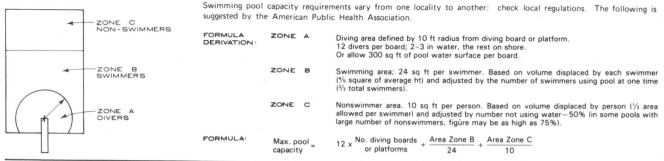

Swimming pool capacity requirements vary from one locality to another: check local regulations. The following is suggested by the American Public Health Association.

FORMULA DERIVATION:	ZONE A	Diving area defined by 10 ft radius from diving board or platform. 12 divers per board; 2–3 in water, the rest on shore. Or allow 300 sq ft of pool water surface per board.
	ZONE B	Swimming area; 24 sq ft per swimmer. Based on volume displaced by each swimmer (⅛ square of average ht) and adjusted by the number of swimmers using pool at one time (⅔ total swimmers).
	ZONE C	Nonswimmer area. 10 sq ft per person. Based on volume displaced by person (½ area allowed per swimmer) and adjusted by number not using water—50% (in some pools with large number of nonswimmers, figure may be as high as 75%).
FORMULA:	Max. pool capacity =	$12 \times \dfrac{\text{No. diving boards}}{\text{or platforms}} + \dfrac{\text{Area Zone B}}{24} + \dfrac{\text{Area Zone C}}{10}$

PUBLIC SWIMMING POOL CAPACITY

Figure 6. Public swimming pool capacity (2).

many people come to relax and enjoy the sun, not necessarily to be in the water most of the time. It is therefore important to design the area around the pool with this in mind. The area around the pool should generally be at least as large as the pool area.

Because outdoor community pools are generally not closely related to changing rooms and toilets, these facilities must be provided at the pool itself. In small community pools these can be quite small, but even so, they should be sanitary and well ventilated. There should always be a shower and foot bath for anyone entering the pool. In larger public pools, the changing rooms are a major element in the arrangement of the pool. They should be so located that they control the entrance to the pool area, which should be fenced in, and have direct access to the pool itself. In determining the size of the pool one must consider the users; that is, swimmers, nonswimmers, and divers. Figure 6 shows a formula suggested by the American Public Health Association.

Because diving is one of the greatest potential dangers in pools and does not mix well with the swimming area, it

is ideal to separate it from the main pool. This also allows the diving area to be deep enough to be safe, while the main swimming area can be quite shallow.

Figure 7 shows a 25 × 75 ft community pool in Lexington, Massachusetts, which was designed to accommodate 30 families, mostly from the immediate neighborhood. Therefore, there is no parking area other than the road, which is a dead-end street. This is not ideal, but probably acceptable when most of the people walk to the pool.

The other extreme for outdoor community pools is an Olympic-size pool with a 3-m diving board and a 10-m platform. Too often these facilities have only minimal lifeguard control—they are almost like large public beaches with hundreds of people and only one lifeguard. In northern climates many pools have been equipped with heated water that can be turned on in the early spring and in the late summer and fall in order to extend the season. This obviously makes more use of the pool and is a partial step toward the indoor pool. It is best in this case to heat the changing and toilet rooms as well. Once the heat of the

Figure 7. Small community pool in Lexington, Mass. Photograph by Richard Morehouse.

summer is gone, the social aspect of the community pools is gone, and it is only the really serious swimmer who will use an outdoor pool in cool weather, so its use becomes marginal.

The requirements for water purification are substantially greater in public and community pools than in private residential ones. This is covered in the section on mechanical and plumbing systems.

Pools for Educational Facilities

As swimming has become an accepted and desirable form of exercise, pools have been increasingly included in educational facilities. In fact, some universities require that everyone must be able to swim at least one length of the pool to graduate.

At the school level, pools may range all the way from training pools for teaching young children to swim, to pools for high schools, which are basically the same as college or university pools. A training pool should be at least 20 × 50 ft with 25 × 60 ft preferred. If used only for training it should be shallow for its entire length, that is from 2 ft 6 in. to 4 ft 6 in. or 5 ft 0 in. in depth. Another alternative is to build a larger pool for more diversified use. Such a pool would be deeper, at least at one end, and should be up to 30 × 75 ft. It is also possible to vary the depth of the pool with the use of hydraulic lifts that adjust to the desired conditions.

For junior high schools, the pool must be designed for a total program, including recreation and competitions, as well as diving and special aquatic programs. The actual size will, of course, be affected by the size of the program as well as the cost and available funds. Table 2 provides guidelines to be used in planning such a facility.

If diving is to be included, there must be a deep end to the pool with depths controlled by the height of the board. It is preferable to have the diving either in an alcove away from the main swimming area or even in a separate pool. In major facilities, it is often desirable to have a separate, entirely shallow pool for those learning to swim, even for older people, similar to the learning pool suggested for elementary schools.

At the university level, the use of the pool for competitions is a dominant factor in the design, and is discussed in the section on competition pools. However, recreation and other aquatic activities must be considered. The development of centralized major natatoria, with both 25-yd cross-pool dimensions, and 50 m-long dimensions, with separate diving areas can provide enough space so that, with proper scheduling, a variety of activities can take place simultaneously.

Table 2. Guidelines for Planning a Pool for an Educational Facility[a]

Feature	Minimum, ft	Desirable, ft
Size	30 × 75	45 × 75
Shallow water	3	3.5
Deep water	5	12
Ceiling height	16	18

[a] Ref. 3.

Pools for Hotels

There has been an increasing recognition of the desirability of having a swimming pool as an added attraction in hotels. In warm climates these are generally outdoor pools. They vary greatly in size and shape because their principal function is recreation. It was noted above that a substantial area should be planned around pools for lounging and swimming, and this is even more important in hotel pools. In fact, pools are often connected with or closely accessible from the bar—which is usually considered forbidden in community pools, partly because of the danger of broken glass. Safety controls and life guarding are much more relaxed in these pools, particularly in foreign countries, which in any case are less strict on matters of safety regulations. As noted above, diving can be one of the principal hazards, and some hotels in the United States are removing diving boards for that reason.

Figure 8 shows a modest pool at a hotel in Cyprus, used as a feature in relation to the building. Increasingly, and particularly in cooler climates, hotels are building indoor pools. Because these are primarily for recreation, there is often a desire to have them appear to be almost outdoors, or in a solarium. Many solutions have been used, ranging from glass walls on both sides (Fig. 9) to geodesic domes. Some companies have specialized in the construction of this type of structure, and have developed methods whereby they can be opened for summer use and to avoid overheating. One example of this in the United States is by Solar Structures (Fig. 10). Just as atria in all kinds of buildings have become popular again, picking up on the great developments along these lines in the nineteenth century, from the Crystal Palace by Paxton in London to railroad stations all over the world, so also are glass-enclosed pools becoming popular again, in the same spirit as the floating pools of the nineteenth century and the great Sutro Baths in California. Although this trend has started primarily in connection with hotels, it may reach much greater use in recreational facilities of all kinds.

Wave Pools

In Europe, pools have been designed for many years with special devices for making waves, and this has become more popular in recent years also in the UK. These are generally in leisure centers or connected to hotels. Because the shape of the pool must be designed to slope up from a moderate depth to nothing in order to create the effect of waves breaking on a beach, this type of pool is highly specialized. It is in effect an artificial beach (Fig. 11).

There are a number of methods of creating the waves, including a swinging arm, compressed air, and the action of falling water. The recent interest in surfing has stimulated the construction of wave pools such as the one in Allentown, Pennsylvania, to be used for surfing competitions in artificial surf.

COMPETITION POOLS

Although many indoor and outdoor pools are used for both recreation and competition, they are treated separately

Figure 8. Pool at Hotel in Cyprus by The Architects Collaborative. Photograph by Wayne Soverns, Jr.

because generally one or the other is the dominant use and controls its design. A pool used occasionally for competition but primarily for recreation need not be so precise in its shape and design and will not need a gallery for spectators. A pool designed for competition cannot compromise.

Some of the great competition pools are outdoor pools, such as the Olympic Pool at Los Angeles used for the 1984

Olympics. These are 50-m pools, 23.5 m wide, allowing nine lanes. A standard of layout for a 50-m competitive swimming pool, is shown in Figure 12. This shows diving in the same area as the main pool. It is preferable to have a separate diving area, or at least a wider space along the side of the pool to avoid conflict. Exact dimensions are, of course, very important in competition pools to assure the validity of record times. Special starting platforms are

Figure 9. Indoor pool in hotel in Yugoslavia by The Architects Collaborative. Photograph by Wayne Soverns, Jr.

Figure 10. Signature Custom leisure pavilion. Courtesy of Solar Structures Division of IBG International.

Figure 11. Decatur Ala. wave pool rendering.

GENERAL NOTES

For judging competitive meets, FINA officials recommend the springboard and diving platform arrangement indicated below in plan. Diving dimensions meet minimum FINA standards. Fifty meters is minimum length for world records.

NOTE

*Length should be 50.03 m allowing an extra .03 m to compensate for possible future tile facing, structural defects and electrical timing panels.

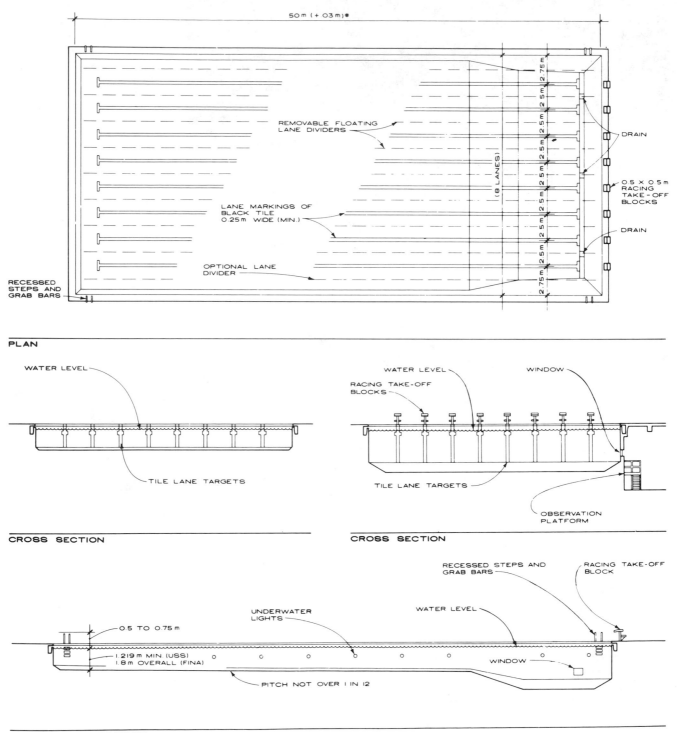

PLAN

CROSS SECTION

CROSS SECTION

LONGITUDINAL SECTION

Figure 12. Fifty-meter competitive swimming pool (2).

LENGTH OF POOLS

25 yards is the minimum length for American records, and meets interscholastic and intercollegiate requirements. (Pool should be 75 ft-1½ in. long to allow for electronic timing panels at one end.)

Standards for international competition are shown on 50 meter pool page.

WIDTH OF POOLS

Drawing below shows 7 ft lanes with pool width of 45 ft (6 lanes). Strictly competitive pools should have 8 ft lanes, with pool width of 83 ft (10 lanes). Minimum widths include additional 18 in. width outside lanes on both sides of pool.

NOTES

Gutters at sides of pool are desirable to reduce wave action in swimming meets or water polo. See lighting standards and diving board standards on other pages of this series for additional requirements for competitive pools.

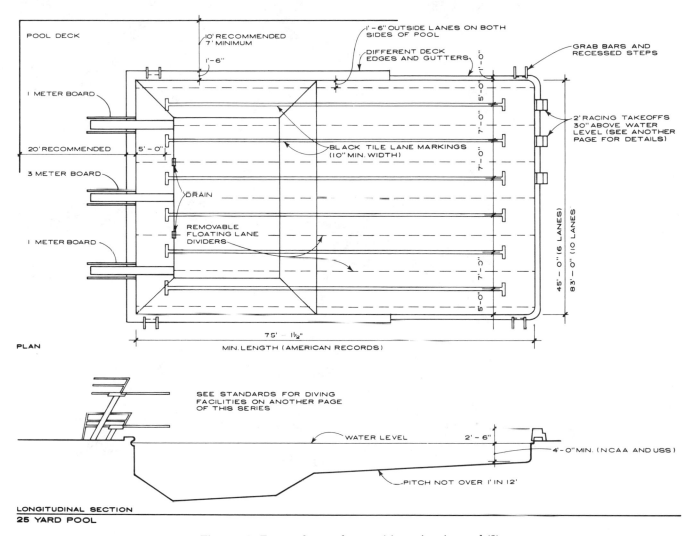

Figure 13. Twenty-five-yard competitive swimming pool (2).

required, and electronic timing panels are sometimes used. In this case, an extra 1.5 in. should be added to allow the panel at one end of the pool. The design of the gutter to avoid waves can increase a swimmer's speed. A number of pool equipment companies in the United States make a full line of pool equipment and fittings, and some actually construct the pool itself. The details are discussed further in the section on Materials.

The typical competition pool in the United States is designed for swimming lengths of 25 yd. Figure 13 shows the layout for a 25-yd competition pool, although for most competitions it should have 10 lanes, with 8 ft per lane, and a total width of 83 ft. Figure 14 shows a 6-lane, 25-yd pool at Smith College, Massachusetts.

Because of the fact that some competitions are swum in meters and some in feet, a variety of pool sizes and shapes have been devised to accommodate both. At the present time, 25 m is not an official competition length. It is either 25-yd, the U.S. standard, or 50 m, the international and Olympic standard. One method of accommodating both lengths is to have a 50-m pool with a moveable bulkhead that can be set at 25 yd. This has the advantage that, assuming there is a spectator gallery, the competitors are always viewed from the same general direction. One example of this arrangement is the new pool at the U.S. Naval Academy. Another arrangement is one in which the width of the pool is 25 yd, and the length 50 m. The new pool at Harvard University is an example of this (Fig.

Figure 14. Pool at Ainsworth Gym, Smith College by The Architects Collaborative. Courtesy of Nick Wheeler/Wheeler Photographics.

15). This pool also has an alcove for diving so as to be out of the swimming area. Another example is the new U.S. Military Academy Pool at West Point, New York (Fig. 16).

Whereas recreational pools need a substantial area for nonswimmers, pools for competitors also need deck area for training, exercises, and swimmers waiting their turn. However, especially in indoor pools, this is not as extensive as the areas in outdoor recreational pools. Competition pools will generally require a spectator gallery, the size depending on the level of competition and potential interest. This is particularly true of Olympic pools. In order to accommodate very large numbers, 10,000 or more seats, the 1984 Olympic Pool in Los Angeles is out of doors. Because the Olympic event requires a seating capacity that will seldom be needed again, some indoor pool stadia have been designed to be contracted after the games are over by removing temporary sections. The German architect Frei Otto designed such a structure for the Munich Olympics in 1972 (Fig. 17). It is important to keep

spectators off the pool deck and separate from the swimmers. This suggests an arrangement with a gallery over the locker rooms and approached from the back, totally separate from the participants.

One of the great concerns in the design of pools is the handling of lighting. Whereas purely recreational pools often have windows or skylights bringing in natural light and giving a relation to the outdoors, most competition pools do not use direct outside light in order to avoid glare. The new Olympic-size natatorium at Indianapolis does bring in natural light through baffled skylights at the peak of the roof over the pool (Fig. 18) in such a way as to avoid glare. Note also the separate diving pool at the end, moveable bulkheads to achieve 50-m or 25-yd swimming distances, and seating capacity for 5000 spectators arranged in a gallery over the locker rooms. Competition pools will generally also involve diving, and this must be integrated into the design. Diving areas are discussed under Special Functions.

Figure 15. Harvard University pool by The Architects Collaborative. Courtesy of Nick Wheeler/ Wheeler Photographics.

SPECIAL FUNCTIONS

Diving

The requirements for diving and for swimming are radically different. This is especially true for high boards or platforms. One might almost say that the only thing they have in common is water. In the early days in Scandinavia and Germany, diving started with swinging out over the water, doing acrobatics in the air, and using the water as a place to land without being hurt. Basically that is true today—diving has more to do with acrobatics than with swimming. Consequently, the depths required are entirely different.

For recommended depths for various heights of boards and platforms, see Figure 19 as recommended by FINA (Federation Internationale de Natation Amateur). If it is

intended that the pool will be used for amateur, collegiate, or international meets, it must have both a 1-m and a 3-m board as well as a diving platform. There are very specific details required for proper design of these boards for safety including a nonslip surface, proper handrails, and adjustments of the fulcrum. Designers should check with an expert in this field. There are a number of companies in the United States, Europe, and the UK that have specialized in the manufacture of diving boards of high quality. Figure 20 shows the approximately 30-in. deflection on a duraflex board. This greater deflection allows the diver to achieve much greater heights and therefore more complicated dives than had been possible with wooden diving boards. Similarly, there are specific heights and dimensions for diving towers and platforms. These are 5 m, 7.5 m, and 10 m. Special note should be taken of the relation of the platforms and diving boards to avoid the danger of

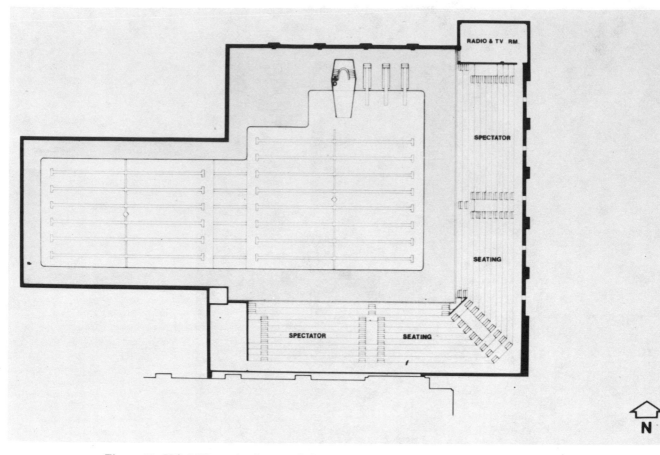

Figure 16. U.S. Military Academy pool plan, Raymond and Rado Architects, Eggers & Higgens, pool consultants. Courtesy of The Eggers Partnership.

hitting a lower board or platforms on the way down. Also, for indoor pools, attention is drawn to the importance of adequate ceiling heights over the platforms, as this can be a major factor in the design of the building.

It is important to design the building so that the diver has the best possible conditions and ability to see. Glare from lights, directly or on the water surface, or from windows should be avoided. Sprays on the surface and bubblers that agitate the surface help to identify the surface of the water. They are required for international competitions.

In order to create a safety cushion for people learning to dive from high boards or platforms, a method of releasing bubbles from the pool floor has been developed that creates a soft, if not precise, surface on which to land. Another safety device is to have a rubber cushion on the pool floor to lessen possible impact. In fact, even though pools are designed for depths appropriate to the height of platforms or diving boards, most good divers reach the bottom with their hands over their heads, flip, and spring back to the surface. Great care and instruction should be practiced in the use of diving equipment.

Figure 21 shows the diving tower used at the Olympics in Moscow in 1980. Note the glass wall between the diving pool and the main swimming pool, which allows a higher temperature in the diving pool but visual contact. Because divers get in and out of the water so much, temperature is very important.

Water Polo

The dimensions of a water polo court have considerable variation from minimum to maximum, and between National Collegiate Athletic Association (NCAA) recommendations and those of the Amateur Athletic Union (AAU). For the designer who is attempting to make double use of a pool, the problem is to find dimensions that accommodate water polo and swimming events. It is evident that water polo will fit comfortably into a standard 25-yd pool, six to eight lanes in width. The recommended depth is 1.8 m or approximately 6 ft minimum for national or international matches. If a 50-m pool or a pool with some L-shaped configuration is designed, it will be necessary to have a removable sideline or bulkhead to define the playing area.

Synchronized Swimming

Synchronized swimming has become much more popular in the United States in recent years and was an event

Figure 17. 1972 Olympic pool in Munich by Frei Otto, Architect. Photograph by R. Jackson Smith.

(unofficially) in the Olympics in Los Angeles. Perhaps part of its popularity derives from water ballet in community pools, an activity in which many can participate and derive enjoyment.

The recommended areas range from 20 × 40 ft to an area of 2000 ft^2 to 3000 ft^2 with a depth of over 6 ft. For beginners, a shallower depth is desirable.

One problem with viewing synchronized swimming is, of course, the fact that so much is below the water level. This requires a high level of illumination, and underwater lights. The spectator gallery should be high enough to look down on the swimmers. Underwater windows are desirable for teaching. It is also essential to have both an air and underwater sound system.

Instruction of Scuba Diving

Increased interest in scuba diving has led to the use of indoor pools for instruction. The principal requirement is that there be some area with a depth of at least 12–14 ft. The area depends on the size of the class; however, the standard competition pool size is best.

POOLS USED FOR HEALTH

As noted in the section on History, pools have been used in connection with health for many centuries. In the UK, the city of Bath is the most famous of watering places to which people have gone for health reasons, and in Europe the bath (or *bad*) involving fresh water and salt water, hot water and mineral water has been used for restoring health and general mental well being. At the present, health spa bathing is being neglected in the United Kingdom; Bath was closed down in 1976. However, spas continue to be used extensively in Europe for health reasons. There are almost 500 bathing towns in Germany, France, and Italy with a variety of mineral springs and thermal hospitals.

In recent times, hydrotherapy has played a major role in healing, particularly in the United Kingdom and the United States. Whirlpool baths and tanks especially designed for the use of invalids and handicapped people are in greater and greater use. The general concern for making all aspects of life more accessible to handicapped people is particularly appropriate to pool design, as being in

Figure 18. Natatorium, Indiana University/Purdue University at Indianapolis by Edward Larrabee Barnes as Architect. Courtesy of R. Greg Hursley.

water eliminates much of the disability people have on land. Therefore, to make a pool accessible for handicapped people is extremely important.

Design of Pools to be Used by the Handicapped

Pools should be accessible to people with a variety of handicaps, including the blind and mentally retarded. They can be of great therapeutic value, but also can be used for pleasure. Swimming is one of the few sports that these people can adapt to well. In designing pools for people in wheelchairs, the following guidelines should be followed.

1. Relation to lockers and showers: lockers for handicapped people should not have benches in front of them. Lockers should be raised off the floor at least 1 ft with space underneath for wheelchair footrests.

2. Showers should have a fixed bench seat with a back. The seat height should be 18–20 in. The shower itself should be removable from the wall to be hand held. The wall mount should be no higher than 4.5–5 ft. The floor of the shower should have a nonskid surface. It should also have grab bars on the wall.

3. Access to the pool itself: the deck around the pool

should be nonskid. There are several ways to make the pool accessible:

- A hydraulic lift with a sling seat (it requires one or two people to operate).
- A manual hand crank lift with sling seat (also requires one or two people to operate).
- A raised wall at one end of the pool 18–20-in. high and at least 16 in. in depth. This would allow a person in a wheelchair to transfer from chair to the wall and then to the water.
- The pool should have a small ledge around the edge of the pool at water level. This ledge should be 4-in. wide. This is useful to hold onto with the hands, elbows, etc.
- A ramp could be constructed at one end of the pool. The slope should be 1/12 and should have hand railings on both sides. This would allow wheelchairs and stretchers to roll directly into the water. It is also a much easier way for an elderly person to enter.
- Steps and ladders into a pool should have hand railings on both sides. The steps should be constructed so that a foot could not slip in between the steps.

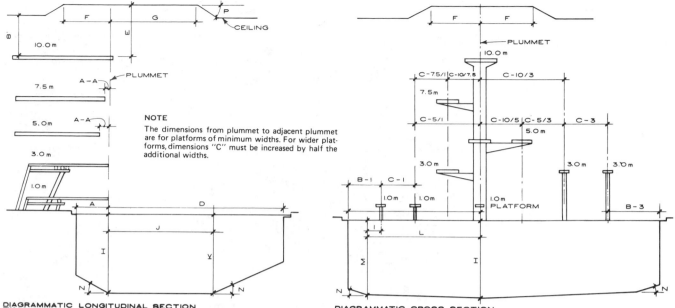

DIAGRAMMATIC LONGITUDINAL SECTION   DIAGRAMMATIC CROSS SECTION

NOTE
The dimensions from plummet to adjacent plummet are for platforms of minimum widths. For wider platforms, dimensions "C" must be increased by half the additional widths.

FINA INTERNATIONAL AMATEUR SWIMMING AND DIVING FEDERATION STANDARDS

			SPRINGBOARDS				PLATFORMS							
			1 METER		3 METER		1 METER	3 METER	5 METER		7.5 METER		10 METER	
DIMENSIONS FOR DIVING FACILITIES		LENGTH	5.0		5.0		4.5	5.0	6.0		6.0		6.0	
		WIDTH	0.5		0.5		0.6	0.8	1.5		1.5		2.0	
		HEIGHT	1.0		3.0		1.0	0.8	5.0		7.5		10.0	
A	FROM PLUMMET: BACK TO POOL WALL	DESIG.	A-1		A-3		A-1 (PL)	A-3 (PL)	A-5		A-7.5		A-10	
		MIN.	1.50		1.50		0.75	1.25	1.25		1.50		1.50	
		PREF.	1.80		1.80				1.50					
A-A	FROM PLUMMET: BACK TO PLATFORM DIRECTLY BELOW	DESIG.							AA-5/1		A-7.5/3		AA-10/5	
		MIN							0.75		0.75		0.75	
		PREF.									1.50		1.50	
B	FROM PLUMMET: TO POOL WALL AT SIDE	DESIG.	B-1		B-3		B-1 (PL)	B-3 (PL)	B-5		B-7.5		B-10	
		MIN.	2.50		3.50		2.30	2.90	4.25		4.50		5.25	
		PREF.	3.00											
C	FROM PLUMMET TO ADJACENT PLUMMET	DESIG.	C-1		C-3	C-3/1	C-1/1 (PL)	C-3/1 (PL)	C-5/3 (PL)	C-5/1	C-7.5/3/1	C-10/7.5	C-10/7.5/3	C-10/3/1
		MIN.	2.40		2.60	2.60	1.65	2.10	2.10	2.10	2.10	2.50	2.75	2.75
		PREF.	2.40		2.40	1.4/3.0								
D	FROM PLUMMET TO POOL WALL AHEAD	DESIG.	D-1		D-3		D-1 (PL)	D-3 (PL)	D-5		D-7.5		D-10	
		MIN.	9.00		10.25		8.00	9.50	10.25		11.00		13.50	
		PREF.												
E	PLUMMET, FROM BOARD TO CEILING OVERHEAD	DESIG.		E-1		E-3	E-1 (PL)	E-3 (PL)		E-5		E-7.5		E-10
		MIN.		5.00		5.00	3.00	3.00		3.00		3.20		3.40
		PREF.								3.40		3.40		5 00
F	CLEAR OVERHEAD, BEHIND AND EACH SIDE OF PLUMMET	DESIG.	F-1	E-1	F-3	E-3	F-1 (PL)	F-3 (PL)	F-5	E-5	F-7.5	E-7.5	F-10	E-10
		MIN.	2.50	5.00	2.50	5.00	2.75	2.75	2.75	3.00	2.75	3.20	2.75	3.40
		PREF.								3.40		3.40		5.00
G	CLEAR OVERHEAD, AHEAD OF PLUMMET	DESIG.	G-1	E-1	G-3	E-3	G-1 (PL)	G-3 (PL)	G-5	E-5	G-7.5	E-7.5	G-10	E-10
		MIN.	5.00	5.00	5.00	5.00	5.00	5.00	5.00	3.00	5.00	3.20	6.00	3.40
		PREF.								3.40		3.40		5.00
H	DEPTH OF WATER AT PLUMMET	DESIG.	H-1		H-3		H-1 (PL)	H-3 (PL)	H-5		H-7.5		H-10	
		MIN.	3.40		3.80		3.40	3.60	3.80		4.10		4.50	
		PREF.	3.80		4.00			3.80	4.00		4.50		5.00	
J-K	DISTANCE, DEPTH OF WATER, AHEAD OF PLUMMET	DESIG.	J-1	K-1	J-3	K-3	J/K-1 (PL)	J/K-3 (PL)	J-5	K-5	J-7.5	K-7.5	J-10	K-10
		MIN.	5.00	3.30	6.00	3.70	5.0/3.3	6.0/3.3	6.00	3.70	8.00	4.00	11.00	4.25
		PREF.		3.70		3.90				3.70		4.40		4.75
L-M	DISTANCE, DEPTH OF WATER, EACH SIDE OF PLUMMET	DESIG.	L-1	M-1	L-3	M-3	L/M-1 (PL)	L/M-3 (PL)	L-5	M-5	L-7.5	M-7.5	L-10	M-10
		MIN.	2.50	3.30	3.25	3.70	2.05/3.3	2.65/3.5	4.25	3.70	4.50	4.00	5.25	4.25
		PREF.		3.70		3.90				3.70		4.40		4.75
N P	MAXIMUM ANGLE OF SLOPE TO REDUCE DIMENSIONS BEYOND FULL REQUIREMENTS	POOL BOTTOM	= 30 Degrees (Approximately 1 ft vertical to 2 ft horizontal)											
		CEILING HEIGHT	= 30 Degrees											

Figure 19. Recommended diving dimensions (FINA) (2).

Figure 20. Duraflex diving board.
Photograph by R. Jackson Smith.

Figure 21. 1980 Moscow Olympic pool and diving towers. Photograph by R. Jackson Smith.

4. Special equipment used by patients include: stretchers, kick boards, floating mattresses, inner tubes, life jackets, arm floats, hand paddles, leg weights, arm weights, fins, goggles, and face masks.

Spas and Hot Tubs

Spas and hot tubs have recently become very popular in the United States. Whether this was the result of the energy shortage, which suggests using a smaller volume of water than a regular pool, or simply the desire for a hot water massage in a potentially friendly situation is not clear. However, according to the National Spa and Pool Institute 1983 Survey, there were 220,000 spas or hot tubs sold in the United States, and this number is certainly increasing. Many of these pools are designed for home use, but they are also used in clubs and hotels in conjunction with a regular pool. In this case they can use the same pool plant. However, the higher temperatures and water turnover through the hydromassage jet inlets requires extra-durable finishes and equipment.

One of the principal aspects of a hot tub is that it has hotter water than a pool; a hot tub also has water jets that can be aerated, which act to massage the body.

Hot tubs are often constructed of redwood (Fig. 22), but are also sold by a number of companies from molded vinyl or other material (Fig. 23).

Hot tubs are generally 1.25-m deep, and vary in diameter from 1.2 to 2.2 m depending on desired use. Deeper pools are also available. The temperature of the hot tub should be able to reach 40°C (109°F).

Figure 23. The hot spring spa. Courtesy of Watkins Manufacturing Corporation.

SUPPORT SPACES

The design and layout of the support spaces related to a pool depend on the type of pool and the functions included. For simple outdoor recreational pools, toilets, showers, and locker rooms are the principal facilities required. For any kind of public pool, these should control the entrance to the pool, and swimmers should go through a shower area to reach the pool itself.

For indoor pools, such as pools for colleges or universities, the circulation pattern becomes more complex. The

Figure 22. The "Caressa" spa by Jacuzzi Whirlpool Bath.

locker area for general recreational swimmers and that of team competition swimmers should be separate, with separate facilities for visiting teams. All lockers, showers, and toilets should be at the same level as the pool deck, as wet steps or stairs are dangerous. The access to the pool should be at a point of sufficient width to avoid accidents with people hurrying out of the locker and shower area. Other support areas will include rooms for coaches, which should have a window directly into the pool at a good control point, a first aid room, and a training room (rub down).

For instruction, it is desirable to have a viewing window below the water level, where it is possible to see swimmers, turns at the end of the pool, and divers entering the pool. Where a pool is part of a general athletic facility, as for example in a school, the lockers are often combined, allowing the participants to go to whatever sport they wish. This is generally not a good idea because of the locational and other special requirements related to pool lockers.

Spectators should be totally separated from the pool deck, and should be in a gallery high enough to overlook the pool at an angle to see swimmers separately in all lanes. This can generally be accomplished in a stadium-type seating arrangement over the locker area. However, to achieve the perfect viewing location for swimming (especially if both Olympic and intercollegiate distances are involved) and diving, if in a separate area, is not easy. Add to this viewing of synchronized swimming, water polo, and other activities, and the problem can be quite complex. The viewing area should be reached through a circulation pattern entirely separate from the participants and should have access to separate toilets. For large pools, there should be a lobby and ticket sales area.

GENERAL STRUCTURAL AND CONSTRUCTION CONSIDERATIONS

Before purchasing a pool or contracting for its construction, the local health and building inspectors should be consulted to find out about health, safety, and zoning restrictions. They are also good sources of information about soil conditions, suppliers, contractors and manufacturers.

Outdoor Pools Built Directly on the Ground

Most residential pool and community pools are built outdoors and must deal with all the problems related to any structure: proper bearing capacity, settlement, drainage around the structure, temperature changes, and so forth. In examining the site, one should look for loose fill below the level of construction; the presence of rock that will require blasting and increase cost; and water conditions, springs, or high water tables. There are additional considerations specific to pools. Because they will be exposed to the weather indefinitely, the exposed surfaces must be as weather resistant as possible. Also, in northern climates the side walls and bottom must be protected from the action of frost. Formerly, it was customary to empty pools in the winter. However, the current practice is to leave

the water in the pool and cover it with a plastic sheet of some kind so that no one can fall in. This protects most of the side walls and the bottom from frost.

Before siting the pool, a few test holes should be made to determine the soil condition and the underground water level. A test hole at each corner of the proposed location is suggested. The holes should be 4 or 5 ft deeper than the planned bottom of the pool. Samples of the soil should be saved to show contractors the type of material that they will have to excavate, if the final decision is to place the pool in the ground, or what type of soil is available to support an above-ground pool. The ideal soil for an in-the-ground pool is a clean, dense, coarse sand, naturally deposited or man-made fill carefully placed and compacted in layers by heavily loaded equipment. Unfortunately, very few sites have an ideal soil condition. If the test holes indicate a rock ledge or large boulders, then an alternative location on the property should be considered or the level of the pool should be raised to eliminate the cost and danger of blasting, the cost of rock removal, and the fear of neighbors that blasting has damaged their property. If peat or other organic materials are found in the test holes, the test hole must be made deeper to determine the distance down to material that is strong enough to support the weight of the filled pool. The compression of the soil beneath the pool will lead to uneven settlement, distortion of the bottom and sides, and cracks in a concrete pool.

Clays, including boulder clays, and silts may be used for bearing in localities that have a constant water level and are not subject to long freezing temperatures. Clays expand when they are wet and shrink when they are dry. This movement will disrupt the pool, causing cracking and leaking. Clays and silts are also frost heave susceptible. As the water in the soil freezes, it expands and causes the top of the soil to heave. Whenever highly compressible materials and frost-bearing materials are found below the proposed bottom level of the pool, they must be excavated and replaced with clean, coarse sand or gravel carefully densified.

Pools may be built of poured-in-place reinforced concrete on structural fill or Gunite concrete sprayed against a form. Concrete should be carefully waterproofed with some product, such as Thoroseal. It is also possible to build a pool from concrete block, precast concrete units, or brick masonry, but these must then receive an interior finish to close the joints and make them watertight. They must also be reinforced laterally to offset any horizontal pressure from the ground around the pool. Aluminum, steel, and fiberglass vinyl pools are also available in a variety of shapes and sizes.

Outdoor Pools Above Grade

It is also possible to build a pool entirely above the ground, or on the roof of another structure. In this case it is often desirable to use a steel, aluminum, or fiberglass shell type of structure to lighten the load to be transmitted to the ground. Even if the pool is directly on the ground, the loads including, of course, the weight of the water, must be transferred to solid bearing, below frost.

Pools Built in Structures

Pools built in structures may vary all the way from a small pool in a house, to a pool in the upper levels of a hotel, to an Olympic-size natatorium built for international competition. From the structural point of view, they have certain things in common that are different from the outdoor pool. They are not subject to outdoor weathering and the extremes of heat and cold or directly to ground action. They do, however, have problems particularly related to their weight and how to transmit it to solid bearing. As noted above, this may suggest lighter methods of construction. If a pool is located fairly high in a tall building in an earthquake zone, the action of the water in an earthquake must be considered in the design. Indoor pools also must be properly heated and ventilated, which is discussed in that section.

Enclosures for indoor pools must meet two special requirements. One is the larger than usual spans for the roof framing; the second is the use of materials to resist the high humidity and water damage. The required span (the distance between supports) is determined by the width of the pool plus its surrounding deck. A 15-ft wide pool with 5-ft decks on each side requires a 25-ft span. This span is greater than the typical house framing, which is usually 14–16 ft long and is too great for economical wooden joists. One economical wooden framing for 20–30 ft spans is prefabricated wooden trusses. The truss members must be connected with heavily galvanized gusset plates and nails. Ordinary steel nails will soon rust and lose their holding capacity. In larger spans over wider pools, steel trusses or beams may be used. It is not economically feasible to galvanize large members so that they must be coated to reduce the rate of rusting. Timber members made up of standard pieces glued together (glued laminated wood or glulam) may also be used. They are made up to the correct size to carry safely the design loads for a chosen span. The pieces must be glued with a water-resistant glue and should be fabricated only by a reputable manufacturer. Precast, prestressed concrete members may also be used. The usual configuration for moderate spans is "double tees"; so called because in cross section they look like two tees with their tips or top flanges touching. They not only support the design loads but also act as the roof decking.

For large spans over public indoor pools, more unusual structures become economically feasible. Perhaps the most popular is the arch. To be effective, the base of the arch must be prevented from moving outward. This is done by providing tie-rods across the bottom of the arch or by building buttresses. In the case of swimming pools, tierods are not practical, so buttresses are used. The arch itself may be made of steel, aluminum, glulam wood, or concrete. The most economical plan for arches is to set them perpendicular to the long axis of the structure. While this is a stable structure in its own plane, the arch needs some bracing to prevent its falling sideways. One method is to place the arches at an angle to the longitudinal axis of the building so that the arches intersect each other. If the intersecting arches are made up of small pieces, the structure is a lamella arch. A growing method

of spanning over large clear spaces is the use of air-supported structures; these are fabrics that are supported by air pressure and are stabilized by steel cables. Unlike usual structures that require a foundation to hold the building up, air-supported structures require a foundation to hold the fabric down. They also require mechanical equipment to supply the air pressure and special accessories such as air locks, heat savers, and lighting supports. Fabrics may be used without internal pressure. There are tent structures also called tension structures. They require tent poles, arches, tension, and compression rings to resist the tension of the fabric. One example of this is the 1964 Olympic Pool in Tokyo, designed by Kenzo Tange. Another is the pool at Regensburg, FRG (Fig. 24).

If the site and the shape of the pool favor a circular roof plan then, in addition to air support and tension structures, domes and space frames can be considered. Domes and space frames may be made of steel, aluminum, or wood. Domes are usually spherical in shape, but they may be elliptical. Space frames are usually in a flat horizontal plane, with only a slight pitch to provide drainage of rain. They are constructed of individual pieces connected so that they carry their loads in more than one direction.

The fact that large pools and their adjacent areas require buildings with large, clear spans, has been a challenge to architects for generations and has resulted in some great architectural achievements. The great barrel vaults over the Baths of Caracalla are an early example. In more recent times, modern technology has turned its attention to this same design problem, producing such results as the Olympic Pool in Munich or the Hallenbad in Landeshamptstadt, Hannover, FRG.

Pool Construction and Equipment Specialists

The specialized design and construction of pools has become a large market, and there are many companies that offer complete packages or standard parts and fittings. Some companies also build (or assist with) large competition pools. Each of these has developed, and sometimes patented, special details for gutters, construction, fittings, starting blocks, and so forth. It is therefore important in making a selection to study the particular details to ensure the most suitable choice. It is not unusual when building a large indoor pool facility for the general contractor to subcontract the pool package to one of the specialized companies.

Pool Materials and Finishes

As noted above, the basic construction of pools may be accomplished in many ways using a variety of structural materials. Some of these are suitable to be left, or simply painted, as the interior of the pool itself. In residential and inexpensive community pools it is quite customary simply to paint the concrete walls and bottom. A "plaster" finish can also be used, consisting of fine cement with a granular component. Similarly, the steel, aluminum, and fiberglass shell type of construction can be painted. (Two coats of chlorinated rubber paint is recommended.) This does require maintenance, often repainting annually. A better finish for the pool area is ceramic tile over waterproofing.

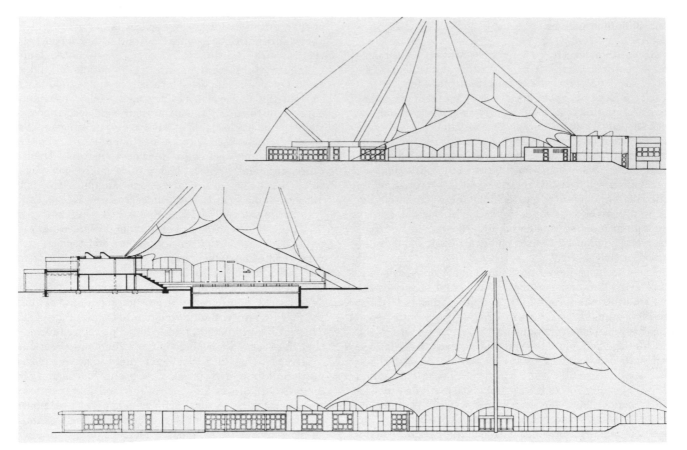

Figure 24. Drawing of pool at Regensburg, FRG.

The deck surrounding outdoor pools can be poured-in-place concrete, precast concrete slabs, or some type of paver. The important thing is that it should have some form of nonslip surface when wet. Some pool decks employ terrazzo ground smooth but this can be dangerous. It is also important, particularly with precast units, that they be laid in a bed that keeps them level, preferably on a subslab, to avoid tripping.

In all pools, outdoor and indoor, all fittings and hardware must be corrosion proof, due not only to the presence of water, but also the chemicals in the water used for purification. In large indoor competition pools, the pool itself is normally lined with tile to give a better and more permanent finish. A principal consideration in the walls and ceiling of pools is the effect of condensation. Because the pool area is apt to have high humidity, the roof or outside wall area must be heavily insulated to avoid a dew point occurring on the interior surface. This can attack, and cause rusting on, metal decks or steel joist construction over a pool, possibly in a concealed area above a hung ceiling.

The exposed surfaces of side walls in a pool area should be easy to keep clean, and not too rough in case people in bathing suits come up against them. Here again, tile is ideal. It is generally desirable to have some acoustically absorbent material on the ceiling of larger pools, as the water is a reflecting surface and the sound level can be high.

One of the key elements in pool design is the overflow or "gutter" system. Several companies in the United States are specialists in supplying and installing their own designs as noted above. These fall into three basic types.

1. The perimeter overflow system.
2. The roll-out or open gutter system.
3. The recessed type.

For details refer to Ref. 2. It is important to work with the athletic department and coaches in choosing which system to use, as each has particular advantages.

Pool Maintenance

There is, of course, a direct correlation between the quality of pool construction, its materials and equipment, and the amount of maintenance necessary. In general, the better a pool was built in the first place, the less maintenance will be required. This is particularly true for outdoor pools with bare concrete paint or plaster finish. These may require patching, repainting, and general repair on a fairly regular basis. Pools with tile finishes should last for years, particularly indoors.

There are, for any pool, certain regular maintenance procedures that must be followed. The quality of the water should be checked daily to be sure that it meets public health standards. Also, all mechanical equipment should be checked regularly to be sure it is operating properly.

Outdoor pools in northern climates must be closed in the winter. They should be cleaned and given a dose of algicide. The water level should be kept just below the outlet drain, and covered with a rubber or plastic sheet. It is also recommended to put logs at the edge of the pool, floating in the water, to avoid the pressure of ice on the side walls. When the pool is opened for use again in the spring, it should be drained and inspected, and thoroughly cleaned before refilling. It is probably a good idea to run the filtration system for a day or two before the pool is used, as even the city water system, when drawn on suddenly in large amounts, can be quite rusty. If there are underwater lights, these should be carefully checked as improper wiring can be very dangerous to swimmers.

For indoor pools, it is important also to check related areas, including the structure over the pool, for possible rust or corrosion due to high humidity or the action of chemicals used in the pool. In particular, for indoor pools, cracks and leaks are of major concern. If these appear, experts should be called in to make repairs immediately.

MECHANICAL CONSIDERATIONS

Plumbing

The design of swimming pools is generally governed by both the Building Code and the Health Code of the applicable area. Before embarking on the design of the filtration system or any portion of the pool, it is essential that all Code requirements be obtained to avoid proceeding with the wrong assumptions. Codes usually distinguish acceptable practices between private-type pools and public-type pools and what is acceptable for one type may not be acceptable for the other. Also, the definitions should be reviewed because wading pools, special-purpose pools, and swimming pools all have specific requirements.

Filtration Systems. The purpose of a filtration system is to remove particulate matter so that the appearance of the water is clean, clear, and inviting. This system is not a purification system and does not treat the water, but serves to maintain cleanliness and sparkle from a purely aesthetic point of view. The filtration system operates continuously 24 h a day, and usually recirculates the contents of the pool over a 6-h period.

Sand Filtration. There are two basic types of sand filter commonly used today: normal rate sand filters and high rate sand filters. These terms also vary throughout the country, but for purposes of this discussion, normal rate sand filters are pressure filters with a filtration rate of 3 gpm/ft² area, and high rate filters are pressure filters with a filtration rate of 15 gpm/ft² area.

Most codes limit the use of high rate filters to small pools because they are newer in concept and therefore must undergo stringent evaluation prior to being accepted by code for large municipal-type pools. These systems have developed a good track record; however, codes are slow in making changes. The advantage of using a high rate filter is to reduce space requirements as well as cost.

Backwashing. As pool water is circulated through the filter and particulate matter is removed, a pressure drop occurs in the filter. This is due to clogging of the sand by the particulates. When this pressure drop reaches approximately 15–20 psi, backwashing is required.

This process reverses the flow through the units, expands the sand bed and wastes the discharge to the drainage system carrying with it all the sediment collected during the filtration process. The backwash process can be accomplished either manually or automatically. The frequency of backwashing is directly dependent on the bather load, which is the major source of dirt in an indoor pool.

Vacuum Diatomaceous Earth (DE) Filters. Diatomaceous earth is a filter media that consists of decomposed seashells. This material forms a coating over a hollow screen and is used to filter water. A vacuum DE filter consists of an open rectangular tank that contains a pipe header on which is mounted a series of hollow leaves coated with DE. A pump draws water from the header, which filters the water in the process. As in the sand pressure filter, as the leaves collect sediment and clogging starts to occur, a pressure drop will indicate that backwashing is required.

Backwashing a vacuum DE filter is accomplished by stopping the filtration cycle, draining the tank and hosing down the filter leaves. In this process, the DE is wasted and must be replaced after each backwash cycle. This differs from a pressure sand filter where the sand is permanent and does not require replacement.

Pressure Diatomaceous Earth Filters. This type of filter in swimming pool applications is usually limited to residential-type pools. It consists of a stainless steel or fiber glass shell that contains DE. It usually comes with a pump and is prepiped, prewired, and skid-mounted complete with controls. Replacement of the DE is required after each backwash.

Disinfection Systems. Pool water must meet specific requirements by Code regarding bacteriological quality. This is to insure a safe condition for the swimmer in the event water is ingested. It also is required to prevent the spread of infection from one swimmer to another.

Treatment by chlorine is the most common method, although other disinfectants such as bromine and iodine are acceptable. Chlorine has an advantage because a measurable "residual" level can be determined by sampling the pool water. When a "residual" level is determined, it is an indication that the water still contains disinfecting potential and the water is at a safe quality level.

Hypochlorinator. A common method of adding chlorine to a pool is by the use of sodium hypochlorite solution and a positive displacement chemical feeder. The chlorine solution is somewhat equivalent to the Clorox bottle one uses in the laundry washing machines.

A residual of 0.6 ppm is a common concentration required where the pH of the water is between 7.4 and 7.8. The pH of the water is a measure of the acidity and a level of 7.0 represents a neutral or balanced water condition. It is best to maintain a slightly alkaline level, which is represented by a level greater than 7.0. A properly balanced pool water, both in pH and chlorine concentrations, will eliminate any odor or eye irritation. It is incorrectly be-lieved that eye irritation is due to an overdose of chlorine. The fact is just the reverse. The odor is the "chloramine" formation that develops when insufficient chlorine has been introduced into the water. It is usually required by Code that the pool water be tested at least 3 times a day for the presence of the required chlorine residual.

Gaseous Chlorination. This system is usually reserved for very large municipal- or public-type pools. Liquid cyl-inders under high pressure are connected to the piping system, and as the liquid chlorine enters the water it va-porizes into a gas and intimately mixes with the water. Because liquid chlorine and gaseous chlorine are highly toxic and dangerous, these cylinders must be kept in a separate room having a noncombustible rating. Gas masks are usually provided adjacent to the room for emer-gency conditions.

Brominators. Bromine is another type of disinfectant and is usually provided in the form of a solid, which is dissolved by the recirculated pool water. The dissolving rate is a little more difficult to control and therefore the residual may have a greater variation than with chlorina-tion. The acidity of the pH of the water must also be con-trolled when using bromine as a disinfectant.

Recirculation Systems. A pool recirculation system con-sists of a series of inlets, drains, and overflow gutters or skimmers, all piped together in a particular method to pass the contents of the pool water through a filtration, disinfection, and heating system. The arrangement of these components are extremely important so that short circuiting of the various processes do not occur.

Skimmers and Overflow Gutters. These devices are used to remove continuously all floating material and dirt that collects at the surface of the pool. Skimmers are restricted for use on small size pools only and are located at specific points on the pool wall at the water's surface. Gutters are continuous around the perimeter of the pool and are de-signed to accommodate 100% of the pool water for recircu-lation back to the filter. See the section on Materials and Finishes.

Surge Tank. In order for a gutter system to be effective it must continually skim the surface of the water. Once a gutter floods it loses the ability to function. Therefore, to accumulate the displaced pool water due to the quantity of swimmers that may enter the pool at any one time, a surge tank should be provided to store this water tempo-rarily. This can be accomplished in a variety of ways: a separate tank, extra deep gutters, or oversize gutter re-turn piping. Codes may dictate the specific method; how-ever, this storage is essential so that the recirculation system can function properly and skimming the pool sur-face is continuous.

Main Drain. All pools must be provided with a drain outlet located at the deepest portion of the pool. This drain must be capable of draining the entire pool contents within an 8-h period. The velocity of the water through the drain grate must be controlled so that a vortex condi-tion cannot occur under any operating condition. This is done to prevent any bathers from being pulled and held at the drain due to the strong pull that could develop due to

high-velocity water flow. Drainage from the pool must be taken indirectly to a sewer to avoid any potential sewer backup and contamination of the pool. While pool drain-age usually is permitted into a storm sewer, filter back-wash is normally required to be discharged into a sanitary sewer.

Inlets. These are submerged adjustable supply fittings usually located flush around the pool wall or floor. Water enters the pool through these inlets after being filtered, disinfected, and heated.

Make-up Water. Due to swimmer removal either by splashing or carry out, or due to evaporation, pool water volume must be maintained. In order to prevent a cross-connection between the potable water supply and the pool water, all make-up water must be supplied through an air gap (indirect connection) or an approved backflow pre-venter. The local Code usually dictates which method is acceptable.

Piping. The recirculation piping system should be con-structed of materials that are corrosion resistant, because pool water, due to the chlorine content required, is highly corrosive. Plastics such as PVC or PP are quite suitable, or even plastic-lined steel pipe. Brass pipe, copper tubing, cement-lined ductile iron, and asbestos cement pipe (ACP) are other common materials for this purpose. Consider-ation must also be given to the materials for inlets, gutter drains, and any other fittings that are surface mounted in the pool. Stainless steel is a preferred material and is a better choice than chrome-plated brass, which has a ten-dency to corrode and turn green due to the chlorine atmo-sphere.

Deck Drains. Most Codes prohibit sloping the deck area around the pool into the pool. Therefore, it is necessary to provide deck drains to keep the area dry. Drainage from the area must be kept separate from the recirculation sys-tem to avoid any unnecessary contamination from outside sources.

Pool Water Heating. Ideally, the pool water tempera-ture for an indoor pool should be adjusted so that a bather leaving the pool does not encounter a chill due to a lower air temperature. Codes usually require an approximate air temperature of 75°F, so that 75°F is also a suitable temperature to maintain for pool water.

Pool water is usually heated indirectly through a heat exchanger using gas, steam, solar, or other heating me-dium as a heat source. Direct injection of steam into the pool is prohibited by Code. Outdoor pools should also be provided with heaters, and temperature settings from 75 to 78°F are common.

Pool Cleaning. Even though pools are provided with fil-tration systems, overflow gutters or skimmers, and hair and lint pump strainers, there are times when there may be visible dirt scum floating on the surface or visible sedi-ment on the pool bottom. Floating material is usually re-moved by long-handled manual strainers when observed by the maintenance staff, and settled materials by the use of vacuum cleaning.

Vacuum cleaning can be provided by a number of methods. One method utilizes a permanently piped system with vacuum fitting inlets located strategically around the perimeter of the pool just below the water surface with a vacuum cleaning pump located in the equipment room. Another method is to use a portable vacuum cleaning unit with integral pump and filter systems. Both these systems require suitable lengths of hose and cleaning heads to reach all surfaces of the pool.

The water from vacuuming can either be discharged to waste or put back into the filtration system to save water. A more recent method is to use a robot device that is placed in the pool bottom and moves automatically back and forth across the pool bottom recirculating water through the unit itself, which contains a filtering component. The choice of which system to use is optional; however, a provision for this type of cleaning should be provided.

Heating, Ventilating and Air-conditioning

Design of swimming pools requires careful attention to construction details and materials used for the room envelopes. The swimming pool generates a highly humid and corrosive environment, resulting from the magnitudes of the water evaporation and the chlorination treatment. It requires the optimization of comfort, energy use, and construction techniques.

Design of the heating and ventilation system for the pool should provide comfort for swimmers and spectators. The higher the humidity and lower the air movement, the lower the evaporative cooling effect on the person emerging from the pool. Natatorium design parameters are usually as follows:

Room Air Temperature: 5°F above water temperature
Relative Humidity: 40–60%
Air Velocity: 20–40 ft/min

Relative humidity is the weight of water present in an air specimen, divided by the weight of water in air fully saturated (100% relative humidity) at the same temperature and pressure. Normal pressure change is minimal and may be neglected. Because the weight of water in saturated air decreases as the air temperature decreases, lowering the air temperature of an air sample results in an increase of its relative humidity to the limit of 100%, beyond which excess moisture precipitates out of the air. This condition is undesirable. It follows that the building construction and ventilation should be designed to preclude low temperature areas and excessive humidity levels.

Building Construction Materials. The construction elements must have insulating values that will permit all interior surface temperatures to remain close to the room temperature, under extreme winter weather conditions. A vapor barrier is necessary to prevent moisture from permeating the building materials and condensing within the construction where the temperature approaches that of the outdoors.

Material and equipment selected for pool construction is of prime importance. The injurious effect of condensation and corrosion from the corrosive and humid pool atmosphere can cause damage and failure of materials and equipment within or serving a natatorium. Unprotected ferrous metals must be eliminated from all areas of pool construction. Insulation at roofs and walls must be protected by a vapor barrier.

Suspended ceilings should be avoided because they provide a high humidity enclosure that requires its own ventilation. Lights, supports, ductwork, registers, and diffusers are subject to corrosion. All components of the heating and air distribution system exposed or indirectly in contact with the pool environment should be furnished in a noncorrosive material, or where unfeasible to do so, protected with a good corrosion-resistant coating. All ductwork serving or adjacent to pool areas should be constructed of stainless steel, aluminum, coated steel, or other corrosion-resistant material. Return or exhaust ductwork should be watertight and pitched to drain points and insulated where passing through cool areas.

All exposed surfaces within the natatorium should be resistant to moisture and corrosion damage caused by the chlorine in the air. The architect–engineer must realize that he or she has little or no control over actual system operation, particularly when the building is not in use. The room night-setback temperature is usually equal to the pool water temperature, and the humidity control should continue to function.

Heating. Heating is required in most climates because there are times when the outside temperature falls below the pool water temperature. Warm wall and floor surfaces increase occupant comfort. Direct radiation, radiant floors, heating a perimeter underfloor tunnel, or warm air curtains are some methods used to offset heat losses through exterior walls, roofs, floors, and windows. In cold climates, the combination of high humidities and the use of glass requires careful design and engineering to avoid condensation problems.

Humidity Control. Relative humidity should not be maintained below or higher than the recommended levels so as to maintain maximum comfort and minimize the deleterious effect of the moisture. This will also permit the least energy use. The humidity level in the room is maintained by introducing sufficient outside air into the natatorium to dilute the moisture concentration. Pool water temperatures vary between 72 and 80°F. The higher the water temperature and the pool activity, the greater the evaporation rate as well as the greater the room ventilation requirements.

Ventilation. Pools require ventilation to control humidity and to maintain comfortable conditions. Pool air handling units are designed to use up to 100% outside air for cooling and dehumidification. The pool area should be maintained at a slightly negative pressure to help prevent moisture from entering other areas of the building. This is accomplished by exhausting more air than is being supplied to the pool area. Increased air motion as well as a separate air supply is desirable for spectator areas, avoiding exhausting or returning humid pool air through the spectator area. Therapeutic pools may require water and air temperatures five to ten degrees higher than those previously listed.

LEGAL ISSUES

The relatively high risk involved with pools and pool users as well as the recent tendency to sue whenever possible have resulted in greater concern for safety in pool design, often the elimination of such elements as diving boards in motel pools, and in greater concern for the design and supervision of the operation of public pools. In the design of swimming pools it is very important at least to meet the legal standards governing the particular situation. Although there are generally accepted standards, laws in different states of the United States vary considerably and, in fact, these laws are often being revised and updated, so it is important to check for specific compliance. In addition to state laws, there are rules and regulations drawn up by state and municipal boards of health. These deal not only with design considerations, but also with standards of maintenance. In the design of pools outside of the United States, it is even more important to check on regulations as standards may differ.

The principal objective in the design of a pool is, of course, to make it work well functionally and to be safe for the users. It is also important to be conscious of the fact that in today's world there are more and more lawsuits involving accidents in pools, and the proper design of the pool is often a factor. In addition to the laws noted above, there are, in the United States, generally accepted standards published by the NCAA and the AAU. In some instances, these cover situations not completely covered in the state regulations, such as detailed dimensions for the depth of pools from various high board or platform diving positions. Even though these have no legal standing, they constitute an accepted standard that will have weight in any litigation.

The simple fact is that pools by their very nature involve some risk for the users. Every care must be used to reduce this risk, but it cannot be eliminated entirely. In addition to the design of pools, their proper use and maintenance is extremely important. Community pools should have regulations, particularly where children are involved. Proper control of water quality is essential. Even maintaining the water level is essential in relation to diving; the effect of dropping the level is doubled, as it not only makes the pool shallower, but also makes the board higher. Finally, it must be recognized that some accidents will occur, and will very probably be followed by lawsuits.

Architects might be advised to call their clients', pool owners', and managers' attention to the inherent dangers and recommend precautions be taken including the following:

1. Safety standards for appropriate pool depths may change from time to time as there is more experience with diving boards and platforms and it will be the owner's continuing responsibility to monitor such changes and to see to it that the pool conforms.

2. A diver not properly instructed as to how to divert his downward course through the water may hit the bottom of a pool designed in accordance with all recommended standards. The owner must see to it that all divers be properly instructed and supervised.

3. Such modifications as a reduction in the water level maintained in the pool or an alteration in the diving board or platform level may have serious consequences as to the safety of the pool. The owner must carefully monitor the condition of the pool, insure compliance with applicable regulations relating to pool operation, and review the effect on safety of any proposed modifications.

BIBLIOGRAPHY

1. J. Dawes, *Design and Planning of Swimming Pools*, John Dawes Publications, Kent, UK, 1979.
2. *Ramsey/Sleeper Architectural Graphic Standards*, 8th ed., John Wiley & Sons, New York, 1988.
3. R. B. Flynn, *Planning Facilities for Athletics, Physical Education and Recreation*, The Athletic Institute, North Palm Beach, Fla, 1985, and American Alliance for Health, Physical Education, Recreation, and Dance, Reston, Va., 1985.

General References

The Encyclopedia Americana, Vols. 3 and 26, Grolier Inc., Danbury, Conn., 1983.
The Encyclopedia Britannica, Vols. I, IX, Micropaedia, Encyclopedia Britannica, Inc., Chicago Ill., 1984.
The New Encyclopedia Britannica, Vol. 17, Macropaedia, Encyclopedia Britannica, Inc., Chicago, Ill., 1984.
Swimming Pool Design Manual, Whitten Pool Systems, Mendon, Mass.
Swimming Pool Weekly is a good general reference.

See also RECREATIONAL FACILITIES

JOHN C. HARKNESS, FAIA
The Architects Collaborative
Cambridge, Massachusetts

The following individuals have contributed to the writing of this article: R. Jackson Smith, AIA, Designer Environment Inc.; David Sheffield, The Architects Collaborative; Herbert L. Panger, Syska & Hennessy; Elizabeth Pillsbury, The Architects Collaborative; Tony Yamada, The Architects Collaborative; Richard Sousa, Partners, Sousa & True.

SYNAGOGUES

The word synagogue is taken from the Greek *synagoge*, meaning "a bringing together." Significantly, its primary definition is "an assembly of Jews for worship and study," with emphasis on the act of coming together for religious purposes rather than on the place. The synagogue itself is not the house of a god, nor is it a holy place, although its role in the life of Jewish communities has made it a revered institution. Indeed, the emphasis on community is central to Jewish religious practice and to the idea of the synagogue. For example, a quorum of 10 men is traditionally required for worship, which can take place anywhere. Furthermore, the individuals in a community govern the life of the congregation rather than a hierarchy of priests or other officials from outside. The synagogue as a building, therefore, derives significance from the activities that take place within.

Essential to the idea of a synagogue are three communal functions: prayer, study, and meeting. Throughout the history of the synagogue, these are the activities that have been the basis of the building program; it is the evolution of these functions in different social and philosophical settings that defines the evolution of the architecture of synagogues. Aesthetically, synagogues have followed styles prevailing in the local culture; the choice of the style of a synagogue only became a design issue in the nineteenth century. At that time eclecticism was a dominant force in architecture and specific meanings were ascribed to different styles. In general, however, unique expression was achieved through the organization of spaces to accommodate Jewish ritual and practice. The ornamentation of the spaces was simple or elaborate, but always based on Jewish symbols. The idea of the synagogue, therefore, is best examined through the evolution of attitudes about prayer, study, and congregating.

THE TEMPLE AND THE SYNAGOGUE

The first Jewish worship took place in sacrificial temples, not unlike the sanctuaries of other semitic peoples (1). While the Jews were special in being monotheistic, they shared a way of life based on agriculture and animal husbandry with their neighbors. Worship involved offerings to a god as well as prayer. The First Temple in Jerusalem, built by King Solomon ca 950 B.C., was, by all accounts, an imposing structure, probably resembling Egyptian buildings. Located on the highest hill in Jerusalem, it was set in a court approximately 265 m square. Entry to the Temple proper was through an entry court, which was the only part of the complex open to women. Men could proceed up steps to an inner court where there was an altar for the sacrifice of animals, areas for the preparation of sacrifices, a large basin of water in which priests would bathe, and other ritual areas. The Temple itself was raised above the court and its entrance was flanked by two large columns, named Jachin and Boas. Inside was an altar for incense and a seven-branched candlestick, or menorah. The menorah sculpted on the Arch of Titus in Rome is thought to have been the one from the Temple, being shown off as war booty. The final room was the Holy of Holies, hidden from view and containing the Ark of the Covenant, which once held the original Ten Commandments (2).

Priests officiated and administered the entire complex, which was the spiritual center of Jewish existence and which represented the faith and power of the Jewish people. In Hebrew called *bet ha-mikdash*, "the House of Sanctuary," the Temple remains to this day a powerful symbol

for Jews and certain of its elements have been used continuously in synagogue design. The intention of building on the highest point in the community, a courtyard as a meeting place, procession upward toward the most holy place, ritual use of water, the ark, the menorah and eternal lamp, and the columns Jachin and Boas evoke the First Temple and demonstrate its persistence as a source of meaning in Jewish observance.

Whereas the Temple was unique for all Jews and a place for offering sacrifices, there were, even in Jerusalem, local synagogues serving small communities as places of prayer, study, and gathering. However, with the destruction of Solomon's Temple in 586 B.C. by Nebuchadnezzar, the synagogue begins its history as the primary focus of Jewish communities. Jews were exiled to Babylon and, chastened by their fall from power and expulsion from their holy city Jerusalem, they turned to the Torah, the Five Books of Moses, as the source of their religious life. While there is evidence that synagogues were in existence from the time of Moses, it is in Babylon that the study and teaching of Torah becomes a primary form of worship. Furthermore, as a minority, the Jews sought an institution that would bring them together and maintain their social, cultural, and religious ties. Sacrifices of animals or other offerings were probably made on a small scale, as a reminiscence of practices at the Temple. In spite of the construction of the Second Temple about 70 years after the destruction of the First Temple, the synagogue, in Hebrew *bet ha-keneset*, "the House of Assembly," grew in importance due to the need of a spiritual center for Jews in exile. After the destruction of the Second Temple by the Romans in 70 A.D., the synagogue became the sole center of Jewish communities. Study of the Torah as an integral part of Jewish practice and as a form of prayer gave a particular character to the life of synagogues, which have been called schools (*schul*) throughout much of their history. Thus, the Jews transformed the concept of a religious building as the house of a god to a place of congregational assembly for study and prayer. The innovation is a fundamental assembly for study and prayer. The innovation is a fundamental one in the history of religion as well as building (3).

SYNAGOGUE PLANNING

The planning of the sanctuary in synagogues is determined by the placement of the ark and the *bimah*. The ark holds the Torah scrolls and is the holiest part of a synagogue. In its earliest manifestations, the ark was a chest that was movable, probably reflecting its nomadic precedents. More pragmatically, the movable ark, the presence of which in a room of any kind made a prayer hall of the room, was useful at a time when synagogues were often simple renovations of other existing buildings. Furthermore, many early synagogues had no special architectural provision for the ark. For example, remains of the synagogue at Ostia Antica, the ancient port city for Rome, show that in the first century the door faced Jerusalem as a symbolic gesture and an inscription indicates that the ark was probably a wooden chest. Later in the fourth century a niche was provided for the ark, which by this time was itself to face Jerusalem (4). Excavations at Dura-Europas, now in Syria, have revealed a synagogue dating from 245 A.D. and traces of an earlier synagogue on the site. A niche for the ark is clearly provided and is placed on axis with the entry to the sanctuary (5).

In general, it can be said that the ark is always placed against one wall, usually opposite the entry to the prayer hall. In form, it has evolved from a portable chest to a permanent feature, integrated to a greater or lesser degree into the architecture of the synagogue, depending on the inclinations of the builder. A curtain often covers the scrolls, a reference to the curtain that separated the Holy of Holies of the original Temple from the congregation. Usually placed on a platform three steps above the sanctuary floor, the ark is often richly decorated, typically incorporating representations of the ten commandments and the pillars of the Temple, Jachin and Boas.

While the ark is the most holy element of the synagogue, it is the bimah that has been most significant in determining the architectural character of sanctuary spaces. The bimah is a raised platform with a desk for the reading of the Torah and is the place from which prayer is directed. As the locus of the main activities of worship services, its location is primary in establishing orientation. The placement of the bimah, its architectural elaboration, and the methods by which it is illuminated reveal differing traditions and attitudes that have developed over the centuries. A study of the evolution of the synagogue plan in response to Jewish practice in various periods of history is, therefore, the most appropriate vehicle for understanding the synagogue as a building type, and style, deriving from the dominant culture, complements this understanding.

ANTIQUITY

The synagogues of classical antiquity were often renovations of existing structures. They were generally simple rectangular rooms, sometimes with stone benches against the walls, as at Dura-Europas. The organization of seating would have created a spatial emphasis on the community of worshipers. The ark would have been a freestanding chest, although an apse may have been provided for it. Basilical plans are also found, the rows of columns giving a focus. For example, the largest known synagogue of the ancient world was at Sardis, in Anatolia (Fig. 1). Sardis was a major city from the sixth century B.C. until the early seventh century A.D.; under Roman rule, the population reached 100,000. The synagogue is a basilical hall, which is part of the Roman bath–gymnasium complex. This close association with an important secular institution reveals the prominence and size of the Jewish community. The complex is over 200 ft long, with a forecourt and a main hall. The bimah was probably placed approximately

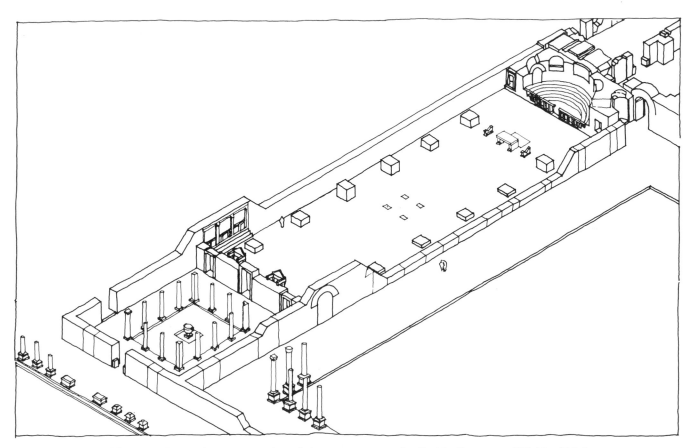

Figure 1. Isometric reconstruction of the synagogue at Sardis (3). Courtesy of Weidenfeld & Nicholson. Drawing by Christena McCabe.

in the middle of the hall and an apse was at the end. Evidence suggests that the Torah scrolls were not installed in the apse, but in shrines against the entry wall, which faces Jerusalem. A large marble menorah was found; numerous representations of menorahs, as well as inscriptions in Greek and Hebrew and elaborate decorations were found in the mosaics, which have been dated to the fourth century A.D. (6).

The formal elegance of the Roman basilica at Sardis represents one aspect of ancient synagogue architecture. A contrasting modesty is found at Dura-Europas, where the synagogue is a renovated private home. Here there is a forecourt and a simple sanctuary room, with ancillary rooms for community use. Most important, however, are the decorations in the sanctuary, where all surfaces are elaborately painted with biblical scenes and Jewish symbols (7).

The synagogues at Sardis and Dura-Europas are alike in that they both are renovations of preexisting structures and in that they share in a tradition of classical architecture with Jewish decoration. There is wide variety in other synagogues of the period. At Capernaum, in Galilee, the synagogue was built in the second or third century A.D. and consists of a forecourt and a rectangular columned room with benches built into the walls. There is no special place for either ark or bimah. The Capernaum synagogue is typical of a group known as Galilean synagogues. Somewhat later, in the fifth to seventh centuries, the Byzantine type develops. At Beth Alpha, also in Galilee, for example, the plan is basilical, with an apse indicating the place of the ark. A forecourt and narthex ritualize entry to the synagogue. Also significant at Beth Alpha are the mosaic pavements, containing depictions of the ark, menorah, and other religious objects, and the lions guarding the ark. The signs of the zodiac are prominent, thought to relate to the twelve tribes of Israel as well as the months of the year (8).

Synagogues of the ancient world also share the use of Roman architectural vocabulary embellished with Jewish decorative motifs. A sanctuary and forecourt are consistent architectural forms. However, one cannot define a distinct building type, due to the enormous variation in how architectural forms are assembled and the lack of consensus on placement of ark and bimah. There was not even a consensus on whether the synagogue need face Jerusalem. However, it is clear that the synagogue is neither a pagan temple nor a church, for synagogues are not houses of gods with priestly officiants. Fundamental ideas about the organization of synagogues are demonstrated in these early buildings and form the basis for subsequent synagogue design.

THE MIDDLE AGES

In the medieval period, two distinct Jewish traditions developed. The Jews of the Iberian Peninsula were called *Sephardim*, a term that later applied to Jews of the East, who followed traditions evolved in Spain. The Jews of Germany, on the other hand, followed different traditions and were known as *Ashkenazim*. As their influence spread across Europe, their traditions were adopted by Jews of the West in general. Each influenced synagogue design in their own ways.

In medieval Spain, Jewish culture reached one of its highest points. Jews and Jewish ideas were disseminated from Babylon to Iran, the Arabian peninsula, Egypt and other centers of North Africa, and finally to Spain. Jews were highly respected by the Muslims who were conquering these areas. As people of "the Book" who had established a tradition of monotheism on which Islam is based, the Jews lived relatively peacefully and freely under Muslim rule. The Moorish conquest of Spain in 711 was the beginning of a long, generally stable period in Jewish history. While reconquest began almost immediately, it was not until the eleventh century that Catholic forces had regained significant territories and only in 1492 was the final expulsion of Moors achieved; Jews were simultaneously expelled.

With the increasing Catholic presence came increasing restrictions on Jewish religious practices. Former mosques were often given to Jews as synagogues. New buildings were plain on the exterior, probably to maintain a certain anonymity. However, interiors were decorated, the ark and bimah receiving the most attention. It was at this time that a strict prohibition against imagery was in force, in accordance with Church proscriptions against painting synagogues, Muslim proscriptions against images, and with respect to the second commandment's prohibition of the worship of images. A separate women's area was the rule after the twelfth century, in the form of balconies or adjacent rooms. Precedent cited was the Second Temple in Jerusalem, which had an upper gallery from which women could observe. The women's gallery, becomes, in fact, one of the particular architectural elements to be integrated into synagogue design.

Because space in the crowded cities was at a premium, synagogues were rather small. Competition for seats was fierce, with the best places going to families of the greatest wealth or social standing. There were also large numbers of synagogues for the same reason; in Seville alone there were 23 synagogues until they were destroyed in 1391. Small interiors crowded by surrounding buildings gave rise to high clerestory lighting for reading the Torah (9).

The synagogue in Toledo, known as "El Transito" from its later Catholic dedication, was built about 1360 and is, in many ways, most representative of the state of synagogue design in medieval Spain (Fig. 2). There are separate entrances for men and women, the women's entrance leading to an upper gallery. The rectangular sanctuary has a niche in the west wall for the ark and high clerestory windows. The bimah was in the center, probably due to the length of the room. In most Sephardic synagogues the bimah would have been toward the end of the room opposite the ark to emphasize the ritual procession of the Torah scrolls to the reading desk and to maintain a balance of focus during services. Elaborate carvings covering the walls and ceilings were executed by Moorish craftsmen. Decoration is typically Moorish in character, often including Koranic inscriptions hidden in arabesques as well as more prominent Hebrew writings. Rooms to the south and north of the sanctuary served as study rooms,

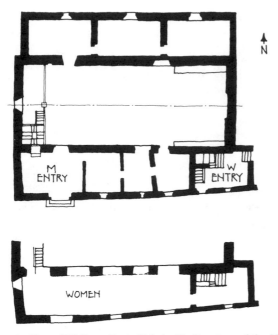

Figure 2. Plan of El Transito in Toledo (9). Courtesy of the University Presses of Florida. Drawing by Christena McCabe.

courtrooms for the settling of disputes, the temporary housing of transients, and other community functions. Therefore, the functions of worship, study, and assembly are all clearly accommodated, along with provision for the presence of women (10).

Jewish communities are also recorded throughout North Africa at a very early date. For example, local tradition on the island of Djerba, off the coast of Tunisia, dates its Jewish population from the time of Nebuchadnezzar, and the scholar Maimonides records a migration of Jews to Djerba in the eighth century (11). The Griba synagogue was built in the early twentieth century on the ancient site of synagogues at the center of the community, but there are no clues to what earlier structures might have been. Built in a Moorish style, with pointed arches and painted tile covering the interior walls, it is related to Sephardic synagogues of the Middle Ages in Spain. Particularly noteworthy is the square sanctuary with three large clerestory windows at the top of each wall, which give the illumination required for reading the Torah. It is said that the twelve windows represent the twelve tribes of Israel. From the exterior, the clerestory rising above adjacent roofs is distinctive and is found on a number of Tunisian synagogues.

In northern Europe, where the first medieval Jewish communities were in Germany, the dissolution of Roman control and institutions after the sixth century meant that Jews came under the authority of local rulers and the Catholic church. The occupations of Jews were restricted to financial affairs and other trades distasteful to Christians, and locations for their communities were also controlled. Jewish quarters were often in undesirable sites within a city, or sometimes in more favorable places close to the ruler who would have brought them in to stimulate the economy. Restrictions on synagogues included the

numbers to be built and their size. In any case, Jews generally preferred to live close together and near their synagogues in order to maintain their social and religious ties. It was prudent that synagogues have a minimal presence on the street and that windows be out of reach of stone-throwing ruffians. Architects or builders were Christian, for until the nineteenth century these occupations were not open to Jews (12).

The earliest medieval European Ashkenazic synagogue of which a clear idea exists is at Worms, in Germany, dating from the late twelfth century (Fig. 3). Although completely destroyed in World War II, it has been restored and can be visited. Entry is through an exterior courtyard, a typical arrangement, which kept the synagogue facade off the street in order to hide its entrance and any assemblies of Jews outside the building. The main sanctuary is constructed of masonry, with two vaulted naves separated by two columns. The bimah was a decorated enclosure in either wood or stone and was placed between the two columns in the center. Women's worship took place in a separate room adjacent to the men's prayer hall. There was no ark or bimah, but women sometimes engaged in their own prayer (13).

In addition to the twin-nave hall, single-nave plans, unobstructed by columns, were employed; the bimah is always placed at, or near, the center. The central placement gives the bimah ritual primacy and is common to Ashkenazic practice. Both types of meeting hall were used in medieval Germany for council chambers or other civic buildings, but not for churches. The long church plan with its focus on an altar was inappropriate for Jewish worship, and the Jews quite naturally would not want to identify with Christian forms (14).

While Spain and Germany have significant medieval synagogues, major Jewish populations were to be found in Italy, France, and England as well. In these countries no large synagogues remain, although there is evidence of significant building activity and some furnishings. Many of the synagogues were in simple buildings, some of which are extant, indistinguishable from other buildings on the outside, but richly furnished inside. A minimal public presence continued to be either mandated or prudent throughout a Europe in which Jews were subject to discrimination or persecution.

At the end of the Middle Ages, significant migrations of European Jews took place. Sephardic Jews were expelled from Spain and Portugal and moved to North Africa, the Ottoman Empire, the Balkans, Italy, Poland, and Palestine (15). From Germany the migration was east to Poland, from France to Alsace and Italy, and from Italy to northern Europe. Many went to Palestine where building traditions of Europe mixed with Byzantine and Islamic traditions. Both Sephardic and Ashkenazic synagogues were built in Jerusalem and surrounding cities in the sixteenth century (16).

THE RENAISSANCE

The next important evolution in the architecture of synagogues takes place in Italy of the sixteenth century. The

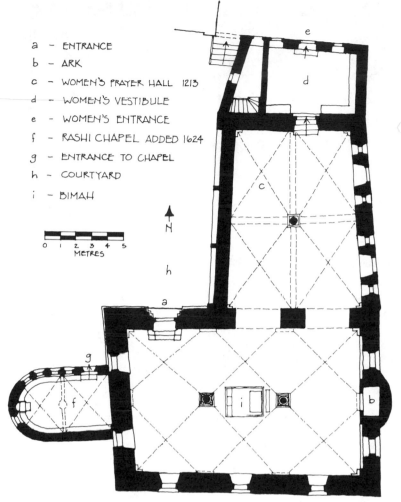

a – ENTRANCE
b – ARK
c – WOMEN'S PRAYER HALL 1213
d – WOMEN'S VESTIBULE
e – WOMEN'S ENTRANCE
f – RASHI CHAPEL ADDED 1624
g – ENTRANCE TO CHAPEL
h – COURTYARD
i – BIMAH

0 1 2 3 4 5
METRES

Figure 3. Plan of the Medieval Synagogue in Worms (3). Courtesy of Weidenfeld & Nicholson. Drawing by Christena McCabe.

Renaissance witnessed a renewed interest in humanistic values and, in particular, in the arts and sciences of classic antiquity. In painting, evocations of classic landscapes and cityscapes were ordered by scientific perspective. In architecture, space and form were to be controlled by systems of mathematical proportion. The use of axial perspectives and hierarchical organization found ample precedent in ancient Greece and Rome, which became sources of the architectural language of the Renaissance.

The Jews participated in the intellectual Renaissance; in particular, it was in this period that scholars worked to clarify Jewish law. Joseph Caro, having been expelled from Spain in 1492, settled in Palestine in 1536 after a stay in Turkey. He defined the code of rabbinic law and practice in the Sephardic tradition. Moses Isserles, who founded a yeshiva in Cracow, Poland, in 1552, wrote a complementary work explaining the Ashkenazic view. While all aspects of Jewish life were considered, for the first time the informal traditions of synagogue design were sorted out and made explicit. Isserles believed that an Ashkenazic synagogue should have the bimah generally in the center of the prayer hall so that the reading of the Torah might be heard equally throughout the room. Separation of ark and bimah was also important in order not to imitate the Christian practice of placing a pulpit

and altar at a single focal point. Seats and reading desks were often freestanding so that they could be moved to address either ark or bimah, as required by the service. Caro did not require a central position for the bimah. In Sephardic synagogues, including those of southern France and Italy, the bimah was near the west wall, with seating along the east–west axis to the ark. Because Sephardic synagogues were generally quite small, there was no problem in hearing the reader (17). There was a greater equality between ark and bimah as foci of attention, as well as a greater emphasis on the unity of the congregation and on the procession of the scrolls.

These differing attitudes toward the organization of the synagogue reflected a long history of accumulated ritual practices. Christian architects of Renaissance Italy designed most of the synagogues there and, working in the prevailing style of the period, they would contribute rational organization of all of the parts of the Italian and Sephardic synagogue. They would also spread the ideas of the Renaissance throughout Europe and affect all of its architecture.

The Spanish synagogue in the Venice ghetto represents a high point in the crystallization of synagogue design (Fig. 4). Established in 1555, its renovation in the seventeenth century is attributed to the architect Baldas-

a – ARK
b – BIMAH
c – ENTRANCE
d – MEN'S BENCHES
e – BENCHES OF THE PARNASSIM
f – LINE OF WOMEN'S GALLERY ABOVE

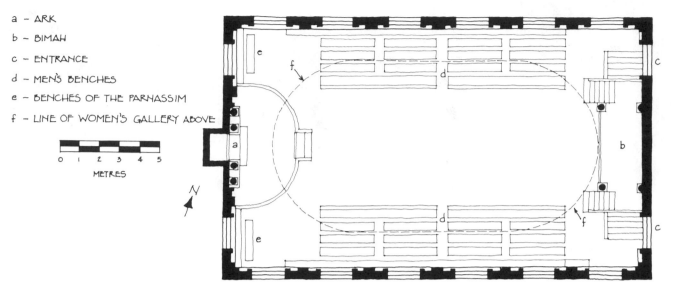

Figure 4. Plan of the Spanish Synagogue in Venice (3). Courtesy of Weidenfeld & Nicholson. Drawing by Christena McCabe.

sare Longhena. Typically, the sanctuary is on the second floor of a building of no exterior distinction. The ark occupies the east wall, balanced by the bimah on the west wall. A large aisle separates them and is flanked by seating for the congregation. Large windows are symmetrically arranged, and the walls and ceiling are elaborately paneled and painted to create proportional harmony as well as richness of effect. An oval women's gallery is above, enhancing the unity of the composition. Two entries flank the bimah, rather than the more usual pattern of entry in the middle of one of the long walls. The plans of the Levantine, Italian, Canton, and German synagogues in Venice are all variations of the same type, even though the latter two serve Ashkenazic communities. The organization has become typical of Sephardic synagogues.

Ashkenazic culture, on the other hand, flourished in Poland and other countries of central and eastern Europe. While Jews are recorded in Poland from the eighth century, beginning in the eleventh century many from western Europe began to migrate to Poland due to increasing restrictions and persecutions. Particularly in the thirteenth and fourteenth century, Polish rulers welcomed the Jews to assist in the economic and urban development of their country. Under the protection of local princes, the Jews were generally not confined to ghettos, although they would group together to be near the synagogue. In the sixteenth century, the Jewish population escalated dramatically, and by the beginning of the seventeenth century Poland contained the largest Jewish community in the world (18).

In 1539, Jews came under the control of nobles in privately owned towns and villages and were allowed to establish self-government. From the late sixteenth century through the middle of the seventeenth century a period of economic and religious freedom gave rise to a flourishing of Jewish culture. At that time the thinking of Moses Isserles was significant in establishing the centrally placed bimah as the primary organizing feature of the prayer hall, a characteristic of orthodox Ashkenazic synagogue design.

Two architectural traditions were important in Polish synagogues. Masonry synagogues were built in the larger congested towns and cities after numerous fires destroyed the wooden buildings of earlier periods. On the other hand, the villages continued to employ less formal wooden construction and developed synagogues that combined local craft tradition with Renaissance ideas of composition. While some masonry synagogues remain, all of the wooden ones were destroyed by the Nazis.

The relative freedom of the Jews in Poland meant that, when space allowed, they could follow Talmudic synagogue requirements with respect to orientation, placement on a high point in proximity to water, and building higher than surrounding buildings, all injunctions derived from the original Temple. The only restrictions were that height must not exceed the height of churches and that the noise of prayer not be audible near churches (19). In terms of exterior appearance, two trends are identifiable. On the eastern borders, some synagogues were built as fortresses to help defend towns against invasions. Otherwise, the style of synagogues kept pace with the evolution of Polish architecture in general, while organization of space evolved uniquely to accommodate Jewish ritual practice.

Some Polish masonry synagogues conformed to the two-nave pattern, as seen at Worms; the Old Synagogue at Kazimierza (near Cracow) is a significant example. The building that now stands is from the sixteenth century. Its bimah, set between the two central columns, is a raised platform enclosed in a wrought-iron cage (20). Single-nave examples are also found, such as the Issac Synagogue of Cracow, built by the Italian architect Francesco Olivieri in 1638–1644. The barrel-vaulted nave is organized symmetrically on the east–west axis; the ark is crowned by a classical pediment and the vestibule on the west end has the women's gallery above (21).

However, the Renaissance in Poland also saw the development of a nine-square plan for synagogues, where the bimah occupied the central square, defined by four columns. If the nine bays were equal, the bimah would be a simple raised platform, surrounded by a balustrade and probably having a canopy, such as at the suburban synagogue in Lvov, built in 1633 (22). A refinement of the idea was to make the central bay smaller and to bring the vaulting lower over the bimah than over the rest of the hall. The bimah was no longer a separate object but was architecturally unified with the composition; light could be introduced into it from above for dramatic effect. Further rationalization of the plan is shown in the placement of the vestibule on the west side, on axis with the bimah and the ark on the east wall. Integration of the women's prayer hall was an architectural problem solved either by placing two adjacent spaces on the north and south walls or by placing a gallery above the vestibule. The plan was efficient in terms of maximum seating capacity, appropriate in terms of the symbolic import of the reading of the Torah, and architecturally elegant in the potential for unified composition and dramatic spatial quality (23).

One of the most impressive of the nine-vault synagogues was built in Pinsk in 1640 (Fig. 5). Both in plan and section, symmetry and hierarchy control the composition. The main vaulted prayer hall is flanked by lower galleries, which allows large clerestory windows to light the interior. The bimah is formed by the four central support pillars and has its own lower ceiling, penetrated by a lantern that focuses natural light into it. The synagogues at Luck, Lublin, and Vilna are other examples of the same type.

While particular site conditions would dictate variations in planning synagogues, there was in the sixteenth and seventeenth centuries in Poland a clearly defined building strategy, which for the first time could be considered uniquely Jewish. Although based on prevalent styles and construction techniques, the spatial organization was such as to differentiate synagogues from preceding building types. The interpretation of these strategies in wood by builders in villages and smaller towns resulted in a particularly evocative group of buildings. Whether executed by local artisans or by sophisticated carpenters, spatial organization was similar to nine-square masonry synagogues. The interiors of prayer halls imitated masonry vaulting, although the flexibility and lighter weight of wood construction and the relatively smaller size of the buildings resulted in considerable freedom to manipulate the shape of the vaulting. Details, too, combined the imitation of masonry with the lightness and delicacy of wood.

The wooden synagogues in Poland for which there is documentation were built primarily in the seventeenth and eighteenth centuries, with some construction continuing into the early nineteenth century. A number of wooden synagogues were also built in Germany in the eighteenth century by Polish craftsmen and artists who had migrated there. Doubtless there were many built earlier that were destroyed. The synagogue at Volpa, from the early eighteenth century, was the most elegant in conception and execution (Fig. 6). The sanctuary was organized on the nine-square pattern, with four columns defining the center and the bimah and supporting an internal cupola above. While at Volpa the central columns were part of the structural system, in many other wooden synagogues they were simply imitative of their more prestigious masonry counterparts; sanctuary spaces were easily spanned with wooden trusses, without central support.

Pairs of columns on the east and west walls of the Volpa synagogue subtly defined the axis from entry to ark. The pairs of columns were repeated on the exterior of the roof gable and were possibly references to Jachin and Boas. Vestibule and women's galleries symmetrically surrounded the sanctuary, and corner towers flanked the entrance. The glory of the building was the sanctuary vaulting, which rose in three octagonal tiers, joined to the square base by pendentives. The tiers became shorter as well as smaller as they rose, a refinement that enhanced the sense of height. Each tier was defined by balustrades, echoed in the decoration of the pendentives and cupola on the interior and in the tower balconies on the exterior (24).

The vaulting and walls in the wooden synagogues were made of wooden planks placed horizontally or vertically, with simply framed windows at the clerestory level. The synagogue at Przedbórz had a barrel vault with elaborate decorative curvilinear strapping applied to its surfaces. More typical decoration was painting applied by itinerant artists in a folk tradition. In addition to Hebrew inscriptions and floral or geometric decoration, biblical subjects, mythical beasts, and local folklore were popular. The representations enlivened the space as they provide a record of the history and collective imagination of the community (25).

The distinctive character and refinement of synagogue planning in Poland was made possible by relative security and prosperity. At the same time, the Jewish community in Poland was unique in Europe in its size and cultural self-sufficiency, which contributed to the intensity of intellectual activity. The implication for synagogue architecture was a synthesis of form and function ideally suited to Ashkenazic Jewish practice. The situation deteriorated sharply when Poland came under Russian rule in the nineteenth century.

In the seventeenth and eighteenth centuries in the Netherlands and Great Britain, significant synagogues were also built. In these countries too, Jews benefited from a relatively open society and liberal views. There was a tendency to integrate culturally in the society, while maintaining Jewish religious identity. Synagogues were built in contemporary styles, using linear basilical plans common to churches; bimahs, however, were centrally placed. Large quantities of glass, which in less tolerant periods of Jewish history would have been destroyed by vandals, flooded interiors with light. Women were still confined to galleries, but the galleries were very open and integrated in the main prayer space. The buildings themselves had significant presence on the street, even if they were entered by a courtyard; they were decorated in accordance with the wealth of the community. In Amsterdam, the Sephardic Synagogue of 1639, the Grote Sjoel of 1671, the Sephardic Synagogue of 1675, and the New Ashkenazic Synagogue of 1752 are particularly noteworthy (26).

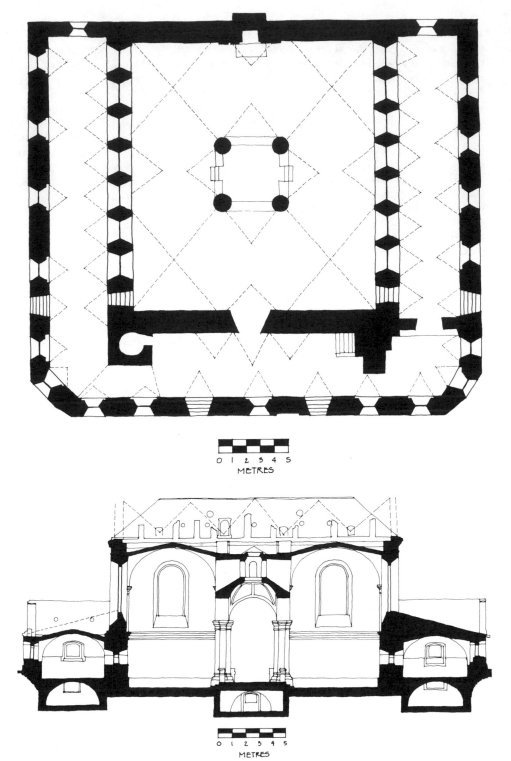

Figure 5. Plan and section of the synagogue in Pinsk (1). Courtesy of Instytut Sztuki. Drawing by Christena McCabe.

In London, the Great Synagogue of 1791 seats 750 and has an interior in the style of Sir Christopher Wren (27).

THE NINETEENTH CENTURY

The French and American revolutions at the end of the eighteenth century were major expressions of general in-tellectual, political, and economic trends to reorder soci-ety. From that time through the third quarter of the nine-teenth century, laws were passed giving Jews of most of western Europe defined legal rights of equality. In the United States, religious freedom was a guaranteed right. While social prejudice against Jews was substantial, they could nonetheless become active participants in society at large in a way never before possible. While some Jews

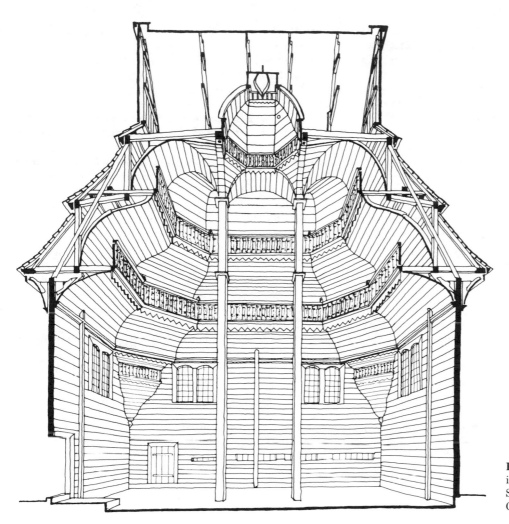

Figure 6. Section of the synagogue in Volpa (1). Courtesy of Instytuk Sztuki. Drawing by Christena McCabe.

held to traditional beliefs and a somewhat insular lifestyle, a larger number considered assimilation into the local culture a desirable opportunity. Secular education became as important as traditional Jewish education, and synagogues tended to imitate the styles of other religious buildings in the local culture.

The Reform Movement of the 1840s gave further impetus to a redefinition of Jewish practice in contemporary terms. The strict observances of Orthodox Jews were considered irrelevant to the progress Jews were making in society. In the synagogue, the entire family could sit together and prayers were in the vernacular. Most importantly, the emphasis changed from the notion of a community of individuals praying and studying Torah to that of a more decorous assembly led in unison prayer. The sermon became an important feature of services, while less ritual surrounded the reading of the Torah. The bimah was no longer central, but was joined to the ark at a single focal point in the sanctuary so that the rabbi could effectively address the congregation. Organs were introduced to accompany musical portions of the service. Stained glass became increasingly acceptable, despite the potential for Christian connotations; the Star of David was a popular motif, especially for rose windows. Thus, the desire for assimilation was reinforced by the Reform Movement, and

the effect on synagogues was to make them very much like Protestant churches. Indeed, Jews who emigrated to the United States often bought churches, which could easily be used as synagogues. Conversely, after World War II, many nineteenth-century urban synagogues were purchased by Christian congregations as Jews left the city for the suburbs. With the transformation of the synagogue into a more generic religious building than it had been, the issue of Jewish character becomes central. Architecturally, the nineteenth century was characterized by stylistic eclecticism, and it is through the choice and manipulation of styles that the Christian and Jewish architects of synagogues sought appropriate formal expression.

The revival of classicism began in the late eighteenth century and, lacking overt connections to Christianity, could be used appropriately for synagogues. The Touro Synagogue in Newport, Rhode Island, built in 1763, is the oldest surviving synagogue in the United States. Designed by the architect Peter Harrison in a neoclassic style typical of the colonial period, the plan is organized around a central bimah. The ark is a two-story pedimented structure integrated into the delicately detailed and well-lit interior (28). Reform synagogues also were built using many varieties of classicism; examples abound in Europe and the United States even to the present. One of the purer neoclassic synagogues is Beth Elohim, built in 1841 in Charleston, South Carolina (29). Gothic was rarely used, due to its strong associations with Catholic churches, but there were exceptions. The styles of Eastern European synagogues were strictly avoided at this time in order not to evoke the *shtetl*, the villages with seemingly regressive traditions and often degraded quality of life under the Czars.

However, classicism and other "pure" Western architectural styles did not convey a specific sense of Jewish identity, which was a concern to Jews increasingly secure in their social positions. Romanesque architecture was seen as proto-Gothic, much as Judaism might be seen as proto-Christian, and therefore appropriate to synagogues. Architects and builders, however, also interpreted Judaism as an eastern religion and turned to Egyptian, Byzantine, and Islamic or Moorish sources. Western involvement in the Islamic world had become extensive, as the French and British, in particular, had established political and economic ties to North Africa, the Middle East, and India. The exotic East was fashionable and the subject of intellectual inquiry. The eclectic combinations of western and eastern styles did, in fact, produce a series of nineteenth-century synagogues associated with Judaism. It must be said, however, that the associations were perhaps more in the minds of the larger Christian society than they were inherent in Jewish belief and practice.

Among Egyptian-style synagogues, Mikveh Israel in Philadelphia, Pennsylvania, was designed by William Strickland and completed in 1825. Its facade has a solidity consistent with the historical durability of Judaism, although the recall of a culture in which Jews were slaves may imply a certain naïveté in this application of eastern style. The interior, however, employs an elliptical dome and central lantern encompassing virtually the entire congregation, which is seated in two semicircular arrays flanking the ark (30). The intention is to reinforce the sense of the unity of the congregation. While Strickland's plan has the inherent centrality of traditional synagogues, this use of the dome is found in many synagogues of the nineteenth century and later to reconcile the desire for a centralized focus on the congregation with the new need for a single axial focus on the ark and bimah.

Moorish–Islamic styles, grafted on to Romanesque or Gothic plans, were the most popular of the eclectic mid- to late-nineteenth–century synagogues. An optimistic interpretation of the trend is that secure congregations were seeking a way to express their unique culture and that the use of Islamic architecture recalled their roots in the East. The use of nonfigurative decoration has precedent in Jewish thinking, and the increasing knowledge of synagogues in Islamic countries reinforced this idea. Furthermore, the Moorish decoration in the Transito and other synagogues in Spain was known to be a manifestation of one of the high points in Jewish history. A less generous view is that European society, through its patrons, building officials, and architects, encouraged the use of "foreign" styles for its Jews to emphasize their difference and imply their inferiority. Whatever the motivation in Europe, the widespread appearance of Moorish–Islamic synagogues in the United States is a stylistic importation.

In the hands of talented designers, the Moorish style was used to build some remarkable synagogues. The Oranienburgerstrasse Synagogue in Berlin was completed in 1866 and was at the time the largest synagogue in the world (Fig. 7). Fronting directly on the street, with a bulbous dome over the vestibule, the polychromed entry facade is flanked by two domed towers. The interior of the prayer hall was basilical in plan, terminating in an apse with bimah and ark. The use of iron in the structure enhanced the sense of spaciousness by reducing the need for large columns and increasing the span of the arches and vaults. The Alhambra in Spain was the inspiration for the decoration, much of which is gilded. The frank opulence accurately reflected the economic and social prominence of the Jewish community (31).

Reform congregations in the United States followed the lead of the Reform Movement in Germany. The Isaac M. Wise Temple in Cincinnati, Ohio, completed in 1866 by James Keys Wilson, is a Gothic basilica in plan. However, its pointed arches and rose windows are all surrounded by rectangular panels, an Islamic device. The facade towers are attenuated to the point of seeming like minarets, although they may also recall Jachin and Boas from the First Temple. Decoration, once again, seems to have been inspired by the Alhambra (32). Also based on a basilical plan, the Central Synagogue in New York City, completed in 1872 by Henry Fernbach, was more Romanesque in its feeling due to the more planar treatment of the dark stone facade. However, the horseshoe arches, bulbous domes on the towers, and distinctive Moorish decoration give it its Eastern character (33). Central domes were used as well as linear basilical plans in Moorish synagogues, because the Moorish style was not necessarily related to plan organization.

The use of a central dome over the sanctuary to express the unity of Jewish belief as well as of the congregation is characteristic of the Byzantine style. Reminiscent of the Holy Land, its round arches and heavy walls were similar to Romanesque architecture, although its textures were generally smoother and its forms more crystalline. The synagogue on Steelerstrasse in Essen, Germany, completed in 1914, combined the two styles in an amalgam that is both European and Eastern; that is, it confirms that its congregation was German, but also distinctly "foreign" (34). Temple Isaiah in Chicago, Illinois, and Tifereth Israel in Cleveland, Ohio, both completed in 1924, are accomplished U.S. examples of the Byzantine style. Although eclectic in form and decoration, they already show modernist tendencies toward functional planning and articulation of massing (35).

THE TWENTIETH CENTURY

The next important phase in the development of the synagogue as a building type takes place in the U.S. suburbs after World War II. While a number of synagogues built in the earlier part of the twentieth century were influenced by the philosophies of the Bauhaus, various revival styles continued to be popular. The Holocaust, however, effectively destroyed major European Jewish communities and

Figure **7.** Oranienburgerstrasse Synagogue in Berlin (1). Courtesy of the Märkisches Museum. Drawing by Christena McCabe.

with them the credibility of styles associated with the older social order. The new modernism was free of historical associations and, in fact, encouraged the definition of new forms based on original interpretations of community needs. At a larger scale, modernism was committed to an urbanism unlike that of the traditional tightly organized European cities; in contrast, U.S. suburbs provided ideal sites for the free planning and abstract compositions of modern building. The Jewish community in the United States was at this time the largest and most affluent in the world. Moving from the declining city centers, Jews joined the large numbers of people who found suburban life congenial to raising families.

The synagogue continued its historical role as a place of prayer, study, and meeting, but each function took on new form in the context of modern life. The greatest challenge in the design of a synagogue is the sanctuary. Orthodox, Conservative, and Reform traditions in Judaism each have attitudes about the proper arrangement of the ark, bimah, and congregation, as well as about the inclusion of choir and organ, stained glass, and other symbolic elements. Furthermore, the autonomy of individual congregations gives wide latitude for interpretation of liturgy.

From a utilitarian standpoint, the size of a sanctuary is the primary issue in Reform and Conservative synagogues, because it is only during the 10 days of the High Holy Days, the New Year and the Day of Atonement, that the entire congregation is served. Daily prayer is a rarity and can be satisfied by a small chapel; likewise, even weekly services are attended by small numbers. Few congregations can afford to build a large sanctuary for the High Holy Days alone, especially because it would lack the intimacy desired by the usual smaller groups. The usual functional solution is to have one or more multipurpose social spaces adjacent to the sanctuary, with removable partitions. Architectural integration of these disparate types of space is a compromise in the best of situations. Nonarchitectural accommodations may include multiple services or the renting of auxiliary halls.

Orthodox congregations do not normally have this particular space problem because attendance is more constant. Furthermore, the prohibition against driving on the Sabbath means that the synagogue must be within walking distance, serving a smaller congregation with a neighborhood orientation. At least one Orthodox congregation provides rental rooms so that worshipers at a distance may stay overnight.

The social activities of a congregation are complex, and facilities must accommodate life cycle events as well as a variety of secular community events. The social hall itself, with related kitchen facilities, takes on proportions to rival the sanctuary in size. For the synagogue is the setting for large-scale weddings, bar and bat mitzvah receptions, and other social and educational functions. Thus, there must be easy access to the social hall from the sanctuary or chapel, as well as the ability to have simultaneous functions. Some congregations use only one space, rearranging it for religious or social occasions, as demand arises. Meeting places for youth are particularly important. Appropriate kitchen facilities, including the double requirements of kosher cooking, and service access must not interfere with more public spaces.

Finally, the educational mission of a synagogue is as primary today as it has ever been in history, serving both children and adults. Programs range from a simple "Sunday School" through daily Hebrew instruction to complete kindergarten through high school curricula. Courses, lecture series, and study groups are available to the community at large as well as to congregation members. A library and office for the rabbi and staff are required; if budgets allow, choir rehearsal space, brides' preparation room, and a nursery are desired.

Erich Mendelsohn, the German expressionist architect

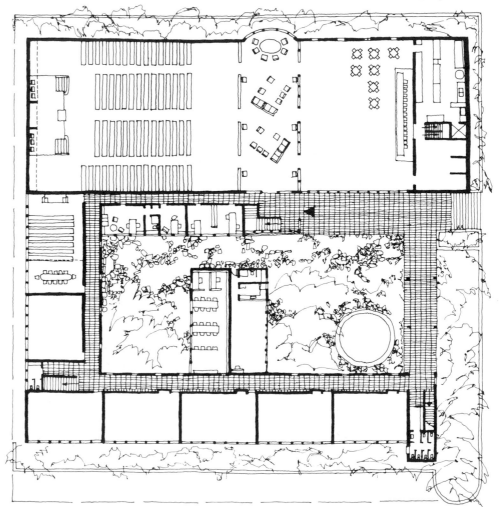

Figure 8. Plan of B'nai Amoona in St. Louis (28). Courtesy of R. B. Wischnitzer. Drawing by Christena McCabe.

Figure 9. B'nai Amoona in St. Louis (28). Courtesy of R. B. Wischnitzer. Drawing by Christena McCabe.

who emigrated to the United States because of the war in Europe, was significant in establishing the fundamental architectural concepts for the new type of synagogue. His design for B'nai Amoona in St. Louis, Missouri, completed in 1946, contains the essential elements of Mendelsohn's reinterpretation of traditional Jewish ideas in their new context (Figs. 8 and 9). In plan, the entry foyer is between the sanctuary and social hall, with walls that can be retracted to accommodate the large congregation that assembles for the High Holy Day services of the New Year and Day of Atonement. The sanctuary space receives dramatic treatment, the roof sweeping down to the ark, which is conceived very traditionally as a chest for scrolls. Light-

ing is indirect from above and behind the congregation. Educational facilities are in a separate wing. The complex is unified by a courtyard, reminiscent in its function more of the The Temple than of the medieval courts that separated the synagogue from the street. A pool of water recalls traditional customs of washing before prayer. Entry is informal and in sharp contrast to the monumentalizing tendencies of many synagogues of the recent past (36).

Mendelsohn understood the Jewish tradition of pragmatic architectural adaptation, and he found an expression as appropriate to postwar United States as it was rooted in Jewish history. Many synagogues followed the lead he established. The New York architect Percival

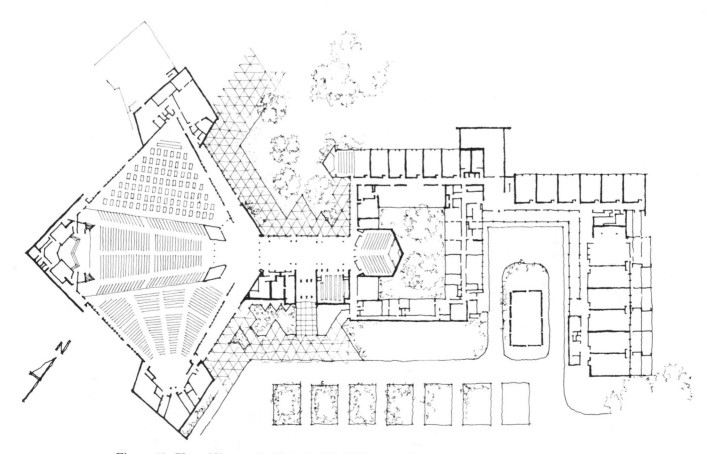

Figure 10. Plan of Shaarey Zedek in Southfield, Michigan. Courtesy of Percival Goodman. Drawing by Christena McCabe.

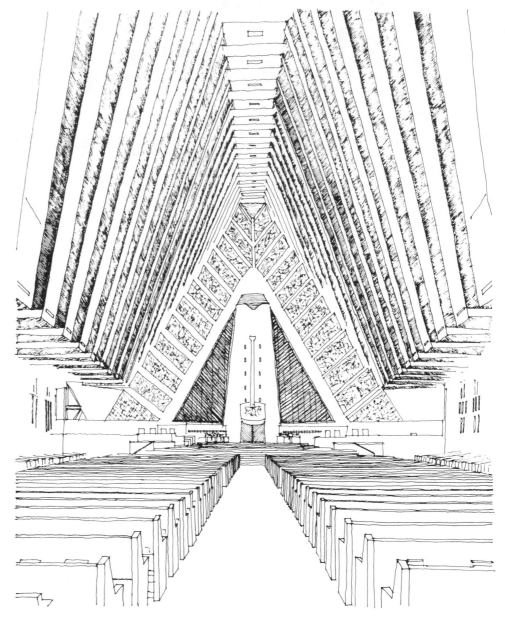

Figure 11. Sanctuary interior, Shaarey Zedek, Southfield, Michigan. Courtesy of Percival Goodman. Drawing by Christena McCabe.

Goodman has built a significant number of synagogues in which he explored not only variations in plan organization, but also the expressive potential of light and the use of sculpture, painting, and stained glass as integrated elements in his compositions. His design for Shaarey Zedek, Southfield, Michigan, dedicated in 1963, is a dramatic synthesis of the pragmatic and symbolic concerns of a large suburban congregation (Figs. 10 and 11). The sanctuary, which seats 1200, dominates the plan and is flanked by two social halls; when the three spaces are combined, a congregation of 3500 is seated with optimized proximity to the bimah. The structure of the sanctuary rises to a height of 100 ft, framing the massive sculpted ark with stained-glass windows and suggesting the form of Mt. Sinai. A chapel is on the axis of the main sanctuary and is the focus of a courtyard, which organizes the rabbi's study, library, and administrative offices. The school

wraps around its own courtyard and can operate independently of the rest of the complex.

Synagogues have been designed by many of this century's leading architects. Frank Lloyd Wright's Beth Shalom, built in Philadelphia in 1954, is a poetic essay in translucent lighting, the jagged pyramidal form of which consciously recalls images of Mt. Sinai suggested by the congregation's rabbi (Fig. 12) (37). In 1968, Louis I. Kahn designed a particularly powerful project for the Hurva Synagogue in Jerusalem. Its centrally focused sanctuary is formed by 16 stone pylons of Jerusalem stone, suggesting ancient ruins (38). The fact that Wright's Beth Shalom also evokes the seventeenth- and eighteenth-century wooden synagogues of Eastern Europe is perhaps a coincidence. But it is no coincidence that Jews of the 1970s and 1980s see in those Polish synagogues one of the most characteristically Jewish building precedents or that Kahn

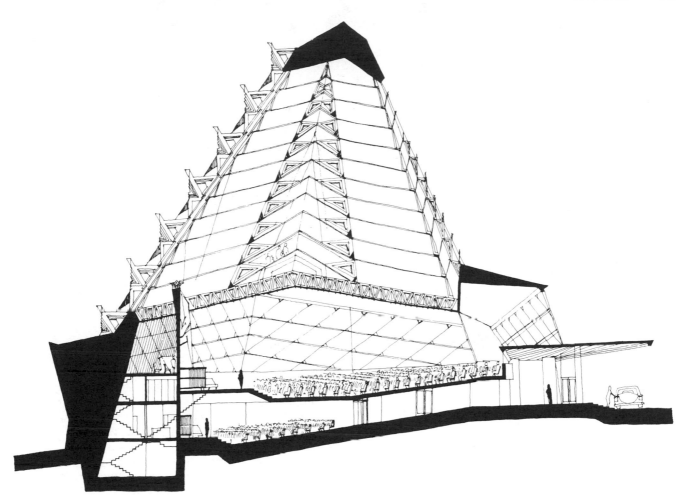

Figure 12. Section of Beth Shalom in Philadelphia (28). Courtesy of the Jewish Publication Society. Drawing by Christena McCabe.

should use forms suggesting the most ancient of building traditions. Indeed, the evolution of the design of synagogues demonstrates that a great diversity of precedents may be found throughout Jewish history.

Contemporary architectural vocabulary of synagogues reflects the multiplicity of attitudes that Jews have toward their religious life. The philosophy of a congregation will be translated into an array of physical requirements that is unique to that congregation, but that shares much with an ancient and diverse tradition of building. It is the interplay of tradition, interpretation, and pragmatic accommodation to unique circumstances that gives synagogue architecture its rich potential.

BIBLIOGRAPHY

1. C. H. Krinsky, *Synagogues of Europe*, The Architectural History Foundation, New York, 1985, p. 5.
2. Thiry, Bennett, and Kamphoefner, *Churches and Temples*, Reinhold Publishing Corp., New York, 1953, pp. 4J–6J.
3. B. de Breffny, *The Synagogue*, Macmillan Publishing Co., New York, 1978, pp. 8–9.
4. Ref. 1, pp. 360–361.
5. Ref. 2, p. 8J.
6. L. I. Levine, ed., *Ancient Synagogues Revealed*, Wayne State University Press, Detroit, Mich., 1982, pp. 178–184.
7. Ref. 6, pp. 172–177.
8. Ref. 6, pp. 15–18.
9. D. A. Halperin, *The Ancient Synagogues of the Iberian Peninsula*, University of Florida Press, Gainsville, Fla., 1969, pp. 19–22.
10. Ref. 9, pp. 49–55.
11. S. Tlatli, *Djerba, l'ile des lotophages*, Editions Ceres Productions, Tunis, Tunisia, 1967, pp. 42–46.
12. Ref. 1, pp. 42–44.
13. Ref. 1, p. 45.
14. Ref. 3, p. 62.
15. Ref. 3, p. 71.
16. Ref. 3, p. 76.
17. Ref. 1, pp. 48–49.
18. M. Piechotka and K. Piechotka, *Wooden Synagogues*, Arkady, Warsaw, Poland, 1959, pp. 9–14.
19. Ref. 18, p. 17.
20. Ref. 1, pp. 200–202.

21. Ref. 1, pp. 203–204.
22. Ref. 1, pp. 215–216.
23. Ref. 18, pp. 29–34.
24. Ref. 18, pp. 35–47.
25. Ref. 3, pp. 125–127.
26. Ref. 1, pp. 387–394.
27. Ref. 1, pp. 415–416.
28. R. B. Wischnitzer, *Synagogue Architecture in the United States*, The Jewish Publication Society of America, Philadelphia, Pa., 1955, pp. 13–15.
29. Ref. 28, pp. 37–39.
30. Ref. 28, pp. 28–32.
31. Ref. 1, pp. 265–270.
32. Ref. 28, pp. 70–73.
33. Ref. 28, pp. 77–78, 80.
34. Ref. 1, pp. 285–288.
35. Ref. 28, pp. 108–114.
36. Ref. 28, pp. 137–139, 149.
37. Ref. 28, pp. 152–156, 166–168.
38. A. Tyng, *Beginnings: Louis I. Kahn's Philosophy of Architecture*, John Wiley & Sons, Inc., New York, 1984, pp. 155–157.

General References

American Jewish Historical Society, *Two Hundred Years of American Synagogue Architecture*, American Jewish Historical Society, Waltham, Mass., 1976.

P. Blake, ed., *An American Synagogue for Today and Tomorrow*, The Union of American Hebrew Congregations, New York, 1954.

A. Eisenberg, *The Synagogue through the Ages*, Bloch Publishing Co., New York, 1974.

Faith and Form, Interfaith Forum on Religion, Art and Architecture, Washington, D.C.

J. R. Fine and G. R. Wolfe, *The Synagogues of New York's Lower East Side*, New York University Press, New York, 1978.

U. Fortis, *Jews and Synagogues: Venice, Florence, Rome, Leghorn*, Edizioni Storit, Venice, 1973.

A. Kampf, *Contemporary Synagogue Art*, The Union of American Hebrew Congregations, New York, 1966.

U. Kaploun, *The Synagogue*, Jewish Publication Society of America, Philadelphia, Pa., 1973.

R. Wischnitzer, *The Architecture of the European Synagogue*, Jewish Publication Society of America, Philadelphia, Pa., 1964.

See also RELIGIOUS ARCHITECTURE

WILLIAM B. BECHHOEFER, AIA
University of Maryland

SYSTEMS INTEGRATION

With the increase of complexity in building as in other fields, the concept of systems developed. It has been written (1):

> Although . . . the word "system" has been defined in many ways, all definers will agree that system is a set of parts to accomplish a set of goals.

A system is also defined (2) as

> a kit of parts with a set of rules to yield some desired behavior.

In this sense all buildings are systems consisting of subsystems. Interrelating these subsystems toward creating a building is systems integration.

Unless strong reasons call for the differentiation of subsystems, throughout this article the word system is used, but subsystem is meant in reality. In the strictest sense, system means the total context under consideration, that is, the assembly of all subsystems needed for a particular project, here with the assumption that the boundaries of the system coincide with the boundaries of the building under consideration.

There are two principal types of systems that relate to building: physical and nonphysical systems. Programming, design methods, cost estimating, and project scheduling are examples of the latter. Such systems are described in Refs. 3–7.

In the following, the context of physical systems in building and their integration is addressed. Nonphysical systems aspects are described only as needed to understand physical systems integration and related implications.

Systems integration may allude to a process or a product. All acts of building are more or less the integration of systems. This abstract definition is value free. How well the integration process is executed, however, determines the quality of the product, the building. Systems integration, therefore, is a thought process leading to a physical process that creates built environments.

Systems integration may be considered from many points of view. In the following sections, its aspects are conceptualized within five subject areas:

1. Function-related integration.
2. Space-related integration.
3. Construction-related integration.
4. Energy-related integration.
5. Aesthetics-related integration.

These subject areas overlap to a considerable extent. Their system and component characteristics are often interdependent.

FUNCTION-RELATED INTEGRATION

Buildings are made to serve particular functions. The better the building systems are coordinated and perform to mutual advantage, the better functional integration has been achieved. For creating systems and predicting their performance, the functions of their subsystems and their combined behavior must be understood.

Figure 1 shows schematically the basic interrelationships of several sets of two subsystems, S_1 and S_2. The

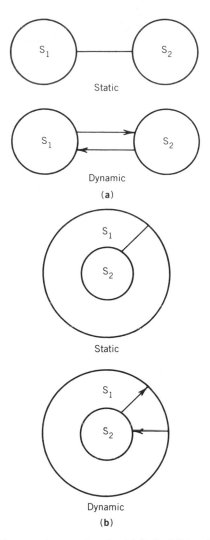

Figure 1. Systems integration for (a) linked (b) and composite performance.

functions of the systems may be static or dynamic, and their interrelationship, represented by links, may be static or dynamic. The function of one system may influence the function of the other, or as is more often the case, the functions of the systems may influence each other. Dynamic action by one system typically causes dynamic response by the other. The functional integration of systems may or may not correspond, however, to a spatial interrelationship, as suggested schematically in Figure 1.

From this, it follows that three principal issues must be understood in selecting and combining systems:

1. The performance characteristics of individual systems.
2. The linkages between systems.
3. The systems interaction.

The interrelationship of subsystems may be close or distant. In any case, functional compatibility is essential. The notion of closed versus open systems is helpful. Closed and open refer to the rules according to which systems operate within their domains.

In a closed system, a particular set of rules governs the makeup and performance within the domain boundaries. In an open system, other systems play a role within the same domain according to an extended set of rules. For example, a demountable partition system in an office building is a rather closed system. It may be open to some extent because of the inclusion of components from other systems, such as integrated furniture, or because of highly adaptive end-joint configurations for interfacing with other systems, such as the load-bearing structure or the building envelope.

Completely open systems in the ideal sense do not exist and are not possible. They would have to accommodate an unlimited number of functions in every respect. The more open systems are, however, the more easily they combine with other systems by connecting, meshing, and interacting. These properties are the basis for systems integration.

Compatibility, as mentioned earlier, is a central issue, particularly with regard to performance. Efforts to integrate subsystems for performance led in the 1950s to complete systems packages and bulk purchasing for many school building projects in the United Kingdom and in 1963 to performance-based bidding for several school districts in California. The latter, the School Construction Systems Development (SCSD), prepared the ground for many other systems integration developments in the United States, for example, in office buildings and health facilities. Figures 2 and 3 show the SCSD systems schematic and its manufacturer's compatibility matrix. These compatibilities are mostly related to the integration of individual subsystem performance, as shown in Figure 1a.

Functional integration for composite performance assigns multiple tasks to a particular subsystem. A simple example of this type is the modular wall closet system that also serves as a partition wall. A more complex example is the air-flow window, which is an exterior wall component, shading device, solar energy collector, and return air duct all in one (Fig. 4).

The most elaborate building systems integration theory to date, especially with regard to the functional aspects of building, is given in *The Building Systems Integration Handbook* (7):

> The theory postulates that four systems are sufficient to completely describe a building . . . structure, envelope, mechanical and interior. . . . The theory also postulates five levels of combination: remote, touching, connected, meshed, and unified." (10)

Figure 5 shows the five levels of integration. One chapter of the Handbook is based on six building performance mandates: spatial performance, thermal performance, air quality, acoustical performance, visual performance and building integrity. The introductory paragraph explains:

> One of the primary motivating forces for systems integration is performance. Such design criteria as energy or resources conservation, functional appropriateness, strength and stability, durability, fire safety, weathertightness, visual comfort, acoustical comfort, and economic efficacy, are only delivered when the entire building performs as an integrated whole. . . . (11).

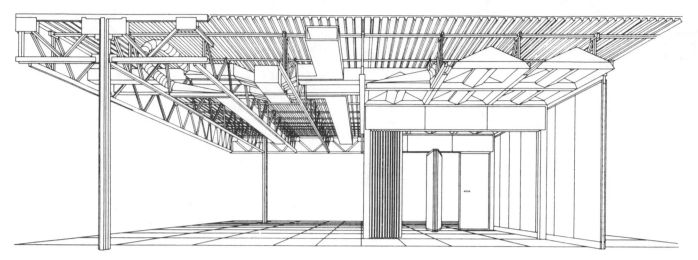

Figure 2. SCSD systems package (8).

Matrix I
Subsystem Compatibility
    Structure
    HVC
    Lighting/Ceiling

LIGHTING-CEILING

| | Armstrong C-60/30 | Armstrong C-60/60 | Butler L/C20,30,GRID | Clg.Dyn. LAMBDA, OMEGA V | Clg.Dyn. MOD II-V, MOD V | Celotex VARI-TEC 800 | Conwed FIVE PLUS FIVE | Donn COORDINATOR | Keene SPEC 10-SPEC 90 | Lok VCR, CUSTOM | Lum. Clg. TEC VI | Nat. Clg. 1000-3000 | O-C DIMENSIONAIRE | Soundlock SOUNDLUME | Sunbeam IS1000-IS6000 | Syncon |

STRUCTURAL

| Butler SPACE GRID | Butler LANDMARK | COMPONOFORM | Dominion Bridge | DYNA-FRAME | Francon RAS | Haven-Busch JOISTRUSS | Macomber V-LOK | PCA DUOTEK-S | Romac MODULOC | Steel Fab. FAB-LOK | Syncon | TrusJoist TJC | Unistrut 5' MODULE |

HEATING, VENTILATING, COOLING

- Acme SERIES "E"
- AAF MZRM
- Carrier 37K,42H,MOD.
- Carrier 48MA
- Chrysler CMS
- Dunham-Bush RTMZ
- ITT RMA 100,400,600
- Lennox DMS-1
- Lennox DMS-2
- Lennox DMS-3
- Mammoth ADAPT-AIRE
- Mammoth ADAPTA-ZONE
- McQuay ROOFPAK
- Schemenauer MULTIZONE
- Trane CLIMATE CHANGER
- York MULTIZONE

STRUCTURAL

- Butler SPACE GRID
- Butler LANDMARK
- COMPONOFORM
- Dominion Bridge
- DYNA-FRAME
- Francon RAS
- Haven-Busch JOISTRUSS
- Macomber V-LOK
- PCA DUOTEK-S
- Romac MODULOC
- Steel Fab. FAB-LOK
- Syncon
- TrusJoist TJC
- Unistrut 5' MODULE

● indicates full compatibility claimed by manufacturers of both products. For requirements of full compatibility, see pages 1-2.

▲ indicates full compatibility claimed by manufacturer of product listed at side of chart but not by manufacturer of product listed at top of chart.

◄ indicates full compatibility claimed by manufacturer of product listed at top of chart but not by manufacturer of product listed at side of chart.

⊕ indicates (a) probable compatibility claimed by one or both manufacturers, and/or (b) probable or full compatibility claimed in previous edition of this report and not revised by manufacturer(s).

┼ indicates compatibility not known or data missing.

■ indicates products incompatible.

Figure 3. Manufacturer's compatibility matrix for SCSD package (9).

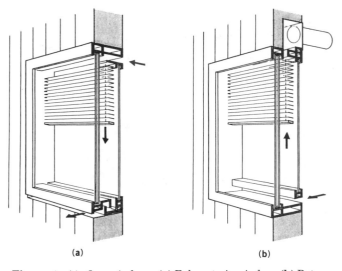

(a)

(b)

Figure 4. Air-flow windows. (a) Exhaust air window. (b) Return air window.

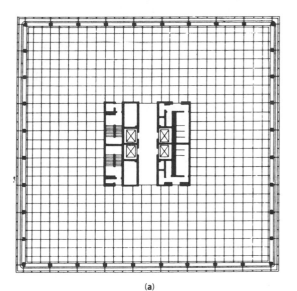

(a)

(b)

Figure 6. Spatial arrangement of vertical egress, structure, and services as internal core of the Occidental Chemical Building, Niagara Falls, New York. (a) Plan. (b) External view. Architect: Cannon Inc.

SPACE-RELATED INTEGRATION

The objective of building activities is to create enclosed space. The materials and systems that are used for this purpose occupy space themselves. Therefore, the assembly of systems and components requires spatial arrangements based on three-dimensional coordination. Space-related integration has a considerable impact on construction processes.

The spatial arrangement during the design stage is an ordering of systems in the vertical and horizontal directions. A building's structure and envelope are developed in response to programmatic and functional space requirements. Column spacings or ceiling spans, for example, are chosen typically according to the needs of particular room utilizations.

Egress requirements may lead to solutions also accommodating structural and service systems. Such integration is often possible at the shafts for stairways and elevators in multistory buildings. The shaft enclosures are designed as principal structural components against hori-

zontal forces. The chases for service systems are frequently part of these vertical penetrations of the building. Variations in the placement of such core elements are shown in Figures 6–8. The cores must be located for easy transitions to areas with horizontal occupancy traffic. Their details must provide connections for horizontal structural components and service system runs.

Extensive requirements for environmental controls and other services lead in certain building types to spaces used only for subsystems distribution. Service towers within or attached to buildings and interstitial floors are now common solutions in hospital and laboratory projects (Fig. 9).

Reasonable distances between the machinery that provides environmental controls and services in large build-

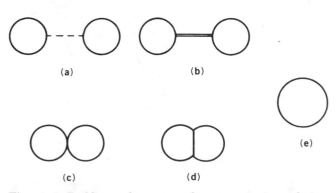

(a)   (b)

(c)   (d)   (e)

Figure 5. Building subsystem and component interrelationships. (a) Remote. (b) Connected. (c) Touching. (d) Meshed. (e) Unified (12).

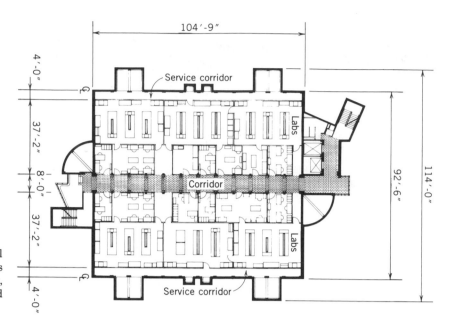

Figure 7. Spatial arrangement of vertical egress, structure, and services as attached cores of the Agronomy Laboratory, Cornell University, Ithaca, New York. Architect: Ulrich Franzen and Associates.

ings require the zoning of such controls and services. The location of equipment rooms often influences the planning and appearance of buildings. In many high-rise buildings, whole stories are provided for equipment rooms in basements and top levels. Intermediate equipment rooms are typically needed for every 10–20 stories (Fig. 10). Depend-

ing on the choice of service systems, particularly for air conditioning, the location of smaller equipment rooms on every story allows for equipment decentralization and short runs for branch distribution.

Systems coordination on the detailed level calls for careful three-dimensional evaluation. The exclusivity of

Figure 8. External view of Agronomy Laboratory, Cornell University, Ithaca, New York. Architect: Ulrich Franzen and Associates.

Figure 9. The service towers and the interstitial floors during construction of the Hennepin County Medical Center in Minneapolis, Minnesota. Architect: Medical Facility Associates.

the location of individual subsystems or components can be simply stated: where one thing is, no other can be. Therefore, integration is additivity in three variations:

1. Subsystems or components may be placed in layers.
2. Subsystems or components may penetrate other subsystems of components.
3. Subsystems or components may enclose other sub systems or components.

Placement in layers is the simplest way of combining systems. In its purest form, zones are designated for the location of particular subsystems. This principle is most frequently found in the so-called integrated ceiling sandwich. The structural ceiling, the suspended ceiling, and the air space in between are the three principal layers. The air space is used for systems distribution. The ceiling itself often consists of several subsystems, such as a metal grid, acoustical panels, air diffusers, and lighting fixtures. Figure 11 shows the zones of a ceiling sandwich used in

Figure 10. Equipment rooms are located at top and intermediate levels in the Civic Center, Toronto, Ontario, Canada. Architect: V. Revell.

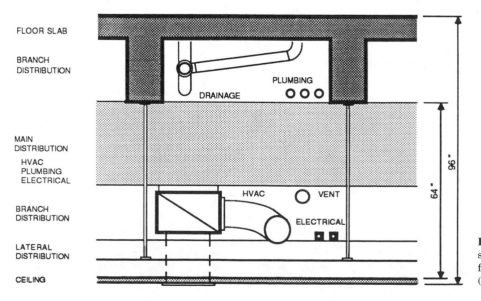

Figure 11. Installation zones between the structural floor and the suspended ceiling for Veterans Administration hospitals (13).

Figure 12. Science Center, Harvard University. **(a)** Assembly of the structural system. **(b)** Interior of laboratories with service distribution penetrating beams. Architects: Sert, Jackson & Associates.

buildings with strong environmental control and service requirements, such as hospitals or laboratories. Similar zoning of services may be applied within vertical chases. Special attention must be given to crossovers for branch connections.

Spatial integration by means of one subsystem penetrating another is most often practiced in connection with structural components. The main reason is space savings.

The penetrating components, such as ducts and pipes, are generally held in place by the structural system. The prefabricated concrete beams of the Harvard Science Center, Cambridge, Massachusetts, feature prefabricated holes that allow the distribution of air ducts, fire sprinkler piping, electrical raceways, etc, within the structural depth of the beams (Fig. 12).

Obviously, the principle of using one system to enclose another has been used in building for a long time. Piping, for example, has been located in wood stud walls or in brick masonry. Various enclosure concepts for vertical systems distribution are used in the CBS tower in New York City (Fig. 13). The main air supply-and-return system is located within shafts of the stair and elevator core. An induction unit system is served by ducts and piping within the facade columns. Another version of this integration has been the enclosure of conduits, either underfloor ducts in concrete slabs or raceways formed by corrugated metal decks, permitting the later installation of power and communication systems and even providing for changes within the enclosure during the lifetime of the building (Fig. 14). The complexity of environmental controls and communication services demands the integration of many functional and spatial aspects at the same time. The rather recently developed raised-floor concept permits the installation and later change of many distribution systems. The Kloeckner Building in Bremen, FRG, uses the floor cavity itself for air distribution and cables

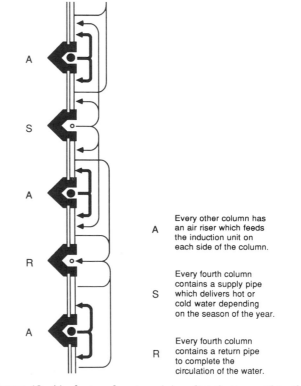

Figure 13. Air duct and water piping distribution within the exterior columns of the CBS Office Building. Architect: Eero Saarinen (14).

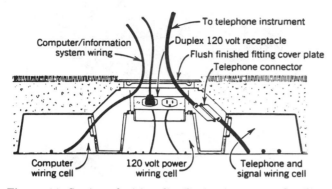

Figure 14. Section of wiring distribution in structural ceiling slab with cables for power, telephone, and computer services. Courtesy of INRYCO, Inc.

of various electronic services. Microclimate control is achieved by means of user-controlled floor outlets and duct extensions to air swivels at desktop (Fig. 15).

A strong potential for spatial integration exists in the rigorous exploration of modular coordination principles. Repetitive dimensional increments have been used since building has been recognized as an additive process. Theories of modular coordination evolved from studies of geometry and proportions. A special aspect developed when mass production became a reality through industrialization.

Successful industrialization depends on the appropriate transformation of building requirements into spatial arrangements that lend themselves to favorable divisibility. The properties of materials used to create space; the

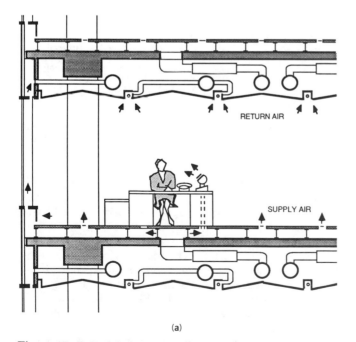

(a)

Figure 15. Raised-floor system, air-flow windows, and furniture-integrated air duct and electronic service extensions provide comfort and microclimate control in the Kloeckner Office Building. Architect: Hentrich-Petschnigg & Partner.

constraints of production, transport, and assembly; and the desire for particular aesthetic expressions also influence divisibility. In 1936, Bemis (15) devised probably the first theory of modular coordination for repetitive dimensional increments, especially for housing. He studied numerous prefabricated housing systems and concluded that 4 in. would be the best basic module. During the 1940s, Neufert (16) used the German brick length of 25 cm, including the mortar joint, as the basic module for his modular coordination standards. Le Corbusier (17) derived "the modulor" from measurements of the human body and the ratio of the golden section.

The largest development in modular dimensioning of whole building systems took place for educational facilities in the United Kingdom after World War II. This coordination effort brought forth bulk purchasing of building components to be used for facilities on various sites. Figure 16 is an isometric of the structure and envelope of the CLASP system (Consortium of Local Authorities Special Programme). Figure 17 shows the modular laboratory wall of the Marburg University Building System in Marburg, FRG. The Marburg System's basic module is 15 cm in the horizontal and vertical directions, with divisions of it for fine details and multiples for planning modules. For the exterior that results from these highly integrated subsystems, see Figure 42, of the chapter on Envelopes, Vol. 2, of this Encyclopedia.

Ehrenkrantz (20) and Dunstone (21) proposed number patterns on which the production of building subsystems and components and their dimensional integration into the building fabric could be based. A principal challenge consists in the step from the preliminary arrangement of building elements with assumed zero thickness, generally on modular planning grids, to the actual three-dimensional condition of the building substance. Brandle (22) investigated the geometries of spaces and procedures for their modularization, the influence of component thicknesses on the selection of modular sizes, and the application of their combinations. Preferred space dimensions and component series for horizontal and vertical application were the result.

Applications of modular coordination principles, with varying degrees of intensity, can be found in many buildings and their systems. The principal applications are in educational, commercial, and industrial projects. Modular coordination is, in conjunction with functional systems compatibility, the basis for the open systems approach and a future comprehensive systems and components market.

CONSTRUCTION-RELATED INTEGRATION

Construction processes basically consist of a three-phase sequence:

1. Building material and subsystems production or procurement.
2. Transportation to the building site.
3. Assembly of the building.

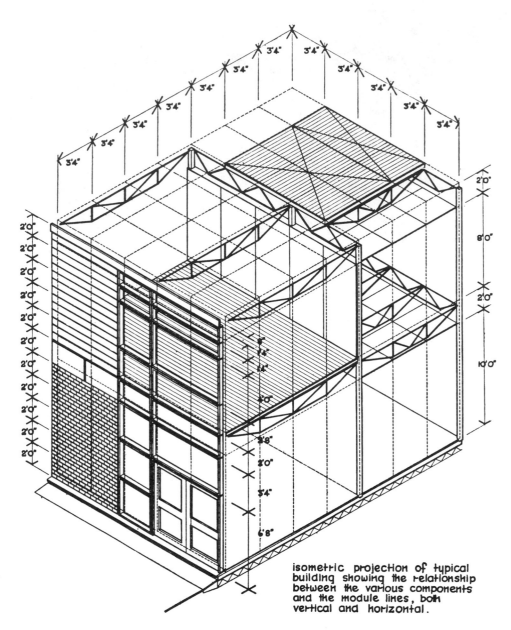

isometric projection of typical building showing the relationship between the various components and the module lines, both vertical and horizontal.

Figure 16. Modular integration of structure and envelope of the CLASP system (18).

The choices of construction processes are made in a complex and ever-changing environment. In addition to the preferences of owners and designers in the project outcome as a functional and aesthetic result, the availability of materials and systems and their costs represent fundamental constraints.

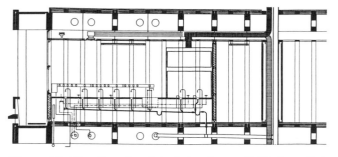

Figure 17. Elevation of modular laboratory wall, Marburg University Building System (19). Architect: H. Spieker.

Each of the three phases of the construction process has its particular influences that must be evaluated and assessed. The decision for a structural system in a multistory building, for example, to be of steel or concrete must be studied with regard to associated effects in every step of the building process. As these steps are highly interdependent, only their combined impact can form a sound basis for decision making, especially about costs.

Of major consequence is the relationship of on-site work vs off-site production. The advances in building technology favor more and more prefabrication and preassembly in manufacturing plants, transport to building sites, component assembly, and, if needed, finishing work. These advances also enhance systems integration off-site, under well-controlled manufacturing conditions. The progress in mechanization and transportation during the past decades has been strong. The sizes and weights of produced and shipped components have increased considerably.

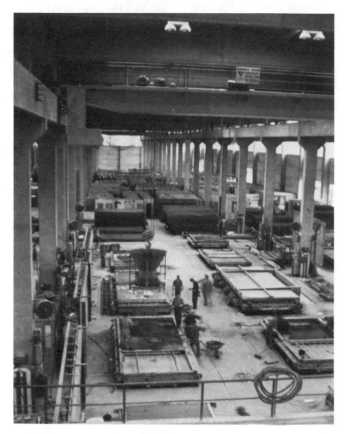

Figure 18. Production of highly integrated concrete wall and ceiling components, Holzmann-Coignet Co., Frankfurt, FRG.

The manufacture and application of large concrete components, packaged air-conditioning units, and plumbing walls are examples of such developments. Figure 18 shows the production of exterior walls and floor slabs in a plant near Frankfurt, FRG, with window frames and electrical conduits installed before the pouring of concrete takes place. The prefabricated plumbing wall in Figure 19

is a result of enclosure and production-related integration. Polyurethane foam holds the pipes, toilet tank, and fixture anchors in place. The form that serves as a container for the foaming process of the wall is used first as a template for the location of the piping and the fixture anchors.

The construction process is organized generally in sequential steps of time. When these steps occur is of crucial importance for the systems integration process. Individual subsystems or component production and integration often happen in parallel steps. Off-the-shelf procurement may be applicable. Careful construction management, including critical path studies for organization and time scheduling, may lead to fast-track sequences that include as a matter of principle the early production and preassembly off-site parallel to assembly on-site.

A simple scenario of this process may be envisioned as the construction of a high-rise housing project by means of prefabricated concrete components. While the load-bearing structure is produced and assembled, the production of the exterior wall components and bathroom modules occurs in a factory. The modules are then shipped to the site and placed through the still-open structure before assembly of the next story's concrete components takes place (Fig. 20). The subsystems production characteristics allow an organizationally and, in time, well-integrated approach. The most elaborate procedure of this kind, so far, was used for one large building, the Hong Kong Bank,

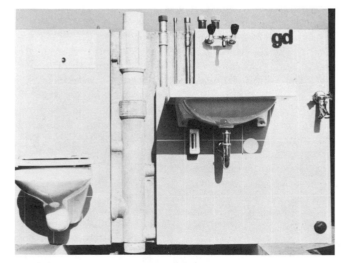

Figure 19. Prefabricated plumbing wall, G. Dziuk Co., Gelsenkirchen, FRG.

Figure 20. Wet core unit placed into concrete structure of housing units in Newark, New Jersey. Descon/Concordia System.

where 139 building service modules were suspended from the main structure, stacked on top of each other (Fig. 10).

Of particular concern for integration is the interfacing of systems. Earlier, functional compatibility was mentioned as a crucial aspect. For the construction process, the physical attributes of the jointing are important. Joint configurations and tolerances must allow easy assembly and provide the desired performance (Fig. 21). For the future interchangeability of subsystems and components, during the design process and possibly even during the building's lifetime, and with it a wide range of choices for integration, a broad-based effort toward systems interface conventions is required, including rigorous dimensional coordination.

Construction process-related integration reaches from the simple placement of thermal insulation in a wall panel to the complete assembly of an emergency clinic as a mobile space module. The most favorable integration intensities within particular levels of the construction process are difficult to generalize. They must be assessed for each project by considering the impact of all design factors on the project outcome, including building costs. This is a rich area for construction research.

ENERGY-RELATED INTEGRATION

Buildings are continuously influenced by exterior and interior environmental factors, such as climatic conditions and occupancy requirements. The influence is dynamic and causes or requires dynamic response. Today's buildings, therefore, include complex energy systems that support and control this response.

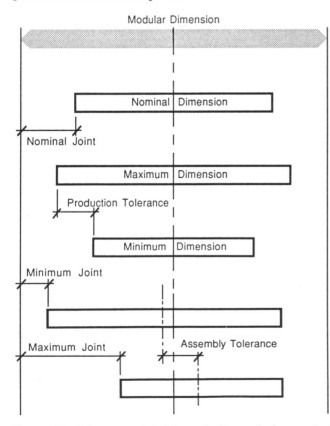

Figure 21. Tolerances related to production and placement of prefabricated components (23).

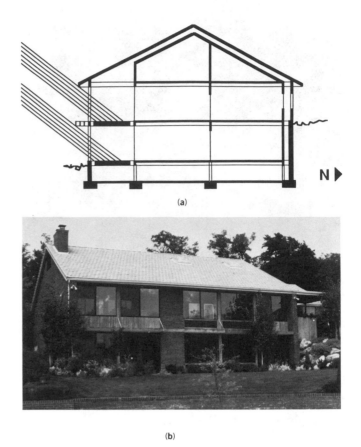

Figure 22. The double envelope of the Plenk Residence, Salt Lake City, Utah, insulates and serves as a duct for the transport of energy by air. The mass of the solarium floors and of the earth below the house provides heat storage capacity. (a) Schematic section. (b) View from the southwest. Architect: Kurt Brandle.

The response may be passive by means of the design, the materials, or the systems of the building fabric. Or it may be active by means of mechanical and electrical systems. With few exceptions, all modern buildings react through combinations of passive and active response. The more active the response, the more it relies on energy consumption. Understanding this fact has profound consequences for a view of systems integration, the operational characteristics of systems, and their interaction.

From the above, it is obvious that the study of passive systems should be directed toward controlling environmental conditions as far as possible through the properties of the building fabric, that is, the location, geometry, and material. A building's systems and components are typically multifunctional. The challenge for the designer is to integrate all characteristics in such a way that functional integrity and energy-effectiveness is achieved. For example, the primary function of a heavy outside wall is to carry structural loads and to separate the interior from the exterior environment. The wall's location, its mass, and the placement of the mass within the wall cross section, however, have a considerable impact on solar heat absorption, storage, and transmission. Passive energy systems require early conceptual integration. Such systems may or may not have a strong influence on the physical appearance of the building.

The residence with a double envelope and a sun space in Figure 22 shows careful integration of site factors such

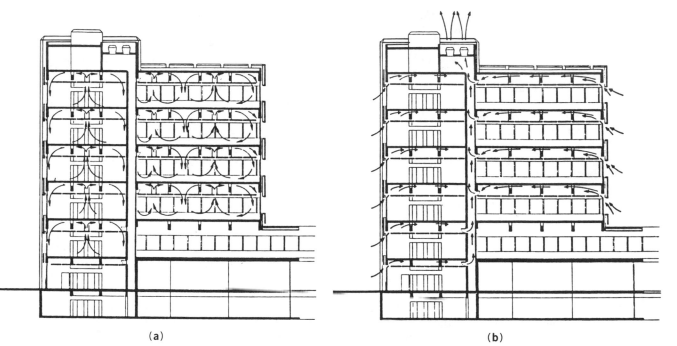

(a)   (b)

Figure 23. Air flow for heat absorption and release in the concrete ceiling structure in the Ziehl-Abegg Office Building, Kuenzelsau, FRG. (a) Section showing daytime loading by internal air circulation. (b) Section showing nighttime flushing with outside air (24). Architect: W. E. Fuchs.

as solar orientation and slope of the site, large windows for solar gain, and the location of mass in the sun space floor for energy absorption. The concrete structure of an office building in the FRG (Fig. 23) absorbs heat gains during the day through internal air circulation supported by small fans in the ceiling. The stored heat is flushed out at night with outside air by means of a central fan. This energy exchange capability, together with ventilation by windows and sun protection as well as daylight control by exterior venetian blinds, makes it possible to operate the building without high levels of artificial lighting and without air conditioning.

The skylight over the atrium of the Tennessee Valley Authority (TVA) Building in Chattanooga, Tennessee (Fig. 24), integrates two important energy-related functions. It serves as a giant solar collector and provides daylight for the interior of this large multistory structure.

The concepts of passive energy systems are well understood. The analysis of their behavior is complicated, however, because of the large number of variables involved and the strong interdependence of variables. Because of the highly dynamic behavior of passive systems, adjustable controls enhance their effectiveness. Examples of such controls are the manually adjusted venetian blinds at windows or the motorized louvers and vents, as in the TVA Building.

Active systems are driven by the utilization of fossil fuels or electricity. They basically consist of four principal subsystems. The primary equipment accepts and often converts the externally supplied energy for its use in the building. Examples are boilers, chillers, or transformers. The distribution system brings the energy to the points where it is needed. Examples are air ducts with fans or electrical raceways with transformers. The terminal

Figure 24. The daylight and solar energy impact of the large skylight in the TVA Building are controlled by motorized louvers and relief fans. Architects: Caudill Rowlett, Scott and Architect's Collaborative.

equipment uses the energy for its intended purpose. Examples are variable air volume boxes for cooling or luminaires for lighting. The control systems activate and adjust the operation of the systems according to functional requirements. Examples are thermometers with activators for variable air volume supply or switches for lighting control.

The fundamental purpose of these active systems is energy transport and diffusion. Energy, especially in the form of electricity, is the medium that translates system control strategies into system activities. Figure 25 represents the development since the early 1970s of large airconditioning systems. Several subsystems are connected and are centrally controlled by a computer program. Most recently, central computer stations have increasingly assumed a coordinating and, where appropriate, control function for most or all operating systems in a building (Fig. 26).

One main reason for the integration of energy-driven systems is the conservation of energy. Because of heat losses, heat gains, hot service water needs, etc, heating and cooling are often required simultaneously in the same building. Energy transfers through heat recovery and storage have proven to be highly effective. The closed water-loop heat pump system (Fig. 27) allows shifting of heat from spaces with cooling demand to spaces with heating demand, for example, in winter, from a building's south-oriented zone with solar gains to its north-oriented zone with heat loss.

Integrated management strategies can reduce energy consumption and costs considerably. Such strategies, for example, collect and interrelate criteria of space utilization, climatic conditions, and system performance characteristics at particular points in time toward energy use optimization. The graph of Figure 28 interrelates occupancy scheduling, exterior temperature fluctuation, heating and cooling operation, and energy consumption for a large educational facility.

Active systems, while providing the desired interior environmental conditions, interact energetically with each other and with the building fabric. Therefore, passive and active systems rarely exist and operate by themselves in an ideal sense. In other words, most environmental control systems are more or less of both. The strong and unavoidable interaction between the building as constructed and energy as an impact factor or operational

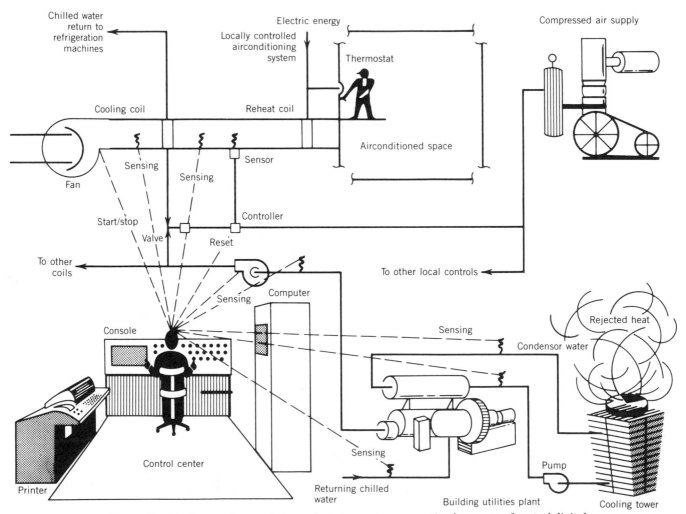

Figure 25. Heating, cooling, and air-conditioning systems operation by means of central digital control (25).

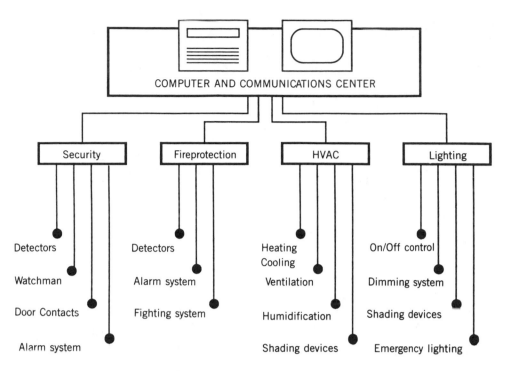

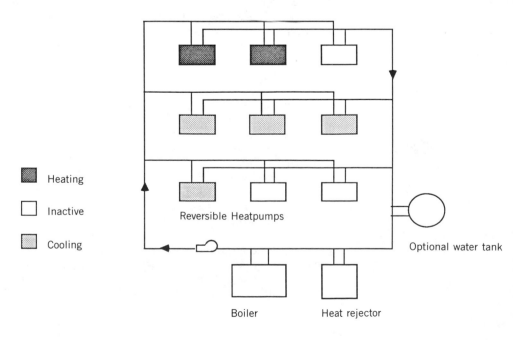

Figure 26. Coordination and control of smart interaction between environmental control and safety systems.

component provides excellent opportunities for integrative design solutions.

AESTHETICS-RELATED INTEGRATION

Throughout architectural history, technology has played a role in the aesthetics of buildings. The Roman aqueduct is an outstanding example. During the industrial revolution, designers and builders began to evaluate systematically a broad range of aesthetic implications of technology. New materials such as cast iron, steel, and reinforced concrete and the conversion of energy for power, illumination, and air conditioning gave the designer not only innovative ideas for solving functional problems, but provided an unprecedented freedom of architectural expression.

The production of subsystems, increasingly by machines off-site, and the mechanization of transport and erection allowed a precision and variety of building assembly formerly impossible. The advent of steel, and later reinforced concrete, fostered visions of daring structures. The machine aesthetic of the Crystal Palace was an early

Figure 27. Closed water-loop heat pump system with some units in heating mode, some in cooling mode, and some inactive. The water loop and the tank serve as the heat storage medium.

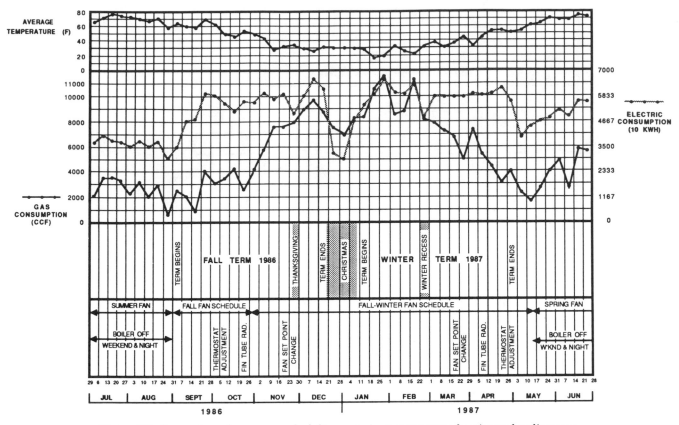

Figure 28. Comparison of occupancy scheduling, exterior temperatures, heating and cooling operation, and energy consumption provide the basis for energy management at the Art and Architecture Building, The University of Michigan, Ann Arbor, Michigan. Courtesy of the Energy Cost Avoidance Project, The University of Michigan.

result. Elevators made the high-rise buildings of Chicago and New York possible. Electrical lighting and mechanical ventilation allowed increased building depth, independent of the access to daylight and air through windows. Integrating into the overall design the systems that make innovations possible became an important issue, and it still is today.

Therefore, during the development of every project, questions arise about how and to what extent the related systems should influence the appearance of the building. The Transworld Airlines (TWA) terminal at Kennedy Airport in New York (Fig. 29), the Equitable Life Assurance

Figure 29. The aesthetic expression of the TWA Building is dominated by the structural shell concept of its building envelope. Architect: Eero Saarinen.

Society Building in Charlotte, North Carolina (Fig. 30), the Hong Kong Bank Building (Fig. 10), and the Provincial Center in Flin Flon, Manitoba, Canada, are examples of recent buildings that integrate particular systems in such a way that they become an important component of visual design.

Not all technology lends itself to visual expression. Many physical and, particularly, operational characteristics of modern building systems cannot or cannot easily be displayed. The distribution of electricity, for example, is difficult to expose, not the least for reasons of safety. Nevertheless, an example of exposing even this kind of system can be seen inside the Centre Pompidou in Paris (Fig. 31). The desire to indicate systems characteristics and exaggerate them led to metaphorical representations. Examples of this kind are the metabolic schemes of Archigram in the 1970s (Fig. 32). More recently, some of the postmodern and deconstructivist projects have used building systems motifs.

A quite different aspect of aesthetic systems integration is the control of characteristics of subsystems and components, not toward systems explicitness or metaphors, but for the reinforcement of general visual expressions. The manipulation of systems attributes such as form, size, proportion, repetition, and color lend themselves to such design manipulation. An example is the

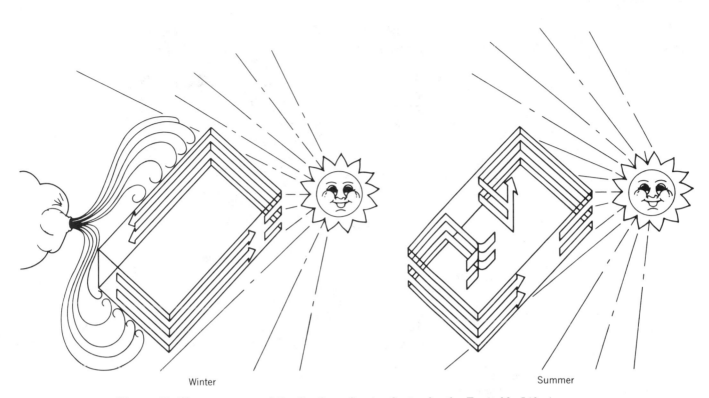

Winter

Summer

Figure 30. The appearance of the Southern Service Center for the Equitable Life Assurance Society results mainly from the glazed ducts in the double envelope that guide solar-heated air to the cool side of the building in winter and cool exhaust air to the warm side in summer. **(a)** Winter and summer air-flow patterns. Architects: Wolf Associates. Courtesy of Wolf Associates.

Figure 31. The air ducts and electrical raceways under the ceiling of the Centre Pompidou are themselves permanent art within the context of this exhibition building. See also article on Envelopes, Figure 43, Volume 2. Architects: Piano and Rogers. Courtesy of Peter Sulzer.

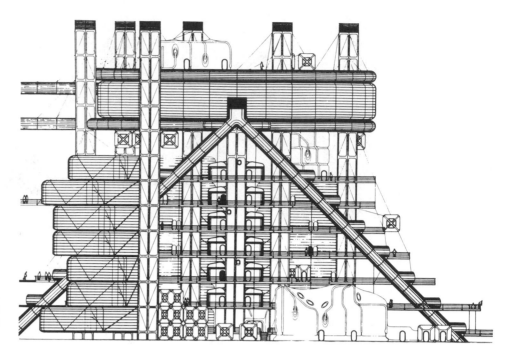

Figure 32. Methaphorical expression of systems in Archigram's Plug-in University Node. Designer: Peter Cook. (26).

choice of bay size for load-bearing columns to achieve a particular visual rhythm of a facade (Fig. 33), or to the contrary, the neglect of such an expression by locating the columns inside a curtain wall (Fig. 34).

In summary, building systems offer technical solutions for design problems. But they also establish constraints. As an activity, systems integration is the effort to combine technological aspects with themselves and with all other aspects of a building. As a result, systems integration contributes substantially to the functional and visual quality of a building.

Figure 33. The particular column bay sizes in the step-down portion of the Harvard Science Center were chosen not only because of structural requirements, but also for visual expression. Architects: Sert, Jackson & Associates.

Figure 34. The curtain wall of the Loop Transportation Center in Chicago, Illinois, receives its lightness of appearance from the invisibility of the load-bearing columns and from the structural glazing of its fenestration. Architects: Skidmore, Owings and Merrill.

BIBLIOGRAPHY

1. C. W. Churchman, *The Systems Approach,* Delacorte Press, New York, 1968, p. 29.
2. M. Brill, lecture notes on building systems.
3. W. M. Pena and J. W. Focke, *Problem Seeking: An Architectural Programming Primer,* 3rd ed., American Institute of Architects Press, Washington, D.C., 1987.
4. C. R. Jones, *Design Methods,* Wiley-Interscience, London, 1970.
5. E. T. White, *Ordering Systems: An Introduction to Architectural Design,* Architectural Media, Tucson, Ariz., 1973.
6. K. Brandle, *The Systems Approach to Building,* Associated Schools of Architecture Learning Package, Graduate School of Architecture, University of Utah, Salt Lake City, Ut., 1974–1976. Distributed to all schools of architecture in the United States and Canada for library location.
7. R. D. Rush, ed., *The Building Systems Integration Handbook,* John Wiley & Sons, Inc., New York, 1986.
8. *SCSD: The Project and the Schools,* Educational Facilities Laboratories, Inc., New York, 1963, p. 59.
9. *Manufacturer's Compatibility Study,* 3rd ed., Building Systems Information Clearing House, Menlo Park, Calif., Sept. 1971, p. 3.
10. Ref. 7, p. 317.
11. Ref. 7, p. 232.
12. Ref. 7, p. 320.
13. G. Agron and J. Borthwick, "Building Systems Research for VA Applied in Both Public and Private," *Architectural Record,* 119 (June 1972).
14. D. Guise, *Design and Technology in Architecture,* John Wiley & Sons, Inc., New York, 1985, p. 173.
15. A. F. Bemis, *The Evolving House,* Vol. III, Technology Press, MIT, Cambridge, Mass., 1936, pp. 73, 217.
16. E. Neufert, "The Standardization of Measurements in Buildings," *Building,* 150–154 (Apr. 1953).
17. Le Corbusier, *The Modulor,* Harvard University Press, Cambridge, Mass., 1954.
18. Ministry of Education, *The Story of CLASP, Building Bulletin No. 19,* Her Majesty's Stationery Office, London, June 1961, p. 33.
19. Marburger Bausystem, Marburg: Staatliches Universitätsneubauamt, Juli 1971, p. 19.
20. E. D. Ehrenkrantz, *The Modular Number Pattern,* Alec Tiranti Ltd., London, 1956.
21. P. A. Dunstone, *Combinations of Numbers in Building,* Estates Gazette Ltd., London, 1965.
22. K. Brandle, "Co-ordinating Dimensions for Building Components," *Build International,* 46–57 (Jan./Feb. 1971).
23. "Modual-ABC," Report No. 4, Sveriges Standardisierungskommission, Stockholm, 1965.
24. W. E. Fuchs, "Beeinflussung des Thermischen Raumklimas in Burogebauden Durch Ausnutzung der Warmespeicherfahigkeit Interner Massen," Doctoral dissertation, Universität Stuttgart, Stuttgart, FRG, 1980, p. 101, 103.
25. J. L. Kmetzo, "When Computers Assume Building Operation," *AIA Journal,* 28 (Dec. 1972).
26. P. Cook, ed., *Archigram,* Praeger Publishers, New York, 1973, p. 42.

General References

"The Integrated House," *Architectural Forum* (Mar. 1943).

K. Wachsmann, *The Turning Point in Building,* Reinhold Publishing Co., New York, 1961.

C. Koch, *Comprehensive Architectural Practice: Architecture and Industrialization, AIA Journal,* 59–71 (Sept. 1963).

T. Schmid and C. Testa, *Systems Building,* Artemis Verlag, Zurich, Switzerland, 1969.

Industrialization Forum (IF), 1969–1976.

E. D. Ehrenkrantz, "The System to Systems," *AIA Journal* (May 1970).

R. Bender, *A Crack in the Rear-view Mirror,* Van Nostrand Reinhold Co., Inc., New York, 1973.

B. J. Sullivan, *Industrialization in the Building Industry,* Van Nostrand Reinhold Co., Inc., New York, 1980.

B. Russell, *Building Systems, Industrialization and Architecture,* John Wiley & Sons, Inc., London, 1981.

J. Bernaden and R. Neubauer, *The Intelligent Building Sourcebook,* The Fairmont Press, 1988.

See also CEILINGS; CONSTRUCTION SYSTEMS; ENVELOPES, BUILDING; MECHANICAL SYSTEMS

KURT BRANDLE
University of Michigan
Ann Arbor, Michigan